Concise Encyclopedia of Preaching

Also published by Westminster John Knox Press

ENCYCLOPEDIA OF THE REFORMED FAITH
edited by Donald K. McKim

THE WESTMINSTER DICTIONARY OF CHRISTIAN ETHICS
edited by James F. Childress and John Macquarrie

THE WESTMINSTER DICTIONARY OF CHRISTIAN SPIRITUALITY
edited by Gordon S. Wakefield

THE WESTMINSTER DICTIONARY OF CHRISTIAN THEOLOGY
edited by Alan Richardson and John Bowden

THE WESTMINSTER DICTIONARY OF CHURCH HISTORY
edited by Jerald C. Brauer

THE NEW WESTMINSTER DICTIONARY OF LITURGY AND WORSHIP
edited by J. G. Davies

THE NEW WESTMINSTER DICTIONARY OF THE BIBLE
edited by Henry Snyder Gehman

Concise Encyclopedia of Preaching

WILLIAM H. WILLIMON
RICHARD LISCHER
editors

Westminster John Knox Press
Louisville, Kentucky

Book design by Publishers' WorkGroup
Cover design by Tanya R. Hahn

First edition

Published by Westminster John Knox Press
Louisville, Kentucky

This book is printed on acid-free paper that meets the American National Standards Institute Z39.48 standard. ∞

PRINTED IN THE UNITED STATES OF AMERICA

00 01 02 03 04 — 10 9 8 7 6 5 4 3

Library of Congress Cataloging-in-Publication Data

Concise encyclopedia of preaching / William H. Willimon,
Richard Lischer, editors. — 1st ed.
    p.   cm.
  ISBN 0-664-21942-X (alk. paper)
    1. Preaching—Encyclopedias. 2. Clergy—Biography—Dictionaries.
I. Willimon, William H. II. Lischer, Richard.
BV4211.2.C583   1995
251′.003—dc20   94–3469

To Our Students

How are they to hear without a preacher?

—Romans 10:14

Preface

We have created the *Concise Encyclopedia of Preaching* as a labor of love for the church's great tradition of preaching. Only after we became deeply involved in the work did we realize how rich and varied that tradition is. It ranges from theological reflection on the meaning of authority in the pulpit to the twinge of anxiety experienced by every preacher who stands to speak. That tradition is as old as the prophets and as modern (or post-modern) as the latest theories of communication. It is as familiar as current resources and as unfamiliar (at least to North Americans) as Scandinavian or Asian developments in homiletics.

Essentially, the book consists of three types of entries: (1) historical, critical, and theological essays on a wide variety of topics related to preaching; (2) practical directions for the production and delivery of sermons; and (3) biographical studies of individuals whose work has deeply influenced the church and its proclamation. Although this is not a book of sermons or sermon ideas, we have supplemented the biographical articles with brief excerpts from sermons that are representative of important preachers or movements in homiletics. The reader will see at once that the most difficult part of the editorial process was the selection of individual persons for study. The encyclopedia was to be "concise," which means that many significant preachers and

thinkers have been omitted. We have tried to choose those persons (1) who were (or are) exemplary preachers, or (2) who were in some way formative for the discipline of homiletics, or (3) who put the stamp of their faithfulness or genius on their generation and, in some cases, upon succeeding generations. Just as we have tried to give "voices" to some preachers by means of the sermon excerpts, so we have also included studies of women and minorities whose voices have not been heeded or appreciated by the dominant culture.

We hope this book will find users among practicing preachers, as well as among academic students of preaching. The former should find refreshment of what they may already know; the latter, instruction and a place to begin their reflection or preaching.

For those who wish to read the *Encyclopedia* systematically according to a field of interest, let us suggest several tracks. In each track, the articles should be read in the following order:

Theology

Theology of Preaching
Word of God
Hermeneutics
Proclamation
Doctrine
Authority
Reason

Homiletics

Homily
Homiletics: Teaching of
Pedagogy of Preaching
History of Preaching
Homiletics and Preaching—
  in Africa
  in Asia
  in German-Speaking Europe
  in India
  in Latin America
  in North America
  in Scandinavia

Many other topics could be included, and the reader may construct his or her own program of study. Considerable overlap exists between tracks, but the multiplicity of perspectives and redundancy of topics also contribute to the richness of the book. Likewise, our many authors cannot possibly represent a single perspective on preaching or a school of homiletics, but we believe this variety also constitutes a strength of the *Encyclopedia*. An asterisk (*) beside a word in an article directs the reader's attention to an article on a related subject elsewhere in the book.

We owe many people our thanks for their help on this book. Early in its development, several scholars in the field of homiletics suggested topics and persons for inclusion. We were fortunate to consult with Elizabeth Achtemeier, O. C. Edwards, Jr., Walter Burghardt, S.J., Thomas Long, James Cox, James Earl Massey, Carol Norén, and Joan Delaplane, O.P. Charles Campbell helped with research in the early stages. Many colleagues—too many to mention—put us on the trail of specialists and appropriate authors for various articles. Finding the right person to write each of the two hundred articles was a bit like detective work. By far the most pleasurable aspect of our work—over and above our own friendship—has been the many contacts and conversations with our authors, especially those we had not known before. These conversations have enriched not only the *Encyclopedia* but also our personal and professional lives.

Finally, we wish to express our thanks to Cynthia Thompson of Westminster John Knox Press for her persistence and editorial guidance; to Jackie Andrews of Duke University Chapel, who helped with the excerpts and permissions to reprint them; and Gail Chappell of Duke Divinity School, who organized our files and prepared the entire manuscript for publication.

Anyone foolish enough to prepare a dictionary or an encyclopedia gives too many hostages to fortune. The possibilities for small errors of fact and large errors of perspective, to say nothing of egregious sins of omission, are endless. Thus we offer this resource to the church's preachers with humility—and with the words of Dr. Johnson who, when asked to explain the errors in his recently published *Dictionary of the English Language*, replied, "Ignorance, Madam, pure ignorance."

WILLIAM WILLIMON
RICHARD LISCHER
Durham, North Carolina

Contributors

Elizabeth Achtemeier
Union Theological Seminary in Virginia
Richmond, Virginia

P. Mark Achtemeier
University of Dubuque Theological
  Seminary
Dubuque, Iowa

Ronald J. Allen
Christian Theological Seminary
Indianapolis, Indiana

John R. Archer
Oakland, California

Mary Christine Athans, B.V.M.
The School of Divinity
The Saint Paul Seminary
University of St. Thomas
St. Paul, Minnesota

David W. Augsburger
Fuller Theological Seminary
Pasadena, California

Raymond Bailey
Southern Baptist Theological Seminary
Louisville, Kentucky

David L. Bartlett
Yale University Divinity School
New Haven, Connecticut

Charles L. Bartow
Princeton Theological Seminary
Princeton, New Jersey

Barbara Bate
General Board of Discipleship
The United Methodist Church
Nashville, Tennessee

Peter Bayley
Gonville and Caius College
Cambridge University
Cambridge, England

Perry H. Biddle
Nashville, Tennessee

Michael W. Blastic, O.F.M. Conv.
Washington Theological Union
Silver Spring, Maryland

Walter R. Bouman
Trinity Lutheran Seminary
Columbus, Ohio

Carl E. Braaten
Center for Catholic and Evangelical
  Theology
Northfield, Minnesota

Walter Brueggemann
Columbia Theological Seminary
Decatur, Georgia

Walter J. Burghardt, S.J.
Woodstock Theological Center
Annapolis, Maryland

John Burke, O.P.
Dominican House of Studies
Washington, D.C.

David Buttrick
Vanderbilt University Divinity School
Nashville, Tennessee

Charles L. Campbell
Columbia Theological Seminary
Decatur, Georgia

Ted A. Campbell
Wesley Theological Seminary
Washington, D.C.

William J. Carl, III
The First Presbyterian Church
Dallas, Texas

Jackson W. Carroll
Duke University Divinity School
Durham, North Carolina

Donald F. Chatfield
Garrett-Evangelical Theological
   Seminary
Evanston, Illinois

Jana Childers
San Francisco Theological Seminary
San Anselmo, California

William Sloane Coffin, Jr.
Strafford, Vermont

John W. Cook
The Henry Luce Foundation
New York, New York

James W. Cox
Southern Baptist Theological Seminary
Louisville, Kentucky

Fred B. Craddock
Candler School of Theology
Emory University
Atlanta, Georgia

James L. Crenshaw
Duke University Divinity School
Durham, North Carolina

Mitties McDonald DeChamplain
Fuller Theological Seminary
Pasadena, California

Joan Delaplane, O.P.
Aquinas Institute of Theology
St. Louis, Missouri

Donald E. Demaray
Asbury Theological Seminary
Wilmore, Kentucky

Dawn De Vries
McCormick Theological Seminary
Chicago, Illinois

Jon T. Diefenthaler
Bethany Lutheran Church
Waynesboro, Virginia

Arlo D. Duba
University of Dubuque Theological
   Seminary
Dubuque, Iowa

Patty Ann T. Earle
Messiah Episcopal Church
Mayodan, North Carolina

O. C. Edwards, Jr.
College of Preachers
Washington, D.C.

Mark Ellingsen
Interdenominational Theological Center
Atlanta, Georgia

Richard L. Eslinger
Trinity United Methodist Church
Niles, Michigan

Gillian R. Evans
Fitzwilliam College
Cambridge University
Cambridge, England

Clyde E. Fant
The Chapel
Stetson University
DeLand, Florida

Al Fasol
Southwestern Baptist Theological
  Seminary
Fort Worth, Texas

Gayle Carlton Felton
Duke University Divinity School
Durham, North Carolina

Joseph Fichtner, O.S.C.
Crosier Community
Phoenix, Arizona

James F. Findlay
University of Rhode Island
Kingston, Rhode Island

David C. Ford
St. Tikhon's Orthodox Seminary
South Canaan, Pennsylvania

Robert V. Friedenberg
Miami (Ohio) University
Hamilton, Ohio

Robert Mikio Fukada
Doshisha University School of Theology
Kyoto, Japan

Reginald H. Fuller
Virginia Theological Seminary
Alexandria, Virginia

Beverly Roberts Gaventa
Princeton Theological Seminary
Princeton, New Jersey

Carol V. R. George
Hobart & William Smith Colleges
Geneva, New York

Peter J. Gomes
Memorial Church
Harvard University
Cambridge, Massachusetts

Catherine Gunsalus González
Columbia Theological Seminary
Decatur, Georgia

Justo L. González
Atlanta, Georgia

David M. Greenhaw
Lancaster Theological Seminary
Lancaster, Pennsylvania

Gracia Grindal
Luther Northwestern Theological
  Seminary
Saint Paul, Minnesota

Eric W. Gritsch
Lutheran Theological Seminary
Gettysburg, Pennsylvania

Nancy Lammers Gross
Eastern Baptist Theological Seminary
Wynnewood, Pennsylvania

Paul W. F. Harms
Trinity Lutheran Seminary
Columbus, Ohio

George W. Harper
Alliance Biblical Seminary
Manila
Republic of the Philippines

Stanley M. Hauerwas
Duke University Divinity School
Durham, North Carolina

Richard B. Hays
Duke University Divinity School
Durham, North Carolina

Susan K. Hedahl
Lutheran Theological Seminary
Gettysburg, Pennsylvania

Richard P. Heitzenrater
Duke University Divinity School
Durham, North Carolina

Jan Hermelink
Martin-Luther University
Halle, Germany

William Hethcock
School of Theology
University of the South
Sewanee, Tennessee

Ann I. Hoch
Duke University Divinity School
Durham, North Carolina

Lucy Hogan
Wesley Theological Seminary
Washington, D.C.

Arthur G. Holder
Church Divinity School of the Pacific
Berkeley, California

Robert G. Hughes
Lutheran Theological Seminary
Philadelphia, Pennsylvania

Willie James Jennings
Duke University Divinity School
Durham, North Carolina

Joseph R. Jeter, Jr.
Brite Divinity School
Texas Christian University
Fort Worth, Texas

L. Gregory Jones
Loyola College
Baltimore, Maryland

John L. Kater, Jr.
Church Divinity School of the Pacific
Berkeley, California

Tsuneaki Kato
Evangelical Church of Japan
Kamakura, Japan

John Killinger
Beeson Divinity School
Samford University
Birmingham, Alabama

William McGuire King
Albright College
Reading, Pennsylvania

Jack Dean Kingsbury
Union Theological Seminary in Virginia
Richmond, Virginia

C. Benton Kline, Jr.
Columbia Theological Seminary
Decatur, Georgia

Gary Kowalski
First Unitarian Universalist Society of
  Burlington
Burlington, Vermont

James N. Lapsley
Sun City, Arizona

George Lawless
Augustinianum
Istituto Patristico
Rome, Italy

William B. Lawrence
Duke University Divinity School
Durham, North Carolina

John H. Leith
Union Theological Seminary in Virginia
Richmond, Virginia

Ralph L. Lewis
Asbury Theological Seminary
Wilmore, Kentucky

Richard Lischer
Duke University Divinity School
Durham, North Carolina

Hugh Litchfield
North American Baptist Seminary
Sioux Falls, South Dakota

D. Stephen Long
Duke University Divinity School
Durham, North Carolina

Thomas G. Long
Princeton Theological Seminary
Princeton, New Jersey

Bradley J. Longfield
University of Dubuque Theological
  Seminary
Dubuque, Iowa

Craig A. Loscalzo
Southern Baptist Theological Seminary
Louisville, Kentucky

Eugene L. Lowry
Saint Paul School of Theology
Kansas City, Missouri

Mary E. Lyons
Vallejo, California

David B. McCarthy
Duke University
Durham, North Carolina

Donald Macleod
Baltimore, Maryland

John S. McClure
Louisville Presbyterian Theological
  Seminary
Louisville, Kentucky

Elsie Anne McKee
Princeton Theological Seminary
Princeton, New Jersey

Thomas R. McKibbens
First Baptist Church
Newton Centre, Massachusetts

George M. Marsden
University of Notre Dame
Notre Dame, Indiana

William Martin
Rice University
Houston, Texas

Conrad Harry Massa
Princeton Theological Seminary
Princeton, New Jersey

James Earl Massey
Anderson University School of Theology
Anderson, Indiana

Robert Moats Miller
University of North Carolina
Chapel Hill, North Carolina

Ella Pearson Mitchell
Interdenominational Theological Center
Atlanta, Georgia

Henry H. Mitchell
Interdenominational Theological Center
Atlanta, Georgia

John M. Mulder
Louisville Presbyterian Theological
  Seminary
Louisville, Kentucky

Roland E. Murphy, O. Carm.
Whitefriars Hall
Washington, D.C.

Lesslie Newbigin
London, England

David Ng
San Francisco Theological Seminary
San Anselmo, California

J. Randall Nichols
Princeton Theological Seminary
Princeton, New Jersey

Morris J. Niedenthal
Lutheran School of Theology at Chicago
Chicago, Illinois

Carol M. Norén
North Park Theological Seminary
Chicago, Illinois

Anne Marie Nuechterlein
Duke University Divinity School
Durham, North Carolina

Stephen A. Odom
University of Southern Mississippi
Hattiesburg, Mississippi

Ronald E. Osborn
Eugene, Oregon

Christine E. Parton
Duke University Divinity School
North Carolina Eye and Ear Hospital
Durham, North Carolina

H. Wayne Pipkin
Moscow Protestant Chaplaincy
Moscow, Russia

Surya P. Prakash
United Theological College
Bangalore, India

Samuel Proctor
Duke University Divinity School
Durham, North Carolina

David James Randolph
The United Methodist Church
Babylon, New York

David H. C. Read
Madison Avenue Presbyterian Church
New York, New York

Charles Rice
Drew University Theological School
Madison, New Jersey

Russell E. Richey
Duke University Divinity School
Durham, North Carolina

Andreas Richter-Böhne
Evangelische Kirche
Nürnberg, Germany

Kathleen L. Riley
Canisius College
Buffalo, New York

Haddon Robinson
Gordon-Conwell Theological Seminary
South Hamilton, Massachusetts

Lucy A. Rose
Columbia Theological Seminary
Decatur, Georgia

George W. Rutler
Saint Agnes Parish
New York, New York

Don E. Saliers
Candler School of Theology
Emory University
Atlanta, Georgia

James A. Sanders
School of Theology
Claremont, California

Gerhard Sauter
University of Bonn
Ecumenical Institute
Bonn, Germany

Robert N. Schaper
Fuller Theological Seminary
Pasadena, California

Quentin J. Schultze
Calvin College
Grand Rapids, Michigan

Jan Schumacher
Free Faculty of Theology
Oslo, Norway

Bernard Brandon Scott
Phillips Graduate Seminary
Enid, Oklahoma

Milton C. Sernett
Syracuse University
Syracuse, New York

Wayne E. Shaw
Lincoln Christian Seminary
Lincoln, Illinois

Bruce E. Shields
Emmanuel School of Religion
Johnson City, Tennessee

Aylward Shorter
Missionary Institute of London
London, England

Craig Skinner
Atlanta, Georgia

Olav Skjevesland
Free Faculty of Theology
Oslo, Norway

William Skudlarek, O.S.B.
St. John's University
Collegeville, Minnesota

Gerard S. Sloyan
Catholic University of America
Washington, D.C.

Christine M. Smith
United Theological Seminary of the
    Twin Cities
New Brighton, Minnesota

D. Moody Smith
Duke University Divinity School
Durham, North Carolina

Jon Michael Spencer
University of North Carolina
Chapel Hill, North Carolina

John M. Stapleton
Washington Street United Methodist
    Church
Columbia, South Carolina

K. James Stein
Garrett-Evangelical Theological
    Seminary
Evanston, Illinois

Richard C. Stern
Saint Meinrad School of Theology
Saint Meinrad, Indiana

Hinrich Stoevesandt
Basel, Switzerland

Harry S. Stout
Yale University
New Haven, Connecticut

Herbert B. Strange
U.S. Army, John F. Kennedy Special
    Warfare Center & School
Fort Bragg, North Carolina

Byron D. Stuhlman
Hamilton College
Clinton, New York

Barbara Brown Taylor
Grace-Calvary Episcopal Church
Clarkesville, Georgia

Gardner C. Taylor
The Concord Baptist Church of Christ
Brooklyn, New York

Richard L. Thulin
Lutheran Theological Seminary
Gettysburg, Pennsylvania

Leonora Tubbs Tisdale
Princeton Theological Seminary
Princeton, New Jersey

Samuel Edward Torvend
Aquinas Institute of Theology
St. Louis, Missouri

W. Sibley Towner
Union Theological Seminary in Virginia
Richmond, Virginia

Joseph W. Trigg
St. Patrick's Episcopal Church
Falls Church, Virginia

Thomas H. Troeger
Iliff School of Theology
Denver, Colorado

Karen B. Westerfield Tucker
Duke University Divinity School
Durham, North Carolina

R. Edward Turner
Annapolis, Maryland

William C. Turner
Duke University Divinity School
Durham, North Carolina

Granville E. Tyson
Coppers Cove, Texas

Arthur Van Seters
Knox College
Toronto School of Theology
Toronto, Ontario, Canada

Dan O. Via
Duke University Divinity School
Durham, North Carolina

Richard F. Ward
Yale University Divinity School
New Haven, Connecticut

Don M. Wardlaw
McCormick Theological Seminary
Chicago, Illinois

Robert P. Waznak, S.S.
Washington Theological Union
Silver Spring, Maryland

Timothy P. Weber
Southern Baptist Theological Seminary
Louisville, Kentucky

Donald Weinstein
University of Arizona
Tucson, Arizona

Timothy J. Wengert
Lutheran Theological Seminary
Philadelphia, Pennsylvania

John H. Westerhoff
St. Bartholomew's Episcopal Church
Atlanta, Georgia

Ewart A. Wetherill
Paoletti Associates, Inc.
San Francisco, California

William H. Willimon
Duke University Chapel
Duke University Divinity School
Durham, North Carolina

Paul Scott Wilson
Emmanuel College
Toronto, Ontario
Canada

James P. Wind
Lilly Endowment, Inc.
Indianapolis, Indiana

Friedrich Wintzer
University of Bonn
Bonn, Germany

Bruce Wollenberg
Idaho Institute of Christian Education
Moscow, Idaho

Catherine A. Ziel
Morgenland Lutheran Church
Orefield, Pennsylvania

Acknowledgments

Bernard of Clairvaux, "Love," from *Bernard of Clairvaux: Selected Works*, trans. G. R. Evans (New York: Paulist Press, 1987), 244–45. Used with permission of Paulist Press.

Bonhoeffer, Dietrich, "The Humanity of the Word," *Worldly Preaching: Lectures on Homiletics*, ed. and trans., with critical commentary, by Clyde E. Fant (New York: Crossroad, 1991), 102. Used with permission of Crossroad Publishing Company.

Buttrick, George A., "The Peace of Christ," preached at Princeton Theological Seminary, August 2, 1953, on a text from John 14:27. Used by permission of the sons of George A. Buttrick.

Cappadocians: "Gregory of Nazianzus on the Son," from *Christology of the Later Fathers*, ed. Cyril Richardson, Vol. III, The Library of Christian Classics, 174–75, Philadelphia, 1954. Used by permission of Westminster John Knox Press.

Coffin, William S., "Alex's Death," preached on January 23, 1983, Riverside Church, New York, N.Y. Used by permission of William S. Coffin.

Craddock, Fred B., "Doxology," from *As One Without Authority*, 3d ed. (Nashville: Abingdon Press, 1979), 165–68. Used by permission of Abingdon Press.

Fosdick, Harry E., "Christ Is Christianity," from *On Being Fit to Live With*, Harper & Brothers, Inc., 1946. Copyright renewed 1974 by Elinor F. Downs and Dorothy Fosdick. Reprinted by permission of HarperCollins Publishers, Inc.

Graham, Billy, excerpt from "John 3:16," copyright Billy Graham Evangelistic Association. Used by permission.

Guibert of Nogent, "The Way a Sermon Ought to Be Given," trans. Joseph M. Murphy, in *Today's Speech* 17:4, November 1969, 48–49. Used by permission of Eastern Communication Association.

Hildegard, "Love Came Down," is reprinted from *Hildegard of Bingen's Divine Works*, ed. Matthew Fox, copyright 1987, Bear & Co., Inc., P.O. Box 2860, Santa Fe, NM 87504. Used by permission of the publisher.

Humbert of Romans, "On the Formation of Preachers," from "Treatise on the Formation of Preachers," *Early Dominicans: Selected Writings*, ed. Simon Tugwell, O.P., *The Classics of Western Spirituality*, New York: Paulist Press, 1982, 187–190.

Luther, Martin, "Preach the Word," reprinted from *Luther's Works*, Vol. 51, ed. John W. Doberstein, copyright 1959 Fortress Press. Used by permission of Augsburg Fortress.

Maier, Walter A., "Nothing Save Jesus Christ and Him Crucified," excerpt quoted from *The Best of Walter A. Maier*, 96–97, by Paul L. Maier. Copyright 1980 Concordia Publishing House, St. Louis, Mo. Reprinted by permission.

McPherson, Aimee Semple, "Bring Back the Ark," excerpts from *Aimee Semple McPherson*. Used by permission of the International Church of the Foursquare Gospel, Los Angeles, Calif.

Ng, David, "Children's Sermon." Used by permission of David Ng.

Peale, Norman V., "A Shoeshiner's Wisdom," from *You Can Win*, copyright 1938 Abingdon Press. Used by permission of Ruth S. Peale, Trustee of the Norman Vincent Peale estate.

Scherer, Paul, "No Easy Gospel," excerpt from *The Word God Sent*. Copyright 1965 by Paul Scherer. Copyright renewed. Reprinted by permission of HarperCollins Publishers, Inc.

Schleiermacher, Friedrich, "The Light of Christ," from *Servant of the Word* by Dawn De Vries, copyright 1987 Fortress Press. Used by permission of Augsburg Fortress.

Sheen, Fulton J., "Folly," from *The Life of All Living: The Philosophy of Life*, New York: Garden City Books, 1950, 154–59. Used by permission of the Estate of Fulton J. Sheen and The Society for the Propagation of the Faith.

Sockman, Ralph W., "Today Is Ours," reprinted with the permission of Macmillan Publishing Company from *Live for Tomorrow* by Ralph W. Sockman. Copyright 1993 by The Macmillan Company, copyright renewed 1967 by Ralph W. Sockman.

Spencer, Jon Michael, three chanted sermons from *Sacred Symphony: The Chanted Sermon of the Black Preacher*, Greenwood Press, copyright 1987 by Jon Michael Spencer. Used by permission.

Spurgeon, Charles Haddon, "Songs in the Night," from *The Protestant Pulpit*, compiled by Andrew Watterson Blackwood, Jr. Copyright renewed 1975 by Andrew W. Blackwood, Jr., James R. Blackwood, Philip T. Blackwood. Excerpted by permission of the publisher, Abingdon Press.

Steimle, Edmund, "And How Does It All End?" reprinted from *From Death to Birth* by Edmund Steimle, copyright 1973 Fortress Press. Used by permission of Augsburg Fortress.

Stewart, James, "The Ascension of Christ," from *The Strong Name* (Grand Rapids, Mich.: Baker Book House, 1941), 50. Used by permission.

Taylor, Barbara Brown, "Dare to Preach," from "Shouting from the Rooftop," preached at Kirkridge Retreat Center, Bangor, Pa., 1990. Used by permission of Barbara Brown Taylor.

Taylor, Gardner C., "We Are Climbing Jacob's Ladder," from "Another Look at the Crucifixion," preached at Rankin Chapel, Howard University, March 8, 1992. Used by permission of Gardner C. Taylor.

Thielicke, Helmut, "The Rich Man in Hell," from *The Waiting Father* by Helmut Thielicke. Copyright 1959 by John W. Doberstein. This book was published in German under the title *Das Bilderbuch Gottes. Reden über die*

Gleichnisse Jesu. Copyright 1957 by Quell-Verlag, Stuttgart. Reprinted by permission of HarperCollins Publishers, Inc.

Tillich, Paul, excerpts from "Born in the Grave," 165–66, reprinted with the permission of Scribner's, an imprint of Simon & Schuster, from *The Shaking of the Foundations* by Paul Tillich. Copyright 1948 Charles Scribner's Sons; copyright renewed 1976 Hannah Tillich.

Weatherhead, Leslie, "The Inevitable Encounter," from *Steady in an Unsteady World: Sermons by Leslie Weatherhead*, ed. John Killinger (Nashville: Abingdon Press, 1975), 25–27. Used by permission of Judson Press.

Willimon, William H., "The Meaning of Worship," *The Eleven O'Clock News and Other Experimental Sermons*, ed. John Killinger (Nashville: Abingdon Press, 1975), 25–27. Used by permission of Judson Press.

Acoustics. Most preachers receive training in public speaking, but few receive much guidance on the effect of the worship space upon speech. Consequently, preacher and parishioner may worship in spaces where speech is poorly experienced. Unless the requirements for good hearing are understood, we build new sanctuaries that perpetuate poor hearing conditions for future generations.

A designer with even an elementary understanding of the requirements for good hearing can attain satisfactory acoustics in either a new or renovated building. These requirements include the creation of a suitably quiet space, adequate loudness of wanted sounds for the entire congregation, control of reverberation, and avoidance of acoustical defects. These qualities are determined by the building enclosure in the following ways.

Quiet. The sanctuary must be quiet enough so that softly spoken words and musical pianissimos can be heard. This requires control of intruding noises from traffic, aircraft, and the ventilation system and avoidance of interference from church school classes or other groups.

Control of outdoor noise may begin with the selection of a quiet building site. If this is not feasible, as is so in many urban or suburban locations, the walls and roof must be substantial enough to reduce outdoor noise to an acceptable interior level. Windows and doors are the paths of most intruding noise, so special nonopening windows and vestibules may be needed. Adequate mechanical ventilation must then be provided, which entails careful control of fan noise and vibration. Design criteria for worship spaces are clearly defined, and the basic requirements for all aspects of noise control are readily available from acoustical engineers. However, few builders or ventilating contractors will address such issues unless specifically instructed to do so.

The essential task for a building committee is to insist that noise control be a basic element of any construction or remodeling work and to stipulate firm noise criteria to be met by the building contractor. This may be as simple as adding a specific statement to the construction agreement that "background noise levels in the sanctuary with the ventilation system in normal operation shall not exceed NC 25." This both defines maximum allowable noise levels and provides for easy verification of compliance.

Adequate Loudness and Distribution of Sound. The building enclosure that shuts out traffic and aircraft noise can also enhance sound from minister and choir and can ensure its proper distribution to the entire congregation. Sounds that would be rapidly dissipated outdoors must be preserved and regenerated by sound-reflecting surfaces in such a way that the reflections reinforce the direct sounds. These hard surfaces will also enhance congregational singing and diminish the feeling of singing alone. However, long-delayed sound reflections from balcony faces and rear walls must be diffused or absorbed so that they are not returned as distinct echoes that would obscure subsequent syllables.

Enhancement of early sound reflections, control of sound distribution to the congregation, and suppression of late reflections are determined by the location and orientation of interior surfaces and by the materials of which they are constructed. For example, surfaces close to the choir and organ should be hard and preferably heavy, made of masonry or thick plaster, while carpeting in or near the chancel should be strenuously avoided. The shape of the space should allow strong sound reflections to reach all listeners—deep under-balcony seating or focused reflections from barrel-vaults or domed surfaces are never desirable. Rear-wall surfaces should be shaped to avoid echoes, or they may be covered with sound-absorbing materials to minimize sound reflections.

Suitable Reverberation. Reverberation is the persistence of sound in a space as a series of overlapping reflections after the source has ceased to produce sound. Reverberation time—the time required for a sound to decay to one-millionth of

1

its initial energy—provides a convenient measurement scale. Reverberation length is determined by the volume of the space and the total amount of sound absorption within it. Increasing room volume will tend to increase reverberation, while increasing the amount of sound absorption will decrease reverberation. A long reverberation time (more than 2 seconds) will enhance organ and choral music as well as congregational singing. A short reverberation time (1 second or less) is appropriate for speech clarity but will not favor music. However, reverberation concerns should never outweigh loudness, clarity, or good distribution of sound.

The greatest amount of sound absorption is provided by the congregation, with the result that a space could be excessively reverberant when empty or nearly empty, but lacking in reverberation when full. It is common practice to design for the desired reverberation time with a full or nearly full congregation and to install pew cushions (preferably seats only, not backs) to control reverberation when only a small group is present.

Carpeting is the most controversial material in worship spaces. Many churchgoers associate carpet with warmth, quality, and absence of distracting footfall sounds. On the other hand, it may add significantly to the total absorption, even with a full congregation, and the added sound absorption in the chancel and front cross-aisles can reduce the loudness and clarity of choral sound. When used under pews, carpet tends to detract from congregational singing, creating the uncomfortable feeling that one is singing alone. One common solution is to limit carpeting to thin, glued-down runners in the front-to-rear aisles for control of footfall noise.

Sound Amplification System. In a worship space that is reverberant enough to enhance organ and choral music, the simplest and most effective way to ensure speech intelligibility (as distinct from loudness) is by the use of an electronic sound amplification system tailored to the acoustics of the space. The amplification system must be carefully designed and competently engineered to a wide range of speaking skills, in addition to allowing for any performance requirements.

Some contractors specialize in the design and installation of high-quality sound systems. However, far too often expensive components are installed in a system that is inappropriate for the space. Select a contractor with a history of successful installations, or preferably, engage an independent consultant to prepare nonproprietary specifications for a system that meets the precise needs of the congregation and that is open to competitive bidding. The consultant also will provide the safeguard of a check on system performance before final payment is made.

Conclusions. When reduced to its elements, church acoustics loses much of its mystery and becomes a rational and manageable aspect of new construction or renovation. There will always be a difference of opinion on sound quality, on the best location for having the choir, and on other acoustical matters. Nevertheless, the primary purpose of worship can be met by adherence to common-sense principles that can be followed by any building committee.

EWART A. WETHERILL

African-American Preaching.

Dr. Martin Luther King, Sr., publicly wondered why seminaries had begun to offer courses in "Black Preaching." There was only one Bible, he declared, not a Black Bible and a White Bible. There was only one Christian gospel. Yet he was surely aware that his own son, Martin Jr., did not preach like his white seminary classmates. "Daddy" King failed to take into account the realities of culture. People hear the good news in their own mother tongue—their own idiom, images, and cultural communication style. It is for this reason that seminary curricula, as well as entries in this encyclopedia, recognize the distinctiveness of African-American preaching.

Yet there is no monolithic preaching style among African Americans. A number of subgroups share the African heritage in varying degrees and are influenced by Anglo culture as well. The preaching preferred among the African-American masses has far more African influence than the preaching preferred among the middle-class minority (*see* Homiletics and Preaching in Africa). Given this fact, this article will deal primarily with the pulpit tradition of the African-American majority, or the masses.

What then are the chief characteristics of preaching in traditional African-American Baptist, Methodist, Pentecostal, and other churches? What is uniquely "black" about this preaching? There is no simple answer, since there is no African-American preaching style that is not closely paralleled in white church pulpits somewhere: Pentecostal, rural Southern Baptist, Appalachian, or otherwise. The main difference is that the more typical elements of mainline African-American preaching have been largely excluded from "mainline" Euro-American pulpit expression.

First among black preaching characteristics is intonation, or "whooping," commonly considered the most stereotypical element of black preaching. Actually, whooping, or "toning," is far from universal, even among the urban masses. While many African-American preachers with professional training claim some competence in toning, the majority of their sermons do not include this form of sermonic celebration. Even among African-American pastors with less training, whooping appears to be on the decline (*see* Folk Preaching [African-American]).

Although there are no statistical studies on the issue, the choice to whoop or not is likely to be made on the basis of the cultural expectations of the congregation and on the cultural formation of the preacher. Apart from the rural South and urban congregations of transplanted southerners, whooping is not required in most churches, and it will not be tolerated in some. There is a general consensus among thoughtful pastors, with and without formal training, that intonation or black-style chanting should be employed only where it is welcome and only by those who can do it with sincerity and cultural integrity. This communal code also requires that traditional chanting carry a vivid biblical message.

In fact, a second and universal characteristic of African-American preaching is not whooping, but spontaneity—the ability to respond to the movement of the Spirit among preacher and congregation and to express deep feeling without shame. Even when the preaching is done from manuscript, traditional freedom of expression prevails. The pattern includes not only the preacher's spontaneity of utterance but also that of the audience. The dynamics of the preaching event include dialogic interaction with the congregation. Quietness among the hearers means one of three things: the sermon is dull and uninspired; the membership is removed from the tradition of the masses; or there is an undercurrent of strife, blocking the presence of the Spirit.

A third characteristic of African-American preaching is its basic structure: imaginative, narrative, and prone to generate experiential encounter. This is in opposition to the Euro-American tradition of cognitive, essay-type sermons, designed to inform and convince by means of logic or reason. In white tradition, the implicit goal has been more intellectual assent than impact on life, even though, in the providence of God, the results may not have been limited to assent. A contemporary trend among academically prominent homileticians moves toward the *experience* of the Word, and in recent years this has brought greatly increased fruitfulness to the dialogue between African-American and Euro-American scholars.

This movement on the part of both traditions should not be mistaken for compromise or downgrading of spiritual goals. The ultimate goal of growth toward the new person in Christ is better fostered among *all* ethnic groups by the biblically well-informed but primarily experiential sermon. The data of faith are encountered holistically: cognitively, intuitively, *and* emotionally. Truth is holistically stored in personal ownership rather than in cold, short intellectual recall. Truth is brought to bear on behavior. The Synoptics report that Jesus himself always taught or preached holistically, in parables.*

This holistic approach includes high emotion, but not emotional*ism*. Faith, hope, and love are primarily intuitive and emotive. Any preacher of any culture ought to address these critically important sectors of human personality. Because of its attention to the *whole* person, African-American preaching has survived amazingly well amid the onslaughts of elitist criticism. The holistic approach also explains why this preaching tradition has served to empower an oppressed people.

Cultural Roots. The cultural roots of the African-American preaching tradition have been widely unknown or ignored until recently. Scholars typically assumed that missionaries taught the Christian faith to Africans in the bonds of slavery, and, with it, a style of preaching. This is grossly in error.

In the first place, Africans brought much of their culture with them. The slavemasters outlawed African drumming (including a sophisticated system of signals), African medicine, and African gatherings for worship. All these prohibitions clearly indicate strong retention of African culture. Otherwise, why outlaw them?

These forbidden externals of culture had deeper counterparts in belief systems and worldview. African traditional religion held that God is omnipotent ("Olodumare" of the Yoruba) and omniscient ("Brekyirihunuade" of the Ashan-ti). Couched in "praise names" such as these, traditional religion declared that the High God of a bureaucratic monotheism is also just and, above all, provident. There are hundreds of traditional proverbs about the justice of God that parallel

Pauline expressions (Gal. 6:7). In effect, African traditional religion paved the way for Christian faith among the slaves.

The notion that Africans were "pagan" animists, worshiping wood and stone, is erroneous. It would be like suggesting that the stations of the cross in a Roman Catholic sanctuary provide graven images for worship. The shrines of African subdeities were holy places for encounter with the divine spirits. The Africans in America continued the tradition with special "praying grounds" where they went to commune with God.

Another misconception concerns the influence of missionaries on the faith of African-American Christians. While there would have been no slave Christians without some form of exposure to white faith, the "Invisible Institution" (underground church) of the South practiced its own African adaptation of that faith—both authentically Christian and unashamedly African American. Slave Christians virtually stole the Bible and the power to read or memorize it. They had their own interpretations to offset their masters' misreadings of the biblical injunction for servants to obey their masters (Eph. 6:5). Many churches of the black masses today have their roots in this underground church and its preaching tradition.

While traditional cultic observances had no sermons as such, African culture was and is permeated with a love of oratory and meaningful narrative in which the whole community takes part. *Aesop's Fables* (by an African slave in Greece) and *The Tales of Uncle Remus* (by an African slave in the U.S.A.) are well-known examples of African folktales used to teach children and promulgate traditional belief. Rich in symbolic meaning and performed with powerful imagination, these cultural resources were awaiting use by the new faith to which Africans were exposed.

The other providential element in the African-American preaching equation is the two Great Awakenings, so important to the religious history of all Americans.

Prior to the arrival of Whitefield* in 1739, Africans in bondage had responded perfunctorily or not at all to the Anglican liturgy of the slaveocracy in Virginia and other southern states. (The response in the North prior to the First Great Awakening had been no better.) Whatever the agenda of the clandestine and unrecorded slave gatherings of the first hundred years, it was mostly prayer and praise from Africa, mixed with English language and increasing bits of Christianity. Then came Whitefield and a whole new approach to the word.

The record here is plenteous: Whitefield employed a great, sonorous voice, reaching outdoor crowds of thousands. He had no inhibitions about passionate proclamation, and his hearers responded with deep emotion. Whitefield's tonality and emotionally powerful expression were especially appealing to Africans, whose native languages were by definition tonal and whose utterance was emotionally unfettered. A seafaring ex-slave from Africa, Gustavus Vassa, reported attending a crowded Philadelphia church around 1765. He was greatly impressed by Whitefield's fervor (Vassa, 99). Herein is the first recorded clue to the rapid development of black preaching.

Whitefield's influence was widespread and can be traced directly to what is usually thought of as the first African-American Baptist Church. Shubal Stearns and his brother-in-law, Daniel Marshall, former Congregationalists who were converted on Whitefield's second visit to New England, soon became Baptists and engaged in missionary work in Virginia, North Carolina, and Georgia. It was out of their work that the African-American Baptist Church at Silver Bluff, Aiken, South Carolina, was established.

Stearns and Marshall were noted for their energetic, emotional appeals. Extending the Whitefield influence, their tumultuous revivalistic preaching was characterized by a "holy whine." This fervor and tonality were most appealing to African slaves, as they validated the kind of preaching of which they were culturally capable and for which their souls longed. They were not taught *how* or *what* to preach, as many have alleged, but they were convinced by the Whitefield model that their natural gifts for preaching were wholly acceptable to God.

The Development of a Powerful Tradition. No detailed descriptions exist of exactly how black preaching evolved or how long it took to happen. There are only early records of African-American preachers who grew in power as they heard or read the Bible, as they heard the preaching of whites, and as they preached and gained experience for themselves. A few sketches of early preachers will illustrate the process:

Related to the Baptist Church at Kiokee was another Baptist Church at Buckhead Creek, Georgia. Soon after the church's founding, its fervor reached George Liele, a slave who was converted in 1772. Hardly a year later he had led worship on nearby plantations so well that he was ordained to preach to slaves on plantations along the Savannah River. Liele was influential in the founding of the African Church at Silver Bluff, which some date as early as 1773, and the First African Baptist Church of Savannah, whence he fled with the British to keep his release from slavery. In 1783, he went to Jamaica, also with the British, and inaugurated the strong Baptist work there.

There is a bit more detail available for tracing the development of Richard Allen* (1760–1831), founder of the African Methodist Episcopal Church. Converted at age seventeen, Allen experienced a call to preach and was licensed in 1782 at Dover, Delaware. After several years of itineration in which he did menial labor and preached, largely among whites, he settled in Philadelphia. When he and his friends were segregated in the St. George's Methodist Church, which they had sacrificed to help build, he withdrew. When the white supply pastors assigned to his black fledgling church proved unsatisfactory, he was elected pastor, later being elected bishop of this new denomination in 1816. There is no record of even an informal tutorship under some clerics, yet Allen became a powerful preacher and leader.

Exactly when a slave named Harry Hoosier, better known as "Black Harry" (1750–1810), started driving the carriage for Bishop Asbury is not known. But by 1782, Asbury was known to ask for Hoosier's services because the crowds were always larger when it was known that Hoosier was to preach afterward. Thomas Coke and others also employed him the same way, and Dr. Benjamin Rush, a signer of the Declaration of Independence, rated Hoosier the greatest orator in America. An impressive variety of leaders of that era, as well as many scholars since, have marveled at the matchless skill of a man whose power as a preacher far exceeded that of any of those from whose preaching he supposedly learned.

One sentence may explain these three new preachers and many others. Referring to Henry Evans, a black shoemaker who settled in Fayetteville, North Carolina, Woodson says, "His preaching became so effective, however, and so many white persons attended his meetings, that the official opposition yielded sufficiently to have a regular Methodist Church organized there in 1790" (Woodson, 48). The key word in the sentence is "became." Without anyone to tutor him, Evans grew in his preaching gifts. He was so revered that even though a white man was later made official pastor in charge, he lived and preached in that church until he died.

The tradition of self-taught preaching geniuses continued through the end of the nineteenth century and into the twentieth, with rare examples found as late as the 1990s. Two such preachers were John Jasper* (1812–1901) and Charles Albert Tindley (1851–1933). Jasper, an ex-slave hod carrier and Richmond tobacco factory worker, received absolutely no formal training. A barely literate friend helped him learn to read the Bible. But in later years, learned clergy, white and black, flocked to hear his powerful depictions of his Jesus, heaven, and the scenes of the Old Testament, as well as the New.

Tindley's training began with his own self-taught ability to read. His efforts never ceased, and though he was never able to enroll in a college or seminary, he learned from tutors, institutes, and correspondence enough to become proficient even in Hebrew and Greek. His powerful preaching made him the most sought-after preacher in Philadelphia, and he was soon in demand in wider circles. His most permanent imprint, however, arises from his being the pioneer writer of gospel hymns, many of which are still highly regarded and widely used.

A contemporary of these two, also lacking formal training, was C. T. Walker (1858–1921), early graduate of Atlanta Baptist College (now Morehouse). His education was no hindrance to his African-American preaching gifts, and he, like Tindley and Jasper, drew huge audiences and built a great congregation, Tabernacle Baptist Church, in Augusta, Georgia. His hearers were known to include President William Howard Taft and John D. Rockefeller, who wintered and golfed nearby.

These preachers illustrate the power of the maturing black homiletic to transcend ethnic and cultural barriers. And it is noteworthy that the one least educated and most supposedly primitive, Jasper, was also the most popular of all across racial lines. Learned whites came to criticize but stayed to cry and worship as they had never worshiped before. These preachers were the best of their day, but their gifts were common to hundreds, if not thousands, of others.

Although men like C. T. Walker added oratorical eloquence to the traditional picture-painting of the black tradition, they never succumbed to the temptation to depend on language as impressive abstraction. Words had concrete reference, and the concrete, like Jesus' parables, had symbolic significance. Ideas were important, of course, but those ideas wore the garb of familiar persons and things.

Theological and Congregational Context. The brilliance of African-American preaching can hardly be ascribed to the preacher alone. It takes place in a congregational setting in which beliefs are held in common. The worshipers enjoy the expectation of unfettered participation, both audible and inaudible. The beliefs held in common derive from the treasury of the Bible. The worshipers' response compounds gratitude for fresh insight into the Bible and antiphonal testimony to the truth and power of the preached word in their own lives. The orientation to the word as power has been nurtured by African traditional religion. The Bible provided the English counterpart to the corpus of holy wisdom that African Americans had lost in the coerced transition from indigenous African tongues. This love of the word was (and is) integral to both preaching and hearing in the African-American pulpit tradition.

The black preacher, then, is more a broker of spiritual power than a teacher. The sermon meets a desperate existential need: the response is laden with gratitude, as well as admiration, for the preacher and his or her gifts.

Indeed, the talents of the preacher must take a very low profile, because the power involved is not the preacher's power; it is God's Holy Spirit.* Thus, when an orthodox white Protestant refers to worship as including the proper proclamation of the word and the proper administration of the sacraments, the issue of propriety cuts across the African-American tradition. Since the talents of many are measured by the criteria of propriety, professional education in prestigious white institutions of higher education has long misfitted blacks for preaching to the masses. It was not until the civil rights movement of the 1960s and beyond that theological training began to recognize the validity of African-American tradition, and so began to prepare ministers for competence in their own culture without insisting on the criteria of propriety and control.

This is not to suggest that black worship is chaos, however. The Holy Spirit is not the author of confusion, and there are ways to understand this both biblically (1 Cor. 14:33) and phenomenologically. In African tradition, where possession by spirits constitutes the ultimate worship, there are unconscious parameters beyond which no person possessed may properly go. These cultural expectations or limits are no less operative in African-American Christian worship. But the propriety and control are in the hands of *God*, who uses unconscious cultural expectations to maintain both a semblance of order and a deep freedom of the Spirit for preacher and hearer.

The Social Relevance of Black Preachers and Preaching. This black pulpit's emphasis on the power of the Spirit may, at first sight, appear to suggest an otherworldly church, fed on a pie-in-the-sky gospel, but the very opposite is true. The Spirit is always ecstasy, but in the best of the tradition, it is always empowerment as well. Thus, however low the level of activism in the majority of the African-American churches of the masses, it is always true that the major advances made in the United States in civil rights were made largely on the initiative of the black churches.

The leadership of Martin Luther King Jr.* in the great civil rights movement of the 1960s was predicated on the power of the gospel and deeply spiritual mass meetings to motivate the people to take unimaginable risks. The church's involvement was not a new phenomenon in the history of the African-American church. Before the Civil War, the leading black Abolitionist orators were nearly all preachers. They included Henry Highland Garnet,* Samuel Ringgold Ward, J.W.C. Pennington, J. W. Loguen, and even Frederick Douglass, who was licensed to preach by the A.M.E. Zion Church early in his career as a freedman. In addition to these notables were thousands more whose faith demanded freedom and whose gospel was nourishment to all the oppressed slaves who craved to breathe free.

Richard Allen, first bishop of the A.M.E.'s, helped with the Underground Railroad and, with the Quakers, organized a boycott of vegetables raised by slave labor. Morris Brown, second bishop of the A.M.E.'s, was pastor of the church in Charleston, South Carolina, most of whose lay officers were hanged for complicity in the Denmark Vesey revolt of 1822. Baptist preacher Nat Turner organized a bloody insurrection in 1831. Every rebellion was in some way related to preachers and churches.

During Reconstruction, schools and colleges were organized and supported by enterprising preachers and their congregations. Preachers held political offices ranging from city councils to the United States Congress. In the constitutional conventions held for the purpose of re-admitting southern states to the Union, black preachers wrote into the law the first public schools of the South, the first voting rights for persons not owning real property, and improved inheritance rights for women; they also sponsored public welfare legislation. Reconstruction was the golden era of social relevance for black preachers. It ended in unspeakable violence after the federal troops of occupation were withdrawn as a political compromise between Northern Republicans and Southern Democrats.

The emphasis on heaven, for which black preachers have been stereotyped for over a century, was at first a positive reponse to the need for hope in an otherwise closed society. In the face of lynchings and the loss of rights, the only viable option to suicide or insanity for the African-American Christian was the certitude of life and justice after death. To survive, much less to stand, in such a society on earth requires the radical hope of heaven. The preaching of Jasper, Tindley, and Walker was carried out under hateful conditions. Such preachers sustained hope until the aftermath of World War II, when the direct militance of the Reconstruction Era resurfaced in the modern civil rights movement.

African-American Preaching and the

Wider World. The African-American homiletical characteristics of spontaneity and experiential encounter are not unique in Christianity. Their relation to white pulpit style has occurred largely outside the mainline denominations. Now, even the mainline pulpit no longer views the sermon as a cognitive idea. The gospel must be encountered holistically. The new emphasis is falling on the emotive and intuitive sectors of consciousness.

The homiletic technique of white Protestantism is moving toward a commonality with the best of the African-American pulpit tradition. Meanwhile, the very discipline required of blacks to articulate their long-loved but seldom analyzed tradition has begun to bear fruit. The dialogue between preachers and scholars in black and white homiletics has made it necessary for blacks to forsake their almost exclusively intuitive tradition of preaching and to entertain other options.

One concrete result of the growing analysis of the African-American preaching tradition has been the increase in cross-cultural discussions. Also, blacks are now eagerly sought to fill faculty vacancies in homiletics in predominantly white seminaries. The day may not be far away when the shared strengths of two major cultures in the preaching of the gospel will so shape worship as to make ethnic inclusivity a common thing, and the church of Jesus Christ a reliable foretaste of the praise services in heaven, where in the presence of God may be found every kindred and people and tongue (Rev. 7:9).

Allen, R., *The Life Experience and Gospel Labors of the Rt. Rev. Richard Allen*, 1960. Day, R. E., *Rhapsody in Black: The Life Story of John Jasper*, 1953. McClain, W. B., *Black People in the Methodist Church*, 1984. Mitchell, H. H., *Black Preaching: The Recovery of a Powerful Art*, 1991. Vassa, G. "The Life of Olaudah Equiano, or Gustavus Vassa, the African," *Great Slave Narratives*, Arna Bontemps, ed., 1969. Washington, J. M., *Frustrated Fellowship: The Black Baptist Quest for*

Social Power, 1986. **Woodson, C. G.,** *History of the Negro Church,* 1972.

HENRY H. MITCHELL

Alan of Lille.

(ca. 1128–1202) Alan first appears as a student in northern France in the schools of Paris and Chartres, probably in the decades of the late 1130s and 1140s when Peter Abelard, Thierry of Chartres, and Gilbert of Poitiers were teaching there. He seems to have stayed on to become a lecturer himself. Alan was not an original thinker or a great stylist, but he was a highly competent eclectic preacher of considerable mental energy.

His writings cover the half century when the medieval universities were coming into being and scholars were working in a fever of intellectual excitement. He wrote systematic theology; a handbook for priests to use in the confessional; one of the first medieval concordances to the Bible in the form of a dictionary of theological terms given in their contexts; scriptural and liturgical commentaries; a treatise on angels; the *Regulae Theologicae* in which he tried to demonstrate the self-evident truth of all Christian doctrine; an epic poem, the *Anticlaudianus,* in which he tells an allegorical story of the world's redemption and the war between good and evil; as well as many sermons and a manual called *The Art of Preaching.*

This *Ars Praedicandi* was a pioneering work. The formal teaching of preaching as a consciously rhetorical art was not to become established in the universities until about 1230. Alan's own experience of the preacher's task is likely to have been limited to the delivery of "university sermons" to academics. Perhaps rather late in his life he may have assisted the work of the Cistercians, as they won converts to the monastic life and tried to tackle the problem of the Albigensian dualist heretics in the south of France. He wrote a treatise, *Against Heretics,* in which he classifies the points an apologist will need to cover to convince Cathars (the anticler-ical Waldensian dissidents in the region of Lyons), Jews, and Moslems.

The *Art of Preaching* begins with a chapter of general practical advice on such points as delivery and the handling of an audience. (Alan advises the preacher who notices tears to stop, "for nothing dries up faster than a tear.") The remainder of the treatise includes a series of schemata, sets of condensed material (quotations, citations, examples) suitable for use in composing a sermon on a given topic, typically one of the virtues or vices. He also designed series for different kinds of audiences (widows, virgins, princes). Thus he provides a handbook from which sermons can be constructed for the seasons of the liturgical year, or for any occasion, on the basis of these topoi or "commonplaces."

His surviving sermons are all in Latin, and for the most part they are academic in character. Usually, but not always, he takes a scriptural text. Alan next seeks to win the interest and attention of the audience in a way that consciously parallels the *captatio benevolentiae* of a classical orator's speech. Next he "divides" the subject in the standard late medieval way. That is, he lists usually three senses or aspects of the key words or themes, and then develops their implications, using many of the classical rhetorician's skills in amplifying and illustrating to argue a case by persuasion. Here Alan was utilizing devices drawn from what was still a very meager stock of classical rhetorical textbooks available to contemporary scholars, chiefly Cicero's *De Inventione* and the *Rhetorica ad Herennium.* He was also adding a third to two recently contrived medieval rhetorical arts, that of letter-writing (from the late eleventh century) and that of poetry (from the twelfth), for which there were already handbooks of practical instruction. He makes free use of aids and illustrations from classical Latin literature, in which he was very well read by comparison with contemporaries, in order to enliven what he has to say and also, no doubt, to win the intellectual respect of an academic audience. But there are stories and images from contemporary life as well. In a sermon for Palm Sunday he describes how certain members of the angelic army, rebelling against their king and ceasing to be loyal to their prince, wanted to rob the lordship of his castle and rule it themselves. His imagery of castle and moat, wall and tower and rampart, brings alive the story of the fall of the angels.

Above all, Alan loved scripture and the intellectual excitement of discovering fresh ways to use scriptural comparisons and illustrations (*see* History of Preaching; Rhetoric).

Alan of Lille, *The Art of Preaching,* trans. G. R. Evans, Cistercian Studies Series, 23, 1981. **D'Alverny, M. T.,** *Textes inédits d'Alain de Lille* 1965. **de Late, R.,** *Alain de Lille, poète du XIIe siècle,* 1951. **Evans, G. R.,** *Alan of Lille: The Frontiers of Theology in the Later Twelfth Century,* 1983.

GILLIAN R. EVANS

Allen, Richard. (1760–1831) Born a slave in Philadelphia to a Quaker lawyer, Benjamin Chew, it was during his years in the Chew household that Richard Allen learned to read and write, something denied most slaves. Richard and his family were later sold to a Mr. Stockeley, living near Dover, Delaware. During this time his mother and three siblings were sold off, leaving Richard and his brother to serve Master Stockeley. Though his years in the Stockeley household were comparatively humane for slave conditions, Richard hated slavery no matter what the conditions and considered it a life goal to see his race freed.

Richard was converted to Christianity under the preaching of Freeborn Garrettson, and in 1777, he joined the Methodist Society. It was this same Freeborn Garrettson whom Allen invited to preach to Stockeley and his household. By having Garrettson preach on the sin of slavery, Allen hoped to secure his freedom. This wish was granted when Stockeley, with repentant and converted heart,

agreed to allow Allen and his brother to buy their freedom. This early event foreshadowed the direction of Allen's life and ministry. Allen was committed to his displaced and oppressed African comrades, as well as to the Christian gospel as it was preached by the Methodist Church. This dual love for Africans in (and out of) bondage and for the church gave content to his life and shaped his preaching.

The contribution of Richard Allen to the field of homiletics, the preaching task, and the church, while not directly accountable to his preaching, is immense. Allen's singular contribution is his redefining of Methodism to address the needs of Africans in the new world of America. Though there were a few ministers of African descent before him, and some his contemporaries, Richard Allen was one of the first African-American models of an effective preacher in a situation of social *and* ecclesial oppression. This contribution can be seen in two areas: (1) his pioneering work in black evangelistic preaching and (2) his ground-breaking work in developing a church and responding to the social needs of African Americans.

Richard Allen was one of the first black evangelists. Allen entered the Methodist Church at the very beginning of its great American legacy of the traveling itinerant preachers. His entrance into the Methodist Church and its ministry stemmed from his early attendance at Methodist meetings. Here he enjoyed the worship, the sense of community among black and white alike, and the simple but powerful preaching of these services. Having bought his freedom from his slave master, Allen desired to become an itinerant preacher for the Methodist Church.

A black itinerant preacher, traveling alone, was almost unheard of. Though preachers themselves, black itinerants normally traveled as "servants" for white preachers. Allen was unique not only in his solo travels but also in his willingness to preach to all who would listen, black and white. Allen understood himself to be a plain, straightforward preacher, relaying the gospel story in simple terms. This modest appraisal of his preaching was not shared by those who heard Allen. In him they found an elegantly simple and deeply moving preacher who had a gift for speaking with great clarity, a clarity appreciated by all. In his preaching and writing, he not only passionately argued for the integrity of the black family and church but he also effectively enlisted the God of the Bible in the struggle. In his inistence that "God himself was the first pleader of the cause of slaves," he established a theological argument that abolitionists and civil rights preachers would repeat for the next two centuries.

Allen soon found a home in the bustling city of Philadelphia. Here he was to move from the traveling preacher to the street-preaching pastor who cared for the downtrodden. Here he would also distinguish himself as the founder of two organizations that would become hallmark institutions for African life in America.

In Philadelphia, Allen, along with other African Americans, was instrumental in renovating the old St. George Methodist Church, the largest Methodist Church in Philadelphia. Yet in 1787, Allen, along with many others, walked out of St. George never to return, having been disrespected and ill-treated a final time by the white congregants, who found the presence of blacks in this church distasteful and annoying. This exodus, however, was the catalyst for Allen in forming first the Free African Society and later the African Methodist Episcopal Church. The Free African Society was formed as an advocacy and improvement agency for black people. This society held members and monitored the situation of oppressed African Americans, serving as a caring canopy over and against the violence and paternalism of white society. Though Christian in character, Allen sought unsuccessfully to keep the Free African Society from becoming a kind of church, because he wanted to reach the masses of black people at the bottom of society, many of whom were not affiliated with any church. This social responsibility

that Allen felt was shaped by his desire to speak a word to all black people in this perilous time.

Allen's forming of the Free African Society was not contrary to his commitment to the gospel, but rather an extension of that commitment. Allen felt from the very beginning that Methodism offered the best religious expression for black people because of its clear and simple message, its radical egalitarianism, and its lack of emphasis on a literate and educated congregation. His commitment to the Methodist Church led him to the development of a church for Africans in this new world. Bethel African Methodist Episcopal Church, dedicated by Francis Asbury and named by John Dickins, underwent much persecution and many attempted takeovers by white leadership in the Methodist Church. Under Allen's leadership and nurturing preaching, however, Bethel survived and thrived. Allen's work in Philadelphia at Bethel did not go unnoticed. Black Methodists in many quarters shared Bethel's experience of oppression. Thus with Allen at the head they sought to consolidate into a united African Methodist Church. Eventually, Allen was to become the first bishop of this church and its defining leader. Allen's preaching served as a source of great nurture and direction for this fragile denomination. Allen became one of the first examples of black pastoral leadership that existed as an unrelenting advocate of suffering black people (*see* African-American Preaching).

Allen, R., *The Life Experience and Gospel Labors of the Rt. Rev. Richard Allen*, 1833, 1960. **George, C.V.R.,** *Segregated Sabbaths: Richard Allen and the Emergence of Independent Black Churches, 1760–1840*, 1973. **Mathews, M.,** *Richard Allen*, 1963. **Richardson, H. V.,** *Dark Salvation: The Story of Methodism as It Developed Among Blacks in America*, 1976.   WILLIE J. JENNINGS

Anti-Jewish Preaching.   After Auschwitz, Christian preachers are compelled to consider the ways in which our preaching, in sometimes subtle but nevertheless tragic ways, fosters contempt for God's people, the Jews. The roots of anti-Jewish preaching lie within the New Testament itself, or rather in our misinterpretations of the New Testament. Even the designations "New Testament" and "Old Testament" imply that one has superseded or negated the other, as if God has now superseded Israel and nullified the covenant with Israel by a new covenant with the church.

In many places within the Christian scripture, we overhear a painful, fierce family debate within Israel about the significance of Jesus. In some instances, we are overhearing a minority movement within Israel (the church) arguing with the religious majority (the synagogue) over who is truly faithful to Torah. It is an interpretive perversion for contemporary Christians, in our majority position, with two thousand years of Christian persecution of the Jews in our past, to align ourselves with New Testament critics of "the Jews" as if the New Testament were taking a superior attitude to Jesus' own people. It is tragic for contemporary Christian preachers to interpret the numerous prophetic rebukes of Israel, all examples of the marvelous self-critical ability of Israel, as if these rebukes were addressed to "the Jews" and not to us.

Some Jews looked at Jesus and saw the Messiah; others did not. Jesus was rejected by a variety of critics, some of whom were Jews. For contemporary Christian preachers to blame all Jews throughout history for the actions of a few of Israel's leaders at the time of Jesus is a sad misreading of history. The Jews did not kill Jesus; crucifixion was a vicious form of Roman punishment. Jesus was one of the many Jews whom the Romans martyred. For later generations of Christian preachers to implicate all Jews throughout history in the death of Jesus, as well as for the church to turn on and persecute Jesus' own people, is an act of Christian apostasy and sin against the people who taught the world to look for the Messiah and gave us God's word to show us the way.

Few Christian preachers would intentionally preach in a way that would hurt the Jews. However, there are many ways in which we are guilty of presenting Judaism in a false light: (1) Preachers will sometimes caricature the Hebrew scriptures, saying that "The Old Testament was full of judgment and wrath; the New Testament is full of love and grace." The God depicted in the Old Testament is the same God rendered by the Christian scriptures. The Hebrew scriptures were the only scriptures Jesus or Paul knew. There is good news in the Hebrew scriptures, just as there is judgment in Christian Gospels. (2) Judaism is sometimes falsely depicted as cold, dead, and legalistic. Jesus' criticism of some pharisees of his day is interpreted as blanket condemnation of all Jews in every age. The gospel is said to have entered a religious and moral vacuum or to have inflamed an otherwise dead religion. These are unfair depictions of Judaism in Jesus' day and in ours. (3) The myth that "the Jews killed Jesus" is perpetuated when contemporary Christian preachers uncritically apply biblical passages about "the Jews" to present situations. Rather than say "the Jews" plotted against Jesus, it is more accurate to say "some of the authorities plotted against Jesus." Rather than say "a group of Jews rioted against Paul's preaching," it is better to say "Paul faced opposition from some of his fellow Jews at this synagogue."

Even though recent biblical scholarship has uncovered the true "Jewishness" of the rabbi named Jesus, the Jew of Tarsus named Paul, and indeed the close dependency of the Christian scriptures to the faith of Israel, Christians do have major theological differences with the Jews. Those differences do not lie in our superior moral or spiritual relation to the Jews, but rather in our differences concerning Jesus. Yet after Auschwitz, after the bitter fruits of centuries of Christian anti-Jewish rhetoric, Christian complicity in the persecution of Jews, and the relative silence of Christians during the Holocaust, faithful, biblical Christian preachers must examine the depictions and renderings of Jews and Israel in our preaching, must ask the God of Israel and Jesus to purify us of our anti-Jewish past, and enable us so to proclaim the gospel in our day that our brothers and sisters in Israel see in us a better reflection of the faith of Jesus, the Jew from Nazareth.

Ruether, R., *Faith and Fratricide: The Theological Roots of Anti-Semitism*, 1974. **Williamson, C. M.**, *Has God Rejected His People?—Anti-Judaism in the Christian Church*, 1982. **Williamson, C. M.**, and **R. J. Allen,** *Interpreting Difficult Texts: Anti-Judaism and Christian Preaching*, 1989.

WILLIAM H. WILLIMON

Anxiety in the Pulpit.

Pulpit anxiety manifests itself in unpleasant feelings of generalized apprehension in response to the preaching task. The word *anxiety* is derived from a Greek root meaning "to press tight" or "to strangle," and the symptoms of anxiety reflect this root meaning in some ways.

Muscles become tense; breathing accelerates; the heart beats more rapidly; there may be sweating or shakiness and an acute sensitivity to the environment. In more extreme situations there may even be gastrointestinal upset, diarrhea, weakness, or faintness. Preachers are often victims of this kind of anxiety.

Fear of speaking or performing publicly is a common anxiety, and it is related to fear of making a mistake in front of others, or of looking foolish or uncertain. It is akin to the "stage fright" often described by performers in other arenas. Some anxiety is natural, of course, and may even make the delivery more effective.

Therefore, anxiety in the pulpit is something of a paradox. Because the presence of some anxiety causes adrenaline to be pumped into the body's systems, one becomes more alert and motivated. When the pressure becomes extreme, however, the effects may be so disconcerting as to interfere with viable delivery.

As the anxiety mounts, the individual may become so involved with overcoming it that energy is depleted and concentration suffers. Under these circumstances the tension present must be reduced in order to think clearly and creatively.

There are ways in which this tension can be addressed and reduced. (1) Before beginning the preparation of a sermon, entrust the content and the delivery to God, asking that God use the sermon to proclaim the truth and that God use the preacher as the vehicle, the instrument, for the delivery of that truth. This relinquishing of absolute responsibility tends to reduce tension at the outset. (2) Thorough preparation of the sermon is the second step in reducing tension. Decide the style of delivery* that suits best. If the fear of delivery stems from concern that some important part of the sermon will be forgotten or delivered out of order, prepare a manuscript with the essential topic sentences underlined or highlighted, and place it on the pulpit for reference. If reading from a manuscript is disconcerting to the congregation, prepare a simple outline on cards that can be flipped unobtrusively but will still keep the preacher on task (*see* Manuscript Preaching). (3) Just prior to the beginning of a service, set aside five minutes of time alone where no interruptions can occur. This time is very important for "fine-tuning the instrument." The essential ingredient is intentional relaxation. Begin by assuming a position that is comfortable, and allow hands to rest in the lap and feet on the floor. Begin with the feet, then legs, then arms, then hands, trunk, neck, face, and finally, shoulders, intentionally tensing each set and consciously relaxing the muscles. Continue until total relaxation has been achieved. (4) Allow breathing to become regular and obvious. Concentrate on the in and out flow of breath until it seems natural. Then, with eyes closed, imagine a blank screen. (5) Then place yourself on that screen, rehearsing mentally each step leading up to the beginning of the delivery. The essential imagining here, however, is visualization of a situation in which you are relaxed, competent and inspired. (6) Offer a prayer of thanks for what God is about to do in this service and through the sermon. (7) Then take three deep and rhythmic breaths, open the eyes, and sit still for about thirty seconds.

Once the sermon is under way, if anxiety has returned, repeat the tensing and relaxing of the shoulders intentionally one time. Do this as often as necessary during the delivery if the problem persists. Practice is essential. The more the process is experienced, the more automatic the assumption of a state of relaxed delivery. Other aids that reduce anxiety in the pulpit include locating several very supportive members of the congregation to whom to direct eye contact. Choose different focal points in the room and imagine that you are engaging in a friendly but serious conversation with each one. Remember that these people want what the preacher wants—for the congregation to hear the Word of God preached.

A visual reminder that God is preaching through the preacher can also help. This can be a card with an injunction such as "Remember that you are an instrument."

Finally, a thank-you to God for what God has done through the sermon is not only appropriate but essential.

Doctor, R. M., and A. P. Kahn, *The Encyclopedia of Phobias, Fears, and Anxieties*, 1989.
PATTY ANN T. EARLE

Apocalyptic.

The literature of the Bible designated by the term *apocalyptic* (Greek: *apokalypsis* = revelation) is a subspecies of an earlier literary genus, prophetic eschatology. All eschatological literature deals with the *eschaton*, the End or Last Day. From Amos onward, the prophets of Israel offered their hearers an unvarying three-part scenario for the future: There will be an *onset* of escalating evil coupled with the announcement of judgment (Amos 5:10–17); this will be followed by the terrifying *Day of the Lord* itself (Amos 5:18–20); finally, a *new age* of peace and prosperity will come into being (Amos 9:11–15). The picture is idealized, yet it can be called realistic, for the promise is that real wolves will live with real lambs here on earth (Isa. 11:1–9) and real children will be born in the new Jerusalem (Isa. 65:17–25).

In its three-part structure, the scenario for the future that apocalyptic literature offers does not differ from that of other eschatological texts, but it has been highly amplified and energized with "mythic" themes. In literature, the term "myth" properly refers to stories about the work of the gods in their own realm at the beginning of time; as such, it is a vital component of creation theology. Four mythic themes drawn from the creation tradition of the ancient Near East are distinguishable in biblical apocalyptic: (1) God engages spiritual enemies in a great cosmic struggle; (2) a world catastrophe ensues; (3) beyond the catastrophe, a new heaven and a new earth replace the ones that have been destroyed; and (4) in that new Eden or new Jerusalem, a new Adam becomes king. As these themes attached themselves to the older prophetic motif of the Day of the Lord, apocalyptic acquired much of its cosmic dimension.

Apocalyptic Texts of the Bible. Based on this distinction between "realistic" or prophetic eschatology and the later, more elaborated form, the following biblical materials can be considered the canon of biblical apocalyptic literature. As one moves down the list, one finds that the genre becomes more and more fully developed.

Isaiah 24—27 (ca. 500 B.C.E.)
Zechariah 9—14 (ca. 550–420 B.C.E.)
Joel 2:28–3:21 (ca. 400 B.C.E.)
Daniel 7—12 (164 B.C.E.)
Various passages in the epistles, including 1 Cor. 15:20–28; 2 Thessalonians 1—2; 2 Peter 3 (ca. 54–90 C.E.)

The "Little Apocalypses" of the synoptic Gospels, namely, Matthew 24—25; Mark 13; and Luke 21:5–36 (after 70 C.E.)

Revelation (ca. 100 C.E.)

In addition to these canonical apocalyptic materials, the deuterocanonical works 4 Ezra (2 Esdras 3—14) and Baruch must be considered important bridges in the development between Jewish and Christian apocalyptic. Many other extracanonical Jewish and Christian apocalypses, including sectarian documents among the Dead Sea Scrolls, also belong to this literary history.

Social Setting and Authorship of Biblical Apocalyptic Texts. Who guided the older tradition of prophetic eschatology toward the elaborated, mythologized genre of apocalyptic? It has long been commonplace to link the appearance of apocalyptic fervor to periods of poverty and persecution. In times of trouble, disenfranchised and dissident groups who found no likelihood of justice in this world turned to the hope that God would intervene to set things right. In recent years, books such as Paul Hanson's *The Dawn of Apocalyptic* have pushed the link between biblical apocalyptic literature and the protests of the oppressed back to the years following the restoration of the Judean community from exile in 538 B.C.E. Taking Zechariah 9—14 as his guide, Hanson believes he can trace an increasingly intense sense of apocalyptic fervor among what he calls "the visionaries," spiritual descendants of the Isaiah of the Exile (Isaiah 40—55), who opposed the elitist polity of the priestly establishment in Jerusalem. Their fervor matures around 420 B.C.E. in the short "apocalypse" of Zechariah 14, wherein hope for the reform of this world yields to a vision of its replacement by a fundamentally different one. Though the authors of these chapters of Zech. are never identified, they are probably the ideological predecessors of those whom, two and a half centuries later, the book of Daniel calls the "holy ones of the Most High" (7:22, 25, 27). This group or sect is held by

many to be identical with the pious Hasidim (the "Saints"), and in 1 Macc. 2:42 to have joined in the Maccabean revolt against their oppressor, the Greco-Syrian king of Antioch, Antiochus IV Epiphanes (175–163 B.C.E.), and eventually to have been massacred for their part in the matter (1 Macc. 7:13–17). It seems likely that among their spiritual descendants were the apocalyptically oriented Qumran community, the earliest Pharisees, and, at least affiliated with the latter, Jesus of Nazareth. In teachings such as the Parables of the Kingdom (Matt. 13:24–53) Jesus' warm expectation of the nearness of the kingdom of heaven matches the vivid immediacy of the "realistic" eschatology of the prophets; however, in the "Little Apocalypses" in the synoptic gospels, Jesus offers a truly apocalyptic vision of the coming (parousia) of the Son of Man in clouds of glory to judge the world at the Last Day.

The Message of Apocalyptic and Its Place in Preaching Today. Contemporary preachers who use apocalyptic materials may do so for several reasons. First, the lectionary* occasionally calls for readings from apocalyptic text, usually for a few Sundays at the end of the Pentecost season. Portions of the book of Revelation are to be read on Sundays eight to thirteen times over the three cycles, which means that worshipers *might* hear an exposition on a lection from the Apocalypse one Sunday out of fifteen or twenty.

Second, because of its deep confidence that the just and good God will not be mocked, biblical apocalyptic literature is sometimes offered as encouragement for those who are crushed under the weight of oppressors. The literature certainly functioned that way in the past, and it continues to do so in places like Latin America.* However, this approach misses the need of many Christians, particularly in western Europe and North America, to be confronted with the ineluctable call of apocalyptic to turn their own lives toward God's future even though they are not at the moment crushed and hopeless. The apocalyptic vision of God's triumph over spiritual evil here and throughout the cosmos is not simply a last-ditch "theology for hard times." It is also a literature for good times, though we who sit contentedly in our armchairs are at risk when we receive the message that God will not be mocked. That message may be our indictment!

Third, some interpreters search the apocalyptic texts for a timetable of the future, confident that with the keys to proper understanding of these cryptic writings, they can discern the "signs of the times" and prepare themselves for the Day of the Lord. Perhaps it is in revulsion against this way of reading apocalyptic literature that many other preachers have abandoned it altogether. Quite aware that timetables of end times, even those given in scripture (Dan. 7:23–27), inevitably fail, the latter groups content themselves with scripture's own so-called eschatological reservation: "It is not for you to know the times or periods that the Father has set down by his own authority" (Acts 1:7). No book written by human beings, not even a book of scripture, can give detailed descriptions of events that will occur centuries ahead, and to say that scripture can do so is to fail to take seriously the incarnate character of the word of God. Yet, to abandon biblical apocalyptic literature—this magnet that can draw us into the future with images that inspire courage and hope—is a mistake.

Fortunately, the value of the apocalyptic writings does not hinge upon their ability to function as a timetable. They have a message more important than simply a prophecy of dates and doom. This introduces a final reason for addressing this literature in preaching: the contemporary reproclamation of its faith. The slogan that would best sum up that faith needs two clauses: (1) "It is near, at the very gates" (Matt. 24:33). God's purpose will reach its consummation. Tyranny, injustice, and death in all their forms will, in God's time, be finally overcome; all faithful obedience, trust, and goodness will be vindicated. Christians see a pre-

view of that consummation in the ministry and resurrection of Jesus of Nazareth. Where Jesus went, the kingdom of heaven was visible already in lives given hope, health, purpose, and victory over death. (2) " . . . But the end is not yet" (Matt. 24:6). This second clause provides the basis for a responsible, world-affirming ethic appropriate for the long, dynamic interim in which we live between the first blush of the new age in Jesus and its full revealing (*apokalypsis*) at the culmination. We have work to do! The goal is not to build a New Jerusalem on earth, as the social gospel thought we could do and as Marxian eschatology claimed it could. Only God does that. God has given us a vision to be our guide. By offering foretastes of the life of this envisioned age, by overcoming sickness, hunger, and injustice here and now, we can make our world more like the world it will be when God completes the work of blessing in it.

Collins, J. J., *The Apocalyptic Imagination,* 1987. **Hanson, P. D.,** *The Dawn of Apocalyptic,* 1975; *Old Testament Apocalyptic,* 1987; and "Apocalypses and Apocalypticism," *The Anchor Bible Dictionary,* ed. D. N. Freedman et al., 1992, 1:279–92. **Koch, K.,** *The Rediscovery of Apocalyptic: Studies in Biblical Theology* 2:22, Naperville, Ill., 1972. **Towner, W. S.,** *Daniel.* Interpretation, 1984.

W. SIBLEY TOWNER

Arts and Preaching.

From its beginnings, Christian preaching has been practiced as an art, first in the Gospels themselves, especially in Jesus' parables, and subsequently in the development of homiletics, beginning with the rhetoric of Augustine.* Though the demands of exegetical and theological inquiry essential to preaching have at times obscured its artfulness, preachers standing within a rich tradition of narrative, story, and image, attempting to communicate that tradition in constantly changing culture, recognize the stake they have in art. The nature of the gospel itself led the first evangelists to speak and write as they did. That, says R.E.C. Browne, has not changed:

> There can be no great preaching whenever the question "Is there knowledge of reality which can neither be perceived nor expressed in propositional form?" is unasked or left unanswered. . . . If the biblical writers are held to be free agents who use their imagination and intelligence in obedience to the divine promptings to say the greatest things about God and man, then the preacher must look on his work accordingly (Browne, 15–16).

Preaching is an art because of what the gospel is and because the forms of its communication are organic to the evangel.

While it is true that the homiletical art has been variously practiced—and that certain movements in the church's history have turned away from art—in the main, Christian witness has exercised imagination in architecture, liturgy, and public speech. The preacher must put into words what is difficult to articulate—Jesus, in his parabolic sermons often proclaimed what the reign of God is *like*, turning to art to communicate. Preachers as various as the prophets, the medieval Dominicans,* and the reformers have done the same. Both the popular and the high arts have a place in the pulpit. Fiction, poetry, cinema, dance, and the plastic arts provide the preacher access to changing culture, and they can provide potent images for the sermon. Preaching always has to do with the *world*, so this demands that television* be included, though some would question calling it even a popular art. If art, however, is the making of images that trap imagination* and so transform life, then the powerful medium of television must be considered alongside the higher arts, especially by the preacher. Television and cinema shape the imagination of the rising generation. The preacher can both learn from and employ these popular arts, as well as good fiction and the works to be seen in museums.

Fiction, some say, is a distinctly Christian art; it pays attention to individuals and makes much of human decision and action. A novel may devote hundreds of pages to the story of a single person, while the short story may detail a small human episode as if it were of ultimate importance. This attention to the individual personality, to the mere vignette, makes for an affinity with some basic Christian ideas: each person matters, people are responsible before God, the divine is manifest in historical events.

This is not to say that writers of fiction "preach," or that they are intentionally religious, though some are. Even a self-confessed Catholic writer such as Flannery O'Connor differentiates between faith and art, but she acknowledges common ground, especially in our culture, with the preacher. O'Connor tells us that her vocation as a writer is to make the experience of God somehow credible, in bold images and unlikely characters, in a culture not attentive to the holy. But even when the writer of fiction is not self-consciously religious, the preacher need not approach fiction as if it were religiously neutral. All literary art worthy of the name is weighted with religious questions, as the theologian Paul Tillich* so clearly understood.

When the preacher reads a novel or a poem, the most important thing is that he or she listen, like a child hearing a story. No work of art opens to the person unwilling to put himself or herself in its power. That is the difference between looking for sermon illustrations and giving oneself over to the power of metaphor. Once the story has taken hold of the reader, then it may have a chance to seize others through the art of the sermon. This internalizing of the text by the preacher is as crucial to reading fiction and poetry as to exegeting scripture.

If the story does take hold and connect with scripture or the liturgy, then the preacher may take one of several approaches: present an image from the book; introduce a character, by way of description and dialogue; have a conversation with the author, even an argument; excerpt a piece of the narrative, a short vignette or manageable episode, and play it out before the congregation. Whatever approach is taken, keep the whole work in view and try honestly to stand inside the world of its characters and action. Failing to do so at the outset will reduce potentially powerful metaphor to wooden illustration. When that happens, the power of fictional art to present the world's tragedy and comedy, and to increase relish for life itself, is lost.

The poem is difficult to bring to the pulpit. Poetry demands close attention, taking time over the words and images, returning to the text. If the preacher does include poetry, it may help to print the poem or an excerpt in the Sunday bulletin.

Cinema is probably the most powerful medium of our time. Next to television, it commands the largest audience. In darkness and anonymity the viewer sits for hours in uninterrupted communication with larger-than-life images and enveloping sound. The moviemaker is able to show us the world with stark realism or, as with no other art form, to distort space and time in order to intensify experience. Film, in fact, is so powerful that it can hardly ever be shown in conjunction with preaching. If, however, the preacher is discriminating in choosing movies, and open to their images, cinema can serve the pulpit well.

Here are some suggestions for going to the movies and bringing this art to preaching. (1) Go to the cinema as the kid at the gas station would, leaving criticism and analysis for later reflection. (2) Soon afterward, make notes on significant characters, moving dialogue, compelling scenes. (3) Note problems, questions, or issues raised by the film. Does the movie evoke something of the biblical tradition, or is there explicit connection with the church and its concerns? (4) As the week moves toward Sunday and as the liturgical calendar unfolds, keep the movie in mind, letting its scenes, characters, and issues connect with text and season.

(5) Discuss the film with someone who has seen it, and try to draw connections—or show contradictions—between the movie and life in the community. (6) Assume, if the film finds its way to the pulpit, that the congregation has *not* seen the movie; replay the scene, show the image, present the character. Tell the story; then trust the images to carry meaning without labored explanation.

Emphasis on the visual—helping people to *see* something—and attention to the mundane are points of similarity between sermon and cinema. Attentiveness to the world, to material embodiment of the actual, is the potential of both picture show and pulpit. From the movies the preacher can learn to be a kind of camera, taking snapshots of a community—or finding images in cinematic art—and holding them alongside the venerable images of Christian tradition.

Television, says Gregor Goethals, "is made for mythologies, stories that help us to understand ourselves, our values, and the events that impinge upon our lives." She believes that the amalgam of religion, politics, and social values that comprise "the American way" finds its icons and priests in television. Although television is commercially driven, it nonetheless provides millions of people with primary images of charismatic leadership, right and wrong, conversion, and sacred objects. The medium occasionally moves toward the prophetic, as in the work of Norman Lear. But for the most part, television is a powerful competing voice that cannot be ignored by the preacher; it may, given a discerning theological eye, provide compelling metaphors of the gospel. As with the movies, the preacher must approach this often debased medium warily but with a susceptible imagination.

The higher arts of sculpture and painting, long the provinces of the church, do not play a large role in the church's life today. As Goethals shows, the art museum offers to many an alternative spirituality, more private and contemplative than corporate Christianity's norm of word and sacrament. These characteristics of the plastic arts make it difficult to transfer the experience of van Gogh's canvases or a work of Rodin to the pulpit: better that the church bring sculpture or painting into the place of worship than that the preacher attempt to describe them from the pulpit.

If a sacramental spirituality is presupposed, then the way opens more easily to the spatial and tactile arts. If, as Goethals assumes, "the world and human relationships give us our meeting place with God" in the particularity of their art, showing us the material world, the painter and the sculptor have much in common with the preacher whose art seeks to embody, here and now, the revelation of God in Christ.

Again, the preacher will be able to bring these arts to the pulpit only if he or she is moved by them. If the holiness that van Gogh saw in a pair of old shoes captures the preacher's imagination, moves the heart, then the painting may find its way into impassioned preaching. Or similarly, a bronze of John the Baptist, if it fascinates the preacher, may appear in a sermon at Advent. These works must so move the preacher that he or she is impelled by the experience to show something of their colors and contours to the congregation.

Preaching is no stranger to dance. In the simplest service of worship, preaching occurs in the context of the most ancient of kinetic arts, liturgy. Preaching is one movement in a kind of communal dance that is the church's worship.

Whether individual dancing can be included in a service of worship depends upon a given community's liturgy. Some liturgies are not porous enough to admit an individual and idiosyncratic performance that might compete with either the preaching of the word or the celebration of the sacraments. On the other hand, liturgical dance has even been presented in place of the sermon, the word choreographed. Preachers might resist this idea, but many would agree that preaching could be more like dance, more physi-cally expressive. The preacher could no doubt learn from the dancer's capacity to internalize and then show in movement the meaning of scripture or sacrament. This parallels closely what the preacher aims for, and in some settings the two might be done together. For example, an individual or group could dance one of the parables, accompanied by a homily.

The arts, like preaching, must be judged finally by the passion of their apprehension of the human situation and their expression of it. For the preacher, Christ's Passion is central; every sermon is finally accountable to the Eucharist. The same could be said of art: Does it apprehend and show the suffering and beauty of the world in a way that leads to meditation, gratitude, and transformation? (*see* Drama; Preacher and Preaching in Literature).

Browne, R.E.C., *The Ministry of the Word*, 1958. **Goethals, G.**, *The Electronic Golden Calf: Images, Religion, and the Making of Meaning*, 1990. **May, J. R.**, and **M. Bird**, *Religion in Film*, 1982. **O'Connor, F.**, *Mystery and Manners: Occasional Prose*, 1969. **Paterson, J.**, *The Novel as Faith*, 1973. **Rice, C. L.**, *Interpretation and Imagination: The Preacher and Contemporary Literature* (Philadelphia, 1970); *The Embodied Word: Preaching as Art and Liturgy*, 1991. **de Rougement, D.**, "Religion and the Mission of the Artist," in *The New Orpheus*, ed. N. Scott, Jr., 1964, 62–63. **Tillich, P.**, *Theology of Culture*, 1959.   CHARLES RICE

Augustine of Hippo   (354–430)

Augustine of Hippo, the Preacher

Sinner and saint, talented theologian, penitent and polemicist, philosopher and monastic legislator, Augustine is well known in the Latin West as conceivably the greatest spokesman for Christianity between Saint Paul and Martin Luther. Yet little attention has been directed toward Augustine as preacher, although more than a third of his work consists in sermons. Augustine was ordained to the presbyterate in January 391 by Bishop

Valerius, after the people themselves actually conscripted Augustine during a service in the local church. Four years later, probably 395 or early 396, Megalius, the Primate of Numidia, ordained Augustine coadjutor bishop of Hippo, a coastal city on the southern shore of the Mediterranean. Augustine went to the congregation at present-day Annaba in Algeria, where he served for thirty-nine years as presbyter and later as bishop.

In a sermon on John 13:10, Augustine lamented the "shortage of preachers" in North Africa. A hitherto unknown letter of Augustine's, published for the first time in Vienna in 1981, refers to some tractates on the Gospel according to John, posted from Hippo to Bishop Aurelius of Carthage, for public use by others in local churches there. Augustine encouraged memorization of sermons and their subsequent delivery by preachers who had difficulty either composing sermons or finding something to say. Augustine and Aurelius gradually extended the task of preaching to their presbyters, while it remained customary for the bishop to speak first. There developed a lucrative market for Augustine's sermons, which eventually became a black market where the bishop's name was falsely linked with myriad sermons whose doubtful authenticity has taxed generations of textual critics in their task of discerning a genuine text from a spurious one.

Augustine is credited with having preached some 8,000 sermons. Only a small number have survived, roughly one in fourteen. In 1990, François Dolbeau, of the Ecole Pratique des Hautes Etudes in Paris, revealed his extraordinary find of nineteen new sermons and seven fragments of sermons by Augustine, which he discovered in the Municipal Library at Mainz, Germany. The latest count, then, of Augustine's extant sermons is 568, exclusive of fragments. Tradition has assigned them the title "Sermons to the People."

Add to the above more than 200 *Commentaries on the Psalms* (in some instances three sermons on a single psalm),

124 *Tractates on the Gospel of John,* and 10 *Homilies on the First Letter of John,* and we have a total of more than 900 authentic sermons. Together with those of John Chrysostom,* Augustine's sermons constitute more than one-half the homiletic material surviving the patristic age.

The terms tractates, sermons, and homilies are somewhat flexible and need not be pressed too far in any technical sense. In a manner reminiscent of the ancient *grammaticus* before Augustine's conversion in 186, he would break up piecemeal the text of the Bible, as the eucharistic bread was broken, and he would nourish people with words, which he frequently described as their "dishes." Of biblical imagery there was no end. He preached the Bible virtually all the time. Its concrete vocabulary was interlaced with finely tuned sounds whose undulating prose rhythms formed unforgettable epigrammatic phrases, which became Augustine's trademark as both catechist and preacher.

Augustine rarely dictated a sermon in the quiet of his monastery. One notable exception in this regard was his extended "Commentary on Psalm 119." With all the imperfections such a style of delivery admits, Augustine's sermons were recorded by secretaries on the spot. Unlike the bishop's books, his sermons exist today in their original unrevised form: exegetical pieces expressed in a homiletic medium of everyday speech. On occasion their extemporaneous character was tested to the limit when the lector read the wrong psalm and the bishop graciously accommodated himself to the mistake.

The Basilica of Peace at Hippo measured a mere 126 feet (with apse, 147 feet) in length, and 60 feet in width, comparable in size to many rural churches. Still Augustine sometimes bemoaned that his voice could not be heard above the muttering crowd, except in complete silence. The winter months he detested because he was highly susceptible to colds, while the summer months brought profuse perspiration and fatigue from the excessive heat. During both seasons Augustine expressed concern for his people because they had to stand anywhere from a half hour to an hour and a half. Meanwhile the bishop remained seated on his official throne. Both chronic hoarseness and a chest ailment vexed him. Yet his remarkable conversational style—reminiscent of the Cynic diatribe and rife with questions directed toward his listeners, his fondness for anaphora, antithesis, and alliteration—frequently elicited vocal response and applause. Over the years his penchant for both numerology and allegory gradually yielded to a more literal approach in his interpretation of the Bible. The bulk of evidence generated by the sermons dispels possible hints of either literary artifice or hagiographical adulation. Possidius, Augustine's first biographer and friend of some forty years, had this estimate of his work: "I believe, however, that they profited even more who were able to hear him preaching in church" (*Life* 31, 4 and 9).

Augustine of Hippo on Preaching. Book Four of *Christian Doctrine* (*De Doctrina Christiana*) concerns itself exclusively with the art of preaching. Its composition during the years 426/7 C.E. has the advantage of reflecting the lifelong cumulative experiences of a seasoned practitioner only a few years before his death in 430 C.E.

The first three books of *Christian Doctrine* were composed in 396/7, shortly after Augustine's episcopal consecration. Book One offers a résumé of Christian doctrine (*regula fidei*) and morality (*praecepta vivendi*). Books Two and Three reveal Augustine's approach to the difficult task of interpreting the Bible, thereby constituting a treatise on the subject of biblical hermeneutics.* Book Four, in turn, functions as a treatise on homiletics. In sum, Augustine highlights the fundamental message of Christianity, how to decode it, and finally, how to communicate it to others.

Book Four of *Christian Doctrine* covers the following range of materials: basic principles of public speaking, I, 1–VI, 10;

samples of Greco-Roman rhetoric* as found in both Testaments of the Bible, VII, 11–XI, 26; the aims of the orator, the genres of oratory, and the styles of public discourse, each with plentiful illustrations from the letters of Saint Paul, Cyprian, and Ambrose, XII, 27–XXI, 50; and, finally, specific guidelines for Christian eloquence, XXII, 51–XXXI, 64.

Both to teach (*docere*) and to sustain attention in a pleasing manner (*placere*) regularly fall within the competence of the preacher; to carry assent into action (*movere*), however, must be left to the generous promptings of grace. All words (*verba*) in the world and, most especially, the incarnate word (*Verbum*), Jesus Christ, are signposts (*signa*) along the way of the pilgrim pointing to the unique reality (*res*) that truly matters, the triune God of love as revealed in Jesus Christ (1, 5, 5). With positive help from preachers, Augustine assigned to Christ as the "Interior Teacher" the dual role of teaching and imparting human understanding of the mystery of God.

When interpreting the Bible, the preacher's moral life counts far more than sublime eloquence (4, 27, 59). The personal comportment of the preacher is a sermon in itself (4, 29, 61). Words ought always to be subordinate to the preacher, not the preacher to words (4, 28, 61). "One ought to pray before one speaks" (4, 15, 32). Six references to prayer form a major consideration for effective preaching in the penultimate paragraph of Book Four (4, 30, 63), which then concludes with a prayer (*see* Character).

Doyle, G. W., "Augustine's Sermonic Method," *Westminster Theological Journal* 39 (1976–1977): 213–38. **van der Meer, F.,** *Augustine the Bishop,* 1961, 405–67.

GEORGE LAWLESS

THE FOUNTAIN OF LIFE
Augustine of Hippo
"Then came the soldiers, and broke the legs of the first, and of the other who was crucified with him. But when they came to Jesus, and saw that he was dead already,

they broke not his legs. But one of the soldiers with a spear laid open his side, and forthwith came thereout blood and water."

A suggestive word was made use of by the evangelist in not saying *pierced,* or *wounded* his side, or anything else, but *opened;* that thereby, in a sense, the gate of life might be thrown open, from whence have flowed forth the sacraments of the church, without which there is no entrance to the life which is the true life. That blood was shed for the remission of sins; that water it is that makes up the health-giving cup, and supplies at once the laver of baptism and water for drinking. This was announced beforehand, when Noah was commanded to make a door in the side of the ark, whereby the animals might enter which were not destined to perish in the flood, and by which the church was prefigured.

Because of this, the first woman was formed from the side of the man when asleep, and was called Life, and the mother of all living. Truly it pointed to a great good, prior to the great evil of the transgression (in the guise of one thus lying asleep). This second Adam bowed his head and fell asleep on the cross, that a spouse [the church] might be formed for him from that which flowed from the sleeper's side.

O death, whereby the dead are raised anew to life! What can be purer than such blood? What more health-giving than such a wound?

> Sermon no. 120, John 19: 31–42, *Homilies on the Gospel of John* in *A Select Library of the Nicene and Post-Nicene Fathers of the Christian Church,* Vol. 7, ed. Philip Schaff (Buffalo: The Christian Literature Co., 1887), 434–35.

Authority. There is no single authoritative definition of the authority of preaching. Every attempt to discuss the authority of the sermon is shaped by the denomination, the experience, the theological biases of the author.

Further, the distinction must be made between de jure and de facto authority. De jure, each preacher preaches out of a set of principles and presuppositions that convince the preacher it is possible to preach at all. De facto, each preacher will have just that amount of authority the listeners grant or acknowledge.

The authoritative preacher authorizes discipleship. The sermon provides the warrants for faithfulness and inspires what it enjoins. People are invited to surprising faithfulness because God's surprising goodness makes it possible.

Authoritative preaching need not be authoritarian. Authoritarian preaching places the word of scripture and the words of the preacher over against the listeners. Authoritative preaching may, however, place the preacher with the listener, sometimes under the word of scripture, sometimes alongside the word, sometimes after it.

Different congregations and different individuals grant authority to different kinds of preaching and to different kinds of preachers. The preacher may of course hold fast to authority unacknowledged. Sometimes that course marks the truest fidelity, sometimes the clearest pride. Most often the preacher will seek to use the words in ways that acknowledge authority—by enticing, inviting, authoring, authorizing.

Most preachers and most congregations acknowledge some combinations of authority for preaching:

1. The sermon has authority because the sermon interprets scripture. The model of the preacher is that of the Matthean scribe who brings forth from the treasure of the Bible that which is old and that which is new, uniquely suited to the interests and needs of the congregation (Matt. 13:52). To claim that the sermon's authority is warranted by the authority of the Bible is not necessarily to affirm any particular doctrine of inspiration. It is to say that the Bible is God's gift to illumine human lives, the human condition, the promise of redemption that can comfort

and urge us on. Though the authority of scripture is not the only authority the sermon can claim, it is not clear that the sermon has any claim to authority without prior commitment to the biblical words. In our time the claim for such preaching has been most clearly represented by Karl Barth* and all those who have been persuaded by him.

2. The sermon has authority because it represents a pastoral word suited to the real needs of the listeners. This kind of authority seems especially well suited to preaching based in a committed, ongoing pastoral relationship between preacher and people. Perhaps the best biblical model is found in the letters of Paul, which vary greatly in tone and concern but are united by a profound concern for the actual lives of congregations and by an attempt to understand the issues of faith and practice that strengthen or discourage believers. A host of preachers of very different theological persuasions base the authority of their preaching centrally on pastoral relationships and insights. Almost all preachers derive some authority from such personal understanding.

3. The sermon has authority because of its place in the liturgy. It is not in the sermon alone but in worship, including word and sacrament, that the promise of God's presence is fulfilled. The preacher here may also be priest, the authority of preaching derived in part from presiding at the table and at the baptismal font. Implicitly, preaching may become sacramental because worship is sacramental, and preaching finds its place in worship. The sixth chapter of John's Gospel provides a model for this combination of word and sacrament.

4. The sermon has authority because it is intellectually compelling. The preacher is not only interpreter of scripture but commentator on the dilemmas and puzzles of contemporary life. The biblical model for such preaching may rest in the Proverbs or wisdom literature, wherein the authority of the sage rests in the ability to see how the world is going and how the structures of the world relate to the wisdom of God.

5. The sermon has authority because of the integrity of the preacher. The preacher is present to the congregation as spiritual guide, as exemplar of God's amazing grace, as fellow pilgrim, or as one who seeks to live the ethics of the faithful life. The Paul of Galatians, 2 Corinthians, and Philippians becomes a model of both suffering Christian and apostolic guide. The Paul of the pastoral epistles is the redeemed sinner urging Timothy and Titus to be moral exemplars for their flock. One need not surrender to homiletical donatism to acknowledge that part of any preacher's authority depends on the life that preacher lives.

6. The sermon has authority because of the rhetorical power of the preacher. The preacher tells the story that illuminates each congregant's story or the story of the congregation itself. The preacher finds the image that fructifies in the hearts of the listeners through the week ahead. The parables become a source for narrative preaching, the Psalms for sermons drawn from images. Because this is a gift not given equally or even generously to all preachers, it is hard to value properly in any theory of authority. In the actual worship of faithful people its power is undeniable.

The authority of preaching is a dangerous gift, easily exploited for personal aggrandizement or self-congratulation. It is also a necessary gift, based on the promise that the Spirit works through the words of scripture, through the words that interpret them, and, most amazingly, through those women and men who seek to preach faithfully (see Theology of Preaching).

Bartlett, D. L., *The Shape of Scriptural Authority*, 1983. Countryman, W., *Biblical Authority or Biblical Tyranny? Scripture and the Christian Pilgrimage*, 1981. Smith, C. M., *Weaving the Sermon: Preaching in a Feminist Perspective*, 1989.   DAVID L. BARTLETT

Baccalaureate Sermon

History. The baccalaureate service and sermon have long been associated with the commencement exercises of American colleges and universities and form one of the last links between these increasingly secular institutions and their religious origins. The term baccalaureate is derived from two Latin words, *bacca*, meaning berry, and *laureus*, which means laurel, and may refer to a crown of laurel with which a newly graduated bachelor was crowned. Some ground for this etymological speculation is to be found in a series of seventeenth-century Scottish baccalaureate sermons titled "Exhortations To The Candidates For Laureation," by Robert Leighton, Principal of the University of Edinburgh. In his Exhortation of 1653, Leighton compared the commencement ceremonies to the most famous councils and public festivals of great men, and their golden crowns with "your crowns of laurel" (Leighton, 259).

English antecedents of the baccalaureate may be seen in the Inception or Commencement Ceremony of the University of Cambridge where the original statutes of ca. 1236–1254 describe a three-part ritual, the second part of which involved a sermon or an address by the candidate's master preached while the candidate "sat with bowed head over which his hood was drawn, a picture of abject humility and utter embarrassment" (Hackett, 127).

The Harvard Commencement of 1642 is the first recorded commencement ceremony in English North America, and in it are to be found recognizable rudiments of its Cambridge ancestor, but no separate baccalaureate sermon is known to have been given. However, as Harvard students were preached at constantly in the seventeenth century, twice daily and twice on Sundays, we may assume that the sermon or sermons nearest the commencement would take the form of a valedictory; yet, we have no extant seventeenth-century equivalents to the Edinburgh "Laureations."

The earliest examples of printed baccalaureate sermons in America are post-Revolutionary and belong to Harvard and Yale. In 1794, David Tappan, Hollis Professor at Harvard, printed "A Discourse Delivered in the Chapel Of Harvard College, June 17, 1794, at the Request of the Senior Class of Students on Occasion of their approaching departure from the University, Preparatory to their receiving its Public Honors." Yale's president, Timothy Dwight,* wrote in the "Advertisement" or Preface to his sermon to the Yale Class of 1797, "In Yale College it is customary for the President or the Professor of Divinity to address a discourse to the candidates for the Baccalaureate on the sabbath preceding the public commencement" (Dwight, 1).

Throughout the nineteenth century, the custom of a baccalaureate service and sermon became a fixed part of the ceremonial life of American colleges and universities. In those places where presidents were also preachers, the duty of preaching the baccalaureate sermon usually fell to them. In the absence of a clerical president, the assignment went to the Divinity Professor and eventually to the school chaplain or even to a lay professor. Rarely was the baccalaureate sermon entrusted to someone not a member of the institution, for the occasion was regarded in some sense as private, the last intimacy between college and students before the public and final act of commencement. In a crude analogy, baccalaureate was to commencement what the pre-game locker room pep talk is to the game.

The Service. In many places in these last years of the twentieth century, the baccalaureate service is considerably less "churchy" than it once was, a result both of the secular spirit of the age and the new religious pluralism. The baccalaureate sermon is now more often than not an address hardly distinguishable from the ubiquitous commencement address, itself the most parodied form of discourse in America. There may be cause for lament here, but these modern circumstances may also generate some useful advantages.

One such advantage may be the actual setting of the baccalaureate service. Today, even the smallest of colleges find their commencements too large to be held indoors; often they are held outdoors or in an athletic or municipal space. Baccalaureate services, however, continue to be held in the chapel, a borrowed church, or the most dignified interior space available to the school. This is a good thing, for not only does space shape function, it also shapes expectations and behavior as well. At the very least, one does not have to contend with the unexorcised secular demons of a stadium or a gymnasium in order to accommodate a solemn assembly.

Just as the "alien space" of the chapel is an advantage, so too is the "alien discourse" of public religion. In the modern American college, it is rare to hear scripture read or public prayer offered. Moral discourse addressed to students is not customary. For these to take place under the auspices of the college will be a new experience for most students. We may assume these students to be uninformed or even mystified, but we should not assume that they will be indifferent or hostile. At this vital and scary stage of their careers, most undergraduates will accept wisdom from whatever source it comes, so the religious dimension of the occasion should not be marginalized.

The form of the occasion is nearly as important as the content of the address. We should remember that in many institutions the baccalaureate service is not only the last occasion for which the entire class is gathered before commencement, but it may well be the first! Hence, splendid music, a sense of ceremony appropriate to institutional dignity, as well as an expressed sense of institutional commitment to its own ideals and those of its young are all very much in order.

The Sermon. While the commencement address may be beyond rehabilitation, there is still some hope for the baccalaureate sermon. Two temptations, however, are to be avoided: the lecture and the Op-Ed piece. No matter how learned or timely these forms of discourse may be, neither is an adequate substitute for the honest work of preaching. To forget this is to court disaster.

What is there left to do? Preach to the students, not to the faculty or the parents, and do so out of the authority of your own tradition. If you are a Christian, do not pretend that you are not. If you are a Jew, do not cease to be one just because you may be preaching to non-Jews. Preach out of your tradition to their condition. You have only one voice that speaks with any kind of authority; it would be foolish to stifle it out of some sense of false deference.

The baccalaureate audience is among the most attentive any preacher will encounter. The young exhibit a surprising willingness to invest in the occasion's potential for good. Thus to treat baccalaureate as a vestigial poor relation of commencement is to make a problem of an opportunity. Thus the preacher must be encouraged to proclaim a truth, a proposition, a conviction, a conclusion, and to do so by the most compelling and clear means available. The preacher should not be afraid to transcend the secular boundaries of the academy or the world itself. Advice, counsel, commiseration, exhortation, encouragement, compassion, the witness of scripture, the teachings of the faith, the examples of virtuous men and women—any or all of these will serve the occasion. Honest preaching addressed to the genuine hopes and anxieties of the young can redeem and revive an ancient occasion for which all can be grateful.

Dwight, T., *The Nature and Danger of Infidel Philosophy,* 1798, 1992. **Hackett, M. B.,** *The Original Statutes of Cambridge University,* 1970. **Leighton, R.,** *Lectures and Addresses Delivered in Latin Before the University of Edinburgh,* 1870.   PETER J. GOMES

Barth, Karl.

(1886–1968) Karl Barth is known not primarily as preacher or even homiletician but more as the outstanding Protestant dogmatician of the twentieth century. His theology was rooted in a twelve-year period as pastor during which the task of weekly preaching became a decisive problem, requiring fundamental reconsideration of his theology.

Barth was the son of a professor of theology, Fritz Barth, of Basel. He grew up in Bern. During his study in Marburg he became a student of Wilhelm Herrmann (1846–1922) and a strong adherent of his liberal theology. In 1909 he became an assistant preacher in Geneva and in 1922 pastor of the village in Safenwil, Switzerland. His long, carefully prepared sermons, usually twelve closely written manuscript pages, were the focal point of his pastoral duties. Immersed in the spirit of liberal theology, he read the Bible from that perspective. He could preach uninhibitedly of a "divine spark" or "the Good, the Divine" in humanity that joins harmoniously with human and cultural progress in history. Social issues appeared on his horizon in the mill village of Safenwil with its great social tensions. Even in the pulpit he sided passionately with the socialist workers' movement without altering his basic theological position or his notion of preaching.

A crisis entered Barth's development during the summer of 1914, shortly before the outbreak of World War I. It became impossible for him to continue to equate the biblical message and the will and action of God with the "good" in humankind. A radical break with liberal theology was in the making. The break was not occasioned by the experience of the war, as a few of Barth's later autobiographical utterances suggest. His preaching became more difficult and simultaneously more important. In place of an optimistically perceived harmony between what he had earlier called "the divine" and "the good" in humankind there emerged a sharp opposition between the word of God as he now (just now!) heard it in the Bible and the religious experience and moral action of humanity, an opposition that deeply troubled the preacher in him. In the sermons of the latter years in Safenwil, the once very obvious references to everyday life and social and political problems receded. Barth's congregations were treated to the hard confrontation with the "wholly Other" of scripture, just beginning to dawn on Barth.

The "difficulty" Barth's preaching presented for him (and for his hearers as well) drove him to search for a different theological foundation for a new reading of scripture. In 1916–1918 he wrote his first book, *The Letter to the Romans*, an unconventional exposition of the Pauline letter. His continuing development of thought was so stormy that he had to write the book once again during 1920–1921, this time strongly under the influence of Kierkegaard and the reformers. The second *Letter to the Romans*, appearing in 1922, was the foundational document of "dialectical theology."

Having become known through his first book, he was called to Germany as professor: in 1921 to Göttingen, in 1925 to Münster, in 1930 to Bonn. Driven from Germany because of opposition to the National Socialist government, he taught in his home town of Basel from 1935 until his retirement in 1962. The theology he developed through teaching does not deny for a moment its origin in the preaching task that had grown so difficult for Barth. In 1923 he shocked his once-revered teacher, the prominent academic Adolf von Harnack, with this statement: "The task of theology is one with the task of preaching. It consists of reception and transmission of the Word of Christ." The formula Barth put together to summarize the common task of theology and preaching became famous: thesis, antithesis, synthesis. "As ministers we ought to speak of God. We are human, however, and so cannot speak of God. We ought therefore to recognize both our obligation and our inability and by that very recognition give God the Glory" (Barth 1928, 186).

The following three statements obtained for the rest of Barth's life, although his thought continued to develop: (1) sermon and theology are founded solely in a commission of God; (2) no human capacity can measure up to that commission, although it becomes increasingly clearer that preaching and theology have a foundation upon which they both can and should stand—God's revelation, i.e., the reconciliation of the world with God in the cross of Jesus Christ; (3) God, and not humankind, is glorified in the clear knowledge preserved in every dogmatic statement by theology and preaching.

The conviction that the task of theology is one with the task of the sermon forms the basis of Barth's gigantic work *Church Dogmatics* (12 volumes, 1932–1967, uncompleted). There it reads: "The normal and central fact with which dogmatics has to do is, very simply, the Church's Sunday sermon of yesterday and tomorrow, and so it will continue to be" (Barth 1936, I, 1, 91). Barth's life work was one grand single meditation on the presupposition of the sermon—not on the (secondary, homiletical) question, "How *does* one do it?," but on the (primary, theological) question, "How *can* one do it?" That is, "How does God enable human discourse about God?"

However, in 1932–1933 Barth did specifically lecture his students on preaching. In two statements corresponding to each other describing the sermon in the perspective of divine commission and human service, the notes of the lecture offer a definition of the sermon and provide a typical example of Barth's "dialectical" thought process (Barth 1991, 44).

Barth the professor preached until four years prior to his death. He preached in various settings, but almost exclusively in a Basel prison after 1954 (Barth 1961). Changes in the style and content of his preaching parallel his theology, which continued to develop into his later years. The older Barth's tone grows warmer and addresses the congregation more person-

ally, assisted by the small size of the prison congregation and his increasing familiarity with it. A constant characteristic of his preaching after 1930 was its close connection with the wording of the biblical texts he interpreted, texts which for him pointed directly and transparently to the central Christ-kerygma. More important to Barth than the historical contingency of the text was the belief that the singular truth of God becomes audible in the word addressed directly to humankind in every age through the medium of the text. The difference in the ages need not be considered, thanks to the proclaimed presence of God. Thus the biblical contexts of the sermonic texts receive little consideration. That is the case both for the longer pericopes that Barth preached in earlier years and most certainly for the briefer texts, usually consisting of a single verse, which he preferred after the 1940s. It is striking that ethical themes increasingly recede in his preaching, whereas political judgments, expressed so vehemently elsewhere by Barth, occur only incidentally. The keynote of the later sermons in particular is the faith, promised unconditionally to the listeners, that God's saving work in Christ has been definitively "accomplished" (John 19:30).

Barth, K., *Deliverance to the Captives*, 1961; *The Doctrine of the Word of God*, Church *Dogmatics*, I, 1, 1936; *Homiletics*, 1991; *The Word of God and the Word of Man*, 1928.

HINRICH STOEVESANDT

Baxter, Richard.

(1615–1691) Although he was a Puritan preacher, pastor extraordinaire, prolific author, and prominent figure in the religious-political controversies of seventeenth-century England, Richard Baxter received informal and inferior schooling. Nevertheless, he excelled as a scholar because of his love for books, his considerable intellect, and his passionate desire to serve God. Baxter's voluminous reading and extensive writings were the foundation of his ministry, and both food for and expression of his convictions.

Baxter served as the vicar of the parish church in Kidderminster for nearly twenty years, where he made his mark as pastor and preacher. Plagued by ill health from boyhood and working in constant pain and anticipation of death, Baxter preached, in his own words, "as a dying man to dying men." His work as both pastor and preacher was motivated by a heart broken by the love of God. The urgency of his method in ministry astounded and inspired other pastors, and he became a shepherd and resource to many beyond his parish.

In May 1662, the "Bill for Uniformity" was passed by both the House of Lords and the House of Commons, and it was given royal assent. The Bill for Uniformity required that all ministers possess episcopal ordination and give unqualified consent and assent to everything in the Prayer Book. Baxter was episcopally ordained, and, in principle, supported the Prayer Book. He could not, however, conform to a church that he thought was established on terms meant to exclude. Branded a nonconformist, silenced, and cast out, Baxter spent the remaining years of his life writing and preaching with varying degrees of official approval, and several times he was imprisoned for defying ecclesial censorship and rejection.

Baxter's style was occasional. He responded to the need or the crisis of the moment. Although he was bound by no formal positions of church or state, he was informed by the mountains of books he read and his study of scripture. When asked by the ministers of Worcester in 1655 to speak to them on the subject of pastoral work, Baxter, unable to address them in person because of illness, responded with a manuscript later titled *The Reformed Pastor*. It became his most enduring essay.

Baxter's preaching and writing were unpolished. Sermon and manuscript preparations were hurried because there was so much to do, and he could spare no time to rewrite. While he read widely, there is no evidence that his reading inspired in him a literary or homiletical theory.

Baxter preached to the common people, leading him to say his language could never be too plain, for "plainness makes it fitter for the ignorant, who are far the greatest number, and have the greatest need." Style,* therefore, should be "mean and vulgar . . . not onely without those subtilties and citations, which might sute it to the pallates of learned men, but also without the conciseness, sententiousness, and quickness which might make it acceptable to the ingenious and acute" (Keeble, 48). Metaphor, allusion, and obscure vocabulary are not found in Baxter's homiletics. Plain preaching for plain people was Baxter's way of being faithful to his flock.

A desire to be understood by his people was not the sole motivation for Baxter's style, however. He was also convinced that employing the rhetorical arts in preaching was an expression of the pride and vanity of the preacher and, therefore, should be studiously avoided. The scriptures were written plainly for simple people, and the goal of scripture is to advance Christ. The only acceptable motivation for the preacher is to advance the gospel of Christ. Above all an evangelist, Baxter sought to save souls more than to please the ears of his hearers.

Realizing, however, that metaphorical language is not altogether avoidable and that God cannot be formally conceived and comprehended by humanity, Baxter did resort on occasion to metaphorical and allegorical forms of expression. He concluded that biblical precedent warrants such expression in moderation, so long as the preacher does not use imagery as ornamentation or to draw attention to itself.

Baxter, R., *The Autobiography of Richard Baxter,* Abridged from the Folio (1696) with Introduction, Appendices & Notes by J.M.L. Thomas, 1925; *The Reformed Pastor,* ed. J. T. Wilkinson, 1939. **Keeble, N. H.,** *Rich-*

ard Baxter: Puritan Man of Letters, 1982. **Orme, W.,** The Life and Times of the Reverend Richard Baxter, 2 Vols., 1831. **Powicke, F. J.,** The Reverend Richard Baxter under the Cross, 1927.   NANCY LAMMERS GROSS

Bede. (ca. 673–735) An Anglo-Saxon monk who in later centuries received the honorific title "the Venerable," Bede was seven when his relatives entrusted him to the double monastery of St. Peter and St. Paul at Wearmouth and Jarrow, in Northumbria. Ordained a deacon at 19 and a priest at 30, he devoted himself to monastic discipline and the work of scholarship. Although English was his native tongue, all his extant works are written in excellent Latin of almost classical purity. Besides the famous Ecclesiastical History of the English People and other historical books, he wrote didactic treatises on grammar, chronology, and geography, as well as on saints' lives, poetry, letters, biblical commentaries, and homilies.

Bede placed such a high value on preaching that he was distressed that some bishops and pastors in his time neglected to proclaim the gospel to people living deep in the mountains and forests of northern England. His historical works provide vivid portraits of great missionary preachers such as Augustine of Canterbury, Columba, Aidan, Chad, and Cuthbert. Believing that Christian pastors were the successors of prophets and apostles who should teach both by word and by deed, Bede never tired of exhorting them to present a wholesome example to the flock.

In his exegesis Bede sought to follow "in the footsteps of the Fathers," especially Ambrose, Augustine, Jerome, and Gregory the Great. He understood enough Greek to conduct textual criticism at a sophisticated level, but his knowledge of Hebrew was limited to what he derived from his reading of Jerome. Although interested in matters of biblical history and philology, he stressed the need to uncover the spiritual sense of the text through allegorical interpretation. In theory, he sometimes identified as many as four levels of meaning in scripture (literal, allegorical, tropological or moral, and anagogical), but in practice he usually distinguished only two, the literal and the "mystical" or "spiritual."

During his own lifetime, fifty of Bede's homilies were collected into two books. These homilies were probably edited versions of those he preached to the monks at Jarrow, either at Mass or in meetings of the monastic chapter. They cover the major events in the liturgical year, including feasts of saints and special occasions such as the anniversary of the dedication of a church. The text for each sermon is the gospel reading appointed for the day in the eighth-century Northumbrian lectionary, which seems to have been derived from that of the church in Naples.

Bede usually commented on the gospel texts verse by verse, though he occasionally skipped over a few verses in the interest of time or paused to elaborate on the biography of a saint or the liturgical customs attendant to a particular feast. Most of the homilies began simply with a reference to "the gospel which we have just heard," followed by an examination of what classical rhetoricians called the "circumstances" of a historical event—those commonplace questions regarding who, where, when, how, and why.

Throughout each homily, and especially at its conclusion, Bede frequently used direct address ("Let us consider this, dearly beloved") to invite his hearers to ponder the hidden meaning of the text as it applied to their own spiritual lives. His emphasis was not on specific issues of moral conduct or contemporary social concerns, but on the familiar universal themes of pride and humility, sin and grace, promise and fulfillment, the certainty of judgment, and the hope of heaven in the life to come.

Bede's approach to scripture was typological; Old Testament happenings foreshadow events in the life of Christ, and New Testament figures correspond to persons in the contemporary church. He was fond of numerology, etymology, wordplay, and the weaving together of biblical words and phrases to create a rich tapestry of interrelated allusions. He also employed syntactic parallelism to contrast Christ's humiliation with our exaltation, as in this line from a Christmas homily: "He whom heaven and the heavens of the heavens do not hold was contained by the narrowness of a small manger so that he might bestow upon us the amplitude of seats on high" (Homily I.6).

Soon after Bede's death, Anglo-Saxon missionaries like Boniface* carried his homilies and biblical commentaries to the Continent. They remained enormously influential throughout the Middle Ages, as numerous surviving manuscripts attest. When Paul the Deacon in the ninth century was instructed by Charlemagne to compile a homiliary containing patristic exegesis suitable for monks to read at the Night Office, nearly a fourth of the material he chose came from Bede. In the twelfth century, substantial portions of Bede's work were included in the most popular medieval compilation of patristic exegesis, which is known as the *Ordinary Gloss*.

Bede, the Venerable, *Homilies on the Gospels,* 2 vols., trans. L. T. Martin and D. Hurst, 1991. **Martin, L. T.,** "The Two Worlds in Bede's Homilies: The Biblical Event and the Listeners' Experience," in *De Ore Domini: Preacher and Word in the Middle Ages,* ed. T. L. Amos, E. A. Green, and B. Mayne Kienzle, 1989, 27–40. **Ward, B.,** *The Venerable Bede,* 1990.   ARTHUR G. HOLDER

Beecher, Henry Ward.

(1813–1887) Widely acknowledged as the most eloquent preacher of his day, Henry Ward Beecher exemplified the changing ethos of nineteenth-century America. His father, Lyman Beecher, had popularized the "New School" theology of his close friend Nathaniel W. Taylor, who attenuated the harsh predestination of New England Calvinism by arguing that human nature was marked not by original sin but by free will. Henry advanced even further in the rebellion against a strict Calvinism by emphasizing an emotional and intuitive faith. For Henry, God's goodness and mercy could be seen as much in the world of nature as in the Bible. Where his Puritan father had denounced the evils of Unitarianism and the immoralities of drinking, gambling, swearing, dueling, theaters, novels, and breaking the sabbath, Henry embraced the spirit of his age. A widely read newspaper columnist, the author of more than thirty books (including the critically panned but best-selling novel *Norwood*), and a popular orator delivering as many as 250 speeches in one year alone on the Lyceum lecture tour, Beecher advocated women's rights, opposed slavery, championed social reform, defended evolution, supported higher biblical criticism, and popularized romantic Christianity.

The seventh of eight living children of Roxanne and Lyman Beecher, Henry Ward Beecher was born June 24, 1813, in Litchfield, Connecticut. Henry's mother died when he was only three years old, and his father soon remarried. Henry and all six of his brothers distinguished themselves in the ministry, and his sisters, Catharine Beecher and Harriet Beecher Stowe, became equally well known. As a child, though, Henry showed little promise of following in his father's footsteps. He often had to repeat himself to make himself understood, and he did not memorize as easily as his older siblings did. Shortly after they moved to Boston in 1826, Henry threatened to run away to sea, but his father persuaded him that even sailors needed an education.

Deemed too deficient in the classics to attend Yale, Henry entered Amherst College in 1830, where he began lifelong interests in oratory and science, leading weekly debates as president of the Athenian Society and lecturing on the new science of phrenology as president of the Natural History Society. In 1832, Henry began a long engagement to Eunice Bullard and, later that same year, Lyman

Beecher became the first president of Cincinnati's Lane Seminary. When Henry graduated from Amherst in 1834, he followed his family west to enroll at Lane, determined to become a missionary.

As a student at Lane, Henry saw his father tried for heresy when a staunch Calvinist "Old School" pastor filed a formal complaint with the Presbytery of Cincinnati. Despite Lyman's eventual exoneration, the ordeal left deep scars on the entire Beecher family. Henry's brother Charles left the ministry, and Henry vowed to avoid all controversy in his own ministry.

Soon after his 1837 graduation from Lane, Henry returned east to marry his fiancée before accepting a call to the First Presbyterian Church of Lawrenceburgh, Indiana, only twenty miles downriver from Cincinnati. A year later, the Oxford Presbytery examined him for ordination and passed him unanimously, but after the presbytery voted to require an oath of allegiance to the Old School, Beecher persuaded his congregation to withdraw from the presbytery. Successful in his preaching but criticized for buying on credit too freely (to support his love of books and "fine living") and for visiting his parishioners too infrequently, Beecher gladly accepted a call in 1839 to the newly established Second Presbyterian Church of Indianapolis.

During Beecher's pastorate, Second Presbyterian Church grew from fifteen members to become the largest Presbyterian congregation in the state, and Beecher's reputation grew with the church. He deliberately changed his preaching method when he realized that the apostles in the book of Acts began their sermons with commonly accepted beliefs (which he called "you all knows"), and he compiled a list of about forty such assumptions shared by his public. With his revised preaching style, he soon became known throughout the state as a successful revivalist, and in 1844 he published a popular Sunday evening sermon series as his first book, *Lectures to Young Men.*

In 1847 Henry Ward Beecher moved east again to become the first pastor of Brooklyn's (Congregational) Plymouth Church, where he spent the rest of his life. Within ten years of Beecher's arrival, Plymouth Church became the largest church in a city known as a "city of churches." Every Sunday morning for decades, hundreds would crowd Manhattan's ferry docks for the short trip to then-suburban Brooklyn.

Widely praised as a popular and powerful preacher and lecturer, Beecher rarely preached from a full manuscript during his later years. His pockets were often full of small scraps of paper covered with random jottings and flashes of insight, and he kept a small notebook of illustrations and sermon ideas not yet "ripened." On Sunday mornings, Beecher retired to his study for an hour after breakfast, where he chose a ripe sermon topic, selected a text, and made a sketchy one-page outline before going to church. Even after the service began, he might change his sermon topic and text before he stood up to preach.

After a large fire in Brooklyn burned Plymouth Church two years after his arrival, Beecher designed the reconstructed church with a much larger sanctuary and no pulpit, providing him greater freedom in his sermon delivery. He preferred a loosely connected sermon form, often stringing together a series of illustrations, which he called "windows in an argument." Notetakers transcribed his sermons verbatim for weekly publication and worldwide distribution, sometimes telegraphing them word for word to Chicago newspapers. In 1871, Plymouth Church member Henry W. Sage honored Beecher by endowing the annual Lyman Beecher Lectureship at Yale, and Henry Ward Beecher gave those lectures for the first three years. Fifty years after his death, textbooks on rhetoric and homiletics still quoted his advice and reprinted his sermons.

Many knew Beecher as a preacher, but still more knew him as a journalist, an avocation first begun in Cincinnati and

Indianapolis as a "recreation" and distraction from preaching. Soon after his move to Brooklyn, Beecher became a columnist for the Congregational *New York Independent*, eventually publishing an anthology of his weekly columns (which earned the name *Star Papers* from Beecher's signature asterisk). From 1861 to 1863, he edited the *Independent*, and in 1870 he became founding editor of the ecumenical *Christian Union*.

Throughout his ministry, Beecher displayed a flair for the theatrical. As early as 1848, he held the first of many mock "slave auctions" in his church, urging his parishioners to put their money, watches, and jewelry in the offering plate, to purchase a young slavegirl's freedom. In another melodramatic effort to keep slavery confined to the south, Beecher supported the colonization of territorial Kansas by antislavery Northerners, campaigning to buy Sharp's rifles (soon known as "Beecher's Bibles") to defend abolitionist Kansas settlers under attack. In the 1870s, while other churches appointed committees to allocate pew seating according to established social criteria (including age, wealth, and social rank) and charged fees that were set accordingly, Beecher's church auctioned its seat assignments to the highest bidder—regardless of social standing or church membership—in a dramatic and highly publicized "pew auction" every January.

As an adviser to presidents and chaplain to an entire nation, Beecher had a hand in shaping America's emergent civil religion. After an 1863 speaking trip to England and Scotland—widely but perhaps wrongly credited with swinging British public opinion from the South to the North—Oliver Wendell Holmes dubbed Beecher "Minister Plenipotentiary." Abraham Lincoln recognized Beecher's leadership by choosing him to address the nation as the Union flag rose once again over Fort Sumter at the close of the Civil War.

Scandal marred the last years of Beecher's career. In 1872, Theodore Tilton publicly accused Beecher of adultery with his wife Elizabeth. A six-month civil trial resulted in a hung jury, voting nine to three in favor of acquitting Beecher. Although the evidence was not entirely clear, the members of Plymouth believed their pastor, and voted to give him $100,000 to help pay for trial expenses. Elizabeth Tilton retreated into isolation; Theodore Tilton retired overseas; and Beecher continued in his pastorate for the remaining fifteen years of his life.

The course of Beecher's life, from the stern Calvinism of his youth to the romantic progressivism of his maturity, paralleled the experiences of many. In his preaching, in his speaking, and in his writing, Henry Ward Beecher served as prophet, guide, and exemplar to an entire generation of Americans.

Caskey, M., *Chariot of Fire: Religion and the Beecher Family*, 1978. Clark, C. E., Jr., *Henry Ward Beecher: Spokesman for a Middle-Class America*, 1978.

DAVID B. MCCARTHY

ADDRESSES TO STUDENTS:
THE NEED OF "A BELIEF"
Henry Ward Beecher

Now a word or two more. You would ask me, "Do not you think that it will be necessary, if we are to preach, that we should be orthodox?" I should like to see a report taken here of what orthodoxy is; I do not believe that there would be two of you that would agree, and it comes back to the old familiar saw, "Orthodoxy is my doxy and heterodoxy is your doxy." But ought not a man to have some distinct system in his own mind? I think he ought. I am not here to dispossess men of intelligence and of rectitude, of the idea that beliefs are unimportant. Every man ought to have a system. He ought to have the high Calvinist view, although it is measured the other way, I think. He ought to have the High Church view in all the different denominations, and the Low Church view, or any of them. Pick out any of them, but see to it that you get the heart right, for the heart is that element that, when it exists in reality and power, corrects all theology practically. Do not think that you have preached everything that you are going to preach because you put a great deal of work into a sermon or a series of them. Be humble, and go on to do the best you can today and the best you can next time, and the horizon will open wider and wider. I laboured under great disadvantages in coming into the Christian ministry. My father was a very eminent theologian and preacher, and that is enough to beat the head in of any son of his that comes after him; because we are all measured by the reputation of the father. I went off out of the city. I went out into the country. I really expected to live and die in Indiana, and it is in my heart to do it yet—I love the state. I went into the woods, and on the prairies, and everywhere. I had very little to say. I had gone through the whole circle of debate and theology, and so on. I had had more than enough of it. I had had a revelation of the nature of Christ, and at first it was no more than a start to me. It grew, however, more and more, but it was not until I had been preaching about four or five years that I had a horizon that extended around the whole circle. I preached in disquietude and in almost discouragement during that time, but at last I came to that feeling—"I do believe that I shall now be a preacher."

From *A Summer in England with Henry Ward Beecher,* ed. J. B. Pond (New York: Fords, Howard, and Hulbert, 1887), 90–98.

Bernard of Clairvaux.   (1090–1153) Bernard was a Cistercian abbot and monastic theologian. His family belonged to the lower nobility of Burgundy, where he was educated by secular canons for a conventional ecclesiastical career. At the age of twenty, however, he entered the austere new reformed order at Cîteaux; three years later he was chosen to found another Cistercian monastery at Clairvaux. As abbot there for thirty-eight years, he proved a dynamic leader for his own monks and for the church at large.

Advisor to popes and counselor to kings, Bernard engaged in many theological and political controversies, which he entered with reluctance but, once involved, prosecuted with extreme zeal. Through his letters and sermons, he was in large measure personally responsible for securing the condemnations of the innovative theologians Abelard and Gilbert de la Porrée and for raising widespread support for the disastrous Second Crusade. Friends and enemies alike agreed that he was an earnest advocate of the truth as he saw it, as well as a compelling speaker; when he preached a sermon on conversion to a group of students in Paris, at least three of them were moved to renounce their studies at once and become monks.

Bernard was the foremost representative in his day of traditional monastic theology, which eschewed the new dialectic then coming into fashion in the cathedral schools. He wrote treatises on monastic reform, the ministry of bishops, the doctrine of grace, and contemplative prayer, as well as several collections of sermons and hundreds of letters. Closely tied to the Bible, the theology of the early church, and the liturgy, Bernard's writings were meditative and reflective rather than logical and scientific in their approach. Although he was certainly capable of subtle reasoning and persuasive argument, he was more concerned to move the affections of his readers to prayer than to convince their minds of the rightness of his point of view.

Bernard preached on many occasions, both to his own monks at Clairvaux and to other audiences. However, there is little we can say with confidence about either the style or the content of those sermons. The sermon texts that have been preserved are highly polished literary works that Bernard dictated to scribes, edited for publication, and then revised repeatedly until the very end of his life. Some of them probably contain the same thoughts and images he used when he actually preached. Many others were originally composed for a reading public rather than a listening congregation, even though they outwardly conform to the conventions of the medieval homiletic genre.

Among Bernard's first published works were four homilies in praise of the Virgin Mary. Bernard's sermons also included many on diverse subjects, some 120 sermons for the feasts of the liturgical year, and his celebrated collection of eighty-six sermons on the Song of Songs, composed over the last eighteen years of Bernard's life. Even so, this great work extends only to the first verse of the second chapter of the Song of Songs because Bernard devoted many sermons to a single verse, and some are topical sermons that do not refer to the biblical text at all. Like his predecessor Origen,* Bernard identified the bride in the Song of Songs allegorically with both the church and the Christian soul.

Bernard's central theme was the love of God as experienced in the interior life of the soul through contemplation. He believed that the ultimate gift of divine grace, received only through ascetic discipline and humble prayer, is the chaste kiss of mystical union with Christ: "an unreserved infusion of joys, a revealing of mysteries, a marvelous and indistinguishable mingling of the divine light with the enlightened mind" (*On the Song of Songs* 2:2). This ardent devotion to the humanity of Christ the Bridegroom influenced much subsequent medieval preaching and piety.

The twelfth century has been called the Age of the Individual. We see this reflected in Bernard's sermons, which pay careful attention to the psychology of devotion. Here style reflects content. His language is warm and intimate, full of references to the subtle variations of affective experience in relationships both human and divine. An extraordinary use of rhythmic phrasing gave his sermons an almost musical quality, enhanced by alliteration, punning wordplay, and surprisingly original references to biblical and liturgical texts. Both the vocabulary and the sentence structure of his Latin were heavily influenced by the French vernacular, which must have given his original audience a sense of being addressed by a lively and contemporary voice. Subsequent generations seeking insight into the realm of spiritual experience have continued to find in Bernard an eloquent and discerning guide (*see* History of Preaching).

Bernard of Clairvaux, *On the Song of Songs,* 4 vols., trans. K. Walsh and I. Edmonds, 1971–80. **Casey, M.,** *Athirst for God: Spiritual Desire in Bernard of Clairvaux's Sermons on the Song of Songs,* 1988. **Gilson, E.,** *The Mystical Theology of St. Bernard,* trans. A.H.C. Downes, 1990.

ARTHUR G. HOLDER

LOVE
Bernard of Clairvaux
But if you love the Lord your God with all your heart, with all your mind, and with all your strength (Mark 12:30), and, leaping in desire beyond that love of love with which love in action is satisfied to the divine love to which it is a stepping stone, you will be wholly on fire with the fullness of what you have received by the Spirit and you will taste God, not as he really is, for that is impossible for any creatures, but certainly to the limit of which you are capable. Then you will love yourself as you are, since you will know that there is nothing to love in you except insofar as you are his. He is all your reason for loving, and you pour all your love out upon him. You will know yourself as you are, I say, when you discover by experience of your love of yourself that there is nothing in you worthy of love except for his sake, you who without him are nothing.

As for your neighbor, whom you ought to love as yourself (Matt. 19:19): To experience him as he is, is the same as to experience yourself, for he is as you are. You do not love yourself except as you love God, so love as you do yourself all those who love him likewise. . . .

Give me a man who above all loves God with all his heart, himself and his neighbor in that they love God; but his enemy as one who will one day love perhaps; his parents who begot him with a warm natural love, but his spiritual teachers the more because of grace. . . . Give me such a man, I say, and I will boldly call him wise, because he recognizes things for what they really are, because he can truly and confidently claim, "He has ordained love in me" (Song 2:4). . . . O Wisdom, stretching from end to end, establishing and ordering everything (Wis. 8:1), and arranging all things sweetly by enhancing feeling and making it orderly, guide what we do as your everlasting truth requires, so that each of us may securely glory in you and say, "He ordained love in me" (Song 2:4). For you are the strength of God and the Wisdom of God (1 Cor. 1:24), Christ, the Bridegroom of the Church and our Lord, God blessed forever. Amen (Rom. 1:25).

From "Sermon on the Song of Songs 50:6–8," in *Bernard of Clairvaux: Selected Works*, trans. G. R. Evans (New York: Paulist Press, 1987), 244–45.

Berthold of Regensburg. (ca.

1210–1272) Although Berthold, a Franciscan friar, was the most renowned popular preacher in Germany during the entire Middle Ages, little is known about his birth or childhood. He received an excellent education, possibly at Magdeburg, and joined the Order of Friars Minor at Regensburg, where he became lector and then preacher. From 1240 until his death, he preached not only in his native Bavaria but throughout the rest of Germany, in Switzerland, Austria, and France as well. In 1263 Pope Urban IV ordered him to assist Albert the Great by preaching a crusade, and he became actively involved as a mediator in various affairs of both church and state.

As a mendicant friar, Berthold followed the common Franciscan* practice of traveling from city to city, preaching as he went. He drew huge crowds that contemporary accounts numbered in the tens, even hundreds, of thousands. Preaching in the open air, he used a wooden pulpit

constructed in front of a church or in the middle of a field and told the crowds to sit downwind so that the sound of his voice would be carried in their direction.

Berthold preached in German, but he arranged for some of his sermons to be set down in Latin because poorly educated monks who were taking notes while he preached often made many errors in their transcriptions. Although five collections of Latin sermons are in existence, most of them have never been printed, and many sermons are of doubtful authenticity. There are also some 125 German sermon texts or fragments attributed to Berthold; no more than thirty-seven appear to be authentic, and even these were based on notes taken by listeners and later edited by others after Berthold's death.

The Latin sermon texts are replete with divisions and subdivisions, and frequent citations of "authorities" such as the church fathers and Bernard of Clairvaux;* this indicates that Berthold was familiar with the homiletic theory found in contemporary manuals on the art of preaching. The German texts, however, lack this kind of systematic organization. Thematic rather than strictly exegetical, many of them are loosely structured around a numerical theme, such as the seven planets, the twelve tribes of Israel, the seven virtues, or the eight kinds of food in heaven; this kind of simple structure must have served the preacher as a useful mnemonic device even as it gave his audience an outline to assist them in following his train of thought.

Berthold's sermons were presented in a simple, informal style in everyday language. He made extensive use of parables, anecdotes, illustrations from nature, satire and other forms of humor, imaginary dialogues (e.g., between God and the devil), and direct address. He had a flair for the dramatic, which he put to good use in his preaching. A favorite device was to suppose that members of his audience were reacting negatively to one of his many moral admonitions, saying something like, "Oh, Brother Berthold, what you ask is too difficult." Then he would respond to his imaginary interlocutors by offering words of encouragement, persuasion, or further rebuke.

The principal themes of Berthold's sermons were those St. Francis had commended to his followers: the vices and the virtues, the pains of hell and the glories of heaven. Berthold continually called on Christians to repent and lead morally upright lives in obedience to the Ten Commandments that they may receive God's mercy and avoid God's wrath. Although he addressed matters of doctrine on occasion, it was usually in order to explain some liturgical or devotional practice or to warn against some spiritual danger found in the teachings of heretics like the Waldensians or the Cathari.

Berthold's stern rebukes fell on clergy and laity alike and on all classes. He inveighed against every kind of vice, vanity, and superstition, but he was especially disapproving of avaricious persons such as those who practiced usury and the corrupt "penny-preachers" who sold forgiveness for a fee. Much of Berthold's moral teaching parallels that found in medieval handbooks of penitence designed to be used by clergy who were hearing confessions, and it is probable that he derived many of his categories of various types of sin, as well as some of his case illustrations, from this source.

Sometimes cited as a forerunner of Luther,* Berthold is better understood as a moral reformer who accepted the doctrine of the medieval church but was appalled by the church's failure to uphold its own standards of conduct and genuine piety. As a preacher, he is remembered for his inventive and dramatic style, for his use of the German vernacular, and for his extraordinary success in capturing the attention and affection of the common people.

Banta, F. G., "Berthold von Regensburg: Investigations Past and Present," *Traditio* 25 (1969), 472–79. Iannucci, R. J., *The Treatment of the Capital Sins and the Decalogue in the German Sermons of Berthold von Regensburg*, 1942. Wailes, S. L., "The Composition of Vernacular Sermons by Berthold von Regensburg," *Michigan Germanic Studies* 5, 1979, 1–24. ARTHUR G. HOLDER

BEWARE OF CATS!
Berthold of Regensburg

No household beast can work such great harm in so short a time as this, most especially in summer: let all take good heed of the cat (*Katze*). She goes away and licks a toad, under some hedge or wherever she may find it, until the toad begins to bleed; then the poison makes her thirsty, and she comes and drinks at the same water where people drink, and defiles it, so that many people are sick for half a year, or a whole year long, or even to their life's end; or it may be that they take their sudden death from it. Or again the cat drinks so greedily that a drop falls from her eye into the water, or she sneezes into it, and anyone who uses that water must taste of bitter death. . . . Wherefore, you people, drive her away, for the breath that comes from her throat is most unsound and perilous. Let her be driven forth from the kitchen or from wherever you may be, for she is deadly unclean. And thence also has the heretic his name of *Ketzer*, since in all his ways he is like no beast so much as a cat. He goes as demurely to other folk, and speaks as sweetly and can bear himself as softly as any cat; and just as suddenly has he defiled people's bodies. He holds such sweet speech of God and the angels, that you would swear a thousand oaths that he is an angel himself; yet he is the devil incarnate. And he promises to let you see an angel, and teach you to see God with your bodily eyes, yet he has swiftly parted you from your Christian faith, and you are lost for evermore. . . . Had I a sister in a country in which there were only one heretic, yet that one heretic would keep me in fear for her, so noxious is he. Therefore let everyone take heed of him. I myself, by God's grace, am as fast rooted in the Christian faith as any Christian person should rightly be;

yet, rather than dwell knowingly one brief fortnight in the same house with a heretic, I would dwell a whole year with five hundred devils! What, heretic! Are you by chance in this congregation! I pray to Almighty God that there be none here present!

> From "Blessed Are the Pure in Heart" German Sermon 25, trans. adapted from G. G. Coulton, "A Revivalist of Six Centuries Ago," *North American Review* 185 (1907): 273–82.

Blackwood, Andrew Watterson.

(1882–1966) Blackwood was the best-known and most widely published homiletician in America in the twentieth century. Born in Kansas of Scottish Covenanter parents, he took his undergraduate education at Franklin College in Ohio and at Harvard and his seminary studies at Princeton Theological Seminary and Xenia Theological Seminary, from which he graduated in 1908. His career as a pastor spanned seventeen years. After ministering briefly in Oklahoma and Kansas, he moved to Sixth United Presbyterian in Pittsburgh, Pennsylvania, First Presbyterian in Columbia, South Carolina, and Indianola Presbyterian in Columbus, Ohio. Then, for thirty-three years he taught: as professor of English Bible and Biblical Theology at Louisville Presbyterian Seminary (1925–1930), as professor of homiletics and later chair of Practical Theology at Princeton Theological Seminary (1930–1950), and as professor of homiletics at the Temple University School of Theology (1950–1958).

From his favorite teacher at Harvard he learned to study Shakespeare intensively, one play at a time, a method that he later employed in teaching his students how to prepare courses of sermons through various books of the Bible. From Harvard's debate coach he learned the principles of argumentation and participated in an experimental laboratory in drama, an approach that he later adapted to his preaching workshops. Because he had been disappointed both at Princeton and Xenia with the quality of his classes in preaching, early in his first pastorate he began an intensive study of the biographies, published sermons, and lectures on preaching by master preachers throughout the ages: Luther, Bunyan, Beecher, Chalmers, Brooks, Spurgeon, Gossip, Truett, Fosdick, Macartney, Stewart, Weatherhead, Barth, and Chappell. Experience strengthened his confidence in the case study method. Thirty years of study about preaching taught him that almost every master preacher had made a study of printed sermons by admired preachers.

Blackwood introduced an imposing number and variety of preaching classes at Princeton: "The Psychology of Preaching," "Preaching from the Old Testament," "New Testament Preachers," "Evangelistic Preaching," "The Art of Preaching," "The Theory of Preaching," "Modern Preachers," and "Modern Sermons." In all of them, however, ran the undercurrents of his twin pedagogical methods: case studies of master sermons and individual coaching.

Blackwood believed that careful writing was essential to improve one's preaching, and he advised his students to strive for something worthy of publication every month. He practiced what he taught. His books became an extension of his seminary classes, giving him an international forum and reputation. He addressed gaps in the general area of pastoral theology with volumes on evangelism, pastoral leadership, public worship, the funeral, and the developing new minister, but he concentrated mainly on helping preachers with their preaching.

The Fine Art of Preaching (1937) and *The Preparation of Sermons* (1948) discuss the theory and practice of preaching. The chapters in *Preaching from the Bible* (1941) set the stage for *Expository Preaching for Today* (1953), *Biographical Preaching for Today* (1954), and *Doctrinal Preaching for Today* (1956). *Special-Day Sermons for Evangelicals* (1961) and his only book of sermons, *This Year of Our*

Lord (1943), provide examples of practical sermons on religious days and biblical sermons on secular days. *Preaching in Times of Reconstruction* (1945), *The Protestant Pulpit* (1947), and *Evangelical Sermons for Our Day* (1959) were designed to make master preachers and worthy sermons available for case studies by today's preachers.

Theologically, Blackwood was an evangelical who embraced the older orthodoxy, and he was called to Princeton partly for that reason. He was not a reactionary, however. He admonished ministers to preach positively because he felt much preaching was too negative, and he urged students to learn their craft from master preachers like Fosdick, whom he admired for the structure and style of his sermons.

Blackwood brought a needed freshness and practicality to traditional homiletics. Basing his theory solidly on classical rhetorical thought, his treatment of topics, structure, supportive materials, introductions, and conclusions was fairly standard, though he included newer forms like induction and narrative. He left it to other departments in the seminary to teach the principles of exegesis and hermeneutics, and he did not deal with how current theological discussions influence the pulpit. What he did he did well. He taught a high view of preaching, urging students to make it their main business. He supplemented classical homiletical theory with careful coaching and case studies of sermons by master preachers. He wrote a variety of helpful books, and he taught hundreds of preachers to preach better.

Adams, J. E., *The Homiletical Innovations of Andrew W. Blackwood*, Vol. 3, *Studies in Preaching*, 1977.   WAYNE E. SHAW

Bonhoeffer, Dietrich. (1906–1945) German theologian and preacher Dietrich Bonhoeffer was martyred by the Nazis at Flossenbürg prison on April 9, 1945, just days before the end of World War II. He had been arrested and imprisoned in 1943 by the Gestapo for his complicity in an unsuccessful plot to murder Adolf Hitler. His principal works, *Communion of Saints* (1927), *Act and Being* (1930), *The Cost of Discipleship* (1937), *Life Together* (1939), *Ethics* (an unfinished work, largely written between 1940–43 and published posthumously), and his *Letters and Papers from Prison*, also published posthumously, have exerted an amazing and continuing influence upon Christian clergy and laity.

Initially Bonhoeffer was regarded as a heroic martyr of the church for his courageous resistance to the Nazis and for his direction of a Confessing Church seminary in opposition to the "German Christians." Subsequently, as his writings and letters were read internationally, he was hailed as the author of a radical new view of the church. His terms "religionless Christianity" and "world come of age," together with his questioning whether the church should or could speak to the world in the future, caused the so-called "death of God" theologians to count Bonhoeffer in their camp. As his works were examined more closely, however, particularly in the context of his life, an altogether different picture emerged. Rather than an opponent of the gathered church and its proclamation, Bonhoeffer was revealed as a dedicated preacher and a significant contributor to the theology of proclamation.

The notes of his lectures on homiletics to the Confessing Church seminary at Finkenwalde on the Baltic reveal three emphases that dominated Bonhoeffer's thinking on preaching: word, church, and world. Each of these is bound to his central emphasis on Christology and serves to explain his most controversial expressions.

According to Bonhoeffer, Christ is the Word of God present in the sermon. With Luther* he believed that the word of God exists both in the Bible and in the sermon but essentially in the latter. The proclaimed word is nothing less than "Christ himself, walking through his congregation as the Word" (*Communion of Saints*, 161).

Similarly, in spite of its imperfections, the church is the visible form of the body of Christ on earth, and it remains the locus of the preached word. "Christ is . . . present . . . as the Word of the Church, i.e., as the spoken word of preaching" (*Christology*, 52). Even the silence of the church, which the falsification of the gospel had forced upon it, was a temporary silence, a humble waiting upon the return of its true Word.

Finally, the world cannot attain its true nature apart from the proclamation of the word. Apart from preaching, the world inevitably deifies itself and its true worldliness—i.e., the world as God intended it, one in which its godlessness is reconciled with God—is lost. "Genuine worldliness is achieved only through emancipation by Christ . . . " (*Ethics*, 295).

Without that emancipation through preaching, the world is enslaved by its own new secular religion, a religion of "alien laws, ideologies, and idols" (*Ethics*, 296). The world has indeed "come of age" (which in German means merely to come to the age of responsibility). But it can only find itself when it leaves its God-of-the-gaps, or its deus-ex-machina, and comes to the gospel. This is "religionless Christianity."

In the practice of this theology of proclamation, Bonhoeffer preached sermons closely bound to the biblical text. In his early preaching he generally used brief texts, but later he consciously turned to longer passages of scripture for exposition. He believed that every text had a center and that every sermon—even thematic sermons and homilies—should proceed along one section of a circle about this center of the text. Bonhoeffer began his sermon preparation, therefore, in prayer over the text. Next he analyzed the text according to concrete questions: What does it tell us about God? about

ourselves? What do I wish to avoid in the text? After repeated questioning and rereading, the preacher begins to see—almost in a mystical way—the meaning of the text.

Bonhoeffer believed in making a clear outline of his thoughts before writing the sermon. Although he invariably prepared a manuscript, he took nothing into the pulpit, not even a sheet of brief notes, which he deemed "a dubious practice." He did not memorize his sermons verbatim but committed the progression of ideas to memory. He believed a sermon that was difficult to commit to memory was not a good one or at least not a clear one. In the pulpit Bonhoeffer spoke with driving energy and direct language. He excelled at graphic description of the biblical and contemporary situations and moved seamlessly between the two. He regarded style as something not to be cultivated. Nothing should be based on the persuasiveness or appeal of the preacher's personality or life story; everything must be committed to the word.

Bonhoeffer's commitment to preaching was lifelong. In the summer of 1940, he wrote that if he knew he had only a short time to live he would want to teach again and "to preach often" (*Gesammelte Schriften*, 1, 7). And so he did. On the last Sunday of his life, he preached a sermon at the insistence of his fellow prisoners. The next day he was hanged by the Gestapo.

Bonhoeffer, Dietrich, *Christology*, trans. J. Bowden, 1966; *Communion of Saints*, trans. R. G. Smith, 1963; *Ethics*, ed. E. Bethge, trans. N. Smith, 1955; "The Proclaimed Word," *Worldly Preaching: Lectures on Homiletics*, ed. and trans., with critical commentary, by C. E. Fant, 1991, 102.

CLYDE E. FANT

THE HUMANITY OF THE WORD
Dietrich Bonhoeffer
The proclaimed word is the Christ bearing human nature. This word is no new incarnation, but the Incarnate One who

bears the sins of the world. Through the Holy Spirit this word becomes the actualization of his acceptance and sustenance. The word of the sermon intends to accept humanity, nothing else. It wants to bear the whole of human nature. In the congregation all sins should be cast upon the Word. Preaching must be so done that the hearer places all needs, cares, fears, and sins upon the Word. The Word accepts all these things. When preaching is done in this way, it is the proclamation of Christ. This proclamation of the Christ does not regard its primary responsibility to be giving advice, arousing emotions, or stimulating the will—it will do these things, too—but its intention is to sustain us. The Word is there that burdens might be laid upon it. We are all borne up by the Word of Christ. Because it does so, it creates fellowship. Because the Word includes us to itself, it makes us members of the Body of Christ. As such we share in the responsibility of upholding one another. Thus the Word of Christ also presupposes Christian fellowship. The Word intends that no one should remain alone, for in him no one remains alone. The Word makes individuals part of the body.

> From "The Proclaimed Word," *Worldly Preaching: Lectures on Homiletics.* Ed. and trans., with critical commentary, by C. E. Fant (New York: Crossroad, 1991).

Boniface of Crediton.　(680–755)
Boniface was a missionary and archbishop who did much to establish the Christian faith in Germany. Born in or near Creedy (or Crediton) in Devon, he was christened Winfrid (or Wynfrith) but took on the name of Boniface either when he entered holy orders or when Pope Gregory II made him bishop of all German lands in 722 or 723.

The region in which Boniface was born was disputed by Celts and Saxons. One contemporary biographer suggests that growing up at the meeting places of two cultures—one of which had only recently become Christian—left a subliminal but powerful imprint on Boniface, equipping him for living among alien peoples in a frontier situation in his missionary work (Tomlin, 14). Boniface was educated at Exeter and Nutsall or Nutsey (now Nursling). There he became head of the abbey school and compiled the first Latin grammar in the country.

In 716, aspiring to enter the mission field, Boniface received his abbot's permission to travel to Friesland. His intent was to assist Willibrord, a Northumbrian monk and missionary bishop of Utrecht. Because of the war between the Frisians and Charles Martel, their work was aborted and Boniface briefly returned to Nutsall. In 718 he set out again, this time to Rome to obtain a letter of protection from Charles Martel, and worked in southern Germany, Thuringia, and Hesse. The fabled episode of cutting down the sacred oak at Geismar occurred during this period. As part of his efforts to eradicate heathen beliefs, he felled a tree that had been regarded as sacred to Thor or Odin.

In 732, Boniface was made archbishop and primate of all Germany. Later he became archbishop of Mainz and papal legate, establishing churches and monasteries throughout the region, including Fulda, his favorite. In 754, he deputized an associate to carry out his episcopal duties and returned to missionary work in Friesland. In June of 755, on a day that there was to be a confirmation, Boniface and several other Christians were murdered by some Frisians who resented the destruction of their idols. The missionary's body was taken to Utrecht but finally interred at Fulda. Boniface is honored in Italy, France, Germany, and the Netherlands, as well as in England. He has been called "the apostle of Germany" for his work in building a united Christian Europe at a time when many lands had been conquered by Muslim soldiers.

Boniface's renown cannot be attributed to the homiletical works he left behind. There are fifteen short, probably genuine, sermons of his written in Latin, though this may not have been the language in which they were preached. The form and content of the sermons suggests they were addressed to nominal Christians rather than delivered in a missionary situation. Among the themes addressed are baptismal vows, the creed, the Lord's Prayer, and the need for virtuous living. They are not lengthy expositions of a text but often relate to the lesson for the day and employ an allegorical method of interpretation. One contemporary biographer claims that Boniface was neither an intellectual like St. Anselm nor a mystic like St. Bernard, but combined a thorough knowledge of the Bible with a zeal for perfection and a puritanical temperament (Tomlin, 34–35).

A more complete picture of Boniface as preacher, missionary, and church leader emerges in his letters that have been preserved. From these we learn that Boniface took a hard line against those who taught false doctrine. This was manifested during the controversy in 745 over two Frankish pseudo-bishops whose teachings were unorthodox. In other instances, however, gentleness and humility are the dominant notes in his efforts to bring people to Christian faith and to discipline those in his care. His concessions to human frailty are evidenced in a letter written in 747 to monks of the Abbey of Fritzlar. It ends with, "Let each one of you strive with all his might to preserve his own chastity and, in your common life, to be helpful to the rest and abide in brotherly love until, God willing, I shall be with you again" (Letter 40). Another letter, written around 738, addresses the listeners with affection, contains several biblical citations, borrows the phraseology of scripture elsewhere, and closes with a benediction that would be equally appropriate for a homily:

We earnestly beseech your brotherly goodness to be mindful of us, who are worth so little, in your prayers that we may be delivered from the snare of Satan the huntsman and from wicked and cruel men, that the word of God may make its way and be glorified. We beseech you to obtain through your holy prayers, that our Lord and God Jesus Christ, "who will have all men to be saved, and to come unto the knowledge of God," may turn the hearts of the pagan Saxons to the catholic faith, that they may free themselves from the snares of the devil in which they are bound and may be gathered among the children of Mother Church. . . .

May the Omnipotent Creator always keep the unity and communion of your affection in power and progress in Christ (Letter 46).

Boniface is remembered not as a powerful preacher or shaper of homiletical theory but as an able missionary and bishop who helped prepare the way for establishment of the church in Germany.

Emerton, E., trans., *The Letters of Saint Boniface*, 1940. Keep, D., *St. Boniface and His World*, 1979. Tomlin, E.W.F., *The World of St. Boniface*, 1981.   CAROL M. NORÉN

Booth, William. (1829–1912) Booth, the third of five children, was born in Nottingham, England, to Samuel and Mary Booth. Apprenticed to a pawnbroker as a teenager, he confronted the specter of grinding poverty blighting the face of England with poor harvests, high prices, and starving thousands. Without the influence of John Wesley's Christian social concern, Booth might have become just another social reformer. Instead he joined the Wesleyan Church in Nottingham and became a local preacher, evangelizing the streets by night and pawnbroking by day.

Moving to London in 1849, he served several church circuits and did evangelistic work with great success. A disciple of John Wesley, his preaching and social consciousness were characteristic of a true Methodist evangelist. Ironically, his success in evangelism caused a falling out with the Wesleyan Church and he joined the New Connection Methodists. After eight years with them, he ventured out on faith as an independent evangelist.

He established an organization called the East London Christian Mission to minister in Whitechapel, the worst district in the city. Whitechapel featured militant atheism, rampant crime, abject poverty, and an alphabet of social ills. For twelve years the Mission carried on a highly successful ministry that spread even into the fashionable West End of London. When Booth changed a publicity piece to read, "The Christian Mission is a Salvation Army," he secured a place in history for a military-type organization admired to this day for its unashamed evangelistic preaching and aggressive ministry to poverty-stricken, homeless, and otherwise troubled people.

Though hindered by respiratory and intestinal problems, Booth was a powerful preacher, an orator who preached without the classical literary bent affecting most preachers of that era. He was plain-spoken yet demonstrated the ability to move his audiences to tears in one moment and to smiles in the next. His faith, his single-minded consecration to God's work, and the natural force of his personality produced his very persuasive and powerful preaching. Yet he recognized the futility of preaching to someone with no money, no home, and no food. He asked, "What is the use of preaching the gospel to men whose whole attention is concentrated upon a mad, desperate struggle to keep themselves alive?" (Bishop, 69).

Booth's major contribution to homiletics was to see the important and unyielding connection between social welfare and spiritual health. Both were equally important to William Booth, who ministered with compassion to the physical needs of fallen men and women and preached eloquently to their souls.

Bishop, E., *Blood and Fire*, 1964. **Collier, R.,** *The General Next to God*, 1965. **Howard, H. C.,** "William Booth and His Army," *The Methodist Review Quarterly* (January 1917). **Page, J.,** *General Booth: The Man and His Work*, 1901.   GRANVILLE E. TYSON

ARE YOU READY?
General William Booth

[Booth is preaching to an immense crowd in the open air.] I think it is a great salvation, and I reckon I am a judge; I have been testing it for fifty-four years. Fifty-four years ago, when Jesus Christ knocked at the door of my heart and told me He had come to save me, I opened the door, fell at His feet, accepted His mercy. He pardoned my sins, and wrote my name in the Lamb's book of life.

It is there today, and the salvation is in my soul today. I have tried it fifty-four years in all sorts of circumstances. I have had my trials, I can tell you; there is nobody in this crowd that has had more to do with the bitterness of this life than I have. And when waves of sorrow have rolled over me, when the cold waters of death have come to my feet, when I have seen the darlings of my heart go over the river, I have proved it a great salvation; and haven't you got some dear ones who think so? Is there nobody who loved you now in heaven who thought it was a great salvation? Ah! you have got mothers and you have got fathers, you have got children and some of you have wives and husbands who thought it a great salvation; and my friends, you will think it is a great salvation some day when you lie on the banks of the river of death and look over its dark waters into the eternal world; you will think it is a great salvation then, whatever you think about it now. God and the angels and the godly people upon the earth and the saints who have washed their robes in the blood of the Lamb in heaven, they think it is a great salvation.

If you are only ready—oh! If you are only ready! If you are only ready, death will be a wonderful gain! You will get away from your temptations. What an awful thing temptation is! Oh, how often I am bewildered with it! There are some men and women whose whole lives are made a torture by the temptations of earth and hell and the temptations of their own flesh. Life is a torture. Cheer up my brother! Cheer up my sister! Hold fast. In the dark and dreary hours don't let go. Stick to Jesus Christ. It will only be for a season; you will soon cross the river, and when you get to the pearly gates you can turn round and bid good-bye to the devil: "Farewell, farewell; I shall never see you any more," and the angels will take you in.

> From J. Page, *General Booth: The Man and His Work* (London: S. W. Partridge and Co., 1901), 73–75.

Bossuet, Jacques-Bénigne. (1627–1704)

Bossuet was one of a group of celebrated preachers at the court of Louis XIV of France and the only one whose work has survived as a classic. His writings have remained a French cultural reference point and a source of literary allusion akin to the King James Bible in the English-speaking world.

As an inspiring orator, Bossuet attracted the attention of fashionable Paris. At a time when high birth counted for much in the French Catholic Church, he came from a relatively obscure provincial legal background in Dijon (Burgundy) and was first educated there at the Jesuit college. He became a youthful canon at Metz when his family moved to Lorraine and he went to study at the Collège de Navarre in Paris. This solid classical education, deployed with exceptional aptness and judgment, underlay his eloquence in the pulpit and swiftly led him to be entrusted with other duties. Consecrated bishop of the small southwestern diocese of Condom in 1669, only a year later he was appointed tutor to the heir to the crown and was elected to the French Academy the year after that. Realizing he would be unable to reside in his see, he resigned in 1671; but when the Dauphin's marriage ended tutorial duties, Bossuet became Bishop of Meaux, a small city close to Paris and to the court at Versailles, where until his death he remained a central figure in the political and theological affairs of France.

Politics and theology were indeed closely entwined in the public life of his day. Bossuet wrote extensively against Protestants (notably the History of the Variations of the Protestant Churches, 1688) at a time when Calvinists were expelled from the kingdom, and yet he corresponded with the German philosopher Leibniz over the possibilities of Christian reunion. He developed for his royal pupil a theory of history (Discourse on Universal History, 1681) and of politics (Politics Drawn from Holy Scripture, posthumously published in 1709), which highlights the intervention of providence in human affairs and supports the divine right of kings while emphasizing the ultimate sovereignty of God.

These ideas naturally recur in his preaching. They are allied to an intense preoccupation with the salvation of the individual soul characteristic of the later Counter-Reformation. As a student in Paris, Bossuet had fallen under the spell of St. Vincent de Paul, the Apostle of Charity whose burning zeal inspires much of the social morality to be found, for instance, in the "Sermon on the Eminent Dignity of the Poor in the Church" of 1659. One of Bossuet's most striking talents is an ability to bring these overarching principles, the love of God and neighbor, the supernatural, and the natural order, to bear on the particular circumstances of a sermon or funeral oration.

Over a long career, these circumstances varied considerably. There was a distinction in seventeenth-century France between brief homilies delivered at Mass and full-dress sermons: the latter marked special events such as patronal festivals and major feast days or were given as a series in Advent and Lent. The central part of Bossuet's output thus consists in panegyrics of the saints, four Lent courses preached before the Court between 1660 and 1666, and two royal Advent courses of 1665 and 1669. Preachers chosen for these occasions, especially in the capital, occupied a place as central as the mass-media celebrities of our day and performed before a critical audience.

Bossuet shows an acute awareness of his hearers, addressing them directly, alluding to their experience, relying on their familiarity with some of his themes, by turns chiding, flattering, even shocking them. In addition, he was in demand as a funeral orator, orchestrating the nation's grief on occasions such as the dramatically sudden death in 1670 of the young Henrietta Maria, sister-in-law of the king, or the state funerals for the queen (in 1683) and for Condé, France's princely military hero (in 1687). He excels at the combination of biography, lamentation, and moral interpretation that the genre demands, remolding each life history so that it yields a direct and often sensational message. These great orations were for the most part printed after delivery; with a single exception, the remainder of his oratory, some of it on the basis of drafts, was published only after his death. This corpus includes addresses to religious and to assemblies of the clergy given as part of his episcopal duties.

The predominant themes of Bossuet's preaching are by definition not strikingly original: His work is a compendium of sound Catholic doctrine as taught between the Councils of Trent and Vatican I, albeit expounded with distinctive order and coherence. His mastery lies in his rhetorical power. To Bossuet, a student of classical antiquity, rhetoric* was not a disparaging term denoting empty verbal tricks but meant the systematic art of persuasion, teaching how to conceive and shape material so as to inspire the hearer with conviction. A typical sermon by Bossuet introduces a topic, divides it into two—often opposed—elements, and in a concluding section synthesizes the elements and forces the message home. This antithetical vision is thus shot through with drama: worldliness wars with austerity, sin with righteousness, death with life. But Bousuet was also steeped in the often paradoxical language of the Bible and the Fathers and used the quotation of authorities both to seal his arguments and to echo his own style. A potentially abstract doctrine became powerfully allied to vivid instances and memorably concrete images. He brought together the physical and the intangible in a way that allowed each to illuminate the other. A constant deployment of controlled verbal ingenuity enables Bossuet to say something and then instantly to gainsay it. To a certain extent these qualities arise from his being heir to a half century of increasingly poised Parisian preaching that aimed to unite delicacy of feeling with spiritual intensity. But ultimately this ability to communicate depended on a penetrating familiarity with his hearers' sensibilities. A paradox can be pushed to its limits, and the shock of an unfamiliar image in a conventional context or of a sudden change of register is effective only in the hands of someone who knows his audience and his genre.

Bayley, P., "The Art of the *pointe* in Bossuet," in *The Equilibrium of Wit: Essays for Odette de Mourgues,* ed. P. Bayley and D. Coleman, 1982. **Collinet, J.,** and **T. Goyet,** eds., *Bossuet: La Prédication au XVIIe siècle,* 1980. **Truchet, J.,** *La Prédication de Bossuet: étude des thèmes,* 2 vols., 1960.

PETER BAYLEY

KNOWLEDGE OF DEATH
Jacques-Bénigne Bossuet

Among the whole range of the human spirit's passions, one of the most intense is the desire for knowledge; and this curiosity leads mankind to strain every mental resource in the search for some arcane secret of the natural world, some original technique of artistic creativity, or some unaccustomed refinement in the conduct of business. But amid these immense yearnings to enrich our understanding by new knowledge, what happens to us is the same as happens to those who, gazing at remote vistas, fail to notice the objects close by them. I mean that our spirit, struggling to encompass far-off things and ranging, so to speak, over the heavens and the earth, passes so lightly over what is immediately present to it that we occupy our whole lives oblivious of what touches us ourselves: and not only of what touches us, but also of what we ourselves are.

Our greatest need is to gather all these wandering thoughts into our hearts. And that is why, my fellow Christians, today I invite you to accompany the Saviour to the grave of Lazarus: "*Veni et vide:* come and see." Come, mortal men, and view the sight of mortal things; come and learn what it is to be a man.

You will perhaps be surprised at my pointing you towards death to learn what you are, and think it strange to portray man in a place where he no longer exists. But, if you strive to understand what is shown us in the grave, you will readily agree that there is no more faithful interpreter, no truer reflection of human things.

The nature of a compound is never more clearly observable than when it is dissolved into its parts. . . . All we need to examine is what death robs us of and what it leaves untouched, what part of our being falls beneath death's onslaught and what other part endures the catastrophe. Then at last we shall understand what man is; and that is why I am bold to affirm that out from the valley of the shadow of death an immortal dayspring lightens the darkness of our ignorance as to our own nature. So hasten forward, mortal men, and see in the grave of Lazarus what humanity is: come and see in one and the same place the ending of all your plans and the beginning of all your hopes; come and see the simultaneous dissolving and renewal of your being; come and see the triumph of life in the victory of death: *veni et vide.*

From "Sermon on Death," delivered before the Court of France Wednesday, 22 March, 1662. *Sermon sur la mort et autres sermons,* ed. J. Truchet (Paris: Garnier-Flammarion, 1970), 130–33, trans. Peter Bayley.

Broadus, John Albert.   (1827–1895)

John Broadus was an author, professor, seminary president, and preacher in the Southern Baptist Convention. The primary focus of his adult life was the establishing and maintaining of a Baptist seminary in the south. He was born in Culpepper County, Virginia. His father, Major Edmund Broadus, was a prominent Virginia politician who strongly supported the Temperance movement. He inspired in John a strong advocacy of missions and, notably, of ministerial education. John, like his parents, was an intricate bookkeeper. At 14 he supervised his busy father's farm and kept careful records of costs of seed, yield per acre, upkeep for slaves, and wages for hired laborers. This fascination with intricate details characterized Broadus in all his ministerial work, especially his writings.

His elementary education came primarily through his parents and his older sister. The Bible, mathematics, grammar, and a limited exposure to Latin and Greek constituted most of his curriculum. Broadus learned to appreciate literature, music, and art from his mother, and he inherited a talent for elocution from his father. At age 12 he delivered a prepared speech for his father, who suffered from laryngitis. He was pleasantly surprised to find the crowd pleased and impressed. At age 16, Broadus became a Christian during a "protracted meeting."

In 1844, he decided to become a schoolteacher. He earned enough money by 1846 to enter the University of Virginia, from which he graduated in 1850 with a reputation for diligence. In that same year he was ordained, and he married Marie Harrison, the daughter of one of his professors. After teaching at the elementary level for two more years, he became pastor of the Baptist church in Charlottesville, Virginia, and an assistant professor at the University of Virginia. He gradually realized that his primary gift was in teaching, and from 1852 to near the end of his life, he was a professor who preached regularly.

In 1859, he became one of four faculty members of a new Baptist seminary in Greenville, South Carolina. He insisted on an elective curriculum in which courses were chosen along the student's own line of interest. The school closed during the Civil War but reopened in the fall of 1865. During the war, Broadus preached to the Confederate troops in Virginia, ministered to rural churches, and wrote articles for various journals. He also began a commentary on Matthew that was finally published in 1886 in the American Commentary series. When the seminary reopened, only one student elected to take Broadus's homiletics course, and he was blind. However, the care Broadus was forced to take in lecturing to the blind man led to the publication of his most significant contribution to the field of homiletics, *A Treatise on the Preparation and Delivery of Sermons*. This book was published in 1870 and has been in constant use ever since, albeit with revisions by three other authors.

The genius of *A Treatise* lies in its view of preaching as sacred rhetoric. As a child, Broadus had studied rhetoric* in the works of Aristotle, Fénelon, and Vinet. Through these influences Broadus placed great emphasis on developing individual style* in preaching. Style, as he saw it, was characterized by what we would call clarity, force, and appeal, developed by a proper use of the special materials of preaching—explanation, application, argumentation, and illustration. Thus, Broadus's book so effectively blended the principles of rhetoric to the practice of preaching that it continues to be a popular resource.

In January 1889, he delivered the Lyman Beecher Lectures on preaching at Yale. Later that year he was elected president of the seminary, which in 1877 had moved to Louisville, Kentucky (now Southern Baptist Theological Seminary). Broadus served as president until his death.

In addition to his commentary on Matthew and his watershed book on homiletics, Broadus also published *Lectures on the History of Preaching*, *Sermons and Addresses*, *Jesus of Nazareth*, the Chrysostom section of *A Select Library of the Nicene and Post-Nicene Fathers of the Christian Church*, and numerous articles and tracts.

He once likened his generation to a little boy standing on his father's shoulders claiming to be tall. Thanks to his life and work, many preachers have stood on the homiletical shoulders of John Broadus.

Broadus, J., *On the Preparation and Delivery of Sermons*, 1870, 1944, rev. ed., 1979.

AL FASOL

Brooks, Phillips.

(1835–1893) Episcopal bishop Phillips Brooks was born in Boston, the second of six boys, four of whom became priests. His parents had Brooks baptized a Unitarian, but when he was four, doctrinal differences brought them and their boys to Saint Paul's Episcopal Church. Brooks attended the Latin School, where in 1856, after graduating from Harvard, he served as a master for an unsuccessful and embarrassing semester. Later that year, quite suddenly and after the term began, he entered the Virginia Theological Seminary at Alexandria. He was impressed by the devout character of its graduates and expected its evangelical emphasis to be accommodating to his own. Leaving seminary in 1859, Brooks went to Philadelphia to serve in turn as rector of the Church of the Advent and Trinity Church. In 1868, he returned to Boston as rector of Trinity Church, remaining for the major portion of his ministry until his election as Bishop of Massachusetts in 1891. After only fifteen months in the episcopacy, a diphtheria-like illness claimed his life at age 57.

Brooks's popularity as a preacher began early in his ministry. In Philadelphia at the Church of the Advent, where lack of attendance had been the cause of despair, parishioners were delighted when the young and winsome preacher began in his first year of ministry to attract crowds. The local press took enthusiastic notice of him, praising his growing reputation as a leading minister in the community. When he finally accepted a call from the vestry of the more affluent Trinity Church, however, they accused him of following wealth and fame. Brooks was an ardent patriot during the war years, having come to despise the practice of slavery he had witnessed while attending seminary in the south. He was loyal to the Union cause, on one occasion uniting the ministers of Philadelphia with shovels and gunnysacks and shaming the citizenry into preparing the city for siege as the Confederate Army was entering Pennsylvania. Brooks's eloquent and powerful address on the death of Lincoln, given in his parish while the slain president lay in state in the city, brought him national attention. In spite of this growing fame, when Brooks later allowed a five-volume publication of his sermons, he included only five sermons from the nine-year Philadelphia period. Brooks's own evaluation notwithstanding, critics consider these five sermons to be as fine as any he wrote. The rich cultural material of his preaching during his Philadelphia years showed his broad literary background as well as his devotion to reading and study. In later years his sermons came to be more theological and practical, dealing forcefully and courageously with current ideas and issues. Still later, his zeal for these concerns came to be matched by his eagerness to stress the centrality of the simple essence of Christianity.

The power of Brooks's preaching lay in his colorful language and vivid images, woven together with easy-to-follow syntax. He was not given to involved illustrations or storytelling. He feared that including poetry and quotations in sermons raised the risk of distracting preachers from revealing their own personalities. He addressed himself directly and artfully to ordinary people in language they relished, moving them to joy or tears, persuading with the transparency of his own commitment and passion. Three times every Sunday, his atypical style easily filled the 1,500-seat Trinity Church in Boston. A private person who disclosed none of himself even to close associates, Brooks preferred to preach before a large impersonal congregation. In this setting, he felt free to open his life and to reveal his inner self in a personal and intimate way.

Brooks wrote out complete manuscripts of his sermons. His final copy was on paper specially cut for the purpose. There were always thirty pages, and he allowed one minute for each page. Brooks filed his manuscripts and showed no hesitation to reuse them without editing. In his later years Brooks began to preach frequently without a manuscript, taking only notes with him into the pulpit and seldom if ever referring to them. Those who heard him in these years remembered the sermons as among his most compelling preaching. Manuscripts of his published sermons were destroyed after they were typeset. He eventually discarded many others himself. Some were given to staff members and after his death to members of his family. Although many of his sermons remain, much of his homiletical material has been lost.

Brooks was clocked by an English shorthand expert, who calculated his speed at 213 words per minute and expressed surprise that anyone could maintain such an uninterrupted flow of rapid articulation. Still, no one seemed lost in this fast-flowing speech. Dissatisfied with himself, however, Brooks sought elocution lessons for a decade during the Boston years. His teacher denied that he suffered from any impediment of speech, asserting instead that "his ideas came faster than his words."

In 1873, Brooks delivered a lecture on preaching at the Andover Theological Seminary, setting forth the major ideas that were to be further developed in the more famous Yale lectures in 1877. Here Brooks set out perhaps most clearly his sense of preaching as joy and adventure. The lectures call on ministers to attend to themselves, allowing the truth of God to invade and inspire them so that they will be prepared for their preaching to communicate the eternal truth. The preacher must authentically "value the human soul," without which value, he said, "preaching is almost sure to become either a struggle for ambition or a burden of routine." From these lectures come Brooks's most frequently quoted words: "Preaching is the communication of truth by man to men. It has two essential elements, truth and personality. . . . Preaching is the bringing of truth through personality."

Much of twentieth-century preaching is contained in Brooks's famous formula. "Truth through personality" at once upheld the truth-claim of Christianity and validated human experience as the theater of God's continuing revelation. The emphasis on personality ushered in the culture's fascination with the personality of Jesus and the resources that this, the greatest of all personalities, makes available to the development of genuine human personalities. Insofar as Brooks located intimations of the divine life in human experience and aspiration, he, more than any other of his century, integrated homiletics and preaching into the liberal project in America.

Abbott, E., *Phillips Brooks: A Memory of the Bishop, an Impression of the Man, a Study of the Preacher,* 1900. **Albright, R. W.,** *Focus on Infinity,* 1961. **Farrar, F. W.,** *Phillips Brooks: The Man, the Preacher, and the Author,* 1989. **Lawrence, W.,** *The Life of Phillips Brooks,* 1930.   WILLIAM HETHCOCK

DESPAIR AND POSSIBILITY
Phillips Brooks
What shall we think about the world? We look around sometimes, and it seems to us as if the world were doomed; as if there could be nothing in the midst of these endless anxieties pressing upon human life by which humanity could be fed and enabled to grow into that image of God, that Divine likeness, immortality, which is set before it. But even in the most material and meagre circumstances of this life there is some power by which God means to build His kingdom on earth. It is souls that refuse to be discouraged by any circumstances, it is those men who are greater than the conditions in the midst of which they live, because their life is in connection with the life of God, who have

laid some stones in the structure of the kingdom of God on earth.

Philip and Andrew will sit down, if they are the only judges of the little supply, and say to the hungry multitude: "There is nothing for you. Here are a few small fishes and a few small loaves. Take them, anybody who pleases; they are of no consequence." But Jesus sees the possibilities where they see no possibilities. So He just goes forward to His miracle, and by-and-by the well-fed multitude go trooping down to the sea again, having eaten a feast in the desert out of the poor little supply— such a feast as they had never eaten when they sat at their loaded tables at home.

I despair sometimes of my circumstances; I despair a thousand times of my soul. What shall come of these wretched disturbances, these passions always running wild, this heart always sinking into stagnation and sloth? What chance is there for my soul? If I see it as I can see it alone, there is no chance. If I see it as God who made it sees it, there is every chance. That is what Jesus came into the world for. Men were despairing. They said: "Let us eat and drink and be merry, for we are good for nothing else." Jesus came and, lo! He taught humanity a different thought of itself. He taught humanity the possibility of glorifying God and saving fellow-men and growing into something divinely genuine. And the power of Christianity has been that it has helped men to see their souls as God sees their souls, and not as they in their poor weakness can understand the mystery.

From "The Feeding of the Multitude," in P. Brooks, *The Spiritual Man and Other Sermons* (London: R. D. Dickinson, 1893).

Bullinger, Heinrich.   (1504–1575) Bullinger suceeded Ulrich Zwingli* in Zurich and was a major leader in early Reformed Protestantism. Born in Bremgarten, Switzerland, Bullinger received his master's degree from the University of Cologne in 1522, where his biblical and patristic studies made him Protes-

tant and shaped his theology for the rest of his life. First a teacher in Kappel (where his biblical lectures emptied the monastery), then pastor in Bremgarten, Bullinger was called to Zurich on December 9, 1531, to take Zwingli's place as preacher at the Grossmünster, where he devoted his life to strengthening the Protestant faith in Switzerland and across Europe.

Bullinger's influence was both personal and theological. He carried on voluminous correspondence with people all over Europe, also welcoming visitors or refugees in Zurich. With John Calvin* he brought together Zwinglians and Calvinists in an agreement on the Lord's Supper (the Zurich Consensus, 1549). Among Bullinger's most important writings are the Second Helvetic Confession (1566), the sermon collection called the *Decades* (1549–51—counterpart to Melanchthon's *Loci Communes* and Calvin's *Institutes*), and *The One and Eternal Testament or Covenant* (1534—influential on Reformed covenant theology). His longevity (he outlived all the major reformers of the first generation) and his considerable gifts as a statesman made Bullinger one of the outstanding Protestant voices of his age. Because his influence waned after the Synod of Dort (1618), his importance among his contemporaries has only recently been appreciated.

For Bullinger, "the preaching of the Word of God is the Word of God. Wherefore when this Word of God is now preached in the church by preachers lawfully called, we believe that the very Word of God is proclaimed, and received by the faithful; and that neither any other Word of God is to be invented nor is to be expected from heaven; and that now the Word itself which is preached is to be regarded, not the minister that preaches" (Second Helvetic Confession, 1). Each part of scripture must be interpreted in the context of the whole, taking into account the rules of love and of faith; all human knowledge (languages, humanities, and especially the teachings of the church fathers) also should be turned to

account, but subordinated always to scripture.

Bullinger practiced what he taught. In the early years in Zurich, he preached six or seven times a week. Later, fears for Bullinger's health led to lightening his load to two or three times a week. Like most Reformed pastors, Bullinger generally followed the continous reading (*lectio continua*) method of biblical exposition. He preached through the greater part of the Old Testament at least once and most of the prophetic books two or three times. He preached through all the New Testament, most of it two, three, or even (in the case of Hebrews) four times. Bullinger's most popular biblical sermons were those on the Apocalypse—sixteen editions of this great "book of consolation"—which is notable because Revelation was not a favorite of most Reformed preachers.

Normally Bullinger preached on biblical texts in Swiss German from Latin notes. (Many of these notes and some sermons in Latin and German remain in manuscript in Zurich archives.) Only a small part of the sermons—about 600 out of 7,000–7,500—were printed, only a few in German. The rest were in Latin. Before 1549, Bullinger's expository works were mainly commentaries; after the *Decades*, he instead published sermon series: 100 sermons on the Apocalypse (1557), 18 on special feast days of Christ (1558), 170 on Jeremiah (1557–61), 66 on Daniel (1565), 190 on Isaiah (1576), plus 24 individual sermons published over the years.

Bullinger also preached in Latin to clergy and ministerial students in the Zurich "Prophezei" meetings for theological education. These sermons, the *Decades* (five books of ten sermons each), were textless or topical* sermons and formed a kind of preacher's handbook, covering all the major points of theology. For contemporaries, the *Decades* (translated into five languages and appearing, whole or in part, in thirty-four printings in the author's lifetime) were probably the most influential of all of Bullinger's writings. The *Decades* served as a theological extension course in England; in 1586 clergy without university training were instructed to read regularly their Bibles and Bullinger's *Decades* and report to neighboring educated ministers on their study.

Bullinger, H., *Decades,* 5 vols., 1849. **Hollweg, W.,** *Heinrich Bullingers Hausbuch: Eine Untersuchung über die Anfänge der reformierten Predigtliteratur,* 1956.

ELSIE ANNE MCKEE

Bultmann, Rudolf Karl. (1884–1976)

Rudolf Bultmann was born in Wiefelstede, Germany, the eldest son of a Lutheran pastor. He received his theological education at Tübingen, Berlin, and Marburg, qualifying in 1912 as a lecturer in New Testament. After holding teaching posts at Marburg, Breslau, and Giessen, he returned to Marburg in 1921 as full professor. He retired at Marburg in 1951. Bultmann was one of the dominating figures in New Testament studies and theology across the middle decades of the twentieth century—perhaps *the* dominating figure.

Bultmann's hermeneutics* is one of his greatest contributions. In his opinion one always interprets texts with a question in mind—however consciously or unconsciously—and that question is shaped by the interpreter's presuppositions. Thus interpretation inevitably incorporates the interpreter's prior understandings. It is then legitimate for presuppositions to govern the *kind* of subject matter that is to be looked for. It is not legitimate for presuppositions to determine the *results* of the exegesis.

In the final analysis there are basically two questions to be posed to a text: (1) the historical question: What does this text tell me about the past? (2) the existential question: What is said here about human beings that can offer a possibility for the interpreter's existence? For Bultmann, although both questions are important, the second is more important. Bultmann challenges the preacher to discover what the biblical text says to contemporary existence yet to remain faithful to the Bible's historical meanings.

For Bultmann one of the tasks of interpretation is what he called *content criticism.* The exegete asks: Is this idea or image adequate or appropriate to the theological intention of the Bible as a whole or of this particular writer?

Bultmann's demythologizing program, which attracted much attention, is a kind of merging of content criticism and existential interpretation. Myth, Bultmann said, is a type of utterance that literally identifies the transcendent God with some object, aspect, or category of the finite world. If the child born to Mary is thought literally to have been conceived from the Holy Spirit, the Spirit is reduced to a powerful expression of the human male procreative principle. Such literal identification of the transcendent with the finite reduces the transcendent to the finite and is not adequate to the Bible's intention to understand God as radically transcendent. The myth, which is not to be taken literally, should be probed for its latent understanding of the meaning of human existence in the world before God.

It has often been thought that Bultmann had an excessively negative attitude regarding our knowledge of the historical Jesus, and it is true that he attributed to the tradition of the early church much that the Synoptic Gospels assign to Jesus. For example, he denied that Jesus thought of himself as the Messiah and therefore that we can know how Jesus interpreted his death. Nevertheless, Bultmann believed in going back to the historical Jesus for a substantive understanding of certain events: exorcisms, polemic against ritual purity and legalism, fellowship with sinners and outcasts, sympathy for women and children, gathering of disciples, proclamation of the eschatological infusion of God's forgiving, demanding rule. The latter justified the church's confession of Jesus as messiah.

Actually more far-reaching theologically was Bultmann's contention that the historical Jesus and the Synoptic narratives about him are historical in the sense that they remain in the past and do not extend into present significance. Jesus' proclamation of the rule of God confronts us with the question of how we will understand our existence and precipitates a crisis of decision. But only the preaching of the death and resurrection of Jesus makes Jesus truly present and brings us through the crisis of decision into faith.

In Bultmann's magisterial *Theology of the New Testament* all the New Testament materials, other than Paul and John, are treated merely historically, as part of our theological past. But Paul and John, while not disengaged from their historical locations, are treated as theological expansions of the proclamation of Jesus' death and resurrection and are interpreted for their present existential significance. Theology is the spelling out of the thought implicit in faith.

In the case of both Paul and John, the broad organizing structure is to present first the plight of humankind and then God's saving action. Human beings in the pursuit of life have wanted to have life on their own terms and out of their own resources. This choice becomes a fate from which they cannot extricate themselves. Sin both estranges the self from God and deforms it. The saving event is the incarnation, death, and resurrection of the Son of God, but this becomes a reality for us only in the proclaimed word, which can move us into a new self-understanding that constitutes a new creation.

Examples of Bultmann's fruitfulness for preaching may specifically be seen in the following themes:

1. The image of Jesus objectively in heaven with God prior to his historic mission is not literally true, but it symbolizes the existential reality that in Jesus something that is decisive comes to us from beyond ourselves.

2. The resurrection of Jesus as a historical occurrence in the flesh is a myth that should not be believed. But we believe in the resurrection of Jesus when we know that God encounters us in the preached word.

3. The notion of the end of the world and Christ's return is a mythological one, and we cannot expect it to happen. But the New Testament's proclamation that the kingdom has both come and is still expected contains an understanding of existence in faith independent of its mythological form. The life of faith transpires within a paradoxical in-between time in which we no longer belong to the sin-fated past yet do not belong to the unequivocally redeemed future.

4. We will not believe in demons that turn the world into darkness. But the symbol of the demonic helps us to understand what is happening when the forces which we seek to possess in the political, social, and technological worlds end up possessing us.

The content and tone of Bultmann's theology is evident in his preaching. In a meditation on Christmas he asks why we light candles at Christmas and take joy in their splendor. We do so to symbolize the eternal light that shines into our dark and uncaring world where we are the victims of forces—economic and political—that the ancients called demonic. This eternal light is never our possession, but in the light of God's grace we are what we are and not what we appear to be in the eyes of the world or even ourselves.

In a sermon on Matt. 11:28–30 ("Come to me all who labor . . . and I will give you rest"), Bultmann points out that even fruitful labor is physically fatiguing and mentally exhausting. Many people become so totally absorbed in their work that they have no other life; therefore, if they experience a failure or become incapable of work they lose the content of their lives completely. Bultmann connects Jesus' promised rest with Sunday's liberation from work and the promise of a new week, a new beginning. On the day of Christ's resurrection the old world broke into the new. On this day God's word offers us the beginning that we cannot give ourselves and assures us that with all our guilt and weakness even now we belong to the new world.

Bultmann's preaching on Mark 13:31–33 ("Heaven and earth will pass away, but my words will not pass away. But of that day or that hour no one knows. . . . for you do not know when the time will come") points up the transitoriness of our lives and our ignorance about the time of our own end. The swift flight of time warns us of the precariousness of life, but what can finally give weight and meaning to our present? How is eternal reality imparted to our present? In part by responding to the call of duty, but that also taxes our inner resources. We need the grace that comes with the assurance that Jesus' words will not pass away. It is by confessing the transitoriness of our lives and surrendering fleeting things that we allow the eternal to come to us as a gift. Thus the future toward which we move becomes God's future. We travel toward the unknown, the darkness, open to what God wills to make of us. It is God's future that gives the present eternal meaning.

Bultmann, R., *Existence and Faith,* trans. S. Ogden, 1960; *Jesus and the Word,* trans. L. Smith and E. Lantero, 1958; *Jesus Christ and Mythology,* 1958; *Theology of the New Testament,* vols. 1 and 2, trans. K. Grobel, 1955; *This World and Beyond: The Marburg Sermons,* trans. H. Knight, 1960.

DAN O. VIA

Bunyan, John. (1628–1688) John Bunyan, author of *The Pilgrim's Progress* and *Grace Abounding to the Chief of Sinners,* was baptized in the Abbey Church of St. Mary in Elstow, England, on November 30, 1628. The exact date of his birth is unknown. The baptismal date was less than a year before Charles I began a period of rule during which he refused to call a Parliament until he was finally forced to do so in April 1640. Bunyan's death on August 31, 1688, was two months before William of Orange came from the Netherlands to save English Protestantism. Bunyan thus lived his entire life during one of the most contentious periods of English history. Charles I was executed in 1649. Oliver Cromwell, the Lord Protector, ruled from 1653–58. The restoration of Charles's son as Charles II in 1660 crushed the hopes of nonconformist preachers such as John Bunyan to speak and to worship freely.

John Bunyan's significance as a preacher is not so much in what he preached but in that he preached at all. He had no formal education or preparation for preaching, and he was imprisoned twice because of his insistence on preaching when refused a license to do so. Bunyan was a tinker's son and learned his father's trade as a brazier by mending pots and pans. He received enough education to learn to read and write, but formal schooling was not available to him. His mother Margaret was his father's second wife, and she died in June of 1644, only to be followed in death a month later by John's fourteen-year-old sister, Margaret, who had been John's companion and playmate. Not quite sixteen years old, he was devastated when his father married again scarcely two months after his mother's death.

When Oliver Cromwell's recruiting officers came to Bedford in the autumn of 1644, John probably had to lie about his age, the minimum age for military service being sixteen, so eager was he to get away from a now unhappy home. He was mustered into the Parliamentary Army and marched the twelve miles to be garrisoned at Newport Pagnell in Buckinghamshire in October 1644.

Such was the early life and condition of a man who was the contemporary of the writers John Milton, Robert Herrick, and John Dryden; of the political thinkers Thomas Hobbes and John Locke; of the scientists Robert Boyle, Sir Isaac Newton, and Edmund Halley; and of the architect Sir Christopher Wren. John Bunyan became the only person of his social class and the only one of his nonconformist religious persuasion to write a classic of English literature, *The Pilgrim's Progress.*

The writings for which John Bunyan is famous were accomplished during his years of imprisonment. Bunyan's *Grace Abounding*, published in the middle of his long imprisonment from 1660 to 1672, is the primary source of information about him for the period following his return to Elstow from military service in 1647 and his reception into membership in the Bedford congregation in 1655. Commentators have described the young Bunyan as morbidly self-centered in his obsessive brooding over the Bible. He was troubled by what he considered his sinfulness in a wide variety of acts and dispositions.

Marriage to his first wife, whose name is unknown, in the fall of 1649 and the birth of his first child, a blind daughter named Mary, seem to have chastened him. He fell in with what he called the "religion of the times" and zealously attended church twice a day. The outward signs of religious commitment did not satisfy him, and he brooded over questions of the genuineness of faith and the uniqueness of the Bible and of Jesus Christ. He viewed as struggles with the tempter the thoughts that "the Turks had as good scriptures to prove their Mohammed the saviour as we have to prove our Jesus is . . . " (*Grace Abounding*).

The resolution of his personal struggle came at the point where he could say, "I saw that I wanted a perfect righteousness to present me without fault before God and that this righteousness was nowhere to be found but in the person of Jesus Christ." Thus *grace* became the powerful theological and personal religious experience that guided all Bunyan's writing and preaching. This emphasis was reinforced by his reading of Luther's *Commentary on Galatians*.

Bunyan became a full member of the congregation in Bedford in 1655. The Bedford Meeting, founded in 1650, was licensed to be a Congregational meeting place. When, under the Act of Indulgence of 1672, it became possible for nonconformist ministers to be licensed and given the legal right to preach, Bunyan was listed in the town records of Bedford as a Congregational teacher.

The Bedford congregation recognized that Bunyan had gifts as a preacher, and he became convinced that preaching was his God-ordained vocation. He preached first in 1656 outside of Bedford and was indicted for preaching in early 1658. His first wife died that year, and in 1659 he married his second wife, Elizabeth. Bunyan was arrested and put in jail in Bedford from 1660 to 1672. He refused to sign an affidavit stating that if released he would not preach.

We know little of Bunyan's preaching technique and have no sermon texts as such, but it is believed that most of his miscellaneous publications were derived from sermons and are likely indicators of his preaching technique.

On Sunday, August 19, 1688, Bunyan preached in a meeting house on Petticoat Lane, London, on the text of John 1:13: "who were born, not of blood or of the will of the flesh or of the will of man, but of God." Two days later he went to bed with a high fever. He had contracted influenza from riding forty miles in a drenching rain, having gone out of his way to bring about a reconciliation between a father and son. He died August 31 and was buried in Bunhill Fields, the only place in the City of London where one could be buried without the ministrations of a priest of the Church of England (*see* Puritan Preaching).

Hill, C., *A Tinker and a Poor Man*, 1988.
Sharrock, R., ed., *The Miscellaneous Works of John Bunyan*, 1976.

CONRAD HARRY MASSA

Burke, Kenneth. (1897–1993) Kenneth Duva Burke, born in Pittsburgh, Pennsylvania, on May 5, 1897, was the most profound and influential rhetorician of the twentieth century. He attended Ohio State University for one semester (in 1916), spent a few years at Columbia University, but became disenchanted with academia's bureaucratic approach to education and dropped out of college without earning a degree. He moved to Greenwich Village, where he began writing essays and poems. This move launched a prolific writing career that spanned more than seven decades.

During the 1920s, Kenneth Burke lectured on literary criticism at the New School for Social Research in New York and at the University of Chicago. He contributed articles, book reviews, literary and musical criticism, and short stories to *The Nation, The New Republic,* and *The Southern Review.* Burke's critical interest shifted toward theory, and he published *Counter-Statement* (1931), his first book of rhetoric. During the 1930s he published two more rhetorical works: *Permanence and Change* (which he wanted to call "A Treatise on Communication") and *Attitudes Toward History.*

Burke accepted his first permanent job in 1946 when he became professor of theory and practice of literary criticism at Bennington College in Vermont. *The Philosophy of Literary Form,* a collection of essays that he had written in the thirties, was compiled and published in 1941. In 1945 he published *A Grammar of Motives,* the introduction to his theory of human motivation based on language and symbolic action.

In 1950, *A Rhetoric of Motives* was published. Burke called this work his philosophy of rhetoric. During the 1960s he published *The Rhetoric of Religion* and *Language as Symbolic Action,* then retired from his post at Bennington College. Following this, he was named Regents Professor at the University of California. He lectured at Harvard, Pennsylvania State, and Emory universities. In 1967, Burke became a member of the American Academy of Arts and Sciences. During the 1970s and 1980s, Burke continued to write essays and to lecture at colleges and universities around the country.

Kenneth Burke dedicated his life to literature and its pursuit, to the development of poetic, rhetorical, and symbolic structures that would enable a better understanding of life, literature, and method through language.

Because of Burke's extensive writing on the subject of rhetoric, his influence moved beyond literary scholars to communication theorists. He wrote an article for *The Quarterly Journal of Speech* (1952) titled, "A Dramatistic View of the Origins of Language," which profoundly interested scholars in speech communication.

Interest in Burke's rhetoric spread to homiletics. Dissertations in the field of homiletics have looked at various aspects of Burke's theories.

Burke's rhetorical theory begins with dramatism, rooted in his understanding of language as symbolic action. Humans express themselves symbolically through language, which in turn leads to action. A newspaper editorial, a play, a song, or a sermon are actions that create an attitude or induce an action in their readers or hearers. Symbolic acts—poems, speeches, novels, or sermons—are symbolic strategies for dealing with the situations that confronted their authors. These symbolic acts are answers to questions asked by the situations in which they arose. Dramatism encourages the creator of a symbolic act to think strategically and intentionally when addressing questions posed by situations.

The implications for preaching are clear. Preaching that is relevant, addressing the real life needs of people, strategically answers questions posed by the preaching situation. The preacher is keenly aware of the needs of his or her hearers, listening to their questions, concerns, hurts, and needs; strategically formulating a symbolic response in the form of a sermon. The sermon is intentionally designed to evoke an action or a change of attitude in light of the biblical revelation being proclaimed. Preaching as symbolic action participates in the revelatory action of God. Jesus Christ, the living word, is made real in and through the preaching event. Dramatism challenges preachers to claim the dynamism available to change lives through proclamation.

The heuristic device for applying dramatism is Burke's pentad: act, scene, agent, agency, and purpose. Every rhetorical act contains each of these elements. A preacher (agent) creates a sermon (act) made up of specific rhetorical strategies (agency) addressed to a particular congregation at a particular moment in time (scene) for a specific reason (purpose). In Burke's method, these elements must be considered jointly. The interrelatedness of the elements is the genius of dramatism.

While dramatism is the key for developing and organizing a rhetorical strategy, the main strategy is identification. Burke believes that rhetoric is concerned with ideal cooperation, which is most effectively achieved through identification. Identification is the normal way humans achieve cooperation. Preachers who live with their hearers, cry with them, experience life as they experience life, becoming one with them, will be heard with joy and acceptance.

Preachers who use the rhetoric of identification attempt to change attitudes and induce actions by identifying their interests with those of the congregation. Congregations hear and respond authentically to sermons when they are convinced that the preacher identifies with their hurts, concerns, sorrows, and life situations. Preaching that embodies the compassion of the gospel is enhanced by Burke's theory of identification.

Logology is another aspect of Burke's rhetorical theory. Because theology deals with ultimate subjects, it becomes Burke's paradigm for words used in their most complete way. The close study of theology and its use of language provides insights into the nature of language itself.

The key term for logology is *god-term*. A god-term is part of an ultimate vocabulary that tries to understand words in the empirical realm based on how words function in theological language. The motivating factor for using god-terms is to achieve the common good, which is the ultimate goal of rhetoric for Burke. Ultimate terms act as unifying devices

around which weighted or motivational vocabularies are developed. Examples of god-terms are faith, forgiveness, hope, love, grace, salvation, redemption, savior, justification, sanctification, peace, good news, cross, and heaven. By understanding a group's ultimate terms, preachers can determine the group's attitude and values. This knowledge is crucial for the preacher in developing rhetorical strategies to address situations that confront the congregation (*see* Rhetoric).

Burke, K., *A Grammar of Motives*, 1945; *A Rhetoric of Motives*, 1950. **Loscalzo, C. A.,** *Preaching Sermons That Connect: Effective Communication Through Identification*, 1992.
                                      CRAIG A. LOSCALZO

Buttrick, George Arthur. (1892–1980) Pastor, preacher, theologian, and teacher, George Buttrick ranks as one of the preeminent homileticians in twentieth-century America. After serving brief pastorates at Congregational churches in Vermont and Illinois, he accepted a call to the pulpit of First Presbyterian Church in Buffalo, New York. In 1927, Buttrick succeeded Henry Sloane Coffin as pastor of Madison Avenue Presbyterian Church in New York City, where he remained for twenty-seven years before moving into academic posts.

Throughout his career, George Buttrick was a mentor to preachers. Approximately 300 clergy subscribed to the Madison Avenue Church newsletter, apparently because most issues included one of Buttrick's sermons. He wrote fifteen books. He served as general editor of *The Interpreter's Bible* and twice delivered the Lyman Beecher Lectures on preaching at Yale. He taught homiletics to generations of seminarians: at Union Theological Seminary during his Madison Avenue years and again during the early 1960s; at Harvard, while he was both minister to the University and professor from 1954 to 1960; and at Garrett and Louisville.

Born in England, the son of a Primitive Methodist clergyman, Buttrick turned aside from the rigid fundamentalism of his father's church and found a spiritual home in Congregational (Independent) circles. After earning honors in philosophy at Lancashire Independent College and Victoria University, he spent a short time with British forces on the continent in World War I. An illness compelled him to return home, where a physician recommended that the climate in North America would be better for his health. Heeding that advice, he traveled to New England, where he met and married the daughter of an English preacher who had made a similar migration.

Buttrick was a disciplined thinker, a careful writer, and a gifted steward of words. His compact phrases and compelling images made him a forceful but not flamboyant preacher. He lacked the voice for pulpit pyrotechnics. While a number of his prominent Manhattan contemporaries (Harry Emerson Fosdick,* Ralph Sockman,* and Paul Scherer,* for example) extended their reach through radio, Buttrick resisted the medium because of his dislike for the way he sounded. Frederick Buechner, who attributes his own spiritual renewal to a 1953 sermon by Buttrick, said he had an "odd, sandy voice, the voice of an old nurse" (*The Alphabet of Grace* 1970, 44). Buttrick's pulpit power lay in what he preached, not in how he preached.

He told his Yale audience in the 1931 Beecher Lectures that the purpose of preaching is to mediate the presence of Christ to people (Buttrick 1931, 141). That mediation occurs through the Bible, Buttrick insisted, for it is in the scriptures that the human quest for God "in its noblest seeking" encounters God's quest for humanity "in its most gracious finding" (Buttrick 1935, 184).

His Bible-centered sermons invariably began with a text, which he envisioned as a word from the Lord brought to earth. The preacher's task was to address that word to the people at their point of need, experience, or understanding; and then, through the sermon, the preacher was to lift the people step by step to the level of the cross for a decision and response. As mediator of the presence of Christ, the preacher does not simply hurl holy, helpful words at people; rather the preacher allows the biblical word to encounter people and to raise them to the point of their redemption. "Great preaching is always a *sursum corda*" (Buttrick 1931, 138).

Buttrick's sermons were always well constructed. His most famous course in his years of seminary teaching was a class in sermon outlines in which he led his students to appreciate the architecture of a sermon. More than once, Buttrick responded to a classroom homily by displaying its outline on the board and rearranging its sections to improve it.

However, he was not merely a homiletical technician. He was an artist whose aesthetic sense shone in more than the literary quotations with which he often illustrated his sermons. He believed that theological language was best interpreted as art rather than as logic. "A poet will always say it better than a theologian," he declared from his pulpit. "We shall never treat our creeds aright until we chant them instead of arguing about them" ("With Us, Yet Unknown," March 6, 1931).

This insight enabled Buttrick to be a Bible-centered preacher without being a biblicist. He could insist on scripture being fundamental without being a fundamentalist. If his parishioners wanted to read a book that was infallible and inerrant, he told them, there was one. "A telephone directory is literally true, and the parable of the prodigal son is not; but the telephone book is not salvation, whereas that story of human folly and divine mercy is like a daybreak on our darkness" ("The Sign of a Savior," December 23, 1928).

He could speak, too, with the courage of a prophet. In the 1960s, when some wealthy churchgoers threatened to withhold their contributions if their pastors preached about civil rights, Buttrick deplored the denominational leaders who "wobbled, when they should have invited these critics to leave the church and take their wretched money with them" (Buttrick 1966, 191). When preachers were told to avoid social issues and stick to the gospel, it usually meant the preacher should "take an anemic Christianity for a Sabbath airing in an ecclesiastical baby buggy" (Buttrick 1951, 126).

What animated Buttrick's preaching was his conviction that faith is a gift that a person receives only by risk and response. His sermons invited listeners to venture into a relationship with Christ, for "in Christ, God is Mother and Father and Friend" ("Nearer Than Hands and Feet," September 22, 1935).

Twenty years after he came to Madison Avenue, his parishioners published a volume of his sermons. Its preface lauded the clarity, honesty, insight, and fearlessness of his preaching, as well as his wise pastoral care in comforting people with the sovereignty and compassion of God.

In the remaining decades of his work, Buttrick continued to be held in high esteem by professional clergy, academic colleagues, and laity. *Life* magazine rated him one of the most influential preachers in the country. A private survey of seminary professors ranked him with Fosdick, Sockman, and Scherer as the most respected pulpit figures of the age. He functioned effectively in academic and ecclesiastical arenas when such versatility was still considered possible. With George Buttrick's death in 1980, an era of great denominational pastors who were great preachers and teachers of preachers had come to a close in America.

Buttrick, G. A., *Christ and Man's Dilemma*, 1946; *The Christian Fact and Modern Doubt*, 1935; *God, Pain, and Evil*, 1966; *Jesus Came Preaching*, 1931; *Sermons Preached in a University Church*, 1959; and *So We Believe, So We Pray*, 1951.   WILLIAM B. LAWRENCE

THE PEACE OF CHRIST
George Arthur Buttrick

But here is Christ saying "My peace I *give* you. It's ours, tonight, for the taking. Now I think perhaps we had better come to terms with the realism. "Not as the world giveth, give I unto you." There is a certain kind of peace that the world can give. Let's try to describe it.

The world, can give what you might call the "fortress" kind of peace. That is to say, men can muster power enough to keep quiet the turbulent realm. Rome in those days had conquered almost all the known world, and they had imposed upon it a certain quietness, a certain absence of strife, which became known as Pax Romana, the Roman Peace. [T]he Roman Peace is always on the brink of coming apart. . . . But mankind still covets this kind of peace: force strong enough to ensure peace. Have you heard it? Have you heard it from the lips of American politicians? "Not as the world gives."

Now there's another kind of peace that the world gives. You can call it if you will the "palace" kind of peace, the prosperity kind of peace. Herod knew it in the day of Christ. But Herod had imprisoned John the Baptist in a dungeon beneath the palace floor. And, for all I know, prosperity always imprisons the prophets. . . . All we need in order to know that prosperity cannot give peace is to talk bluntly to ourselves. So, will you let me talk bluntly?

Somebody here tonight with a poignant sorrow, somebody here tonight stricken in memory with a blunder that he cannot forget. . . . Now if this person be a woman, all she needs is a mink coat in the winter, and if this person be a man, all he needs is a Cadillac car. And all both of them need is a luxury trip to Europe. That's all they need! The very idea is an insult, isn't it? But this is what the world calls peace. We call it in America "a high standard of living," and it isn't very high, and I hope it never becomes standard, and I doubt very much if it's living. "Not as the world gives."

Now there's another kind of peace that the world can give. It's the peace of escapism. . . . If we wish to forget that at this moment in Calcutta there are one million people lying homeless on the sidewalk, we can have peace. . . . The proper name for it is selfishness, tricked out with a little psychology and varnished with less religion. . . . "Not as the world gives."

So we have to make up our minds, I suppose, what kind of peace we want: a low peace with the soul within us crying; or a high peace with some surgical pain.

And perhaps I ought to say to you bluntly about this peace of Christ that He didn't cancel Roman taxes, and he did not drive the Romans from his land, and he did not make people finally immune from sickness, and he did not outlaw death. And as for escaping the actual sorrows of the world, he carried them to a cross. . . .

The peace was his last will and testament. It had something to do with his dying. The accent is on "my"—it is absolutely his. And by sheer gift it is ours. This is the mystery and miracle of Christ. . . . "My peace I bequeath to you."

When a man is at peace with God, he is in the beginnings of being at peace with his fellow man. And once more if a man is at peace with God, the lesions in his own heart can be mended. . . . The only reason we can accept ourselves, to use the psychological phrase, is that God in love made known in Jesus accepts us. And if we receive the gift of peace, the inner lesions are healed, the tensions and conflicts are stilled, so that quickly or slowly they disappear. "Peace I bequeath unto you, my peace I give unto you."

You can't get it. You can *receive* it. This way. You can receive it now. This minute. Sermon on John 14:27, delivered August 2, 1953. (Transcribed from an audiocassette purchased from Princeton Theological Seminary.)

Call. A call or calling is central to the Old and New Testaments and is integral to understanding Christian discipleship. Theologically, call is closely related to the doctrines of providence and election and the concepts of conversion and vocation. Since the Reformation, call has also been associated with the Christian understanding of work.

In the Bible, a call is both a summons to a relationship with God and a commissioning to a particular task. This call is both corporate and individual. In the Old Testament, the people of Israel are chosen for a covenant with God and appointed to be "a light to the nations" (Isa. 42:6, 49:6). In the New Testament, the church is the *ekklesia*—people who have been united with God through God's grace in Jesus Christ and sent out as witnesses to the gospel. Similarly, in the Old Testament individuals are called for specific roles to demonstrate the power of Yahweh. In the New Testament, as well, God calls forth individuals to be messengers of God's word.

The biblical treatment of the call rests on a confrontation with God—a basic emphasis throughout all of scripture. It is God who issues a call to a people and individuals; it comes from beyond one's self and one's culture; it is not something people invent to justify their own desires and ambitions. A call comes from God, and it is often disturbing, frightening, and awesome (Ex. 3:1–4:17; Isa. 6:1–8).

Underscoring the theme of divine initiative is a subtheme of human resistance. Moses protests that he does not have the authority to speak to Pharaoh and that he is slow of speech and tongue (Ex. 3:1–4:17). The people of Israel, delivered from oppression, seek to return to Egypt (Ex. 14:10–18). Sarah laughs when she is told she will conceive and become the mother of a great people (Ex. 17:15–22). Jeremiah declares he is too young (Jer. 1:1–10). Luke's Gospel records the following: "To another he says, 'Follow me.' But he said, 'Lord, let me first go and bury my father.' And Jesus said to him, 'Let the dead bury their own dead; but as for you, go and proclaim the kingdom of God'" (Jer. 9:59–60). On the road to Damascus, Saul is admonished not to "kick against the goads" (Acts 26:12–18). In virtually every confrontation with God and in every call lie the barriers of human fear, weakness, and resistance. But equally important is the emphasis that God will be present and will provide strength to those who are called (Jer. 1:1–10; 2 Cor. 4—5, 11—12).

A call comes from God. It radically redirects the path of life and is usually resisted and initially rejected. Those who are called are often unlikely prospects to be the special agents of God's will—the outcasts, the poor, women, foreigners, enemies, youth—but God's choice of the unlikely demonstrates the power of God over the assumptions and expectations of the world (2 Cor. 1:26–31).

Biblically and theologically, a call is also a commission. To be called to God is to be sent. Sometimes it is a journey—for example, from Ur of the Chaldees or from Egypt to the Promised Land or from Jerusalem to Damascus. More often a call means being commissioned to bear witness to the love of God—as prophets or apostles or teachers. Central to the idea of a call is to be turned toward God and then back to the world (2 Cor. 5:11–21).

In the early and medieval church, the concept of call was focused on the monastic ideal—the disciplined and sacrificial communal life seeking purity and union with God. Luther* and Calvin,* as well as other reformers, rejected this concept of call and extended the Christian understanding of vocation to all of human life and to all areas of work. In contemporary Christian thought, both Protestants and Catholics embrace the affirmation of call in every aspect of human endeavor.

Calvin differed from Luther in arguing that there was an external and internal call. An external call was the preaching of the word, while an internal call was the hearing of the word through the work of the Holy Spirit. In contrast, Luther insisted that the word as preached and the word as heard constitute one call.

The Protestant movement has also stressed the call to preach. This emphasis has been characteristic of all branches of Protestantism, but it has been particularly strong in African-American* churches and Pentecostal* and charismatic denominations. The preacher is called by God to proclaim the gospel. That call is a compelling, urgent summons. The preacher must speak because God has provided a message. There is no other choice. As Martin Luther King, Sr., said of his famous son, "The boy was called to preach. He had to, he could do no other."

In the modern period, the idea of call interacted with the rise of nationalism—particularly in England, Germany, and the United States. Both political and religious leaders transferred Israel's call from God to the nation—making it "the elect nation" or "God's new Israel." In American history, it has been a summons to be a moral example to the rest of the world. Martin Luther King Jr.'s* speeches and sermons are filled with this exhortation. On the other hand, the call has also been the foundation for notions of manifest destiny and the moralistic imperialism that has scarred the history of the United States and Western nations.

When Luther and Calvin extended the call to all occupations, it contributed to what Max Weber identified as the Protestant ethic, which had a profound influence on the development of capitalism. At its best, the call encouraged people to see the value and significance of their work in God's eyes and to defer the gratification from their toil and sacrifice for the benefit of others. However, it has also contributed to a form of righteousness, as well as the equation of work with moral worth. The latter has distorted understandings of poverty, race, class, and gender.

Drawing on scripture and the doctrine of the church, a contemporary understanding of call would include an emphasis on the summons to listen, to receive God's steadfast love and grace in Jesus Christ, and to become the bearers of that good news into all the world (2 Cor. 5:11–21). A call is an invitation to be with God and to bear witness to God's love and justice. To use Paul Minear's image, a call is both a map and a compass, for it shows people the direction of their lives and then offers them the way—the path to salvation and service.

Calhoun, R. L., *God and the Common Life*, 1935. Hardy, L., *The Fabric of This World: Inquiries into Calling, Career Choice, and the*

Design of Human Work, 1990. **Johnson, C. H.,** *God Struck Me Dead: Religious Conversion Experiences and Autobiographies of Ex-Slaves*, 1969. **Minear, P. S.,** *To Die and to Live: Christ's Resurrection and Christian Vocation*, 1977, 3–35. **Nelson, J. O.,** ed., *Work and Vocation: A Christian Discussion*, 1954. **Winn, A. C.,** *A Sense of Mission: Guidance from the Gospel of John*, 1981.

JOHN M. MULDER

Calvin, John. (1509–1564) Calvin thought of preaching as the primary means by which God's work is accomplished in individual life and in the community. As a churchman, Calvin relied on preaching to create a godly public opinion in the community and to be a means of grace in the life of the church. Preaching took priority over discipline as a means of social change as well as of strengthening the life of the church. Insofar as Calvin created a "new civilization" or a "new man," he did so in large measure by preaching. The sheer volume of Calvin's preaching is impressive. At first (after his return to Geneva in 1541) he apparently preached twice on Sunday and then on Monday, Wednesday, and Friday. In 1542, in response to demand, every second week he preached twice on Sunday and each workday.

Calvin's sermons were recorded after 1549 by an excellent group of secretaries, headed by Denis de Raguenier, who sought to record them just as Calvin preached them. In Raguenier's catalog (1549–1560) 2,042 sermons are listed. An additional 263 were recorded later. Today we know the texts of 1,460 sermons, which means that about 1,000 have been lost. At the time of Calvin's death, or shortly thereafter, 780 sermons had been printed. A total of 872 sermons were printed in the *Corpus Reformatorum*, and five volumes of sermons, containing 206 sermons, have been printed since 1961 in the *Supplementa Calviniana*. Richard Stauffer estimates that the known sermons constitute about one third of the Calvin corpus. The addition of the lost

sermons would make the sermons one half of Calvin's total writing. Even this estimate does not include sermons that were preached without any record.

Calvin lived in Christendom, a society that was in its official commitments Christian. He preached in a community in which preacher and congregation shared a common context of intelligibility, a common "apperceptive mass" of biblical knowledge, symbols, images, and visions of human life and society. This shared way of looking at things and understanding them was rooted in the homogeneity of the society and its history. Calvin and his hearers shared an awareness of the holy. The sense of the reality of the creator and source of all things, the feeling of the objective presence of God, a sensitivity to the activity of God in life in general and in worship in particular, left an imprint on everything Calvin did or wrote.

We have little information on how John Calvin learned to preach. The tradition of his preaching at Bourges, perhaps as early as 1529, is reported by Calvin's friends and biographers Theodore Beza and Colladon, but the information is not reliably elaborated. We know that he came to Geneva in 1536 with the ability to preach.

Calvin learned to preach out of the Christian tradition—in particular, from the practice of the ancient church and the Christian humanists. The Christian humanists taught him to return to the sources and trained him in the skills of interpretation and communication. They also taught him and the early reformers to preach. Jacob Wimpfeling, John Geiler in Kaisersberg, and Johann Ulrich Surgant of Basel are preeminent examples of preaching in the style that became common in Zurich, Strasbourg, and Geneva. A second source of guidance in the art of preaching was the ancient church. He prized Augustine,* above all others as a theologian. It was from John Chrysostom,* whom Calvin judged a poorer theologian than Augustine but a better exegete, that Calvin and others learned much about preaching.

First, Calvin understood preaching to be the will of God for the church. The justification for preaching is not in its effectiveness for education or reform. It is not a practice for which other practices may be substituted should they prove to be more popular or more useful. Preaching is rooted in the will and intention of God. Its purpose is first of all the honor of God.

Calvin had no illusions about the impact of preaching. He knew, as he said in one sermon, that there were as many people in the tavern as at the sermon. He knew that preaching would create problems and difficulties. It kills as well as makes alive; it hardens as well as renews. The validity of preaching does not depend on the response it elicits. It is a witness or a testimony that God wills to be made in the world even if all reject it.

This emphasis on the foundation of preaching in the will of God should not obscure Calvin's practical concern for edification. He wanted preaching to edify, to convince. Certainly on the human level he had confidence in its power.

Second, Calvin understood preaching to be a sacrament of the saving presence of God. Stauffer suggests that preaching for Calvin was not only a moment of worship, not only a task of the church, but also something of a divine epiphany. When the gospel is preached in the name of God, it is as if God spoke in person. In preaching, the Holy Spirit* uses the words of the preacher as an occasion for the presence of God in grace and in mercy. In this sense, the actual words of the sermon are comparable to the element in the sacraments. The word in preaching accomplishes nothing apart from the work of the Holy Spirit, who illuminates the mind. (For Calvin, preaching is sacramental in the context of the order of salvation and as a means of grace and not in the more general sense by which all creation may be sacramental. The distinction is important for

Calvin, though he never explicated the meaning. The sense in which "common grace" may be saving is a modern question, not an issue in which Calvin was interested.)

The power of preaching is the act of the Holy Spirit that makes the words, their sound and their meaning, the occasion of the voice of God. "If the same sermon is preached, say to a hundred people, twenty receive it with ready obedience of faith, while the rest hold it valueless, or laugh, or hiss, or loathe it." Yet the ultimate difference in the response does not reside in the sermon, the sound of the words, the rhetoric or the meaning, but in the electing grace of God.

Calvin's sacramental doctrine of preaching enabled him both to understand preaching as a very human work and to understand it as the work of God. The characteristic perspective that pervades all of Calvin's theology, which on the one hand emphasizes the transcendence of God and refuses to identify the transcendent God with any finite and determinate object and on the other hand asserts the immanence of God in creation, and more particularly in the means of grace, has particular application to preaching. The sermon is a human work. From one perspective the human work of the sermon is critically important. The sermon's fidelity to scripture, the skill of the syntax and rhetoric,* the liveliness of the delivery,* are of a fundamental importance that should not be minimized. From another perspective a sermon is a work of the Spirit of God, which may make a "poor" sermon the occasion of God's presence and a brilliant sermon barren of power. Calvin unites the work of God and the work of humanity in the sacrament and in preaching without separation, without change, and without confusion. In practice he may have claimed too much for the minister and for the words of the sermon. Yet in doctrine he knew that the words of the sermon are at best frail, human words but words that can by the power of the Holy Spirit become the occasion of the presence of God (see John 14:26; Ezek. 2:2; Isa. 29:11). For Calvin as for Luther (*Lectures on Hebrews*), the "ears alone are the organ of the Christian man." Hearing the Word of God makes one worthy of the name "Christian."

Calvin, as a homiletician, understood preaching to be the explication of scripture. The words of scripture are the source and content of preaching. As an interpreter, Calvin explicated the text, seeking its natural, its true, its scriptural meaning. "The true meaning of Scripture is the natural and obvious meaning; and let us embrace and abide by it resolutely. Let us . . . boldly set aside as deadly corruptions, those pretended expositions which lead us away from the natural meaning" (Gal. 4:22).

Calvin, according to Ford Lewis Battles, was a superb explicator of scripture because he was a master of paraphrase. He could paraphrase scripture with precision and clarity, translating it into the language of the common human discourse of his own time. This skill was based on his humanist learning and also on his theological and spiritual depth and insight. Understanding and confidence concerning the things of Christ are "not acquired in a natural way" and are "not attained by mental capacity but [depend] entirely on the revelation of the Spirit" (1 Cor. 2:12).

Thus Calvin substituted the *lectio continua*, the continuous preaching through a book, for the selections of the lectionary* or for the individual choices of the minister. Following this method, for example, he preached 200 sermons on Deuteronomy from March 20, 1555, to July 15, 1556, and 159 on Job from February 26, 1554, to March 1555.

When Calvin came to Geneva in 1536, no festivals were celebrated. In 1538 four festivals (the circumcision, the annunciation, the ascension, and Christmas Day) were reinstated in the same edict that expelled Calvin and Farel. These festivals were abolished again in 1550 without Calvin's knowledge. Calvin was not unhappy with the abolition of festivals, though this was an issue he did not consider of sufficiently critical importance to do battle over. On Wednesday, December 25, 1550, when preaching through Micah, Calvin took note of the large number of people present because it was a feast day. He declared that, while it was good to remember that Jesus Christ came into the world, and to recite the history of the Nativity, this would be done on Sunday. In the creation of a festival, an idol, the product of human fantasy, was forged in the name of God. While Calvin was willing to compromise to maintain peace and freedom of practice, there is no reason to be surprised that some thought he wished to do away with Sunday as well, except as a means of ordering the life and worship of the Christian community.

Calvin established the practice of preaching from the New Testament on Sunday and the Old Testament on workdays. On Sunday afternoons he also preached on texts from the Psalms.

Calvin's purpose in preaching was to render transparent the text of scripture itself. For this reason, Calvin made little use of the fathers of the church in his preaching. Likewise, he found little need for secondary aids to confirm the meaning and significance of scripture. Hence he is content with an analytical method that interprets and evaluates verse after verse, word after word. Calvin had a deep awareness that scripture has an integrity and a coherence of its own. His insistence that scripture must be interpreted by scripture enabled him to integrate problematic texts into his preaching and into his theology.

For the reformers, generally, method grew out of the reality of what they were doing. Bullinger's* summary in his sermon "Sense and Right Exposition of the Word of God" is an exception to this silence concerning method. Bullinger's principles were (1) the rule of faith; (2) love of God and neighbor; (3) the historical situation; (4) scripture interpreted in the context of scripture; (5) a heart that loves God and continually prays to God for the Holy Spirit. This is also a fair summary of Calvin's own hermeneutical principles.

Preaching is not only the *explication* of scripture but also the *application* of scripture. Just as Calvin explicated scripture word by word, so he applied the scripture sentence by sentence to the life and experience of his congregation. Hence his sermons always have a strong note of reality. They move directly from scripture to the concrete, actual situation in Geneva. Calvin spoke vigorously concerning issues from the dress and cosmetic concerns of women to international issues, including war.

What were the characteristics of Calvin's preaching? First, his style was consistently marked by an emphasis on simplicity, brevity, and clarity. For Calvin, simplicity was very close to sincerity, to the sense of reality. The pretentious, the ostentatious, the pompous, and the contrived all cover up reality. The simple exposes reality. For Calvin the message was and is the medium; therefore, the medium must not distort the message.

Calvin did not use illustrations* in the modern sense. Yet his sermons are replete with metaphors, comparisons, proverbial images, and wisdom that appeal to the imagination.* He made use of drama, of personal address, of antithesis, of gradation of emphasis, of exclamations, of appeals to the absurd and irony. Calvin provided the craftsmanship that established a relationship between the sermon and the congregation.

Second, Calvin's sermons are marked by a didactic quality. He intended to instruct. This concern for instruction explains and justifies the repetitions. It is also the basis for Calvin's constant use of the interrogative by which he engaged his congregation.

A third quality of Calvin's sermons is their liveliness. They are frequently dramatic, placing God and the devil in opposition to each other, the protagonist and the antagonist. He dramatized the battles and crises with which his hearers were familiar. This lively concern is also seen in the intrusion of his own personality into the sermons, as well as in his challenge to his hearers by use of interrogations.

A fourth quality of Calvin's sermons is their polemical stance. He attacked the Muslims, the Nicodemites, and the fanciful who substituted their own inspirations for the revelation of God. His greatest polemic is directed toward the Roman Catholic Church, a polemic that he carried on to the end. Calvin was the advocate of Christian faith, of what he believed to be God's Word, and in this way he was an adversary. Even in sermons he could speak of his opponents as "these barking dogs," "these vile goats," "these ravenous wolves." While Calvin understood his struggle in global terms, his polemical stance came to a sharp focus in the congregation. In a sermon on Titus 1:10–12, he characteristically exclaims, "If these vain talkers and deceivers be let alone, if we take no notice of them, what will become of the church? Will not the devil win all? . . . It [is] the duty of those who are called to preach the word of God to use plainness, and point out the errors of the faithful." Calvin was a person with a mission to accomplish, and this sense of mission, of responsibility to build up the Christian community, and to fulfill the purposes of God in human history, comes through in most of his sermons. He thought of the world as a battlefield, and he found military metaphors appropriate for the Christian life.

Fifth, Calvin's preaching was serious and solid. "We come together in the name of the Lord. It is not to hear merry songs, to be fed with wind, that is, with a vain and unprofitable curiosity, but to receive spiritual nourishment. For God will have nothing preached in his name but that which will profit and edify" (sermon on 2 Tim. 2:16–18). Our nature, Calvin believed, is such that we take great pleasure in novelty and speculations that seem subtle. The sermon is not entertainment. Calvin spoke against those "who make a pastime of the Word of God and recreate themselves thereby." Preaching inhered in the substance, not in the rhetoric, the subtlety, or the entertainment quality of the sermon (*see* History of Preaching).

Stauffer, R., *Dieu, la création et la providence dans la prédication de Calvin,* 1978.
Parker, T.H.L., *Calvin's Preaching,* 1992.

JOHN H. LEITH

Cappadocian Fathers.

For the greater part of the fourth century, the church struggled to reach consensus on the issue that Arius had raised and the Council of Nicaea (325) attempted to resolve—Can we speak of Christ as God in the same sense in which we speak of the Father as God? The battle to uphold the Nicene answer that Christ is "of one Being with the Father" was first taken up by Athanasius, patriarch of Alexandria. The final victory, however, can be attributed to the work of three natives of Cappadocia (a Roman province in modern Turkey): Basil the Great (ca. 330–378), Bishop of Caesarea, his brother Gregory (ca. 335–ca. 394), Bishop of Nyssa, and his friend Gregory of Nazianzus (ca. 330–390), for two crucial years the orthodox Bishop of Constantinople.

All three were members of the provincial aristocracy. Basil and Gregory of Nazianzus received the best education available in their day. After initial schooling in the provincial capital of Caesarea, they studied rhetoric and philosophy in Athens for several years in preparation for sharing in the administration of their family estates and taking their place in the affairs of their regions as civil servants. Soon after their return from Athens, however, both turned to God and took up the ascetic life. Together for several years in ascetic retreat at one of Basil's family estates at Annesi, they devoted themselves to prayer and the study of scripture, taking Origen as their guide. Their anthology from Origen's works, the *Philokalia,* preserved his wisdom for the church when his works themselves began to be destroyed under suspicion of her-

esy. Basil's brother, Gregory of Nyssa, went no further in his education than the schooling he received in Caesarea, but Basil's tutelage and his own study made him, in fact, the most philosophically acute of the three of them.

Basil took the leadership in the defense of the Nicene cause. His anti-Arian efforts, represented by his treatise *Against Eunomius,* the late Arian who took Arius to his logical extreme and made the Son *unlike* the Father in all things, rallied the church to the orthodox position. Basil's tract *On the Holy Spirit* asserted the deity of the Holy Spirit as well, and the three Cappadocians together forged the technical language for the doctrine of the Trinity adopted at the Council of Constantinople in 381. Consecrated bishop of Caesarea, Basil dragooned the two Gregories, his friend and his brother, into undertaking episcopal duties to support the cause—duties they took up unwillingly and with mixed results. We have a modest collection of Basil's sermons—most notably his sermons on the six days of creation, collected in the *Hexaemeron,* but Basil's greatest gifts were those of an administrator in church affairs—particularly in establishing the pattern for the monastic life in the Byzantine church in his *Shorter and Longer Rules* and in forging the coalition in support of Nicene orthodoxy.

Gregory of Nyssa reinforced his brother's ascetical work by providing a theological rationale for it in a series of treatises, perhaps the most notable of which are *On Perfection* and *On Virginity.* After his brother's untimely death he continued the fight for Nicene orthodoxy with his four works, *Against Eunomius,* and completed the exegetical work of the *Hexaemeron* with his *On the Making of Man.* Many of Gregory's sermons were preached to ascetics—especially his homilies *On the Lord's Prayer, On the Beatitudes, On Ecclesiastes,* and *On the Song of Songs.* We also have a short collection of his liturgical homilies for various occasions, the most famous of which is no doubt his sermon *On the Feast of Lights*

(Epiphany), which focuses on the baptism of Christ.

The greatest preacher of the three by all accounts was Gregory of Nazianzus. The most famous of his forty-five extant sermons (orations) is the series of five known as the *Theological Orations*. In 379, Gregory was coopted by the small orthodox minority in Constantinople to lead its cause in a city that was predominantly Arian. He served as their bishop for two years, and by the time he resigned the see during the Council of Constantinople the cause of Nicene orthodoxy had triumphed not only in the city but in the church at large. In large measure his success in the cause was due to his skill as a preacher. *The Theological Orations* demolished the case that the Arians had made and set forth with consummate skill the orthodox doctrine, devastating the logic-chopping Eunomians with superior logic and rhetorical skill. These sermons can still be read profitably today. Though we are likely to be wearied with the intricacies of the debate, Gregory rises to considerable eloquence in his ringing affirmations of the orthodox confession.

All three Cappadocians are capable in their more formal sermons, which follow the standard pattern of exordium, encomium, and conclusion, of utilizing all the devices of late antique Greek rhetoric*—metaphor, comparison, ecphrasis, Gorgianic figures, and parallelism—with great skill; but are also capable of plainer style when occasion demands, and this we find particularly in the exegetical homilies of Basil and Gregory of Nyssa. In his exegesis,* Basil tries to remain close to the literal sense of the text (the *historia*). Gregory of Nyssa, on the other hand, follows the lead of Origen in devoting much attention to the deeper meaning (the *theoria*), and out of this reflection develops the understanding of the three stages of our pilgrimage to God that would become commonplace in later literature—the way of purgation, the way of illumination, and the way of union. His understanding of the perfection toward which the Christian strives as one of perpetual progress is a theme which many twentieth-century Christians have found attractive, even if the exegetical basis that he sets out for it seems artificial to the modern reader of the Bible.

Basil, *Exegetical Homilies,* trans. Sister Mary Agnes Way, 1963. **Bouyer, L.,** "Erudite Monasticism: The Cappadocians," *The Spirituality of the New Testament and the Fathers,* 331–368, 1963. **Gregory of Nazianzus,** *Select Orations,* trans. C. G. Browne and H. E. Swallow, 7, *A Select Library of Nicene and Post-Nicene Fathers,* 1980. **Gregory of Nyssa,** "On the Baptism of Christ: A Sermon," trans. H. A. Wilson, 5, *A Select Library of Nicene and Post-Nicene Fathers,* 1980. **Quasten, J.,** *Patrology,* vol. III, 216.   BYRON D. STUHLMAN

ON THE SON
Gregory of Nazianzus

[Christ as an infant] was wrapped in swaddling clothes—but he took off the swathing bands of the grave by his rising again. He was laid in a manger—but he was glorified by angels, and proclaimed by a star, and worshiped by the Magi. . . . He was baptized as man—but he remitted sins as God—not because he needed purificatory rites himself, but that he might sanctify the element of water. He was tempted as man, but he conquered as God; yea, he bids us be of good cheer, for he has overcome the world. He hungered—but he fed thousands; yea, he is the bread that gives life, and that is of heaven. He thirsted—but he cried, "If anyone thirst, let him come unto me and drink." Yea, he promised that fountains should flow from them that believe. He was wearied, but he is the rest of them that are weary and heavy-laden. . . .

He prays, but he hears prayer. He weeps, but he causes tears to cease. He asks where Lazarus was laid, for he was man; but he raises Lazarus, for he was God. He is sold, and very cheap, for it is only for thirty pieces of silver; but he redeems the world, and that at a great price, for the price was his own blood. As a sheep he is led to the slaughter, but he is the shepherd of Israel, and now of the whole world also. As a lamb he is silent, yet he is the Word, and is proclaimed by the voice of one crying in the wilderness. He is bruised and wounded, but he heals every infirmity. He is lifted up and nailed to the tree, but by the tree of life he restores us; yea, he saves even the robber crucified with him; yea, he wrapped the visible world in darkness. . . . He lays down his life, but he has power to take it again; and the veil is rent, for the mysterious doors of heaven are opened; the rocks are cleft, the dead arise. He dies, but he gives life, and by his death destroys death.

He is buried but he rises again; he goes down into hell, but he brings up the souls; he ascends to heaven, and shall come again to judge the quick and the dead.

> From "Third Theological Oration—On the Son," in E. R. Hardy, ed., *Christology of the Later Fathers* (Philadelphia: Westminster Press, 1954), 174–75.

Character. The character of the preacher has been of prime importance throughout the history of Christian preaching. A great preacher is one whose witness to the gospel is reflected in his or her manner of life. Character also becomes a crucial issue when the preacher's message and lifestyle radically diverge— as in the fictionalized description of the preacher in *Elmer Gantry.*

The character of a speaker traditionally has been described as "ethos." Contemporary use of the word designates the mood or persona of a society. From a homiletical perspective, however, ethos must be defined as "the image held of a communicator at a given time by a receiver—either one person or a group" (Anderson and Clevenger, 59).

The concept of the proclaimer's ethos is rooted in ancient Greek rhetoric.* While this is useful as a starting point, there are differences, similarities, and tensions between the homiletical and rhetorical definitions of ethos.

Aristotle defines three artistic forms of proof (evidence) provided by the speech.

Of these—the logical (logos), emotional (pathos), and ethical (ethos)—Aristotle says, "moral character, so to say, constitutes the most effective means of proof" (*Rhetoric*, I, ii). Over the centuries, moral character as a form of proof indicates the following qualities: "trustworthiness, intelligence, knowledge or expertise, good will or identification, power or charisma" (Golden and Coleman, 217).

When the Romans adapted and reworked Greek rhetorical theory, qualities of character were not only considered essential impressions for the listeners at the time of the speech but were applied to the speaker's entire life. The ideal orator—the *vir bonus*—was described at some length by the Roman rhetorician Quintilian in his *Institutes of Oratory*, a work that later became an important part of Christian rhetorical education through the Middle Ages and the Renaissance.

While these foundational rhetorical ideas carry over into contemporary homiletical training, the primary source for homiletical theories about ethos is the Bible and, in particular, Paul's assertions about proclamation. Paul was trained in Roman rhetoric, and his sermons and homiletical pronouncements reveal the contradictions between a rhetorical and homiletical understanding of ethos.

Paul repeatedly asserts that he will not be the focus of attention: "For I have decided to know nothing among you except Jesus Christ and him crucified" (1 Cor. 2:2). Yet several of his writings carefully detail his personal sufferings and demand attention to the ethical claims his own witness to Christ offers the listener: "Join in imitating me . . . " (Phil. 3:17). Even if the preacher is to be merely an iconic channel for the presence of Christ, there still remains the problem of the preacher's own personality.

A paradoxical diminution of the role of ethos in sacred discourse became part of Augustine's* homiletical work *On Christian Doctrine.* While repeating the necessity of focusing on God's truths in proclamation, Augustine's reworking of Ciceronian rhetorical principles still honored the importance of ethos.

During the Reformation, pastoral ethos dominated homiletical practice precisely because of its negation. Luther,* for example, continually emphasized the power of the word alone (*sola scriptura*) while simultaneously achieving for himself a popular reputation as a great preacher.

Tension over the rhetorical and homiletical functions of ethos persisted in American homiletical theory. The virtue of Christian humility in the pulpit vied with the need for well-prepared sermons delivered by qualified, charismatic speakers.

Homiletical constraints on the centrality of ethos resulted in various views of the doctrine of sermonic inspiration. To what extent was the preacher dependent on self or the movement of the spirit for preaching well? During the nineteenth and early twentieth centuries, concern with the preacher's image resulted in an emphasis on performance. Elocution colleges, aids, and journals were employed by preachers of many denominations. While this was particularly useful for an immigrant population attempting to learn American speech patterns, elocutionary training was sometimes carried to extremes. One teacher showed the preacher thirteen ways to use the eyes and eyebrows for dramatic effect. Others erred on the side of complacency, omitted any preparation, and decided to "let the Spirit do it all."

One of the most significant assertions about the function of homiletical ethos occurred in the Lyman Beecher Lectures in 1877, when Phillips Brooks* said, "Preaching is the communication of truth by man to men. It has in it two essential elements, truth and personality."

Brooks's statement echoed through homiletical literature and instruction for decades following. His statement signaled the growing preoccupation with issues of ethos that continues today—often at the expense of the listeners and the text.

With the advent of television* preachers, ethos remains a central reality for viewer and image-makers alike. The lack of personal contact between preacher and congregation makes it almost impossible to evaluate the speaker's ethos with any accuracy. Image rather than character predominates.

A devaluation of the role of ethos is actually at work in television preaching. Religious programming often stresses overall context, thus diverting any critical assessment of character through emphasis on beautiful music, attire, setting, and a reassuring mix of secular and religious symbols and clichéd speech.

The local parish, however, continues as the primary area for assessments of ethos. Undoubtedly, the central response to any sermon emerges from the listeners' perception that preachers either do or do not believe in their own witness. Parishioner interaction with the preacher and parish life during the rest of the week will only confirm the judgment.

Whatever the shape of the sermon, congregational responses exhibit the truth of Aristotle's observation: *Who* preaches is the most essential component for receptivity of the gospel (*see* Rhetoric; Personality).

Anderson, K., and **T. Clevenger, Jr.,** "A Summary of Experimental Research in Ethos," *Speech Monographs* 30, June 1963, 59–78. **Aristotle,** *The Art of Rhetoric,* trans. 1982. **Brooks, P.,** *Lectures on Preaching,* 1877. **Golden, B.,** and **R. J. Coleman,** eds., "Rhetoric as Value: Ethos and Image," *The Rhetoric of Western Thought,* 1978, 219–26.
                                    SUSAN K. HEDAHL

Children's Sermons.

Children's sermons are messages presented during worship primarily to children under the age of twelve years. Such sermons intend to include children as participants in the service of the Lord's Day through an event that uses language, concepts, and activities within the developmental capabilities of children (usually those between the ages of three and nine years). The message can be presented in a variety of forms including a sermon, story, conversation with the children, drama, or demonstration using visual aids. Three to five minutes is the usual length of the presentation, and often the children are invited to come forward to receive the message. The congregation seeks to say to the children that each of them is important to God and to the congregation and is included in the central activity of the people of God. Further, God's word is addressed to children, and they are called to respond in gratitude and dedication. However, as with every element of corporate worship on the Lord's Day, even while focused on young children, this activity involves the entire congregation gathered for worship.

Principles and Practices. Children's sermons are a recent development not mandated by tradition or order. Congregations may discover the unwitting separation of children in the life of the church. Children's sermons, then, are used to include children as a part of the family of God gathered for worship. This practice has become popular in recent years, especially in churches with less prescribed liturgical traditions. What must be included when a congregation considers the use of children's sermons in corporate worship? In children's sermons a basic principle is that this activity should enable the entire congregation to worship God. It then follows that the children will be enabled to worship God (and not merely be led in an educational activity) and that the relationship of the worshipers with God will be enhanced with opportunities to experience God's grace, to encounter and respond to God's word, and to receive the gifts of the Holy Spirit* and community in Christ. The availability of worship leaders able to execute the activity with skill, artistry, and integrity is important.

Precautions. Children's sermons are addressed to the entire congregation while using language, images, metaphors, analogies, synonyms, and definitions children can grasp. Usually one concept or main idea per sermon is suffi-cient. Abstractions and symbols are to be avoided. While persons thinking at an adult level may find a symbol edifying (a butterfly to symbolize resurrection or a cross to symbolize suffering, sacrifice, crucifixion), young children find most symbols beyond their cognitive ability and often confusing or even misleading. A variety of activities can be used, such as storytelling, dramatic or musical activities, and audiovisual aids appropriate to the age of the participants. In every instance the activity can be simple, brief, and presented with warmth and affection; humor* can be used if it is not abstract, forced, or at the expense of children. The presenter must respect the children and never manipulate or exploit them or force on them unwarranted moralisms. Most pastors know from experience that presenting a children's sermon that is appropriate and attractive, imaginative, compelling, and faithful to the teachings of the Bible and tradition calls forth every bit of skill, artistry, and integrity the presenter can offer.

Considering the principles, practices, and precautions listed above, worship leaders and congregations do well to ask these questions: Is a children's sermon an element of corporate worship that can be justified in terms of liturgical tradition, benefits to the congregation and the children, and availability of leaders to execute the activity with integrity and effectiveness? If the fundamental goal is to incorporate children into the worship, work, and witness of the community of faith, is a children's sermon the way to do it? Is this the only way to do it? Are there other ways or better ways? These evaluative questions may help a congregation realize its goals in the ministry with children. They may also help children themselves minister in the congregation. In addition, these questions may cause other goals to surface that should be addressed outside of worship. A congregation may realize that the incorporation of children into the worship and witness of the congregation involves much more than providing a children's sermon. Sometimes children's sermons give a false impression that the needs of children in the congregation are being met when a more effective strategy might be pursued.

Worship leaders and congregations must have the honesty and integrity to identify clearly what they wish for their children and the courage to decide how these goals can be met. Children's sermons, if they are done at all, must enable children and the entire congregation to worship God and to respond to God's word in gratitude and commitment.

Coleman, R. J., *Gospel-Telling: The Art and Theology of Children's Sermons*, 1982. **Ng, D.**, and **V. Thomas**, *Children in the Worshiping Community*, 1981.   DAVID NG

GROWING UP MEANS GETTING
READY TO SERVE GOD
David Ng
(*Read the story of David and Goliath from 1 Samuel 17 in the Bible.*) Good morning everyone! I want to talk about the Bible passage which has just been read, and I invite all the children to come forward so you can be a part of this presentation.

Good morning, boys and girls. We are glad you are here. When you listened to the reading of the Bible passage that told the story of David and Goliath, what did you think about? Did you think about great, big Goliath? How big was he? As tall as a house? He was perhaps seven feet tall—or maybe even ten feet tall! That's about this tall, and more! (*Lift a hand as high as possible and reach up on tiptoe.*) Goliath was very, very big, and he was a powerful soldier. Everyone was afraid of him, and no one dared to fight him. They were afraid they would lose.

When the story of David and Goliath was read to us, maybe you thought about David. At that time he was a young boy— maybe a little bit older than you who are sitting here. You might be four, or six, or nine years old. David might have been eleven or twelve at the time he came forward to fight the giant Goliath. You are probably thinking, David might have been this tall (*indicate with a hand a person about five feet five inches*) and Goliath was this tall (*indicate about seven or more feet tall*) or taller! No one had ever beaten Goliath before in a fight. How could little David possibly beat Goliath?

But it was very important that David beat Goliath. Goliath and his people had belittled God—made fun of God and said bad things about God. David and the people of God wanted to stand up for God and to stop Goliath and his people from belittling God.

The people of God were afraid and thought that the only chance David might have in his fight with Goliath was to put on the king's armor. The king's armor was a heavy and strong leather chest protector and a metal shield. Maybe this might protect David in his fight against Goliath. Maybe the king's sword might be just the weapon David could use against the giant. But young David said, "No—I do not want the king's armor. I will not wear it and I will not use the king's sword."

You remember the story: David stood in front of Goliath, with no armor, and with no sword. David took out his slingshot— the same little slingshot that he had used so many times when he was tending his family's sheep. This was the little slingshot that he had used so many times to protect the sheep and to fight off attacking animals. You know the rest of the story: David brought down Goliath with his slingshot! (*Hand and arm motions of slinging.*)

When the people of God needed David, he was ready, even though he was only a very young boy. But as a young boy protecting his family's sheep, David had used his slingshot many times. He was well prepared to use a slingshot. What might have happened if David had put on the king's armor—the heavy suit of leather that was too big for him? What might have happened if David had tried to hold the king's heavy metal shield? Or used the king's sword? Many others had tried to beat Goliath while wearing heavy armor, and a big shield, and a sword. But David did not try to do what he as a young boy could not do. Instead, he did what he knew how to do. He used the weapon that was right for him, that he was prepared to use—his slingshot. And for the sake of the people and for God's sake, he won.

For David, his talent or skill was in using the slingshot. As a child he learned how to use it. When the time came for him to serve the people and serve God, he was ready. What are the talents or skills you are developing? When the church and God call on you to serve, will you be ready?

This week, think about the story of David and Goliath. Think about how David was ready to serve the people and serve God. And think about how you are developing your talents and skills, so that you too will be ready to serve the church and serve God in your own special way. Thank you for coming up here this morning.

Written by David Ng in September 1993 to illustrate an effective sermon for children.

Chrysostom, John. (ca. 347–407)

John Chrysostom is one of the most beloved of the saints in the Eastern Orthodox Church, and he is considered to be one of the three greatest hierarchs of the church, along with St. Basil the Great and St. Gregory of Nazianzus (*see* Cappadocian Fathers). In the Roman Catholic Church he is honored as one of the four Doctors of the Eastern Church and as the patron saint of preachers.

From 386 to 398, Chrysostom was a priest in Antioch, where he had the principal preaching duties in the Great Church. During the next six years he was Archbishop of Constantinople, where he continued his emphasis on frequent preaching. Due to his personal austerity, the moral rigor of his sermons, and his various efforts at reforming church life in the capital city of the empire, he incurred the opposition of many clergy and especially that of the emperor and empress,

Arcadius and Eudoxia. This led to his deposition and forced exile in 404.

For the next three years he lived under house arrest in the obscure town of Cucusus in eastern Asia Minor. Nevertheless, he was able to receive visitors and to maintain a vigorous correspondence with his supporters in Constantinople—especially with his closest confidant, St. Olympias the deaconess. His continuing influence provoked the imperial authorities to take him by forced march to a more remote place of exile to the north. While on this march, he collapsed from exhaustion and ill treatment at the hands of his military escort. He had to be carried to the nearby shrine of the early Christian martyr, St. Basiliscus, in the town of Comana, where he died on September 14, 407. In 438, his remains were brought back to Constantinople in triumph.

John was given the surname "Chrysostom" ("Golden-Mouth") shortly after his death, in reference to the eloquence of his sermons. He had learned the art of rhetoric* from the great pagan orator Libanius of Antioch, but he realized early in his preaching career that he must not let his eloquence obscure the clarity of his message. And he never forgot the purposes to which he had dedicated his rhetorical skills—the instruction, edification, and exhortation of his flock. Sometimes his congregation would erupt into applause for the beauty and power of his speech, but he would quickly remind them that their praise meant nothing unless they put into practice what he was urging them to do. For his sole aim was the spiritual and moral growth of his listeners; as he would say to them, "If I see you living in piety, I have all I wish" (Homily VI on the Statues).

Typically, Chrysostom delivered sequences of expository sermons on various books of the scriptures. Sometimes, such as during Great Lent, he preached daily. While he preached through much of the Bible, his homilies on Genesis, the Gospels of Matthew and John, Acts, the

Pauline epistles, and portions of Isaiah and the Psalms are all that survive. These sermons, probably preached without notes, were recorded by stenographers, who later wrote them out for publication. They have served as the most popular biblical commentaries in the history of the Eastern Church.

Chrysostom is sometimes criticized for being primarily a moralist. But his sermons nearly always demonstrate insightful meditation upon the scriptures as he expounds orthodox doctrine from them. This theological foundation then becomes the fountain from which flow his moral exhortations to his flock to live a life of "orthopraxy"—in accordance with, and empowered by, the doctrines of the Christian faith.

Usually in the second half of a homily he draws moral lessons from the passage of scripture which he has explicated verse by verse in the first half. Sometimes these exhortations are loosely based on the scriptural text at hand, since he always tried to relate his preaching to the immediate needs of his flock. Among his favorite themes were almsgiving, simplicity of life, repentance, free will, love, humility, prayer, the glory of the celibate life dedicated to Christ, and the beauty of Christian marriage.

Chrysostom usually preached in an engaging conversational style, creating a strong rapport with his listeners. For instance, he frequently anticipated objections, stating them in the form of "But you may say . . ." and then answering accordingly. Often he asked rhetorical questions. He also used rhymes and wordplays that cannot easily be conveyed in English translation.

He loved to use vivid imagery drawn from almost every realm of nature and everyday life, of which he was a keen observer. For example, observing that "bees will never settle down in an unclean vessel" but only in "wicker baskets . . . sprinkle[d] with fragrant wines, and all other sweets," he then says that "Our soul is a sort of vessel or basket, capable of receiving the swarms of spiritual gifts; but if there [is] within it gall, and 'bitterness and wrath,' the swarms will fly away" (Homily XV on Ephesians). In reference to his gleaning as much meaning as possible from a certain passage of scripture, he compares himself to a farmer harvesting grapes, saying, "Since, therefore, even now I see, as if hidden under leaves, some thoughts still concealed under the letters [of the passage], come now, let us harvest these also very thoroughly, using this sermon in place of a sickle" (Homily IV on Lazarus and the Rich Man). With elaborate flourish he describes a life of sin as "groveling on the ground," the church as "the real palace," and a beggar as "the altar of God" upon which to offer the sacrifice of alms.

Chrysostom was always ready to make dramatic use of contemporary events in his preaching. When Eutropius, a court eunuch and the "man behind the throne" of Emperor Arcadius, suddenly fell from favor and sought asylum in the Great Church of Constantinople, the next day, a Sunday, as Eutropius clung to one of the columns supporting the high altar, John preached to great effect on the vanity of riches and the transience of earthly fortune.

He was loved not simply for his rhetorical brilliance but also because the people saw Chrysostom living what he preached. They experienced his love personally and saw the care with which he organized and directed his church's many works of charity—providing for 3,000 widows, feeding hundreds of others daily from the church's kitchens, and establishing hospitals and hospices.

His most frequent theme in all his preaching was that of bearing tribulation and suffering with patience, gracefulness, and dignity. In the final years of his life, he was able to act upon his own advice in the face of the injustice, malice, and cruelty that led to his deposition, exile, and martyrdom. His last words were "Glory to God for all things! Amen" (*see* History of Preaching).

Attwater, D., *St. John Chrysostom, Pastor and Preacher,* 1959. **Baur, C.,** *John Chrysostom and His Time,* 1959. **Schaff, P.,** ed., *Works of St. John Chrysostom,* in *Nicene and Post-Nicene Fathers,* first series, IX–XIV, 1983. **Vandenberghe, B. H.,** *John of the Golden Mouth,* 1958.   DAVID C. FORD

HOLY SPEECH

John Chrysostom

Do not say, "It is nothing if I say something abusive, if I insult someone. . . ."

You call God "Father," and then you immediately revile your brother? Reflect a moment—how is it that you can even refer to God as "Father"? Is it from nature? You could never say this. Is it from your virtuousness? You could not say this either. . . . No, this has been given to us purely by God's great love, and tenderness, and the mercy which He has for humanity. . . . Do not, therefore, disgrace that which you have received from God's lovingkindness by treating your brethren cruelly.

You call God "Father" and yet you revile? But this is not what the Son of God did. For His work was to forgive His enemies, to pray for those who crucified Him, to pour out His blood for those who hated Him. This is worthy of the Son of God: to take His enemies—the thoughtless, the dishonest, the reckless, the treacherous—and to make them brethren and heirs, and not to treat contemptuously, as slaves, those who have become brethren. . . .

Think what your mouth touches, what it tastes, of what manner of food it partakes [in the Eucharist]! Do you still think that you are doing nothing when you speak against your brother? How, then, can you call him "brother"? But if he is not your brother, how then can you say "Our Father"? For the word "Our" indicates many people.

Think with whom you stand at the time of the Holy Eucharist—with the Cherubim and Seraphim! The Seraphim do not revile; rather, their mouths fulfill this one purpose—to sing the hymn of praise, to glorify God. How is it possible, therefore, that you say with them, "Holy, holy, holy," and yet you use your mouth for insults? . . .

Why then do you defile and contaminate yourself? You stand in Heaven, and yet you revile? Your citizenship is with the angels, and yet you revile? The Lord has deemed you worthy of His kiss, and yet you revile? God has graced your mouth with so many great things—with angelic hymns; with food, no, not angelic, but more than angelic; and with His own kiss—and He has wrapped you in His embrace, and yet you revile?

Oh, no! I implore you! Vast are the evils from this source. Let it be far from a Christian soul.

From Homily XIV on Ephesians 4:25–30, J.-P. Migne, ed., *Patrologiae Cursus Completus* (Paris: J.-P. Migne, 1862), vol. 62, col. 104–5, trans. David C. Ford.

Church Architecture.

Church architecture plays an active role in the act of preaching, one that is significant for the preacher as well as for the congregation. The architectural environment in which preaching occurs not only houses the event but shapes the way it is heard, seen, and perceived. That environment is the context in which proclamation occurs, and while the context is secondary to the hearing of the word, the architecture has the ability to enhance or interfere with the purposes and results of preaching. Church architectural planning and design is therefore, by extension, related to and significant for the act of preaching.

The architecture of the central worship space of the church building can place the preacher and the sermon in direct communication with the congregation. It can hold them aloof from the congregation. It can make it difficult to see or to hear, and it can detract from or obscure what should be clear and accessible.

Preaching occurs in a variety of settings: street corners, open spaces, arenas, coliseums, as well as in homes and other places through the media of radio and television. However, the emphasis here is on the traditional setting for the Christian sermon within the context of worship in a church building. Current theological and pastoral studies in preparation for ministry do not emphasize the role that architecture plays in the act of preaching or, for that matter, the role it plays in the everyday life of ministry, lay and ordained. Architecture designed and built for the purposes of the church becomes part of the so-called "material culture" of the church. The material culture is all the accumulated artifices that have been created by the church in the process of making itself known in the world. Architecture constitutes some of the most valuable and meaningful material culture that the church has created. Reflection upon that material culture in relation to the tasks of religious ministry within a theological and pastoral context is seldom encouraged, however. What is more evident in a church's ministry than its building and place of worship? It is routinely within the "life" of the material culture of Christianity as it serves ministry, witness, and worship that decisions concerning the role and appropriateness of architecture are necessary. Therefore, one of the roles of the pastor-priest-leader of congregations is to include the world of architecture within the opportunities and tasks of ministry.

Church architecture is one of the ways the witness of the church expresses itself to the world. Church architecture is a symbolic language of the church's message expressed in material, functional, and environmental ways. The building and its worship spaces constitute a sermon in material form. Church building types say something visually and symbolically about the institutions they house. They speak a symbolic language to the communities in which they reside, a language made up of forms, scale, proportions, and function. Although the language of church architecture is an abstract language, unlike that which is verbally spoken, it nevertheless expresses a value system, and through sets of symbolic references gives off visual codings that constitute messages.

Church architecture speaks its message through the iconography of architecture. Church buildings also express their values through various attributes. For instance, the scale of the church building or buildings within a neighborhood of buildings is a factor in how the church is perceived. The way a building participates in its environment affects perception. The style of its form makes a statement. Accommodation to vehicular and pedestrian traffic patterns expresses accessibility. Avenues of access that invite and facilitate participation imply the institution's interest or lack of interest in the public.

When planning a new building, it is preferable for the local congregation and the necessary judiciaries to study the priorities and goals of the congregation before an architect's design stage is considered. The architect will want as clear a statement of vision and goals as possible. The expertise of an architect is necessary for good church architecture to be achieved, and the architect occupies a unique position in the process. The result of collaboration will put in the hands of the architect the task of embodying, translating to material form, the vision and message of a particular congregation. The responsibilities placed on both sides—that of the congregation and of the architect—are serious. In relationship to preaching, the architect is a participant in every instance of preaching by virtue of his or her planning and design decisions.

Good church architecture is not hurriedly achieved, and in congregations where the process and results are carefully considered, the experience is often healing and reviving. Once built, new church buildings are a responsibility and opportunity. Ongoing maintenance and upkeep should be planned in the budget for construction. Attention to design, construction, upkeep, and maintenance is a moral obligation because of the investment by the community and because of the role that architecture plays in the realization of ministry. The preaching ministry of a church is especially influenced by the architecture due to the complex relationships of material properties, issues of scale, acoustical concerns, sight lines, and symbolic significance.

Renovation of church buildings is equally if not more important than new construction because more buildings are being repaired and renovated than are being newly built. Renovation can be a more responsible decision than new construction because it may save a good building as well as eliminate the higher cost of new construction. Renovation also allows a building to be retrofitted for functional, educational, and liturgical needs. These projects need a professional architect as much as any building project in which a church may become engaged. While liturgical renewal is often the stimulus for church renovation, care must be taken not to diminish the place and role of preaching in the results.

In the latter half of the twentieth century four major factors that have specific relevance for preaching have emerged as priorities in building churches. First, liturgical renewal has influenced all churches and has brought increased need for spaces that encourage active participation of the worshipers in liturgical services. Second, multiple-use spaces and flexibility of usage are valued. Therefore, there is interest in portability and changed-use possibilities in worship centers, as well as in other parts of the building. Third, more community services are incorporated in space usage in churches, and full-time midweek use of church spaces is encouraged. Fourth, there is renewed interest in the aesthetic possibilities of church buildings. While no church building need be ugly, beauty in construction need not be costly. Any community, poor or wealthy, that can afford to build or renovate a church can respect the need for beauty within the context of ministry. Each of these priorities is significant in relation to preaching and should be evaluated in relation to ways in which preaching is to be enhanced.

Good architecture does not guarantee good preaching. The environment for preaching is important, but preaching itself requires renewed attention to the theology of the word, the life of the word among the people of God, and the unique place proclamation has within the tradition. Although preaching may take place anywhere at any time, it regularly and actually happens in church buildings where people worship. The worship center within the church building is the community's place where the ongoing encounter with the living God takes place. The architecture of that place is an intimate participant in the event of preaching (*see* Pulpit).   JOHN W. COOK

Church Year and Preaching

Preaching and the Origins of the Church Year. The New Testament both reflects and transforms the observance of the year in first-century Judaism. This observance had as its main locations the Temple festivals and their scriptural traditions, the synagogue sabbath service with its developed structure of lessons and occasions, and the Jewish household with its hospitality, meals, and the "table-talk" of Jesus. In each of these settings, scripture served both to shape the observance and to invite reflection, commentary, and preaching. With regard to the Temple festivals, for example, it has often been noted that the Gospel of John revolves around three passovers, each with its signs and relationship to Christ's "hour" when he is lifted up in crucifixion/exaltation. What is overlooked, however, is that the scriptural readings at each festival are assumed to be within the reader's knowledge as John deals with Jesus' words and actions at the time of that festival.

With regard to the synagogue, by the first century, two cycles of readings were in place, the first from the Pentateuch (*Torah*) and the second from the prophets

(*Haftarah*). Gradually, by virtue of this lectionary, the sabbaths of the year received names derived most typically from the opening portions of one of these two lessons. Each was in turn read and commented upon, Jesus' reading from Isaiah 61 and his short proclamation in Luke 4:16–21 being the *locus classicus* of this practice. The context of the Jewish household also seems now to be the origin of much of what the synoptic Gospels portray as the public preaching of Jesus— "table-talk" now elevated to mountaintop discourse. Thus, observance of the Jewish year, seasons, festivals, sabbaths, and days, provided the context for the New Testament witness to Jesus Christ.

The preeminent Christian alteration to the "liturgical year" of Judaism in the New Testament was the emergence of Sunday as the day of worship. This first day of the week was for both Jews and Gentiles a workday with little or no cultic expression. Only as the followers of Jesus experienced the risen presence of their Lord did that day become "first" in a normative sense; those Christians worshiped on the Lord's Day because the Lord appeared to them on that day in the breaking of bread. The Emmaus narrative (Luke 24:13–35) embodies this understanding and provides an intersection for those aspects of Jewish worship and piety that were undergoing transformation. Christ is risen, marking his passover from death to new life (the Temple festival transformed). The two sojourners heard the kerygma from the Stranger as he interpreted Torah and the prophets concerning himself (the sabbath/synagogue transformed) and finally was "made known to them in the breaking of the bread" at table in their home (the Jewish household transformed). Now, each Lord's Day will follow this pattern of scripture read and proclaimed and of bread taken, blessed, broken, and shared. This first day reenacts the mystery of Christ's death and rising, gathers a new community in Christ, and is a sign of the great "Day of the Lord," of Christ's return in glory (Searle, 17).

It was not until about the middle of the second century that the Christian community began to celebrate the Lord's Day as the Sunday of Easter. While every Lord's Day proclaims the death and resurrection of Christ, the paschal feast became centered on the Easter Vigil. Here, on the night of nights, as the Lord makes his passover from death to new life, the community gathers for prayer and fasting, for the baptism of converts from the pagan world, and at cock's crow, joyously celebrates the Easter Eucharist. Expanding eventually to incorporate Good Friday and Holy Saturday as well—the Triduum—this Vigil retained its unified character through at least the fourth century. The great Three Days were an anamnesis of Christ's death and resurrection as a type of passover. Quite naturally, therefore, certain lessons and psalms gravitated toward their new home in the Vigil. Among the factors at work in this process were the baptismal nature of the Vigil, the interpretation of Psalm 118 as prophecy and as doxology, and the resurrection narratives of the Gospels.

The present shape of Lent seems to have originated from at least two component practices, each with distinct though complementary purposes. On one hand, the Great Week from Palm Sunday through Easter centered on reenactment of the Holy Week drama as observed in Jerusalem (as witnessed and reported by the Spanish pilgrim Egeria during the years 381–384). On the other hand, a variety of liturgical centers in the early church devoted different periods of time to a final instruction of and formation in the faith of those seeking baptism. Fourth- and fifth-century developments saw a gradual dominance of a "forty days" motif to these preparations, though they were counted differently in the East and West. A parallel development was the absorption of the Great Week within the Lenten forty days. In all of the above, the emergence of these liturgical occasions was organically related to the assignment of specific lections. Perhaps it might be more accurate to say that the selection of those scriptural texts really gave birth and distinction to the occasion. Of course, with the giving of the text, the church also preached its gospel.

The other festival cycle that erupted into the ordinary sweep of Sundays of the year was that of Christmas. In the West, Christmas can be quite precisely dated in its inception to the year 336 in Rome. Lections forming the focus and piety of the liturgies of the feast involved the Lukan Christmas story at the Mass on Christmas Eve and the prologue of John on Christmas Day. In the East on January 6, the festival of the Incarnation (Epiphany or Theophany) was a multivalent occasion, celebrating Christ's birth, Magi, baptism, and the first sign at Cana. Gradually, East and West borrowed each other's Christmases, with the former shifting birth to December 25th and the latter adopting the January 6th Epiphany but only regarding the Magi. In the Western church, the period of preparation for Christmas and its twelve days of rejoicing varied as much if not more than the various origins of Lent. Here, there was no baptismal occasion to structure a forty days. However, the season of Advent was finally ordered as a four-week observance, as practiced by the Latin Church. The texts once more gave the Sundays their distinctive orientation—Advent I focusing on the Parousia, II and III on the Baptist, and IV on Mary and the events immediately preparing for the birth of Christ. The shape of the Incarnation cycle, therefore, resembles that of the Paschal cycle with each having a season of preparation (Advent and Lent), the feast day related to each respective cycle (Incarnation and the Paschal Mystery), and a protracted season of celebration with a distinctive observance at its conclusion (Epiphany and Pentecost).

Preaching and Its Functions within the Church Year. The church year is a sequence of Sundays in ordinary time interrupted by the Christmas and Easter cycles, each with its own internal structure of seasons, rites, and lections. "Preaching the church year" is not simply a question of determining the seasonal context and theme of the day. A far more complex and dynamic relationship between preaching and the liturgical year may be detected, especially in understanding the origins of the year. There are three homiletic possibilities:

1. Preaching *about* the occasion: Much of preaching in the early church functioned first to recount the biblical event in which the liturgical event was grounded. The fullest early expression of this homiletic attending to the church-year occasion is seen in the sermons of Leo the Great (d. 480) and the homilies of his mentor in rhetoric, Augustine* (d. 430). A survey of the Augustinian homilies written for specific days within the Advent-Christmas-Epiphany and Lent-Easter-Pentecost cycles discloses a consistent approach best described as narrative preaching. The scriptural narrative at the heart of the observance is retold in detail and in many cases the lection's story and its attendant imagery were then applied to the context of the hearers, using typological interpretation. Cassian Folsom comments:

> For Augustine, what happened once for all in time, in order that our life be renewed, is celebrated every year, in order that our memory be renewed. Again and again he repeats that the yearly feast renews in our minds the memory of our salvation. In fact, it renews the memory in such a way as to re-present, as it were, the day of the historical event itself (Folsom, 19).

Leo the Great takes a similar approach while emphasizing even more than his mentor the organic, even sacramental relationship between the feast day and the scriptural text. In his liturgical sermons, Leo speaks of the particular mystery celebrated at the feast as always (*semper*) existing for the faithful, but now (*sed nunc*) brought near, seen by eyes of faith, and experienced anew. Notice, however, the distinction between this homiletic approach of anamnesis with its interest in "bringing near" the scriptural foundation of the occasion and the tendency of some "liturgical preachers" today to "explain" the occasion and perhaps the components of the liturgy proper to its observance.

The contemporary recovery of the church year with its texts appropriate to the occasion offers the church the opportunity for observance and for scripture to regain the sacramental unity found in the preaching of Augustine and Leo. Within the context of the reformed liturgy of Word and sacrament, hearing a topical, discursive sermon following the reading of the lessons is experienced as oddly disconcerting. The lectionary* with its implied year as well as the reformed Sunday liturgy are two of the most powerful factors inviting preachers toward a more biblical and sacramental approach to the practice of their vocation today.

2. Preaching *at* the occasion. Days and seasons of the church year have been explained generally with regard to their thematic designation. While some amount of such discursive summarization is both helpful and inevitable—Easter *is* about resurrection, after all—it may be more accurate to speak of a season's performative intention. Thus the Lenten season may be described as having a vested interest in the formation of catechumens and, in fact, the lections for the Easter Vigil are rather incomprehensible unless the baptism of those catechumens into Christ's death and rising is seen as the primary purpose of the Night of Nights. One of the marks of faithful preaching in the early church, then, is this fidelity to the vested interest of the homiletic location with the year of grace. Cyril of Jerusalem (315–386), Ambrose of Milan (339–397), and, of course, Augustine, are examples of preachers who had a clear sense of their vocation in preaching the vested interest of the day and the season.

3. Preaching *toward* the occasion. Before there were feast and fast days or the seasons of the church year, there were the narratives of scripture and there was preaching. In fact, conventional descriptions of the church year typically under-

estimate or even ignore the homiletic interest in the biblical event that gives rise to the liturgical event. The present issue in the churches centers on the recovery of either the church year itself or the kind of preaching as anamnesis appropriate to the liturgical context. This tends to obscure that an essential factor in the emergence of the church year was homiletic attention to certain scriptural narratives at a time that was fitting to their hearing.

A recent example of this dynamic of preaching toward the occasion may be seen in the homiletic interest women preachers devoted to Luke's narrative of the Bent Woman Made Straight (Luke 13:10–17), omitted by the three-year lectionary in both its Roman Catholic and various Protestant expressions. These mostly women preachers accorded the story sufficient homiletic attention to recover the text for many of the churches. It now has its fitting place within the Sundays after Pentecost in Year C of the Revised Common Lectionary.

The situation today in many American churches regarding preaching and the church year, however, remains one in which the interwoven unity of time, text, occasion, and preaching has become disrupted if not fractured. In the name of reformation, several church traditions had swept away the days and seasons of the Christian year, trusting only in the witness of scripture and the sabbatarian Sunday as the time for worship. Into this symbolic vacuum, however, the days and seasons of the American civil religion insinuated themselves ("Memorial Day," "Independence Sunday," and perhaps the most benign civil religion feast, the American Thanksgiving). Ironically, the intention of reform has led to a subversive co-optation of the church year by the civil religion's year, a captivity desperately in need of reform in a substantial number of churches and traditions.

On the other hand, the so-called liberal denominations filled the symbolic vacuum with a new calendar of denominational special days on behalf of good causes: "Human Relations Sunday,"

"Laity Sunday," "Rural Life Sunday." A host of other promotional occasions have clogged the year of the old-line Protestant churches as badly as had the overfunctioning saints' calendar in the medieval church. One distinction prevails, though, when the two practices are placed side by side. The denominational special days promote a thematic and works-righteousness approach to preaching; the sanctoral calendar in its reformed expressions celebrates grace and attends to scriptural narrative.

In contrast to these contemporary examples of the need for reform, those communties of faith ordering time by means of the three-year lectionary are discovering a remarkable "surplus of meaning" (Ricoeur) in the course of their recurring "ordinary" observances.

The church year is once more becoming essential to Christian identity. The Christian community can be sustained in these times only by attending to its own narratives through its own year of grace (*see* Liturgical Preaching; Homily).

Adam, A., *The Liturgical Year*, 1981. **Folsom, C.,** *The Liturgical Preaching of Leo the Great*, 1990. **Jones, C., G. Wainwright,** and **E. Yarnold,** eds., *The Study of Liturgy*, 1978. **Searle, M.,** ed., *Sunday Morning: A Time for Worship*, 1982. **Talley, T.,** *The Origins of the Liturgical Year*, 1986.

RICHARD L. ESLINGER

Civic Occasions. Once we differentiate between state and cultus, religious utterance on public occasions or in civic space gains a special—sometimes ceremonial, often intrusive—quality. Then cultus reclaims a public hearing, a relationship to the state, a claim over political leadership. The Hebrew Bible considers such intrusive, even critical preaching as prophecy, as one of its constitutive strands of witness and expression. The prophet spoke to the occasion, invoked God's covenant promises, and recalled the people to law and righteousness.

Kings and even the people did not always welcome these words from God.

Civic preaching, then, is as old as preaching itself and has had its distinctive forms, as well as its specific occasions. The Christian movements generated a variety of relations to the civil order (of Christ to culture) and therefore different modes of civic preaching. Here, too, most clearly remembered are the prophets,* sometimes as upholders of orthodoxy, sometimes as reformers, even heretics. Civic preaching in the United States derives from these older traditions—Old Testament prophecy, Greek patterns of civic discourse, modes of Christian preaching. Of particular importance in the latter regard are styles and understandings rooted in the sixteenth-century Reformations and their repoliticizing of preaching, reclaiming of the vernaculars, and pressing toward persuasion. These styles—Protestant and Catholic—prospered in the political chaos in Europe, as well as in missions and situations of colonization. The subset of such preaching that proved most influential in the United States came through the Reformed or Calvinist movement and was worked into Puritan political fabric, social understandings, and mythology.

Although Puritans distinguished carefully between state and church; relegated much of the religious life specifically to congregations or families; and complained of Anglican and Roman confusion of the two realms, they understood both commonwealth and church to be in covenant with God and therefore looked to God's spokespersons, the ministers, for insight on particular occasions and in times of crisis. On days of fasting or thanksgiving, elections, fires, wars, and other weekday civic occasions, the clergy spoke self-consciously to magistrates and citizens, not sinners and saints. Like the prophets, they spoke to the occasion; they recalled the covenant; they spoke for a jealous God who made promises, gave commandments, and demanded righteous obedience; they knew this God to govern nations and order the world; they read adversities as betokening God's providence and favor. To the prophets but also to the whole Bible—Old and New Testaments—the ministers looked to understand what New England experienced. They rendered providential, typological readings of political events and spoke in jeremiadic judgments. Ancient Israel prefigured new Israel's story.

One can overstate the importance of Puritanism in American history, but it is difficult to overstate the importance of Puritan contributions to civic preaching (see Puritan Preaching). The jeremiad readily gathered to itself the powerful republican motifs and liberal "truths" so that revolutionaries sounded like preachers, and preachers sounded revolutionary. And the new nation—heir to covenant and promises, the hope of the world, God's new Israel—heard jeremiads on Fourths of July, during elections, and on days of fast and thanksgiving. Such preaching served national cohesion. Civic preaching could, and doubtless did, generate moments of civic or civil religion. But civic preaching also served, as it always had, to judge cohesion bought with unrighteousness and human misery. Civic preaching, jeremiads, and calls to republican virtue came for abolition, women's rights, and temperance. These and other reforms, resisted in churches as well as congress, moved of necessity into public space and created new civic occasions—special events, special voluntary institutions—for the cause at hand. Sectionalism and the Civil War generated new occasions for civic preaching—to call forth troops and to call down divine aid. Both North and South appointed fasts and demanded to know the will of God. After the war the bloody flag called forth preaching that would reenact and legitimize each side's glorious cause. And both North and South established memorial days, civic holy days, to remember their dead. Thanksgiving, another civic holy day, was fixed by that war.

In the twentieth century, wars and crises have continued to create weekday oc-casions for civic preaching. Reforms, particularly temperance, labor rights, peace, and civil rights, produced prophets who effectively claimed the civic pulpit. The greatest of these, Martin Luther King Jr.,* drew on the traditions of American civic discourse but also on themes and resonances of African-American* preaching. After him and with the breakup of the older Protestant mainline establishment and the Supreme Court's succession of "wall of separation" decisions, two paradoxical patterns have emerged: (1) Preachers and politicians have eroded the line between sabbath and weekday, the religious and the civic. Television time honors no such boundary, and evangelicals, specializing in preaching in that forum, move easily from the civic to the religious and back. (2) The court, on the other hand, distinguishes the civic from religion, federalizes every locale, and extrudes preaching, praying, and crèches from public space. Both trends undercut civic or prophetic preaching by managing its content and insisting on politically correct or incorrect prophetic words.

Bellah, R. N., *The Broken Covenant: American Civil Religion in Time of Trial,* 2d ed., 1992. **Carter, S.,** *The Culture of Disbelief,* 1993. **Holifield, E. B.,** *Era of Persuasion: American Thought and Culture, 1521–1680,* 1989. **Noll, M. A.,** ed., *Religion & American Politics,* 1990. **Stout, H. S.,** *The New England Soul: Preaching and Religious Culture in Colonial New England,* 1986. **Wilson, J. F.,** *Public Religion in American Culture,* 1979.   RUSSELL E. RICHEY

Claude, Jean.

(1619–1687) Jean Claude was an important Reformed preacher and apologist in French Protestant history. Born in La Sauvetat, he was the son of a pastor who trained him in theology and literature. He was known as a faithful man and dutiful pastor who possessed an impeccable character and keen intellect.

Claude began his pastoral duties at the small church at St. Afrique in southern France where he devoted much time to

his own studies. In 1654 he went to
Nîmes as pastor and also taught theology.
In 1661, when Claude presided over the
Synod of Nîmes, his career took a turn
toward controversy. At that provincial
meeting, an alliance with the Roman
Catholic Church was proposed that
Claude declared intolerable to Protestant
principles. Later, he was forbidden to
continue his ministry in the Languedoc
region and went to Paris, where he became a pastor in 1666. Until the Revocation of the Edict of Nantes in 1685,
Claude was at the center of conflict with
the Catholics. During this time he published his famous *Defence of the Reformation* and debated eloquently with priest
and orator Jacques-Bénigne Bossuet.*
Claude was banished from France at the
Revocation and went to The Hague,
where he preached to the exiles until his
death (Dargan, 124–25).

As a homiletician, Claude offered an
expanded Reformation view of preaching. His *Essay on the Composition of a
Sermon* was concerned particularly with
preaching method, and he addressed the
relationship between scripture and sermon. He agreed with Calvin's three ways
of treating a text (explication, exhortation, application) and developed a theological concept of preaching:

Some say preaching is designed only to
make scripture understood, and therefore they take a great deal of text, and
are content with giving the sense, and
with making some principle reflections: but this is a mistake; for preaching is not only intended to give the
sense of scripture, but also of theology
in general; and, in short, to explain the
whole of religion (Claude, 3).

Claude emphasized preaching in a
framework of theology, wherein the use
of scripture goes beyond textual analysis
and exposition to the derivation of a subject from the text and discussion of it on
its merits and its application to the life of
the hearers. He introduced the category
of propositional preaching and asserted
that it allows the preacher greater free-

dom and more extensive theological development in the sermon. The focus of
propositional preaching is not to treat
only the text but

those *subjects* which you have chosen
from several contained in the text. The
way of explication is most proper to
give the meaning of Scripture; and this
of systematical divinity. The way of application rather regards practice than
theory; but this, which we call the way
of propositions, or points, is more
proper to produce an acquaintance
with systematical divinity, and it will
equally serve theory and practice
(Claude, 200).

The method in Claude's *Essay* was classic and more literary in style than that of
the Reformers, and it exercised influence
over preachers for more than two centuries after its publication. The British Baptist Robert Robinson first translated the
work from French to English in the eighteenth century. Then, in 1833, Charles
Simeon, an Anglican instructor at Cambridge, attached an improved translation
of Claude's essay to his own sermon outlines and Old and New Testament commentaries and published it as *Horae
Homileticae.* The homiletical tradition of
Jean Claude contributed to the shape of
preaching in English-speaking Protestantism in both England and America
(Brilioth, 179).

Few of Claude's sermons have survived.
The one preached at the time of the Revocation of the Edict of Nantes, based on
Genesis 17:7–8, was transcribed after it
was delivered. He was exiled shortly
thereafter.

Brilioth, Y., *A Brief History of Preaching,*
trans. K. E. Mattson, 1965. **Claude, J.,** *An
Essay on the Composition of a Sermon,* trans.
R. Robinson, 1823. **Dargan, E. C.,** *A History
of Preaching,* Vol. 2, 1912.   ANN I. HOCH

GOD IS LEAVING YOU
Jean Claude
My beloved brethren, you have asked
for this exhortation; I give it to you with all

my best wishes; it was conceived in haste and in the greatest distress of my grief, but as I perceived by the torrent of tears which it brought from you that it was blessed, I scrupled in publishing it to make any change. It is not a regular explanation of the text; grief did not suffer art and method. . . . God is leaving you; this is the plain proof of it; here is the break: "I will not spare them longer; he that dieth, let him die." And whither should they go, Lord? "He who is appointed for death, to death; he who is appointed for famine, to famine; he who is appointed to captivity, to captivity." . . . You will be without pastors, but you have for pastor the Great Shepherd of the sheep, whom you will hear in His Word. . . . You will have no more a temple, but the Sovereign does not dwell in temples made by hands. . . . Holy family of my Father, dear heritage of my God, sacred flock of my Divine Master, if I do not preach to you in this place I shall gather you in my heart; if I do not bless you from this pulpit I shall bless you in my heart, and there you shall be the main subject of my joy or of my grief. . . . Holy Father, keep them in Thy Name! . . . O! that we may be able at that great and last day to see them all at the right hand of Jesus Christ, and that they may be our joy and our crown in the day of the Lord! Amen.

> Preached in Paris at the Revocation of the Edict of Nantes, 1685, in E. C. Dargan, *A History of Preaching,* Vol. 2 (New York: Franklin, 1912).

Coffin, William Sloane, Jr. (1924–)

William Sloane Coffin, Jr., was born in New York City. He studied music with Nadia Boulanger in Paris and at Yale. World War II interrupted his studies, which he completed in 1947. During the Korean War he worked for the CIA training anti-Soviet Russians for operation within the Soviet Union. Returning to America he studied at Yale Divinity School, receiving his Bachelor of Divinity degree in 1956. For a brief period he served as chaplain at Phillips Academy

and Williams College. Coffin came to international attention, however, during his eighteen years (1957–1975) as chaplain of Yale University, a period in which he became known for his participation in the civil rights movement and the Clergy and Laity Concerned for Vietnam, an organization of which he was a cofounder. In 1977 he became senior minister of Riverside Church in New York City, where he established the church's Disarmament Program. In 1987 he left Riverside Church to start SANE/FREEZE, the largest peace and justice organization in the United States.

In his preaching William Sloane Coffin, Jr., reunited evangelism and social concern, two great themes that had been separated in the nineteenth century. He believed that since most personal problems that surface in counseling sessions have social origins, pastors ought to try to change society. As Yale chaplain and as Riverside pastor he attempted to merge both the personal and social dimensions in every sermon. His faith in God and his study of the radical claims of Christ in scripture led him to speak out. Influenced by his uncle, Henry Sloane Coffin, author of the pamphlet titled "The Practical Aims of Liberal Evangelicalism," and by Reinhold Niebuhr,* who believed that "it was not inconsistent to be theologically right of center and politically left," Coffin regularly attacked what he called the "privatization of Christianity," which tries to separate "homo religiosus" from "homo politicus." To him, abandonment of the public domain leads to a joyless, authoritarian, narrow-minded trivialization of the Christian faith. That is one reason that most of his sermons, grounded in the Bible, often address contemporary issues and questions. His ministry at Yale and Riverside was radical in the sense of getting back to the root of the gospel, especially as it is seen in the Luke-Acts tradition, where sharing the good news of salvation is always seen side by side with care for widows, orphans, and strangers and where the good Samaritan plays a prominent role.

Like the Old Testament prophets,* Coffin was something of a *conservative revolutionary* whose social criticism both in and out of the pulpit was not designed to destroy society but to preserve it even if it meant radical change. He was not anti-institutional but spoke as a "patriot" who had "done his time" during World War II and with the CIA. He spoke as a conservative theologian with a fresh, healthy piety and a deep faith in God. There was nothing of the nineteenth-century liberal announcing that things were getting better and better or the prophet of doom haranguing the crowds with "The end is near!" Coffin often expressed his sense that he had been "coerced by a vision of truth," one that he could not hold back. He also understood that preachers earn their right to be prophetic by first being steadfastly pastoral. As with the prophets of old, pastoral sensitivity undergirded his sermons. What motivated Coffin was not a desire to attack the status quo but his desire for his people to live rightly and to do justly under God.

Coffin's sermons were often given in the context of a global moral imperative. He took on large, controversial subjects but insisted on bringing the biblical vision to bear on public life and policy. He believed that preachers who leave their religious turf are the ones who get into trouble. "I always spoke as a Reverend," said Coffin once, "even at the Rotary Club." His poignant humor usually disarmed his opponents in tense political situations. There was always a kind of swashbuckling rambunctiousness about his sermons. (See pp. 161–62 below.)

Some believe that he oversimplifies with his sweeping analyses of complex moral problems and that on occasion he plays fast and loose with the scripture in his more topical offerings as a way of forcing his global and moral hermeneutic, but Coffin's bold speech and defiant trust in God's providence echo his Uncle Henry's belief that "back of both protest and programme is the living God," and that, with God, what should be shall be.

Coffin, W. S., Jr., *The Courage to Love,* 1982; *Living the Truth in a World of Illusions,* 1985; *Once to Every Man,* 1977.

WILLIAM J. CARL, III

Communication.

The subject "preaching and communication" contains a paradox: preaching is a form of human communication; but on theological grounds most would also say that preaching is a divine event whose essence cannot be explained by or reduced to "communication." Preaching's relationship to communication dynamics, study, and theory is always bound by some version of that paradox.

H. Grady Davis* found in 1961 that among teachers of homiletics across a wide theological spectrum there was a noticeable uniformity of assumptions about the preaching event. He reported his findings in six succinct propositions: (1) True preaching is a form of the Word of God. (2) True preaching is biblical in the sense of making the Bible a truly living document. (3) True preaching centers on Jesus Christ as God's redemptive act, the restoration of broken humanity. (4) True preaching is itself, contemporaneously, part of the divine redemptive event. (5) The message of preaching is in collision with the thought, cultural habits, and concerns of the times. (6) Preaching is a unique kind of speaking, a special language, a dialogical interaction between God and hearers. Approaching the subject from the perspective of human communication theory means taking these theological affirmations seriously and integrating them with knowledge of communication. It does not entail the dualistic assumption that divides all knowledge between science and revelation. At no time does the transcendent render scientific study superfluous.

History of Communication Study. Although in some sense the study of communication is as old as ancient rhetoric,* modern communication theory and research is largely a post-World War II phenomenon. The war-generated interest in telecommunications and propaganda called forth both a new communication technology and a new interest in understanding and theorizing about the dynamics of the entire communication process. Shannon and Weaver's original "mathematical theory of communication" (1949) was an attempt to understand and more efficiently produce the flow of information along telephone lines. Social psychologists entered the communication field with their interest in how attitude formation and change was influenced by messages, particularly in persuasive communication such as propaganda, advertising, or indoctrination. The increasing importance of mass media in the postwar years, with the rise of television,* created its own niche in communication study. Marshall McLuhan's* popular and creative book *Understanding Media* paved the way for broad cultural and psychological interest in the role of human communication.

During the postwar period the field of human communication struggled to emerge as an academic discipline in its own right. Controversy continues to exist over whether there *is* such a "field," with its own definition, research methodology, and unique phenomena for investigation. One school of thought maintains that communication study is inextricably linked with the particular operations in which communication is key (mass media, interpersonal relationships, advertising, social relations, education, and information processing) and cannot be studied in its own right apart from these contexts or applications. An alternative school of thought believes that the central core of a "discipline" of communication can be defined and studied in principle without limitation to particular applications or contexts. What might be called first-generation scholars of communication typically came from other fields: journalism, speech and rhetoric, linguistics, cultural anthropology, social psychology, neuropsychology, political science, systems theory. Writings in the field of human communication continue to display a sometimes bewildering variety of disciplinary foci and assumptions in their backgrounds.

Approaches to the Study of Communication. A variety of different descriptions have been offered to organize the wide diversity of approaches to the systematic study of human communication. G. Gerbner broadly distinguishes between "tactical" and "strategic" approaches to communication study (Gerbner 1967a). By the former he refers to studies of the internal mechanisms of the transmission of information (how codes are created and operate, how communication channels and networks behave, what effects messages have on their recipients, and how communication knowledge is applied in practice). A tactical interest in communication is concerned with visible, measurable, and often pragmatic phenomena: what makes for intelligibility in messages, how messages influence people to respond in different ways, and how institutions use communication in their work.

By the "strategic" Gerbner means an interest in less visible and more indirect phenomena, such as how human beliefs and values are shaped and cultivated by communication experience and, by extension, how those belief and value expectations influence human behavior in complex social settings. A "strategic" interest in communication is concerned primarily with the ways in which human worldviews or consciousness of reality are molded, maintained, and influenced in and through communication experience. In the world of advertising, for example, the tactical approach would apply to how influential an advertising message is in changing a population's buying habits or persuading them to do whatever the advertisement aimed for. By contrast, a strategic approach would investigate how the same message affected its recipients' worldview or sense of what is real, what is important, or what is right (Gerbner 1967b).

Another approach to studying communication is offered by B. Aubrey Fisher (1978), who divides the field into four perspectives, each with its own methodology, model, and research interests: the mechanistic (the way information operates), the psychological (the internal experience of participants in the communication process), the interactional (the ways communication participants relate to each other), and the pragmatic (the dynamics of the communication experience in terms of systems theory). Since communication behavior is universal and ubiquitous, it is not surprising that any approach to its systematic study faces the challenge of defining for its purposes what is *not* communication.

Preaching's Relationship to Communication. Preaching's interest in communication has typically shown three dimensions: (1) the creation and delivery of messages, (2) the maintenance of community, and (3) the cultivation of worldview.

The earliest attempts to apply insights about communication to preaching consisted largely of pragmatic efforts to "apply" communication knowledge to the construction and delivery of religious messages in hopes of making them more persuasive, intelligible, or personally relevant—a distinctly tactical approach, in Gerbner's terminology. The superficial semantic resemblance of the terms "communication," "community," and "communion" often provided a symbolic, if not analytic, rationale for preachers' being interested in communication and at times made this "secular" science acceptable to the high and mysterious purposes of preaching—perhaps represented by the phrase "communication of the gospel."

Attention to the community-developing or "public-forming" dimension of the communication process (Stephenson 1967; Nichols 1980, 1987) has been enhanced in part by the pastoral care* and counseling movement with its interest in the role of communication in regulating human interactions and building human relationships. More recent interest has focused on family and other systems' dynamics and the ways they are carried out in communication behavior. Understood from the perspective of communication, preaching is therefore seen as having a primary effect in the development of the faith community and of interpersonal relationships within it.

The third approach has in more recent years been the study of theology and communication in preaching in a more "strategic" perspective, having to do with such subjects as the role of communication in faith development, religious awareness, spiritual formation, and worldview. Such an approach focuses less on how to structure effective religious messages and more on the outcome of communication in the faith experience of the participant. In this dimension there is an intimate relationship of communication to the study of hermeneutics.* Welsh (1974) argued, for instance, that the significance of communication in preaching could be seen not so much in providing religious information as in influencing the way people found meaning, including ultimate theological meaning, in the information they were already experiencing in unprecedented amounts. Nichols (1980, 1987) believed that the role of intrapersonal conflict in creative experience was key to understanding the communication process in theological perspective. McClure (1991) has recently proposed a schema in which different religious codes in preaching create different realities or "intertexts" for their participants.

Example of a Communication Approach to Preaching. In discussing communication it is important to differentiate among three categories that are sometimes spoken of interchangeably: model, theory, and principle.

Communication *models* are pictorial representations of the communication process as it is defined by the particular researcher. A model serves to depict a complex process in recognizable form and is therefore primarily a way of organizing data.

Communication *theory* is a statement

of how the communication process is believed to work, given a certain definition and variables. The classic (some would say only) theory of communication is Shannon and Weaver's mathematical theory of information (1949). A communication theory for preaching must account for both human and theological dimensions of the process. The application to preaching for heuristic purposes of one or another model of communication should not be confused with the development of a theory of communication for preaching.

Communication *principles* are statements of implication about the communication process, given a certain theoretical understanding of its dynamics. Principles serve as a conceptual bridge between theory and practice and are different from either.

What follows are six *principles* of communication process or dynamics that may guide a preacher's reflection on his or her communication work.

1. *Communication is a receiver phenomenon.* Although much of traditional homiletics focuses on the preacher's work in constructing a sermon, a communication approach recognizes that communication is an inherently *constructive* process in which the receiver of messages actively builds meaning on the basis of information at hand, both from signals provided by the sender and from existing or ambient information in the receiver's field. Meaning is not delivered by messages but is rather constructed (or reconstructed) at the receiving end. The process is governed by various assumed or stipulated rules of the symbolic process involved. When the meaning intended by the sender of a message and the meaning reconstructed by its receiver are similar enough, the participants agree that communication has been successful. "Feedback" is the term used to describe data provided by the receiver to the sender that are used to "check" the "fit" between the message sent and the message received. It is important to recognize, however, that the isomorphy between intention and construction is seldom if ever perfect; there will always be some difference between the two, and the degree of difference is commonly held to be a measure of the effectiveness of the process. By implication, therefore, whatever communication behavior best facilitates the reconstructive process is "good communication" in this functional, rather than rhetorical, perspective.

2. *Communication can be defined as the "transgeneration of experience" as well as the "transmission of information."* Given the constructive viewpoint of the preceding principle, it follows that the aim of the communication process is for some experience of the sender of a message to be replicated in the experience of the receiver. That experience is "encoded" in the information of messages, dismantled into component parts, and reassembled at the receiving end. Transmission of information alone is not the endpoint of the process. The information must create in some acceptable form the same phenomenon in the experience of the receiver as was present in and intended by the sender. The experience can therefore be said to be "transgenerated" by the interaction.

3. *Messages in communication contain both "report" and "command."* Any message consists of two separate ingredients: the information of the message (the report) and some form of instruction, verbal or nonverbal, about what to *do* with that information (the command). The command aspect of a message is sometimes referred to as "metacommunication," or communication about communication. The structure of grammar itself often carries the command component. For instance, in the imperative mood, the sentence "Close the door" clearly conveys both a report—a door needs adjusting— and a command—you do it. Problems arise in communication when the command aspect is either neglected or overemphasized. With neglect, it is unclear to receivers what they are being asked to *do* with the information they are getting or why they are getting the information to

begin with. With overemphasis, so much attention is given to the coded instructions that the basic content is lost.

An example of neglect would be the sermon in which the aim of the preacher is never stated and the information conveyed therefore connects to no point or purpose that the receiver can identify. An example of overemphasis would be a person struggling to say something difficult and repeating over and over how hard this is to understand or how potentially upsetting it may be but never quite getting around to *saying it*. Metacommunication overshadows the content of the communication itself. In preaching, a formal and highly structured piece of metacommunicative "command" is what has been referred to (Nichols 1980) as the "contract" between preacher and congregation for what a particular sermon is aiming to say and accomplish.

4. *All communication establishes some form of relationship among its participants.* Stephenson (1967) and Nichols (1980) have referred to the "public-forming" work of communication, meaning that the command aspect of any message poses for a receiver the implied question, "Who or what must I be to be hearing this message and responding this way?" Some form of relationship between sender and receiver is implied in the communication, and the possibilities are virtually endless—teacher and student, entertainer and customer, doctor and patient, judge and felon, and so on. Perhaps more pertinent for preaching, consistent exposure to a pattern of messages establishes among receivers acquiescence to a corresponding identity of themselves so far as the communicative interaction is concerned. The relationship-defining or public-forming property of communication process is one of the sources of its considerable power in shaping people's basic expectations about the real world, including, of course, their theological beliefs and values.

5. *All communication relies on a text or message and is thus inherently a form of symbolic interaction.* The communication process relies on a "code" and the process of codification (Ruesch and Bateson 1968) for the content of its messages. The experience of human communication is thus representational and symbolic in its very essence. As soon as any experience is encoded in a message, it has become a text, and the process of decoding the message is inherently a hermeneutical one. The process of representation or encoding is necessarily a selective one, with the encoder choosing some aspects of an experience or object to be encoded and leaving others behind. Communication may therefore be said always to reveal and to conceal aspects of the experience that is the subject of its messages.

6. *Communication depends for effectiveness on an optimal degree of difference between sender and receiver.* Though it is somewhat counterintuitive, a theoretical principle of communication is that the frames of reference, levels of understanding, modes of discourse, and degrees of comfort or familiarity between sender and receivers should *not* be identical, but slightly askew. Communication is a tensive process (Wheelwright 1962), and the aim is not for the absence of tension but for an optimal degree of tension. This principle is very different from the erroneous popular stereotype that communication is most effective when it perfectly matches a receiver's understanding, language, or expectations. If the message is perfectly consistent with and familiar to a receiver's expectations—if the frames of reference between sender and receiver are identical—no information will be generated, and the outcome will be redundant, leading to an "I've-heard-it-all-before" response. At the other extreme, if the frames of reference are too divergent, there will not be enough common ground for understanding, and the outcome will be random, articulated in the reaction, "I don't know what you're getting at." The flow of information (which is defined in communication theory as "the reduction of uncertainty") is compromised at either extreme—on one end because there is not enough uncertainty to be reduced and at

the other because there is too much. This principle leads the communicator to seek an optimal balance between the general and the particular, concrete and abstract, personal and global, familiar and novel, certain and uncertain, or complex and simple.

The use of communication principles such as these may aid the preacher's reflection on the human communicative experience in service to greater understanding of the complex and mystifying phenomena for which the high theological claims of preaching are traditionally made. Communications theory is most helpful to preachers who believe that only when human phenomena are clearly understood are we free to make theological constructions about the incarnate work of God in such an event as preaching.

Davis, H. G., "The Teaching of Homiletics: The Present Situation in American Seminaries," *Encounter* 23, Spring 1961. **Fisher, B. A.,** *Perspectives on Human Communication,* 1978. **Gerbner, G.,** "An Institutional Approach to Mass Communications Research," Lee Thayer, ed., *Communication Theory and Research,* 1967a; "Mass Media and Human Communication Theory," F.E.X. Dance, ed., *Human Communication Theory: Original Essays,* 1967b. **McClure, J. S.,** *The Four Codes of Preaching: Rhetorical Strategies,* 1991. **McLuhan, M.,** *Understanding Media: The Extensions of Man,* 1964. **Nichols, J. R.,** *Building the Word: The Dynamics of Communication and Preaching,* 1980; *The Restoring Word: Preaching as Pastoral Communication,* 1987. **Ruesch, J.,** and **G. Bateson,** *Communication: The Social Matrix of Psychiatry,* 1968. **Shannon, C.,** and **W. Weaver,** *The Mathematical Theory of Communication,* 1949. **Stephenson, W.,** *The Play Theory of Mass Communication,* 1967. **Welsh, C.,** *Preaching in a New Key: Studies in the Psychology of Thinking and Listening,* 1974. **Wheelwright, P.,** *Metaphor and Reality,* 1962.   J. RANDALL NICHOLS

Congregation.

Congregation. One of the marks distinguishing Christian preaching from other speech is that preaching is liturgical and communal. Preaching ordinarily takes place within a congregation, a gathering of people who have pledged to live out their faith in community, and who come together on a regular basis for worship in Jesus' name.

Preaching, then, is a highly particular and incarnational word event. A sermon is not a talk addressed "to whom it may concern" but a proclamation addressed to a distinctive and local body of believers. A sermon is not a pithy and inspiring message crafted by the pastor in isolation but an address that arises out of the common life shared with a people of faith—an address that forms and reforms that community according to the scriptures. A sermon is not simply God's eternal Word funneled through the mouth of the preacher; it is an incarnate word, clothed anew in the flesh-and-blood language and experience of a local congregation and the world it inhabits. As Fred Craddock* asserts,

> Sermons should speak *for* as well as *to* the congregation. The Bible is the church's book, not the minister's alone, and therefore a proclamation of its affirmations is the church's word to itself and to the world (Craddock, 26).

In order to speak both for and to a congregation in preaching, the pastor needs skill in exegeting the congregation as well as in exegeting the scriptures. As Augustine* recognized, the significance of congregational makeup for the preacher

> likewise makes a great difference . . . whether there are few present or many, whether learned or unlearned, or a mixed audience made up of both classes; whether they are townsfolk or countryfolk or both together. . . .
>
> For it cannot fail to be the case that different persons should affect in different ways the one who intends to instruct orally and likewise the one who intends to give a formal discourse . . . (Augustine, *The First Catechetical Instruction,* 2).

Pastors have long recognized the truth of Augustine's words and have attempted to preach in a manner that is fitting for their particular congregations. However, it has only been in recent decades—with the emergence of academic disciplines such as cultural anthropology, sociology, and (more recently) congregational studies— that pastors have gained access to the knowledge and tools essential for deepening congregational understanding in a more systematic manner.

Phillips Brooks* recognized over a century ago that when pastors speak possessively of "my congregation" they are, in part, witnessing to the truth that each local congregation exhibits a distinctive corporate "character":

> [The congregation] is to the minister a unit of a wholly novel sort. There is something in the congregation which is not in the men and women as he knows them in their separate humanities, something in the aggregate which was not in the individuals, a character in the whole which was not in the parts (Brooks, 183).

For Brooks, however, the primary value of that corporate congregational character is its ability to provide the preacher with a glimpse of humanity as a whole. In facing a congregation, said Brooks, the pastor is "looking the [human] race in the face" (Brooks, 188). Consequently, he urged pastors to preach occasionally in congregations other than their own so that their view of humanity could be expanded and they could avoid the creeping parochialism that comes with preaching week-to-week in the same community of faith.

Yet Brooks also recognized that the pastor "who would bear fruit everywhere for humanity should root himself into some special plot of human life and draw out the richness of the earth by which he is to live at some one special point" (Brooks, 190). It is toward the goal of such local "rooting" that authors in the emerging field of congregational studies encourage pastors to attend more closely to congregations in their particularity.

James Hopewell sees congregations as subcultures, each with its own particular idiom, worldview, ethos, and values. By attending carefully to the distinctive stories and symbols, history and heritage, rituals and practices of congregational life, the pastor's understanding of the congregation can be deepened. Such knowledge can also have a profound influence upon the pastor's ability to craft sermons that are—in their theology, language, and form—"incarnate" for a particular people.

African-American homiletician Henry Mitchell has claimed that the success of African-American preachers has been due, in part, to their ability to preach— theologically and communicationally—in a style consonant with the subculture of their hearers. Mitchell urges white preachers to take a lesson from the black tradition of preaching as folk culture:

> Whether in the Black ghetto, the affluent suburb or the uttermost parts of the earth, the deepest and most meaningful cultural heritage of persons must be identified, respected, and built upon. . . . Preaching that makes meaningful impact on lives has to reach persons at gut level, and it is at this level of communally stored wisdom and cultural affinity that such access to living souls is gained (Mitchell, 29).

While the dialogue between the fields of homiletics and congregational studies is only beginning, the ongoing conversation holds promise for assisting preachers in crafting sermons that—in their theology and their art—attend more closely to the "folk culture" of the congregations for and to whom they are preached (see African-American Preaching; Lay Response to Preaching).

Brooks, P., *Lectures on Preaching,* 1877. **Carroll, J., C. Dudley, W. McKinney,** eds., *Handbook for Congregational Studies,* 1988. **Craddock, F.,** *Preaching,* 1985. **Grierson, D.,** *Transforming a People of God,* Melbourne, 1984. **Hopewell, J.,** *Congregation:*

Stories and Structures, 1987. **Mitchell, H.,** *The Recovery of Preaching*, 1977. **Van Seters, A.,** ed., *Preaching as a Social Act: Theology and Practice*, 1988. **Willimon, W. H.,** *Integrative Preaching: The Pulpit at the Center*, 1981.

LEONORA TUBBS TISDALE

Coughlin, Charles E. (1891–1979)

Father Coughlin was a Roman Catholic priest well known for his radio sermons in the United States in the period between the world wars. Born in Ontario, Canada, of parents of Irish ancestry, Coughlin studied at St. Michael's College, Toronto, joined the Basilian Congregation, and was ordained a priest in 1916. From 1916–1918 Coughlin taught psychology, English, and logic and directed the dramatic society at Assumption College in Ontario on the Canadian border near Detroit. In 1923 he moved to Michigan and became incardinated into the diocese of Detroit. In 1926 Bishop Michael J. Gallagher asked him to build a new parish in a Detroit suburb known as Royal Oak. The parish was named for Thérèse of Lisieux, who had recently been canonized and was affectionately known as "The Little Flower." In an effort to raise funds, Coughlin negotiated for his first radio program, which aired on October 17, 1926, over WJR in Detroit. With the advent of the Depression, Coughlin changed his format from sermonizing and spoke more of the frustration of the people. By 1930, CBS picked up his program nationally, gaining him an audience of an estimated forty million listeners. Short wave from Philadelphia soon carried his voice all over the world on "The Golden Hour of the Little Flower."

Coughlin was an ardent supporter of Franklin Roosevelt in the early 1930s and hoped to have a place of influence in the new administration. He promised Roosevelt that he would use his influence on the air waves to support his campaign and coined the expressions "Roosevelt or Ruin," and "The New Deal is Christ's Deal." President Roosevelt, however, did not look to Detroit for advice. Coughlin

felt rejected, and his antagonism grew into enmity. In 1936, the same year he founded his weekly newspaper, *Social Justice*, Coughlin joined the heir apparent of Huey Long's program, Reverend Gerald L. K. Smith, and Dr. Francis Townsend of California, to form the Union Party to oppose Roosevelt in his bid for reelection. Coughlin lost credibility during this period of theatrical tactics and inappropriate language; he called the President ("Franklin Double-Crossing Roosevelt") a liar and betrayer. Even the Vatican sent word to Bishop Gallagher that Coughlin should be curtailed.

By December of 1938, Coughlin had become radically anti-Semitic, relying on the infamous forgery, *The Protocols of the Elders of Zion*, and on the writings of an Irish theologian, Father Denis Fahey, C.S.Sp. He was sympathetic to Hitler and described Nazism as "a defense mechanism against Communism." With the advent of the war, Coughlin had his mailing privileges revoked for *Social Justice*, and President Roosevelt sent word to Archbishop Edward Mooney of Detroit that if Coughlin was not curtailed he would be indicted under the Espionage Act of 1917. Coughlin's emotion-laden rhetoric on political issues ceased in the summer of 1942. He remained pastor of the Shrine of the Little Flower Parish until his retirement and did some writing until his death in 1979.

Popularly known as "the radio priest," Coughlin was second only to President Roosevelt as a radio orator in the 1930s. It has been said that on Sunday afternoons in the summers one could walk down many a city street and never miss a word of his sermons. His deep voice had a warm, resonant, mellifluous quality that created an atmosphere of personal relationship, and people felt an intimate bond with this priest who, especially in the early days of the depression, conveyed compassion and communicated hope. In large assemblies, such as in Madison Square Garden, he often stirred up the crowd by playing on its fear of godless Communism.

The content of Coughlin's speeches was often framed in terms of scholastic philosophy and theology and reflected the neo-Thomistic revival popular among Catholics at that time. Coughlin was also influenced by the papal social encyclicals *Rerum Novarum* (1891) of Leo XIII and *Quadragesimo Anno* (1931) of Pius XI. Both supported the rights of the working class to fair treatment and wages. Coughlin is credited with popularizing the papal social encyclicals through his radio addresses—ideas welcome to people suffering during the depression.

As Coughlin placed emphasis on the political rather than the priestly, his radio addresses became more angry and vitriolic. He sought scapegoats, especially the Jews. His use of exaggeration when pronouncing Jewish names and his constant references to "turning the money changers out of the temple" coupled with anti-Semitic innuendo led to his being labeled as one of the "demagogues of the depression."

Coughlin, largely self-taught, was a powerful speaker. His charisma created an emotional response on the part of those who admired him and those who despised him. Some suggest he was a precursor of the televangelists in the later twentieth century (*see* Radio Preaching; Television and Preaching; Anti-Jewish Preaching).

Athans, M. C., *The Coughlin-Fahey Connection: Father Charles E. Coughlin, Father Denis Fahey, C.S.Sp., and Religious Anti-Semitism in the United States, 1938–1954,* 1991. **Bennett, D. H.**, *Demagogues in the Depression: American Radicals and the Union Party, 1932–1936,* 1969. **Brinkley, A.,** *Voices of Protest: Huey Long, Father Coughlin, and the Great Depression,* 1983. **Marcus, S.,** *Father Charles E. Coughlin: The Tumultuous Life of the Priest of the Little Flower,* 1973. **Tull, C. J.,** *Father Coughlin and the New Deal,* 1965.

MARY CHRISTINE ATHANS, B.V.M.

AM I AN ANTI-SEMITE?
Charles E. Coughlin
Tolerance, then, becomes a heinous vice when it tolerates the theology of atheism, the patriotism of internationalists, and the justice of religious persecution. No matter, then, what ties of blood and common parentage bind the God-fearing Jews in New York with the atheistic Jews in Moscow, those ties must be severed for God, and for country and for the preservation of the teeming masses of Jews in America who have been victimized by the silence of their leaders and the propaganda of the press. . . . But, remembering that godlessness is the poisoned spring whence Communism originates; remembering that this United States was founded by Christians, pioneered by Christians and developed, in great part, by Christians with no more than four million Jews claiming residence amongst our 130 million population, why do the local Jewish Community Councils cooperate with others in imposing their policies, their constitutional policies, of opposition to Christmas and Easter practices? Why do they propagate that policy through the agency of a law that is on their side? Why do they boast in their publications that they have sown seeds—what shall I call them—seeds of godlessness? . . .

Therefore, I appeal to the General Jewish Council and to the local Councils. I ask you: Even though you are within your constitutional rights; even though we dare not protest legally—why have you closed the minds of our children to the beautiful story of Bethlehem and the Messias? Was not that an act of poor judgment? Why have you blotted out the cycle of the Easter story with its Pilate's hall, its crucifixion, and its glorious resurrection of the Victim of mob violence and hate? We Christians—we have no constitutional redress. We should not even complain because you are within your rights. But, I repeat, it appears that you are injudicious.

Even if you Jews and gentiles in great number consider that these practices are idle dreams and poetry—why not leave us with our dreams, our poetry—dreams and poetry that we learned at our mother's knee; dreams and poetry which were carried here by Columbus in his Santa Maria.

. . . Oh, my fellow citizens, it was the dreams and poetry born in the crib of Bethlehem and spoken from the pulpit of the Cross that made this country the land of the free and the home of the brave.

> From "A Chapter on Intolerance" (Broadcast December 11, 1938), in *"Am I an Anti-Semite?": 9 addresses on Various "ISMS" Answering the Question* (Royal Oak, Mich.: Radio League of the Little Flower, 1939).

Court Preachers. Without access to the seats of power, Jesus of Nazareth had no opportunity to preach in court; on trial he barely spoke to the governor and stood silent before the king. By contrast, the ideal missionary strategy of the book of Acts pictures the apostle Paul boldly addressing Roman governors and King Agrippa.

Though the imperial court remained closed to preachers of the illicit Christian sect, Justin Martyr (ca. 100–165) cast his *First Apology* as an oration addressed to Emperor Antoninus Pius and his son Marcus Aurelius. Generations of martyrs, including such eloquent bishops as Ignatius (ca. 35–107), Polycarp (ca. 70–156) and Cyprian (ca. 200–258), bore faithful witness before officials of Caesar's court. When persecution abated, Christian preachers seized the opportunity to speak openly. In Antioch, the Empress Julia Mammaea, mother of Emperor Alexander Severus, invited the renowned preacher Origen* (ca. 185–254) to expound to her the Christian faith.

With the grant of toleration by the Edict of Milan (313), Christian preaching came fully into the open. Bishop Eusebius of Caesarea (ca. 263–339?), "father of church history" and a counselor at the court of Constantine, cast his orations in general philosophical terms (e.g., logos) without mentioning the name of Jesus Christ, thus commending to a still largely pagan audience policies befitting a Christian emperor. Like later court preachers he praised the ruler in extravagant language; having seen Christians die for their faith, he doubtless considered it wholly deserved:

> No longer as formerly do the babblings of godless men fill the royal chambers, but rather priests and celebrants of God now keep solemn festival with hymns to the royal piety. The One God Himself, the Universal Sovereign, is proclaimed to all, and the joyous word of His benefits binds the race of mankind to the Ruler of All, bringing the good news that the Heavenly Father is gracious and loving to His sons on earth. . . . Together with those who live in the East, those allotted to the West are trained in His teaching at the same moment of time, and with those in the South those allotted the Northern sphere sing out a harmonious strain: to pursue the pious life under the same customs and laws; to praise one God who is over all; to acknowledge one Only-Begotten Savior, the cause of all good things; and to recognize also one sovereign, rector of the earth, and his sons beloved of God ("In Praise of Constantine," Drake, 102).

In Antioch, the eloquent John Chrysostom* (ca. 347–407) enjoyed the court's favor until the Empress Eudoxia sent him to exile. In the Western capital of the Empire, Bishop Ambrose of Milan (ca. 340–397) personally chastised the young Emperor Theodosius on issues of governmental policy and stood ready to preach on them if necessary: "I have done what I could do honorably, that you might hear me in the palace rather than make it necessary to hear me in the Church" (*Letters,* Vol. 26, 19).

Missionaries from the Bishop of Rome or Christian rulers went as ambassadors to the courts of peoples they sought to convert. Pope Gregory the Great (590–604) sent Augustine of Kent to the Angles; the Venerable Bede* (673–735) pictures the preacher and his retinue approaching the court in liturgical procession, bearing a silver cross and an icon of Jesus Christ.

Charlemagne brought the English

preacher and scholar Alcuin (735–804) to his court, and succeeding Holy Roman Emperors adorned their palaces with preachers of eloquence and Christian humility.

Throughout the Middle Ages papal legates were sent to recalcitrant monarchs to deliver demands in sermons. Thus Peter Damian (1007–1072) preached to the hostile court of Emperor Henry IV, making clear that Rome would not grant the divorce the young king desired. The fateful sermon of Pope Urban II, which launched the First Crusade in 1095, was preached to the Council of Clermont, an assembly of kings and barons from across western Europe. Preachers of later crusades aimed their rhetoric at feudal lords.

The age of Renaissance and Reformation brought heightened prestige to eloquence. In Florence, Girolamo Savonarola* (1452–1498) thundered in judgment, enraging Lorenzo the Magnificent and Pope Alexander VI; as the political tide turned, the preacher of penitence was tried and burned at the stake.

On the island of Hispaniola, in 1511, the Dominican Antonio de Montesinos denounced the conquistadors' exploitation of the original inhabitants. When the governor, Diego Columbus, complained of the preaching to King Ferdinand, Montesinos and Bartolomé de Las Casas sailed for Spain to plead the Indians' cause.

Affected by the sermons of Martin Luther* (1483–1546), Frederick of Saxony, gave crucial support to the Protestant Reformation. To uphold the historic church, Ignatius of Loyola (1491–1556) founded the Society of Jesus. Their strategy sought a place for Jesuits as confessors and preachers in the royal courts. In Scotland, John Knox* (ca. 1513–1572) struck terror into the heart of the young Catholic Queen Mary, and the Reformed Kirk chose the Calvinist path.

In England, Hugh Latimer (ca. 1492–1555) pleaded the plight of the poor and pressed upon the boy-king Edward VI his religious duties.

But wherefore shall a king "fear God, and turn neither to the right hand nor the left?" Wherefore shall he do all this? . . . "That he may reign long, he and his children." Remember this, I beseech Your Grace. And when these flatterers and fibbergibs another day shall come and claw you by the back and say, "Sir, trouble not yourself. What should you study? Why should you do this or that?" Your Grace may answer them thus and say, "What, sirrah? I perceive you are weary of us and our posterity. Doth not God say in such a place that a king should write out a book of God's law and read it, learn to fear God? And why? That he may reign long. I perceive now thou art a traitor" ("Second Sermon before Edward IV," *Selected Sermons of Hugh Latimer*, 84).

Court preaching reached its climax in the seventeenth century. In London, Lancelot Andrewes (1555–1626), John Donne* (1572–1630), and John Tillotson* (1630–1694) spoke boldly to king and court. Louis XIV of France adorned his palaces by bringing eloquent pulpiteers to Paris and Versailles. Considered most powerful among the French court preachers were Jacques-Bénigne Bossuet* (1627–1704), Louis Bourdaloue (1632–1704), and Jean-Baptiste Massillon* (1663–1742).

Mourn then that great Captain, and weeping say—"[I]n his silence, . . . his very name . . . warns us, that to find, at death, some rest from our toils, and not arrive unprepared at our eternal dwelling, we must with an earthly king, yet serve the King of Heaven." Serve then that immortal and ever merciful King, who will value a sigh or a cup of cold water, given in his name, more than all others will value the shedding of your blood. And begin to reckon the time of your useful services from the day on which you gave yourselves to so beneficent a Master . . ." (Bossuet, "Funeral Oration for Louis Bourbon, Prince of Condé," Turnbull, 46–47).

In colonial New England, where power centered in the royal governors and their courts, annual election sermons gave instruction on the duties of magistrates and subjects. The preachers exegeted the scriptures in accord with John Locke's writings on civil government. As a result, the claims subsequently advanced in the Declaration of Independence became "self-evident."

Though the disestablishment of religion removed the possibility of court preaching in the United States, various denominations have built "national cathedrals" in Washington, D.C., and have gloried as their particular edifice became for a time "the president's church." Richard Nixon regularly scheduled Sunday services in the White House and issued invitations to favored ministers to preach. Evangelist Billy Graham* (1918–) became spiritual consultant to presidents from Eisenhower to Bush.

Preaching to power is fraught with ambiguity, as the apparent opportunity for prophetic utterance or spiritual counsel is drastically constrained by the august presence of the person who embodies the majesty and might of the nation. Given the demands of protocol and the human tendency to ingratiate oneself to one's sponsor, the court preacher is tempted to toady. Only when secure in the countervailing power of the church, as the medieval preachers were, or in the security of the Word of God, as the reformers were, is one free to declare divine judgment and costly grace.

Few authentic prophets have earned their living by preaching or have won favor in palaces. Given the hazards of the occupation, the "court preachers" here named acquitted themselves with faithfulness to match their eloquence.

Ambrose, *Letters,* trans. M. M. Beyenka, O.P., *Fathers of the Church,* Vol. 26, 1954. **Chester, A. G.,** ed., *Selected Sermons of Hugh Latimer,* 1968. **Drake, H. A.,** *In Praise of Constantine: A Historical Study and New Translation of Eusebius' Tricennial Orations,* Classical Studies, Vol. 15, 1976. **Giles, J. A.,** ed., *The Venerable Bede's Ecclesiastical History of England,* 1849. **Hanke, L.,** *The Spanish Struggle for Justice in the Conquest of America,* 1949. **Plumstead, A. W.,** ed., *The Wall and the Garden: Selected Massachusetts Election Sermons, 1670–1775,* 1968. **Turnbull, R.,** *The Pulpit Orators of France and Switzerland: Sketches of Their Character and Specimens of Their Eloquence,* 1848.

RONALD E. OSBORN

Craddock, Fred B.

Craddock, Fred B. (1928–) Fred Craddock has been one of the most creative and influential voices in homiletics in the latter third of the twentieth century. A native of Humbolt, Tennessee, Craddock is an ordained minister of the Christian Church (Disciples of Christ) and a popular preacher and lecturer across the United States. In 1993 Craddock retired from his position as Bandy Professor of Preaching and New Testament at the Candler School of Theology at Emory University, which he had held since 1979. Prior to coming to Candler, Craddock was Professor of Preaching and New Testament at the Graduate Seminary of Phillips University.

In the mid-1960s, shortly after coming to the seminary at Phillips, Craddock began to develop his distinctive approach to preaching. The period was one of social, political, and religious turmoil, and preaching was in decline. Along with other activities associated with institutions and tradition, the Christian pulpit was generally viewed as an anachronism in a visually oriented, socially active, antiauthoritarian culture. In addition, there was a growing frustration with historical-critical biblical scholarship, which seemed to create a distance between the Bible and the pulpit. In this context Craddock sought to take seriously the cultural revolution of the 1960s while maintaining his commitment to preaching informed by serious biblical scholarship. This dual commitment is evident in Craddock's publications, which consist of homiletics texts, biblical commentaries, and lectionary aids.

Craddock focused his attention on the hearers and the methods of preaching. His goal was to effect a new hearing of the gospel in a culture suspicious of authority. Language, communication, and particularly sermon form received his primary attention. In his most important book, *As One Without Authority*, these concerns coalesced and were given practical shape by his "inductive method"* of preaching.

Rhetorically, Fred Craddock's inductive method represents a challenge to traditional deductive preaching, which announces general, propositional conclusions and then breaks them down into various points and exhortations. As an alternative, Craddock's method begins with the particulars of human experience and takes the congregation on a journey toward the often surprising conclusions of the gospel. In this process the preacher doesn't simply deposit conclusions in the hearers' minds but enables the congregation to participate actively in the movement and meaning of the sermon. Inductive movement encourages listeners to think their own thoughts, feel their own feelings, draw their own conclusions, and make their own decisions, with the result that they take a measure of responsibility for the message. Preaching becomes the shared activity of preacher and congregation.

Craddock's own sermons provide excellent examples of his method. The sermons are exercises in concreteness and particularity, often consisting of little more than a series of anecdotes that move with minimal abstract reflection to a point at which the hearers must draw their own conclusions and make their own decisions. In good inductive fashion, the general emerges from close attention to particulars.

On the biblical side, Craddock's homiletic emphasizes the particularity of the biblical text. Craddock not only rejects topical preaching but highlights the various rhetorical functions that biblical texts perform. Although the parables serve as the primary biblical model for the induc-

tive method, Craddock has consistently stressed that the various rhetorical forms in scripture should shape the form and function of the sermon. A doxological text should not be reduced to informational points but should move the congregation to praise. In his appreciation for the rhetorical variety in scripture, Craddock's dual concern for the biblical text and homiletical communication converge.

Four major influences shaped Craddock's method. First, his own exegetical work served as a paradigm for sermonic movement. Rather than beginning the sermon at the point of conclusion, Craddock seeks to replicate the inductive movement of exegesis in the sermon itself. Second, Craddock drew upon the educational philosophy of John Dewey, which focused on "helping persons arrive at conclusions, rather than depositing conclusions in their mind"—precisely what Craddock hopes to accomplish through inductive preaching. Third, Craddock undergirded his method theologically with an individualistic interpretation of the doctrine of the priesthood of all believers. The inductive sermon gives individual "priests" the freedom and responsibility to draw their own conclusions and make their own decisions. Finally, Craddock's method was informed by the existentialist philosophy and theology of Gerhard Ebeling and Søren Kierkegaard.* Influenced by Ebeling's New Hermeneutic, Craddock emphasized the linguistic dimensions of the sermon, the importance of Jesus' parables, and the oral, experiential, and event character of preaching. Kierkegaard's theory of indirect communication provided a concrete example of the inductive method and a paradigm for creating an existential event through the sermon. Kierkegaard's cultural theory of Christendom's immunity to direct proclamation also underlay Craddock's reflection. Although none of these pieces were new, even in the homiletical literature, Craddock shaped them into a clear, coherent, and practical method of preaching.

Craddock's *As One Without Authority* virtually set the agenda for homiletical reflection in the two decades that followed its publication. His work helped to place sermon form at the center of the homiletical enterprise, where it has remained during the latter part of the twentieth century. Craddock also helped turn the attention of homileticians to the linguistic dimensions of preaching, particularly the oral, evocative, and performative character of homiletical speech in contrast to positivistic, informational understandings of language. In addition, Craddock's insights into the concrete, indirect character of narrative communication contributed to the development of "narrative preaching."* His focus on the biblical text influenced recent trends toward more biblical approaches to preaching. Finally, Craddock's emphasis on the holistic character of preaching, which involves the emotions as well as the mind, has continued to be a central concern of recent homiletical thought.

Craddock, F. B., *As One Without Authority,* 1979; *Luke,* 1990; *Overhearing the Gospel,* 1978; *Preaching,* 1985.

CHARLES L. CAMPBELL

DOXOLOGY

Fred B. Craddock

I was leading a group of students in a study of Paul's letter to the Romans. The class soon discovered, however, that in this weightiest and most influential of all Paul's letters, the argument was often interrupted by Doxology. . . . After a very lengthy treatment of the tragic situation concerning the Jews from whom came the Christ but who had not believed in Him, Paul breaks off his argument suddenly and begins to sing:

O the depths of the riches and wisdom and knowledge of God! How unsearchable are his judgments and how inscrutable his ways. . . .
For from him and through him and to him are all things.
To him be glory for ever. Amen.

Time and time again Paul breaks the line of thought with a doxological reservation. . . .

Is there ever a time or place when it is inappropriate to say, "For from him and through him and to him are all things. To him be glory for ever. Amen."?

It was from the class on Romans that I was called to the phone. My oldest brother had just died. Heart attack. When stunned and hurt, get real busy to avoid thought. Call the wife. Get the kids out of school. Arrange for a colleague to take my classes. Cancel a speaking engagement. And, oh yes, stop the milk, the paper, the mail; have someone feed the dog. . . . "I think I packed the clothes we need," the wife said as we threw luggage and our bodies into the car.

All night we drove, across two states, eyes pasted open against the windshield. Conversation was spasmodic, consisting of taking turns asking the same questions over and over. No one pretended to have answers. When we drew near the town and the house, I searched my mind for a word, a first word to the widow. He was my brother but he was her husband. I was still searching when we pulled into the driveway. She came out to meet us and as I opened the car door, still without that word, she broke the silence:

"I hope you brought Doxology."

Doxology?

No, I had not. I had not even thought of Doxology since the phone call.

But the truth is now clear: if we ever lose our Doxology, we might as well be dead.

"For from him and through him and to him are all things. To him be glory for ever. Amen."

From "Doxology," in *As One Without Authority,* 3d ed. (Nashville: Abingdon Press, 1979), 165–68.

Cross-Cultural Preaching. Preaching is a cultural event. No sermon is acultural, apolitical, asexual, aeconomic, or aracial. Every sermon occurs in a complex of cultural diversity with contrasting

values on family, individual, age, gender, race, community, and differing views of destiny, freedom, agency, responsibility, honor, and dignity.

All preaching is cross-cultural as it seeks to bring the multiple, strange world of the Bible and the Christian heritage to bear on our own. Biblical hermeneutics* must be universally responsible while locally relevant; theological ethics must address issues ranging from international to individual concerns; theological reflection must apply to the translocal as well as the local. To view individual problems as separate from their context is to misunderstand them; they need to be seen in the system, network, society, and culture where they lie embedded if they are to be realistically understood. Individual problems are manifestations of systems that extend far beyond one's personality, family, and locality; individual salvation and healing is a subset of the church's larger concern for the salvation of the world.

Preaching *within* a culture calls for cultural *adjustments*, for ongoing change, transformation, or gradual evolution toward greater faithfulness. Preaching *between* cultures calls for cultural *adaptation* as each becomes more sensitive to dialogue, more open to each other's styles, concerns, values, and unique nuances. Preaching *beyond* culture points to those universals that connect us at the root, such as the sense of alienation, the capacity for awe and wonder, the needs to belong, to have meaning, to be secure, to enjoy novelty, to experience growth.

Effective preaching in a multicultural context, which our urban and increasingly our rural churches inhabit, requires that the sermon must be contextually congruent with the context in which it is given. It must also have multicultural clarity exemplified in the use of a second culture's perspective and the inevitable variability in understanding and application. A sermon embodying only one culture is blind to culture; one sees when there is sufficient light to provide contrasts, feels when there are differing pressures on the nerve, smells when fragrance is new. Culture, like the atmosphere one inhabits, must be lifted to awareness by use of contrast in context.

A theology of incarnation calls the preacher to enflesh the message in authentically human flesh, not just in her or his own experience. A theology of redemption empowers the preacher to challenge and reduce barriers, to diminish and to dismantle walls whenever possible. A theology of resurrection draws the preacher to live on the boundaries, preach from the boundaries, invite the listeners to become a boundary-crossing people.

All cultures and subcultures are shaped by particular myths (stories) that make life more meaningful and intelligible, that unify the culture, and that promote the values of the society or group. Thus the preacher in any context, but especially in cross-cultural contexts, is best understood as a storyteller or narrator who creates bonds of *identification* between the sacred text of scripture and the particular text of the community addressed. The efficacy of cross-cultural preaching may be understood in terms of its "mythic adequacy," that is, the degree to which a sermon reveals the preacher as an authentic character, constitutes a responsible representation of biblical and cultural reality, and represents an effective articulation of the mood of the group addressed.

The Preacher as an Authentic Character. The first measure of mythic adequacy grows out of the universally acknowledged idea that matters of character* have always been central to persuasive discourse. The truth of the gospel is mediated through personality (Brooks*). A believable sermon presupposes a believable storyteller, a preacher whose demonstrated intelligence, integrity, and good will merit audience response. Is the preacher known as one who embodies in life what is preached in the message? Does the person of the preacher ring true? Is the preacher good news?

A Responsible Representation of Biblical and Cultural Reality. The second measure of mythic adequacy is aimed at answering two essential questions: Is the sermon a faithful reflection of the meaning of the biblical text? And is the sermon true to the basic facts of life within the particular cultural setting in which it is uttered? Fidelity to scripture is most certainly indispensable to all Christian preaching. Nonetheless, the preacher's assertions of biblical truth will be received as true only if this truth is not falsified by the conditions of life. In short, a sermon's truthfulness will be jeopardized unless it possesses both biblical and cultural intelligibility.

An Effective Articulation of the Mood of a Congregation.   The final measure of mythic adequacy relates to evaluating the overall efficacy of cross-cultural preaching. Do the language and thought of the message constitute a fitting response to the images, ideas, beliefs, and values of the cultural setting? Does the sermon adequately conform to the expectations of the group for what communication ought to look like? Is the sermon successfully and sensitively adapted to the pressing concerns of a congregation? Does the sermon take into account the real mind of the listener? Does the sermon identify the ways of the gospel and the ways of the preacher with the ways of the congregation? (*see* Communication; Missions).

Augsburger, D. W., *Pastoral Counseling Across Cultures,* 1986. **Fisher, W. R.,** *Human Communication as Narration: Toward a Philosophy of Reason, Value, and Action,* 1987. **Gudykunst, W. B.,** and **Young Yun Kim,** *Communicating with Strangers: An Approach to Intercultural Communication,* 1992. **Kraft, C. H.,** *Communication Theory for Christian Witness,* 1991.

DAVID W. AUGSBURGER
MITTIES MCDONALD DECHAMPLAIN

Davis, Henry Grady.   (1890–1975)

Grady Davis was professor of Practical Theology at the Chicago Lutheran Theological Seminary (the Lutheran School of Theology at Chicago) from 1937 to 1967.

He is known primarily as the author of *Design for Preaching,* one of the most widely used textbooks in homiletics in the last thirty years. Many contemporary issues in homiletical thought and research may be found in embryonic form in Davis's work.

Foundational to Davis's understanding of a sermon and of preaching is his insistence that content and form* are not two separate entities. Although theological substance does not receive thorough discussion in his writings, Davis's homiletical thought was shaped by theological concerns. He was influenced by the biblical theology movement of the 1950s and the neo-orthodox traditions of the Word of God represented by Emil Brunner, Karl Barth,* Joseph Sittler, and Reinhold Niebuhr.* Davis largely accepted the conclusions of their work and did not feel compelled to explicate his own understanding of the content of Christian proclamation.

The biblical text was the source of Christian preaching for Davis. But the form, he believed, needed to be congruent and organic with the idea or theme of a sermon, which in turn arises from reflection on a biblical text. An organic form is a structured, living organism. Davis criticized notions of sermon preparation as sermon *construction,* preferring the concept of *design* for its functional associations.

How does a germinal idea expand out of its own energy? The analogies Davis uses for sermon design he drew from nature and living organisms. "The relation of substance and form in the communication of thought is the kind of relation that exists between living tissue and organism. All life, every living thing we know, comes in some organic form" (Davis 1958, 1). Not only his poetic sensibility but also his awe at the incarnation of the Word was the fundamental ground of Davis's organic view of preaching.

The organic forms, however, are dependent on the germinal sermonic idea. The anatomy of an idea thus becomes essential in the consideration of form.

Davis insisted that no person could tell another person how to preach. He believed that he could render his best service by asking the right questions about a sermonic idea and the sermon itself.

The questions he asked were simple. He insisted that the mastery of plain tools and elementary observations are indispensable to a master craftsman, artist, and preacher. His questions to the preacher were these:

1. What are you talking about?
2. What are you saying about it?
3. What do you mean?
4. Is it true? Do you believe it?
5. What difference does it make?

Thus the characteristics of a good sermon idea were these:

1. The subject must be narrow enough to be sharp.
2. It must have in it a force that is expanding.
3. It must be true.
4. It must be loaded with the realities of the human heart.
5. It must be one of the many facets of the gospel of Christ.

Organic forms for the sermonic idea that Davis proposed are: (1) a subject discussed—an incomplete thought that the sermon completes; (2) a thesis supported or a proposition maintained and developed; (3) a message illuminated—without argument or proof; (4) a question propounded, where inquiry, not assertion, is essential; and (5) a story told—narration of events, persons, and actions. A germinal sermonic idea may assume these forms.

Substance or content and form are inseparable. That was Davis's central conviction and the motivation for his homiletical proposals. Latent in his writings, however, are themes and concerns that contemporary homileticians continue to develop—for example, genres in relation to preaching, narrativity, images, metaphors and poetic language, form, and movement of thought, especially inductive preaching.* These themes are illustrated in Davis's own words (1958, 15):

Design for a Sermon

A sermon should be like a tree.
It should be a living organism:
  With one sturdy thought like a single
      stem
  With natural limbs reaching up into
      the light.
It should have deep roots:
  As much unseen as above the surface
  Roots spreading as widely as its
      branches spread
  Roots deep underground
    In the soil of life's struggle
    In the subsoil of the eternal Word.
It should show nothing but its own unfolding parts:
  Branches that thrust out by the force
      of its inner life
  Sentences like leaves native to this
      very spray
    True to the species
    Not taken from alien growths
  Illustrations like blossoms opening
      from inside these very twigs
    Not brightly colored kites
    Pulled from the wind of somebody
        else's thought
    Entangled in these branches.
It should bear flowers and fruit at the
    same time like the orange:
Having something for food
  For immediate nourishment
Having something for delight
  For present beauty and fragrance
  For the joy of hope
  For the harvest of a distant day.
To be all this it must grow in a warm
    climate:
  In loam enriched by death
  In love like the all-seeing and all-
      cherishing sun
  In trust like the sleep-sheltering
      night
  In pity like the rain.

Davis, H. G., *Design for Preaching*, 1958; "Dimensions of the Word," August 5–8, 1963, four sound cassettes, Reigner Recording Library, Union Theological Seminary, Richmond, Virginia.

MORRIS J. NIEDENTHAL

Delivery of Sermons. The delivery of sermons begins with the speaking of the texts upon which those sermons are based. This is so because the texts of scripture themselves, for the most part, are texts of oral discourse. They are meant to be heard, felt, and acted upon. The stories of scripture are recorded oral narratives. The poems of scripture are songs waiting to be sung. Even the more discursive texts of scripture such as Paul's letters contain poetic and narrative elements. It can be argued that they are better thought of as sermons meant to be preached and heard than as bits of didactic correspondence to be read quietly or in a detached, reflective manner. Stories, poems, and sermons require embodiment, for they are *poiemata*, ethical-aesthetic works, made of the stuff of life. To be fully known they must be performed.

Many texts of scripture are works of oral-aural, face-to-face communicative art. Narrative works live as they are told. A poem "survives / In the valley of its saying . . . it survives, / A way of happening, a mouth," says W. H. Auden. Sermonic texts likewise manifest their power as living speech when they are preached. To treat texts of scripture only as documents for study according to the rules of exegesis* and historical criticism, therefore, is to distort them. Such study provides needed information about texts. However, to know texts in terms of what they can do to those who read them, the texts have to be said. They require a human voice and body.

To speak texts is to be changed by them. Preaching is what happens as a result of that change. Paul Ricoeur, for instance, can lead one to see how preaching is a rhetoric of testimony (Ricoeur, 119–54). Literary theorist and critic Stephen Prickett has made a strong case for viewing all literature—and especially sacred literature—as a manifestation or confirmation of previous experience of the subject under consideration in the literary text (Prickett, 149–95). Scripture texts bear witness to the confirming/disconfirming experience of God's self-disclosure. Therefore, to speak texts of scripture is to enter into a moment of confirmation/disconfirmation of previous experience of God.

Even the so-called neo-orthodox theologians, who have not been noted for emphasizing the human character of divine speech, have indicated that preaching participates in God's self-attestation. This is what gives preaching its theological import. Scripture is God's human speech in that, with it, God, by the power of the spirit, takes preachers—and their congregations—as they are and presses them into the service of what God would have them be.

Connotation (emotional content) thus is wedded to denotation (logical content) from the very beginning, for what a text asserts cannot be separated from what it effects in those who speak it and preach from it. Consequently, if sermons seem to be lifeless when they are spoken from the pulpit or if what liveliness they have appears to be artificial and forced, the cause very possibly may be the preacher's lifeless reading of the text.

In rhetorical terms, preaching includes: (1) invention—the discovery of something to say; (2) arrangement—the organization of what is to be said; (3) style*—the preacher's diction or way of using language; (4) memory*—the preacher's internalization of what needs to be said; and (5) delivery—the preacher's act of bringing thought to expression. These five dimensions of the rhetoric* of preaching should not be separated. Since delivery of the text is crucial to the impact of the text as an event of God's self-disclosure, delivery skills clearly play a role in invention. Also, since arrangement of sermonic material has to do with how one most clearly and winsomely may bear witness to God's Word, skill in delivery has an impact upon the ordering of the sermon. Furthermore, if style has to do with a preacher's distinctive use of language in light of the demands of subject matter and setting, then questions about self-expression in body and voice must have stylistic import.

Finally, one cannot keep in mind the matter of the speech without giving due consideration to how it is to be expressed. Whether one uses a full manuscript,* notes, or no notes at all when preaching, skill in delivery is crucial for making the sermon memorable. Thus sermon delivery skills play an important role in the homiletical process from beginning to end. They do not merely enable preachers to say things well. They help preachers determine what they are to say. Sermon delivery skills have epistemological and hermeneutical significance.

What, then, are the skills of sermon delivery? They are skills of thinking, feeling, and doing. Technical skill in sermon delivery involves the clear perception and expression of denotative and connotative meaning. Consider Ezekiel's statement: "The hand of the Lord was upon me, and he brought me out by the Spirit of the Lord, and set me down in the middle of a valley; it was full of bones" (Ezek. 37:1). Such a statement is qualitatively different from that a cartographer might make concerning a Middle Eastern plain. It is a statement of vision, not of mere sight. It is figurative, a metaphor. The bones are "the whole house of Israel" (Ezek. 37:11). A cartographer seeks to remove mystery from any landscape. The prophet's words, on the other hand, fill the landscape with profound mystery.

What is needed to bring that sense of mystery and the awful presence of God to consciousness is empathic speech. Empathy means to feel with others and to enter into what seems to be foreign territory. It is the opposite of self-absorption. Empathic speech also enables preachers to lead others into an exploration of imaginative, even strange, worlds. This is not what is commonly called "getting in touch with your feelings." To the contrary, it is getting in touch with feelings which are precisely *not* one's own. Nor is empathic speech a matter of faking emotions that one really does not have. One really does have the emotions but in response to a literary stimulus. Emotions grounded in experiences with litera-ture may be different from emotions grounded in experiences of some other type, but they are no less real. To express those emotions in voice and body, therefore, is not to put on an act. It is not to be artificial. In fact, to refuse to express them is to cheat others of the connotative aspect of meaning.

Preachers initially may *feel* artificial as they attempt to lead others into the exploration of imaginative, word-created worlds. However, focusing on that feeling of artificiality or trying to say the words with a connotation of neutrality and detachment only exacerbates the problem. It shifts the focus of attention from the experience to be explored to the experience of the self. The preacher then becomes a servant of the self instead of a servant of the word. To speak emotion-packed words without appropriate response is to misspeak them. The alternative is to focus on the experience evoked by the text instead of on the experience of the self. Sermons, like passages of scripture, are word-created worlds of meaning. Despite the impediment of self-consciousness, sermons must be delivered with full attention to denotative and connotative meaning.

In connection with empathy it should be borne in mind that both voice and body play a part. The voice should be supple, exhibiting suitable variety in quality, rate, pitch, and volume, so that what is felt by the preacher may be sounded as clearly as possible. The body should respond to what is thought and felt so that there may be congruence between the inner form and outer form of the experience being shared. For the listener, physical gesture is more crucial than vocal gesture in stimulating empathic response. As preachers change their posture—as their muscles tense or relax, as their facial expression changes—covertly at least, the listeners react kinesthetically. The spoken word of the preacher is not only heard but seen, felt, and done. For that reason, preachers need a discipline of thought, subjectivity, voice, and body. Just as no musician thinks of performing on a poorly maintained and untuned instrument, so no preacher who is wise neglects the instrument with which she or he preaches. The preacher's voice and body require tuning and wise use (*see* Voice).

In addition to empathic response, the preacher must be aware of the movement of thought implicit in the words spoken. Too many sermons seem to lack directed movement. In sermon delivery a failure of progression in thought manifests itself in a sameness of rate, pause, and intensity only for the sake of variety. The variation needs to be in accord with the development of thought. Preachers need to be aware of the comparative size and quality of thoughts, the relationship of thoughts to one another, and how thoughts in succession build to a climax.

The psalmist's words, "The earth is the Lord's and all that is in it, the world, and those who live in it . . . " (Ps. 24:1), express a very large idea. The idea demands a lengthening of vowel sound and flow as well as suitable volume and intensity. There could be a brief pause between "Lord's" and "and" and perhaps a slightly longer one between "it" and "the world." However, the pauses should not be long and drawn out. Psalm 24:1 should not be rushed, but there can be no dawdling with it either. The pauses taken give the speaker of the text a millisecond or so to catch a breath so that vocal and physical vitality can be sustained to the very end of the line. Pauses, rightly handled, are not dead spots. They are like rests in music. They contribute to the progression of thought. They do not halt that progression.

There are instances when longer pauses are needed in order to sustain progression of thought. When a thought is weighted with heavy emotional freight—grief, pain, or anger so deep that it hardly can be expressed—it may be necessary to slow down and to stop speaking entirely for a second or two, maybe even longer. The psalmist's cry, "How long, O Lord? Will you forget me forever?" (Ps. 13:1a), fairly begs for a substantial pause after "O Lord." In fact, a quick pause or no pause

at all would seem ludicrous. It takes time to ingest the pain implicit in such a statement. The thought progresses inward through the preacher and the listener during the pause. Returning to the figure of music, the rest in the line, "The earth is the Lord's and all that is in it" might be the equivalent of a sixteenth note. The pause after, "How long, O Lord . . . ," on the other hand, might be the equivalent of a whole note. It might even be preceded by a *fermata* or "hold" on the word "Lord." In other words, progression in scripture reading and sermon delivery is not synonymous with "hurry." Instead, progression involves suitable variation in rate, pause, and intensity according to the demands of the particular thoughts being spoken and their relationship as understood by the preacher.

Pauses, no less than the speaking of words in a sermon, also necessitate physical reaction to the thought just stated and anticipation of the thought coming up. Just as the mind must not go blank during a pause, so also the face must not go blank, and the body must not become disengaged. If congregations are to wait *with* preachers and not simply *for* them, preachers' physical involvement with the thoughts and experiences being delivered must be sustained. Whether preachers' eyes are focused on a manuscript, notes, the congregation, or ideas inwardly held, preachers' eyes must actually see something, and preachers' faces and bodies must react to what is seen. If that does not happen, people in the congregation, because of the empathic power of kinesthetic cues, will lose a measure of contact with the thoughts and experiences being expressed. In other words, when there is a conflict between word and action, it is the action that is believed, not the word. The preacher may say: "This is a matter of life or death!" But if the preacher's body says: "Don't you believe it," the congregation won't believe it.

When Demosthenes was asked what rhetoric was all about, he replied: "delivery, delivery, delivery." In a sense, this is also true of preaching. Plainly, exegesis,* careful textual interpretation, theological reflection, sermon design, and composition are crucial homiletical tasks. As a professor of speech once put it, "You can't say 'nothing' well." However, sermon delivery skills inform the way exegesis, interpretation, theological reflection, sermon design, and composition are done. But these tasks are preparation for preaching, not preaching itself. Preaching is a matter of speaking *and* hearing. And the preacher is a listener who speaks in order to help others listen.

One question remains: To what end is all this disciplined effort in sermon delivery expended? The answer, of course, is that its purpose is the proclamation of God's Word. Through preaching, God registers a divine claim upon preachers and congregations alike. In the spoken word of the sermon, God in Christ, by the power of the Holy Spirit, at any moment may choose to make the divine presence known and felt. And God, by doing so, may stir human beings to think again about who they are and what God would have them be and do. A mood of expectancy, therefore, ought to pervade the sermon from beginning to end. Yet some preachers seem to saunter through their sermons "like Mohawks along a strand of scaffolding who have long since forgotten their danger" (Annie Dillard, 60). Years ago, in an effort to put an end to such "sauntering," a professor of homiletics said this to his students: "What is the purpose of preaching? The purpose of preaching is to raise the dead!" The preacher exists for the sake of God's Word, that it may be heard. And in the end, by the power of the Spirit, it is the church—preachers and congregations together—that proclaims the Word of God. So those who are about to deliver sermons pray: "Let the words of my mouth and the meditation of our hearts be acceptable to you, O Lord, our rock and our redeemer. Amen" (Ps. 19:14).

Bartow, C. L., *The Preaching Moment: A Guide to Sermon Delivery*, 1980; *Effective Speech Communication in Leading Worship*, 1988. **Bozarth-Campbell, A.** *The Word's Body: An Incarnational Aesthetic of Interpretation*, 1979. **Dillard, A.,** *Holy the Firm*, 1977. **Prickett, S.,** *Words and the Word: Language, Poetics, and Biblical Interpretation*, 1986. **Ricoeur, P.,** "The Hermeneutics of Testimony," *Essays on Biblical Interpretation*, ed. Lewis S. Mudge, 1980. **Stevenson, D. E.,** and **C. F. Diehl,** *Reaching People from the Pulpit*, 1958. **Ward, R. F.,** *Speaking from the Heart: Preaching with Passion*, 1992.

CHARLES L. BARTOW

Doctrine. Doctrine is the glue that holds *every* sermon together and determines whether the words uttered from the pulpit are in fact Christian proclamation. Occasionally, as in the case of "teaching sermons," Christian doctrine may play this role explicitly, when the exposition of a particular doctrine receives express attention as the sermon's theme. More typically, however, the essential role of Christian doctrine in the sermon is less explicit.

Jaroslav Pelikan asserts that "doctrine is what is believed, taught, and confessed" by the church; thus every sermon is an expression of Christian doctrine (Pelikan, 3). This is not to say that every sermon should include explicit exposition of doctrine or theological propositions. Christian doctrine is not identical with the proclamation of the gospel. Doctrine serves proclamation, enriches and enhances it, largely in a *critical* role, as a criterion for determining that what the church proclaims today is in harmony with scripture and its tradition, that it is truly human language *about God* and not about the latest spiritual trend or social ethical passion.

Another way of making this point about the role of doctrine in every sermon is to note the obvious distinction between the often rarefied language of theological discourse and the first-order language of faith used by most Christians. There is a parallel intimate relationship between the rules of English grammar and ordinary American English discourse (Lindbeck, 80–84).

Not all discourse that employs Christian vocabulary is proper Christian discourse any more than a sentence using nothing but English terms, such as "He don't do no wrong to nobody," qualifies as a proper English sentence. Of course the impropriety of the preceding example of an English sentence is immediately recognizable. Yet a recognition of its impropriety is not intuitive. We have come to recognize its impropriety as a result of our mastery of the rules of English grammar and our use of these rules to criticize and evaluate the sentence. In much the same way, Christian doctrines should function to criticize discourse that flows from the pulpit.

It is possible, for example, to proclaim from the pulpit that "Because God has given us his commandments, we are capable of fulfilling them." But the doctrine of original sin and the Conciliar condemnations of Pelagius rule against the legitimately Christian character of such proclamation. It violates the rules (grammar) of the Christian faith.

Preachers need to concern themselves with doctrine, then, in every sermon that they preach, just as authors need to attend to grammatical rules when writing. Just as the rules of subject-verb agreement inform the writing of this paragraph, so the Trinity doctrine must inform the way preachers speak when referring to God as Father, Son, and Holy Spirit, reminding them that their discourse does not imply that Christians believe in three gods.

Given its subordinate role as a kind of servant to actual Christian proclamation, doctrine need not receive much explicit attention in most sermons. Likewise, it should not typically (except in the case of the occasional "teaching* sermon") receive much attention in the early stages of sermon preparation. The subject of proclamation* is God and his word (primarily as revealed in scripture), not doctrine. But if express doctrinal/theological issues

are habitually introduced too soon in the sermon preparation process, this focus may be lost, and the sermon may take the form of a mere lecture on theology.

For those working in denominational traditions committed to the Reformation *sola scriptura*, a systematic commitment to introducing theological or doctrinal reflection in the early stages of biblical exegesis* would represent a compromise of one's own doctrinal heritage. Indeed, faithfulness to this heritage entails an openness to the possibility that particular theological or doctrinal categories may be corrected by the insights of scripture. That commitment can most readily be honored if we do not impose such categories on our exegesis but first endeavor to formulate an exegetical summary that can subsequently function in a critical dialogue with our own doctrinal commitments.

Of course, these suppositions do not represent an admission of the unimportance of doctrine for homiletics. After completing the initial exegetical work and summarizing the conclusions, preachers should proceed to analyze their exegetical summaries in relation to certain relevant doctrines (their relevance to the season of the church year, or their relevance to the situation the preacher is addressing). Such self-conscious attention to doctrine at this stage of sermon preparation can offer at least three potential contributions.

First, attention to doctrinal themes can help preachers order their material and help them see things in a text they might not otherwise have seen. For example, the temptations Jesus experienced in Matthew 4:1–11, the hunger he felt, stand out in sharper relief when this pericope is assessed in light of the Nicene doctrine of Christology and its insistence on the full humanity of Jesus of Nazareth. Likewise, it might be quite easy to interpret Romans 13:8 as an exhortation by Paul for Christians to love. But an analysis of the pericope in light of the doctrine of justification by grace through faith helps the preacher to recognize that Paul is not suggesting that we can save ourselves by such love.

Second, in addition to helping preachers see things in texts they might not otherwise have seen, self-conscious attention to Christian doctrine in the later stages of sermon preparation can help preachers in ruling out exegetical errors they might have made. Conflict between one's exegetical conclusions and classical doctrinal commitments may be a warning sign. Preachers are obligated to account for it, or else they may need to conclude that they are in error (*see* Exegesis).

Finally, self-conscious reliance on doctrinal reflection provides categories for preachers to assess the overall impact of their preaching. If, for example, analysis reveals that the doctrine of redemption surfaces in virtually every one of a preacher's sermons, with scant reference to the doctrine of creation, it is easy to see why that preacher may be nurturing an individualistic spirituality among the flock.

The preceding comments have offered reflections on how doctrine functions in most sermons (usually behind-the-scenes). However, on occasion in "teaching sermons," doctrine may be the subject of the sermon. At least three possible approaches to such a sermon may be identified. Sometimes, a biblical text may be the primary source for a doctrine so that, in preaching on the text, one cannot responsibly avoid expounding the doctrine. For example, one could hardly think of preaching on 1 Corinthians 11:17–34 without taking up an explanation of the doctrine of the Lord's Supper in the sermon. This approach to teaching sermons works best when the sermon is essentially an exposition of the biblical text, as with any other sermon. Explicit exposition of doctrines could best emerge as transitional clarifications of what is going on in the text.

A second approach to "teaching sermons" on doctrine is simply to devote the whole sermon to the exposition of a single doctrine, to start out by asking the congregation what they think of it. Unless the doctrine in question is highly controversial or of immediate existential significance for the context (predestination, the resurrection from the dead, just war—at least during the Persian Gulf crisis—the Trinity, and the like), such a sermon too easily degenerates into a lecture. To avoid this, preachers must endeavor to help hearers not just to understand the doctrine in question, but to see how it can help them interpret their everyday experience and make sense of the world.

A third possible approach, a species of the second, is to begin not with the doctrine as such but with a question or existential dilemma the doctrine will address. For example, reflections on how sometimes we feel inadequate, guilty, or do not really like ourselves, could be used to precede a sermon on the doctrine of justification by grace through faith. Once again, the aim in such a sermon would not be merely to teach about the doctrine but to help one's hearers experience the gospel through the doctrine in order to interpret their daily lives.

As social analysts continue to remind us of the withering of cohesive communities that formerly provided authoritative standpoints from which to organize experience, it is essential that the Christian community be very clear about its identity. More than ever, the church needs to be sure that its members both know what they believe and know how to use what they believe in coping with daily life. The need for more doctrinal catechesis in our era is readily apparent. The pulpit is clearly a place for undertaking this task. Indeed, because any sermon that unwittingly instructs the faithful falsely about the nature of the Christian faith compromises Christian identity, preachers must critically assess the doctrinal implications of every sermon they preach. Doctrine and Word must always be inseparable.

Carl, W. J., *Preaching Christian Doctrine*, 1984. Duke, R. W., *The Sermon as God's Word: Theologies for Preaching*, 1980. Ellingsen, M., *Doctrine and Word: Theology in the Pulpit*, 1983; *The Integrity of Biblical Narrative: Story in Theology and Proclamation*, 1990. **Lindbeck, G.,** *The Nature of Doctrine*, 1984. **Lischer, R.,** *A Theology of Preaching: The Dynamics of the Gospel*, rev. ed., 1992. **Ott, H.,** *Theology and Preaching*, 1965. **Pelikan, J.,** *The Emergence of the Catholic Tradition*, 1972.   MARK ELLINGSEN

Dominicans (Order of Friars Preachers).

The Order of Friars Preachers began modestly with the vigorous preaching of St. Dominic de Guzman (ca. 1170–1221), a son of minor Spanish nobility, and a small group of his followers from 1205–1215 in the Languedoc region of Southern France. Their immediate motive for such intensive preaching was to counteract the harmful influence of a sect called the Cathars or Albigenses. The Albigenses preached a doctrine of Manichaean-like dualism, which they disguised as Christianity.

Because the Albigensian preachers practiced great physical austerity, they were immensely popular and won many adherents from among the common people, who were generally poor.

Encouraged by the results of his ministry, St. Dominic went to Rome in 1216 and secured a bull of confirmation from Pope Honorius III on December 22, officially establishing his small band of followers as the Order of Preachers. Until this time, doctrinal preaching was reserved to the bishops of the Catholic Church. Today the Order of Preachers remains uniquely distinguished in being a religious community whose members have been given the office of preaching as auxiliaries to the bishops.

In establishing his Order in this way, Dominic made two significant contributions to the life of the Catholic Church. First, he significantly expanded the role and importance of preaching, and second, he gave a new direction to traditional monasticism.

Since Dominicans from the beginning were specially dedicated to the preaching office, Dominic immediately began to train his followers in theology so that they could preach orthodox Catholic doctrine. As a result, study for Dominicans has replaced the manual labor common to the monastic traditions of the Catholic Church. Along with the observance of the evangelical vows of poverty, chastity, obedience, and living according to monastic discipline, study not only prepares Dominicans to preach, it is one of the principal means of their personal sanctification.

Because the Order was founded to combat erroneous views of the Christian faith, an exceptionally well-developed understanding of the scriptures, theology, and the teaching of the church universal has always marked Dominican preaching.

One of the great Dominicans was St. Thomas Aquinas (ca. 1225–1274). His writings cover many volumes, but one of the best known is his *Summa Theologiae*, a concise summation of all Catholic theology. Thomism, which is based on Aristotle's hylomorphic theory, has been the mainstay and clearest articulation of Catholic theology since the thirteenth century.

Many of the popular devotions of the Catholic Church owe their origin to the zealous preaching of the Dominican friars. Perhaps the outstanding example is the rosary. In the United States, Dominicans also promoted the Holy Name Society for laymen, to which most Catholic men belonged during the middle of this century. Many members of the Dominican family, furthermore, have over the centuries been especially noted for theological writing and the mystical life of deep contemplation.

Up until Dominic's time, monks seldom left their monasteries and engaged in the active life of ministry only occasionally. With Dominic's friars, the monastery cloister was enlarged to enclose the whole world.

From the beginning, the Dominican Order has been exempt from direct control by the bishops; instead, it is responsible for its own governance and ministry under the immediate supervision of the pope himself. Its constitution and organization was one of the most advanced and highly systematized forms of government in the Middle Ages. Although amended over the centuries, the primitive constitutions continue to govern the Order today.

Each community is responsible for undertaking those activities that bring sufficient income for it to continue its ministry. Since income is severely restricted, the lives of the friars of the Order of Preachers are characterized by poverty and dependence on the Lord.

Presently, there are four provinces of Dominicans in the United States, creating a total of about 1,000 friars. While the vast majority of Dominicans are ordained priests, there are some who are called cooperator brothers. While not ordained to the priesthood, these friars take the same vows as the priests and live according to the same rule of life. They are active in a variety of ministries such as teaching, administration, and health care. In addition, many congregations of religious women have been founded on the teachings and inspiration of St. Dominic.

The Dominican Friars are known colloquially as the Black Friars, referring to their official garb (habit): a white tunic with narrow white mantle (scapular) and white hood (capuce), over which they wear a black, hooded cape (cappa) on formal preaching occasions. This characteristic clothing goes back to the earliest days of the Order when St. Dominic was part of a cathedral chapter, and whose members wore this garb as they prayed, taught, and assisted the local bishop.

Laypersons also participate in the life of the Order as members of the Dominican Laity. It has its own rules that bind its members to regular prayer and apostolic action, primarily some sort of proclamation of the Word of God (*see* Lay Preaching).

Many members of this broad Dominican family have been declared saints by the Catholic Church because of the holiness of their lives and the profundity of their teaching; among these are St. Albert (ca. 1200–1280)—called the Great even in his own lifetime—teacher of St. Thomas Aquinas; St. Hyacinth (ca. 1200–1257), patron saint of Poland; St. Vincent Ferrer (1350–1419), a great preacher; St. Catherine of Siena (1347–1380), a mystic who argued with popes during the Avignon Papacy (1308–1378); and St. Martin de Porres 1579–1639), a black cooperator brother who worked among the poor in Lima, Peru.

Joret, F.-D., O.P., *Dominican Life,* 1937. **Hinnebusch, W. A., O.P,** *The Dominicans: A Short History,* 1975. **Mandonnet, P., O.P.,** *St. Dominic and His Work,* 1948. **Vicaire, M.-H., O.P.,** *St. Dominic and His Times,* 1964.   JOHN BURKE, O.P.

Donne, John. (1572–1631) For the last ten years of his life, John Donne was dean of St. Paul's Cathedral, London. The second half of the twentieth century has seen a revival of interest in his preaching, due in large part to the publication of his 160 extant sermons between 1953 and 1962. His preaching is significant today because of his mastery of the art of rhetoric* and his blending of metaphoric language, personal experience, biblical themes, and inductive* or narrative* form.

Donne brought to his preaching his gifts as a poet and a student. He was the most prominent of the Metaphysical poets, whose trademark is the outlandish, startling conceit or figure of speech. In his preaching one finds the same passion, ingenuity, and careful attention to language that characterize his poetry.

As a student, Donne received early instruction from a private tutor, attended Oxford, and studied law in London. According to his earliest biographer, he was an avid student all his life, rising at 4:00 A.M. and remaining in his study until 10:00 P.M. five days a week. His sermons evidence a familiarity with Hebrew, the classical languages, and the writings of the church fathers, as well as mathematics, science, business, law, geography, natural history, and medicine.

Donne's fusion of intellect and passion won the admiration of T. S. Eliot in the early 1920s. Eliot's rediscovery of Donne and the other Metaphysical poets catapulted them into the literary limelight of the 1930s and 1940s after more than two centuries of neglect and paved the way for the rediscovery of Donne's sermons at mid-century.

The time was ripe for Donne's reemergence. The seventeenth and twentieth centuries have much in common. In both centuries the previous intellectual and religious consensus was disintegrating, society was deeply and dangerously fragmented, and questions of method, form, and language pressed to the forefront: By what method does one discern truth and meaning? What language, what literary forms can express and anticipate the emerging understandings struggling to arise from the decay and collapse of past certainties? Donne's response to these challenges included his concern for personal experience, language, and form. Similar concerns have characterized the homiletical literature of the second half of the twentieth century.

Of particular interest for homiletics today is Donne's use of metaphor. Donne's sermonic metaphors function both to enhance the sermon's emotional and intellectual impact and to contribute to the sermon's movement as an unfolding drama or argument. This use of metaphor contrasts on the one hand with the Spenserian tradition in which figures of speech were merely ornaments and on the other hand with the plain, controlled style of both the Puritan preachers and the poet Ben Jonson. Since the late 1950s many homiletical scholars have rejected traditional theory, which values clarity as the dominant virtue in preaching and denigrates metaphor as ornamental. Instead, they have highlighted the ability of a well-constructed metaphor to jar hearers out of their ordinary modes of perception and to open them to the transforming power of the gospel (see Figures of Speech). Those who wish to explore how metaphors can serve the task of preaching would profit from reading Donne's sermons. Donne's sermon on Psalm 63:7, for example, includes an elaborate metaphysical conceit:

If you look upon this world in a Map, you find two Hemisphears, two half worlds. If you crush heaven into a map, you may find two Hemisphears too, two half heavens; Halfe will be Joy, and halfe will be Glory, for in these two, the joy of heaven, and the glory of heaven, is all heaven often represented unto us. And as of those two Hemisphears of the world, the first hath been knowne long before, but the other, (that of America, which is the richer in treasure) God reserved for later Discoveries; So though he reserve that Hemisphear of heaven, which is the Glory thereof, to the Resurrection, yet the other Hemisphear, the Joy of Heaven, God opens to our Discovery, and delivers for our habitation even whilst we dwell in this world (VII, 1, 69).

A second characteristic of Donne's preaching relevant for today is his use of personal experience. Donne's numerous sermonic references to himself allow his listeners (to borrow a phrase from Fred B. Craddock*) to "overhear" as Donne prays, describes an experience, or wrestles with an idea. For example, in the sermon on Ps. 63:7, Donne quotes God's promise in Ezek. 11:19 and 36:26—*I will take away your stony hearts, and give you hearts of flesh. . . .*" He follows this quotation with his personal prayer—"And, Lord let mee have a fleshly heart in any sense, rather then a stony heart" (VII, 1, 55). Overhearing the prayer, the hearers perhaps find themselves adding their own "Amen. That is my prayer as well."

A third significant characteristic of Donne's preaching, inductive or narrative form, is congenial to contemporary homiletics. Some of Donne's most powerful sermons are "inductive" or "narrative" in their movement from the tensions of life to resolution in Christ. Donne's sermon on Ps. 63:7 invites the hearers first to recognize life's "waight, and burden, and heaviness, and oppression," then to remember God's activity in their personal lives, and finally to affirm and celebrate God's promise of joy. Long before contemporary homiletical discussions of inductive and narrative movement, Donne constructed this sermon on Ps. 63:7 as a journey for the hearers toward rejoicing as faith's answer to the burdens of human existence.

Donne, J., *The Sermons of John Donne*, 10 vols., 1953–62. Davis, W. R. "Meditation, Typology, and the Structure of John Donne's Sermons," in *The Eagle and the Dove: Reassessing John Donne*, ed. by C. J. Summers and T.-L. Pebworth, 1986. Partridge, A. C., *John Donne: Language and Style*, 1978.

LUCY A. ROSE

THE RESURRECTION OF THE BODY
John Donne
There are so many evidences of the immortality of the soule, even to a naturall mans *reason,* that it required not an Article of the Creed, to fix this notion of the Immortality of the soule. But the Resurrection of the *Body* is discernible by no other light, but that of *Faith,* nor could be fixed by any lesse assurance then an *Article* of the *Creed.* Where be all the splinters of that Bone, which a shot hath shivered and scattered in the Ayre? Where be all the Atoms of that flesh, which a *Corrasive* hath eat away, or a *Consumption* hath breath'd, and exhal'd away from our arms, and other Limbs? In what wrinkle, in what furrow, in what bowel of the earth, ly all the graines of the ashes of a body burnt a thousand years since? In what corner, in what ventricle of the sea, lies all the jelly of a Body drowned in the *generall flood?* What coherence, what sympathy, what dependence maintains any relation, any correspondence, between that arm that was lost in Europpe, and that legge that was lost in Afrique or Asia, scores of years between? One humour of our dead body produces worms, and those worms suck and exhaust all other humour, and then all dies, and all dries, and molders into dust,

and that dust is blowen into the River, & that puddled water tumbled into the sea, and that ebs and flows in infinite revolutions, and still, still God knows in what *Cabinet* every *seed-Pearle* lies, in what part of the world every graine of every mans dust lies; and . . . he whispers, he hisses, he beckens for the bodies of his Saints, and in the twinckling of an eye, that body that was scattered over all the elements, is sate down at the right hand of God, in a glorious resurrection.

From "A Sermon Preached *At the Earl of Bridgewater's house in London at the marriage of his daughter . . .* November 19, 1627," in *Donne's Sermons: Selected Passages* (Oxford: Clarendon Press, 1919), 214–15.

Drama. The gospel is inherently dramatic. Dorothy Sayers is unflinching: "Not Herod, not Caiphas, not Pilate, not Judas ever contrived to fasten upon Jesus Christ the reproach of insipidity; that final indignity was left for pious hands to inflict. To make of his story something that could neither startle, nor shock, nor terrify, nor excite, nor inspire a living soul is to crucify the Son of God afresh and put him to an open shame. . . . Let me tell you, you Christian people, an honest writer would be ashamed to treat a nursery tale as you have treated the greatest drama of history" (in Scherer, 134). Jaroslav Pelikan writes: "In its drama rather than its philosophy the Greek mind came to grips with the deepest and bitterest realities of human existence. It is strange that early Christianity, with its profound sense of tragedy and redemption, should have paid so little attention to Greek tragedy and so much to late Greco-Roman philosophy. Greek tragedy embodied the best that Greece was able to discover about the paradox of human life and its relation to the ultimates under which it lived" (Pelikan, 119).

For a moment in the Middle Ages, drama in the form of Mystery and Miracle plays involved both church and community. The interrelationship of drama and liturgy has been clearly established. But for the most part, drama in the church is more honored in the breach than in the keeping.

God enfleshed divine messages in the prophets.* They then bodied them forth: Isaiah in his nakedness, Jeremiah with a yoke, Gideon with trumpets and ceramic jars, Moses with his staff, Jonah and the gourd, Hosea with a prostitute, John the Baptist with locusts and wild honey. John's vestments were not Pierre Cardin. Christ embodied message, action, reaction, interaction. He acted. He enacted. He performed. What he performed was "God among us." Jesus evoked a sense of immediacy, of amazement, of astonishment, but never of boredom. Boredom is to crucify the Son of God afresh.

What makes for boring preaching of the nonboring Christ? It is this: Listeners do not sense a commitment to God, to the message, or to them. There is no embodiment of message. The preacher is as bored in preaching as the congregation is in listening. To be effective, as Christ was effective (note, not successful—crucifixions are not successful), the congregation must sense the caring in the preaching.

This is not to impugn the preacher's faith. Just because Robert Frost, Wallace Stevens, and T. S. Eliot read their poetry aloud poorly does not mean they did not understand their poetry. Understanding alone helps neither poets nor preachers.

The preacher en*acts* doxology as Olivier enacts Hamlet, Richard III, Henry V, and King Lear. He "actions them out." Olivier's experience of these characters enables us to experience them. To enable people to experience Christ, the preacher experiences the sermon, thus engaging the hearer in the fullness of God.

If *King Lear* cannot survive phlegmatic actors, neither can preaching survive phlegmatic preachers, whose spineless embodiment ravages the sermon. Even after requisite labor, the sighting, the sounding, the gesturing—90 percent of the sermon still needs enacting.

Preaching differs radically from print, as Hebrew does from English, as Greek differs from Chinese. Preaching orchestrates timbre, pitch, pause, pace, timing, volume, intensity, and silence. As Mozart's *Flute Quartet in G Major* elicits the full response of flute, cello, violin, and viola, so the sermonic text excites the full orchestra of the preacher. The text clamors for "vivid realization of the idea at the moment of utterance." No "vivid realization" can make up for "death from the larynx down." Preaching then degenerates into laryngeal sounds, like the clatter of a printer, unvarying, no matter what its content.

The actor Alec McGowan astonishes hearers. How? His text is the 2,000-year-old Gospel of Mark, King James Version no less. Shakespearean actors astonish hearers. Their texts are 400 years old. Their language is no longer current. The plots are known. How do they do it?

The actors strive to see what the text sees and feels and how the text feels about what it sees and feels. This "truth behind the words" invites the actors (preachers) to realize the truth in the moment of utterance. Drama enables the realization, then the communication of the intention of poem, play, sermon through a series of sights, sounds, and gestures in a continuity of time.

Sermons in a book, unpreached, are like pages of printed music unplayed. Preaching has more in common with the performance of Bach's *Mass in B Minor*, Bernstein's *West Side Story*, the Beatles' *Let It Be*.

Both preaching sermons and performing music seek to be responsive. Like musicians and actors, preachers strive to embrace the text. Preparing for *King Lear* yet again, seventy-five-year-old Sir Lawrence Olivier stands in awe of the text. Thus, aged Lawrence Olivier gives *King Lear* a sense of first-timeness and of last-timeness. The moment is epiphanic.

Olivier incarnates the text. While Shakespeare is dead, through Olivier these fictive characters live—King Lear, Richard III, Henry V, Othello, and Hamlet. The responsible preacher likewise incarnates the sermonic text, thus making

Christ present in the preaching. Life and death matters insist on a "life and death manner." Not the dry bones of Ezekiel but the enfleshment of Christ is the preacher's goal (*see* Delivery).

Benedetti, R., *The Actor at Work*, 5th ed., 1990. Harms, P.W.F., *Power from the Pulpit*, 1977. Kelber, W. H., *The Oral and Written Gospel*, 1983. Lee, C. I., and T. Gura, *Oral Interpretation*, 8th ed., 1992. Ong, W. J., *Orality and Literacy*, 1982. Pelikan, J., *Fools for Christ*, 1953. Scherer, P., *For We Have This Treasure*, 1943.   PAUL W. F. HARMS

Dwight, Timothy.

(1752–1817) Timothy Dwight was admitted to Yale at age thirteen. There he committed to serious study for fourteen hours a day after first wasting two years in compulsive gambling, revelry, and the loose moral climate common to students of that period. He earned his baccalaureate with high honor at the age of seventeen. At age nineteen Yale called him back from school teaching to serve six years as a tutor. There he was greatly appreciated for his thoroughness, and he completed his masters degree at twenty. To support relatives after his father's death, he managed the family farm for several years while also filling local pulpits each Sunday. He accepted the pastorate of Greenfield Congregational Church, in Connecticut, serving there twelve years, refusing nominations for the state legislature and congress to do so. During this period he published many sermons, papers, and addresses, leading Princeton University to confer a doctorate in his thirty-fifth year.

Unanimously elected to the Yale presidency in 1795, Dwight found the college church virtually extinct and students committed to licentiousness and secularism. Many, disillusioned about the course of the nation, affirmed high interest in the philosophies and political ideas of classic antiquity. Others responded to Jefferson's Deism with enthusiasm. As unbelief moved across the Atlantic through the writings of skeptics associated with the French Revolution, popular philosophical positions either favored naturalism or Unitarianism. An enormous edition of Tom Paine's *The Age of Reason*, published in France, was shipped to America and sold for just a few pence per volume. Where these could not be sold they were given away. Many students so admired the arguments advanced that they adopted new names for themselves, such as Voltaire or Rousseau, and delighted in mounting cynical and scornful attacks on the Christian faith. In the meantime, alcoholism and rowdyism became the common order on campus. Departing from the traditional faculty stance, which insisted on the truths of the Christian faith authoritatively, Dwight immediately opened up his classes to no-holds-barred debates, allowing open discussion of all relevant theological and philosophical issues.

As a preacher, Dwight possessed a strong resonant voice and the ability to deliver dramatic sermons with excitement and vigor. Due to poor eyesight, he worked through an amanuensis, to whom he first dictated his ideas in full. He used brief, large-lettered notes to present a weekly chapel series of theological lectures. These continued over four years, resulting in many outstanding conversions and initiating a movement of spiritual revival which spread throughout the North. Dwight bent his large learning (which made him almost a university in himself) to the task of preaching rational, apologetic, and inspirational sermons focused on the challenges of the day. In these he outlined a whole system of theology through which he demonstrated how the radical ideas of infidelity destroy the foundations of morality and possess no means for restoring vision or promoting virtue. He proved how the Deists maliciously distorted some of Calvinism's tenets and answered attacks on orthodoxy by presenting the reality of a personal faith in Christ as the only effective antidote to godlessness, anarchy, and despotism. His well-applied addresses argued for the mainline doctrines of grace and focused clearly on the reality of Christ's substitutionary atonement. In general, Dwight followed Jonathan Edwards* (whose grandson he was) but presented a moderated Calvinism that avoided extreme positions so that, instead of urging seekers to wait for supernaturally initiated conviction, he invited them to seize a salvation already procured through the cross and now available to all through repentance and faith.

Dwight brought a freshness to faith but set it within the balance of reason, carefully directing its realities to fit the educated, literate, and disciplined contexts of the North. During the late eighteenth century, because of its intellectual and political leadership, New England was the dominant force in the social culture of the United States. President Dwight thus initiated an authentic movement of spiritual revival known as the Second Great Awakening, which swept back and forth across the nation for two generations after 1800. In 1802 his preaching and fatherly counsel led one-third of the Yale student body to experience religious conversions so profound that nearly all of these entered the ministry. Between 1812 and 1837 alone, no less than thirteen distinct periods of religious awakening were documented on the Yale campus in addition to many other special times of unusual religious interest. The new students demanded the establishment of the early seminaries such as the schools at Andover, Yale, Princeton, and Union in Virginia, all of whom owed their birth to the sudden appearance of a new theological wave. Not only did Dwight's preaching foster a fresh generation of young and fiery preachers, it also was important for the work of Asahel Netteton, Lyman Beecher, Henry Ward Beecher,* Charles G. Finney,* and other later evangelicals.

Dwight, T., *Theology Explained and Defended in a Series of Sermons . . . , 1845.*

CRAIG SKINNER

A WARNING
Timothy Dwight

To him who stands on the brink of the grave, and the verge of eternity . . . and who, at the same time, is disposed to serious contemplation, all . . . things become mightily changed in their appearance. . . . Particularly have I coveted reputation and influence to a degree which I am unable to justify. . . . But in the circumstances to which I have referred, all these things were vanishing from my sight. . . . They could not relieve me of pain; they could not restore me to health, they could not prolong my life; they could promise me no good in the life to come. What then were these things to me? . . . Let me exhort you, my young friends, now engaged in the ardent pursuit of worldly enjoyments, to believe that you will one day see them in the very light in which they have been seen by me. The attachment to them, which you so strongly feel, is unfounded vain, full of danger, and fraught with ruin. You will one day view them from a dying bed.

But no acts of obedience will then appear to you to have merited, in any sense, acceptance with God. . . . Those acts of my life, concerning which I entertained the best hopes, which I was permitted to entertain, those, which appeared to me the least exceptionable, were nothing, and less than nothing.

The mercy of God, as exercised towards our lost race, through the all-sufficient and glorious righteousness of the Redeemer, yielded me the only foundation for hope beyond the grave. . . . I had ample opportunity to survey this most interesting of subjects on every side. As the result of all my investigations, let me assure you, and that from the neighborhood of the eternal word, confidence in the righteousness of Christ is the only foundation furnished by earth, or heaven, upon which, when you are about to leave this world, can safely, or willingly, rest the everlasting life of your souls. . . . You will then be at the door of eternity: will be hastening to the presence of your Judge; will be just ready to give up your account of the *deeds done in the body;* will be preparing to hear the final sentence of acquittal or condemnation, and will stand at the gate of heaven or of hell.

From sermon on Ps. 94:17–19, delivered June 2, 1816 (after four months of life-threatening illness). In T. Dwight, *Theology Explained and Defended in a Series of Sermons, with a Memoir of the Life of the Author in Five Volumes* (Cheapside, London: Thomas Tegg, 1845), xxxix–xliii.

Education. In 1990, the Search Institute analyzed the faith maturity of members of the mainline denominations (Benson and Eklin 1990). A survey was used to evaluate persons in terms of "both a life-transforming relationship to a loving God—the vertical theme—and a consistent devotion to serving others—the horizontal theme." The findings are disturbing. Less than one-third of the adults exemplified a faith that integrated the vertical and horizontal dimensions. Thirty-six percent had an undeveloped faith, meaning that they evidenced maturity in neither dimension. When the faith development of teenagers was the focus, the results were even more alarming. Sixty-four percent revealed an undeveloped faith. Rather than strengthening during these formative years, the faith maturity of teenagers, especially boys, declines sharply after the eighth grade in the mainline denominations using the confirmation process—a practice that realistically functions for many as graduation from the church. Persons in mainline congregations in the United States are living lives in which their Christian commitment is largely inconsequential, and their churches are doing little to address this dilemma.

The findings of the Search Institute project support the conclusions of other researchers stimulated by the pioneering work on faith development by James Fowler (1981). Although Fowler's work continues to undergo modification and refinement, most scholars in the field agree that many persons never progress beyond the stage of "synthetic-conventional" faith, which he associates with adolescence. This faith stage is characterized by conformity in thought and action, by dependence on conventional understandings, and by the absence of critical examination. Persons in this stage cling to a secondhand faith accepted through the authority of others, rather than moving on to choose reflectively values and beliefs of their own that define them in distinction from others. If this "individuative-reflective" stage is attained, the maturing person of faith is to go on to the "conjunctive" stage in which there develops a keen awareness of the contextual nature of truth perceptions. The self-constructed system of beliefs and values is recognized as the product of a limited personal and cultural perspective; the person becomes more open to differing experiences and contrasting views. There is a willingness to leave some issues unresolved and to tolerate the existence of paradox and mystery.

The ultimate stage of development—"universalizing faith"—is rarely achieved. Universalizing faith involves the recognition of a transcendent source of reality in which all varieties of truth are grounded. Persons in this stage are able to relate to all others; they are committed to striving for the realization of universal community. Because of the depth and breadth of their vision, such persons are in general uncomfortable with the limitations of mundane existence. They look beyond *what is* to *what could be.* This highest stage of faith development accords with the Search Institute's description of persons with mature or integrated faith. Such persons are critical of their society, unorthodox in their views, inclusive in outlook, and courageously nonconformist.

The preaching ministry must enhance the development of mature Christians. Preaching is not to be limited to the proclamation of the good news of salvation available through Jesus Christ, or even to the exhortation of persons to accept saving grace. Preaching must also nurture, train, and edify persons in the faith. For many churchgoers, the sermon may be their only opportunity to learn what it means to be Christian. The report of the Search Institute project is replete with evidence of the need for such teaching and learning. More than two thirds of the adults surveyed understand salvation to be a matter of keeping commandments and rules, rather than a gift of divine grace. Areas that are problematic for many people include seeking spiritual growth, including prayer and Bible reading; sharing one's faith with others; helping others who are in need; and involvement in social justice efforts. The preacher must make clear what Christians believe. The gospel message has content, and doctrine is fundamental to faith. Church members need to know how to read and interpret the Bible and how to apply the eternal truths of divine revelation amid the trappings of unfamiliar cultural contexts. The preacher must explicate how Christians live. There are ethical imperatives that guide the life of Christian discipleship in both its personal and corporate aspects. The community of faith must comprehend its identity if it is to grasp its purpose and fulfill its mission. The preacher calls and carries the community to ever-deepening commitment and more faithful praxis.

Such preaching can be done most effectively when it is informed by understanding of the faith characteristics of congregations and by clarity about desired outcomes in the faith development process. Preachers need to study their hearers so as to design sermons that will engage them where they are in the journey of faith and enable them to progress in faith maturity. This challenge is complicated by the evident reality that rarely are all members of a congregation at the same stage. For example, the preacher should know that at all ages women tend to be more mature in their faith than men. Recognition of the relatively underdeveloped nature of the faith among most mainline church members is fundamental. This is by no means to assert that these persons are devoid of commitment, integrity, or spirituality. It is, rather, to contend that there is a depth of Christian experience and a richness of Christian living that are seldom appropriated. It is the task of the preacher to help make these possibilities into realities.

Benson, P. L., and **C. H. Eklin,** *Effective Christian Education: A National Study of Protestant Congregations: A Summary Report on Faith, Loyalty, and Congregational Life,* 1990. **Fowler, J. W.,** *Becoming Adult, Becoming Christian,* 1984; *Stages of Faith: The Psychology of Human Development and the Quest for Meaning,* 1981.

GAYLE CARLTON FELTON

Edwards, Jonathan.

(1703–1758) Jonathan Edwards was the most influential American-born preacher of the eighteenth century. After graduating from Yale College and briefly serving as a pastor in New York, in 1726 Edwards became assistant to his renowned grandfather, Solomon Stoddard, in the Congregational church in Northampton, Massachusetts. Upon Stoddard's death in 1729, Edwards became sole pastor, preaching regularly until his dismissal in 1750. He then served as a missionary to Native Americans in Stockbridge, Massachusetts. He died in 1758, shortly after becoming president of Princeton College.

Edwards's fame arose from continuing a tradition of revival preaching initiated by his grandfather. In 1734 and 1735, an awakening in Northampton surpassed all New England precedents. Three hundred new members joined Edwards's congregation within a six-month period. When in 1737 Edwards issued *A Faithful Narrative of the Surprising Work of God,* describing the remarkable events, his works helped spark excitement about awakenings throughout the English-speaking world. George Whitefield,* whose tour of

the colonies in 1739–1740 set off awakenings throughout the American colonies,
viewed Edwards as a close ally. As a settled pastor, Edwards stayed close to
home, but along with Whitefield, became
associated with what eventually came to
be called the Great Awakening. In 1741,
in nearby Enfield, Connecticut, Edwards
preached the most famous sermon of the
Awakening, "Sinners in the Hands of an
Angry God."

In this sermon Edwards accentuated a
technique that he used regularly, but more
sparsely, in the rest of his preaching. He
painted vivid verbal images that could excite the affections. In wilting paragraphs of
the application, Edwards piles up image
upon image. Just a few of these are:

> Your wickedness makes you as it were
> heavy as lead, and to tend downwards
> with great weight and pressure towards
> hell; and if God should let you go, you
> would immediately sink. . . . There are
> black clouds of God's wrath now hang-
> ing directly over your heads, full of the
> dreadful storm and big with thunder
> and were it not for the restraining hand
> of God, it would immediately burst
> forth upon you. . . . The wrath of God is
> like great waters that are dammed for
> the present; they increase more and
> more, and rise higher and higher. . . .
> The bow of God's wrath is bent, and the
> arrow made ready on the string, and
> justice bends the arrow at your heart,
> and strains the bow.

With each of these images sustained for
perhaps a minute, the effect could be
overwhelming, as it was to some of the
original hearers.

The power resided in the words. Edwards spoke calmly with clear modulation and, until his later years, from a fully
written text. Though he was occasionally
turning the pages of the sermon notebook
he held in one hand, he reputedly seemed
to be staring at the bellrope at the back of
the church as he delivered his carefully
chosen words. His view of the power of
words in sermons was closely connected
with his view of true religion.

Essential to Christianity, he argued,
were proper religious affections. Either
our loves and desires were directed toward God as revealed in Christ, or they
were directed elsewhere. For one's heart
to change, one's affections must be
changed. Only God could change the
heart. What the preacher could do, however, was help provide the occasion for
sinners to get a glimpse of what God was
like. This knowledge of God was not just
intellectual, although it involved essential
intellectual content. True knowledge,
however, was affectionate knowledge,
knowledge that touched our loves or desires. The preacher could help spark such
affections by arguments, which formed a
large part of Edwards's preaching; but
images, especially those that related to
the hearers themselves, were most effective in generating affective knowledge.
Since God had created the entire universe
as an expression of his love, even the
mundane things in it were rightly seen as
images and shadows of divine things.

Although Edwards occasionally preached hellfire, since fear was a valuable human emotion, the center of this theology
and his preaching was the love of God.
God's love and beauty were at the heart of
creation and were constantly being declared in it. Humans, because of their sin,
were blinded from seeing this love and
beauty and perversely loved infinitely
lesser and more trivial things. Yet God
withheld his judgment and revealed his
love most perfectly in Christ's sacrifice
for these totally undeserving creatures.
Sinners could not change their own
hearts; nonetheless, their hearts could be
changed by gaining a glimpse of Christ's
perfect love. As one's will may be overwhelmed by a beautiful person or work of
art and be drawn to it, so one's will can be
changed, yet changed voluntarily, by a
glimpse of the love of Christ. God's revelation is essential. We must be given eyes to
see and ears to hear.

The preacher's task is to be the occasion for this revelation, displaying the
love of God and the human condition as
revealed in scripture. Careful exposition

of scripture is absolutely essential to this task, since only there is the revelation complete. Edwards backed away from preaching that was geared simply to play on the emotions by sensational means, dramatics, and shouting—techniques that became popular during the awakenings. His *A Treatise Concerning Religious Affections* (1746), originating as sermons, provided a careful analysis of how to distinguish true religious affections from sensational excesses.

Edwards did not write another sermon like "Sinners . . . " More typical of his preaching is "A Divine and Supernatural Light," perhaps Edwards's most concise statement of his views. Characteristic of his sermons is the Puritan style of a careful exposition of points and subpoints making it easy for notetakers to follow. While vivid images are often used, the style is spare and otherwise unadorned (*see* Puritan Preaching).

A Doctrine:

. . . . There is therefore in this spiritual light. 1. A true sense of the divine and superlative excellency of the things of religion; a real sense of the excellency of God and Jesus Christ, and of the work of redemption, and the ways and works of God revealed in the gospel. . . . He that is spiritually enlightened truly apprehends and sees it, or has a sense of it. He does not merely rationally believe that God is glorious, but he has a sense of the gloriousness of God in his heart. There is not only a rational belief that God is holy, and that holiness is a good thing, but there is a sense of the loveliness of God's holiness. There is not only a speculatively judging that God is gracious, but a sense how amiable God is upon that account, or a sense of the beauty of this divine attribute. . . .

Thus there is a difference between having an opinion, that God is holy and gracious, and having a sense of the loveliness and beauty of that holiness and grace. There is a difference between having a rational judgment that honey is sweet and having a sense of its sweet-

ness. A man may have the former, that knows not how honey tastes; but a man cannot have the latter unless he has an idea of the taste of honey in his mind. So there is a difference between believing that a person is beautiful, and having a sense of his beauty . . . (in Simonson 1970, 72–73).

An engaging sample of Edwards's preaching can be found in *Charity and Its Fruits*, a series on 1 Corinthians 13. Some 1,200 of Edwards's manuscript sermons survive, many of which are now being published by Yale University Press.

Kimnach, W. H., ed., *The Works of Jonathan Edwards,* Vol. 10, *Sermons and Discourses, 1720–1723,* 1992. **Piper, J.,** *The Supremacy of God in Preaching,* 1990. **Simonson, H.,** *Jonathan Edwards: Theologian of the Heart,* 1974; and *Selected Writings of Jonathan Edwards,* 1970. **Westra, H. P.,** *The Minister's Task and Calling in the Sermons of Jonathan Edwards,* 1986.   GEORGE M. MARSDEN

SINNERS IN THE HANDS OF AN ANGRY GOD
Jonathan Edwards

The God that holds you over the pit of hell, much as one holds a spider, or some loathsome insect, over the fire, abhors you, and is dreadfully provoked: his wrath towards you burns like fire; he looks upon you as worthy of nothing else, but to be cast into the fire; he is of purer eyes than to bear to have you in his sight; you are ten thousand times more abominable in his eyes, than the most hateful venomous serpent is in ours. You have offended him infinitely more than ever a stubborn rebel did his prince: and yet, it is nothing but his hand that holds you from falling into the fire every moment. It is to be ascribed to nothing else, that you did not go to hell the last night; that you was suffered to awake again in this world, after you closed your eyes to sleep. And there is no other reason to be given, why you have not dropped into hell since you arose in the morning, but that God's hand has held you up. There is no other reason to be given why you have not gone to hell, since you have sat here in the house of God, provoking his pure eyes by your sinful wicked manner of attending his solemn worship. Yea, there is nothing else that is to be given as a reason why you do not the very moment drop down into hell. . . .

And now you have an extraordinary opportunity, a day wherein Christ has thrown the door of mercy wide open, and stands in calling, and crying with a loud voice to poor sinners; a day wherein many are flocking to him, and pressing into the kingdom of God. Many are daily coming from the east, west, north, and south; many that were very lately in the same miserable condition that you are in, are now in a happy state, with their heart filled with love to him who has loved them, and washed them from their sins in his own blood, and rejoicing in the hope of the glory of God. How awful it is to be left behind at such a day! To see so many others feasting, while you are pining and perishing! To see so many rejoicing and singing for joy of heart, while you have cause to mourn for sorrow of heart, and howl for vexation of spirit! How can you rest one moment in such a condition? Are not your souls as precious as the souls of the people at Suffield, where they are flocking from day to day to Christ?

From "Sinners in the Hands of an Angry God," *The Works of Jonathan Edwards, A.M.,* Vol. 2 (London: Southgate, 1839), 10–11.

Epistles. Because early Christian epistles stand close to central tasks of pastoral ministry, one might reasonably expect they would lend themselves readily to preaching. While not themselves sermons, they provide glimpses of the instruction, correction, and comfort that lie at the heart of early Christian preaching. They address the real struggles of particular congregations over questions of leadership (1 Tim. 1:5–9), worship (1 Cor. 14), theology (Phil. 2:5–11), ethical standards (Rom. 12—13), community life (2 Thess. 3:6–13), and the future (1 Thess. 4:13).

Sometimes the tensions and struggles seem to leap from the page to address contemporary situations so that preachers and congregations readily sense their immediacy and relevance.

Despite these potential benefits, the epistles pose a number of difficulties for preachers. Reading an epistle provides access to only one side of dialogues for which there were at least two partners. Read apart from the context of the larger dialogue, however, interpreters may be tempted to treat the epistles as essays rather than as elements of conversation. The concreteness and immediacy evaporate into abstract discussions of theological themes (unity in Ephesians 2, love in 1 John). The problem becomes even more acute because preachers cannot easily preach the whole of an epistle but must slice into it, addressing only one moment in one side of a discussion.

Understanding the other conversation partners and their positions is important if the letters are to come to life for contemporary congregations, but even a quick glance at the history of interpretation demonstrates the difficulty of such reconstructions. Even 1 Corinthians, which addresses some problems explicitly and *seriatim* ("Now concerning the matters about which you wrote . . . "; 1 Cor. 7:1), lends itself to multiple reconstructions. Other epistles, such as Ephesians or Colossians, provide few hints as to context, making it even more difficult to identify what prompts the letter.

Several developments in the study of New Testament epistles can help the preacher to hear (and therefore also to proclaim) the epistles once again as genuine exchanges between people. First, attention to the practice of letter-writing in the ancient world gives preachers and therefore their congregations a sense of both the conventions in which early Christian letters participate and their innovations on those conventions. A student away from home writes to his father: "Aurelius Dius to Aurelius Horion, my sweetest father, many greetings. I make supplication for you every day before the gods of this place" (73). Early Christian letters that begin with assertions about prayer (Phil. 1:3; Col. 1:3; 3 John 2) sound less stilted and foreign alongside this commonplace family letter. At the same time, however, Paul's salutations often elaborate the simple conventions into full-fledged claims about apostolic vocation (Gal. 1:1–2) and even into an epitome of the gospel itself (Rom. 1:6). Letters of various common genres—friendship, praise, exhortation, and blame, to mention a few—exert their influence in the letters of the New Testament.

A second development that may put flesh and bones on epistles that otherwise appear to consist entirely of disembodied ideas is the reinvigorated study of the social world in which Christianity emerged. 1 Peter's language about "aliens and exiles" takes on specificity when understood within the context of the social, legal, and economic dislocation of Christians in Asia Minor at the end of the first century. The question in 1 Corinthians about whether Christians should eat meat that has been sacrificed to idols becomes frightfully practical if it is understood that many had virtually no access to meat unless that meat had first been sacrificed in a temple. Paul's discussion of the Lord's Supper in 1 Corinthians 11:17–34 becomes more compelling when it is understood that Paul responds theologically to what many would view as a merely social problem.

These developments in the study of Christian epistles do not constitute an alternative to attending to the theological argumentation within the letters. What they do suggest is that letters written by early Christians conform to the letter-writing conventions of their contemporaries. They also suggest that the conflicts reflected in the letters are not solely theological conflicts but also reflect the differing social locations and situations among early Christian congregations.

Thoughtful preaching from the epistles will also enter into careful reading and analysis of the way the writers argue their case. Sensitivity to context is important to all exegesis,* of course, but in the epistles it is absolutely essential to trace the bends and turns in the argument. Without discerning how each statement builds on the one that precedes and anticipates the one that follows, the temptation to make a letter over into an essay on an abstract theme can become overwhelming. To follow, as best one can, the developing theological reflection of the writer allows the preacher to understand not just what topic is under discussion but why it is important and how the writer works with it.

While it is never possible to peek "over the shoulder" of the first-century Christian in the act of writing an epistle, the preacher who attempts to do so comes closer to proclaiming the gospel in continuity with the way in which it was first proclaimed in an epistle to an ancient Christian community.

Meeks, W., *The First Urban Christians: The Social World of the Apostle Paul,* 1983. **Stowers, S.,** "Greek and Latin Letters," *Anchor Bible Dictionary,* ed. D. N. Freedman, 1992, and *Letter Writing in Greco-Roman Antiquity,* 1986. **Theissen, G.,** *The Social Setting of Pauline Christianity,* 1982.

BEVERLY ROBERTS GAVENTA

Ethics.

The movement from theology or faith to moral behavior requires *systematic* ethical reflection. This is especially urgent in a world that thinks in fragments and is morally adrift. Congregations today are listening communities rooted in such a world, and they are less and less sure of what they believe. On many issues of morality Christians are deeply divided. Preachers therefore rightly turn for assistance to contemporary Christian ethicists who have identified and discussed basic elements of Christian morality.

The systematic dimensions of ethical reflection have been variously named but can be summarized as follows: Grounded in *authoritative sources, basic convictions* shape *moral character* and *moral norms and standards* within a given *situation* set in a larger *social/cultural context* (Anderson 1992). In recent literature on preaching a number of these themes have been explored, though somewhat indirectly and not yet as thorough processes of ethical reasoning.

Authoritative Sources. The sermonic phrase "the Bible says" is viewed by many as a rhetorical device that no longer carries the weight it once may have had. James Gustafson maintains that "the Bible remains the charter document" for Christian ethics, but he outlines different ways (usually reflecting different literary forms) in which the Bible may be used: prescriptive statements, ethical principles, analogous descriptions of behavior (some exemplary, others not), and a theological understanding of the world, human nature, and God (Gustafson, "The Changing Use of the Bible in Christian Ethics," in Curran and McCormick, 133). There is extensive writing today on the complex issue of the use of the Bible in ethics, but preaching still has a crucial hermeneutical task, especially in the use of narrative texts, of forming communities that seek to live under the word.

Both preachers and congregations recognize yet other authoritative sources in addition to scripture and accord them differing degrees of importance. These include tradition, reason, and experience. Lisa Sowle Cahill speaks of four complementary reference points: foundation texts, the community's tradition of faith, theology and practice, philosophical accounts of the human, and descriptions of what is or has been lived experience (Cahill, 5). Since the Enlightenment, Western culture's respect for scripture and tradition has declined steadily, while reason and especially experience (bolstered by the dominance of empirical study) have increased. Preaching will, of necessity, root itself more deliberately in scripture and tradition, but it cannot communicate effectively without serious attention to the experience of the people of God in the world. Each concrete moral dilemma addressed in a given sermon will require varying uses of these sources.

Basic Convictions. Speaking and listening take for granted operative assumptions about reality. Such beliefs infuse our narratives. Theologically, the basic conviction, "Jesus is Lord," is expanded by Lesslie Newbigin to mean that he is Lord not only of the church but of the world, not only in the religious life but in all life, not merely over some peoples but all peoples (Newbigin 1991, 33–34). This elaboration may seem startling even in sermons because it runs counter to the pervasive thought patterns of Western society.

Preaching is also being influenced by the imagistic nature of contemporary culture. Images often tend to hide convictions. They may obscure the deeper realities that guide our moral reasoning. For example, fostering individualistic thinking ("each person is entitled to his or her own opinion") creates confusion and a false sense of autonomy.

By contrast, a central assumption from baptism is that Christians are bound to each other and to Christ. Christian convictions are communally formed and are publicly expressed in worship. Personalistic preaching, which leaves each listener to formulate merely individual beliefs, reduces the significance of the sermon for moral decision-making.

Moral Character. "If one experiences the reality of God, . . . there ought to be consequences for the sort of person one becomes morally" (Gustafson, in Curran and McCormick, 80). How Christian convictions shape the moral life is bound up with the formation of Christian character, particularly, says Stanley Hauerwas, within the community of faith. Because Christian convictions have a narrative quality, biblical narratives, specifically, shape the church's self-understanding and can transform its view of the world (Hauerwas 1983, 24–30).

The recent emphasis on narrative* preaching may reflect too much the influence of an entertainment culture, but it may also play a formative ethical role.

When the gospel story is related to other human stories, Christians can be formed in character. A communal identity created through narrative discourse can also overcome some of the erosion of genuine community that marks Western society.

Virtues like love and hope in turn fundamentally affect behavior positively while anxiety, dishonesty, and fear do the opposite. Who Christians are profoundly influences what they do. Sermons that sensitively and concretely interpret the church's own behavior in terms of character have significant potential.

Norms and Standards. Israel's understanding of its covenant identity required an extensive elaboration of norms summed up in the Ten Commandments. Jesus, for all his pungent, iconoclastic stories, also articulated obligations (e.g., "Love your neighbor as yourself") and specified the implications of discipleship (Mark 10:17–22 and Matt. 5:27–48).

James Childress points to the necessity of moral deliberation in reflecting on Christian responsibility (Childress 1980, 371–80). Preachers often either seem naively bold in quoting biblical injunctions without adequately connecting them with biblical principles and perspectives or flee all imperatives, preferring the safe haven of the indicative. But thoughtful engagement with legal passages (see Calvin's "third use of the law," *Institutes* 2.7.12), prophetic denunciations, and epistolary directives arrest attention and sharpen the cost of discipleship in a broken and self-deceptive world. Limitation of sermon time and structure probably requires some additional forum for extended exploration on application, especially on complex questions like war, abortion, or the provision of health care.

Situation and Context. Moral decisions are made in specific situations that require careful discernment. Such enquiry may even be hazardous, especially in relation to controversial issues such as those noted above. The art of discerning includes gathering information, exploring underlying social patterns, and assessing the significance of the situation with reference to some larger frame of meaning. Also, knowing the influence of the larger societal context helps clarify affective and systemic dimensions that push and pull on human inclinations.

These situational factors and societal reflections are too complicated to be explored in a sermon. They demand an expertise beyond what any one person can command. They require an invitation to others to share in the task and analytical skills better developed through such exercises as case studies. But the preacher's attention to this dimension of ethical reflection can prevent simplistic preaching on complex issues (*see* Prophetic Preaching).

Anderson, T. R., *Walking the Way: An Introduction to Christian Ethics,* 1992. **Cahill, L. S.,** *Between the Sexes: Foundations for a Christian Ethics of Sexuality,* 1985. **Childress, J.,** "Scripture and Christian Ethics . . .," *Interpretation* 34:4, 1980, 371–80. **Curran, C. E.,** and **R. A. McCormick,** *Moral Theology No. 4: The Use of Scripture in Moral Theology,* 1984. **Hauerwas, S.,** *The Peaceable Kingdom: A Primer in Christian Ethics,* 1983. **Newbigin, L.,** *Truth to Tell: The Gospel as Public Truth,* 1991.

ARTHUR VAN SETERS

Evangelism.   All evangelism originates in the heart of a God who calls people in a thousand ways: by scripture (the story of redemption), through nature (Rom. 1:19–20), music, art, and the flow of daily life. All events carry in some way God's message of grace, sometimes both judgment and grace.

St. Augustine* asserted that our hearts are restless until they find rest in God. Pascal complemented Augustine's statement when he observed that in every person is a God-shaped vacuum. God's very creation of us demonstrates the yearning to put persons into right relationship with God. Authentic evangelistic preaching recognizes the divine yearnings and reflects in some measure their expressions.

Basic Principles. Evangelistic preaching proclaims the gospel in the Spirit's energy and drawing power, with the intention of bringing people to repentance and belief in Christ as Savior. All Christian preaching does this in some measure; certain sermons focus wholly on bringing the unsaved to the feet of Christ.

The first principle is *compassion*. The evangelistic preacher who communicates genuine concern gets through to the hearts of the hearers. Listeners often identify that compassion by the words of the sermon but also by unspoken features: body language, spiritual preparation, tone—all of which have potential for projecting earnestness, reality, and genuineness. Urgency born in heaven makes contact with needy souls.

The second principle is that the sermon *must stem from scripture.* Herein lies a secret of authority.* "My" words cannot save anyone; the Word of God has power to rescue any and all. The Word and the Spirit of Christ come together to bring conviction of sin, light to the mind, faith to the attentive heart, and new creation to the total being (John 16:8–11; Rom. 10:14–17; 1 Peter 1:23, 25b; 2 Peter 1:3–4).

The third principle is to speak so *people can understand* (2 Cor. 1:12–14). The secular character of today's society means that what preachers comprehend many who come to church cannot understand. Wise homilists focus on a single evangelical truth, visualize the message by illustrations* to which people can relate, get to the point with a sense of timing, speak with consistency.

The fourth principle is to announce the good news in such a way as *to make people say,* "That means me." " . . . we entreat you on behalf of Christ, be reconciled to God" (2 Cor. 5:20b). Evangelistic preachers will, at appropriate times, relate their own conversion stories; this helps hearers identify with both the evangelist and the message. The sermon must assure all persons that they can indeed come to the kingdom of God (most feel unworthy and tend to disbelieve that God really wants them). Listeners often respond to inspiring stories of conversion (see, for example, Hugh T. Kerr and John M. Mulder, *Conversions*, 1983, for fifty conversion stories with analyses). A great Bible account like the conversation between Jesus and Nicodemus (John 3) drives home the necessity of personal conversion.

The fifth principle is to *call for decision*. Gospel communicators know for certain that those who sincerely come to God get a divine response because "Everyone who calls on the name of the Lord shall be saved" (Rom. 10:13; cf. Joel 2:32 and Acts 2:21). That knowledge generates confidence to demand a verdict. St. Paul spoke with this urgency toward decision: "See, now is the acceptable time; see, now is the day of salvation!" (2 Cor. 6:2b; Isa. 49:8a).

Preaching: Gospel Vehicle. Jesus stands as our supreme model. He came "proclaiming the good news of God, and saying, 'The time is fulfilled, and the kingdom of God has come near; repent, and believe in the good news'" (Mark 1:14–15; cf. Matt. 4:17). Jesus preached the gospel by telling stories—the synoptic writers record over thirty parables*) (*see* Narrative Preaching). Jesus' parables of the lost sheep, the lost coin, and the lost son (Luke 15) demonstrate his passion to save the lost.

Preachers know from early Acts the power and effectiveness of inspired preaching (Acts 2:37–47; 6:1, 7; 8:12; 9:31). The history of preaching is replete with examples of energized proclamation.

The content of preaching, too, carries enormous significance. Evangelistic preaching is kerygmatic (the *kerygma* is the saving gospel). St. Paul declared he must preach Christ crucified and resurrected (1 Cor. 1:18–25; 1 Cor. 15). Billy Graham,* early in his career, did not in one campaign see so many come forward to accept Christ. An older, wiser man told Graham why: You did not preach the cross as much as you usually do.

Limits and Warnings. The evangelistic preacher can never entertain the illegitimate pride that says preaching is God's only means of bringing people into divine communion. Preaching is *one* means—a major means, to be sure, but complementary to God's many methods of speech. This understanding saves preachers from egocentricism, greed, the itch for power, and vanity. Misplaced focus and the fakery of some fallen televangelists and pastors show up vividly against the standards of the Bible and the God-honoring gospel proclaimers (*see* Television and Preaching).

Preachers need help. No single pastor or evangelist can convert all the people in his or her assigned arena. Thus, we have a need for teaching laypersons how to serve on the evangelism team. Moreover, one-on-one approaches often lead to decision (John 4:1–42).

The tone of evangelistic preaching finds its model in Jesus,* who spoke prophetically and forthrightly but never committed assault and battery on human emotions. Negative, unreasoned, evangelistic preaching—capitalizing on emotionalistic devices—hurts individuals, sometimes permanently. Biblical and historical preaching—balanced, thoughtful, and sensitive—creates what Thomas Long calls an "environment of respect" (Long, 78). In such an environment, repentant souls can make solid decisions for Christ. Compassion, not assault, tells people the evangelist cares and lets men, women, and children sense God's caring nature.

Most especially, preachers must stay free of money and status as motivations. The New Testament comes across clearly at this point: "Now when Simon saw that the Spirit was given through the laying on of the apostles' hands, he offered them money, saying, 'Give me also this power so that anyone on whom I lay my hands may receive the Holy Spirit.' " Peter's response must have terrified Simon—Peter commanded that Simon's silver perish with him! (Acts 8:17–21).

Summary and Motivation to Preach Evangelistically. Evangelistic preaching must begin with God. John 3:16 focuses on God's love for all people. The Apostles' Creed, its three paragraphs centering on the Father, Son, and Holy Spirit, spells out the saving gospel.

The evangelistic preacher finds motivation in the Great Commission (Matt. 28:18–20) and knows the saving revelation of God comes to best expression in the scriptures (2 Tim. 3:16–17; 4:2). Those scriptures must come to clear exposition in stories, visual material that facilitates hearer identification with the passion of God's heart to bring human beings to God.

Special days—e.g., Easter, Christmas, Pentecost—provide rich opportunity for the call to decision. These Sundays in the church year by their very nature herald the *kerygma*. So-called revival efforts (*see* Finney, Charles Grandison) have their place too, and require concentrated and prayerful planing by pastors and people. But every sermon should, in some way, communicate the saving gospel (*see* Revivals).

Evangelistic preachers work from motivational assumptions: all have sinned and come short of God's intentions (Rom. 3:23); all can experience salvation from sin by grace through faith, the free gift of God and God alone (Rom. 1:16–17; Eph. 2:8); whoever will respond to the offer of grace and faith will come to peace (Matt. 11:28; 18:14; John 3:14–16; 7:37–38; Phil. 4:6–7; Rev. 22:17); the gospel call comes to individuals (Luke 15—a single sheep, one lost coin, one son); judgment and grace are realities; Christ wants to give eternal life (John 3:16; Rom. 14:10; 2 Cor. 5:10); Christian preachers stand accountable to Christ, scripture, and the church for faithfully and responsibly announcing the good news and inviting sinners to say yes.

Green, M. B., *Evangelism in the Early Church,* 1970. **Jones, E. S.,** *Conversion,* 1959. **Kerr, H. T.,** and, **J. M. Mulder,** *Conversions,* 1983. **Long, T.,** *Preaching In and Out of Season,* 1990. **Sangster, W. E.,** *Power*

in Preaching, 1958. **Stewart, J. S.,** *Heralds of God,* 1972. **Stott, J.R.W.,** *Between Two Worlds: The Art of Preaching in the Twentieth Century,* 1982. **Willimon, W. H.,** *The Intrusive Word: Preaching to the Unbaptized,* 1994.
DONALD E. DEMARAY

Exegesis

The Purpose of Exegesis. Exegesis of the Bible is the foundation of Christian preaching. If the sermon is not informed by careful study of scripture, the preacher is likely to offer the congregation recycled common sense rather than the proclamation of the Word of God. It is the primary task of preaching to unfold the message of scripture, not to explain it away or to trim it to fit the patterns of conventional wisdom; hence, there is the need for rigorous exegesis.

The word "exegesis," despite its dauntingly technical connotations, means simply "interpretation." Every close reading of a text—any text—is an act of exegesis. When the Supreme Court interprets the Constitution, that is exegesis; when a woman pores over a long-awaited letter from her absent lover, that is exegesis. So, also, the preacher pores over scripture, seeking to read its message rightly.

The preacher's task of exegesis, however, is made more challenging by the historical distance between the present time and the biblical texts. These documents were written in the Hebrew and Greek languages in ancient cultures, written for communities whose customs and assumptions differed dramatically from our own. Consequently, when the Bible is read in church, the congregation is listening in on a communication originally intended for readers long ago and far away. Thus, preachers are charged with two distinct tasks: exegesis and proclamation. They must understand the historical and literary contexts within which the biblical text becomes intelligible and then reflect imaginatively on the way in which that text might speak to a congregation in a

very different historical setting. The more precise the exegesis, the more focused the proclamation will be (*see* Hermeneutics).

Two widespread misconceptions about exegesis hamper effective use of the Bible in preaching. The first is that the primary aim of exegesis is to limit interpretation: exegesis tells the preacher what *may not* be said about the text. Of course, there is some truth to this view: disciplined exegesis would forbid the preacher to claim that the message of Romans 5 is that "God helps those who help themselves." Nonetheless, it is wrong to think of exegesis only as posing constraints on meaning. No exegesis can provide the single definitive interpretation that excludes all others. Rather, *the principal effect of the exegetical process is to stimulate the imagination.** Sustained attention to the text leads the reader into a richly visualized account of the world of the text, "the strange new world of the Bible," as Karl Barth* called it. Encountering a world of different values, assumptions, and possibilities, the preacher is encouraged to envision God's dealings with humankind in new and surprising ways. Exegesis expands, rather than narrows, the preacher's homiletical horizons.

The second misconception is that exegesis is an arcane discipline that can be practiced only by highly trained experts with large libraries and unlimited time at their disposal. Preachers, according to this view, have neither the competence nor the time to do exegesis; they can only depend on secondary aids and summaries produced by certified specialists. On the contrary, *serious exegesis can and should be done by the preacher on a regular basis as a generative source for the sermon.* This is not to say that all preaching must be expository;* rather, whatever form the sermon may finally take, it must emerge from the preacher's serious wrestling with the Bible.

Exegetical Procedure. Because exegesis is an art rather than a science, no single mechanical procedure can be prescribed. Each preacher will have to find the most effective way of engaging the text. The following suggested procedure offers one way to approach the exegetical task.

First, the preacher should read the text carefully, without recourse to commentaries or other aids, observing how the passage fits into its wider literary context. Those who have studied biblical languages should prepare their own translation of the passage; the process of working through the Hebrew or Greek text *slows down* the interpreter, who may therefore notice important details otherwise overlooked. Those who have not studied the languages should compare several different translations. Following this preliminary close reading, the next task is to outline the passage, giving a brief schematic view of its structure. Here, for example, is an outline of Mark 2:1–12.

A. Healing story: beginning (2:1–5a)
   1. narrative setting: crowds in Capernaum (1–2)
   2. presentation of problem: paralytic lowered through roof (3–4)
   3. Jesus responds to the faith of the paralytic's friends (5a)
B. Controversy dialogue (2:5b–10a)
   1. Jesus pronounces forgiveness of sins (5b)
   2. Scribes question Jesus' authority (6–7)
   3. Jesus discerns their doubt, poses rhetorical question (8–9)
   4. Author's parenthetical comment to reader (10a)
C. Healing story: conclusion (2:10b–12)
   1. Jesus gives healing command (10b–11)
   2. evidence of healing and crowd response (12)

Then, before proceeding further, the preacher should jot down notes about questions raised by the text: What is the main point? What seems odd or puzzling? What problems are left unresolved? How does the passage challenge prevailing ideas and customs? Only after this preliminary process of reflection should the preacher begin to consult secondary sources.

The second stage in exegesis is a more detailed study of the text, drawing upon reference tools and sources as necessary. Even at this stage, the emphasis ought to be not so much on finding a single "right" meaning as on *raising questions* that will stimulate the preacher's reflection. The following checklist offers some categories that will facilitate a careful reading of the passage, using Mark 2:1–12 for purposes of illustration.

Boundaries and Placement of the Pericope and Function of the Passage in Its Context. Where does the unit begin and end? Has the lectionary omitted some verses that are integral to the passage? If so, why? Would different partitioning of the text affect its interpretation? Does it belong to a wider grouping of materials (such as a collection of parables or controversy stories)? If so, is its placement within this grouping significant? What role does the passage play in the development of the narrative or argument? Does the passage reflect characteristic themes and emphases of the writer?

The delineation of Mark 2:1–12 as a unit seems clear: both in 2:1 and in 2:13 we find narrative links announcing Jesus' movement to a new scene. This pericope introduces a series of five controversy discourses grouped together in 2:1–3:6. Why is it placed first in the series? How are the other controversies related thematically to this one? Note, for example, that the last controversy (3:1–5), like the first one, centers on a healing. The first controversy (2:1–12) deals with forgiveness of *sins,* and the second (2:13–17) concerns eating with *sinners.* All five controversies deal in some way with Jesus' *authority* to defy social/religious norms. Do the other stories in the series clarify the primary emphasis of 2:1–12?

Textual Problems. Do some ancient Greek manuscripts provide significant variant readings? How are the variants to be explained? What do they tell us about the earliest interpretation of the text?

What is the probable original reading? Commentaries on the Greek text will contain this information, or the preacher may consult Bruce Metzger, ed., *A Textual Commentary on the Greek New Testament*.

The few variant readings in the manuscript tradition for Mark 2:1–12 are of minor importance. Note, however, the variations in the tense of the verb in vv. 6 and 9. Does Jesus tell the paralytic that his sins "are being forgiven" (*aphientai*, present tense) or "have been forgiven" (*aphentai*, present perfect tense)? One suspects that the perfect tense might reflect later liturgical use of the story. In other passages, text-critical problems are crucial. For example, in Luke's story of Jesus' last meal with his disciples (Luke 22:14–23), some ancient manuscripts lack vv. 19b–20. The interpreter must decide whether to treat these words as a part of the passage.

Translation Problems. Are there ambiguities or syntactical difficulties in the text? Compare several English translations and try to determine how and why they differ. Consider the following examples:

1. In Mark 2:2 ("he was preaching the word [*ton logon*] to them") does the term "the word" carry its quasitechnical early Christian connotation (the gospel), or does the expression simply mean, as it might in ordinary Greek discourse, "the message" or "the report"? See Mark's use of "the word" in the interpretation of the parable of the sower (4:14–20).

2. In 2:10, how should *ho huios tou anthropou* ("the Son of Man") be translated? It is a very odd expression, not idiomatic Greek. Is it merely a circumlocution meaning "I"?

3. In 2:10, Jesus seems to change addressees in midsentence, creating a syntactically awkward piece of narration. Note how different translations handle the mechanics of this problem. Should the words about the Son of Man in v. 10a be read as a continuation of the words of Jesus (as in most English translations) or

as an aside from narrator to reader? (For other instances of this narrative technique in Mark, cf. 7:3–5; 7:19; 13:14.)

Analysis of Key Words. Using Bauer's *Greek-English Lexicon of the New Testament and Other Early Christian Literature*, Kittel's *Theological Dictionary of the New Testament*, and a concordance (such as Morrison's *Analytical Concordance*), investigate the meanings of important words in the passage. Are any of the terms used in the passage thematic keys to interpretation? Which ones? Why? Consider the following examples:

1. "Faith" (*pistis*, 2:5): a key emphasis in synoptic healing and miracle stories (Mark 5:34; 10:52; 4:40; 11:22). In these stories, the term seems to refer to *trust* in the person of Jesus, rather than to belief in doctrines about him. Jesus "sees" the faith of the paralytic's friends in their action (2:3–4).

2. The "scribes" (2:6) appear frequently in Mark (more than twenty times), often linked with "chief priests and elders" (e.g., 8:31; 10:33; 11:18, 27; 14:1, 43, 53; 15:1, 31) as enemies of Jesus. (Interestingly, Mark connects them with the Pharisees only in 7:1, 5.) Jesus' authority was already contrasted to that of the scribes in 1:22.

3. "Sins" (*hamartiai*, 2:5, 7, 9, 10): surprisingly, a minor emphasis in Mark (besides this passage, only in 1:4–5; 3:28–29—in the latter text, the word is *hamartemata*). A similar observation applies to "forgive." The contrast with Matthew and Luke is striking. Is the relative scarcity of these terms in Mark significant?

4. "Blasphemy/blaspheme" (2:7): linked with forgiveness (but differently) in 3:28–29; cf. 15:29. See also 14:64.

5. "Authority" (*exousia*, 2:10): significant theme in Markan controversy discourses and exorcism stories (1:22, 27; 3:15; 6:7; 11:28–33). The word can connote both "freedom" and "power." Is it possible to distinguish which sense is primary here?

6. "Son of Man" (2:10): Note the connection with blasphemy in 14:62–64. The

term appears in Mark primarily in Jesus' predictions of his passion/resurrection (8:31; 9:9, 12, 31; 10:33, 45; 14:21, 41) or of his future coming in glory (8:38; 13:26; 14:62). The exceptions to this pattern are found only in chapter 2 (vv. 10, 28). Should these early appearances of "Son of Man" be read as suggesting the eschatological significance that the term acquires later in the narrative?

Form-Critical Issues. Does the text belong to a typical literary form (such as "miracle story" or "pronouncement story") with standard formal characteristics? If so, does this provide insight into the meaning of the passage? Has the author in some way significantly modified the standard form?

Has Mark spliced together two different traditional stories in Mark 2:1–12: a healing story (vv. 1–5a, 10b-12) and a controversy dialogue (vv. 5b-10a)? See the outline on p. 123. This hypothesis would explain a number of otherwise peculiar features of the text: the awkward syntax of v. 10, the abrupt introduction of the issue of forgiving sins in v. 5b and of "the scribes" (not previously mentioned in the story) in v. 6, the absence of any specific description of the scribes' reaction to the healing, and the mixed formal type of the story (healing and controversy). If Mark has indeed spliced two traditions here, why or to what effect? The juxtaposition reveals a characteristic Markan redactional emphasis: an apparently simple story of miraculous power becomes the occasion for emphasizing Jesus' confounding of expectation and resultant conflict with religious authorities.

Why does Mark draw our attention not to the faith of the paralytic but to the faith of those who had brought him? This contrasts to other healing stories, which tend to emphasize the faith of the person who receives the healing (cf. 5:34).

Use of Sources. Does the passage quote from other sources (for example, the Old Testament)? Does the writer employ traditional material from other early Christian sources (confessional or liturgi-

cal formulae, hymns, catechetical traditions)? A special instance of the source question is the problem of the literary relationship among the Gospels: has one of the evangelists used another as a literary source? Where traditional materials are used, *how* are they used and for what purposes? How are they modified and why? Consider the following examples:

1. Does the title "the Son of Man" (2:10) come from Daniel 7:13–14? Was there an established expectation within first-century Judaism of a messianic "Son of Man" figure?

2. Do the healing story and the controversy story about forgiveness originally come from separate pre-Markan sources?

In other passages, questions about the use of sources may be of major importance. For example, any preacher dealing with Rom. 10:5–13 must wrestle with Paul's use of OT texts, especially his strange reading of Deut. 30:12–14. Likewise, a sermon on Phil. 2:1–13 should reckon with the likelihood that in vv. 6–11 Paul is quoting an early Christ hymn.

Cultural Background. Does the passage reflect images, motifs, or ways of thinking that must be understood against the background of Jewish or Greco-Roman culture, religion, and philosophy? Commentaries will often provide helpful insight on such matters. For example, consider the following issues in relation to Mark 2:1–12:

1. Did Jews ordinarily regard sickness as a punishment for sin? What is the evidence that they did?

2. Could Jesus' act of proclaiming sins forgiven apart from the temple sacrificial system be construed as a revolutionary challenge to the dominant religio-economic order?

Relation to Other New Testament Texts. Are there themes and motifs here that occur elsewhere within the New Testament, or is the passage distinctive within the canon? Does it express a theological perspective that might be illuminated by—or stand in tension with—other New Testament texts? The preacher should be careful not to conflate the message of the passage with the message of other texts; indeed, parallel texts may prove most helpful in highlighting what the passage does *not* say.

The synoptic parallel between Mark 2:2 and Luke 5:17 is revealing: where Luke stresses the presence of the healing power of God in Jesus, Mark simply stresses the proclamation of the word. Forgiveness of sins, a favorite theme of Luke and Matthew, generally receives less emphasis in Mark. There is a loose but fascinating parallel to this story in John 5:1–18, which opens out into a lengthy revelation discourse on Jesus' authority (John 5:19–47). According to Matt 18:15–35 and John 20:19–23, Jesus confers the authority to forgive sins upon the community of his followers; in Mark, however, there is no clear evidence of this authority transfer (cf. 6:6b–13).

Problems of History.   Such issues arise at two different historical levels. First, does the text narrate events "as they really happened," or must the historian reconstruct a different account of the history behind the text? Second, how does the text illuminate the history and characteristics of the *community* within which it was produced and used? How has the historical context shaped the text? It is rarely wise for the preacher to preach on a hypothetical historical reconstruction rather than upon the story as told by the text; nonetheless, there are occasions when it is both helpful and necessary to consider such issues. For example, the vehement anti-Jewish rhetoric of John 8:31–59 is best understood not as a report of what Jesus of Nazareth actually said but as a construction of the Johannine community after their painful experience of expulsion from the synagogue in the latter part of the first century. In Mark 2:1–12, the following questions illustrate historical problems:

1. Did the historical Jesus really make the sort of claims for himself that this text presents him as making? Did he in fact antagonize religious leaders by performing healings and/or claiming to forgive sins? Did he claim to be "the Son of Man"? Why does this title appear in the Gospels *only* in quotations from Jesus (unless 2:10, 28 are exceptions)?

2. Was Mark writing for a community within which the claim of Jesus' authority to forgive sins was being questioned? Do the scribes stand as ciphers for some opponents confronted by Mark in his own time? Did Mark's community practice healing?

Synthetic Literary and Theological Observations.   Having examined the passage in light of the above categories, it is important to take a step back and look at the larger picture: how does the unit fit into the literary and theological framework of the text in which it appears? In the case of Mark 2:1–12, one might consider reflections such as the following:

1. Note the use of irony and dramatic foreshadowing in verse 7. The scribes' complaint ("No one can forgive sins except God alone") is ironic in light of Mark's Christology: the reader of the story has known since 1:1 that Jesus is "God's Son" (cf. also 1:11). The scribes' "questioning" here develops into a hardened opposition (3:6), and Jesus is ultimately convicted on the charge of blasphemy (14:64), first raised at this point in the narrative (2:7).

2. What is the answer to Jesus' question in v. 9? It looks like a purely rhetorical question (note that it receives no answer from the scribes), but which way does the question cut? Does it mean (a) "Forgiveness is hard but healing is easy; here, I'll show you"; or does it mean (b) "Talk about 'forgiveness' is easy, but now I'll do something harder (healing) in order to prove to you that I really do have the authority to forgive"? The question remains an enigmatic riddle, not easily answered. This is consistent with Mark's portrayal of Jesus as an enigmatic figure who eludes easy comprehension and challenges conventional categories (cf. 4:10–12; 8:14–21; 9:30–32; 11:27–33; 12:13–17; 12:35–37).

3. The emphasis of the passage lies on the authority of Jesus. He has burst upon

the scene "as one having authority," unlike the scribes (1:22). Such authority, in a world gone wrong, evokes opposition and conflict (cf. 1:21–28). Thus, Jesus' forgiveness of sins in Mark 2:1–12 is an apocalyptic sign, an indication that the eschatological power of the Son of Man is breaking the power of the old age, overcoming its paralyzing inertia (*see* Literary Criticism).

From Exegesis toward the Sermon. Few preachers will be able to work thoroughly through all these exegetical issues for every sermon. This example illustrates a range of possiblities; the preacher will learn to pick out interesting or significant questions for investigation. Of course, no sermon can possibly deal with all the issues that emerge from the exegesis. The detailed exegesis will, however, provide numerous stimuli for the homiletical imagination. Furthermore, the close reading should lead toward an informed overall construal of the text's meaning. After working carefully through the exegetical process, the preacher should begin to ask questions concerning the significance of the text for theological reflection and for the congregation.

What understanding of God, Jesus, the church, and the world is presented in the passage? What would it mean for the community of faith to treat this passage as normative for its life and witness? At what points will the community find itself already in agreement or disagreement with the teaching of the text? How are the points of tension to be interpreted or acted upon?

To raise such questions is to take up the hermeneutical task of bringing scripture into critical dialogue with the congregation's world. In order to promote such dialogue, it is often helpful to ask what works of literature, art, or music—or what current events—might be read in counterpoint with the passage in order to bring its message into perspective.

The following questions illustrate some of the issues that a sermon on Mark 2:1–12 might seek to address: (1) What is the relation between sin and sickness? Is sin a cause of illness? (2) What is the relation between faith and healing? Can people be healed on the basis of someone else's faith? Should we pray for healing? How are forgiveness and healing related? (3) Who is Jesus? Mark portrays him as the Son of Man who has the authority to heal and to forgive. Are the scribes right that only God has such authority? What does that tell us about Jesus' claim? Do we accept that claim? (4) Do we have the authority to pronounce the sins of others forgiven? (Consider the controversy surrounding President Reagan's visit to Bitburg cemetery in the late 1980s.) (5) In this passage as in many others throughout this Gospel, Mark portrays Jesus' words and actions as generating controversy, conflict, and resistance. Why? Is this an inevitable response to the proclamation of the word? Does our proclamation provoke such a response? Should it? (6) Is the gospel always most offensive to persons in positions of religious authority?

However the preacher chooses to address these themes, the foregoing analysis suggests that all preaching on Mark 2:1–12 must emphasize *Jesus' authority* to forgive. A sermon dealing with forgiveness must not lose the christological focus; to do so would be to distort Mark's message. This illustrates how exegesis can serve to provide guidelines for proclamation without imposing narrowly prescriptive limitations (*see* Authority).

It cannot be stressed too strongly that the preacher's imaginative task of bringing scripture and congregation into dialogue can occur only through direct wrestling with the text. Commentaries and lectionary aids may prime the pump of the imagination, but they cannot substitute for direct encounter with the word.

Craddock, F. B., *The Gospels,* 1981. **Fee, G. D.,** *New Testament Exegesis: A Handbook for Students and Pastors,* rev. ed., 1993. **Furnish, V. P.,** "Some Practical Guidelines for New Testament Exegesis," *Perkins School of Theology Journal* 26 (1973): 1–16. **Hayes, J. H.,** and **C. R. Holladay,** *Biblical Exegesis: A Beginner's Handbook,* 1982. **Keck, L. E.,**

and **G. M. Tucker,** "Exegesis," *Interpreter's Dictionary of the Bible, Supplementary Volume,* 1976, 296–303. **Steinmetz, D. C.,** "The Superiority of Pre-Critical Exegesis," *Theology Today* 37 (1980): 27–38.

RICHARD B. HAYS

Experimental Preaching. "Experimental preaching" is a term coined in the 1960s and 1970s to apply to a bold, often fragmentary kind of homily offered in the more open or radical pulpits of the time as an antidote to the traditional sermon. Theoretically, it derived from the efforts of the experimental artists, musicians, and dramatists of the earlier part of the century—the Impressionists, Dadaists, Expressionists, Absurdists—to break the stranglehold of traditional patterns and release creative energies through risky and unexpected new approaches to what they were doing. Theologically, it was grounded in a strong awareness of the grace of God, which permits great latitudes in worship and expression, and in the doctrine of creation, which encourages human beings to express themselves as imaginatively as God does.

Underlying attempts at such a departure from the homiletical norm was an academic interest, somewhat shortlived, in the "theology of play," deriving from such seminal books as Johann Huizenga's *Homo Ludens* (Man Playing), Sam Keen's *To a Dancing God,* and Jürgen Moltmann's *A Theology of Play,* which emphasized the importance of wit, spontaneity, playfulness, and creativity as ways of catching glimpses of the divine intention and imitating the divine activity.

Several religious publications of the period, led by the Methodist student magazine *motive* and the strongly satirical *Wittenburg Door,* published articles, cartoons, and composite photos that could only be characterized as probing, rebellious, fanciful, and impudent, criticizing the conservative viewpoints and methods of most churches, seminaries, and ministers. For a brief, shining time they were among the most admired and imitated American religious journals (*see* Humor).

Into this *Zeitgeist,* or out of it, came two zany representatives from the National Council of Churches' Department of Worship and Culture, Roger Ortmayer and Ed Summerlin. Ortmayer, a former editor of *motive,* carried the collegiate spirit of fun and games over into his work with Worship and Culture, visiting churches and campuses across the country to stage worship events, "happenings," with people wearing paper sacks on their heads to symbolize their failure to relate to persons around them and sailing paper plates out of sanctuary balconies as signs of the Holy Spirit's call to freedom and exuberance. Summerlin, a jazz saxophonist trained at Eastman School of Music and teaching at a New York university, imparted a Boots Randolph seductiveness to classical old hymns as well as popular new choruses. Controversial among many older Christians, the two were nevertheless like Pied Pipers of mirth and frivolity among the younger set, especially on university and seminary campuses.

All across the United States at this time, one began to hear of innovative homiletical efforts with which ministers were daringly replacing the old-fashioned sermon, including playlets, dramatic monologues, dialogue sermons, enigmatic parables, mime shows, clown acts, and multimedia presentations. In few places did they become the staple offering on Sunday mornings. Instead, they were occasional interludes, primarily in college and seminary pulpits or in the chancels of university-related churches. They were part of the extraordinary general ferment of the years that contained not only the war in Vietnam but the onset of the drug culture and the rise of the flower children, when Allen Ginsberg was reciting and John Cage was performing his four minutes and thirty-three seconds of silence in Carnegie Hall. The radical departures that characterized the arts seemed appropriate for the gospel as well.

As a young professor of preaching at

Vanderbilt Divinity School who had always had a vital interest in the arts, I began to offer an annual seminar called "Experimental Preaching." Out of this seminar came *Experimental Preaching* and *The 11 O'Clock News and Other Experimental Sermons.* I am astounded at the freshness many of these sermons still exhibit and the power with which some evoke almost visceral reactions in a time when such efforts are out of fashion.

Among the most memorable are Patterson D. Ellis's "Parable of a Parable," in which a learned preacher is interrupted in his pedantic exposition of the story of the good Samaritan by the news that someone has been injured and needs assistance in the church parking lot, but the preacher manages to dismiss the interruption and continue with his sermon; Thomas B. Martin's "2001: The Church Revisited," with its futuristic world under a dome and people removing their oxygen masks at communion to breathe on each other as Christ breathed on the first disciples; Virginia Morgan's "Corinth and the Creeping Crud," a play about God and ecology; and Jerry L. Barnes's "A Christmas Eve Letter," pieces of correspondence between a young Christian in Vietnam and his parents at home, who work for a munitions factory—the play climaxes with a telegram from the War Department about the death of the son.

It is also fascinating to see the names of the contributors to these two volumes, many of whom are well-known contributors to this *Encyclopedia:* Charles Rice, William Willimon, Perry H. Biddle, Jr., and Don E. Saliers.

What was the effect of this mini-wave in homiletical theory and practice? Did it vanish with the dawning of the 1980s and the advent of the Reagan years? Largely, perhaps, but not without leaving in its wake a taste of freedom and imagination for the homileticians who would follow. Just as the plays of Samuel Beckett, Eugene Ionesco, and Arthur Adamov left their mark on subsequent theater, so that it would never return entirely to its pre-absurdist days, the experimental sermons

of the heady, courageous 1960s and 1970s prepared the way for the freer, more colloquial narrative, confessional, and other kinds of sermons popular in the 1980s and 1990s.

Killinger, J., *Experimental Preaching*, 1973; and *The 11 O'Clock News and Other Experimental Sermons*, 1975.

JOHN KILLINGER

THE MEANING OF WORSHIP
William H. Willimon
(*This sermon is a dialogue between Pastor and a clown figure. Clown is dressed in white overalls and his face is painted in traditional makeup.*)

PASTOR: Today I'd like to talk with you about what it means to worship God—

CLOWN: Hold it! Hold it! (*Walking down aisle*) Sorry I'm late. Let's see, where's a good place to sit? Oh, there are plenty of good seats up here in front. (*Looks up at preacher*) Why are they all sitting back there? There are plenty of good seats up here in front. Oh, well. (*Takes seat*)

P: (*Continues very nervously*) As I was saying, today we are going to talk about what it means to worship.

C: Go right ahead. You've got the floor. You talk about anything you want to. (*Looks back at congregation*) We won't stop him, will we? You go right ahead!

P: (*With some disgust*) Thank you.

C: Don't thank me! They gave you the pulpit, not me. They're paying the bills. If it had been up to me, I'd have preferred a movie or a play or something with a little more zip to it, but they asked you, so you go right ahead.

P: I will!

C: I thought you would.

P: (*Loudly*) Today we are going to consider what it means to worship God. For true worship is more than just gathering here in these beautiful surroundings and—

C: Say! This place is pretty nice! Who owns this place anyway? Is this your building? Is that why you're standing up there? I noticed that your name was on the sign out front.

P: No. Of Course not.

C: Then they own this place, right? (*Gestures to congregation*) Which one of you picked this color for the carpet?

P: No. It sort of is their place but not exactly.

C: Who paid for it?

P: Well, we did.

C: Then you must own it.

P: No, no. You can't own a church!

C: (*Laughs*) I bet if they paid for it, they think they own it. Right, out there? Just try up-setting some of 'em and you'll find out who owns this place! There'll be a new face looking down from up there!

P: This is God's house. This is his church.

C: Oh. God runs this place. Have we been invited!

P: Yes, of course. We are here to worship him.

C: Worship him, worship him. What does that mean?

P: I'm glad you asked that. Now if you will sit down I will continue with the sermon I had intended to preach and tell you what that means!

C: Okay, okay.

P: To worship, in the words of the West-minster Confession, means to "glorify God and enjoy him forever."

C: You've got to be kidding! What a laugh! Enjoy him? Ha! Look at that crowd out there! (*Gestures to congregation*) Do they look like they are enjoying anything? Man, look at those faces! If that's enjoy-ing yourself. I'd say you people have an odd way of having a good time! Why, you should have heard your singing a few minutes ago! (*Moving to center of chan-cel and mimicking in slow, dull tones*)

Praise God, from whom all blessings flow;
Praise Him, all creatures here below;
Praise Him above, ye heav'nly host;
Praise Father, Son, and Holy Ghost.

Why, I've heard more joy than that at a wake!

P: Perhaps if you showed a bit more dignity and reverence you might have gotten more out of it.

C: (*Moving toward pulpit*) Dignity? Good Lord, you've sure got dignity! I agree with that. If God likes stiffness and dullness and (*lifts nose*) D-I-G-N-I-T-Y, I bet he loves this! (*Goes to lectern and turns pages of Bible*) But how about this? (*Reads loudly and with spirit*)

Praise the Lord! Praise God in his sanc-tuary;
Praise him with trumpet sound, praise him with lute and harp.
Praise him with timbrel and dance.
Praise him with strings and pipe! Praise him with loud clashing cymbals!
Let everything that breathes praise the Lord!
Praise the Lord!

Now that doesn't sound so dignified to me. I wish I'd gone to that church this morning. It may not be too dignified, but I bet it's a lot of fun!

P: Then maybe you would be happier else-where. I've had enough of your carrying on. We are not used to this kind of behav-ior at our church. I should call the ushers and have them take you—

C: Oh-oh-oh! (*Shaking a finger at Pastor*) Not so fast! Can't do that.

P: And why not? This is my church. I'm in charge here.

C: Oh, well, then maybe you can. But I thought you said before that this place belonged to God?

P: Well, yes, but—

C: You're just the bouncer here, right? Better be careful who you go tossing out of this place. After all, they threw him out once too.

P: Him?

C: Yeah. You know him. (*Goes to Bible and reads from Luke*)

"Then Jesus went to Nazareth, where he had been brought up, and on the Sabbath Day he went as usual to the synagogue. He stood up to read the scriptures. . . ."

From J. Killinger, ed., *The Eleven O'Clock News and Other Experimental Sermons* (Nashville: Abingdon, 1975), 25–27.

Expository Preaching. "Exposi-tion" means bringing out what is there. The word exposition derives from the Latin word *expositio*, which means "setting forth" or "making accessible." The expository sermon is a sermon which faithfully brings a message out of scripture and makes that message accessible to contemporary hearers.

The Bible provides many examples of expository preachers. Ezra exposited the Law to the returned exiles (Neh. 8:8). Jesus* was an expositor of the Hebrew scriptures (Luke 4:16–21). Peter exposited scripture, especially in his sermon in Acts 2:14–36. The theme of Paul's letter to the Romans, that "the just shall live by faith" was taken by Paul from Habakkuk 2:4. Philip's sermon to the eunuch in Acts 8:26–35 is expository in method.

Commonly noted examples of expository preaching prior to the Reformation include the sermons of Cyprian, Athanasius, Chrysostom,* Augustine,* the Venerable Bede,* Bernard of Clairvaux,* and Wycliffe.* During the Reformation, expository preaching underwent a revival. Zwingli,* Bullinger,* and Calvin* preached through entire books of the Bible (lectio continua) as a way of increasing biblical literacy in the church. Karl Barth* and Helmut Thielicke* have done much to underscore the importance of expository preaching in the twentieth century.

The central principle for expository preaching is the authority* of scripture in the pulpit. Scripture must clearly "authorize" the preacher's message. This means two things for homiletical method. First, preachers must assess, from time to time, their prejudices, biases, and perspectives. Second, preachers should make a determined effort to "respect the otherness" of the biblical text. This means that the preacher strives to understand the text on its own terms, apart from personal or doctrinal agendas. The biblical text must be carefully studied in its original historical context, and every effort must be made to modify sermon ideas, purposes, or forms to agree with scripture. Lectionary* preaching also helps to assure that the agenda of scripture is heard from the pulpit (see Exegesis).

The second principle of expository preaching is clarity in communication. Since the purpose of expository preaching is to make scripture accessible, subtle forms of communication are usually eschewed in favor of simple, clear forms of language and logic. For this reason, expositors are often wary of inductive* and narrative* forms of logic and urge the use of deductive propositions and arguments. Stories or images are used only if they help the preacher illustrate an idea (to apply or inform) or assist the preacher to "convict" and "convert" (to persuade).

Although there are a variety of expository methods, the two principal types are verse-by-verse exposition and thematic exposition. In verse-by-verse exposition, or "running commentary," the preacher divides a larger biblical pericope into smaller units of thought. The sermon moves in a serial fashion through these smaller units, asserting and applying ideas derived from each one separately. These ideas are connected together in order to achieve the same unity of thought in the larger pericope.

In thematic expository preaching, the preacher derives the sermon theme from the biblical text but unfolds that theme in whatever way seems necessary or appropriate to the task of making that message accessible to the hearer. The sermon will move in and out of the biblical text in a fashion that is not necessarily verse-by-verse.

Other homiletical possibilities sometimes considered expository are: textual preaching, or preaching on a shorter scriptural passage (so long as the larger context is not overlooked), biographical sermons on biblical characters or authors, expository studies of biblical contexts or words, exposition of scripture in relation to confessional statements or doctrines, exposition of related passages in a series, continuous exposition through a book of the Bible or through the entire Bible, and the exposition in a single sermon of a central message from an entire biblical book.

The techniques of several preachers have influenced the shape of contemporary expository preaching. Alexander Maclaren* helped to popularize textual preaching. He would use a smaller text as a pathway into the exposition of a larger text. F. B. Meyer reversed this technique and would move through his exposition of the larger biblical text toward a smaller pivotal text which would provide a crucial turning point in the development of the sermon. Perhaps the best exemplar of the running commentary method was Harry A. Ironside of the Moody Church, Chicago. The forerunner of many television expositors, Ironside was less interested in careful biblical exegesis than he was in provocative application and illustration. A. T. Robertson and William Barclay, on the other hand, were forerunners of more scholarly approaches to expository preaching today. Both preachers made the intricacies of Greek word studies and historical analysis lively and imaginative for the hearer. The preaching of James Forbes often demonstrates how scriptural exposition can help the preacher take the hearer beyond customary interpretations of the biblical text. In recent years, several scholars and preachers have suggested that biblical exposition can include not only the thematic content of the biblical text but also its literary form.

The primary weakness of expository preaching is that it can constrict a preacher's engagement with culture and human experience from the pulpit. Since the expositor sees daily life as an arena in which the scriptural message is "applied," the preacher can develop a utilitarian approach to scripture.

Another potential weakness is the tendency toward authoritarianism. This is the result of an often unconscious identification of biblical authority with the preacher's authority. This can be remedied only by recognizing the influence of personal doctrinal preunderstandings in determining what is "there" in scripture.

The great strength of expository preaching is that it reinforces the authority and centrality of scripture in the life of the church. It is a homiletical method that teaches scripture and enhances the knowledge and understanding of the Bible for both preacher and congregation. More than any other genre of preaching, expository preaching honors the desire of the hearer to understand and claim the meaning of the scriptures for life in today's world.

Liefeld, W. L., *New Testament Exposition: From Text to Sermon*, 1984. **Robinson, H. W.**, *Biblical Preaching: The Development and Delivery of Expository Messages*, 1980. **Whitesell, F. D.**, *Power in Expository Preaching*, 1963. **Nixon, L.**, *Calvin—Expository Preacher*, 1950.   JOHN S. MCCLURE

Extemporary Preaching. Television* has made everyone more alert to the means and techniques of contemporary communications.* Many of the traditional characteristics of public speaking have been chastened by the strictures exerted upon us, either indirectly or unconsciously, and by the successes or failures of professional communicators. Probably more than is realized, the Christian pulpit has been affected, fortunately for the better, by the new breed of speakers who communicate hourly with all levels of the listening public. Indeed, no preacher can presume any more to communicate adequately the timely message of the gospel to the world of these times in the manner of the old time. As Lowell rightly observed, "New occasions teach new duties."

What type of preaching has been affected the most by the communications media of this electronic age? The extemporary preaching method. Why? Because "impact" has become the litmus test of successful communication, especially since the struggle and competitiveness to gain a "hearing" is the concern of every communicator today as never before. The occupant of the Christian pulpit must face an inevitable question regarding every sermon: "What was its impact upon the men and women waiting upon God for the word?"

Kinds of Extemporary Preaching

There are two main types of extemporary preaching, and preachers have either risen or fallen according to their understanding or discovery of the one that works for them. Television has its Nielsen ratings; the pulpit has its full or empty pews. Under the word "extemporary," Webster has two meanings: (1) "Done or made with little or no preparation; composed or uttered on the spur of the moment" and (2) "Carefully prepared but delivered without note or text."

The first of these definitions one associates mostly with street or open-air preachers or the more informal liturgical patterns of contemporary sects. This method has built-in weaknesses that are detected or felt according to the hearing or learning capacities of the congregation. Such "off the cuff" presentations are marked often by the following shortcomings: poorly framed sentences; meaningless gestures; inaccurate word choices; repetition of ideas and incomplete handling of others; vague foci and progression, if any at all, of thought; and the tendency to address people *en masse*. This latter weakness was Fosdick's* concern when he said: "When I get into that pulpit I say to myself, 'There is in this congregation one person who needs what I'm going to say. Oh, God, let me get to him! So I can forget the crowd.' " The poorer side of this type of extemporary preaching, then, is the preacher's tendency to be mindful only of the crowd and to avoid talking one to one.

The second type of extemporary preaching is certainly the more preferable because it holds the secret to real impact, although it exacts a price. Perhaps no better description of the nature, method, and demand of this second type is given than in Fénelon's* *Dialogues on Eloquence:*

A man who is well instructed and who has a great facility of expressing himself; a man who has meditated deeply in all their bearings upon the principles of the subject which he is to treat; who has conceived that subject in his intellect, and arranged his arguments in the clearest manner, who has prepared a certain number of striking figures and of touching sentiments which may render it sensible and bring it home to his hearers; who knows perfectly all that he ought to say, and the precise place in which to say it, so that nothing remains at the moment of delivery but to find words to express himself—such is the extempore speaker" (Fénelon, 106–9).

What are the strengths and possible dangers of this method?

Strengths

(i) *Fullness:* The old cliché has it: "He knows whereof he speaks." The preacher is equipped with solid facts, in-depth knowledge of the subject under consideration and, like any competent researcher, brings forward treasures new and old.

(ii) *Authority:** No worthy impression is made upon hearers by a dogmatic mien, emotional shouting, a parade of scholarship, a series of name-dropping, or "I've been there" of the travelogue. Rather, in the words of R.E.O. White, "real authority is most clearly felt when truth is spoken plainly and quietly in a manner that permits no arguments" (White, 21).

(iii) *Immediacy:* The element of "nowness" must be an ingredient of the preacher's concern. Gerhard Ebeling, the German scholar, says: "Let the text become God's Word again." And Charles Kingsley, leaning over the pulpit, said to his people: "We are here today to discover what the Gospel has to say to our hearts NOW!" This sense of immediacy has impact; however, it is caught by the hearer only when the preacher's attitude and bearing indicate that he or she has been grasped by the truth of scripture and by its dynamism shares its effect with hearers.

(iv) *Freedom:* The extemporary preachers, in their preparation, should avoid memorizing words; rather they must grasp ideas, put them into a mentally visible framework, and thereby carry their hearers along with them. Fosdick was a master of transitions: "We have seen . . . Now we go onto . . ." Incidentally, this is the missing technique with modern impressionist preachers. Their sermons are a stream of reactions to life's diverse stimuli without a concrete goal or purpose.

(v) *Persuasion:* Preaching a sermon is not an end in itself; if it were, it would belong to the genre of entertainment. The *raison d'être* of a sermon is to persuade people to accept and lead a new life. Hence, as John Henry Jowett* urged, the ultimate objective of preaching is "to move the will." Preaching is for a verdict. Fosdick asked himself tirelessly: "What do I propose to do this morning?" That meant: What conviction does the preacher wish to convince his hearers of before God? Will the contagion of the sermon emerge with the impact of the Pauline: "This one thing I know . . . I believe . . . I do"?

Weaknesses

(i) Detailed memorization of every word and punctuation mark leads to an academic affectation and—as my speech colleague used to say—thereby "sounds prepared."

(ii) It gives the impression of a mental struggle to remember the script, while the audience agonizes lest the preacher should forget.

(iii) It lacks a strategy that has become the preacher's own homiletical methodology, and hence the preacher remains uncomfortable with the whole presentation (*see* Memory).

The following men, in their day, excelled as extemporary preachers: Howard Thurman,* Fulton J. Sheen,* and D. T. Niles.

Fénelon, F., *Dialogues on Eloquence,* trans. W. S. Howell, 1951. **White, R.E.O.,** *A Guide to Preaching,* 1973.   DONALD MACLEOD

Feminist Preaching.   Feminist preaching is religious proclamation that seeks to address the oppression, violence, and inequity created by the social reality

of gender injustice. Women and men who preach from various feminist perspectives share a belief that many dimensions of the Christian tradition contribute to this injustice and therefore stand in need of liberating transformation. How one understands the nature of the social and ecclesial transformation that is needed varies according to the preacher's social location, severity of her or his feminist critique of the Christian tradition, and the preacher's vision of a different world. Even with these differences, feminist preaching is by nature transformational.

Preaching is a public act of theological naming. It is also an act that interprets and constructs social reality. With this in mind, there are two primary tasks in feminist preaching: (1) to rethink the theology that undergirds and permeates one's preaching ministry, and (2) to examine the connections between women's oppression, sexism, gender injustice, and all the other expressions of oppression in our day.

Feminist preaching relies on feminist theology because articulating and creating social, theological, and ecclesiastical change is feminist theology's primary aim. In an effort to proclaim and create this transformation, preachers place the traditional discipline and craft of homiletics in constant dialogue with the critique and vision of feminist theological thought. Feminist preaching is the integration of feminist theology and homiletical practice.

Feminist theology and feminist preaching share some basic commitments and principles. Feminist theology begins with women's experiences of oppression and marginality. The feminist theologian then draws upon those experiences in order to transform and to reshape theological categories, ethical paradigms, biblical hermeneutics, the reconstruction of church history, and the practice of Christian ministry.

Beverly Wildung Harrison describes the breadth of the feminist theological critique and vision with challenging words:

The critique we feminists make of Christianity involves a long agenda for theological change. It requires an extended and profound rethinking of all the language, images, and metaphors central to Christian theology, a revisioning that will surely not be exhausted soon (Harrison, 227).

Similar work faces those who embrace feminist preaching. Feminist preachers commit themselves to rethinking the entire preaching task in relation to gender justice. God language, biblical interpretation, christological doctrine, and all theological categories need to reflect an awareness of women's distinctive experience and oppression. Special attention is given to gender-inclusive God language in scripture and images of God that emerge from within women's experience. A different kind of biblical hermeneutics* is needed. Preachers will interpret the scriptures with a keen eye toward women's invisibility (Hagar in the story of Sarah, Abraham, and Hagar in Genesis), subtle and blatant expressions of violence against women found within the texts (Jephthah's daughter in Judges), accounts of women's leadership (Samaritan woman and her apostolic witness in John 4), and stories of women's strength and vision. Feminist preachers also need to consider the implications of their Christologies and how doctrine about the historical Jesus and the Christ of faith shape our common understandings about normative humanity and divine possibility. Ethical paradigms and theological assumptions must be evaluated and critiqued for their impact on women's lives. Joanne Carlson Brown and Carole R. Bohn move into the heart of the theological challenge that confronts the feminist preacher in a book that addresses the relationship between Christianity and abuse:

The central image of Christ on the cross as the savior of the world communicates the message that suffering is redemptive. If the best person who ever lived gave his life for others, then, to be of value we should likewise sacrifice ourselves. Any sense that we have a right to care for our own needs is in conflict with being a faithful follower of Jesus. Our suffering for others will save the world (Brown and Bohn, 2).

Preachers who preach from a feminist perspective will critically look at the ways traditional theological assumptions perpetuate women's suffering and oppression, and then seek to construct theological understandings that liberate.

Feminist preaching assumes a very broad agenda for its transformational work. In addition to the explicit theological task, feminist preaching attempts to make connections between women's oppression and all other forms of human injustice. Sexism is fundamentally connected to classism, North American imperialism, ageism, handicapism (the oppression of persons with disabilities), racism, and heterosexism (the oppression of gay men and lesbians). A preacher's awareness and knowledge of these connections influence the pastoral, hermeneutical, and theological content of proclaimed sermons (see Theology of Preaching).

Feminist preachers will examine economic realities and assumptions that pervade our common life. North American superiority will be challenged. Sermon illustrations* will draw upon the wisdom of older adults and the distinctive worldviews of persons with disabilities. Preachers will help communities understand the relational commitments and realities of gay men and lesbians, and white supremacy will be indicted. In a book about the moral and ethical agency of African-American women, Katie G. Cannon names the essential work of making connections in another way:

Moral agents must evaluate every situation as to whether it contributes to or impedes the growth of human personality and genuine community. . . . Ethical living requires an intolerance of civil arrangements that result in the horrors of racism, gender discrimination, economic exploitation and widespread cruelty. The interdependency of the "beloved community" projects a "constructive equality of oneness" (Cannon, 173).

Feminist preaching proclaims a religious and ecclesiastical vision that assumes the fundamental equality of all creation, and it seeks theological and ethical language that will reflect the diversity and truth of all human experience.

Feminist preaching weaves together theology and social analysis at every turn. Indeed, feminist preaching does commit individual preachers to the critical and constructive task of rethinking every aspect of the pastoral, hermeneutical, theological, and social dimensions of proclamation. Within its demands and challenges, contemporary preachers might discover again the radical nature of God's mandates for our lives and the transformational power of the gospel (see Women as Preachers; Inclusive Language).

Brown, J. C., and **C. R. Bohn,** eds., *Christianity, Patriarchy, and Abuse: A Feminist Critique,* 1989. **Cannon, K. G.,** *Black Womanist Ethics,* 1988. **Fulkerson, M. McC.,** *Changing the Subject: Feminist Theology and Women's Discourse,* 1994. **Harrison, B. W.,** "The Power of Anger in the Work of Love," in *Making Connections: Essays in Feminist Social Ethics,* 1985.   CHRISTINE M. SMITH

Fénelon, François Salignac de la Mothe.

(1651–1715) Priest, mystic, preacher, and theologian, Fénelon was born of an aristocratic family in the southwest region of France known as Perigord. Although he did not write or preserve many of his sermons, he has long been regarded as a devout and godly man who sought to lead the souls of his parishioners to the holy presence of God. He was ordained to the priesthood at the age of twenty-four in Paris, after being educated at schools there and in Cahors. His spiritual influence in his stated opinions about Quietism (mysticism) came into

conflict with Jacques-Bénigne Bossuet,* priest, orator, and bishop, who enjoyed a favored position with King Louis XIV. As a result, Fénelon was forced to recant some of his views. He became known for teaching children, performing acts of kindness, maintaining a conciliatory position with Protestants, and later was made archbishop of Cambrai.

During Fénelon's life, France was home to a distinguished group of Roman Catholic preachers that included Bossuet, Bourdaloue, and Massillon.* In contrast to Bossuet's flamboyant eloquence and Bourdaloue's methodical logic, Fénelon appealed to his auditors' sentiment and religious feelings (Dargan, 91). *Dialogues on Eloquence,* probably written before he was thirty years old, contains a thorough treatment of preaching and criticizes his contemporaries' practices. Most notably he was concerned with affectation that arose from a misuse of rhetorical eloquence and an abuse of scripture that derived from superficial uses of the text.

His *Dialogues* is divided into three parts, each dealing with an aspect of Fénelon's theory about eloquence. The ideas are advanced by means of conversations among three characters: A conveys the author's viewpoint; B is a young preacher who wants to improve his preaching but is greatly influenced by the popular style of the time; and C does little except offer occasional questions and remarks and generally agrees with A.

Fénelon, demonstrating thorough knowledge of Plato and Cicero, argues in the first dialogue that the rhetorician's skill is to serve the hearers' intelligence and morals rather than call attention to the speaker's manner and display (see Style). His advice to B is:

Consult yourself if you would know whether the speakers you hear are doing well. If they make a living impression upon you, if they render your mind attentive and sensitive to the things they say, if they warm you and raise you above yourself, then you may believe without fear that they have reached the goal of eloquence. If instead of moving you or inspiring strong feelings in you, they only act to please you and to make you admire the brilliance and the nicety of their thoughts and expressions, tell yourself that they are false speakers (Fénelon, 87).

His assessment of the aim of preaching stood in contradiction to what he observed in his well-known colleagues.

The second dialogue develops the concepts of *prouver*—to prove, *peindre*—to portray or picture, and *toucher*—to move or strike. These principles of oratory serve to help the preacher appeal to the hearers' reason, imagination, and sentiment. Eloquence, according to Fénelon, consists not only in proof or convincing but also in arousing passion or persuading. He contrasts the metaphysician and orator: the former gives "a bare demonstration that does not go beyond theory," and the latter "will add everything capable of arousing your sentiments, of making you love demonstrated truth" (Fénelon, 89). Passions are aroused by portraying them: "Not only to describe things but to represent their surrounding features in so lively and so concrete a way that the listener imagines himself almost seeing them" (Fénelon, 92–93). Extemporaneous* delivery,* moreover, adds to the ardor one hopes to kindle. The scholar Wilbur Samuel Howell notes that Fénelon adapted the meaning of persuasion in Cicero and Augustine* to refute Ramus and Talaeus whose rhetorical theories were popular in his day (*see* Rhetoric; Form).

His third dialogue, in ways similar to Augustine's *On Christian Doctrine*, consists of a discussion of scripture. The epistles, according to Fénelon, demonstrate St. Paul's ability as a philosopher and orator, but "his preaching . . . was founded neither upon human arguments nor human persuasions. His was a ministry whose strength came entirely from on high" (Fénelon, 127). He suggests the eloquence of scripture, in its simplicity, liveliness, and persuasion, should be copied by preachers. The gospel is all that needs to be explained, but too often, in Fénelon's opinion, the orator's pride leads to inventiveness and ingenuity antithetical to the gospel. He is convinced that the success of the church and the promotion of the gospel do not require the way of eloquence and wisdom found in human philosophy but need to be founded upon the spirit and power of God. He closes his work with a quote from St. Jerome:

When you teach in the church, do not stir up applause; stir up lamentations in the people. Let the tears of your listeners be your praise. The discourses of a preacher must be full of the sacred Scripture. Don't be a declaimer, but a true teacher of the mysteries of your God (Fénelon, 153).

Brilioth, Y., *A Brief History of Preaching,* trans. K. E. Mattson, 1965. **Dargan, E. C.,** *A History of Preaching,* Vol. 2, 1912. **Fénelon, F.,** *Dialogues on Eloquence,* trans. W. S. Howell, 1951. **Fish, H. C.,** ed. and comp., *History and Repository of Pulpit Eloquence,* 1856.   ANN I. HOCH

Figures of Speech.

The subject of this entry is suspect. Common parlance discounts the truth of a statement that is "merely a figure of speech." In a culture dependent upon science and rational analysis, there is a tendency to be suspicious of language that works by way of analogy and an appeal to the imagination.* If something cannot be empirically or literally expressed, then its actuality is in doubt.

Yet philosophical and linguistic studies have shown that figures of speech are essential to human communication.* Research on common American usage has revealed "that metaphor is pervasive in everyday life, not just in language but in thought and action. Our ordinary conceptual system, in terms of which we both think and act, is fundamentally metaphorical in nature" (Lakoff and Johnson 1980, 3).

In ancient times the term "figure of speech" was derived from any shape or form—any figure—that was visible to the eye. Once it became a category of speech, the term took on increasing subtlety and complexity. Classical rhetoric* provided precise definitions of the various types of figures that a speaker could employ. Although some early Christian writers on homiletics (most notably Augustine* in Book IV of *On Christian Doctrine*, used these definitions to analyze passages of scripture), there was in the church a general distrust of figures of speech. This may have been because the invention of figures of speech is part of conscious rhetorical work and that is not the emphasis in scripture: "Some practical recognition is given to natural ability, but the Judeo-Christian orator, at least in theory, has little need of practice or knowledge of an art as required by the orator in the classical tradition" (Kennedy 1980, 122). Figures of speech were suspect as the creation of the human imagination rather than as the inspiration of the Spirit (*see* Style).

The three Cappadocian* fathers of the fourth century—Gregory of Nazianzus, Basil the Great, and Gregory of Nyssa—illustrate the ambiguity toward figures of speech that continues to this day: "Virtually every figure of speech and rhetorical device of composition can be illustrated from their sermons, treatises, and numerous letters . . . Yet all three are repeatedly critical of classical rhetoric as something of little importance for the Christian . . ." (Kennedy 1980, 143).

That early suspicion of figures of speech in preaching has continued to haunt the history of Christian homiletics. It can be seen, for example, in the way the Puritans disparaged the preaching of the Anglicans as being too poetical and in the reservations about becoming too imaginative that continue to be voiced by many pastors today.

Despite the history of resistance to figures of speech, they have proven to be an inescapable part of Christian preaching for a number of reasons. First and foremost is the fact that the Bible is filled with them. Water, flame, wind, rock, bread, fortress, servant, lamb—the list of images through which scripture invokes the divine is rich and diverse. No one preaching from the Bible is able to avoid figures of speech.

Second, effective preachers have long known what modern communications studies have revealed about the receiving capacities of listeners: namely "that verbal, abstract expression is the province of a few, whereas the visual, sensory, and imagery filled discourse is accessible to virtually everyone. . . . This fact does not mean that preaching is only about the physical world or is confined to what we see and hear. But effective preaching is rooted and focused in the physical and sensory" (Wilson-Kastner 1989, 13).

The natural propensity of listeners to be more responsive to preaching that engages their sensory capacities has been heightened by the impact of the mass media, especially on the younger generations, whom Pierre Babin describes as "audiovisually oriented people" (Babin with Iannone 1991, 4). Effective communication with the "audiovisually oriented" requires giving people a "picture" of what is being said, and that inevitably involves the use of figures of speech.

Third, the development of new sensitivities to the experience of women, persons of color, those with physical disabilities, and other marginalized groups has increased our consciousness of how figures of speech can include or exclude others from our preaching. We are becoming aware how the figures of speech that we use can be tantamount to a statement of who is in power and how that power is expressed (*see* Feminist Preaching; Liberation Preaching).

For all three reasons, then—biblical usage, more effective communications, and an amplified awareness of those who have been marginalized—it is imperative that preachers become adroit at understanding how figures of speech have been employed in the past and how they can now be used in preaching.

A helpful place to begin is to define the major figures of speech that were recognized by ancient practitioners of rhetoric and the preachers who followed them. As with any list of definitions, especially about the terms of language, nothing is absolutely precise and one figure of speech can often blend into another. Nevertheless, here is a basic repertoire of figures, all of which can be found in the Bible and all of which have been used in the history of preaching.

Hyperbole is an exaggerated form of speech, an overstatement. An example: " 'You strain out a gnat but swallow a camel' " (Matt. 23:24b).

Image is any term that evokes "sense-impressions by literal or figurative reference to perceptible or 'concrete' objects, scenes, actions, or states, as distinct from the language of abstract argument or exposition" (Baldick 1990, 106). Image is a broadly inclusive term that covers several of the figures listed below. An example: "Now you are the body of Christ and individually members of it" (1 Cor. 12:27).

Metaphor uses an image from one realm of thought or experience to stand for something else. Unlike *simile*, it does this without any intervening word of comparison. An example of metaphor: "The Lord is my shepherd" (Ps. 23:1). An example of simile: "He will feed his flock *like* a shepherd" (Isa. 40:11). The qualifier lessens the literalism of the comparison, creating a sharper consciousness of the joining together of different realities.

Metonymy is a figure of speech in which one term stands for another with which it is closely associated. For example, the "right hand of God" frequently stands in the Bible for God's power and authority.

Unlike all the other figures that are listed here, a *symbol* does not compare one discrete object to another or use one image to stand for another. A symbol usually is a visual sign—bread, wine, table, cross—that has an indeterminate number of meanings. For example, the church has been preaching about the cross for two thousand years but its meaning is not yet exhausted.

A symbol also can accrue different meanings and interpretations over time and may even awaken radically different meanings according to its context. Thus, the Bible associates water with the depths of chaos (Gen. 1:1, 2) as well as new life springing up within the believer (John 4:14).

This list does not begin to exhaust all the figures of speech found in scripture or the history of homiletics, but it is adequate to raising our awareness of how pervasive and effective figures of speech are to preaching.

It is important for preachers to become attentive to the figures that are present in the primary texts of scripture and of their tradition, especially the fixed prayers of their rituals and their most frequently used hymns. But it is also essential that preachers become aware of which figures their sermons and public prayers tend to favor and which they tend to exclude. Preachers have an obligation not to monopolize their congregation's religious imaginations with the limited repertoire of figures that are their personal favorites.

There are fundamental issues of justice and pastoral care at stake in the choice of figures. If images of darkness become the dominant expression of evil, then this casts aspersions on persons of color. If images of masculinity dominate the figures for God and humanity, then the full humanity of women is undercut. In sum, figures of speech are never *merely* figures of speech. By virtue of their vivid, memorable impact upon listeners they often become the chief carriers of theology, the theology that shapes the religious imagination of people and thus informs how they see the world and how they decide to act. One of the preacher's main rhetorical tasks is to provide figures of speech that expand the sense of God's compassion and justice, that strengthen the image of God in all people, and that stir listeners to deeper prayer and more faithful action.

Babin, P., and **M. Iannone,** *The New Era in Religious Communication,* 1991. **Baldick,**

C., *The Concise Oxford Dictionary of Literary Terms*, 1990. **Kennedy, G. A.,** *Classical Rhetoric and Its Christian and Secular Tradition from Ancient to Modern Times*, 1980. **Lakoff, G.** and **M. Johnson,** *Metaphors We Live By*, 1980. **Troeger, T. H.,** *Imagining a Sermon*, 1990. **Wilson-Kastner, P.,** *Imagery for Preaching*, 1989.

THOMAS H. TROEGER

Finney, Charles Grandison. (1792–1875) Finney enjoyed a wide and varied career as a teacher, lawyer, pastor, theologian, and college president, but he is best known as the father of American revivalism. He stands as the bridge between Jonathan Edwards* and Dwight L. Moody,* Billy Sunday* and Billy Graham.* If American theological thought resembles a series of footnotes to Edwards, then American evangelistic methods are a series of footnotes to Charles Grandison Finney.

Finney was born in Warren, Connecticut, and when he was two his family moved to central New York State. He acquired a high school education and then taught school in the area. In 1818, he enlisted as an apprentice in a law office. His legal textbooks frequently referred to the Mosaic law code. These references aroused enough curiosity in Finney to prompt him to purchase a Bible.

He attended the Presbyterian church in his community. Although Finney found the pastor's preaching boring and his rigid Calvinism unconvincing, in October 1821 he felt he must settle the question of his soul's salvation. One morning on his way to the law office, he turned aside into the woods at the edge of town. He knelt on the ground and wrestled with God throughout the afternoon. That experience was so profound that at an advanced age he could still recall the "waves of liquid love" that swept over his body.

His dramatic conversion changed his life. Finney gave up his legal career, convinced he had received a "retainer from the Lord Jesus Christ to plead his cause." He was ordained in 1824 as a Presbyte-

rian minister and commissioned as a missionary by the Female Missionary Society to a revival ministry among the settlers in the small towns of upstate New York.

In 1825, under his stern, rough preaching, a series of revivals* broke out in several small communities and in the larger towns of Utica and Rome, New York.

During these New York revivals, Finney used several "New Measures" that upset some of the established clergy. Particularly offensive were his practices of allowing women to pray in mixed gatherings; using an anxious bench at the front of the church—special seats for people who felt concern about their salvation; holding protracted meetings—daily services—rather than regular weekly meetings; employing colloquial language in sermons and in his prayers; pressing for decisions; and immediately admitting new converts into church membership.

Between 1827 and 1832 community-shaking revivals under Finney swept cities such as Philadelphia, New York, Boston, and Rochester; and news of his successes made headlines in both the religious and secular press. The evangelist emerged as the champion of revivalism. Lyman Beecher, an original opponent of Finney and his methods, later described the six-month Rochester revival as "the greatest work of God, and the greatest revival of religion, that the world has ever seen in so short a time."

Although Finney promoted and led revivals throughout his lifetime, even traveling to Britain for that purpose twice in the 1850s, those early years were the zenith of his revivalist ministry.

In 1832, forced to curtail his travels because of illness, Finney served briefly as the pastor of two congregations in New York City. His life then took another turn when he became professor of theology at Oberlin College in northeastern Ohio. He remained at the college for forty years until his death and served as its president from 1851 until 1866.

Charles Finney was a powerful preacher and a commanding presence in the pulpit. He took his legal training with him into ministry, and his preaching reminded listeners of a lawyer pleading a case in court. In contrast to most ministers of the period, who composed oratorical sermons supported with classical illustrations, Finney spoke extemporaneously in a conversational tone. His delivery was blunt, sometimes crude, always impassioned, and he hounded his audiences as a prosecuting attorney might press a jury. His "great searching eyes," witnesses reported, maintained unrelenting eye contact with his hearers.

Finney usually preached topical* sermons based on a single verse or phrase from the Bible. After introducing his text, he would announce the outline of his message and then go back and expound each separate point. His conclusions consisted of a series of as many as thirty somewhat disconnected ethical appeals or practical applications arranged under the general heading of "remarks."

In the body of his sermons, Finney often stressed the moral government of God, and in contrast to the severe Calvinism of his time, he emphasized the ability of every person to repent. He came to believe that human nature could be perfected and that converted men and women could change society and establish Christ's kingdom on earth. Christians must, therefore, apply their faith to daily living. In practical terms, this meant winning others to Christ and getting involved in causes such as temperance and antislavery. Finney did not believe that the cause of abolition should be a major focus of preaching, even though he so opposed slavery that he refused to serve communion to slave holders in his congregations.

More than a century after his death, historians and scholars still jeer or cheer Charles Finney. Critics blame him for introducing some of the more controversial techniques into mass evangelism.* His supporters reply that he did what he had to do to shake clergy and laity out of their apathy so that they would take the gospel seriously. One fact is certain: Charles G. Finney was an attorney pressing the case

for Jesus Christ, and he did whatever he thought necessary to win the verdict for his client.

Harman, K. J., *Charles Grandison Finney,* 1987. **Rosell, G. M.** and **A. G. Dupuis,** eds., *The Memoirs of Charles G. Finney,* 1989.
                                    HADDON ROBINSON

O, SINNERS!
Charles Grandison Finney
What infinite madness to rest on excuses which you dare not bring before God now? How can you stand before God in the judgment, if your excuses are so mean that you cannot seriously think of bringing one of them before God in this world? Oh, sinner, that coming day will be far more searching and awful than anything you have seen yet. See that dense mass of sinners drawn up before the great white throne—as far as the eye can sweep they come surging up—a countless throng; and now they stand, and the awful trump of God summons them forward to bring forth their excuses for sin.

Ho, sinners—anyone of you, all—what have you to say why sentence should not be passed on you? Where are all those excuses you were once so free and bold to make? Where are they all? Why don't you make them now? Hark! God waits; he listens; there is silence in heaven—all through the congregated throng—for half an hour—an awful silence—that may be felt; but not a word—not a moving lip among the gathered myriads of sinners there; and now the great and dreadful Judge arises and lets loose His thunders. O, see the waves of dire damnation roll over those ocean masses of self-condemned sinners. Did you ever see the judge rise from his bench in court to pass sentence of death on a criminal? There, see, the poor man reels—he falls prostrate—there is no longer any strength in him, for death is on him and his last hope has perished!

O, sinner, when that sentence from the dread throne shall fall on thee! Your excuses are as millstones, around your neck as you plunge along the sides of the pit to the nethermost hell!

> From Charles G. Finney, 1876. *Sermons on Gospel Themes* (Manchester: J. Robinson), 100.

Folk Preaching (African-American).

When a black preacher delivers a sermon in a traditionally folk manner, the first utterances are generally rendered in a normal speaking voice. As the sermon picks up momentum and rhythm and the congregation becomes involved in the preaching by giving affirmative responses, an atmosphere of heightened spirituality is corporately generated. In order for the preached word to keep pace with that heightening atmosphere of spirituality and for the delivery to express the surplus of spiritual meaning in the word that cannot be communicated through the speaking voice alone, the preacher may begin to chant or sing the sermon. As worship becomes even more spiritually excited and there remains spiritual surplus in the message that cannot be communicated by singing alone, the preacher will sometimes stop articulating altogether and commence "dancing the sermon." "Danced religion" is the height of worship in the traditional black religious experience. It reveals the kinship between African and African-American religious ritual.

Not all preachers who continue to practice the traditional black folk style of preaching go so far as to "dance" the sermon. But it is very common today to hear even academically educated black preachers maintaining the tradition of sermonic chanting or singing. Looking back at accounts of antebellum slave preaching documented in the journals and diaries of southern planters and their wives, we can see that a correlation has always existed between black folk preaching and the antebellum black spiritual. In fact, it is most probable that a substantial number of spirituals actually evolved through the preaching event of black worship. Although it is likely that, apart from wor-

ship, slave preachers and other individuals worked at "composing" the songs that later came to be called "spirituals," it is probable that the more frequent development of these folk songs came from extemporaneous preaching (and praying) that intensified little by little into intoned utterance. This melodious declamation, delineated into quasi-metrical phrases with formulaic cadence, was customarily enhanced by intervening tonal responses from the congregation. Responsorial iteration of catchy words, phrases, and sentences resulted in the burgeoning of song, to which new verses were joined. What facilitates this contemporaneous composing is that black sermons and prayers have been traditionally comprised of formulaic units that include repetition, extension, variation, sectional transition, tonal modulation, and thematic recapitulation.

Spirituals created in such a manner were likely remembered and perpetuated through oral transmission. There is no telling, then, how many of the spirituals sung in churches today might have spontaneously evolved out of the event of preaching in the antebellum "invisible" and institutional black church. What is certain, however, is that traditional black preaching is itself musical and shares in common with the spirituals certain melodic, rhythmic, and textural traits.

That which is variously referred to in contemporary black preaching circles as whooping, intoning, chanting, and tuning is none other than the *melody* that was heard in antebellum black preaching. This melody is made up of a series of cohesive pitches that have continuity, tonality, quasi-metrical phraseology, and formulary cadence. The principal melodic mode that from antebellum times continues to be employed by black preachers in their traditional "tuning" is the pentatonic, a scale common not only to uncountable black spirituals but also to African folk song.

Rhythm, which has always been a seminal element in African music and language, is the single ingredient that gives the melodiousness of black preaching its momentum. Scholars who have written on black preaching have generally concurred that rhythm is the fundamental musical component of this vocal genre. Black preachers who are knowledgeable of the spiritual and aesthetic value of traditional rhythmic usage generally seek to become skillful at fitting their sermonic phrases and sentences into quasi-metrical units. This is accomplished by squeezing together and stretching out words in the same way that modern rap artists do; they are the linguistic kin of black preachers. Preachers often simultaneously accompany this quasi-metered delivery of their text by striking the lectern or stomping the foot. Thus, the rhyme of traditional black preaching (like black rapping) includes kinetic, linguistic, and metric manifestations.

When the congregation participating in such a sermonic event gets involved in the rhythm of the preaching, the verbal responses coming from the congregation increasingly fall within the intervals where the preacher metrically pauses to take a breath. This call and response, a practice also rooted in African musical and verbal tradition, is a crucial texture found wherever traditional black oratory occurs. It is the responsorial event itself that is partly responsible for making black oratory so inspirational.

As a worship experience heightens in a responsorial setting, worshipers do more than simply acknowledge the preached word with "amen" and similar brief responses; they actually preach back to the speaker. As the inspiration continues to heighten, the exchange between a preacher and members in the congregation is often surpassed in musical intricacy by what is best described as a contrapuntal texture. This contrapuntal texture involves the preacher's intoned delivery weaving its way through a context of congregational response, response that is often itself tonal and melodic. The musical threads of the contrapuntal fabric may be so intricately interwoven that when a preacher dramatically breaks off the chant, a congregation-

al response is sometimes right there to complete the musical phrase and cadence. The intertwining of a congregation's sung phrases and nonarticulated sounds (moaning and humming) establishes a kind of symphonic musicality. Thus, traditionally black folk preaching, with its emphasis on African-rooted melodic, rhythmic, and textual patterns, can be best described as "sacred symphony" (see African-American Preaching).

Davis, G. L., *I Got the Word in Me and I Can Sing It, You Know: A Study of the Performed African-American Sermon*, 1985. **Mitchell, H. H.,** *Black Preaching*, 1970. **Rosenberg, B. A.,** *Can These Bones Live?: The Art of the American Folk Preacher*, rev. ed., 1988. **Spencer, J. M.,** *Sacred Symphony: The Chanted Sermon of the Black Preacher*, 1987.
                                      JON MICHAEL SPENCER

SERMON EXCERPTS
(From sermons preached by E. V. Hill, John R. Bryant, and Z. D. Harris, respectively.)

A Sleeping Church

As we drove on in the taxi,
We went by the Groovy Green
And the cars were ev'rywhere.
We came down Downing Street
And we passed two fights,
And all of the saloons were wide open.
A sleeping church and a roving lion
Is a bad thing for any town.
With the church resting
And the devil working,
This is not a safe town.

Sampson Died Alive

Sampson pushed and he pushed,
And the record said
   that the building collapsed,
And his enemies were destroyed;
And Sampson died.
But my brother and my sister,
His death was not a tragedy;
His death was a victory.
Sampson died alive;
I feel sorry for folk who died dead.
When I die, I want to die alive.

For those who die dead will die forever;
But those who die alive will live again.

Just Hold On

Let me lift the curtain of the future
And show you about my people.
They may suffer down here,
But I got a better place
  on the other side.
Ain't you glad about it.
So I wanna say to you:
  If trouble comes, just hold on.
  If trials come, just hold on.
  If darkness flow, just hold on.
God Almighty has promised you
That I will make a way.

From *Sacred Symphony: The Chanted Sermon of the Black Preacher* (New York: Greenwood Press, 1987), 106, 58, 114. © by Jon Michael Spencer. Used by permission.

Form. The issue of sermon *form* has to do with the way in which the content of a sermon is proportioned and arranged. A sermon's form is the shape given to the clay out of which the sermon is molded, the structure by which the material of the sermon is organized.

A preacher faces numerous questions about form in the creation of every sermon. How many sections, points, or moves should the sermon contain? Should the sermon be opened with a quotation from literature, a discussion of the biblical text, an illustrative story involving a personal experience, or the posing of a provocative ethical dilemma? Does the sermon flow best when patterned as a logical argument, as a narrative, or as a dialogue? Should the sermon remain open-ended, leaving matters somewhat unresolved at the finish, or should it tie things together, providing a firmly laced concluding summary?

All of these are examples of questions about the form of a sermon, and how such questions are answered makes a great difference in a sermon's overall impact. "The power of a sermon," observed homiletician and preacher H. E. Luccock, "lies in its structure, not in its decoration" (Luccock 1944, 118).

Controversies over Sermon Form. The issue of sermon form admittedly seems rather tame, even mundane, but it has actually been a chronic source of controversy throughout the history of preaching. This recurrent debate has been at once *theological*, focusing on the basic question of how appropriate it is for preachers to be concerned about a sermon's rhetorical form, and at the same time *practical*, asking more strategic questions about the principles involved in the construction of effective sermons.

On the theological side, there has always been the nagging suspicion, surfacing forcefully from time to time, that it is unbecoming, perhaps even faithless, for a preacher to allow the sermon in any sense to become a literary product, an object of art, and, thus, to be concerned in a significant way about the sermon's design. Since the purpose of a sermon is not to be beautiful, but to be faithful, not to draw attention to the preacher or to itself, but rather to point to the gospel, does it not follow that matters of form should be suppressed in favor of matters of substance? Witnessing to the gospel, some argue, is like water finding its own path as it flows across the land; it seeks its own natural forms and, therefore, sermon form ought to be so matched to the character of the gospel that it need not be a matter of planning or rhetorical tactic.

Advocates of this theological view often point to the example of the apostles and the gospel writers of the New Testament, claiming that they did not fret about such matters as points, divisions, illustrations,* or transitions. They had urgent news to tell, and they told it, the form of their telling springing forth from the nature of the news itself. Like a theater usher who discovers that the building is on fire and who needs no lessons in rhetorical form to point to the exit and cry, "Hurry! That is the way out!" a preacher needs only to be faithful to the gospel message. For the preacher of good news, function is all-consuming, and form follows function.

The problem with such arguments is that history will not fully support them. There is now considerable evidence that the writers of the New Testament were not at all indifferent to questions of form and poetics, but employed numerous literary and rhetorical strategies in their compositions. The texts of the Bible have been skillfully shaped to accomplish their purposes. Likewise, many of the earliest Christian preachers evidently patterned their sermons after those heard in the synagogue, which were quite cunning in terms of structural strategy and sophisticated in communicational design. From the very beginning, then, there has been a self-conscious artfulness in preaching. There never was any pristine period of unmeditated, intuitive witness, but from the outset preachers have been concerned not only with what to say but also with how to say it.

This is not to say that the argument against form is without merit. Indeed, it serves as a theological corrective and a reminder that questions about sermon rhetoric, including form, should not be made apart from the character of the gospel message. There are, to be sure, some forms more suited than others for proclamation. A sermon's form is not theologically inert; the shape of a sermon can be expressive of the gospel, but it can also undermine its message by being manipulative or deceptive or by serving as a magnet for its own artiness. "I swear," vowed Reinhold Niebuhr,* "that I will never aspire to be a preacher of pretty sermons. I'll keep them rough just to escape the temptation of degenerating into an elocutionist" (Niebuhr 1929, 15).

Indeed, the suspicion about sermon rhetoric, including form, emerges over and over in the history of preaching and, fortunately, seems to take hold precisely in those moments when it should, namely those seasons when sermon art has drifted dangerously close to artifice.

For example, no movement was more critical of a preacher's concern with sermon form than the neo-orthodox movement of the first half of the twentieth century. In one of his lectures on sermon preparation, Karl Barth* rejected most of the traditional homiletic categories having to do with form, including introductions, conclusions, and division of the sermon into sections or parts. "There is no need," he said, "to consider the problem of what should come first, second, and third. The preacher has only to repeat what the text says . . . " (Barth 1991, 121).

Barth's disavowal of communicational and formal concerns grows, of course, out of his larger theological conviction that human beings can do nothing to establish the freely given Word of God and should not attempt to do so (fiddling with the design of a sermon to make it more effective is a *prima facie* case of such human arrogance), but his position is also a reaction to the artsy, pious, and psychologically manipulative preaching of many of the preachers in the turn-of-the-century religious establishment. Barth was remaining consistent with his broad theological program, but he was also wagging his finger at some poor pulpit practice. Indeed, his view, as representative of a stream that flows through the history of the theology of preaching, works better as a correction of excess than as a prescription for normal practice.

Perhaps Augustine* struck the proper balance when he pointed to the excellence of the biblical writers in terms of their eloquence—their skills in matters of rhetoric, poetics, and form—and remarked that eloquence "seems neither lacking in them nor ostentatious in them" (Augustine 1958, 124). The same is true for Barth as a preacher. He was certainly not ostentatious in terms of the art of sermon language and form, but he was not lacking in that department either. Whether he would acknowledge it or not, even Barth's own sermons had form—introductions,* conclusions, structure—and decisions about such aspects of a sermon must be made according to some criteria.

Because this is true, homiletical literature has given much attention to the practical aspects of sermon form.

Traditional Structure: The Presentation of an Idea. Throughout the centuries, preachers have been extraordinarily inventive in regard to sermon form. Sermons can assume, and have, an almost endless variety of forms. Forms move in and out of fashion and, in any given era, there is a reciprocal relationship between those sermonic forms preferred by preachers and the forms in popular use more generally in public rhetoric.*

For example, the movement in American preaching after the Civil War toward storytelling forms, with sermons designed to feature experiential anecdotes, occurs simultaneously with the emergence of similar styles in the popular lectures given throughout the land in lyceums and Chautauquas and with the rise of the popular, romantic novel. While fashions change in regard to the popularity of types of sermon form, no single design formula can claim normative status.

Contemporary homiletics has been deeply attentive to the question of form, and homileticians have advanced many innovative proposals regarding sermon design. These can best be seen against the backdrop of what can be called the "traditional" approach to sermon form—that is, the style of sermon design that was in vogue in the first half of the twentieth century and prevailed in the homiletics classrooms and pulpits of the last generation.

Briefly, in the "traditional" approach a sermon's form is crafted on the basis of the assumption that the task of a sermon is to present to the hearers a clear elaboration of some important idea or thesis. Indeed, the sermon is often viewed as a kind of sustained argument, a logical case, for this central idea. In terms of sermon form, the implications of this assumption are fairly easy to see. The central idea of the sermon is divided into its essential parts, and these would become the major divisions, or points, of the sermon. These points are then further divided into subpoints and arranged according to some principle of internal logic (for example, moving from the lesser to the greater) to create the overall sermon design. This produces a sermon design, or outline, like the following:

Central Sermon Idea

I. First Point or Division
   A. Subpoint 1
   B. Subpoint 2
   C. Subpoint 3
II. Second Point or Division
   A. Subpoint 1
   B. Subpoint 2
III. Third Point or Division
   A. Subpoint 1
   B. Subpoint 2
   C. Subpoint 3

In this approach to sermon form, a good sermon design displays characteristics like the following (Abbey, 61–164):
1. *Unity*—Each of the points grows out of the central idea and serves to support it.
2. *Order and Proportion*—The points are fairly equal in terms of length and importance, and they are expressed in parallel construction.
3. *Movement and Climax*—There is a logical development from point to point resulting in a growing impact upon the hearers.

Though it has often been criticized for leading to predictable, "cookie cutter" sermon patterns (thus the old jokes about sermons with "three points and a poem"), the traditional approach to sermon form actually yields an impressive variety of sermon configurations.

One of the best treatments of the traditional approach to sermon form can be found in H. E. Luccock's classic textbook *In the Minister's Workshop* (Luccock 1944, 118–47), in which he discusses ten major types of sermon structure. What Luccock recognized was that the central idea of a sermon could be presented and organized around various logical patterns. A sermon could be arranged, for example, as a persuasive argument, each point of the sermon building reasonably upon the previous ones. Luccock named this structural type the "ladder" sermon, since the sermon invited the hearers to move from point to point, like climbing the rungs of a ladder. Or, again, the sermon could expose various facets of the central idea, one after the other (Luccock dubbed this the "jewel" sermon), or it could pose a question and ask the hearer to guess the answer. (Is it this? No. Is it this? No. Is it this other thing? Yes.) Luccock's name for this structure was the "chase" sermon.

In all, Luccock described nearly a dozen kinds of sermon forms, all variations of traditional rational argument. In addition to the "ladder," the "jewel," and the "chase," Luccock described the "skyrocket," "Roman candle," "classification," "analogy," "surprise package," and "rebuttal" sermons. Far from being predictable and uniform, the traditional approach to form, in skillful hands, produced a remarkable array of sermon structures.

Even though the traditional approach allowed for a multitude of variation, the constant that held them all together was the notion of the sermon as an idea, or proposition, and sermon form as the expression of the internal structure of that idea.

The Sermon as Organism: The Idea Grows. In 1958 the book *Design for Preaching* was published by H. Grady Davis,* a Lutheran professor of homiletics. Its appearance was notable in several ways. First, it was extraordinarily well received and influential, quickly becoming among the most widely used preaching textbooks in North American seminaries and divinity schools, a distinction it held for two decades. Equally significant, the volume was also almost entirely devoted to the question of form; other matters of sermon development received little or no attention in Davis's text. As such, *Design for Preaching* was the first raindrop in a fast-moving thunderstorm of homiletical books and monographs on sermon form. Attention to the category of

form, perhaps even preoccupation with it, is a mark of contemporary homiletical literature, and Davis's work was the precursor of this trend.

Design for Preaching was a bridge spanning the gap between the traditional approach to form and those developments yet to come. On the traditional side, Davis still described the sermon in ideational terms. "A well-prepared sermon," he claimed, "is the embodiment, the development, the full statement of a significant thought. . . . So it seems natural to speak of *the idea* of a sermon" (Davis 1958, 20).

Where Davis departed from the traditional approach—and where he made his original contribution—was in his understanding of the sermon as an "organism." To Davis, a sermon's structure was not simply the subpoints of a main point arranged in a logical sequence, as the traditional approach had maintained; it was a living unity, an organism with "parts or members in structural and functional relation to one another and to the whole" (Davis 1958, 23). Davis did not think of sermon form being created by dividing the main idea into its component parts; rather, he visualized the main idea of a sermon as a generative thought, growing a form like a seed producing a tree.

The traditional approach to sermon form suggested that any given sermon could take on one of a number of structures. A preacher could, for instance, imagine the same main idea being embodied in a "ladder" sermon or a "jewel" sermon or a "chase" sermon, to use Luccock's labels. Sermon forms could be tried on like sweaters. Not so with Davis. A sermon's "form is inherent in the idea itself," he argued. In other words, every sermon has contained in its central idea, like a DNA code, the pattern for its own ideal form. In Davis's view, good sermons are not given a form; they *take* form. Wise preachers do not force the sermon into a form; they discover the form embryonically present in the germinating idea.

Davis undeniably strengthened the practice of preaching through his notion of the organic unity of sermon form. He enabled preachers to think of sermon structures as totalities, each part interacting with all of the others. There was, however, something vaguely Platonic about this view. Davis's notion of pure forms shimmering inside sermon ideas was abstract, even ethereal. His vision of profound sermon ideas sprouting into ideal organic structures seems more suited to the greenhouse than to the backyard, where real sermons actually grow. What Davis gave to the field of preaching was a persuasive account of the union of substance and form in sermons. What is largely missing from Davis's equation, however, is the somewhat messier actuality of the listening context. Though he acknowledges, of course, that there are people out there listening to sermons, the way they listen—bending and reshaping the information that comes toward them, pushing the sermon through the grids of their own listening styles—was simply not a factor for Davis and thus counts for little in his theory of form.

It is, however, precisely to the hearer's side of the preaching moment and toward an understanding of how patterns of listening affect sermon form that homiletical theory moved after Davis. Davis was the bridge; homiletical theory has crossed over to the other side, and the primary category is no longer the structure of the idea, but the dynamics of the ear.

Sermon Form as Listening Event: Inductive Preaching.* In the late 1960s, affected by interaction with modern rhetoric and communication science, teachers of preaching began prompting their students to ask some new questions: What are the "shapes" of human listening, and how can the forms of sermons match those patterns? This way of posing the issue of sermon form constituted a revolutionary turn from the traditional approach. Instead of conceiving of a sermon as a solid mass of information needing to be arranged into an orderly system, now a sermon was considered to be a series of linguistic strategies designed by the preacher to produce a compatible listening event for the hearers. So, instead of

looking at a block of sermonic marble and seeing a beautiful sculpture already there waiting to be revealed, the preacher now wondered about others' expectations of beauty.

The metaphors employed to describe sermon form and design began to shift. Instead of solid and static concepts, such as sermon "construction" and "outlining," homileticians now began to speak more of the sermon "flow" and "movement." Sermon structures were less and less compared to buildings and more to kinetic events and those with arranged temporal progression, such as dance, symphonic music, and drama.

This change had theological as well as practical implications. Rather than understanding a sermon as an essay or a tightly constructed doctrinal argument, the emphasis fell upon the capacity of a sermon to create an event for the listener, to provoke at the ear an experience of the gospel. Suddenly, the rather nuts-and-bolts question of how to structure a sermon moved to center stage in the theology of preaching,* and word-event theologies, especially those with roots in the Reformation, were invoked to support various theories of sermon design.

A milestone in the literature of this period was the appearance in 1971 of Fred B. Craddock's* *As One Without Authority.* This little book, largely devoted to sermon form, was the leaven in the loaf, the timely yeast for a preaching movement ready to ferment. Craddock managed to pull together the threads from a variety of parallel developments in the preaching field, to add his own original contributions, and to state the issues in ways that connected to the concerns of preachers struggling to transform their preaching approaches. *As One Without Authority,* first modestly published by a small academic press, went through several editions, multiple printings, and remained in print for over twenty years.

In this book, Craddock's villain was the traditional approach to sermon form, which he termed "deductive" preaching. "Homiletically," he said in an apt and succinct description of the traditional approach, "deduction means stating the thesis, breaking it down into points or subtheses, explaining and illustrating these points, and applying them to the particular situations of the hearers" (Craddock 1971, 54). The problem with this, in Craddock's view, is what it does—or, more accurately, does *not* do—for the hearers. "There is no democracy here," he charged, "no dialogue, no listening by the speaker, no contributing by the hearer" (Craddock 1971, 55).

The way out of this dilemma, according to Craddock, was to introduce into sermon form an alternative pattern of movement, namely induction, which is congruent to the experience of listening. Instead of creating sermons with deductive movement (breaking a central idea down into smaller components and presenting these ideas systematically from the larger to the smaller—a logical pattern that does not reflect the way people really think, discover, and learn), preachers, Craddock urged, should employ inductive forms that reverse the logical flow by moving from the smaller to the larger. Deductive sermons state a claim and then defend it; inductive sermons build, piece by piece, toward a claim.

In a somewhat playful section of his book, Craddock even suggested turning traditional sermon structure on its head:

Instead of this *(deduction):*	*this* *(induction):*
I.	1.
	2.
A.	A.
1.	1.
2.	2.
B.	B.
1.	
2.	
	I.

In inductive preaching, the preacher doesn't announce a sermon's thesis at the beginning; preacher and hearer move together through the sermon to arrive at the sermon's insight at the end. Indeed, when skillfully done, the preacher doesn't actually finish the sermon at all; the hearers do. In a truly inductive sermon, Craddock argued, the listeners complete "the thought, movement, and decision-making within the sermon itself. The process calls for incompleteness, a lack of exhaustiveness in the sermon" (Craddock 1971, 64).

Craddock said that the very process by which preachers develop sermons is itself inductive. The preacher does not suddenly apprehend next Sunday's sermon on Monday morning. The preacher gathers bits and pieces of knowledge, plays hunches, follows trails, collects clues, tries out various possibilities, gradually building toward the culmination of the sermon. Craddock argued that effective sermon form results when preachers replicate imaginatively the movement of their own creative process in the sermon.

The idea that sermons could be built inductively was not new to homiletics; homileticians W. E. Sangster* and H. Grady Davis, among others, had described inductive logic as a sermon design possibility years before Craddock. Craddock, however, transformed induction from an abstract principle of internal sermon organization to a guiding concept built upon the phenomenon of human communication and experience. Indeed, the most important feature of Craddock's book, and of the trend in sermon form it represents, is the major role given to the psychology of listening. Craddock built his theory on an assumption about what is happening inside the heads of sermon listeners—that people think and pattern their experiences inductively—and preaching, therefore, should do the same. He claimed that "inductive movement in preaching corresponds to the way people ordinarily experience reality and to the way life's problem-solving activity goes on naturally and casually" (Craddock 1971, 66).

Beyond Induction: Narration and

Moving Pictures. It was almost inevitable that an interest in inductive preaching would lead to a passion for narrative* preaching. Preachers have always known the power of a good story, and the notion of the preacher as a "storyteller," relating biblical narratives and stories of revelatory human experience, found a natural companion in inductive theories of sermon form. A story moves from the lesser to the greater, just like inductive form. A story gradually builds toward a moment of disclosure; so does an inductive sermon. It was a short jump from the concept that effective sermons should be inductive and include stories to the more complex claim that through induction sermons could possess narrative structure—that is, they could have narrative *plots.* Through induction, preachers could not only tell stories in their sermons, they could also design their sermons to move *like* stories.

What does a plotted sermon look like? What is narrative form in preaching? One possibility, of course, is that the sermon itself is a story, a long and presumably complex version of a sermon "illustration." So-called "first person" sermons, in which the preacher takes on the role of a certain (usually biblical) character and then speaks autobiographically, would qualify as examples of this type of narrative form.

Homileticians, however, have usually pointed to quite a different conception of narrative form. Narrative sermons are not "story sermons"; they are sermons that have structures analogous to stories. "Sometimes when writers in the field of preaching speak of *narrative sermons,*" states Eugene Lowry, himself a proponent of narrative form, "people think they mean either, one, that every sermon ought to be chock full of stories, or, two, that every sermon ought to be one long story. But there is another option" (Lowry, 25). This other option is that sermons, instead of being divided into points or themes, consist instead in a sequence of dramatic movements leading toward a denouement.

How do narratives move? Simply put, narratives have beginnings (where the stage is set and something intriguing is introduced), middles (where matters become more complicated), and endings (where resolution is achieved or anticipated). So, too, for narrative sermons. In place of traditional points, narrative sermons have plot developments, beginning with the posing of a problem or a disclosure of some ambiguity in human experience, proceeding to explore that discrepancy, moving on toward a resolution, hopefully arrived at simultaneously by preacher and hearer. Lowry is somewhat more particular about the plot stages of a narrative sermon, claiming that sermons ought to follow the narrative sequence of "opening conflict, escalation, reversal, and proleptic closure" (Lowry 1989, 25).

Narrative sermon form, as described by Lowry and others, sometimes appears to be a version of an older and often-used sermon pattern, the "problem-resolution" sermon (describe a problem, explore its ramifications, disclose the resolution), and it shares certain affinities with the "law-gospel"* sermon especially favored in the Lutheran tradition (moving from a description of the human predicament—that is, the law—to the divine response of grace—namely, the gospel).

In a larger sense, both inductive and narrative preaching are seen to be aspects of a more general approach to sermon structure, one in which each portion of a sermon is designed to allow the sermon to interact with the hearers' listening tendencies and to make certain things happen in the consciousness of the listeners. David Buttrick elaborated this approach in his *Homiletic: Moves and Structures,* in which he develops what he calls a "phenomenological" approach to preaching, an approach built, in part, upon the phenomenon of human consciousness and the psychology of listening.

Buttrick's approach to sermon form, though uniquely his own, is in many ways typical of the prevailing view of form in contemporary homiletical theory. According to Buttrick, "Sermons involve an ordered sequence. . . . [and] are a movement of language from one idea to another, each idea being shaped in a bundle of words" (Buttrick, 23). Exegeting this theory-packed sentence, we find three major claims about sermon form:

First, Buttrick claims that sermon form is the embodiment of a logical sequence. That is, the components of a sermon are logically connected, each section of a sermon building upon all prior sections to accomplish its communicational impact upon the listeners. Thus, what Davis and Craddock criticized—the possibility of a sermon with three or four disconnected points, each hanging like a Christmas ornament from the limbs of the sermonic tree—Buttrick comes close to calling a communicational impossibility. Preachers may try to build sermons nonsequentially, but hearers don't process information that way. They hear this, and then they hear the next thing in the context of what they have just heard. Sermons will be heard in this orderly pattern, whether preachers realize it or not, and good sermons are formed to match this communicational fact of life.

Second, Buttrick claims that the sequence of a good sermon is not just orderly; it also exhibits movement. Sermon insights do not simply stand in single file, one after the other in a rational pattern; they move and develop, causing bursts of energy in the consciousness of the hearers. Indeed, Buttrick names the individual sections of a sermon "moves."

Finally, Buttrick develops what could be called the "quantum mechanics" of sermon form. In the same way that modern physics asserts that light consists both of particles and waves, Buttrick claims that sermon form is both movement and units of information. Even though there is sequence and movement in sermon form, it happens through packets or units of thought. Each idea is "shaped in a bundle of words," which causes the idea to register in the consciousness of the hearer, to make an image on the film of the hearer's mind.

Put together simply, Buttrick presents good sermon form as a sort of well-crafted filmstrip, moving sequentially and logically from frame to frame, each frame casting light on a key insight, all of the frames working together to achieve the total communicational impact of the sermon.

The emphasis in contemporary homiletics, then, in regard to form, is upon movement and experiential impact upon the hearer. Preachers are beckoned, not to arrange the information in a well-ordered outline, like a sophomore planning a term paper, but to the more demanding task of creating a communicational event for the ears of the listeners. Sermon form becomes more than the static mold into which the molten sermon material is poured; it becomes rather a communicational assembly line along which the sermon is progressively assembled in the minds of the hearers.

What is underplayed, of course, in the more recent understandings of sermon form is exactly what was emphasized in the traditional models: ideational content and didactic purpose. Ironically, the future may hold a renaissance of traditional sermon form as the pulpit increasingly faces a church unaware of its tradition and woefully lacking in knowledge of the basic content of the faith (see Reason; Sermon; History of Preaching).

Augustine, *On Christian Doctrine*, trans. D. W. Robertson, Jr., 1958. **Barth, K.,** *Homiletics*, 1991. **Buttrick, D.,** *Homiletic: Moves and Structures*, 1987. **Craddock, F. B.,** *As One Without Authority*, 1971. **Davis, H. G.,** *Design for Preaching*, 1958. **Lowry, E. L.,** *How to Preach a Parable: Designs for Narrative Sermons*, 1989. **Luccock, H. E.,** *In the Minister's Workshop*, 1944. **Niebuhr, R.,** *Leaves from the Notebook of a Tamed Cynic*, 1929.   THOMAS G. LONG

Forsyth, Peter Taylor.

(1848–1921) A Congregationalist minister and a "preacher's theologian," P. T. Forsyth has been called the first great evangelical of this century. Often thought of as a forerunner of Karl Barth,* he worked against the grain of the liberal theology of his day and pioneered what came to be known as "crisis theology." Born in Aberdeen, he attended university there, taking a semester off to study in Germany with Albrecht Ritschl. Afterward, he enrolled briefly at Hackney College, but fragile health forced him to withdraw. He was ordained in 1876 and served several important English churches before assuming the role of principal at Hackney College (now New College, London) in 1901. A prolific author, he produced twenty-eight books and hundreds of articles during his career.

Caught between the orthodox biblicism and the liberal optimism of his day, Forsyth bowed to neither. Instead he wrote a "positive" theology that focused on an objective view of the atonement, the centrality of grace, and the holiness of God. Athanasius, Paul, and the reformers were his chief influences and the power of the cross his favorite theme. In an age of great prosperity and optimism, an age caught up in belief in the inevitability of human progress, Forsyth wrote compellingly of sin and of humanity's inability to save itself:

Christ came to redeem us from our last strait; and this deep distress was neither blindness nor sickness of spirit, neither darkness nor disease—it was guilt. The difficulty was not our attitude to love alone—it was not coldness needing warmth—it was our treatment of holy love. . . . The redemption Christ brought was not from our stupidity, nor from our feebleness—it was from our sin (Forsyth 1949, 305).

The Power of the Cross. Forsyth's "positive gospel" focused on the work of the cross. He believed that God's full and final forgiveness, given for Christ's sake, is the source of every aspect of and all energy in the Christian life. Against those who argued that human achievement has a role to play in salvation or who saw Christ as some kind of cosmic ombuds-

man, Forsyth insisted that the atonement represents *God's* offering to humanity. Although he actually taught that the cross's action has two meanings, an act of God and "an act done in humanity," he emphasized the first, speaking of salvation as work that only God can do.

In Forsyth's view, sin (humanity's radical alienation from God's holiness) is atoned (covered) by God's own self-sacrifice. The relationship between God and humanity is restored as Christ, representing the human race, affirms God's holiness and accepts God's judgment. Forsyth's understanding of the power of the cross brings together three atonement theories: satisfaction theory, victory theory (or the "classic" view of the atonement), and regeneration theory.

Forsyth's gospel, theology, sermons, and lectures share a common method that can only be described as christological. For Forsyth, everything begins and ends with Christ. All knowledge (of self, God, and world) arises from the miraculous divine-human encounter that Christ makes possible, he believes. It is in the light of this encounter that human beings come to know God as "Holy Love" and themselves as "creatures of the will." (Forsyth prefers the category of "will" or "personality" to that of "mind" for describing what is essentially human.)

Against the relationalists of his day, Forsyth vigorously defended the right of theologians to use a method appropriate to the nature of their subject matter. He refused to accept the popular opinion that theology should seek to be more "scientific." "To begin with the world is to become dubious about the Word; whereas to begin with the Word is to become sure about the world" (Forsyth 1907, 249). So Forsyth reasoned from revelation, not philosophy, from God's decisive act in Jesus Christ, not from the Bible's words, and from the miraculous divine-human encounter, not from empirical evidence. The starting point of all of Forsyth's theory is a very personal claim based in his own mid-career "conversion" from the shallow liberalism of his day to what was to become neo-orthodoxy:

> It pleased God also by the revelation of his holiness and grace, which the great theologians taught me to find in the Bible, to bring home to me my sin in a way which submerged all the school questions in weight, urgency and poignancy. I was turned from a Christian to a believer, from a lover of love to an object of grace (Forsyth, 1907, 282–83).

The Power of the Word. It is not for nothing that Forsyth is often called the "preacher's theologian." His view of preaching, his homiletical theory and his homiletical skill, rank him as one of preaching's staunchest allies. To say that he held a "high view" of preaching is hardly saying too much. The first of his 1907 Beecher lectures began with these words: "It is, perhaps, an overbold beginning, but I will venture to say that with its preaching Christianity stands or falls."

Forsyth's "positive preaching" is, in origin, historical, sacramental by nature, and kerygmatic in character. Its purpose is the mediation of the Word of God. The theological principle of grace forms the core of such preaching. That is, what is mediated is personal, objective, and consistent with the nature of grace, and it is in this "objective personal content of faith" that the authority of preaching lies.

If Forsyth holds a high view of preaching and of preachers, he cannot be accused of undervaluing the role of the listener. "Every great true sermon is a great true sacrament . . . in which the people participate as really as the preacher. . . . On every such occasion those who hear in faith are not simply present, do not simply listen, they assist in the service" (Forsyth, 1899, 217–18).

"The preacher's theologian," a "prophet for today," a "Barthian before Barth," P. T. Forsyth is perhaps best remembered as a theologian of the cross whose theology "preached." Generations of preachers

owe him the underpinnings of their craft, and many owe him more (*see* Theology of Preaching).

Brown, R. McA., *P. T. Forsyth: Prophet for Today,* 1952. **Forsyth, P. T.,** *The Church and the Sacraments,* 1917, 1947; *Positive Preaching and the Modern Mind,* 1907, 1980; *Rome, Reform and Reaction: Four Lectures on the Religious Situation,* 1899. **Hunter, A. M.,** *P. T. Forsyth, Per Crucem ad Lucem,* 1974. **Miller, D. G.,** et al., *P. T. Forsyth: The Man, the Preacher's Theologian and Prophet for the Twentieth Century,* 1981.   JANA CHILDERS

THE EXCLUSIVENESS OF CHRIST
P. T. Forsyth

Nowhere apart from Christ do we find faith identical with the spirit of sonship, as a constant habit of new life. We find flights of aspiration and fits of faith, longing, guesses, glimpses, visions. But these are no more than, as it were, paying occasional calls. Faith is indwelling. It is living in the Father's house. It is constant, confidential intercourse. It is sonship as a standing relation habitually realised.

That is what Christ meant by coming to the Father. It is really coming into the Father, and going no more out. When we speak of a man coming to himself we do not mean only that he has occasional gleams of consciousness or sanity. So of coming to the Father. It means returning to a habitual state—not to gleams and glimpses, dotted over a great tract of life dark or unsure.

And in this sense of sonship, of coming to the Father, in its sense as a new life, it has not been had, and cannot be had, apart from Christ and His ever-living personality. "Through Me" means, not simply "by My acts, My words, My intercessions," but "through Myself, My personality," which *is* the revelation, the meeting place of God and man. . . .

I am afraid we must part with the idea that there is no narrowness in Christianity. There must be. We can only take care that it is the right kind. Strait is the gate and narrow the way that leads to life. . . .

The gospel is as narrow as Christ, and

Christ is as narrow as the Cross. It is not by a religious idea we enter in—either by a vague one or an exact one. Even an exact idea is not narrow enough. An idea, or even a truth of any kind, is a loose, vague thing compared with the existence of a person, a living soul and will. And it is by no idea or even sentiment of fatherhood, but by something so narrow as Christ's filial *will,* that we enter to the Father. That individual will, straitened to the Cross, is the one channel to a habitual life with the Father. That will, not imitated or reflected, but trusted. The way to the infinite God, the infinite Heart, the way to absolute *certainty* about it, and to continual *life* in it, is the narrow way of the historic man Jesus Christ crucified.

From "The Exclusiveness of Christ," in *Missions in State and Church: Sermons and Addresses* (Cincinnati: Jennings & Graham, 1918), 200–203.

Fosdick, Harry Emerson. (1878–1969)

Harry Emerson Fosdick was America's most prominent liberal Protestant preacher when religious liberalism knew its finest, though not unchallenged or unflawed, hour. Born in Buffalo, Fosdick was raised in a devout but not dour Baptist home. He graduated from Colgate, then studied at Hamilton Theological Seminary under William Newton Clarke, the leading liberal Baptist theologian. Hungry to know a wider world, Fosdick transferred to Union Theological Seminary in New York City. Barely surviving a first-year suicidal nervous breakdown, he graduated in 1904 with his earlier commitment to liberalism sealed.

Fosdick's first major pastorate at the First Baptist Church in Montclair, New Jersey, assured him local repute, and his national speaking engagements heightened his reputation, but his widening fame rested principally on six devotional books, especially *The Meaning of Faith* and *The Meaning of Prayer.* Collectively, these slim volumes enjoyed scores of reprintings, translation into over fifty languages, and millions of sales, meriting for

him a place in the pantheon of gifted Christian apologists. Called to a professorship at Union in 1915, for the next three decades he quickened the minds and honed the preaching skills of several generations of grateful students. His three major books of progressive biblical scholarship, drawing on his Union lectures, may now seem dated, but they were enormously influential in their day, especially to laypersons and "working" parsons who appreciated the accessibility of *The Modern Use of the Bible, A Guide to Understanding the Bible,* and *The Man from Nazareth.* Fosdick's pioneering of psychological pastoral counseling resulted in the best-selling *On Being a Real Person.* The horrors he witnessed during a half-year tour of duty in France with American doughboys in 1918 converted him to a pacifism that remained unshaken even by Pearl Harbor. Returning from France, Fosdick accepted an invitation to become Preaching Minister of New York's historic First Presbyterian Church. In 1922, Fosdick felt driven to preach his most famous and provocative sermon, "Shall the Fundamentalists Win?" which was distributed, thanks to the largess of John D. Rockefeller, Jr., to every ordained Protestant minister in the country. He immediately became the central symbolic figure in both the Presbyterian and the Baptist escalating denominational wars pitting fundamentalists (or conservatives) against modernists (or liberals or moderates). Unwilling to accept an "invitation to become a Presbyterian or permit the continued racking of the First Presbyterian congregation," in 1925 he accepted a call from the Park Avenue Baptist Church with the understanding that the congregation, led by Rockefeller, in time would erect a great new interdenominational sanctuary. In 1931, the Riverside Church on Morningside Heights was raised, and from its pulpit and from guest lecterns worldwide and over the National Vespers Radio Hour, Fosdick's voice, year after year, reached millions of perplexed believers and inquiring unbelievers. He also reached audiences as author or editor of nearly fifty books and a thousand printed sermons and articles. Additionally, the hymns he composed became beloved, notably "God of Grace and God of Glory."

Fosdick believed that by keeping faith and reason in creative tension it was possible to be a Christian in the twentieth century without throwing one's mind away, and he wished to help others make that same discovery for themselves. Despite the epithet "Modernism's Moses" volleyed at him by conservatives, he in fact belongs within the evangelical tradition, warming and winning the hearts of thousands, giving point to Rabbi Stephen S. Wise's thoughtful judgment: "Fosdick—the least hated and best loved heretic that ever lived." In a real sense, throughout his ministerial career, Fosdick preached from a single text: though astronomics (theologies) change, the stars (faith) abide. It was his historic mission to be the faithful's guide to the new astronomies while convincing doubt-plagued souls that the stars abide. Even while seeking to touch the hearts and quicken the minds of his audiences, Fosdick sought to spark their consciences as well. In full agreement with Rauschenbusch's* dictum, "We rarely sin against God alone," his preaching placed under God's judgment the sins of racism, hunger, exploitation, greed, and, for Fosdick, the supreme evil, war.

As a servant of the word, Fosdick was aware of the awfulness of his commission, and never long absent from his consciousness was Paul's anguished cry, "For necessity is laid upon me. Woe to me if I do not preach the gospel." Legend has it that he spent one hour of preparation for each minute of sermon delivery—and in this case, legend approximates the fact. He kept his morning hours sacrosanct from intrusive invasion, and during these sternly guarded hours he read and wrote with intense concentration, agreeing with J. H. Jowett's* warning, "If the study is a lounge, the pulpit is an impertinence." Long periods each summer were spent in an isolated study on his Maine island re-

treat. He was a voracious reader of wide-ranging material. Biography was a clear favorite and, of necessity, also heavy works of biblical scholarship and theology. Still, he excessively conned jejune material for homiletic purposes and, as all preachers do, borrowed illustrations from the sermons of others. Although his memory was near-photographic, he prudently marked up books he read and filed sermonic materials in crammed notebooks made accessible by an elaborate index. Fosdick judged pastoral counseling essential to preaching, providing him with "clairvoyance" into the hopes and fears of worshipers in the pews. Inevitably, of course, Fosdick drew from his personal experiences. To be sure, if a preacher refuses to glean ideas from books, he will probably be guilty of solipsism; yet there is an aridity about ideas known only objectively, never existentially. But aside from his breakdown at Union and the scenes of hell on the Western Front and the tragedies afflicting kin, his life was blessed. Until his death he enjoyed honors, family love, obedience, troops of friends and admirers. There were terrors and tears of existence foreign to his own life and, therefore, perhaps inevitably, unsounded in his sermons. Many passages might be cited from his sermons to evince his tragic sense, but there is, finally, an irreducibly sunny, nostalgic, Norman Rockwell cast to his preaching and a late-Victorian aura to his moral pronouncements.

Unlike some preachers, Fosdick prepared his sermons week by week; he did not have a comfortable backlog, and this insecurity was a matter of some anxiety. (Also, only rarely did he preach the same sermon more than once—this, too, compounding his labors.) Usually the sermon preparation was begun on Monday morning and completed by noon Friday. Without exception, every word of every sermon was handwritten with meticulous care and many corrections. "I do not see how," he observed, "anyone can keep strength of thought and the variety of language and illustration if he does not discipline himself to the severe task of writing everything he says." On Saturday morning he sat down to rethink the whole sermon as if the congregation were before his eyes so that he might honor the prayer he once lifted up: "Whoever stands in a pulpit, bless thou his spirit and touch his lips with a coal from off the altar that he may speak thine everlasting gospel, carrying the truth far into the hearts and consciences of those who hear." At the outset of his career, Fosdick prided himself on not taking any scrap of paper into the pulpit. One Sunday his vaunted memory failed him, and he began the practice of arming himself with an outline, having reviewed the written manuscript until it was in his mind and heart. In later years he decided to experiment with a full manuscript before him, in the hope that it would take less out of him in delivery. The experiment was a success, for as he explained, "Just as one can *write* for listeners, so one can *read* for listeners, combining the advantage of a manuscript's careful preparation with the freedom of face-to-face address" (*see* Preparation; Manuscript Preaching).

If Lincoln in fact admired the preacher who looked like he was fighting a swarm of bees, he would not have been happy in Fosdick's churches. His posture was soldierly. The gestures were few and restrained, the hands gripping the folds of the robe. Never did he point a finger at the hearers because it suggested scolding. Occasionally, he lifted a single arm to drive a point home or extended forward an open, upturned, inviting hand. His eyes maintained a very direct contact with the audience. Rather than turning the pages of the manuscript, he slipped them across, one on top of the other, to avoid giving the impression of reading. His facial expressions were restrained, but never masklike, and they conveyed his emotions perceptibly, especially through his habit of snapping his teeth down on his lower lip. The voice was not the rotund, rich, or melodious voice of the "orator." In fact, it was hoarse, raspy, metallic, with a kind of vibrato. But at least the

pronunciation was clear, the articulation exact, and the voice carried well. His whole being radiated an intense aura of *disciplined* power.

Fosdick once described the "essential nature of the sermon as an intimate, conversational message from soul to soul." His statement misleads. He was too much the evangelist, too much concerned to preach for a verdict, to preach so cozily. Vigor, vividness, drama, power, warmth, concreteness, and beauty are all there. He favored strong, hearty Anglo-Saxon words and eschewed technical ones. Gritty colloquialisms, epigrammatic flashes, and gnomic flavoring kept the listener on the alert. Fosdick shunned the bombastic but not the impassioned. Who converses in the splendid diction of the rolling periods he employed? Who in conversation gives voice to these hallmarks of a Fosdick sermon: "O my soul!", "Ah, Jerusalem," "For see!", "Ah Christ!", "Aye!", "O knightly youth!"? Yet perhaps "intimate conversation" is not entirely misleading, for other hallmarks of a Fosdick sermon are: "Friend, listen," "But, my friend, that does not account for the facts," "Let us say this to ourselves!" "There may be someone here who . . . ," "We are to think together today . . . ," "I speak to someone like this today as though we two were alone in this church."

Fosdick's people wanted dignity and reason in the sermons of their minister, and in that sense they were modernists; but they were also heirs of nineteenth-century evangelism in that they did not want these qualities at the expense of a heartwarming experience. The ultimate court of appeal for every Christian remained this: "Whereas once I was blind, now I see." The essence of Fosdick's appeal is that his sermons helped bewildered people in the first half of a whirling and calamitous century to open their eyes and hearts without insisting that they close their minds (*see* History of Preaching).

Crocker, L., ed., *Harry Emerson Fosdick's Art of Preaching: An Anthology*, 1971.

Fosdick, H. E., *The Living of These Days*, 1956. **Miller, R. M.**, *Harry Emerson Fosdick: Preacher, Pastor, Prophet*, 1985.

ROBERT MOATS MILLER

CHRIST IS CHRISTIANITY
Harry Emerson Fosdick

This Christmas season finds us a rather bewildered human race, facing a confused world, man's wild behavior dangerously out of control. No neat formula from anywhere can solve our problems or allay our anxiety, but today we turn to one man in the New Testament who lived in an age not unlike our own, and who carried on with hope and confidence. He wrote the letter to the Hebrews. In his time, too, the world was shaken. . . . Confusion reigned, and as for his own people, only a few years before he wrote Jerusalem had been laid waste, the Holy Land desolate, its population slain or scattered. . . . [But the writer] adds the affirmative factor that for him changes the whole perspective of his outlook: "What we do see is Jesus. . . . "

In saying this the writer was not turning from realistic facts to a beautiful ideal; he was turning from one set of facts to another fact. Jesus, too, was a fact. He had actually come. That life had been lived. If we are to base our lives on facts, must we not take that fact in too? As this writer saw him, Christ was a towering, challenging, revealing fact, and to see him changed his whole outlook on life. On the threshold of our Christmas season we try today to share that experience. . . .

In all confused eras such as this, what does human nature do? It always looks, not so much for something as for someone to believe in. So Germany believed in Hitler and said, He is the answer! So Italy believed in Mussolini and said, He is the answer! We say that people believe in imperialism, nationalism, democracy, communism, and all the rest. Granted! We need not belittle the importance of these abstract beliefs. But we never get to the bottom of the matter until we see how inevitably we humans believe at last, not in isms but in incarnations. It is they who make abstractions real and powerful. Re-

member Marshal Foch's saying, "It was not an army that crossed the Alps; it was Hannibal."

Christmas means this at least: a personality has come into the world concerning whom millions believe that he is the answer. Even Paul never said, I know what I have believed. The mystery of life so deep, the confusion of the world so great, he sometimes did not know what he believed. What Paul said went deeper: "I know him whom I have believed." That is Christianity! . . . I am inviting you to see Christ . . . and so seeing him, to say, He is the answer! Cannot we see whither the contrary answers are plunging the whole world now? He is the answer! That is the everlasting truth!

From "Christ Himself Is Christianity," in *On Being Fit to Live With* (New York: Harper & Brothers, 1946), 185–93.

Francis de Sales. (1567–1622)

Francis de Sales was a Roman Catholic bishop, spiritual director, and leader in the Counter-Reformation. The child of minor French nobility, he studied law in Paris and Padua in preparation for a life of high public office. After being admitted to the bar, he had a spiritual experience that confirmed his longstanding sense of religious vocation, and he abandoned his secular career for the priesthood. He rapidly became known for both his diplomacy and his piety and was consecrated Bishop of Geneva in 1602. His friendship with Jeanne Frances de Chantal led him to found the Visitandines, a contemplative order for women, to which he remained a mentor and spiritual father.

Francis was active during one of the lowest points in the history of Christian preaching. The Counter-Reformation produced few noteworthy, much less great, preachers. In fact, it has been suggested that even Francis might be revered more for his piety and earnestness than for his preaching. Nonetheless, preaching was central to his ministry and was the means by which he sought to carry out what he believed to be the most pressing part of his work: winning back Geneva from the Calvinists. His method was not to preach explicitly against Calvinism but simply to preach with love, believing that to be a more powerful weapon than the denunciation of heresies. In this he enjoyed much success, being credited with 8,000 conversions in one two-year period.

Francis's understanding of homiletics is set forth in a letter of advice to a friend written in 1604 and published after his death under the title *On the Preacher and Preaching*. This letter makes clear that the person of the preacher played a crucial part in Francis's view of preaching. Personal faith is fundamental to being a good preacher, he argued: "Our Lord did not ask St. Peter, 'Are you learned or eloquent?' in order to tell him, 'Feed my sheep,' but 'Do you love me?' To love well is sufficient for speaking well." The preacher must not only be free of mortal sin but must avoid even certain venial sins, such as drinking or hunting, which might give the appearance of moral laxity.

But Francis did not reject all concern with technique in preaching. He was solidly traditional in insisting that sermons must begin from and focus upon scripture. His interpretive method used the classical fourfold approach of looking at a text literally, allegorically, anagogically, and tropologically. Having studied rhetoric* and the humanities as a young man, Francis did not hesitate to employ them as tools in service to delivering his message. He urged the use of illustrations from various sources including the church fathers, the lives of the saints, and events from history. While he saw illustrations as an important way to shed light on the subject, he warned that the preacher needed to avoid "worthless, flabby descriptions" and should beware of long quotations from the fathers. Quotations that were used, if given in Latin, should always be repeated in French, or they would be of no value to the people.

Preaching had two goals as Francis understood it. Following tradition again, he saw the function of a sermon as first to instruct and then to move. That is, the first half of a sermon should enlighten the intellect, while the second half should contain affective passages to stir the will. While acknowledging that some believed preaching to have a third goal, that of delighting, Francis disagreed at least in part. Delight, he argued, is valuable only as it follows upon learning and the movement of the will. It should never be sought purely as a response to technique.

To someone just entering upon the ministry of preaching, Francis offered simple advice on how to learn, saying that "Preaching makes preachers."

CATHERINE A. ZIEL

Franciscans. The Franciscan movement is composed of a variety of communities of men and women, religious and secular, who find their inspiration in the life and teaching of Francis of Assisi (1182–1226) and Clare of Assisi (1193–1253). Francis underwent a dramatic conversion, which led him to turn from ambitions for glory and fame to identify with the suffering humanity of Jesus Christ in the embrace of a leper and to receive a mission from the cross to rebuild the church that was falling down. In the process, Francis was joined by men who desired to associate their life with his, discovering together their rule of life in the life of the gospel. Innocent III gave verbal approval to Francis's and his brothers' way of life in 1209, including with his approval a mandate to preach penance to all.

Clare had been living a penitential life in the home of her parents when the example of Francis's conversion gave direction to her own religious yearning. On Palm Sunday in the year 1212, Clare left her home and joined Francis and the brothers at the little chapel of the Portiuncula, where she was received into their community. Eventually she would be joined by other women including members of her own family. They took up residence at the church of San Damiano, living a life of poverty, humility, and care for one another, their life together providing a vivid example of gospel living.

By 1217, the young order of brothers undertook mission expeditions into Hungary and Germany and rapidly spread beyond the borders of Italy throughout both western and eastern Europe. In 1219, Francis traveled to Syria in the hope of winning martyrdom—the highest form of imitation of Christ—at the hands of the Saracens. Present in the crusaders' camp and witnessing the defeat of the Fifth Crusade in the summer of 1219, Francis made his way to the camp of the Sultan, Melek el Kamel, who was struck by the example of this simple Christian man. Francis's positive impression on the Sultan won him and his brothers safe passage in Muslim territory with the condition that they not preach against the Prophet Mohammed.

Upon his return to Assisi, Francis and the brothers worked on finalizing the Rule, which was approved by papal bull on November 29, 1223, by Honorius III. Eventually Francis would retire from leadership of the movement and concern himself with providing an example of gospel-living, modeling Franciscan life for his brothers.

From the outset, Francis's chief intention was to live the gospel by "following in the footsteps of Jesus Christ," as he would write in the Rule. This life of poverty, humility, and simplicity in imitation of Christ impacted both the style and content of early Franciscan preaching. Employing gesture and symbolic actions in the proclamation of the gospel—Francis himself danced while he preached before the pope—the Franciscan sermon aimed at capturing the attention of the listener so that the words might penetrate to the heart, thus effectively engaging the whole person in the message. The most famous sermon of Francis's is his Canticle of Brother Sun, which he had the brothers set to music so that it might be sung as they traveled about the world. When sung in the presence of the bishop and mayor of Assisi, who were engaged in a bitter

feud, it immediately touched their hearts and effected reconciliation.

Unlike Dominic and his brothers, for whom poverty and a simple lifestyle were primarily the means for legitimating a preached message, for Francis and his brothers, poverty and a simple lifestyle were the message, and the life itself preached (see Dominicans). Even though not every brother would be authorized to preach theological sermons, Francis insisted that all the brothers preach through their deeds. Since all the brothers worked with their hands in order to support themselves, they were in close contact with lay men and women in the world on a daily basis, and in this context preaching by example was most effective.

By the time Bonaventure became general minister of the brotherhood in 1257, the office of preaching was already clericalized. Since the purpose of preaching was conversion of life and repentance, the full effect of the sermon was its completion in sacramental confession. The effect was to limit the preaching office to the ordained brothers. Even with this development, however, Franciscan preaching through the centuries continued to be characterized by its simplicity (closeness to ordinary human experience), concreteness (examples taken from observable behavior and the natural processes of creation), immediacy (the engaging of the imagination to picture the real possibility for change within the given social and economic context and limits), and affectivity (direction to the heart so as to move the will to action).

Franciscans produced their own model sermon collections, beginning with the first and most famous of Anthony of Padua (d.1231), whose Sunday and Feastday Sermons is still extant. A very popular and influential text in the later middle ages was the fourteenth-century Meditations on the Life of Christ, now attributed to the Franciscan John of Caulibus. Bonaventure himself taught theology to the friars at the University of Paris with the clear purpose of preparing them for their preaching ministry. His gospel commentaries, especially his *Commentary on the Gospel of Luke*, are a classic example of how the exegetical skills of his day were marshaled for the purpose of preaching the Word of God. Other famous Franciscan preachers include Bernardino of Siena (1380–1444) and John of Capistrano (1386–1456) in the fifteenth century.

The ministry of preaching continues to be central to the Franciscan mission today in various settings such as the liturgy, retreat work, and parish missions. Today Franciscans employ modern means of communication such as television, radio, and other media, including the graphic and performing arts, in order to further their mission of preaching the gospel in word and example.

Armstrong, R., and I. Brady, *Francis and Clare: The Complete Works*, 1982. d'Avray, D. L., *The Preaching of the Friars: Sermons Diffused from Paris Before 1300*, 1985. Lesnick, D. R., *Preaching in Medieval Florence: The Social World of Franciscan and Dominican Spirituality*, 1989. Manselli, R., *St. Francis of Assisi*, 1985. Short, W. J., *The Franciscans*, 1989.

MICHAEL W. BLASTIC, O.F.M. Conv.

Funeral Sermon.

Funeral Sermon. The tendency of some pastors and priests to omit the preaching of the word from the funeral liturgy is a candid admission of the difficulty of preaching in this context. In some Christian traditions it has been common to rely on the liturgy alone for help and comfort. Psychologically, it is clear that survivors are shaken by their loss and attend to the sermon with difficulty. Attention spans are short. Listener expectations in some churches, such as the desire to have the pastor "preach the person into heaven," further "load" the occasion. The leave-taking that sometimes concludes the liturgy may preoccupy mourners. Finally, it is difficult to preach effectively when either the deceased or the mourners (or both) are strangers to the preacher.

At the same time, the recognition that a sermon is integral to a complete worship service has become normative for most Christians. These persons will feel cheated and offended if the sermon is omitted. They know instinctively that funeral preaching is therapeutic in purpose—that is, it aims to heal those who hear and believe. Effective funeral sermons sustain and support the bereaved psychologically while communicating the gospel, which heals at the deepest levels. Specifically, the announcement of the victory of Jesus Christ over death and the grave is the fundamental good news for those who have lost someone through death, and only the proclamation of this gospel can enable survivors both to face the reality of death and to hope for the new life God has promised.

Designing the Funeral Sermon. As with any sermon, one can begin with biblical text or human situation. It is axiomatic that both should be taken seriously. While the good news of Jesus' triumph over death can be proclaimed apart from a particular biblical text, the text gives the message authoritative roots and concrete focus. While the human situation may not be overt in some other types of sermons, a particular group of grieving mourners is the obvious audience of the funeral sermon.

How does the funeral sermon negotiate between the reality of death and the hope of resurrection and new life? One reality is that mourners are preoccupied with thoughts of the dead loved one. Minds drift back to the death itself. The coffin may be open before them. Listeners are ready to hear about their loved one. Using the person's name while recounting a few significant events and activities of the deceased, of course without embellishment, helps to establish a firm sense of reality.

Another important reality is the particular emotions and questions of mourners. To take these seriously in the sermon, it must first be asked what these immediate survivors are feeling and thinking. Are they angered at the circumstances or suddenness of death? If so, likely targets of blame are God, particular caregivers, the deceased, or even themselves. Self-condemnation will be experienced as guilt. Mourners will wonder what they did to deserve this loss or if they were responsible in some way for the loved one's death. Typically, depression evokes questions of God's absence, while other emotions have their own attendant questions. The pastor will listen actively in an attempt to address real concerns.

Of course, while proclamation may begin with the reality of death and grief, the heart of any sermon should testify to God's gracious activity. A helpful way to avoid eulogy and shape the sermon around a single issue is to initiate sermon design with the question *What is God doing here?* The answer, framed as a crisp declarative sentence, focuses on God's activity. Thus God, Christ, or the Holy Spirit should be the subject of the sentence. Action centers on the verb. What is God saying or doing, first in the text and then today? Likewise, God's activity has a particular referent in both past and present tense. For the sermon, it is crucial to underscore what God is doing *here*, in this specific situation of loss and grief. For example, the theological message of Luke 24:13–35, the story of bereaved disciples on the road to Emmaus, might address the loss of a close friend in this way:

> In the situation of the loss of Robert, the risen Christ comes to despairing friends on the way, revealing himself in word and meal, and strengthening them in the community of the church.

Though this sentence will never appear in the funeral sermon, it both focuses the message and provides a possible progression.

The first major move of this sermon might well focus on the death of a friend and the hopelessness of the mourners. The situation of Jesus' friends ("We had hoped that he was the one to redeem Israel") has an obvious counterpart in the feelings of Robert's friends. The second major design element in the sermon would center on the surprising presence of Christ in the midst of grief, by means of word and meal, and the consequent re-birth of hope within the community of believers. Certainly other design elements are possible, but this sequence underscores the good news of Christ's vital and renewing presence.

Experienced pastors testify to the power of images to break through the bewilderment of grief and to linger in the minds and imaginations of the bereaved. Persons who are dazed find it easier to see pictures than to follow rational arguments. In this passage, the image of a lonesome road or the positive images of sacred text and sacred meal offer homiletical possibilities. Persons who find it difficult to attend, who flit in and out of even short messages, find a helpful continuity in a centering image that recurs throughout the sermon.

The funeral sermon is most effective as a key public response in a continuing pastoral relationship. Significant contact with bereaved persons, both before the funeral and following it, give the sermon a pastoral as well as a liturgical context and enhance the possibility that the word will take root and grow (*see* Pastoral Care and Preaching).

Hughes, R., *A Trumpet in Darkness: Preaching to Mourners,* 1985.

ROBERT G. HUGHES

ALEX'S DEATH
William Sloane Coffin, Jr.

As almost all of you know, a week ago last Monday night, driving in a terrible storm, my son Alexander—who to his friends was a real day-brightener, and to his family "fair as a star when only one is shining in the sky"—my twenty-four-year-old Alexander, who enjoyed beating his old man at every game and in every race, beat his father to the grave.

Among the healing flood of letters that followed his death was one carrying this wonderful quote from the end of Hemingway's *Farewell to Arms:* "The world breaks everyone, then some become strong at the broken places." My own broken heart is mending, and largely thanks to so many of you, my dear parishioners; for if in the last week I have relearned one lesson, it is that love not only begets love, it transmits strength.

Because so many of you have cared so deeply and because obviously I've been able to think of little else, I want this morning to talk of Alex's death, I hope in a way helpful to all.

When a person dies, there are many things that can be said, and there is at least one thing that should never be said. The night after Alex died I was sitting in the living room of my sister's house outside of Boston, when the front door opened and in came a nice-looking middle-aged woman, carrying about eighteen quiches. When she saw me she shook her head, then headed for the kitchen, saying sadly over her shoulder, "I just don't understand the will of God." Instantly I was up and in hot pursuit, swarming all over her. "I'll say you don't, lady!" I said. (I knew the anger would do me good, and the instruction to her was long overdue.) I continued, "Do you think it was the will of God that Alex never fixed that lousy windshield wiper of his, that he was probably driving too fast in such a storm, that he probably had had a couple of 'frosties' too many? Do you think it is God's will that there are no streetlights along that stretch of road, and no guardrail separating the road and Boston Harbor?"

For some reason, nothing so infuriates me as the incapacity of seemingly intelligent people to get it through their heads that God doesn't go around this world with his finger on triggers, his fist around knives, his hands on steering wheels. God is dead set against all unnatural deaths. And Christ spent an inordinate amount of time delivering people from paralysis, insanity, leprosy, and muteness. Which is not to say that there are no nature-caused deaths (I can think of many right here in this parish in the five years I've been here), deaths that are untimely and slow and pain-ridden, which for that reason raise unanswerable questions, and even the specter of a Cosmic Sadist—yes, even an Eternal Vivisector. But violent deaths, such as the one Alex died—to understand

those is a piece of cake. As his younger brother put it simply, standing at the head of the casket at the Boston funeral, "You blew it, buddy. You blew it." The one thing that should never be said when someone dies is, "It is the will of God." Never do we know enough to say that. My own consolation lies in knowing that it was *not* the will of God that Alex die; that when the waves closed over the sinking car, God's heart was the first of all our hearts to break.

Preached on January 23, 1983, at Riverside Church, New York City.

Garnet, Henry Highland. (1815–1882) Presbyterian minister, orator, teacher, political activist, and writer, Garnet was born in the dismal web of slavery in New Market, Kent County, Maryland. He was the grandson of a Mandingo prince, a slave named Joseph Trusty. At the age of nine, Henry and his family escaped slavery, arriving finally in New York City. In the North, Henry attended a host of "experimental" schools set up to integrate slaves into the larger society and to prove the capabilities of Africans for intellectual advancement. From his matriculation at the New York African Free School through his time at the New York City High School for Colored Youth, and the Noyes Academy in Canaan, New Hampshire, to his completion of studies at the Oneida Theological Institute, Garnet learned the cultural importance and political purpose of education. During his early years, there was an attempted recapture of his family. This event, along with his physical disability (a diseased and later amputated leg), helped to solidify the character of his life and preaching. Both were shaped in the crucible of slavery and the painful struggle to make free all enslaved Africans.

Raised with Alexander Crummell as a close friend, Garnet also knew from his youth such notables as George T. Downing, Isaiah De Grasse, Ira Aldridge, and James McCune Smith. Long noted for his association with re-emigration impulses in America, Garnet was an eloquent spokesman for an emerging black nationalism. Garnet's radical positions in these areas, along with his advocacy of John Brown and his opposition to many of the positions of Frederick Douglass and William Lloyd Garrison, show his keen intellectual vitality.

Garnet's contributions to preachers, the field of homiletics, and the church must be seen at two levels: materially and formally. Materially, he combined keen analytical skills, eloquence in oratory, and a high level of cultural refinement to establish himself not only as a brilliant debater but also as one of the preeminent preacher-speakers of his generation. Celebrated for his oratorical cunning, he was a master of repartee, which was essential for public debate, given the great danger in speaking against not only slavery but the concomitant forms of oppression surrounding that hated institution. In the face of slave society and racial oppression, Garnet exemplified an oratorical style that was an apologetic for African-American intelligence and a polemic against the violence inflicted upon Africans in the new world. Clothed in a rhetorical genius matched by few, Garnet's was a radical political vision. He demonstrated the need for mastery of the intellectual forms of public discussion as a basis for effective preaching and speaking. He also showed the importance of cultural awareness for public presentation of ideas.

At a formal level, Garnet embodied what has now become a hallmark of African-American ministry and preaching: he understood himself as both ecclesial steward and public servant, demonstrating African transcendence of Western dualism of the secular and the sacred. He sponsored public policy through his preaching, and he preached radical transformation of society through his public declarations. From his position as pastor of Liberty Street Presbyterian Church in Troy, New York, and (later) as pastor of New York's Shiloh Presbyterian Church, as well as from his association with the abolitionists, Garnet's ministry displayed three hallmark characteristics of African-American preaching and prophetic speaking: First, he was intimately aware of the horror of slave existence and was deeply involved with freeing slaves and helping them adjust to freedom. Few among his contemporaries were closer to those who were moving from slavery to freedom. Thus, Garnet spoke out of an unbreakable connection to the pain of his people—slaves and ex-slaves—a connection that gave focus and intensity to his words.

Second, Garnet clearly understood the economic context of slavery and oppression. In ways consistent with (though more radical than) his colleagues, he understood the connection between slavery and land monopoly. Slaveholders were landholders; thus, long before the reality of emancipation, Garnet saw that no freedom for the slaves could be sustained without a radical change in the structure of land and wealth distribution. Therefore, Garnet was a strong proponent of land ownership for slaves, encouraging slaves to attain as much land as possible. However, Garnet also challenged laws that favored only those who owned property, thereby excluding the vast majority of African Americans. Seeing the complex matrix of obstacles to freedom, Garnet moved away from general public pleading for an abstract freedom on the basis of merely moral grounds and sought to posit the need for freedom within the concrete capitalist structures of his generation. This required both courage and a radical vision for the conversion of an economy that had been birthed with an addiction to free slave labor.

Third, Garnet grasped early the pervasive and persistent nature of racist ideology that made slavery not only possible but a reality in many nations. Garnet realized the connectedness of Africans enslaved throughout the world and the tremendous profit being gained from this racist mechanism, as well as the racist vision sustained by slavery. Thus, before many others, Garnet recognized the inevitability of violence to break the hold of slavery over the modern world. Through his speeches and sermons he advocated slave revolt and various forms of nationalism for freed slaves, either in America or elsewhere—primarily Cuba and Jamaica. For this advocacy he was roundly criticized by slaveholders and abolitionists alike. However, Garnet's radicality was rooted in sensitivity to the way racism permeated American society and especially the white church in America, which he himself often criticized. Thus Garnet's preaching and public speaking embodied a consciousness of the ways people in a given society are deceived by the ideological rhetoric of a nation-state. Garnet understood that radical preaching and prophetic speaking have a demystifying function that reveals forms of oppression often hidden by the opinions of those who have dominant political and social power. Garnet, as lecturer and preacher, prophetically exemplified this threefold hallmark of African-American ministry. As a forerunner of Pan-African nationalism, he is also an example of one who understood the ecclesial and political effect of prophetic preaching (*see* African-American Preaching; Prophetic Preaching).

Ofari, E., *Let Your Motto Be Resistance: The Life and Thought of Henry Highland Garnet*, 1972. **Schor, J.,** *Henry Highland Garnet: A Voice of Black Radicalism in the Nineteenth Century*, 1977. **Stuckey, S.,** *Slave Culture: Nationalist Theory and the Foundations of Black America*, 1987.

WILLIE JAMES JENNINGS

AWAKE!
Henry Highland Garnet
Brethren and Fellow-Citizens:
Your brethren of the North, East, and West have been accustomed to meet together in national conventions to sympathize with each other, and to weep over your unhappy condition. In these meetings we have addressed all classes of the free, but we have never, until this time, sent a word of consolation and advice to you. . . .

Slavery! How much misery is comprehended in that single word. What mind is there that does not shrink from its direful effects? Unless the image of God be obliterated from the soul, all men cherish the love of liberty. The nice discerning political economist does not regard the sacred right more than the untutored African who roams in the wilds of the Congo. Nor has the one more right to the full enjoyment of his freedom than the other. In every man's mind the good seeds of liberty are planted, and he who brings his fellow down so low as to make him contented with a condition of slavery, commits the highest crime against God and man. Brethren, your oppressors aim to do this. They endeavor to make you as much like brutes as possible. When they have blinded the eyes of your mind—when they have shut out the light which shines from the word of God—then, and not till then, has American slavery done its perfect work. . . .

Brethren, it is wrong for your lordly oppressors to keep you in slavery, as it was for the man-thief to steal our ancestors from the coast of Africa. You should therefore now use the same manner of resistance, as would have been just in our ancestors, when the bloody footprints of the first remorseless soul-thief was placed upon the shores of our fatherland. The humblest peasant is as free in the sight of God as the proudest monarch that ever swayed a scepter. . . .

Brethren, arise, arise! Strike for your lives and liberties. Now is the day and the hour. Let every slave throughout the land do this, and the days of slavery are numbered. You cannot be more oppressed than you have been—you cannot suffer greater cruelties than you have already. Rather die freemen than live to be slaves. . . .

It is in your power to torment the God-cursed slaveholders, that they will be glad to let you go free. If the scale was turned, and black men were the masters and white men the slaves, every destructive agent and element would be employed to lay the oppressor low. Danger and death would hang over their heads day and night. Yes, the tyrants would meet with plagues more terrible than those of Pharaoh. But you are a patient people. You act as though you were made for the special use of these devils. You act as though your daughters were born to pamper the lusts of your masters and overseers. And worse than all, you tamely submit while your lords tear your wives from your embraces and defile them before your eyes. In the name of God, we ask, are you men? Where is the blood of your fathers? Has it all run out of your veins? Awake, awake; millions of voices are calling you! Your dead fathers speak to you from their graves. Heaven, as with a voice of thunder, calls on you to arise from the dust. Let your motto be resistance! resistance! resistance!

> From "An Address to the Slaves of the United States of America," in Carter G. Woodson, *Negro Orators and Their Orations* (Washington: The Associated Publishers, 1925).

Gospels. The canonical Gospels have long been a rich source for Christian preaching, as the lectionaries suggest. There is always a Gospel lesson. Since the Gospels present themselves as accounts of Jesus' ministry and of Jesus as preacher,* it is hardly surprising that they have played a large role in the worship and preaching of the church.

While Christians have for good reason taken the Gospels to be reports of Jesus' activity, modern scholarship has shown that to view them simply as history or biography does not do them justice. Papias (early second century) characterized Mark as a rendition of Peter's preaching that was "not in order," presumably meaning historical order. His characterization has fared well, particularly in the twentieth century, as form criticism (or tradition history) and redaction criticism have called attention to the community origin and proclamatory and theological nature of the Gospels. Martin Dibelius, one of the founders of form criticism, emphasized the churchly, communal matrix of the Gospel material, pointing out

that it was shaped by the needs and functions of the community. Although he did not deny that the Gospels contained deeds and words of the historical Jesus, he argued that they were not simply reflected, as in a mirror, but refracted through the lens of the church's life. More than any other scholar, Dibelius insisted upon the importance of preaching as a key to the content and purpose of the Gospels. "In the beginning was the preaching" correctly characterizes Dibelius's position, if one recognizes that he believed the reality and impact of Jesus Christ himself was best and most faithfully presented in preaching.

Such a presentation is, however, at odds with the expectations of modern people accustomed to biography, not to mention the film media. For one thing, contrary to what the reader might assume, the framework of the Gospel narrative, particularly Mark, was determined more by the early Christian preaching and theology than by canons of biographical narrative or chronological history. For another, the individual Gospel narratives, parables,* and sayings (or sayings collections) tend to recur in definite patterns or forms, which form critics such as Dibelius and Rudolf Bultmann* believed could be correlated with their function in the church. (While Dibelius put preaching at the center, Bultmann proposed a number of other settings or purposes.) In either case, the Gospel material was seen to fall into discrete units that are not integrally related and for the most part do not require, on internal, substantial grounds, the order in which they now occur in the Gospels. C. H. Dodd argued in *The Apostolic Preaching and Its Developments* that the Gospels, particularly Mark and John, are expansions of the early Christian kerygma or preaching. Whether his thesis is adequate or accurate may be debatable, but it is nevertheless not misleading. The structure of the Gospels has more to do with theology and preaching than with modern concepts of biography or history.

Although the Gospel tradition had its earliest life in the worship and mission of the church, the role of the individual authors as preachers and theologians must not be overlooked. Each evangelist has created out of remarkably similar materials Gospels that differ in shape and purpose. Redaction critics such as Willi Marxsen recognized the achievement of form criticism but insisted that the Gospels could not be properly understood as the products of community and tradition only. Rather, one must take into account the accomplishments of the evangelists.

The working assumption of form and redaction critics alike was the two-document hypothesis, according to which Mark was the earliest of the synoptic Gospels, and probably the earliest Gospel written. His achievement in expressing the Christian message in narrative form was taken to be an event of epoch-making proportions. Mark was, in due course, used by Matthew and Luke independently, each of whom also employed similar collections of Jesus' sayings (often called the Q-source), which had previously been assembled for church use. (The order of events and narrative of Matthew and Luke have, then, no clear, independent historical value apart from Mark.) The Gospel of John is, of course, another matter, and its character and relation to the synoptics remain a matter of debate among scholars, although its theological character is obvious (cf. John 20:31) and sheds light on the nature of the Gospels generally. The fundamental insight of source criticism about synoptic relationships helps the reader to see the unique contributions of Matthew and Luke, who used the same two principal sources but employed them along with other materials in distinctively different ways for their own ends.

More recent literary criticism* has called into question the efforts of form and redaction critics to identify the historical settings of the Gospel traditions and Gospels in order to make such determinations fundamental to exegesis* and, ultimately, to preaching. They remain, after all, hypothetical. At the same time, there has been a renewed appreciation of the literary character of the Gospels and of the qualities they share with other literature. In a certain sense, the Gospels are ancient religious biographies or at least would have been read as such in antiquity. The kinds of literary analysis of character, plot, and so forth, that have been applied to fiction and other literature can be illuminating for the interpretation of the Gospels. Even those New Testament interpreters who are skeptical of the results of form and redaction criticism acknowledge, however, the communal, churchly origin and shaping of the Gospel tradition.

When all is said and done, the pulpit of the church, rather than the desk of the literary critic or historian, is the place where the exegesis of the Gospels finds its proper home, for preaching and related church functions gave rise to the Gospel traditions and the Gospels in the first place. It is probably not coincidental that the pericopes or lessons of the synoptic Gospels are rounded off in such form and size as to be convenient texts for preaching. In all likelihood they were in the first instance preached. Contemporary preaching can profit from this fact, but at the same time should take note of the total literary and theological context of each pericope—that is, of the Gospel of which it is a part. How a parable or miracle story functioned in the context of pre-Gospel tradition must in the nature of the case remain a moot question. How it functions in the canonical text of each Gospel is easier to discern and perhaps the more important question for preaching.

If synoptic pericopes may be thought of as originally texts for preaching, the longer complexes and discourses of the Fourth Gospel appear initially to be something quite different. Yet even there, one frequently finds the story of a miracle (the man born blind in chapter 9) or a chance encounter (the woman of Samaria in chapter 4) developed into a lengthy discourse or dialogue that has sermonic features. One may therefore imagine that the Gospel of John presents not just texts for preaching but in a real sense texts and preaching. In any case, because all the Gospels are grounded in the church's preaching, they afford rich resources for the contemporary preacher and invite the development of sermons.

Dibelius, M., *From Tradition to Gospel,* trans. Bertram Lee Woolf, 1935. **Dodd, C. H.,** *The Apostolic Preaching and Its Developments,* 1936. **Keck, L. E.,** *The Bible in the Pulpit: The Renewal of Biblical Preaching,* 1978. **Marxsen, W.,** *Mark the Evangelist: Studies on the Redaction History of the Gospel,* trans. James Boyce, 1969. **Smith, D. M.,** *Interpreting the Gospels for Preaching,* 1980.
                                          D. MOODY SMITH

Graham, William Franklin ("Billy")

(1918–   ) Billy Graham has been for nearly half a century the dominant figure in the worldwide movement of evangelical Christianity and, at least in terms of numerical response, is the most successful evangelist who ever lived. A native of North Carolina, he has become a citizen of the world. He has preached in person to more than eighty million people in more than eighty countries and has seen more than two million respond to the invitation at the end of his sermons. He has spoken to countless millions more on his radio and television programs, which were major foundationstones in what has come to be called the electronic church. He founded *Christianity Today,* the flagship publication of evangelical Christianity. He has befriended scores of world leaders, including ten U.S. presidents. He was the first Christian to preach in public behind the Iron Curtain since World War II, and he has played an important role in increasing the scope of religious freedom in the former Soviet Union and its satellite states. International conferences he has sponsored—in Berlin in 1966, in Lausanne in 1974, and in Amsterdam in 1983 and 1986—have helped create an international evangelical coalition of remarkable vitality and influence. Despite his detractors, such accomplishments have made Billy Graham quite possibly the best-known and most-admired religious figure of the twentieth century. In a 1978 *Ladies Home Journal* survey, only God earned more points than he did in the category, "achievements in religion."

While a student at Florida Bible Institute in the late 1930s, Graham decided to become an evangelist and began to develop his preaching skills in earnest, imitating the gestures and rhetorical styles of the fabled fundamentalist warhorses who visited the school, practicing borrowed sermons on snakes and alligators in the Hillsborough River, and serving as a "supply preacher" to little churches within driving distance of Tampa. He was ordained a Southern Baptist minister in 1938. After graduating from the unaccredited Florida school in 1940, he enrolled as a freshman at Wheaton College in Wheaton, Illinois, where he met and married Ruth Bell, who had been reared in China as the daughter of Presbyterian medical missionary L. Nelson Bell.

After graduation from Wheaton, Graham served briefly as pastor of a small Baptist church in neighboring Western Springs, his only stint in that capacity. The church grew under his leadership, but both he and his staunchest supporters, not to mention his critics, acknowledged that he was not well suited for the pastorate. His real interest lay in evangelistic preaching, in casting his net as widely as possible every time he preached. A stint on a popular Sunday-evening radio program gave him wide exposure in the Midwest. Not long afterward, he resigned his post to become a field representative for a fledgling movement called Youth for Christ International. Graham traveled throughout the U.S. and to many places in Europe, speaking at large rallies that combined wholesome entertainment and earnest evangelical preaching, teaching local ministers how to continue such meetings on their own, and establishing a network of loyal friends who would support his revivals in the years that followed.

Graham came to national attention while holding a revival in Los Angeles in 1949, when William Randolph Hearst instructed the editors of his newspaper chain to "puff Graham." The wire services picked up the story immediately; Henry Luce's *Time* and *Life* magazines followed suit a few weeks later, and Billy Graham was suddenly the most talked-about preacher in America. Within a short time, he established the Billy Graham Evangelistic Association; launched his radio, television, and motion picture ministries; and perfected the organization and mechanics of extended revival campaigns, which he conducted throughout much of the free world. He also began to cultivate friendships with presidents and other prominent political leaders, who recognized that Billy Graham's presence at their side could bestow a valuable symbolic blessing upon them and their causes. By the end of the 1950s, evangelical Christianity was flourishing as it had not for more than forty years, and Billy Graham was undeniably its chief spokesperson.

In the early years, Graham usually began his sermons by relating a few warm-up jokes to let his listeners know that, despite the hard things he had to say, he was really a good fellow not much d'fferent from themselves. He then shifted gears and set about to create a high level of tension by running through a catalog of problems—adultery, divorce, crime, alcohol abuse, suicide, materialism, greed, general moral decline, and the growing power of godless Communism—that threatened to bring down the awful judgment of God upon individuals, cities, and nations if they did not repent their evil ways.

These pronouncements flashed like a fusillade from an automatic weapon. Indeed, Graham's basic mode of preaching in these early years was assault. To keep entire arenas alert and at bay, he stalked and walked and sometimes almost ran from one end of the platform to the other, his body now tense and coiled, now exploding in a violent flurry. His arms slashed and crushed, his hands chopped and stabbed and hammered, his fingers pointed and sliced and pierced. His clenched fist descended with such power and fury that none could doubt he had made the wrath of God his own. And his words kept coming—a stream of arresting, often violent and frightening images. He never faltered, never groped for a word, never showed the slightest doubt that what he said was absolutely true and, as he repeatedly proclaimed, holding the limp-backed book high overhead or drawing his hands down like lightning to where it lay open on the pulpit, because "the *Bible* says . . . !"

When he had his listeners mentally cowering in terror, aware that all the attractively labeled escape routes—alcohol, sexual indulgence, riches, psychiatry, education, social-welfare programs, increased military might, the United Nations—led ultimately to dead ends, Graham called on his auditors to accept God's offer of grace and mercy, made possible by Christ's atoning death on the cross, and to turn their lives over to Jesus, who is able to answer their deepest needs. That offer, he stressed, will not forever be available. Even if Christ does not soon return, each individual's life is of brief and uncertain span. How can anyone be sure he or she will be alive a year from now? What about a week? a day? How easy it would be to die in an automobile accident on the way home from the service, and then face God at the judgment, having missed one's final opportunity. Graham did not ply such themes for the anxiety and fear they might inspire, but seldom did he let a sermon pass without mentioning them. Finally, when he felt the time was right, he offered the invitation: "I'm going to ask you to get up out of your seats and come and stand in front of the platform, and say, 'Tonight, I want Christ in my heart.'" And then, he stopped talking, closed his eyes, rested his chin on his right fist, cradled his right elbow in his left hand, and waited for the

Holy Spirit to move, for men and women and boys and girls to decide that *this* would be the day of their salvation.

For all his vitality and carefully honed technique, Graham is far from flawless as a preacher. Members of his own team, who have heard him preach countless times, do not regard him as a remarkably gifted pulpiteer, volunteering that "Billy's sermons are quite ordinary, even subordinary," or that "he'd be the first one to tell you there are lots better preachers." Graham himself has often insisted he is no scholar or intellectual, and his sermons have provided garish justification of his modesty. Still, frequent gaffes, anachronisms, overstatements, and simple errors of fact have detracted hardly at all from the quality that has given his preaching its strength and power: the unmistakable authority of his proclamation. The source of his authority, of course, is the Bible and his absolute confidence in its truth. He understands intuitively that countless multitudes—not everyone, to be sure, but far more than enough to fill the largest arena in any city—want to be told what to believe by someone who believes it himself. He has advised ministers to hide whatever doubts they might have and to preach what they do believe with full conviction. "People want to be told authoritatively that this is so," he has stated, "not be given pro and con arguments. . . . The world longs for finality and authority.* It is weary of theological floundering and uncertainty. Belief exhilarates people; doubt depresses them." Because he has no discernible doubts himself, he is able to convey in his voice, his gestures, and his absolute forthrightness a personal authority that bolsters and exemplifies the authority of scripture. He does not defend his belief; he proclaims it in clear and perfectly intelligible language, so that no one can doubt or misunderstand what he wants them to do. It is this trusting simplicity that makes Graham so effective as a preacher. Whatever his audiences may think about his intellectual acumen, they view him as utterly sincere about what he says in the pulpit.

Over the decades, Graham's theology has moderated a bit. Though he remains loyal to traditional formulations, he has made room for more liberal views than his own on such questions as evolution, the virgin birth, even the literal inspiration of scripture. In keeping with these developments, both the style and content of his preaching have altered. Though he still preaches regularly on the same topics, his sermons are shorter and less densely packed than in earlier years. He also uses a much calmer and quieter style, a change fostered not only by age but also by the demands of the cooler medium of television. He still attacks the complacency of his listeners by confronting them with their fears and discontents, but the focus has shifted from the flames of hell and nuclear holocaust to the chillier discomforts of loneliness, emptiness, guilt, and the fear of death, and to such high-profile threats to society as drugs and AIDS. Graham freely acknowledges his use of fear as a motivator for conversion, but the anger critics saw in his early preaching now seems mostly absent. Certainly, Graham hopes it is gone. "We need to preach with compassion," he told a group of aspiring evangelists. "People should sense that you love them, that you are interested in them. Even when you preach about hell, you need to convey that both the author [God] and the messenger speak from a broken heart."

In keeping with his own advice, Graham displays a more tolerant attitude toward human frailty than he once did. He increasingly recognizes differences between cultures and stresses forgiveness more than judgment. During the 1960s, he took a cautious but courageous stand against racial segregation, though he regarded changing individual hearts and minds as the most promising route to racial harmony. More recently, he has developed an increased appreciation for the need to change social structures and conditions as well. His exposure to the full range of the world's political and economic systems has made him less confident that Western-style free-enterprise capitalism is the only economic system Christians can support. The inequity between the rich and poor, including disparities between wealthy and developing nations, he has observed, "is going to have to change somehow, whether voluntarily or by law. There is a crying need for more social justice. . . . As a Christian, I believe God has a special concern for the poor of the world, and public policy should in some way reflect this concern. I believe God has a special concern for things like peace, racism, the responsible use of Earth's resources, economic and social justice, the use of power, and the sacredness of human life" (Charlotte *Observer*, Feb. 7, 1977; April 25, 1982). Since the early 1980s, he has gained high praise from former critics by calling repeatedly for the elimination of all nuclear and biochemical weapons of mass destruction.

These late-life alterations in the famed evangelist's interests and preaching are less a renunciation of earlier positions or harbingers of a new phase in his ministry than they are evidence of a capacity for continued growth, one of Billy Graham's most attractive personal characteristics. "I do not plan to be a leader in a peace movement or organization," he has written. "I am an evangelist. But I am a man who is still in process" (*see* Evangelism; Revivals; Television and Preaching).

Martin, W., *A Prophet with Honor: The Billy Graham Story*, 1991. WILLIAM MARTIN

JOHN 3:16
Billy Graham
"For God so loved the world, that he gave his only begotten Son, that whosoever believeth in him, should not perish, but have everlasting life."

. . . .

The first phrase says, "For God." It brings us right at the start to the subject of God. Does God exist? . . .

What is God like? . . . The Bible tells us what God is like, because God has revealed himself to us. . . .

First, the Bible teaches that God created the universe. . . .

[T]he Bible tells us God also is a spirit. . . .

The Bible also says God never changes. . . .

The Bible teaches as well that God is a holy God. . . .

The Bible also says that God is a God of judgment. . . . There are three things you cannot escape. . . . First, we cannot escape being born. . . . Second, we cannot escape death. . . . The third thing you cannot escape is the judgment of God. . . . The moment you are born your name is written in the book of judgment, and all the sins that you commit are in that book. When you receive Christ, all of those sins are wiped out because of what Christ did for you on the cross. . . .

Now, what does God require of you and me? . . .

First, you must repent of your sins. . . .

Second, you must come by faith and trust to Christ as your Savior and Lord. . . .

The Bible says, "Now is the accepted time; behold, now is the day of salvation." You may be closer to God at this moment than ever before in your life. You may never be this close again. Tonight is the night to receive him, and to put your whole weight on Christ. . . . Whatever your background, come to him by faith and make your commitment to him now.

© Billy Graham Evangelistic Association. Used by permission.

Gregory the Great. (ca. 540–604) Gregory became pope in 590. A member of the Roman aristocracy, Gregory displayed his administrative talents as prefect (governor) of Rome in the years 572–574. After the death of his parents, he resigned the office of prefect, sold most of the family estates, and turned his own residence into a monastery where he pursued an ascetic life. In 574, however, he reluctantly accepted ordination as one of the seven regional deacons of Rome who oversaw the administration of the church's charitable work, and shortly thereafter he went as papal legate (*apocrisiarius*) to the imperial court in Constantinople. Not long after his return, he was elected pope.

His papacy came at a time when imperial rule in Italy, which Justinian had reestablished earlier in the sixth century after the fall of the Western Empire to the Goths, was too weak and ineffective to withstand the new invasion of the Lombards. In this political vacuum Gregory made the church the one stable institution in the West, effectively organizing its charitable relief, reforming its clergy, and establishing a missionary strategy to Arian and pagan elements among the barbarian heirs of Roman authority in the West. He gave strong support to monasticism, and his *Dialogues* (a series of popular reflections on the Christian life) established Benedict of Nursia as the primary Western authority on the monastic life. Gregory's administrative skills served him well in meeting the challenges that faced the church in this period of social collapse, but the role in secular affairs that the church assumed out of pastoral necessity at this time laid the foundation for the political role the church played during the Middle Ages and beyond—a role that was to lead to the corruption triggering both the religious protest known as the Reformation and political resistance to papal claims.

Gregory served as one of the principal architects of Christian society in the coming centuries and as a bridge by which the patristic heritage was mediated to the Middle Ages. Unlike earlier Christian authors, he was little concerned with major doctrinal issues: he presupposed the consensus established by the first four ecumenical councils. He devoted his energy instead to the practical, moral, and ascetical implications of the Christian faith. His moral and ascetical concerns come to the fore in his *Pastoral Care*, a treatise on the pastoral duties of bishops (and, by exten-

sion, parish clergy). This work is a guide to the minister's role as preacher and teacher. Much of it is devoted to the differing approaches appropriate for addressing a long series of such contrasted groups in the congregation as men and women, young and old, those in authority and those under authority. It also addresses the ascetic discipline needed to give the preacher both the self-discipline and the moral and religious authority required for the task of effective preaching. *Pastoral Care* became a standard work on pastoral ministry during the Middle Ages and is probably the book for which Gregory is best known.

A course of sermons on the Gospels for many of the Sundays and feasts of the church year provide concrete evidence of Gregory's work as a preacher. These *Homilies on the Gospels* exercised considerable influence on clergy in later centuries because they were excerpted as readings for matins in the Roman breviary. Indeed, the present *Liturgy of the Hours* remains the easiest place to find these sermons in translation. Gregory also gave a series of meditations on particular books of the Bible in his *Moral Reflections on Job* and his *Homilies on Ezekiel*. The *Moral Reflections on Job* were originally delivered to his companions in the ascetical life; the *Homilies on Ezekiel* were directed to much the same audience but were delivered in public to all who came.

Gregory's sermons and exegetical homilies reflect the primary foci of his ministry—the moral life of Christians in the world and the spiritual life of ascetics, or the active life and the contemplative life. They reveal the practical character of Gregory's pastoral ministry—both a strength and a weakness. The earlier fathers had seen heaven impinging on the ordinary events of world history, but on the whole they avoided claiming that we can discern the causal links between what would later be called the natural and the supernatural. Gregory, to a large extent, dissolved the boundary between heaven and earth and integrated the action of

God, the angels, and the saints into the ordinary course of human events. Gregory's treatment of the practical impact of the eucharistic sacrifice, of the miraculous powers of holy persons, relics, and similar phenomena, and of the patronage exercised by saints and angels is often likely to strike us as a descent into popular superstition. These are features of medieval Christianity that met with the fiercest attack at the time of the Reformation. Religion became practical but lost a large measure of its transcendence.

Gregory's allegorical interpretation of the scriptures, while aimed at practical ends and illustrated with popular examples, often bears little relation to the text that is his starting point. In his concern to discover the practical implications of that text, Gregory at times uses it as the basis for reflections that bear little relation to its original meaning. This is sometimes evident in his homilies on the Gospels. Details in the nativity Gospels, for example, such as the fact that Jesus' birth occurred during a census, on a journey, and at Bethlehem, take on meanings for Gregory that bear little relation to the biblical narrative. Such an approach becomes much more evident in Gregory's interpretation of Job and Ezekiel, where he can discern no evident historical meaning, and he bases his allegorical exposition of the text on moral and ascetical concerns of his own day.

Gregory understood himself and was understood by others as the interpreter of the earlier church fathers (particularly Augustine) to his times. His success was that of a popularizer rather than of an original thinker. But his popularized version of Augustinian thought in fact modifies and distorts it. Gregory emerges from the pages of history as an example of both the necessity and the danger of popularizing the Christian gospel to relate it to the concerns of the day in preaching.

Gregory the Great, *Pastoral Care*, ed. and trans. H. Davis, 1978; Ancient Christian Writers 2. **Leclercq, J.,** "The Teaching of St. Gregory," in L. Bouyer et al., *The Spirituality*

of the Middle Ages, 3–30, 1968. **Richards, J.,** *Consul of God*, 1980. **Straw, C.,** *Gregory the Great: Perfection in Imperfection*, 1988.

BYRON D. STUHLMAN

Guibert of Nogent. (1053–1124) A Benedictine monk and abbot, Guibert was a prolific author, producing works of history, controversy, and biblical scholarship. He became abbot of Nogent-sous-Coucy in his early fifties. His best-known writing is his autobiography, *De vita sua*. It is an important source for the church and social history of the period. His other works include a history of the First Crusade, a treatise highly critical of the cult of relics, polemical volumes against Berengarius and against the Jews, and tropological interpretations of Genesis, Hosea, Amos, and Lamentations.

The significance of Guibert for the history of preaching is that he prefaced his ten books of *Moralia in Genesim* with a treatise titled *Liber quo ordine sermo fieri debeat* ("A Book about the Way a Sermon Ought to Be Given"). This was one of the earliest homiletical treatises ever written, the first one having been Augustine's* *De doctrina christiana*. Gregory the Great's* *Pastoral Care* is largely concerned with preaching, but the only other treatment prior to that of Guibert is a section of Rabanus Maurus's early ninth-century volume, *On the Training of the Clergy*, lifted largely from Augustine. Indeed, preaching had gone through a crisis of self-confidence when clergy assumed that it would be presumptuous of them to add anything to the biblical interpretation of the great church fathers. The work of Guibert, then, represents a resurgence of confidence in the church. Theologians may have agreed with Bernard of Chartres that they were like dwarfs standing on the shoulders of giants, but they recognized that this vantage point permitted them to see further than their predecessors. There was still hesitancy on the part of some, though. When Guibert's abbot at St. Geremar discovered that a monk of his who was barely thirty-two years old was presuming to imitate Ambrose in commenting on the Six Days of Creation and was even claiming to do the sort of moral interpretation of Genesis that Gregory the Great had done of Job, he was aghast and forbade him to continue. The extent of Guibert's monastic obedience in this case, however, was merely to proceed with his work in secrecy, thus completing it in 1084, shortly after the death of his abbot.

The fact that Guibert's thoughts about preaching were a preface to a biblical commentary shows the reciprocal relation he perceived between exegesis* and homiletics. Biblical commentary was prepared as a resource for preaching, and the style of preaching in vogue was still the expository homily. In his treatise Guibert provides one of the earliest statements of the state of exegesis at the time. As early as the age of Origen, most biblical interpretation had been allegorical. By the time of Gregory the Great there were thought to be three senses of scripture: the literal, the typical (allegorical interpretation for doctrine), and the moral. Guibert was one of the first to state clearly the medieval assumption that there were four senses in which the Bible could be understood:

> There are four ways of interpreting scripture; on them, as though on so many scrolls, each sacred page is rolled. The first is *history*, which speaks of actual events as they occurred; the second is *allegory*, in which one thing stands for something else; the third is *tropology*, or moral instruction, which treats of the ordering and arranging of one's life; and the last is *anagogy*, or spiritual enlightenment, through which we who are about to treat of lofty and heavenly topics are led to a higher way of life (Guibert of Nogent, 49).

In actual practice, however, sermons seldom dealt with more than one sense. On the whole, the literal, historical sense was of little interest; nor were the doctrines that grew out of allegorical interpretation in the strict sense thought appropriate matter for preaching. The real concern was the daily life of Christians and thus the tropological sense was emphasized, the sense on which Guibert concentrated in his commentaries.

More than the first quarter of Guibert's treatise is devoted to an examination of the reasons people who should preach do not. The impression is that the duty of preaching should not be confined to bishops or abbots or even to priests but should be extended to all who "live virtuously and continently" who "have acquired knowledge of the sacred page." A young monk like Guibert is unlikely to have had much practical experience of preaching. Thus what he says about biblical interpretation is more specific than his words about preaching as such.

Yet his advice on preaching is worthy of being followed by those who stand in the pulpit in any age. Preachers are advised to begin their sermons with prayer so that their own devotion will kindle the hearts of their hearers, "for a tepid sermon, delivered half-heartedly, cannot please even the preacher." Sermons that are not going well should not be allowed to run on too long; indeed, even the best should be brief since repetitions and irrelevancies anger the audience and cause them to forget the good they have heard. Only after spiritual and intellectual preparation should the preacher give thought to issues of style. The preacher, however, should always keep in mind those who will hear the sermon. "Though he preaches simple and uncomplicated matter to the unlettered, at the same time he should try to reach a higher plane with the educated." Preaching should be a way in which the preacher shares what he has learned of the life of the spirit both through reading the masters and through personal experience. Just as tales of battle are told very differently by those who have been in battle and those who have not, so preaching about moral struggle profits from an obvious existential involvement. Thus Guibert gets the new writing about homiletics off to a good start.

Benton, J. F. ed., *Self and Society in Medieval France: The Memoirs of Abbot Guibert of Nogent*, 1970. **de Nogent, G.,** "A Book about the Way a Sermon Ought to Be Given," trans. Joseph M. Miller, *Today's Speech* 17:4 (Nov. 1969), 45–56.   O. C. EDWARDS, JR.

SHORT SERMONS
Guibert of Nogent

Let a prayer always precede the sermon, so that the soul may burn fervently with divine love; then let it proclaim what it has learned from God so as to inflame the hearts of all hearers with the same interior fire which consumes it. For a tepid sermon, delivered half-heartedly, cannot please even the preacher; wonder of wonders, then, if it should please anyone else. And how can a mangled or stammered phrase serve to inspire others, when we know perfectly well that speech of that kind does not usually soothe the minds of listeners, but rather oppresses them with boredom and seriously irritates and angers them. For this reason, when we recognize that our intellectual acumen is not at its best, and that what we ought to be saying simply does not come and that the workings of the mind are under a heavy cloud, then, as I see it, we know that no real usefulness can result from a sermon drawn out to great length in these circumstances.

After all, if a sermon ought not be given at excessive length when the words come easily and the fluency is pleasing to the heart, how much less when the memory fails, the delivery is halting, and the mind is sluggish. As St. Ambrose said, a tedious sermon arouses anger; and when the same things are repeated over and over, or when unrelated topics are dragged in during the sermon, it usually happens that the hearers lose everything from the sermon equally, because of their boredom, the beginning, the conclusion, and everything in between. Where a few ideas might have been presented effectively, a plethora of ideas presented at too great a length leads to apathy and even, I fear, to hostility.

We know that when food is taken in moderation it serves to nourish the body, but when taken in excess it works to the detriment of the body and even provokes vomiting. Or, again, a man who uses his seed properly in the marital act generates offspring, while he who masturbates accomplishes nothing good and only befouls his body. So a preacher who abuses words interferes with what is already planted in the hearts of his hearers, what he should be helping to grow. For this reason, if the preacher has a great fervor of spirit and has mastered all his material, then he can add the possibility of eloquence and style to the essentials, his own virtues. Let him think of those who must listen in silence to pompous inanities, and he will realize that it is much better for them to hear a few things well presented than a great many things from which they will retain almost nothing. Then he will not delay making an end to one sermon so that, when he preaches another, his audience will be eager rather than resentful.

From "The Way a Sermon Ought to Be Given," trans. Joseph M. Miller, *Today's Speech* 17:4 (Nov. 1969), 48–49.

Hamilton, J. Wallace. (1900–1968)

Hamilton was the minister of the Pasadena Community Church in St. Petersburg, Florida, for nearly forty years. This church was noted for its "drive-in" congregation which often numbered in the thousands. Born in Pembroke, Ontario, Canada, the son of farmers, Hamilton graduated from Moody Bible Institute in 1924. He toured with a quartet, singing around the country. When the quartet disbanded, he accepted his first pastorate at Baileytown, Tennessee. In 1927, he began the new work of the Trinity Methodist Church in St. Petersburg, Florida. In 1929, he added to his duties the work of the Pasadena Methodist Church, a church struggling to survive.

Early in his ministry at the church, many could not get into the crowded sanctuary to hear Hamilton preach. To accommodate them, loudspeakers were installed so they could sit in their cars and listen. That was the beginning of the drive-in congregation, which would often number as many as 3,000 cars.

Hamilton and the church reached an agreement that allowed him to preach at the church for eight months and then be free to preach around the country the remaining four. He was the Methodist preacher for "The Protestant Hour" series twice. He also published ten books of sermons. In the last twenty years of his life, Hamilton preached to an average of 5,000 people weekly.

What was the secret of Hamilton's appeal? One of his strengths was his relevancy. His major theme was the abundant life, a life that could only come when a person surrendered to Christ as Savior and Lord. He believed that if people were Christians, out of love for Christ they would work to make the world a better place to live for all people. His sermons dealt with the major doctrines of faith and discipleship. He faced the personal problems others had, often applying the insights of the new discoveries in psychology. Social issues, such as war, ecology, prejudice, secularism, science, and Communism, were challenged and discussed.

Hamilton's preaching was enhanced by a variety of homiletical approaches. Many different outline types appear in his sermons, each very clear to follow. Some of these forms were problem/solution, biographical studies, chase outlines, question-and-answer approaches, and effect-to-cause outlines. His sermons had a clear focus and flow.

Perhaps the most distinctive characteristic of Hamilton's sermons was his use of illustrations.* In a study of 170 of his sermons, an average of 21 illustrations per sermon was found. He used a variety of illustration types. His favorites were the brief quotation, story, and poetic verse. He often included short, humorous anecdotes. Once he wrote: "A little boy in Cape Kennedy, about to say his prayers and troubled about all the missile shooting, said, 'I hope they don't kill God.' Not much danger of that. The divine order is not likely to be dislodged by firecrackers." The use of effective illustrative material made Hamilton's sermons highly interesting and desirable for copying by countless preachers of his era (e.g., Martin Luther King's* famous sermon, "Drum Major Instinct," was taken from Hamilton's sermon).

Hamilton's final strength was his use of language. He used clear, vivid, interesting, and forceful language. He avoided the use of long sentences and words. Such a clear style did not come easily. He struggled painstakingly to find the right words and to make the right use of them.

The longevity of Hamilton's ministry in St. Petersburg—and his ability to draw large crowds throughout that ministry—point to the effectiveness of Hamilton's preaching. After his death, Norman Vincent Peale* wrote: "In my opinion Wallace was one of the greatest preachers who ever gave expression to the gospel in this country. I do not know that he had any peers at all."

Hamilton, J. W., *Horns and Halos in Human Nature,* 1954; and *Where Now Is Thy God?,* 1969. **Litchfield, H.,** "An Analysis of the Homiletical Method of J. Wallace Hamilton," 1971.   HUGH LITCHFIELD

Hermeneutics

Meaning. Hermeneutics in general terms is the art of understanding. More specifically, it refers to the method and techniques used to make a text understandable in a world different from the one in which the text originated. The word derives from the Greek noun that came to mean "understanding," which was in turn based on a verb that had apparently meant "say" or "speak."

Hermeneutics pertains to the world of communication among humans and with the divine. Speech is the act of formulating thoughts coherently and expressing those thoughts in a way that communicates them to another or others orally or in writing. Hermeneutics is the art of understanding such an expression in the world of the hearer or reader. The

hermeneut, engaging in the act of understanding, is also a text, as it were, and the
encounter between the two is an act of
intertextuality. Every text read or heard is
already an interpretation of earlier texts
incorporated into it, exhibiting its own
hermeneutics of understanding those earlier texts.

Early History. Aristotle treated the
art of understanding as a branch of logic,
and so it was understood, for the most
part, until the work of Friedrich Schleiermacher* (1768–1834), who perceived
that there had to be a clear understanding
of general hermeneutics before developing a specific hermeneutic for reading the
Bible. No person or community had privileged access to the Bible through some
special hermeneutic accorded it. Schleiermacher thus gave expression to the break
with the past that had begun with the
Enlightenment.

Ancient communities that viewed the
Bible as inspired or sacred usually
claimed they had by special revelation the
key to understanding the Bible. At
Qumran the key was called *raz;* in the
New Testament it was called *mysterion* or
kleis (key). The word "sect" is usually used
to designate such communities today.
Schleiermacher challenged all such
claims. In doing so he brought to fruition
a process of understanding the Bible that
began in the Enlightenment and culminated in the view that the Bible was a
human product claiming divine revelation; the most that could be said was that
the Bible is a record of human responses
to divine revelations.

The Bible itself is a textbook, so to
speak, of biblical hermeneutics; it is full
of itself. Not only does the New Testament constantly cite and echo the Old,
but within the latter are many examples
of alluding to and echoing earlier biblical
thinking. To this observation we shall return in discussing canonical hermeneutics.

The early church engaged in various
forms of rejecting the Old Testament
while trying to understand the New Testament in increasingly Hellenistic and Roman cultural and philosophic terms. The
concept of supersessionism gained expression early on in the Christian division
of scripture into Old and New Covenants
or Testaments; it came to full expression
in Marcion's desire to eliminate the Old
Testament from the Christian Bible.
When it or portions of it, such as the legal
material, were not rejected, they were often spiritualized. In Alexandria the spir-
itualizing hermeneutic came to be expressed as allegory. Origen* did for the
whole of scripture what Philo of Alexandria had done for the Septuagint. By contrast Antioch developed a school of
thought that insisted on literal and historical meanings of the texts.

In the fourth and early fifth centuries,
Jerome and Augustine* largely set the
stage for how the Bible was to be understood for centuries to come. Jerome was a
philological giant who gave the last thirty
years of his life, in Bethlehem, to creating
an understanding of the Old Testament
that was as close to his concept of *Hebra-
ica Veritas* as possible; the Old Latin,
which had been a translation of the Septuagint, was eventually to be displaced by
Jerome's Vulgate. Jerome's commentaries, however, often exhibit the spiritual-
izing tendencies he had learned during a
short visit to Alexandria. Even where the
literal/historical sense was stressed, the
concept of the *sensus plenior* (fuller
sense) of scripture allowed for recognition of dimensions of scripture beyond it.
Augustine consciously resisted spiritual-
izing but saw the Bible, especially the Old
Testament, as a struggle between two cities, the heavenly and the earthly, offering
a kind of dialectic in which one could
understand the earthly in the light of
God's will and purpose. In the thirteenth
century, Thomas Aquinas reconciled the
spiritual and literal by distinguishing between moral laws, which resonate with
natural law, and the peculiarly cultural,
ceremonial, and judicial laws bound to a
particular historical era. Sacrifices in the
Old Testament would be seen not only as

guards against idolatries of the time but also as spiritual pointers to Christ's passion.

Enlightenment and Reformation.

With the invention of the printing press in the fifteenth century came a surge of enlightenment in Europe that gave rise to the Reformation. Luther* took clues from Augustine's concept of the two cities and developed the idea of two kingdoms, the heavenly and the earthly—the church and the world in which it witnessed. He also used other dichotomies such as law and gospel,* promise and fulfillment. He expressed these in a hermeneutic for text criticism he called *res et argumentum*, in which *res* was essentially that which truly mattered about the Bible, the gospel of Jesus Christ, and *argumentum* was any and everything else that scripture addressed, which either pointed to the gospel or did not matter. Where there were differences among manuscripts, the Christian scholar would choose the term that best witnessed to God's work in Christ.

John Calvin,* by contrast, stressed the unity of scripture. The Old Testament was to be read in its historical or literal sense but in the light of his belief that the gospel was to be found in both testaments, latent in the one and patent in the other. The law was to be taken seriously and reread and applied in the light of the whole of scripture culminating in the gospel. Calvin countered Luther's two-kingdoms hermeneutic by stressing the obligation of Christian civil authorities to apply the law in the world in the light of the gospel.

These efforts to take the Enlightenment seriously issued in the birth of biblical criticism, which called for the literal and historical understanding of scripture in terms of the historical contexts of the biblical authors. Spinoza, in his *Tractatus Theologico-Politicus* (1670), argued that the truth of the Bible could not be found until a critical history of the formation of biblical literature was written. Spinoza's influence on the thinking of those that followed him was considerable, whether they cited him or not.

One such follower was Richard Simon, a Parisian Catholic, who in 1678 argued for a new translation of the Old Testament based on a thoroughly critical edition of the Hebrew Bible. Rejecting traditional views of biblical authorship, Simon introduced the idea of scribal schools in place of seeing Moses, Samuel, David, or other known figures, as authors. The Catholic, he argued, was free to be as critical as need be toward writing a history of formation of the text because of the equal authority of the magisterium of the church. Simon argued that biblical authority lay not in the intention of individual authors but in the inspiration of scripture by God's Holy Spirit, who used the imagination and intention of the authors to include meanings in *sensus plenior* for times later than theirs. Thus two senses of a passage could be discerned, the literal/historical and the spiritual—a brilliant amalgam of the old Antioch/Alexandria distinction. Simon advocated careful study of Jewish understandings of scripture: The history of Jewish interpretation of scripture was essential to a true understanding of Christianity because God had never retracted the authority he once conferred upon Moses and the Elders of Israel.

With the eighteenth century came the primacy of reason. With this, in part, came a form of retreat into pietism, where the individual's personal experience came to mean as much as tradition or doctrine. John Wesley's* so-called quadrilateral gave scripture, tradition, reason, and experience equal weight in the quest for authority. By the beginning of the nineteenth century, historical criticism was fully launched. Between the work of W.M.L. De Wette at the beginning of the century and that of J. Wellhausen at its end, there had developed a critical view of the formation of the Pentateuch, which formed a response to Spinoza's call.

Schleiermacher. Friedrich Schleier-

macher shifted the focus of hermeneutics to the presuppositions that make understanding possible. Misunderstanding is a human problem, generally, that threatens all communication among humans. Language presupposes shared conventions and pre-understandings, but the problem lies in the baggage the individual brings to the text, the anticipations that demand satisfaction. His insights have been carried forward in the areas of ontology and existentialism by philosophers dependent on him, such as Dilthey, Heidegger, and Gadamer, who saw that the art of understanding is an act of intertextuality between text and reader, between past and present, between two quite different horizons encountering and interpreting each other. Karl Barth* and Rudolf Bultmann,* as different as their approaches were, both stressed that the act of engaging a text in order to understand it brings one to realize that the reader is also being interpreted. Language, that peculiarly human engagement, whether spoken to others or used to order thoughts, came to be seen as the home of human being; faith was seen as a speech event. Because of human limitations, the quest for truth is a never-ending dialectical process.

The twentieth century has seen a number of movements that have challenged theories of source criticism, each attempting to delve more and more deeply into the origins and formation of the text—form criticism, tradition criticism, redaction criticism, archaeological/philological analysis, structuralism, modern literary criticism,* cultural anthropology, and the social sciences (see Exegesis). The second half of the century has seen an emphasis on praxis over theory and hence the rise of special-interest hermeneutics such as liberation* and feminist* readings of the texts. Finally, there has developed a canonical approach to scripture, the one (Brevard Childs) focusing on the final form of the text and its synchronic intertextuality and the other (James Sanders) on the canonical process and its diachronic intertextuality.

Intertextuality. The term intertextuality refers to three basic textual relationships: the interplay between two bodies, small or large, of texts of differing provenance (synchronic); the function or interplay of an older text or tradition cited, alluded to, or echoed in a new text (diachronic); and the interplay between a text and its reader(s). This last signifies recognition that humans bring a whole complexity of individual or communal backgrounds to the encounter with a text and must be aware, as Schleiermacher stressed, of the presuppositions, pre-understandings, and expectations they bring to reading a text. Jews and Christians usually bring, with their cultural givens, some form of faith and the expectation that a biblical text will address their needs.

Academic study of religion attempts to bracket such a stance but inevitably replaces it with other pre-understandings. Critical study of the Bible brings some distancing from it, which is essential and good but may induce a hermeneutic either of consent or of suspicion. The synchronic focuses on the hermeneutic moves within a complex but stable text, such as the Bible, that take place between various contributions within it, such as differing sources within a single book, or the chemistry that takes place because disparate writings are bound together in something called a canon; the focus is on the final form of the text with minimal attention to historical contexts that gave rise to the parts of the text. The diachronic focuses on the hermeneutics of the canonical process that takes place when older texts or traditions are called on to function in a new text for a new historical context or situation; the focus is on the never-ending process of repetition/recitation/reapplication, which gave rise to the formation of biblical texts in antiquity and continues in believing communities today. The latter is exactly what preachers do today. In either case, the Bible is read critically with appreciation for the many contributions to the formation of the text, whether indigenous to

Israel and church or from other cultures surrounding it. The Bible is full of international wisdom from many sources. What is exciting is to discern the hermeneutics by which such wisdom was adapted and claimed.

Canonical Hermeneutics. The history of hermeneutics actually begins with the earliest biblical text. In the text itself and its early social context are clues for discerning canonical hermeneutics—that is, the hermeneutics that provide keys to unlock the power of the critically read Bible today.

The Bible is full of unrecorded hermeneutics that lie among the lines of scripture wherever an earlier tradition is adapted to a text addressing a new situation. Even the earliest datable literature in the Bible is intertextual—has earlier traditions in it. Sometimes in the prophetic literature it is given the name *massa*, which is often mistranslated "burden" but actually designates a prior revelation or insight reapplied to a new situation. This phenomenon occurs far more often in the prophets than in the word.

Sometimes an earlier passage is cited with an introductory formula ("As Isaiah said . . ."), often without such a formula. Newer compositions wove earlier phrases and sentences into the new fabric; in fact, nearly all early Jewish literature, including the New Testament, was written scripturally. Allusion to earlier events and figures is frequent. Paraphrase is very common; often the earlier language is archaic or esoteric and needs clarification by use of more common, later terms meaning the same thing. Two very common modes of intertextuality are what might be called echoes of the earlier, familiar passage and imitation of earlier compositions, such as rewriting an early book in a more fulsome style or writing a new composition following the structure of an earlier one.

Three Factors in Intertextuality. Whenever one discerns any such occasion of intertextuality, one needs to work with three major factors: the text or tradition being cited or woven into the passage studied, the socio-political context the new passage addressed, and the hermeneutics by which the tradent wished to make a point. According to Luke 10:26, Jesus was asked what one should do to inherit eternal life. In good Jewish fashion, Jesus answered by asking, "What is written in Torah and how do you read it?" What and how? What passage pertains to the issue? And by what hermeneutics do you understand the passage? Those are two of the three factors. The third is the socio-political situation addressed, both originally and whenever the passage is reread. The social location of the person or persons addressed or reading the passage largely determines the perception they have of reality, of the law, of justice, indeed of the issues addressed.

The prophets* and Jesus,* as well as other biblical speakers and authors, often called upon earlier texts and traditions to challenge the leaders and those with power in society, even the very texts that the leaders thought by their constitutive hermeneutics supported their point of view. The prophet Amos (2:9–3:2) called upon Israel's most precious identifying traditions of God's earlier gracious acts in the exodus, wanderings, and entrance into Canaan to challenge the claims the supposedly faithful leaders interpreted favorably to themselves. Amos was then able to say that the tradition that claimed Israel was the only family God knew was the authority by which he pronounced God's judgments on his generation. Such shocking interpretations of Israel's precious traditions were the hallmark of the ministries of the prophets and of Jesus and the principal cause of their rejection by their own.

Jesus also used the same traditions to comfort powerless sinners. James Crenshaw, following Eva Osswald and Martin Buber, put it well: "The true prophet must be able to distinguish whether a historical hour stands under the wrath or the love of God" (Crenshaw, 54). But the era is not the only factor; social location is as important. In Ezek. 33:24, the prophet rejected the effort of the elders who argued after the fall of Jerusalem in 586 B.C.E. that because Abraham was only one person when he inherited the land and they were more numerous (and supposedly faithful), they would inherit the land that Babylonia had just captured and largely destroyed. In Isa. 51:2–3 the prophet advanced the same argument as true that Ezekiel had earlier rejected as false.

Why? Not only the time factor of Isaiah addressing Jews in exile forty years later but social location. In the time of Ezekiel, the elders still had not gotten the point that Babylonia was the instrument of God's judgments of his own people; they still were making claims on the promises without acknowledging the judgment. By the time and situation of the Second Isaiah the scene had changed; many Jews were defecting and assimilating to the dominant culture of the time. They had come back around to the social location of the powerless slaves in Egypt whom Moses led out of bondage. Hosea and Jeremiah had earler pointed out that Israel's sinning began when the Israelites crossed the Jordan (Hos. 9:15; Jer. 21:8)—that is, when they received the promise and thereby gained some power. Blessing, said the prophets, was occasion for sin; and it was their duty to point it out to folk whose consciousness of reality had become corrupted and who saw their blessings as evidence of divine favor and God as their guarantor.

Canonical hermeneutics indicates two basic worldviews on the part of biblical tradents who adapted earlier traditions or international wisdom: belief in the essentially fragmented and competitive nature of reality or belief in reality's having ontological and ethical integrity—that God is One. The first derives essentially from accepting limited, human, inductive views of the way reality appears to work; the second derives from accepting by faith the wisdom that reality has integrity despite human experience and reason alone. The latter does not deny that human experience and reason are important in discerning truth. Far from it, it simply also accepts by faith the general witness of scripture that God is one and filters experience and reason through that faith perspective.

Two Modes. Study of intertextual hermeneutics within the Bible indicates that within the monotheizing thrust of canonical hermeneutics there are two major modes whereby biblical tradents adapted earlier traditions and wisdom: the *constitutive* or comforting, and the *prophetic* or challenging. By one, the biblical speaker or author applied the earlier tradition or insight to the new situation constitutively—that is, favorably to the situation addressed; by the other, the tradent applied it prophetically—that is, as a challenge to those addressed, and it was often the very same tradition with no difference in wording. The same word that, read constitutively, comforts the afflicted may, read by prophetic critique, afflict the comfortable. In the skillful hands of the Isaiah of Jerusalem even the Davidic traditions were applied prophetically: God's promises are sure, but the route to their fulfillment may be rough indeed, according to the people's need for judgment. Isaiah reached the height of theological genius when he affirmed in 701 B.C.E. that God could convert even an Assyrian siege stone being hurled at Jerusalem into a precious cornerstone of a new foundation; one who had true faith and believed, not only in God's promises but also in the freedom and power of God eventually but surely to convert evil into good, would indeed not be in a frenzy (28:16).

The true prophet held in creative tension the view that God was both creator and redeemer, both free and committed, not just one or the other. As redeemer, God is the faithful promiser, but as creator of all peoples God is free to judge his own people as well as to express grace to others. Focus on God as redeemer alone leads to denominational hermeneutics wherein the concept of God is tribalized and made into an idol. And while focus on God as creator alone may lead to an irrelevant deism or flaccid universalism, it is essential as a guard against the concept of God becoming a denominational idol. A major reason the New Testament must be read in its full canonical context is that the New Testament alone emphasizes Christology, or God's work as redeemer in Christ, and is easily subject to polytheistic and idolatrous readings.

Even a passage like John 14:6—"No one comes to the Father except through me"—can be read constitutively or prophetically. Read in the constitutive mode, focusing on God as redeemer, the readers may assume they are upheld by or in Christ, and for young, struggling churches or movements that are not at all sure of survival, such a reading may be indicated. But for readers with power that corrupts their consciousness, such a reading can be falsely understood as saying that no one has access to God except through their Christ. Read in the prophetic mode, the passage may be a challenge to assumptions about denominational concepts of the incarnation. In fact, the whole New Testament can be read understanding Christ to be God's Christ, hence, to some degree, a stranger in our midst and not the church's Christ or idol.

What one perceives in pursuit of canonical hermeneutics is that the Bible as a whole exhibits a monotheizing thrust. God is not a Christian, a Jew, or a Muslim, male or female. God is God. The power in the concept of the incarnation is that the one God, creator of all the world, chose not only to sojourn with the people of Israel in weal and in woe but climactically to live fully the life of one Galilean member of the Abraham-Sarah family under Roman oppression.

The question, then, is whether it is canonically fair to read the parts in light of the whole. Is it fair to read tribalizing passages in light of the canonical monotheizing thrust? The Bible, beginning in the Torah, stresses that God is the God of death as well as life, of fallings as well as risings, of woe as well as apparent well-being, of apparent failure as well as apparent success. It confronts the human mind with the challenge of whether it can be ultimately sure of human judgments about what is truly good or evil. The first

three commandments may well be the greatest challenge to the human mind in all of literature. They prohibit polytheism, idolatry, and the co-opting of God's name for one point of view, whether in a court of law or in theology. They challenge humanity to affirm the integrity of reality, ontologically and ethically, to affirm the Oneness of God.

The unrecorded canonical hermeneutics throughout the Bible, wherever indigenous traditions or international wisdom was adapted, displayed a depolytheizing and monotheizing thrust. And while the Bible as a whole may not be a consistently monotheistic piece of literature, it has a distinct monotheizing thrust that should be continued by hermeneuts and tradents today in the never-ending canonical process.

Preachers Are Tradents Too.   In preaching on a text the current tradent is heir to the goodly fellowship of tradents who formed and shaped the Bible as the Book of Life. They believed it continued to have life and that it should be given to those who searched the scriptures for their identity. The preacher should keep in mind three hermeneutic H's: honesty, humility, and humor.

To read the Bible honestly is to theologize any passage before moralizing on it. To moralize first is to stress the mores of the Bronze to the Hellenistic Ages, the cultural traps and trappings of the eras in which a given passage is expressed. The current tradent should first ask what the passage indicates God can do with the likes of us reflected in the text and then, in light of that reading, form a program of obedience.

To read the Bible with humility is to read it dynamically rather than statically—that is, to identify in reading a passage not only with the so-called good folk in it but also with those we do not like. Committed Christians today would do well to identify occasionally with the committed Pharisees and other religious leaders of Jesus' time. At one point in his ministry Jeremiah became angry with some slaveholders who took their slaves back after a jubilee year during which the owners had obediently released them (Jeremiah 34). It turned out that the owners had released them just to fight on the ramparts of the city against the Babylonian invaders. Jeremiah told them that the next time they read Genesis 15 (or heard the tradition in it recited) they should by dynamic analogy identify not with Abraham in God's establishing the covenant with him but with the halves of the carcasses of the sacrificial animals through which the fire pot and torch had passed, for God was proclaiming jubilee release to Nebuchadnezzar's sword to return and cut them in two (Jer. 34: 18–20).

The normal tendency for readers of these texts is to identify with the favored one in the passage, and sometimes that may be right according to the social location of the readers. The Bible's imprecatory prayers that embarrass comfortable people may be very much appreciated by those on the bottom of the social scale. Nathan told David (2 Samuel 12) that he should have by dynamic analogy identified with the rich man in the parable Nathan recited in court and not with the poor man whose sheep was stolen since he, David, had stolen Uriah's wife. In reading Christ's parables it is always good to identify with different elements in them in order to gauge the appropriate message for the situation, the message that will encourage listeners to continue on the pilgrimage of affirming the integrity of reality, the oneness of God. Whenever our reading of a biblical passage induces self-righteousness, we can be confident we have misread it.

To read the Bible with a sense of humor* is to take God a little more seriously and ourselves a little less so than we normally do. Belief in the oneness of God who, unlike an idol, is never quite in our grasp or understanding is an act of profound, even divine humor.

Reading the Bible with the three H's induces believers old and new to walk in the way of pilgrim folk toward the threshold of truth. In this way the Bible, read critically but faithfully, is actualized into the present tense as the prophetic yet ultimately hopeful voice the church and synagogue so desperately need to hear.

Crenshaw, J. L., *Prophetic Conflict*, 1971. Fishbane, M., *Biblical Interpretation in Ancient Israel*, 1985. Hays, R. B., *Echoes of Scripture in the Letters of Paul*, 1989. Jeanrond, W. G., "History of Biblical Hermeneutics," *The Anchor Bible Dictionary* 3, 1992, 433–43. Lategan, B. C., "Hermeneutics," *The Anchor Bible Dictionary* 3, 1992, 149–54. Ricoeur, P., *Essays on Biblical Hermeneutics*, ed. L. S. Mudge, 1980. Rogerson, J. W., "Interpretation, History of," *The Anchor Bible Dictionary* 3, 424–33. Sanders, J. A., *Canon and Community*, 1984; *From Sacred Story to Sacred Text*, 1987; and "Canon," *The Anchor Bible Dictionary* 1, 1992.   JAMES A. SANDERS

Hildegard of Bingen. (1098–1179)

Abbess, mystic, and musician, Hildegard is one of the earliest women* preachers of whose work there is written record. Born at Böckelheim/Bermersheim on the Nahe, she was the youngest of ten children and the daughter of a knight. She was educated at home until her eighth year when, perhaps because of her religious visions, her parents took her to the Benedictine monastery of Mount St. Disibode to be tutored by Jutta von Sponheim, an anchoress attached to the double monastery. At the age of eighteen, Hildegard decided to take holy orders and joined the community. Upon Jutta's death in 1136, Hildegard was made the leader of the dozen or so women in the community.

Her spiritual awakening and subsequent writings began in 1141. She had a vision in which God commanded her, "Write what you see and hear! Tell people how to enter the kingdom of salvation!" The work in which most of her visions are recorded is *Scivias* (Know the Ways). As the foreword to *Scivias* notes, the work was still four years from completion when the Trier Synod convened in late 1147. Pope Eugene III read a portion of the work to the assembly and encouraged

Hildegard to continue writing. Her correspondence with Bernard of Clairvaux* was also crucial during this phase of her work; he convinced Hildegard of the integrity of her visions and writing at a time when she lacked self-confidence. A letter to Bernard demonstrates her initial diffidence: "I am greatly troubled by this vision which has appeared to me through the inspiration of divine mystery. I have never seen it with the outer eyes of the flesh. Wretched as I am (and more than wretched in bearing the name of woman), I have seen, ever since I was a child. . . . Most true and gentle Father, answer in your goodness, your unworthy maidservant" (*Hildegard of Bingen*, 127).

By 1150, Hildegard had drawn so many followers that her community outgrew its space at Mount St. Disibode. Using her own money and the dowries of other women in the community, she built a new convent at Rupertsberg, near Bingen. Because she had the backing of the Archbishop of Mainz and the protection of the emperor, she could risk the disapproval of her former abbot in this move toward relative autonomy. In 1160, Hildegard began preaching publicly in Trier and other cities and villages along the Main. Her preaching tours over the next twelve years extended as far afield as Paris and Constanz and included cathedrals in Bamberg, Trier, Ingelheim, Cologne, and Bonn. She called herself a prophetess, and contemporaries, who likened her to Deborah and Jeremiah, requested copies of the sermons from her secretaries. In 1165, the growing community at Rupertsberg needed more space, so Hildegard established a second foundation at Eibingen, across the river from Bingen.

The last twenty-five years of Hildegard's life were the period of her greatest literary output. In addition to 300 letters, her writings include two scientific works: *Physica* (Natural History), about natural remedies, including the use of rocks and jewels to aid healing, and *Causae et curae* (Causes and Cures), a medical book. Commentaries on lectionary Gospel readings, the Athanasian Creed, and the Rule

of St. Benedict are from the period 1158 to 1163, as are her biographies and *The Thirty-Eight Questions*, a doctrinal discourse. Hildegard's final visionary work, *De operatione Dei* (Book of Divine Works) was begun in 1163 and finished about ten years later.

When Hildegard died in 1179, traditions and legends about her death sprang up almost immediately. Her formal canonization process was never completed, though in 1324 Pope John XXII gave permission for her "solemn and public cult" (Bowie, 14–15). Her work and life have been rediscovered in recent years by feminist theologians and advocates of creation-centered spirituality.

Scivias is Hildegard's best-known and most often studied work. It is generally assumed that the core of her preaching was taken from the record of her visions. Studied as the basis for proclamation, the visions employ a method common in medieval sermons: the preacher begins with a nonbiblical story or image—either mundane or fantastic—and does an allegorical interpretation that may eventually draw in biblical or doctrinal material to substantiate its assertions. For example, "The First Vision of the First Part" begins: "I saw a great mountain which was iron colored, and a certain person of very great brightness was sitting upon it." After completing the depiction of the vision, the preacher starts to explicate it: "That great mountain which is iron colored signifies the strength and stability of the eternal reign of God, which cannot be banished by some impulse to change and decline" (*Scivias*, "The First Vision of the First Part"). Biblical phrases and images abound in the discussion of the vision's meaning, although there is only one text citation. The exposition of the first vision concludes with a characteristic exhortation: "whoever has knowledge in the Holy Spirit and wings in faith, let that person not pass over my warning. . . . " In addition to telling listeners/readers about the visions in *Scivias*, Hildegard supervised paintings of each one.

Scivias also has homiletical significance as a "salvational encyclopedia." It is divided into three main sections, corresponding to the Trinity, with a varying number of chapters or visions per section. What sets Hildegard's writings apart from those by other mystics is not theological innovation so much as her use of symbolic forms and images that were unknown in her time. Matthew Fox and other contemporary scholars have emphasized Hildegard's affinity with creation-centered spirituality in contrast to traditional Western fall/redemption spirituality. Hildegard coined the term "viriditas" or greening power as a metaphor for the divinely given life-force manifest in all creation. "Drying up" and shriveling, on the other hand, correspond with sin or ignoring one's vocation to cooperate with greening power. Though Hildegard's writing does celebrate the goodness of God's creation in a way that resonates with contemporary environmental concerns, the imagery in *Scivias* does not supplant or negate the traditional cosmology and ecclesiology of that age.

Bowie, F., ed., *Hildegard of Bingen: Mystical Writings,* 1990. **Fox, M., O.P.,** *Illuminations of Hildegard of Bingen,* 1985. **Hozeski, B.,** trans., *Scivias,* 1986.   CAROL M. NORÉN

LOVE CAME DOWN
Hildegard of Bingen
Humility caused the Word of God to be born from the Virgin, where humility was neither in envious surroundings, nor in the beauty of the flesh, nor in earthly riches, nor in golden ornaments, nor in worldly honors. But the Word of God was placed in a manger because the Word's mother was poor. Furthermore, humility always sighs and destroys all crimes because that is its work. Whenever the devil wishes to capture something, that object should protect and arm itself with humility because Lucifer certainly fled from humility, even as the serpent hides itself in a cave whenever humility is present. . . .

Love or charity also brought the Only-Begotten Word of God from the bosom of God in heaven and placed the Word in the womb of a mother on earth. She scorned neither sinners nor publicans, but instead strained in childbirth in order that all people might be saved. She also softened the fountain of tears falling from the eyes of the faithful, often leading away the hardness of their hearts. Humility and charity are clearly virtues; they are like a soul and a body; strong people have the forces of a soul and the members of a body. What does this mean? Humility is like a soul and charity is like a body; they cannot be separated by some internal change, but they work together.

Similarly, neither the soul nor the body would be strong if they were separated from each other, but they work together as long as a person lives in a body. And just as various powers of the various members of the body have been subjugated to the soul and to the body, so also the other virtues in accordance with justice work for humility and charity. Therefore, people, follow humility and charity for the glory of God and for your salvation. Armed with humility and charity, you do not need to fear the snares of the devil, but you will possess everlasting life.

Whence whoever has knowledge in the Holy Spirit and wings in faith, let that person not pass over my warning, but let that person lay hold of it by embracing it in the enjoyment of the soul.

From *Hildegard of Bingen's Divine Works,* ed. M. Fox (Santa Fe: Bear & Company, 1987).

History of Preaching

The Early Church
The New Testament.   There are several genres of Christian preaching, including at least the *missionary* or evangelistic, the *catechetical,* and the *liturgical.* Since texts of missionary preaching have not survived from the early church, nor have catechetical sermons from before the great series of Cyril of Jerusalem and Ambrose in the late fourth century, the liturgical sermon is the only genre to be considered in the earliest Christian

centuries. Such a sermon may be defined as a speech delivered by an authorized person applying some point of doctrine, usually drawn from a biblical passage, to the lives of the congregation with the purpose of moving them to accept that application and to act on the basis of it (*see* Education; Evangelism; Liturgical Preaching).

Clearly there is little in the New Testament that can be identified according to these criteria as Christian preaching. There is, of course, a larger sense in which everything in it is preaching. The major forms one encounters in the Christian canon are proclamation (*kerygma*) and exhortation (*paraenesis*), the indicative that declares the history of the Christ event and the imperative that spells out the implications of that event for living. Yet in the strict terms of the definition, there are probably no sermons as such in the New Testament, no texts that had been delivered orally to an assembly for evangelization, instruction, or worship.

The preaching of Jesus* could be thought to provide an exception, but it fails to on at least two counts. First, since its content was the breaking in of the reign of God and it refers only by implication to its proclaimer's role in that inauguration, it is not, strictly speaking, Christian preaching. Second, while the Gospels contain long speeches that are placed on the lips of Jesus, scholars doubt that any of them represents exactly what he said on any single public occasion. Even the beloved Sermon on the Mount— or maybe especially the Sermon on the Mount—cannot be accepted as composed exclusively of the *ipsissima verba* of Jesus. Thus, while it is certain that preaching was the main form of communication employed by the founder of Christianity, Jesus' preaching is not available to be studied for insight into the nature of Christian preaching.

Nor is it likely that any of Paul's sermons *as such* have survived. Paul makes it very clear that he had a strong sense of vocation to preach the gospel of Christ crucified and risen to the Gentiles, but he nowhere gives any indication of a similar sense of vocation to write letters to distant congregations. Yet the letters are what remain and not his missionary, catechetical, and presumably liturgical sermons. While a certain amount of overlap might be expected between the contents of the two kinds of effort to communicate, it cannot be assumed that what he delivered orally was the same as what he wrote.

A considerable portion of the Acts of the Apostles is taken up with speeches of one sort or another, many of them claiming to be the missionary sermons of Peter, Paul, or another representative of the primitive church. All of these missionary sermons, however, have the same outline: they begin with what is taken to be a prophecy from the Hebrew Bible, go on to claim that the prophecy was fulfilled in and by Jesus, document that claim by saying that the apostles were witnesses of its fulfillment, and call upon members of their audience to repent and believe the gospel. The unlikelihood that all of these preachers always followed the same outline means that the reports in Acts cannot be taken as transcripts of actual sermons. Indeed, since they present in a few short verses discourses that could have taken hours to deliver, their resemblance to real speeches is evidence not of their historicity but of Luke's extraordinary literary skill in creating such convincing scenes. Thus, if the sermons convey any information at all about preaching in the early church, they tell what Luke thought the missionary preaching of his own day ought to be like.

Some scholars do believe that at least two New Testament books contain material that originated in oral proclamation: 1 Peter and the Epistle to the Hebrews. Even if those claims are justified, however, there seems to be little reason to think that the shape of Christian preaching in the New Testament period can be reconstructed. This is to say that, while true Christian preaching began much earlier, the *history* of Christian preaching cannot be traced back earlier than the middle of the second century. There are, however, at least two movements of immense importance for the development of Christian preaching: Jewish synagogue preaching and Greco-Roman rhetoric, which began earlier and need to be looked at now to acquire an understanding of why Christian preaching developed the way it did.

Ancient Jewish Synagogue Homilies. Little is known about the earliest history of the synagogue, its services, and the preaching that occurred there. The current tendency of scholars is to date the origin of synagogues more recently than was done in the past. Instead of the exile, the first or second century B.C.E. is now considered to be the time when synagogues emerged. Ironically, some of the earliest evidence about synagogue services and preaching occurs in New Testament passages such as Luke 4:16–21 and Acts 13:15–16.

Both of these passages show that after readings from the Torah and Haftarot (the Law and its "completion" in the Prophets, the first two divisions of the Hebrew canon) there could be commentary on one or both passages that would apply their teaching to the lives of the people. Here already, then, is what has been the most distinctive characteristic of Christian preaching through the ages: the explication and application of biblical texts, an activity for which no provision was made in classical rhetoric.

Jewish* sermons have been preserved from as early as the Tannaitic period (70–200 C.E.), but the majority are from the Amoraic period (200–500 C.E.). There are many sermons that preserve the form of comment on the lections at the service, a sort of sermon that has been referred to as "an exposition of the first verses of the Pentateuchal section." The formal characteristics of this genre, which were relatively loose, are:

1. The sermon begins with a quotation of the first verse in the passage or at least several words from that verse.
2. A key word or words are explained and emphasized throughout the sermon.
3. Other words and phrases from the rest of the passage are also explained and repeated in the sermon.
4. Verses from elsewhere in the Bible are cited to illustrate points already made or to introduce others.
5. Illustrations are drawn from contemporary life as well as from the Bible.
6. When biblical stories are retold, there are frequently imaginative additions to the text.
7. A word or words from the opening text are repeated at the conclusion to show that the sermon has ended.
8. The main thrust of the sermon is frequently summarized in the conclusion.

This commentary sort of homily was used on festival days and on Sabbath (Saturday) afternoons, but as early as 70 C.E. there developed a shorter homiletical form called the *proem* that was used for daily services. The proem was an introduction to the lection that was about to be read. Unlike the commentary form, however, direct influences of the proem on Christian preaching are hard to detect.

Greco-Roman Rhetoric. Another influence from the environment of the early church that through the centuries was to prove almost as powerful a force in shaping Christian preaching as the textual commentary of synagogue sermons was the oratorical tradition of classical culture. The information that follows on Greco-Roman rhetoric* is not so important in its own right as it is for introducing concepts and vocabulary that would recur in the history of Christian preaching, especially in the golden age of the Fathers, when all of the great preachers had been trained as rhetoricians, and in the Renaissance and Reformation, when the recovery of classical rhetoric had considerable influence on preaching.

Most cultures in the history of the world have produced great oratory. The difference between the ancient Greeks and the others is that Greece also developed a technical vocabulary about oratory that facilitated analysis of it. This conceptualization of public speaking was a result of there being no professional lawyers in Greece. Citizens had to argue their own cases in court, and some were better at it than others. By the fifth century B.C.E., little handbooks on effective rhetoric techniques began to appear. The great synthesis of Greek thought on the subject was the work of Aristotle, who defined the aim of rhetoric as the discovery of the available means of persuasion. While many others also wrote on the topic, the Roman appropriation of rhetorical theory is best seen in the compilations of Cicero and Quintilian.

The three sorts of occasions on which Athenians might be called upon to speak in public were in the courts of law, in the legislative assembly, and at ceremonial events. Each required its own appropriate manner of speaking (what the Romans called its *genus dicendi*). The law courts, for instance, had to decide what had happened in the past; the *boule* had to agree upon what ought to be done in the future; and ceremonial occasions called for praising or blaming someone or something. These three types of oratory came to be called, respectively: forensic, deliberative, and demonstrative or "epideictic."

Classical thought divided the task of preparing to speak into five stages: invention (figuring out what to say to make one's case), disposition (the outline the speech should follow), elocution (style, especially in the sense of deciding what figures of sound and thought would best contribute to making one's case), memory (preparation for delivery), and delivery itself. Invention recognized the existence of three kinds of "proof": the trustworthiness of the speaker (*ethos*), reason (*logos*), and appeal to the emotions (*pathos*). Each of these seemed generally more appropriate to one part of a speech than another: *ethos* should be established in the introduction, *logos* was necessary for the body, and *pathos* was most effective in the conclusion. Cicero also spoke of the duties of the orator to prove (*probare*), to delight (*delectare*), and to stir or move (*flectere*). Each of these

could be connected with one of the levels of style: the plain for proof, the middle for pleasure, and the grand for moving. The grand is not the most flowery; that is the middle, which is intended for the pleasure of the audience. The grand style aims at moving the audience to believe or do what the speaker is calling upon it to believe or do.

The final concepts from classical rhetoric that need to be introduced are those related to elements thought to be required for each type of speech. Since the forensic speech was taken as normative from the beginning, the textbooks normally did not discuss in such detail the outline of either of the other types. The six parts a forensic speech was expected to have were introduction, narration, partition, confirmation, refutation, and conclusion. In the introduction the speaker must make the audience well-disposed toward the speaker, attentive, and receptive. The narration sets the facts of the case before the jury. In the partition, the audience is told what is to follow in a list of either the points of disagreement or the points the speaker will try to prove. In the confirmation, those points are made, and in the refutation, the opponent's case is attacked. The conclusion involves a combination of summarizing what has been said and arousing feeling against the opponent and in favor of the speaker. The appropriateness of such a pattern for arguing a case in court at a time when each of the two speakers was given only one opportunity to state a case is immediately apparent. What is not so apparent is that this pattern would be helpful to a preacher trying to write a sermon. That does not mean, however, that there would not be many homiletical authorities in the future who would insist that preachers should follow it exactly without recognizing the distinctiveness that explication of biblical text gives to the rhetorical form of Christian preaching.

The Oldest Known Christian Sermons. That there was preaching at Christian assemblies for worship from the earliest days is suggested by a description of such assemblies written by Justin Martyr in the middle of the second century:

> On the day called Sunday there was a meeting in one place . . . and the memoirs of the apostles or the writings of the prophets are read as long as time permits. When the reader has finished, the president (*proestos*) in a discourse urges and invites us to the imitation of these noble things (*1 Apol.* 67).

After that the Eucharist continues. Something of what that preaching must have been like can be known from two works from the mid-to-late second century that meet the criterion of texts written for oral delivery to a Christian congregation assembled for worship. Thus they are the oldest known Christian sermons.

The first has been known since the fourth century as the *Second Epistle of Clement to the Corinthians* under the belief that it was written by Clement of Rome. Stylistic analysis shows that Clement was not the author. Instead, explicit references in the text identify *2 Clement* as a sermon—for example, ". . . at this moment while we are being admonished by the presbyters" (17.3). This sermon, which fills about ten pages of a modern book, is preached on the the text of Isa. 54:1, and it is understood here as it is in Gal. 4:27 to refer to the relative situations of the church and Israel. With that, however, the parallels between *2 Clement* and Paul cease, since the sermon comes close to preaching salvation by works rather than by grace.

While the argument rambles a bit, there is a relatively clear thread of thought that is developed by frequent quotations from scripture. The sermon ends with a doxology:

> To the only invisible God, the Father of truth, who dispatched to us the Savior and prince of immortality, through whom he also disclosed to us the truth and the heavenly life—to him be glory forever and ever.

Different scholars have assigned the provenance of this sermon to every major center of the early church, but they do agree that it was written in the middle of the second century. This makes it the oldest surviving Christian sermon.

While the oldest sermon seems a little banal, the next oldest is a tour de force. Known only by title and unidentified fragments before 1940, the *Paschal Homily* of Melito of Sardis has become widely recognized for the light that it sheds on the early history of the Christian calendar and liturgy. During the last third of the second century Melito was bishop of a church in eastern Asia Minor mentioned in the Revelation. He was the author of around twenty works that are still lost and was regarded by his contemporaries as one of the "great luminaries" of Asia. Tertullian admired his prose style. Beyond his membership in the Quartodeciman party, little else is known of Melito except what may be deduced from his homily.

The sermon dates from the period when the paschal mystery was celebrated as a unified event including everything from trial to resurrection and ascension, so the exact occasion on which it was preached according to the Christian calendar of today cannot be fixed. The way it is developed, however, resembles much that was to become familiar in later liturgical formulas. Essentially, the sermon is an interpretation of the account of the Passover in Exodus as a type of the death and resurrection of Christ. It begins with a long account of salvation history, showing the necessity for a redeemer. That is followed by a statement of the principles of typological interpretation, which leads into an identification of the salvation wrought through Christ with all that was prefigured in the exodus, especially the Passover. Next comes an extended apostrophe to Israel in which Israel is blamed for rejecting Christ and necessitating the crucifixion. The peak of emotional intensity occurs when Melito speaks in the voice of Christ, proclaiming and offering the salvation he brings. After that follows an almost creedal summary of the work of Christ that leads into the doxological conclusion. The homily shows both the influence of the Septuagint, especially the poetic books, and also that of the sort of rhetoric with which professional orators were dazzling Asia Minor at the time. Most of the figures of sound and thought are there. One can easily find, for instance, anaphora, antithesis, apostrophe, and personification. From this point on, classical rhetoric would be an influence on Christian preaching (*see* Style).

Interpreting the Word in Alexandria. Several Latin homilies have come down from the early third century, mostly of pseudonymous attribution. The most influential homiletic development of the early church, however, was to come from Greek-speaking Egypt. Alexandria, the third largest city of the Roman empire and its intellectual capital, the place where the Hebrew Bible had been translated into the Greek of the Septuagint and Philo had labored to state his apology for Judaism in the vocabulary of Greek philosophy, was the natural place for Christian preaching to settle into a pattern that would remain influential until the modern period.

The earliest sermonlike document from Alexandria is a delightful piece produced by Clement of Alexandria near the beginning of the third century. Many scholars consider it a homily because it is a verse-by-verse analysis of Mark 10:17–31 that seeks to provide an answer to the question, Who is the rich man who shall be saved? It even ends with a wonderful legend about St. John. But one cannot know whether it was delivered orally to a congregation and thus whether it was truly a sermon.

Credit for creation of the classical form of the homily has to go to the one who is also known as the first Christian systematic theologian, Origen.* Origen's father was a priest who was martyred when his son was seventeen. A precocious boy, Origen became a teacher to support his mother and the younger children. In addition to this secular instruction, he also began to teach interested pagans about Christianity. Philosophically gifted, he was eventually to acquire a reputation in the church for being more given to speculation than to the life of the Christian community, but modern research shows that to be an erroneous impression. His main interest was in biblical interpretation: most of his writings were detailed studies of biblical books, using the word-by-word analysis that Greek grammarians had developed for the study of classical texts.

Even though he was devoted to biblical study, Origen did not preach often until he was almost fifty. After the bishop of Caesarea made him a priest in 232, Origen moved to Palestine and began his preaching ministry. At the weekday morning services, only a lection from the Hebrew Bible was read; a book was read straight through, two or three chapters at a time. It was at these services that most of the two hundred surviving sermons of Origen were delivered. At the Sunday liturgy, short homilies were preached on each of the three readings—Old Testament, Epistle, and Gospel—and it is for these occasions that Origen preached his *Homilies on Luke*, the only New Testament series that has been preserved.

Origen stood to deliver these homilies extemporaneously after he had prepared himself exegetically, and they were taken down by a stenographer. He went through the pericope a verse at a time, explaining it literally and then applying it to the lives of the people. To the extent that the word homily* is a technical term, it means a sermon that does such verse-by-verse exegesis in applying a biblical passage to the lives of a congregation.

His methods of application he called moral and mystical. The moral sense looked for the meaning of the passage for the soul, and the mystical sense sought what the passage meant in regard to Christ and the church. At other times Origen would refer to the letter and the spirit, a distinction he borrowed from Paul (2 Cor. 3:6).

While the accusation of arbitrary biblical interpretation has followed Origen down to the present century, several things need to be said to set such evaluations in perspective. The first is that Origen's mystical sense is very much like the typological method all New Testament writers use to discover prophecies of Christ in the Hebrew scriptures. Next it can be pointed out that history as the term is understood today—the verifiable reconstruction of past events—is an invention of the nineteenth century. When the Reformers, for instance, called for literal instead of allegorical biblical interpretation, they still assumed that the Christian creed was the hermeneutical key to the Hebrew Bible. Further, since the historical meaning of biblical passages is always in reference to their first readers, the only way that any preacher has ever been able to transfer those passages to the lives of latter day parishioners has been to assume that there were analogies between the original situation and the situation in the contemporary congregation. Analogical application is not very far from allegorical application.

Finally, to treat all allegorical application as invalid is to excommunicate most of the preaching in the history of the church. While it is true that allegorical interpretation cannot be used to prove Christian doctrine, it was seldom ever used for that purpose. More often it was used to illustrate Christian beliefs that had been arrived at on the basis of other evidence. Mostly it was a tool for extending the meaning of biblical passages to the lives of Christians of later periods. The impetus for it both in the time of Origen and later was the basic assumption of biblical inspiration, the belief that God gave the Bible to the church as the main hermeneutical instrument for understanding its own life. Thus the preaching of Origen furnished the model for biblical interpretation that was to dominate for many centuries to come.

The Golden Age of the Greek Fathers. The next major development of Christian preaching occurred about a century and a half after the time of Origen. By the late fourth century Christianity had achieved a privileged position in the Roman empire as a result of the conversion of Constantine. This was a period in which many of the administrators of the empire were members of the landed class whose preparation for this work was rhetorical training. Bishops were often chosen from the ranks of those who had trained as rhetors. Certainly, the greatest preachers (who were also the greatest theologians) among the church fathers had received such an education.

The Cappodocians* were such fathers. Gregory of Nazianzus, who received his elementary education in his home town, went to the provincial capital of Cappadocia, Caesarea, for his secondary schooling, and then, in the manner of the day, began seeking out famous teachers, first at Caesarea in Palestine and then at Alexandria. Finally, he spent the decade of his twenties at Athens studying rhetoric and philosophy. During a good bit of this long educational program, he was a fellow student with his best friend, known to history as Basil the Great.

Gregory's sermons are not called homilies but discourses (*logoi*), even though a few of the forty-four preserved were obviously preached at regular Sunday worship. Some of them are theological treatises; indeed, the "Five Theological Orations" (27–31) did much to formulate the great Eastern statement of trinitarian orthodoxy on the eve of the Council of Constantinople, and it is because of them that their author is referred to as "St. Gregory the Theologian." His Second Oration is a justification for his flight to avoid ordination and is one of the greatest and most influential manuals of pastoral care from the early church.

Quite a few of the orations, however, are encomia—especially eulogies of family members and friends—and there are even invectives (against Julian the Apostate and against the Arians). These discourses obviously belong to epideictic, the classical genre of praise and blame. Gregory followed closely the criteria for such speeches laid down in the rhetorical handbooks. While most of the sermons of the other two Cappadocians, Basil the Great and Gregory of Nyssa, were in the traditional form of the homily, the epideictic of Nazianzus is an indication of how completely all three of them were shaped homiletically by their years of rhetorical training.

John Chrysostom* was another church father. He is generally regarded as the greatest preacher of the early church, and Pope Pius X referred to him as the patron saint of Christian preachers. Born in the middle of the fourth century into an educated upper-class family in Antioch, John was brought up by his mother Anthusa after his father's early death. He studied under one of the greatest rhetoricians of the age, Libanius, and seemed destined by his talent for a brilliant career in the law or civil service. He felt drawn, however, to the Christian ministry during his teens and began to study scripture under the Bishop of Antioch, Meletius. Before ordination, he first tested his vocation as a monk.

Ordained a priest in 386, he spent a decade in Antioch during which he produced the bulk of his many sermons that have survived. Most of his expository homilies are on consecutive sections of entire biblical books rather than on pericopes appointed for the liturgical lectionary. The books treated include Genesis, Matthew, John, Romans, 1 and 2 Corinthians, Ephesians, and the Pastoral Epistles. These are especially prized by later scholars since John practiced literal, grammatical, historical exegesis in the tradition of Antioch rather than that of the allegorical tradition of Alexandria. During this period he also preached series of topical sermons against the Arians and Judaizing Christians, the latter unfortunately proving a mine for later Christian anti-Jewish preaching.* The most famous topical series, however, was the twenty-one sermons *On the Statues*

that he preached when statues of the emperor and his family were overturned by mobs in protest against new taxes.

After being appointed as Bishop of Constantinople in 398, John discovered that pastoral and spiritual zeal were no protection against getting caught up in church and state politics. Being harmless as a dove did not automatically make him as wise as a serpent. After serving in Constantinople for six years he was deposed by two stacked councils on trumped-up charges and spent his few remaining years in exile.

This man of superb training and native genius used all his skill to mold the development of the distinctive Christian genre of public address, the homily. As noted already, the homily was constructed around the explication of a biblical text, and thus it had a shape and purpose that was different from anything discussed by the classical rhetoricians. It took a person so reflexively eloquent as Chrysostom to show what superb oratory could be practiced in this crude new genre.

The High Tide of Preaching in the Western Church. There were distinct differences in ethos between Eastern and Western Christians from the beginning, the most basic being the theoretical and theological orientation of the Greek church in contrast with the more practical and ethical concerns of the West. Originally, however, these cultural differences were not reflected by a difference in language. Rome in the early days of the Christian era was such an international city, and the Romans themselves had so much respect for Greek culture, that the language of the church in the capital of the empire remained Greek for several centuries, and Christian Latin was developed in North Africa. Thus it is at the end of the fourth century that the first major homiletical documents in Latin were produced, those of Zeno of Verona and Ambrose of Milan. Neither of these bishops, however, was distinctive enough in his preaching to merit extended consideration here. For all practical purposes, the history of Christian Latin preaching begins with a convert of Ambrose who was not only its *arche* but also its apogee.

The facts of the life of the future bishop of Hippo, Augustine,* are well known, not least from his *Confessions*. Born in 354 in Thagaste in the Roman granary of North Africa to a Christian mother and pagan father, Augustine was sent to study rhetoric at Carthage. There he achieved such proficiency as a teacher of rhetoric that he was able to move first to Rome and then to Milan, where he was appointed to an imperial chair at what was then the administrative capital of the empire. In Milan he fell under the influence of Ambrose and underwent the conversion he narrates so powerfully in his *Confessions*. From that time on, he began to practice the life of a Christian ascetic in the company of friends, returning the next year to his home in North Africa. Although he remained a monk, he was made a priest in 391 and a suffragan bishop four years later. Succeeding to the see the year after that, he continued as bishop of Hippo until his death in 430. One of the greatest theologians of all time, he is known for his controversies with the Donatists and Pelagians, for his treatise on the Trinity, and for his great apology for Christianity, the *City of God*.

Even though he was influential throughout North Africa during his lifetime, most of his more than 500 surviving sermons were preached to his own congregation at Hippo. Many of his sermons were preached at the regular liturgical assemblies and show signs of this setting not only in their themes but also in their brevity. Yet others were continuous expositions of biblical books, most notably the Psalms and the Fourth Gospel. All are spoken very directly to his people, urging upon them the necessity of understanding their lives in the light of the gospel and of conforming their lives to it. At times they have a simplicity and apparent artlessness that masks the consummate artistry of one of the greatest orators who ever lived; he was, after all, preaching not to impress his people but to lead them to heaven.

Augustine's pastoral concern rings in every line.

In addition to being a great practitioner, he was one of the first theoreticians of homiletics, his *De doctrina christiana* being the earliest textbook on the subject. The standard translation of the title, *On Christian Doctrine*, is misleading, suggesting as it does that the treatise concerns the content rather than the activity of Christian pedagogy. His topics, then, are, as one authority put it, "hermeneutics and homiletics"—what to say and how to say it effectively so that people will hear and act.

> There are two things necessary to the treatment of the Scriptures: a way of discovering those things which are to be understood, and a way of teaching what we have learned (I, 1.1).

The first three of the four books are dedicated to the first of these two topics. Book I establishes the hermeneutical key by which one can recognize the correct interpretation of a biblical passage:

> Whoever, therefore, thinks that he understands the divine Scriptures or any part of them so that it does not build the double love of God and of our neighbor does not understand it at all (I, 36.40).

In Books II and III Augustine puts forth his method for biblical interpretation in a discussion of signs that sounds curiously modern. Then he moves on to state his Christian rhetoric. He does not bother with the principles of secular rhetoric on the assumption that they have been acquired earlier at school. The aim of specifically Christian eloquence is not to impress the audience but to make it possible for the audience to understand and accept what is taught. That is done by fulfilling all three of the duties of a speaker listed by Cicero: teaching, delighting, and moving. Each has its role in the strategy of Christian persuasion, and each of these duties is related to one of the three levels of style. The plain style is used for teaching, the middle for delighting, and the grand for moving. The Christian teacher cannot be persuasive, however, unless his life proclaims what his preaching does. Unlike Aristotle's ethos, this trust in the speaker is not created by the speech but outside of it in daily life. Such is Augustine's theory of preaching, a theory that has been very influential ever since he wrote it.

The occasion of the writing of Augustine's *City of God* was the sacking of Rome by Alaric in 410. The barbarian invasions that were to bring the western Roman empire to an end sixty-six years later were already well under way. Roman culture was almost as endangered as Roman rule. Yet at least one pope remained who would achieve rhetorical brilliance as well as theological influence: Leo I, who occupied the chair of Peter from 440–461. Known both for his theological orthodoxy and for his strengthening of the claims of the papacy, Leo the Great also used his eloquence to persuade Attila not to invade Rome and Gaiseric to do so less violently. He has importance in the history of preaching for several reasons. He was a master rhetorician who, unlike Chrysostom and Augustine, used the full power of his style in preaching. As a student of his style has said:

> Leo's Latinity is a grand parade of rhythmic alliteration and assonance employing sonorous and majestic word patterns, interogative and emphatic as well as discordant phrase-making, that utilizes the Latin language's inestimable power and regality as well as pathetic potency (F. X. Murphy, C.S.S.R., "The Sermons of Pope Leo the Great: Content and Style," in *Preaching in the Patristic Age*, 1989, 186).

So sensitive was he to the formal cadences of Latin that his style became the model for the Middle Ages. Then too his preaching was more closely tied to the liturgical calendar and lectionary than that of any of his predecessors. Leo also showed a deep passion for social justice.

Catechetical Preaching. From the second half of the fourth century there are a number of examples of a kind of preaching that must have been going on for a couple of centuries even though earlier examples have not been preserved. These are didactic sermons instructing those who are to be initiated into the Christian community. Relatively complete sets of such sermons by Cyril of Jerusalem, Theodore of Mopsuestia, John Chrysostom, and Ambrose of Milan exist. These show what would be a startling similarity in the pattern of preparation for initiations—if Hippolytus had not claimed that the same pattern had been normal in Rome during his youth (ca. 200 C.E.) and that it was ancient then.

By the fourth century, baptism was often postponed even by those who were associated with the church out of fear that it would be impossible to have later sins forgiven. Thus adult baptism became the norm even for those like Augustine who were enrolled as catechumens in infancy. During Lent, catechumens were instructed by daily sermons dealing with basic Christian faith, especially as that was summarized in a baptismal creed (such as the Apostles' Creed) that they had to memorize. Baptism and first communion were administered at the Easter Vigil and Eucharist. Custom varied from place to place so that in some places the explanation of baptism and the eucharist occurred before the reception of the sacraments, while in other places it came afterward. At some point the Lord's Prayer was also taught and explained as were other general matters of Christian behavior.

Late Patristic Latin Preaching. After the fall of the empire in the West, the infrastructures that promulgated Roman culture fell into disarray. Thus the rhetorical training that had equipped so many bishops for the technical side of their preaching ministry became far rarer. A leader of the church in the West during this embattled period is Gregory I,* bishop of Rome from 590 to 604. The son of a senator who had become prefect of Rome, he sold his vast property, gave the money to the poor, founded a monastery, and entered it himself. From this life of detachment from the world that he loved, he was called first to be the pope's representative to the imperial court at Constantinople and then later to be pope himself. Since Italy was no longer effectively protected by imperial troops, the bishop was left with the responsibility for relations with the invading Lombards, for much of the civic administration of the peninsula, and for the feeding of the people who were under siege. During all this he sent Roman missionaries to Britain and wrote a number of what were to be among the most influential books during the Middle Ages. Small wonder that later generations know him as Gregory the Great.

Until recently, however, scholars have failed to recognize the importance to Gregory of preaching. In addition to his *Homilies on the Gospels*, which he preached on the liturgical lectionary, his *Moralia on Job* and *Homilies on Ezekiel* originated as preaching, and his other biblical commentaries seem related to preaching. The importance that he placed on preaching may be seen in his allegorical interpretation of the book of Job, in which he understood the sons of Job to stand for the apostles, whose distinctive work was preaching. Indeed, he found references to preaching wherever he looked in the Bible. Furthermore, his treatise on pastoral care is largely about preaching. About two thirds of the book is devoted to instructions on how to preach to the various types of people who might be found in the congregation. Another section deals with the temptations that come to a preacher after a sermon is delivered, and the remaining two sections have particular relevance to preaching. Finally, his *Dialogues* about the miracles of Italian saints contain six stories that he had already used in his homilies and were an important source for the *exempla* used to illustrate late medieval sermons. Indeed, Gregory was one of the first to use nonbiblical narratives to illustrate points made in his sermons, a practice that has been emulated ever since.

The shape of the future, however, can be seen even more clearly in one who, although he came two generations before Gregory, lived nearer the rim of Roman influence. Caesarius was archbishop of Arles, the primatial see of Gaul, during the first four decades of the sixth century, a period that has been described as "a time of political and spiritual revolution and ferment." A monk, he was devoted to the ascetic ideal but much involved in the life of the church and society. Although trained in rhetoric by Julian Pomerius, his preaching was popular preaching in the language of the people. Two hundred thirty-eight of his sermons have been preserved, including liturgical homilies and other genres as well. Caesarius was devoted to the ideal of preaching at every liturgy and believed that if the bishop were not there to preach, a presbyter should be. If there was no presbyter, then a deacon could read a sermon written by someone else. Providing sermons to be read for such occasions was one of his reasons for assembling his collection. These in turn borrowed from the sermons of the great preachers among the church fathers, especially Augustine. Thus, in the sermons of Caesarius there is a sample of things to come, a foretaste of the homiliaries of the early Middle Ages when classical culture would have eroded so that no preacher dared to have opinions or even words of his own.

One has the sense of having come full circle from a beginning of Christian preaching outside the areas of high culture, through a period in which the best-trained minds of the civilized world were proclaiming the gospel, to a time when the lights of culture were going out in the West. The light of the gospel, however, was not going out. Vigorous new peoples were being won for the faith who would create the Gothic culture of the High Middle Ages, a culture that made Christian presuppositions its core.

The Middle Ages

Homiliaries. While the concept of the "Dark Ages" has been discarded by historians of the early Middle Ages because of the great cultural vitality of the period, it is nevertheless the case that after the abdication in 476 of the last Roman emperor in the West, Romulus Augustulus, there was a marked decline of specifically Roman culture in the Latin-speaking areas of the empire. The Greek-speaking half of the empire centered around Constantinople continued, of course, for another thousand years until the Turkish conquest. In the West, however, most infrastructures had collapsed under the trauma of the movement of peoples known as the "barbarian invasions." Since the preaching of the Western church had been so intimately connected with Roman culture, a time came when no one had the confidence any longer to compose entirely new sermons. All authentic Christian proclamation was felt to have taken place in the past golden age of the Latin Fathers. The result is that the only new homiletical materials created during the period were not new sermons but collections of patristic sermons called homiliaries by later scholars.

"Homiliaries" are obviously collections of homilies, of verse-by-verse expositions and applications of scriptural readings from the liturgical lectionary. Such reflections on the biblical passages for the particular day in the church's calendar were the most common form taken by the preaching of the Latin Fathers. Homiliaries were not devoted to the sermons of any single one of the Fathers, nor were they arranged topically. Rather, they were anthologies following the liturgical year and incorporating sermons by a number of different preachers. At this time bishops were still regarded as the normative preachers, but there were towns and villages without bishops, where presbyters and sometimes deacons would preach—or at least read sermons from the Fathers. While some clergy might read one of these homilies to their congregations on the appropriate day, others would use them as sources of materials for sermons of their own composition. Such volumes could also be used for private devotions. Their main use, however, was to provide readings for the night office or at meals in monasteries; the Rule of St. Benedict calls for such readings at those times.

The compilation of homiliaries seems to have begun in Africa in the middle of the fifth century and to have been taken from there to Naples and Arles by exiles. From there the form was diffused throughout western Europe. Some of the more important homiliaries, designated either by the name of their collector or that of the provenance or locality where the manuscripts appear, are: St. Peter of Rome, Verona, Fleury-sur-Loire, Wolfenbüttel 4096, Vatican lat. 3828, Vienna 1616, Toledo, Agimond, Alan of Farfa, Paul the Deacon, Alcuin, and Ottobeuren. It was by such documents that the light of the proclaimed word was kept alive in what at least homiletically appears to have been a dark age.

The Carolingian Reform. While Charlemagne was doubling the size of the kingdom of the Franks during the last half of the eighth century, he encouraged a renewal of learning among the clergy, expected his conquests to be accompanied by evangelization among the subject people, and used clergy a great deal in his administration. The renewal of learning was necessary if the clergy were to do the evangelization and also if they were to help administer the empire. In this program, preaching was thought to have a strategic importance because it was the medium through which recently converted pagans were to receive their catechetical formation as Christians. Thus there was both civil and ecclesiastical support for a renewal of preaching that is reflected in such documents as Charlemagne's *Admonitio generalis* (789) and the canons of the Council of Arles (813). These called for sermons in all parish churches on every Sunday and holy day, sermons that were to be delivered in the language of the people. For congregations of such new Christians, it was necessary that the instruction communicated through these sermons be very basic.

An interesting example of Carolingian catechetical preaching is Rabanus Maurus, a disciple of Charlemagne's adviser Alcuin who became abbot of Fulda and then Archbishop of Mainz. His two efforts at collecting homiliaries were separated by a period of forty years. The later collection was intended for the private devotions of the emperor, but the first was assembled to provide parish clergy with sermons to deliver to their congregations. The purpose of these sermons was to instruct the people in how to observe the main feasts of the church year and about virtues, vices, and doctrinal errors. They provide an exposition of the gospel for the day, followed by exhortation on whatever topic the passage suggested to the particular Father who wrote the sermon.

Anglo-Saxon Catechetical Preaching. Hrabanus's goal of producing texts for the socialization of new peoples into the Christian faith was realized more fully in England 150 years after his death. After the Anglo-Saxon invaders had driven the Celtic-speaking British people into what is now Wales, Ireland, and Scotland, they occupied England and developed the culture that is called Anglo-Saxon and the language that is known as Old English. Involved in this process was a monastic expansion similar to the contemporary Cluniac reform on the continent except that it did not establish isolated monasteries so much as develop cathedral chapters as monastic communities. These cathedral cloisters became great centers of learning, and they began to take on the responsibility for the catechesis of the people in their native language. Such basic instruction had become necessary for all families, not only those who were new Christians, because the establishment of infant baptism as the norm meant that pre-baptismal catechesis of adults could no longer be presupposed.

This task of catechetical preaching was greatly assisted by Aelfric (ca. 955–1020), a disciple of monastic reform who became Abbot of Eynsham. While he was still a monk at Cerne Abbas, he issued two sets of homilies in English, the first dealing with the feasts of the liturgical year and the second with doctrine and church history. The context in which such sermons were to be preached was the office of Prone. A sort of "service within a service," Prone occurred after the Gospel at Mass. Since the eucharistic liturgy was in Latin, Prone became a vernacular insertion in which the Gospel was translated, announcements were made, homilies were preached, and bidding prayers and other devotions were offered. When that office ended, the Latin liturgy was resumed. Aelfric provided two complete cycles of sermons to be preached at Prone on a bi-weekly basis. Of those, the sermons for Rogationtide are the most explicitly catechetical (*see* Teaching and Preaching).

Early Medieval Textbooks. Although there are many patristic writings that contain teaching of one sort or another about preaching, the closest the early church came to producing a full-fledged homiletics textbook was in Augustine's *On Christian Doctrine.* The first medieval work to have any similar claim was the effort of Rabanus Maurus to write a one-volume curriculum in pastoral theology, which he called *De clericorum institutione.* The third book concentrates on the related topics of biblical interpretation and preaching. It shows the age's lack of confidence, however, because it consists exclusively of long verbatim quotations from the fourth book of Augustine's work.

The first original medieval work on homiletics is a product of the renaissance of the eleventh and twelfth centuries. Guibert of Nogent* began in 1084 to write a commentary on Genesis to which he added when it was finally completed what he called "A Book About the Way a Sermon Ought to Be Given." It begins with a long excursus about the reasons why people try to avoid preaching. His advice on preaching is that sermons should begin with prayer and they should be short; the preacher needs to prepare spiritually and intellectually before giving thought to questions of style; and the congregation who will hear the sermon should never be far from the preacher's mind. Guibert then goes on to discuss biblical interpretation, giving one of the earliest clear statements about the four senses of scripture (historical, allegorical, tropological, and ascetical or anagogical). His own strong preference was for sermons preached on the tropological or moral sense.

In the century that elapsed before the next surviving textbook was written, the revival of learning and restoration of confidence had made great strides. The initiative was passing from monasteries to cathedral schools, and dialectic came to dominate theological discussions. Thus Alan of Lille's* *The Art of Preaching* already contains hints of what the preaching manuals of the great revival of preaching in the thirteenth and fourteenth centuries would be like. Alan, who had taught at Paris and Montpellier before becoming a Cistercian monk, was such a polymath and wrote in so many fields that he was known in his time as "the universal doctor." In his *Art* he gives the first definition of preaching in the history of the church:

> Preaching is open and public instruction in faith and behavior, whose purpose is the forming of men; it derives from the path of reason and from the fountainhead of authorities.

Then he moves to an allegorical interpretation of Jacob's ladder as stages in the development of the perfect person. These he sees to be: confession, prayer, thanksgiving, Bible study, consulting more learned biblical scholars, expounding the scripture, and preaching. This exalted evaluation of preaching was to become common in the High Middle Ages.

One of the ways in which Alan's *Art of Preaching* most resembles the treatises that are to follow is in his insistence that every sermon should develop from a theological authority.* For practical purposes, this means that sermons should be based on biblical texts. An "authority" is a quotation that authorizes an assertion a speaker or writer makes, functioning almost as a proof text. The most authoritative "authorities" are Bible verses, but these may also be backed up by other statements from the fathers and these, in turn, by tags from pagan classics. After centuries of expository preaching in patristic homilies, textual preaching now emerges, reflecting as it does the preoccupation of the age with argument and proof. When an authority was taken as the text for a sermon, contemporary usage referred to it as a "theme." Alan's treatment of the way the theme is developed homiletically is different from what was soon to become standard in that he does not advocate a system of dividing the text into its component parts and developing each of these subdivisions separately. In his own surviving sermons, Alan shows himself to be a good and, at times, eloquent practitioner of the principles he enunciates.

Monastic Preaching. There was a great renewal of monastic life during the eleventh and twelfth centuries, and preaching was one of the main media through which that renewal was communicated. The monastic life at its best was always a way presented to souls so in love with Christ that they wanted to leave all and follow him. Its preaching, therefore, was counsel in how that might be done most efficaciously. In this period, the Rule of St. Benedict was standard for most Western monasticism. It enshrined a pattern by which souls could draw near to God through a daily routine of corporate prayer, work, and meditation on the Bible or other spiritual reading. Corporate prayer was spread throughout the day and night in seven services in which the entire Psalter was recited weekly and the rest of the Bible read in the course of a year. The work that was performed—all manual labor at first, although it was later extended to include such activities as copying manuscripts—was considered to be as important spiritually as prayer. Time not spent in chapel or in work, eating, or rest was spent in *lectio divina*, spiritual reading that also involved meditation and memorization. Silence was maintained much of the time.

Preaching was the main way the abbot had of teaching monks how to advance in their spiritual life. He would preach twice a day: in the morning before work began and in the evening when it was finished. These sermons generally took the form of homilies in which biblical passages were interpreted anagogically to apply to the spiritual life. In this they were much more like the homilies of the fathers than they were like the thematic sermons that were soon to characterize university preaching.

Since there was essentially one monastic theology, it is possible to survey monastic preaching in the work of its greatest practitioner, Bernard of Clairvaux* (1090–1153). Born into a family of minor nobility near Dijon, he received a good education before deciding at the age of twenty-one to become a Cistercian monk. When he did decide, however, he took thirty others along with him. He helped revive the flagging new order and was sent off after only three years to found a new monastery at Clairvaux. By the time of his death, the order had grown to 350 houses, almost half of which were under his authority. His reputation as a spiritual teacher grew until he was one of the most influential men in Europe and was called on to advise popes and kings, not to mention monks and scholars. He preached the Second Crusade and refuted the teaching of French heretics. A century later, Dante had Bernard introducing him to the Blessed Virgin Mary in *The Divine Comedy*. He well deserves the accolade of Mabillion, his great seventeenth-century editor, who called him "the last of the Fathers."

Almost two thirds of the 3,500 pages of the standard edition of his work consists of preaching material. The question arises of the extent to which anything that has survived represents what Bernard delivered orally to his monks. Most of his works have come down in three different manuscript traditions. The shortest may represent no more than the outlines from which he spoke; the second was the first written form he prepared for publication; and the third was a finely polished revision of all his works that he made near the end of his life. All of these appear to be his own work—with whatever secretarial assistance he may have used—representing a spectrum from oral to written communication. Even the most polished forms observe the conventions of homilies, including asides and practical announcements. The homilies come in series and the series are so interconnected that even a genius like Bernard could not have achieved that degree of integration in his essentially extemporaneous delivery. No system of shorthand was in use at the time. Yet the form and the content permit an idealized view of monastic preaching, showing what it always hoped to be.

A look at the major works of Bernard indicates which books of the Bible formed monastic spirituality and the homiletical conventions by which they did so. The collection called *Sentences* seems to represent sermon outlines, while the *Parables* represent the sort of illustrations he used—mostly allegories. In their present edited state, the *Sermons Through the [Liturgical] Year* represent treatises on the seasons of the church calendar, but behind them lies the sort of week-in, week-out preaching on the lectionary* that was the stock-in-trade of Bernard and all other abbots. The Sermons on the Psalm "Whoso dwelleth" are reflections on Psalm 91 (Vulgate 90) that constitute the Lenten series of the sermons for the year; they have been preserved both as a part of the larger collection and in separate editions. This work shows how the Psalter lay at the heart of monastic spirituality. *Sermons on Diverse Subjects* are what the name implies, individual sermons that have been preserved through a number of channels. Bernard's acknowledged masterpiece, his *Sermons* *on the Song of Songs,* follows a tradition of mystical interpretation that goes back through Origen in its Christian form to rabbinic exegesis. The passionate yearning of the soul for God finds apt expression in the human erotic vocabulary of such verses from the Canticles as "Let him kiss me with the kiss of his mouth" (1:2). The *Four Homilies in Praise of the Virgin Mother,* based on Luke's account of the Annunciation, reflect the sort of monastic Marian devotion that came to contemporary architectural expression in the cathedral at Chartres. The conversion at issue in the *Sermons to Clergy on Conversion,* preached to students at the University of Paris, is not so much the evangelization of pagans as it is the discovery of monastic vocations. Thus, in all these topics it can be seen that the difference between the preaching of Bernard and that of other abbots was not in biblical texts chosen nor in what was said about them but was rather the difference between the work of an authentic genius and that of lesser mortals.

The Outpouring of Preaching in the Thirteenth and Fourteenth Centuries. While the popularity and effectiveness of preaching have waxed and waned throughout the entire history of the church, few periods compare with the late Middle Ages for the quantity of preaching that was done, the enthusiasm with which it was heard, and the sheer volume of "helps" created to assist it. Something in the neighborhood of 80,000 sermons in manuscript form survive from the two centuries following 1150. Furthermore, most of these were intended to be preached not only more than once but also by more than one preacher. A number of factors were involved in creating the conditions under which this outburst occurred, beginning with the network for travel and trade that had been expanding since the First Crusade (1096–99). The trade also caused cities to multiply, and their populations necessitated new ways of evangelization that were met by the founding of religious orders. The members of these orders,

called friars rather than monks, did not live in secluded monasteries but traveled around preaching in the cities while living off alms. These mendicants prepared themselves for their preaching by studying at the new universities being founded. All of these factors contributed to the creation of a complex infrastructure for preaching.

The two largest orders of Friars, the Franciscans* and the Dominicans,* reflect the personalities of their founders. Francis of Assisi was a charismatic figure still in his twenties who had a deep desire to imitate the disciples as he understood them in a simple, direct, and apparently naive spirituality. Dominic, on the other hand, was an Augustinian canon in his forties, a well-trained scholar engaged in helping his bishop in a crusade against the Albigensians, who discovered that it was impossible to compete with the heretics without matching their example of apostolic life. Preaching was at the center of Dominic's mission from the very beginning, but for Francis it was only one apostolic activity among others and more important as an example to be imitated than in its own right. Thus, from the beginning, the Dominicans demonstrated the appropriateness of their being named the Order of Preachers, while only the "little brothers," the Friars Minor, explicitly licensed by Francis, were permitted to proclaim the word. Very quickly, however, as both orders grew and began to seek the education that effective preaching was believed to require, they began to assimilate to one another.

With the preaching of the friars there developed the first real homiletical form* that was not just a shapeless verse-by-verse comment on a passage from the Bible. Each sermon was constructed on the basis of a single verse of the Bible that was broken down into its component parts. A manuscript illumination from the time sees an analogy to the development of a sermon in the branching of a tree. The text or theme of the sermon was divided into a number of parts, usually three, and these were, in turn, subdivided into three subpoints. The initial division of the theme was generally preceded by an introduction that was in effect a mini-sermon on another theme making the same point as the main one. Each of the affirmations made in the sermon was expected to be backed up by the quotation of authorities, biblical first, then patristic and classical. Each subdivision had to be "dilated" or developed using established techniques, including illustration by *exempla*. This type of sermon has been given various designations, such as artistic and modern. Later scholars have called them university, scholastic, or school sermons, but thematic seems to be less misleading than any of the other designations. It has been thought by some that the thematic structure would be appreciated only by a learned audience, but surviving popular sermons show that the form had great appeal to ordinary people as well.

The existence of so technical a standard for sermons meant that textbooks were needed to inculcate the method for preparing and preaching them. These are referred to as "Arts of Preaching" (*Artes praedicandi*), but *ars* here is used not so much in its modern aesthetic sense as it is as a synonym of the Greek *techne*—a skill or method. Several hundred of these survive, often showing great dependence on one another. The earliest, that of Alexander of Ashby, goes back to about 1200, but the most developed examples of the genre, such as those of Thomas Waleys and Robert of Basevorn, come from a century and a half later. While so intricate a form might suggest artificiality of content, a reading of these manuals shows the spiritual seriousness of those who composed them. The taste for thematic sermons reflects the excitement over dialectic that characterized European consciousness after the logical works of Aristotle had been acquired from the Arabs.

Artes praedicandi were not the only tools, or even the most important ones, for preaching developed in the High Middle Ages. The needs of the great movement in preaching led to the development of a number of types of preaching aids, especially reference books in which a topic could be searched. Indeed, many of the conventions of searchable reference works that have been employed ever since were developed for the preaching aids of this period. These include concordances and collections of "distinctions" that indicate all of the different senses in which a word is used in the Bible. There were also *florilegia*, "gatherings of flowers," collections of authorities to support whatever point the preacher wished to make. Then too there were sets of sermons on virtues and vices that could be mined for the materials from which to construct new sermons on the same subjects. Perhaps the most important sort of tool was a collection of model sermons, often in no more than outline form and bound as a small volume. Such an aid would assist busy friars rushing from one preaching engagement to another to be ready always to organize a sermon that would not only "give a reason for the hope" that is in them, but to do so in the form that was currently admired (*see* Resources for Preaching).

The sort of preaching aid that has attracted most attention, however, has been collections of *exempla*, medieval "cyclopedias of illustration." An *exemplum* has been defined as "a short narration given as truthful and intended to be inserted into a speech (usually a sermon) to convince an audience by means of a salutary lesson." These stories not only had the intrinsic interest of all good tales and the concreteness of all analogies, but they also functioned as authorities because they quoted the writings of authoritative persons. While the church had the example of Jesus' teaching by parables, Gregory the Great was the first to use stories to illustrate sermons to any great extent, and it was not until the thematic sermon that the practice became pervasive (*see* Illustrations).

The existence of so many preaching aids suggests that the preaching of the friars enjoyed enormous popularity among both learned and popular audiences. Itinerants such as Berthold of Regensburg,* for example, drew crowds fully as large as those of Wesley* and Whitefield* during the Evangelical Awakening or Billy Graham* today, often in smaller towns and under less promising circumstances. A spirituality based on the obligation to preach was written by Humbert of Romans* for his fellow Dominicans under the title of *The Formation of Preachers*, another sign of the extensiveness of the phenomenon.

The Rhineland Mystics.* This is not to say, however, that all of the preaching done by friars was thematic. Some Rhineland Dominicans in the early fourteenth century developed a highly effective means of communicating the ideal and practice of mystical spirituality through preaching. This spirituality, proclaimed to nuns and lay groups as well as friars, was based on the cultivation of the life of prayer rather than on the obligation to preach, as Humbert's spirituality was. The movement may be studied in the lives of two of its most effective practitioners, Meister Eckhart and his disciple John Tauler. Eckhart, who was born in 1260, rose high in the Dominican order, and for a number of years seemed to alternate responsibilities at the University of Paris with others in his native Germany. The type of mystical experience that he preached came close to being unitive, and, toward the end of his life, he was accused of heresy.

He taught his views by sermons that followed the pattern of a homily, with continuous exegesis of a passage, and the exegesis was very allegorical. While this could sound like the monastic preaching of Bernard of Clairvaux and the other abbots, the different spirituality it inculcated gave it quite a different feel from the earlier preaching.

Tauler, who was born in 1300, eight years after the death of Eckhart, was able to preach a modified form of Eckhart's doctrine in sermons so clear that they are among the sermons of the period that are easily accessible to modern readers.

While these, like Eckhart's, are in the form of homilies, their exegesis does not seem farfetched. Instead, the sermons are down to earth, practical, and compelling in their devotion. They were a major influence on the *Theologia Germania* and thus on Luther.

John Wycliffe.* There came a time, however, when the charisma of the friars became routinized, and some members of the mendicant orders no longer had their founders' zeal for souls or practiced the spirituality of either Humbert or the Rhineland mystics. The worldliness to which some of them succumbed is well known to readers of Boccaccio and Chaucer. Protest was also made by a theological writer contemporary with these authors, John Wycliffe (ca. 1330–84). The nature of his protest, however, has been greatly distorted by the polemics of later controversy, and his place in the history of preaching cannot be determined without some consideration of his career and thought. Most of Wycliffe's life was spent as an Oxford don whose brilliance in scholastic logic made him one of the most influential members of the university. When he was in his forties, the simultaneous taxing of English clergy by the king and the pope to finance wars in which they were engaged led Wycliffe to decide that no church official in a state of sin had a right to obedience, although he believed that civil governors had it, whatever the condition of their souls. This view made him popular with John of Gaunt, son of the king and one of the most influential men at court.

It also raised for him questions of authority in the church, and he concluded that the supreme authority was the Bible and that it should be open to all people to interpret. Although he wrote a learned commentary on the entire Bible, his interpretation of it was nearer to that of the patristic than the Reformation age: he continued to use allegorical interpretation and to understand scripture primarily as holy law. He then went on to define the church as consisting of those who were predestined to salvation. Yet he recognized that those so elected may not be in a state of grace at a particular moment, while those not elected may be in that state. Since he had already determined that only those church officials in grace should be obeyed, he came to the ironic conclusion that some who did not belong to the true invisible church should be obeyed and some who did should not. This left him in a condition of protest against the papacy, a protest fueled by his conviction that the hierarchy lived in luxury when it should be caring for the poor and feeding the hungry. He also believed that the validity of sacraments depends on being in grace. His own form of scholastic logic then led him to deny not the real presence of Christ in the Eucharist but the manner in which it was upheld in the doctrine of transubstantiation.

Up until that point, Wycliffe, a secular priest, had the support of the friars, who practically controlled the university at the time. When he was declared heretical in his eucharistic doctrine and forced to withdraw from his position at the university, however, he began to attack the friars, being especially critical of their preaching. He held that their *exempla* were often told more for entertainment than for edification and were sometimes off color and that the friars favored thematic sermons over the patristic form of homily that he preached. His retirement from the university allowed him to devote the final three years of his life to serving as parish priest in nearby Lutterworth, a benefice he had held in absentia for many years. He also continued to issue polemical writings and to edit his Latin sermons. While some of these were preached at the university earlier and contained no distinctive teaching, those he preached at Lutterworth are filled with his polemics.

He seems not actually to have done the two things for which he is most often remembered, translating the Bible into English and sending out "poor preachers," Lollards, to evangelize the country. He probably did inspire two English translations made in those final three years of his life, a stilted version by Nicholas of Hereford and a more idiomatic work by John Purvey. In time, congregations did come into existence that took his teaching as their guidelines. There is, in fact, a collection of Wycliffite sermons in existence, a set of 294 English homilies on the Epistles and Gospels for the church year. These, however, appear to have been written by his followers rather than by Wycliffe himself. The extensive manuscripts in which they have survived suggest that they constituted the official teaching for congregations who adopted this position and that clergy in the congregations read these sermons instead of composing their own. Few, if any, Lollard priests went out during his lifetime, but those who later did were inspired by him. It is ironic that descriptions of them suggest nothing so much as the early friars whose latter-day descendants Wycliffe treated with such contempt. Lollard groups remained underground in England until the Reformation. They had great influence on the movement in Czechoslovakia led by John Hus, which similarly opposed the hierarchy, claimed the Bible as its supreme authority, and used allegorical interpretation to discover holy law in it.

Girolamo Savonarola. Another preacher, this one a friar, is also often regarded as a precursor of the Reformation. Specialists in the life and thought of Girolamo Savonarola (1452–98), however, see him more naturally as reflecting life in Italy before the Reformation or within the movement of medieval apocalypticism. Intended originally for a career as a physician, Savonarola ran away from home to join the Dominicans at the age of twenty-two. It was ten years before he began to attract attention by his preaching, and then only after he began to receive what he regarded as revelations. The content of these was that the church was to be scourged, but that it would then be renewed, and all of this was to happen very soon. Early on, he made some political predictions that came true, and this added considerably to his prestige. His influence in Florence was so great that he was able to create a theocratic democracy there, but it functioned almost like a dictatorship driven by his own highly ascetic ideals. In his puritanical preaching he was critical of the laxity of the church hierarchy. Eventually these attacks led to his excommunication by the pope, Alexander VI. His response was to begin to urge secular powers to call an ecumenical council to depose an unworthy pope. He was taken into custody, tortured, made to confess, and executed. His sermons, rather than being in the usual thematic pattern of the friars, were verse-by-verse exegesis of passages taken continuously from the same biblical book rather than appointed for the liturgical occasion. Although his method of interpretation involved the traditional four senses of scripture, he also used the revelations he received concerning the contemporary fate of Florence. So confident was he of these that he could say that God had prepared the particular passage of scripture specifically so that it would apply to that time and those events.

The various protest movements show that the great outburst of preaching that dominated the thirteenth and fourteenth centuries was beginning to fade. New impulses from the Renaissance and Reformation would propel the next great preaching movement.

Renaissance and Reformation

Erasmus and the Humanists. By the beginning of the sixteenth century, the medieval synthesis which had bound Europe together in a universal western Catholic culture had begun to dissolve. The dissolution can be seen in what happened to the papacy. After a high tide when even emperors had to submit to the Holy See, there was a continuous ebbing of influence occasioned by popes functioning as secular monarchs, rival claimants to the throne of Peter, and the rise of indulgences to finance vast building projects. Another factor in the breakup of the medieval synthesis was the change in scholarly method brought about by the rediscovery of classical antiquity. The scholars

involved were known as "humanists" because of their concern for the "humanities," the liberal arts of grammar, rhetoric, poetry, history, and moral philosophy. Of these, none was more influential than classical rhetoric. As a distinguished scholar has said, what united the humanists was "a conception of eloquence and its uses." Since preaching was the main form of public speaking in renaissance culture, it immediately began to reflect the rediscovery of eloquence.

The first major effort to apply classical rhetoric to preaching, the *Ecclesiastes* of Desiderius Erasmus, has deservedly been called "the great watershed in the history of sacred rhetoric." The last and longest book that Erasmus wrote, *Ecclesiastes* sets forth both his understanding of the importance of preaching and his theory about how preaching ought to be done. He considered teaching to be the most important duty of priests and regarded preaching chiefly as a means of teaching (which gave him a moralistic understanding of the task). Since preaching is so important, he said, it should be done well: "If elephants can be trained to dance, lions to play, and leopards to hunt, surely preachers can be taught to preach."

Erasmus believed that the adversarial nature of forensic oratory made it inappropriate for Christian preaching, but that both deliberative and epideictic sermons could be preached. In fact, he subdivided the deliberative genus into four types: persuasive, exhortative, admonitory, and consolatory. These, along with epideictic, constituted five proper types of preaching. Since these terms refer to content more than form, however, they really say little about what a sermon ought to be. A greater sense of that is gained from Erasmus's designation of a sermon as a *concio,* a form of deliberative oratory prepared not for a legislative assembly but for a boisterous audience of common people.

While there are promising aspects to that idea, it still fails to take into account the sermon's reliance on a biblical text. Even though Erasmus propounded a theology of scripture and ministry in the first of his five books, his preoccupation with pagan rhetoric in the rest of the work resulted in his leaving his practical advice untouched by theological theory. Thus, important as it was, even *Ecclesiastes* does not deal with the principal problem of all who would build a homiletic on classical rhetoric, the lack of guidelines for accommodating explication of the biblical text in an oratorical *genus*.

The Reformation Preaching of Luther and Melanchthon. Few people in the history of preaching have had more influence than Martin Luther,* yet it must be admitted that his followers did not imitate his style and that his own preaching has not been much studied. His preaching and his theology were largely shaped by his personal experience. As an ascetic monk he was unable to quiet his conscience. To divert him, his superior assigned him the tasks of earning his doctorate and becoming a professor of scripture. After he began teaching he had his "tower experience" in which all his doubts were resolved in the realization that "the justice of God is that righteousness by which through grace and sheer mercy God justifies us through faith." It was some time after that, however, that he saw that this insight militated against the medieval view that the good works of the saints could be transferred through the treasury of merit by means of indulgences offered by the pope to reduce the time others spent in purgatory. His posting on the door of the church at Wittenberg of "Ninety-five Theses" for debate against this doctrine is generally regarded as the beginning of the Protestant Reformation.

Luther's Theology. It is impossible to understand what Luther thought about preaching without knowing the overall dynamic of his thought. He believed that the Word of God has three manifestations: God the Son (the incarnate Word), the Bible (the written Word), and preaching (the proclaimed Word). Because of the intimate relation between the Son and the Bible, Luther believed that the whole purpose of scripture was to reveal Christ. Discovering that proclamation in any passage, then, is the key to biblical interpretation. The guidance of the Holy Spirit* is necessary if one is to do that. Proclamation has two aspects, God's moral requirements for human beings (law) and the good news that Christ justifies sinners unable to meet those requirements who turn to him in faith (gospel). Sinners are justified (regarded as righteous) when they hear the gospel of God's good will toward them and accept it by trusting entirely in Christ and claiming no merit of their own. The work of preaching is thus to proclaim the gospel in such a way that those elected to salvation may hear it and appropriate it through faith (*see* Law; Law and Gospel; Proclamation; Word of God).

Because of the role of preaching in the justification of the elect, Luther considered preaching to be the most important job in the world. Thus he took his own preaching very seriously and did it regularly, sometimes as often as four times a day. For him preaching was the medium of salvation because it was not a merely human activity but the very Word of God proclaiming itself through the preacher. This does not mean that the human voice of the preacher is unimportant, however, because the word of preaching is essentially an oral encounter with God.

Luther was convinced that every sermon should contain both law and gospel. Hearing the law leads people to know their need for the gospel and opens them to hear its word of grace and forgiveness. Thus the basic content of all Christian preaching is the forgiveness of sins. Yet, again, it is the Holy Spirit who allows people to hear that word and to be saved by it. (On the other hand, it is not to be expected that those who are saved will cease to sin: they are *simul justus et peccator*.)

While this necessary task of preaching was the most important work of clergy, Luther believed that members of the laity could preach also. Indeed, he regarded the religious teaching done by schoolmasters and heads of households, among others, to be preaching. He even held open the possibility that under certain circumstances women could preach. Thus he had a very encompassing understanding of the Word of God. Yet preaching did require talent and education; he felt that his doctorate authorized him to preach. Furthermore, the preacher must have a call from God, interpret the Bible correctly, and live consistently with the message for his preaching to be authoritative. Even then, the response to it may not always be positive; Luther was often disappointed in the results of his sermons.

Luther's Homiletical Practice. More than half of the over 4,000 sermons Luther preached have been preserved and published. The church at Wittenberg had three services on Sunday at which sermons were preached on the different lections appointed for the day. Course preaching on the various biblical books and the catechism was done on weekdays. Luther was not the pastor of the church and was only one of several who preached there, but obviously he was one of the more frequent preachers and certainly the most authoritative.

From the surviving sermons it is possible to trace the development of his style. Beginning with medieval thematic sermons, he went on to develop a form that was unique. It resembles that of patristic homilies but concentrates not so much on individual verses as what he considered to be the "center of meaning," the "heart point," or the "kernel" of the passage. Having identified that, he would develop an outline that would enable him to get the point across. Yet he did not prepare by writing out a manuscript; instead, he immersed himself in the text and then preached extemporaneously, beginning with a statement of the *Herzpunkt* and going from there to extract that meaning from his text. In the pulpit he would have no more than a brief outline of what he meant to say, his *Konzept*, but he departed from that often enough for some-

one to say that the structure of his sermons was one of "heroic disorder." His most common principle of organization was an antithesis.

Since he considered preaching to be an eschatological struggle in which Christ would elect individuals and save them from the enemy, his preaching was powerful. Some of the power came from his popular, conversational style; he considered it more important to be heard by the young people in the congregation than by the many scholars who attended. From his scholastic background he understood preaching as a pedagogical art that used dialectics for persuasion. This gave him an understanding of preaching that was not far from Erasmus's classification of the sermon as a form of *concio,* a deliberative speech addressed to a popular assembly.

While the revival of rhetorical learning had little to do with the form of Luther's preaching, it had a good bit to do with the content. During the Renaissance, the principles of rhetoric came to be used not only for the construction of speeches (primary rhetoric) but also for the analysis of speeches and other efforts to persuade written by others (secondary rhetoric). This moved the work of the rhetorician closer to that of the grammarian, the one traditionally charged with teaching literature, using a line-by-line analysis of texts. It is in this area that the influence of humanism on Luther was strongest, giving him his tools for the biblical exegesis he regarded as basic to the preacher's task.

Melanchthon's Influence on Lutheran Preaching. While Luther wrote no treatise on preaching (although he did have much to say about it in his *Table Talk* and elsewhere), his close associate Melanchthon* wrote several textbooks on preaching and rhetoric. Called at the age of twenty-three to teach Greek at Wittenberg, Melanchthon quickly became associated with Luther, who had already been on the faculty for ten years. By the time of the Diet of Augsburg, he was a leading figure and the principal author of the Confession produced there. No less important was his educational work. He devised an essentially rhetorical educational system that is the basis for his reputation as "the preceptor of Germany."

His most influential work on preaching was in his basic textbook on rhetoric. Devoted to the revival of classical rhetoric, he dealt with the difficulty of fitting the explication of the biblical text into the three classical genera by creating a fourth, called *genus didascalicum*, which grew out of Luther's understanding of preaching as doctrine and exhortation. This genus made use of the dialectical *loci* for dealing with simple and complex questions. With the help of these, the preacher can "invent" (discover) what needs to be said about every biblical topic. Melanchthon also taught that the deliberative genus of the legislatures could be used in preaching if it were broken into two subgenera: the epitreptic, which exhorts to faith, and the paraenetic, which exhorts to good morals.

The homiletical forms devised by Melanchthon had more influence on subsequent Lutheran preaching than the *concio* pattern of Luther. This is to say that polished rhetorical forms reflecting humanistic consciousness and taste eclipsed the eschatological battles waged in conversational language that were the mark of Luther's preaching.

The Early Reformed Tradition. Luther's Reformation succeeded in spreading only to other Germanic countries. The form that was to influence the rest of the world began in Switzerland. Its pioneer was Ulrich Zwingli,* but he had little influence on the history of preaching beyond making two innovations that became standard in many places: he did course preaching through biblical books exclusively rather than basing his sermons on the liturgical lectionary, and he devised an order of worship that placed the sermon rather than the Eucharist at its center.

The Radical Reformation. As radical as Zwingli appeared in comparison to Lu-

ther, he did not go far enough to satisfy some of his fellow citizens of Zurich. While they and others who had similar convictions came to be known as Anabaptists because of their practice of believer's baptism, their original controversy with Zwingli was over the Eucharist, especially over his willingness to allow the town council to make decisions about it. The medieval synthesis, in which the civil and religious community were two aspects of the same reality, had broken down, and a complete separation of church and state was called for. Thus the term Anabaptist is a misnomer on two grounds, the first being that what occurs is not rebaptism, if what was administered in infancy was not baptism, and the second that there were many more issues at stake than the nature of one sacrament. More recent usage employs the term "radical Reformation" to refer to three kinds of supporters of adult baptism (revolutionary, contemplative, and evangelical), three kinds of spiritualists (revolutionary, evangelical, and rational), and evangelical rationalists.

Previous scholarship has tended to lump these groups together in spite of their considerable variety. It has also interpreted them not in terms of their own writings but in terms of those who opposed them, notably Lutherans and Calvinists. They have often been dismissed as revolutionaries and *Schwärmer* ("enthusiasts"). The evangelical Anabaptists began from the assumption that the apostolic age was the golden age of the church from which it fell in the time of Constantine, when baptism came to be administered indiscriminately. This was the beginning of state coercion of religious conformity. The radical reformers understood themselves to be living in the eschatological age. In those last days they were called upon to restore Christianity to its New Testament pattern. They established a pattern of pacifism that was an invitation to martyrdom. Their beliefs, combined with a missionary zeal extraordinary for the period, resulted in rapid growth.

It was evangelistic activity that was initially responsible for most Anabaptist preaching as such. Anabaptist worship had little more affection for the centrality of preaching than for the centrality of the Mass. Instead, it was characterized by informal teaching, prayer, and mutual exhortation, with many worshipers taking an active role. The notions that church members were unconverted and in need of evangelization or that one main person should lead worship were equally repugnant. Thus, what preaching there was at these assemblies consisted in admonition to the congregation by its own members on the basis of the Bible, life experience, and inspiration by the Holy Spirit.

The impromptu nature of such preaching militates against the survival of written records of it. Certainly an exception to this pattern developed in Prussia and Russia where for a time sermons were written out. But the composition of new sermons came to be regarded as a mark of pride. Preachers were to read written sermons from the past. This practice, reflecting attitudes similar to those of early medieval homiliarists, was followed until the middle of the present century in Hutterite congregations in Canada and the Northwest. Eventually, sermons came to be collected and printed, but these were used mainly in family devotions. Thus, what must have been an impressive movement in the history of preaching has left few traces for those who would reconstruct it.

Calvin and the Reformed Tradition. When Luther posted his Ninety-five Theses on the door of the Wittenberg church on All Hallows' Eve, 1517, John Calvin* was an eight-year-old boy. His notary father had probably already decided that the priesthood offered the best opportunity for advancement to his precocious son, and within four years he would procure for him several benefices that would finance his education. At the age of fourteen, John began his study at the Sorbonne. Before he could be ordained, however, his father's quarrels with church authorities caused the young man to turn to the study of law. During his university training, he fell under the influence of

such humanists as Erasmus and Jacques Lefèvre d'Etaples, the great biblical scholar of St. Germain-des-Prés. Their influence enabled him to publish his first book, a commentary on Seneca's *De clementia*, about the time he completed his legal studies. His humanist teachers were critical of abuses within the Roman Catholic church while remaining loyal to it, and Calvin's support of such criticism necessitated his flight from Paris in 1533.

It is not clear from the sources at what point Calvin decided that he must make a break with Rome, nor is it certain that he ever experienced the sort of conversion that Luther had. At some time near his departure from Paris, however, he appears to have realized that his principles of evangelical humanism were inconsistent with remaining under papal obedience. Probably that prompted his surrender of his benefices in 1534. For the next two years he traveled in France and Italy and also produced the first edition of his great instruction in the Reformed faith, his *Institutes*, a work that he would revise and expand continually until the time of his death. Its publication gave him an instant reputation as a leader. When he was on his way to Strasbourg, where he hoped to find a quiet place to continue his study, thinking, and writing, he was reluctantly persuaded by Guillaume Farel, a pupil of d'Etaples, to stay in Geneva and help promote the Reformed cause. After only two years, however, the Geneva town council, which had invited them, expelled Farel and Calvin, thus permitting Calvin to go to Strasbourg. But after three idyllic years there, he was recalled to Geneva, where he remained the rest of his life, making it the mecca and model for all who desired to see Reformed principles put fully into operation.

Under Calvin's rule, Geneva had a rich diet of preaching: the two larger churches had three sermons, and the third had two on Sundays, while there were also sermons on Mondays, Wednesdays, and Fridays (which eventually became daily). Of these it has been estimated that Calvin himself preached an average of 290 per year. Many of these have been lost, however. It was not until 1549 that arrangements were made for Denis Raguenier to take down Calvin's extemporaneously delivered sermons in shorthand. Only 800 of these were published during the preacher's lifetime, and only slightly less than 1,100 are in the modern scholarly edition; it is estimated that over 1,000 have been lost.

While Calvin's doctrine of preaching was very high, it was not identical with Luther's. He believed, for instance, that preaching becomes revelation when and if God decides to add to it the Holy Spirit.* Yet preaching is the ordinary channel through which the Spirit speaks, although the Spirit does not say through preaching anything that has not already been said in scripture. Thus, preaching may be said to be the Word of God only in the senses that it expounds and interprets the Bible and that proclaiming the Word of God is what the preacher is called to do. Even though Calvin believed that it took the ratifcation of the Spirit to make a sermon the Word of God, believed in double predestination, and had a generally low view of human activity, he nevertheless considered the qualifications of pastors to be a matter of high importance. These qualifications should include technical competence in theology and biblical interpretation, personal fitness in way of life, and the charisma of teaching. Preaching was understood as "the constituting essential of the ministry."

No one exemplified Calvin's ideal of preaching better than he did himself. In addition to having all the qualifications listed above to an extraordinary degree, he also had his own native rhetorical ability greatly sharpened by his humanistic training. This is not to say, of course, that his ability is immediately apparent to modern readers. He did preach extemporaneously, which always makes for better oral than written communication. And the sort of verse-by-verse interpretation that he did of passages taken in sequence from biblical books would seem to many like reading aloud from a commentary. Yet he thought that only such preaching would do justice to biblical revelation as he understood it.

Such a sermon would begin with a prayer, move on to a brief recapitulation of the previous sermon, then to exegesis of the structural members of the passage one by one, followed by reconstruction of the passage's original meaning with an application to the life of the congregation and an exhortation to obedience. Then the next member would receive the same treatment. The sermon concluded with a bidding prayer that summarized the sermon. What he says is always very clear but without any verbal ornament, imagery, or illustration. The sermons were marked by cogency of thought and the preacher's passionate conviction that his words were the instrument by which the Holy Spirit called some to election and others to damnation.

Calvin's humanistic training made him an extraordinarily well-equipped exegete for his day. His deep knowledge of biblical languages enabled him to go, as he said, *ad fontes*. His idea of what constituted the original meaning of a passage, however, was very different from modern post-Enlightenment presuppositions. His belief in the unity and perfection of the scriptures, for instance, meant that he assumed that christological interpretations of Old Testament passages revealed their inspired and only true meaning—the one the Holy Spirit had both given to the sacred writer and revealed to the faithful interpreter. Thus, while he was opposed to allegorical interpretation and insisted on the literal, grammatical sense of scripture, his understanding of that would be very different from a modern historical-critical view.

Like Luther, Calvin had a theological understanding of the message to which all of the Bible bore witness. For him, the Bible proclaimed the salvation of the elect through grace. While true preaching publishes this message, its efficacy depends on the Holy Spirit's gift of faith to the elect believer. Justification and the communication of this knowledge of the mercy of God are one and the same thing. The preaching of the Bible also communicates the knowledge of the creator as it is imparted by the Old Testament. This too is necessary knowledge; otherwise, the Spirit would not have revealed it. It is the knowledge of faith, however, that is saving knowledge. Since it is communicated by preaching as well as directly to the heart by the Spirit, it is no wonder that Calvin preached with such earnestness and solemnity.

The Preaching of Catholic Reform.

In an age of ecumenical church historiography, it is increasingly recognized that the spirit of reform operated in those who remained within the Roman communion as well as in those who separated from it. In fact, the traditional term for the Roman Catholic movement, Counter-Reformation, is now rejected for its purely negative and reactionary implications.

The part played by preaching in Catholic Reform may be seen in four of its most important channels: religious orders in general, the Jesuits in particular, the Council of Trent, and missionary activity. Already in the fifteenth century strong reforming movements existed within the older orders, yet these were more concerned with developing the lives of their members than with renewing the church at large. New orders would have to be created for that, and they were not long in coming.

Of the orders founded, several placed great emphasis on preaching, especially the Barnabites and the Capuchins. These orders display what one historian has called the single theme running through the Catholic Reformation—"the quest for a more adequate clergy." No other group was more important in this respect than the Society of Jesus. The founder of the Society, Don Iñigo de Oñaz y Loyola, was a thirty-year-old soldier recuperating from wounds in both legs, who found himself in a situation in which the only reading material available was devotional literature. Converted by it, he took the dress of a beggar and began a year's retreat during which he wrote the initial draft of the devotional classic that was to shape the consciousness of his order, the *Spiritual Exercises.*

At the University of Paris, Loyola began to acquire the necessary followers to found his order. They left Paris to go on a missionary crusade to the Holy Land, but when war made that impossible, they went to Rome resolved to put themselves directly under the pope. There they began to encourage more frequent devotions, including confession, communion, and preaching. Though they were viewed with suspicion, their new order and rule were recognized in less than two years.

The preaching of these early Jesuits quickly began to attract attention and crowds. They preached in church at the liturgy, in the open air, and in their own genre, the sacred lecture. In cities where they were conducting missions, the Jesuits would devote Sunday afternoons or some other convenient time either to course preaching on biblical books or to lectures on catechetical issues or cases of conscience. In every way they were eager to instruct the faithful.

The third channel of Catholic Reform in which the importance of preaching may be seen is the Council of Trent. Paul III called a council to meet in 1545 at Trent, a town in the Italian Alps. It took several sessions over the course of eighteen years for the council to complete its work, but when it was over, Roman Catholicism had the essential appearance that it maintained until the Second Vatican Council. Essentially, the church reasserted its medieval theological positions against Protestant revision and took steps to curb reforming abuses in practice.

Most of these practical reforms can be understood as part of the quest for a more adequate clergy. Included in these provisions was a considerable emphasis on preaching, which was designated as "the principal duty of bishops." All with a cure for souls were called upon to preach at least every Sunday and major feast day. Sanctions were specified against those who failed to do so. Provision was also made to train clergy in preaching and to establish seminaries.

The last channel of Catholic Reform in which the importance of preaching may be observed is missionary activity. Foreign missions were far more characteristic of the Catholic than the Protestant Reformation. As always in the history of Christian missionary activity, preaching was an important medium for spreading the faith (*see* Missions).

A happy coincidence of the ideals of Trent and the humanistic revival of ancient rhetoric resulted in the production of homiletical textbooks that shaped Roman Catholic preaching for two centuries. A key figure in this movement was Charles Borromeo, the Archbishop of Milan, who may be regarded as an example of how the decisions of Trent moved from policy to practice. In the area of homiletics, Borromeo was an indefatigable preacher who issued an instruction to his clergy about their obligation and encouraged others to write treatises on preaching. While his own preaching and the instruction to his clergy were marked by a moralistic emphasis, he nevertheless helped focus attention on the role of preaching in the life of the church. More significantly, however, he sponsored the production of good textbooks in homiletics, such as those of Agostino Valier, Luis de Granada, and Diego de Estella. Thus, Borromeo has been identified as the chief promoter of the enthusiasm for preaching that was as characteristic of sixteenth-century Roman Catholics as it was of Protestants.

Upheaval in Britain. Beginning with the English Reformation, the remainder of this article will focus on preaching in the English-speaking world. That shift will not yield a simple picture because the essential ecclesiastical orientation of Great Britain has varied considerably over the centuries. The changing religious orientations of monarchs has meant that the ecclesial complexion of the country has varied more than that of other states.

Henry VIII wanted no more change in religion than the replacement of papal with royal authority. The protectors during the reign of Edward VI moved the English church in a Calvinist direction, but under Mary Tudor papal obedience was restored. It was during the long reign of Elizabeth I that what has become known as the Anglican *via media* between Romanism and Protestantism set the basic pattern for the future. Even that was interrupted by the Civil War and Interregnum when first Puritans and then Independents called the tune. Shortly after the Restoration, a number of social and cultural factors produced a Latitudinarian emphasis that was in turn modified by the Evangelical Awakening, Catholic Revival (Oxford Movement), and modernism.

The shift from the thematic preaching of the Middle Ages to other forms began during the reign of Henry VIII and had at least two inspirations, the rise of humanism and the influence of Luther. Of the two, the former was more significant. Erasmus taught in England and was a great influence there. Much of the reforming spirit during the reign of Edward VI was shaped by his vision, but when Mary came to the throne, the revival of classical rhetoric was more determinative for Catholic preaching than for thematic preaching. In England, as in both Catholic and Lutheran countries, the dominant sermon pattern resembled a patristic homily with an even greater accommodation to the classical *dispositio* in order to permit the explication of a biblical text.

The influence of Erasmian humanism is easily observed in the reign of Edward. When the power of the crown was placed behind the Reformation, two things were obvious: the new doctrines had to be taught in a wholesale way, and most of the clergy were not trained well enough to teach them. To meet this need, *The Book of Homilies* was published. It was a collection of topical sermons written by Thomas Cranmer, Archbishop of Canterbury, and other leaders of the Church of England. This program for the catechesis of the country reflected convictions acquired from Erasmus.

But prefabricated sermons to be read repeatedly were not as effective as new ones composed by well-trained clergy for their own congregations. Some clergy were educated enough to do such preaching from the very beginning, and the ideal of the Erasmian reform can be seen in them, especially in their best representative, Hugh Latimer (ca. 1485–1555). The brilliant son of a yeoman farmer, Latimer was well launched on an academic career at Cambridge when the influence of Erasmus and Luther began to be felt there. Some date the English Reformation from his preaching from the pulpit of St. Andrew's Church in Cambridge. Along with Thomas Cranmer and Nicholas Ridley, Latimer became one of the most notable martyrs under Mary. In his *Book of Martyrs*, Foxe says that Latimer's last words when he was burned at the stake were these: "Be of good comfort, master Ridley, and play the man. We shall this day light such a candle, by God's grace, in England, as I trust shall never be put out." The power of Latimer's preaching can hardly be suggested by a description. In some ways he was more like Luther than any other great preacher of the period. He used the homily form and spoke in colloquial, racy language without appearance of outline other than the verses of his text. Unlike Luther, however, he did not reduce the purposes of preaching to a single task. He was not above using any trick of the popular communicator—jokes, stories, horrible puns, or neologisms—in order to share the passionate faith for which he was willing to die.

During the reign of Elizabeth, England was filled with theologians who had fled to Geneva during the reign of Mary and who had returned with a vision of a church thoroughly reformed according to the insights of Calvin. While most English clergy operated out of a Calvinistic theological framework, there were some who yearned to see the established church completely remodeled according to the more scriptural pattern of Geneva. These were called Puritans. Their convictions were shared and supported by many of the laity. When they could not get the preaching they considered essential from the incumbent of the parish church, they hired clergy of their own persuasion to serve as lecturers or readers, preaching Calvinist sermons at times other than those of the regular services.

Ordinary Puritan* preaching was built on the Calvinist ideal of public exegesis. The classical form of the Puritan sermon both in England and America was stated simply by William Perkins in *The Arte of Prophesying* (Latin 1592, English 1607):

1. To read the Text distinctly out of the canonical scripture.

2. To give the sense and understanding of it being read by the scripture itself.

3. To collect a few and profitable points of doctrine out of the naturall sense.

4. To applie (if he have the gift) the doctrine rightly collected to the manners of men in a simple and plain speech.

As simple as the formula sounds, sermons based on it could last several hours, during which every shade of the meaning of the text was explored, doctrines were extrapolated, and each was applied to the lives of the faithful. The number of divisions and subdivisions could be enormous.

Anglo-Catholic preaching during the age of Shakespeare developed its own appropriate patterns, patterns that owed much to England's greatest poets and prose stylists who were among its practitioners. This school of preaching is called "Metaphysical" because it included Metaphysical poets such as John Donne.* It is also called "witty," in the contemporary understanding of the word as referring to "facility in discovering resemblances between the most disparate things, especially when one of these happened to be of a religious character."

Such preaching did require a learned audience and its greatest practitioners certainly satisfied that criterion. Those who heard Donne when he was Dean of St. Paul's Cathedral in London appreciated the intricacy of what they heard, and those who listened to Lancelot Andrewes in the court of James I were even better equipped to do so. Persons trained in rhetoric and Latin, many of whom wrote poetry and read serious theology themselves, were addressed in a way that delighted their minds and refreshed their souls.

It is difficult to imagine a preaching style more different from that of the Puritans than that of Lancelot Andrewes, whose glories were admired by T. S. Eliot. Inevitably, the two preaching styles and the theological positions out of which they grew came into conflict. A Parliament dominated by Puritans put to death Charles I and his Archbishop of Canterbury, William Laud, and instituted the Commonwealth first under Presbyterian and then Independent inspiration. The Restoration of Charles II in 1660, however, also meant a restoration of Anglicanism. That, however, represents the end of the era of the Reformation and the beginning of the modern era, a time when forces other than humanistic and biblical ideals would shape preaching.

The Modern Era: From the Restoration to World War II

The Restoration and the Age of Reason. There are periods in history in which it is possible to discern a shift in consciousness, moments when the whole world suddenly awakens to a new vision. One such moment occurred in Europe in the late seventeenth century. After the wars of religion that followed the Reformation, Europe was exhausted by bloodshed and devastation and would have been willing to live under any religious system or none rather than continue in destruction. At the same time, Francis Bacon and Isaac Newton were doing scientific experiments and producing extraordinary results. Philosophers such as

Spinoza and Descartes had ceased to presuppose revelation and had begun to depend on human reason alone. A rising mercantile class had taken priority over those of the nobility and royalty. The culture of Christendom that was conceived with the conversion of Constantine had now begun visibly to disintegrate.

In Great Britain, when Richard Cromwell proved in 1660 to be lacking in his father's great ability, Presbyterians joined with royalists to recall Charles II to the throne. Although Charles himself had little interest in religion, under him the royalists succeeded in excluding Puritans and Independents from the established church. Thus, for the first time, one can speak of the Church of England as Anglican (although the term is of later coinage) and note that there were dissenting churches in the realm, the Presbyterians and Congregationalists. Charles's brother, James II, who succeeded him, had a great deal of religious commitment, but it was all Roman Catholic. When the "Glorious Revolution" against him in 1688 brought in his daughter Mary with her husband, William of Orange, a leader of Dutch Protestants, it became inevitable that dissent should be tolerated. For the first time it was recognized in England that the country could be politically united and yet religiously divided.

Inevitably, this shift was reflected in preaching. It expressed itself as a growing distaste for the styles of either Anglo-Catholics or Puritans. The basis for this change of taste was expressed originally in terms of exclusively homiletical and rhetorical values, without reference to the cultural changes that occasioned the shift. The first person to articulate the new homiletical values was Robert South, a staunch Anglican. In 1660 he preached a sermon to ordinands at St. Mary's Oxford, in which he protested against two kinds of bad preaching. Without naming them, he accused the Anglo-Catholics of being "such as disparage and detract from the grandeur of the gospel, by a puerile and indecent levity in the discourse of it to the people" because of their use of "all vain, luxurious allegories, rhyming cadences of similar words." The more extreme Puritans and Independents he described, also anonymously, as "such as depreciate and . . . debase the [gospel], by a course, careless, rude, and insipid way of preaching the great and invaluable truths of it." Eight years later, at the cathedral in Oxford, he set forth his own standard of what preaching should be like: "plain, natural, and familiar."

The plain style advocated by South had much in common with the sort of prose being advanced at the time by members of the newly formed Royal Society for the communication of the results of their scientific investigations:

> They have extracted from all their members a close, naked, natural way of speaking, positive expressions, clear sense, a native easiness, bringing all things as near the Mathematical plainness as they can, and preferring the language of Artizans, Countrymen, and Merchants, before that, of Wits or Scholars.

Their goal, in short, was to deliver "so many *things* almost in an equal number of *words*." Yet, while some of the people calling for the change in preaching style were involved in the formation of the Royal Society, it seems that both movements were responses to the same social forces rather than that one was an outgrowth of the other.

The person who succeeded in making this plain style of preaching the norm was John Tillotson (1630–94), who was Archbishop of Canterbury for the last three years of his life. Having been a Puritan in his youth, he yearned for a more inclusive, less sectarian sort of Christian theology and preaching. He was an early disciple of Bishop John Wilkins, whose *Ecclesiastes* was the first homiletics text to set forth the new ideal. The style of Tillotson has been described by Bishop Gilbert Burnet, his eulogist, in this way:

> Neither did his Thoughts sink nor his Stile swell: keeping always the due Mean between a low Flatness and the Dresses of false Rhetorick. Together with the Pomp of Words he did also cut off all Superfluities and needless Enlargements: He said what was just necessary to give clear Ideas of things, and no more: He laid aside all long and affected Periods: His sentences were short and clear: and the whole Thread was of a piece, plain, and distinct. No affectation of Learning, no squeezing of Texts, no superficial Strains, no false thoughts nor bold flights, all was solid and yet lively, and grave as well as fine (in W. F. Mitchell, *English Pulpit Oratory from Andrewes to Tillotson*, 1932, 1962, 334–35).

This new style of preaching is called neoclassical by some scholars because it has much in common with the great homiletical movement of that name in France at the same time, a movement with which are connected such names as Bossuet,* Fénelon,* Bourdaloue, and Massillon*— although there are significant differences between the movements in the two countries. One of the qualities that makes the adjective neoclassical appropriate is the authority of classical manuals of rhetoric. It was assumed, for instance, that a sermon of the period—or "discourse" as it was often called—should follow with slight amendment the structure of a forensic speech: exordium, explication, proposition, partition, argumentation, application, and conclusion. Inevitably, such sermons were topical, constructed around the need to discuss a subject rather than to expound scripture. All it would take to turn many of these sermons into essays would be to lop off the text and its explication (which took the place of the narration in the forensic speech) from the beginning and the application from the end.

Tillotson's popularity has been explained as an anticipation of the British taste that would develop in the next century. There can be no doubt of his popularity; his sermons were published, widely read by the laity, and repreached by the clergy for quite a long time. Soon the plain style of sermon became the only style preached by any cleric of any denomination. In content, neoclassical sermons were more concerned with correct behavior than correct belief. Or, as one historian has put it:

> As recast by Tillotson, the sermon lost its heroic note, and became a moral essay, the vehicle of a sober, utilitarian, prudential ethic, rather than a proclamation of the gospel of the Kingdom of God (Smyth 1940, 160).

The theology of Tillotson and of most of the clergy of all denominations who followed him during the next century was Latitudinarian. Rather than believing in the wrath of God toward all not elected to salvation, the clergy believed in the divine benevolence toward not only Christians but all human beings. Even those without the benefit of revelation enjoyed a universe that proclaimed its Creator by its design, a world in which reason could arrive unaided at the benefits of virtuous conduct. Nevertheless, human will had been enfeebled by the Fall so that redemption was necessary to make it possible for human beings to petition for the grace they would certainly be given. Only part of that grace had already been given in the revelation of eternal reward for the righteous and punishment for the evil.

Modern readers find neoclassical preaching as hard to appreciate as the Restoration congregations found the sermons of the Metaphysicals and the Puritans. To contemporary ears it has a sound of smugness, self-satisfaction, comfort in the universe, and ease in Zion that many would find uncongenial. Its serene good taste and abhorrence of enthusiasm make it guilty of breaking the eleventh commandment for all public speakers: "Thou shalt not bore!" Yet neoclassical Latitudinarian preaching fit the consciousness of its time like a custom-tailored garment. It was the style of preaching developed during the Enlightenment, a time when Christianity was very much on the defensive. In an atmosphere in which Deists were attacking the roots of the faith, neoclassical preaching may have offered as much of the gospel as could be heard.

The Age of Feeling. During the same period, Europe saw the development of a number of religious movements that found their criterion of authenticity in religious experience. Early British manifestations of the movement may be seen in strains of seventeenth-century Puritanism, Scots-Irish revivalism, and the Quakers. Yet these represent only local phases of a trend that transcended national and ecclesiastical boundaries alike. This "religion of the heart" appeared not only in the Reformed Pietism of the Netherlands, Lutheran Pietism in Germany, and the Moravian movement but in Roman Catholic Jansenism and Quietism, Russian Orthodox schismatic groups, and Jewish Hasidism. According to a scholar who has studied them together,

> the religion of the heart movements arose simultaneously . . . among Europeans of widely different confessional traditions who, disgusted with what corporate Christian states had done to each other since the Reformation, and disillusioned with "objective" appeals to scripture and tradition, turned inwardly to a more individualistic and (in a certain sense) "subjective" appropriation of the Christian faith (Campbell 1991, 177).

Inevitably, this new emphasis and the movements that expressed it called for new methods of preaching. In Britain and later in America, the major method developed was evangelistic. While the beginning of such preaching is often associated with the work of Whitefield and the Wesleys in the eighteenth century, many elements of it were present in Scottish and Northern Irish Calvinism in the 1620s and 1630s. This preaching grew out of an essentially Calvinistic and Puritan understanding that the election of those predestined to salvation generally occurs when the Word of God is opened to a congregation through preaching. Although it was God's eternal decree that effected salvation, it was nevertheless preaching that was the usual medium of conversion.

For some time Presbyterians had taken the reception of Holy Communion seriously and, in order to ready themselves for its proper reception, they had adopted the custom of preparing for it with preaching at sacramental meetings. In Scotland during the 1620s, such meetings became occasions when many fell under conviction of sin and were converted. Soon the phenomenon spread to Northern Ireland.

What had begun spontaneously came to be cultivated. Soon revivalistic preaching became standard fare at sacramental meetings. Attendance at such occasions became so great that congregations could not be contained in churches and were forced outside into the open air. By the time of the Restoration, when Anglicanism was imposed on Scotland and Ireland, Presbyterians were forced to carry on the tradition of sacramental meetings illegally. After the "Glorious Revolution" in 1688, legal sanctions disappeared, but a basic format for revivalistic preaching had already been established that would be near to hand when the Evangelical Revival of the next century began.

The Preaching of the Great Awakening. Although the evangelical awakening is usually associated with John Wesley in England and Jonathan Edwards* in America, the link between the two movements is George Whitefield.* An Anglican priest with a Calvinistic theological orientation, it was he who anticipated the Wesley brothers in undergoing conversion, in beginning an itinerate evangelistic ministry, in field preaching, and in the formation of "religious societies" in Church of England parishes. And while Jonathan Edwards's congregation in Northampton, Massachusetts, had already experienced "Surprising Conversions," it was Whitefield who transformed the understanding of a revival from an occasional work of grace sent by the Holy Spirit in God's own good time into something that could occur on a reg-

ular basis. For thirty years he toured England, Scotland, Ireland, and America, preaching several times a day to congregations that usually numbered in the tens of thousands, always moving them to emotional response, and usually leaving large numbers of converted.

Whitefield created the basic pattern of evangelistic preaching. The sermon was usually based on a short text and, after an introduction and some background, there was an announcement of the points that would be made. After that, the sermon developed topically, with each of the heads having several subheadings, all leading to a conclusion.

So far, the evangelistic sermon followed neoclassical lines. But the greatest dread of the neoclassicists was "enthusiasm." Emotional appeals may be necessary, but they were never to exceed the bounds of good taste. What Whitefield was aiming at, however, was conversion, and he believed that could occur only when people were brought under conviction of their sins, when they were brought to believe in the depths of their own sin and their need of God's intervention. Most of his sermons are driven by that conviction. They amass overwhelming evidence against the hearer whose rescue depends on the free gift of God's mercy. Whitefield himself was frequently in tears, as were most of his hearers. Often the emotional response in his audiences was more extreme.

In addition to creating a formula, Whitefield also possessed extraordinary personal gifts. His voice carried to larger audiences more than any other; he was the envy of actors because of his ability to convey heartfelt emotion by voice, face, and gesture. To these abilities he added other techniques of popular speakers. One student has enumerated them thus:

the element of surprise; travellers' tales; anecdotes to lighten the strain or point a moral; the selection of the dramatic parts of scripture for his most successful expositions; such rhetorical devices as the formal introduction to an imaginative flight, antithesis, the intermingling of long and short sentences, and the enforcing of a point by a pithy saying; counter-attacks upon his critics by way of declamations; the comic interlude in which wit, satire, and whimsy, humor, and even puns are used; the direct form of address to individuals or to groups in the auditory and particular applications in the exhortations of his sermons; the great range of his appeal to sentiment, arousing pity (he was a master of pathos), indignation, or terror; the use of homely and telling illustrations; and the employment of topical references and impromptu illustrations (Davies 1963, 162f.).

Later Evangelistic Preaching. Although the established church in England had originally reacted negatively to the nascent Methodist movement of Whitefield and the Wesleys, soon clergy within it were captured by its aims. While the Methodist founders remained Anglican priests until they died, they had been forced to carry on most of their work outside the official structure of the Church of England. This new group of Anglican Evangelicals, however, succeeded by the middle of the nineteenth century in making their movement one of the most effective forces in their communion. In their zeal to bring the saving news of Christ to all people, some of them preached in unconventional locations, but most of their preaching was done from their own pulpits in parish churches of the establishment.

One of the great evangelical leaders was Charles Simeon (1759–1836), fellow of King's College, Cambridge, and vicar of Holy Trinity Church. He did not believe that he learned to preach until he discovered the homiletics manual of the French neoclassical Protestant divine, Jean Claude.* To help his disciples learn, he shared his insights with them at "conversation parties." He also revised and annotated the English translation of Claude and published *Horae Homileticae*, twenty-one volumes containing 2,536 outlines of sermons on every text of the Bible.

In America, Whitefield had already begun to transform revival as a surprising work of grace sent by the Holy Spirit to a work that could be accomplished by human endeavor. In his case, the endeavor was to have him come and preach. Revivalism increasingly became a matter of techniques that could be learned and practiced by anyone. This was apparent in the Second Great Awakening of the early nineteenth century. Its first outbreak was on the raw frontier of Kentucky, where the camp meeting developed, characterized by extreme emotionalism as evidenced in such religious "exercises" as falling, running, jumping, and jerking. At about the same time, Yale president Timothy Dwight* was fighting "infidelity" among students with a more sedate form of revival. His students went out to the parishes of New England to convert those who had become "formal" in their religion, but they did so in a way that avoided the so-called excesses of the first awakening.

The third phase of later evangelicalism combined features of the first two and succeeded both. It was led by a converted lawyer of western New York, Charles G. Finney* (1792–1875). He introduced such innovations into the techniques of revival as the anxious bench, the inquiry room, and protracted meetings. He also recognized that the very act of holding a revival brought into question the strict Calvinism of Whitefield as well as New England double predestination. He believed that the unconverted were justly doomed to a burning hell because of their willful persistence in sin. The purpose of his preaching was to awaken a horrified awareness of sin in his hearers so that they might repent and be saved. He said that he preached like a lawyer trying to persuade a jury to return a verdict of guilty. His sermons, therefore, were long treatises with many subdivisions based on careful logical distinctions, with the Bible treated as a legal contract. His purpose was to hammer away relentlessly until he overcame resistance, until, as he said, the sinner was "broken down" and "slain."

Finney's milieu was the small towns along the frontier of western New York and Ohio. The next important innovator in revivals and evangelistic preaching was destined for the bustling life of cities in the middle of the nineteenth century. Like many of the most successful evangelists to follow him, Dwight L. Moody* (1837–1899) was a layman. A farm boy who went to Boston to make his way as an entrepreneur, he soon moved to Chicago and began to live the script of a Horatio Alger novel. He undoubtedly would have succeeded had he not been converted before he left Boston. In Chicago he began to pour as much of his vast energy into the cause of religion as he did into his business activities. He started a church school class for slum children. It grew so fast that it became a separate congregation. He did similar work with the YMCA.

Eventually he began preaching. He and song leader Ira Sankey spent two years in Great Britain conducting a series of revivals that met with an enormous response. Back in the States, they continued to find the same success. Finney preached like a lawyer, but Moody's ideal for a sermon was the report of one businessman to others. He kept it short and simple, much more concerned with practical realities than theoretical niceties. He would make a short series of points and support them with long, homely, often sentimental anecdotes illustrating the principles. His theology was very different from Finney's; he had become convinced that the love of God was the main truth to be communicated. His job was to persuade people to accept it, and he went about it as he would present a product to a customer. Instead of an order, however, he hoped to get a commitment symbolized by a card completed by the hearer. He went about acquiring commitments like the good businessman he was, seeing to it that every detail was prepared and organized for success.

Moody's revivals were thus as far re-

moved from the "surprising work of God" in Jonathan Edwards's parish as they were from the flamboyant crusades of Billy Sunday* (1862–1935), the ex-baseball star, who invented a style of preaching that made the revivalist a celebrity and entertainer who could deliver conversions to depopulated congregations at so much per head. Despite the variations in revivalist technique that evolved over the years, the basic pattern of evangelistic preaching set by Whitefield can still be recognized. Nor was the evangelistic style confined to revivals. It remained the characteristic pulpit fare in many congregations until World War II and after (see Revivals).

Rhetorical and Homiletical Developments in Britain. Although preaching has always been influenced by rhetoric, this was never truer than in Great Britain from the end of the seventeenth through the middle of the nineteenth century when so many notable orators were members of the clergy. English education had always been rhetorical education, but in this period even greater attention was paid to the question of what makes oral communication effective.

Neoclassicism. At the beginning of the period the main school of thought was the neoclassical, which taught that speech should be natural and meet the criteria of Greek and Roman rhetoric. There is a sense in which that had been the norm all along, especially after the rise of humanism, but during this period it came to be invoked explicitly for written as well as oral communication. Rhetoric was extended to include literature and criticism in addition to oratory. Among the most influential neoclassicists were Dryden, Pope, and Swift, leading Augustan stylists. Since Swift was also Dean of the Anglican cathedral in Dublin, he was a preacher as well as a writer and was the author of a short treatise on preaching. The English neoclassical school was greatly influenced by the French. The spirit of this movement can be seen in the preaching of Tillotson and the Latitudinarians.

The Belles Lettres Movement. The insights of the classical rhetoricians, however, were quickly supplemented by the rediscovery of a classical work on rhetoric that took a different approach from that of most previous writers. In 1674, the French neoclassicist Boileau published a translation and a commentary on a work written around the first century, *On the Sublime*, by Longinus. This author asserted that the goal of the speaker was not so much to persuade the listeners (the goal of the three classical genera) as to "transport them out of themselves" into an experience of the sublime.

This idea was consistent with the emphasis on feeling that was characteristic of the evangelical awakening. It also fit in with other motifs in the thought of the time. Francis Bacon, for instance, introduced the concept of "faculties psychology," the idea that the human mind has several different parts: reason, imagination, memory, and appetite. In light of these distinctions, he went on to say that "the duty and office of Rhetoric is to *apply Reason to Imagination* for the better moving of the will." Thus a distinction was introduced between convincing and persuading. Reason alone would suffice to change people's minds, but the involvement of their emotions was necessary to cause them to act on that belief.

Faculties psychology, with its emphasis on moving the will, also fit in with another cultural development of the eighteenth century, which was a theory of art that still prevails. *Ars* in Latin, or *techne* in Greek, possessed the sense of a skill. An understanding of art as the creation of beauty, of "art for the sake of art," entered Western consciousness in the period under discussion through the French beaux arts movement. The appropriation of Longinus's understanding that the function of rhetoric was to enable an audience to experience the sublime made it possible to think the rhetor could function as an artist and even as a genius (in the sense of one who has "extraordinary capacity for imaginative creation, original thought, invention, or discovery," another new concept of the time). When rhetoric was expanded to include writing and criticism along with oratory, its aim came to be understood as the creation of belles lettres.

The leading exemplar of that movement was Hugh Blair, minister of the High Kirk in Edinburgh and Regius Professor of Rhetoric and Belles Lettres at the university there. After his retirement in 1783, he published his *Lectures on Rhetoric and Belles Lettres*, which proved so popular that it has been said that half of the educated English-speaking world studied it for the next century. Believing that persuasion worked through the imagination to move the will, Blair combined the forensic and deliberative genera into "the eloquence of the public assembly" and included "pulpit oratory" in that genus (*see* Imagination).

The Elocutionary Movement. Alongside the emphasis on emotion in persuasion there developed a new concern with delivery, the Elocutionary movement. It grew in part out of a conviction that one of the reasons the Methodists were drawing members away from the established church was the liveliness of their delivery in comparison to "the cold, artificial manner" with which so many clergy read their notes from the pulpit. (Hogarth's prints depict the deadliness of the one and the extravagance of the other.) Actors like David Garrick were attracting attention by the naturalness with which they were able to communicate the emotions of their characters using gesture and facial expression. The Elocutionary movement adapted these techniques to oratory. Its leading proponent, Thomas Sheridan, father of the playwright Richard, was convinced that both the pulpit and the bar would profit enormously. The success of George Whitefield was a strong argument in favor of the thesis. The theorists believed that the whole art could be reduced to a set of rules and even diagrams that showed what stances and expressions one assumed to communicate each emotion.

From the movement's excesses came conventions of the Victorian theater that have been parodied ever since.

The Epistemologists. A more profound influence on rhetorical theory in the late eighteenth and early nineteenth centuries was the epistemological thought of such philosophers as John Locke and David Hume. In 1776 a Scottish Presbyterian minister and educator, George Campbell, published his *Philosophy of Rhetoric*, which combined faculty psychology, the laws of association, sympathy, moral reasoning, and common sense. On this basis he constructed a theory of persuasion that saw it moving through four steps: instruction, imagination, passions, and motivation of the will. The movement through imagination was key because it permitted the mind to conceive of things with which it was not familiar. It is to that faculty that fables, parables, allegories, and poetry are addressed. Thus it is through the imagination that the emotions are engaged. In this way Campbell understood persuasion to depend on a combination of strong rational arguments and closely related appeals to the passions. His understanding of reasoning was not the classical dependence on syllogisms but a more empirical approach consistent with developing scientific thought. In many ways, Campbell's work demonstrated the growing acuteness of psychological analysis and its necessary role in any adequate rhetorical theory.

His work was further advanced by a book on rhetoric by an Oxford don and Anglican priest, Richard Whatley, who eventually became Archbishop of Dublin. Whatley, who also wrote a major book on logic, limited his discussion of rhetoric to argumentation. For him the speaker does not have to "invent" things to say but starts out with a proposition to be advanced. The proposition is advanced progressively as a number of different kinds of testimony are invoked to support it. The presumption always sides with the position taken by the majority of the audience. The burden of proof is on those who would bring that position into question. Whatley's motivation for the development of his theory of argumentation was his desire to defend the Christian faith at a time when it was under attack.

Newman and Robertson. Knowledge of these developments is necessary for understanding the development of preaching in Britain during the nineteenth century, especially the preaching of two of the pulpit giants of the period, John Henry Newman* and Frederick W. Robertson.* Newman was a pupil of Whatley at Oxford and is credited with being the anvil on whom Whatley hammered out his thought. In at least one respect Newman departed from the method of his teacher because he continued to think of invention as the key to rhetoric, generally taking two "topics" (*loci communes*) that represented the extremes of the controverted positions and using those as a hermeneutical device for arriving at the full range of possibilities in the discussion. That this method was used as a progressive argument to produce probability and that presumptions were taken seriously is clear to any reader of Newman's sermons or any of his other writings. His sermons also exhibit the psychological acuity that the rhetorical theory of Campbell called for. According to one scholar, the reason these sermons are still read is "chiefly for their penetrating understanding of human nature and destiny, and for their moral guidance and spiritual illumination, which are admirably expressed in the economy of nervous and subtle English prose."

Robertson, whose preaching is usually described in superlatives, fell under the influence of Newman while he was at Oxford. Soon, however, he returned to the evangelical circle in which he had grown up. Later he was to leave that, too, and to cease to be wholly acceptable to any party, even the Liberal, although he was very concerned about the implications of science for religion and the needs of the poor. As he said, "My tastes are with the aristocrats, my principles with the mob." During his life he attracted little attention and held no posts of distinction. Most of his sermons were preached in one parish, Trinity Chapel, at Brighton, and he died at the age of thirty-seven after only thirteen years of active ministry. Yet seventy-five years after its first publication, the American edition of his complete sermons had been continuously in print—a record unequaled by any other religious book published by Harper's.

Analysts have difficulty deciding whether to treat Robertson as a great biblical preacher or a great pastoral and psychological preacher. The reason for the dilemma is clear. He identified a personal or spiritual problem on which he thought he ought to preach and then wrote the sermon as a study of a biblical character who suffered from it. In this way he brought the issue so to life that his hearers could recognize themselves and their own situations and be given insight accordingly. The theory is aptly stated in a comment about Robertson written anonymously:

> I think one great need in our pulpit ministrations is naturalness. . . . Many are miserable in their inmost hearts, who are light-hearted and gay before the world. They feel that no heart understands theirs, or can help them. Now, suppose a preacher goes down into the depths of his own being, and has the courage and fidelity to carry all he finds there, first to God in confession and prayer, and then to his flock as some part of the general experience of Humanity, do you not feel that he must be touching close upon some brotherman's sorrows and wants? . . . Does not the man feel that here is a revelation of God's truth as real and fresh as if he had stood in the streets of Jerusalem, and heard the Saviour's very voice? (F. W. Robertson, *Sermons Preached at Brighton*, 1877, Preface, ix).

American Preaching. A Swedish historian of preaching, Yngve Brilioth, has described the most recent homiletical history of American Christendom as "an impenetrable forest to the outsider." The response of an insider is to wonder why he confined his description to the most recent period. It is true that before the Great Awakening most preaching was of the Puritan variety described above and that after the Awakening evangelistic preaching became the norm in many places. Beyond that, the most that can be done is to point to a few broad categories to which the majority of the rest of American preaching can be assigned before World War II.

The first must reflect the rationalistic preaching that began in England in the late seventeenth century, which went beyond the rationalism of Tillotson and the Latitudinarians. Deists who persisted in religious observance became Unitarians. While the American Unitarian movement came later than the English and was not directly connected to it, it was still a response to many of the same cultural stimuli. In America the original concern was not so much with the number of divine persons as it was with an optimistic evaluation of human nature in reaction to Calvinist convictions of total depravity. As time went on, the influence of such "liberalism" spread to most mainline Protestant denominations. Many discussions of "science vs. religion" were to take place in the pulpit. A naturalist/supernaturalist controversy was one expression of the issue and the liberal/fundamentalist controversy was another. Topical sermons, many of them taking one side or the other on a controversial issue, became a favorite homiletical form.

Another trend that developed early was preaching on social issues. This practice was a by-product of the Awakening. Evangelists became preoccupied with how conversion was to be lived out in society. The Temperance movement is a prime example, but evangelical zeal also came to call for decisions on other issues of personal morality. While many of the causes they preached have come to seem trivial to later generations, social-issue preaching also played a crucial role in the effort to have slavery abolished. Later, before and during both world wars, there was preaching that supported both pacifism and the war effort. By the turn of the century, the social gospel movement was beginning to raise moral issues about social as well as personal morality and to call into question institutions and structures that militated against justice.

These general categories represent the types of preaching with which Americans supplemented the Sunday task of instructing the faithful. An overview of late nineteenth-century preaching can be gained from looking at a homiletics textbook that was first published in 1870 and continued in revisions for over a century, *The Preparation and Delivery of Sermons* by John A. Broadus.* Broadus recognized four kinds of sermon subject matter: doctrinal, moral, historical (especially biblical history), and what he called "experimental," that is, pertaining to religious experience. For the presentation of these subjects he acknowledged the existence of three kinds of sermons. (1) "Subject" or topical sermons undertake to present an analysis of a subject, the analysis being subdivided on the basis of logic rather than being derived from a biblical text. (2) Text sermons derive their structure from the biblical passage on which they are based. (3) Expository sermons have no sharp distinction from the other two and may analyze anything from a part of a single verse to several verses or a chapter. What distinguishes expository sermons, however, is that they have as their basic purpose the explanation of the meaning of the passage under consideration. All these types of sermons are familiar from the earlier history of the church. The homily form used by church fathers from Origen on and by Jewish preachers before them is expository. The thematic sermon of the High Middle Ages was textual, while the neoclassical sermons of Tillotson and other Latitudinarians tended to be topical.

Yet the limitation of preaching to four kinds of subject matter and three patterns of development did not mean that creativity had gone out of preaching. The varieties of outline listed by Halford E. Luccock during World War II (*In the Minister's Workshop* 1944, 134–47) shows how inventive preachers continued to be in trying to find the most effective means of communicating the Word of God. Some of these were

1. the Ladder sermon, in which one point follows another in a necessary sequence;
2. the Jewel sermon, the development of which consists in "turning one idea around as one might turn a jewel in his fingers, allowing different facets to catch the light";
3. the Classification sermon—"based on dividing people and things into different classes or types."
4. the Skyrocket sermon, which "begins on the ground, rises to a height, then breaks into pieces and comes down to earth again";
5. the Twin sermon, "setting forth opposing or contrasting aspects of one truth or one word of scripture";
6. the Roman Candle sermon, "a succession of statements or observations which follow without any particular design except that they are all related to the subject" (*see* Form).

And so it goes, picking up along the way the Analogy, Surprise-Package, Chase, and Rebuttal patterns. There are even two types to be avoided; the Elephant sermon, which has a long introduction and a very short tail of a conclusion, and the Magellan sermon, in which the preacher circumnavigates the globe every Sunday. While these terms may suggest superficiality, they are valuable nevertheless because they are easily remembered; sermons are actually constructed in all these ways; and they indicate the process by which each sermon is developed according to its own interior logic. A combination of Broadus and Luccock shows where preaching in America had arrived after it had been shaped by post-Reformation rationalism, on the one hand, and "religion of the heart," on the other, as Christians of all traditions sought to proclaim the Word of God in response to the challenges of modernity.

The Period after World War II

The last half century has seen as many changes in the basic understanding of the meaning and practice of preaching as in the previous two-and-one-half centuries. These changes reflect the increasing pluralism of Western and especially American culture during this period. The trends are varied and even at times competitive. Thus the most that can be done is to list what appear to be the major trends and to characterize them briefly.

The Biblical Theology Movement. This preaching movement, like several of the others to be noticed, has antecedents from well before World War II. The most obvious beginning of this one is in the work of the Swiss theologian Karl Barth.* A pastor during World War I, Barth came to regard the regnant liberal theology of the German universities as a totally inadequate basis for ministry to people experiencing the traumas of war. Inspired by the reformers, especially Calvin, but inspired also by the existentialism of Kierkegaard,* Barth emphasized revelation at the expense of any achievements of human reason. His theology of the Word of God* is referred to variously as crisis or dialectical theology. In the U.S., the broad movement that he initiated was called neo-orthodoxy. A perspective similar to Barth's lies behind Gerhard Kittel's multivolumed *Theological Dictionary of the New Testament* and may also be seen in the Old Testament theology of Gerhard von Rad. The movement became prominent in Britain, especially Scotland, during the 1930s and was the dominant school of theology in the U. S. after the war. In America the work of Reinhold Niebuhr* was regarded as having similar emphases.

The biblical scholarship developed in Germany, Great Britain, and the United States under the inspiration of dialectical theology assumed that there was a consistent perspective throughout the Bible that made it possible to speak of the theology of the whole Bible. One of this theology's characteristics was a narrative orientation centered upon "the God who acts" in redemption history (*Heilsgeschichte*). In the same period C. H. Dodd drew the distinction between *kerygma* (proclamation) and *didache* (teaching), and insisted that preaching, if it was to follow the model of the New Testament, should consist exclusively of the former. Preaching was a divine-human encounter that elicited a decision on the part of the hearer. Two prominent British publications on homiletical theology during this period were *The Servant of the Word* and *God and Men* by H. H. Farmer, a Cambridge theologian. No single homiletics textbook, however, dominated the field on either side of the Atlantic.

The Liturgical Movement. In the nineteenth century the abbot of the Benedictine monastery of Solesmes, P.L.R. Guéranger, began the revival of plainsong that would be the basis for a new emphasis on the participation of the congregation in the Mass. The modern liturgical movement is generally thought to date from that effort, although it was not until World War II that the movement exercised any influence on parochial life. By then, however, there was already developing within the Roman Catholic Church a call for dialogue masses (those in which the congregation made the responses), the use of the vernacular rather than Latin, celebrations in which the priest faced the people, and other usages that have become standard since the Second Vatican Council.*

For these innovations (or, actually, restorations) to be successful, it was necessary for the laity to be better instructed in the liturgy. Thus, it became common for homilies to emphasize the season of the liturgical year and the theme of the particular Sunday or feast. Simultaneously, Roman Catholic biblical scholars were adopting the historical-critical method in their exegesis, and preachers began to make use of their findings. This amounted to a rediscovery of the pulpit by Roman Catholic priests first in Europe and then in America.

In time the movement began to affect other traditions—at first liturgical communions like the Anglicans and Lutherans, and then others as well. Its impact can be seen in such phenomena as much more widespread use of the liturgical year, preaching based on the lectionary, and the conviction of many in free church traditions that the Eucharist ought to be the main service on Sundays. The result is more liturgical preaching in both Catholic and Protestant churches (see Liturgical Preaching).

Pastoral Care from the Pulpit. While many preachers throughout history have intended to help parishioners deal with various kinds of problems, a new era began in 1928 when Harry Emerson Fosdick,* the famous founder of Riverside Church in New York City, published an article in *Harper's Magazine* called "What Is the Matter with Preaching?" The method of preaching he recommended in the article has been variously described as "life-situation" or "problem-centered," but he referred to it as the "project method." He stated his basic position this way:

> Every sermon should have for its main business the solving of some problem— a vital, important problem, puzzling minds, burdening consciences, distracting lives—and any sermon which thus does tackle a real problem, throw even a little light on it and help some individuals practically to find their way through it cannot be altogether uninteresting (July 1928).

Not all of the problems Fosdick dealt with in his sermons were matters of pastoral care, but many were. His method of evaluating a sermon was to see how many who heard it arranged to meet him later for counseling.

The influences on Fosdick's thought were the social gospel, modern psychology, and the learning theory of John Dewey. As time went on, it was to be the psychological element that would most influence the pulpit. After World War II the American people came to accept psychology as the new orthodoxy, and pastoral care was often reduced to one-on-one pastoral counseling. In this cultural climate, Fosdick's example of doing pastoral care from the pulpit was greatly imitated. The movement has not been so pervasive in Britain as it has in the States, but there have been preachers there who brought psychological insight into their preaching, the most notable being Leslie D. Weatherhead,* Minister of London's City Temple from 1936 to 1960 (see Pastoral Care and Preaching).

Developments in Evangelistic Preaching. Shortly after World War II, the United States became aware of a new mass evangelist, Billy Graham,* who has remained at center stage ever since. Since his first big crusade in Los Angeles in 1949, he has corrected all that had gone bad in revivalism and attempted to restore its integrity—for example, by insisting on financial disclosure within his organization.

His ministry has been characterized by ready adoption of modern media techniques. For instance, the electronic amplification of his voice has meant that he has been heard by congregations of over 100,000. His ministry was quickly expanded to include a network radio broadcast, "Hour of Decision," and a nationally syndicated newspaper column, "My Answer." He has made movies and, when television became an effective medium, he began telecasting his crusades. As a result, his ministry is credited with over a million "decisions for Christ." One scholar writes, "No other preacher in history has proclaimed the gospel to more persons or seen more lives committed to the Christian faith under his ministry than has William Franklin Graham" (in Fant and Pinson, Vol. 12, 282).

Graham's use of television paved the way for more intensive exploitation of the medium by other evangelists. Most of the "televangelists" preach the necessity of a personal conversion experience. Television has multiplied the evangelists' influence. Air time is expensive; thus a good deal of their total effort focuses on raising money to continue telecasting. In a secularized society many know little more of the Christian church and its preaching than what they see on religious television. An investigation of how preaching has been affected by being filtered through this medium remains to be made (see Television and Preaching).

Contemporary evangelism has also taken the form of the so-called "megachurches." These vast congregations gather to hear the gospel proclaimed in the idiom of contemporary secularized culture rather than the traditional vocabularies of Christianity. They have also generated their own form of evangelistic preaching, which is characterized by an expository, practical style.

Preaching on Social Issues. While Christian preaching has always been concerned with social conditions, it has tended until the present century to present those conditions as issues of personal morality and has thus aimed at changing individuals rather than institutions. Although a change began to occur at least as early as Walter Rauschenbusch's* efforts to proclaim the "social gospel," a whole new era was inaugurated in the 1960s with the civil rights movement, the peace movement, the student movement, the women's rights movement, and the war on poverty. Social activism became the criterion by which many congregations or their clergy assessed the seriousness of their Christian commitment.

Two simultaneous responses to these movements occurred in the area of homiletics. One was the hermeneutics of suspicion, which was directed at all forms of public speaking. The 1960s witnessed a declining respect for the spoken word in general and for preaching in particular. The second response was a new homiletical genre, the "prophetic" sermon. It drew on the words and examples of the proph-

ets of the Hebrew Bible. At its best, the prophetic medium was a powerful tool for social change. The sermons of William Sloane Coffin* at Riverside Church, for instance, were stirring calls to live out the implications of the gospel. While times have changed, prophetic preaching continues in less publicized forms.

Particular manifestations of prophetic preaching occur within the African-American church (see below) and wherever liberation theology exercises influence. One particular genre of liberation* preaching is the corporate homily, developed in Latin American base communities, reported in Ernesto Cardenal's The Gospel in Solentiname.

African-American Preaching.* What is now known as black preaching probably goes back to the time of the Second Great Awakening, the first period in which large numbers of African-American slaves were converted to the religion of their white owners. Before that time there had been conversions and even the founding of black denominations. But the form of preaching that is usually associated with the African-American tradition is a development of the chanted sermon still performed by some white preachers in Kentucky, Tennessee, and elsewhere in the South. The form is traceable to the Second Awakening. It has been compared to the oral literature of the Homeric epics, Beowulf, African chant, and the Serbo-Croatian guslars. It also has much in common with the Welsh folk preaching to which the First Awakening can be traced. However the form began, in the African-American church there has developed a virtuoso tradition of oral art in which practitioners regularly "commit poetry" and preach the gospel powerfully at the same time (see Folk Preaching [African-American]).

For most of its history this preaching has been little known in the white community. Literally, the tradition was awakened by the publication in 1927 of God's Trombones: Seven Negro Sermons in Verse by James Weldon Johnson. Next came Green Pastures, the 1930 Broadway hit and later Hollywood film, based on Roark Bradford's efforts to retell Bible stories in the manner of the black pulpit. While the latter came to be regarded as demeaning, the two works together nevertheless made it necessary for educated white people to take black preaching seriously.

It was in the civil rights movement of the 1960s, however, that the country was exposed to the most eloquent black preaching. The "I Have a Dream" speech of Martin Luther King Jr.,* at the March on Washington in August 1963, functioned as a black sermon to the nation. Since then, others have begun to make an impression outside the African-American community proportionate to the one they made within it. Gardner C. Taylor* was a Beecher lecturer at Yale. James Forbes has taught preaching at Union Theological Seminary, given the Beecher lectures, and become senior minister at Riverside Church. James Earl Massey has contributed to the literature of homiletics as well as that of New Testament studies.

Henry Mitchell and others have described the distinctive elements of preaching in the African-American tradition. Mitchell, Jon Michael Spencer, and Evans Crawford comment on the musicality of black preaching. The silences before and between the words are as important as the words themselves; the rests are as necessary as the notes. The pauses establish the timing and the rhythm. "Talkback" responses—what Crawford calls the "participatory proclamation"—occur (see Response to Preaching). The efforts of human speech to utter the ineffable are discussed in terms of "hum." The articulation of the sermon in language that is consonant with the congregation is spoken of as "pitch," and the new theological and ethical themes being developed within the tradition are designated by the jazz term "riffs." With these terms and others, African-American homileticians provide insights into the power of the tradition.

The 1960s saw a growing presence of other racial and ethnic groups within American society, especially Hispanics and Asians. Within the latter group the Koreans have been most active in the formation of Christian congregations. There is also a tradition of Native American preaching that goes back several centuries. While it is very likely that distinctive homiletical traditions have developed within these groups, they have not yet been sufficiently studied to permit easy description.

The Preaching of Women, Feminists, and Womanists. While many of the trends discussed began before World War II, the preaching of women is rooted in the earliest days of the church. Patriarchal suppression, however, has kept the preaching of women from being an obvious part of the mainstream. However, the Gnostics and Montanists, the Albigensians, and others recognized the preaching gifts and call of women. Occasionally within the heart of the establishment there have been those like Hildegard of Bingen* whose preaching has been valued (*see* Women as Preachers).

Women have been preaching in America since the seventeenth century. The preaching of Anne Hutchinson caused controversy in Puritan Massachusetts. Although the Quakers of the time did not ordain ministers, they were the only denomination fully to accept the preaching of women in the seventeenth century. By the eighteenth century, others began to open themselves to this ministry as well, but all were outside the mainstream: Shakers, Universalists, and Unitarians. In the nineteenth century, Freewill Baptists, Free Methodists, and, as one authority has put it, "factions connected with the holiness and deeper-life movements" pulled down the barriers. Congregationalists, Disciples of Christ, and American Baptists began to ordain women around the turn of the century.

Only since World War II have the largest denominations begun ordaining women: Methodists and northern Presbyterians in 1956, southern Presbyterians in 1964, major Lutheran groups in 1970, and Episcopalians in 1976. The two largest groups in the country, the Southern

Baptists and the Roman Catholics, have demonstrated the greatest resistance to the preaching of women.

Women are gradually developing homiletical models of their own. These have been sharpened by some (but not all) women preachers into a feminist homiletic. A feminist homiletical literature is only now appearing, yet efforts at identifying its various strands are being made. One scholar has characterized feminist preaching as rooted in the Bible and the quest for justice:

Other elements that constitute a feminist perspective are these: (1) the use of gender-inclusive or mutual language for humans and for God; (2) the modification of theological, especially Christological assumptions; (3) the use of a feminist or liberation hermeneutic for interpretation of the biblical text; (4) the manner in which imagery is used, particularly images of God. . .; (5) the evidence of a relational or communal approach to authority; (6) the use of personal story . . . (Edwina Hunter, Introd., *And Blessed Is She: Sermons by Women*, 1990, 94f.).

Within the African-American community there are those who describe their own efforts as womanist rather than feminist. By the distinction they wish to indicate that racism continues as a companion to sexism and that their own homiletic will continue to battle both (*see* Feminist Preaching).

Toward a New Homiletic? One trend appears to be reaching across boundaries and affecting much of the homiletic enterprise. A shift is occurring from deductive preaching to inductive* preaching. The difference between the two is usually stated as a contrast between sermons that begin with a general rule and move toward particular examples and sermons that begin with concrete experience and move toward wider principles. Inductive preaching assumes that a change of consciousness has occurred. What has

changed is the rhetorical ground of persuasion.

This change of consciousness is attributed to a number of different causes. One group of theories points to the first television generation coming to maturity. Since television tells a story far better than it transmits data, narrative may have become the reflexive way of processing reality. In *Eloquence in an Electronic Age*, Kathleen Hall Jamieson (1988) argues that political speeches given on television have to forsake what were formerly regarded as the conventions of manly speech and move toward a manner of speaking that used to be regarded as feminine. Its style is intimate, self-disclosing, and conversational. It also makes great use of narrative and metaphor. In theory, it appears that what is effective on television will be effective in communicating with people whose consciousness has been formed by television.

Writers who favor the inductive approach disagree among themselves about the best rhetorical strategies for exploiting it. Most, however, are convinced that effective preaching today will display a narrative quality. How that is done will vary from theorist to theorist. For some, narrativity refers mainly to the quality of the sermon as unfolding in time. For others, storytelling will dominate the entire sermon. There are mediating strategies as well, not to mention others that focus on metaphor and image. In every case, what is advocated is very different from the linear, deductive sermon that was characteristic of the biblical theology movement (*see* Narrative Preaching).

After 2,000 years, homiletics seems to have arrived at inductive preaching, but the journey is not over. The shape of the immediate future in homiletics is not clear. The one thing that can be relied upon, however, is that women and men who are called to proclaim the Word of God to their generation will find effective ways of doing so, just as all the doctors and saints who have preceded them in this glorious calvalcade have done. The

Word of God will remain living and active and sharper than a two-edged sword as long as the church remains in its pilgrim state on earth.

Brilioth, Y., *A Brief History of Preaching,* trans. K. E. Mattson, 1965. **Campbell, T. A.,** *The Religion of the Heart,* 1991. **Dargan, E. C.,** *A History of Preaching,* 2 vols. (1905–12), 1968. **Davies, H.,** *Varieties of English Preaching, 1900–1960,* 1963. **Edwards, O. C., Jr.,** *A History of Preaching,* 2 vols. (forthcoming). **Fant, C. E., Jr.,** and **W. M. Pinson, Jr.,** *20 Centuries of Great Preaching: An Encyclopedia of Preaching,* 13 vols., 1971. **Kennedy, G. A.,** *Classical Rhetoric and Its Christian and Secular Tradition from Ancient to Modern Times,* 1980. **Lischer, R.,** *Theories of Preaching: Selected Readings in the Homiletical Tradition,* 1987. **Petry, R. C.,** *No Uncertain Sound: Sermons That Shaped the Pulpit Tradition,* 1948. **Schütz, W.,** *Geschichte der christlichen Predigt,* 1972. **Smyth, C.,** *The Art of Preaching: A Practical Survey of Preaching in the Church of England, 747–1939,* 1940. **Turnbull, R. G.,** *A History of Preaching,* Vol. 3, *From the Close of the Nineteenth Century to the Middle of the Twentieth Century . . . ,* 1974.

O. C. EDWARDS, JR.

Holy Spirit and Preaching. The work of the Holy Spirit in preaching does not refer to any particular understanding that serves to distinguish some Christians from others. Preaching is a charismatic act that relies utterly on the grace given by the Spirit to speak for God and bring the hearer into the presence of God. Preaching and all acts pertaining to the ministerial office flow from the work of the Spirit.

An appropriate place to start is with the most fundamental image of the Spirit's procession from the Father and the Son. We begin with the trinitarian image because this is the mode in which the Spirit is revealed. Unlike the figures of the Father and the Son, no roles associated with human relations are offered for assistance in understanding the Spirit. This may well be a great service in that it compels a movement beyond easy transposi-tion in the quest for knowledge of the Spirit.

Thoroughly clothed in mystery, the nature of the Spirit underlies all that can be said about God and the things of God. Intersecting the invisible and the visible, the Spirit is not restricted by the laws and boundaries acknowledged in the physical world (John 3:8). Yet, without the Spirit, living objects have no body with which to fill space (Gen. 2:7). Searching the deep things of God, the Spirit bears the divine life to the destination God wills (1 Cor. 2:10). This is the sense in which it is correct and essential to say that preaching is the work of God the Spirit. Like all other acts of worship, to be acceptable it must be done in spirit and in truth.

The Spirit's going forth like wind or breath is fundamental to the origin and nature of the Spirit. Movement, vitality, life, and energy are what we are offered in these images. In Genesis, this image meets us from the onset, as the Spirit hovers over the deep (the *tehom,* the unformed chaos), prior to the word that calls forth light and order (Gen. 1:2). Again and again, the Spirit is spoken of as wind (*ruach*) or breath—blown into Adam, coming upon judges and prophets. In the most definitive word spoken concerning the Spirit's origin, the Spirit proceeds from the Father at the request of the Son on behalf of disciples living in a hostile environment (John 15:26, 18).

As the message from God (the Word of God*), preaching must be accompanied by divine authority* for it to be more than mere human speech. This dimension of preaching is amply attested to in the commissions to preach in the New Testament and the church. Those called by Christ are ordained and given authority to preach in his name. In the name of Jesus they were to heal the sick, cast out devils, and proclaim that the kingdom was at hand (Mark 3:14). The investiture of this ministry includes a decisive moment of pneumatological empowerment.

The Spirit authorizes preaching in Jesus of Nazareth—the Christ, the Messiah, the One anointed by God. Luke is careful to disclose the pneumatological dimensions of this pattern. Beginning the account of Jesus' inauguration to the Messianic office, reliance on the Spirit is depicted in the descent of the dove and the testimony of the Father. What follows is a period of preparation, during which Jesus, led and filled by the Spirit, overcomes the temptations of Satan. Only following victory in the wilderness does the Son return to Galilee in the power of the Spirit (Luke 4:1–14).

Preaching in the synagogue is the direct consequence of the Spirit's anointing. This preaching is good news that God has declared release for the captives and liberty for those who are bruised; it is proclamation of the acceptable year of the Lord. Those who heard could not remain indifferent to the proclamation's power. Conviction brought on by the Spirit forced self-identification through the word and rejection on the part of those not prepared to accept it. Prophetic anointing takes the human vessel as the channel through which God's grace and power flow into those who respond in faith (Luke 4:18ff.).

Standing in the line of the Hebrew prophets, Jesus declared the fulfillment of the scriptures, which promised the salvation of the Lord. By the Spirit, Christian preaching points to Christ as the anointed one in whom the promises of God find their Amen. The Christ who preached in Nazareth preaches to those who receive the testimony of the Spirit, declaring that the time of God's favor is present.

The Johannine account contains the promise of the paraclete who will be with the people to teach them and to lead them into all truth (John 14:25). The fulfillment of the promise is seen when the risen Christ appears behind closed doors, breathes the Spirit upon them, and grants authority to forgive sins (John 20:22–23). In the Lukan account, the disciples are instructed to wait in Jerusalem for the promise of the Father—the Holy Spirit—who would clothe them with power (Luke 24:49). The fulfillment comes on the Day of Pentecost when they are filled with the Spirit and speak the gospel with boldness so that people from all nations can understand their account (Acts 2:4–6).

Setting apart and sending forth those who preach the gospel of Christ as representatives of the church is punctuated by the calling down of the Spirit (Acts 13:2–3). In the early church, fasting and praying preceded the acts of choosing and setting apart those who were to be ordained. Hands were laid upon them as a sign of the Spirit's gifts for the office they were to assume. Such prayer was accompanied by a charge and, on occasion, by prophetic utterance (1 Tim. 4:13, 14; 2 Tim. 1:6). The practice continues, with the primary elements in ordination being the laying on of hands and prayer for the outpouring of the Spirit for effective execution of the office. In sum, the act of preaching in the Christian church is utterly meaningless unless accompanied by the Spirit.

The pneumatological dimension is inseparable from all communication from God. The Spirit is God going forth into the creation dispensing life, vitality, energy. The Spirit is the very life (breath) of God that accompanies the Word of God, permitting the response for which God calls. It is not the case that God is everything and everything is God—as with pantheism. Yet God is not alien from the creation, as is implied in a deistic understanding. Rather, while remaining distinct from the world, God nevertheless remains active within the creation, ever able to effect a response. This is made possible by the Spirit, who intersects the visible and the invisible.

This pattern of God's dealing with the world is shown most clearly in the sending of the Son—the occasion for Christian preaching—and in the creation of the church, the primary locus of the Spirit. The Spirit's work in the incarnation is to prepare the body of the Son—the instrument of the Son's obedience. The Holy Ghost came upon Mary, and the power of the Most High overshadowed her. The holy thing conceived in her is to be the Son of God (Luke 1:34–35). In a real way, this work of the Spirit is the paradigm for preaching as the act of implanting faith within the heart of the hearer.

The efficacy of preaching relies on the correspondence between the Spirit's participation in the saving work of Christ and the work of the Spirit in the believing heart. By the Spirit, Christ performed mighty acts, doing good and healing those who were oppressed by the devil. The Spirit sustained the Son on the cross as he became sin and endured being forsaken by the Father (2 Cor. 5:21). Through the Spirit, the Son offered himself without spot as a sufficient sacrifice, securing eternal redemption (Heb. 9:14). In the Spirit, he preached to captive souls and broke the power of death (1 Pet. 3:19). Believing that the Father raised Jesus from the dead acknowledges the power of the Spirit to raise all who trust in Christ from the deadness of sin to walk in newness of life (Rom. 1:4; 10:9).

By the Spirit, Christian preaching is witness to these saving acts accompanied by conviction. It is testimony that declares the gracious love of God in sending the Son and the saving work of the Son in obeying the Father for all creation. The Spirit causes the word of preaching to be more than formal propositions or claims to which the hearer can be indifferent. Like an eyewitness in the courtroom, the Spirit testifies to the hearer, verifying the truth of what is claimed in preaching. The consequence is to force a verdict of belief or disbelief. This is what John Calvin* referred to as the internal testimony of the Spirit. The very capacity to believe is the result of grace given by the Spirit who moves within the believer as the power of God (Rom. 10:14–17). This inward work of the Spirit is the preparation for believing in and receiving Christ and being united with Christ in the Spirit body—the church.

Preaching relies on the Spirit in every aspect. Only by the Spirit is the word present within the scriptures. The Spirit communicates that living word to the preacher and fashions it as a vital address to the hearer. The Spirit works in sermon preparation and delivery to discern the heart and the situation of those who hear preaching and to guide their spiritual walk. This includes not only bringing persons to faith but also nurturing and deepening faith, which itself is a gift of the Spirit imparted through preaching (*see* Theology of Preaching; Pentecostal Preaching).

Comblin, J., *The Holy Spirit and Liberation,* 1989. Forbes, J. A., *The Holy Spirit and Preaching,* 1992. Heron, A., *The Holy Spirit,* 1983.   WILLIAM C. TURNER

Homiletics and Preaching in Africa.

In Africa, contemporary preaching in the mainline churches follows the doctrinal, liturgical, and social purposes of preaching in the various world communions. In the Reformation churches, it occupies a central position and possesses an avowedly evangelistic purpose. In churches with a Catholic or Orthodox tradition, preaching is typically liturgical, being subordinated to the demands of the context of worship. In the new religious movements and African independent churches, there is considerably more originality of doctrinal content, form, and style. In these churches there is often an order of preachers that constitutes the main form of ministry. Despite these differences between the churches, African preaching possesses many common characteristics, and it is probably still true to say that the most important theological work of Africans is to be found in the living voice of sermons and in the act of preaching itself.

The African preacher tends to adopt the hermeneutical methods favored by the New Testament, imparting a typological function to biblical events and traditions and reinterpreting these in relation to contemporary existence. Historicity is played down, while emphasis is placed on symbolical and allegorical explanations. This is because African thinking is traditionally mythical and because, in Africa, the world of created nature has a transparent or symbolic quality. This tendency also gives the African preacher an interest in myths of origin. The Old Testament is not merely a work of reference but a source of remembrance, and the preacher feels an affinity with the primordial images and archetypes of the Bible.

The African preacher likes to use folk tales, proverbs, and material from oral tradition and from daily life in the rural areas as illustrations and examples for understanding the biblical message. Popular themes are liberation and Christ's victory over evil. To an outsider, these applications and elaborations may appear anachronistic and contrary to the data of historical criticism, but they represent an effective appropriation of scripture. An important religious tradition in Africa concerns the links between the living and the dead. The interest of Africans in soteriological and eschatological doctrines has often been pointed out. In much of the Christology of African preaching, the mystery of Christ is frequently understood in relation to the theological role of ancestors. This is understandable, since ancestors are the essential mediators between God and humanity in African traditional religion and since the churches teach that Christ is now the unique mediator and channel of forgiveness. It is therefore natural that in African preaching ancestor veneration should help elucidate the doctrine of Christ, as well as provide substance for a Christian understanding of the communion between the living and the dead.

News and events from politics, current affairs, and technology play an important part in African sermons. These references help to relate biblical history to the modern community and contribute to African involvement in the biblical story itself. For example, Africa provided a shelter and a help to Jesus Christ in the first and last days of his life. It was in Africa that he found shelter when persecuted by Herod, and on his way to Calvary he found a helper in the African Simon of Cyrene.

Thus, Africa has been involved in the salvation story of humanity, and it may be that Africa now has a special message to give to the rest of the world (see Burkle).

Although mainline Christianity introduced monologic preaching in Africa, this form is far from congenial to African congregations. The African preacher uses direct address to hearers, so that they become participants in the sermon and actors in the biblical story. Congregational participation is achieved in a variety of ways, sometimes through poetry, sometimes through a direct invitation to the congregation to answer a question or complete a phrase, and sometimes through the singing of hymns during the sermon.

A more complex approach to preaching in Africa is the use of the choric story form. Many African folk tales and etiological stories take this form, in which the audience is made to participate in the telling of the story by singing a refrain at specified intervals. The sermon may be constructed as a choric story and may make use of themes from oral literature, amplifying them in light of biblical teaching and Christian doctrine. An African theme is thereby developed into a Christian one. The choric form has affinities with an ancient oriental practice of the fifth century. The *kontakion* was a metrical homily set to music and rendered by a preaching-cantor with the choir or congregation singing a refrain.

Many churches in Africa have adopted dramatized forms of Bible reading. Bible stories are acted out before the congregation with a great deal of local color and humorous anachronism. Such plays have a parallel to the miracle plays and mystery plays of medieval Europe. In some cases the sermon is a commentary on the drama itself.

In the African independent churches preaching is part of a total event, often lasting many hours. This is especially the case with the great pentecostal gatherings that take place in the open air. Lacking a public address system, the preachers run up and down between the lines of worshipers, shouting their message. Indeed, shouting is the characteristic style of preachers in these churches and is regarded as a sign of forceful preaching in the power of the Spirit (*see* Pentecostal Preaching).

During such an event, there may be a number of sermons. These are interspersed with dance and song, ecstatic experiences, prophecies, and communal prayer in which everyone prays in unison or as moved by the Spirit. Pastoral conversations may take place between the sermons and other liturgical acts. Sermons are regularly interrupted by prophetic messages or faith healings. To a Western observer, this preaching may appear somewhat chaotic. In fact, preachers operate within strict and conventional guidelines.

Preaching in Africa is far from a purely intellectual encounter between the Word of God and the African world. It is an encounter with the stark realities of life and death on the continent, with the rich oral traditions of African peoples, and with the themes and tenets of traditional religion. The sermon also demonstrates the African love of celebration and total communal involvement. Comparisons have been made between African preaching and the sermons of some of the early church fathers. Certainly, they share a love of symbolism and allegory, but such comparisons should not in any way detract from the specific genius of Africa that is present in its preachers.

Preaching in Africa is popular and can even be said to possess considerable entertainment value. Informal preaching is a common activity in urban and industrial areas, where it may also be a vehicle for political or social protest. It remains to be seen whether preaching can withstand competition from the increasing influence of the mass electronic media in the growing towns and cities of Africa (*see* African-American Preaching; Folk Preaching [African-American]).

Burkle, H., "Patterns of Sermons from Various Parts of Africa," *African Initiatives in Religion*, 1971, 222–31. **Éla, J.-M.,** *My Faith as an African*, trans. J. P. Brown and S. Perry, 1988. **Mbiti, S. J.,** *Bible and Theology in African Christianity*, 1986. **Shorter, A.,** "Form and Content in the African Sermon: An Experiment," *African Ecclesial Review* 2, 1969, 265–79. **Turner, H.,** *Profile Through Preaching: A Study of the Sermon Texts Used in a West African Independent Church*, C.W.M.E. Research Pamphlets, No. 13, 1965.   AYLWARD SHORTER

Homiletics and Preaching in Asia

The Christian Church in Asia.   Asia is huge. Its history, culture, and social environment differ according to each area and nation. Thus, it is extremely difficult to speak in general of the Christian church or Christian preaching in Asia. Nevertheless, while recognizing these differences, we can also find similarities.

The Protestant presence has a short history in the countries of Asia. Whereas Roman Catholic societies had already initiated mission work in Asia in the sixteenth century, it was not until the eighteenth century that the various Protestant mission* organizations first turned their attention to the whole of Asia, becoming especially active during the second half of the ninteenth century.

The Philippines, formerly a colony of Spain and where today the majority of the citizens are Roman Catholic, is the only nation in Asia that may be regarded as a Christian nation. Only in Korea does the percentage of Protestants surpass ten percent of the total population. Christians constitute a small minority in all other Asian nations, including India, with its long history of receiving mission activity.

Almost all Protestant denominations are active in mission to Asia. However, central among these have been the Anglo-Saxon churches, especially the American churches. Evangelicals and representatives of the revivalist movement have been prominent. Missionaries sent out by established churches did not merely transplant the patterns of worship and church life from their own countries, but they encouraged simpler rites and doctrines more suitable to the mission field. This emphasis was in keeping with the Asian people's inclination toward simplicity, and consequently it took root. Today Protestant worship services are simple, and the Bible is accorded the highest value in both teaching and life. There is less emphasis on traditional doctrine and church polity than in the Western churches.

Western Protestant mission to Asia coincided in time with the colonization of Asian lands by Western nations and the effort to modernize by independent Asian nations. Christianity, especially Anglo-Saxon Protestantism, was often linked in the minds of people with the colonizing efforts of modern Western culture and also with the culture and civilization that was thrust upon those countries aspiring to become modern nations. Many became Christians, thinking they were becoming civilized and cultured in a Western sense by doing so, and many valued Christianity as a representative of a superior Western culture. This kind of thinking only appeared to facilitate mission work, but in reality it impeded the establishment of any deep roots by Western Christianity in Asia. It was difficult for the gospel to permeate those Asian nations having pronounced Asian religious views and cultures as well as a strong ethnic awareness. Where ethnocentric patriotism opposed Western colonialism, an anti-Christian attitude was also strengthened that further impeded mission advance.

The immediate post–World War II years witnessed the retreat of colonialism, an increase in the number of independent nations, and a decrease in the number of missionaries from Europe and America. Moreover, Western churches encouraged Asian churches to become independent and emphasized a partnership type of relation with the younger churches in Asia. Consequently, Asian churches developed their own theologies and education, emphasizing the truth of a gospel rooted in Asia.

Preaching in the Protestant Churches of Asia. It is even more difficult to generalize when speaking about preaching in Asia. First, there is almost no documentary research material available on homiletics. Therefore, it is impossible to make a scientific survey of what kinds of sermons are preached at present. Theological study and education by Asians has progressed somewhat only since the end of World War II, but here too practical theology is underdeveloped. Even if sermons were to be published in each nation's tongue, it is almost impossible for them to become the common property of all Asian churches, for there is no common language in Asia. Collections of sermons thrive in Japan and Korea, but on the whole, homiletics in Asian nations is carried out in isolation.

In India and the Philippines, which were colonies for many years, English, the language of the rulers, became the official language and also the language of education and culture. Mission work in English was easily carried out, and theology in English was accepted. However, independent nations such as China, Japan, and Korea, with high levels of culture, built up their modern culture through the use of their own languages. In churches, the Western languages required translation, but also the gospel itself required transculturation into the thought patterns of the people. In the midst of the reality of the life of those who hear, the language of the listeners must be utilized. The indigenization of the gospel has occurred primarily by means of the sermon. Moreover, it has happened in a different way in every Asian country (*see* Cross-Cultural Preaching).

Asian churches, which always find themselves to be a minority, must continue in mission. In Asia, the worship service is a means of evangelism. The sermon in the worship service is always an evangelistic message. Salvation in Christ is its central theme. The sermons must be understood by those who do not know the historical tradition of the Christian church. The preacher must have an understanding of the Asian religious, cultural, and social context and must confront the anti-gospel elements included in that context. The preacher has to address animism, shamanism, and pantheism. This struggle continues today. Various religious elements are inseparably intertwined with the social system customs of those who hear the gospel. Asian preachers do not want to be the mouthpiece of Christian or Western triumphalism, but rather by understanding human sin, anxiety, suffering, and religious needs that are hidden there, the preacher must preach the word to overcome all forms of idolatry. Here too the sermon must speak the language of Asia.

Patterns of Preaching in Asia. What the early Protestant missionaries implanted in the process of forming churches set a pattern not only for general church life but for Christian preaching. The early missionaries emphasized an evangelistic zeal common in nineteenth-century North America, aiming at a life of a strict ethical standards and a passionate piety.

The missionary emphasis of Protestantism was quickly taken over by Japanese Christians, many of whom came from Samurai background. The dominant preaching style was an unadorned, serious, biblical exposition, based upon a systematic exegetical analysis of scripture, avoiding, as much as possible, emotionally charged expressions. Much emphasis was given to the ethical implications of the text.

The introduction of Protestantism to Korea is generally dated at 1885, some thirty years later than the arrival of missionaries to Japan. The general character of the missionaries, whether in Japan or in Korea, was similar, but the Korean context had a stronger Confucian orientation. Also distinct in Korea was the composition of early churches by less educated people, while the opposite was true in Japan. Another element affecting the preaching in Korea was the translation of the Bible into Hangul, an indigenous Korean writing form. This translation made the Bible accessible to everyone and made the Old Testament especially a popular source for preaching, particularly during the movement for independence in the early twentieth century.

The term for preaching in Japanese, *sekkyo*, comes from a Buddhist background and denotes the exposition of sutra for general public instruction in a temple. At times, the priest told stories based upon sutra with a freely composed tune or melody.

With this term, transplanted into the Christian context, preaching has come to mean "to expound and teach." The conceptual base for preaching, especially in the Protestant sector of Japan, stands in the Reformation tradition of the sermon as the Word of God.*

While Korean preaching is predominantly carried out in a topical style, Japanese preachers tend to rely on biblical exposition. A sermon in Japan often runs from thirty to forty minutes, while a Korean preacher tends to take a shorter time.

Japan has produced a number of effective preachers. Not all were eloquent preachers in the popular sense, but they were effective teachers of the Bible. Korea and Taiwan have also produced skillful preachers with deep religious commitment who affected not only individual souls but entire communities. Surveying the wider Asian context, one is able to note a significant number of well-known preachers. It is important, however, that in the Asian context in general sermons are to be heard in specific cultural and social situations, though the value of printed sermons is not to be discredited. Books of sermons do not sell well in Japan. The only exception is the collection of sermons by Karl Barth,* which demonstrates a theological interest among Japanese preachers. Asia is intricately complex and has within it diversified languages and cultures. The history of Christianity also differs from one country, or area, to another. Even within the southeastern segment of Asia, though there is a common heritage of missionary activity, what developed in each church is unique. In Thailand, for instance, Christian preaching reflects the Buddhist cultural and linguistic environment. It has an objective and sacramental character similar to a priest's exposition of Buddhist sutra, with much emphasis laid upon the historical figure of Gautama Buddha. Although the format may be similar to a Buddhist exhortation, Christian preaching retains its distinctive message of salvation through faith in the historical event of Jesus Christ.

"Church," in *The Japan Christian Quarterly*, Vol. 49, Nos. 3–4, 1983. **Elison, G.,** *Deus Destroyed: The Image of Christianity in Early Modern Japan*, 1973. **Elwood, D.,** ed., *Asian Christian Theology*, 1980. **Kitagawa, J.,** *The Christian Tradition: Beyond Its European Captivity*, 1992. **Yoshinobu, K.,** and **D. L. Swain,** *Christianity in Japan*, 1971–90, 1991.

ROBERT MIKIO FUKADA
TSUNEAKI KATO

Homiletics and Preaching in Germany and German-Speaking Europe

Homiletics since Schleiermacher. In modern times homiletics in Germany was given a fresh impetus by F.D.E. Schleiermacher.* He argued for the institution of the parish-related sermon and defined his understanding of homiletics against the orthodox instructional sermon and the lecture-oriented sermon of the Enlightenment. Schleiermacher's description of sermon preparation was the "homiletical triangle," according to which the sermon acts as mediator between preacher, scripture, and congregation. From the beginning, Schleiermacher's homiletical theory was grounded in a theory of worship. The sermon serves a particular congregation. Its scholarly claim consists in the establishment of principles of the sermon that exceed mere pragmatic advice.

In the first half of the nineteenth century, homiletics was influenced by Carl Immanuel Nitzsch, who interpreted the sermon as "continued proclamation of the gospel for the edification of the church of the Lord . . . in relation to current conditions and by means of called witnesses." In general, the nineteenth century still practiced the traditional rhetorical preaching structure, consisting of introduction, scripture reading, declaration of the topic, and various parts of the sermon. This theory, based on ancient rhetorical principles, is found throughout German homiletical literature. At the beginning of the century Claus Harms, the great preacher of Kiel, combined Reformation theology with romantic theories of preaching.

In the nineteenth century, homiletics was affected by the pulpit's competition with political speeches. The language of preaching strove to gain coloration and to avoid generalities. It was Reformed theologian Paul Drews who promoted the concrete and specific type of sermon that grew increasingly popular. He contrasted the homiletic practice of Pietism, which was oriented toward the fundamentals of the Christian faith, with the homiletics of the Enlightenment and pointed out the effectiveness of the situational sermon above the general. At the same time, the need for moral and social sermons was on the rise. But social preaching required new forms of social ministry as well.

The liberal theologian Friedrich Niebergall emphasized the ecclesial dimension of preaching and education within the parish. He insisted that the sermon offer nurture for the believers' faith and life. Of the three sides of the "homiletical triangle" (preacher, text, congregation), Niebergall emphasized the role of the addressee and did research on the target group in terms of sociology and religion-related psychology.

Since Niebergall, the psychological dynamics of the homiletical communication have been intensively explored. By the end of the nineteenth century, the Great Awakenings of previous centuries had lost their influence on the sermon. New voices were pleading for attention to communication, for greater clarity, and for the consideration of the parish's concrete situation. The social gospel sermon constituted one distinct response to the crisis of abstraction in German theology. Many saw in the crisis of preaching a challenge to traditional homiletical understanding. The theological school of Albrecht Ritschl emphasized the pedagogical task of the sermon. Following Schleiermacher, others pressed for the homiletical concept of preaching as the special language of worship. Reform of the sermon would lead to the reform of the service in general (Julius Smend). Others insisted on a decisively kerygmatic sermon. By 1900, the sermon was the object of many competing claims and calls for reform.

Twentieth-Century Homiletics. Homiletic thinking in Germany in the twentieth century owes its special quality and its abundant variety to two particularities. First, ever since the Lutheran Reformation the German word for preaching, *Predigt*, has always had two different meanings: In pastoral practice, *Predigt* is the speech based on a biblical text and delivered in a service. But, since God reveals himself in the word, the act of *Predigt* is in addition the only way in which God creates faith, building the church. Understood dogmatically, preaching is the Word of God itself. So homiletics, the theory of preaching, in German tradition not only deals with the practical problems of delivering a sermon but also regularly addresses dogmatical and hermeneutical considerations of *the* preaching, thereby mirroring contemporary theology.

The double meaning of *Predigt* results in the common opinion that weekly preaching is nothing less than the very center of the minister's theological existence. This may explain why the dramatic changes that shook the foundations of Christian life in modern times first became visible in the professional experience of preachers. This is the second feature of German homiletics in the twentieth century: There is always a sense of crisis connected with preaching. So homiletics

assumes a kind of therapeutic quality, understanding itself as an effort to treat the so-called "crisis of preaching."

To deal with that crisis, the successive schools of twentieth-century German homiletics give priority to either the dogmatic question or the pragmatic problems of *Predigt*. In consequence, they recommend different practical resources to overcome the preacher's dilemma.

The Movement of "Modern Preaching." Since about 1890, the declining relevance of preaching in public and private life has become a major homiletic subject. Influenced by liberal theology (Ritschl, Herrmann) with its emphasis on individual experience, several practical theologians, such as Friedrich Niebergall (1866–1932), Paul Drews (1858–1912), and Otto Baumgarten (1858–1934), linked the exterior dilemma of preaching to an interior deficit: Captivated by traditional, formal rhetoric with its obsolete theology, many preachers lost contact with ordinary life. "They answer questions nobody is asking, and they don't answer the questions everybody asks," said Niebergall.

So the new homiletic movement started by asking "How do we preach to modern man?" as Niebergall's main work (1905–1921) is called. Homiletic theory cannot be deduced from dogmatic principles but must be constructed inductively, utilizing empirical observations from contemporary life conditions (*see* Inductive Preaching). Therefore, Niebergall and his colleagues took great interest in religious psychology. With a similar intention, Drews attempted to describe the religion of ordinary people. The background of all these empirical studies is the modern interpretation of the gospel. Modern preaching of the gospel has to be special preaching: Sermons in a village are different from sermons in a city; preaching to educated listeners is unlike preaching to the working class. Instead of reflecting *the* sermon, homiletics has to deal with a broad spectrum of various practical demands. This emphasis on particularity is also reflected in the way the movement of modern preaching gives concrete support: For the most part, the relevant publications review the contemporary practice of preaching, or they offer paradigmatic sermons for different situations. Through these models, individual preachers are supported in finding their own way, appropriate to their situation and personality.

Basically, the homiletic authors adopt an educational perspective: Preaching aims to educate the congregation and to help the listener to master his or her problems of life, addressing spiritual values or motives, namely, peace, joy, and freedom. This explicitly immanent view of preaching is, however, in constant danger of simplifying biblical and theological traditions and of sweeping aside their spiritual demands.

Preaching as a "Service to the Word of God." In the shadow of World War I, the Swiss ministers Karl Barth* (1886–1968) and Eduard Thurneysen (1888–1974) found a different reason for the crisis of their preaching and pastoral existence. The thorough focus given to the audience's situation in fact uses the word as a means to serve human purposes, ignoring the word's revolutionary power. So the problems of preaching must be interpreted strictly in theological terms, namely in terms of dialectical theology.

From this new perspective, the preacher's position between the Bible and the congregation reveals nothing less than the fundamental crisis of humanity when confronted with God. So the preacher must destroy all security that threatens to hinder the listeners' reliance on God. Focusing on that, he or she is to avoid any rhetorical diversions, to ignore completely the audience's situation and needs. "The death of all human affairs is the subject of preaching. Therefore, one has to preach not construction but reduction" (Thurneysen, 114).

But how is a mortal and sinful human capable of preaching the Word of God at all? The relationship of God's Word to human words has been the central homiletic question since the 1920s. Barth's answer is a double definition given in a homiletic seminar in 1932:

1. The sermon is the Word of God spoken by Himself by means of an explanation of a biblical text to contemporaries . . . delivered by a person called by the church. 2. The sermon is the ordered attempt of a called person . . . to serve the Word of God itself by explaining a biblical text to contemporaries as an announcement of what they have to hear from God himself (Barth, 30).

The human task of preaching is defined and controlled by a dogmatic framework. While Barth made use of the christological doctrine of the two natures, other homiletic authors referred to incarnation (Bonhoeffer*) or law and gospel* (Bultmann*). But these deductive approaches regularly tended to overburden the concept of *Predigt*. So Wolfgang Trillhaas in his homiletical textbook (1935) defined preaching merely as "service to the Word of God."

Generally, the theological claim for preaching corresponds to the emphasis on the Bible as God's Word. The practice of preaching is no more and no less than to interpret a biblical text, as if "the listeners are contained in the text," as the Swedish Lutheran G. Wingren sums it up. It was adherence to the Bible that enabled many German preachers to withstand the temptation of fascist church policy after 1933.

The practical result of this orientation has been the increased use of the so-called "preaching-meditations," made popular by Hans Joachim Iwand* (1899–1960). For every Sunday, there is a specific interpretation of the assigned text, focusing on its exegetical and existential aspects.

Preaching as a Problem of Communication.* Since the 1960s, the dogmatic perspective on preaching has been criticized because it fails to cover the varieties of practice. The homiletic dilemma is now seen as the constant problem of how the preacher can communicate to the respective listeners' reality. This impetus also comes from Bultmann's hermeneutical effort to consider the specific situation of modern man. In 1968 Ernst Lange (1927–1974) suggested a new homiletic starting point: "The *homiletic situation* is to be understood as the specific situation of the listener through which the church, remembering its mission, is challenged to a concrete act of preaching to meet this situation" (Lange, 22).

Unlike liberal homiletics, Lange does not refrain from interpreting the situation in theological terms as a place where the promise of God is to be realized. But the theological assertion must relate to the empirical circumstances of the concrete "homiletic act." In practice, preaching then appears as an integral part of the whole parish's task to "communicate the gospel." Lange's approach gained influence through the invention of a dialogical type of homiletic meditation in which two authors, one an advocate of the text and the other of the listener's situation, confront each other.

The interest in the pragmatic complexity of preaching also led to a strictly rhetorical perspective: Every sermon "is a piece of language in the act of public speech," constituted by the interrelation of form and content (M. Josuttis, 12). The use of rhetoric is also advocated by Gert Otto who relativizes the significance of the Bible and of theological traditions by naming many other homiletic factors, for example, the poetic dimension of language and the social situation of the sermon's audience. In the wake of contemporary political theology, some authors also analyze the public effects of preaching.

While Otto Haendler's Jungian analysis of the preacher's task (1941) has remained isolated, in the 1970s the preacher's personality became a homiletic topic. "The crisis of preaching is the crisis of the preacher," said H.-C. Piper, and this problem is to be handled by the various psychological methods of pastoral counseling. Most important, Piper and others elaborated *methods of sermon analysis* through group-dynamics, determining the subjective factors in a sermon and also distinguishing various types of preachers and listeners.

Altogether, the understanding of preaching as a problem of communication resulted in large amounts of detailed empirical research, using various theoretical backgrounds to describe the conditions and effects of the preacher's practice. However, this pluralistic approach tended to neglect the question of how this practice is to be interpreted and controlled by theology.

Catholic Contributions. Until the 1950s, Catholic homiletics had been scarcely more than a collection of pragmatic rules for the priest's individual study. By formulating a theology of God's Word and by opening the Mass to local practices, Vatican II* increased the importance of preaching. As a consequence, Catholic research not only adopted the dogmatic type of homiletics, emphasizing biblical exegesis and the church's authority, but after the failure of this approach also turned to the question of communication in preaching.

Even more thoroughly than Protestant homiletics, Catholic authors analyze sermons by psychological, linguistic, and sociological means. Using learning and creativity theories, they have adopted much of the rhetorical tradition for homiletic training (see Zerfass).

Although the cooperation between Protestant and Catholic homiletics has grown quite close, especially in Germany and the Netherlands, there remain some fruitful differences. Catholicism tends to understand preaching as an institutional act by which the church's doctrine is spread. More than Protestantism, Catholic preaching focuses on secular philosophies and ethical problems. Apart from the Bible, the sources of Catholic preaching include material from the church fathers, the saints' legends, and various spiritual traditions. Finally, preaching is seen in interrelation with liturgy: The sermon actualizes the Eucharist, and the sacrament integrates the spoken word.

A New Integration of Theology and Practice. The publications of recent years indicate on the one hand a gradual relativizing of preaching. As with Catholic preaching, Protestant preaching often becomes part of the liturgy. Also, other occasions of Christian speech are taken into consideration, thereby widening the perspective to the whole of pastoral work. Preaching appears as a dimension of the liturgical,* catechetical, and pastoral endeavors of the church.

To reintegrate the theological and the pragmatic aspect of *Predigt,* several authors have adopted pneumatological patterns (Bohren, Rothermundt) or the Lutheran dogma of justification (Josuttis, Gräb). Thereby homiletics again focuses on the preacher, reflecting on his or her sociological, biographical, and pastoral circumstances as well as on the makeup of his or her own faith, which is communicated through the sermon.

The perennial insistence on sound theological reflection on preaching is, as the latest publications again suggest, the most important contribution of German homiletics to a comprehensive theory of preaching.

Barth, K., *Homiletik: Wesen und Vorbereitung der Predigt,* ed. G. Seyfferth; Zürich: Theologischer Verlag, 2d ed. *Homiletics,* trans. G. W. Bromiley and D. E. Daniels, 1991. **Bohren, R.,** *Predigtlehre,* 4th rev. and enl. ed., 1980. **Gräb, W.,** *Predigt als Mitteilung des Glaubens: Studien zu einer prinzipiellen Homiletik in praktischer Absicht,* 1988. **Josuttis, M.,** *Rhetorik und Theologie in der Predigtarbeit: Homiletische Studien,* 1985. **Lange, E.,** *Predigen als Beruf: Aufsätze zu Homiletik, Liturgie und Pfarramt,* ed. R. Schloz, 2d rev. ed., 1982. **Niebergall, F.,** *Wie predigen wir dem modernen Menschen?* 3 vols., 1905–1921. **Thurneysen, E.,** "Die Aufgabe der Predigt," in *Aufgabe der Predigt,* ed. G. Hummel, 1971. **Wintzer, F.,** *Die Homiletik seit Schleiermacher bis in die Anfänge der 'dialektischen Theologie' in Grundzügen,* 1969; ed., *Predigt: Texte zum Verständnis und zur Praxis der Predigt in der Neuzeit,* 1989. **Zerfass, R.,** *Grundkurs Predigt,* 2 vols., 1987, 1992.   JAN HERMELINK
                                       FRIEDRICH WINTZER

Homiletics and Preaching in India.

Christian preaching continues to occupy the foremost position in the ministry of the church on the Indian subcontinent. The church continues to preach, and the people continue to show their interest in good preaching. The church finds itself in a pluralistic context surrounded by many religions. Although preaching is done on Sundays as in every country, because of its multireligious background there is a marked difference in India. The phenomenon of Christian preaching by preachers who are independent of the institutional or established churches is one of the chief features of Protestantism in India. Along with the missionaries, pastors, catechists, evangelists and Christian teachers, individual Christians, especially converts, have also carried on evangelistic preaching as independent preachers.

Independent Preachers. The practice of independent preaching both within and outside the church came into existence mainly for two reasons. First, as the churches began to grow in size, more preachers and teachers were needed, but not enough theologically trained persons were available. Independently, preachers and teachers began to share the responsibility of teaching and preaching. Second, independent preaching began with the avowed intention to live and preach the gospel in an Indian way (*see* Cross-Cultural Preaching; Missions). Independent preaching and teaching of faith and practice belongs to the Indian religious tradition. There have always been wandering sadhus and friars among the Hindus and other religions. Therefore, converts from Hinduism or Islam to Christianity carried over this tradition to the church.

Some of the best-known converts who became independent preachers are Pandita Ramabai Sarasvati (1859–1922) and Chandraleel (b.1860), both women converts from Hinduism, Paul Kadambha-vanam (b.1887), and Sadhu Sundar Singh (1888–1929). They all preached the gospel of Christ independently of the established churches among Christians and non-Christians, following the Indian tradition of religious teaching by wandering sadhus. The importance of this phenomenon of independent preaching to the Indian church has been rightly pointed out as follows:

One of the signs evidencing the desire of the indigenous church to be free is the presence of the independent religious worker or preacher. There are now scores of indigenous Christian preachers who belong to no denomination, but are like the wandering friars or *sanyasis*, untrammelled either by dogmas or forms of worship, and free to interpret Christ in their own way ("Indian Christians," Madras, 1928, 338).

The beginning of this century saw a new move toward nationalization in administration and management and a new awareness of the indigenous form of worship and witness. Many of the practices and values inherited from the Western missions came under scrutiny. Efforts were made to free the churches from "the Latin Captivity." Solomon Raj points out: "Slowly the Indian Christians have got rid of their hesitation to express their faith in truly indigenous forms" (Raj, 2). As part of the movement to free Christianity in India from its "Latin Captivity," Christian preachers appeared on the scene zealous to adopt Indian forms of expression and practice. Since then, Christian preaching by independent persons has become one of several indigenous forms of expression among the Protestant churches.

Independent preaching takes place at three levels. First, a number of Christian preachers go from place to place, mainly visiting Christian families and conducting prayer meetings in small groups. They have no fixed plan or itinerary. Therefore, they are usually called wandering preachers (*see* Itinerant and Open-Air Preach-

ing). They make a vital contribution to the ministry of Christian religious education by their preaching and teaching. Their contribution is recognized by Bishop Azariah:

Preaching seems to be the chief form of *Christian teaching* in rural congregations. This is done periodically and sporadically by pastors, both trained and untrained, by elementary school teachers—mostly working as voluntary teachers, catechists, and also by itinerant preachers both official and also frequently unofficial wandering evangelists (*Witnessing in India Today*, Madras 1983, 40).

Yet sometimes these preachers are considered a nuisance to the churches because of their emphasis on personal and group prayers over the liturgical worship in the church. Second, revival preachers are often invited by congregations to hold revival meetings at least once a year. Independent preaching here takes place at the level of a particular congregation. Third, sometimes a number of churches in big cities and towns organize revival meetings jointly at an ecumenical level. Such meetings are called Christian Conventions, Good News Festivals, New Life Festivals, Gospel Festivals, or simply Revival meetings (*see* Revivals; Evangelism).

The independent preachers are of two types: There are those who are full-time, voluntary, independent preachers or evangelists without any other professional commitment. Sadhu Amarendernath Sarkar from New Delhi and Brother Prabhudass from Nellore, Andhra Pradesh, are contemporary preachers who can be placed in this category.

There are other preachers who are professionally associated with independent Christian organizations. Among the popular preachers in this category are Dr. Abdul Akbar Haqq, an Indian Muslim convert and a long-standing Associate Evangelist of the Billy Graham Evangelistic Association, Minneapolis, Minnesota, and others.

The above-mentioned types of preachers are normally called revival preachers. This independent preaching has contributed to the indigenous form of the theological thought and expression of the gospel in India. Such preaching offers a different kind of religious experience, a kind that is not commonly emphasized by the mainline churches.

The church as an institution or a community of believers and its theology and sacraments are given only secondary importance by the independent preachers. The social, political, economic, and even cultural situation of the people is almost totally neglected by the independent preachers. Their emphasis is on faith and practice at the individual level. Therefore, their understanding and interpretation of the Christian faith can be called personal Christianity. One of the weaknesses of the revival preachers is that they go only to the members of the established churches, whereas the independent wandering preachers, especially converts, go to non-Christians also.

In recent years, Christian preaching by independent preachers has increased, becoming a regular feature in the Protestant churches irrespective of denomination. Thus preaching is never confined only to the institutional or the historical churches in India. It has always been carried on both by the full-time workers of the various churches, such as pastors and evangelists, and by voluntary Christians.

The evangelical preaching characteristic of independent preachers is carried on also in the theological colleges with an evangelical bent. It differs markedly from that which goes on in liberal theological colleges and seminaries. The latter is oriented to social issues and matters of justice and equality. By and large, preaching is given lesser importance than theology in the liberal theological colleges.

The Lectionary Preachers. Churches such as the Church of South India, the Church of North India, and the Lutheran churches have lectionaries* for the Christian year. Normally, a theme for the day is also suggested along with the Old Testament, Epistle, and the Gospel readings. Preachers try to find in the texts supporting ideas. The result is that they often preach thematic sermons, using the texts to illustrate them. Exegesis is usually neglected or given only a secondary place in the preparation of sermons. Roland Gierth, who made an intensive study of Christian life and work in South India, makes the following observation regarding preaching in the churches: ". . . it should be remembered that text-centred, expository preaching occurred quite seldom, whilst the sermon often came to life because of the preacher's personal emotional engagement, which is rooted in a very vivid faith and the acquaintance with almost all listeners in the church" (Gierth, 337).

The Reference/Concordance Preachers. There are many preachers who in a single sermon trace one subject, one theme, or one word through the entire Bible. This may be called reference/concordance preaching. Such preaching is mostly found among the sectarian groups.

The Sermon in Indian Christian Worship. The sermon occupies a unique place in Christian liturgy and worship in India. Many of the Indian religious traditions do not have the practice of a religious discourse during worship. In many Christian denominations, preaching is not seen as simply one of the elements of worship but as *the* important element (although in some traditions the celebration of Holy Communion is of equal importance). The preaching of the Western missionaries and the Indian tradition of religious gurus (teachers) making discourses to their disciples are the antecedents of contemporary Indian preaching. Both in form and content Western preaching continues to influence preaching among the Indian churches in urban areas. However, indigenous forms are used in preaching in the villages.

Indian Methods of Preaching. A variety of methods has been adopted in the preaching of the gospel among rural congregations on the subcontinent. First, there is drama—Indians have a deep love for drama. Numerous itinerant groups go from place to place enacting the stories from both Christian and other scriptures. These groups portray religious and spiritual truth through homely dialogues, spontaneous actions, and appealing folk songs. Then there are *Bhajans*—all religious groups in India love to sing bhajans, short lyrics sung by a leader and repeated by the worshipers. Every word of the song is meant to stir the deep spiritual commitment of the worshiper. Sometimes bhajans are lyrical presentations of the gospel story, especially parables. The leader of the bhajan will sit in the center of the stage or sanctuary surrounded by his or her group, consisting of musicians and singers. Finally, there are *Kirtans*—narration of stories from the Bible similar to bhajans. The head singer will have hand cymbals for rhythm, and he or she will be assisted by one or two others who provide music by beating a *dakki* (drum) and repeating the song. This acting is also viewed as a dance. It is called by various names, such as *Kalakshepam, Katha-Kalakshepam, Harikatha,* or *Burrakatha* in different parts of the country (*see* Homiletics and Preaching in Africa).

Christian Preaching and Other Religions. In the midst of a pluralistic society, Christian preaching is seen as bearing witness to the saving power of the gospel in Christ Jesus. It has two important elements—calling for a faith commitment to Jesus Christ as Lord and Savior and edifying the community of believers in the faith and practice of the church. The presence of other religions influences Christian preachers to adopt both cultural and religious elements that can be effectively used for the preaching of the gospel.

Amalorpavadass, D. S., *Preaching the Gospel Today: Main Problems in Mission Lands,* 1973. **Boyd, R.H.S.,** *India and the Latin Captivity of the Church,* 1972. **Gierth, R.,** *Christian Life and Work at the Pastorate Level and Practical Theology in South India,* 1977. **Niles, D. T.,** *The Preacher's Task and the Stone of Stumbling,* 1958. **Raj, P. S.,** *A Christian Folk-Religion in India,* 1986. **Spivey, R. V.,** *Preaching the Word,* The Students' Christian Library No. 40, Christian Literature Society, 1967. **Wijngaards, J.N.M.,** *Communicating the Word of God: Practical Methods of Preaching the Biblical Message,* Theological Publications in India, 1979.

SURYA P. PRAKASH

Homiletics and Preaching in Latin America.

Preaching in Latin America exhibits as broad and rich a diversity as the history and practice of Christian faith in that part of the world. Roman Catholic priests accompanied the *conquistadores* from Spain to the New World on the early voyages of discovery and conquest, and preaching played a role in the efforts by which the Spanish and later the Portuguese imposed their control over the peoples of the Americas.

Mostly members of the Franciscan* and Dominican* orders, those first preachers understood their task as first baptizing the "pagan" and "idolatrous" natives of America, then explaining the basic elements of Christian faith. Ignorance of the American cultures and an unquestioning faith in the superiority of their own religion led them to assume that nothing of the native people's religion was worth saving, even as a starting point. Rather, they considered their subjects to present a tabula rasa, on which their preaching could write the essentials of Christian belief. Because their very presence depended upon the Spanish colonial power, their preaching also assured their hearers that submission to Christ included obedience to their new masters. Christian faith was all too often reduced to a set of rituals, mechanically repeated and only vaguely related to biblical faith, helping form a "popular piety" that depended very little on the preached word—a piety still found in many parts of Latin America.

Many of the missionaries preached against the mistreatment of the native converts by their conquerors. As early as 1511, Father Antonio de Montesinos warned his hearers, "You are all living in mortal sin, and you will live and die in sin because of the cruelty and tyranny with which you abuse these innocent people." His preaching so moved one of his hearers, Bartolome de Las Casas, that he dedicated the rest of his life to struggling on behalf of the *conquistadores'* victims.

In the colonial cities, the descendants of the Spanish *conquistadores* heard sermons reflecting the great issues of European Christianity. The passions of the Spanish Counter-Reformation found their way to the Americas; famous preachers such as Peru's Juan de Espinosa Medrano used their often highly developed rhetorical skill to show off their verbal flourishes even as they urged their hearers to demonstrate the zeal of their faith by strict adherence to the church's teachings. Preachers also used their sermons to warn of the dire consequences of heresy, a warning reinforced by the all too visible presence of the Inquisition.

The historical ties between the church and the ruling political circles were not entirely broken, even when the former Spanish colonies became independent early in the nineteenth century. Sermons continued to urge believers to an unwavering faith in God, which often included exhortations to accept the rule of those placed over them.

In the nineteenth century, the emerging middle class, eager to share the modern world's commercial and industrial "progress," sought to create a social climate more like that of the United States and Europe by opening their countries to other influences and traditions. A number of Protestant churches and organizations took advantage of this opportunity to enter what had previously been a continent-wide Roman Catholic enclave. Their presence brought a new emphasis on preaching to Latin America.

The early work of ecumenical organizations like the Latin American Mission sought primarily to translate Protestant hymns, theology, and worship into the languages of Latin America, with little concern for the enormous cultural differences that separated them from their hearers. Just as the preaching of the first missionaries had seen in the native peoples a tabula rasa, Protestant sermons were designed to impose the gospel on a continent they considered to be ignorant of it. Latin America needed conversion, and preaching was one of the main ways by which it would be accomplished. Preaching was a call to reject the past, including Roman Catholic practices judged to be incompatible with Protestant faith; it was also an exhortation to maintain that faith, usually affirmed by a commitment to a particular style of personal morality.

The first generations of Latin American Protestant leaders were often sent for training in North America, where they learned to copy the preaching of conservative, often fundamentalist evangelical churches. Although this style was foreign to Latin American culture, a great deal of Protestant preaching in the region continues to draw on this heritage.

In the last forty years, another important movement has arrived from the north: the pentecostal movement. While its appearance depended upon missionaries from the United States, it quickly took root among Latin Americans and may represent a majority of the population of several countries by the year 2000. Scholars note that the style of preaching among Latin American Pentecostals, while still stressing the need for personal conversion, offers hearers an intense and joyful experience of faith. The highly emotional and spontaneous preaching style favored by Pentecostal* preachers makes faith accessible to the most marginalized among the population, while its spontaneity makes it seem more authentically rooted in Latin American culture than the more reserved heritage of North American Protestantism. Many cities in Latin America have Pentecostal churches numbering their members in the tens of thousands, but the success of the movement has been aided even more by small neighborhood store-front congregations and, more recently, by the mass media. Borrowing techniques from their North American counterparts, Latin American pentecostal preachers reach millions of hearers, many of whom live far away from population centers. Those who live in cities can take part in the great preaching crusades, often accompanied by campaigns for healing, that are now a fixture in Latin American religious life (*see* Revivals).

But many Christians, both Catholic and Protestant, have grown dissatisfied with earlier emphases and styles of preaching. Under the direction of figures like the Cuban Rubén Lores, important ecumenical institutions such as the Seminario Bíblico Latinoamericano in San José, Costa Rica, have sought ways to take the reality of Latin America, with all its hopes and pains, as the raw material of preaching and of all pastoral ministry. The goal of preaching is no longer understood as proclaiming the gospel to an alien setting but articulating the gospel in such a way as to challenge the death that pervades so much of Latin America and to offer hope for the transformation of the whole of life.

For many, this implies that the most effective preaching takes the form of a dialogue between the gospel and the world and between the preacher and the hearers. In "base communities" of poor believers found throughout the continent, the sermon is no longer delivered by a professionally trained preacher; rather, it is an extended conversation, in which special training might be useful to provide information and to facilitate the exchange, but the reflection on the relationship between gospel and reality is shared by the community (*see* Liberation Preaching).

Those responsible for the future of preaching in Latin America know that such a task calls for new skills in communication, including expertise in new technologies as well as a deepened awareness of their impact on modern culture. The contribution of the social sciences as a source for understanding the milieu in which the gospel is preached is taken more seriously. Preachers need to learn how to facilitate dialogue and the ex-

change of information and ideas. They need to become experts in the communities of which they are part and to learn to discern the sources of the violence, misery and death that are ever-present realities. They also need to learn how to proclaim Christian hope in the face of such widespread death. And if faith is to make a difference in the future of Latin America, then Pentecostal preachers whose appeal brings joy and emotional warmth must be brought into the ecumenical community, where the basic issues of life and death are discussed and where the implications of faith are not merely private and otherworldly but allow the faithful to participate in the transformation of this world. At important centers of theological reflection and education, such as the Seminario Bíblico Latinoamericano in Costa Rica and Argentina's Instituto Superior Evangélico de Estudios Teologicos, such explorations are already taking place.

Future preaching will no doubt invite Christians to an active and hopeful faith that seeks to change the realities of Latin America and makes them not only hearers but participants in that project, overcoming the passivity and ignorance of the biblical story that have been a part of some traditional Latin American Christianity.

If the gospel is indeed to be heard as good news by the peoples of Latin America, it is clear that the place of preaching will continue to gain in significance, even as it becomes more diverse with the growing diversity of the Christianity of the continent.

Cardenal, E., *The Gospel in Solentiname*, Vol. 1, 1976. Dussel, E., *A History of the Church in Latin America*, 1981. Galeano, E., *Memory of Fire: Genesis*, 1985; *Memory of Fire: Faces and Masks*, 1987.

JOHN L. KATER, JR.

Homiletics and Preaching in North America.

The history of homiletics in North America corresponds to

four cultural eras in North American history. In each of these epochs, homiletical theory evolved from shifts in theological climate induced by the ebb and flow of cultural change.

1639–1800:
Guided by Distant Voices

Shortly after 1639, the year printing began in America, printers were turning out copies of American ordination sermons that offered extensive advice about how to preach effectively. Candidates for parish ministry turned to these ordination sermons to supplement their apprenticeships with working pastors. Aspiring preachers in the mid-seventeenth century in New England substituted for formal homiletical training the close mentorship of experienced pastors.

By contrast, preachers who had arrived earlier in New England, soon after the Mayflower, were learned and articulate graduates of Oxford or Cambridge in England. The average Protestant parson in the early colonial days was *the person* in his community by virtue of education and standing, expected not only to expound biblical truth but also to announce and interpret news of the community and country. The generation of preachers to follow, however, born and raised on colonial soil, with many educated at Harvard, had only apprenticeships and several ordination sermons to prepare them for their pulpits. By the eighteenth century a few reprints of English homiletical works and some volumes of sermons by English notables joined the collections of American ordination sermons to form a meager early American homiletical literature.

Preaching with a Rationalist's Rhetoric.

The sermon of this period in North America bears the marks of Enlightenment scholasticism. For instance, as Cotton Mather suggested in 1726 in his homiletical text *Manuductio ad Ministerium*, the preacher is foremost a scholar who turns out a "well-studied sermon." For Mather, worthy preaching presupposes a knowledge of Latin, Greek, and Hebrew, if not additional passing acquaintance with Syriac and French. Further, the minister needs to be familiar with mathematics, natural philosophy, astronomy, and music—"if you fancy it."

Many preachers of that period ordered their discourses about Christian doctrine with the detached air of rationalistic rhetoric. William Cook, in an ordination sermon in 1756, put the purpose of preaching in terms of "bringing Mankind to the Knowledge of the Things necessary to their Salvation." Preachers expounded on those "necessary things" using an established threefold rhetorical design, *subtilitas intelligendi, subtilitas explicandi, and subtilitas applicandi:* understand the text, explain it theologically, and then apply it.

Elaborate Sermon Structures.

Sermon structure in the eighteenth century was a monument to reason. Rather than form the sermon around a single theme or purpose, the Enlightenment preacher presented an elaborate biblical or doctrinal exposition that unfolded in an extended series of divisions and subdivisions. Jonathan Edwards,* arguably one of the greatest American preachers, typified this rigid formality with sermon conclusions that sometimes contained thirty-one subdivisions. Mentors of preaching in this Age of Reason gave sermon style little more than passing thought. Matters of sermon delivery were taken for granted: Preachers simply read aloud the written material as clearly as possible. Well-reasoned substance was all-important. Style, whether written or spoken, was at best the handmaid to reason.

1800–1928:
Awakening to Our Own Landscape

At the dawn of the nineteenth century the gathering energies of Romanticism stirred homiletics to a new concern for imagination, feeling, and common humanity, awakenings that became the first distinctive North American voice in homiletics. Where seventeenth- and eighteenth-century preaching concentrated primarily on the truth to be communicated, nineteenth- and early twentieth-century homiletics focused on the communication of that truth.

This passion for reaching ordinary people with the gospel sparked for the first time in North American homiletics an interest in rhetoric.* In 1802, John Witherspoon, in his "Lectures on Eloquence," bridged scholastic and romantic homiletics. On the one hand, Witherspoon kept company with his eighteenth-century colleagues by devoting less than two pages to sermon delivery. A sermon in the late eighteenth century was not so much an oral/aural experience as it was a series of propositions in print. The preacher either voices the print from paper or from memory. Yet, unlike his predecessors, Witherspoon anticipated the changes coming in homiletical theory when he made written style as essential for effective preaching as the preacher's personal piety. Witherspoon turned to Cicero for help in his plea for the art of simplicity, openly embracing classical rhetoric as an indispensable ally in preaching. Thus began an allegiance to rhetoric that would preoccupy homiletics for years to come.

The Accent on Rhetoric in Seminaries. With the founding of theological seminaries throughout the U.S. and Canada in the first half of the nineteenth century, leading Protestant denominations for the first time had the capacity to teach homiletics systematically. This instruction, in addition to its reliance upon classical theological disciplines, depended heavily upon the rhetoricians, both ancient and modern. Students often studied in their original languages Aristotle, Plato, Horace, Demosthenes, Cicero, and Quintilian, while also exploring English rhetoricians of their day; Campbell, Blair, and Whately. The names of academic chairs for teachers of preaching are instructive: Henry Ware was Professor of Pulpit Eloquence at Harvard; Ebenezer Porter, Professor of Sacred Rhetoric at Andover Theological Seminary. Since exegesis relegated sermon matter to predictable biblical and doctrinal themes, homileticians devoted much of their energies to communication of those topics.

Concerned to Connect with Common People. By mid-century, homileticians pressed for preaching that connects with ordinary people. As early as 1824, Henry Ware at Harvard questioned sermon delivery that was oriented to the eye. Teachers such as Ebenezer Porter at Andover Seminary and Henry Ripley at Newton Seminary published texts that combined exegetical and theological concerns with chapters on rhetoric and speech, all in the service of effectively reaching the person in the pew. William Russell's *Pulpit Elocution* and John Dowling's *The Power of Illustration* went to great lengths to demonstrate the ways that language, voice, and body-use can capture the attention of the hearer. The scholastic method of shaping a sermon in a complicated sequence of divisions and subdivisions gave way to the single thought and natural speech.

Rhetoric and Homiletics Split. With the establishment of the annual Lyman Beecher lectures on preaching at Yale in 1871, homiletics in North America began to discover its own voice. Almost as many books on preaching appeared during the two previous decades as were published in the two centuries prior to 1850. The study of rhetoric enlarged in many seminaries to the point that by 1879 separate divisions of speech or rhetoric were established alongside departments of homiletics.

This parting of homiletics and rhetoric occasioned a significant split between leading teachers of preaching over the appropriate point of departure for homiletics. The most famous of the rhetoricians was John Broadus,* whose textbook *A Treatise on the Preparation and Delivery of Sermons*, was a North American favorite for 80 years. Broadus, along with Franklin W. Fisk, Francis L. Patton, and William G. T. Shedd, taught that homiletics is a species of rhetoric. He defined preaching in terms of rhetoric's historic intent to instruct and persuade.

The second group, Henry Ward Beecher,* A.J.F. Behrends, Phillips Brooks,* Daniel Kidder, E. G. Robinson, and

Henry van Dyke, while acknowledging the corollary value of rhetoric, understood homiletics as a species of theology and designated the sermon an instrument of the "divine plan of salvation." Perhaps the most telling clue in distinguishing between the two groups was that the rhetoricians were all seminary professors, while the interpretation group was comprised, with the exception of Robinson, of parish ministers. To the rhetoricians, the sermon differed from secular rhetoric only in terms of subject matter and the authority of the speaker. To the interpreters, preaching involved much more than applying truths or doctrines to people with the help of ancient principles of composition and speech.

Secularism and the Religious Consciousness.

Much of the impetus for the pastors' stress on the preacher as interpreter stemmed from their preaching regularly to congregations amid the kind of radical social changes that require strategies more complex and profound than the applied rules of classical rhetoric. By the end of the nineteenth century, secularism was noticeably eroding the religious culture, putting the old Sabbath in retreat, bringing on what Henry van Dyke called "an age of doubt." The rising scientific, critical spirit challenged Christian orthodoxy through burgeoning interest in biblical archaeology, evolution, and psychology. Economic and social problems began to mount in an increasingly urban culture, with its antagonisms of labor, shifting immigrant populations, and economic combines. P. T. Forsyth,* in his Beecher lectures of 1907, wrote, "The age, and much of the Church, believes in civilization and is interested in the Gospel, instead of believing in the Gospel and being interested in civilization" (Forsyth, 133).

In the face of cultural upheavals and the longing for a theological base, the influence of classical rhetoric upon homiletics began to wane. As late as 1937 Andrew Blackwood would still claim Cicero's aims as the goals of the Christian preacher (*The Fine Art of Preaching*), but

such volumes would be the exception. Student rhetorical societies that flourished in the 1890s were virtually extinct by 1920.

The Threat of Materialism to the Pulpit.

In the early part of the twentieth century, many preachers turned their pulpits into battle stations in the fundamentalist-liberal combat over evolution. Yet the less dramatic but far more profound challenge to preachers was not how to address a scientific ideology such as evolution. Rather, as Conrad Massa notes, preaching's "greatest battle [was] to be against the . . . *technological achievements* whereby materialism . . . [was] deeply rooted in American life" (Massa, 245). In 1908 only one in 1,788 people owned a car; a little over a decade later, one in *eight* people owned one. The roar of the printing press, with its secular sermons by journalists, dramatists, novelists, poets, and statespeople, threatened to drown out the pulpit. Most of the populace was no longer satisfied with preachers who could merely repeat biblical doctrines. They wanted a realistic word to help them deal with the issues raised by a growing technological culture.

New Fascination with the Arts and Human Sciences.

Anxious to maintain a hearing amid an increasingly profane culture, many preachers slipped loose from their biblical moorings and began drawing inspiration from books and poems, seeking the "spiritual message" in the literary arts. They also turned to educational philosophy and psychology to bolster both their communication and personal authority. The work of John Dewey, Freud, and Jung, among others, began to be influential in homiletics. "Psychology," wrote Charles Parkhurst in his Yale lectures, "is as essential as theology to the proper presentation of pulpit truth" (*The Pulpit and the Pew*, 1913, 48). Preaching swapped its textbooks on rhetoric for manuals on psychology. With this new pulpit aesthetic fashioned by a meld of literary arts and human sciences, homileticians sought ways to make inroads upon the new secular consciousness.

World War I left the Western world grieving the loss of an innocence that romantic idealism could never restore.

1928–1960:
A New Union with Scripture

By the late 1920s, however, the psychologically and socially directed preaching of the past three decades was wearing thin. Craving a more trustworthy word than humanism, the homiletical world was ripe for rediscovering its biblical roots. Two currents of biblical studies converged at this hour to inaugurate a renaissance of scriptural authority in the pulpit. The first was evolutionary, resulting from over a century of the historical-critical approach to biblical exegesis. Already in the 1920s, the historical-critical approach put in many preachers' hands modern translations of scripture that shed new light on the texts. But more important, critical exegesis changed the way many preachers viewed the Bible as a vehicle of revelation. Against a horizon of earlier idealism that understood scripture primarily as a deposit of abstract theological propositions, biblical scholars by the late 1920s were teaching that revelation in the Bible comes primarily through scripture's witness to historical events. God is revealed in scripture through a series of acts in history—exodus, Sinai, exile—that culminated in the Christ event. Biblical preaching testifies to the Bible's witness to these mighty acts of God and in so doing recapitulates this unique, historically grounded revelation for the contemporary faith community.

Karl Barth's* Impact on Preaching. The second reformation in biblical studies in the late 1920s was more revolutionary than evolutionary. It came like a trumpet blast from Switzerland in the form of Karl Barth's theology of the Word of God. With his publication of *The Word of God and the Word of Man,* a theological study that began as a marginal note on preaching, Barth inaugurated the reaction against nineteenth-century liberalism that, in turn, led homiletics into a new kind of alliance with scripture. While Barth accepted the results of critical biblical scholarship, he was equally convinced that sinful humans do not have the capacity to discover God's presence within the realm of history. Hence, his dialectical theology (and Brunner and Bultmann's* versions) at once asserted God's presence in history while admitting that such transcendent mystery is accessible only through God's Word in scripture. From this "crisis theology" came Barth's high view of preaching that insisted that the preacher in expounding scripture is little more than a mouthpiece for God. "Proclamation," Barth wrote, "is human language in and through which God himself speaks, like a king through the mouth of his herald" (*Church Dogmatics,* I, 1, 57).

Rediscovering Early Church Preaching. In 1936 in England the New Testament scholar C. H. Dodd published *The Apostolic Preaching and Its Developments,* a landmark study for the new biblically based homiletics. Dodd declared that preaching intends not moral instruction but *kerygma,* the proclamation of the gospel—the good news of Christ crucified, risen, and coming again to transform human affairs. Preaching Christ extends the Christ-event into the lives of the faithful. Moral instruction, or *didache,* takes its cues from *kerygma* but never supplants it. Dodd's work shed valuable light on the unity of the New Testament, the nature of the church, and christology. His work lent theological fiber to an emerging cluster of books on preaching by such North American pulpit stalwarts as Henry Sloane Coffin, George Buttrick,* Paul Scherer,* Halford E. Luccock, and Gerald Kennedy. These homileticians declared amid the trauma of the Depression and World War II that the hope sermons offer must be a transpersonal assurance rooted in God's eternal word and borne through faithful biblical witness.

The Cold War and the Age of Anxiety. The exuberance in the 1950s surrounding the postwar economic boom only partially masked a deep fear aroused by the ever-present possibility of nuclear conflagration. The cold war was on. The

Communist bloc and Western nations stood poised with their fingers on nuclear triggers. W. H. Auden rightly christened these days "The Age of Anxiety": cultural conformity set in as an unconscious defense against dread. Homiletical literature in this apocalyptic decade reiterated the Barthian dialectic.

1960 to the Present:
Homiletics Beginning to Come of Age

If the previous era in North American homiletics was formed by the biblical theology movement, this present epoch, by comparison, was affected by shifts in sensibilities that have released new, more dynamic homiletical theologies. The 1960s and early 1970s experienced several social upheavals: civil rights battles; the assassinations of the Kennedys and Martin Luther King Jr.;* the war in Vietnam; urban riots; the politicization of ecological concerns; the emergence of feminism; Watergate; and the resignation of Richard Nixon.

The raw energy released in these social earthquakes testifies to upheavals loosed in the depths of the cultural consciousness. In the 1960s, cultural change was symbolized by computer technology and televised images. Instant televised connection with peoples around the world ushered pluralism into every family den. In this new cosmopolitanism, people all over the world stirred to commonly shared aspirations. Women and people of color began singing in their own voices in protest against dehumanizing, male-dominated hierarchical systems of power. Above the revolution was the sacred canopy that held together and blessed the old civil and religious authority structures. Now the canopy was swaying in the wind.

Shifting Hermeneutical Ground. Joseph Sittler wisely observed, "Homiletics is up for grabs today." By the early 1970s, the hermeneutical ground beneath homiletics had begun a radical shift. This move shook the foundations of the historical-critical method, which for a generation seemed the citadel for preachers' exegesis. Biblical scholars such as Brevard

Childs (*Biblical Theology in Crisis*) and Walter Wink (*The Bible in Human Transformation*) asked if interpreters can ever objectively locate God in historical events behind texts, much less restrict God's mighty acts to the salvation history pictured in the Bible. While the Bible remained no less authoritative for the pulpit, its immediacy as revelation was experienced by many interpreters more as an encounter with the literary dynamics of the text than as a reconstruction of the history behind it. A dizzying array of rhetorical approaches to texts is now surfacing: redactionist, structuralist, reader-response, deconstructionist, phenomenological, and psychological (*see* Literary Criticism).

With the erosion of history, rationalist assumptions about objective revelation in scripture have begun to collapse. By the mid-1960s the philosopher Paul Ricoeur was leading conversations in hermeneutics* that focused on the way language functions in consciousness. Enlightenment notions about the static nature of words gave way to the sense of the tensive or dynamic actions of language. Scholars like Ernst Fuchs and Gerhard Ebeling spoke of language performing or intending meaning. Metaphor, with its offspring—parable, simile, narrative, and myth—took on new importance in hermeneutics and biblical studies. An image has the power to mediate mysteries in ways that sequentially oriented, denotive abstractions cannot have (*see* Language, Theories of; Figures of Speech).

The shift from a rational to an aesthetic hermeneutic carries with it two important side effects for interpretation. First, the new criticism invites a reaffirmation of the imagination.* From the Middle Ages until the nineteenth century, imagination in the Western mind was suspect as an agent of ambiguity and unpredictability. At best, imagination could serve as the decorator of rational thought. Today in hermeneutics, however, with the myth of objectivity laid to rest, the relativities of language and the psychosocial perspective of the interpreter beg for an agent of synthesis to make sense of texts. Interpreters have rediscovered imagination as the mind's meaning maker, the intellect's integrative capacity. In so doing, they honor the high view of imagination that began emerging a century ago.

A second crucial side effect of the revolution in hermeneutics is derived from the rise of liberation and feminist theologies in the 1960s and 1970s. With Juan Luis Segundo of Uruguay (author of *Liberation of Theology*), the hermeneutical circle must include the social and political environment of the interpreter. A group of farm laborers studying the Bible in a base community in Guatemala, for instance, began to discover that scripture was written from the perspective of the poor and oppressed—a view alien to generations of North American scholars who have read texts through the lens of privilege and power. With Phyllis Trible (*God and the Rhetoric of Sexuality*) or Elisabeth Schüssler Fiorenza (*In Memory of Her*), the interpreter's loop must include the additional suspicion that the biblical materials were originally filtered to the faithful through a patriarchal consciousness that must be transcended if today's believers are to hear a liberating word (*see* Liberation Preaching; Feminist Preaching).

Homiletics Coming of Age. The new hermeneutical ventures in the 1960s and 1970s catalyzed a revolution in North American homiletics in the 1970s and 1980s. Discussions focusing upon rhetoric, imagination, and social analysis began to fill the agendas for most gatherings of homileticians. The time was ripe to institutionalize these explorations. In 1965 Donald Macleod, with William Thompson, David Randolph, and a dozen other homileticians, anticipated new conversations in homiletics by founding the Academy of Homiletics. By the 1970s seminaries began considering homiletics a discipline in its own right. Chairs in homiletics were no longer automatically reserved for veteran parish preachers or for versatile faculty members trained in other fields. Publications by

homileticians dramatically increased, while graduate programs in preaching began to appear across the continent. In 1976, *Homiletic*, a semiannual review of publications in homiletics and communication, was launched by the Academy of Homiletics and the Religious Speech Communication Association. In 1977, the members of the Academy of Homiletics began planning their annual meetings more around their own scholarly contributions than around offerings by non-homileticians (*see* Homiletics: Teaching of).

Sermon Models Grounded in Rhetoric. Of the three capital concerns in the homiletical revolution of the 1970s and 1980s—rhetoric, imagination, and social analysis—the most active and extensive discussion focused on models for sermons grounded in rhetoric, particularly narrativity and imagery. In the 1970s, when theology as narrative was capturing the church's imagination, homileticians found in narrativity the basis for a major revolution in preaching theory. Fred Craddock* in 1971 sparked the reformation by recasting the sermon's traditional Aristotelian, deductive mold into an experience of inquiry whose flow functions like a developing story. In his *As One Without Authority*, Craddock argues that the sermon needs to unfold inductively, emulating the narrative-like process of inquiry the preacher experiences in exegesis for preaching (*see* Narrative Preaching).

While Craddock and others reversed the flow of logic from deductive to inductive along the avenue of argument, other teachers of preaching pressed for sermons that actually assume the story form. In 1977 Henry Mitchell, in *The Recovery of Preaching*, held up the traditional African-American sermon with its story form as a model for vital preaching. Through the African-American preacher's artful storytelling ability the oral traditions that underlie the sacred writings in scripture are released again to immediacy for contemporary hearers. Story also serves as a crucial vehicle for the "transmittal of the transconscious," a Jungian deep corporate consciousness that bears a people's religious symbols and values (*see* African-American Preaching).

Imagery Emerging as the Rhetorical Key. But not all homileticians by the mid-1980s preferred to shape their sermons on narrative lines. Several thinkers found imagery closer to the rhetorical heart of postmodern homiletics than story. The novelist-theologian Frederick Buechner, in his Beecher lectures in 1977, *Telling the Truth: The Gospel as Tragedy, Comedy, and Fairy Tale*, hinted at the supremacy of imagery over story as a vehicle of revelation. While the title of his lectures reflects the story metaphor in vogue, his writing as well as his sermons convey images that tell stories in and of themselves quite apart from plots.

In 1987, David Buttrick deepened the discussion regarding the significance of imagery in the new homiletics. His *Homiletic: Moves and Structures* turns to a phenomenology of language to explore, among other things, how image functions in the consciousness of congregations. Buttrick uses the idea of plot to track the action of language rather than of story. The language of the biblical text moves not in patterns of deductive reasoning but in plots analogous to structures in consciousness. Since the Bible "thinks" in images, parables, analogies, and metaphors, the image is the catalyst within each sermon move that enables the life of the text to happen in the hearers' awareness.

Embodiment as Rhetoric. Other voices stressed the importance of connecting with the original oral-aural setting of biblical texts in order to experience their meaning. Since Walter Ong's study in 1967 on the orality involved in the transmission of scripture (*The Presence of the Word*), many interpreters now recognize that the energy of biblical texts belongs either to the moment they were originally shared orally by the faith community or to community life infusing the literary dynamics of the passage. These texts, now locked into print, beg for rerelease to realize their spirit-life through

public embodiment and utterance. Homileticians like Thomas Troeger have been quick to pick up on the importance of acoustical and kinesthetic space for preaching. In his *Imagining a Sermon* (1990), as well as his earlier *Creating Fresh Images for Preaching* (1982), Troeger stresses the cruciality of the preacher's sensory appropriation of the life of the text if that text is to come to fruition in the preaching event (*see* Oral Communication and Preaching).

Sermon Models Infused with Imagination. The second major focus for dialogue in the new homiletics centers on the role of imagination in preaching. The pulpit has always celebrated the difference imagination can make in preaching. In 1988, Paul Wilson (*Imagination of the Heart*) and Thomas Troeger (*Imagining a Sermon*) explored how imagination works in the pulpit. Both authors locate imagination at the heart of the preaching enterprise. Both find imagination at the juncture of human spirit and Holy Spirit, channeling divine creativity through human creativity to fashion new visions of the kingdom. Walter Brueggemann in his Beecher lectures, *Finally Comes the Poet: Daring Speech for Proclamation*, joined the dialogue by declaring that only with the imagination of the poet can the preacher offer scripture's alternative consciousness to the trivialities of our prose-flattened world.

Sermon Models Informed by Social Hermeneutics. The third principal center for conversations in postmodern homiletics features sermon models informed by social hermeneutics. Until the 1980s little attention was paid to the sermon as a social act. In every generation prophetic preaching cried out against social ills. But with the emergence of liberation and feminist theologies and with the rise of social analysis in theological and biblical studies, the social quality of preaching has become a discrete and decisive category for dialogue.

Catherine and Justo González in 1980 anticipated the discussion with their *Liberation Preaching*, in which they point out that oppression is a fundamental human condition that all preaching must address. Arthur Van Seters, as editor in 1988 of *Preaching as a Social Act,* helps sharpen preachers' awareness of the social realities that both shape and challenge their preaching. Van Seters's book points up the prevalent privatism in North American preaching that addresses individuals as if they were separable from their corporate reality. Such preaching also privatizes God by ignoring the importance of tradition and the common good and by promoting the church as a closed community. By contrast, a growing number of homileticians now work from a social hermeneutic that features preaching as the interface of two social worlds, that of the biblical text with that of the contemporary preaching moment.

During the 1980s, as women and people of color announced their own versions of the social nature of preaching, they discovered common ground in their homiletics. Both parties express their pulpit genius through passion and story, perennial ingredients of oppressed people's response to prejudice, bigotry, and hatred. In the past, women endured by telling stories while sharing a common task like quilting or spinning. By the 1980s women had become a formidable force in seminary student bodies; many were searching for an alternative to the rational, sequential sermon model associated with men. In *Weaving the Sermon: Preaching in a Feminist Perspective,* Christine Smith explains how women tend to weave stories, images, and metaphors around a controlling theme rather than arguing in rational fashion along a sequential line. Similarly, as Henry Mitchell reminds us in *Celebration and Experience in Preaching,* African-American slaves turned for centuries to biblical stories in preaching as the bearers of a collective "transconsciousness" or "stored insight" that enabled them to trust in God's rule. The celebratory climax of the African-American sermon at its best affirms like a victory shout God's saving grace for people used to living under the lash.

In contrast with the African-American pulpit, Hispanic homileticians in North America discovered in the 1970s and 1980s that they must first shed an Anglo model of preaching before they can discover their own voice. Ruben Armendariz describes how white, Protestant, American missionaries in the nineteenth century imposed upon Mexican proselytes a sermon paradigm that was anti-Roman Catholic in sentiment, grounded in biblicism, and fired with evangelical, puritanical fervor ("Emerging Issues with Latino Students in the Teaching of Preaching," unpublished paper for the Academy of Homiletics, December 1977). Such preaching promoted an escapist mentality that was incapable of addressing the ecojustice issues involved in the Anglo oppression of Hispanics in the United States. Today new sermon models are being formed in the matrix of liberation theology. The sermon can now transcend narrow pietism to become the word's gracious call for social justice (*see* Homiletics and Preaching in Latin America).

On the Horizon:
Homiletics Claiming Its Identity

Homiletics in North America has come of age. Historical studies of preaching both reflect and offer the sense of tradition needed to give stability and context to the discussions. From its established sense of identity, North American homiletics will soon pause on the threshold of a new century and new millennium to assess its agenda. One can expect from this traditionally eclectic field more concerted attempts at a common language to unify its inquiries into such diverse disciplines as hermeneutics, poetics, language theory, and social analysis. In theological education homiletics may well find itself moving closer to the center of curriculum formation, modeling by its nature and purpose the praxis expected of seminary graduates.

The list of subjects for future investigation is as prismatic as homiletics itself. Yet several concerns will likely top the agenda. One relates to the discussion of rhetoric and poetics that is still gathering momentum, especially with the ongoing debate about authorial intent and reader response. A second involves the phenomenology of language, particularly with how symbols form and work in the unconscious as well as consciousness to effect transformation. A third discussion will seek a more profound understanding of the dynamics of the congruency between preacher and sermon at the moment of delivery. A fourth explores that murky frontier between pastoral and prophetic preaching, searching for an authentic fusion to replace the false dichotomy between the two. A fifth ventures into multiculturalism to discover what it means to preach to a pluralistic society. A sixth turns to liturgy and to how the sacraments, music, prayer, and architecture write their own homiletical theologies. A seventh delves into ecclesiology to deepen understanding of the essential corporateness of preaching. Yet another discussion opens to the visual and literary arts to gain new revelations for the aesthetics of the pulpit. These are but a few of homiletics' concerns as it faces the twenty-first century.

Buttrick, D., *Homiletic,* 1987. **Davis, H. G.,** *Design for Preaching,* 1959. **Eslinger, R.,** *A New Hearing: Living Options in Homiletical Method,* 1987. *Homiletic* (periodical), 1976– . **Lischer, R.,** *Theories of Preaching: Selected Readings in the Homiletical Tradition,* 1987. **Massa, C.,** *Toward a Contemporary Theology of Preaching,* Ph.D. Diss., Princeton Theological Seminary, 1960.

DON M. WARDLAW

Homiletics and Preaching in Scandinavia.

Christianity in Scandinavia was influenced by the Lutheran Reformation during the sixteenth century. The national churches became state churches under the supremacy of the kings. The Swedish church got its own blend of Protestantism through certain historical links with Anglicanism. In the centuries after the Reformation, Scandi-

navian theology—including homiletics—developed through the distinctive periods of Lutheran Orthodoxy, Pietism, Enlightenment, and the revival movements of the nineteenth century. In the post-Reformation period specific homiletical literature was meager in Scandinavia. Some textbooks and manuals were published from time to time, but they were often strongly influenced by the dominant German homiletics. Thus independent Scandinavian contributions to this field of research were few. Scandinavian preaching has been more or less a function of the predominant theological concepts and influential preachers of the various periods. Yngve Brilioth, the Swedish theologian and bishop, was probably right when he said that we should not exaggerate the impact of homiletical teaching. Homiletics has reflected the conventions of church life more than it has made new contributions to the formation of preaching and teaching.

Sweden. The first homiletics of major importance was Laurentius Petri's *Hypotyposes,* stemming from a synod in Uppsala, 1566. This small book defines the task of preaching according to the theological fundamentals of the Lutheran Reformation. The purpose of preaching is to proclaim the gospel purely without adding anything to it or omitting anything from it.

A number of "Metodus concionandi" were published in the Age of Pietism, but homiletical contributions were meager in the period of the Enlightenment. A certain influence on Swedish homiletics came from two translated books: The Danish *Collegium pastorale practicum,* written by Erik Pontoppidan (see below), and Christian Palmer's *Homiletik* (German orig. edition 1842).

The new era in Swedish homiletics dawned when the discipline of practical theology was established at the University of Uppsala in 1807 (Lund in 1809). These professorships had from the beginning no scholarly pretensions, and only practical and technical qualifications were required of their holders. The main emphasis was placed on practical utility in the Age of Enlightenment. After Schleiermacher's* influential survey of the study of theology (1811), practical theology gradually modified its ambitions and self-understanding. According to the Royal Ordinance of 1831, the professor of practical theology was given a twofold task: to lecture on "one or more aspects of pastoral theology" and, together with the teachers involved in practical training, "to hold homiletic, catechetic, liturgic, and declamatory exercises."

Scholarly work on homiletics in the twentieth century began with J. O. Quensel's *Homiletik* in 1901. Quensel, an outstanding scholar of the historical school, was appointed as permanent professor of practical theology in 1909. His book was based on intensive studies in the history of preaching. He defines preaching as the free homiletical, nonritual side of the cult. Preaching in a narrow sense is "the proclamation of the gospel within the worshiping congregation."

During these first decades of the twentieth century, a Swedish school of homiletics was established. In this period a number of studies were published using the *loci* method, in which one defines the main dogmatic ideas in certain historical and homiletical material. These studies often were titled "[Name] as preacher."

Since World War II, the historical emphasis on homiletical research has gradually been weakened. The systematic theologian Gustaf Wingren published his major study *Predikan* in 1949. This work, influenced by Ireneus, Luther,* and Karl Barth,* has played an important role in the international homiletical discussions (German ed. 1955). In recent years, Professor Wingren has more and more intensely criticized historical and analytical research in the field of homiletics in Sweden. He proposes a more kerygmatic and hermeneutical understanding of homiletical efforts.

The latest Swedish textbook in the field is by Martin Loennebo (*Homiletik* 1977). In his inclusive way of thinking, Bishop Loennebo has drawn on impulses from many theological traditions—Lutheran, Greek Orthodox, and revivalism. He recommends many variations in the art of preaching, placing strong emphasis on both dramatic forms and different kinds of meditative preaching.

In 1979 practical training for the ministry of the word was institutionally organized in two pastoral seminaries (Uppsala and Lund) under the administration of The Council on Education, Church of Sweden.

Denmark-Norway (1537–1813); Denmark and Norway (1813–)

Lutheran worship was established in the double monarchy of Denmark-Norway by the Church Ordinance of 1537. Theological education in Denmark-Norway was fundamentally revised during the seventeenth century. In a royal ordination of 1629, it was stated that no person had access to the pulpit in the Church of Denmark-Norway without having a theological degree from the university.

From 1635 a "dismissory sermon" was demanded at the end of theological studies. The final test should prove the candidate's qualifications for (1) reading and expounding the biblical texts (*lectio biblica*) and (2) the knowledge of Lutheran dogmatics on the basis of the *loci* method (*loci communes*). This reformation of pastoral education took place in the period of Lutheran Orthodox theological consolidation.

The most important figure in Danish-Norwegian pastoral theology in the era of Pietism was Erik Pontoppidan (d. 1764). His *Collegium pastorale practicum*, originally given as lectures at the University of Copenhagen, was published in 1756. In chapters 14–32 he deals with the problems of preaching. He conveys his homiletical ideals in a warm and counseling way. He discusses the pastor's personal and spiritual qualifications for preaching. The main purpose of preaching the gospel is "the salvation of the souls," and the basis for salvation is to know the only true God and Jesus Christ whom he has sent. Since the way to salvation in Jesus

Christ follows a number of stages, the *ordo salutis*, the predominant task of the preacher is to preach the word of God, taking into account the various degrees of spiritual maturity in the congregation.

The first Danish homiletics in the modern sense of the word was written by Christian Bastholm (1775). His presentation of "the clergyman's way of speaking" bears the theological characteristics of the Enlightenment—a positive affirmation of the richness of human life, an apologetic tone, and a rational argumentation for the credibility of the Christian message. His work demonstrates a remarkable will to accommodate the gospel to the modern, critical mind.

Preaching and the whole of church life were soon influenced by theologians breathing the new air of Romanticism, especially J. P. Mynster (1775–1854) and N.F.S. Grundtvig (1783–1872). Although no homiletic work was written in the nineteenth century, general theological thinking also was related to the task of preaching. At the end of the Enlightenment, preachers had to face a dilemma: The listeners of that time felt the objective message (the concern of Lutheran Orthodoxy) irrelevant, and the accommodation to the modern mind (the concern of rationalism) threatened to undermine the integrity of the gospel.

The solution was to focus neither on the message nor the listener but on the messenger. Preaching was now no longer understood as a theoretical teaching but as a self-experienced testimony. Both the message and the listener as he receives it unite in the preacher's own person.

Søren Kierkegaard's* ascetic and paradoxical understanding of Christianity is quite different from Mynster's Christohumanism and Grundtvig's preaching of the Holy Spirit, the church, and the sacraments. In a number of aesthetic-philosophical works, he promoted a preaching characterized by deep devotion to God, concentration on the individual and the existential choice, the "paradox," and the imitation of Christ. Only the devoted individual can enter into a relationship with God and experience true existence.

These intensive theological discussions in the nineteenth century, accompanied by a deep popular revival, gave birth to some distinctive groupings within the Danish church, many of which are living traditions in Denmark today:

1. a mainstream, conservative Grundtvigianism
2. a left-wing Grundtvigianism with post-Bultmannian elements
3. a faction focusing on theology of creation (K. E. Loegstrup)
4. The Inner Mission Movement (pietistic but loyal to the folk church)
5. a low-church, lay movement

Karl Barth's influence on Danish theology and preaching has been considerable. In L. Broendum's homiletic *Praedikenen og dens forberedelse* (The Sermon and Its Preparation, 1975), the heritage from Barth is clear.

Two contributions to Danish homiletics were made by A. F. Noerager Pedersen. In 1980 he published *Praedikenens idéhistorie* (History of Homiletical Ideas), in which he searches for "the category of preaching," summarized as biblical narration with application. This ideal he finds in the apostolic preaching and in Luther. Some years later, his book *Den kunst af predike* (The Art of Preaching) appeared, modeled on the tradition of classic rhetoric.

When the University of Oslo was established in 1813, new possibilities for independent Norwegian theological education were created. The professors at the Faculty of Theology gave homiletical courses from time to time. Ordinary training for ministers, organized in a pastoral seminary, was established in 1848. No homiletics was published in Norway in these years.

At the beginning of the twentieth century, there was a felt need for less dogmatic preaching. Thv. Klaveness and J. J. Jansen designed a new way of preaching—closer to people's everyday life, more inclined to dialogue, and with a new psychological sensibility. J. J. Jansen's homiletics *Forkyndelsen* (Homiletics), published in 1906, was used at other Scandinavian universities.

Karl Barth's* influence on Norwegian theology was rather limited. But Barth's "Word-of-God" theology inspired J. Smemo, dean of the Pastoral Seminary at The Free Faculty of Theology (1933–46), to write his important book *Er predikenens tid forbi?* (Is Preaching Obsolete?) in 1938. Smemo argues strongly that preaching is still an indispensable part of God's will for his church.

Smemo's book is a principal study, and so in 1951 was C. Fr. Wisloeff's *Ordet fra Guds munn* (The Word from God's Mouth). In the central chapter of his book, Wisloeff emphasizes the homiletical importance of the dialectic between law and gospel*.

In the 1980s, O. Skjevesland in his homiletics *Broen over 2000 år* (Bridge Over 2,000 Years) and T. Aukrust's book *Exodus* have tried to give both a foundation in principle for preaching and practical guidelines for the preparation and delivery of sermons in the Age of Communication.

Finally, it may be noted that practical theology still has no status among the classical theological disciplines in Norway. Practical theology since 1848 has mainly been linked to practical training at pastoral seminaries. But curricular reforms at the end of the 1980s seem to inaugurate a shift in this situation.

The Future Agenda. The discipline of homiletics in Scandinavia is in a state of reorientation. It is difficult to predict scholarly development in the years to come. Probably, there will be no common, inclusive direction because there are so many different tendencies and contradictory voices in the present discussions.

Today's Scandinavian situation reflects a great deal of experimentation in preaching, giving attention to the various literary forms of the Bible. Both narrative* and meditative-poetic preaching are much discussed, but the result appears to be mixed.

Confusion in scholarly discussions has a lot to do with the decline of the historical-critical method in biblical exegesis. New methods appear on the exegetical scene: structuralistic methods, other forms of literal and rhetorical reading, socio-historical reading, and others. Perhaps a stabilization of exegetical methods is needed before we can predict the homiletics of tomorrow.

Brilioth, Y., *Predikans Historia,* 1962; *A Brief History of Preaching,* trans. K. Matson, 1977.   OLAV SKJEVESLAND

Homiletics: Teaching of, Graduate Study, Professional Associations.

Instruction in homiletics in the seventeenth and eighteenth centuries was carried out largely by means of ordination and installation sermons in which the nature of the minister's call, the rights of the congregation, and the purpose and nature of preaching were articulated. Relatively little attention was given to style, and the appeal was to reason. A scholastic method of division and subdivision, with the formal application at the end, was the usual form of the sermon. One sermon by Jonathan Edwards* concludes with six inferences broken down into sixteen subdivisions.

What is probably the first book on preaching written by an American, published in America in 1726, was Cotton Mather's* *Manuductio ad Ministerium* (Directions to a Candidate for the Ministry). Mather includes in his directions the proper foundation for the ministerial candidate, emphasizing the need for the preacher to be a scholar who turns out a "well-studied sermon." A knowledge of the classical languages was to be supplemented by a study of natural philosophy, mathematics, astronomy, and music—"if you fancy it."

The beginning of the nineteenth century saw the publication of John Witherspoon's *Lectures on Eloquence*, which signified changes to take place in the century to follow. No similar full treatment of style* for preaching had ever been published in America.

The establishment of seminaries by leading Protestant denominations early in the nineteenth century provided both the need and the means for teaching homiletics systematically. From the beginning, some form of instruction in preaching was felt to be necessary to the seminary curriculum. Instruction depended heavily on the rhetoricians, both ancient and modern. The second third of the nineteenth century brought an increasing number of works devoted to homiletics proper, and entire books were devoted to the specific application of the principles of rhetoric* to preaching and to the use of illustration.

By the mid-nineteenth century, a debate had arisen about the teaching of homiletics by seminary professors who had no experience as pastors. Gradually, the actual work of the pastor, including preaching, which had been the background, the concern, and the interest of the whole faculty, tended to become the narrower concern of the incumbent of a Chair of Sacred Rhetoric or Pastoral Theology.

Increasingly, in the later nineteenth century, the importance of the context in which preaching was to take place became recognized. Biblical criticism was receiving wide attention by the 1880s, and social problems were being talked about as significant issues of religious concern. Churches built in the late nineteenth century bore a strong resemblance to lecture halls. The pulpit* became central and was sometimes replaced by the lectern or reading stand comparable to that of the secular lecturer.

Teachers of preaching articulated the difference between the written interpretation of the printed page and the "living interpretation" by the spoken word. They differentiated between "secular" and "sacred" rhetoric in terms of the subject matter and the person (authority or position) of the preacher. Some homiletics teachers continued to emphasize the sermon as a rhetorical work, while others began to stress the interpretive function of preaching. The latter group was strengthened by the establishment of the Lyman Beecher Lectures on preaching at Yale Divinity School, the first of which was given by Henry Ward Beecher* on January 31, 1872.

Beecher emphasized that the sermon is not preached for the sake of any system of truth but in order to reconstruct the life of the hearer. Preaching was not to be thought of as the application of rhetorical principles to biblical or doctrinal material or as an explanation from some deposit of divine truth. Preaching was to be an interpretation of the hearer and the hearer's situation, and the preacher could not wait "for the latest theory propounded at Tübingen or Berlin." The scholarship of the preacher required universality—with politics, law, and social reform becoming part of the preacher's knowledge and vocabulary.

The teaching of preaching in the twentieth century confronted increasing religiously illiterate individualism. A significant switch occurred from dependence on rhetorical principles to dependence on psychological insight. Charles H. Parkhurst in his Yale lectures in 1913 said, "Psychology is as essential as theology to the proper presentation of pulpit truth." The nineteenth century had made this kind of statement about rhetoric.

Homileticians attempted to teach preaching as an event in which the dynamic was not simply the relationship of form and content in the older textual-rhetorical pairing. The dynamic event was the relation of biblical-theological and the psychological-sociological aspects of human existence. While the first three decades of the twentieth century saw the preacher turning to sources other than the Bible, by mid-century a renewed emphasis on "expository preaching"* had taken place. The development of emphases in worship included a recovery of the use of the lectionary* for preaching.

When leading churches adopted a common lectionary, a new possibility for homiletical teaching and writing was created. Series of volumes on preaching from the lectionary appeared and continue to be developed.

By 1935, "practice preaching" came into the classroom as a recognized procedure for teaching and brought preaching into a closer link to the rest of the theological curriculum. For the most part, teachers of preaching continued to be outstanding preachers, and some continued to serve significant congregations while engaging in their teaching. By the late 1950s, seminaries recognized the need to have appropriately trained persons as professors of homiletics (see Pedagogy of Preaching; Homiletics and Preaching in North America).

Six doctoral programs in homiletics now exist but differ from one another considerably in regard to their methodology and content. The critical academic issue is whether homiletics can be regarded as a theological discipline appropriate for a research doctoral program.

The Divinity School of Drew University has offered a Ph.D. in homiletics by combining it with either liturgical, biblical, theological, or religious studies. Candler School of Theology at Emory University offers work in homiletics as a collateral track for those enrolled in some other theological discipline. The Graduate Theological Union at Berkeley admits doctoral students to a program titled "The Arts, Worship, and Proclamation," which requires the student to work in all three of the areas indicated and give attention to the interfacing of those areas. At Princeton Theological Seminary, the doctoral program in homiletics is a subspecialty of Practical Theology called, "Theology and Communication in Preaching." Princeton Seminary emphasizes practical theology as an interaction between theology proper and a cognate discipline in the human sciences. The Southern Baptist Theological Seminary in Louisville combines the doctoral student's emphasis in homiletics with a minor emphasis in another theological discipline and some university study in a cognate area. The Divinity School of Vanderbilt University divides the student's curriculum between homiletics proper and some other area of biblical or theological work.

The leading professional association for the teaching of homiletics is the Academy of Homiletics, which was founded in 1965. It holds an annual meeting, usually in early December, sometimes with a single emphasis and sometimes with papers on a variety of aspects of homiletics. The Academy brings teachers of preaching together in working groups for the discussion of precirculated papers that attempt to identify current and future emphases in the teaching of homiletics. It publishes the semiannual journal *Homiletic*.

Recently an international organization of teachers of preaching, *Societas Homiletica*, was chartered in Oslo, Norway. *Societas Homiletica* originated in a conference on preaching held in Heidelberg in 1986. It currently numbers members from about fifteen countries, including the United States and Canada.

CONRAD HARRY MASSA

Homily. In current Roman Catholic usage, homily is a category of sermon which (1) flows from and follows immediately upon scriptural readings and (2) leads into the celebration of sacraments. Recent research and experience stress four facets of the Catholic homily that wed traditional approaches and fresh insights.

1. The homily is *scriptural*. Reversing a centuries-long medieval and post-Tridentine stress on doctrinal instruction with little or no reference to the liturgy's biblical texts, the Second Vatican Council declared that "all the preaching of the Church must be nourished and ruled by Sacred scripture" (Constitution on Divine Revelation 21). For it is in scripture and the liturgy that the preacher discovers the substance of what is to be preached: "a proclamation of God's wonderful works

in the history of salvation" (Constitution on the Sacred Liturgy 35).

Significant developments since Vatican II reveal how important it is for effective preaching to supplement the historical-critical methodology of scriptural interpretation blessed by the council with other biblical methods—for example, social-scientific models, feminist hermeneutics, literary criticism,* and narrative* criticism. Further, the National Conference of Catholic Bishops argued in 1982 that "the preacher does not so much attempt to explain the scriptures as to interpret the human situation through the scriptures" (*Fulfilled in Your Hearing*, 20). Indispensable is the preacher's ability to read the signs of the times and focus their significance through biblical lenses on the lives of the people.

2. The homily is *liturgical.** Reacting to a long-standing aberration wherein the homily was seen as an interruption unconnected to the liturgy proper, Vatican II insisted that the homily is "part of the liturgical action," is "part of the liturgy itself" (Sacred Liturgy 35 and 51). The homily is not only part of the Mass; it is part of all sacramental celebrations. The homily is not an extraneous activity inserted into something more accurately designated as liturgy. The liturgy of the word and the liturgy of the Eucharist make up one unified liturgical celebration, one single act of worship. The homily is liturgical prayer—a prayer of praise and petition, of gratitude and contrition.

The homily not only comments on the paschal mystery, the dying-rising of Jesus, in light of the liturgical texts; it draws the faithful into the mystery, helps them unite their lives to the mystery, helps make the mystery of Christ "present and active within us" (Sacred Liturgy 35). The living word has to transport the age-old, rather rigid universal symbols of the liturgy to this time, this place, this people. It personalizes what the rite expresses in a common, general way.

3. The homily is *proclamation.** The idea harks back to the New Testament kerygma, the preaching of the apostles in Acts 2, 3, and 10. Because the homily, like the rest of the liturgy, does not simply recall God's saving works, does not merely remember the mystery that is Christ but must make the history and the mystery "present and active within us," sheer exposition or straightforward catechesis is insufficient. The homily should be evocative, help the believer to open up to God speaking now. Not a cold intellectual assent to a proposition—"I believe that God's only Son took flesh for my salvation"; rather, a totally selfless, "What do you want from me, Lord?"

How is such a response effected? Not primarily by indoctrination, which plays upon a single faculty of the human person, the intellect's ability to grasp ideas, concepts, propositions. It is effected by imagination*—stories (parable, allegory, myth), symbols, the fine arts—an approach that is more open-ended than the concept (*see* Arts and Preaching). Sheer indoctrination pays little heed to an old scholastic axiom, "Nothing is present in the intellect that was not previously present in the senses." Our ideas are triggered by sense experience. The more powerful the sense experience, the more powerfully an idea will take hold. If I want a congregation to "see" the Holocaust, I do not simply assert, "Six million were exterminated"; I let them visualize the gas ovens, the mountains of human bones. It is not enough to show you the score of Handel's *Messiah;* you must drink it in with your ears. It is one thing to hear "I love you," quite another to experience love's touch.

4. Does a homily call for a specific *style?** It is often asserted that the homily should be informal, popular, familiarly conversational. The thesis harmonizes with the Greek origin of the word (*homilia*), with much (but not all) early Christian preaching, with hints in various official documents, and with some contemporary preferences. In consequence, some disparage a traditional, deductive, expository* method of homilizing in favor of the inductive* and narrative, allegedly more appropriate to the homily's

function, to contemporary culture, and to the needs of the people.

For all its genuine contributions, the thesis is in danger of introducing too sharp an opposition between deductive and inductive, exposition and narrative; it often fails to see that the solution is not an either-or but a both-and, not adherence to a preconceived definition but this preacher and this congregation in this cultural situation. Here there are few universals.

Finally, to preach effectively in the context of scripture, the liturgy, and contemporary living, homilists would do well to incorporate five of the qualities that Abraham Joshua Heschel has unearthed in the Hebrew prophets: Homilists (1) should be extraordinarily sensitive to evil and injustice; (2) must feel fiercely and at times shock rudely but always lovingly; (3) ought ceaselessly to challenge the idols that lurk within sacred and not-so-sacred institutions, beliefs, and persons; (4) will find themselves frequently lonely and frustrated; (5) release words that are charged with divine power because they have experienced a God intimately involved in history and have experienced a God who is living care.

Fuller, R. H., *Preaching the Lectionary: The Word of God for the Church Today* (rev. ed.), 1984. **Heschel, A. J.,** *The Prophets,* 1962. **National Conference of Catholic Bishops,** *Fulfilled in Your Hearing: The Homily in the Sunday Assembly,* 1982. **Waznak, R. P., S.S.,** "Homily," *The New Dictionary of Sacramental Worship,* ed. P. E. Fink, S.J., 1990, 552–58.   WALTER J. BURGHARDT, S.J.

Hospital Chaplaincy.

Hospital chaplaincy often focuses on one-to-one pastoral care with patients rather than on worship or preaching. In fact, most books and articles on hospital chaplaincy fail to mention worship or preaching. This article examines the ways in which hospital chaplains can strengthen their preaching when they give close attention to both the context and content of their sermons.

People admitted to hospitals have tended to be too sick to attend chapel. However, many hospitals offer worship services through closed circuit television. Even though the number of worshipers in the chapel or on closed circuit television may be small, hospital patients have profound needs to experience the best worship possible.

Context. Chaplains benefit from being attentive to the specific context of hospital preaching. The worship service participants tend to be older persons, those hospitalized for nonmedical reasons, families, and staff members. Older people are often engaged in a review of their lives and therefore benefit from reflective sermons. Other worshipers include patients in alcohol and drug rehabilitation, physical therapy, or psychiatric units. Such persons need sermons that relate to their particular recovery needs. Hospital chaplains must be cognizant of who their participants are and sensitive to their feelings in this critical time. They must fashion their sermons accordingly. The preaching challenge is not to find a common denominator to which one can speak but to focus on the particular people gathered. Those who might be listening on closed-circuit television will take the sermons seriously because they see the chaplain taking the needs of the worshipers seriously.

Hospital chaplains also need to be attentive to the informality of the context. The worshiping congregation may include those who are not fully alert or those who are in the midst of recovery from a serious psychiatric or addiction problem. The worshipers will appreciate sermons that lift up the most reassuring and familiar messages about God's love and presence.

This informality also lends itself to preaching in a spontaneous and extemporaneous manner. Chaplains may interact and join more with their worshipers when they are flexible in their style and use an outline rather than a formal manuscript. To be a chaplain who works on being spontaneous in preaching is haps the pastoral equivalent of a good bedside manner in a physician.

Hospital chaplains minister to a pluralistic group that includes many faith groups. Their preaching is enhanced when they express sensitivity for the religious and cultural diversity of their worshipers, as well as when they use eye contact and a participatory worship style. While chaplains attempt to reach out to a wide variety of faith groups, they also need to honor their Christian identity and speak out of their theological formation and religious heritage.

Although the setting is more informal and the worshipers are perhaps less theologically and physically alert than at a traditional parish, chaplains do well not to be misled into thinking that their sermons can therefore be less substantive. Hospital chaplains have the opportunity to preach to people who are often asking themselves challenging, difficult questions about their own spirituality. In such a context, hospital chaplains need to proclaim a biblical message of comfort and hope in the midst of pain.

Content. In preaching, hospital patients and their families need their chaplain to identify with their experiences and with their feelings of hurt, fear, anger, sorrow, and loss. They yearn for the chaplain to know who they are and what they are experiencing. They hunger for personal, concrete, and realistic sermons.

Spiritual needs are especially prominent during times of sickness and hospitalization. Patients and their families often wonder how God is present in their experiences. They long to hear sermons that present God's love for them in Jesus Christ. They want to hear a clear, comforting message of God's healing presence, powerful love, and forgiveness. Their faith has to be grounded in scripture and their hope rooted in prayer.

The theology of the sermon needs to be portrayed in real-life examples and experiences. Patients value sermons with which they can identify, such as sermons rich in the imagery and narratives of scripture. In such sermons, patients find

themselves immersed in the story, and the story sustains them as they grapple with their current struggles. When chaplains preach narrative sermons, there is more potential for keeping the sermon structurally simple. In addition, the chaplain needs to talk about theological concepts in very personal and down-to-earth ways.

Preaching about their identity in Christ gives hospital patients and their families emotional strength and resilience. In this way, the impact of specific problems or setbacks is diminished or at least set in a broader perspective. In addition, sermons that focus on listeners' identity in Christ help them believe in themselves and work toward specific goals. If progress toward their goals is obstructed, a strong sense of identity helps them consider other alternatives to defeat and hopelessness. Sermons about God's presence and love for them may enable them to face their struggles and overcome their emotional and spiritual crises. When hospital patients and their families hear sermons about their identity as loved, forgiven people, they are often renewed in their faith and moved to hope.

Key components in hospital preaching, therefore, include attentiveness to the specific context of hospital preaching, identification with the feelings and experiences of patients and their families, and help in the formation of their identity in Christ Jesus. Through such preaching, hospital patients and their families are able to face their struggles, trust in God's presence and love, and move toward emotional and spiritual healing (*see* Pastoral Care and Preaching).

Holst, L. E., *Hospital Ministry: The Role of the Chaplain Today*, 1985. **Moore, T.,** *The Care of Souls*, 1992. **Nouwen, H.,** *The Wounded Healer*, 1972.

ANNE MARIE NUECHTERLEIN

Humbert of Romans. (1200?–1277)

Humbert was born at Romans (Dauphiné, France) during a time of critical

change in western European history. As
the feudal age ended with the decline in
monastic, agrarian, and rural centers of
influence, new forms of life and thought
appeared: Cities emerged, universities
were established, trade opened to the
east, mercantile guilds and banks were
founded, Aristotelian philosophy won
great admiration, and new groups of
wandering preachers appeared in profu-
sion.

In response to such social, religious,
and economic ferment, Francis of Assisi
founded the Order of Friars Minor (1209–
1210), and Dominic of Guzman established the Order of Preachers (1216). In
1224, Humbert entered the Preachers
(Dominicans*) and served his religious
brothers as provincial of France (1244).
An adept administrator, Humbert set
about consolidating the essential structures of the Preachers' life: the revision of
the Dominican liturgy, the preparation of
a new edition of the friars' constitution,
and the promotion of a new missionary
effort supported by centers of biblical,
linguistic, and oriental research.

In the history of Christian preaching,
Humbert's contributions include his pop-
ularization of biblical *exempla* in preaching on moral issues to various groups of
listeners and his masterful treatise *De er-
uditione praedicatorum* (*On the Formation of Preachers*). The latter work elaborates both his theology and spirituality of
preaching and reveals the particular insight that his religious order offers the
history of preaching: The minister is
identified as a preacher of the word; all
other ministerial and liturgical tasks flow
from and return to this primary task. In a
time when ministry was understood as
monastic prayer and education or parish
liturgical celebrations, the identification
of the minister as a preacher appeared
novel. Likewise, Humbert's writings underscore the universal nature of the evangelical project: the preacher must proclaim the word to *all* social classes, in all
circumstances, to the believer, the skep-
tic, and the nonbeliever.

Concerning the preacher's formation,
Humbert offers a simple yet demanding
course. The preacher's training cannot be
limited to biblical, theological, and philosophical studies. If the preacher is to be
effective, he or she will have intimate
knowledge of the other "texts" that reveal
the word: the "books" of nature, daily human activity, and the artistic and literary
works that shape and express human
need and aspiration. In this regard, Humbert insists that a life of active ministry is
preferable to and yet incomplete without
the contemplative.

What does one need to be a preacher?
Humbert asks. First, one must have enthusiasm for the job, an authentic desire
to preach. Second, one must have the requisite skills to preach: knowledge, the discipline to prepare a sermon, the ability to
speak persuasively in public. Merchants
and teachers may have enthusiasm and
the ability to speak in public, but the
preacher needs a third element, and that
is the "grace of preaching." This grace,
writes Humbert, is given by the Spirit and
discerned by the church. These three elements serve as the foundation of his or
her spirituality* of preaching, which is
directed toward the goal of being useful
for others.

Preaching, Humbert argues, is a *specu-
lum animae*, a "mirror of the soul" set
before the listener. Without preaching, he
contends, people will make foolish assessments of the value and purpose of life
unless guided by a spiritual vision. And
without good works, which preaching intends to promote, a dearth of goodness
and charity will come into existence. Using a variety of vivid images, Humbert
writes that preaching heals the soul with
a medicine, namely the Word of God. It is
a fire that rekindles the flames of faith
and hope, a strong wine full of rich blessings, a powerful soap of cleansing forgiveness, and a small yet potent seed that
bears much fruit in the life of the Christian.

Humbert's singular devotion to the
preacher's mission is rooted in the scriptures, the sermons of the preaching bishops of the early church, and the patristic

and medieval commentaries on preaching (Ambrose, Augustine,* Gregory the Great,* John Chrysostom*). His consistent demand that preaching take place among all classes and types of persons heralded a shift in religious consciousness that no longer identified the apostolic life with monastic seclusion but with the popular demand to hear the word and live the Christian life in the newly emerging urban centers of western Europe.

Brett, E. T., *Humbert of Romans: His Life and Views of Thirteenth-Century Society,* 1984. "On the Formation of Preachers," in *Early Dominicans: Selected Writings,* ed. S. Tugwell, *Classics of Western Spirituality,* 1982.

SAMUEL EDWARD TORVEND

ON THE FORMATION OF PREACHERS
Humbert of Romans
Without preaching, which sows the word of God, the whole world would be barren and without fruit. If the Lord of hosts had not left us a seed (the word of God, that is), we should have like Sodom (Isa. 1:9), a land which is altogether barren and bears no fruit. . . .

If there were no preaching, the hearts of men would not be stirred to hope for heavenly blessings. "If he holds back the waters, everything will be dried up" (Job 12:15). Gregory comments on this: "If the knowledge of the preachers is withheld, the hearts of people who could have burgeoned with eternal hope will shrivel up instead. . . ."

Without preaching the church would never have been established. "Where were you when I laid the foundations of the earth?" (Job 38:4). Gregory says: "When scripture refers to foundations, we understand the preachers, who were the first to be established in the church by the Lord, so that the whole structure which follows rests on them. . . ."

The church would collapse without preaching. "I will make glorious the place of my feet" (Isa. 60:13). The Gloss explains: "It is preachers who are called the feet of the Lord, because they support the whole body of the church." So the church

stands because of them, just as the human body stands on its feet. . . .

Furthermore, the apostle (Paul) says to some people, "You were once in darkness, but now you are light in the Lord" (Eph. 5:8), because men who lack preaching are like men in the dark. At the beginning of creation, we are told that the abyss was covered with darkness, but once light was created, all that matter was illuminated. In the same way men are illuminated by preaching. "On those who dwell in the region of the shadow of death, light has dawned" (Matt. 4:16), which means, according to the Gloss, the light of preaching. So preaching is the world's lighting. . . .

So God, seeing how necessary preaching is in the world, for reasons we have been considering, has from the beginning never stopped sending preachers, one after the other, nor will he ever stop until the end of time. Gregory says: "The head of the household hires laborers to cultivate his vineyard at the third hour, the sixth hour, the ninth hour and the eleventh hour, because from the beginning of this world until its end, the Lord does not give up assembling preachers to be sent to instruct his faithful people."

From "Treatise on the Formation of Preachers," in *Early Dominicans: Selected Writings,* ed. S. Tugwell, O.P. *The Classics of Western Spirituality* (New York: Paulist Press, 1982), 187–90.

Humor. In a sermon on humor, Reinhold Niebuhr* allowed humor a role in our worship, but a limited one:

Humor is a recognition of incongruity. But the sense of humor remains healthy only when it deals with immediate issues and faces the obvious and surface irrationalities. It must move toward faith or sink into despair when the ultimate issues are raised. . . . [T]here is laughter in the vestibule of the temple, the echo of laughter in the temple itself, but only faith and prayer, and no laughter in the holy of holies (Niebuhr, 130–31).

The history of Christian preaching and evidence within the Bible itself challenge Niebuhr's characterization of humor as valuable only as a prelude to faith or consideration of the ultimate issues. Humor is near to faith itself.

Sermons provoking laughter have biblical precedent. The story of Balaam's ass exemplifies biting, biblical satire (Num. 22:5–31). Elijah ridicules the prophets of Baal (1 Kings 18:27), and Isaiah makes fun of those who use half a log for a fire to cook meat, the other half for an idol to whom to pray, "Save me, for you are my god!" (Isa. 44:14–17). Humor is a primary prophetic weapon against idolatry. Luke depicts a slapstick scene in Acts 12:1–19, where the power of God first makes fools of Peter's Roman jailers and then even pokes fun at the myopic church. Examples of biblical humor suggest that wherever the divine touches the human, conditions are right even for God to laugh (Ps. 2:4).

Wit, satire, irony, sarcasm, puns, and ridicule perform the same functions in sermons as in everyday speech. As Niebuhr noted, humor deals with life's incongruities. Human weaknesses are named, sometimes exaggerated in humor. A speaker's humor can unite an audience and reveal the speaker's humanity. Comic relief reduces tension within a speech. Aristotle said that humor is often linked to aggression. Therefore, speakers must use humor with care. Humor can be an effective weapon of the oppressed. There is more than a hint of aggressiveness present when, in humor like satire, the pompous and proud are put down or the lowly and powerless are freed from the grip of present arrangements. Humor is always at someone's expense. Homiletical humor is less dangerous when the price extracted by humor is paid by the preacher.

Even though John Wesley* advised his preachers, "Let your whole deportment before the congregation be serious, weighty, and solemn," humor appears in the preaching of the past. Luther often provokes a smile in the listener when he notes, with biting irony, our pitiful attempts to make ourselves right with God. Henry Ward Beecher* may be credited with making humor one of the distinctive characteristics of North American preaching. Preachers, particularly nineteenth-century Methodists in polemics against Baptists and Calvinists, borrowed heavily from Beecher's quips and barbs like, "DOCTRINE is nothing but the skin of Truth set up and stuffed." Lyman Beecher and Timothy Dwight* were also known for their pulpit humor, particularly polemical humor used to good advantage in the numerous nineteenth-century theological controversies.

Evangelical preaching, as it developed in the nineteenth century, provided many opportunities for the preacher to engage in humorous comments and to seek congregational reaction through jokes and banter. When the aim of the sermon is conversion and acceptance of the preacher's message, humor is the preacher's natural ally. In the midst of an impassioned oration, Henry Ward Beecher was interrupted by a drunk man in the balcony who began waving his arms and crowing like a rooster. Beecher stopped, took out his watch, and said, "What—morning already? I wouldn't have believed it, but the instincts of the lower animal are infallible" (Weisfeld, 36).

Dwight L. Moody* and Charles Finney* pioneered the practice of retelling biblical stories in contemporary, humorous style. Preaching on Luke 14:16–24, Moody said of the first man's excuse:

I can imagine this man was a very polite man and he said, "I wish you would take back this message to your Lord, that I would like to be at that feast. Tell him there is not a man in the kingdom that would rather be there than myself, but I am so situated that I can't come. Just tell him I have bought a piece of ground, and that I must needs go and see it." Weird time to go and see to land, wasn't it? Just at that supper time (Moody, 105).

The prominence of humor in African-American* preaching can be traced not only to nineteenth-century models but also to the way in which humor is effective in uplifting the downtrodden and deflating the proud. Because humor often arises in dialogue between persons, the dialogical quality of much African-American preaching is a natural birthplace for pulpit humor. When, early in his career, an attempt was made upon the life of Dr. Martin Luther King,* a newspaper account noted that if Dr. King had sneezed before he arrived at the hospital, he would have died. Dr. King seized upon the event as an illustration of the fragility of life. He picked up the phrase, "If I had sneezed," and in dialogue with the congregation, noted how he hung between life and death with nothing between the two but a sneeze. Humor enables us to treat deadly serious subjects without deadliness.

Sermonic humor is sometimes accused of being in bad taste or inappropriate to the serious intentions of Christian preaching. Because humor is powerful, preachers must use it with care. Jokes for the sake of jokes are rarely appropriate in sermons. Ridicule of ethnic groups, jokes about women, humor with sexual overtones—in short, what the world regards as funny—is not funny in church. Christians are most interested in humor that arises as a gracious by-product of our never-ending task of taking God a little more seriously and ourselves a little less so.

Humor is most effective and justified in preaching when (1) it arises out of interaction of the biblical text with the preacher and the congregation, (2) it is natural for the preacher's own style and personality, (3) the effects of the humor are congruent with the purposes of Christian communication, and (4) the liturgical, congregational, context is not violated by the humor.

Adams, D., *Humor in the American Pulpit from George Whitefield Through Henry Ward Beecher*, 1975. **Moody, D.**, *The Great Redemption*, 1888. **Niebuhr, R.**, *Discerning the Signs of the Times*, 1946. **Weisfeld, I. H.**, *The Pulpit Treasury of Wit and Humor*, 1950. **Willimon, W. H.**, *The Laugh Shall Be First: A Treasury of Religious Humor*, 1986; *The Last Laugh: A Second Treasury of Religious Humor*, 1991. WILLIAM H. WILLIMON

Illustrations. The master of sermonic illustration in the nineteenth century was Henry Ward Beecher,* founder of the famous lecture series at Yale in honor of his father Lyman Beecher. Henry Ward gave the first of those lectures at the peak of his career. At that time, he said to the ministers,

I can say, for your encouragement, that while illustrations are as natural to me as breathing, I use fifty now to one in the early years of my ministry. For the first six or eight years, perhaps, they were comparatively few and far apart. But I developed a tendency that was latent in me, and educated myself in that respect; and that, too, by study and practice, by hard thought, and by a great many trials, both with the pen, and extemporaneously by myself, when I was walking here and there. Whatever I have gained in that direction is largely the result of education. You need not, therefore, be discouraged if it does not come to you immediately (Beecher, 175).

Contemporaries of Beecher, Phillips Brooks* and Charles Haddon Spurgeon* were skilled illustrators in their own right. There are few famous twentieth-century preachers who are not also masters of the art of sermon illustration.

People like sermons that are well illustrated. Abstract, unadorned sermons tend to put audiences to sleep. Illustrations are important for their entertainment value, for they can capture and sustain interest in what the preacher has to say. At the same time, they can inform and help to explain; they can convince; they can inspire; and they can move to action.

The term *illustration* is a popular word

generally used to refer to the major forms of support for the ideas or assertions in sermons, although technically illustration is only one type of supportive material. In this article, illustration is used in the broader, popular sense.

Stories can be illustrations. Some stories are examples of the preacher's main assertions. By relating the factual incident of Rosa Parks's refusal to sit in the back of a bus because she was black, one might illustrate the assertion that an ordinary person can make a difference for social change. Other stories are comparisons, like the parable of the prophet Nathan that caused King David to face up to a sin that he had committed.

Preachers like Brooks, Fosdick,* and Theodore Ferris made extensive use of the hypothetical example. This illustration is made up: An imagined person exhibiting certain traits or attitudes in an imagined situation demonstrates the point the preacher is attempting to make. The preacher indicates that it is not an actual person or event described by introducing the example with such words as, "Here is a man who . . ." or "Consider a young woman who . . ." or "All of you have known youth who . . ."

The parables* of Jesus were of a special genre. They were stories, but they did not normally make one-to-one comparisons: their uniqueness lay in the surprise ending. Jesus' parables, as Frederick Buechner has said, were a kind of "holy joke." Unlike the illustration of a point, however, the true parable operates as a metaphor, which combines likeness and unlikeness. The disjunction of the two produces a shock in the hearer.

Some illustrations are as swift as an arrow. They may be only a sentence, a phrase, or even one word. But like an arrow that has reached its target, they stick. We remember *similes* such as, "Though your sins are like scarlet, they shall be like snow" or "The angry father bore down on his trembling neighbor like a Mack truck." An extended simile, an explicit comparison, or an *analogy* helps to clarify something with which it is compared, using several points of comparison, such as, "The human body is like a machine: It has to have fuel; it must be lubricated; it responds to atmospheric changes; it needs repeated fine-tuning." Similes and analogies are explicit comparisons.

Metaphors, also, are comparisons, but they are implied comparisons, like "The headline screamed its message" or "He was caught up in a maelstrom of memories."

In the same way, analogy is related to both simile and *allegory:* In allegory there are several points of implied comparisons. A well-known example is John Bunyan's* *Pilgrim's Progress,* which shows Christian's pilgrimage from the City of Destruction to the Celestial City.

General examples and specific examples can demonstrate the content of an idea or assertion more or less concretely. *General examples* describe the meaning of this sentence: Different people look for different things when buying a car—some are attracted by name and reliability; others, by color, speed, economy, safety, or profile." *Specific examples* ground an idea more deeply in reality by citing names, dates, times, places, and incidents. The sentence "The eighteenth century was a time of creative national turbulence" can be exemplified (or illustrated) specifically in this way: "General George Washington led the colonists to victory in the American Revolution of 1776. About the same time, the French entered a new era with their slogan 'Liberty, Equality, Fraternity.'" There is no absolute line of demarcation between the general and the specific: They often merge.

Testimony may play a desirable supportive role when used to bolster an argument, to avoid a debate, or to say something more graphically, more movingly, or more memorably. Testimony may range from a brief pithy statement like General Sherman's words "War is hell" to an article in the Constitution of the United States of America or a stanza from "Amazing Grace." Two criteria should rule: recognition by the hearers of the authority of the person quoted in a line of argument and appropriateness to the subject when testimony is used for purposes other than argument.

Illustrations should be chosen to suit the dominant aim of the sermon. A sermon designed to explain or inform will employ similes, analogies, and examples—all with the purpose of achieving understanding. A sermon designed to convince will employ the same types of illustrations in order to gain clarity of understanding *plus* belief or conviction. A sermon designed to inspire or comfort will employ stories of struggle and triumph, of faith and hope—specific instances—that touch the emotions. A sermon designed to motivate toward overt action or commitment may need the armamentarium of types of illustration.

In using illustrations, the preacher ought to observe these caveats: Never tell another person's experience as if it happened to you. Never represent as true any story that is not true. Avoid thinly veiled true stories that might hurt or embarrass people in the present or in a former parish. Always check your facts. When using fiction or fantasy as illustration, be sure that the material possesses verisimilitude—likeness to truth—so that the hearers can identify with the material.

Where can the preacher find good illustrations? This question usually refers to stories, but it should include various types of material. The Bible is the most obvious source. Georges Polti, citing Goethe, identified thirty-six types of plot in literature. All thirty-six dramatic situations can be found in the Bible. Also, personal experience and observation, reading, and pastoral work are rich resources. It is important to keep a journal or file of these treasures. Elaborate indexing is not necessary, but faithful, regular recording of illustrations *is* necessary. Preachers lose thousands of potential illustrations simply because they do not write them down.

Every generation tends to have its own stylistic preferences in the use of illustrations. Some preachers, however, with open and discriminating minds have enriched their sermons by studying the techniques that succeeded in previous times. Fosdick* reported on how he learned to preach:

I . . . began to see how much the old preachers had to teach us. At their best they did achieve results. Their sermons were appeals to the jury and they got decisions. They knew where the great motives were and appealed to them with conclusive power. I began studying sermons of men like Phillips Brooks—not merely reading them, but analyzing sentence by sentence the steps they took toward working in their auditors the miracles they often did achieve . . . (Fosdick, 100).

Fosdick, however, went beyond his mentor Brooks, as every apprentice preacher must do. Exegesis of the audience is as important as exegesis of the biblical text. Illustrations should be in tune with the times and with the personality of the congregation. Beecher considered it desirable to use a variety of illustrations in order to reach different classes of people in the same audience.

If there is a difference in the types of illustrations today, the difference is likely to be weighted toward illustrations more suitable to inductive* sermons than to deductive sermons. In any case, the way illustrations are used is largely a matter of taste, and that criterion is established by the preacher's total intellectual, spiritual, and cultural experience (*see* Figures of Speech).

Beecher, H. W., "Rhetorical Illustrations," *Yale Lectures on Preaching*, 1872. **Cox, J. W.,** *Preaching: A Comprehensive Approach to the Design and Delivery of Sermons*, 1985. **Ferguson, C. W.,** *Say It with Words*, 1939. **Fosdick, H. E.,** "Learning to Preach," *The Living of These Days*, 1956.

JAMES W. COX

Imagination. Imagination is a valuable asset to a preacher, a way of knowing, or a type of creative thought that is in contrast to the creativity of logic. Rather than proceeding in linear fashion ("if *a* and *b*, then *c* "), imagination proceeds by making a lateral leap from one point to another (for instance, discerning similarity in dissimilarity or dissimilarity in similarity). All preachers have imagination, but some may not trust it or know how to develop it.

Imagination for preaching is best understood in at least three ways: prophetic, ethical (or communal), and poetic (or interpretive):

1. In its prophetic function, imagination discerns the discrepancy between God's intentions for the world, as revealed in scripture, and the world as it actually is. Prophetic imagination has a delimiting function, refusing to accept the limits the world holds as absolute or the limits we would place on God's power, seeking the possible in the impossible and the actual, the new in the old, the breaking in of God's realm in the midst of the mundane.

Walter Brueggemann has argued that prophecy need not be restricted to the big issues of the day but may be recognized whenever an alternate to the *status quo* is imagined. Similarly, prophecy should not be conceived narrowly as the pronouncement of doom. Every Sunday is a celebration of the resurrection. Preaching that employs prophetic imagination will dream the dreams of the church, not simply portray events and people as they are. By envisioning the reality God wills, in the manner of Martin Luther King Jr.,* in his "I Have a Dream" address, reality begins to happen (*see* Prophetic Preaching).

2. Ethical (or communal) imagination allows people to empathize with others, respecting who they are and entering into their suffering. Jesus spoke of this in the great commandment (Mark 12:29–31). The needs of others become one's own, and genuine community of the self-giving sort that Christ enables becomes possible. Even as ethical imagination opens responsible living, it has a limiting function. It places community limitations on individual appetite or an individual com-

munity's appetite for the benefit of all God's children. It shatters individual illusions and self-obsession. It refuses to allow present actions to be disengaged from past and future, projecting onto both consequences of actions and required healing or prevention. Ethical imagination in preaching points to ethical boundaries or the results of those boundaries having been crossed. It is at the same time compassionate expression with wide-open spaces of salvation (*see* Ethics).

3. Poetic (or interpretive) imagination may be understood more technically as a language process that creates (or discerns) a particular act of juxtaposition within language such as is found, for instance, in metaphor, simile, symbol, paradox, and parable (*see* Figures of Speech). Imagination is the bringing into relationship of two ideas that normally would not be connected. In doing this, a spark of new meaning is produced. In 1 Corinthians 15:55, the ideas of death and serpent are creatively united in the metaphor "Where, O death, is your sting?" In most of Jesus' parables,* the idea of the realm of God is brought together with a simple story about mundane reality.

Samuel Taylor Coleridge, the romantic poet and theologian, called this process of imagination, "the reconciliation of opposites." He influenced Horace Bushnell, who said that language is completely metaphoric; that strictly literal interpretation of the Bible is impossible (which anticipates Paul Tillich); that biblical texts have many meanings; that imagination is essential for theology; and that Christ is "the metaphor of God's last metaphor" (Cherry, 101). Sallie McFague has called Jesus "*the* parable of God" (McFague, 78).

The growing appreciation of the parables of Jesus has helped stimulate recent theological and homiletical interest in metaphor, parable, and story. Another source of homiletical ferment is the theory of organicism in art, which is traceable to the early nineteenth-century romantic movement. To the romantics, poetry is not content that fills a predetermined form like a sonnet. Rather, art grows according to its own internal principles of unity. It has a life of its own. Form and content are related to one another under the guidance of the poet's imagination.

The implications of the organic theory of art for preaching were enormous, although they took almost 150 years to be fully felt. Sermon form* and structure were assumed to be an adaptation of the Puritan "plain style" sermon, moving from brief exposition of the biblical text (often just a verse) to development of the doctrine in propositional manner to application. The Lutheran homiletician H. Grady Davis* pioneered the view that the central idea of the sermon is an idea that grows and the entire sermon develops organically like a tree. Underpinning Davis's organic sermon theory was the insight that biblical pericopes often have organic unity and that texts need to be understood in relation to their contexts and culture.

Charles L. Rice advocated a sermonic form that was heavily weighted toward narrative and art. Fred Craddock* identified the new approach as inductive* rather than deductive, and called for greater equality of emphasis on form and content. Eugene L. Lowry encouraged preachers to understand sermons as plot with their own specific internal movements.

In recent years, there has been increased attention to metaphor, parable, and particularly to the function of story in evoking experience and bringing people to an encounter with each other and with God (*see* Narrative Preaching). Much less attention has been paid to how imagination functions in nonnarrative sermonic forms. Idea-centered preaching is in need of reform but in some homiletical theory is rejected outright. This rejection is unwarranted because imagination or creativity is not limited to one genre. Similarly, not all use of story form demonstrates imagination. Much more work on imagination is needed to disclose new opportunities within a wide array of sermon forms.

Preachers wanting to increase their own use of imagination in preaching might begin with the three types of imagination, paying attention to some of the following:

1. Preaching is an action God uses to put right the world. Our preaching is most appropriate when events of the entire world are deemed worthy of bringing into focus before God's Word. Preaching that concentrates too much on the individual, on the congregation, on the local region, or even on the nation has two effects: (a) it narrows Christian imagination, and (b) it presents God as small and powerless before the tumult of our times.

2. Prophetic imagination not only names the sin but also moves toward hope. Often the former is easier than the latter. It may be difficult to find the right story or illustration* to help present the truth of the gospel. Preachers in such circumstances can act responsibly and creatively by painting a picture for the congregation of what a situation might look like if God's will were being done.

3. Excessive abstraction can be a sign of imagination that is stifled. Preaching ethics as intellectual ideas or preaching a remote, abstract God can be the result. One way of avoiding excessive abstraction can be to think in terms of human relationships and interaction. Preaching is incarnational. Through the words of the preacher, people who are involved in tough ethical situations can be introduced to the congregation (protecting identities where necessary). Preachers who imaginatively empathize with the worst persons in stories help to open pastoral relationships with those who also identify with the worst.

4. Poetic imagination, when applied to the interpretive task, looks at every biblical text as having many possible meanings, correct and incorrect, strong and weak, determined largely by one's faith and traditions. Similarly, when considering for sermonic use any situation in the world, there are many ways of seeing or

describing what takes place. The recognition that every story is about many things can be the starting place for exciting links between the biblical text, the world, and doctrines that will facilitate an experience of God through preaching.

Cherry, C., ed., *Horace Bushnell: Sermons*, 1985. **Kearney, R.,** *Poetics of Imagining: From Husserl to Lyotard*, 1991. **Lowry, E. L.,** *The Homiletical Plot*, 1980. **Lynch, W. F., S.J.,** *Christ and Apollo: The Dimensions of the Literary Imagination*, 1975. **McFague, S.,** *Speaking in Parables*, 1978. **Riegert, E. R.,** *Imaginative Shock: Preaching and Metaphor*, 1990. **Rice, C. L.,** *Interpretation and Imagination*, 1970. **Troeger, T. H.,** *Imagining a Sermon*, 1990. **Wilson, P. S.,** *Imagination of the Heart: New Understandings in Preaching*, 1988.   PAUL SCOTT WILSON

Inclusive Language.

Inclusive language is a term used since the 1970s to denote language that does not denigrate or relegate to lower hierarchies of being those who are neither white nor male. "Inclusive" means language that gives women an equal status with men. Guidelines for inclusive language always also warn against using language to denigrate other races and cultures. Until the latter part of the 1970s, it applied mostly to language that referred to human beings, but since the 1980s, it has tended to cover imagery and pronouns about God as well. The words "man," "men," and "mankind," defined by prescriptive dictionaries (before *Webster's Third International Dictionary*) as meaning both men and women, no longer are taken by many to mean both. Furthermore, studies have demonstrated that the traditional "he" pronoun, the singular personal pronoun that tradition claimed to refer to both men and women in the group, did not evoke females in the minds of listeners or readers. In English it is possible to use feminine images for human beings or God and then, by the old rules, have to resort to the male pronoun, as in "Man is the animal that hunts, gathers, and breast-feeds his children." Analysts of language would say

that all of these terms, even pronouns, had been used metaphorically—as in synecdoche, a figure of speech* that uses a part for the whole—to refer to both males and females in the past but with the rise of feminist consciousness, were no longer heard metaphorically but literally.

Since the 1970s the case has been made more vigorously than in the past, though it is not the first time speakers and writers of English have noticed this problem, especially in regard to the word "he" as a common referent to both male and female. From Chaucer on, English writers have struggled with this difficulty. The *Oxford English Dictionary* records that many distinguished writers of English, from Chaucer to Shakespeare, through Dryden and George Bernard Shaw, dispensed with formal prescriptive grammar when using the personal pronoun for both male and female and resorted to the common plural pronouns "they," "them," and "their" to refer to one person, as in "Would everyone pick up their needles?" This would not pass muster with strict grammarians, especially after the Enlightenment and the triumph of a logical grammar in English largely imposed by men with a notion of grammar that they had learned in Latin studies. These rules, however, have fallen by the wayside, especially with the rise of descriptive grammars and dictionaries that describe the actual language usage in practice rather than prescribing the ideal, correct language.

At first, efforts to change church language were focused on liturgical and hymnological resources, resulting in massive revisions of hymnals and liturgical services, especially in regard to the naming of human beings and for the name of God. The original criticism was of the notion of God the Father, but this has broadened for some feminists who can no longer find themselves within the Christian family, given the male nature of God in Christianity. For most Christian feminists, this discussion, however, has subsided since the mid-1980s when the United Methodist hymnal committee chose not to dispense entirely with the traditional name. Preachers can, because of the nature of their craft, explore a wider range of images for both humans and God than are possible in traditional, printed formulas because preaching is always for the oral occasion.

Those who are serious about using inclusive language should understand its various levels and the strong feelings the use or nonuse of inclusive language in the pulpit can engender. Most agree today that "men" and "brothers" no longer work as synecdoches for both men and women since it is understood that "he" no longer embraces (as the old grammarians once said) both male and female. "Mankind" is frowned upon by many, especially feminists, though *The New York Times* and other such arbiters of taste and language do not shun this word.

In order genuinely to engage the lives and attentions of all of their listeners, preachers attempt to use illustrations and stories that show how the gospel makes sense for both men and women. Thus, the preacher will not always use only images from traditionally male or female occupations and interests—for instance, sports images to appeal to men and housekeeping images to appeal to women. These stereotypes are changing, and the criteria for judgment are in flux.

One can use a variety of images for God that surprise and evoke new and different feelings in the hearers. Yet there are dangers here as well. If mothers are always gentle and fathers always strict and commanding, and these images are used to describe God with no critical imagination, one will have succeeded only in projecting sexual stereotypes into the cosmos.

All speakers want to reach their audiences. In using images and parables to describe God, the preacher has opportunities to explore the character of God by creating images that are not expected or usual. The greatest remaining difficulty is the pronoun for God. Many feminists reject "he" for God; others accept it only in traditional texts. Those opposed to femi-

nist concerns will insist on the use of "he." In some ways this has become a new shibboleth, and preachers are well advised to discover what the norms are in the congregation (which may have strict rules on this). Individual congregations and publishing houses, as well as national denominations, frequently have inclusive-language guidelines to be followed by the members of the organization. Every preacher would be wise to inquire after them (*see* Feminist Preaching).

Eller, V., *The Language of Canaan and the Grammar of Feminism*, 1982. **Jenson, R.,** *The Triune Identity: God According to the Gospel*, 1982.   GRACIA GRINDAL

Inductive Preaching.

Inductive preaching is a method of preaching popularized by Fred Craddock* that has exercised significant influence on homiletical theory and practice since the 1970s. As a form of communication, the inductive method represents a challenge to traditional "deductive" preaching, which announces general, propositional conclusions and then breaks them down into various points and exhortations. As an alternative to this kind of deduction, the inductive method begins with the particulars of human experience and moves toward the often surprising conclusions of the gospel. In this process the preacher does not simply deposit conclusions in the hearers' minds but enables the congregation to participate actively in the movement and meaning of the sermon. Inductive movement encourages the listeners to think their own thoughts, feel their own feelings, draw their own conclusions, and make their own decisions so they will have ownership of the message. Preaching becomes the shared responsibility of preacher and congregation (*see* Form).

The term "inductive" is thus not used with scientific or logical precision in contemporary homiletics. Rather, "inductive method" simply highlights a specific kind of movement in the sermon—a movement from particular experiences to general conclusions. The central image of the sermon is that of a trip on which preacher and congregation travel together toward an eagerly anticipated destination, in contrast to deductive preaching, wherein the preacher authoritatively announces the destination at the beginning of the sermon and excludes the congregation from the trip altogether.

Understood in this broad sense, inductive preaching has influenced the development of narrative* preaching and is closely related to it. Stories specialize in the particular, which is central to inductive preaching. Moreover, inductive preaching, even without the presence of specific stories, tends to move like a good story, inviting the congregation to travel along with the preacher. Consequently, although inductive and narrative preaching should not be equated, there are important affinities between them.

Behind the inductive method lies the issue of authority. Craddock developed the method during the 1960s at a time when the traditional authority of the Christian pulpit was being seriously challenged in American culture. Most significant was the issue of the preacher's authority, as the title of Craddock's book, *As One Without Authority*, reveals. In inductive preaching, authority is not located with the preacher, making conclusive, authoritative pronouncements from the pulpit. Rather, authority is located in the interaction between the congregation and the biblical text. However, with inductive preaching's emphasis on human experience and individual response, the danger always exists that the biblical text will become secondary and the real authority will become the experience of individual hearers, which both precedes and verifies the message of scripture.

Biblically, Jesus' parables* are often cited as the primary exemplars of inductive preaching. Like inductive preaching, the parables begin with the concrete particulars of human life, move like a story, invite the participation of the hearers, and require the hearers to draw their own conclusions. Obviously, there are similarities between inductive preaching and the parables. However, the dissimilarities are also significant. At the heart of the parables, unlike in inductive preaching, there is often a radical *discontinuity* between Jesus' message and human experience. In addition, in contrast to inductive preaching, the parables are intimately related to the authority of the speaker, Jesus, apart from whom the parables are frequently little more than nonsensical. Any simplistic equation of the parables with inductive preaching would be inappropriate.

Although inductive preaching marked a new direction in contemporary homiletics, the inductive method is not new, even in rhetorical and homiletical practice. The roots of inductive preaching lie most immediately in modern science. Describing the modern scientific method as one of "inductive inquiry and personal verification," Deane William Ferm has in fact provided a nice description of inductive preaching (Ferm, 60). Using the inductive method, the preacher invites the hearers into a kind of "inductive inquiry" that moves toward "personal verification" of the sermon's message. Indeed, Craddock's method was shaped by his own practice of scientific, historical-critical exegesis, which he sought to recapture in the movement of the sermon. In addition, over two centuries earlier a homiletical method with similarities to inductive preaching can be found in the first modern rhetoric, the *Dialogues* of François Fénelon,* which was influenced by the development of seventeenth-century experimental science. Although inadequately examined, the relationship between modern science and inductive preaching is significant.

In light of changes in scientific thought in recent years, which have emphasized the communal paradigms or frameworks within which purportedly inductive inquiry takes place, some rethinking of inductive preaching is required. Naive confidence in individual experience and verification is no longer a possibility. Rather, the larger theological, ecclesial, and cultural paradigms within which both exegetical and homiletical induction occur require further exploration.

Rhetorically, inductive movement has also existed in some form for a long time. As was already noted, in the early eighteenth century François Fénelon proposed a homiletical method which, while stopping short of contemporary inductive preaching, nevertheless possessed some similarities to this newer homiletical method. Moreover, two thousand years earlier, Aristotle, in his *Rhetoric*, had developed a form of inductive rhetorical movement. According to Aristotle, rhetorical argument always begins with the *endoxa*, the "common sense" or common beliefs of the hearers; rhetoric begins, in contemporary idiom, "where the people are." Grounded in these common sense truths, rhetorical argument moves inductive fashion to new conclusions through a form of argument that emphasizes probabilities more than rigid syllogisms. Although Aristotle's emphasis on rational argument and persuasion is very different from the more experiential emphasis of inductive preaching, the seeds of inductive preaching can be found in Aristotle's own rhetorical theory (*see* Rhetoric).

Although some critical issues remain for inductive preaching, this homiletical method unquestionably helped revive the theory and practice of preaching at the beginning of the 1970s. By highlighting the communicative significance of sermonic movement, the centrality of particularity and concreteness, and the importance of congregational participation in the sermon, inductive preaching has made and continues to make an important contribution to homiletics today.

Aristotle, *Rhetoric,* trans. W. R. Roberts, *The Rhetoric and the Poetics of Aristotle,* ed. F. Solmsen, 1954. **Craddock, F.,** *As One Without Authority: Essays on Inductive Preaching,* 3d ed., 1979. **Fénelon, F.,** *Three Dialogues on Pulpit Eloquence,* trans. S. J. Eales, 1717, 1909. **Ferm, Deane William,** "American Protestant Theology, 1900–1970," *Religion in Life* 44 (Spring 1975).

Lewis, R., and **G. Lewis,** *Inductive Preaching: Helping People Listen,* 1983. **Lischer, R.,** *Theories of Preaching: Selected Readings in the Homiletical Tradition,* 1987.

CHARLES L. CAMPBELL

Introductions and Conclusions

Introductions. The advice of Cicero about introductions has often been embellished but hardly improved: "Arouse interest, secure favor, and prepare to lead." The advice is basic and appropriate because if the "lead statements" to the sermon do not induce the hearer to desire more and remain open for more, then the hearing is foiled, and the point of it all fails. A well-prepared and strategically handled introduction stirs listener interest, establishes a relation between preacher and hearer, and offers promise for the agreed togetherness.

In seeking to arouse interest, the preacher can take a cue from the nature of the occasion, suggest a question raised by the textual basis of the sermon, or perhaps relate how and why the text was chosen. Projecting a sense of initiative, the preacher can create a mood of anticipation by launching into an illustration that will bring the text into focus, by using a literary reference that brings some aspect of the text into clear view, or perhaps by referring to a previous sermon. There are other ways to begin, but whatever method is utilized, the introduction should establish contact with the hearers and give promise that "the best is yet to be." Aptly planned, briefly fulfilled, stimulating in effect, the *introduction* should do what the term suggests— provide an initial clue to the aim and direction of the sermon. It can be related to the logic of the text and/or the subject or theme being treated. If the form of the sermon is the preacher's plan for what is to be said, then the introduction to the sermon should reflect some aspect of that plan; it should provide directional focus as the sermon begins.

Among the many types of introductions

on record in the long history of the preaching task, several provide promise when planned wisely:

1. a window-view into the text, either by reference to comparable circumstances or comment on the nature of the textual form;
2. life-situation tie-in, by which the dynamic of a text is highlighted for eager hearers;
3. simple orientation, with a brief but pointed statement of *why* the text was chosen;
4. raising of a question that needs to be answered from biblical wisdom;
5. dramatized exposition in which predetermined materials are represented, moving from story levels to applied insights;
6. directional announcement about the "journey" to be taken in dealing with the text or theme;
7. propositional statement that voices a prophetic concern;
8. statement of human need to which the announced text offers hope and help;
9. historical account that leads to the wisdom and timeliness of the biblical text;
10. reference to current happening (local, national, international) that excites interest in the biblical message.

All of the types listed above lead to treatment of scripture that is basic for Christian preaching and for sustained Christian living. Whatever type is preferred, it is important that the introduction be pertinent, grant perspective, and lead to the main issue of the sermon itself.

Conclusions. The conclusion is that part of the sermon that rounds out and completes the line of purpose that runs through it. If there are any loose ends left, the conclusion should tie them together. If there is an action or response sought through the sermon, the conclusion should seek to gain it. The conclusion takes what has been launched on the sea of the hearers' thoughts and brings it all to port, tying it to the dock of their will.

A sermon conclusion should be related to what the sermon was designed to do. Specific sermons have immediate goals, and these goals determine the focus and form of individual sermons at a given time. A sermon can be preached to offer a *solution* to a problem. A fitting conclusion to such a sermon will give that solution final focus for ready use. If a sermon is preached to *instruct* in an essential doctrine, then the meaning and import of that teaching should be highlighted to effect the hearers' understanding and faith. If a sermon is preached to *prescribe a cure* for some spiritual or social ill, then the sermonic conclusion may be an appeal for trusting acceptance of what has been prescribed, with added caution voiced about the dangers of neglect or delay in doing so. A sermon may be preached in *support of a cause*, in which case the conclusion should be an arousing call to action. Still another sermon will be preached to *strengthen* people who are burdened; an apt conclusion would generate a mood of encouragement and an awareness of renewed inward strength and courage to "keep on keeping on." The particular purpose of any sermon should be reflected in the design used to achieve its end, and an apt conclusion is part of that design.

The conclusion of the sermon provides the preacher with the final opportunity for applying its truth to the hearers' lives. A rightly shaped sermon will have application points scattered throughout, but the final application of truth is usually expected as the sermon concludes. Preaching is deliberative: It uses both information and inspiration to achieve its end, which is *persuasion.* All rightful handling of truth in preaching is in the end motivational.

Given the motivational concern in preaching, the final application of truth can be shared by using any one or a combination of several methods. The sermon may end with a pointed statement or an applied call, or it can seek its end by the recital of some gripping illustration or testimony. Usually, the motivational concern is shared by creating a *climax of impression* that brings the hearers into a high state of awareness about the meaning of what has been heard and experienced. In this way, persuasion engages the hearers at the levels of reason and emotion, since preaching at its best is a whole-person action that makes a whole-person claim upon others.

There are several rhetorical levels on which a sermon may be brought to a conclusion. One is the *simplified* conclusion, which involves a direct statement about the significance of acting on the message one has heard. Another level is the *amplified* conclusion, which reinforces the point of the message by dramatic examples of outcomes. A third is the *dignified* conclusion, a method characteristic in the African-American* preaching tradition. The dignified conclusion involves planned cadence of hymn verses, strategically ordered words, and climax-building phrases, so that the sermon may crescendo in a passionately felt mood of involvement with the truth.

The cadence ending dignifies the conclusion of the sermon. Whether the preacher has treated an argument, theme, story, or single text, the use of cadence at the end heightens the emotional impact of the event. It appeals to the imagination by means of engaging recitation and rhythmic impact. The cadence ending also heightens the impact of the sermon because it allows the sermon insight to be sensed at a new level of consciousness. Facts, faith, and feeling all blend at a point beyond argument. The result is an intensely felt experience of religious celebration. Rightly achieved, the cadence is not an obstruction but an outgrowth of the sermon theme. It is not an appendage but a celebrative response by the preacher to the truth which has been shared. The cadence intensifies dramatic action with dignity and depth, leaving much that is remembered by the *total* self (*see* Form).

Buttrick, D. G., *Homiletic: Moves and Structures*, 1987. Demaray, D. E., *An Introduction to Homiletics*, 2d ed., 1990. Mitchell,

H. H., *Black Preaching: The Recovery of a Powerful Art*, 1990.   JAMES EARL MASSEY

Itinerant and Open-Air Preaching.

Itinerant preaching denotes the custom of preaching by traveling (*itinerans*) evangelists or preachers, and open-air preaching denotes the closely related custom of preaching outside of the context of Christian churches or other regularly appointed places for worship.

Although Jesus sometimes spoke in synagogues (Mark 6:2) as he "went about among the villages teaching" (Mark 6:6), he also spoke in the open air, as on the occasion of the Sermon on the Mount. Jesus explicitly sent his disciples out to proclaim the good news of the kingdom, with specific instructions on how they were to conduct their itinerant ministry (Mark 6:7–13). The ministry of the apostle Paul shows a similar pattern of teaching while journeying about the Mediterranean, sometimes speaking in synagogues (Acts 18:4; 19:8) but on other occasions speaking in the open air or marketplaces (Acts 17:16–34).

The Pauline epistles consistently refer to the offices of apostles and prophets (Rom. 12:6; 1 Cor. 12:28; Eph. 4:11), both of which seem to have denoted traveling teachers, as indeed Paul's own self-understanding as apostle suggests. Some early Christian communities gave preference to the local offices of deacons and presbyter-bishops (the Pastoral epistles), and these developed in the early second century into the threefold orders of deacons, presbyters, and bishops (seen clearly in Ignatius of Antioch). But in other communities the itinerant offices of apostles and prophets persisted into the second century. The so-called *Didache* or *Teaching of the Twelve Apostles* illustrates this model of community, in which traveling teachers were to be carefully tested (*Didache* 11) but, once tested, had a degree of authority over local deacons and presbyter-bishops (*Didache* 10, where the instructions for the Eucharist conclude with a note that prophets may celebrate Eucharist as they will).

The Montanist movement (late second and early third centuries) also had itinerant prophets who understood themselves as fulfilling the ancient offices mentioned in the New Testament. But the identification of Montanism as eccentric (at best) or even heretical shows that by the end of the second century local offices had prevailed over itinerant ones, and from this time itinerant and open-air preaching grew rare in the life of the church. One could argue that the continuing office of *chorepiskopos,* a bishop assigned to rural areas, functioned in some senses as an itinerant teacher beyond the third century.

Both itinerant and open-air preaching emerged in Europe in the Middle Ages with the rise of a number of religious movements in the twelfth and thirteenth centuries. Such twelfth-century groups as *Humiliati* and Waldensians spread through southern France and northern Italy by wandering preachers. A similar pattern appeared early in the thirteenth century with the rise of the mendicant orders of Dominicans* (the "Order of Preachers") and Franciscans.* Both of these groups held itinerant preaching and teaching to be part of their distinctive missions. Since preaching was not customary in parish churches in the Middle Ages, the presence of itinerants at fairs or market days provided one of the few occasions when laity could be exposed to Christian teaching.

Because the earliest of Protestant Reformers tended to focus on the reform of specific principalities and their existing churches, itinerant preaching as such did not appear among Protestants through the middle of the sixteenth century. Late in that century, however, English Puritans* began to sponsor itinerant lecturers who would give talks, sometimes in parish churches but often in homes or in the open air. A distinct tradition of open-air preaching emerged among the Presbyterians of Scotland and Northern Ireland in the 1630s, associated with quarterly Eucharists, "sacramental seasons," where the "order of salvation" would be rehearsed through several days of preaching. Because of the size of the crowds at first, then because of the closing of parish churches to Covenanters during the Interregnum, these Scots-Irish celebrations were often carried on in large barns or out of doors.

A new tradition of itinerant and open-air preaching was born in the eighteenth century and characterized the Evangelical Revival of that age. The first three itinerants of the eighteenth-century Revival were Anglicans. Beginning in late December of 1735 with the cottage teaching of Welsh schoolmaster and layman Howell Harris in Trevecka, the practice was emulated early in 1739 by George Whitefield,* who began to attract considerable crowds and raised itineracy to the level of a transatlantic phenomenon. Whitefield's earliest open-air preaching, near Bristol, was directly observed by John Wesley,* who on April 2, 1739, also took up the practice. Itinerant preaching, including preaching by laypersons (1740s) and women (1770s) became a distinctive characteristic of the Methodist movement and allowed the Methodists considerable flexibility in following the movement of British society to new industrial cities and suburbs growing as a result of the Industrial Revolution.

In North America, both the traditions of open-air preaching associated with Scots-Irish Presbyterian "sacramental seasons" and the tradition of Anglican Evangelical itinerants appeared in the first "Great Awakening" of the eighteenth century. Presbyterians in the Middle Colonies would carry on preaching at sacramental celebrations, leading in the 1790s to the development of "camp meetings" on the Appalachian frontier. George Whitefield preached itinerantly throughout the American colonies, and by the 1760s Methodist itinerants appointed by John Wesley were active in North America. Just as itinerant preaching had given

British Methodists the flexibility to follow the Industrial Revolution, so it gave American Methodists an important degree of flexibility to follow the expanding American frontier. By the early nineteenth century, these two strands of open-air and itinerant preaching had merged, with Methodists adopting camp meetings enthusiastically. Late in the nineteenth century, with increasing urbanization in North America, frontier camp meetings gave way to urban revivals, although revivalists such as D. L. Moody* (now with elaborate evangelistic associations) could be considered itinerants. At about the same time, North American Methodists, now more settled than earlier, began more and more to "station" their preachers, leaving "itineracy" as a term that expressed only their unique system of appointing pastors but no longer referring to the preachers' literally traveling weekly from one place to another.

In the twentieth century, itinerant and open-air preaching have been associated with the rise of Pentecostalism in the developing countries of less industrialized nations. There have been some attempts to revive older traditions of itinerant and open-air preaching, such as the public speaking of Methodist Donald Soper* in Speaker's Corner in London. With the transition to a video-oriented culture and the widespread availability of radio and television broadcasting, though, itinerant and open-air preaching seem now to be relics of a bygone era (see History of Preaching; Evangelism; Revivals).

TED A. CAMPBELL

Iwand, Hans Joachim. (1899–1960) Hans Iwand was a leading Luther scholar and theologian of the "Confessing Church" in the German church struggle from 1933 on. After that, he was theologically close to Karl Barth,* although he also criticized Barth, reminding the theological community of Martin Luther's* distinction between law and gospel.* In 1935, Iwand was dismissed from his teaching position in Riga. He then educated theologians of the "Confessing Church" in an illegal seminary. Forbidden to speak in public, Iwand was arrested and later served as a pastor in Dortmund until the end of the war.

In 1945 he was called to Göttingen as Professor of Systematic Theology, and in 1952 to Bonn. In 1945, he founded the "Göttingen Sermon-Meditations" ("Göttinger Predigt-Meditationen"/GPM). These printed resources were to help the pastors who had lost their books during the war or, through being forced to flee, were searching for a new spiritual orientation. Iwand—who was himself a charismatic preacher—believed preaching to be the most important and most difficult task of the church: the preaching of the promise and the directive of God to guide the Christian community in the spiritual and political situation of this time. Iwand understood his "sermon-meditations" as guides for preaching. The sermon-meditation is founded on a short exegesis* and is explicated as a thorough systematic-theological (dogmatic and ethical) reflection. It then makes suggestions for the shaping of worship, not to remove the responsibility of the pastor for preparation but to enable the pastor to be theologically responsible in his or her preaching. The historical-critical exegesis is accompanied by practical devotional exegesis. The meditation reflects the biblical text in its theological context and perceives it as God's address to the people. The sermon-meditation is therefore not founded on psychological techniques of soul-searching and contemplation, nor does it strive to provide the listeners with a religious experience. Rather, it reflects on the text's own character, which leads to its proclamation. Therefore the sermon meditation concentrates on what the text has to say (narrating, teaching, encouraging, and warning) and on that which God wishes to mediate to the people of today with the "Word within the words."

The biblical texts to be meditated upon are from the designated lectionary for the German Protestant Church. The bond with the lectionary favors "text-preaching" as opposed to "theme-preaching," in which an attractive motto is linked to a chosen text. The preference for text preaching goes back to dialectical theology's critique (Karl Barth,* Rudolf Bultmann,* Emil Brunner) of the theme-preaching of liberal theology. In dialectic theology, all theology is in itself a way from text to sermon. It is a combination of theological exegesis, insights from church history, systematic theology, and practical theology. This theological integration is concentrated in the sermon-meditation as Iwand understood and promoted it.

Iwand could create the sermon meditation because of the consensus in the theological faculty of the University of Göttingen. The department at that time (Gerhard von Rad, Günther Bornkamm, Joachim Jeremias, Ernst Wolf, Otto Weber) was totally committed to dialectical theology. Thus, a noteworthy theological unity was reached in the early issues of the preaching-meditations, which enabled Iwand to call on his colleagues in the department. Later those making contributions to the preaching-meditations were expanded to include numerous theologians who were close to this concept of theology and preaching: Hans Walter Wolff, Walther Zimmerli, Ernst Käsemann, Hermann Diem, Helmut Gollwitzer, and others. The list of contributors to the GPM is still representative of the kerygma-oriented German Protestant theology today. Iwand had worked since the end of World War II for the overcoming of political divisions, especially for the reconciliation of the Germans with their eastern neighbors. Therefore, he also attracted contributors from Czechoslovakia, Hungary, and Estonia.

From 1954 on, the GPM was distributed in the German Democratic Republic, the only theological journal that could legally reach through the iron curtain.

Iwand welcomed this as a symbol of theological cooperation crossing political borders and as a political sign. "We hope that the meditations will help to strengthen our old program—the unity of the message of the *one* gospel in the flux of state and society forms." Later difficulties led to the parallel publication of an East German journal *Protestant Sermon-Meditations* (published in East Berlin), in which particular articles from the GPM were published. Since 1990 these preaching-meditations have again been united with the GPM.

From 1939–1960, Iwand wrote 150 sermon-meditations of which about 110 appeared in the GPM. After his death, they were collected into 2 volumes—his most important theological legacy.

Iwand, H. J., *Ausgewählte Predigten*, ed. H. Esser and H. Gollwitzer, *Werke* III, 1963; *Predigt-Meditationen*, 2 vols., I, 1963–1984; II, 1973.   GERHARD SAUTER

Jasper, John.

(1812–1901) James Weldon Johnson's portrait of "the old-time Negro preacher" as "an orator, and in good measure an actor" might have had in mind the former slave and freed preacher John Jasper, of whom a contemporary wrote, "He was a theatre within himself, with the stage crowded with actors. He was a battlefield—himself the general, the staff, the officers, the common soldiery, the thundering artillery and the rattling musketry. He was the preacher" (Hatcher, 9). Like George Whitefield* a century earlier, Jasper captivated huge audiences with his ability to dramatize the characters and events of the Bible; unlike Whitefield, who merely overcame his own humble origins and the connivance of his opponents, Jasper, an uneducated black man, won the approval and respect of nineteenth-century black and white southern audiences.

Jasper's story was typical of the slave and later freed preachers in the South. The son of an exhorter, Jasper grew up on a Virginia plantation. He was a slave, working in a tobacco factory in Richmond, when he underwent a classic conversion in which he became a "God-made" preacher. At the encouragement of his master, he began to preach around Richmond, Virginia, twenty-five years before the coming of freedom. At the age of sixty he fulfilled his life's ambition of building and pastoring a church, Sixth Mount Zion Baptist Church in Richmond, where he served until his death.

Although his grammar was, in his biographer's words, "a riot of errors," his ability to paint the picture of a biblical story was unparalleled among his peers. His narrative and metaphoric genius featured outrageous elaborations of the biblical account and an uncanny knack for dialogue. His biographer remembers Jasper's rendition of the first temptation:

"Nice garden you got there," he say in a admirin' way. "You got heap of nice apples over there." "Oh, yes, indeed," Eve replies. "We got lots of 'em." Eve spoke these words like she was proud to death 'cause the serpent like the garden. . . . "Can you eat all the apples you got over there?" "No, indeed," says Eve, "We can't eat 'em all. We got more than we can destroy to save our lives. They gettin' ripe all the time; we have just hogsheads of 'em."
"Oh, I didn't mean that," spoke the serpent, as if shocked by not being understood. "My point is, is you allowed to eat 'em all? . . ."
For a minute the woman jumped same as if somebody struck her a blow. The cold chills run down her back, and she look like she want to run, but somehow the eye of the serpent done got a charm on her. There was a struggle, a regular Bull Run battle, goin' on in her soul at that moment (Hatcher, 52–53, spelling altered).

His most famous sermon was "The Sun Do Move," which he preached around the country no fewer than 250 times. In it he "proved" that the sun rotates around the earth on the basis of Joshua 10:12–14 and, more important, that God is the Lord of all "laws." He told his audiences, "The sun was travelin' along there through the sky when the order come. He hitched his red ponies and made quite a call on the land of Gibeon" (Hatcher, 138, spelling altered; cf. Mitchell, 71). He concludes with a traditional evocation of heaven, which lies beyond the sun and stars: "The chariot that will come to take us to our Father's mansion will sweep out by them flickerin' lights and never halt till it brings us in clear view of the throne of the Lamb. Don't hitch your hopes to no sun nor stars; your home has got Jesus for its light, and your hopes must travel up that way" (Hatcher, 149, spelling altered).

This great folk preacher is a legend of the church. He was admired by whites because he entertained them and because their own preachers were incapable of vivifying the scripture as Jasper did. However popular he was, Jasper was more than an entertainer. Both as a slave and a freed preacher, he performed a necessary ministry of sustenance to his own people when Richmond was in shambles and more revolutionary tactics were impossible. The manner in which he told the biblical stories reminded his hearers, especially his black hearers, that the Bible is filled with *our* stories. They therefore witness to the importance of all God's creatures and not merely to the rich and powerful of this world.

Even the ritualized otherworldliness of the traditional sermon was more than the opium of an oppressed people. For in times of suffering or unrelieved want, the otherworldly symbol assumes a mysterious power to actualize its own content. The Negro's experience of the "Lord's victory" in the timelessness of worship will hasten the coming of that day in history. Gayraud Wilmore sagely observes, "Oppressors have never been able to relax in the presence of this kind of otherworldliness" (Wilmore, 51).

Like the other great Negro storytellers, Lemuel Haynes, Uncle Jack, Henry Evans, and C. R. Walker, Jasper sometimes "voiced" the story in such a way that the preacher indirectly made the points that he or she could not overtly express. As the last sentence of the sermon excerpt shows, even the most entertaining narrative might convey a subtle critique of the ruling powers. In retelling the Bible's stories of the conflict between the powerful of this world and God's downtrodden chosen ones, the Negro folk preacher found plenty of ammunition in the battle for his people's dignity (see African-American Preaching; Folk Preaching [African-American]).

Hatcher, W. E., *John Jasper*, 1908. Johnson, J. W., *God's Trombones: Seven Negro Sermons in Verse*, 1927. Mitchell, H., *Black Preaching: The Recovery of a Powerful Art*, 1990. Pipes, W. H., *Say Amen, Brother! Old-Time Negro Preaching: A Study in Frustration*, 1951. Wilmore, G. S., *Black Religion and Black Radicalism*, 2d ed. rev., 1983.
                                                       RICHARD LISCHER

FROGS, FROGS, FROGS
John Jasper

I tell you, my brethren, this scheme did the business for Pharaoh. He come from ridin' one day, and when he get in the palace the whole hall is full of frogs. They is scamperin' and hoppin' round till they fairly cover the ground, and Pharaoh put his big foot and squashed 'em on the marble floor. He run into his parlor trying to get away from them. They was all around; on the fine chairs, on the lounges, in the piano. It shocked the king till he get sick. Just then the dinner bell ring, and in he go to get his dinner. Ha, ha, ha! It's frogs, frogs, frogs all around! When he sat down he felt the frogs squirmin' in the chair; the frogs on the plates, squattin' up on the meat, playing over the bread, and when he pick up his glass to drink the water, the little frogs is swimmin' in the tumbler. When he tried to stick up a pickle his fork stuck in a frog; he felt them runnin' down his back. The queen, she cried and 'most fainted and told Pharaoh that she would quit the palace before sundown if he didn't do somethin' to clear them frogs out'n the house. She say she know what is the matter; 'twas the God of them low-down Hebrews, and she wanted him to get 'em out of the country. Pharaoh say he would, but he was an awful liar; just as they tell me that most of the politicians is.

From "Sermon on the Plagues," William E. Hatcher, *John Jasper* (New York: Fleming H. Revell, 1908), 164 (spelling altered).

Jesus as Preacher. The most common form of the historical Jesus' preaching was dinner conversation, although the Gospels picture Jesus preaching in a variety of situations. The Greek word for "to preach" (*kerysso*) also means to cry out loud, announce, proclaim, or herald and is used almost synonymously with saying, witnessing, or teaching (see Proclamation).

Only one scene in the Gospels pictures Jesus preaching at a liturgical celebration (Luke 4:16–30). Jesus' inaugural sermon at the synagogue in Nazareth is programmatic for Luke's Gospel, announcing the themes of Spirit, preaching to the poor, and rejection. This scene is unique to Luke's Gospel and does not describe a typical preaching action of Jesus. Furthermore, Jesus does not exhibit the style of midrashic preaching based on scripture characteristic of the synagogue. Matthew's portrayal of Jesus in the Sermon on the Mount,* preaching to large crowds in the open air, is undoubtedly imaginary, conforming Jesus to the image of Moses or famous Hellenistic rhetors.

The most likely situation for Jesus' actual preaching is table fellowship, which forms the context for many Gospel scenes. It is used in several of his own parables and is the most probable situation for a Jewish peasant. The Jesus of the Gospels possesses neither the literacy of a synagogue preacher nor the powerful presence of a heroic Moses-like figure. The contrast between John the Baptist and Jesus makes this point explicitly. John was an ascetic, and his contemporaries said he had a demon. But Jesus characterizes himself as one who "has come eating and drinking, and you say, 'Look, a glutton and a drunkard, a friend of tax collectors and sinners!'" (Luke 7:34). Such a saying represents a popular impression of who Jesus was and how he behaved. It imagines him at a party where everyone is invited, even those who are not supposed to be invited (Gospel of Thomas 64; Luke 14:16–24).

Most frequently, the Gospels picture Jesus as a wandering charismatic missionary. All four Gospels and the oral tradition picture Jesus in this way. The Q-gospel mission speech (Luke 10:2–12) demands of the disciples that they "carry no purse, no bag, no sandals; and greet no one on the road. Whatever house you enter, first say, 'Peace to this house!'" (Luke 10:4–5). As a wanderer, Jesus is homeless: "Foxes have holes, and birds of the air have nests; but the son of man has nowhere to lay his head" (Luke 9:58). This is a deliberate strategy in his preaching, and it sets him apart from the brokerage system of the ancient world. As a homeless one he cannot become a patron for his disciples or those he cures or heals. Because he is homeless he comes into conflict with his family and village, as Mark 3:20–35 reflects. A homeless preacher must always find a new place to preach and to eat.

The term *charismatic* characterizes not only Jesus' preaching, but also his deeds. Jesus was probably best known to his contemporaries as an exorcist and healer, but the controversies over his healing indicate a challenge to the source of his power. His opponents attribute his activity to Beelzebub, while he claims that he works by the power of the spirit. "But if it is by the finger of God that I cast out the demons, then the kingdom of God has come to you" (Luke 11:20). Jesus identifies his healing activity with the spirit and the coming of the kingdom. Jesus' speech should also be viewed as part of his charismatic activity. This is why he is viewed as speaking with authority in contrast with the scribes (e.g., Mark 1:22). Furthermore, his legal sayings do not call on tradition or legal precedent and are cast in an aphoristic form that burlesques the formality of legal code. For example, in the series of aphorisms deduced against the *lex talonis* in Matthew 5:39–42, one is to turn the other cheek only if the right is struck; one must surrender also the cloak if sued for one's coat, or go

two miles if a soldier forces one to carry his baggage. Such legal interpretation would leave one black and blue, naked, and embarked on a long journey as a porter. Such legal sayings are not meant to prescribe what to do but to jolt the hearer into the new reality of the kingdom, where life is not onerous but free.

The notion that Jesus was a wandering charismatic missionary notes that he had a mission toward Israel, and that mission can be summarized under the heading of kingdom of God. Since the *basileia* in the ancient world was the Roman empire with its authoritarian and oppressive domination, a contrast and conflict with Rome is always implicit in any other usage of *basileia*. "Empire of God" also points out how ironic Jesus' usage of the symbol is. A debate has raged in scholarship about whether the kingdom of God is future (apocalyptic) or present (sapiential). In the apocalyptic model, Jesus preached the coming end of the world and its final judgment. The conclusion that Jesus was such a preacher is now being challenged on several fronts. The aphorisms and parables of Jesus appear to find their proper context within the Jewish wisdom tradition and are not apocalyptic ciphers. Likewise, in the efforts to work out the various layers of the Synoptic tradition, Luke and the Gospel of Thomas point to wisdom sayings as the core of the Jesus tradition and to apocalyptic sayings as later.

The principal forms of Jesus' preaching are aphorisms and parables. They employ ordinary language and draw on the life experiences of a Galilean peasant. But his wisdom demonstrates a sophisticated oral artistry and the concentration of language characteristic of poetry. There is little explicit reference to religion, Torah, or God, although God is implicit. Jesus' primary opponent appears to be conventional wisdom, the dominant, taken-for-granted way things are in the world. Within second-temple Judaism, conventional wisdom can be summarized as a lawgiving God or the politics of holiness. The strategy of conventional wisdom is dictated by the overwhelming and threatening presence of the Roman empire. Judaism began to understand itself as holy in the sense of separate and set apart. Since God was holy and pure, his people also should be holy and pure and thus set apart. Jesus' healing, exorcisms, table fellowship, and preaching all cohere at this point. The empire of God demands not holiness but sympathy. All the boundaries are broken down—Jesus is homeless, his healings and exorcisms make the unclean clean, he eats with everyone, the kingdom come is now, and his preaching in aphorism and story jolts the hearer into this new kingdom. In his parables and aphorisms the father comes out to welcome both the younger and elder sons just as they are (Luke 15:11–32); the kingdom is more like leaven (corruption) than purity (Luke 13:20–21); and the dead should bury their own (Luke 9:60). Jesus does not preach about this, which is why his language is not prescriptive. His preaching is an empire of sympathy and not power.

Borg, M. J., *Jesus, A New Vision: Spirit, Culture, and the Life of Discipleship,* 1987. Crossan, J. D., *The Historical Jesus: The Life of a Mediterranean Jewish Peasant,* 1991; *Jesus: A Revolutionary Biography,* 1994. Koester, H., *Ancient Christian Gospels,* 1990. Mack, B. L., *The Lost Gospel: The Book of Q and Christian Origins,* 1993. Scott, B. B., *Hear Then the Parable: A Commentary on the Parables of Jesus,* 1989.

BERNARD BRANDON SCOTT

Jewish Preaching.
Jewish preaching was born out of the destruction of the kingdom of Judah, its capital Jerusalem, and the seat of its religion, the ancient Temple, in 586 B.C.E. With this destruction, Jewish leaders felt that their faith in the Torah could best be preserved by combining prayer with instruction. Hence, worship services soon began to include sermons that served to instruct. Though precise dates are difficult to pinpoint, the Jewish preaching tradition is an ancient one predating Christianity.

The Talmudic Period. The earliest Jewish sermons may have been translations of Hebrew scripture, and embellishments upon those translations, into the Aramaic vernacular for those who could not follow Hebrew. Such sermons provided basic information concerning the content of the Torah to diaspora Jews who had little knowledge of Hebrew, enabling them to better understand their faith. Moreover, as the rabbis translated and explained the Torah, they of necessity also provided interpretations, often applying the Torah to contemporary problems.

In most communities, sermons were delivered during Sabbath services. However, other customs concerning the treatment of the sermon differed from community to community during this period. While customs differed, a frequent practice was to have a brief sermon explicating the Torah reading, immediately following that reading. In some communities, the rabbi delivered the sermon himself. In others, deference was paid to the rabbi by having other individuals read his sermon to the congregants. In some communities it was customary for the audience to raise questions and for the rabbi to respond to those questions immediately.

The predominant sermon form of this period was to open with a quotation from scripture, though not from the passage to be read on that day. Through the use of other quotations, interpretations, and stories, this quotation would then be linked to the opening section of the daily passage. The opening section typically was then explicated to summarize the entire passage. The conclusion of the sermon often either thanked God for giving the Torah or contrasted the troubles of this world with the happiness of the next world.

The Middle Ages. The sermons of this period were virtually always based on scripture or rabbinical works such as the Mishnah, the Talmud, or works by Rashi, Maimonides, and others. The sermon enabled rabbis to stress the principles of the Torah while responding to the issues of the day. Given the anti-Semitism encountered by so many Jewish communities during this period, the sermon was a vital way of reinforcing the faith and providing reassurance and hope.

This period saw the rise of itinerant* preachers who traveled from community to community, often supplementing the efforts of the local preacher. Some rabbis, especially the itinerant preachers, regarded preaching as their principal responsibility and delivered sermons of considerable artistic merit.

Typically sermons were based on scripture, the Talmud, Midrash, and other Jewish sources. The Hebrew word for sermon, *drashah*, derived from the verb to search, to investigate, to interpret, well characterized the sermons of this period, which were searches, investigations, interpretations of the deepest meanings of scripture. However, sermon forms and practices differed among German, Spanish, and Mediterranean Jewish communities. Particular concern in most Jewish communities was paid to making the sermons intelligible to even the least educated members of the audience in order to strengthen the faith.

During the Middle Ages, Jewish sermons tended to center on three basic themes: first, the majesty of God; second, the grandeur of the Torah; third, the unique destiny of Israel. God, Torah, and Israel, the keystones of Jewish thought, have been the preeminent sermon topics throughout the history of Jewish preaching.

The Birth of Modern Jewish Preaching. Although preaching had been characteristic of Judaism for centuries, it gradually began to disappear from Jewish services in large parts of Europe at the outset of the eighteenth century. Since the reasons varied from community to community, it is impossible to ascribe a single reason to the decline in Jewish preaching. Among the reasons that contributed to the decline may have been local resentment of itinerant preachers and stricter regulation of Jewish life by non-Jews.

Nevertheless, the birth of German Reform Judaism, particularly in the first three decades of the nineteenth century, saw a rebirth of Jewish preaching. The German Reform movement altered a variety of Jewish customs. It advocated a more relaxed observance of both the Sabbath and the rules of Kashruth. Moreover, it made a variety of reforms in the service itself. Among the major changes advanced were shortening the services, replacing much of the Hebrew with German, seating women with men, adding organ music to the service, and perhaps most important, adding a vernacular sermon to the normal sabbath and holiday service.

The addition of vernacular sermons to the service was a consequence of a variety of influences. Among them were the use of addresses during "devotional hours" in Jewish schools, the model of the Christian community, the influence of civil authorities who in some areas of Germany and France required rabbis to know the vernacular language and preach in it, and the popularity of the first Reform preachers, who generated imitators.

In a little over two decades, between 1808–1830, sermons became a common feature of German Reform services. Moreover, this period witnessed the publication of the first significant Jewish works in homiletics, Leopold Zunz's *Sermons of the Jews* and the works of Ludwig Philippson. Moreover, the popularity of preaching in German Reform Judaism spurred its growth among more Orthodox Jews and the Jewish communities of other nations. For example, on November 19, 1817, Tobias Goodman delivered what is generally accepted as the first English-language sermon as part of a service in Great Britain.

American Jewish Preaching. Sermons were not a part of the normal sabbath or holiday services of early American Jews. Those Jews who migrated to America in the 1700s came from a European Jewish tradition that did not include sermons as a part of normal services. Additionally, the scarcity of Jews and the lack of a professionally trained rabbinate contributed to the lack of preaching in early American Jewish services. Nevertheless, Jewish preaching did take place in colonial America. Typically, the motivation for delivering sermons from Jewish pulpits during the colonial period did not come from within the Jewish community. Rather, colonial Jewish sermons were often motivated by the civil authorities. For example, civil authorities suggested that the houses of worship sponsor days of thanksgiving, often in response to epidemics or military events, and Jewish synagogue leadership, as with the other houses of worship in the community, voluntarily complied.

Such occasions gave rise to the first sermons delivered from Jewish pulpits in what would become the United States, of which we have records. Those sermons were delivered by the Reverend Joseph Jeshurun Pinto, the hazzen or chanter of the religious service for New York's Congregation Shearith Israel, who preached several times during the 1760s in response to events of the French and Indian wars. The fact that Pinto's sermons were parts of special services, not normal sabbath or holiday services, is important. For this was typical of American Jewish preaching until 1830. Events such as special days of thanksgiving and prayer called by civil authorities and special services occasioned by the visits of rabbis from Europe or the holy land, often seeking charitable support for some venture, gave rise to most Jewish sermons in early America.

The outstanding Jewish preacher in prerevolutionary and revolutionary America was Gershom Mendes Seixas, who served Jewish congregations in New York City and Philadelphia. Seixas gave a variety of patriotic sermons during the Revolutionary War, as well as sermons on civil holidays such as Thanksgiving. Moreover, he gave yearly sermons devoted to stimulating charitable contributions and works. Nevertheless, though perhaps the most active Jewish preacher in the nation at this time, it is fair to say that because he did not deliver sermons as part of a normal religious service, he probably delivered fewer sermons in his lifetime than would an active Christian minister in a year.

It was not until June 2, 1830, that Isaac Leeser, hazzen of Mikveh Israel Congregation in Philadelphia, began to deliver sermons on a regular basis during normal sabbath services. Initially, Leeser prepared and delivered an English-language sermon every two weeks and on some special occasions.

The introduction of vernacular sermons into the sabbath service was not an occasion for great controversy in the American Jewish community, as it had been in Europe. In Europe, the use of vernacular sermons was intimately bound to the Reform movement. Typically, vernacular sermons were part of a large group of changes by which Reformers effected both the manner of observing Judaism and some of the principal tenets of Jewish belief.

But in the United States, the English sermon was introduced into the service by Leeser, a staunch defender of the Orthodox tradition. He did so primarily to aid in Jewish education. Within thirty years of Leeser's pioneering efforts, English-language sermons had become commonplace in American Jewish services. Typical of many of his initial followers, Leeser's sermons were midrash in the traditional sense: They were attempts to explain God's word as given in the Torah. Though subsequent Jewish preachers were to rely on a wide variety of Jewish sources, Leeser, who was not ordained or widely versed in Jewish sources but who prepared the first English translation of the Torah, relied almost exclusively on the Torah as a source of evidence. Significantly, while their Christian contemporaries were often preaching on the issues of the day, most notably slavery and abolition, contemporary public issues were rarely treated from the Jewish pulpit.

In October of 1875, the First rabbinical seminary in the United States, Hebrew Union College, opened its doors. Founded by Rabbi Isaac Mayer Wise—a strong proponent of good preaching—Hebrew

Union College, the Reform seminary, stressed the importance of preaching and provided students with considerable training in preaching. Wise perceived preaching to be of exceptional importance, for he felt that a well-educated rabbinate composed of individuals with outstanding preaching abilities would not only help American Jews understand their faith but would also serve as models for the Americanization of immigrant Jews. Wise greatly admired the work of the Scottish clergyman-rhetorician Hugh Blair. Blair's *Lectures on Rhetoric and Belles Lettres* was frequently recommended by Wise to his students.

By the opening of the twentieth century, Zionism became a frequent topic in Jewish sermons. Discussions of Zionism from Jewish pulpits opened the way for the advocacy of a wide variety of social and political issues. In the first decades of the twentieth century, the American Jewish pulpit still shied away from treating social and political issues. But to preach on Zionism, a well-informed rabbi had to examine and discuss a wide variety of secular topics, including the history and development of the foreign policy of the United States and a variety of other nations. From treating topics necessary to discuss Zionism intelligently, it was but a short jump for most rabbis to preach on other important issues of the day. So, for example, in contrast to the abolitionist movement a century earlier, the civil rights movement of the 1950s and 1960s was heavily supported by the Jewish pulpit.

By the late twentieth century, American Jewish sermons were taking many forms. Though American rabbis now preach on an enormous range of topics, perhaps the most common sermon remains a text-based sermon in which the rabbi typically opens with a text from the Bible, midrash, or similar source and explicates that text, trying to suggest its meaning and applicability for current life. The growing presence of women in Reform and Conservative pulpits has often injected subtle changes on the issues treated from the pulpit in addition to providing a new perspective on old issues.

Though a host of organizational patterns are found in contemporary sermons, perhaps the most frequently found pattern is the use of topical organization, stressing three major points. Though this tradition is still common, a variety of other organizational patterns are being used. Indeed, many rabbis are making use of entirely new forms, such as dialogues with the audience. Eloquence in language, such as that which characterized the preaching of many outstanding American Jewish pulpit speakers during the first half of the twentieth century, still characterizes outstanding Jewish preaching. However, the national decline in eloquence is reflected in the contemporary Jewish pulpit, where masters of oral style are not as frequently found as they were earlier in the century. In sum, as the twentieth century draws to a close, Jewish preachers, like their Christian counterparts, are frequently drawing upon the teachings of their faith to preach upon a wide spectrum of personal, ethical, and moral issues as well as a vast number of the nation's concerns. In doing so, they utilize an extensive variety of rhetorical techniques.

Bettan, I., *Studies in Jewish Preaching: Middle Ages,* rev. ed., 1987. **Friedenberg, R. V.,** *"Hear O Israel" The History of American Jewish Preaching,* 1989. "Preaching," *Encyclopedia Judaica,* Vol. 13, 994–1007, 1971. **Saperstein, M.,** *Jewish Preaching 1200–1800: An Anthology,* 1989.

ROBERT V. FRIEDENBERG

Jowett, John Henry. (1863–1923) "The Preacher, what is he?" This question, with which J. H. Jowett opened an address called "The Secrets of Effective Preaching" in 1901, led him to four answers: herald, evangelist, logician, and conversationalist (Jowett, 263). These terms characterized the thirty-three-year preaching ministry of this man, who was easily the best-known preacher of his day in the English language. His ministries in England and America (1889–1922) spanned the era between Spurgeon,* Brooks,* and Moody* on the one side and Fosdick,* Macartney, and Studdert-Kennedy on the other.

A serious, self-disciplined student, he grew up in Halifax, England, in a pious family and was mightily influenced by the parish preacher of the town's Congregational Church, Dr. Enoch Mellor. While honing his debating skills in meetings of the Young Men's Society, he preached his first sermon at a local chapel at age seventeen. His decision to study for the ministry was made at the brink of his entering an apprenticeship with a local attorney. While studying at Airedale College, Edinburgh University, and Oxford, he sharpened his scholarly skills and found great encouragement in the preaching of the likes of Alexander Whyte, George Matheson, and Henry Drummond.

On the strength of his student sermons, Jowett was called to the pulpit of St. James Church, Newcastle, where he preached to increasingly larger and more enthusiastic crowds for six years. In 1895 he moved with his wife and adopted daughter to Birmingham, where he succeeded R. W. Dale in the pulpit of the Carr's Lane Church. The example of Dale's years of preaching on heavy doctrinal issues encouraged the young Jowett to increase the substantive nature of his sermons. His sixteen years at Carr's Lane left a deep impression on the congregation, the city of Birmingham, and the Congregationalists and other free churches of Great Britain.

After several years of trying, the Fifth Avenue Presbyterian Church of New York City finally convinced Jowett to become its preacher in 1911. His only stipulation was that they pay him a salary no greater than his income in Birmingham. Jowett's effectiveness and fame in England were matched in New York. Soon people were being turned away regularly because of lack of space in the 1,500-seat sanctuary at Fifth Avenue. World War I made it emotionally taxing for Jowett to remain an ocean away from his beloved home-

land, and in 1918 he succeeded G. Campbell Morgan* in the pulpit of Westminster Chapel, London. Even though he continued to preach regularly in London, anemia weakened him steadily, finally causing his retirement in 1921. His final sermon was preached at Westminster on December 17, 1922. He died just a year and two days later.

Jowett was a single-minded individual who was never distracted by controversy or current fads. In a time of great upheaval in the churches over science, critical approaches to the Bible, and the social gospel, he continued to preach on the great issues of Christian theology. The primary content of his preaching was redeeming grace. He had no time to trifle with secondary considerations. This attitude was clearly stated in his Lyman Beecher lectures of 1912, titled *The Preacher: His Life and Work.*

If Jowett had a hobby it was words. His use of the English language was impeccable, and he was always on the lookout for better ways of clarifying the themes he treated in his preaching. One is impressed not so much by his marvelous vocabulary but by the clarity of his statements. Because of the care with which he prepared to preach, he was always a manuscript preacher, though people who attended his services found the manuscript no hindrance to communication. He told a friend that when he saw the first words on a page, he knew the rest, since he reviewed the thoughts of his manuscript and not just the words (Poritt, 269f.).

In his own words, Jowett was "a *herald*, a public crier, a man with an imperial proclamation, charged with a message which must be announced from the housetops with all the urgency of a sovereign command." Jowett was "an *evangelist*, with a message which is almost a song, full of sweetness and of light, the speech of the wooer, laden with tenderness, and bright with the promise of gladsome days." He was "a *logician*, engaged in strenuous reasonings, seeking to gather together the loose and incoherent thoughts of men, and bind them into firm and well-knit spiritual decision." And Jowett was "a *conversationalist*, who sometimes lays aside the spacious function of the public ministry, and, discarding the formalities of linked and well-connected discourse, engages in homely intercourse, in fireside speech with his fellow-men" (Jowett, 253).

Fant, C. E., Jr., and **W. M. Pinson, Jr.,** eds., *Twenty Centuries of Great Preaching,* Vol. 8, 1971. **Jowett, J. H.,** *Apostolic Optimism,* n.d.; *The Preacher: His Life and Work,* 1912; *The Whole Armour of God,* 1916. **Poritt, A.,** *John Henry Jowett,* 1925.

BRUCE E. SHIELDS

THE SHIELD OF FAITH
John Henry Jowett

Paul wanted a shield, not against failure; that might come or stay away. But he wanted a shield against the pessimism that may be born of failure, and which holds the soul in the fierce bondage of an Arctic winter. Paul wanted a shield, not against injury; that might come or stay away; but against the deadly thing that is born of injury, even the foul offspring of revenge. Paul wanted a shield, not against pain; that might come or might not come; he sought a shield against the spirit of murmuring which is so frequently born of pain, the deadly, deadening mood of complaint. Paul wanted a shield, not against disappointment; that might come or might not come; but against the bitterness that is born of disappointment, the mood of cynicism which sours the milk of human kindness and perverts all the gentle currents of the soul. Paul wanted a shield, not against difficulty; that might come or might not come; but against the fear that is born of difficulty, the cowardice and the disloyalty which are so often bred of stupendous tasks. Paul did not want a shield against success; that might come or might not come; but against the pride that is born of success, the deadly vanity and self-conceit which scorch the fair and gracious things of the soul as a prairie-fire snaps up a homestead or a farm. Paul did not want a shield against wealth; that might come or

might not come; but against the materialism that is born of wealth, the deadly petrifying influence which turns flesh into stone, spirituality into benumbment, and which makes a soul unconscious of God and of eternity. The apostle did not want a shield against any particular circumstance, but against every kind of circumstance, that in everything he might be defended against the fiery darts of the devil. He found the shield he needed in a vital faith in Christ. . . . The ultimate concern of faith is not with a polity, not with a creed, not with a church, and not with a sacrament, but with the person of the Lord Jesus Christ. And therefore the first thing we have to do if we wish to wear the shield of faith is to cultivate the companionship of the Lord. . . . Faith-life cultivates the friendship of Christ, and leans upon it, and surrenders itself with glorious abandon to the sovereign decrees of His grace and love.

From "The Shield of Faith," *The Whole Armour of God* (New York: Fleming H. Revell Company, 1916), 86–89.

Søren Kierkegaard. (1813–1855)

Throughout his brief life, Søren Kierkegaard was usually introspective, even melancholy, often compared to Shakespeare's brooding Dane, Hamlet. No doubt this orientation of his life and thought was fed by the periods of isolation due to poor health, a physical appearance that made him an easy mark for caricature, and the death of both parents, a brother, and two sisters. His pained genius was fueled by conflicts with himself, his father, the church, and God. He was engaged but not married, theologically educated but not ordained.

The literary achievement of Kierkegaard consists of thirty-five volumes of philosophy, theology, aesthetics, and ethics. However, by his own admission, he pursued but one question; how to be a Christian within Christendom. He saw Christendom with its buildings, clergy, public rituals, canonized writings, and social, even governmental approval as an illusion of Christianity, not the genuine faith of Jesus Christ. True faith is without the guarantees and approval of Christendom. Christian faith is a risk without certainty, a trust without proof, a leap without a net. In a life of faith, conclusions are premature; one believes in God afresh every morning.

But how can one introduce Christianity into Christendom? Kierkegaard clearly understood his problem to be one of communication. Christianity is not a piece of information to be transmitted from one person to another; it is not a system of thought superior to other systems. "Truth is inwardness," he often said. The task of Christian community, therefore, is to generate a hearing, a wrestling, an arrival at faith in the other. It was this struggle, this effort to move Christ past the closed doors of minds content with the illusion of Christianity, that has made Kierkegaard important for preaching.

On the streets of Copenhagen and in social circles, Kierkegaard's method of communication was Socratic, engaging and drawing out his auditors. In his writings, likewise, he used an amazing display of dialectic to make conversation partners of his readers. Through the use of pseudonyms and with erratic, unpredictable, and elusive personal behavior and relationships, he sought to conceal himself, thinking thereby to set his readers free to engage not him but the subject matter and eventually themselves. Convinced that the eyes and ears of Christendom were closed to the call to genuine faith, he determined to enter the minds and hearts of his listeners or readers indirectly. This meant finding a way of communicating that entered through the back door or a window or down the chimney; as he put it, "sneaking up from behind." To move past the reader's defenses he used many devices of indirection such as irony, exaggeration, and stories.

A favorite form of indirect communication was the parable.* As many after him came to realize, the parable will "tease the mind into active thought" (to borrow a line from C. H. Dodd) and in so doing lead the hearer to take responsibility for his or her own thought and faith. He wrote scores of parables in the service of communicating the gospel. The genius of this method was that the parable, as is true of all stories, puts the listener in the position of overhearing. Stories are not confrontational; on the contrary, they cause the hearer to relax and drop resistances because they are about someone else, somewhere else. In addition, they are interesting; they have entertainment value. However, once the story, especially a parable, is heard it begins its work, and if it is told in the service of the gospel, the auditor cannot escape its ultimate claims. As did Jesus' hearers, "they perceive he was talking to them."

Kierkegaard was further persuaded of the effectiveness of this method of overhearing when he recalled powerful and life-changing experiences of his own. He remembered when as a child he overheard important conversations between his father and guests in the home. Extremely influential was an occasion of overhearing in the cemetery. While on a walk through the graveyard, he heard from beyond the hedgerow an old man talking of life and death to a young boy while they stood beside a fresh grave, obviously that of the boy's father, the old man's son. Not being directly addressed in either case, Kierkegaard did not resist listening, and once one listens, what is heard begins to do its work. The power of the message does not lie in the authority of the speaker or in the relation of the speaker to the hearer but within the message itself.

This is not to say that Kierkegaard discarded direct communication. He directly communicated in many of his writings, especially those bearing his own name. In fact, in *The Point of View for My Work as an Author* he speaks directly about his indirect method. He knew that without occasions of direct and straightforward speech, indirection would become a clever game, no longer in the service of the gospel. He longed for the time when resistance to hearing the gospel would die away and everyone could communicate directly. Until that day, however, he understood he could best fulfill his God-given assignment by using indirection, slipping past illusions and false assumptions to the heart where faith again could be born. This meant, of course, that he could not aspire to become a great writer or a great speaker but only a servant of the Word, bending his own gifts into whatever shapes necessary to effect a hearing of the gospel (see Inductive Preaching; Craddock, Fred).

Craddock, F., *Overhearing the Gospel,* 1978. **Diem, H.,** *Kierkegaard: An Introduction,* 1966. **Hamilton, K.,** *The Promise of Kierkegaard,* 1969. **Willimon, W. H.,** "Kierkegaard on Preachers Who Become Poets," *Worship,* 1975, 107–12.

FRED B. CRADDOCK

King, Martin Luther, Jr. (1929–1968) "In the quiet recesses of my heart," Martin Luther King Jr. often said, "I am fundamentally a clergyman, a Baptist preacher. This is my being and my heritage for I am also the son of a Baptist preacher, the grandson of a Baptist preacher and the great-grandson of a Baptist preacher" (*Ebony,* August 1965, 77). The usual context of these words was King's justification of his radically prophetic ministry to America. But they also help explain his lifelong confidence in the power of the Word of God to change the hearts of all who hear it. King's confidence in the word was born in the African-American church, particularly his father's congregation in the heart of Atlanta's "Sweet Auburn." After graduation from Morehouse College at age 19, he received his theological education at Crozer Seminary in Chester, Pennsylvania (graduating first in his class), and Boston University where he earned a Ph.D. in theology. After completing his course work at Boston, he accepted the pastorate of Dexter Avenue Baptist Church in Montgomery, Alabama. In 1960 he joined his father as associate pastor of Ebenezer Baptist Church in Atlanta.

While at Dexter, he was catapulted into the leadership of the successful Negro boycott of the segregated city bus system. By the age of 28, he was widely recognized not just as the leader of a local protest but as the most eloquent spokesman for Negroes in the United States. At thirty-five he was awarded the Nobel Peace Prize. With his colleague Ralph David Abernathy and others, King was a founder of the Southern Christian Leadership Conference under whose auspices he led civil rights campaigns in Atlanta, Albany, Georgia, Birmingham, Selma, Chicago, Memphis, and other cities. As his concerns expanded from desegregation to voting rights, open housing, antiwar activities, and the problems of the poor, his influence as a preacher became more widespread. In the course of a brief but intensely controversial career, his preaching and ministry transcended the boundaries of Ebenezer Church and helped transform the social and political structures of American life. He was assassinated in Memphis on April 4, 1968, while defending the rights of city sanitation workers. On April 7 the first sentence of the *New York Times* editorial was a fitting epitaph: "Martin Luther King was a preacher, a man from Georgia. . . . "

King was trained to preach in the black church. Like most young Negro preachers, he learned by imitation (see African-American Preaching). His father, Martin Luther King, Sr., and William Holmes Borders of the neighboring Wheat Street Baptist Church, modeled for him the captivating authority of the pulpit, while his teachers and mentors, Benjamin Mays, Howard Thurman,* Mordecai Johnson, Gardner Taylor,* and his pastor during the Crozer years, J. Pius Barbour, demonstrated the compatibility of academic learning and homiletical eloquence. With those voices he blended the influences of personalist and liberal theology, especially as it was given expression by the popular preachers of his day. The phrases of nineteenth-century bishop Phillips Brooks,* along with those of Harry Emerson Fosdick,* George Buttrick,* Halford

Luccock, J. Wallace Hamilton,* and others appear regularly in King's sermons.

In the convergence of many voices, he developed his own distinctive style* and message. The King style relied on the skillful manipulation of memorized set pieces organized in classical fashion around topics that he inserted as needed into any sermon or speech. The set piece might be as brief as a Homeric-like epithet, "the iron feet of oppression," with which he habitually evoked the familiar tyrannies of segregation. Or it might be a more lengthy assemblage of materials, including passages from other preachers or poetic verses. In black churches, but rarely in white, King extended his use of homiletical set pieces to include gospel and spiritual formulas with which he brought his sermons to a thunderous climax and his services to the prescribed altar call. For example, in one of his Ebenezer sermons he exalts the name of God: "I know him because He's the Lily of the Valley. He's the bright and morning star. . . . He's my everything. He's my mother and my father. He's my sister and my brother." Such formulas, along with most topical references and other typically African-American religious expressions, have been omitted from his major volume of printed sermons, *Strength to Love*.

A second, related element of King's style was his use of metaphor and poetic language. The prophetic image of the dream, which he immortalized in his 1963 address in Washington, D.C., and the "drum major for justice" by which he described his own ministry shortly before his death, are vivid and unforgettable. He spoke with a natural poetic cadence that included alliteration, repetition, internal rhyme, anaphora, epistrophe, antithesis, and many other rhetorical devices.

King's sermonic delivery was inextricably tied to the power of his language and the urgency of his message. In the black congregation, particularly, his baritone would begin low and slow, quicken, come up, rise, soar, and hit the highest imaginable peaks of ecstasy only to rise higher to

an extemporized exaltation of God's greatness. His voice was characterized by unusual range and control. As ecstatic as were his cries of deliverance ("March, children, don't ya' get weary . . . "), his voice never broke or lost control of the speech's content. A second characteristic of his voice was its pathos. Its heartfelt tremolo rarely degenerated to sentimentality and never to demagoguery. His voice seemed to echo both the weariness and hope of African Americans as well as the speaker's own history of conflict, imprisonment, and suffering.

In order to understand King's message, it is necessary to identify his most important principles of biblical and theological interpretation. The master key to King's message is found in no one biblical story, although the exodus underlay all his theological and social thought. In King's sermons the master story is the saga of the enslavement of African people in North America, their continued oppression and humiliation, and now the stirrings of freedom at work among them. This story has unfolded in a universe governed by God who is grieved by the suffering of his people and whose will it is that they should ultimately triumph. The deliverance of black people will occur, however, only if its vehicle, the Movement, is perfectly aligned with the loving nature of Christ's ministry and the redemptive character of his death. In most of his sermons, King addresses the issues common to midcentury liberalism—personal anxiety, nuclear war, love of neighbor, self-esteem, and the like. But ultimately, every sermon moves to the master story of liberation and turns on its principles.

Throughout his brief career, King preached, refined, revised, and reused a small canon of sermons. Much of the material in these sermons found its way into his mass meeting speeches and his civil addresses. Because his sermons eventually created many audiences, the question of their effect is a complex one. Among African-American Christians King managed to identify the suffering and rage of his people as few had done before him.

The nobility of his style and his eloquent appeal to the precedent of history filled his black audiences with courage and self-respect. King himself modeled a new role for the black preacher and a new militancy for the black church in the south. When speaking to ministers he never tired of urging them to a more prophetic ministry.

King wanted his white audiences to recognize the best of American religious and political ideals in the mirror of his message. Through the breadth of his appeal to Western values and his creative use of the Judeo-Christian tradition, his rhetoric helped create a fragile and temporary consensus among people of good will in America. This priestly office of the word also entailed a prophetic* confrontation with evil. His prophetic words were complemented by prophetic actions—marches, pray-ins, and arrests—the purpose of which was to isolate and expose the evil of American racism. To describe his own prophetic vocation, King employed a figure used by Jonathan Edwards two centuries earlier, that of lancing an overripe boil.

As a preacher, King demonstrated unflagging perseverance in his vocation even in the face of personal danger. He was faithful to the black preaching tradition and to the values of political and theological liberalism. He thereby produced a unique if temporary synthesis of traditions in America. Like no preacher in the twentieth century, King transposed the great Judeo-Christian themes of love, suffering, deliverance, and reconciliation from the sacred shelter of the pulpit into the arena of public policy and behavior.

King, M. L., Jr., *Strength to Love*, 1963, 1981. The Martin Luther King Jr. Center for Nonviolent Social Change, Archival Collection: Sermons, speeches, correspondence. **Lischer, R.,** *The Preacher King: Martin Luther King Jr. and the Word That Moved America*, 1995. **Miller, K. D.,** *Voice of Deliverance: The Language of Martin Luther King Jr. and Its Sources*, 1992. **Mitchell, H. H.,** *Black Preaching*, rev. ed., 1990.

RICHARD LISCHER

Knox, John. (ca. 1513–1572) Born in Haddington, Scotland, John Knox was raised in a rigorous tradition of classical theological scholarship, studying at the universities of Glasgow and (probably) St. Andrews. He received minor orders and may have been ordained to the priesthood, but he was soon enlisted in the rapidly growing Protestant movement. He was destined for the practice of law, becoming a notary in his native town, but he soon left to become a private tutor. About this time (1544), under the influence of the Lutheran George Wishart, Knox was decisively converted to the tenets of the Reformation. Soon his exceptional pulpit gifts were recognized, and in 1547 he became preacher to the beleaguered Protestant forces at St. Andrews, sharing in their fate when the castle was captured by French forces, after which he spent nineteen months as prisoner, including many weeks as a galley slave. His experience in St. Andrews confirmed his conviction that he was called to preach the liberating gospel in defiance of all the dangers that threatened him, thanking God that he had come in the thick of the battle and proclaiming that "A man with God is always in the majority."

On release from prison in France, Knox went to England and in 1551 was made chaplain to the king. His reputation was growing, and on the accession of Queen Mary, who fiercely attacked the Protestants, Knox had a hand in the revision of the Second Prayer Book of the Church of England. He fled to the Continent, where a meeting with Calvin* at Geneva had momentous consequences for the Scottish Reformation and his future career. After pastoring English refugees at Frankfurt, he returned to Scotland in 1555. There, his preaching and writing had an enthusiastic response, but within a year, to the distress of his friends and the scorn of his enemies, he accepted a call of service to the English congregation in Geneva. This move gave him the chance to carry out the fight by means of the written word and to study doctrine and church polity under the inspiration of Calvin, whom he revered. He returned finally to Scotland in 1559, where he composed the "Scots Confession," still to be found, for instance, in the Book of Confessions of the Presbyterian Church U.S.A. (1983). With the arrival of Mary, Queen of Scots, Knox was at once embroiled in the violent political and theological struggle that ushered in the establishment of the Church of Scotland as the national church based on Reformed doctrine and Presbyterian polity. During this tumultuous time he had constantly attacked Mary from the pulpit of St. Giles and in harangues in the royal Holyrood House. When she abdicated, he preached the sermon at the coronation of King James. After the murder of his chief supporter, Lord Murray, his influence waned, but he carried on the struggle through pulpit and pamphlets and died knowing that his cause would triumph. At his funeral the Regent, the Earl of Morton, pronounced his epitaph: "Here lies one who neither feared nor flattered any flesh."

Few preachers have had a greater influence on the politics and destiny of a nation, yet he maintained vigorously that his sermons were based on the Word of God and proclaimed the sovereignty of Christ alone over this church. His critics have questioned his use of scripture, notably his constant use of Old Testament texts in his attacks on Mary (his favorite being the stories of Jezebel and Ahab), and both friends and foes have deplored the vehemence of his preaching style. Yet none could doubt the sincerity of his beliefs as he sought to be an instrument of God's Word at a critical moment in the history of the Kirk. It was this quality of his preaching that earned him the contemporary compliment, "I assure you the voice of one man is able in one hour to put more life in us than five hundred trumpets continually blustering in our ears."

Knox, like Luther,* was a master of the language of his day, both standard English and occasional pithy Scots, and greatly influenced the style of Scottish preaching in subsequent years. He was also a model for preachers who wrestle with a task of relating the Word of God to specific political controversies as he sought to fulfill Calvin's ideal of a godly nation. He was, more than any other, responsible for the presbytery tradition (in Scotland and later in North America and other lands to which Scots emigrated in large numbers) of a theologically trained clergy and an educated people. He was one of the first to advocate a system of nationwide compulsory schooling—as well as measures to relieve poverty and provide for the sick, which foreshadowed the modern welfare state.

On the political scene, Knox faced the uproar caused by the clash of traditional loyalties and the new revolutionary ideas fostered by the Reformation. He had to help steer Scottish foreign policy away from the century-old alliance with Catholic France since he needed the support of Protestant England. Yet his skill as a statesman is seen in his cultivation of strong ties with France and tactful treatment of Queen Elizabeth of England. He had to deal with arrogant nobles seeking to back the winning side. When he preached in St. Giles, he had in mind the common people but was conscious of the presence of men and women of political power and ambition—and not in the least afraid to speak his mind in exhortation or rebuke (the familiar picture of his haranguing Mary doesn't depict a sermon at St. Giles—where she would not have been in attendance—but a private service in the palace of Holyrood House).

The drama of Knox's clash with his queen has been the theme of many novels and plays, and it must be admitted that Knox's reputation has suffered by the contrast so often highlighted between the beautiful, gifted, and attractive young queen and the fierce, fanatical preacher, determined to browbeat her into submission to the Reformed Kirk and outmaneuver her in the political game. A truer picture of the antagonists can be formed by reading Knox's account in his "History of the Reformation in Scotland"—one of the masterpieces of its kind. The man is there, with all his bias and dogmatic assurance and roughness of speech but also with his deep sense of divine calling, his liveliness and, at times, his humor. Mary was no saint—and Knox was no Puritan, in the popular meaning of the word. His message could be summed up in his reply to Mary when she asked, "What have ye to do with my marriage? Or what are ye within this Commonwealth?" His answer: "A subject born within the same, Madam, and albeit I be neither Earl, Lord, nor Baron within it, yet God hath made me (however abject that ever I be in your eyes) a profitable member within the same."

It has been said that modern democracy was born in his answer.

McLeod, G. F., *John Knox and Today,* 1959. Reid, W. S., *Trumpeter of God: A Biography of John Knox,* 1974.   DAVID H. C. READ

Language, Theories of.

The word "language" indicates both the sounds or signals that signify certain meanings and the system by which sounds and meanings are related. We both "speak" a language, and we "know" a language. Theories of language, therefore, focus on both the actual performance of language (utterance, speech, communication) and on the system of language itself (grammar, syntax, cultural context, semantic categories).

Linguistics is the study of language. The Western predecessors of modern linguists are the philosophers and grammarians of ancient Greece and Rome and the rhetoricians and philologists of Europe and America. Modern theories of language are drawn from behavioral sciences such as cultural anthropology, psychology, and sociology and from modern philosophies of language such as logical positivism, logical empiricism, and philosophical hermeneutics.

Two major cross-disciplinary theories of language have had a significant impact on contemporary homiletics and preaching: empirical theories and phenomenological theories.

Empirical Theories. Since the late nineteenth century, there has been a general trend, especially in Britain and North America, toward empirical, naturalistic, and mechanistic theories of language. Empirical linguists define language in terms of the behavioral interaction between the language user and the environment. The rules for language and for the creation of meaning are bound to rules of behavior and to physical laws. The meanings of words are linked to behavioral effects. Language, and therefore human knowledge, is tied closely to the physical world.

American linguist Leonard Bloomfield (*Language,* 1933) rejected any theory of language that attributed nonphysical explanations to verbal behavior. Under his influence, American linguistics developed into an empirical science, focused on careful observation of verbal sounds and rules of syntax.

The philosophical writings of Bertrand Russell (*An Outline of Philosophy,* 1927) paralleled attempts by linguists to bind language to physical and verifiable reality. Russell held that figurative or metaphorical language was problematic in communication, reducing clarity and precision. Words and their various configurations must help us picture something in the physical environment. Logical positivist A. J. Ayer (*Language, Truth and Logic,* 1936) went one step further by asserting that the meaning of any proposition must be empirically verifiable.

Ludwig Wittgenstein, in *Philosophical Investigations* (1953), softened the perspective of logical positivism by introducing the concept of situational "language games." He asserted that different language games produce different sets of language rules. These rules generate different behavioral effects. In the same way, the "speech-act" theory of J. L. Austin distinguished between the cognitive, referential function of language and the interactive, "performative" function of language in ordinary use (*How to Do*

Things with Words, 1962). The work of Wittgenstein and Austin subordinated the referential meaning of language to its communicative "force" in a particular language-game. Similarly, functionalist and structural-functionalist anthropologists in Britain and America narrowed the locus for linguistic meaning to the shared semantic knowledge of particular cultures or subcultures (see also Bronislaw Malinowski, Edmund Leach, and Clifford Geertz).

Theologians holding narrow empirical assumptions about language asserted that religious words could only be understood as statements focused, however indirectly, on human behavior. Ian Ramsay asserted that religious language was "odd" and had effects that were different from the cognitive effects of logical propositions (*Religious Language: An Empirical Placing of Theological Phrases,* 1957). Likewise, Paul van Buren, in *The Secular Meaning of the Gospel* (1963), examined some of the observable effects that religious language has on believers.

More recently, George Lindbeck, following the lead of Wittgenstein and Geertz has bracketed "cultural-linguistic" approaches to Christian theology as those that locate religious meaning within the text or language-game of religious faith (intratextuality), rather than outside the language system in "objective realities" or in experience. According to Lindbeck, "meaning is constituted by the uses of a specific language rather than being distinguishable from it" (*The Nature of Doctrine: Religion and Theology in a Post-Liberal Age,* 1984, 114).

Empirical theories of language typically have three effects on homiletics and preaching.

Denotative style. Preachers with denotative styles strive to achieve clarity of language and logic. They use clear, common language and are less inclined to use figurative language such as metaphor, image, or symbol. They prefer deductive forms of logic or forms that have cultural and communal precedents.

Hermeneutics of Equivalence. Preach-

ers with empirical views of language attempt to achieve clarity and accessibility in biblical interpretation. In order to accomplish this, they seek accurate substitutions or equivalencies that will faithfully reproduce the original meaning of the biblical text. Hidden meanings from behind, beneath, or in front of the biblical text are less important than the "plain sense" of the biblical language in its historical context.

Since the late 1970s, some scholars have focused attention on the "performative" and "cultural-linguistic" aspects of biblical language. They are concerned that preachers learn accurately to reproduce not only what the biblical text *says* but also what it *does* (Leander Keck, *The Bible in the Pulpit: The Renewal of Biblical Preaching,* 1978).

Catechetical Preaching. Preachers with empirical presuppositions about language are more inclined to preach prescriptive forms of theology and theological ethics. They are concerned with the relationship between the language of preaching and the task of forging an unambiguous communal identity and clear norms of behavior. Catechetical preaching assists hearers to learn the grammar and language of scripture and of doctrine in ways that will inform their decisions and lifestyle. In some instances, this may mean asserting the "oddness of Christian discourse" and the unique and separate claims of the Christian language-game in opposition to culture at large (Stanley Hauerwas and William Willimon, *Preaching to Strangers,* 1992, 11; William Willimon, *Peculiar Speech: Preaching to the Baptized,* 1993).

Phenomenological Theories. For the phenomenologist of language, the denotative use of language is the weakest and least significant use of language. Phenomenologists give priority to metaphor and symbol in understanding the nature and function of language. The purpose of language is not to illumine the physical world and yield behavioral effects but to disclose the hidden ground from which the physical world proceeds.

In the twentieth century, existentialist and phenomenological theorists of language introduced a strong primitive movement into language study. Fred Craddock embraced this movement as "an attempt to recover the power possessed by words before they were smothered by a scientific and technological culture . . . " (*As One Without Authority*, 3d ed., 1979, 34).

In the behavioral sciences, structural linguist Noam Chomsky developed transformational rules to relate "deep," hidden structures of meaning to "surface" structures of sound and syntax (*Aspects of the Theory of Syntax*, 1965). Social anthropologist Sir James Frazier (*The Golden Bough*, 1922) and structural anthropologist Claude Lévi-Strauss (*Structural Anthropology*, 1958) attempted to discover primitive archetypes or universals that undergird surface cultural grammars.

Phenomenologist of religion Mircea Eliade (*The Sacred and the Profane: The Nature of Religion*, 1959) attempted to achieve a sympathetic participation in distant or primitive experiences and events, to return to the point where symbols begin to "give back" what they symbolize. Philosophical hermeneuticist Paul Ricoeur spoke of symbols that "plunge us into the shadowy experience of power" (*Interpretation Theory: Discourse and the Surplus of Meaning*, 69). Experiential realists, such as John E. Smith (*Experience and God*, 1968) and Bernard Meland (*Fallible Forms and Symbols*, 1976), reasserted the origins of religious language in prelinguistic experience. Likewise, process philosophers and theologians have insisted on the need to keep religious language open to and informed by what Alfred North Whitehead called "naive experience" (*Science and the Modern World*, 1929, 90).

Theologians such as Paul Tillich, John Macquarrie, and Walter Ong, S.J., embraced this theory of language. According to Tillich, religious language is symbolic and disclosive of ultimate reality (*Systematic Theology*, 1951). Macquarrie asserted that "God-talk" is rooted in the "fundamental openness" of human existence to its own "being-in-the-world" (*God-Talk: An Examination of the Language and Logic of Theology*, 1981, 78). Ong was attracted to a primitive "oral-aural" mode of human existence in which human vocalizations generate a sense of mystery that connect the hearer with a shared existential awareness of meaning (*The Presence of the Word*, 1967).

The phenomenological approach to language has had a threefold impact on homiletics and preaching.

Connotative Style. Preachers with connotative styles use language and forms of logic that promote ambiguity and subtlety in communication. They use image, narrative, dialogue, metaphor, and symbol to keep hearers "on the hook" and in pursuit of ideas or meaning. Narrative, inductive, and conversational homiletical theories promote connotative styles.

Hermeneutic of Discovery. Preachers with a phenomenological approach to language are interested in discovering the hidden symbolic references of biblical language, Meanings are not *in* the text, but come *through* the text. Some preachers are drawn toward meanings that reside *behind* the text in the cultural, historical, and redactional context. Others try to discover the hidden kerygmatic or existential "claims" of the biblical text that require a decision and reorientation of human existence (Gerhard Ebeling, *Theology and Proclamation: A Discussion with Rudolf Bultmann*, 1966, 28–31). Still others employ a contextual hermeneutic or a hermeneutic of suspicion, looking for trajectories of hidden meaning that require our own historicity, experience, and interests to be discovered (*see* Hermeneutics).

Priestly Preaching. Preachers with a phenomenological understanding of language are more inclined to preach descriptive forms of theology and theological ethics. Preachers assume a priestly posture, assisting parishioners in the act of "naming grace" in the ordinary fabric of their lives (*see* Mary Catherine Hilkert, "Naming Grace: A Theology of Proclamation," *Worship* 60, Sept. 1986). They attempt to find language that is adequate to articulate the hidden presence of God in various kinds of human experience. Instead of using language to forge a community of common identity and behavior, preachers use language to provoke theological insight or to support an ongoing theological conversation in which what it means to be faithful takes diverse shapes.

Special Applications

Feminist Applications. Feminist studies of language have raised an awareness of the oppressive usage of language. Feminist homileticians use both empirical and phenomenological theories of language to analyze women's ways of speaking and preaching (Christine M. Smith, *Weaving the Sermon: Preaching in a Feminist Perspective*, 1989).

Strategic Applications. Making use of structuralism, semiotics, cultural anthropology, and philosophical hermeneutics, homileticians are beginning to explore the strategic, long-term function of the language of preaching in congregational and social contexts. Several homiletical efforts in the late 1980s and early 1990s point in this direction. (See J. Randall Nichols, *The Restoring Word: Preaching as Pastoral Communication*, 1987; David Buttrick, *Homiletic: Moves and Structures*, 1987; and John S. McClure, *The Four Codes of Preaching: Rhetorical Strategies*, 1991.)

Dramatist Applications. The idea that the language of preaching is primarily "performative" language has attracted the attention of homileticians. Drawing upon speech-act theory, reader-response criticism, Ong's "oral-aural" theory of communication, Burkean rhetoric, and kinesthetics, homileticians are investigating the nature of preaching as an embodied language-event (*see* Oral Communication; Rhetoric; Burke, Kenneth).

Fowler, R., *Understanding Language: An Introduction to Linguistics*, 1974. **Hamilton, K.**, *Words and the Word*, 1971. **Tilley, T. W.**, *Talking of God: An Introduction to Philosophical Analysis of Religious Language*, 1978.   JOHN S. MCCLURE

Law. "Law" is a phenomenon that applies to all dimensions of life, including the physical laws of nature, the positive laws of society, the imperatives of human morality, the ritual codes of religion, and the divine laws of revelation. The study of each dimension is conducted by a variety of specialized disciplines, such as physics, sociology, jurisprudence, ethics, history of religions, and theology. This brief article will limit itself to a *theological* understanding of law on the basis of the Holy Scriptures and the history of the Christian tradition.

The Biblical Understanding of Law. Torah is the Hebrew word for "law." In Judaism it came to refer specifically to the Pentateuch, the first five books of the Old Testament. Torah conveys the revealed will of God, prescribing the kind of attitudes and behavior appropriate to sustain the covenant that God made with his people, Israel. In the New Testament, and in the Christian tradition generally, particularly in Lutheranism, the word "law" was often used to refer to the entire Old Testament (e.g., John 15:25; Rom. 3:19; 1 Cor. 14:21).

The interpretation of the law in the New Testament is extremely complex and the subject of much dispute in contemporary biblical studies. The attitude of Jesus the Rabbi of Nazareth toward the law seems to have been ambivalent. On the one hand, Jesus showed great respect for the law, declaring the inviolability of every "jot and tittle" of the law (Matt. 5:18) and scolding the scribes and Pharisees for neglecting "the weightier matters of the law" (Matt. 23:23). On the other hand, Jesus was criticized for placing himself above the law, breaking the Sabbath laws and the rules of cleanliness, declaring all foods clean (Mark 7:19).

The law functioned as a major theological category in the writings of Paul* the apostle. For Paul, the law was "holy" and "good" (Rom. 7:12, 16), showing sin to be sin; its purpose was to show the need for the coming of the Messiah to redeem his people. And while Paul could say, "we uphold the law" (Rom. 3:31), he could almost in the same breath announce, "Christ is the end of the law" (Rom. 10:4). In his letter to the Romans and the Galatians, Paul even relegates the law to the past; at the present time the law has given way to a new age in which the promises of God have been fulfilled in Christ, when believers live by faith and not by the works of the law. "Therefore the law was our disciplinarian until Christ came, so that we might be justified by faith" (Rom. 3:24).

The question whether Christians were still obligated to keep the law became the first great theological problem in the early church. Paul's teaching that contrasted the righteousness of faith to the righteousness of works was opposed by some Jewish Christians. James 2:14, 24 expresses the feelings of many Jewish Christians who could not understand Paul's idea of justification by faith: "What good is it, my brothers and sisters, if you say you have faith but do not have works? . . . You see that a person is justified by works and not by faith alone." The crux of the issue focused on whether Gentile Christians would be required to observe the Jewish law of circumcision. The Apostolic Council at Jerusalem determined that what is required of Jews—namely, the obligation to observe the law, such as circumcision—does not necessarily apply to Gentiles. It is proper for Jews who become Christians to observe the law; Gentiles who become Christians are free from the law. This settlement was bound to cause friction between Jews and Gentiles and to keep the problem of the relation of the Jewish law to the gospel of Jesus Christ a continuous source of controversy in the future of the Christian mission to the nations (see Anti-Jewish Preaching).

Law in the History of Christianity. The ancient church struggled over the question of the role of the law in the history of salvation. Jewish converts to Christianity tended to keep the law as an essential condition of salvation. Their Christology moved within the framework of the law, picturing Christ not only as its perfect fulfillment but also as one who enables Christians to "fulfill the law of Christ" (Gal. 6:2) and to "look into the perfect law, the law of liberty." The law was integral to the way of salvation—no clear distinction was made between law and gospel. The Ebionites in the early church most clearly exemplified this synthesis of Christ and the Torah.

Marcion, influential heresiarch in the second century, is the clearest example of the opposite view. He launched a protest against Judaizing Christianity, calling for a radical separation of the gospel from the law, the New Testament from the Old, the God who redeems from the god (demiurge) who created the world, the freedom in Christ from bondage under the law. His movement embodied an extreme dualistic form of Paulinism and thus a misinterpretation of Paul's subtle dialectics of law and gospel.*

First Tertullian and later Augustine* became the architects of a synthesis of law and gospel that prevailed in medieval Catholicism. They combined a strong affirmation of the new order of divine grace brought about by the saving work of Christ with a description of the way of salvation that could be administered by an ecclesiastical system of sacramental graces and meritorious works. The explosion set off by Martin Luther* in the sixteenth century shattered the medieval synthesis of grace and works via a return to Paul's distinctions between law and gospel in Galatians and Romans. For Luther it takes the greatest theological skill properly to distinguish law and gospel, with respect to both the doctrine of justification through faith alone and the interpretation of scripture. The worst theological errors result from commingling law and gospel, confusing their differences in origin, content, purpose, form, and effect. The law commands; the gospel promises.

The law tells us what to do; the gospel gives what we lack. The law addresses us on account of our sin; the gospel announces forgiveness on account of God's love. The law is the letter that kills; the gospel is of the spirit that gives life. Luther's biblical commentaries, sermons, and lectures are saturated with such contrasts between law and gospel modeled on the Pauline epistles.

The Theological Problem of the Law.
The problem of the law has remained a subject of controversial theology from the Reformation to the present time. The chief point in dispute bears on the functions of the law. It has been customary in Protestant dogmatics to distinguish three uses of the law—the political, the evangelical, and the didactic.

The political use of the law refers to the way in which the living God works in the world, in nature, history, and personal life. God exercises rulership in the world through the law written into the structure of things. In the medieval tradition this was called "natural law"; Protestant theology has preferred to call it the "law of creation." In the ordering of human society this means that kings, dictators, presidents, and parliaments are instruments God uses for carrying out world-governing purposes, whether they acknowledge it or not.

The idea of God's acting through the law in the natural life of humanity does not mean that God's law can be equated with any particular set of positive laws, not even with codes of laws in the Old Testament. That would amount to a biblicistic legalism. On the other hand, the second table of the Decalogue given to Moses on Mount Sinai summarizes an elementary knowledge of revealed law that is universally valid in human life and that can be known apart from any special word of revelation in the Bible. Such a constant core of human morality is a sign that God is universally active in human society.

The living God is the driving force behind the demands that human beings make upon each other as they live in community. The test whether laws are good or right is rooted in the ideal of justice. The core of justice is care for the neighbor and the common good. Justice is the form that love takes in social life. The whole law is summarized in the words: "Thou shalt love thy neighbor as thyself." A law is good when it functions in the care of human beings in society, suppressing evil deeds and rewarding good deeds.

We have been describing the political use of the law, often called the first use of the law. The second use of the law has been called the evangelical or pedagogical use. It confronts human beings with the naked truth about themselves in relation to God, the world, their neighbors, and themselves. The purpose of the law is diagnostic—to make sick people aware that they need a physician. The law that commands people to act simultaneously accuses them, burdens their conscience, and drives them to despair. Luther said, "the law always accuses."

The accusatory purpose of the law is fulfilled when people are driven to seek their help in Christ. Just as Christ is the fulfillment of the Old Testament Torah, he is the fulfillment of the law at work in each individual human life. The accusing function of the law is teleologically connected with the consoling voice of the gospel. Neither one can accomplish its purpose without the other. But it would be a mistake to bind this evangelical function of the law so closely to the office of preaching the Word of God, as though the church were the sole custodian of God's law, hidden and anonymously at work within the conscience of of all human beings. The law in all its scope and force must assuredly be preached by the church, but there is also a silent preaching of the law searing the conscience of human beings apart from the church.

The third use of the law, the didactic, relates to its applicability to regenerate believers, to instruct them concretely how to live the Christian life in the power of the Spirit. At the time of the Reformation there were "spiritualists" who taught that the law has no validity among the "born again." True believers are guided by the Spirit and not the law. Those who teach this are called "antinomian," meaning "against the law." Both Luther and Calvin rejected the antinomian teaching as an unrealistic, romantic idea untrue to both scripture and the Christian experience.

Each use of the law is subject to abuse. Critics of the third use of the law fear the legalizing of the gospel, throwing the believer back into bondage to the very law that Christ has fulfilled and from which he has brought deliverance. On account of the perennial danger of legalism in the Christian life, perhaps we should speak of the new obedience to which believers are summoned through the preaching of the whole counsel of God, law, and gospel. The new obedience is not conformity to an external code of principles but to Christ, who is an example, "so that you should follow in his steps." (1 Peter 2:21) (see Theology of Preaching).

Dunn, J.D.G., *Jesus, Paul and the Law,* 1990. **Walther, C.F.W.,** *The Proper Distinction Between Law and Gospel,* 1928. **Wingren, G.,** *Creation and Law,* 1961.

CARL E. BRAATEN

Law and Gospel.
The theological theme of law and gospel came to prominence in the teaching of Martin Luther.* Increasingly influenced by the language of Paul through his lectures on Romans (1515–1516) and Galatians (1516–1517), Luther's understanding of law and gospel received typical formulation in this comment on Romans 10:15:

> The preaching of the Gospel is something lovable and desirable for those who are under the Law.* For the Law shows nothing but our sin, makes us guilty, and thus produces an anguished conscience; but the Gospel supplies a longed-for remedy to people in anguish of this kind. Therefore the Law is evil, and the Gospel good; the Law announces wrath, but the Gospel peace. The Law says: "Cursed be everyone who does not abide by all things writ-

ten in the book of the Law and do them" (Gal. 3:10). But no one continues in them to do them, as it is written in the same place: "For all who rely on works of the Law are under a curse." But the Gospel says: "Behold the Lamb of God, who takes away the sin of the world" (John 1:29). The Law oppresses the conscience with sins, but the Gospel frees the conscience and brings peace through faith in Christ" (*Luther's Works,* 25, 416).

There are differences between the thought world of Luther and that of Paul. For Paul, "law" meant primarily the Jewish Torah, and "gospel" meant the news that Jesus is the Messiah of Israel. For Luther, "law" meant encounter with the "hidden God," the God whose mercy is hidden in those dread-filled dimensions of existence that require human beings to justify their existence. "Gospel" meant that God's justification of human beings is both grounded and revealed in Christ. "Sin" meant that human beings do not trust God's justification. Instead they trust their own religious and moral works. Paul and Luther do, however, share the conviction that human beings need to be set free from the religion and piety evoked by law and converted to faith in Jesus Christ.

In his defense of the 1530 Augsburg Confession, Luther's colleague, Philip Melanchthon,* made law and gospel a hermeneutical key to understanding the Christian scriptures:

> All Scripture should be divided into these two chief doctrines, the law and the promises. In some places it presents the law. In others it presents the promise of Christ; this it does either when it promises that the Messiah will come and promises forgiveness of sins, justification, and eternal life for his sake, or when, in the New Testament, the Christ who came promises forgiveness of sins, justification, and eternal life. By "law" in this discussion we mean the commandments of the Deca-

logue, wherever they appear in the Scriptures (*Apology of the Augsburg Confession*, IV, 5–6).

There is potential here for grounding the authority of the scriptures in the gospel as contrasted with the law rather than in the claim of unique divine inspiration for the biblical documents.

That path, however, was followed neither by seventeenth-century Protestant scholasticism nor by the Protestant pietism that has been such a factor since the eighteenth century. In Protestant scholasticism, law and gospel were presented as the content of preaching. In Protestant pietism law and gospel became a description of the experience of conversion and hence the content of evangelistic preaching. The preaching of the law meant bringing about in hearers a conviction of sin by demonstrating that they had not kept the divine commandments perfectly. The preaching of the gospel meant proclaiming Christ's cross so that hearers accepted him as personal Savior and thus received salvation.

The theme of law and gospel has been influential in twentieth-century neoorthodox theology. It informs the basic structure of Paul Tillich's* correlation of philosophy (uncovering the fundamental questions of existence) and theology (the revelation that addresses those questions). Rudolf Bultmann* used the insights of existentialist philosophy to identify life under the law as inauthentic existence and obedience to the gospel as authentic existence. Anders Nygren singled out self-giving love (*agapē*) as the distinctive motif of Christianity in contrast to the law motif (*nomos*) of Judaism. Werner Elert insisted on a radical, mutually exclusive antithesis between law and gospel as central to Christianity. Opposing him, Karl Barth* charged that the sequence and antithesis of law and gospel in preaching does not do justice to the christological character of revelation and the ethic built into that revelation. Gustav Aulén criticized the scholastic and pietistic use of law and gospel because it set the Christian gospel into a legalistic and moralistic framework.

The theme of law and gospel will have contemporary power for preaching only if the terms law and gospel are defined appropriately. Law means whatever can be enforced with coercive power. Gospel as a translation of the Greek *euangelion* means good news, news that something beneficent has taken place. Law can be understood as a word of God only if that which is coercively enforced is experienced as ultimate, final. Gospel can be understood as a word of God only if a claim of ultimacy or finality can be made for it. Thus "gospel" will displace "law" as having "the last word."

Existential analysis such as that given by Ernest Becker in *The Denial of Death* (1973) discloses the law because it reveals that the encounter with death raises the ultimate question of the justification of life. There are finally only two responses to that ultimate question. Either human beings live destructively with the illusion of self-contrived justification, Becker's "vital lie." Or they live despairingly with the self-hatred born of oppression, abuse, and victimization. The law discloses the bondage of sin not because human beings misbehave or break commandments (although that also occurs) but because human freedom is misused to trust something other than God's gospel.

That gospel is truly news, an announcement that something has happened that promises to have created an ultimate, eschatological alternative to the power of death and sin. Jesus* announced the good news that in his words and deeds the reign of God had "come near" (Mark 1:14–15). The earliest disciples of Jesus announced the good news: Jesus of Nazareth is the Messiah of Israel because he has been raised from the dead! (*see* Jesus as Preacher).

Paul, a servant of Jesus Christ, called to be an apostle, set apart for the gospel of God, which he promised beforehand through his prophets in the holy scriptures, the gospel concerning his Son, who was descended from David according to the flesh and was declared to be Son of God with power according to the spirit of holiness by resurrection from the dead (Rom. 1:1–4).

The disciples of Jesus experienced his resurrection as a final, eschatological event. They encountered Jesus as raised to the final future of the kingdom of God. The future of the universe belongs to him and to no other (1 Cor. 15:20–28; Eph. 1:17–23). "Death no longer has dominion over him" (Rom. 6:9). He can therefore make promises no longer conditioned by death and send his disciples on an eschatological mission (Matt. 28:18–20). The reign of God, not the power of sin and death, will have the last word. Hence the disciples live as those who have seen the outcome of history (*see* Apocalyptic).

The proclamation of the resurrection of Jesus creates freedom for the unconditional future of God. "Law" means the future as bound by death. If death has the last word, then the only thing to do with the future is hold off death as long as possible. To protect one's self for as long as possible at the expense of others is to live under the bondage of sin fueled by the power of death. But if the future belongs to Jesus, then there is more to do with one's life than to preserve it.

The proclamation of the resurrection of Jesus creates freedom for the truth about Jesus. In light of his resurrection, the disciples of Jesus were able to reappropriate his cross as the saving event of God (2 Cor. 5:17–21). They were able to recognize that the God who created a universe became vulnerable to the suffering of the universe in that creating act. Because God the Father and God the Son have undergone ultimate alienation (Jürgen Moltmann, *The Crucified God*, 1983), all alienation and evil have been overcome. The cross and resurrection of Jesus thus create a new eschatological future of which the Holy Spirit is the "down payment" (2 Cor. 1:22; Eph. 1:13–14). The church is both the location and the experience of the Holy Spirit to the extent

that it lives in anticipation of the coming reign of God.

The proclamation of the resurrection of Jesus frees those to whom it is announced for attention to the truth and meaning of their own history. Because Jesus has the power of the future, the gospel is God's justification of all persons and all of history. The appropriate sequence is not confession followed by forgiveness. Rather, the proclamation of the gospel frees for confession, for the death of the sinful illusion of self-justification, and/or for renouncing the sinful despair of self-hatred. The proclamation of the gospel frees persons for authentic self-affirmation and therefore for the authentic affirmation of other persons and of the whole creation. The apostolic *paraenesis* (exhortation) is descriptive of the way persons want to be and want the world to be if the gospel is true.

The New Testament can speak of the gospel as a power, as a liberating and life-giving word (Rom. 1:16–17; 4:17–21). The grammar of the gospel is the opposite of the grammar of the law. Because Jesus has been raised from the dead you are free to love your neighbor as yourself; you are free to serve the future of the reign of God. "The law of the Spirit of life in Christ Jesus has set you free from the law of sin and of death" (Rom. 8:2). (*See* Theology of Preaching.)

Bouman, W. R., "The Concept of the 'Law' in the Lutheran Tradition," *Word and World* III, No. 4 (Fall 1983), 413–22. **Forde, G.,** *The Law-Gospel Debate,* 1969; and *Theology Is for Proclamation,* 1990. **Lischer, R.,** *A Theology of Preaching,* 1981, 2d ed. rev., 1992.

WALTER R. BOUMAN

Lay Preaching. The controversy that has surrounded lay preaching is fundamentally a debate about the criteria by which the church determines who may teach or exhort the community in an official capacity and speak in its name.

In the earliest years of Christianity, the

ministry of the word was shared by apostles, prophets, evangelists, and teachers (see Eph. 4:11 and 1 Cor. 12:28). The *Didache*, dating from the early second century, emphasized the importance of prophets and teachers in the community by setting them apart from and in some sense over bishops and deacons (15:1–2).

As early Christian communities became more organized, prophetic preaching gradually disappeared, and the ministry of the word became a teaching office restricted to bishops and priests. The first formal prohibition of lay preaching is found in a letter of Pope Leo I to Bishop Maximus in 453: "Apart from those who are priests of the Lord, no one may dare to claim for himself the right to teach and preach, whether he be monk or layman, one who boasts a reputation for some learning" (Pope Leo I, *Letters*, 1957, 207f.).

The spiritual awakening that swept through Europe in the eleventh and twelfth centuries gave rise to various lay preaching movements, especially in southern France and northern Italy. What they had in common was their insistence that the "apostolic life" of preaching demanded that preachers be holy by imitating the poverty of Jesus and the apostles and, conversely, that poverty rather than an ecclesiastical commission was the sign that one was "sent" to preach. The most famous of these movements traced its origins back to a layman from Lyons, Valdes, known as Peter Waldo (d. 1217), whose followers became known as the Waldenses or Waldensians. Pope Innocent III agreed with the Catholic theologians of his day who appealed to Romans 10:15 ("And how are they to proclaim him unless they are sent?") to show that preaching could not be justified simply by appealing to the holiness of life. However, he was careful not to make ecclesiastical authorization ("sending") the basis for the right to preach. What grounded that right, he wrote in a letter to the prelates of Poland in the year 1206, was a *divine* call and mission.

Innocent III failed in his attempt to keep the Waldensian lay preachers within the Roman church. His policy of cautious acceptance of lay preaching movements, however, proved much more successful with the followers of another apostolic lay preacher of the time, Francis of Assisi. Rome's insistence on ensuring the doctrinal orthodoxy of lay preachers, however, led to the rapid clericalization of Francis's little brotherhood.

The insistence of the sixteenth-century reformers that the doctrine of the priesthood of all believers meant there was no essential difference between the ordained and the rest of the baptized might seem to suggest that lay preaching is a moot question in the Protestant tradition. However, both Luther* and Calvin* insisted that while the church as a whole is called to proclaim the good news of salvation, the normal way it fulfills this ministry is by designating ("ordaining") those individuals who by charisma and training are called by God to exercise the office of preaching.

The eighteenth-century religious revival known as Methodism had its inception in lay preaching. In his determination to reach all people with the message of universal salvation, John Wesley* relied on a company of lay preachers who lacked formal academic training and were therefore all the more likely to speak out of their personal experience of God in a language appropriate to the unlettered people of the industrial cities of England and the American frontier (*see* Itinerant Preaching).

According to its revised Code of Canon Law promulgated in 1983, the Roman Catholic Church now allows for participation by the laity in the preaching mission of the church (can. 766). However, it continues to restrict the eucharistic homily to one who is ordained, normally to the priest or bishop who presides at the celebration, but increasingly to deacons. Because of the declining number of Roman Catholic priests in most parts of Europe and North America, it is becoming more and more common for lay people to preside and preach at Sunday celebrations that are not the Mass (*see* Vatican

II). Many dioceses are just beginning to deal with the question of determining whom to call to this ministry and how to prepare them for it. The practice of lay people preaching at "liturgies of the word" is widespread in the base Christian communities of Latin America, though the format is more often one of shared reflection than of an address given by an individual.

Foley, N., ed., *Preaching and the Non-Ordained*, 1983. **Palard, J.,** "Prédication des laïcs et pouvoir d'interprétation dans l'église catholique," *Foi et Vie* 85 (April 1986), 143–56.   WILLIAM SKUDLAREK, O.S.B.

Lay Response to Preaching.

African-American* preaching is noted for its tendency to foster an ongoing dialogue between preacher and congregation. In the typical African-American congregation, the preacher need only listen for the spoken "Amen" of the congregation to know if he or she is being heard.

For other preachers, lay reaction to preaching is difficult to obtain. Even African-American preachers who desire to probe beyond the occasional "Amen" in order better to discover how preaching is being received may find that perceptive, reliable, honest lay evaluation of preaching is elusive.

In order to grow in our preaching, preachers need informed lay evaluation. How do we move beyond the haphazard, "Nice sermon, Preacher" and avoid becoming victims of the merely chronic complainers?

Some laypersons are reluctant to criticize preaching. Many assume that since the pastor has been called by God to preach and because the pastor has studied preaching for many years, lay comments are inappropriate. Other laypersons, in their loyalty to their congregation, may feel that negative reactions to sermons reflect negatively upon their church. Does the preacher really desire lay reaction? Few people desire criticism. Laypersons, realizing how awesome the

responsibility of the preacher is, may be hesitant to add to the preacher's sense of insecurity by making critical comments.

Yet over time, and with repeated urging from the pastor, laypersons can become able evaluators of preaching. While lay reaction is not the only measure of a sermon's effectiveness, it is one means of measurement that preachers should seek.

In recent years, preachers have experimented with many means of receiving lay reaction to preaching. Some pastors have formed sermon discussion groups from among the members of the congregation. These groups meet, either with or without the pastor, to discuss sermons. The pastor then attempts to listen, in as open and nondefensive a way as possible, to the group's evaluation of sermons. Sometimes this method can be made even more fruitful, for both pastor and laity, if the group meets before the sermon, reads the proposed scripture, discusses possible approaches for the sermon, and then convenes after the sermon for evaluation.

The challenge to obtain informed, helpful, lay reaction to preaching can also be aided by the use of a Sermon Reaction Questionnaire. Dr. Boyd Stokes developed such a questionnaire by first asking scores of laypersons what they listened for in a "good" sermon. He then selected the criteria most frequently cited and formed a questionnaire from their responses. (See the Sermon Reaction Questionnaire that follows.)

The Sermon Reaction Questionnaire has a number of advantages. It enables the preacher to focus on specific aspects of preaching such as delivery or biblical interpretation. Results are quantifiable. Quantification enables the preacher to compare scores on various items over time to see if the listeners note improvement. The questionnaire enables the preacher to measure how different age and gender groups within the congregation respond to sermons. The questionnaire yields either a total reaction score or a score on each item. Perhaps the greatest advantage of the questionnaire is that it can be completed in a few minutes, either immediately after the sermon or at the end of the service.

The questionnaire may be given to a selected group of laypersons for a couple of weeks. Then, a few months later, if the questionnaires are given to the same group, the pastor can measure change. A randomly selected group of laypersons might agree to attend worship every Sunday for a couple of months, complete the questionnaire at the end of each service, and meet with the pastor at the end of the time period to discuss the results.

Note in scoring the results of the questionnaire that some items are stated negatively in order to keep respondents from simply going through the questionnaire and mindlessly checking off the same number on every question. Scores for items numbered 3, 5, 7, 8, 9, 10, 13, 19, 20, 21, 23 need to be reversed when tallying the total scores in order to unify the results of the questionnaire. For instance, a score of 1 on question 3, "I was not inspired," should be tallied as if it were 5. That way, all the results "move" in the same direction.

Preachers who use the questionnaire over a period of time may notice that some of their scores actually go down as a result of laypersons becoming more astute listeners. Through the use of this questionnaire and other systematic attempts to obtain lay reaction to preaching, preachers will grow in abilities and will better understand the impact they make upon listeners. The congregation will gain a new appreciation for the challenges involved in faithful Christian proclamation.   WILLIAM H. WILLIMON

Sermon Reaction Questionnaire

Please supply the following information. Do not sign your name.

A. Sex
   (1) male _____   (2) female _____
B. Age
   (1) up through   (2) 20–29 _____
   19 years _____
   (3) 30–39 _____   (4) 40–49 _____
   (5) 50–59 _____   (6) above 59 _____

Please indicate whether you agree or disagree with the following reactions to the sermon you have just heard. This includes both the content and the delivery of the sermon. Indicate your reactions on the scale as follows:

Circle 1 for Strongly Agree, 2 for Agree, 3 for Uncertain, 4 for Disagree, 5 for Strongly Disagree.
Your honesty and frankness are appreciated.

The preacher/The sermon

1. maintained my interest
   1   2   3   4   5
2. integrated the sermon into the total service of worship
   1   2   3   4   5
3. did not inspire me
   1   2   3   4   5
4. involved his or her personality in the message
   1   2   3   4   5
5. did not both deal with and illumine the scripture chosen as the text
   1   2   3   4   5
6. used words and thought patterns in present-day usage
   1   2   3   4   5
7. did not evidence a personal confession of faith
   1   2   3   4   5
8. lasted too long
   1   2   3   4   5
9. was not very well understood by me
   1   2   3   4   5
10. looked at or read his or her notes too often
   1   2   3   4   5
11. projected an attitude of love for us
   1   2   3   4   5
12. spoke to some of my personal needs
   1   2   3   4   5
13. did not sufficiently emphasize the greatness of Christ
   1   2   3   4   5
14. was made more meaningful by the reading of the scripture
   1   2   3   4   5
15. showed self-confidence
   1   2   3   4   5

16. was more readily accepted by me because of my previous feelings for the minister

1   2   3   4   5

17. was made more meaningful by the appearance of the worship setting

1   2   3   4   5

18. made me feel a oneness with him or her

1   2   3   4   5

19. seemed to speak down to us

1   2   3   4   5

20. did not have a sufficiently forceful conclusion

1   2   3   4   5

21. did not initiate an encounter between God and me

1   2   3   4   5

22. contained points that were easy to remember

1   2   3   4   5

23. did not make me eager to serve God any more than I have up until now

1   2   3   4   5

24. led me to accept the message

1   2   3   4   5

Lectionary. A lectionary is an "orderly sequence of selections from scripture to be read aloud at public worship" (Reumann, 116). The selections may be set out in full or listed in a table of "pericopes." They may be selected in three ways: as continuous readings, as semi-continuous readings skipping certain verses, or as isolated passages chosen for a specific occasion. They presuppose a calendar or church year.* They may be intended to provide preaching texts or simply for use as readings for cultic purposes.

Origin. The reading of the law and prophets is already attested in Judaism at the time of Christian origins (Luke 4: 16–30; Acts 13:14). It is disputed how far these readings were already fixed in synagogue usage. At all events, it was from the synagogue that the early church derived the idea of using selected portions of the Old Testament, to which it added readings from its own literature, the Apostolic writings, and the Gospels.

Development. In early Christian usage there were several readings, but in the course of time these were reduced, first to three (Old Testament, Apostolic writings, and Gospel) then to two. As the church year developed, certain readings became fixed for special occasions, though in nonfestal seasons ("ordinary time") continuous readings selected by the officiant were still the norm. In addition to festivals, other factors led to the fixing of specific readings. They included the agricultural year, proximity of saints' days, station masses (at Rome), preparation for baptism (Lent), post-baptismal instruction (Eastertide). Traces of earlier semi-continuous reading survive. In the West, the development of the lectionary was highly unsystematic. Alcuin is credited with having given it some sort of order, though local variations and ad hoc additions continued until the eve of the Reformation.

The Reformation. The Lutheran and Anglican Reformations basically retained the traditional Western lectionary, though with slight variations between theirs and the Roman Missal. In addition, Cranmer provided a lectionary for daily morning and evening prayer based on the civil calendar, with two lessons, one from each Testament. The Reformed churches sometimes retained a lectionary of Gospel readings only, but the radical Reformation abolished lectionaries altogether, allowing the preachers liberty to select their own text, usually on the principle of continuous reading.

Post-Reformation Changes. The Church of England revised its office lectionary slightly in 1871 and produced a new office lectionary in 1923 to conform with the church year. It also produced minor revisions of the eucharistic lectionary in 1928. Similar developments took place in the American Episcopal Church. The German Lutherans produced four alternative sets of pericopes, including Old Testament readings. Generally, Lutherans adhered strictly to the lectionary in preaching, while Anglicans often chose their texts independently from the lectionary.

Vatican II* and Its Results. The Constitution on the Sacred Liturgy (1963) stated that "The treasures of the Bible are to be opened up more lavishly" with a wider selection of readings over a cycle of years. In response, a new lectionary was devised and published in 1969. This was based on a three-year cycle with Matthew (Year A), Mark-John (Year B) and Luke (Year C) providing a semi-sequence of Gospel readings in ordinary time. Each mass had three readings: Old Testament (including the Apocrypha or deutero-canonical writings, in addition to the Epistle and Gospel reading, and a responsory psalm for each occasion). Like the Gospels, the epistles were to be read semicontinuously in ordinary time. The Old Testament reading was selected to match the Gospel (prophetically or typologically) except in Lent, when a series of special readings highlighted Israel's salvation history. A two-year cycle was also provided for weekday masses. A conservative revision of the calendar gave special place to the fifty days of Easter (when Acts replaced the Old Testament and in one year when Revelation replaced the epistle). The Sundays after Epiphany and Pentecost became "Sundays of the Year." Meanwhile, the Church of England in concert with the Free Churches had developed a two-year lectionary on thematic principles.

The Common Lectionary. The three-year lectionary was widely adopted in North America, each denomination producing its own adaptation of the Roman form. The need for greater uniformity, together with certain defects of the three-year lectionary that became apparent from experience, led to the setting up of an interdenominational committee (North American Committee for Calendar and Lectionary, or NACCL). This committee completed its work in 1983. The major innovation was the provision of a series of semicontinuous readings from the Old Testament for the Sundays of ordinary time after Pentecost. This change was designed to allow the Old Testament to speak for itself rather than being subordinated christologically to the Gospel reading (*see* Liturgical Preaching; Homily).

Bower, P. C., ed., *Handbook for the Common Lectionary*, 1987. **Consultation on Common Texts**, *Common Lectionary*, 1983; revised ed. 1992. **Hessel, D. T.**, ed., *Social Themes of the Christian Year: A Commentary on the Lectionary*, 1983. **Reumann, J.**, "A History of Lectionaries: From the Synagogue at Nazareth to Post-Vatican II," *Interpretation* 31:2 (1977): 116–30.

REGINALD H. FULLER

Lectionary Preaching. Lectionary usage may be examined under seven headings. Each of the features is fundamentally positive, although care must be taken to safeguard against certain liabilities.

Scriptural Comprehensiveness. By providing three stipulated readings (Old Testament, Epistle, and Gospel) for use over various cycles of years, lectionaries attempt to give voice to the entire canon of scripture by ensuring that representative lessons are heard and interpreted. Semi-continuous readings, as with the Gospel and Epistle lections during Ordinary Time (Sundays after Epiphany and after Pentecost), permit large sections of books to be read in their fullness. Even so, not all of holy writ can be included in the cycles of readings; some books, such as Ezra, Nahum, and the second and third Johannine epistles, are often omitted altogether from contemporary lectionaries. Sometimes the material that is included has been subjected to editing, or the scriptural units (pericopes) have been abbreviated, thereby distorting the text.

Placement of the three lessons in combination can bring to the fore the continuities and discontinuities within the sacred text. The relationship of parts to the whole canon may become clearer by juxtaposing texts, although such a synthesis or connection risks being false or strained.

Lectionaries for Christian worship are organized with a christological orientation in which the person and work of Jesus Christ is understood as the key to the scriptures. The Gospel lesson functions as the principal text that is complemented by the other two lessons. Such a disposition of texts raises the question of whether a canon within the canon is created; in other words, must the Old Testament be interpreted in light of the New Testament, or can it also stand legitimately on its own?

Scriptural Primacy. Reliance upon the lectionary, rather than dependence upon the preacher's subjectivity and selectivity, allows the message of the scripture to take rightful precedence over the message of the preacher. By beginning with the text and allowing the text to speak, both preacher and congregation are placed under the judgment and grace of the text. Working with established lessons helps to counteract idiosyncrasies and avoids the danger of forced readings when a text or texts are chosen ad hoc to address a specific topic or occasion.

Liturgical. Lectionaries are designed to provide shape and coherence for the church's annual calendar and for the weekly Lord's Day service. The predominance of the Gospel lesson proper to the day provides a linkage with the story of God's work of salvation in and through Jesus Christ as told throughout the liturgical year. The Gospel may shed light on the accompanying lessons (and vice versa), though pressing Old Testament and Epistle lessons into service of the Gospel theme of the day or season of the Christian year may refocus the original intention or purpose of those texts. Given the limitation in the number of readings provided to tell the story of salvation, it is important to examine if the lectionary used recounts the whole story or if there are significant omissions.

In furnishing a structure for Sunday worship, the lessons can govern the whole of the liturgy and not just the preached word, which stands as one part of the worship service. Lectionaries generally presuppose a weekly Eucharist, and connections are often made between the readings and the proper preface of the eucharistic prayer. Established texts aid in the celebration of a unified liturgical event.

Practical. Besides easing the task of sermon text selection, employment of a lectionary enables long-range planning and preparation for the sermon and for the entirety of the worship service. Coordination of the sermon with music (congregational, choral, and instrumental) and other liturgical acts and ministries is facilitated by advanced knowledge of the texts for the day.

Arising circumstances or concerns within a congregation may require that the intentions of the lections be reexamined in order to speak to such situations or may suggest the need for alternate texts. Departure from the lectionary may be needed, on occasion, for purposes of biblical and theological instruction, as when examining large portions of a single biblical work (thereby utilizing continuous readings or *lectio continua*) or developing an exposition upon an ecumenical creed (employing isolated scripture passages).

Instructional. Because they provide a regular course through selected portions of the Bible, lectionaries invite biblical, theological, and liturgical literacy for both preachers and congregations. Liturgical reading of the day's lectionary selections (even if all the lessons do not constitute the basis for the sermon) ensures that the congregation hears, at least on a weekly basis, a wide range of texts from both the Old Testament and New Testament. Repetition of the lessons in their regular cycles encourages familiarity with the biblical material and allows associations of particular texts with days and seasons of the liturgical calendar.

Theological reflection is promoted by systematic investigation of the tensions and connections in the three designated texts, by exploration of the content of the texts in relationship to the theological issues of the liturgical year, and by examination of the theological assumptions that undergird the construction of the lectionary itself.

Congregational. Advanced publication of the designated texts grants an opportunity for congregations to prepare for the experience of corporate worship, thus allowing for active hearing and participation. Since the readings belong to the entire community and are not simply the prerogative of the preacher, representatives from the congregation may readily participate in the planning of sermon and worship. Lectionaries also provide an easily accessed resource for directed study of the scriptures and can serve as a guide for disciplined devotion and prayer.

Ecumenical. Use of a lectionary within a denomination and across the churches attests that the Bible is the basic source of revelation for all Christian people. Common readings remind congregations that they exist as part of the church and serve as a visible sign of unity to the still-fractured body of Christ.

KAREN B. WESTERFIELD TUCKER

Liberation Preaching.

Although the category of "liberation" should be applicable to all preaching that aims to liberate its hearers from the bondage of sin, the name of "liberation preaching" is usually reserved for preaching informed by the various theologies of liberation that have evolved in recent decades. This includes Latin American liberation theology, black theology, feminist theology, Hispanic-American theology, and other theologies developed from the perspectives of the nonindustrialized nations or of ethnic and cultural minorities in the so-called developed world.

The distinguishing characteristic of liberation preaching is not its content but its hermeneutics.* In other words, liberation preaching is not preaching *about* liberation but preaching that approaches its hermeneutical and homiletical tasks from a perspective of liberation. Since liberation preaching is not *about* liberation, but rather about gospel as a liberating power, it deals with all the traditional themes of Christian preaching, although from a perspective of its own—a perspective that varies according to the situation in which the preacher stands and the group that she or he represents.

A common denominator of these theologies is that they are being developed by persons and groups that have traditionally been disenfranchised from the mainstream of theological dialogue and discourse. Furthermore, traditional theologies have often provided the justification for such disenfranchisement—women are by nature defective human beings; third-world peoples are the recipients of mission and will remain such until they fully appropriate traditional theology; the typically Western and masculine ways of doing theology are the only legitimate ones; the poor and the unlearned are not sophisticated enough to do theology, and so forth.

Another common denominator is that these theologies understand salvation in a holistic way, as liberation from all powers of oppression. This includes both what has traditionally been called the spiritual oppression of sin and the political, economic, and social oppressions that these various groups suffer and that are also manifestations of sin.

As a result, liberation preaching seeks to recognize the political dimensions present in the Bible. In some cases—notably, that of some feminist theologians—this means that the Bible, or at least portions of it, must be regarded as reflecting an oppressive society and must therefore be rejected or at least corrected. In most cases, however, the Bible is seen as the record of God's liberating activity for men and women and as a call to join God in that activity. From this perspective, the

Bible is first of all a historical narrative (or a series of interrelated narratives) that provides the inspiration and the direction for present-day commitment to liberation. This is often related to a typological interpretation in which creation, the exodus, the exile, the incarnation, and Pentecost play a central role.

Liberation preaching also must take the setting of the sermon very seriously. Preaching is itself a political act in which there are relations of power and dependence. For this reason, some liberation preachers prefer situations in which the hermeneutical task is performed by the community as a whole, in dialogue, and not exclusively by the preacher from the pulpit. Others—particularly women and ethnic minorities—are aware that their preaching must vary according to who their audience is: A woman will preach differently to a group of women than to a mixed audience, and the message of an African-American preacher to a white congregation will not be the same as to an African-American audience.

Liberation theology is often closely related to liberation movements that include in their membership those who have no relationship to the church or perhaps have even a hostile reaction to it. There is then a borderline on which there may be those who relate to liberation theology but not to the church. However, when one speaks of liberation preaching, it is quite clear that those who engage in such activity are closely related to the Christian community, thus defining the meaning of liberation more precisely in a theological direction.

Social groups in which there are liberation movements, however, are not the only locus for such preaching. The liberating power of the gospel is needed for all people, though it is also specific to each setting. Those who are poor need liberation from their poverty as well as from the sense of shame that often accompanies poverty. Those who are rich need liberation from the reliance on wealth—which may mean liberation from wealth—and the false sense of self that goes with it.

Liberation preaching does not think of itself as totally new. It finds parallels in the early preaching of the church, when the Christian community was itself a despised group. It finds the demise of this preaching in the Constantinian period when the church became closely associated with the powerful of the Roman Empire and its successors in Western European civilization.

To the degree that hermeneutics* after the Enlightenment stressed the historical-critical method that depended upon modern scholarship and a scientific mentality, it is not surprising that Christians who are not part of this mindset—perhaps through lack of such education—and who are immersed in the biblical story, find it easier to read scripture in postcritical terms. When such groups are also oppressed by social and political structures, a liberation hermeneutic readily develops. We can see this particularly in the preaching of the African-American churches and in the base ecclesial communities in Latin America. Precisely because of its origins in traditionally marginalized groups and the fact that it is not based on the methodologies of critical scholarship, such a hermeneutic has often been dismissed as naive by the academy. However, in more recent years, liberation hermeneutics has been given a wider hearing. This is due to the lessening of the hold of the historical-critical method in the academy itself, as well as the dominant churches finding themselves marginalized by an increasingly secular culture. As the traditionally powerful churches lose their status, they are more open to learn from congregations that have long been accustomed to the margin (*see* Homiletics and Preaching in Latin America; African-American Preaching; Feminist Preaching).

Cardenal, E., *The Gospel in Solentiname*, 3 vols., 1976–79. González, C. G., and J. L. González, *Liberation Preaching: The Pulpit and the Oppressed*, rev. ed., 1993. González, J. L., ed., *Proclaiming the Acceptable Year: Sermons from a Perspective of Liberation*,

1982. **Segundo, J. L.,** *The Liberation of The-*
ology, 1976.   JUSTO L. GONZÁLEZ
                    CATHERINE GUNSALUS GONZÁLEZ

Literary Criticism.   Contemporary
literary criticism is a diverse and complex field. Structuralism, New Criticism,
reader-response criticism, post-structuralism, deconstruction, psychoanalytic
criticism, and political criticism all offer different and frequently conflicting
approaches to the study of literature. Indeed, no consensus even exists concerning what counts as "literature." Consequently, any uniform understanding of
literary criticism is impossible today, as
is any monolithic treatment of the relationship between literary criticism and
preaching. Indeed, one of the challenges
facing the homiletical appropriation of
literary criticism lies precisely in the diversity of approaches from which to draw
and the different, often contradictory, implications of the various approaches.

Despite this diversity, however, one general trend can be discerned in the development of literary criticism during the twentieth century. The focus of criticism has
shifted from an *author-centered* approach
characteristic of the nineteenth century to
a *text-centered* approach (e.g., structuralism, New Criticism) to, most recently,
a *reader-centered* approach (e.g., reader-
response criticism). Although these general approaches often shade into each
other, particularly in the literary criticism
of the Bible, the text-centered approaches
have to this point exercised the most influence upon preaching.

Although homileticians have not adopted any one specific theoretical stance,
several aspects of text-centered literary
criticism have proven especially significant for preachers, primarily by offering
new ways of interpreting scripture. First,
in contrast to the historical-critical
method, literary criticism has focused on
the final form of the text. Rather than
going "behind" the texts to examine earlier sources, historical references, or authorial intent, textual criticism encour-

ages preachers to examine the final form
of the biblical texts themselves—the
"world" created by the language of the
Bible. In this respect, this kind of literary
criticism is closely related to "canonical
criticism," which focuses on the present,
canonical form of the church's scripture.
Such a primary engagement with the text
itself, rather than with a host of secondary historical-critical materials, has not
only narrowed the gap between exegesis
and the sermon but has also helped to
make scripture once again an imaginative
and creative source for preaching (*see*
Hermeneutics; Exegesis).

Second, text-centered literary criticism
has stressed the integral relationship between the form* and content of texts. The
message of scripture is not something
that can be abstracted from the forms in
which that message is embodied. Rather,
the various literary forms in the Bible are
essential to the meaning of scripture.

This emphasis on the inseparability of
form and content has contributed to a
virtual revolution in homiletics. Rarely
today are sermons simply fitted into
some abstract predetermined structure,
whether that structure be the classical
rhetorical argument or the traditional
"three points and a poem." Rather, the
form of the text itself—whether parable,
story, dialogue, poem, or argument—has
come to play a vital role in shaping the
form and function of the sermon. In the
wake of developments in literary criticism, a new appreciation for sermon
form has emerged and a variety of new
sermon forms have arisen in the practice
of preaching. Scripture and sermon have
been brought formally into closer relationship.

Finally, text-centered literary criticism
has generally presupposed the unity of
the biblical text. Rather than breaking the
biblical text into its smallest component
parts, a method characteristic of historical criticism, textual literary critics have
explored larger blocks of biblical material, stressing the connections and creative tensions among various parts of the
biblical text. This approach has led to a

new appreciation for the narrative character of much of scripture. In particular, the Gospels have been extensively examined as unified narratives, spawning a new branch of biblical study called "narrative criticism."

It is at this point, in the interpretation of narrative, that literary criticism has made its most significant impact on contemporary preaching and continues to hold much promise for preachers. The categories of narrative criticism, such as plot, character, setting, and point of view, offer preachers some valuable tools for exploring narrative texts and relating their exegetical work directly and imaginatively to their preaching.

Most fully explored to date has been the element of plot. Drawing on studies of narrative, some homileticians have argued that sermons should no longer consist of logically organized information but rather should take the form of a plotted movement through time—a "homiletical plot," as Eugene Lowry has called it. A sermon, in short, should move like a good story. Rather than constructing a sermon from a central idea abstracted from a narrative text, the preacher explores the text's movement from initial conflict to final resolution and then seeks to recapture that movement in the sermon. the plot of the story directly shapes the sermon's development. In this way a category of literary criticism has helped redefine the nature and form of the sermon. Indeed, the genre of "narrative preaching"* has been shaped largely by considerations of plot.

Less fully explored has been the matter of character. A careful examination of the characters in a story offers a creative way to enter exegetically and homiletically into the biblical narratives. One helpful method is for the preacher to "stand in the shoes" of various characters in a story to better understand each character's point of view. The parable of the good Samaritan, for example, looks and feels different when one stands respectively with the religious leaders, the good Samaritan, or the person lying beside the road. Such an exploration of character

can help clarify the point of view from which the sermon will be preached, including the desired impact upon the hearers. In addition, with reference to the gospels, a focus on character highlights the centrality of Jesus. The Gospels invite preachers not simply to take the place of various characters in the story but to focus particularly on the person of Jesus, whose identity is rendered by the interplay of character and incident in the Gospel narratives.

Like plot and character, the setting of a story, which is often symbolically or metaphorically significant, can be rich with homiletical possibilities. For example, in the Gospel of John one reads that Judas left the last supper, and "it was night" (13:30). Because "night" is a significant theological metaphor in John, the image of the church depicted by this setting is a poignant one: Jesus and his disciples gathered together in a lighted room, surrounded by a world of darkness. One picture speaks a thousand words, and the categories of narrative criticism can help preachers explore these pictures through careful attention to narrative settings.

Even such an apparently insignificant literary matter as the pace of a story—the quickness or slowness of its movement—can be exceedingly helpful to preachers. When the presentation becomes more detailed and the pace slows down, the preacher can be sure that important material is present. Examples can be seen in the careful description of John the Baptist's dress in the story of Jesus' baptism (Matt. 3:4); in the slow, detailed account of John the Baptist's execution, which follows a rapid series of brief vignettes in the Gospel of Mark (6:14–29); and, most obviously, in the account of Jesus' Passion itself. Here again, a literary approach to scripture can alert preachers to particularly significant material for sermons.

Homileticians have thus drawn fruitfully on some specific dimensions of literary criticism, primarily those focused on the text itself and those related to narrative. However, whereas secular literary criticism has moved in recent years from a text-centered to a reader-centered approach, the homiletical implications of these newer forms of criticism have not yet been seriously examined. Although some recent homiletical theories have emphasized the preacher's "experience" of texts in sermon preparation and the congregation's role in completing the sermon's message, homileticians have not yet examined carefully the homiletical significance of reader-response criticism, which stresses the reader's active role in creating the text and its meaning. Similarly, although some feminist* and liberation* theologians have begun to develop the implications of their work for preaching, political criticism, which uncovers the socio-political dimensions of both texts and interpretation, has not yet made a significant impact on contemporary homiletics. Likewise, the implications of more radical forms of criticism, such as deconstruction, which emphasizes the instability of texts and the lack of foundations for interpretation, have not been examined in detail by homileticians.

It now remains to be seen if and how these more recent trends in literary criticism will bear fruit in homiletical theory and practice. The possibilities are varied and far-reaching. For example, reader-response criticism offers a variety of theoretical and practical directions for exploring the dynamic relationship not only between the preacher and scripture, but also between the sermon and its hearers. And recent studies of the role of "interpretive communities" in reading texts suggest a more intimate relationship between church and scripture than is frequently recognized in the homiletical literature. Post-structuralism and deconstruction may also open up new, and possibly perilous, avenues for preaching, calling for sermons that are more open-ended and destabilizing than anything heretofore imagined. In addition, contemporary political criticism suggests directions for exploring the role of power and ideology in both the reading of texts and the preaching of sermons. Finally, all of these reader-centered approaches raise important questions about the authority of scripture in the church, which is always of concern to preachers.

Thus, although homileticians have drawn on some specific aspects of literary criticism in fruitful ways, they have only scratched the surface of this rich and complex field. Much more ground remains to be cultivated.

Alter, R., *The Art of Biblical Narrative*, 1981. Barton, J., *Reading the Old Testament: Method in Biblical Study*, 1984. Eagleton, T., *Literary Theory: An Introduction*, 1983. Fish, S., *Is There a Text in This Class? The Authority of Interpretive Communities*, 1980. Long, T. G., *Preaching and the Literary Forms of the Bible*, 1989. Lowry, E., *Doing Time in the Pulpit*, 1985. Moore, S. D., *Literary Criticism and the Gospels: The Theoretical Challenge*, 1989. Powell, M. A., *What Is Narrative Criticism?*, 1990.

CHARLES L. CAMPBELL

Liturgical Preaching. It is tautological but at the same time helpful to say that liturgical preaching is preaching that takes place during the liturgy or formal, public worship of God. The terms "sermon"* from the Latin *sermo* and "homily"* from the Greek *homilia* describe an exposition of scripture or a development in Christian faith or practice delivered within the framework of public prayer. This exposition is made chiefly at the Lord's Supper and other sacramental rites, less frequently as part of the night and day hours (the divine office). To this should be added marriage and Christian burial for the churches that do not celebrate these events sacramentally. In some communions the sermon came after Bible reading and in effect became the worship service. To this proclamation of the word, hymnody and prayers of praise and petition were added. This may be termed preaching as liturgy rather than preaching in liturgy. It is called "liturgical preaching" only to the confusion of those who engage in it.

The classic form of liturgical preaching is the "homily" occurring within the rite after the proclamation of the gospel. The "sermon" only very slowly emerged as distinct from it. A second, transferred sense of homily in the *Oxford English Dictionary* (1933) defines it as: "A serious admonition, exhortation or counsel; a lecture; a tedious moralizing discourse." Originally, the homily (meaning converse or discourse, from *homilos*, an assemblage or crowd) expounded a pericope or paragraph of the scripture(s) just read. It may have been "moralizing" but in intent, at least, it was merely hortatory. A homily attempted to confirm Christian hearers in the faith they held and exhort them to even greater fidelity in their following of Christ. Homilies may be tedious. They may also be too long, a quite different matter. Neither is of their essence. The homily is the form of discourse most characteristic of liturgical preaching. It is directly related to the biblical passage or passages just proclaimed and does not depart too far from them. The sermon, on the other hand, has come to describe a discourse that develops a specific theme. Examples would be a local church observance, a particular virtue, or the praise of a person or ideal. The true liturgical homily is integral to the text of the rite and partakes of its character of prayer or praise.

This genre of preaching is first testified to in St. Justin Martyr's first *Apology* (ca. 155), where he speaks of the presider at the ritual meal of Christians as "urging and inviting us in a discourse to the imitation of these noble things [from the writings of the prophets or memoirs of the apostles]" (67). The origin of this oral form may have been the commentary on the Torah portion read in synagogue services. It was, however, shortly seen as an application of the text to Christian living rather than as a didactic commentary on the text. Origen* of Alexandria (d. 254) is credited with being the first to distinguish between the *logos*, or sermon in the style of classical oration, and the *homilia*, as above, which took its rise from a popular exegesis of scripture.

Liturgical preaching may derive from one of the two (weekday) or three (Sunday and feastday) readings in Western lectionaries* (some of the Eastern rites having as many as five). An early pattern seems to have been continuous reading out of successive biblical books. This gradually came to be a matter of readings selected for their appropriateness to a particular feast or season such as Easter's fifty days or the Epiphany. Since psalmody was widely used in Christian ritual for entrance processions, at the solemn transfer of the Gospel book, the preparation of the gifts, and the Communion rite, references to or citations from the psalms of the day became part of liturgical preaching (*see* Psalms). Similarly, the feasts that the Bible texts were chosen to illustrate and the songs of Christian poets such as Romanos Melodos, Sedulius Scotus, and Rabanus Maurus that were incorporated into the rites were the subjects of exposition.

Preaching in the liturgy may have an instructive function, but this is not primary. One recalls the lengthy homilies of the patristic and medieval periods in which whole books of the Bible were expounded successively, presumably in a liturgical context. There the exegetical was always subordinated to the hortatory or the edifying. The paradox is that the moral life, or the life of Christian perfection, is normally encouraged more successfully by illustration and instruction than by direct appeal.

The modern homilist in a liturgical setting is hampered by widespread ignorance of the Bible and postbiblical tradition. This includes confinement of festal observances to the churches, whereas once they had meaning in the broader culture. The folkloric counterfeits of the Christian feasts work actively against a faith understanding of them. This means that the liturgical homily must itself supply what in another day could have been assumed.

In sum, liturgical preaching is biblical, it is ecclesial, and it is eschatologically oriented. This makes it integral to the worship experience rather than an interruption of it. When nonbiblical writings are cited they are usually the work of classic commentators on the scriptures, whether from the patristic or later ages. None of this renders liturgical preaching archaic. Its chief concern is modernity in the sense that the lives of worshipers provide the direction any commentary on the inspired and other texts must take. In the churches described as "liturgical," their lives are lived in the rhythm of the church's year* and not just the rhythms of work or family, economic or recreational existence. This means that liturgical preaching takes its lead from people's experience, to which homilists must be attuned, as much as from the classic texts they expound. The one must speak to the other and conversely. Otherwise there is a merely "churchy" exposition going on in pulpit or ambo. It may be at a higher level than normal pulpit discourse, but it will be no more effective than the preaching that seldom manages to get out of the confines of the church building.

Congregations that celebrate the church's liturgy well are rarely inclined to report that they have a "great preacher." However gifted the person may be, they are more likely to say that they have a great experience of worship from one Sunday to the next, of which the homily is a part.

Martimort, A. G., "The Word of God in the Assembly," I. H. Dalmais et al., *The Church at Prayer*, I, *Principles of the Liturgy*, 1987, 133–42. **O'Shea, W. J.,** "Homily," *New Catholic Encyclopedia*, VII, 113–15. **Sloyan, G. S.,** *Worshipful Preaching*, 1984.

GERARD S. SLOYAN

Luther, Martin. (1483–1546) Luther was an ordained member of the Augustinian Hermits and a professor of biblical theology at Wittenberg University from 1513. Preaching was an integral part of his assigned duties. He started preaching at the monastery and continued at the university, frequently at the Town Church, and at times on the road or on assigned tours. It is estimated that he preached between 4,000 and 10,000 times; 2,300 sermons are extant, the bulk of them recorded by listeners rather than by his own hand. In 1528, he preached 195 sermons in 145 days, focusing on catechetical instruction. In 1529, he preached 121 times, twice a day for forty days, again concentrating on the catechism. At that time he could look back to four years of marriage, resulting in three children; he had been condemned by church and state as a heretic and outlaw; and he was the leader of a speedy reform movement in and beyond Germany.

All stages of Luther's life and work are mirrored in his sermons. He attacked the abuse of forgiving sins through money ("indulgences") in sermons before he drafted his famous "Ninety-five Theses" in 1517, calling for a debate of the abuse. His journey to the Diet of Worms in 1521 was a preaching tour. When the Diet condemned him and he was concealed at the Wartburg Castle, he produced, among many other literary items, a collection of sermons and homiletical aids for the preachers of the reform movement and for German households without access to preaching. In 1522, Luther returned from the Wartburg Castle, violating the mandate of Elector Frederick to stay, and preached every day for a whole week in Wittenberg, where there were riots and unrest caused by radicals. All of Luther's liturgical and catechetical reforms were expounded in sermons. "Let everything be done so that the Word may have free course" (*Luther's Works*, 53, 14, hereafter cited LW). Luther viewed the mission of the church as making the Word of God come alive in oral and sacramental communication. "Whoever has the office of preaching imposed on him has the highest office in Christendom imposed on him" (LW 39, 314). There is a "real presence" in the preached word just as there is in the Eucharist. For where the preacher speaks, God speaks. A true sermon must disclose the eschatological battle between Christ in whom God battles sin, death, and evil. "Preaching continues the battle begun by the saving event and is itself the saving event" (LW 51, xx). Otherwise, preaching is just smart rhetoric. In 1540, Luther threatened "to write a book against artful preachers" but never did (LW 53, 384). He himself was frequently frustrated by the task of preaching. His work as interim pastor at the Town Church, at one time for two years (1537–1539), made him aware how difficult it was to change people through the Word of God. On a preaching tour in Saxony in 1545, Luther decided to retire and quit preaching altogether since his audiences seemed to resist everything he proclaimed. His wife Katie, his friends, and the Saxon court persuaded him to return to his post in Wittenberg. Luther's last sermon conveys how difficult it was for him to balance the divine and human work of preaching. "This and much more might be said about this Gospel [Matt. 5:25–30], but I am too weak and we shall let it go at that" (LW 51, 392).

Luther began preaching in the style of medieval scholastics, enumerating all his points, at times twenty or more. His early sermons often begin with a proposition, which then is analyzed in the sermon. But he soon switched to expository* preaching, expounding scripture according to pericopes from the liturgical tradition according to the church year, highlighted by Advent, Christmas, Epiphany, Lent, Easter, and Pentecost. Year after year, Luther preached on the same texts, usually with fresh insights from exegesis and contemporary experience. All worship services included preaching. There were three public services on Sunday for the 2,000 inhabitants of Wittenberg: from five to six in the morning with a sermon on the Pauline epistles; from nine to ten on the Gospels; and in the afternoon or evening on the catechism. Luther frequently added Old Testament texts, favoring Genesis, the major prophets, and Jonah. He was also part of the Wittenberg preaching team, staffed by pastors, professors, and deacons who would conduct weekday services: Mondays and Tuesdays offered sermons on the catechism; Wednesdays on the Gospel of Matthew; Thursdays and Fridays on the pastoral epistles; and Saturdays on the Gospel of John. Luther hardly ever used a manuscript for preaching but preached from an outline. Friends and other listeners then wrote down what they heard him preach, using a mixture of Latin and German, even though Luther preached in German. The recorded sermons were collected in "postils" (from the Latin for "according to these words of Holy Scripture—*post illa verba sacrae scripturae*," the traditional way of starting a sermon in Luther's day). The postil contained whole sermons, at times with outlines, notes, or other homiletical aids. Luther's Advent, Christmas, and Lenten postils were widely used (see the collection for Christmas and Epiphany in LW 52 and John N. Lenker, ed. and trans., *Sermons of Martin Luther*, 8 vols., 1989, reprint of editions of 1907 and 1909). An American postil of Luther's Christmas sermons shows how Luther made the story of Christ's birth palatable to his German audience: The Holy Land becomes Thuringia; the distance from Nazareth to Bethlehem is the distance form Saxony to Franconia; and the childbirth takes place in a German medieval home (Roland H. Bainton, *Martin Luther's Christmas Book*, 1948).

Luther's method of preaching concentrates on the core of the biblical text, a main point from which everything flows. When that point is clearly made, the sermon has accomplished its task. Whenever Luther preached on Jesus' entry to Jerusalem, he would concentrate on "Behold your king comes to you." The rest of the sermon dealt with the tension between opposites: law and gospel,* good and evil, sin and grace, freedom and bondage, always stressing that God is revealed in opposites, be it as a baby and crucified man or as the power that is strong in the weak. That is the main theme, the leitmotif, of Luther's preaching: that sinners are made right with God, justified not by what they can earn as divine credit for human works but as believers who trust God in Christ alone. The rest of preaching has to do with the proper and best use of one's talents and skills. Luther's "table talks" offer varied advice to preachers, ranging from a good voice to suffering for what is preached. When asked to be brief he replied that one must learn to go up to the pulpit, i.e., to have a divine call; to stay there for a time, i.e., to preach good doctrine; and to get down again, i.e., preach no more than one hour (LW 53, 393).

The preacher Luther is well portrayed in a painting of Lucas Cranach the Elder for the Wittenberg Town Church in 1547. It shows Luther in the pulpit pointing to the crucified Christ at the altar as the focus of the sermon for the congregation on the other side of the altar. As he told a fellow friar in 1516, "Learn [and preach] Christ and him crucified. . . . Meditate on this love of his and you will see his sweet consolation" (LW 48, 12,13) (see History of Preaching).

Grimm, H. J., "The Human Element in Luther's Preaching," *Archiv für Reformationsgeschichte* 49 (1958), 50–60. **Kiessling, E.,** *The Early Sermons of Luther and Their Relation to the Pre-Reformation Sermon,* 1935. **Lischer, R.,** "Luther and Contemporary Preaching: Narrative and Anthropology," *The Scottish Journal of Theology* 36 (1983), 487–504. **Meuser, F. W.,** *Luther the Preacher,* 1983. **Pelikan, J.,** and **H. Lehmann,** eds., *Luther's Works,* Amer. ed., 55 vols., 1955–1986.   ERIC W. GRITSCH

PREACH THE WORD
Martin Luther

I will preach it [the Word], teach it, write it, but will constrain no man by force, for faith must come freely without compulsion. Take myself as an example. I opposed indulgences and all the papists, but never with force. I simply taught, preached, and wrote God's Word; otherwise I did nothing. And while I slept [cf. Mark 4:26–29], or drank Wittenberg beer with my friends Philip [Melanchthon] and

[Nicholas von] Amsdorf, the Word so greatly weakened the papacy that no prince or emperor ever inflicted such losses on it. I did nothing; the word did everything. Had I desired to foment trouble, I could have brought great bloodshed upon Germany; indeed, I could have started such a game that even the emperor would not have been safe. But what would it have been? Mere fool's play. I did nothing; I let the Word do its work. What do you suppose is Satan's thought when one tries to do the thing by kicking up a row? he sits back in hell and thinks: Oh, what a fine game the poor fools are up to now! But when we spread the Word alone and let it alone do the work, that distresses him. For it is almighty and takes captive the hearts, and when the hearts are captured the work will fall of itself. Let me cite a simple instance. In former times there were sects, too, Jewish and Gentile Christians, differing on the law of Moses with respect to circumcision. The former wanted to keep it, the latter not. Then came Paul and preached that it might be kept or not, for it was of no consequence, and also that they should not make a "must" out of it, but leave it to the choice of the individual; to keep it or not was immaterial [1 Cor. 7:18–24; Gal. 5:1]. So it was up to the time of Jerome, who came and wanted to make a "must" out of it, desiring to make it an ordinance and a law that it be prohibited. Then came St. Augustine and he was of the same opinion as St. Paul: it might be kept or not, as one wished. St. Jerome was a hundred miles away from St. Paul's opinion. The two doctors bumped heads rather hard, but when St. Augustine died, St. Jerome was successful in having it prohibited. After that came the Popes, who also wanted to add something new and they, too, made laws. Thus out of the making of one law grew a thousand laws, until they have completely buried us under laws. And this is what will happen here, too; one law will soon make two, two will increase to three, and so forth.

Let this be enough at this time concerning the things that are necessary, and let us beware lest we lead astray those of weak conscience [1 Cor. 8:121].

> From "The Second Sermon, March 10, 1522, Monday after Invocavit," *Eight Sermons at Wittenberg,* 1522, ed. and trans. J. W. Doberstein, *Luther's Works,* American Edition, 55 vols., ed. H. T. Lehmann (Philadelphia: Fortress Press; St. Louis: Concordia Publishing House, 1959), 51:77–78.

Maclaren, Alexander. (1825–1910)

Although born in Glasgow, Scotland, Alexander Maclaren spent his entire ministry in England, first at Portland Chapel, Southampton, for nine years and then for 45 years as pastor of Union Chapel in Manchester. He was a Baptist, but his brilliant expository* sermons, published on both sides of the Atlantic, served as models of eloquence and devotion to Christians of many denominations.

Maclaren was chiefly noted for his strict expository style, often stating three points. From his earliest years as a young minister in Southampton, he established a systematic method of study and sermon preparation to which he clung tenaciously throughout his ministry and that enabled him consistently to produce sermons of depth and clarity. He normally rose at dawn and worked steadily for nine or ten hours with only a short break for lunch. In the middle of the afternoon he visited the sick, but in the evening he was in his old-fashioned rocker with a clay pipe in one hand and either a Greek Testament or a Hebrew Bible in the other.

He became a master of the biblical languages, frequently finding a nuance of meaning or an alternative translation to be the doorway to truth. He urged all young ministers to become students of the biblical languages: "Unless you are competent students of the original . . . you will be having to expound a book which you cannot read" (Maclaren 1925, 166). Unlike his contemporary, Charles H. Spurgeon,* Maclaren did not reject the higher criticism of the Bible, but considered it a blessing not to be neglected.

"Whatever the Higher Criticism has done," he claimed, "it has not touched the main substance of the Gospel which we have to preach, nor do even its most advanced positions seem to me seriously to affect the homiletic worth of Scripture" (Maclaren 1901, 12).

When Maclaren moved to Manchester at age thirty-two, he found himself preaching to a large and well-educated congregation. Within a few years after his arrival, the church membership more than doubled, and the need for a new building became obvious. In 1869, a new chapel that could seat 1,500 people was completed, and when extra seats were brought in, it could accommodate 1,800. Soon, however, 2,000 people would pack themselves into Union Chapel, some seated behind and around the pulpit.

Throughout his long ministry, Maclaren devoted himself to his task in Manchester, frequently turning down invitations to preach or lecture in other cities. "My first duty," he would say, "is to my own congregation." With that reasoning he turned down an invitation to give the Lyman Beecher Lectures on preaching at Yale University, and later an invitation to leave Manchester to become University Preacher at the University of Chicago.

John Brown, in the Beecher Lectures at Yale University in 1899, referred to Alexander Maclaren when he said, "If ever a prophet of God stood in the midst of our modern nineteenth-century life with the burden of God upon his heart . . . this preacher of whom I am speaking is that prophet" (John Brown, *Puritan Preaching in England,* 1900, 271). Maclaren's Manchester sermons were widely published, and after his retirement, his commentaries (largely in sermonic form) were published under the title *Expositions of Holy Scripture.*

Although Maclaren never spoke or wrote at length on his approach to preaching, his sermons themselves reveal a Christ-centered sermonic form, with all texts leading eventually to Christ. "The essence of the whole," he said in one sermon, "is not the intellectual process of assent to a proposition, but the intensely personal act of yielding up a heart to be a living person" (Maclaren 1905, 3).

Almost all his sermons followed a three-point outline. One of the members of his congregation in Manchester commented that Maclaren served the bread of life on a three-pronged fork. He managed to find three points in a text even if the text did not lend itself to three points. His method of delivery was to use sketchy notes from the pulpit but never a manuscript. He was especially gifted in forming exquisite literary sentences as he spoke, so that his sermons were attended not only by people seeking religious instruction and inspiration but also by literary people desiring to hear his exemplary eloquence of speech. Upon his retirement, he was presented an honorary degree of Doctor of Literature, and it was stated by a college Chancellor that " . . . for forty-four years [Maclaren] has devoted in this city his exact theological scholarship, his charm of literary form and freshness, his fervid eloquence and his intense conviction . . . " (Williamson, *The Life of Alexander Maclaren*, 1945, 166).

Maclaren's devotion to the preaching task was so focused that a fitting motto of his life might be "This one thing I do." He limited his outside speaking engagements, his administration of the church, even his attendance at church activities so that he would have what he considered the required amount of time to prepare for his sermons. In his later life he limited his preaching to once a week and left the Sunday evening service to an assistant, refusing even to attend himself.

His simplicity of style and penetrating insights into biblical texts still serve the modern preacher well.

Maclaren, A., "Counsels for the Study and Life," *Review and Expositor* 22 (April 1925); *Expositions of Holy Scripture,* 1942; "An Old Preacher on Preaching," *The Baptist Handbook for 1902,* 1901; *Sermons Preached in Manchester;* and *The Holy of Holies,* 1905.

THOMAS R. McKIBBENS

THE PREACHER AS TEACHER
Alexander Maclaren

But the preacher has to be a Teacher as well as an Evangelist. . . . And the first thing that I desire to lay stress on is, that the educational is never to be separated from the evangelistic office. True, "there are diversities of operations"; and idiosyncracies and spiritual gifts, which for the most part follow in their line, may mark out one man more especially for the one kind of work, and another for the other. . . . Still, it remains true and important to keep in view, that the truest teaching must be evangelistic, and the truest evangelizing must be educational. The web is made up of warp and woof. The evangelism which appeals to emotion only is false to the Gospel; for God's way of moving men is to bring truth to their understandings, which shall then set their emotions at work, and so pass on to move the will, the directness of the man, and thus at last affect the actions. . . . The evangelist who is not a teacher will build nothing that will last. And not less one-sided, and therefore transient, will be the work of the teacher who is not an evangelist. He will give husks instead of the bread of life, notions that may rattle in skulls like seeds in dried poppyheads, but not convictions which burn all the more because they are light as well as heat. . . .

All knowledge may come into his sphere. There is room for the widest culture. The teacher may elaborate his theme with the closest thought, or may adorn it with poetry and imagination. There is room for all gifts in the building of the great temple. Bezaleel was taught by the Spirit of God to execute his works of artistic beauty, and Hiram's workmen had to hew logs in Lebanon. But the wider the teacher sweeps his circle, the stronger must be its centre. The more he lengthens his cords, the more must he strengthen his stakes, and the middle prop that holds up the tent is the Cross with Christ upon it. "Him first, Him last, Him midst and without end." All that the teacher has to teach is summed up in one word—Christ. His whole theme is "the truth as it is in Jesus."

From "An Old Preacher on Preaching" (London: Baptist Tract and Book Society, 1901).

Maier, Walter Arthur. (1893–1950) Maier was a minister in The Lutheran Church–Missouri Synod and a professor of Old Testament Interpretation at its Concordia Seminary, in St. Louis. Born in Boston of German immigrant parents, he followed a pretheological course of study at Concordia Collegiate Institute, Bronxville, New York, went on to complete the requirements for a B.A. at Boston University, and then received his theological education at his denomination's seminary in St. Louis. Ordained in 1917, Maier spent the next three years serving as an assistant pastor to a Boston congregation and doing graduate work in Old Testament and Semitics at Harvard University, where in 1920 he was awarded an M.A. and in 1929 a Ph.D. In 1922, he returned to St. Louis to join Concordia Seminary's faculty and remained there until his death in 1950. It was as the regular preacher during the 1930s and 1940s on "The Lutheran Hour" that Maier achieved his greatest recognition. This radio program was in fact the weekly pulpit from which he addressed a worldwide audience of listeners.

Maier was quick to see radio as a potent medium for transmitting the Christian gospel. He used his position as editor of a youth magazine to raise the funds necessary to establish Concordia Seminary's own radio station, KFUO, and by 1930, succeeded in gathering enough support from his Synod's "Lutheran Laymen's League" to launch the first broadcast of "The Lutheran Hour" over the CBS and Don Lee networks. Financial difficulties forced a suspension of the program after eight months. Yet Maier refused to let the Great Depression bury "The Lutheran Hour," and once the Mutual Broadcasting System agreed to run the program in 1935, it became the world's largest radio broadcast.

"Bringing Christ to the Nations" was as much the aim of Walter Maier's preaching as it was the theme of his radio program. When no revival of religion materialized during the depths of the Depression, he repeatedly attacked the modernist versions of American Protestantism and accused its "termite" preachers of undermining the authority of the Bible, reducing faith in God for salvation to a theology of human accomplishment and character, and turning the Sunday-morning homily into nothing more than a personal commentary on a particular social or political issue. Real hope of change, he insisted, lay at the foot of the cross in the atonement Christ accomplished for the sinfulness of which every human being stood convicted. Although hesitant during the 1930s to recognize the threat to world peace posed by Nazi Germany, Maier openly supported the Allied cause, once America entered World War II. His messages clearly linked "Christ" with "country," and he offered his listeners a "pledge of allegiance," which made the following addition to the one repeated at civil ceremonies:

I also pledge allegiance to the Cross of Jesus Christ and to the faith for which it stands, one Savior-King eternal, with grace and mercy for all. So help me God (Maier 1963, 223).

On the other hand, Maier did not advocate blind patriotism. He regarded war as a manifestation of God's outrage over human contempt for divine obligations, and America's redemption, as he saw it, lay in the pardon and power promised by Christ to a repentant nation. The Cold War years served to vindicate the consistently uncompromising stand Maier took in his sermons against Communism. Already in 1930, he labeled it "the world's greatest away-from-the-Bible and away-from-God movement" in history and thereafter continued to describe it in Manichaean terms as the most formidable enemy of Christianity and of the American institutions it was aggressively and relentlessly seeking to infiltrate. Faith in the God whose existence Communism openly denied, he liked to argue, was the foundation for all forms of human integrity and ethics.

Maier's sermons followed the classical Lutheran pattern of law and gospel.* After a brief introduction designed to get the attention of listeners, he usually launched into a lengthy discussion of a human problem or dilemma that he interpreted as evidence of humankind's sinful tendency to violate God's law. While appeals to emotion were not lacking, Maier more often chose to argue in attorney-like fashion, stacking up documentation, statistical data, and testimonies from past and present witnesses in order to support his case. His goal was to exhaust every subject he treated, and for this reason his office contained a filing system of twenty-five steel, four-reference-drawer cabinets filled chiefly with newspaper and magazine articles. On the other hand, every Maier sermon was balanced by a presentation of the gospel of God's grace toward an undeserving humanity and the hope of reconciliation and redirection occurring because of Christ's incarnation, death, and resurrection. Here, as elsewhere in his text, he made liberal use of biblical phrases, and at least one direct quotation of a Bible passage appeared on nearly every page of a typical sermon manuscript. Being a Lutheran, Maier did not conclude his sermons with the "altar call" used by other Protestant preachers. But unbelievers were invited to accept Christ, and his pattern was to employ a question ("Will you not rally to the cause of the Crucified? . . . ") or an imperative ("Come to Him in his Word. . . . Take the sacred Book . . . and let God's Spirit work in your hearts") in order to enjoin the members of his audience to consider acting upon what they had heard.

One radio network executive called the Maier style of preaching "the soap-box delivery of a Harvard manuscript." His manner of speaking was unusually rapid-fire, tending to reach an optimum rate of 130 to 170 words a minute. Without stopping to catch his breath, he could, in fact, complete marathon sentences that sometimes approached one hundred words. Devoted listeners, however, did not find this pace of delivery distracting or overwhelming because Maier expressed himself with absolute sincerity and conviction about the truth of his message. Experience as a religious editor and writer also helped him become a gifted wordsmith, one who made creative use of alliteration ("the fatal folly of fighting Christ"), metaphor, and other word pictures. He was able, therefore, to assert the same point in a sermon three or four different times without sounding repetitious. In addition, he carefully avoided expressing his commitment to the unchangeable essence of the Christian faith in sterile, doctrinal terms, and he made generous use of anecdotes, stories, and illustrative nuggets mined from the pages of history, science, literature, and the news media (see Radio Preaching).

Seen in retrospect, Walter Maier was a twentieth-century pioneer who effectively used the medium of radio to reach a weekly congregation much larger than that of any preacher before him. Yet, during a period when mainline Protestantism in America was undergoing controversy and reassessment, he eschewed any mediating role. As a Lutheran committed to a more classical version of the Protestant faith, he was as proficient as members of the emerging neo-orthodox movement in attacking modernism. His view of the Bible as infallible and his complete aversion to the use of higher criticism in interpreting it, however, kept him from forging any alliance with the neo-orthodox. Maier also repudiated the social gospel and insisted in his sermons that the conversion of individuals to Christ, rather than social justice, was the chief objective of Christianity. Hence his audience, apart from Lutherans, was composed largely of fundamentalists and other conservative evangelicals, many already alienated from the Protestant mainstream, and after his death, prone to gravitate to the young Billy Graham.* At the same time, it was Maier's preaching that helped to bring his own Lutheran denomination, the Missouri Synod, out of its immigrant cocoon, and to stimulate America's "return to religion" after World War II (*see* Radio Preaching).

Maier, P. L., *A Man Spoke, A World Listened: The Story of Walter A. Maier and the Lutheran Hour,* 1963; *The Best of Walter A. Maier,* 1980. **Rudnick, M. L.,** *Fundamentalism and the Missouri Synod,* 1966.

JON T. DIEFENTHALER

NOTHING SAVE JESUS CHRIST
AND HIM CRUCIFIED
Walter A. Maier

. . . Unfortunately a class of clergymen is abroad in the land who, ill informed as they may be, insist upon knowing a hundred things in preference to the Crucified. They must speak on banking systems, presidential policies, inflated currency, and allied subjects, which exclude the Savior of men from His own sanctuary. Long ago have they banished from their sermons the high-priestly Christ, who declared with blessed finality, "It is finished!" They want to finish the task of saving men—if indeed we must be saved, and they can only plunge desperate souls into deeper dismay, only offer new versions of age-old delusions that place men before the impossible task of earning heaven. . . .

No wonder that millions in America are trying to live without Christ and have willfully rejected the grace of the Crucified. Too many want a bread-and-butter paradise here on earth. Too many are ready to welcome the Christ of the loaves and the fishes but spurn the Christ of the thorns and nails; for His cross, an imperishable monument to God's hatred of sin but to His greater love for the sinner, makes no appeal to selfish affections and self-indulgent ambitions. . . .

How blessed, by contrast, is the joy of peace, the patience of hope, the strength of spirit which comes to those who commit themselves to the Redeemer's care! Once you regard Jesus as the apostle did, *in that intensive focus which beholds only "Christ and Him crucified,"* you need nothing else to help you discover a cheer-

ing, sustaining answer to every problem of life. When your soul is cleansed, your conscience stilled, your heavenly Father reconciled, then are you prepared to meet the best or the worst that life may hold for you. Let the avalanche of human miseries sweep over you; if you know the Crucified, you will hear His sustaining *"Let not Your heart be troubled."* Let whirlwinds of disaster blow the high towers of your hopes into shapeless ruins; over the wreckage Christ's voice will ring clear: *"Behold, I make all things new."* Let the ravages of incurable disease, the feebleness of old age, the terrors of approaching death shake the foundation upon which life itself rests; your Savior's stabilizing pledge declares: *"Thou shalt be steadfast and not fear."* Let heaven and hell raise their charges against you; if you have Christ as your *"Advocate before the Father,"* you need nothing else to assure you of God's pardon.

From "Nothing Save Jesus Christ, and Him Crucified!" Delivered at the beginning of the third "Lutheran Hour" season, in the fall of 1935, in Paul L. Maier, *The Best of Walter A. Maier* (St. Louis: Concordia, 1980), 96–97.

Manuscript Preaching. The term "manuscript preaching" supposes two actions: a carefully written product and its effective delivery. Both are of crucial importance, but the second has often spelled the doom of the first. "We want," writes Walter Russell Bowie, "a preacher to speak straight to us with nothing in between" (206). Harold Cooke Phillips, noted Baptist preacher, deplored the presence in the pulpit of "the paper curtain." And there was the Scotsman who gasped in despair, as the new preacher set a full manuscript on the pulpit, "He reads!"

To begin: Why must we write our sermons? The reasons are multiple, all of them positive. First, there is the need to cultivate continually the processes of disciplined thinking as one wrestles with great ideas. Then there is the matching of one's vocabulary with the need for accuracy, relevance to one's audience, and contemporary freshness (not slang). A news commentator said of Winston Churchill's vocabulary, "His nouns are pictures and his verbs work." George Buttrick spoke of the preacher's "doing words," for "words are deeds—the deeds of the lips" (Buttrick, 156). Other advantages from a carefully prepared manuscript are: constantly improving one's literary style; sharpened focus of ideas; clear terminal facilities—no drag out; and—as someone said—"the pen is a marvelous magnet to draw the thoughts out of the brain."

There are, however, detractors who claim that the written sermon counteracts the impression of "first-time-ness," the impact of free delivery, and the power of creative vitality. Yet, most of the truly great preachers of the Western world have been unfailing contributors to the literature of the pulpit. John Henry Newman* wrote each sermon three times because he was never satisfied with the first two drafts. Such a procedure gives each sermon a second chance to have its creator ask, How can I say this more effectively? Where can I excise every trace of unreality? Have I written—as Fosdick warned—for readers and not for hearers?

The manuscript preacher must give absolutely careful attention to delivery, even without the manuscript in hand. Some of the masters of manuscript preaching have been Thomas Chalmers, Phillips Brooks,* William Sloane Coffin,* George A. Buttrick,* and Harry Emerson Fosdick.* They were experts of impact because the written sermon had been made part of their own being. Their handling of it seemed as if they were thinking aloud. Each of them avoided stilted and lifeless vocal phrasing, the tendency to pontificate, and the sanctified moan. Their own personality dominated the whole exercise because theirs was an "I-Thou" continuum. And, like Bunyan's* Interpreter, they stood "as if they pleaded with men." George Herbert once said that every sermon must be "informing and inflaming."

The preacher who puts her or his whole self into the sermon preparation and its delivery will inform hearers in the evangel and inspire them to live it (*see* Extemporary Preaching).

Bowie, W. R., *Preaching*, 1954. **Buttrick, G.,** *Jesus Came Preaching*, 1970.

DONALD MACLEOD

Massillon, Jean-Baptiste.   (1663–1742) Massillon was a member of the French academy and Bishop of Clermont. Born in Hyères in Provence, the son of a royal notary, he is regarded as one of France's most distinguished preachers. A member of the Oratorian order, Massillon is especially remembered for his Advent and funeral sermons, his preaching in the French court, and his annual conferences to the priests of his diocese. He was taught philosophy by the Oratorians at Hyères and Marseilles and studied theology at Arles.

Despite his order's prediction that he would become a brilliant preacher, Massillon insisted that he was unfit for the pulpit. He spent several years teaching Moral Philosophy. Finally, out of obedience to his Oratorian superiors, he agreed in 1691 to be ordained a priest. He was chosen to preach at the funerals of MM. de Villeroy, Archbishop of Lyons, and de Villars, Archbishop of Vienne. When these funeral orations were declared brilliant successes, the praise so frightened the young priest that he withdrew to the Cistercian Monastery of Sept-Fons for several months in 1696. When Massillon returned to his order, he was appointed a director of seminarians at Saint-Magloire in Paris from 1696 to 1698. It was then at the Oratory on Saint-Honoré Street, that he returned to preaching.

He began to acquire a name for himself through a series of Lenten and Advent sermons. During Advent of 1699 and the Lenten seasons of 1701 and 1704, he was called to preach before King Louis XIV at Versailles. It was a formidable appointment because the king was at the height of his power and glory; the "grand monarch" of Europe was accustomed to the flattery of court preachers but not to the challenge of the gospel. But Massillon was able to touch the conscience of the king without offending him. Louis XIV once remarked: "I leave my chapel very often pleased with my preachers but after hearing Father Massillon, I always leave dissatisfied with myself."

When Louis XIV died, Massillon was appointed to preach the funeral oration. In the exordium, he stood still after giving the text, stared at the funeral pomp, and finally raised his eyes and palms to heaven, and declared, "My brethren, God alone is great!" It had a profound effect. Even Massillon's theological opponents congratulated him.

When Louis XIV died in 1715, he left as his successor a nine-year-old boy. Two years later, Massillon was nominated to the Bishopric of Clermont in Auvergne. But before he took possession of his diocese, the Regent Orleans appointed Massillon to preach the *Petit Carême* (Little Lenten program) in the royal pulpit. The Regent wanted to reach the heart of the boy king.

Massillon took part in the theological debates that followed the papal bull *Unigenitus*, which was aimed at stamping out Jansenism, and actively prepared a compromise to end the ecclesial crisis. In the height of these debates, Massillon remarked that "it is easier to convert sinners than to get theologians to agree." In 1721 he left the court and retired to his diocese, where he remained until his death on September 28, 1742. It is remarkable that during these years as bishop of Clermont he would not preach. His spent most of his time ministering to peasants, erecting local hospitals, introducing cotton spinning, and improving the sanitary conditions of the villages.

Although he did not preach to his people, he held long conferences with his priests during annual synods. He sharply rebuked them for negligence and exhorted them to prayer and simplicity of life.

Massillon was less Roman and more common in appeal than his famous predecessors, Bossuet* and Bourdaloue. He strove to simplify the doctrines he preached. His letters reveal a man embroiled in the theological debates of his day yet committed to a policy of *détente*. His sermons, however, reflect spiritual and pastoral concerns rather than theological controversies.

D'Alembert characterized Massillon's oratorical style as "modest and reserved . . . without exaggerated movement and almost without gestures, but animating . . . by a touching sensitive voice." When he refused to preach like the great orators of his age, the actor Baron told Massillon, "Continue, Father, to preach in the same way. You have a manner which is your own; leave the rules to others."

He wrote out the complete text of his sermons and recited them without changing a word. Because he was careful about the details of his composition, some consider Massillon more a literary than an oratorical figure. His writings were greatly admired by Voltaire.

Massillon's sermons reflect his moralistic temperament. His moral judgments have been criticized as harsh and tending toward Jansenism. However, others have praised his preaching for its call to interior conversion and its pastoral sensitivity to the needs of the listeners. His sermons reveal both the evangelical call of the missionary and the tender care of the pastor (*see* Court Preachers).

Auvray, P., *Dictionnaire de Spiritualité*, Tome X, 1980, 753–56. Massillon, J.-B., *Oeuvres de Massillon*, Tome premier, deuxième, 1860; *Sermons by Jean-Baptiste Massillon*, Vols. 1 and 2, 1889; and *The Ecclesiastical Conferences*, Vols. 1 and 2, 1825.
ROBERT P. WAZNAK, S.S.

Mather, Cotton.

(1663–1728) Cotton Mather was a Congregational minister, religious scholar, civic leader, and preeminent voice for Calvinist orthodoxy in colonial Massachusetts. Named for his maternal grandfather, the learned John Cotton, Mather early displayed unusual intellectual prowess, mastering Latin, Greek, and Hebrew as a child and graduating from Harvard College at the age of fifteen. Having experienced conversion while still a teenager, he elected to follow his father, Increase, and both his grandfathers into the Christian ministry. Although he received offers from a number of congregations, his most determined suitors were his father's own parishioners at Boston's North Church, where in 1685 he was ordained and installed as Increase's associate.

Regrettably, the one event most closely associated with Mather's name today is the outbreak of witchcraft in Salem village in 1692 and the subsequent trial and execution of twenty alleged witches. Yet Mather himself never attended the trials, and although he wrote in their defense, he also denounced the basis on which the prosecution was conducted. More reasonably, he is recalled for his hand in the revolt of 1689 that ended the autocratic rule of Sir Edmund Andros, for his scientific pursuits that led to his induction into Britain's Royal Society, for his farsighted advocacy of inoculation against smallpox that brought him so much derision during the epidemic of 1721–1722, and for the hundreds of books he authored on topics ranging from theology and the supernatural to medicine and local history. He deserves to be remembered above all, though, for the vocation that consumed most of his waking hours, for his arduous labors on behalf of the gospel.

Mather was not so much an ecclesiastical pioneer as a creative synthesist, with the Januslike ability to look forward and backward at the same time, allowing tradition and innovation to buttress one another. His supreme achievement lay in drawing on the perspectives of English Puritans like Richard Baxter* and German Pietists like August Hermann Francke to forge a distinctively American spirituality. Like Baxter and Francke, he wrote early and often on pastoral care, urging the importance of neglected practices like catechesis and visitation. Also like them, he put his words into practice, pursuing an aggressive program of house-to-house calling. Moreover, he seized on the religious society, a time-honored tool that had fallen into disuse, employing it as a lever to empower the laity and thus multiply the effectiveness of his ministry. The results were evident in North Church's robust health under his 43-year pastorate.

The same synthetic impulse was evident in Mather's preaching. Traditionally the Puritan sermon had been cast in the "plain style," rejecting rhetorical artifice and flowery prose in favor of razor-sharp logic and visceral thrust, the better to drive home the claims of Christ. But Mather was a devotee of the baroque who laced his homilies with classical citations as readily as he powdered his wig. In his *Manuductio ad Ministerium* (1726), a handbook for pastors-to-be, he urged that they too embellish their sermons with *"Profitable References,"* so that the text became a sort of *"Cloth of Gold, . . .* stuck with as many *Jewels,* as the Gown of a Russian Embassador." Moreover, Mather's own "Jewels," his endless citations and rhetorical flourishes, were harnessed to a vision of God's work that moved beyond narrow sectarianism to embrace fellow laborers from other orthodox Protestant communions: "Let the *Table* of the Lord have no *Rails* about it, that shall hinder a Godly *Independent,* and *Presbyterian,* and *Episcopalian,* and *Antipedobaptist,* and *Lutheran,* from sitting down together there." Although his sermons, like those of his forebears, depicted New England as a "city on a hill," the diverse citizenry of Mather's rendering made it seem quite a different place.

Still, the points of continuity, both formal and material, remained strong. Most obviously, Mather continued to structure his sermons in the time-honored tripartite fashion, first examining the particulars of a biblical passage, then drawing out its doctrinal dimensions, and finally exploring its "use," its implications for the disciple's daily life. More significant, he maintained and even heightened the stress on Christ that had always characterized the best of Puritan preaching. His words of counsel to would-be ministers, set down in *Manuductio ad Ministerium*, caught the spirit of his own sermons: "Among all the Subjects, with which you *Feed* the People of GOD, I beseech you, Let not the true *Bread of Life* be forgotten; but exhibit as much as you can of a Glorious *Christ* unto them: Yea, Let the *Motto* upon your whole Ministry be, CHRIST IS ALL." In his Christocentric preaching as in so many other aspects of his ministry, Cotton Mather served as a bridge between what had been—New England Puritanism—and what was to be—nineteenth- and twentieth-century American Evangelicalism (*see* Puritan Preaching; History of Preaching).

Lovelace, R. F., *The American Pietism of Cotton Mather: Origins of American Evangelicalism,* 1979. **Silverman, K.,** *The Life and Times of Cotton Mather,* 1984.

GEORGE W. HARPER

McLuhan, Marshall. (1911–1980) Marshall McLuhan graduated from the University of Manitoba in 1934 and received a Ph.D. from Cambridge University in 1942. In 1946 he became a member of the Department of English at St. Michael's College at the University of Toronto, and in 1963 he became Director of the University's Centre for Culture and Technology. His interests ranged from the literature of the Renaissance to that of the modern period, from rhetorical patterns and intellectual processes to communications media. McLuhan's best-known slogan, "the medium is the message," is the title of the first chapter of his most influential book, *Understanding Media: The Extensions of Man* (1964). Because of this volume, McLuhan was catapulted into prominence. His work was subsequently discussed, debated, lauded, criticized, and even ridiculed.

McLuhan's claim that "the medium is the message" is contrary to what is even now the popular understanding of the communication* process. There is a common tendency to believe that what is communicated is a message and that the medium of transmission is merely that, a channel through which the message passes. McLuhan called attention to the medium itself and insisted that it is the medium rather than the content (or the use to which the medium is put) that is the crucial element. McLuhan insisted that every medium introduces something different into human affairs, something that "shapes and controls the scale and form of human association and action" (*Understanding Media,* 24). It is such "shaping" that is the medium's message. For example, he claimed that the message of the medium of electric light is change. The electric light has no content, but it has power to change every structure it penetrates: it turns night into day; it allows buildings without windows; it permits travel in the dark (and thus transforms time and space).

Every interpreter of McLuhan runs quickly into a major difficulty. If it is the medium that is the message, then McLuhan should be read and experienced firsthand. In other words, readers of this brief article would do better to go straight to McLuhan's books. His books are not like most other books. Many are filled with photographs, drawings, cartoons, headlines and quotations, each juxtaposed with another and with McLuhan's own commentary. Even those writings that are limited to prose exhibit a peculiar style. They are aphoristic and epigrammatic. There are discontinuities in picture and prose that invite, even demand, participation. They offer probes rather than points of view, tentative explorations usually stated dogmatically and in the extreme.

According to McLuhan, there are "hot" media and "cool" media. As printed word, the typical book is what McLuhan labeled a hot medium. It extends a single sense, the eye, and diminishes the roles of the other senses. As a hot medium, the usual book is intense with visual data (print) that can be repeated without limit. So much information is offered to a single sense that relatively little participation is required by the reader. In his own written work, McLuhan worked at turning the book from a hot medium into a cool one. The reader must complete what McLuhan offers. The aphorism, the epigram, the discontinuity of picture and prose appeal to more than the eye, and their very incompleteness requires the reader to fill in what is missing.

Whether McLuhan was right or wrong in his analysis of media temperatures, the distinction he made points to what is central in his work. McLuhan was interested in the special effects and character of media. From his perspective, media include not only books but television, roads, clothing, automobiles, housing, weapons, and anything else that is an extension of some human faculty. He viewed the wheel as an extension of the foot, the book as an extension of the eye, and clothing as an extension of the skin. Of necessity, human beings embrace such extensions of themselves in material form and undergo the psychic and social consequences that result. He insisted that the embrace of any medium has effects that are unavoidable and are so subliminal as to be overlooked completely. He insisted also that a critical change occurred with the appearance of electronic technologies and the ebbing of the mechanical age of typography and the printed word. The mechanical age was visual, an age in which the human eye was extended in material form. In sharp contrast, the electronic age is nonvisual. It is an age of acoustic space and wraparound sound. The new media have altered the sensory mix. Today it is not the human eye that has been extended by print; it is the human nervous system that has been extended by electric circuitry. It is this change of ages and alteration of senses that McLuhan attempted to examine in his cool-medium books.

McLuhan wrote a good deal about the historical changes that result from major shifts in communications. The tribal ear-world of speech was drastically altered by the introduction of the phonetic alphabet and print. As has been noted, McLuhan believed also that the environment fostered by the visual and orderly medium of print has been drastically altered by the introduction of electronic technologies. McLuhan provocatively suggested that the effect of the new high-speed electronic media is a kind of retrieval. In the electric age human beings reenter the tribal village. The entire globe has become an extended nervous system. Today's culture is one of total involvement.

Toward the end of his life, McLuhan concentrated on isolating the factors that are common to all media. One is the notion that every medium is the extension of a human faculty (as print is the extension of the eye). A second factor is the idea that the heightening of one human faculty, by extension, diminishes the others. (In a visual age the human ear is exchanged for an eye.) A third is the notion of retrieval. (Electronic media recover the simultaneity of oral culture.) A fourth factor, that of reversal, suggests that any medium eventually engenders another that is basically different.

From the earliest, McLuhan's probes had an impact on preaching. McLuhan's claim that the medium of communication is more crucial than the content encouraged greater variety in sermonic form, especially in the use of dialogue, mixed media, and multimedia. His verdict that the electronic age is an age of acoustic space and wraparound sound called attention to preaching as an oral event and fostered new impetus for the oral* manuscript and for extemporaneous* preaching. His distinction between "hot" and "cool" media promoted a consideration of narrative proclamation as the key to listener participation.

More lasting, perhaps, than the sermonic experiments McLuhan's work stimulated is the reaction to his insistence that messages are changed when the medium changes. This caution continues to raise questions about the use of certain media, particularly the medium of television. As is the case with any medium, television* has its own bias, and it is one many consider to be antagonistic to gospel proclamation. ("The TV image . . . does not afford detailed information . . ."; "Speech on television must not have . . . careful precision . . ." *Understanding Media*.) As is the case with any medium, television carries its own message and it does so quite apart from any specific programming. McLuhan refers to this message as an "all-inclusive *nowness*" that is a "disaster" for a literate, specialist culture (*Understanding Media*). Many warn that preaching on television does little more than yield the gospel to television's own message.

The greatest significance of McLuhan's work for preaching may be in its invitation to carry on the investigation of the special effects and character of media. It is an invitation to accept the postulate that the electronic age has changed the perceptual habits of human beings, as well as the scale and form of human association. It is an invitation to take seriously the caution that any medium can impose its assumptions on the unwary. McLuhan's structural analysis of media offers a way for preachers to understand more fully themselves and their audiences and the cultural matrix they share.

McLuhan, M., *The Mechanical Bride: Folklore of Industrial Man*, 1951; *The Gutenberg Galaxy: The Making of Typographic Man*, 1962; *Understanding Media: The Extensions of Man*, 1964; and *The Medium Is the Massage* (with Quentin Fiore), 1967.

RICHARD L. THULIN

McPherson, Aimee Semple

(1890–1944) McPherson was an independent Pentecostal evangelist whose spectacular national and West Coast ministry helped to found the fellowship known today as the *International Church of the Foursquare Gospel*. She was born Aimee Kennedy in Ontario, Canada, of Salvation Army background. At seventeen, after a spiritual conversion under lay evangelist Robert Semple, she married Semple and joined him in missionary service in Hong Kong. In 1918, after his early death and the failure of a second marriage, she launched herself into a passionate itinerant gospel ministry. During the next five years, she crossed the United States eight times, using tents, theaters, and churches to conduct huge evangelistic and healing campaigns in major centers including Philadelphia, San Francisco, Baltimore, San Diego, Washington, D.C., Denver, Indianapolis, and St. Louis.

She settled into a permanent Los Angeles pastorate, founded a Bible school, and welcomed other churches into her movement. McPherson emphasized conversion, Holy Spirit baptism (the initial evidence of which she believed was "speaking in tongues"), healing as a gift available within the atonement, and she advocated a major focus on Christ's imminent return.

On New Year's Day, 1923, McPherson dedicated what was then the largest house of worship in the world, reminding her followers that she had first arrived in Los Angeles five years earlier "with only ten dollars and a tambourine." Through campaigns in selected cities, she raised funds for the huge church building, gathering $40,000 in St. Louis and $70,000 in Denver. The Temple featured two balconies, crowned by the largest unsupported dome in North America, with stars spangled over its blue ceiling to suggest the sky.

At her death in 1944, 50,000 mourners viewed her body over three days while it lay in state. This was a response to her generosity during the Great Depression when she served thousands of the poor and hungry through Temple-sponsored soup kitchens and other social ministries. Her Temple's 2,000 worshipers today still support a program that feeds 750 in its downtown "commissary" every week and an additional 7,000 off-premises.

An organizational genius, McPherson often delivered illustrated sermons, supported by scenery, footlights, platform pageantry, tableaux, and other theatrical elements, which regularly kept the Temple's 5,000 seats filled for over twenty years. She composed and directed spectacular musical extravaganzas, and "sacred operas," often clothed in pulpit costumes ranging from those of police and firemen to biblical characters such as "Pharaoh's daughter."

Always dressed in the height of fashion, she became the darling of the news reporters (who said that "she put hallelujah in the headlines"). She appeared to capitalize on constant media attention arising from litigation over charges of financial fraud and other scandals associated with her ministry. (Over one two-year period, the Los Angeles press counted no less than 45 separate civil lawsuits for unpaid bills, charges over fraudulent IRS records, and other court dispute claims, which totaled well over one million dollars.)

During these times, she successfully raised huge sums from her congregations, appealing for jewelry and even for gold teeth to be donated for her legal defenses. Her lawyer died under mysterious circumstances, and a superior court judge was impeached as a direct result of his associations with her. Her apparent mismanagement of huge sums of money from Temple funds was never proven but never fully explained.

The popular evangelist caused a major sensation on May 18, 1925, when, supposedly drowned while swimming at a Los Angeles beach, she returned after five weeks with a wild tale of abduction by kidnappers, a story that police believed to be a coverup for her involvement in a romantic scandal. This and a cluster of fraud and bribery questions finally led to a grand jury indictment for conspiracy to perpetrate a hoax and cause a public nuisance. Nothing immoral or dishonest could be proven, but publicity arising from the constant media attention undoubtedly stimulated extra interest in her ministries.

The evangelist was unembarrassed by her visions and controversies. She claimed to support a disciplined and non-excessive Pentecostalism,* but she also defended some of the unorthodox physical manifestations of "the Spirit's power" that accompanied her meetings. These included "healings," "tongues-speaking," praise shouting, shaking, dancing, and prostrations, as well as other "signs and wonders"—practices that seemed so abnormal to many that they led to the loss of most of her initial interdenominational support.

McPherson's place in evangelism history has been recognized by the inclusion of her life in the Billy Graham Center for World Evangelism at Wheaton, Illinois. When Sinclair Lewis based his novel *Elmer Gantry* loosely on her life, he portrayed her with sympathy and cast those associated with her as responsible for her bad experiences.

Blumhofer, E., *Aimee Semple McPherson: Everybody's Sister,* 1993. **Cox, R.,** *Aimee: Life Story of Aimee Semple McPherson,* 1979. **Hall, G. L.,** *The Sawdust Trail: The Story of American Evangelism,* 1964. **Thomas, L.,** *Storming Heaven: The Lives and Turmoil of Minnie Kennedy and Aimee Semple McPherson,* 1970.   CRAIG SKINNER

BRING BACK THE ARK
Aimee Semple McPherson

While those who have lost the anointing and are lacking spirituality may not even miss the old-time power of the Spirit, and are contented with the superficial imitation of a card-signing, hand-shaking, oyster-suppering, moving-picturing religion; nevertheless the Lord's "Davids," who have the anointing, and are in real touch with Heaven, realize the lack of power in their midst and are filled with determination to bring back the Ark and put it in its rightful place. . . .

Casting aside the advice of those who urged for a more modern method, and disregarding the criticism of some of his contemporaries, David set out again, to bring back the Ark, in the old-fashioned way. Minister, Teacher, Christian worker of today, do you dare to take the bold, uncompromising stand which David took?

Your pews empty, your altars deserted, your hearts hungry! . . . You know that none other than the original Pentecostal experience will satisfy, for you have tried all the twentieth-century methods. Standing only upon the teachings of God's word, setting aside the jeers of the ungodly, and the criticism of the misunderstanding Michals who mock, will you join hands and hearts and go forth to bring back the Ark into the sanctuary of the Church, as did David of old? . . .

With psalter, sack and harp! With timbrel, cymbal and praise unconfined. See it coming—the Ark of the Covenant. Too long has it lain in the household of doubt! Too long in the corner of the wayside hut! Bring it back to the House of the Lord, even as David brought the Ark of the Covenant to the Tabernacle and enshrined it in the heart thereof. Bring back the Holy Spirit into His rightful place in the heart of the Church. . . .

Let the ministers leap with joy. Let the altars be heaped to overflowing with the fullness of the Spirit's grace. Let Davids dance with all their might and timbrels loudly ring. Let new songs spring from yielded lips and hallelujahs rock the sky. . . .

Bring back the Ark! Bring it back with shouting, with tears and with song. Bring back the Pentecostal power!

> From "A New Beginning" in *Fire from on High* (Los Angeles: [Angeles Temple] Foursquare Publications, 1969), 215–19.

Melanchthon, Philip. (1497–1560)

Philip Melanchthon was professor at the University of Wittenberg, Germany, from 1518 until his death in 1560. Called there as an instructor in Greek at the recommendation of his great-aunt's brother, the famous Hebraist Johannes Reuchlin, Melanchthon quickly came to teach in both the Arts and Theology faculties. His defense of Martin Luther* after the Leipzig Debates of 1519 and the publication in 1521 of the first textbook on evangelical theology, the *Loci communes the-*

ologici, secured his status as speaker for the Reformation. He also wrote opinions on behalf of the theological faculty for Saxony's electors. His biblical commentaries and books on theology, rhetoric,* dialectics, and philosophy became standard texts at many universities and Latin schools of Central Europe and earned him the nickname "Preceptor of Germany." As Luther's coworker in church reform, he represented the evangelical cause at various imperial diets, including the Diet of Augsburg (1530), where he was chief author of the *Augsburg Confession* and its defense, the *Apology* (1531). After Luther's death in 1546, he continued to dominate the Wittenberg theological faculty and was embroiled in a series of disputes over adiaphora, the role of the human will and good works in salvation, and the Lord's Supper, which involved other evangelical theologians whom he mockingly called "genuine Lutherans" (gnesio-Lutherans).

As he admitted in a 1536 letter to Johannes Brenz, reformer of Württemberg, Melanchthon did not have permission to preach in public worship. Nevertheless, through books on rhetoric, occasional pieces on preaching, and his own postils, he exercised considerable influence upon the shape of Protestant preaching in the sixteenth century. He linked preaching to rhetoric and dialectics and used commonplaces (*loci communes*) widely in interpreting scripture and organizing sermons.

The Preaching Genre. As evangelical theology developed in Wittenberg in the 1520s and beyond, Melanchthon's understanding of the relation between rhetoric and homiletics developed as well. Whereas in his early books on rhetoric Melanchthon subsumed preaching under rhetoric, in his later textbook he barely mentioned the subject, and in his occasional pieces on homiletics he differentiated the two.

Books on Rhetoric. In 1519, Melanchthon published his first book on rhetoric, *De rhetorica libri tres.* Two years later his lectures on rhetoric at Wittenberg were published as the *Institutiones rhetoricae*. In 1531, he produced his own textbook, the *Elementa rhetorices* and revised it slightly in 1542. In 1519, Melanchthon still divided speeches the traditional way into three types: demonstrative, deliberative, and judicial. Demonstrative speeches included a subcategory of didactic speech that employed dialectical questions. In his discussion of preaching, Melanchthon categorized sermons as falling under either the didactic part of the demonstrative or the deliberative (also called persuasive) category. In 1521, Melanchthon separated the didactic from the demonstrative, creating an entirely new genre called the dialectical. Although his textbook on rhetoric from 1531 contained no separate section on preaching, it did include a discussion of this fourth genre. He insisted that this type not be overlooked, given its crucial importance for the church, where not only persuasive sermons but, more important, dogmatic teaching using dialectics must be delivered. This approach to preaching came to dominate the sermons of Protestant orthodoxy.

Occasional Pieces on Homiletics. In 1535, fragmentary comments on preaching by Melanchthon from as early as 1529 were published without his knowledge under the title "De officiis concionatoris." In 1540, his comments on 1 Tim. 4:13 appeared first in a commentary by Caspar Cruciger, Sr., and later in works by George Major (1570) and Andrew Pangratius (1571). In 1551, Melanchthon published his own lectures on 1 Corinthians and 1 Timothy, both of which contained expanded comments on preaching.

In these works Melanchthon defined more precisely the relationship between rhetoric and preaching. He excluded the demonstrative and judicial genres, mixing instead the didactic and deliberative and emphasizing both teaching and personal impact (*affectus*) in preaching. Sermons not only instruct but also move listeners to fear and faith in God and to good works. Melanchthon transformed the technical terms of rhetoric to describe the genres of preaching (1535: instruction, encouragement, and paraenesis; 1540: doctrine and exhortation). According to Uwe Schnell, this shifted his understanding of preaching to biblical categories and emphasized the Lutheran distinction between law and gospel.*

The "Loci" Method. Building on the work of Rudolf Agricola and Erasmus of Rotterdam, Melanchthon made *loci communes* the centerpiece of his exegesis and homiletics. Melanchthon believed that grammar, rhetoric, and dialectics helped explain the biblical text. Commonplaces, derived in dialectics from the relation between genus and species, defined the basic points of scripture so the interpreter could relate passages to one another. They were a crucial hermeneutical tool to assist the preacher in determining the basic theological categories of the text. Commonplaces also provided the preacher with the basic structure and organizing principle of the sermon itself. Thus for Melanchthon, 1 Tim. 4:13 moved from interpretation of the text to catechesis, or instruction, in basic Christian doctrine. These *loci,* most clearly outlined in Romans, included not moral topics, as Erasmus had insisted, but central Christian truths: justification by faith alone, the distinction between law and gospel, and Christian freedom. Melanchthon held catechesis for foreign students (from the 1530s until his death in 1560) at 6 A.M. on Sundays, basing it on the appointed texts for the day. Later preserved in his postils, this classroom "preaching" clearly demonstrated his use of *loci communes.*

Because Melanchthon insisted that Christian preaching and teaching move from doctrine to effect, he tied the dialectical category of definition (*loci communes*) to the impact of this teaching on the hearer. On the one hand, because faith rests on certainties, dialectics and *loci communes* must be employed in preaching to obtain true and trustworthy statements. On the other, because faith involves the heart and will (*affectus*), preaching must effect fear of God and trust in God (repentance and faith) in the believer. This same movement from doctrine to affect also shaped his understanding of a sermon's genre.

Melanchthon learned much about preaching from his own experience. In a letter to a former student written November 9, 1544, he concludes his description of the good preacher, who balances biblical doctrine with proper movement of the soul to fear and faith, by recollecting, "I remember hearing such from Luther in the past."

Manschreck, C., *Melanchthon: The Quiet Reformer*, 1958. Schneider, J. R., *Philip Melanchthon's Rhetorical Construal of Biblical Authority: Oratio Sacra*, 1990. Schnell, U., *Die homiletische Theorie Philipp Melanchthons*, 1968. Wengert, T. J., *Philip Melanchthon's "Annotationes in Johannem" in Relation to Its Predecessors and Contemporaries*, 1987.   TIMOTHY J. WENGERT

Memory. Memory, or the lack of it, presents a unique and often frustrating challenge to preachers. Since the sermon is built upon detailed analysis of a scriptural text and careful study of the contemporary situation of the hearers, the end result can be a bewildering aggregation of ideas. Even when reduced to a logical arrangement on paper, the question of the method of delivering the material to an audience remains. Should the problems of remembering the sermon be eliminated by the writing and reading of a manuscript? Or should notes alone, whether extensive or meager, be taken into the pulpit and memory be trusted for the balance? Or should written materials be avoided altogether in delivering the sermon? And if so, should the sermon be memorized line by line from a previously written manuscript? What place, if any, should memory play in the delivery of a sermon?

Since memory can be notoriously unreliable, and since public speaking itself is such a fear-arousing experience, it is little wonder that many preachers opt for the reading of a prepared script. One bad experience of trusting in memory for the sermon can outlive positive memories of a lifetime. When Charles R. Brown, Dean of Yale Divinity School, first attempted to preach without notes, he spoke for exactly eleven minutes and ran completely out of ideas: "I could not think of anything more that could be said on that particular text or upon the general subject of the Christian religion" (Brown 1922, 85). George W. Truett, pastor of the First Baptist Church in Dallas, was even less fortunate. After preaching for only seven minutes on "Ye are the light of the world," he said, "My little light went out." Both of these preachers recovered from their trauma to go on to preach largely from memory. Many others never survive that initial shock (*see* Manuscript Preaching).

Why, then, should anyone bother to trust memory in the first place? Why not simply read a prepared text and eliminate the tension and fear of failure?

Numerous studies in oral communication* theory have shown that audiences respond better to authentically oral* presentations than to the reading of written manuscripts. Listeners find oral speeches to be more understandable, more interesting, more informative, and superior in style (Capp, 212ff.). Persuasive communication seems to lose some of its effectiveness when read from prepared copy. Lawyers, for example, never deliver closing arguments to a jury from a manuscript. Christian preachers, likewise, have noticed the importance of directness in delivering their messages. Even so meticulous an expositor as Alexander Maclaren* relied almost wholly upon memory and rebuked himself after once attempting an address from a complete manuscript: "A failure because I read it. Again and again I was tempted to fling the paper from me . . ." (Maclaren, 100ff.).

The list of preachers who have relied to a great extent upon memory in sermon delivery is as surprisingly varied as it is long. Among the more historically notable: Augustine,* Aquinas, Luther,* Zwingli,* Calvin,* Knox,* Whitefield,* F. W. Robertson,* Phoebe Palmer,* Henry Sloane Coffin,* Alexander Maclaren,* Maggie Newton Van Cott, R. W. Dale, T. DeWitt Talmage, Charles Haddon Spurgeon,* Sojourner Truth,* Frances Willard,* Paul Scherer,* Dietrich Bonhoeffer,* D. T. Niles, Billy Graham,* and Martin Luther King.* But if preaching without a full text is such a daunting task, how did these preachers do it? How, and to what extent, did they rely upon memory?

Some of the preachers who did not use a manuscript seemed not to rely on memory at all in the strictest sense of the word. Their remarks were not prepared for a specific sermon but stemmed from general comments made on many other occasions. Evangelists whose sermons were delivered in many different places—such as George Whitefield, Billy Graham, and Maggie Newton Van Cott—likely relied on many stock expressions and formulas in their sermons (see Extemporary Preaching).

Expository preachers and others who preached textual homilies preached largely out of the "overflow" of their lengthy textual studies. Calvin, for example, who had a prodigious memory, relied on his never-ceasing exegetical studies for his textual homilies (286 of which he preached in one year, according to Beza). The same approach was true of Alexander Maclaren, although he did write some notes to aid his memory.

Only a very few preachers seem to have memorized their sermons verbatim. T. DeWitt Talmage was one of those. He had a great gift of memory but also for writing a manuscript in such a natural (oral) way that his sermons sounded extemporaneous. For most speakers, however, the regular pressures of preaching each week are severe enough without the increased anxiety of a memorized text. For that reason, almost all preachers have relied on writing at some point in the process of sermon preparation. Even those who carry no notes into the pulpit usually prepare a written outline, if not a full manuscript. Others prepare the first and last sentences of the sermon and/or the transitional sentences between major ideas.

Augustine, for example, composed by mental preparation, committed his major points to memory, and left the details to the moment. Spurgeon, after careful textual study, thought out his sermon on lengthy walks about London. He carried only a small page of outline into the pulpit. F. W. Robertson brought only a few notes with him, which he frequently crumpled in his hand once in the pulpit. Nevertheless, he believed that careful preparation was the key to memory in the sermon:

> Now, without method, memory is useless. Detached facts are practically valueless. All public speakers know the value of method. Persons not accustomed to it imagine that a speech is learnt by heart. Knowing a little about the matter, I will venture to say that if anyone attempted that plan, either he must have a marvelous memory, or else he would break down three times out of five. It simply depends upon correct arrangement. The words and sentences are left to the moment; the thoughts methodized beforehand: and the words, if the thoughts are rightly arranged, will place themselves" (Brooke, Vol. 2, 126).

The crucial relation of clear sermon structure to memory has been emphasized, with variations, by practically all who preach without a manuscript or those who teach such a method. Dietrich Bonhoeffer wrote, "A sermon that is difficult to learn is not a good one, or at least it is not a clear one." Paul Scherer stressed the simple development of a central sermon idea and outline as essential to sermon memory. His method was to develop first the theme, then the simple outline, then the manuscript, then a few notes to take with him in the pulpit.

In summary, there seems to be no great secret to the art of those who preach largely from memory, no clever devices to aid in memorizing the sermon. Certain elements, however, recur in the comments of the preachers known for the accomplished delivery of sermons apart from a manuscript: detailed exegesis; careful outlining; mental preparation of sentences and ideas (sometimes aloud) frequently aided by writing out key sentences (the first, last, and transitional); and the repeated reading and review of this material.

The minister then presents to the congregation the sermon that fills his or her thoughts, trusting that the directness and creativity of the sermon event will overcome whatever lack of precision is caused by the absence of a manuscript. Such sermons are delivered in the hope that this very absence of an essaylike compaction of ideas will aid the memory of the listeners, who, unlike the preacher, will have only their memories to retain the preached word.

Brooke, S. A., *Life and Letters of Frederick W. Robertson*, 2 vols., Vol. 2, 1865, 126. Brown, C. R., *The Art of Preaching*, 1922. Capp, G. A., *How to Communicate Orally*, 1961. Maclaren, A., "An Old Preacher on Preaching," *The Baptist Handbook for 1902*, 1901. CLYDE E. FANT

Military Setting Preaching

Preaching in a military context is in many respects no different from preaching in a civilian one. The essential task is the same—the proclamation of the Word of God. The preacher is called to be a prophetic voice to the hearers for the time and the situation in which they live. What distinction does exist between military and civilian preaching is bound up primarily in the situation in which the sermon occurs. It is, however, an important distinction, and must be clearly understood if one is to be effective in preaching within that context.

Danger is an inherent part of the military lifestyle, whether one is involved in training or on a mission. There is always the risk of injury, wounding, maiming, or death. Military parishioners and their families have a focus that is decidedly different from that of their civilian counterparts. The fragile nature of human existence is never far from their thoughts.

While they may share in this awareness, not all military parishes are the same. The military worship setting is as diverse as the population which it serves and the physical situations in which it exists. Depending on the particular military installation, this may include services of both Christian and non-Christian religious groups. Within the Christian tradition, most installations will likely have Roman Catholic and Protestant services. Some of these may be ethnically or linguistically focused (e.g., Samoan, Hispanic, or Korean). Many installations may have specific denominational services—Episcopal, Lutheran, Pentecostal—which in form and content will duplicate what is found in civilian life. On larger installations one may also find Orthodox services.

Within the Protestant Christian tradition, the "typical" military worship setting is the "collective Protestant" service. It is here that many of the distinctions between the military and civilian settings are most clearly in evidence. Unlike most civilian parishes, the collective Protestant congregation* displays a striking demographic mixture—multidenominational, multiracial, multiethnic. It will likely display a socioeconomic composition ranging from the lowest-ranking enlisted person to the general or admiral commanding the installation. The collective nature of worship means that the preacher cannot endorse specifically denominational programs or be verbally negative toward the beliefs and practices of denominations other than his or her own. The preacher must focus on themes that are Christian in the most inclusive sense. The sense of unity in the Protestant service derives from the worshipers' shared experience in service to the nation.

Although most collective Protestant congregations can claim this unity in diversity, there are a number of factors that may distinguish various congregations within this general type.

Main Post versus Unit Chapel. As often as not, the "main post" chapel service tends to be relatively formal or liturgical in nature, whereas other chapels generally employ a more free-church approach. The length, themes, and delivery of the sermon vary in accordance with the type of service and the style of the individual preacher. The main post chapel tends to have a fairly large percentage of high-ranking officers, enlisted people, and retirees from similar positions. Unit chapels are normally attended by service members and families who have current or past association with the particular unit—engineers, infantry, airborne, and special operations.

Training Base versus Permanent Party. As a result of a week of arduous training activity, the attention span of soldiers in training tends to be relatively short. The sermon delivered in the chapel of a training unit will generally be shorter and simpler than one delivered in a "normal" chapel setting with a permanent party congregation. The usual 20–30-minute sermon of several neatly ordered points must of necessity give way to a ten-minute (or shorter) homily with one or two easy-to-remember emphases, focusing on the ways in which reliance on God can help soldiers in their training.

Garrison versus Field/Deployment. Services held in a permanent chapel building will by nature of their setting be more formal than those held in a field environment. In the field a stack of ration boxes may become a pulpit, and the hood of the nearest vehicle may serve as the altar. Field services are generally shorter, with less formal liturgy and with a briefer, more focused sermon. The structure, subject matter, and delivery of a field sermon are often determined by the type of field duty during which the service is held—a training exercise, a mission deployment, or a war-time scenario with imminent threat of attack. Due to mission requirements, field services are often at-tended in smaller numbers, and multiple services may be required. The smaller group setting provides an excellent opportunity for more personal interaction with those in attendance.

Variety in Chaplains. The number of chaplains assigned to a particular chapel and who preach from its pulpit will vary. In some chapels one chaplain may have sole responsibility for the entire service every week, while at others two or three (or more) chaplains may rotate the homiletical duties. The decision about who preaches and how often generally resides with the senior chaplain. Since military chaplains, like their collective Protestant congregations, come from a variety of denominational backgrounds, each will have his or her own style based on education, denominational standards, and personal preference. Such diversity adds a rich variety to the worship experience. It also poses the danger of inconsistency, which creates discontent within the congregation. Coordination and cooperation are essential to avoid this latter result.

Preaching in a military setting requires the same basic skills as preaching in a civilian one—dedication to the task, preparation for the task, practice of the task. It is in understanding that the *audience,* by God's grace, must become a *congregation* that the preacher will take special care to deliver the necessary word at the right time.

From *Military Chaplains' Review,* Winter 1986 and Summer 1992.

HERBERT B. STRANGE

Miracles. A miracle is an event that manifests power in an extraordinary way. The purpose of the miracle is to effect change (normally positive) in the affairs of the human or cosmic communities and to demonstrate the power of the agent responsible for the miracle. The miracle worker hopes to win or confirm the trust of those who witness the miracle. A miracle story narrates a miracle. The purpose of the miracle story is ordinarily to win or confirm the trust of those who hear or read the story in the power that performs the miracle in the narrative. The miracle story also reveals possibilities for the human and cosmic realms that result from the presence of the power in the world. The miracle story does not present details that explain the miraculous happening as such, but simply presumes its occurrence.

Miracle stories are found throughout the Bible. In scripture, God is ordinarily the power who performs miracles. When Jesus performs miracles, he is typically God's agent. However, persons unrelated to God can perform dramatic acts (Acts 8:9–13; 13:4–12), and Satan and Satan's representatives can work miracles that parallel those of God (Rev. 13:11–15). Miracles and miracle workers were commonplace in many cultures and religions in antiquity. A fundamental issue for the biblical writers is the interpretation of the miracle: Does the miracle encourage confidence in the living God and does it reveal God's intentions for the world, or does it serve some lesser end, perhaps one that is even idolatrous or destructive?

Biblical writers are not troubled by the bifurcation of the natural and the supernatural that has plagued humankind since the Enlightenment. In the premodern view of the biblical writers, the cosmos is a single sphere, where the divine presence and power are manifested in many ways, of which miracle is one. While the biblical writers assume the factuality of miracles, they do not work to establish the likelihood that miracles occurred. That is a modern concern. Instead, the biblical authors use the miracle stories to help their communities understand the effect of the divine presence, purposes, and power in the world.

Preachers today are properly agnostic with respect to whether or not the biblical miracles occurred as described, for there is no way for contemporary research to confirm or deny the occurrence of such events. Today's hearers, however, are often concerned about these matters. What can the congregation affirm about miracles that coheres with what they otherwise believe to be true of the world and of God? How does this affirmation encourage the community's understanding of God and its response to God's word?

For example, a preacher might assert that miracles of the kind depicted in the Bible are outside our normal experience. However, in the context of the ancient worldview, the miracles witness to God's presence, trustworthiness, and will. Listeners need not accept the historicity of the miracles in order to be conscious of God's presence, trustworthiness, and will. The congregation can be aware of God's relationship with the world through means which are as familiar in today's setting as the miracles were in antiquity.

The preacher who takes this approach must reckon with contemporary reports that sometimes parallel the miracles of the Bible. How does the preacher interpret the case of the terminal patient who is unexpectedly (at least from the standpoint of modernity) restored to health? Can the congregation count on God to act this way for all? If so, does the congregation need to alter its view of how God works in the world? If not, what does the preacher say to those whose illnesses continue their ravaging path? How do we speak of miracles today?

Scholars have analyzed the functions of the miracle stories. Antoinette Wire identifies four kinds of miracle stories that show how divine action breaks open closed, oppressive life systems: (1) Provision miracles (e.g., the manna in the wilderness) portray divine provision in the midst of want. The preacher might ask, How does God provide similarly today? (2) Exorcisms (e.g., the Gerasene demoniac) represent God's displacement of arbitrary, restrictive, even violent powers with freedom for the possessed. The preacher might ask, What similar powers bind people today and how does God exorcize them? (3) Controversy miracles (e.g., the healing of the withered hand on the sabbath) picture God's intent to release the community from a variety of social and moral restrictions. The preacher might probe ways in which God is releasing today's society from arbitrary social and moral laws. (4) Request miracles (e.g., the woman with the issue of blood) are initiated at the request of the person or group who feels physically or psychologically impotent but who responds to the presence of divine power by requesting a miracle. When the request is granted, potency is restored. The preacher might identify such persons and situations in our setting and indicate how contact with the divine power can offer them renewal (Wire, 83–113; *see also* Theissen).

Literary criticism* stresses that the miracle stories must be considered in light of their place and purpose in the complete narratives in which they occur. For example, how does the sign at Cana function in terms of plot, character development, atmosphere, and theological point of view in the Fourth Gospel? Further, literary critics stress that the miracle stories create a narrative world. We encounter the meanings of the story as we imaginatively enter its world and follow its plot. Indeed, the story itself may provide a structure for the sermon. This suggests that the preacher may not so much want to explain the miracle story as to create a sermon in which the congregation experiences the world of the narrative and then considers how that world can inform its own (*see* Narrative Preaching).

Allen, R, J., *Our Eyes Can Be Opened: Preaching the Miracle Stories of the Synoptic Gospels Today*, 1982. Kee, H. C., *Miracle in the Early Christian World*, 1983. Keller, E. and M.-L., *Miracles in Dispute*, 1969. Theissen, G., *The Miracle Stories of the Early Christian Tradition*, 1983. Wire, A., "The Structure of the Gospel Miracle Stories and Their Tellers," *Semeia* 11 (1978), 83–113.

RONALD J. ALLEN

Missions. Homiletic theory and practice in the Western world normally assume that the audience knows the name of Jesus and recognizes that the Bible has some kind of authority. Missionary preaching can make no such assumptions. "Jesus" is a new word—perhaps the name of a new deity? Quoting from scripture evokes no resonance.

The preacher has, of course, to begin by learning the language, using words that are freighted with meaning, often with profoundly evocative meanings, derived from the mental world of the hearers. The preacher uses, and must use, words that have a meaning for the hearers different from the preacher's intention. There is no escape from this. Words like God, sin, and salvation derive their Christian content from the entire experience of sharing in the Christian tradition.

People nourished in a tradition wholly alien to the Christian tradition come to share the Christian understanding of these words by becoming familiar with the Bible. It is impossible for people to understand who Jesus is without a deep insertion into the mental world of the Old Testament. The widely practiced custom of making sections of the New Testament available many years before the complete Bible was translated has had far-reaching consequences, especially in Africa, where the separation of independent groups from the churches founded by missionaries has been in direct proportion to the unavailability of the Old Testament.

The missionary preacher must be deeply involved in the mental world of the hearers. A preacher, for example, who claims to offer eternal life to an audience of Hindus is offering them exactly what they are trying to escape. If he or she offers the gift of salvation in Christ to those who are strangers to the Bible, they will assume that he or she is offering them something like the benefits of the welfare state.

A great preacher of the gospel to Hindus, the Scottish missionary A. G. Hogg, used the phrase "challenging relevance" to describe what is needed. The preacher must be heard as addressing real issues. But the word must probe behind the unquestioned assumptions of the hearers with a call to new allegiance. In his book

Karma and Redemption, Hogg illustrated his principles by taking the Hindu doctrine of karma as the frame for a sharp presentation of the atoning work of Christ. But the supreme examples of missionary preaching are those to be found in the writings of St. Paul and St. John, who use the philosophical terms and concepts of their Greek readers to communicate a message that calls these concepts into radical question.

The work of foreign missions during the "Great Century" (Latourette's phrase) of Anglo-Saxon missionary outreach has had effects in the preaching of the sending churches. The reports of missionary success have provided material for preachers. It can be candidly said that while missionaries were all too aware of their own failures and disappointments, it was expected that they would report their successes, and these reports provided encouragement to preachers looking for evidence of the truth and power of the gospel. The reports helped to nourish a mood of triumphalism. It must also be admitted that this sense of triumph could become a dangerously syncretistic mixture of a proper Christian glorying in the cross with an improper nationalist glorying in the achievements of "our people." Such concepts as those of British Imperialism and American Manifest Destiny were too easily nourished by a particular genre of missionary reporting.

The elements of falsehood in this mixture were unmasked when in the late twentieth century large numbers of the peoples to whom missionaries had been sent ("the heathen") became neighbors of Christian congregations in the cities of the Western world. Guilt over Western imperialism infected the church's mandate with the result that in many Christian circles it came to be regarded as improper to preach the gospel to the adherents of the world religions. "Dialogue" became the preferred option. This development overlooks: (1) that dialogue in the sense it is understood in the Western society that inherits the Greek tradition is foreign to the world religions and (2) that no dialogue can replace the communication of factual news, which is what preaching in the biblical sense is.

The impact of missionary experience on preaching in the Western world is likely to be of a different character in the next decades. The long syncretistic relation between Christianity and Western culture has now developed into a situation in which the specificity of the gospel is almost lost, absorbed into the relativism, individualism, and narcissism of Western culture. It is now necessary for preachers in the Western world to recognize that they are in a missionary situation where the Bible is no longer authoritative scripture, and the name of Jesus, freely used in swearing, does not refer to any well-known person. Many preachers in Western society feel like missionaries to their own cultures, cultures that were once allegedly Christian. Unlike the nineteenth-century missionary, today's preacher does not have to make a deliberate effort to immerse himself or herself in the mental world of the hearers. That has already been accomplished. The task is to recover the full meaning of the words used in Christian discourse, and that can only happen when the Bible in its canonical wholeness recovers its place as scripture. Preaching is the announcing of news; the telling of a narrative. In a society that has a different story to tell about itself, preaching has to be firmly and unapologetically rooted in the real story (*see* Cross-Cultural Preaching).

Newbigin, L., *Foolishness to the Greeks,* 1986.   LESSLIE NEWBIGIN

Moody, Dwight Lyman.   (1837–1899) Moody was the most widely known and respected American revivalist of the last third of the nineteenth century. Born in the small town of Northfield, Massachusetts, he left there as a teenager to go first to Boston and then to Chicago, where he worked as a boot and shoe sales-

man and as a lay evangelist until 1873. In that year he went to Great Britain and launched his now-famous career as an urban revivalist, conducting extended "campaigns" in the principal cities of Scotland and England. Moody returned to the United States in 1875, with his revival techniques and preaching style well developed and his reputation as a successful "fisher of men" (and women) firmly established. In the fall of 1875, he initiated a series of lengthy, large-scale revivals in major American cities, which continued until about 1880 and confirmed his reputation as a popular national religious leader.

Unlike revivalists who both preceded and followed him, Moody did not possess charisma as a preacher. He lacked the intellectual acumen of Jonathan Edwards,* the piercing eyes and the lawyer-like sharpness of Charles Finney,* the baseball-player showmanship of Billy Sunday,* the matinee-idol good looks of Billy Graham.* His was an ordinary charisma that appealed to the people of America's late nineteenth-century urban centers precisely because he seemed so much like them. His medium height, stocky build, carefully trimmed beard, flat, almost nasal voice, and conservative black suits produced the image of a respectable businessman in an age when business was triumphant. Always a layperson, possessing little formal education (at most through the primary grades) and no formal theological training, Moody invited his hearers to identify quickly with a revivalist sprung from the common people. Revivalism in America, especially in the nineteenth and twentieth centuries, was thoroughly mixed with democratic social tendencies, and Moody illustrated well this interdependence.

The atmosphere of the mass meetings also helped Moody cast his spell over his audience. He created the machinery of mass revivalism, and it is no accident that his techniques remain at the base of the revival practices of all his twentieth-century successors, including Billy Graham.

The sheer size of his meetings—usually audiences of 5,000 people or more—evoked a sense of awe among participants. Mass choirs, a platform crowded with both secular and religious dignitaries, antiphonal singing within the audience—all created a great stir and excitement. Moody's "musical assistant," Ira B. Sankey, also added an important element. Sankey's untrained but sweet and airy tenor voice (ruined by the late 1800s from overuse), the muted, organlike sound of his portable harmonium, and the rollicking, catchy gospel tunes he played and led the crowd in singing, all served as essential preparation for Moody's preaching. Hints of traditional church services were present, but the dominant atmosphere reflected the rapidly secularizing culture of the cities in which Moody conducted his revivals.

When Moody preached to his large audiences, he did not "convict" them by the force of overpowering logic and a carefully prepared text. He always spoke informally; he never wrote out in exact detail an entire sermon. The documentary remains of his sermons consist of envelopes filled with scraps of paper containing scribbled anecdotes, biblical citations, and key phrases and thoughts to be used in his talk. Many of these sermons were repeated over and over in different cities (he meticulously recorded the places and dates of delivery on the outside of the sermon envelopes). In published form, usually verbatim accounts written down by newspaper reporters and stenographers at his revivals, his sermons do not read well. They lack logical coherence and, more important, the emotion that accompanied the actual presentation. Moody's sermons were most effective as they were preached. A master storyteller, he presented to audiences steeped in personal study of the Bible a spiritual message intimately tied to biblical stories he and they knew by heart. He stressed a simple message of a God of love, not of a God of wrath and judgment. His sermons often evoked the vivid, comforting images of thrifty, sober, moral Victorian families living in small-town or rural America, the place of origin of many in his audience.

In every sermon, Moody conveyed his own deep evangelical religious commitments. Even in the huge downtown auditorium buildings where he held his revivals,* he was able to convey the immediacy of his personal religious convictions. He possessed the special power of nineteenth-century evangelical revivalists to touch the common people. This is the power that transcends the gimmickry and crowd manipulation that were a part of his work and of the American revival tradition since his time. After 1880, Moody developed other public interests besides his work as a revivalist. Beginning in 1879 and continuing into the next decade, he founded three schools. First came two private secondary academies: Northfield School for Girls and the Mt. Hermon School (for boys), opened in his hometown in western Massachusetts. Today they are known as the Northfield Schools. In the 1880s he created a school for lay evangelists in Chicago, which eventually became Moody Bible Institute. Moody also established a series of summer institutes or "conventions" for adults and college students on the campuses of the schools in Northfield, which he conceived as rallying points for evangelicalism. These gatherings eventually reflected the early division between liberals and conservatives that helped to precipitate the fundamentalist movement of the twentieth century. These endeavors suggest that in his later years the evangelist was searching for ways, in addition to mass revivalism, to energize American evangelical Protestantism.

Brereton, V., *Training God's Army: The American Bible School, 1880–1940,* 1990. **Findlay, J. F.,** *Dwight L. Moody: American Evangelist, 1837–1899,* 1969. **McLoughlin, W. G.,** *Modern Revivalism: Charles Grandison Finney to Billy Graham,* 1959. **Marsden, G. M.,** *Fundamentalism and American Culture: The Shaping of Twentieth Century Evangelicalism, 1870–1925,* 1980.

JAMES F. FINDLAY

O, BACKSLIDER
Dwight L. Moody

But there is another class I want to speak to—that is the backslider. Now, I will venture to say in this congregation there are scores, maybe hundreds of men and women that once knew the Lord; that were once in fellowship with Him; once delighted to go to the house of the Lord and sit down at the communion table; once had a family altar; once delighted to be with His people. All that is gone now. Perhaps I can tell you how you got away from Him. It may be that you were converted down there in some little town in the state and identified yourself with the church there. You knew everyone that belonged to the church; they knew you and helped you. At last perhaps your business brought you to Cleveland, and you were among strangers. You went into this and that church, and they did not seem exactly like the churches in the country. There was no one to shake hands with you or take any interest in you; and you began to think you didn't like the Christians here in Cleveland. They were not so warmhearted as they were down in the country where you came from. You can't find a church like that where you were converted. The trouble was you went to the churches, but didn't make yourself known. You didn't tell them who you were, and where you came from. If you had done that they would have gathered around you and took your hand and given you a warm welcome. You went to the public services; no one spoke to you and you thought they were very cold. I have always noticed when a man is himself cooling off he always thinks other people are cooling off likewise. When he is cold he thinks every one else is cold. Before you came to Cleveland you had a family altar, you prayed to the Father to protect you from sin; but the family altar has been broken down. O, backslider! I want to ask you tonight, where art thou? If God should summon you into eternity, what would become of your children?

I never saw a man that could give a reason for leaving the Lord. A backslider is one who has backslidden from the Lord. It is not backsliding from the church, because the church don't save us. . . .

O, backslider, hear the voice of the Shepherd this night calling to you from the dark mountains of sin, and say as the Prodigal did, "I will arise and go to my father." You know, Peter backslided. He denied the Lord, I will tell you what won him back. It was the loving look of his Master. It broke his heart when Christ turned and looked at him. O, may the tender loving look of Christ fall upon your heart tonight, sinner, and may you go out and weep bitterly, as Peter did.

> From "Where Art Thou?" in *Moody's Great Sermons* (Chicago: Laird & Lee Publishers, 1899), 31–34.

Morgan, G. Campbell. (1863–1945)

George Campbell Morgan was the preeminent conservative biblical expositor of the English-speaking world during the first half of the twentieth century. The son of a Baptist preacher in Tetbury, Gloucestershire, Morgan was raised in Wales, where he absorbed the great tradition of Welsh preaching.

Morgan was educated at home and in private schools. He never attended college or received a formal theological education. But he preached his first sermon at the age of thirteen and some 25,000 more before his death at the age of 81. He taught as a young man and then applied for the Wesleyan Methodist ministry. He was rejected as a candidate by the Methodists for showing "no promise as a preacher."

Following this rejection in 1888, Morgan became a Congregationalist, was ordained, and served two village congregations. During his early pastorates, the young preacher discovered his vocation to study and teach the Bible. His models were Moody,* Spurgeon,* Dale, and Gipsy Smith. In 1893 he moved to Birmingham and in 1897 to London where he became the pastor of the historic New Court Church, counting among his predecessors the venerable Richard

Baxter.* Morgan accepted a call to Westminster Chapel in the heart of London in 1904. The congregation there had fallen on hard times. But it was soon revived under the preaching and thorough organizational work for which Morgan was famous. The activities most associated with Morgan's London ministry were the Friday night Bible studies, where his reputation as an expositor of scripture soared. He served Westminster until 1917 and would return a second time in 1933, when he was 69 years old.

The Expositor.   Morgan's biblical work and the preaching that grew out of it were expository.* His father had taught him only one book, the Bible. When he encountered critical books as a young man, they threw him into a spiritual and intellectual tailspin. Finally, he took all the books he had, locked them in the cupboard, bought a new Bible, and determined from that day to live for one thing: to preach the teachings of the Bible alone. From that time he remained little interested in historical-critical questions, preferring instead to concentrate on the content of scripture. He chose the fundamentalist side of the controversy with the modernists, but he was not an absolute fundamentalist. In fact, he often came to the defense of ministers and teachers who were accused of doctrinal infidelity. For Morgan, the key to scripture was Christ. He interpreted all scripture christologically. For example: "There is no answer to Job till we find it in Jesus." Morgan published more than 60 books, almost all of them dealing with scripture. Many included his expository sermons, which reached a wide audience and helped shape the homiletical method of a generation of conservatives.

Morgan's expository work might strike some contemporary listeners as pedantic. His classic work *The Analyzed Bible* is a clue to his method. He divided and analyzed books of the Bible, categorizing and numbering themes and ideas. His exposition was straightforward and sometimes unimaginative. When writing about Jesus' use of parables, he said, "I freely confess my own inability to such form of teaching. I dare not attempt a method so delicate and so beautiful" (Morgan 1907, 15–16).

The Missioner. The word "missioner," often used interchangeably with missionary or evangelist, designated a traveling preacher who conducted preaching missions. In his day, Morgan had no peer as a missioner. His greatest achievements took place in the United States and Canada. He made his first trip to America in 1897 at the invitation of Dwight L. Moody and crossed the Atlantic some 43 times in the next 28 years.

In 1919, he decided to devote himself to itinerant preaching in North America. From his base in Athens, Georgia, he traveled hundreds of thousands of miles and preached thousands of sermons over the next thirteen years. His travels were interrupted by several sojourns: at the Northfield Conferences in Massachusetts founded by Moody; as a lecturer at the Bible Institute of Los Angeles and Gordon College in Boston; and in brief pastorates at the First Presbyterian Church of Cincinnati and the Tabernacle Presbyterian Church of Philadelphia. Morgan returned to England in 1933 and once again assumed the pastorate of the Westminster Chapel, finally retiring again in 1943.

Preaching. Morgan believed that "the supreme work of the Christian minister is preaching." His method of preparation was "work; hard work; and again, work." He studied the text extensively, prepared a sermon brief that allowed for freedom of expression, and then preached for at least 45 minutes. He spoke longer than most preachers and was aware of it. He once announced, "The evening meeting will begin at eight o'clock and will conclude . . . when I'm through."

Campbell Morgan was tall and gaunt, with wavy hair and an intense, almost sad, face. His voice was resonant though not powerful. He believed that the essential elements of preaching are truth, clarity, and passion (Morgan 1955, 14). Alexander Gammie sums up his gift of preaching this way:

He will not attempt to overpower you with rhetoric, or entertain you with ancient anecdotes, or surprise you with dexterous illustrations, or dazzle you with brilliant quotations. Not at all. But he will—for nearly an hour—build up a solid, sustained carefully thought out and apparently unanswerable argument, which you would not think to be irresistibly attractive. Still, people crowd to hear it, from Los Angeles to London . . . (Fant and Pinson, 13).

Fant, C., and W. Pinson, "G. Campbell Morgan," *Twenty Centuries of Great Preaching*, Vol. 8, 1971. Morgan, G. C., *The Analyzed Bible*, 1964; *Parables of the Kingdom*, 1907; and *Preaching*, 1955.

JOSEPH R. JETER, JR.

Mott, John R. (1865–1955) By his message of evangelism and ecumenism, his promotion of the role of the laity in preaching, and his extraordinary effort on behalf of world peace, John Mott was a shaper of twentieth-century Christianity. He was the corecipient of the Nobel Peace Prize in 1946 in recognition of his life's work and especially his efforts at reconciliation between the world wars. Mott was "the inspirer and founder of the World Student Christian Federation . . . , the man who, if any deserves the title, may be called the pioneer of the modern ecumenical movement" (Rouse and Neill, 331). Mott is an inspiration and point of reference a century after he initiated the movement that committed mainline Protestants to a vigorous presence in America's colleges, making a witness that is closely related to the intellectual issues of higher education.

Mott made a decision for the Christian life under the guidance of J.K.E. Studd while he was a student at Cornell University, from which he graduated in 1888. Upon graduation, he became General Secretary of the Student Y.M.C.A. and Chairman of the Student Volunteer Movement for Foreign Missions. Missions* were the passion of his life from

1886, when he joined the Student Volunteer Movement at the Mount Hermon Conference. From his student days, he saw the connection between mission and ecumenism. In 1895, he set out on the first of many world tours of universities and colleges and took the lead in founding the World Student Christian Federation. His evangelistic work with students brought to Christ many hundreds of those who became leaders of Life and Work and Faith and Order.

He chaired the Edinburgh World Missionary Conference in 1910, the first of the global missionary conferences. He chaired the International Missionary Conference in 1921, the Oxford Conference on Church, Community, and State in 1937, and the Westfield Conference in the same year. He became the honorary president of the World Council of Churches in 1948.

Mott led the way in involving the Eastern churches in the ecumenical movement. The W.S.C.F. Conference in Constantinople in 1911 was significant chiefly in that it drew these ancient churches for the first time into the emerging ecumenical movement. This conference not only extended the Student Christian Movement into the Near East from Turkey to Egypt but it brought many of the leaders of East and West together with far-reaching consequences.

Mott was active in the work of international reconciliation during both world wars, working through issues related to German missions before, during, and after World War I, though this was one of the most controversial of his activities. His work with students kept some communication open between students of the different nations and contributed later to the rebuilding of Europe.

Of Mott, Kenneth Scott Latourette wrote:

In an unusual degree he combined a dignified, commanding presence, deep religious faith, evangelistic zeal, the capacity to discern ability and promise in youth and to inspire it, wide-ranging vision, courage, tact, administrative ability, power over public assemblies as a presiding officer, and compelling, convincing speech (Rouse and Neill, 356).

Mott was a Methodist who won the cooperation of many thousands of men and women of many churches, races, and nations. Not theologically trained, he was able to win the support of many who were.

He used only his native English for conversation and public address but communicated with people all around the world. A constant traveler, he sought to win people to Christ and to service in his name. His dreams and actions were devoted both to individuals and movements that would affect nations and humanity as a whole. He had a gift for attracting outstanding persons to the enterprises in which he was involved.

"The evangelization of the world in this generation" was the watchword of the Student Volunteer Movement with which Mott was associated. It may appear at this point in history that the goal was too grandiose and doomed to failure. Yet Mott and his purpose are not easily dismissed. Evangelization for Mott meant "giving every person an adequate opportunity to know Jesus Christ as personal Savior and Lord. It does not mean converting every person in the world in this generation" (Mott, 80). To be sure, Christian faith may be understood differently today (especially in relation to other world religions), and the world itself continues to change dramatically. The individual and small group work that Mott stressed must be supplemented with new methods.

However, John R. Mott's statement of the supreme purpose of the Christian church stands as a judgment where even it is not accepted as a summons: "The supreme purpose of the Christian Church is to make Jesus Christ known, trusted, loved, obeyed, and exemplified in the whole range of individual life—body, mind, and spirit—and also in all human relationships. This is incomparably the most important work for every Christian" (Mott, 7).

Mott, J. R., *The Larger Evangelism*, 1944.
Rouse, R., and S. C. Neill, eds., *A History of the Ecumenical Movement 1517–1948*, 1954.
DAVID JAMES RANDOLPH

Narrative Preaching.

The field of narrative preaching involves a cluster of related foci, including narrative homiletics, narrative hermeneutics, and narrative theology. Central to the first focus, narrative homiletics, is the issue of *sermonic shape*. Primary attention to the specific matter of sermonic shape can provide both clarity of definition as well as access to questions of underlying theoretical considerations.

A *narrative sermon* is any sermon in which the arrangement of ideas takes the form of a plot involving a strategic delay of the preacher's meaning.

Typically, narrative preaching will embody a storylike process, moving from opening conflict, through complication, toward a peripetia or reversal or decisive turn, resulting in a denouement or resolution of thought and experience. This plotted movement, nuanced differently depending on the particular text, theme, and sermonic purpose, is shaped toward maximizing a growing sense of expectancy and culminates in the final experience of the sermon on the part of the listeners. Such a sermon may or may not actually involve any particular story.

The complication of its plot may be occasioned by the juxtaposition of conflicted ideas, rational/discursive argument, and metaphorical exploration, or by the use of an extended illustration. The means are varied, the purpose is singular—namely, to provide the context of heightened expectation in preparation for the evocation of the sermon's experiential meaning.

The peripetia (often occurring fairly late in the sermon) may involve a polar reversal of thought or a more modest yet decisive turn somehow not quite expected. Whether the turn is modest or radical depends upon the content and genre of the biblical text and the treatment of the homiletical theme.

The denouement or resultant resolution, in ways parallel to the narrativity of a musical score, may build to a grand finale or return to a knowing reprise. The focus on movement is motivated in part by concern for how the meaning can best be grasped. Delay of meaning born of suspense will maximize the power of its hearing.

Sometimes a narrative sermon will actually consist of one long story told—biblical or otherwise. In this case the sermon, like other literary plots, will actually involve such narrative elements as setting, characters, action, and tone—all moving the plot line from opening disequilibrium toward final resolution. Such a sermon is best described as *story preaching* and can be viewed as one form of the larger category of narrative preaching. All story sermons (defined as a sermon consisting entirely of a single story) are narrative sermons; only some narrative sermons are story sermons. Conversely, many sermons that contain stories may not be narrative sermons because the entire sermon is not shaped into narrative form.

A sermon based entirely on an elaboration of the "prodigal son" story *and* following the plot of the parable would be a story sermon. A sermon utilizing the parable of the lost coin as one of several ingredients may or may not be a narrative sermon—depending entirely on whether all the ingredients are shaped into narrative form. The overall shape of the sermon is key to the definition of narrative preaching. Again, the inclusion of illustrative material involving stories does not constitute a narrative sermon. Nonnarrative sermons often include story-type ingredients. Narrative *shape* is the defining factor. Unlike the majority of narrative sermons, a story sermon may likely focus less on discursive thought and rely more on aesthetic presentation of image, metaphor, and parable.

Closely related and sometimes nearly identical to narrative preaching is what is known as *inductive preaching*,* which takes its name from the movement of ideas beginning with the particular and moving toward the general (in contrast to deductive movement from the general to the particular). Whether inductive preaching and narrative preaching are similar or identical in shape will depend upon the preacher and the particular sermon. For example, inductive reasoning is one way to complicate a narrative sermon plot, but not the only way. Likewise, the result of inductive logic often is complication of the plot, but not always. In either case, the conclusion is delayed until close to the end of the preached sermon. One may observe also that a narrative sermon may sometimes shift briefly into deductive movement once the decisive homiletical turn occurs.

Another form of narrative may be titled *episodal preaching*. Such a sermon consists in episodes or separable vignettes only implicitly connected, but which then find explicit closure by means of a conclusion that brings unity to the whole. Such a design may utilize metaphor rather than linear development as the means by which expectancy grows toward the homiletical meaning. For example, one can imagine a set of three stories or parables told, the interconnections of which may not be fully grasped by the listener until the conclusion of the third story. At that point, a gestalt of meaning may sweep backward around the three stories, and for the first time explicit homiletical unity becomes known. Indeed, this description is appropriate for understanding the movement of Luke 15 in which Jesus tells the three stories of lost sheep, lost coin, and lost sons.

Finally, another variation on the theme of narrative sermonic shape can be described as the *phenomenological move*

sermon. This type of sermon consists of a sequence of plotted ideational units culminating in the sermonic conclusion. The goal here is to establish a phenomenological field in the consciousness of the listener. Just how narrative-like this structure appears depends on the text and the intention of the preacher. But, as in the case of each of these variations, there is a narrative principle at work that involves the delay of meaning until the end of the preached sermon.

Once one asks questions about why meaning is delayed, or why expectancy or mounting tension or conflict is important, or why inductive movement is effective—in short why this attention to plot—the focus of narrative preaching expands beyond sermonic shape to sermonic purpose, narrative hermeneutics, and narrative theology. Converging upon the preached sermon and its shape are concerns born of many disciplines and issues nurtured by diverse interests and points of view. That the sources of influence are not singular, results of course in multiple understandings of what a narrative sermon is—or ought to be.

Among these converging concerns are the following:

1. the basically inductive movement of biblical exegetical work;
2. the power of narrative shape as experienced in such literary forms as drama, short story, and the novel;
3. the essentially narrative shape of human experience;
4. the power of story as the primary vehicle of revelation;
5. the essentially narrative shape of the canon (with even nonnarrative passages serving the larger biblical story);
6. the connection of imagination and theological worldview by means of such narrative elements as metaphor and image;
7. the increasing role of narrative criticism in biblical studies;
8. the significant shift of understanding of the purpose of preaching from

conviction by means of rational argument toward transforming event-in-time by means of participation, identification, and engagement;

9. the changing sense of authority as it relates to the preaching office;

10. the increasing emphasis within the field of biblical hermeneutics upon the question of what a text is intending to *do*, rather than the central idea to be abstracted.

One can readily perceive other rich and diverse issues that may bear upon the questions of sermonic shape and purpose. Clearly, one motivation behind narrative homiletical shape is fueled by the question of how the sermon can best become an event-in-time, rather than simply an elaborated explanation thematically shaped or deductively outlined.

The shape of a narrative sermon may appear radically different from the traditionally organized structure involving a move from exegesis and interpretation to final application. Yet, the substance of a narrative sermon is seldom radically different from the traditionally shaped sermon. Rather than perceiving an either-or mentality, one may discern a figure-ground shift in this important homiletical development. The shape of traditional homiletics is an outgrowth of rhetorical principles that go back to Aristotle's *Rhetoric*. Narrative preaching is informed additionally by his *Poetics*. With the exception of some story or parable sermons, the central difference is not so much *what* is said, as *how* it is said. Rather than utilizing a sermonic envelope governed by rhetorical principles with narrative components inside, narrative preaching provides a narrative envelope in which rhetorical components reside (*see* History of Preaching; Form; Literary Criticism).

Beardslee, W. A., *Literary Criticism of the New Testament*, 1970. Buttrick, D., *Homiletic*, 1987. Craddock, F. B., *As One Without Authority*, 1971. Crites, S., "The Narrative Quality of Experience," *Journal of the American Academy of Religion* 39 (September 1971), 291–311. Frei, H. W., *The Eclipse of Biblical Narrative: A Study in Eighteenth and Nineteenth Century Hermeneutics*, 1974. Lowry, E. L., *How to Preach a Parable*, 1989. Scholes, R., and R. Kellogg, *The Nature of Narrative*, 1966. Wilder, A., *Theopoetic: Theology and the Religious Imagination*, 1976.
EUGENE L. LOWRY

Newman, John Henry. (1801–1890) Newman was a Cardinal of the Roman Catholic Church and one of the greatest prose stylists in the history of English letters. Born in London of Anglican parents, he was influenced by the Evangelical school within the Church of England. He studied at Oxford, where he was a Fellow of Oriel and Vicar of the University Church of St. Mary the Virgin. There his sermons of increasingly High Church sentiments attracted large numbers of undergraduates while distracting university officials. As a principal figure in the Oxford Movement, which promoted a more Catholic understanding of Anglicanism, his researches, especially into the Arian question of the fourth century, moved him to join the Roman Catholic Church in 1845. Throughout a long life whose trials were commensurate with fame, his virtues were so heroically lived that he is a popular candidate for sainthood.

Newman's spiritual, theological, and literary genius places him in the company of the most eminent Victorians. When Catholics suffered defamation, the Cardinal's integrity won the respect and even devotion of countless numbers not of his religion. As a theologian, his *Essay on the Development of Doctrine* and *Essay in Aid of a Grammar of Assent* have attained a venerability less than only the works of the early fathers and the canonical Scholastics. Recent popes have regarded him as a prophet of the Second Vatican Council, particularly in understanding the role of the laity. The *Idea of a University* is the most lapidary modern exposition of educational theory, and the *Apologia pro Vita Sua*, which is indispensable for understanding the moral and intellectual formation of Newman as a preacher, is widely recognized as one of the finest autobiographies in the English language. While his verse is generally less distinguished, "The Dream of Gerontius" places him second only to Dante as poet of Catholic eschatology, and hymns like "Lead, Kindly Light" still are universal favorites.

The essential Newman was a preacher, and he followed the Patristic tradition of making sermons the primary vehicle for theology. He opposed the reactionary mood when it held suspect attempts to express eternal truths in images accessible to the grasp of the age; but his life's work was to contradict what he called the spirit of liberalism in religion, the definitive infidelity of the day that rigidly believes in unrigid unbelief. Liberalism assumes that revealed religion "is not a truth, but a sentiment and a taste; not an objective fact; not miraculous: and it is the right of each individual to make it say just what strikes his fancy."

So he spoke in the "Biglietto Speech" of 1879 when being created a Cardinal; the words were identical in sentiment to those preached as an Anglican in his twenties. Pulpit oratory is sacred because it is for the sanctification of souls, and sanctification is impossible if it is not the work of truth leading individuals to truth. His was a personalism where others offered individualism, for the individual is not saved apart from the body of Christ. Salvation perfects and does not destroy, as does sin, the integrity of each human person. Newman preached this to the elite of the university, to farmers in nearby Littlemore, and later to the poor immigrants of the Birmingham tenements in whose midst he established an Oratory of St. Philip Neri.

It was said that as his preaching moved from Anglican pulpits to Catholic pulpits, its rhetorical diction shifted from Doric to Corinthian, finding Ionic repose as it matured in the idiom of Catholic life. The mental architecture can be traced in the many volumes of his collected sermons principally *Parochial and Plain Sermons* (1834–1843), *Discourses Addressed to*

Mixed Congregations (1849), and *Sermons Preached on Various Occasions* (1857). Yet not once did he alter the conviction chiseled in *The Idea of a University:* "Talent, logic, learning, words, manners, voice, action, all are required for the perfection of a preacher; but 'one thing is necessary,'—an intense perception and appreciation of the end for which he preaches, and that is, to be the minister of some definite spiritual good to those who hear him." The theme located itself in his cardinalitial motto, adapted from the early seventeenth-century counsel of St. Francis de Sales: "Cor ad cor loquitur" (Heart speaks to heart). As Matthew Arnold recalled from his undergraduate days, it was already a moral fact when the young Oxford vicar dimmed the gaslight in the pulpit and began to read from a carefully scripted text in a silvery voice that seemed aimed at a solitary hearer.

Newman's character, and the scope of interests to which he applied it, made him the embodiment of the church's economy of prophetic, priestly and kingly offices. Sacred rhetoric must resonate within the framework of a solid ecclesiology if it is not to ring hollow. Conscious of a sacramental dignity attached to preaching, the preacher preaches substantial doctrine through the accidents of worthy character. Personal holiness unites the objectivity of the truths preached and the subjectivity of those receiving the sacred words, making the proclamation an act of worship beyond edification. The pulpit becomes one of the "two tables" of the Eucharist, leading to the altar where the Living Word is sacrificed. Grace cannot be underestimated in the exchange: " . . . the Apostles argued not, but preached, and conscience did the rest," he says in the *Sermon Notes*. He says in the *Idea:* "Nothing that is anonymous will preach. . . . Thought and word are one in the Eternal Logos, and must not be separate in those who are His shadows on earth."

In a characteristic phrase, Newman argued for the superiority of Cicero who "wrote Roman" when others like Livy and Tacitus "wrote Latin." Cicero was the pagan version of Christian Newman for whom "Definiteness is the life of preaching. A definite hearer, not the whole world, a definite topic, not the whole evangelical tradition; and in like manner, a definite speaker." None of this can be had without a civilized familiarity with history and the diverse arts that history records. But this would be pedantry without obedience to the revealed truths of God that are not the inventions of any culture. Devotion to history may help to explain Newman's spare use of allusions to nature, so dear to romantic oratory. Otherwise, he was the most careful of Victorian artists, maintaining that "elaborateness in composition is no mark of trick or artifice in an author." If he admired Cicero, he venerated St. John who held with all the greatest preachers one of the tenets of the *Apologia:* the mysteries of the church "are but the expression in human language of truths to which the human mind is unequal."

Cragan, D. B., *A Rhetorical Analysis of Five Sermons of Cardinal Newman with Special Reference to Aristotle's Rhetoric,* 1943. **Jaki, S. L.,** ed., *Newman Today,* 1989. **Newman, J. H.,** *The Idea of a University Defined and Illustrated,* 1873.   GEORGE W. RUTLER

THE GLORY OF THE CHURCH
John Henry Newman

And let him say to those about him: "I see a bleak mount, looking upon an open country, over against that huge town, to whose inhabitants Catholicism is of so little account. I see the ground marked out, and an ample enclosure made; and plantations are rising there, clothing and circling in the space. And there on that high spot, far from the haunts of men, yet in the very center of the island, a large edifice, or rather pile of edifices, appears, with many fronts and courts, and long cloisters and corridors, and story upon story. And there it rises, under the invocation of the same sweet and powerful name which has been our strength and consolation in the Valley. I look more attentively at that building, and I see it is fashioned upon that ancient style of art which brings back the past, which had seemed to be perishing from off the face of the earth, or to be preserved only as a curiosity, or to be imitated only as a fancy. I listen, and I hear the sound of voices, grave and musical, renewing the old chant, with which Augustine greeted Ethelbert in the free air upon the Kentish strand. It comes from a long procession, and it winds along the cloisters. Priests and Religious, theologians from the schools, and canons from the Cathedral, walk in due precedence. And then there comes a vision of well nigh twelve mitred heads; and last I see a Prince of the Church, in the royal dye of empire and of martyrdom, a pledge to us from Rome of Rome's unwearied love, a token that that goodly company is firm in Apostolic faith and hope. And the shadow of the Saints is there; St. Benedict is there, speaking to us by the voice of bishop and of priest, and counting over the long ages through which he has prayed, and studied, and labored; there, too, is St. Dominic's white wool, which no blemish can impair, no stain can dim: and if St. Bernard be not there, it is only that his absence may make him be remembered more. And the princely patriarch, St. Ignatius, too, the St. George of the modern world, with his chivalrous lance run through his writhing foe, he too sheds his blessing upon that train. And others, also, his equals or his juniors in history, whose pictures are above our altars, or soon shall be, the surest proof that the Lord's arm has not waxen short, nor His mercy failed—they, too, are looking down from their thrones on high upon the throng. And so that high company moves on into the holy place; and there, with august rite and awful sacrifice, inaugurates the great act which brings it thither. What is that act? It is the first Synod of a new Hierarchy; it is the resurrection of the Church.

From "The Second Spring," in *Sermons Preached on Various Occasions* (London: Burns, Oates & Co., 1874), 175–76.

Niebuhr, Reinhold.   (1892–1971)

Reinhold Niebuhr was one of the dominant theological voices of the twentieth century. His influence was immense not only in ethics but in every aspect of theology and church life. Many sermons embody Niebuhrian themes, even though the preacher may never have read Niebuhr. Niebuhr's way of conceiving Christian existence has become so pervasive we are all, in some sense, Niebuhrians.

In a critical essay on Niebuhr, Noam Chomsky observes that Niebuhr in his many writings and activities remained a preacher. Chomsky writes:

> The persuasiveness of his contributions is not to be judged, or to be explained, in terms of the way he uses factual or documentary evidence, or reaches the heart of the positions of his adversaries, or provides sustained argument for his conclusions. Rather, his writings are a form of exhortation, which, at best, brings to our attention ideas and perceptions that we recognize as valid or worthwhile from our own experience, or on the basis of our own intuitive judgments, but might have missed without stimulus to our thought; and at worst, provides rationalization for the interests he emphasized but often failed to recognize (Chomsky, 209–10).

That Niebuhr always worked in sermonic fashion is not surprising, given his background. He was the son of an Evangelical minister and spent his early life in the church. He also grew up with German, the language of his church. He later worked to free the Evangelical Synod of its use of the German language in order to increase its appeal to a wider public, which was but one aspect of his lifelong commitment to the American project.

Niebuhr spent his adolescent years in Lincoln, Illinois, before being sent to the church's small boarding school, Elmhurst College. From there he went on to seminary at Eden Theological Seminary, graduating in 1913 at the age of 20.

Niebuhr continued his schooling at Yale Divinity School, working with Douglas Clyde Macintosh. He discovered that his schooling to this point had been quite deficient as he was yet unable to write English in a manner that would satisfy his new teachers. However, by dint of hard work and extraordinary energy, he was able to receive in 1915 the B.D. and M.A. They would remain Niebuhr's most advanced degrees.

In 1915, he was called to Bethel Evangelical Church in Detroit and served there until he was called as professor of social ethics at Union Theological Seminary in New York in 1928. Although Niebuhr was deeply involved in pastoral tasks, his energy took him in many directions. While in the pastorate, he became a sought-after speaker and writer. It is sometimes suggested that Niebuhr's church in Detroit was a working-class church. In fact it was relatively affluent. His commitment to the cause of labor in Detroit was in some ways in spite of, rather than due to, the constituency of his church.

Niebuhr's theological position during his ministry was liberal. He had little use for the "supernaturalism" of traditional orthodoxy, and he was committed to the understanding of the Bible characteristic of the great German historical critics and theologians. He shared the commitments of the social gospel's attempt to work to establish the kingdom of God. His subsequent attack on the social gospel and his stress on the significance of sin for understanding the human condition has created the impression that he abandoned his liberal theological presuppositions. Yet Niebuhr remained throughout his life deeply committed to the structure of liberal theology, particularly in the assumption that Christian theology is fundamentally anthropology. In fact, he later took pains to distinguish his position from Barth,* whose account of the Christian faith he considered obscurantist.

When he left his church in Detroit, he published his reflections on the ministry in his *Leaves from the Notebook of a*

Tamed Cynic (1929). The book is full of the striking insight and honesty characteristic of Niebuhr's subsequent work. In it he reflects on why preachers are so seldom prophetic. He notes that it is not because, as so often is believed, the minister is financially dependent on the people of the church. Rather, as Niebuhr wrote,

> The real clue to the tameness of a preacher is the difficulty one finds in telling unpleasant truths to people whom one has learned to love. To speak the truth in love is a difficult, and sometimes an almost impossible, achievement. If you speak the truth unqualifiedly, that is usually because your ire has been aroused or because you have no personal attachment to the object of your strictures. Once personal contact is established you are very prone to temper your wind to the shorn sheep. It is certainly difficult to be human and honest at the same time. I'm not surprised that most budding prophets are tamed in time to become harmless parish priests (74).

Niebuhr, however, was quite critical of those preachers who build their congregations around their pulpit eloquence. "What kind of fundamental ethical questions can a man be eloquent about when he draws that much cash, particularly since a Croesus or two usually has to supply an undue proportion of it?" (85) He believed the "modern pulpit" has failed to preach repentance. Its estimate of human nature is far too romantic to give people any appreciation of the brutalities of life. Niebuhr had no use for those "prophetic* preachers" who assert their egoism by criticizing yours. "A spiritual leader who has too many illusions is useless. One who has lost his illusions about mankind and retains his illusions about himself is insufferable" (112).

Niebuhr's preaching did not cease when he became a professor at Union. He simply became the preacher to the nation. His ceaseless activity and his many writings catapulted him into the forefront of the church's life and the public life of the nation. In spite of his criticism of the social gospel in his Rauschenbusch lectures, *The Interpretation of Christian Ethics,* Niebuhr remained committed to the social task of Christianity. His "realism" about social power as articulated in *Moral Man and Immoral Society* in no way qualified his political and economic commitment to the creation of a more equitable social order. He did, however, become increasingly more concerned with politics and international relations rather than the economic issues more characteristic of the social gospel.

Niebuhr taught at Union until his retirement in 1960. His life consisted in a torrid round of churchly and political activities. Niebuhr was originally associated with the socialist party and its leader Norman Thomas. Later, after World War II, he generally identified with the left wing of the Democratic party. In 1947, along with Hubert Humphrey, he helped establish the Americans for Democratic Action. In 1948 he was pictured on the cover of *Time* magazine, honored not only for his theological accomplishments but also for his anti-communism.

Like many preachers, Niebuhr was not attracted to systems of thought. He was a polemicist who dealt with large themes and generalities. This does not mean that his thought was haphazard but rather that he was willing to take large risks in the presentation of his thought. The most sustained presentation of his position is found in his Gifford lectures, *The Nature and Destiny of Man,* delivered in the spring and fall of 1939 and published in two volumes (1941, 1943). These lectures not only provided him a forum for his position, but through them he educated himself in the classics of Christian theology. Niebuhr's increasingly political realism forced him to seek in orthodoxy more profound accounts of the human condition.

There can be no question that Niebuhr's account of the inevitability of sin expressed as pride and sensuality resonated in those who endured the horrors of war. His influence extended not only to those who were explicitly Christian but to many whose self-understanding was explicitly secular. The latter often found Niebuhr's account of human nature and the possibilities and limits of politics compellingly accurate.

In many ways, the themes Niebuhr developed in *The Nature and Destiny of Man* were anticipated in his 1937 book *Beyond Tragedy*. This book is particularly important for understanding Niebuhr as a preacher since he described the book as a series of "sermonic essays" (ix). Each of the "essays" was originally a sermon that was not written at the time of delivery but was later transcribed. What is striking is how similar the essential ideas of *Beyond Tragedy* are to themes in *The Nature and Destiny of Man*. Larry Rasmussen suggests that the play of Niebuhr's mind was most evident when he preached. "Here Niebuhr the dramatist of theological ideas for public life was perhaps most at home." He was most at home because the sermon gave him the opportunity to make associations at once striking and illuminating.

Niebuhr's sermons are not rigorously exegetical. He had no use for close readings of texts, but rather the texts were occasions to illustrate his prior theological notions. As he says in *The Nature and Destiny of Man*, it is "important to take Biblical symbols seriously but not literally" (II, 50). Indeed, for Niebuhr it is the great strength of the "Biblical myths" to depict the paradoxes of human existence without trying to explain them by a more inclusive philosophical system. The fundamental dialectic of the infinite and the finite that lies at the heart of "biblical religion" cannot be overcome if we are to do justice to the character of our existence. For Niebuhr, the strength of Christianity is that it supplies an account of human existence that is free of illusory rationales for self-justification.

It is not surprising, therefore, that Niebuhr begins *Beyond Tragedy* with a sermon on 2 Cor. 6:4–10, titled "As Deceivers, Yet True." In it Niebuhr calls attention to the "deceptive symbols"

through which the Christian faith expresses the dimension of eternity in time (4–5). Thus, we cannot take the myth of the Fall as something that happened in time, but rather what Christianity means by the Fall can only be known by introspection (12). This is but a restatement of Niebuhr's often-repeated theme that there are two facts about the human condition:

> The obvious fact is that man is a child of nature, subject to its vicissitudes, compelled by its necessities, driven by its impulses, and confined within the brevity of the years which nature permits its varied organic form, allowing them some, but not too much, latitude. The other less obvious fact is that man is a spirit who stands outside of nature, life, himself, his reason and the world (*Nature*, I, 3).

That humans are so constituted accounts for our anxiety, which leads to our attempt to secure our own redemption and security.

For Niebuhr, sermons are not so much proclamation of a news that would not otherwise be known as the occasion to clarify the human condition. Indeed, in many respects the power and influence of Niebuhr's work has much to do with the startling honesty and candor with which he allows us to see ourselves. Thus, in a sermon on David and the ark and another on Solomon and the temple, both from the book of Chronicles, Niebuhr reflects on our inability to separate civilization from the injustices on which it is built to secure the good. Those who cry for peace too often forget that pacifism may be a luxury of nations and classes that already have what they want (*Tragedy*, 59). No culture, nation, church, or person can be perfect in this life. Our task is to work for more nearly equitable justice in a world where the very achievement of relative justice cannot help but create further injustice.

Like his great social gospel predecessor, Walter Rauschenbusch,* the eloquence of Niebuhr's style and the energy with which he delivered his sermons helped account for his extraordinary influence. If he is the last great public theologian in America, his status was due in part to the hegemony of Protestant Christianity. Many were still capable of responding to a good sermon, whether it appeared as a sermon or a serious book of theology. For Niebuhr, the two were not distinguishable. That they have become so for us is an indication that we cannot and should not try to copy Niebuhr's extraordinary achievement.

Chomsky, N., "Reinhold Niebuhr," *Grand Street* (Winter 1987), 197–212. Niebuhr, R., *Beyond Tragedy*, 1937; *Leaves from the Notebook of a Tamed Cynic*, 1929; *The Nature and Destiny of Man*, 2 vols., 1941, 1943. Rasmussen, L., *Reinhold Niebuhr: Theologian of Public Life*, 1991.   STANLEY M. HAUERWAS

Old Testament Preaching.

When Matthew began his Gospel with the words, "Jesus Christ, the son of David, the son of Abraham," he acknowledged the fact that Christ cannot be understood apart from the Old Testament. The same is true in Luke: Jesus is the fulfillment of "the law of Moses, the prophets, and the Psalms" (24:44). Indeed, the course of Jesus' life is "according to the scriptures" (1 Cor. 15:3–4) of the Old Testament (Mark 14:21; Matt. 26:56; Acts 13:29), and the New Testament understands the whole of Old Testament hexateuchal, royal, prophetic, and wisdom theology to be gathered up and incarnated in Christ's person as the Word made flesh. "All the promises of God find their Yes in him," writes Paul (2 Cor. 1:20), and the two testaments are bound together by the promises of God in the Old Testament, which God then fulfills in his Son in the New. It follows, therefore, that in order fully to proclaim the good news of Jesus Christ, preachers must preach from the Old Testament as well as from the New. Otherwise, congregations cannot truly know who their Lord is.

Apart from the Old Testament, they also cannot know who they are as the church of Christ. In the New Testament, the Christian church is understood as "the Israel of God" (Gal. 6:16), "the true circumcision" (Phil. 3:3), the wild branches grafted into the root of Israel (Rom. 11:17). Those who believe in Christ are the "descendants of Abraham" (Gal. 3:7) who have inherited all of God's promises to Israel (Gal. 4:7) and become members of his people (Eph. 2:11–21; 1 Peter 2:9–10). But to understand who they are as the new Israel in Christ, congregations must hear the story of Israel from the Old Testament and understand that it is also their story—that they, like the Israel of old, have been redeemed from slavery, brought to the table of covenant, given God's commands for their new life as God's chosen people, set on a pilgrimage toward a promised place of rest, and accompanied on the journey by the presence of their God.

Necessary to a congregation's understanding, too, is the Old Testament's view of the natural world, of history, and of human beings. It is from the Old Testament that we learn that God is not identified or bound up with anything in all creation, that God is "holy," totally other from everything that God has made (Deut. 4:15–19; Hos. 11:9; Isa. 31:3; 40:25–26), just as it is from the Old Testament that we first learn that God's rule encompasses the whole of human history that had its beginning in God's purpose and that will find its fulfillment in the creation of new heavens and a new earth (Gen. 1:1–12:3; Isa. 65:17). And it is from the Old Testament that we learn that human beings are made in the image of God and cannot fully be understood apart from their relation with God (Gen. 1:26–27). In short, the Old Testament provides revelation apart from which the New Testament's message cannot properly be comprehended. Preachers must preach from the Old Testament as often as they preach from the new, if they would preach the gospel.

When preaching from the Old Testament, however, homileticians should pair the Old Testament text with one from the New Testament, for the Old Testament is not complete in itself. It ends with the promises of God unfulfilled, and congregations need to know if God kept his word. They also need to realize that it is only through Jesus Christ that Israel's story has become their story and the promises given to Israel their promises. If a preacher uses only an Old Testament text, the sermon is usually made Christian only by a general presentation of the gospel at the end of it. The gospel, however, is not given us in general but through the specific deeds and words handed down to us in the New Testament. Specific New Testament texts need to be paired with some Old Testament texts.

The three-year lectionary* furnishes the preacher with such pairing, although its joining of texts need not be slavishly followed, and there are often better pairings to be made. In addition, large portions of the Old Testament that are absolutely necessary to the full proclamation of the gospel are not in the lectionary.

Old and New Testament texts may be paired in one of several ways. They may be joined on the basis of promise and fulfillment (Gen. 12:3 with Gal. 3:8). There may be common motifs that bind them together (e.g., "yoke" in Jer. 2:20 and Matt. 11:29; "living water" in Jer. 2:13 and John 7:38; cf. 4:14); the control of the chaotic waters in Gen. 1 or Ps. 46:1–3 and Mark 4:35–41). There are hundreds of such common motifs running throughout the scriptures. They can be located by consulting a biblical concordance or a cross-reference Bible, and the use of them adds greatly to the power of a sermon.

Sometimes legitimate contrasts can be drawn between a text in the Old Testament and one in the New (e.g., between Gen. 4:10 and Heb. 12:24, or between Jer. 25:15–16 and 1 Cor 10:16). In these instances, however, the preacher must be sure that the contrast is legitimate and that the Old Testament's revelation is not being discarded in favor of the New. Both testaments make up our canon. Both mediate the Word of God to us, and there is

no sense in which the Old Testament has now been superseded by the "higher spiritual truths of Christianity"—a view that was popular among biblical scholars at the turn of the century and that is still ignorantly held by some preachers and lay people.

The most common method of pairing Old and New Testament texts is that of analogy. That is, Israel's life with God forms an analogy or prefigurement or foreshadowing of the church's life with its Lord. For example, the same words said to Israel at Sinai, in Ex. 19:6, are pronounced to the church in 1 Peter 2:9, and the church has become the New Israel in Christ. Likewise, attitudes marking the people of Israel are found also in the church (cf. the ingratitude of the Israelites in Num. 11:4–6 with that in the story of Luke 17:11–19 or with our contemporary lack of thankfulness for God's sustaining gifts). Similarly, incidents in the Old Testament may prefigure events in the life of our Lord. For example, the sacrifice of Isaac in Genesis 22 has often been seen as the prefigurement of Christ's death on the cross, just as Moses' lifting up of the bronze serpent in the wilderness (Num. 21:8–9) is understood in the fourth Gospel as a type of Calvary (John 3:14–15). In the same manner, Elisha's feeding of one hundred men (2 Kings 4:42–44) prefigures Jesus' feeding of the 4,000 and 5,000 (Matt. 14:15–21; 15:32–38). That which binds the two testaments together is the action of God, and that which God has promised or done in the history of Israel is often that which God has fulfilled or done also in the life of the church. By pairing Old and New Testament texts, the preacher witnesses to the unity of the one history of salvation that God is working out in his creation.

Further, by pairing texts, the preacher prevents his or her hearers from wandering into grave theological errors with regard to the nature of Jesus Christ. According to the New Testament itself, our Lord was not some mysterious figure suddenly dropped from the blue. Rather, he was and is the completion, fulfillment, and reinterpretation of God's two thousand years of working with Israel. And he can properly be understood, as the New Testament understands him, only by knowing the Old Testament history. Indeed, apart from his relation to Israel, Jesus of Nazareth could have been understood in the first- to the third-century Mediterranean world as just another mythical savior in a mystery religion or gnostic sect. And still today, without his connection to the Old Testament, he is understood by some simply as a symbol or sign or metaphor of the divine. But the fact that he is revealed as the historical fulfillment of a concrete-specific sacred history prevents his person and work from becoming the subjects of such speculation and superstition. Jesus is, the New Testament writers assert in all their differing ways, tied to a concrete history of the past which has been completed in concrete events in the writers' age. And it is that concrete history, the New Testament writers say, which alone defines Jesus Christ.

The perils of neglecting Old Testament preaching can be illustrated from history. Between 1875 and 1933, the Old Testament was considered by many European biblical scholars to be nothing more than an interesting historical record of Israel's religious development from primitive animism and sacrificial worship to the higher ethical ideals of the prophets, which then found their highest form in the teachings of Jesus of Nazareth. In short, if one had the New Testament, the Old had become unnecessary, just as the people of the Old Testament, the Jews, had become unnecessary: Hitler's Third Reich could eliminate them with impunity (see Anti-Jewish Preaching).

Similarly today, when the Old Testament has become virtually unknown in many branches of the church and is systematically neglected by some preachers in some denominations—black preaching still serves as a stunning exception—the God and Father of our Lord Jesus Christ has been reduced to an identification with some numinous spirit inhabiting all nature and persons or to a feeling of eros and love within human relationships. The result is a dreadful idolatry, in which human beings have become their own gods and goddesses, unbounded by any divine demand beyond their own will and desires. Indeed, even where a vestige of the biblical understanding remains, the view often is of a God who exists but does nothing. Only a culture that has lost the Old Testament and never hears it preached from the pulpit can entertain such perverted understandings of the nature of the God of the Bible. We will preach from the Old Testament, or we will lose the biblical faith (see Psalms; Prophets, Old Testament).

Achtemeier, E., *Preaching from the Old Testament,* 1989. von Rad, G., *Old Testament Theology,* 2 vols., 1962, 1965.

ELIZABETH ACHTEMEIER

Oral Communication and Preaching.

Preaching as oral communication can be distinguished from the literary object called "the sermon" in terms of three qualities, each with implications for both theory and practice. First, preaching involves immediacy, the physical presence of speaker and hearers in a corporate communication event called worship. Second, it entails an interdependence of participants, since the persons in the pews count on someone to preach and the person in the pulpit counts on someone to listen to what is said. Third, preaching involves indeterminacy; it cannot be a finished product before it is heard; its hearing and application are decided in various ways by those present in worship.

The immediacy of preaching means that people are present to each other in a physical, social, intellectual, and spiritual context that they have agreed to share for a period of time. This many-layered presence places a premium on the oral communication skills of the preacher, who will be integral to the message preached, whether intentionally or unintentionally. Because listeners can choose among many communicators in the religious and secular mass media, the so-called personality* of the preacher carries substantial weight in the perceptions of those who attend worship.

The preacher's voice, facial expressions, and body movements can reinforce, complicate, or even contradict the words being spoken. When the preacher's implied assumptions, language, and physical behaviors are consistent, the preaching event conveys the message that the person speaking to others in worship is both congruent as a person and committed to the communication process. Trust in the preacher as a guide depends on the perception that the person preaching believes and is influenced by the words being spoken at that moment (*see* Delivery of Sermons; Character).

Less often emphasized in discussions of preaching is another aspect of immediacy, the preacher's capacity to experience the persons in a given congregation* as particular individuals even while they are behaving as a corporate body during worship. Pastors who can maintain a sense of their congregation as lively, concrete, and active contributors to worship tend to avoid preaching general or generic sermons that are directed to any listener anywhere and to no one in particular.

The second quality of preaching as oral communication, interdependence, derives from the first. Preachers need persons listening actively from the pews, just as those who come to worship need to have words spoken to and meant for them. In traditions in which preaching is the central event in worship this second factor may be deemphasized. But where the worship context itself involves a pattern of call and response, corporate prayer, and singing interwoven with individual reading and preaching, the very rhythm of worship serves to reinforce the interrelatedness of the worshiping community (*see* Lay Response to Preaching).

Preachers who can maintain relatively frequent eye contact with their listeners receive important feedback about whether their pulpit speech is clear or confusing, interesting or boring, affirming or discouraging, through visual and oral cues provided by those in the pews. Preachers who read from their manuscripts during worship often miss these nonverbal signals in their efforts to adhere to the exact words on the printed page. The use of computer-generated preaching manuscripts has offered pastors more freedom while composing messages, but the existence of well-formed pages of print can lead preachers to feel bound to their own typed words rather than free to participate fully in the preaching moment (*see* Manuscript Preaching).

Linguist and communication theorist Walter J. Ong has described oral communication of the late twentieth century as "secondary orality," because it depends on print and technology rather than on the active memories and shared culture of its listeners. In a context of secondary orality preachers cannot assume that worshipers will know a large number of scripture passages, proverbs, or formulas by heart. Worshipers tend to retain concrete sensory images and well-told stories rather than long trains of reasoning or complex theoretical language. The condition of secondary orality is problematic when preachers are trained to produce scholarly theological papers but not to organize their thoughts into accessible oral messages for a wider community.

The third quality of preaching as oral communication, its indeterminacy, can be restated in terms of both the preacher's intention and the listeners' power. Preachers are rhetorical communicators in that they intend their messages to have the effect of leading listeners toward discipleship. But only listeners can accomplish that goal of preaching through the participation of their senses, their capacity for imaginative connection and identification, and their decision to act on what they experience in worship. The open-ended quality of preaching is both a blessing and a curse for preachers, who may decide that a particular pulpit message was unsuccessful but later hear that it has had a major impact on some of its hearers. This is evidence that the skills and perceptions of the preacher are essential to but not the whole of the communication* event called preaching.

Recently translated writings by the Russian literary scholar Mikhail Mikhailovich Bakhtin underscore from a different perspective the open-ended or dialogical quality of preaching. Bakhtin discovered in studying novelists such as Dostoyevsky and Tolstoy that even literary works can be engaged in dialogue, open and capable of interaction with those who encounter and interpret them. This dialogic quality emerges when the source of the verbal message sees it as a contributor to a communication process, not as a finished product unavailable to human scrutiny, evaluation, or recreation. If literary works of art can be seen as never finished, preaching as oral communication may be considered as both formed and forming.

Adopting a perspective on preaching as immediate, interdependent, and indeterminate can help preachers to consider themselves not as isolated sources of authoritative words from God but as co-creators in the ongoing work of God among human communities.

Bakhtin, M. M., "The Problem of Content, Material, and Form in Verbal Artistic Creation" (1919), trans. in *The Architectonics of Answerability,* 1977. **Clark, K.,** and **M. Holquist,** *Mikhail Bakhtin,* 1984. **Ong, W. J.,** *Orality and Literacy: The Technologizing of the Word,* 1982.   BARBARA BATE

Origen. (ca. 185–253) Origen was the first systematic theologian in the Christian tradition and an influential theorist of biblical interpretation and of asceticism. His more than 200 surviving homilies provide the only evidence of preaching in the ante-Nicene period.

Reared in a Christian family in Alexandria, Origen evidently received a superb education in the Bible and in Greek literature and philosophy. He also had a life-long interest in Jewish learning. He committed himself to a life of severe austerity and began catechetical teaching in Alexandria as a young man, during the persecutions under Septimius Severus, in which his father was martyred. He was soon sought after as a teacher. A wealthy patron, Ambrosius, whom he had converted from Gnosticism, provided him with stenographers and copyists so that he could write books. He moved to Caesarea in Palestine in 231, probably because of tensions with his bishop. It was there that he preached, after having been ordained a presbyter. He also continued to teach more learned students. His death was hastened by tortures suffered in the Decian persecution.

In addition to his sermons, he wrote letters and dialogues, learned treatises, and the Hexapla, a massive work that placed all Greek versions of the Old Testament in parallel columns. Because of their sheer bulk and his subsequent condemnation as a heretic, most of these works have perished, but many still survive. Only two of Origen's letters and one dialogue are left. His best-known surviving treatises are *On First Principles,* his work of systematic theology; *Contra Celsum,* the refutation of an attack on Christianity by a pagan philosopher; and *On Prayer,* a seminal work on the spiritual life. The treatises also include massive commentaries, of which those on Matthew and John survive most fully. These, together with the homilies, constitute the first attempt to comment on the whole Bible. Most of Origen's surviving homilies, like *On First Principles,* come to us in fourth-century Latin translations by Rufinus and Jerome. Twenty homilies on Jeremiah and one on 1 Samuel survive in Origen's Greek.

As a theologian, Origen was devoted to the Christian tradition as it had achieved self-definition in opposition to Gnosticism, and he was committed to full investigation of that tradition. In *On First Principles,* he sought to make coherent the relationship between the data of revelation in the Bible as interpreted by the church's rule of faith. The problem of evil, raised by Marcionites, led him to explore the relationship between the free will of created rational beings and God's goodness and providence. *On First Principles* helped form Christian understandings of the Trinity and of the nature of Christ; criticism that Origen was the spiritual father of Arius is unfair and anachronistic. His discussions there of cosmology and eschatology have fared less well. Heavily dependent on Platonism, even if by no means divorced from the Bible, they have made him suspect of heresy from his own time to the present.

On First Principles also contains the first extended theoretical treatment within the Christian tradition of principles of biblical interpretation. There Origen argues that the Bible has a spiritual meaning reached by interpreting passages allegorically. This method can produce outlandish interpretations, far from the original intent of the text. Nonetheless, the reader of Origen's extensive exegetical works must be impressed by his consistency in the treatment of biblical images and by his close attention to the biblical text, which he approaches not just with awe and humility but with considerable critical sensitivity (*see* Hermeneutics; Exegesis).

Translation aside, Origen's homilies represent his actual preaching at Caesarea during the liturgy of the word that preceded the Eucharist. They vary widely in length, but some must have taken well over an hour. He exhibits a high doctrine of the word, preached as well as written, and a strong sense of responsibility. For him, the preacher was a priest, mediating between the congregation and God; a hierophant, initiating them into the mysteries of God's word; a prophet, warning them of God's judgment; and a teacher, instructing them in how to live and believe.

Origen's homilies are exegetical, patiently expounding verse by verse a lesson from the Bible that had just been read. In this way, they are like his commentaries. He was, nonetheless, acutely aware of the difference in content between a learned treatise and a sermon to a largely unlearned congregation. In his sermons he avoids technical discussions and theological speculation, seeking, rather, to improve his hearers' morals and to guard them from heresy. He probably preached much as he taught. His style is thus homiletic in the root sense of the word—that is, conversational and extemporaneous. He often raises hypothetical questions and addresses his congregation in the second person singular, as if he were speaking individually to each person before him (*see* Homily; Expository Preaching).

He sought to confront his hearers personally with God as a fire that does not simply illumine the understanding but also purifies the will. He therefore preached for conversion, understood not as a ritual act or a sudden personal experience, but as a slow process of personal transformation brought about by continual immersion in Holy Scripture. If the Red Sea corresponds to baptism, the abrupt renunciation of idolatry and sin, Christian maturity is not possible without slow progress, beset by temptation, through the wilderness. He often speaks of fighting demons and receiving angelic assistance, but he never loses sight of personal responsibility. In the thriving maritime commercial center of Caesarea, he singled out avarice and fornication as the most pervasive vices of his congregation.

Origen was not altogether well received as a preacher; he often appears querulous or defensive. He himself attributed the hostility and inattention he complained of in his congregation to the members' unwillingness to be reprimanded for their sins and to their hidebound attachment to the traditional Septuagint text. For all his attempts to suit his preaching to his listeners, we may suspect that Origen's moral advice was not particularly relevant to people who could not abandon the concerns of the world as he did and devote themselves to ascetic discipline and Bible study, and thus his critical approach to the Bible may have threatened them.

No doubt Origen's homilies were in many ways *sui generis*. We may, though, reasonably conclude from Origen's work and from the testimony of such authors as Justin Martyr that preaching was a vital part of early Christian worship and that the roots of the Christian sermon are at least as much in the school lecture as they are in the public oration.

Castagno, A. M., *Origene predicatore e il suo pubblico*, 1987. Crouzel, H., *Origen: The Life and Thought of the First Great Theologian*, 1989. Origen, *Homilies on Genesis and Exodus*, trans. R. A. Heine, *Fathers of the Church*, Vol. 71, 1982. *Homilies on Leviticus*, trans. G. W. Barkley, *Fathers of the Church*, Vol. 83, 1990. Trigg, J. W., *Origen: The Bible and Philosophy in the Third-century Church*, 1985.   JOSEPH W. TRIGG

Palmer, Phoebe Worrall.

(1807–1874) Phoebe Palmer, the mother of the Holiness Movement, is one of America's most influential yet forgotten religious figures. Born and raised in New York City, Palmer's ministry was firmly grounded in the evangelical fervor of nineteenth-century revival movements. Palmer's lectures took her all over the United States, Canada, and the British Isles, and her prolific writings extended that reach even further.

In 1827, she married physician Walter Palmer, and their early married life was haunted by tragedy with the deaths of their first three children. In 1836, Phoebe's sister, Sarah Lankford, invited Phoebe to become a part of the women's Bible study meetings Sarah had started a few months earlier. Known as the Tuesday Meeting for the Promotion of Holiness, it became the starting point for Palmer's illustrious and influential career. Based on the Methodist class meeting, the Tuesday Meeting, primarily populated by women, was a combination of prayer, Bible study, and testimony. The meeting provided those women with a safe place in which to find and develop their voices, so long kept silent by church strictures.

Although Palmer had been raised in a Methodist home and attended the Tuesday Meetings, it was not until July 26, 1837, that Palmer finally experienced holiness. As she recorded the following day, "Between the hours of eight and nine— while pleading at the throne of grace for a present fulfillment of the exceeding great and precious promises . . . *I received the assurance that God the Father, through the atoning Lamb, accepted the sacrifice;* my heart was emptied of self, and cleansed of all idols." With that assurance granted in a moment she later came to call the "day of days," Palmer began the way of holiness.

Influenced by Methodist pietism and by the evangelical enthusiasm of the second Great Awakening, the way preached by Palmer, which became the title of her first and perhaps most popular book, *The Way of Holiness* (1843), offered people a path to sanctification: "consecrate all upon the altar of sacrifice to God, . . . believe that the sacrifice became the Lord's property." At that moment, according to Palmer, one experienced holiness even if one did not experience the feeling of holiness. Although Palmer put a premium upon the direct experience of the Holy Spirit,* this experience was always held up against the critical light of the Bible.

According to Palmer, once an individual had experienced the blessings of the Holy Spirit, it was crucial for that person to testify to the experience, and testify Palmer did. Like most women of her generation, Palmer never received a formal, institutional education. But that did not stop her from a prolific output in the service of the holiness movement. Palmer spoke to tens of thousands of people during her thirty-year career. Likewise, in addition to the *Way of Holiness*, Palmer published numerous volumes promoting Holiness: *Present to My Christian Friend on Entire Devotion to God* (1845), *Faith and Its Effects* (1854), *Israel's Speedy Restoration* (1854), *Incidental Illustrations of* the Economy of Salvation (1854), Promise of the Father (1859), and Four Years in the Old World (1867).

Palmer's inclusion in an encyclopedia of preaching is somewhat ironic. In spite of the decades of speaking and the thousands of people converted by her messages (including WCTU leader Frances Willard*), Palmer never claimed to be preaching. Rather, she was "bearing witness," "prophesying," or "exhorting." Palmer contrasted preaching as "oratorical display, onerous titles, and pulpits of pedestal eminence" with preaching as "explaining the teachings, enforcing the commands, of Christ and his apostles." And it was the latter in which she encouraged women and men to engage.

In Promise of the Father, Palmer argued that women should be allowed to proclaim the good news in the same way that all men were permitted, making her, as Thomas Oden argues, one of the leading protofeminists in the church. Palmer believed that as long as the church suppressed the preaching of women it failed to live up to the full pentecostal commission and that the church and the world suffered because of that failure. Palmer never sought ordination in the Methodist Episcopal Church, of which she remained a lifelong member, nor did she argue for the ordination of other women. Nevertheless, her efforts to secure a place in the church for the preaching of women eventually led to the ordination of women, and The Promise of the Father laid out the fundamental biblical arguments employed by the women who followed her in the struggle to enlarge women's sphere of influence.

Following her death in 1874 in New York City, the legacy of Palmer's Holiness Movement could be seen in numerous pentecostal denominations indebted to her revelations, as well as in her profound influence upon women's status in the church (see Pentecostal Preaching; Women as Preachers).

Oden, T. C., ed., Phoebe Palmer: Selected Writings, 1988. Raser, H. E., Phoebe Palmer: Her Life and Thought, 1987. White, C. E., The Beauty of Holiness: Phoebe Palmer as Theologian, Revivalist, Feminist, and Humanitarian, 1986.   Lucy Hogan

THE WAY OF HOLINESS
Phoebe Worrall Palmer

"I have thought," said one of the children of Zion to the other, as in love they journeyed onward in the way cast up for the ransomed of the Lord to walk in; "I have thought," said he, "whether there is not a shorter way of getting into this way of holiness than some of our brethren apprehend?"

"Yes," said the sister addressed, who was a member of the denomination alluded to; "Yes, brother, there is a shorter way! O! I am sure this long waiting and struggling with the powers of darkness is not necessary. There is a shorter way." And then, with a solemn feeling of responsibility, and with a realizing conviction of the truth uttered, she added, "But, brother, there is but one way."

Days and even weeks elapsed, and yet the question, and solemn bearing, rested upon the mind of that sister. She thought of the affirmative given in answer to the inquiry of the brother—examined yet more closely the scriptural foundation upon which the truth of the affirmation rested—and the result of the investigation tended to add still greater confirmation to the belief, that many sincere disciples of Jesus, by various needless perplexities, consume much time in endeavoring to get into this way, which might, more advantageously to themselves and others, be employed in making progress in it, and testifying, from experimental knowledge of its blessedness.

How many, whom Infinite Love would long since have brought into this state, instead of seeking to be brought into the possession of the blessing at once, are seeking a preparation for the reception of it! They feel that their convictions are not deep enough to warrant an approach to the throne of grace, with the confident expectation of receiving the blessing now. Just at this point some may have been lingering months and years. Thus did the sister, who so confidently affirmed "there is a shorter way." And here, dear child of Jesus, permit the writer to tell you just how that sister found the "shorter way."

On looking at the requirements of the word of God, she beheld the command, "Be ye holy." She then began to say in her heart, "Whatever my former deficiencies may have been, God requires that I should *now* be holy. Whether *convicted,* or otherwise, *duty is plain.* God requires *present* holiness." On coming to this point, she at once apprehended a simple truth before unthought of, i.e., *Knowledge is conviction.* She well knew that, for a long time, she had been assured that God required holiness. But she had never deemed this knowledge a sufficient plea to take to God—and because of present need, to ask a present bestowment of the gift. . . . Deeply conscious of past unfaithfulness, she now determined that the time past should suffice; and with a humility of spirit, induced by a consciousness of not having lived in the performance of such a "reasonable service," she was enabled, through grace, to resolve, with firmness of purpose, that entire devotion of heart and life to God should be the absorbing subject of the succeeding pilgrimage of life.

From *The Way of Holiness* (London: Alexander Heylin, 1843), 1–5.

Parables of Jesus.

Despite the countless numbers of books and articles that have been written about the parables of Jesus, it is not easy to say what a parable is. That is part of the power and effectiveness of the genre. A parable refuses to be pinned down.

Two streams of tradition flow into the parables of Jesus. The main one is the usage of the term *mashal* in the Old Testament. While the primary meaning of that word is proverb (as in Prov. 1:1), a short saying grasping the shape or order of a certain area of experience, it also takes on a number of other connotations, such as commonplace saying (1 Sam. 24:13), figurative saying (1 Sam. 10:12), taunt song

(Isa. 14:4), and byword (Jer. 24:9). Especially important for the New Testament meaning is the association of the *mashal* with the words for riddle, enigma, or dark saying (Prov. 1:6; Ps. 49:3–4; 78:1–3). It seems that the genre *mashal* in the Old Testament, however, did not contain narrative parables, which are so characteristic of Jesus. It is also important that the Hebrew verb that is cognate with *mashal* means "to be like" (Ps. 143:7). For the most part, the Septuagint translates the Hebrew *mashal* by the Greek *parabolē* with which, of course, the English word *parable* is cognate.

The place of *parabolē* in Greek rhetoric* goes back to Aristotle (*Rhetoric* 2.20). Aristotle argued that there are two means of persuasion common to all types of rhetoric: *example* and *rhetorical syllogism*. Examples of these, in turn, fall into two subtypes: *parallels from facts of history* and *invented parables*. The latter again are subdivided into *parables or comparisons* and *fables.* An example of a parable would be to say that choosing politicians by lot is like choosing athletes by lot rather than for their ability.

It is hard to say whether Greek rhetoric had any impact on Jesus and his audience. But it was deeply embedded in first-century culture and would have had at least an indirect influence on the evangelists and their first readers and hearers. The Hebrew and Greek traditions clearly agree on the element of comparison.

At this point, a tentative definition of parable might be offered. A parable is a brief figurative or connotative utterance making a fundamental use of comparison and hiding its meaning or revelation in an enigma that the reader/hearer must penetrate. Parables are not simple sayings or stories that make meanings obvious. This definition is not too far from Irving Howe's recent description of the short short story. The latter is a condensed account of a single incident exploding into a burst of revelation or illumination and bearing a symbolic weight (Donahue, 20).

The purpose of Jesus' parables is rather shockingly stated in Mark 4:10–12 as being to *prevent* understanding in order that the hearers might *not* repent. This is indeed the purpose according to the Gospel of Mark. Whether some version of this saying can also be traced back to Jesus (as argued by Joachim Jeremias in *The Parables of Jesus*) is debatable (Scott, 22–25). In any case, for Mark, concealment is the penultimate purpose of the parables, but the concealment exists for the ultimate purpose of illumination (Mark 4:21–23). It is appropriate to Jesus' parables as a whole in their historical context to say that their purpose is not to be obscure for the sake of obscurity but to be sufficiently enigmatic and sufficiently suggestive to provoke the hearer to work to penetrate the darkness and come to an understanding of the parable by understanding herself or himself in a new way.

Jesus' parables are closely associated with the kingdom of God (Mark 4:26; Matt. 13:24, 31, 33). But where exactly in the parable is the meaning to be found that illuminates the kingdom by comparing it to something? From New Testament times until the beginning of the twentieth century, the parables were mistaken as allegories, and the meaning was found by giving all the details of the parable independent symbolic significance. This can already be seen in the allegorical interpretation (Mark 4:13–20) given to the parable of the sower (Mark 4:2–8). Then, during most of this century, the parables were held to have *one* point of significance, and that was to be understood in light of Jesus' historical situation.

Since the 1960s, a more literary approach has been gaining ground that maintains the meaning is located not in one point but in the parable as a whole—in the totality of the content as shaped by the form. All the parts are important but not as independent symbols. Rather, the parts are connected to each other by the integrating power of the form (*see* Literary Criticism).

Probably the forms or literary categories that have proved most useful and fruitful are metaphor and plot (*see* Figures of Speech; Narrative Preaching). A metaphor is an utterance that creates semantic tension by comparing or juxtaposing areas of meaning not usually thought of as belonging together. The upshot is that the world is defamiliarized and redescribed. The one-liner parables create metaphorical tension by comparing the kingdom to something unexpected—an image and/or a rudimentary story. The leaven (Matt. 13:33) defamiliarizes the religious world by connecting the kingdom to leaven, which in ordinary usage was usually an image of evil and corruption. The longer narrative parables are metaphors within themselves in that they unexpectedly interweave everyday reality (a father and two sons and a farm) with the extravagant or extraordinary (the father's unanticipated forgiving love, Luke 15:11–32). As a result of the realism and indirection of a parable it does not tell us what the kingdom of God is like in itself but what human existence is like when it is intersected by God's rule.

In the narrative parables metaphor is extended into plot. These stories manifest plots composed of beginning, middle, and end, which have temporal and causal connections. Some plots move downward in a tragic way, while others move upward in a comic way. The one-talent man moves from an action that is self-interested and apparently safe through a crisis of questioning to the unexpected loss of everything (Matt. 25:14–28). The dishonest manager moves from a crisis through shady dealings to unexpected praise (Luke 16:1–8a).

It matters whether the interpreter pays attention to the plot. Attending to the plot, for example, turns a parable that has customarily been interpreted as being about grace into a parable about the kind of self-understanding that rejects grace (Matt. 20:1–14a) (*see* Jesus as Preacher).

Dodd, C. H., *The Parables of the Kingdom,* rev. ed., 1961. **Donahue, J. R.,** *The Gospel in Parable,* 1988. **Jeremias, J.,** *The Parables of Jesus,* trans. S. Hooke, 1962. **Ricoeur, P.,** "Biblical Hermeneutics," *Semeia,* 1975.

Scott, B. B., *Hear Then the Parable*, 1989.
Via, D. O., *The Parables*, 1967.

DAN O. VIA

Parker, Theodore. (1810–1860)
Born in Lexington, Massachusetts, Theodore Parker graduated from the Harvard Divinity School in 1836. He then served the Unitarian church in West Roxbury, Massachusetts, for nine years until called in 1846 to be minister of the newly formed Twenty-Eighth Congregational Society, which met in Boston's Music Hall and eventually grew to include 7,000 names on its parish rolls. Regarded as dangerously radical even by his Unitarian brethren, Parker agitated fiercely for an agenda of social reform that included temperance, women's rights, and the abolition of slavery, crossing the country on a punishing schedule of lecturing that ultimately undermined his health. On doctor's advice, with his wife, Lydia, he traveled to Europe, where he died in Italy. His headstone in Florence calls him "the Great American Preacher."

In his final letter to his congregation, Parker reflected on his own homiletic style. "In my preaching I have used plain, simple words," he said, "and counted nothing unclean because merely common."

> In philosophic terms, and in all which describes the inner consciousness, our Saxon speech is rather poor, and so I have been compelled to gather from the Greek or Roman stock forms of expression . . . and hence, perhaps, have sometimes scared you with "words of learned length." But I have always preferred to use, when fit, the everyday words in which men think and talk, scold, make love, and pray, so that a generous-hearted Philosophy, clad in common dress, might more easily become familiar to plain-clad men (Parker, 163).

Parker strongly identified with common folk. As a boy, he helped manage the family farm and knew what it was to plant and plough. He resisted those who urged him to use "more elegant and sonorous language" in the pulpit, drawing his similes instead from "trees, grass, oxen, and stars, moonlight on the water . . . the gambols and prattle of children, and the common work of blacksmiths, carpenters, wheelwrights" (164), for these were the things he naturally loved best.

Yet underneath Parker's apparent simplicity lay vast erudition. He had mastery of Italian, Portuguese, Dutch, Swedish, Danish, Persian, Arabic, and Coptic, and familiarity with several other languages, in addition to Hebrew and Greek. He published dozens of translations and articles introducing American readers to the discoveries of German biblical scholars such as Schleiermacher, Eichorn, and De Wette. His private collection of books, the largest in the United States, was bequeathed at his death to form the nucleus for the Boston Public Library. While using plain words and familiar illustrations in his sermons, Parker also delivered substance, noting that he had "not feared to treat philosophic matters with the rigor of science" (166). His addresses were often long and closely reasoned but sustained the attention of listeners eager for intellectual and spiritual depth.

Parker's most famous sermon may be "A Discourse of the Transient and Permanent in Christianity." Like his Transcendentalist comrades Ralph Waldo Emerson and George Rippley, Parker believed that religious and moral truths are self-evident and innate to human consciousness. According to this view, the imperative of love to God and love to humankind, which Parker identified as the enduring teaching of Jesus, in no way depends upon the authenticity or authority of scripture, which is merely a transient record of human experience and interpretation. Parker's "Transient and Permanent" sermon of 1842 made him a theological outcast among Unitarians and within the larger Christian fold; years later, when invited to speak at Harvard Divinity School by the graduating class, he was forbidden to do so by the faculty.

Parker's preaching provoked the political establishment no less than the religious, and his most thunderous condemnations were reserved for the institution of slavery. Like his grandfather, Captain John Parker, who led the Minute Men into battle at Lexington, Theodore had a profound love of liberty and a daring taste for confrontation. He defied the Fugitive Slave Law and was arrested for advocating civil disobedience. He helped fund John Brown and wrote his sermons with a loaded pistol on his desk when slave-catchers threatened to kidnap freed blacks from the streets of Boston. Words were vain, in Parker's mind, unless tied to action. But it was as a communicator that Parker soared and made his greatest impact.

Theodore Parker's eloquence inspired American Orators from Abraham Lincoln to Martin Luther King Jr. As minister of one of the largest congregations in the United States, Parker's words touched thousands, and as a lecturer and writer, his ideas reached mass audiences. More than any other figure of his generation, he deserved his epitaph of "the Great American Preacher."

Commager, H. S., *Theodore Parker: Yankee Crusader*, 1982. Parker, T., *Experience as a Minister*, 1859.   GARY KOWALSKI

THE LAW OF GOD
Theodore Parker
It is plain to me that it is the natural duty of citizens to rescue every fugitive slave from the hands of the marshal who essays to return him to bondage; to do it peaceably if they can, forcibly if they must, but by all means to do it. Will you stand by and see your countrymen, your fellow citizens of Boston, sent off to slavery by some commissioner? Shall I see my own parishioners taken from under my eyes and carried back to bondage, by a man whose constitutional business it is to work wickedness by statute? Shall I never lift an arm to protect him? When I consent to that, you may call me a hireling shepherd, an infidel, a wolf in sheep's clothing, even a

defender of slave-catching if you will; and I will confess I was a poor dumb dog, barking always at the moon, but silent as the moon when the murderer came near.

I am not a man who loves violence. I respect the sacredness of human life. But this I say, solemnly, that I will do all in my power to rescue any fugitive slave from the hands of any officer who attempts to return him to bondage. I will resist him as gently as I know how, but with such strength as I can command; I will ring the bells, and alarm the town; I will serve as head, as foot, or as hand to any body of serious and earnest men, who will go with me, with no weapons but their hands, in this work. I will do it as readily as I would lift a man out of the water, or pluck him from the teeth of a wolf, or snatch him from the hands of a murderer. What is a fine of a thousand dollars, and jailing for six months, to the liberty of a man? My money perish with me, if it stand between me and the eternal law of God!

From "The Function of Conscience," in *The Slave Power*, ed. J. K. Hosmer (Boston: American Unitarian Association, 1910), 304.

Pastoral Care and Preaching

Preaching's purpose is the proclamation of the Word of God. Yet while a pastor is preaching, the pastor is also caring for the congregation. The relegation in many pastors' minds of pastoral care to pastoral counseling is unfortunate. Every time the preached message confronts and forms personal need in the light of the gospel, pastoral care occurs.

Rigid distinctions between the gentle pastor who empathetically cares for the flock and the bold prophet who speaks the truth are due more to modern stereotypes than to biblical portrayals of the servants of God. Paul, for instance, saw himself as a preacher (1 Cor. 1:17) and as a caring nurse for fledgling Christians (1 Thess. 2:7). First Timothy urges early church leaders to preach the word *and* to tend the flock (1 Tim. 2:1–6:1).

Most pastors have therefore agreed

with Phillips Brooks* who in his *Lectures on Preaching* said to those who thought it impossible to be both preacher and pastor, "I assure you you are wrong" (76). As the pastoral care movement gained momentum in American churches beginning in the early 1920s, many mainline protestant pastors wholeheartedly embraced pastoral psychology as an aid in preaching. Harry Emerson Fosdick* said that his great discovery as a young preacher was that a sermon begins

> with the real problems of the people. That was a sermon's specialty, which made it a sermon, not an essay or a lecture. Every sermon should have for its main business the head-on constructive meeting of some problem which was puzzling minds, burdening consciences, distracting lives, and no sermon which so met a real human difficulty, with light to throw on it and help to win a victory over it, could possibly be futile (Fosdick, 94).

Fosdick went so far as to describe preaching as "counseling on a group scale," and made the personal problems of his listeners central to his "life-situation preaching."

Twentieth-century pastoral care took as one of its assignments the affirmation of the individual and developed techniques for empathetic, nonjudgmental listening. Preaching appeared to many practitioners of pastoral care as pastoral counseling's polar opposite. They criticized traditional preaching for its typically authoritarian, moralistic, biblically simplistic, and judgmental approach to human problems. Pastoral counseling courses captured the interest of seminarians, and the work of the pastor seemed to shift from the pulpit to the one-to-one counseling session.

Yet by the mid-twentieth century, when American preachers were wholeheartedly embracing the insights of psychology and directing their sermons to the needs of people, critics charged these latter-day practitioners of "life situation preaching" with forsaking the biblical text in their often facile use of psychological answers to problems that may be as much theological as psychological in nature. In a therapeutic, psychologized culture, as many claimed North America had become, preaching that always tried to offer psychology-based pastoral care was criticized for playing into the hands of some of the most provincial, limited aspects of our radically subjectivized society. Karl Barth* dismissed modern attempts to reduce preaching to psychological therapy: "Preaching is not intended to be simply a clearer and more adequate explanation of life than can be arrived at by other means. . . . The congregation is waiting for the meaning of life to be illumined by the light of God" (Barth, 53).

Each area of pastoral work has its own inherent values and its own integrity. While preaching is not "pastoral care on a group scale" (Fosdick), and pastoral care is not psychotherapeutic preaching, the two distinct pastoral activities can mutually enrich one another. Parish pastors, in their work, do not make rigid distinctions between the various modes of ministerial activity. Preaching is a public, corporate, traditional, proclamation-oriented pastoral function. Pastoral counseling, while not limited to individuals, tends to be more personal, one-to-one, and problem-oriented than preaching. In preaching, the pastor is not merely speaking to human problems but is rather proclaiming the faith of the church whereby our problems are addressed in a peculiarly Christian way. In pastoral care, human problems are informed by the psychological perspective in a personal, direct, and caring way that can both enrich and challenge the theological and biblical perspective.

Pastoral care aids preaching by giving the preacher a respect for listeners in their individual struggles. In counseling troubled parishioners, preachers are with their people in intimate, personal, face-to-face encounters. The preacher who is also a pastor is therefore less likely to make sweeping, generalized, universal judgments about the human condition.

Before making pronouncements from on high about human problems, the pastor will see specific human faces, the lives of individual members of the congregation who are struggling with these problems. Thus pastoral care provides a necessary context for faithful preaching.

Kierkegaard* urged preachers "to present a human being as he is in daily life" rather than as some abstracted, ideal type: "The speaker who does not know how the task looks in daily life and in the living-room, might just as well keep still, for Sunday glimpses into eternity lead to nothing but wind. . . . in the living-room the battle must be fought. . . " (*The Point of View for My Work as an Author*, trans. W. Lowrie, 1962, 27).

Pastoral care activities, like pastoral counseling, not only provide the preacher much information about the lives and struggles of parishioners but also build rapport between the preacher and the people. In one-to-one or small-group counseling experiences, people have the opportunity to relate to their preacher in a personal way. Surely this dynamic was what Paul had in mind when he blended the preaching and the counseling ministry in saying, "So, being affectionately desirous of you, we were ready to share with you not only the gospel of God but also our own selves" (1 Thess. 2:8). People make themselves available to pastors who have made themselves available to the people. People listen to preachers who demonstrate that they have listened to their people.

Preaching can enrich pastoral care. Recent critics of contemporary pastoral counseling have noted the need for pastoral care to make clearer what is specifically Christian in its care. What is the difference between pastoral counseling and secular counseling? Preaching helps to identify the pastor as representative of the church and its witness. In preaching, human problems are named and contextualized as concerns related to discipleship and faithful witness, not just personal psychological dilemmas. In coming to a pastor with personal problems, peo-

ple realize that they are also coming before a preacher who has a sacred responsibility, through ordination, to witness to the historic faith of the church, to urge parishioners to lay their lives alongside the story that is the gospel, not simply to be psychologically caring and sympathetic.

Preaching is also precounseling activity. Parishioners are present with their pastor in greater numbers for a more extended and focused time in preaching than in any other pastoral function. A sermon might be the only contact many people in the congregation will have with the pastor. What impressions will the people receive from their preacher? Will the preacher be experienced as someone who is sufficiently open and empathetic to the discussion of tough, personal issues? Or is the preacher the sort of person who always has an easy answer to every problem on the tip of the tongue?

Preaching can open the door for counseling. When a preacher tackles some tough subject in a sermon, listeners may learn that the preacher is willing to discuss this problem with them in a more personal, individualized setting. Therefore, pastors ought intentionally to address certain personal issues in their sermons.

As important as the pastoral care of individuals is, preaching is more important. Preaching places our care in its proper context; it articulates the divine judgment and the divine grace whereby individual struggles are set within the framework of the continuing story of God's gracious dealings with God's people. Without the weekly demands of the preaching office, the pastor's care easily degenerates into mere care with little else to inform or to form that care than the latest psychotherapeutic trends. Without the weekly attendance upon the preached word, the individual's desire for care easily degenerates into narcissistic craving for personal affirmation, bereft of repentance, forgiveness, or vocation. Thus, preaching is pastoral care's criterion for fidelity, that abiding norm whereby our care is rendered truly pastoral care, explicitly Christian.

Barth, K., *The Preaching of the Gospel,* trans. B. Hooke, 1963. **Browning, D. S.,** *The Moral Context of Pastoral Care,* Philadelphia, 1976. **Willimon, W. H.,** *Integrative Preaching: The Pulpit at the Center,* Nashville, 1981; *Worship as Pastoral Care,* Nashville, 1979.

WILLIAM H. WILLIMON

Peale, Norman Vincent. (1898–1993) Clergyman, author, publisher, and public personality, Norman Vincent Peale is best known for his 1952 bestselling book, *The Power of Positive Thinking.* He was as popular in the secular world as in the religious community. He is frequently credited, along with Billy Graham,* with leading the revival of religion in the 1950s. From 1932 to 1983 Peale served as senior minister of the Marble Collegiate Church (Reformed Church in America) in New York City, where his popular sermons packed the church and attracted tourists, many lining up hours before the service in hopes of gaining a seat. Business groups and civic organizations were also interested in his motivational messages, and he was much in demand as a public speaker. His celebrity peaked in the post-World War II decades, then settled to a more modest level after 1960. Politically conservative and excited by partisan politics, he experienced a decline in public acclaim after 1960 because of his identification with a group of evangelicals determined to thwart the election of John F. Kennedy to the presidency. From that time on, he focused his work around his personal ministry, anchored in the Peale Center for Christian Living, Pawling, New York.

Peale was born in Bowersville, Ohio, to Anna DeLaney and Charles Clifford Peale, both devout Methodists, his father a Methodist clergyman. His early life conformed to that of a "preacher's kid" in rural Ohio: Family life was centered in the church and warmed by the fires of Prohibitionism with its political and soci-

ological implications. Like many Methodist clergy families, the Peales moved often, a factor he later explained contributed to his sense of personal insecurity and inferiority, qualities he thought made him an ideal candidate for the message of positive thinking. He enrolled in Ohio Wesleyan University in 1916 and graduated four years later, equipped, he said, with the formative influences on what would become his personal message of positive thinking, namely the ideas of Marcus Aurelius, Ralph Waldo Emerson, and William James. He dabbled in journalism and newspaper work, and then in 1921, heeded a call to the ministry and enrolled in Boston University School of Theology. The school was then in the grips of the philosophical idealism of Borden Parker Bowne, creator of the concept known as Personalism, and Peale easily grafted the basic outline of Personalism on to his inherited Methodism and his developing notion of positive thinking. They provided the seeds for his popular message of positive thinking that flowered in the later 1940s and beyond.

Peale served briefly as the student minister of a Methodist church in Berkeley, Rhode Island, and then from 1924 to 1927 pastored King's Highway Methodist Church in Brooklyn, New York, where the congregation experienced phenomenal growth, thanks to his leadership style and enthusiastic preaching. He worked a somewhat similar magic at University Methodist Church in Syracuse, New York, between 1927 and 1932, despite having his efforts hampered financially by the Depression. It was in Syracuse, too, that he met Ruth Stafford, also a Methodist parsonage child, whom he married in 1930. In 1932, he accepted the call to the fiscally attractive but membership-poor Marble Collegiate Church.

In New York he honed his preaching ability to a polished art. While in Syracuse, he had been advised by a University dean attending his church to forgo manuscript preaching.* He continued to follow that advice in New York, making seemingly extemporaneous preaching* one of the hallmarks of his style. His technique, he said, was to develop a very full outline for his sermon or talk (he insisted that in giving a sermon he was "speaking," not "preaching") and then commit it to memory. He said he would "picturize," or create a mental image, of the address in his mind, then visualize it as he spoke to his audience. Since he did not use notes, he did not need a lectern and usually did not use one, except on rare occasions when it provided something on which to lean. He swept his audience up in a warm verbal embrace, with many members observing that they felt he was speaking personally to them.

His speaking style was folksy and familiar and reflected his roots in rural Ohio. Although he lived most of his adult life on the Upper East Side of Manhattan and was a world traveler, he retained an unpretentious manner in his speech, a sort of spiritual Will Rogers. He left the final "g" off verbs, called a fellow a "fella," and described the color of the sun as "yella." His modest and self-effacing style was noticed even by his many critics and appreciated by his vast audience. His arms and hands cut the air when he spoke, although his feet never left the appointed spot. His timing when telling a story equaled that of the best public performers.

Peale described his message as "practical Christianity," and his sermons became practical lessons for daily living. Every sermon had a text, which provided a general thematic background rather than serving as a vehicle for close textual analysis. From about 1945 on, Peale's sermons followed a standard formula, which consisted of three stories loosely organized around the theme of the text. Peale was at his oratorical best when he told these anecdotes. He painted word pictures with great skill and had an uncanny sense of timing. Shy in a group and ill-at-ease with individuals, he flourished on the platform, revealing an enthusiastic, charismatic personality. His anecdotes were homely accounts of individuals triumphing over the disappointments and disabilities of daily life, human interest stories with which members of his congregation could readily identify. They recounted the problems of businessmen and homemaking women, of individuals struggling with limitations that were physical, emotional, or financial. The stories—or parables—were sad or humorous or thrilling, and frequently memorable. They were also intended to be motivational.

According to Peale, the motivation derived from his Methodist sense of the preacher's duty to seek conversion. What was latent in his thinking, he therefore suggested, was the need to have his listeners do something, mindful of the "presence" of God—to believe, to pray, to change. What was manifest to many of his hearers, however, was a motivational challenge to improve in some area of their lives. It was this motivational challenge, considered by his critics to have more in common with secular "success" techniques than traditional Christianity, that left him open to charges of providing shallow preaching and bowdlerized psychology to his national audience.

Peale spent most of his adult life at the center of a storm of controversy, derided by his critics—drawn largely from mainstream Protestant churches, seminaries, universities, and the press—for his conservative politics and unconventional message. Despite the critics, he reached a vast national, and even international, audience, numbering over 30 million weekly at the height of his popularity in the 1950s. He was most successful on the platform, as preacher and public speaker, but he also did well on the radio, while generally faltering on television. In later life, he developed a school for ministers at his center in Pawling, offering a weeklong opportunity to the clergy to learn Peale's preaching style. There ministers learned to speak without notes, to "picturize" their sermons, and to perfect the art of telling meaningful anecdotes. What could not be taught was Peale's inimitable style, which perfectly combined self-effacement with charisma, practical advice with biblical references. His public style was a product of his personality, and although it encouraged many imitators, its success derived from his unique qualities.

George, C., *God's Salesman: Norman Vincent Peale and the Power of Positive Thinking,* 1993. **Peale, N. V.,** *The Power of Positive Thinking,* 1952.   CAROL V. R. GEORGE

A SHOESHINER'S WISDOM

Norman Vincent Peale

I recently had occasion to witness the truth of this principle, sitting in a shoeshining parlor. While the proprietor of that institution worked on my shoes and I read the paper we discussed various items in the news—among other matters a crime which was then prominent in the public print. We were led into the query as to why such things happen. Giving a flick to his cloth, the shoeshiner opined, "I have noticed that in all these affairs somebody or some people were doing what they should not be doing and," he continued, "most people get into trouble simply because they do not behave themselves." Then he concluded with what I regard as a wise piece of philosophy: "If you do right," he vigorously declared, "usually things will be right." I was struck by that, and it occurred to me it had a strangely familiar ring. It did not sound quite original and I felt I must have read it somewhere, so I went home and got out an old Book in which I have found more wise truth about the business of living than in any other source. Sure enough, there it was—and this is what I found: "And thou shalt do that which is right and good in the sight of the Lord: that it may be well with thee, and that thou mayest go in and possess the land which the Lord sware unto thy fathers." In effect, what the Bible is saying is that if you do that which is right and good in the sight of God, it will be well with you and you will come into possession of the good land—which is to say, the good life. Do right and life will yield to you its richest fruits. This old writer of the book of Deuteronomy stated a truth which wise men in the common run of life in every generation discover by hard experience—that if you do right, things will be right.

From *You Can Win* (New York: Abingdon Press, 1938), 52–53.

Pedagogy of Preaching.

Despite the overwhelming amount of literature on preaching in the Christian church—handbooks, theories, methods, and sermon collections—until quite recently, little has been written specifically about teaching preaching. Historically, there seems to have been little self-conscious attention to the matter of theoretical pedagogy within homiletics. One can infer some early methods from the Gospels and Epistles. The vast collection of manuals written since the early centuries of the church suggest more about theory than pedagogy. One can examine the pedagogy employed in university education of the time; theological training has often taken place in or alongside this setting. These sources provide some minimal historical perspective on the teaching of preaching.

Prior to Origen there was little formal theological training for preachers. From the time of Origen, however, there were schools dedicated to theological training, including preaching. Transcribed sermons were circulated for study by preachers and preachers-in-training. Many, if not most, of the eloquent preachers of the early church received training in classical rhetoric* either before or during their theological training. Examples include Cyprian, Basil, Chrysostom,* Augustine,* and many others. There were doubtless other master preachers who developed a following and formed schools to educate those who sought to emulate that master's style. The model was very much that of apprenticeship in the crafts.

The rigor and sophistication of education in preaching has varied. How preaching was taught has depended somewhat on who was being taught. From the early centuries of the Christian church into the twentieth century, when those with a thorough secular or theological education approached the preaching task, they typically did so with a working knowledge of classical rhetorical principles. However, when those with less education approached the same task, they were often provided model sermons, sample illustrations, and outlines from which they could borrow or after which they could model their own work (Brilioth, 14). The emphasis on preaching in a curriculum seems to follow the ebb and flow of the quality of preaching. After periods of decline, such as the Middle Ages, new seminaries or new curricula have attempted to reverse the trend by placing renewed emphasis on preaching.

Teaching Preaching and Spiritual Formation. There has been a steady increase in homiletic methods: expository,* narrative,* inductive,* phenomenological, and transactional. What does not always accompany these methods is a clarity about the underlying theology. Each theory or method makes implicit assumptions about scripture, the purpose of preaching, the role of hearer, and the definition of preaching. The need for clarity about these factors has much to do with seeing homiletics as an occasion of spiritual and theological formation and not simply as a skill or as speech education for religious personnel. Certain homiletic methods may be incompatible with some theologies. The theological underpinnings of methods should receive careful attention as they are taught and as they are used.

Homiletics includes developing an awareness of the interrelationship of scripture, the preacher, and the hearer. Much recent homiletics literature acknowledges this interrelationship. How do preachers see themselves in relationship to the canon? How do they define the Word* of God? preaching? their role as preacher? the role of the hearer? As the preparation of a sermon has come to be perceived as more than the construction of an argument, as the recreation or evocation of an experience based on the intention of the text, methods of teaching

need to become more creative and interactive as well. The roles of instructor and student necessarily become softer, less defined, more mutual. The instructor facilitates the students' awareness of the theological issues of homiletics as much as teaches a method of sermon preparation. Indeed, whereas at one time a single approach—familiar to the instructor—was taught, emphasis on enabling students to develop their own method needs to be consciously attended to in designing preaching courses. This is a matter relating to the theology* of preaching.

Satellite Disciplines. While the narrowest study of homiletics would provide a lifetime of work, there are satellite disciplines that have been and will continue to be of value to the preacher and the teacher of preachers. Although the emphasis on liturgy varies from denomination to denomination, it nevertheless is vital that the preacher understand how the sermon functions within the larger liturgical setting. Failure to address this concern can result in giving undue weight to the sermon in contrast to the broader proclamation of the word or ignoring the relationship of the other elements of the worship service such as the Eucharist, which often follows the sermon (*see* Liturgical Preaching; Sacraments and Preaching).

Preaching historically has been enriched because of the influence of other disciplines of study and practice. This is especially true in the case of rhetoric* and speech. The apostle Paul refers to the training that other evangelists had received in speech (from the Greek root, *logos*), training that he did not have. The influence of the five canons of classical rhetoric (invention, arrangement, style, memory, and delivery) is prevalent. Indeed, some recent homiletic methods seem merely updated versions of these classical canons.

Human communication* theory has influenced the teaching of preaching with its insight into the active role of the hearer in the sermon event. A significant shift has taken place, which acknowledges the hearer as the cocreator of meaning in a communication event. This move from an actional to a transactional understanding of communication is evident in many current theories of homiletics, although less evident in practice. Several authors, such as Fred Craddock,* and before him Harry Emerson Fosdick,* encourage the preacher to *begin* with an analysis of the hearer before turning to the text. It is important, then, for the homiletics instructor to develop teaching strategies that illustrate and model this shift that identifies the hearer (and the student) as active participants, not simply passive receivers of information.

The tools of literary analysis can also be of help in determining the workings of a text. The greater the understanding of how a scripture passage works literarily, the more likely the text will be adequately represented in the sermon (*see* Literary Criticism).

Expanding theories of teaching and learning offer many options to the homiletics instructor beyond the traditional lecture format. There is growing concern that the various learning styles of students be addressed within the classroom. Methods for teaching creativity, especially in creative writing, offer many techniques for using language to fully and accurately express the preacher's thoughts.

Some Promising Contemporary Approaches. Traditional methods such as lecture and practice sermons will likely continue. New theories of learning, however, call for acknowledgment by the instructor of differences in the ways individuals learn. Using the style most comfortable or familiar for the instructor may not be to the students' best advantage. Attention to the uniqueness of adult learners has grown in particular.

Videotape is already widely used to analyze students' delivery style and content, perhaps ironically, affording opportunities for more personal and individualized analysis with the instructor. Videotape can also be used to present sermons of those whose methods are being studied. Because the sermon is primarily an oral/ aural medium, seeing and hearing a sermon delivered by a preacher is superior merely to reading an example.

Many exegetical and preaching resources are already available for use on computer: translations, concordances, word studies, text analysis, etc. As these become easier to use and more readily available, they can be presented as yet another tool for sermon preparation (*see* Resources for Preaching).

Although certainly not widespread in teaching preaching and probably abhorrent to the minds of some, computer-based instruction also offers opportunities for students to examine varying methods of sermon preparation. Interactive design would allow students to develop a sermon from text choice to final draft according to one or a series of methods. Key questions along the way with frequent feedback would highlight a method's features. Computer programs already developed for teaching writing could provide models for use in preaching classes.

Another developing approach to teaching preaching is contextualization. Because of the burgeoning need for ministers to be alert to issues of multi- and cross-cultural* communication, it is important to equip students with awareness while they are in seminary. Students should be encouraged to be sensitive to the varied settings in which they might preach and be provided with opportunities to preach in multi- and cross-cultural settings. Another option is to invite representatives of other cultures to join the class for a discussion of issues related to preaching to members of that culture. Short of this, the use of well-developed case studies can highlight the issues involved in preaching in various situations. The case study provides an opportunity as well to integrate homiletics with other theological disciplines that might provide insight into the situation.

Contemporary Pedagogical Problems There are several contemporary realities with which homiletics instructors must cope. One is the previously noted diversity of students. The average age of seminarians is rising. An increasing number of students come after leaving well-established careers to begin education for new careers in ministry. A significant number of students come with little background or history in the denomination in which they desire to minister. They may not have been enculturated in that or any denomination. These trends are true for both Roman Catholic and Protestant seminaries. In many Protestant seminaries, women represent a significant percentage of the student body. Developing courses that can accommodate this tremendous diversity is a major challenge for any instructor.

A second impact on teaching homiletics is the influence of media, especially television,* on both preacher and hearer. Many factors, including attention spans and expectations of hearers concerning sermon style and content, have changed as a result of electronic media. This is true in general because of our sustained exposure to electronic media. It is true in particular because of the influence of certain styles of *religious* communication that are prevalent in electronic media—televangelists, for example.

If it is true that students read less, how can knowledge transfer be effectively accomplished? Perhaps even the manner in which one processes information has changed because of the heavy reliance on image-oriented, mediated electronic communication. What methods are available to teach preaching? Does the traditional sermon fit anymore? How can it adjust to new contexts? The need to teach preachers the fundamentals of audience and sociological analysis along with the traditional theological disciplines is obvious and critical.

The pedagogy of preaching is an understudied activity that has drawn on and benefited from many sacred and secular disciplines. As it develops its own integrity as an arena of study and practice, it can also continue to enrich its sibling theological disciplines. (*See* Homiletics: Teaching of.)

Cram, R. H., and S. P. Saunders, "Feet Partly of Iron and Partly of Clay: Pedagogy and the Curriculum of Theological Education," *Theological Education* 29 (Spring 1992), 21–50. Donica, D. R., "Traditional and Contemporary Methodologies in the Teaching of Homiletics," Diss., Boston University School of Theology, 1962. Stern, R. C., "Communication Perspectives in Teaching Preaching," Diss., Northern Illinois University, 1990. Wardlaw, D. M., ed., *Learning Preaching,* The Academy of Homiletics, 1989.   RICHARD C. STERN

Pentecostal Preaching.

Pentecostalism is a twentieth-century revival movement within the church. The American version, largely responsible for its spread throughout the world, is rooted in revival movements of the nineteenth century. Notable among these antecedents were the Holiness Movement and the African-American church. Pentecostalism's chief doctrine teaches that the necessary initial evidence of Spirit baptism is speaking with tongues. It is taught that this speech, not produced by the powers of human reason and intellect, occurs by the direct inspiration of the Spirit and is the distinctive sign that the Spirit has taken full control of the believer.

The distinctive doctrines, clearly articulated by Charles Fox Parham and popularized by William J. Seymour, fostered their own patterns of worship and preaching. Drawing on elements already present within the larger body of American evangelicalism, leaders and adherents adopted forms consistent with their understanding of the Spirit and the Spirit's work within the believer and the church. Largely a reaction to the more subdued forms produced by modern culture that emphasized reason (science, history, and rejection of primitive manners), Pentecostal worship featured freedom in the Spirit. Preaching came to be characterized by its spontaneity and its ability to evoke the charismatic responses (dancing, speaking with tongues, healing) for which Pentecostalism was chiefly known.

Two key hermeneutical principles for

Pentecostals must be clarified from the outset: first, the position that the mode of the Spirit's presence remains constant from the Apostolic Age; second, the conviction that the testimony to the Spirit's work in Acts is not merely descriptive but normative. The most contested derivative of this perspective is the tongues-doctrine.

A primary textual battleground for the contest is 1 Cor. 13:8: " . . . where there are tongues they shall cease . . . " This passage is interpreted by Catholic and Reformation orthodoxy to mean that certain modes of the Spirit's operations were proper for the Apostolic Age. Necessary for the establishment of the church, tongues were given as proof that God had granted salvation to the Gentiles. Unusual and extraordinary measures were required to convince Jews that Jesus of Nazareth, whom they rejected, was truly the Messiah sent from God, whom God had raised from the dead.

Moreover, these same extraordinary means were required to break down the strongholds of a religious world filled with mystery, awesome claims for the deities of popular cultures, and great expectations of the people. No case for the gospel was plausible if its bearers had no more power than priests and specialists devoted to other gods. Charismatic manifestations were the proof that the kingdom of God had advanced against the kingdoms of this world (the kingdom of Satan) and that the final judgment of God was near at hand (Matt. 12:28). On the cross, the cosmic powers had been overthrown and disgraced. Death, hell, and the grave had been taunted by the victorious Christ. Captivity had been made captive in the exaltation of Christ (Col. 2:15). Wondrous speech in language inspired by the Spirit and known only by those upon whom the Spirit moved, words of wisdom and knowledge, miracles of healing, and preaching that yielded deliverance demonstrated to the world of sensible experience what God was doing in the spiritual realm.

With the triumph of the gospel and the victory of the church, these extraordinary manifestations were no longer necessary. Preaching became a more reasoned account of those things believed among Christians and instruction to those who had exercised faith. What is more, in the baptized nations where the children of believers received grace for the sake of believing parents, preaching was essentially a matter of catechesis. Again, preaching served an apologetic function, showing how the faith was consistent with what people already knew and believed about God or how their own culture was preparation for the gospel. Under such conditions, extraordinary gifts ceased out of lack of their necessity.

Pentecostal preachers, on the contrary, rejected this view of history. Their argument was that any changes seen in the world are essentially cosmetic. Demonic strongholds remain, and the need for signs and wonders is as strong as ever. But more to the point, the continuation of the charismatic gifts does not rest on the foundation of necessity: they show the nature and power of God who is the same yesterday, today, and forever. Any cessation of the gifts reflects not a change in God's way of dealing with the world but the condition of unbelief and apostasy within the church. Tongues and other prophetic gifts will cease only when "that which is perfect has come," and that will take place in the kingdom of God.

Pentecostals insist that the world remains open for the entrance and movement of the deity. This worldview, not limited by the boundaries imposed by science and historical consciousness, is radically theistic. God the Spirit has immediate access at any point within creation. The acts of God rather than laws of nature create the primary order in which the true believer lives. As was the case for the ancient Hebrew prophets, the word is accompanied by sufficient power to perform whatever claim is made in the name of God. It will not return void (Isa. 55:10–11).

Pentecostals believe that preaching is authorized and commissioned by Christ as the instituted means by which the truth of God is made known in every generation. Preaching forces a decision that yields belief or unbelief in a confrontation that cannot be avoided. The Pentecostal understanding extends to the view that the Spirit will work in preaching in sensible ways that give conclusive evidence of what has been wrought.

Hence the affections of the preacher and the hearer are regarded as manifestations of the Spirit's presence. Speaking with tongues as initial evidence of Spirit baptism is the most specific instance of this correspondence. Other instances of tongues-speaking, weeping, and bodily exercises are understood as evidences of the Spirit in the experience of the believer. The birth of modern American Pentecostalism at the Azusa Street Mission in Los Angeles, 1906–1909, was described by one participant as a "cyclonic" manifestation of the Spirit's power: "Suddenly the Spirit would fall upon the congregation. God himself would give the altar call. Men would fall over the house, like the slain in battle, or rush for the altar en masse, to seek God. The scene often resembled a forest of fallen trees. Such a scene cannot be imitated" (Lischer, 322).

Pentecostal worship is charged with the expectation that conversion, Spirit baptism, healing, and other works of the Spirit will be ingredients in the preaching event. Such signs and wonders are regarded as demonstrations (apodeixis, proof) of the gospel's truth. In some instances, these demonstrations are even considered to be proof of the Pentecostal message. With this understanding, the Pentecostal preacher is not armed with an argument only: there is also the reinforcement of personal and communal experience, part of which is constituted in demonstrations.

Identifying themselves as Protestants, Pentecostals tend not to specify precisely the elements in their liturgy. Hence, much of the ritual integral to Pentecostal worship is considered part of the preaching event. Preaching is a Spirit-filled, Spirit-charged event that is not grounded in proclamation of objective truth alone. This attitude toward preaching is consistent with the Pentecostals' protest against Protestantism in the search for the higher life, the second blessing, and the full gospel.

Understood in this light, preaching amounts to an invocation of the Spirit. As an act of epiclesis, it summons the Spirit to be present and to perform whatever is claimed for God. Further, to the extent that the delivery of the message is enveloped in a ritual, preaching is a means by which grace is extended to those who receive it, thereby taking on sacramental dimensions.

Initially an interracial witness, Pentecostalism and its preaching cannot be properly understood apart from its roots in African-American* religion. Indeed, it was the three-year revival at Azusa Street in Los Angeles, led by W. J. Seymour, a black holiness preacher, that brought the emerging movement to the attention of the nation and the world in the early twentieth century. From Seymour and his African roots came what Gayraud Wilmore calls a hierophantic sense of historical experience. That is, rather than being a closed system of laws characterized by natural causes and effects, history is essentially open to the manifestation of the sacred and the arena in which the will of God is executed. The task of the preacher is to safeguard that openness and to declare where the divine intervention occurs. Even where there have been disagreements on social and political implications, strong affinities have remained among Euro-American and African-American Pentecostal preaching, and the black church in general on the matters of preaching style and concern for the dispossessed.

From the outset, Pentecostal preaching set a high priority on winning converts to Pentecostalism. Nearly as much attention in this effort was directed to Christians as to non-Christians. With the growth of Pentecostal denominations, the emphasis has shifted to denominational development and to the retention of faithfulness among those within the fold. Pentecostalism also witnesses to the larger culture within which Pentecostals exist. One result is that many characteristic Pentecostal themes and much of its fervor can be found in nearly every church tradition.

Each of the Pentecostal denominations has its outstanding preachers. Some have gained notoriety outside their narrow circles. In his book *All Things Are Possible*, David E. Harrell discusses the career of some of the better-known revivalists of the 1950s, '60s, and '70s. Others have lately risen to national prominence, such as James Forbes assuming the pulpit of the world-renowned Riverside Church in New York City (*see* Holy Spirit and Preaching).

Anderson, R. M., *Vision of the Disinherited*, 1979. **Bartleman, F.**, "Pentecostal Preaching," in R. Lischer, *Theories of Preaching*, 1987, 320–25. **Bruner, F. D.**, *A Theology of the Holy Spirit*, 1970. **Harrell, D. E., Jr.**, *All Things Are Possible*, 1975. **Synan, V.**, *The Holiness–Pentecostal Movement in the United States*, 1971. **Wilmore, G.**, *Black Religion and Black Radicalism*, 1973.

WILLIAM C. TURNER

Personality. Personality is a term in common but imprecise use. Although many definitions have been attempted, it has defied precise definition. In general, it refers to the configuration of human characteristics possessed by or presented by an individual. Some definitions of characteristics possessed by an individual, including many theological ones, have emphasized the inner organization of the rational, conative (willing, striving, wanting), emotional, and relational aspects of the individual. Definitions of characteristics presented by an individual have emphasized the external effects of human beings upon others, following the etymology of the Latin *persona*, a mask, such as those used in classic Greek drama. In an article in a volume devoted to preaching, the external effects must be in focus, but the internal organization cannot be totally neglected. Tension among definitions that emphasize the rational, motivational, emotional, and social-relational aspects of human beings must also be acknowledged.

Only the personality of the preacher is in view here. Personality factors in hearers are of legitimate interest to the preacher but beyond the scope of this article except as they may interact with some preaching styles. This focus on the personality of the preacher has an affinity with the definition of preaching that Phillips Brooks,* the nineteenth-century Episcopal preacher and bishop, proposed in his Beecher lectures at Yale in 1876, which he stated in two ways: "Preaching is the communication of truth by man to men. It has in it two essential elements, truth and personality. . . . Truth through personality is our description of real preaching. The truth must come really through the person, not merely over his lips, not merely into his understanding and out through his pen. It must come through his character, his affections, his whole intellectual and moral being" (Brooks, 5, 8).

In spite of its fame, this definition has not been greatly amplified in the literature in the more than a century since its formulation. Among many personal factors in preaching, the following are some of the more important. (1) *The impossibility of being impersonal.* This basic point goes back at least to Horace Bushnell. The preacher's personality will have an impact on the congregation even though she or he, consciously or unconsciously, attempts to suppress it, or the effort of suppressing will itself have impact on it. Body language, inflection, tone, pitch, cadence all give it away. (2) *Self-involvement.* Hans van der Geest urges preachers to be self-revealing, frequently using the pronoun "I" (not "we," which he thought was a sign the preacher was hiding something), to provide security for the hearers (Van der Geest, 39–41). J. Randall Nichols distinguishes between self-disclosure and self-display, with the latter being a wallowing overpresentation of self (Nichols, 114). Not whether to disclose oneself, but when, what, and how much are the questions for the preacher. (3) *Artless integrity in tension with role taking*. Integrity comprised of "deep personal piety" (Brooks, 38), "whole intellectual and moral being," uprightness, and freedom from self-consciousness have been emphasized by Brooks and many successors. "No man ever yet thought whether he was preaching well without weakening his sermon" (Brooks, 51). Nevertheless, preaching seems to entail role taking closely related to that needed by actors in the theater (the *persona* or mask). The preacher needs to be able to transcend the mood of the moment, to have enough flexibility of personality figuratively to "don the motley" with Canio in *Pagliacci*, who must play the clown, though his heart is breaking with rage and despair (*see* Character). (4) *Authority in tension with prophetic reporter*. Preaching requires the acceptance of authority* without authoritarianism, which is a denial of accountability. Authority coexists with prophetic reporting of what another has said (in scripture or other basic text) in a figure-ground relationship in which first one then the other is dominant as an attitude that must be personally expressed. (5) *Identification with audience*. Preachers need to be able to identify with their hearers, without over-identifying with them. (6) *Use of personality*. Preachers need to use both conscious and unconscious aspects (after they become known to her or him) of personality. The unconsious can be a problem for the preacher if unknown, as it may lead the preacher to try to solve personal problems through preaching, such as taking vengeance on father figures in the congregation. But if known, as Wayne Oates has said, it can be used positively as an identification facilitator with paradigm figures from the past, especially in identifying with Christ (Oates, 441).

Although there is no one configuration of personal characteristics that is ideal for a preacher, the following are some principal personal traits or qualities needed in preaching. (1) *Empathy*. The ability to convey in word, gesture, body, and vocal inflection that one understands or is attempting with care to understand the experience of another is *de rigueur* in pastoral care, but no less important in preaching. Comfort with appropriate self-disclosure is an important factor in empathy. (2) *A sense of knowledge and wonder in the presence of the mysteries of the divine*. The preacher needs to convey an impression of treading on the edge of light and darkness. Piety and knowledge emphasized by Brooks are important in this, but the "second naiveté" discussed by Paul Ricoeur is a more contemporary way of expressing the attitude involved. The preacher knows much, but conveys also the limits of knowledge and a sense of what is beyond. Van der Geest's statement, "The preacher's own astonishment is fundamental" in conveying the gospel of deliverance captures the core of this trait (van der Geest, 75). (3) *Firmness without authoritarian oppressiveness*. This provides most hearers with a sense of confidence, although some congregations containing a preponderance of obsessive-compulsive hearers may be more comfortable with authoritarian preaching, as Jackson says (Jackson, 52–53). (4) *Flexibility of expression*. Preachers need to be able to experience a full range of emotions, including especially joy, anger, and sadness, and to be able to express them appropriately. Integrity of personality is expressed through such flexibility of emotional life (role taking), not by the denial of the emotions. (5) *Self-awareness*. The unconscious may become continuous with consciousness, enabling empathy and preventing projection and displacement of feelings in preaching.

Some common personality problems of preachers include a narcissistic preoccupation with voice, delivery, or thought, a tendency to complain about personal insults or injustices, rigidity and narrowness, and self-indulgent habits of excusing poor preparation and delivery.

In summary, the preacher needs to be integrated, transparent to mystery, self-aware, empathic, open to self-disclosure, firmly authoritative, and flexible in expression of emotion. If he or she cannot be all of those things, empathy alone will go a long way (see Pastoral Care and Preaching).

Brooks, P., *Phillips Brooks on Preaching,* 1964. Furgeson, E. H., "Preaching and Personality," *Pastoral Psychology* 10 (October 1959), 9–14. Jackson, E. N., *A Psychology for Preaching,* 1981. Nichols, J. R., *The Restoring Word,* 1987. Oates, W., "The Preacher and His Relation to the Unconscious," *Review and Expositor* 42 (1945). van der Geest, H., *Presence in the Pulpit: The Impact of Personality in Preaching,* 1981.

JAMES N. LAPSLEY

Plagiarism. The subject of plagiarism brings chills to most writers and speakers, and scholar-preachers are no exception. This fear is not without good reason. Such stellar literary artisans as Aristotle, Milton, Coleridge, Dickens, Byron, and Shakespeare have suffered charges of purloining the ideas and words of their sources. More recently, Dee Brown and Alex Haley have been accused of borrowing heavily from the work of others. Politicians of the stature of Disraeli and Churchill used the words of others without attribution.

The clergy have not escaped the temptation to steal sermons and illustrations. King James found plagiarism so widespread in Elizabethan England that he issued a decree that every preacher should deliver at least one original sermon per month. Famous preachers such as Cotton Mather, Peter Marshall, and Martin Luther King Jr. have been publicly accused of borrowing freely from others without crediting them.

Preaching, because of the great demand for material, presents the perfect setting for dependence on others. The special purpose of Christian proclamation and the nature of Christian theology further frustrate the performer who seeks to be pure and original. The church's fidelity to a tradition has never promoted originality; its ideal of the common life in the body of Christ has never offered special protection to the ownership of ideas.

Like Tennyson's "Ulysses," preachers are a part of all they have met and heard in their personal pilgrimages. Halford Luccock argued that the temptation to borrow could be avoided by refusing to read other people's sermons. The purist would have to extend the prohibition to the reading of books of theology, biblical studies, philosophy, and fiction. Strands of sermons and lectures heard and volumes read are assimilated until it is sometimes difficult to know where an idea or phrase of the sermon had its origin. It is sometimes possible to identify the period and place of a minister's education by hearing a sermon that includes remnants of thought by professors who dominated a particular institution at a given time. Plagiarism must be distinguished from streams of thought or *Zeitgeist* that shape the thinking, speaking, and writing of individuals.

Lack of originality is not plagiarism. Preachers would be better off not to struggle to be original when the possible result may be obscurity or, worse, a distortion of Christian theology. The books written and sermons preached over two millennia make originality difficult. Harold Bloom argues that poets are so influenced by other poets of past generations that none can be considered original. It has been said that there are only 120 original ideas in the history of humankind. The creative preacher looks for the best biblical and human plots for the needs of a particular time and audience as the basis for sermonizing. Ethics require that one not *claim* originality for such plots.

Plagiarism is the willful representing of the ideas or words of another as one's own. Deceit is intentional, and the motivation is usually personal gain of money or acclaim. In the case of preachers, laziness may also be a prime motive. Attribution is the vital issue. Ministers too often use the first person for stories that they have heard from others; indeed, old stories that have been passed down for generations are often "modernized" and told for the "first time."

A sermon is not a scholarly paper that requires detailed documentation. The typical congregation is quickly bored with attribution to unknown sources or labored technical identification. One can, however, with little distraction, note that a "biblical scholar has written" or "the story is told" or "a minister has noted." Care should be taken that originality is not claimed for the work or experience of another.

Most preachers are delighted to have their ideas, outlines, and illustrations used with integrity by other preachers. The notion that ideas and insights are personal property is a curious one, particularly in the context of the church that strives for mutual sharing. This borrowing should not extend to verbatim use of sermons without permission or attribution or to publication for profit. The preaching of the sermons of others may be desirable under certain circumstances. People may be delighted to hear a good sermon preached by someone other than their minister rather than a poor original one. Augustine recognized that some were better theologians and writers than others and that those not good at preparing sermons should preach the sermons of others. Yet surely if one is delivering the sermon of another, at least attribution can be made.

Circuit Rider, Thematic Issue: "Preaching: When Does Borrowing Become Stealing?" (Oct. 1993), 4–8. **Shaw, P.,** "Plagiary," *American Scholar* 51 (Summer 1982).

RAYMOND BAILEY

Powell, Adam Clayton, Jr. (1908–1972) Adam Clayton Powell, Jr., was born in 1908 in New Haven, Connecticut, where his father was the pastor of the Emmanuel Baptist Church. He inherited an imposing physique and a legacy of

oratorical flair. His father was a product of Virginia Union University of Richmond, an institution that established itself as a principal source of trained black Baptist ministers by the turn of the century. It had been founded by the American Baptist Home Mission Society.

As a graduate of Virginia Union, his father, Adam Clayton Powell, Sr., was a part of a group of black pastors who followed the black migration from the rural south to the urban north and established large, influential congregations.

Young Powell was born into this dynamic social movement, the urbanization of the emancipated blacks in the north. Because his father belonged to this fraternity of educated black pastors, he was exposed to ideas and movements that few young blacks knew or understood at this time.

As an infant he was brought to New York City, where his father assumed the pastorate of the Abyssinian Baptist Church, on 40th Street in mid-Manhattan. This church was established in 1808, when Jefferson was President. A small group of blacks in the First Baptist Church in downtown Manhattan refused segregated seating and were joined by a group of Ethiopian seamen who happened to be in the Port of New York. Under the leadership of a Baptist missionary, they organized a black church and called it Abyssinian, an alternate biblical name for Ethiopia.

When Powell's father came to Abyssinian, it was already one hundred years old and a center of black life in New York City.

When young Adam was 13 years old, in 1921, his father led the church into an imposing Gothic edifice seating 2,000. The membership soared to 10,000 by 1940. This was where Adam spent his youth, in the parsonage of an influential church at the vortex of major social change and the unrelenting struggle of blacks for justice and equality.

During his youth, the NAACP and the National Urban League organized and began their crusades for the amelioration of the black condition; lynchings were frequent and widely publicized; blacks were denied access to public facilities, hotels, restaurants, libraries, parks, and churches. Many blacks sought relief by migrating to Europe, but more found refuge in nationalist movements in America. In Harlem, the black Renaissance in literature and music attracted national attention as the music, poetry, and drama of black artists gained respect and recognition. It became popular for blacks to express their rage and indignation and to arouse a new consciousness on such matters among blacks and whites.

Meanwhile, young Adam attended college at City University and later graduated from Colgate. In the early 1930s, he began preaching and gradually assumed a position as his father's assistant. Throughout this process, he was attracted to social activism, and by 1938 he was elected the first black New York City Councilman; in 1944 he was elected to the House of Representatives. By 1960 he had emerged as the powerful chairman of the House Committee on Education and Labor. He was a strong ally of the Johnson administration's Great Society agenda, and 67 pieces of social legislation came through his committee.

As a preacher, his sermons reflected the times, the pivotal role of his father as a civic leader, and the church as a center of black life and culture in New York and in America. When Paul Robeson was denied a place to sing, the Abyssinian sanctuary was open to him.

Adam pursued a master's degree in religious education at New York University, but he bypassed a theological degree at the Union Theological Seminary a few blocks from the church. His sermons, therefore, reflected the social themes of the eighth-century prophets of Israel and Judah and the deliverance themes found in the lives of Moses, Joshua, David, Elijah, Daniel, Esther, Jesus, and Paul, rather than traditional doctrinal messages.

His sermons were written down but not published, and at his death his personal papers, including several notebooks of his manuscripts, were unavailable to the public. His book *Adam by Adam* is autobiographical and deals more with his political career than his ministry.

When Powell died in April of 1972, he had not been the pastor of Abyssinian Baptist Church since July 8, 1971. It is rumored that he and the church had come to an impasse, for his pastorate ended abruptly at that time. His funeral, however, was conducted as though he had remained the pastor until his death. This may explain why the many materials on his stellar career remain unpublished.

Moses and the deliverance of the Israelites from Pharaoh's yoke was his favorite theme. Over and over, Powell preached about the rod in Moses' hand (Ex. 4:2) and used that as an analogy of the power that blacks had in their hands, the power of the ballot and of protest.

His sermons were a blend of God's power to deliver and the people's power to resist oppression. Rarely did he preach on anything other than liberation themes.

One of his targets was conservative blacks, those who accommodated a strategy of gradual change. He had few close friends or political allies. His strength lay in the people of Harlem, with the church and the pulpit as his base. His sermons, therefore, resembled protest rallies and campaign appeals. Considering the task that was paramount, he found no better use of sermons than these liberation themes.

When Powell spoke in the chapel of Virginia Union University in 1940, he charged black leadership with being too conservative. He asked: "Why be conservative when you don't have a damn thing to conserve?" The chapel froze in shock. But Powell saw his mission as a preacher to be an iconoclast, to shatter the mold of injustice and of complacency.

Alexander, E. C., *Adam Clayton Powell: A Black Power Political Educator,* 1983.

Hamilton, C. V., *Adam Clayton Powell, Jr.: The Political Biography of an American Dilemma*, 1991.   SAMUEL PROCTOR

Prayer. In Jewish and Christian traditions, prayer is essential to the divine-human relationship. Luther once observed that faith is "prayer and nothing but prayer." Both encounter and dialogue with God, prayer listens as well as speaks. Such listening and speaking includes praying together, as in public worship, and praying alone. In its fullest range, authentic prayer is a way of knowing God and a way of being known by God. Thus, any proclamation of the Word of God rests upon prayer as acknowledgment of receptivity toward and wrestling with God.

Within the biblical traditions, we may distinguish specific types and themes of prayer. The psalms express praise, thanksgiving, lament, confession, supplication, trust, and instruction. In one form or another, the psalms have been the common song or recited prayer book of God's people. All the great themes of the scriptures are found there in address to God: creation, covenant, sin, prophecy, messianic hope, and wisdom. Much of the language of Christian and Jewish liturgy is permeated by the imagery and rhetorical forms of psalms and biblical canticles (*see* Psalms).

The Bible is also filled with a wide variety of praying people—from Abraham to Moses and Miriam, through Mary and Jesus to St. John the Seer—whose ability to speak about God is grounded in their address to God. Preaching that is not grounded in praying the scriptures is therefore theologically and pastorally impoverished. The preparation for preaching by "living into" and interpreting biblical texts is itself a prayerful activity.

The activity of praying, liturgically or alone, is theological. That is, God is imaged, addressed, and meditated upon. Prayer forms and expresses human beings in ways to speak about God, as well as in modes of relating to God in life. The very attempt to address God, even in mystical prayer, carries with it a way of picturing and articulating the divine, even if by negating human idolatrous images. Various names and metaphors for God, such as "Almighty," "Holy One," "Heavenly Father," "Shepherd of Israel," or "Loving Spirit," all show how human language both does and does not grasp the divine. Some early Christian writers claim, "If you pray truly, you are a theologian." The theological indicative or imperative of preaching is thus made resilient and self-critical by being grounded in the practice of the vocative—the language of vulnerable address to God in human names and metaphors.

Prayer has always been influenced by theological debate and forms of preaching as well as by shifts in social-cultural sensibility. This is seen within the biblical literature itself. A significant theological shift occurs when the earliest Christian communities offer prayer to the God of Abraham "in the name of Jesus." This was itself grounded in the proclamation that "Jesus is Lord." Liturgical prayer and devotional practices underwent radical changes during the Reformation period when specific theological doctrines, forcefully preached, collided and reshaped "right" or "true" prayer to God. And for good and for ill, the tradition of the "pastoral prayer" in Protestantism has often developed into sermonizing. The form and style of praying is always in mutual interaction with proclamation and theological debate (*see* Theology of Preaching; Liturgical Preaching).

In the nineteenth and twentieth centuries, increasing attention has been given to the anthropological and, more recently, the psychological and social dimensions of prayer. The theology expressed by prayer is always and everywhere culturally embedded and embodied. Responsible thinking about the practice and meaning of prayer now confronts this complexity and ambiguity. In recent years, great interest has developed in a variety of forms of meditative and contemplative prayer, many of which are drawn from so-called Eastern spirituality and from secular forms of spirituality as well. Spiritual practices that involve bodily posture, breathing, imaging, movement, and the like show a marked tendency to give less importance to verbal language. This noncognitive or nonconceptual concern, while seemingly less explicitly theological, raises important questions for preaching. At the same time, feminist and liberationist theologies have raised questions about the inadequacies of much traditional prayer language (*see* Feminist Preaching; Liberation Preaching).

Four basic modes of prayer remain at the heart of preaching, liturgy, and life: praise and thanksgiving, confession, petition, and adoration. The offering of "thanks and praise" is foundational to the acknowledgment of God. Hymns of praise are common to all traditions, liturgical or "free." Praise explores God's own being as well as what God does. This may be given great solemnity, as in the *Te Deum*, or may express ecstatic states of joy, as within the charismatic or traditional Pentecostal patterns. Praise shades into thanksgiving when the works of God are recited, as in the eucharistic or baptismal prayers that have been reformed and restored to most Protestant traditions in the twentieth century. Praise and thanksgiving are God-oriented rather than human-oriented. The prayers of Great Thanksgiving, however, combine address to God in praise and thanksgiving with supplication while at the same time being *proclamatory*. The recital of the mighty acts of God are intimately related in these particular prayer forms to "proclaiming the mystery of faith." It is no accident that powerful forms of preaching in the early church were *doxological*, as in St. John Chrysostom's homilies.

Confession focuses upon self-awareness before God and is crucial to the struggle for truthfulness about ourselves. Confession of sin is part of the larger pattern of repentance: personal, communal (general), and sacramental. There is an intimate link between self-examination before God and truthfulness in liturgical participation. Proclamation needs such truth-telling to keep the preacher from presumption.

Petitionary prayer or supplication—the making of specific requests to God—is the most widely practiced form of praying. At the heart of the church's vocation is the calling to be a community of prayer for others. Thus intercessory prayer shapes acts of mercy and service. What we ask God for, whether for ourselves or for the world, tells us much about both our conception of God and our moral sense of human responsibility. Preaching is deepened by attending to and addressing what and for whom we pray; the sermon is more discerning when there is mutual intercession between preacher and congregation.

Adoration is sometimes regarded as the highest form of prayer—the contemplative beholding of God or of the created order. Praising and thanking God may begin with human language and move toward a wordless "resting" in the divine, as with the mystics. Despite the tension between prophetic and mystical forms of faith, contemporary preaching that seeks to include the insights and experience of both contemplative and active prayer will avoid being one-sided in either a prophetic or pastoral direction.

Proclaiming the gospel of Jesus Christ requires a life of prayer not only for the spiritual maturation of preaching and the congregation but also for the theological and pastoral integrity of the act itself.

Barth, K., *Prayer*, ed. D. E. Saliers, 1985. **Jennings, T. W., Jr.,** *Life as Worship: Prayer and Praise in Jesus' Name*, 1982; "Preaching the Word," *Liturgy* 8:2 (Fall 1989). **Saliers, D. E.,** *The Soul in Paraphrase: Prayer and the Religious Affections*, rev. ed., 1990. **Westermann, C.,** *The Living Psalms*, trans. J. R. Porter, 1989. DON E. SALIERS

Preacher and Preaching in Literature. Although clergy and their fate

are not favorite topics in the realm of *belles lettres*, modern literature offers a sizable gallery of memorable portraits, many more than a brief essay can cover. For centuries, clergy have been shown in favorable and unfavorable light, sometimes with the nobility of Archbishop Jean Marie Latour in Willa Cather's *Death Comes for the Archbishop* or the valiant French curé in Georges Bernanos' *The Diary of a Country Priest*, sometimes with all the flaws of the whiskey priest in Graham Greene's *The Power and the Glory*.

Viewed together, this gallery unveils many dimensions of the inner struggles of clergy at the same time that it chronicles their changing social circumstances. Each literary portrait teaches us about the burdens, temptations, and, occasionally, joys, of bearing religious traditions and their truth in the modern age. Like the rest of humanity, the clergy depicted in literature commit all seven of the deadly sins—pride, avarice, lust, envy, gluttony, anger, and sloth—but they do so with public religious consequences that seem to make their failings more egregious and more revelatory.

A special collection within this impressive gallery of portraits is devoted to American preachers, a species within the larger genus called clergy. No work of American fiction has played a larger role in shaping our imaginations about preachers than Nathaniel Hawthorne's *The Scarlet Letter*. This short work, written in 1850 but telling a story of Puritan Boston near the end of the seventeenth century, provides us perspectives on preachers from two different eras simultaneously. The well-known tale, now an American classic, recounts the mortal agony of the Reverend Arthur Dimmesdale, a promising young preacher known for his eloquence and tangled in a dark web of partially revealed adultery. Hester Prynne, his partner in the affair, is a public sinner, sentenced by church and state always to wear a scarlet letter A prominently on her clothing. Dimmesdale is the private sinner, crushed under the weight of public expectations and personal cowardice, who conceals his paternity at great cost to Hester, her daughter Pearl, the community, and himself. His unconfessed sin festers beneath the surface of the story, involving the preacher in acts of hypocrisy as he participates in the public examination of the adulteress, in decisions about the fate of his illegitimate daughter, and in a powerful experience of exaltation and humiliation as he preaches Boston's Election Day Sermon (the equivalent of the invocation at a presidential inauguration today) to great acclaim, only to follow it by publicly confessing his sin and tearing away his clerical garb to reveal his own scarlet letter, one burned into his flesh by the weight of his sin and guilt. His movement from community apotheosis to public ignominy releases an entire community from the burden of this one unconfessed sin at the same time that it ends his life.

Lest the reader miss his point, Hawthorne states the moral of his tale directly: "Be true! Be true! Be true! Show freely to the world, if not your worst, yet some trait whereby the worst may be inferred!" (222). Hidden guilt and the evil that accompanies it are lethal occupational hazards for clergy. Caught in the untenable position of embodying a tradition that relentlessly seeks to expose and forgive sin at the same time that it seeks to elevate the good, the true, and the beautiful, preachers are trapped between expectations of perfection and the reality of deep fallenness. In their own flesh they embody the paradox of saints who are simultaneously sinners. Perhaps they do not bear physical stigmata like Dimmesdale's accusing scar, but they nonetheless manifest signs of bearing the Christian burden for all the public to see, to mock, or to revere. All too often they attempt to resolve their vocational paradox by embracing a lie that leads them and their followers into catastrophe.

Hawthorne's classic statement of this fundamental ministerial dilemma in many ways sets the theme for an unfolding tradition of American novels about clergy.

The centuries, circumstances, and forms of betrayal vary, but again and again preachers are caught in destructive deceptions. They fail to "be true!"

Writing less than half a century later, Harold Frederic focuses attention on a preacher who faces the sophisticated temptations of dawning modernity. *The Damnation of Theron Ware*, a period piece of great popularity at the time of its publication in 1896, tells the story of a young Methodist preacher, whose pulpit gifts lead him to prominence and then downfall. Called to his third charge in the midwestern town of Octavius, the Reverend Theron Ware is suffocated by the narrow rigidity of congregation members who gossip about his wife's hats and nickel and dime him during discussions about salary and parsonage needs. Down the street blows the fresh air of knowledge and culture embodied primarily in the presence of the urbane Father Forbes, rector of the Catholic parish, who no longer preaches because his historical knowledge and sophistication will only confuse his parishioners. Forbes's friend, Dr. Ledsmar, devotes his life to studying the implications of Darwin's theory, and a third figure, Celia Madden, embodies the world of wealth and art. These three figures represent worlds that Ware knows nothing of, but as he tastes their claret, dines late into the evening on heavenly food unmentioned in the scriptures, discusses whether or not the biblical figure Abraham ever existed, and listens to Chopin, he succumbs to their seductiveness.

As Frederic tells the story of this social-climbing cleric, a rich and sad irony unfolds. Reverend Ware feels he is being invited to citizenship in another world. The more he tastes the higher life, the less his vocation (as preacher and husband) holds him. His ministry becomes a career rather than a calling. Even as he improves his homiletical prowess, his identification with traditional Methodism diminishes. Matters of personal salvation (even his wife's) become of little interest. Viewing his own transfor-

mation as a process of illumination, Ware is brought to a bruising downfall when he confesses his love to Celia, only to suffer the rebuff that he has become an inauthentic bore. Her dismissal of what he had become—"What you took to be improvement was degeneration" (327)—hurls him into professional and personal breakdown, resulting finally in Ware's exit from the ministry.

In Frederic's novel, it is possible to see how different the ministerial situation has become from the Puritan days described by Hawthorne. Settled ministries where clergy stay in one spot for a lifetime have given way in the American environment to the ministerial career with its series of appointments. Instead of being an authority figure by virtue of office as Dimmesdale was, Ware must attract and hold the loyalties of a clientele. Preaching and pastoral calling become means toward professional success rather than means of grace. Professionalism, which will become a much larger fact of ministerial life in the twentieth century, shows early signs of influence.

If the Reverend Ware seems to fall naively into the trap of envy, avarice, and pride and if his basic failure to tell the truth seems to be due to his own self-deception, Sinclair Lewis's *Elmer Gantry* pursues these and the other deadly sins with breathtaking intentionality. No other portrait in this collection is as unsparing in its criticisms of ministerial behavior than Lewis's. Published in 1927, it, like *The Scarlet Letter*, has reached the status of classic, bequeathing an indelible image to future generations. From the opening sentence of his novel ("Elmer Gantry was drunk" [9]), to the closing scene where Gantry once more dupes his listeners through rhetorical manipulation and takes another step toward his goal of national power, Sinclair Lewis is relentless in showing how religion, especially preaching, can become merely instrumental in the hands of gifted, cynical, and unscrupulous entrepreneurs. Gantry, whose collegiate nickname is appropriately "Hellcat," has prepared for the ministry as football captain, class president, and chief carouser of Terwillinger College in Kansas. A Baptist in love with his own voice and the power it has to move people, Gantry fakes his experience of the Call and sets out on a career of self-promotion. Abusing women, colleagues in ministry, and anyone who steps in his way, the Reverend Gantry climbs the ecclesiastical success ladder, serving small churches, assisting one of the leading traveling evangelists of his day, Sharon Falconer, leading campaigns of vice suppression, and gradually coming to hold one of the most prominent pulpits of his time.

As he makes his relentless climb, Gantry falls numerous times. Distorting, manipulating, blackmailing, and deceiving whenever the truth threatens to undo his plans, Gantry becomes the self-made religious superstar. Always a hairsbreadth from scandal, Gantry preaches his way to national power. Unprincipled enough to pass off even the great infidel Robert Ingersoll's thoughts as his own in his sermons, Gantry overwhelms truth with rhetoric, showmanship, and bravado. He is a salesman who sells himself.

Much more than a portrait of one clergyman, *Elmer Gantry* is a rich tableau filled with a variety of clergy portraits, many rich descriptions of congregational and seminary life in the early twentieth century, and broad-brush landscapes of American protestantism as it began to polarize into liberal and fundamentalist parties. Above all, it reveals how entrepreneurial American religion had become, most especially its preachers. Part of the sardonic quality of Lewis's novel is the gullibility of the believers, who seem unable to distinguish between religious salesmanship and the substance of the Christian tradition. Here the problem of clergy truthfulness is much more severe than an inability to tell the truth about a sexual trespass, or naive social climbing. Gantry is a charlatan preacher for whom the truth is an obstacle, even an enemy.

At mid-century, novelist Peter De Vries provides comic relief while continuing to work at the question of clergy truthfulness. In *The Mackerel Plaza* (1958), the Reverend Andrew Mackerel is pastor of People's Liberal Church, Avalon, Connecticut, the "first split-level church in America." Ministering in the new affluence of suburbia, where food drives result in vichyssoise and artichoke hearts rather than the plain dishes of an earlier era, Mackerel feels called to battle for truth against the tide of revivalism sweeping the land in the 1950s. The liberal Mr. Mackerel is revolted by the piety of his parishioners and strives to build "a church designed to meet the needs of today, and to serve the whole man. This includes the worship of a God free of outmoded theological definitions and palatable to a mind come of age in the era of Relativity." In one sermon he preaches that "It is the final proof of God's omnipotence that he need not exist in order to save us" (8).

Suspected of being a Communist by some and struggling with congregational expectations about how long he should remain unmarried after the death of his much-admired wife, Mackerel struggles to extract the truth from an enormous cultural captivity. His vocation is undermined when he begrudgingly leads his congregation in a prayer for much-needed rain, and the prayer is answered with a storm, what he glibly calls "Jehovah's wetness" (254).

De Vries provides a true comic twist with a countercultural preacher who deliberately goes against conventional mores in the pursuit of truth (unlike Dimmesdale or Ware or Gantry). The *coup de grace* comes when the truth that the preacher is committed to is undone by an "act of God."

In 1974, John Updike twisted this tradition of portraits once more in *A Month of Sundays*. His nondenominational preacher/protagonist identifies himself simply as "a Christian minister and an American" (7), a telltale sign of the shifting religious ground traversed by clergy. The Reverend Thomas Marshfield is met not in the customary congregational setting but in a special treatment center for troubled clergy. Exiled to this center by his bishop and board of deacons, Marshfield's therapy/penance is to spend a month writing about his experience. Marshfield has committed Dimmesdale's sin—repeatedly and with a variety of members of his staff and congregation. Updike's twist is to treat Marshfield's adultery explicitly and to give his preacher opportunity to preach four sermons from his therapeutic wilderness. Beginning where Hawthorne left off, Updike has Marshfield write and preach to one reader, Ms. Prynne (Hester redivivus?), the keeper of his prison/retreat center.

Marshfield's "confessions" lay bare the soul of an American religion that has lost its moorings. The "piety of the full belly" (122) has overwhelmed the specific substance of the Christian message, replacing it with a "pornography of faith" (246). His congregation had not provided evidence of even one grain of faith that can explode its walls. His colleagues in ministry are part of the conspiracy that has left American churches with a dangerous case of "anorexia" (193), a lack of hunger for real spiritual food. "From the pulpit we with our good will and wordy humanism lean out to tempt our poor sheep from those scraps of barbaric doctrine, preserved in the creed like iguanodon footprints in limestone, that alone propel them up from their pleasant beds on a Sunday morning" (248).

From his humiliating exile, this preacher clarifies a diagnosis of American religion at the time of Watergate, identifies a life-giving rumor that is still alive in 1973 "that something mitigating has occurred" in the Christian story, and recovers a sense of vocation that clergy exist to stand as "emblems" whose station it is "to be visible and to provide men with the opportunity to profess the impossible that makes their lives possible" (249). Unlike the other clergy in this gallery of portraits, this preacher publicly acknowledges his sin, redeems it, and prepares to take up his ministry once again, with the paradox of his saintly sinnerhood only intensified.

There are, of course, many more clergy portraits, including recent ones by Frederick Buechner of Reverend Leo Bebb, and by Walker Percy of Father Simon Smith, both of whom minister in extreme, perhaps even apocalyptic, circumstances. These clergy and all their other fictional colleagues illuminate the enduring predicament at the heart of the ministerial vocation. They are all expected to bear grace and lead holy, exemplary lives in the impossible circumstances of finitude and fallenness. They fail, but as Updike has Marshfield discover, in the parched deserts of their experience there still are gracious signs of life, enough to keep the Christian tradition alive, even if just barely (*see* Arts and Preaching).

Bernanos, G., *The Diary of a Country Priest,* 1936. **Buechner, F.,** *The Book of Bebb,* 1990. **Cather, W.,** *Death Comes for the Archbishop,* 1927. **De Vries, P.,** *The Mackerel Plaza,* 1958. **Frederic, H.,** *The Damnation of Theron Ware,* 1896. **Hawthorne, N.,** *Great Short Works of Nathaniel Hawthorne,* 1967. **Greene, G.,** *The Power and the Glory,* 1940. **Lewis, S.,** *Elmer Gantry,* 1927. **Percy, W.,** *Thanatos Syndrome,* 1987. **Updike, J.,** *A Month of Sundays,* 1974. **Wind, J. P.,** "Clergy Ethics in Modern Fiction," in J. P. Wind, R. Burck, P. F. Camenisch, and D. P. McCann, eds., *Clergy Ethics in a Changing Society: Mapping the Terrain,* 1991.

JAMES P. WIND

Preparation. An effective preaching ministry involves two unavoidable claims: long-range and immediate preparations, an overall lifetime activity requiring a balanced recognition of the necessity for both. These twin prerequisites can be put concisely as: preparation for preaching and preparing to preach.

Preparation for preaching may begin while a person is still in his or her early stages of Christian growth. Seeds are sown possibly in one's home life, Christian education training, regular attendance at worship, all culminating in a decision to confess one's faith in Christ and an acceptance of the rite of confirmation. Then that venture of faith is nurtured by the disciplines of Christian living, including Bible study, prayer, personal witness, and faithful involvement in the church as the Body of Christ. Occasionally this way of life leads to a commitment to full-time professional ministry with ordination. With this decision comes the realization that service in such a capacity will mean a constant drain upon one's spiritual resources. A distinguished minister gave this advice to a young ordinand: "Spend the first ten years of your ministry in an in-depth study of the Bible and along with it keep your wits sharpened by reading, for example, Marcus Aurelius." This process is self-cultivation and develops capacities academic training docs not always give. It helps the pastor become a servant of the Word and not merely knowledgeable about the Word.

The second responsibility—preparing to preach—comes as an immediate and necessary assignment every week of the Christian year. As such it is an exhaustive appointment that can be sustained only to the degree that one's long-range preparation has been faithfully cultivated. For every preacher must speak out of a large range of thought. As Gounod used to say to his students: "Be wider than your calling." Early each week one faces the inevitable question: what to preach? This can be mitigated by either of two systems or a confluence of both: One may follow the lectionary pericopes of one's denomination or spend a month during the summer in charting a preaching program for the year, taking into account the needs of the people, the festivals of the church year, the national and civic occasions, and denominational issues requiring congregational attention.

All preachers face a further and equally critical question: how to preach? Whatever choices or habits are made early, they are subject inevitably to changes, for we learn by doing. One or two basic monographs on homiletical theory should be read carefully. It is dangerous to select any one model; it is better to read constantly sermons by preachers of high reputation, both past and present. Sermons, sermonic studies, articles in respectable religious journals, contemporary literature of real worth should be read and notations made on index cards for filing. Each year a preacher should read one or two books about preaching—an old one (e.g., Brooks,* Forsyth,* Grady Davis,* Stewart,* etc.) and a new one. In such a study, one will find guidelines for the pursuit of biblical preaching in a diversity of methods: narrative, thematic, expository, textual, all the rest.

Immediate preparation becomes in time a second-nature process: a scripture passage or text is chosen, and one's preliminary step is a brooding session upon it in every available translation (including one's own) during which notes are taken. The "brainstorm" is imperative, for it gives the sermon its stamp of originality. Then one reaches for commentaries in order to answer the five W's: who wrote it, when, where, why, and what? Another page or two of notes is now on hand. The preacher broods over the material until the central idea arises from this miscellaneous mass. With an "Aha!" the central idea is framed into a succinct statement that becomes the main thrust of the sermon and its organizing and coordinating principle. Is it something the congregation ought to hear and live by? If so, it must be faceted under several movements in which logical and psychological factors (i.e., good sense, climax, etc.) play a developmental role. Now comes the need to fill out the sermon's substance with auxiliary ideas, which involves a resort to accumulated index files, apt illustrations, personal experiences, and biblical and theological resources. All this finished, the preacher writes out the sermon in full, keeping in mind that he or she is writing for hearers, not readers, and that imagination must supplement reason and give wings to solid concepts and ideas.

In reflecting upon the completed message, the preacher must apply the litmus tests of objective and subjective criticism: Is this sermon interesting enough to hold the congregation's attention? Does it grapple with ultimate issues? Does it stand on the side of truth? Does it convey the church's faith endorsed by the preacher's own assent? Is there a tendency here to talk *at, above,* or *under* the hearers rather than *to* them and *for* them? If these criteria are well met, then the message must be disengaged from the paper and become a living entity in the preacher's mind. This is every preacher's "secret stairway," for it involves who and what he knows himself or herself to be and to do. W. E. Sangster spoke well: "The secret power of preaching is to know the truth of what you are saying and to believe it utterly."   DONALD MACLEOD

Proclamation. Sometimes the term "proclamation" is regarded as a fancy synonym for preaching. Indeed, in the Greek of the Christian scriptures, *kerysso,* "to proclaim" or "to herald," is often used interchangeably with *euangelizo* "to preach." But the noun *kerygma,* "proclamation," has taken on special significance in the twentieth century.

In 1936, C. H. Dodd published his lectures, *The Apostolic Preaching and Its Developments.* Reprinted again and again, the little book was remarkably influential. Dodd argued that the Christian scriptures sharply distinguish teaching, *didache,* from proclamation, *kerygma.* Drawing together declarative passages from Galatians and 1 Thessalonians, Dodd believed that the early Christian *kerygma* could be summarized as such:

The prophecies are fulfilled, and the new Age is inaugurated by the coming of Christ.
He was born of the seed of David.
He died according to the scriptures, to deliver us out of the present evil age.
He was buried.
He rose on the third day according to the scriptures.
He is exalted at the right hand of God, as Son of God and Lord of the quick and the dead.
He will come again as Judge and Savior of [people].

Turning to the sermons in the Acts of the Apostles (for example, Paul's speech in 20:18–35 or Peter's several sermons in chapters 2–4), Dodd discerned the same patterned *kerygma.* In subsequent chapters, Dodd proceeded to argue that the synoptic Gospels embody a similar kerygmatic structure as does the Gospel of John.

Finally, Dodd outlined the basic proclamation of early Christian communities, a message that he claimed is found throughout Christian writings, underlying the idiosyncrasies of separate authors, such as Paul or Luke or John.

1. "The age of fulfillment has dawned." All that has been foretold by prophets is now realized; the Messianic Age has begun.
2. "This has taken place through the ministry, death, and resurrection of Jesus." A summary of the events of Jesus Christ usually included his Davidic descent, his ministry, his death on the cross, and his resurrection by God's power.
3. "By virtue of the resurrection, Jesus has been exalted at the right hand of God, as messianic head of the new Israel."
4. "The Holy Spirit in the Church is the sign of Christ's present power and glory."
5. "The Messianic Age will shortly reach its consummation in the return of Christ."
6. "The *kerygma* always closes with an appeal for repentance, the offer of forgiveness and of the Holy Spirit and the promise of 'salvation,' that is, of 'the life of the Age to Come,' to those who enter the elect community."

Dodd's research, though controversial, was addressed by scholars in biblical fields and homiletics. The rising Biblical

Theology Movement welcomed the notion of one essential message underlying all the Christian scriptures and, therefore, one message in every age for the church to proclaim. Preachers were called to be "kerygmatic"; they were "heralds" who should deliver the same message that apostles once declared. From the 1940s until the 1990s, scarcely a book on homiletics appeared that did not refer to Dodd's *The Apostolic Preaching* and the idea of a primitive *kerygma*.

Of course, Dodd's work was questioned. Is preaching to be nothing more than the recital of an early Christian credo? After all, are there not more than thirty words in Christian scriptures used to describe what we call "preaching"; do not these other words—e.g., witnessing, prophesying, exhorting—convey a wider ministry? Surely preaching is more than the bald announcement of an evangelical *kerygma;* cannot preaching include ethical instruction, doctrinal explication, or congregational encouragement, all of which are also found in early Christian writings? And what of Dodd's sharp separation of proclamation and education, preaching and teaching: Is such a distinction appropriate? Though Dodd's work was brilliant, it may have encouraged a kind of pulpit arrogance. In a secular age, when terms such as "Messianic Age," "resurrection," "right hand of God," and so forth, may not mean much of anything, can the pulpit merely *announce*, or must preaching include explanation and even some modicum of what Rudolf Bultmann* labeled "demythologizing"?

What the term *kerygma*, "proclamation," does is underscore the character of the gospel as *news*, good news of a new state of affairs in our world. Preaching is not merely shouting the name Jesus a few times. According to dictionaries, the word "proclamation" refers to "an official formal public announcement." So the word promotes the gospel as announcement of a radically new human situation inaugurated by God. The gospel is "public" because it speaks of a new social order. It is "official" because it is from God.

It is "formal" because it is of ultimate significance. In every age, preaching is proclamation.

Bultmann, R., *Theology of the New Testament,* Vol. 1, trans. K. Grobel, 1951. **Dodd, C. H.,** *The Apostolic Preaching and Its Developments,* 1949. **Worley, R. C.,** *Preaching and Teaching in the Earliest Church,* 1967.

DAVID BUTTRICK

Prophetic Preaching.

"Prophecy" is listed as one of the necessary charisms for the functioning of the church in the letters of Paul. Paul does not let us know exactly what this charisma accomplishes. But the gift of prophecy is associated with faith (Rom. 12:6), as well as with learning and encouragement (1 Cor. 14:31). Although the term prophetic is often associated with a divinely inspired ability to predict future events, the scriptural witness is much more concerned with the unity of the body of Christ and its edification.

In some important early documents of the church, the prophets are portrayed as traveling charismatics who bring a word of truth to the community of faith. Evidently, these prophets created some problems for the early church. Thus the *Didache*, which some scholars date as early as the late first century, set principles by which the community of faith could discern a true from a false prophet.

> When a prophet speaks in the Spirit you should neither put him to the test nor interpret what he says: for every sin shall be forgiven except this one. Yet not everyone who speaks in the Spirit is a prophet: only he who walks in the ways of the Lord. From his ways therefore the false prophet can be distinguished from the prophet. . . . And if a prophet teaches the truth but does not follow it himself, he is a false prophet (11:7–10 in Burtchael, 302).

A letter known as the *Shepherd of Hermas,* usually thought to be a mid-second-century document, states:

Test the man who has the divine Spirit by his life. First, he who has this spirit is gentle, tranquil and humble, and abstains from the wickedness and vain desire of this world, and treats himself as inferior to others, and does not give prophetic answers to people's questions, nor does he give utterance in private (the Holy Spirit does not speak on demand), but speaks when God prompts him. Next, when the man with the divine Spirit comes into an assembly of righteous men who have faith in a divine Spirit, and intercession is made to God from this gathering, then the angel of the prophetic spirit, who abides with him, fills that man and he, filled with the Holy Spirit, addresses the group as the Lord wishes. In this way, then, the Spirit of God shall be manifest. This is the power of the divine Spirit of the Lord (11:7–16 in Burtchael, 302).

These early accounts of prophetic preaching place it within the context of the worshiping community but also understand it as a charisma that comes directly from God mediated through the prophet.

Current usage of the term *prophetic* often diminishes this earlier emphasis on the divinely inspired aspect of prophecy along with its ecstatic, albeit orderly, manifestations. Currently, the phrase "to be prophetic" is often reduced to either mere prognostication ("he was prophetic about the rise in interest rates"), or it is associated with moral exhortation. While such exhortations are certainly one part of prophetic preaching, it should not be reduced to moral denunciations on the whole. Prophetic preaching is a charisma, divinely inspired, which either seeks to recover a faithful word from within the Christian tradition against corrupt practices or seeks to discover a necessary word in new situations that threaten the rule of God.

Another important interpretation of the prophetic charisma grew out of historical studies in the nineteenth century that set this charisma in opposition to the institutional offices of the church. There is good reason for this interpretation. Prophetic preaching often appears antagonistic to the community of faith and to the wider environs within which that community resides. Amos's denunciations of Israel for its injustices and reliance upon violence appear to set him in opposition to his own community of faith (*see* Prophets). Likewise, Martin Luther King Jr.* denounced the moderate approach to the civil rights struggle by many of the church's clergy in a well-known and prophetic passage from his "Letter from Birmingham City Jail" in which he suggests that Black freedom was in greater jeopardy from white moderates who sought an "absence of tension" than from the violent aggression of Ku Kluxers. Coupled with his confession that he was discouraged by the white church and its leadership, Martin Luther King Jr.'s prophetic words set him in opposition to the church's acquiescence to racial injustice. Yet we misunderstand prophetic preaching if we merely contrast it with the institutional church. For those who have the charisma of prophetic preaching, promoting such an opposition is a temptation that should be resisted.

In his *Economy and Society*, Max Weber placed the term "prophetic" in opposition to the terms "tradition" and "institution." To be prophetic is to repudiate the past with its routinization and institutionalization of an originally free charismatic activity. This original activity becomes burdened by its institutional practices. Such routinization may be necessary for the continuance of the original activity, but the true charismatic essence will require prophets to speak against the institutional restrictions. Thus the prophet is placed over and against the institution and its commitment to tradition. As James Burtchael suggests, Weber's account of the prophetic finds an inevitable process of rationalization, where "the prophet customarily is replaced by the priests, who then convert revelation into dogma, fit timeless oracles into a tradition, and moderate the radical ethic into pastoral care" (Burtchael, 139).

We would be foolish to deny the truthfulness in Weber's important analysis of prophecy: that charismatic leaders who bring a prophetic word are often replaced by persons who then institutionalize that prophetic word and, in so doing, often reproduce the specific practices against which the prophetic word was originally spoken seems descriptively true in many instances. Franciscans become worldly. Protestants become dogmatically committed to tradition. Methodists become pragmatists and embrace slavery. The list goes on and on. But in the tradition established by Weber, the prophet and the priest are placed in a *necessary* antinomy. We should question the *necessity* by which the charisma of the prophet is set against the office of the institution. When this is read as a necessary feature of prophetic preaching, two results follow. First, prophetic preaching in the present is captured by an inappropriate antagonism to the community of the faith. Second, we fail to stand in continuity with prophetic preachers of the past, and thus become incapable of truly hearing their words.

The Antagonistic Captivity of Prophetic Preaching. The antinomy between prophet and priest appeared most forcefully in the work of Weber, but it was not unique to him. The great historian Adolf von Harnack set charismatics in opposition to institutional offices. The Harnack-Weber consensus also influenced the work of Ernst Troeltsch. The hold of this consensus upon preaching is evident in the assumption held by many preachers that to preach prophetically is to side for justice against charity, to be prophetic against being pastoral.

Recently this dominant consensus has been called into question by New Testament scholars, sociologists of religion, and theologians. The consensus was questioned because of a lurking Protestant theological assumption that the Word of

God is most authentic when it speaks for itself and is not beholden to rules, institutions, and traditions. Scholars of the dominant consensus read the main threat to the Christian faith to be the "Judaizers" against whom Paul wrote. The free and charismatic essence of the gospel was first threatened by a Judaism that sought to place it under the burden of the law. Then it was threatened by Roman Catholicism with its rules, offices, and rituals. Catholicism is viewed as a threat to the gospel analogous to the threat of Judaism. As Albert Schweitzer and others suggested, Jesus called for the kingdom and got the church instead.

Because of the power of this dominant consensus, many preachers who have had the courage to speak truthfully and boldly on important social and historical events have labored under a false notion of the prophetic. When the prophet is placed in a necessary opposition against tradition and institution, several false assumptions follow. Prophets become representatives of a charismatic authority that looks to the future. Priests represent traditional and institutional authority grounded in the past. Once this occurs, then, to be prophetic requires either a lack of appreciation for the traditions and institutions that make such preaching possible or even a contempt toward them. The prophetic word is taken to represent an unencumbered freedom, and the priestly word a form of legalism. Preachers will be forced to choose between this false alternative. The result is that preachers who represent the institutional office forego proclaiming the prophetic word, while preachers representing the prophetic charisma equate obedience to the traditions of the institutional church with compromise of the prophetic message.

The dominant interpretation of the prophetic stemming from the Harnack-Weber consensus leads to these three false notions.

1. Prophetic preaching sets the preacher against the faith community.
2. Preachers must decide whether they

will be prophetic or pastoral. These are different callings. The pastoral office is rooted in charity, while the prophetic office is rooted in justice.

3. Prophetic preaching points to the future. It seeks to "move the church forward."

There are reasons for these three notions. The church often suffers from an inability to hear a prophetic word. Those who have spoken prophetically have often paid great costs, even their very own lives. The repetition of this pattern throughout time is well attested in the common book of saints, the anabaptists' *Martyrs' Mirror* and the *Book of Martyrs*. These stories certainly lend support to an apparent opposition between the prophetic preacher and the community of faith. But what is lacking in the dominant consensus is the acknowledgment that those who bring a prophetic word to the community of faith speak from *within* that community. If we assume they are opposed to it, then we cannot hear what they say.

Hearing Prophetic Preaching. Prophetic preaching is not heroic. The hero is an isolated individual who is self-sufficient and does not need the community of faith for the truthfulness of his or her words. The hero speaks a word in opposition to a stubborn people who receive it with initial resistance. Only after some dramatic event, usually involving threats to the hero, does the community gradually accept the words. The community begins to be transformed, and once this process has begun the hero can leave. The hero is vindicated by the community's transformation, but basically she or he remains unaffected by the process of resistance, gradual acceptance, then transformation.

The place of the hero is strongly embedded in Western culture. But preachers should not be seduced by the image of the hero. The prophetic preacher should never conceive of her or himself as the *isolated* individual standing against the community of faith trying to move the community of faith into a future it stub-

bornly resists, seeking to create for it a new future.

Prophetic preaching seeks to discover what *is*, not to create that which is *not*. This theological definition of prophetic preaching assumes the all-sufficient merit of Christ's life of obedience, his death, and his resurrection. Jesus Christ is the fully realized sign of God's creating and redeeming activity. This sign lacks nothing. The preached word cannot add any merit to it. Yet as an all-sufficient sign, it is not self-interpreting nor limited to one universal meaning. Christ as our sign yields inexhaustible significations. Prophetic preaching repeats this sign in various circumstances, allowing people's sufferings to be taken up into the sufferings of Christ, and thereby redeemed.

Because of this theological definition of prophetic preaching, the following notions provide an alternative to the dominant consensus:

1. The prophetic preacher stands under the community of faith; he or she is not set over and against it.

2. To be prophetic is not in opposition to being pastoral. Prophetic preaching is the most pastoral of activities.

3. Prophetic preaching is never discontinuous with the past but finds resources internal to the tradition of the community of faith to call that community to its true identity.

What follows is but one example of prophetic preaching:

Bishop Richard Allen* preached in a time of great apostasy. He witnessed firsthand the dissolution of the Methodist church's prohibition against slaveholding. Having witnessed discrimination against Africans and African Americans in Old St. George's Methodist Church in Philadelphia, Richard Allen, a Methodist preacher, was forced out of an apostate church. However, he did not leave the church, not even the Methodist church. He recognized that the persons who sat in the pews were the ones who had left the Methodist church. Richard Allen then established the African Methodist Episcopal Church. He was not seeking to create something new; he was seeking continuity with the Rule of God that the Methodist church as it existed had lost. Commenting upon these activities, Bishop Allen proclaimed, "I am well convinced that the Methodists have proved beneficial to thousands and ten times thousands. It is to be awfully feared that the simplicity of the Gospel that was among them fifty years ago, and that they conform more to the world and the fashion thereof, they would fare very little better than the people of the world. The discipline is altered considerably from what it was. We would ask for the good old way, and desire to walk therein" (Allen, 145). Notice that Bishop Allen did not seek to create a new movement. He sought faithfulness with a vision that the dominant church could no longer see. In his prophetic words and actions, he did create something new, but only when we view it as an effort of continued faithfulness to the Rule of God will we truly hear his words.

Allen, R., "Life Experiences and Gospel Labors" in *Afro-American Religious History: A Documentary Witness*, ed. M. Sernett, 1985. **Burtchael, J. T.,** *From Synagogue to Church*, 1992. **King, M. L. Jr.,** "Letter from Birmingham City Jail," in *Testament of Hope: The Essential Writings of Martin Luther King Jr.*, ed. J. M. Washington, 1986.

D. STEPHEN LONG

Prophets, Old Testament.

The prophets of the Old Testament are a peculiar and inexplicable phenomenon, embodying what is most poignant in the faith of ancient Israel.

The prophets sound an odd voice, presenting to Israel a distinctive and uncommon vision of reality, subverting a more common and established perception of reality. The *subject* of their speech is a convergence of three characteristic themes: (1) They bear witness to a holy God who is terrible in power, free in sovereign actions that bear upon the success or failure of the human community. (2) They give voice to a moral quality of his-

torical reality, whereby the practice of justice and righteousness determines the future, overriding the significance of power, money, or arms. (3) They articulate an alternative future for their community and for other peoples, anticipating trouble for seemingly successful communities, promising well-being for communities in despair. They join together the holiness of God, the moral quality of historical reality, and a counter-future for the world, to render the world in a quite unexpected and evocative way.

The *form* of their speech is characteristically highly stylized poetry laden with daring images and metaphors. Only very late do the prophets of Israel speak in prose, likely under the influence of Deuteronomic theology or scribal modes of discourse. Only then do the prophets speak in ways that might be regarded as "sermonic." More characteristic are poetic utterances that utilize tightly controlled forms in most imaginative ways. The use of metaphors from every sphere of human experience and from nature serves to shatter conventional categories of perception, political and religious.

Primary attention has in the past been given to the *persons* of the prophets. In the course of Israel's history, there is a sequence of such powerful, disturbing personalities that reaches from the time of David (1000 B.C.E.) until the time of Malachi (perhaps 460 B.C.E.). It is difficult to determine the source of their uncommon power and authority, both in terms of their own claim, and in terms of the seriousness with which they were taken. On the one hand, there is evidence that these persons were open to powerful, psychological experiences, which are taken as ecstatic moments of invasion by God. The evidence for this peculiar experience is offered in passages concerning "prophetic call." On the other hand, recent sociological and anthropological studies suggest that the prophets occupied a social role (not to say office) in society that was respected or feared and accepted as a voice outside conventional arrangements of social power. Powerful, established officials were not free in that society to ignore these voices. This role of course does not preclude the fact that some of the prophets are judged "false"—that is, capable of misreading and misrepresenting social reality in the interest of preferred or officially sanctioned ideology.

In varying ways, the work of the prophets indicates that (a) they were deeply rooted in the most authoritative and treasured traditions and memories of their community; they insist that those old traditions are still alive in ways that illumine and redefine present reality; (b) they were acutely aware of present social reality and capable of discerning social criticism. They were able to speak concerning both the complexities of international politics and the subtle realities of internal communal policy and practice. Their comment on social reality made bold connections between the reality of God and the shape of social relations; and (c) they were convinced that God had in store for Israel, for other nations, and for creation an alternative future that could be neither impeded nor produced by human action or policy.

The prophets, however, are not to be understood simply as traditionists, or as social critics (a liberal temptation), or as future-tellers (a conservative temptation). Rather, their imaginative appropriation of past memory and future possibility converges into an artistic utterance that lets the present moment be perceived as the focus of God's dangerous purpose in the world. Their characteristic work is to voice a "metahistory," that is, to witness to the power, pain, purpose, and presence of God in human affairs, a reality that is usually not noticed by those otherwise preoccupied. "Metahistory" suggests that there is a quality, texture, and resolve in, with, and under human effort that cannot be disregarded or overcome.

More recent attention has turned away from the *person* of the prophets to consider prophetic *books*. We no longer have simply the raw, unfettered words of these odd personalities. What we have of their words has now been remembered, preserved, selected, transmitted, and shaped to make a second-level formulation of prophetic utterance. This canonizing process has taken remembered words (mostly oral) and has transformed them into "sacred books." Moreover, the canonizers are not simply neutral collators, but they themselves are interested theologians who through the process make their own statement, which itself must be judged as "prophetic."

Each of the prophetic books is edited and shaped in its own distinctive way. In general, however, we may observe two tendencies. On the one hand, the "oracles of judgment" that threaten, warn, and condemn, mostly uttered in anticipation of the destruction of Jerusalem in 587 B.C.E., are taken as God's enduring, sovereign judgment upon those who resist God's intentions for the world. On the other hand, the oracles of promise, mostly uttered after 587 B.C.E. in the midst of exile, are taken as God's powerful intention to create "a new thing" in a situation of despair. These accents of judgment and hope have served to thematize much prophetic utterance so that the prophets are concerned with the dismantling of a faithfulness community and the formation of a new community. While such themes pivot around 587 B.C.E., in their canonical form these actions of dismantling and forming are taken as God's characteristic actions. In subsequent reflection upon the canon, these themes concern God's capacity to unmake and remake for God's own purposes. In Christian categories, these themes have come to refer to the crucifixion and resurrection of Jesus as a model of God's characteristic way in the world, of reducing "to nothing the things that are" (1 Cor. 1:28), and calling "into existence the things that do not exist" (Rom. 4:17).

The canonizing process thus has produced a *text* (well removed from the original personality who uttered it) that has come to have a life and authority of its own as "Bible." This accent on *book* rather than *person* has important implications for contemporary preaching. It suggests that prophetic preaching does not require or permit the preacher to replicate the person of Amos or Jeremiah but to exposit faithfully the text of Amos or Jeremiah, thereby witnessing to the "metahistory" they affirmed, which must not be disregarded in the present.

The most recent scholarship has focused on "intertextuality," the practice of later texts quoting earlier texts and reinterpreting them. The practice of intertextuality is an early example of "preaching" from a prophetic text. In this way "prophetic preaching" is a process of taking a text already reinterpreted through the canonical process and interpreting it yet again for contemporary utterance. When faithful, each reuse of the original text moves against and subverts a world arranged without the God of Israel. It offers an alternative in which the threat and promise of this God decisively reconfigure all reality—cosmic, political, and personal.

The persecution of prophets (cf. Matt. 5:12) is the fearful effort to eliminate this demanding alternative voice. As the fearful king Jehoiakim learned, the prophetic word, despite all book burning, has a resilient, reassertive power (Jer. 36:32). No amount of coercion or intimidation has been able to silence this shattering, healing oddity of prophetic poetry (*see* Prophetic Preaching).

Blenkinsopp, J. A., *A History of Prophecy in Israel: From the Settlement to the Hellenistic Period*, 1983. Brueggemann, W., *The Prophetic Imagination*, 1978. Koch, K., *The Prophets* I, *The Assyrian Period*, 1982; *The Prophets* II, *The Babylonian and Persian Periods*, 1984. von Rad, G., *The Message of the Prophets*, 1972.

WALTER BRUEGGEMANN

Psalms.   Ancient Israelites understood the first two divisions of their Bible as divine instruction, whether proclaimed in legal statute, as in the Torah, or in prophetic oracle. The diverse material in the Torah and the Prophets readily lent itself to proclamation as God's will for human guidance. Not surprisingly, early Christian preachers, following Jesus' practice, drew heavily from Deuteronomic texts and from selected prophetic teachings. They did not altogether neglect, however, the major work from the third division of the Hebrew Bible, the Writings; for the book of Psalms, representing the human response to God's declaration of the divine purpose, contained a vast storehouse of knowledge about the human condition in the presence of its maker.

Two descriptive terms, prayer and praise, indicate that the composers and compilers of the book of Psalms thought the requests for help, as well as the hymns about the wonders of the universe and the mighty deeds on Israel's behalf, were appropriate human responses. The scope of these fervent hymns and laments extends from private meditation to communal worship so that they embody the best, and sometimes the worst, religious sentiments over a long period of time. Later preachers can extract from these texts, among other things, powerful insights concerning (1) life's brevity, (2) the wonders of the created order, (3) God's providential care, (4) human sinfulness, and (5) the chosen divine representative on earth.

The initial division of Psalms 1—41 roots all meditation in the real world, one where good people often encounter resistance and sinners flourish. True, life is short and adversity often threatens its quality, but God takes care of those with weak elbows and pure hearts. These psalms and similar ones in the other four divisions (42—72, 73—89, 90—106, 107—150) acknowledge that human beings merely travel life's journey like pilgrims making their way toward the holy city on a hill. Sooner or later most people are afflicted in one way or another, necessitating cries for help. The perennial question "How Long?" links humankind over the ages, making the ancient psalms thoroughly modern. Psalmists vocalize their deep longing to stand before God, and they make no secret of their profound trust in one who hears their prayers and collects their tears lest any fall in vain.

The frailty of men and women becomes all too obvious in light of the majesty of the universe and the grandeur of its creator. Numerous hymns extol the beauty and mystery of the heavens and earth; indeed, the universe proclaims, without speech, the wonders of its maker. Similarly, God's deliverances on behalf of Israel, who viewed them as miracles and signs, moved the psalmists to elaborate praise. Sometimes that expression of adulation took the form of liturgical instruction of the community, graphic reminders of previous unforgettable moments in sacred story. The whole world was bursting over with mystery, whether it was the birth of the universe or that of a tiny child. Millennia later, these sources of awe and wonder have not diminished at all.

Again and again, psalmists marveled at the fact that the creator of this vast universe took notice of creatures shaped from flesh and blood. Metaphors abound for this solicitous guardian of widows and orphans, who never succumbs to sleep. Shepherd, rock, king, fortress, refuge, shield, portion, father, warrior, light, and salvation—such metaphors indicate that Israel's singers of praise looked to every domain of existence for apt expressions of God's relationship to humankind. Occasional psalmists could not suppress their desire to reside under the shelter of the divine wing, to dwell in the vicinity of the Lord's house just like a lucky bird nesting under the portico of the temple. In these psalms, the distant God, typical of myths of creation, and the near God, characteristic of patron deities in the ancient Near East, are merged into one, uniting transcendence and immanence. Believers today have even more reason to ponder the ways of God in a world threatened by its own inhabitants, some of whom persist in using the old images of a benevolent ruler (*see* Figures of Speech).

That threat, not altogether new, made itself known to the writers of many psalms. Radical honesty compelled them to confess their own base thoughts and actions, knowing that by their doing so the one to whom they unveiled their souls gained no new knowledge. Sin often seemed to concentrate in the tongue, if not even deeper within the vehicle of thought. After all, the psalmists frequently experienced slander from enemies who wished to do them harm, so they were fully acquainted with malice, their own and that of others. Awareness of their sinful state complicated the issue of divine justice, which the psalmists puzzled over at great length. Apparent injustice threatened traditional beliefs, calling into question creedal affirmations transmitted from parents to children. Close scrutiny of their own motives, together with reflection on the consequences of surrendering to crippling doubt, prompted at least one psalmist to reconsider and to rejoin the community of the faithful (73). By facing their doubts and acknowledging their weakness, Israel's psalmists led worshipers to adopt a stance of complete honesty before God, for entrance to the Lord's house demanded purity of thought and deed. That policy and the conditions leading to it are timeless. Those believers today who examine their lives in light of God's holiness find themselves at one with their earlier counterparts whose ruthless honesty survives as a testimony to their integrity.

In every group, a few individuals stand out as exceptional. Some of them seem to enjoy divine favor above and beyond ordinary blessings. The ancients viewed kingship as ordained by God, and despite less than optimal experience with their anointed officials, the psalmists kept alive the hope that one of them would, like an idealized David, follow God's directives for the chosen people. This hope survived frequent disappointments, and with each one it grew in scope until an expectation of an anointed one—a messiah— emerged, promising deliverance for the oppressed. Christians boldly asserted that this hope had been fulfilled in Jesus of

Nazareth. Yet their confidence that in him God was at work among women and men did not bring an end to this hope, which modern believers proclaim like their predecessors. Together with them, Christians await the coming of God's anointed and the final eradication of evil with the establishing of God's kingdom.

Anderson, B. W., *Out of the Depths,* 1983. **Kraus, H.-J.,** *Psalms,* 2 vols., trans. H. C. Oswald, 1988, 1989. **Westermann, C.,** *The Living Psalms,* trans. J. R. Porter, 1989; *The Praise of God in the Psalms,* trans. K. R. Crim, 1965.   JAMES L. CRENSHAW

Pulpit. Speaking the truth of the gospel is central to the practice of the church and to the role of ministry. The place from which that truth is proclaimed has assumed a special priority in the Christian tradition. While the idea of the pulpit brings to mind a few places and shapes, the tradition has created a great variety of pulpit types throughout the centuries, and each in its own way reflects the esteem with which the church has always held both the role of preaching and the one who preaches.

Throughout the ages, the physical location for preaching has had various degrees of status within liturgical structures. That is to say, preaching has been central in some traditions, has been a major factor within the context of worship but not the highest priority, and in some instances preaching has had a minor role. Today in some traditions the sermon is the single focal point of all worship, and sermons may be lengthy, a half hour or more. In others, a ten- to fifteen-minute sermon may be considered sufficient within the context of a highly structured liturgical service. Historically, there have been great differences. Sermons were central and lengthy in Reformation Germany in the sixteenth century, while the two- to three-hour worship services in the Byzantine tradition at Istanbul, for instance, gave little place to the role of preaching. Regardless of the length of sermons and their relative place within the context of worship, the place for the act of proclamation was architecturally designated, given material and physical presence.

The word pulpit has more than one meaning. It may refer to a professional clerical position within a parish or a congregation. It may refer to a professional collective—those who represent the clergy may be called the pulpit in a manner similar to that in which lawyers are referred to as the bar. The word pulpit has also been used to refer to a small area at the front of a boat, an area defined by a safety rail that extends around the bow of the craft. In this article, the word is used in reference specifically to the architectural entity that is a part of the liturgical furnishing of a worship space, the object or area of proclamation.

Pulpits have been platforms at the front of small rooms; chairs centered on the top rung of semicircular stepped platforms, called synthronons; niches opened in transept walls; large rectangular boxes raised on columns; sculptured stone bemas; exterior balconies; speakers stands; reading desks; and ornate wooden receptacles. In modern times, communications technology has provided the opportunity for radio and television pulpits to be identified.

The physical object that is the place of proclamation in church buildings is seldom studied or critically evaluated in terms of its appropriateness for the task that it houses. After a pulpit is designed to be in the correct visible and auditory location for functional purposes, there are questions concerning its symbolic and theological character. Understated, barely visible, and timid characteristics of pulpits inappropriately symbolize what the proclamation of the gospel is to be in the context of the church's activities. Overwhelming, menacing, and oligarchical characteristics of pulpits symbolically misrepresent the prophetic, priestly, and servant role of the message and messenger. Flimsy speaker's stands are less appropriate than sturdy places for speaking that have a sense of stability. Good pulpit design represents the tension between a place for speaking that enhances the authority of the word on the one hand and the Word preached as an invitation to the accessibility of truth and the presence of the Divine on the other. Pulpits that create a wall between the preacher and the people or that box the preacher in a tight, restricted place are more inappropriate than places that lift up the messengers, make them more accessible, and allow them to move, gesture, and be easily heard.

Most preachers inherit the pulpit from which they and others preach within their communities, and in some instances it is difficult to make physical changes that more appropriately serve the function of preaching. However, the theological and spiritual integrity of preaching should not be diminished or misserved by the place from which it happens.

The pulpit is a place, one that can be configured in all sorts of material and styles, but a place where the Word is made *voice*. It is a place to be honored, respected, never entered into lightly, nor trod upon as anything less than a sacred opportunity. A pulpit can be a practically constructed, functional piece of furnishing, and it can be a wondrous work of art wrought by the greatest skills of the designer and craftsperson. In either case it has its role within the economy of worship. The preaching tradition insists that the pulpit be made and used with the greatest theological and spiritual insight possible.   JOHN W. COOK

Puritan Preaching. By all accounts Puritan New England represented a unique departure in New World settlements. Among other distinguishing characteristics, its government was entirely located on American shores; its inhabitants included women and children, making it the first "folk" migration in North American history; and its settlement patterns were confined within tight, nucleated towns in which most inhabitants were landowners and voters. At the center of every town was a Congregational church with a self-proclaimed mission to be a "beacon" or "City Upon a Hill" to a lost world. Such was the power of these Congregational churches on the lives of the inhabitants that the terms "Puritan" and "New England" were virtually synonymous. Puritanism, more than any other seventeenth-century movement, bequeathed to America a rich vocabulary that was mythic and messianic; words that called for heroic, self-sacrificing action in defense of religious ideas. The type of heroism Puritanism evoked was universal; every man and every woman was called to a battlefield that began within the self and extended out to engage the American wilderness. Even today, the language of Puritan discourse can be heard in literature, political discourse, and religious campaigns for a "Christian America."

For generations, historians have pointed to various factors to explain the uniqueness of colonial New England. But one formative power stands out above all others: the Puritan sermon. The sermon, of course, was hardly original with Puritan New England. But never before (or perhaps since) did it assume such uncontested sway over the hearts and minds of its listeners as it did in colonial New England.

To appreciate the unique position and power of the sermon, it is helpful to begin with some broad statistics. Collectively, over the span of the colonial era, New England ministers delivered something on the order of five million sermons, each sixty to ninety minutes long. On a more individual basis, the average New England twice-weekly churchgoer (and all were required to attend church) would have listened to something on the order of 7,000 sermons in a lifetime, totaling up to 15,000 hours of concentrated listening. If compared to hours spent in a modern university classroom, this figure would correspond roughly to receiving ten separate undergraduate degrees without ever repeating the same course. While lacking in formal education, colonial New Englanders were hardly unschooled. Through the sermon, they were introduced to ideas and arguments that made many the theological equals of ministers and professors today.

But even more significant than the frequency of sermon delivery was the fact that the sermon, considered a medium of public communications, had no competition. Unlike the plurality of modern mass media, where every day individuals are subjected to a bombardment of competing messages and images all promising meaning and happiness, New England Puritans invested the sermon with a monolithic voice that spoke authoritatively to every significant event in the life of the community. Even on election days, next to Sunday the most important in the life of the community, audiences were graced not with a governor's state-of-the-union address but with an election sermon delivered by local pastors. Sermons supplied the answers not only to the great religious questions of life, death, and eternity, but also, in special weekday or "occasional" sermons, to temporal questions regarding corporate purpose and the meaning of present circumstances. In terms of public communications, then, the Puritan sermon functioned simultaneously as prophet, newspaper, video, advertisement, community college, and personal therapist. Inhabitants might not have liked or approved everything they heard, but there were no other public voices to be heard and, for the most part, they remained silent before its demands and explanations. Such was the range of its influence on all aspects of life that even the power of contemporary television pales in comparison to the Puritan sermon.

If these summary facts suggest something of the range and influence of the Puritan sermon, the explanation for its power remains unclear. How did sermons become so powerful and all-embracing in the first place? Part of the explanation lies in the open spaces of the New World environment that separated the colonists from competing voices of authority in England. As every group of town settlers discovered open lands "abounding with rich and goodly meadows," they encountered a blank space on which they could etch a new destiny. These open spaces signalled not only material opportunities but, more important to the Puritans, spiritual opportunities for cultural and moral innovation. And chief among these innovations was the creation of a church-centered society subordinate in all respects to the Word of God interpreted through the sermon. In the Old World, sermons necessarily stood in the shadows of older rival institutions of church, state, military, and nobility. In the New World, society began—literally—with the creation of local churches, and all else would be made to conform to their dictates.

Besides the open spaces offered by the New England environment, the other crucial ingredient in the sermon's power was the Puritan inhabitants themselves. For the voice of the sermon to dominate, there had to be a sufficiently homogenous, like-minded people, willing to subordinate themselves to a common speaker. From first settlement to the waves of Irish Catholic immigrants in the 1830s, New England was composed of such a people. After the first generation of settlement, there was hardly any immigration into New England; virtually all growth in population took place through natural increase, as each generation replicated itself and discouraged "outsiders" from settlement. Unlike William Penn's "Holy Experiment," the Puritans' "New England Way" was not an experiment in religious liberty and pluralism but an experiment in disciplined submission to a shared worldview. Uncooperative and dissenting inhabitants were told in no uncertain terms that their "liberty" extended no further than the liberty they had to leave New England.

At the core of this discipline of like-minded, self-perpetuating New England "saints" was the colonial church. The New England churches were Congregational, meaning that all authority resided in the local congregation. This also enhanced the power of the spoken sermon, for it meant that there would be no higher synod or episcopacy imposing its will (or words) on the local congregation. Rather, all authority was retained in the congregation and institutionalized through the simple but profoundly important mechanism of a common pledge or "covenant" between the congregation and their pastor(s). Through acts of "covenanting," congregations promised that they would honor the sermon as if it were God speaking, and ministers promised to preach nothing but the Word of God. With that simple act, the religious institution was complete. Seldom in the history of New World settlement was so much invested in so little as a man and a woman's promise to commit themselves to one another and submit to the Word of God as expressed in the sermon. And seldom was a form of religious governance more perfectly suited to the wide open, blank environment in which it found itself than in Puritan New England.

Once covenanted and ordained by lay elders in the congregation, the forms of voluntary selection and lay ordination ceased, and the ministers became, in the words of the Rev. Samuel Stone, a "speaking aristocracy in the fact of a silent democracy." The ministers' responsibility was to translate the printed Word of God into a living voice whose pronouncements would be as reliable and authoritative as if God was speaking. Typically their sermons would be preached in a plain style that moved inexorably from biblical *text* to *doctrine* to application or use. Greek and Latin tags, popular in Anglican metaphysical preaching, were studiously avoided in an effort to bring all discourse within the world of ordinary hearers. At the same time, those hearers were told in no uncertain terms that the words they heard were neither of human origins nor mere opinions; they were the very words of God given without regard to popularity or public approval.

By uniting democratic and aristocratic

forms, the Puritan communities believed they had reached the ideal mean or balance that would maintain order without sacrificing the voluntary commitment of the people. Soon after their arrival, the Rev. John Cotton explained to his Boston congregation that their church was: "in respect of Christ the head, a Monarchy, and in respect of the [Elders] and Pastors . . . is an Aristocraty [sic], or rule of the best men; and in respect that the people are not secluded . . . it is a Democraty, or popular state." Through such balancing of powers and interests, the New England churches succeeded in avoiding both tyranny from above—the plague of Old World societies, and anarchy or indifference from below—the plague of many New World societies.

Through the formative words of the sermon and the pledge of the church covenant, New England society evolved outward to embrace families, schools, economy, and state. All these institutions were patterned after the model of church covenants and balanced powers and existed to support the word preached and to uphold its authority in the life of the community. Sunday was public ritual day not only for the church but for society as a whole. It marked the only regular (weekly) occasion for the people to assemble and receive information from which they could construct a common identity and interpret the meaning of life's events. Fathers and mothers in the household, teachers in the schools, merchants in the shop, and rulers in the commonwealth all remained silent before the pulpit. Their calling was not to speak to the people in public assembly but to uphold the voice of God's prophets.

That the sermon survived at the center of New England social life was owing in no small measure to the talents and abilities of the ministers to sustain their special status as God's prophets. Above all, they were rhetoricians trained in the art of leadership through persuasion, first at English universities and later at Harvard and Yale. At Harvard and Yale, rhetoric* dominated the curriculum according to the dictates of the French Huguenot logician Peter Ramus, who taught students how to harness all of knowledge—and all of scripture—to the task of popular communication.

In their Sunday and occasional weekday sermons, the ministers drew the populace into a spiritual world that was more compelling and immediate than the physical wilderness surrounding them. In this rhetorical world, events were perceived not from the human vantage point but from God's. It was a world of providential design in which things were not as they might appear. Here, all events, no matter how mundane or seemingly random, were parts of a larger pattern of meaning that the ministers described in terms of "providence." The outlines of this pattern were contained in scripture. Under the discerning eye of their pastors, New England congregations saw themselves referred to in biblical prophecy as the "New Israel," endowed with a sacred mission that destined them as lead actors in the last triumphant chapter in the history of redemption. Europeans might ignore them or revile them as "fanaticks," but through the sermon they knew better. Better to absorb the barbs of English ridicule than to forget the glorious commission that set them apart as a people of providence.

Puritan sermons were all-inclusive and existed to assist the people's orientation in the invisible world of providential design. They taught not only the way to personal salvation in Christ according to traditional Calvinist theology but also the way to temporal and national prosperity as God's chosen people. Through the sermon, particularly occasional fast and election sermons, New England audiences learned to perceive themselves not as a ragtag settlement of religious exiles and eccentrics, but as a special people of God who were planted in the wilderness so that they might bring light to the world. They were not only individuals elected by God to membership in the invisible church of Christ but also a collective people bound in a federal or national covenant with God patterned after the ancient nation of Israel. And, like Israel of old, they would bring forth a redeemer, a second coming of Christ, who would triumph over evil and rule over a millennium of peace and perfection.

Seen from a twentieth-century vantage point, it is clear that the rhetoric of Puritan sermons would outlive its creators. Once sounded it would never disappear, and it continues to articulate for many Americans the innermost meaning of the nation. In that sense, we continue to live in a world fashioned by the Puritan sermon (*see* History of Preaching).

Bercovitch, S., *The American Jeremiad,* 1977. **Miller, P.,** *The New England Mind: From Colony to Province,* 1953. **Stout, H. S.,** *The New England Soul: Preaching and Religious Culture in Colonial New England,* 1986. **Winslow, O. E.,** *Meetinghouse Hill, 1630–1783,* 1952.   HARRY S. STOUT

Radio Preaching.

Radio preaching began almost as soon as radio did in the early 1920s. On January 2, 1921, the Calvary Episcopal Church broadcast its regular Sunday service over KDKA in Pittsburgh. Almost immediately, religious leaders and institutions recognized radio's potential for spreading their message. As a result, there was an explosion of religious radio stations during the 1920s. By 1924, one out of every fourteen radio stations was operated by a local church. For example, in 1922 the National Presbyterian Church in Washington, D.C., and the Calvary Baptist Church in New York City licensed their own radio stations; and in 1924 Aimee Semple McPherson's* Angelus Temple began broadcasting over KFSG in Los Angeles.

Religiously affiliated educational institutions also discovered radio early. Moody Bible Institute and the Bible Institute of Los Angeles started their own radio stations during the 1920s and thereby created enormous supporting clienteles. Other Bible colleges and institutes also came to the conclusion that radio was an indispensable part of their own missions. Between 1924 and 1925, the number of stations owned by religious educational institutions grew from twenty-nine to seventy-one.

Most of these stations founded by religious institutions during the twenties were controlled by Protestant fundamentalists who increasingly felt marginalized by the religious mainstream. Cut off from denominational power, these entrepreneurial and innovative fundamentalists found in radio an effective tool for building their own institutions and constituencies. At first, programming consisted of broadcasting regular church services, but station operators quickly learned how to create a variety of appealing and even entertaining programs. By 1924, Aimee Semple McPherson's KFSG claimed to have the second largest radio audience in Los Angeles. In addition to her own lively preaching, it broadcast music programs, amateur talent shows, and even a dramatic series, "Jim Trask, Lone Evangelist."

Despite the growth of different kinds of religious programming, the mainstay of religious radio during the 1920s was the sermon. In 1924, Lutheran Pastor Walter Maier* began the "Lutheran Hour" from St. Louis and quickly attracted a national following with his biblically centered gospel message. More controversial were preachers like "Fighting Bob" Shuler, the fundamentalist Methodist from Los Angeles, and J. F. "Judge" Rutherford, the leader of the Jehovah's Witnesses in Brooklyn, whose sermons lambasted Catholics, the U.S. government, and all those who disagreed with them.

By the late 1920s, many mainline Protestants complained that the airwaves had been taken over by narrowminded and sectarian preachers and decided to take to the radio themselves. In 1927, Harry Emerson Fosdick,* liberal Baptist minister from New York, became the featured speaker on the "National Vespers" program that was nationally broadcast over the new NBC network. In the following year, S. Parkes Cadman, the eminent

Congregationalist pastor from Brooklyn, began preaching on the Sunday afternoon program sponsored by the Federal Council of Churches. Unlike some of the more combative fundamentalists, such mainline Protestant radio preachers aimed at a more inclusive and less sectarian audience. According to Fosdick, "Nothing narrow, sectarian, exclusive and merely partisan will do. He [the radio preacher] must strike a universal note and deal with elemental human problems" (Harry Emerson Fosdick 1956, 226).

Radio preaching was greatly influenced by the Federal Radio Commission, established by Congress in 1927. The FRC was given the authority to grant radio licenses, assign frequencies, and determine hours of broadcasting. New licensing standards resulted in the closing down of twenty out of the seventy already-operating religious radio stations. Those that remained were often forced to shift frequencies, share them with other stations, or broadcast at odd hours. In 1929, the FRC categorized all religious stations as "propaganda stations" and thereby denied licenses on the basis of too narrow and partisan interests. Using such criteria, the FRC refused to renew the license of "Fighting Bob" Shuler in 1931. Some religious radio stations managed to survive the new regulations; but many preachers and their programs found themselves suddenly off the air.

These new restrictions did not eliminate all religious broadcasting, however. At the urging of the Federal Council of Churches, the national radio networks adopted policies that favored mainline Protestant programming. The Federal Radio Commission mandated that licensed stations reserve so much free time for "public service" programming, which almost without exception went to mainline Protestant preachers. NBC agreed to sell radio time only for nonsectarian and nondenominational religious programs; and CBS refused to sell time to any religious program, though it did give free time to preachers with good Federal Council of

Churches connections. The new Mutual Radio Network took a different approach. It decided that there was a huge market for paid religious programs and quickly found one-quarter of its annual revenues coming from that source.

Fundamentalist preachers and programs were quickly back on the air. They figured out ways to syndicate their programs on independent local stations, thereby creating their own national "networks." Eventually they were able to buy more time on the regular networks, after NBC and CBS began moderating their policies in light of Mutual's profitable experience. Naturally, when radio preachers were forced to pay for expensive commercial time, they had to engage in on-air fund raising. Mainline preachers, who often were given free air time, found these money-raising appeals unseemly and frequently condemned certain other radio preachers as con men because of too much stress on raising money. Nevertheless, fundamentalist radio preachers soon located loyal audiences that were willing to foot the bill.

During the 1930s, then, paid religious programming came into its own. By 1939 Walter Maier's "The Lutheran Hour" was carried by every one of Mutual's 178 stations. In addition, other programs attained huge national audiences: the Radio Bible Class, the Back to the Bible broadcast, and the Back to God Hour. Father Charles Coughlin,* the fiery Catholic priest from Detroit, electrified his hearers (and dismayed his superiors) with his attacks on Jews, Communists, and New Dealers. In 1930, Father Fulton J. Sheen,* who would later become one of the early stars of television, began preaching on the "Catholic Hour," which was sponsored by the National Council of Catholic Men. But no one could rival the following of Charles E. Fuller, whose "Old-Fashioned Revival Hour" had the largest national distribution of *any* prime-time radio program in 1939.

By the end of the 1930s, many people were still concerned about the tenor of much religious broadcasting. In 1939, the National Association of Broadcasters revised its standards to support only nonsectarian and noncontroversial religious programs. Though directed at extremists like Rutherford and Coughlin, such standards could be used against a wide range of radio preachers. As a result, evangelicals connected to the newly established National Association of Evangelicals formed the National Religious Broadcasters in 1943 in order to look out for their own interests.

Mainline religious interests were served by the inauguration of "The Protestant Hour" in 1945. Through its interdenominational framework, a cooperative effort of the Episcopal Radio and Television Foundation, the Evangelical Lutheran Church in America, the Presbyterian Church (U.S.A.), and the United Methodist Church, "The Protestant Hour" continues to be one of the largest and longest-running radio preaching series.

It is clear that from the 1920s to the advent of television, no preacher in America could hope for a real national following without going on the radio. In the 1950s and 1960s, Oswald Hoffmann (Maier's replacement) on "The Lutheran Hour" and Billy Graham* on "The Hour of Decision" drew large radio audiences. Oral Roberts started broadcasting his healing revivals on television in the early 1950s, but his first venture into electronic media was his radio program "Healing Waters."

It is difficult to generalize about the nature of radio preaching, especially since the advent of paid religious programming. There are about 1,400 religious radio stations in the U.S. today (out of a total of 9,000). In some regions, it seems, every local preacher has his or her own fifteen-minute broadcast. Nevertheless, it is possible to say that radio preaching has been a great equalizer in American religious life, affording charismatic communicators the opportunity to bypass ecclesiastical and educational elites to build popular clienteles of their own. In a free-market religious system in which the audience is sovereign, radio preaching can be the road to religious celebrity and power (*see* Television and Preaching).

Armstrong, B., ed., *Directory of Religious Broadcasting* (annual). **Fosdick, H. E.,** *The Living of These Days,* 1956. **Fuller, D. P.,** *Give the Winds a Mighty Voice,* 1972. **Parker, E. C.,** *Religious Radio: What to Do and How,* 1948. **Shultze, Q.,** "Evangelical Radio and the Rise of the Electronic Church, 1921–1948," *Journal of Broadcasting and Electronic Media* 32 (Summer 1988), 289–306.

TIMOTHY P. WEBER

Rauschenbusch, Walter.

(1861–1918) Walter Rauschenbusch was one of the most articulate and influential exponents of the Protestant social gospel movement in America. Born and raised in Rochester, New York, by German immigrant parents who had joined the German Baptist faith, Rauschenbusch studied in Germany and at Rochester Theological Seminary, where his father was the director of the German mission department.

Rauschenbusch followed his father into the ministry, despite theological differences with him. As the young Rauschenbusch wrote to a close friend, "I want to be a pastor, powerful with men, preaching to them Christ as the man in whom their affections and energies can find the satisfaction for which mankind is groaning" (Hudson, 53). Turning down more prestigious offers, Rauschenbusch chose to accept a call in 1886 from a small German Baptist mission church on 45th Street in New York, a working-class neighborhood bordering on some of New York City's worst tenement districts, where he hoped to immerse himself in the life of the working people.

In 1897, deafness forced Rauschenbusch to resign his pastorate, a difficult and sad decision for both him and his congregation. He returned to Rochester Theological Seminary, where he became Pettengill Professor of Church History, a position that enabled him to develop further his thoughts on the social gospel.

Rauschenbusch's writings, lectures, and speeches in the last twenty years of his life captured the imagination of a younger generation of church leaders and catapulted him into a position of national prominence as the spokesperson for the social gospel. He influenced later generations of American preachers, including individuals as diverse as Reinhold Niebuhr,* Harry Emerson Fosdick,* and Martin Luther King Jr.*

Briefly stated, the social gospel asserted that the social realities of the modern industrial age required a reformulation of evangelical Christianity. It protested the increasing privatization of religious piety and the dominant social ethic of competition and profit-seeking because they deformed human relationships and institutions, especially in the areas of family, church, government, and industrial relations. Returning to biblical sources, social gospel proponents characterized Christianity as a "social religion," based on a faith in the spiritual truths of social solidarity, cooperation, and personal sacrifice for others.

Rauschenbusch wrote that solidarity with others—especially with the impoverished outcasts of society—could become a way of experiencing God's presence in human life and history. These convictions led Rauschenbusch and others to build bridges between the churches and the labor movement and also to develop a cooperative communitarian ethic to express pragmatically the social focus of Christianity. Jesus' concept of the "kingdom of God," Rauschenbusch taught, united personal religious experience and practical social ideals.

Although deeply involved in the social gospel movement as a young pastor, Rauschenbusch's early sermons seldom emphasized social concerns directly. They were in German and stressed the spiritual transformation and personal holiness that he hoped would broaden eventually into moral concern for neighbor and country. After 1897, however, his sermons, lectures, and addresses focused directly on the social dimensions of the Christian faith.

Rauschenbusch's homiletical preparation included writing out sermons beforehand, usually in a shorthand script that he invented for himself, and delivering them without notes. A typical example from his sermon notes (converting his shorthand into standard English) would be:

Usual evangelism hits coarse personal sins. Leaves the master iniquities untouched. Sins of the rich and respectable. Jesus reversed the attitude of the Church. Trust his judgment more. Little on drink and vice, much on mammon and hypocrisy. . . . Come out of the world of extortion and hardness into world of justice and fraternity ("The Minister and the Church in Evangelization," delivered at Garden City, N.J., April 19, 1914; Box 21, American Baptist Historical Society, Rochester, New York).

Later, if he planned to publish the sermon, he would expand such notes.

Rauschenbusch's style tended to be a bit on the didactic side, in contrast to the florid rhetoric and flourishes of the leading "princes of the pulpit" of that period. He focused on a single theme and often relied on biblical texts to support his argument. In doing so, he was quite willing to "contemporize" the text to discover its social application. He did not often rely on metaphors or figures of speech; but when he did, he used them to great emotional and dramatic effect. Such images were often "plain," in the sense of being drawn from the experiences of everyday life. Thus, he suggested to his fellow preachers in the Baptist Congress that they should speak of salvation, not in legal terms but "in terms borrowed from the simpler relations of life in the family or in neighborly intercourse" (Rauschenbusch, "Ethical versus Forensic Conceptions of Salvation," *Eleventh Annual Session of the Baptist Congress*, 1893, 77). In addition to similes drawn from domestic relations, he enjoyed using horticultural metaphors, perhaps because his beloved Rochester had been the nation's "flower capital." The images of patient cultivation and sudden blooming seemed to him to capture the challenge and excitement of the social hope.

After publication of *Christianity and the Social Crisis* (1907), Rauschenbusch was in constant demand as a preacher and lecturer on social gospel issues, a task he relished despite the pain his loss of hearing caused him. He never lost interest in preparing preachers for the pulpit. He regarded the pulpit as a forum "to make men see things as Jesus Christ saw them, or as he would see them if he were walking among us today" (Rauschenbusch, "The Pulpit in Relation to Political and Social Reform," *Tenth Annual Session of the Baptist Congress*, 1892, 127). The purpose of a sermon, Rauschenbusch believed, was not so much to articulate abstract truths as to motivate persons, to help Christians discover the spiritual resources within themselves for living a daring faith. His social gospel did not rely on a naively optimistic belief in human nature or social progress. In its stress on "revolutionary Christianity," it foreshadowed contemporary liberation theology (*see* Prophetic Preaching).

Hudson, W. S., ed., *Walter Rauschenbusch: Selected Writings*, 1984. **Minus, P. M.,** *Walter Rauschenbusch: American Reformer*, 1988. **Rauschenbusch, W.,** *Christianity and the Social Crisis*, 1907, 1992; *Dare We Be Christians?* 1914, 1993; and *A Theology for the Social Gospel*, 1917.

WILLIAM MCGUIRE KING

Reason

Question: Is reason a suitable topic for an encyclopedia article on preaching?

Objection 1. It seems that reason is not a suitable topic for preaching. For the apostle Paul specifically indicates that Christian preaching is foolishness rather than wisdom. "Has not God made foolish the wisdom of the world? For since, in the wisdom of God, the world did not know God through wisdom, God decided, through the foolishness of our proclamation, to save those who believe" (1 Cor. 1:20b–21).

Objection 2. It seems that an article on reason is mistaken, for it confuses the purposes of academic lectures and theological orations and the purpose of preaching. The former involves the reasoned explication of Christian faith, but the purpose of the latter is to communicate the significance of Jesus Christ in a way that stirs listeners to a commitment to follow him. It is not difficult for most people to recall miserable occasions when a preacher sought to instruct rather than proclaim the Word of God. Hence reason, which is crucial to theological argument, ought not be given much attention in the art of preaching.

Objection 3. Furthermore, preaching ought to stir a commitment of the whole person, including both the mind and the passions. Few people have been stirred to commitment to follow the crucified and risen Christ by theological argument alone. But focusing on reason means that the emotions will be given little if any significance. Thus, an article on reason in an encyclopedia on preaching mistakenly emphasizes the cognitive element of the faith at the expense of the passions and the call to conversion.

Objection 4. Preaching is an activity whose success depends on the guidance of the Holy Spirit,* not the achievement of rational argument. An uneducated yet Spirit-filled preacher is much to be preferred to an educated preacher deaf to the promptings and guiding of the Holy Spirit. Indeed, some great preachers have been known more for their stirring, emotional rhetoric than for their theological insight. Hence reason is not an important topic for preaching.

On the contrary, reason is important to the art of preaching. But it ought not be confused with rationalism. For, as Cardinal John Henry Newman* has suggested

(97–98), "Rationalism is a certain abuse of reason; that is, a use of it for purposes for which it never was intended, and is unfitted."

I answer that, the neglect of reason in discussions of preaching has been a serious omission, particularly in the time since the Enlightenment in Western culture. In recent decades, Christians have too often thought of preaching simply as a technique; likewise, there has been a tendency to reject or ignore the importance of reason for preaching by conflating it with rationalism. While reason is not the only or even the central element in proclamation, its thoughtful and appropriate use is crucial.

A rational component is internal to the Christian faith. It is not the same conception of reason as may be found in other traditions; Christian reason operates within the revelation of God in Jesus Christ. Thus, while a Christian understanding of reason may subvert other standards of human reason, it is not irrational. For example, Jesus' parables* subvert people's expectations, but they do so in order that people may glimpse more clearly the true reason and wisdom of God. Likewise, an encyclopedia article in this form (borrowed from Thomas Aquinas) may subvert people's expectations, but it does so as a reminder that there is more than one way to deploy reasoned reflection. So preachers need to recognize that there is more than one way to deploy reasoned reflection in the craft of preaching. The crucial decision the preacher makes is how reason is deployed, ensuring that it is appropriate to Christ, the Logos, the wisdom of God; whether it ought to be used in preaching should be an unquestioned presumption.

Reply to Objection 1. St. Paul continues in that same chapter, "For Jews demand signs and Greeks desire wisdom, but we proclaim Christ crucified, a stumbling block to Jews and foolishness to the Gentiles, but to those who are the called, both Jews and Greeks, Christ the power of God and the wisdom of God" (1 Cor. 1:23). By the *world's* understanding of reason, Christ's cross (and, likewise, Christian preaching) is foolishness; but Christ is the wisdom of God. And, as Alasdair MacIntyre has argued, there is no one standard of reason; we need to ask "which rationality?" Thus the task for preaching is to deploy reason in a manner consistent with Jesus Christ, the Logos, whom we proclaim.

Reply to Objection 2. A sermon is not an academic lecture or a theological oration. Further, it is perhaps even less difficult for most persons to recall sermons that—far from being too dry and academic—lacked any reasoned reflection at all. Random musings or emotional diatribes are not appropriate as proclamation of the Christ who is the wisdom of God. Christian preaching need not, and ought not, be directed only to the educated; but reasoned reflection on the text of the sermon can play an important role in stirring people to follow Jesus Christ.

Reply to Objection 3. There is no good justification that reason ought to seem either exclusive of or in competition with the emotions. Further, those who believe that the wisdom of God is not separable from the love of God ought to recognize that reason and the emotions are very closely related. There is a passionate dimension to Christian reason and a rational component to Christian emotions.

Reply to Objection 4. The Holy Spirit can work through human minds, as well as in spite of them. Education alone does not make a preacher; but that does not mean education and reasoned reflection ought to be disparaged in preaching. The Spirit's guiding, inspiring work has shone through people whose rhetoric was more stirring than theologically illuminating; but it has also shone through the preaching of such theologians as John Chrysostom,* Augustine,* Wesley,* and Newman.* Even though not all preachers are given great theological insight, all are called to proclamation, which allows the Holy Spirit to guide and inspire faithful witness to the word. Reasoned reflection

on and reasoned proclamation of that word ought not be ignored (*see* Theology of Preaching; Authority).

MacIntyre, A., *Whose Justice? Which Rationality?,* 1988. **Newman, J. H.,** *The Essential Newman,* ed. Vincent Ferrer Blehl, 1963. **Wolterstorff, N.,** *Reason Within the Bounds of Religion,* 2d ed., 1984.

L. GREGORY JONES

Resources for Preaching.

There are two classes of preaching resources I describe in this article. The first are those video "workshops" and exercises that review the basic elements of preaching. The second are the variety of print resources that stimulate the preacher's preparation through exegesis of biblical texts, illustrative material, theological reflections, and even complete sermons. Many preachers subscribe to print resources because they provide focus and direction to the limited time available for sermon preparation. Each one puts the preacher into a lively conversation with scholars, theologians, literary figures, and other preachers.

As popular as these aids are, some words of caution are in order. (1) The study of the resources may displace a preacher's own reading and study of the Bible; (2) the engaging voices of the commentators in these resources may lead the preacher to mistrust or devalue his or her own insights; (3) for the most part, these print resources encourage only silent reading and reflection. Oral reading stimulates the imagination by calling attention to the rhetorical and experiential aspects of the texts themselves; (4) since these resources usually focus on specific pericopes, the preacher needs to build into his or her own life of study some attention to an entire Gospel, a book from Hebrew scripture, or an epistle. Otherwise, the preacher's library becomes smaller and the Bible fragmented.

Video Resources. These productions represent experimentation in the teaching of preaching. Each is designed as a "self-directed workshop" for individuals or groups of preachers who want to revisit the basic elements of the preparation and delivery process.

The Preaching Preference Profile (Takestock Ministries, 1988) presents brief sermon excerpts from twenty different preachers. The viewer watches the sequence twice. On each viewing, he or she marks a score sheet that treats aspects of the sermon's content and style. The exercise is designed to begin a group discussion on the question "what is good preaching?" and identify some goals for self-improvement for the preacher (*see* Lay Response to Preaching).

Crisis in Preaching: A Four-Part Video Workshop is produced by the Academy for Preaching of the United Methodist Church. Donald Davis, a professional storyteller and ordained minister, challenges three assumptions: (1) that sermons must be prepared one Sunday at a time; (2) that sermons move from concept to illustration and supportive material; (3) that writing a manuscript or preparing an outline are the best preparations for the oral event of preaching. In these videotaped lectures, Davis stresses that preaching is *oral** communication.

Lifetime Scholar (Logos Publications) is a series of video tapes and workbooks for preachers. Course 1 consists of sermons by six preachers with evaluative comments by William H. Willimon. The commentary explores issues related to the move from text to sermon.

A Guide to Improving Your Preaching (Broadman Press, 1990) is a set of two tapes that emphasize (1) techniques of biblical exegesis in sermon preparation and (2) the sermon as oral communication. The homiletics faculty of Southern Baptist Theological Seminary presents a panel discussion on ways to make the biblical text come alive for the listener. Preachers must learn to look at texts with fresh eyes and within the context of the whole Bible's theology.

In addition to the discussion, the panel presents videotaped excerpts of sermons that illustrate these principles. One added feature of this video workshop are interviews of laypersons who comment on what "effective" preaching is.

Preaching by Fred Craddock (Abingdon Press, 1986) is a set of four, thirty-minute tapes that are designed to accompany Craddock's textbook on preaching. Situated in a seminary classroom, Professor Craddock* outlines a method for sermon preparation that emphasizes "movement" into a text and then out toward the listener. To receive a message, the preacher listens attentively to both text and congregation. Craddock illustrates his process by "talking through" a biblical passage (John 19:31–37) with his eye on the pulpit. The entire process is embedded in a concern for the quality of a preacher's study life. There are suggestions throughout about how a preacher might improve habits of preparation.

Print Resources

Lectionary-Based Resources. Some publications are primarily organized around the new Common Lectionary. Each assumes that the preacher is familiar with the lectionary,* understands its strengths and weaknesses as a preaching resource, and attempts to enliven the preacher's study of the selected texts by establishing different emphases.

For example, *Proclamation: Aids for Interpreting the Lessons of the Church Year* accents the preacher's work with the text itself. Authors in this series attempt to build a bridge between exegesis* and homiletical interpretation. Biblical scholars here understand that a preacher's task is to listen to texts with the ears of her or his congregation.

Each author issues a brief statement that relates the cluster of texts to the liturgical season, then sets up conversations with the texts themselves. Dissonance among the texts is acknowledged; congruity is not forced. There are enough rough edges and loose ends in these entries to prompt the preacher's interpretive, pastoral work.

Lectionary Homiletics pushes beyond concern with the text to include a variety of articles treating theological themes, pastoral implications, the arts as resource, sermon reviews, and some options for developing the sermon. This expansive approach offers some clear advantages for the preacher. A very close verse-by-verse exposition of the texts is balanced by a broader discussion of traditional theological concepts. A section on "pastoral implications" for the sermon closes the distance between the text's original audiences and the preacher's congregation; the section on the arts awakens the preacher's visual sensibilities. Though it is impossible for the preacher to have a primary experience of visual or aural arts in the medium of print, an essay that links text to the arts teaches the preacher to value artistic expression as a resource for preaching.

Sermon reviews, sermons, and an article on "preaching the lesson" all put the preacher in conversation with others who have preached or plan to preach on this set of texts. The effect of a team of writers, each of whom is looking at the text from a different angle, is to enlarge the preacher's conceptual world. However, such an extensive treatment may result in the loss of a focus for a sermon. *Lectionary Homiletics'* approach may contribute to sermons that are much too large or try to do entirely too much.

Pulpit Resource is similar to *Lectionary Homiletics* in format, but its content is not as densely packed. Here too are sections that treat different aspects and implications of lectionary texts. The author introduces each lesson with a suggested focus or direction for all of the material, gives a synopsis of each text, and even writes out a prayer that the preacher can use as a personal or liturgical resource.

Exegetical information is presented as "encounter" with the text. The questions that are offered for reflection do give shape and direction to that study and encourage candor and honesty in relating to the text. "Proclaiming the text" and "Relating the text" both give the preacher some hints on how to move from the study to the pulpit. The lively and engaging style of writing that characterizes these entries reminds the preacher to at-

tend to the communicative values of a sermon throughout the process of preparation.* Anecdotes, quotes, and literary selections punctuate these articles to feed the preacher's reflection on his or her own style and experience.

One distinguishing feature of this publication is the "Five-Minute Preaching Workshop." It is one of the few places in this kind of literature where communication* issues are related to the craft of preaching. Here the author reminds the preacher that the sermon is an oral event for both preacher and listener and gives some practical advice to the preacher for cultivating oral communication skills.

Non-Lectionary-Based Resources. There are a number of publications where the primary focus shifts from the lectionary itself to sermons or topics. An example is *The Living Pulpit.* The emphasis in each issue is on a specific topic or theme (such as "anger" or "the Earth"). Among the contributors are essayists, poets, and activists, as well as theologians and preachers. Different genres are included in the format: biblical exegesis and commentary appear alongside stories and historical essays. There are excerpts from imaginative literature and book reviews as well as sermons preached on the theme. The effort is to involve as many voices as possible in the discussion of critical issues for the church.

The effect is to inspire the preacher to think as a prophet but not to go it alone. There is material enough here to encourage the preacher to depart occasionally from the lectionary in order to address troubling social issues that require careful discussion and responsible community action. Preachers who speak on these issues outside the context of worship will also find a good deal of help in this publication. The authors assume that the preacher must be in conversations about these issues outside of the church building and settings of worship.

Another advantage of this publication is that it closes the distance between the preaching and educational ministries of the church. Each issue is a resource for social action groups, intergenerational discussion, or community outreach. *The Living Pulpit* is valuable because it brings together many of the "publics" that a preacher serves and points him or her to a pulpit. By thoroughly developing themes and topics, *The Living Pulpit* expands the horizons of a preacher's social concern.

Preaching is another issue-based resource for preachers. Like *The Living Pulpit*, it includes a section that treats the lectionary, but its emphasis is more broadly defined. For example, articles address theological issues related to the craft of preaching, some practical concerns, and interviews with resource persons. Many sermons are published here, as well as book reviews, ideas for children's sermons, and material for sermon illustrations. Women are conspicuously absent in this publication, and the theological parameters are narrowly defined.

Biblical Preaching Journal and *Pulpit Digest* are examples of publications that assume there is value in reading the sermons of others. Just as a preacher will profit by reading other works of the imagination, so will that preacher profit from reading sermons as a form of literature. Preachers who are not able to hear anyone else preach tend to grow weary of the sound of their own voices. Through an encounter with a sermon in print, a preacher may get a new sense of what is possible in the pulpit ministry. He or she will be refreshed by another's treatment of a familiar text or by the stylistic devices that characterize a sermon. The medium of print creates a kind of preaching peer group in which one can see how others handle sermon introductions and conclusions, difficult textual matters, or pastoral issues in preaching. In any case, the practice of reading the sermons of others helps create a safe place where the preacher can, in the privacy of his or her own experience, hold the preaching ministry up for scrutiny and review.

Yet this kind of resource is limited because it does not further open up the process of preparation. The reader can see only one set of choices that a preacher made on a particular occasion. The *Biblical Preaching Journal* does expose some of the undergirdings of well-made sermons by providing each published preacher some space for exegetical interpretations of the selected biblical texts. Even so, since the reader cannot be a part of the interaction between the preacher and the congregation, nor hear the sound of the preacher's voice, nor experience his or her pastoral presence, the value of this resource is limited.

Craddock, F., *Preaching*, 1985. *Biblical Preaching Journal* is published quarterly by Biblical Preaching Institute, 695 Craigs Creek Road, Versailles, KY 40383-8909. *Lectionary Homiletics* is published monthly by Lectionary Homiletics, Inc., 13541 East Boundary Road, Suite 113, Midlothian, VA 23112. *The Living Pulpit* is published quarterly by The Living Pulpit, Inc., 5000 Independence Avenue, Bronx, NY 10471. *Preaching* is published bimonthly by Preaching Resources, Inc., P.O. Box 7728, Louisville, KY 40257-0728. *Proclamation* is a quarterly publication by Fortress Press, Box 1209, Minneapolis, MN 55440-1209. *Pulpit Digest* is published bimonthly and *Pulpit Resource* is published quarterly, both by Logos Publications, Inc., P.O. Box 240, South St. Paul, MN 55075-0240.

RICHARD F. WARD

Revivals. Revivals are times of intense preaching and personal religious experience that usually center on conversion and renewal. While revivals are usually localized affairs, at times they have become more generalized and have been called "awakenings" because they have played a major role in cultural change. Though revivals have often been considered unexpected outpourings of divine grace, they have now become a regular and even scheduled part of evangelical church life.

Revivals in American History. While periods of religious renewal have occurred throughout the history of Christianity, revivals and revivalism (the system that promotes them) are most characteristic of evangelical Christianity since the eighteenth century. In America, evangelicalism grew out of the convergence of Continental Pietism and New England Puritanism and stressed the "new birth," holy living, and the need to evangelize others. Colonial churches experienced many "harvest times" when conversions increased membership and religious vitality surged. Usually these early revivals occurred without altering normal church activities or calling in a special preacher. In the 1730s and early 1740s, there was an unprecedented Great Awakening, which Jonathan Edwards* declared "a surprising work of God." Itinerants like George Whitefield* and Gilbert Tennent preached to thousands by ignoring parish boundaries and denominational labels. When they openly criticized some clergy for being indifferent to the awakening and unconverted themselves, many religious leaders fought back, condemning the spread of "enthusiasm" and the breakdown of ecclesiastical authority. Edwards admitted some excesses but argued that the awakening was an authentic work of God; he used theology (Calvinism) and philosophy (John Locke) to show the centrality of the affections in authentic Christian living (see Puritan Preaching).

The older Calvinism did not so easily survive the Second Great Awakening of the early nineteenth century. From orderly revivals at Yale and Princeton to raucous Kentucky camp meetings, American churches rebounded from the religious depression of the Revolutionary years. The Methodists and Baptists, who embraced the revival, quickly became America's largest denominations. Charles Grandison Finney,* the most famous revivalist of the era, preached an "arminianized Calvinism" that taught that anyone who wanted to could be saved. In 1835, he published Lectures on Revivals of Religion, a how-to manual in which he claimed that revivals were not divine miracles, but took place whenever people followed Bible-based procedures and prac-

tices. Thus believers could work revivals up as well as pray them down. Finney also developed controversial "new measures"—"protracted meetings" (i.e., services held nightly for two or three weeks), the anxious bench (located in the front, where people seeking salvation came for prayer and counsel), rather sophisticated advertising, gospel music used to heighten emotions, and previously unseen levels of organization and planning.

Not everyone approved. John Williamson Nevin (The Anxious Bench) and Horace Bushnell (Christian Nurture) challenged his methodology and view of conversion, but in the long run, more people copied than criticized Finney. Even Roman Catholics in the last two-thirds of the nineteenth century adapted Protestant revival practices. Popular preachers from the religious orders conducted one- or two-week "parish missions" to win back lapsed Irish and German immigrants. But Catholic converts did not come forward to the anxious bench. They went to the confessional, where they reaffirmed their baptismal vows and reconnected with the sacramental life of the church.

After Finney came hundreds of professional evangelists who traveled the country conducting revivals in local churches or seeking larger venues in towns or cities. Dwight L. Moody* was the best-known revivalist after the Civil War in what some historians have called the Third Great Awakening. A successful businessman before entering full-time YMCA work, Moody and his chorister Ira Sankey entered the world of professional revivalism in the 1870s. After successful revivals in Great Britain, the Moody-Sankey team returned home to concentrate on big cities, where they used more sophisticated organizing and financing techniques. Never a sensationalist, Moody tried to "love them in" by preaching homey and sentimental sermons that held out the hope of heaven more than the threat of the fires of hell.

Around World War I, America's best-known revivalist was Billy Sunday,* a former hard-drinking professional baseball player who entertained urban audiences with his athletic pulpit antics, slangy preaching style, and scathing but humorous attacks on liberals and evolutionists. The "Sunday Party" was revivalism's biggest bureaucracy, with "advance men," musicians, tabernacle builders, and an assortment of other specialists. He proved, at least for a while, that revivalism could compete with big-city amusements and distractions, though many people complained that Sunday's theology was anemic and that those converts who "hit the sawdust trail" in response to his invitation rarely turned into regular churchgoers.

From the mid-twentieth century on, Billy Graham* became America's—and the world's—leading evangelist. He continued the Moody-Sunday urban revival tradition of mass meetings but early on employed other means of getting the message across: radio, television, and even motion pictures. Starting in the 1950s, a Pentecostal faith-healing revival began, with people like Oral Roberts and Kathryn Kuhlman also utilizing television (*see* History of Preaching).

Revivals as Expected Religious Practice. Over the years, revivals have become standardized and quite predictable. In the early nineteenth century, the Methodists institutionalized the frontier camp meeting and made it a normal part of summertime church life. Many churches in the Holiness, Pentecostal, Baptist, and Church of Christ traditions made fall and spring revivals a regular part of their yearly schedules. By the 1990s, hundreds (maybe thousands) of professional revivalists still itinerate from church to church, putting on special meetings or local crusades. In fact, some denominations ordain revivalists to their work and publish how-to manuals for organizing, promoting, and conducting church-based revivals.

Because such meetings are so intentional and frequent, they contain very few real surprises. In many churches, the annual revival is considered the best time for the children of church members to make their own faith commitments and for church members to invite lapsed or unchurched neighbors, relatives, or acquaintances. Therefore, most people who attend revivals are already connected to churches in some way and consider themselves believers. As "insiders," they prepare carefully for these meetings; and those who attend almost always know what to expect. Revivals feature a tradition of singing, testifying, and preaching that creates, as historians of religion might say, a sacred time and place. Accordingly, one could argue that revivals are highly ritualized events that not only seek new converts but confirm the already-converted in their faith. Revivals strengthen the group's identity and at the same time add to its size. They also provide the permission and the context for powerful and expressive experiences that may seem inappropriate at other times. In short, revivals are where people can make initial commitments to Christ, rededicate their lives, re-establish life's priorities, or validate their own conversions by seeing them duplicated in others. These experiences vary enormously in intensity and long-term results. Some are highly emotional; others are not. Some have remarkable, transformational staying power; while others seem to diminish rapidly.

One of the most distinctive components of revivals is their preaching. Revival sermons are characterized by their fervor, straightforwardness, and persuasive appeal. Though they vary widely in style and their use of rhetoric, revivalists invariably must create in their hearers a sense of sinfulness and personal need, a desire for the offer of grace in the person and work of Jesus, and the resolve to receive it through an act of repentance and faith. As a result, revival preaching usually touches on some of the major themes of Christian theology: sin, forgiveness, grace, atonement, justification by faith, and the hope of eternal life. Revivalist preachers often use vivid and concrete imagery and employ stark contrasts: heaven and hell, salvation and loss, eternal life and eternal punishment. But mainly they preach to persuade, often by arousing intense emotions, including fear of the consequences of unbelief (*see* Evangelism).

Blumhofer, E., and R. Balmer, eds., *Modern Christian Revivals*, 1993. Butler, J., *Softly and Tenderly Jesus Is Calling*, 1991. Dolan, J. P., *Catholic Revivalism*, 1978. McLoughlin, W., *Revivals, Awakenings, and Reform*, 1978; and *Modern Revivalism*, 1959.
TIMOTHY P. WEBER

Rhetoric. The word *rhetoric* is often misconstrued because of pejorative use in contemporary contexts. News commentators often describe a speech that lacked substantive content as "mere rhetoric." In this usage, the implied definition of rhetoric is "insincere or grandiloquent language" used to confuse or mislead an audience (see "rhetoric" in *Webster's Ninth Collegiate Dictionary*). In colloquial speech, adjectives that precede *rhetoric* often color its general meaning: *fiery* rhetoric, *empty* rhetoric, *political* rhetoric, *foolish* rhetoric. Language is a dynamic symbol system; words gain meaning by their usage. Although *rhetoric* is frequently used pejoratively, its actual meaning transcends modern usage. Sound definitions of *rhetoric* include "the art, study, or skill of using language effectively and persuasively," "the art of speaking or writing effectively," and "skill in the effective use of speech." The Greek *rhema* (word) and *rhetor* (a teacher of speech) stem from the verb *eiro*, which means, "I say." *Rhetoric* stems from the Greek *rhetorike techne*, which is "the art of the rhetor or orator" (Corbett, 20).

The following article begins with an overview of rhetoric's roots. This survey is representative, not exhaustive. Then rhetoric's early influence on preaching is considered, followed by a more detailed discussion of rhetoric's later influence on preaching. The next section deals with the renaissance of rhetorical studies in the early twentieth century, followed by a look at movements taking place in contemporary rhetorical studies. The final part discusses preaching's continued debt to rhetoric. The weaving of the discussions of rhetoric and preaching is intentional to show how interrelated the two subjects are.

The Roots of Rhetoric. In the classical Greek period, rhetoric was understood as the oral art of persuasion, with its main function to train people adequately to defend themselves in courts of law. Rhetoric's province was to discover *what* needed to be said in a particular case and to prescribe *how* to say it. Aristotle (ca. 384–322 B.C.) in the *Rhetoric* defined rhetoric as "the faculty of discovering in the particular case what are the available means of persuasion" (I). He wrote that rhetoric was an art not limited to particular subject matter. If a subject lent itself to oral address, it resided in the purview of rhetoric. For him, rhetoric was a teachable discipline, easily systematized; thus, rhetoric could guide a speaker in the effective composition and delivery of a speech. However, Aristotle's *Rhetoric* has been characterized as descriptive and not prescriptive; that is, he described what he saw as effective devices in the persuasive speeches he witnessed more than he prescribed theories of rhetoric that had not been measured experientially. Aristotle was concerned with both the content of a speech and with the way its parts were arranged for persuasive effect. He was also, however, interested in the way the character of the speaker affected what the speaker said. He emphasized the speaker's knowledge of his or her audience and how audience emotions might be *ethically* aroused to effect communication and persuasion.

Unlike his teacher Plato, who argued that ideal rhetoric ground itself in philosophy, Aristotle saw rhetoric as the counterpart of dialectic. Plato's concerns reemerged at various times throughout rhetoric's history. Characteristic of his view was Peter Ramus's (1515–1572) division of rhetoric. He placed invention and organization under the rubric of philosophical inquiry and relegated style and delivery as subjects befitting rhetoric. Aristotle rightly argued that the discovery of truth (dialectic) and the discovery of the available means of persuasion (rhetoric) were not only compatible but were counterparts. Subsequent rhetoricians, such as Ernesto Grassi, also argue that rhetoric and philosophy are anything but diametrically opposed.

Later, Latin rhetoricians expanded Aristotle's foundation. Cicero (ca. 106–43 B.C.) wrote at least seven works on rhetoric. He broadened the scope of rhetoric by insisting that the effective orator was well schooled in a variety of subjects. He argued that the study of rhetoric was a major portion of a liberal education. The function of rhetoric, according to Cicero, was to persuade an audience to respond to truth that had been discovered by reason (Cicero, *De Inventione*). Like Aristotle, Cicero saw a connection between dialectic (the pursuit of truth through dialogic process, such as the Socratic method) and rhetoric. Cicero observed that some speakers surpassed others in their ability to effectively move an audience. This excelling was due to rhetorical skills the speaker had learned and developed.

Cicero was more systematic in his understanding of rhetoric than was Aristotle. By Cicero's time, five principles or canons of rhetoric were well established: invention, arrangement, style, memory, and delivery (Cicero, *De Inventione*). Cicero outlined a method by which a speaker should produce a speech: the speaker discovers what should be said (invention); the speaker arranges the speech in a particular order based on purposeful intention (arrangement); the speaker clothes thoughts with language (style); the speaker secures the speech in memory; and the speaker effectively delivers the speech (Cicero, *De Oratore*, I, 31). Cicero's writings strongly influenced nineteenth-century preaching in the United States as evidenced by John A. Broadus's* reliance in *A Treatise on the Preparation and Delivery of Sermons*. This homiletics text is a training manual in rhetorical skill applied to preaching.

Quintilian's (ca. 40–95 C.E.) work *Institutio Oratoria* represents a synthesis of the body of rhetorical study that preceded him. Like Cicero, he felt that the effective orator was a diligent student of liberal arts, one not afraid of hard and exhausting work. Quintilian's orator was a good person, speaking well. Like Cicero, he broadened the scope of rhetoric beyond persuasion to include instruction and giving pleasure.

Rhetoric's Early Influence on Preaching. Rhetoric's relationship with preaching has early roots. John Chrysostom* and Augustine* of Hippo, both trained rhetoricians and preachers, recognized an integral alliance between the two disciplines. Chrysostom studied rhetoric in preparation for a law career. As his clerical vocation developed, he saw the value of the power of effective speech for priests. This power could be developed by applying rules of rhetoric to the task of preaching. In his work *On the Priesthood*, Chrysostom argued that Christianity was being attacked on all sides by pagan views through the effective application of rhetorical skill. The church could counter such attacks because rhetorical skills should not only be relegated to the enemies of the church. However, he saw the use of rhetoric not only for defending the faith but for use in ministering to the difficulties that plagued the souls of people.

Augustine, having attended Latin schools of rhetoric, was heavily influenced by Cicero's works. Augustine himself became a teacher of rhetoric before he pursued his call to the service of the church. Many of his contemporaries disdained rhetoric because it emphasized style and because pagans used it to advance their arguments against Christianity. Augustine wondered why Christians did not employ the same deftness in rhetorical skill to defend the faith as pagans did to refute it. Augustine succinctly stated his position in *On Christian Doctrine*:

While the proponents of error know the art of winning an audience to good will, attention, and open mind, shall the proponents of truth remain ignorant? While the [sophist] states facts concisely, clearly, plausibly, shall the preacher state them so that they are tedious to hear, hard to understand, hard to believe? While the one attacks truth and insinuates falsehood by fallacious argument, shall the other have too little skill either to defend the true or refute the false? (IV, 2).

Augustine reclaimed the classical aim and definition of rhetoric and applied it to Christian purposes. Between A.D. 396 and 426 he wrote the four books of *De Doctrina Christiana*, the fourth of which could rightly be called the first handbook of Christian rhetoric. In it, he emphasized rhetoric as a means of persuading Christians to lead a holy and righteous life. Augustine's thesis declared that knowledge of truth alone did not ensure effective communication of the truth. He borrowed Cicero's categories of style but associated them exclusively with the literary styles of the Bible. In so doing, he created the church's first homiletic and set the canons of Christian rhetoric for more than a millennium.

Preaching Reclaims the Art of Rhetoric. The eighteenth century was characterized by intense intellectual fervor, marked by an avid interest in the classics. Empirical sciences flourished, and the study of human nature made its way onto the intellectual stage. Thinkers began asking questions about the origins and functions of language and how humans, from an anthropologic basis, were communicating beings. The stage was set for the revaluation of rhetoric as a tool for such studies.

The primary proponents of rhetoric during this period were the British clerics and rhetoricians George Campbell (1709–1796), Hugh Blair (1718–1800), and Richard Whately (1787–1863). The burgeoning psychological and philosophical ideas of the day greatly influenced their formulations of rhetoric. Being both rhetoricians and clerics, they understood rhetoric to be an effective tool for preparing Christian preachers in both the defense and presentation of the faith. They understood rhetoric's multidisciplinary nature as a means of communication. They recognized the relationships among rhetoric and literature, psychology, science, language studies, and theology. Though their knowledge of the social and behavioral sciences were naive compared to today's available awareness, their interest in these subjects shows how forward-looking they were in their rhetorical theories. Their approaches demonstrated an interest in the audience, which has carried into contemporary approaches to rhetorical theory.

Scholars identify George Campbell's *Philosophy of Rhetoric* as the most important treatise on rhetoric since the classical period. Relying on classical definitions, Campbell saw rhetoric as intentional or purposive discourse. He expanded the definition, though, to move beyond only a suasive end. He saw four aims of speaking: to enlighten the understanding, to please the imagination, to move the passions, or to influence the will. He also broadened the understanding of the *function* of rhetoric by noting an essential relationship among the speaker, the hearers, and the subject matter. This emphasis foreshadowed the work of twentieth-century rhetoricians, such as I. A. Richards and Kenneth Burke.* While the classical writers were unnerved when it came to discussions of the emotive effect of rhetoric, Campbell emphasized that rhetoric should engage the whole person—intellect and emotions.

Hugh Blair's *Lectures on Rhetoric and Belles Lettres* (1783) was widely used during the latter part of the eighteenth century in America for teaching public speaking. In this three-volume work, he discussed such subjects as taste, beauty, sublimity, a history of oratory, legal rhetoric, and rhetoric for the pulpit. With a rather circuitous tone, he defined rhetoric as "the Art of Speaking in such a manner as to attain the end for which we speak." Like Campbell, Blair felt that speakers, whether in the court of law or from the pulpit, should have some end in view: to inform, to amuse, to persuade are all within rhetoric's purview.

Richard Whately presented his rhetorical theory in four parts: (1) appeal to the reason or understanding, (2) appeal to the will, (3) style, and (4) delivery. Whately saw rhetoric as indelibly related to logic; argument more than anything else persuades.

During the nineteenth century in America, John Broadus wrote of the importance for preachers to use all the available ethical tools for preaching the gospel. For him, rhetoric was one important tool. Broadus relied heavily on Aristotle, Cicero, Quintilian, and Whately. In following Cicero's exhortation, Broadus beseeched, "All who preach eminently well . . . will be found, with scarcely an exception, to have labored much to acquire skill" (Broadus, 24). Such skill is the province of rhetoric adapted to preaching. Broadus' book, which for many years was used throughout the United States as a primary text for homiletics' classes in colleges and seminaries, challenged preachers to hone their rhetorical skills. For Broadus, rhetoric provided the basic tools necessary for preachers to discover what to say and how to say it. His homiletics class was as much a class in classical rhetoric as it was a course in preaching.

Phillips Brooks,* in his Yale lectures on preaching, sounded the same chords. When he called for "as eloquent a man as can be found or made," Brooks implied that there is no worthier goal than to become a more effective preacher of God's truth.

In this century, Ronald Sleeth taught both rhetoric and preaching. He intrinsically wed the two:

. . . the heroes and writers of the Bible were advocates. They were not sophists employing rhetorical skills for the sport of it. They had convictions, with a burden to convince others that what they believed was true and righteous. . . .

It is no wonder, then, that in every age, those who preach the gospel under Christ's commission . . . should seek the most effective way to communicate the Word so that those who hear might believe (*Persuasive Preaching*, 1956; 1981, v).

These homileticians believed that the methods of preaching, including theological inquiry (invention) can be taught and learned—hence, the weaving of rhetoric and preaching. Like rhetoric, preaching is an art, with principles—theological, philosophical, and practical—that can be learned. Rhetoric emphasizes the purposeful use of oral discourse with stress on intent and effect; such is also within the purview of preaching.

Early Twentieth-Century Rhetorical Studies. In the early 1920s, Cornell University established a seminar studying the rhetorical theories of Aristotle, Cicero, and Quintilian. This seminar pointed toward the renewed study of classical rhetoric in this century. A review of the indices of *The Quarterly Journal of Speech* reveals that numerous articles on rhetoric were written in the 1930s and 1940s. Mortimer Adler's *How to Read a Book* boosted interest within academic circles in the study of rhetoric. The contemporary rhetorical theories that developed during this time not only profited from this new-found interest in the ancients, but also built on psychology, semantics, motivational research, communication theory, and other behavioral sciences. Rhetoricians were eclectic in their interests, reminiscent of Cicero's admonition that orators be well educated in the liberal arts.

In 1936, I. A. Richards wrote *The Philosophy of Rhetoric*. Richards thought classical rhetoric with its emphasis on persuasion had serious limitations. To confine rhetoric to the persuasive aspects of language, he argued, was to neglect rhetoric's full scope. His target was primarily Richard Whately's design to confine rhetoric to argumentative discourse.

Richards preferred George Campbell's theory because of its concern for the psychology of the audience. Richards' interest was to determine how language *worked* to produce understanding. His definition of rhetoric reflects this concern: "Rhetoric . . . should be a study of misunderstanding and its remedies. We struggle all our days with misunderstandings, and no apology is required for any study which can prevent or remove them" (Richards, 31).

Kenneth Burke* displayed more reverence for classical rhetoric than did Richards. However, Burke also saw the possibility of extending the scope of rhetoric beyond persuasion. Persuasion theory emphasized deliberate design; Burke stressed the new rhetoric's interest in unconscious factors of appeal.

Like others writing at this time, Burke was heavily influenced by insights provided by philosophy of language, psychology, anthropology, and the behavioral sciences. The sociological aspects of language and its function in human communication processes probably influenced Burke more than any of the other factors (*see* Language, Theories of).

Movements in Contemporary Rhetorical Studies. Contemporary rhetorical studies have broadened the definition of rhetoric beyond analyses of persuasion and general theories of human communication. Contemporary definitions move rhetoric beyond seeing language as the mere medium for discursive interaction. While Greek and Latin rhetoric presupposed *spoken language*, and while the *belles lettres* movement of the eighteenth century predicated itself on *written language*, contemporary scholars of rhetoric see *purposive symbolic action* in such diverse subjects as art, architecture, creative dance, and modern music. The visual arts have become fertile ground for the study of rhetorical effect. Contemporary society, so profusely influenced by visual media, will be sorely misunderstood if rhetorical scholars fail to consider the rhetorical effects of the visual use of symbols on communicative processes.

Nevertheless, language and linguistic studies still form a major concern for contemporary rhetorical theorists. Burke and Richards grounded their theories in the study of language and the way humans construct language to make sense of their worlds. Burke viewed the uniqueness of humans as symbol-using animals who can talk about their world in both positive and negative terms. The linguistic ability to express in negative terms is found nowhere in nature; it is strictly a human construct. Burke also understood language as the primary medium for the expressing and forming of human attitudes. Humans understand their world and prove that understanding by the way they *name* things. The biblical story of Adam naming the animals is paradigmatic for Burke of the human process of making sense out of the world through *naming*. The ability to name one's reality is a rhetorical process.

The major rhetorical theories—in classical, modern, and contemporary times—are grounded in Western modes of thinking and communication, often dominated by male theorists and rhetors. Rhetorical studies are currently expanding and will continue to expand to consider woman rhetors, the role women have taken in forming rhetorical communities, the particular ways that women communicate that differ from traditional norms, and other questions that have been missed by male-dominated rhetorical studies. Feminist rhetoric is a major field of study that is quickly gaining recognition and appreciation among the academic community (*see* Feminist Preaching).

Gender issues are not the only direction that rhetorical studies are taking. Communication is culturally biased and controlled. For example, *persuasion* in the Aristotelian model would be considered brash to many Asian theorists. Asian rhetorical studies must differentiate between the various Asian cultures, realizing that Thailand is not China, and China is not Japan, and Japan is not Korea. Communication and rhetorical strategies in each of these cultures have had a long, indigenous history, perhaps even predating Aristotelian rhetorical strategies. Western critics have tended to view their rhetorical approaches and strategies as normative. Rhetorical studies in the future must recognize the distinctive features that make up rhetorical stances for a variety of rhetorical communities. Rhetorical theories, to truly represent cultural realities, must be sensitive to the particular communicative affinities represented in a particular culture's social norms. This sensitivity is necessary if one is studying the rhetoric of Asian, Spanish-American, African, or any other culture.

In the United States, African-American rhetoric is another area of study that represents a burgeoning area of potential. African-American rhetoric is grounded not in the Western tradition but in cultural roots with a rich history of its own. An example of a rhetorical technique often used in African-American rhetoric is seen in the worship of African-American Christians. Old Testament metaphors of exodus and exile are often used to represent the situation faced by contemporary congregations. The rhetorician intentionally creates an identification between his or her hearers and the issues faced by the biblical characters or peoples in their historical situations. The rhetorical strategy is based not on syllogisms but on the narrative movement of the story.

Movements in contemporary theories must continue this broadening of understanding that rhetoric, in general, is not gender or culture specific but also that specific rhetorical theories are not a one-size-fits-all enterprise. Rhetoric is concerned with the effective use of discourse. It is interested in the way materials—the subject matter—are organized for clear and persuasive communication.

Preaching's Continued Debt to Rhetoric. Renewed interest in rhetoric and rhetorical studies is growing among homileticians. This attention is spawned by the widening scope of rhetorical studies into areas of audience analysis, linguistics, gender-based communication, cultural biases in communication, as well as

the more traditional purviews of speech studies. Biblical scholars' use of rhetorical-critical methods for interpreting texts also provides impetus for preaching scholars to pursue rhetoric as an area of study. This influence is reciprocal as biblical scholars have acknowledged the debt homileticians have paid to rhetoric.

"What a good rhetorician can do," writes David Buttrick, "is to tell us how speakers can speak and people hear in any generation. No wonder that century after century, preachers have learned from rhetoricians" (Loscalzo, 10). Rhetoric reminds preachers and those who study preaching that certain interrelated questions must continually be asked if preaching is to be effective: What must be said? How do we discover what must be said? What determines the parameters of what must be said? These representative questions, which imply biblical inquiry and historical, theological, and philosophical reflection, can be answered, for preaching, rhetorically. Aristotle would have linked such questions to dialectic and the invention step of rhetoric. Contemporary rhetoricians look to the questions to formulate rhetorical strategies that adequately address the situations in which such inquiries are framed and to which such questions are addressed. In other words, the beginning of a rhetorical strategy is discovering what needs to be said.

Once one has chosen what to say, the question becomes, In what order should it be said? For example, many preachers give away too much too soon in sermons. Rhetorical awareness reminds preachers to consider such things as suspense, surprise, irony, expectations, and fulfilling of expectations. In other words, deciding what needs to be said first before moving to what needs to be said second—strategic decisions that must not be haphazardly chosen—is rhetorically important. Conversations move in a stream-of-consciousness fashion, often rather unintentionally. Because preaching has some goal in mind, preachers must decide what they will say before they move on to say something else. Unlike viewing a painting, in which the viewer has the freedom to look at the whole, speech communication comes to hearers in a serial medium; that is, one word follows another, one thought follows another, one image follows another, and so on. Though conversational *style** should often be employed while preaching, the "sermonic conversation" is not unintentional but strategic. Words said, ideas framed, images evoked, and thoughts considered all create an impact on preaching's hearers. Effective preachers remain aware of that impact and anticipate it. Such is rhetorical awareness. In 2 Samuel 12, Nathan keenly anticipated his story's effect on King David. It is a grave understatement to say that Nathan was aware that the parable he told to the king would have some impact. Nathan's action was not only intentional; it is apparent from the passage of scripture that he awaited the outcome. Nathan's approach demonstrates the intentionality of rhetorical strategies being described here.

Some preachers might chafe at the idea of being so intentional about determining the goal of a sermon; letting the Spirit move, for some, seems more theologically correct. While that might be an honorable goal, the damage to preaching is often not reparable. Boring sermons, lack of direction, and the sense that the preacher is wasting the hearer's time are often the results of preaching that lacks the dimensions of intentional movement, design, and arrangement, all aspects that rhetoric helps to define, order, and enhance.

Rhetoric directs preaching also on how to say what needs to be said. In the classical rubric, this aspect is known as *style*. Words portray images; language creates worlds. The right word can open doors; the wrong word can build walls of resistance that might never be removed. Finding the right words to invoke the right images, to elicit desired responses, to remove imbedded biases, to unlock hidden fears, is making use of rhetorical skill. Kenneth Burke drew attention to this issue in his quip: "The rich person's prayer

is not the poor person's prayer." Being aware of idioms within a rhetorical community, attempting to evoke meaningful images for both males and females, and taking the particular preaching event into consideration are signs of rhetorical awareness and responsiveness.

Preaching also looks to rhetoric for help in the delivery* of sermons. Delivery, which is the one canon that everyone has always considered within the realm of rhetoric, must not be neglected. A preacher can have the most profound insights into theology, the most imaginative approaches to interpreting the Bible, the keenest sense of artistry in composing the sermon, yet the sermon will never take flight if it is poorly delivered. Traditional rhetorical issues concerning delivery include proper word pronunciation, rate of speech, tension and pitch of voice, volume, body tone, and gestures. Contemporary rhetorical issues about delivery include these as well as matters of staging (whether or not a pulpit is used), the use of microphones, presence, eye contact, and timing. For example, contemporary preaching relies heavily on the use of stories—biblical and modern. Timing is crucial to the storyteller's art. Miss an appropriate pause or misphrase a story's punch line, and the rhetorical effect of the story can be lost. The delivery of the sermon is as rhetorically significant as the discovery of what needs to be said.

Harry Emerson Fosdick* described the preacher's task, perhaps unknowingly, rhetorically:

The preacher's business is not merely to discuss repentance, but to persuade people to repent; not merely to debate the meaning and possibility of Christian faith, but to produce Christian faith in the lives of his listeners; not merely to talk about the available power of God to bring victory over trouble and temptation, but to send people out from their worship on Sunday with victory in their possession. A preacher's task is to create in his congregation the thing he is talking about.

(Harry Emerson Fosdick, *The Living of These Days*, 1956, 99)

The preaching task is an intentional one. The strategies preachers choose are rhetorical. Preachers will move to recognize that the analytical and logical structures so often associated with Aristotelian rhetoric will be modified when categories of women's rhetoric and multicultural rhetorical issues are recognized and codified. This broadening is refreshing as rhetoricians become more inclusive in their understanding of how language works to create communities. The five classical canons of rhetoric need not be abandoned but expanded. Preaching owes a debt to rhetoric; rhetoric's influence on preaching will continue (*see* History of Preaching).

Aristotle, *The Rhetoric*, trans. L. Cooper, 1932. **Augustine,** *On Christian Doctrine*, trans. D. W. Robertson, Jr., 1958. **Broadus, J.,** *A Treatise on the Preparation and Delivery of Sermons*, 1870. **Cicero,** *De Inventione*, trans. H. M. Hubbell, 1949. **Cicero,** *On Oratory and Orators*, trans. J. S. Watson, 1970. **Corbett, E.,** *Classical Rhetoric and the Modern Student*, 1965, 1990. **Foss, S., K. A. Foss,** and **R. Trapp,** *Contemporary Perspectives on Rhetoric*, 2d ed., 1991. **Loscalzo, C. A.,** *Preaching Sermons That Connect: Effective Communication Through Identification*, 1992. **Richards, I. A.,** *The Philosophy of Rhetoric*, 1936.   CRAIG A. LOSCALZO

The Rhineland Mystics. The term "Rhineland Mystics" is applied to the preaching activity among the Nuns' Convents and extends to the Beguines and lay bourgeois circles, carried out by some outstanding members of the Dominican* order during the fourteenth century. Their activity centered around Cologne and Strasbourg. During the thirteenth century, the obligation to supervise the growing number of nunneries in Germany had been imposed on the Dominican friars. The movement included three major preachers and writers, Meister Eckhart (ca. 1260–1329), Johannes Tauler (1300–1361), and Heinrich Suso (ca. 1295–1366), along with a host of others of lesser rank. Their numerous sermons and tractates presupposes a large circle of readers far beyond conventuals.

In the early years of the Dominican order, meditation and contemplation were synonymous with the study of theology, and the friars' contemplative life was not something to be sought as a goal in its own right but as a means to become better preachers. Accordingly, the term "mysticism" should not be taken in the modern, rather narrow sense. A more fruitful angle is to use it in a much wider sense as circumscribing the development of the theology within the Dominican order prompted by the needs of the German nuns for religious instruction in the vernacular language. This development had been anticipated in the preceding century by Cistercian nuns and by Beguines in Flemish and German areas, whose spirituality reflected the contemporary growing urban culture. Of fundamental importance was the incipient recording of spiritual experience in the vernacular, supplying a vocabulary for spiritual experiences until then confined to the Latin language within monastic circles.

Meister Eckhart spent his entire life within the Dominican order. His activity as preacher was concentrated in 1313–26, years Eckhart spent as visitor and spiritual director in Strasbourg and Cologne. Eckhart's writings fall into two groups according to the language in which they are written. They grew out of his duties as a learned teacher within his order and his pastoral care among nuns and ordinary people. In his own words, Eckhart's intention with his Latin writings was to "explain the teachings of the holy Christian faith and of the Scriptures with the help of the principles of philosophy." These writings include two sermonic expositions of passages from Ecclesiasticus preached at the Provincial chapter. Eckhart's vernacular writings encompassed mainly homiletic material—nearly one hundred sermons, not to mention several tracts dominated by pastoral themes. Among the latter ones, the tract *Of the*

Nobleman, centered on Luke 19:12, stands out as the most concise summary of Eckhart's pattern of humanity's way to unity with God. To what extent the written form of these German sermons is attributable to Eckhart himself has been disputed. Many of the sermons were probably copies by nuns, and some of them were circulated in lay circles. However, this does not rule out the possibility that Eckhart had a hand in transferring the spoken words into written prose.

During the last years of his life, his career was disturbed by the proceedings undertaken against him by the archbishop of Cologne with assistance from theologians from the Franciscan order. The case against Eckhart's alleged deviation from orthodoxy did not reach a decision until after his death, and the question whether he was a heretic has been disputed since. From a homiletic point of view, the process against Eckhart is interesting as an illustration of the tension between the linguistic idioms of *dogma* and *sermo.* Eckhart's sermons are the results of a twofold effort to translate Scholastic phraseology into spiritual direction and the language of the Christian-Platonic tradition into a German vernacular that lacked abstract words and was not adapted for the use of a scholar. Eckhart's German works are therefore outstanding illustrations of linguistic innovation. By adapting Latin terms, creating new German ones, or by adding new meaning to already existing words, Eckhart became the creator of a vernacular prose scarcely to be found elsewhere in Europe at the beginning of the fourteenth century.

In one of his German sermons, Eckhart did recapitulate his main homiletical themes in four items:

When I preach, I am careful to speak about detachment (*Abgeschiedenheit*) and that a person should become free of self and of all things. Secondly, that one should be reformed (*wiedereingebildet*) in the simple good that is God. Thirdly, that one should think of the great nobility (*Adel*) which God has

placed in the soul, so that a person may thereby come to God in a wonderful way. Fourthly, concerning the purity (*Lauterkeit*) of divine nature—there is such brilliance in it that it is expressible.

Additional topics in Eckhart's sermons are the spark of the soul, the abyss of the soul, and resignation (*Gelassenheit*).

In Eckhart's sermons the theme of detachment emerged as an application of the monastic theme of evangelical poverty to the interior life, reflecting how fourteenth-century spirituality was challenging the marked borderline between monastic and lay secular life. Detachment amounts to the freedom for which the whole creature is yearning and which is an affirmation of the unity inherent in the creaturely status of human beings.

Both creation—described in neoplatonic terms—and incarnation are existentially applied in Eckhart's sermons as paradigms for the unifying coming of God to humanity. The narrative of the Savior's birth in Bethlehem is applied tropologically when God's coming is expressed as God giving birth to God in the soul of a person. When describing this re-creation, Eckhart deliberately steered clear of extraordinary spiritual experiences. Instead, he emphasized the loving presence of God through the events of ordinary experience, including even the vestiges of God in creation and in the church's Book, sacraments, and ordinances.

For Eckhart the "nobility of the soul" and "detachment" come to the same thing. Only in the soul's emptiness is God present as fullness in the "abyss." This is the setting for Eckhart's teaching of the "spark" (Funke). But detachment even includes the willing acceptance of God's absence in God's presence. In this way the human being comes closest to the divine nature's own "purity," of which natural man is an image.

Johannes Tauler.   To a certain extent, Eckhart's preaching may be characterised as God-centered, even if he in his sermons eagerly admonishes his listeners to imitate both creation and incarnation in their lives. With *Johannes Tauler,* the first impression when reading his sermons is of a heavier pervasion of christocentric themes; or to put it in Tauler's own words: "One can never go beyond the image of our Lord Jesus Christ."

Born at the beginning of the fourteenth century, Tauler entered the Dominican Order at the early age of fifteen. During the 1330s, he was active as preacher in and around Strasbourg. Some years he spent in Basel, and he traveled to the Netherlands, where he probably became acquainted with Jan van Ruysbroeck. He had close contacts with lay circles around Strasbourg. Perhaps these "friends of God" are the originators of the widely circulated belief that the learned doctor Tauler had been converted through the directions of a spiritually gifted layman.

Tauler defended Eckhart and tried to prevent his listeners from misunderstanding Eckhart's teachings. Perhaps Tauler's marked christocentric bias could be taken as a hermeneutical key even for Eckhart's sermons, the former making explicit what is more implicit in the latter, namely how the christological pattern forms the framework within which the theory of spiritual growth is enfolded.

As a preacher, Tauler has been characterized as more attuned to time, place, and to the hearer's concrete earthly existence. As for the theme of detachment, Tauler's sermonic method consists of vividly describing the course of this life as a place where one suffers all kinds of temptations, but in and through this muddle, God still works in a mysterious way.

Heinrich Suso's life ran its course primarily in Constance, although he was trained as a lector at the Dominicans' house of theology in Cologne. For the last thirty years of his life, his work was dedicated to pastoral care, a task that brought him to Switzerland, Alsace, and the Rhineland. Suso collected and edited his writings in the so-called *Musterbuch,* comprising treatises, letters, and an autobiography in addition to sermons. In his autobiography, his preaching and coun-

seling activity is interpreted in mystical terms as an abandonment or *Gelassenheit.* He gave up the confinement of his cloister in order to devote himself to a pastoral care in which the whole world was to be his parish.

Suso's sermons have been characterized as more consciously literary than both Eckhart's and Tauler's. He is the troubadour among the Rhineland Mystics. It could also be said that Suso as a preacher moves closer to the point where the preacher makes himself superfluous. He even extended the genre of the sermon to the point where it crosses the border into literature.

Succeeding generations, however, did not think of Suso's literary skill as superfluous. Among the works collected in the *Musterbuch,* the *Book of Eternal Wisdom* became most popular during the late Middle Ages.

Eckhart, M., *The Essential Sermons, Commentaries, Treatises and Defenses,* Classics of Western Spirituality, 1981. **Kieckhefer, R.,** *Unquiet Souls: Fourteenth-Century Saints and Their Religious Milieu,* 1984. **Tauler, J.,** *Sermons,* Classics of Western Spirituality, 1987.   JAN SCHUMACHER

Robertson, Frederick William

(1816–1853) The story of Frederick William Robertson is one of the most remarkable in the history of preaching. All but unknown during his life, his influence upon preaching grew after his death until he would be called "the most influential preacher in the English-speaking world" (Blackwood, ix). Such a tribute would have astounded Robertson, who died a sad and early death.

Born in London to a military family, Robertson sought a military career himself. His devout father had urged him toward ministry, but Robertson demurred: "Anything but that; I am not fit for it" (Robertson 1964, 3). After a brief unsuccessful fling at law, he yielded and entered Oxford in 1837 to study theology. He was an able student, but preferred the quiet of books to the noise of debate.

The English church was entering a time of theological storm. German philosophy and biblical criticism fueled conflicts between liberals and conservatives. Robertson moved away from his own evangelicalism because he thought the movement had degenerated into a kind of scholasticism. Nor did he accept the high church views of the Tractarians. He stood between them and apart from them. As a result, he would be attacked for the rest of his life by both sides.

Ordained in 1840, he first served as curate among the poor of Winchester, then as curate among the elite of Cheltenham. His health, never good, frequently failed him, and he had to take long periods of rest. During this time, he also married and had three children, one of whom died at birth. In 1847 he became rector of Trinity Chapel in Brighton where, in six short years, he established a homiletical reputation that would long outlive him. Brighton was a resort town where the grand and well-to-do existed next to the poor and needy. All manner of folk soon found their way to hear Robertson: "Lady Byron and other members of the literary class, the aristocracy, the servants, the working men, the young, the old, the agnostics, the devout—all thrilled at his message, though all did not agree with his views" (Fant and Pinson, IV, 365).

Besides the Sunday morning sermons, it was also Robertson's custom to give "expository lectures" on Sunday afternoons. These lectures attracted a large following and engendered much controversy. He began with the book of 1 Samuel. As he addressed the political nature of the text, including the intrigue of the Davidic court, similarities between the biblical events and the upheaval in Europe in 1848 were noticed, and Robertson was accused of being a radical, a revolutionary, a socialist. He denied any political implications in his work but did say that he believed in progress.

After Samuel, he worked his way through Acts, then Genesis, and finally 1 and 2 Corinthians. On June 5, 1853, he gave his last lecture on the text, "Finally, brethren, farewell" (2 Cor. 13:11), and his voice was never afterward heard from the pulpit of Trinity Chapel (Robertson 1883, x). In his physical weakness he sought a curate to help him, but an unfortunate disagreement with his bishop precluded that, and Robertson went home to die.

With his death began Robertson's greater ministry. His sermons were collected and published and have remained in print for over a hundred years. His lectures and letters were also collected by Stopford Brooke, who added an impressive biography to the collection. Soon preachers on both sides of the Atlantic were marveling at the words of this obscure preacher. Such Americans as Luccock, Bowie, Fosdick,* and Blackwood counted Robertson their mentor in preaching.

What made Robertson's preaching so impressive, so useful? First, his preaching was distinctively biblical. He was well grounded in biblical languages. He understood the historic landscape of scripture and approached the hermeneutical task with fervor. "He brought to the scriptures talents of scholarship, imagination, 'logic on fire,' and a sensitive awareness that in these pages God was speaking to his condition" (Blackwood, 186).

Second, Robertson had gifts of language that he used to good benefit. He was a great reader. He loved history, biography, and especially poetry. He lived with Dante, Shakespeare, Milton, Coleridge, Wordsworth, and Tennyson. He lectured working people on the importance of poetry, telling them that poetry's wonders were just as much for them as for men of leisure: poetry was "of the people and for the people" (Robertson 1906, 13). The poet's eye and ear influenced Robertson's preaching as well. His hearers remarked about his spiritual presence in the pulpit, his voice that was quiet but laden with feeling, his rhythmic pace, and his beautiful imagery.

The broad appeal of Robertson's sermons may also rest in the broadness of his spirit. He worked with and loved the poor. He worked with and loved the well-to-do. As he once said, "My tastes are with the aristocrats; my principles are with the mob" (Blackwood, 184). He aligned himself with no theological or political party, and, though attacked for indecisiveness, this was consistent with his theology and homiletic. He outlined his principles as follows:

First. The establishment of positive truth, instead of the negative destruction of error. Secondly. That truth is made up of two opposite propositions, and not found in a *via media* between the two. Thirdly. That spiritual truth is discerned by the spirit, instead of intellectually in propositions; and therefore, Truth should be taught suggestively, not dogmatically (Brooke, 315).

Of the first principle, Robertson's son would comment years later that this was the reason so many turned to his father's work: It was constructive and not destructive.

The second principle formed the basis of Robertson's seminal method: the two-point or bipolar sermon. He was ahead of his time in looking for truth in the dialectic or polar structures of the text. He was more interested in encountering the tensions within a text than in trying to harmonize them. When most preachers of his day were laying dogmatic templates upon texts, his method anticipated the direction of biblical scholarship by more than a century.

His third principle is at the forefront of homiletical discussion in the 1990s. His "suggestive" approach is the foundation upon which inductive* and narrative* preaching have built. It is astonishing to realize that these principles were penned 150 years ago. Robertson has had great influence because his biblical, linguistic, and homiletical methods have been more at home in the twentieth century than during his own time, because his winsome character and pastoral concern are timelessly evocative, and for one additional reason: Most of his brief ministry

was performed in pain. His understanding of the Christ whose sufferings set us free was wrought of his own experience. His sympathy with those who suffer was real and genuine, not secondhand.

Where many saw confusion, Robertson saw truth. Where many saw suffering, Robertson saw Christ. The marvelous "failed" preacher of Brighton continues to guide the church and its preachers.

Blackwood, J. R., *The Soul of Frederick W. Robertson,* 1947. **Brooke, S.,** ed., *Life, Letters, Lectures and Addresses of Frederick W. Robertson,* 1870. **Fant, C. and W. Pinson,** "Frederick W. Robertson," in *Twenty Centuries of Great Preaching,* Vol. 4, 1971. **Robertson, F. W.,** *The Preaching of Frederick W. Robertson,* ed. G. Doan, Jr., 1964; *Sermons Preached at Brighton,* 1883; *Expository Lectures on St. Paul's Epistles to the Corinthians,* 1883; and *Sermons,* 1899.

JOSEPH R. JETER, JR.

ON THE LONELINESS OF CHRIST
Frederick Robertson

There is no thought connected with the life of Christ more touching . . . than the solitariness in which He lived. Those who understood Him best only half understood Him. Those who knew Him best scarcely could be said to know Him. On this occasion the disciples thought—Now we do understand, now we believe. The lonely spirit answered, "Do ye now believe? Behold the hour cometh that ye shall be scattered, every man to his own, and shall leave me alone." Very impressive is this trait in His history. He was in the world alone. . . . But He added, "The Father is with me."

Be sure that often when you say, "I am alone," the real correcting thought is this, "Alone, but the Father is with me; therefore I can live that lonely conviction." . . . The practical result and inference of all this is a very simple, but a very deep one— the deepest of existence. Let life be a life of faith. Do not go timorously about, inquiring what others think, what others believe, and what others say. It seems the easiest, it is the most difficult thing in life, to do this—believe in God. God is near you.

Throw yourself fearlessly upon Him. Trembling mortal, there is an unknown might within your soul which will wake when you command it. The day may come when all that is human, man and woman, will fall off from you, as they did from Him. Let His strength be yours. Be independent of them all now. The Father is with you. Look to Him, and He will save you.

From "The Loneliness of Christ," in *Sermons Preached at Brighton* (New York: Dutton, 1883), 170, 176–77.

Sacraments and Preaching.

In many Christian traditions, the relationship of sacraments, rites, and ordinances to preaching is juridical, a matter of church law or government. Also, in many Christian denominations, the relationship between word and sacrament is a theological as well as a practical issue. We shall first look at these two subjects.

Church Law and Proclamation. In most denominations and church traditions there is a constitutional relationship between the celebration of the sacraments and the preaching of the word. In virtually all Protestant denominations, it is mandated that preaching shall accompany—usually precede—the observance of celebration of either Baptism or the Lord's Supper.

The order of the liturgy in the Roman Catholic Church, in place since the Second Vatican Council, mandates that the scriptures shall be proclaimed in homily or sermon at every eucharistic service and strongly suggests that baptisms take place at a regular liturgical assembly with the preaching of the word. Preaching is not mandated with reference to the other five sacraments, unless they are observed as a part of a eucharistic liturgy (*see* Vatican II). The same rules basically apply within churches of Eastern and Oriental Orthodox traditions.

A form of words is a necessary accompaniment of any sacrament or sacramental act. The Words of Institution, usually from 1 Cor. 11:23–26, or possibly from one of the synoptic Gospels, are used in relation to the celebration of the Lord's Supper in virtually all Christian groups. Similar words, usually a warrant or institution formula from scripture, are prescribed for every sacrament authorized to be celebrated by any denomination.

While church rules do not ordinarily mandate that a sermon or homily be preached on these passages, nonetheless it has become the custom, especially in those churches that celebrate the Lord's Supper infrequently, to have the sermon based on a passage of scripture that pertains to the Lord's Supper, when the supper is celebrated. This same close correspondence between the celebration observed and the sermon preached is ordinarily true for all sacramental acts and for the ordinances of the church. A study of such usage may be approached from a juridical point of view by studying church manuals or from a study of the practices of each denomination or church tradition.

Word-sacrament may be considered from a *theological* and *biblical* point of view. There is theological and practical consensus that the Word of God preached entails a response. The Word of God demands proclamation and obedience. Some churches name the response "sacrament"; others name it "ordinance." In either case, there is concurrence that actualization is a necessary part of all proclamation, whether expressed as altar call, a call to the Lord's Table, intercessions, deeds of love and mercy, mission, evangelism, or outreach.

This article deals with the complimentarity between the word preached and the word celebrated in the sacraments and ordinances of the church. First, we survey the history of these relationships, beginning with the biblical basis for proclamation in both word and act. Then we will deal with theological issues arising out of the Word-Sacrament relationship. In this article, sacrament is defined as the visible and experiential manifestation of divine communication, most commonly in Baptism and the Lord's Supper, though not confined to these.

History

The Biblical and Early Church Period. In the pre-Constantinian period there was a unity of word and sacrament. In the writings of the early church it is difficult to differentiate between word and sacrament. Sacrament had not yet been defined. This unitive understanding of the Word of God comes from the Hebrew understanding of *dabar* (word), which means not simply speech as the English language understands speech but a deed, a happening, an event. When God spoke at creation, creation took place. The word itself is active, achieving that for which God intends it (Isa. 55:10–11). This understanding pervades the entire Old Testament and carries over into the New, where Luke equates Jesus' word with the Word of God (Luke 5:1; 4:32; 8:11) and where Paul says that the power of preaching is the power of God (Rom. 1:16 and 1 Cor. 1:25).

In the New Testament, Jesus' word and work are seen together. In the story of the healing of the paralytic (Matt. 9:2–8), the words "stand up, take your bed and go to your home" must be seen in the context of Jesus' preceding words. Jesus' miracles are the empirical accompaniments of Jesus' words (*see* Jesus as Preacher). This same principle can be seen throughout the book of Acts. If we utilize the post-sixteenth-century definition of sacrament as "the outward and visible sign of inward and invisible grace," we observe that the aural and the visible always stand together, with neither word nor sacrament of higher rank. The New Testament makes clear that hearing that does not lead to sacramental, visible change in real life is not full encounter with God.

Justin Martyr (ca. 150 C.E.), in providing an account of worship in the early church, says, "After the reader has finished [reading the scriptures], the one who is presiding addresses us and exhorts us to imitate the examples of virtue we have heard" (*1 Apol.*, 67). In the Latin, the two verbs are *admonitio*, interpretation of texts, and *adhortatio*, application to concrete life situations.

For Irenaeus (115–190), making known the mystery of the gospel equally included proclamation and celebration. God's word is more than mere utterance or intellectual discourse. It is rather God's self–communication that is efficacious and performative. The early church clearly understood this unity of word and action, a complimentarity of what later came to be distinguished as word and sacrament.

Origen* (185–253) differentiated between the *logos* or *sermo* and the *homilia* or *tractatus*. The *sermo* followed the shape of classical rhetoric in convincing and persuading. The *homilia* or *tractatus*, on the other hand, arose out of the total liturgical action. It flowed directly from the scripture and was a free and popular exposition *and* application of scripture and liturgical action. This rationale accounts for the contemporary preference among Roman Catholics for the word "homily"* instead of "sermon."*

The Age of Christendom. A change in understanding can be identified after the Edict of Milan in 313. With Augustine* (353–430), one begins to observe the development of a distinction between word and sacrament, though Augustine speaks of the sacraments as "visible words," with a very lively complimentarity. This period sees the rise of thematic and doctrinal preaching that may have taken place apart from the liturgical assembly. There was a formalizing of the catechizing function apart from worship.

In the twelfth century, the Franciscan* Order was established as a lay movement, dedicated to the proclamation of the gospel. The permission to preach, without concomitant permission to celebrate the sacrament, granted by Pope Innocent III in 1209, marked the final dissolution of the unity between the word preached and the word celebrated as sacrament in the gathered community.

The Reformation. In the Reformation period, there was an explosion of preaching. At the same time, there were uniform

attempts by the major reformers to reunite preaching and sacraments. All
maintained that preaching shall accompany the Lord's Supper, and most were
successful in establishing this practice.
They were generally not successful in
their attempts at a complete unification
of word and sacrament. Protestant
churches emphasized preaching and
came to be known as churches of the
word, while the Roman Catholic Church
was known as the church of the sacrament.

Since the Second Vatican Council, the
Roman Catholic Church has been moving
progressively to reintegrate preaching
into Sunday worship, and the churches of
the Reformation are moving toward more
frequent communion, with some striving
for the celebration of the Lord's Supper
whenever the word is preached (see History of Preaching).

Theological Issues regarding Word and Sacrament

Dabar: Word-Act. The Word of God*
is performative—it accomplishes what it
proclaims. It is revelatory in providing
knowledge, and it is powerful. The Word
of God preached leads to the enactment
of sacraments, which are signs of and
lead to changed lives.

The Incarnation. The Christian faith
as an incarnational faith demands that
proclamation become embodied. The
aim of proclamation is to present the
story of the gospel so that both teller and
hearer experience the presence of God
and experience (and appropriate) the
power of God. The aim is change of life,
transformation into the body of Christ. In
the worship of the church, the sacraments and ordinances are occasions for
the demonstration of the enfleshment of
the gospel. There the word is acted out,
made visible.

Sermon and Demanded Response.
Some say that the two major sacraments,
Baptism and the Lord's Supper, contain
within them all themes of theology and of
the faith and can provide illustration for
every sermon. It is also said that the end
of the sacraments is not to be realized

only within the church building but in
daily life. Sacraments, like incarnation,
speak of the materiality of Christian life
and labor. Thus, sacraments, ordinances,
and visible, observable Christian (sacramental) responses to the gospel are demanded by the Word of God. The unity of
the word proclaimed and the word demonstrated is modeled within the service of
worship itself when sacraments and ordinances are celebrated. Both sermon and
sacrament must provide entrance into,
not escape from, earthly reality.

*The Preacher as Proclaimer and Ac-
tor.* Although it is not a popular concept
among clergy in our time, the concepts
being dealt with here presume that the
one who proclaims the Word of God will
also be the bearer of a spirituality* (or
piety or lifestyle) that manifests the
power of the word. This is modeled in
most church orders by assigning the tasks
of preaching and/or presiding at sacramental celebration to the ordained minister or priest. The minister carries responsibility for being a leader in community
enactment as well. All who are baptized
and who are members of the priesthood
of believers, witness to the gospel by assisting in its proclamation and through
their sacramental life in the world (see
Liturgical Preaching).

Baillie, D. M., *The Theology of the Sacraments,* 1957. **Cooke, B.,** *Ministry to Word
and Sacraments,* 1976. **Schwarz, H.,** *Divine
Communication: Word and Sacrament in
Biblical, Historical and Contemporary Perspective,* 1985.   ARLO D. DUBA

Sangster, William Edwin. (1900–
1960) Will Sangster came from good
working-class stock in the city of London
and was proud of it all his life. His parents
were members of the Church of England,
but when he was ten he joined Radnor
Street mission, loosely attached to
Wesley's Chapel. There he found his
home and along with it his conversion
and his call to ministry. His experience
teaching the poor children of the neigh-

borhood in the mission helped him relate to persons throughout his ministry. At seventeen he became a local preacher. Even then he was rigorous, bold, and completely confident.

On his eighteenth birthday he was called up and joined the Queen's Royal Regiment. Rising rapidly in rank, he was offered a commission as education officer, but then the offer was hastily withdrawn. A man who treated religion seriously and was a teetotaler might spoil the atmosphere of the officers' mess hall.

This disappointment was perhaps the most bitter of his life. He longed for the opportunity to continue his studies. He was accepted for the Methodist ministry and reported to Handsworth College, still in uniform, as soon as his army days ended.

Sangster moved to Richmond for four years where he learned to preach to his fellow students. His first sermon was not a success. He had vigor, warm appeal, and deep earnestness, but his delivery was spoiled by a cockney accent so strong it seemed comic.

He would not have his message marred by a laughable dialect. He was so humiliated by his listeners' response that he enlisted a fellow student to tutor his speech.

His personal gifts grew—his determination, zest for hard work, stewardship of time, and winsome personality all contributing to his gift for preaching. This was his first method of evangelism* as he took his message outside his church to preach, as earlier evangelicals did—in the open air, in the fields, on the docks—anywhere people congregated.

At Aintree, he launched his popular Sunday Evening services. He read every word of each sermon to his wife and struck any idea or phrase or word she did not consider absolutely simple and clear. There is a curious parallel here with Wesley, who read his sermons to a simple old servant of his and changed any word she did not understand. Many today believe a ten-minute sermon is sure to attract a congregation by its brevity, but

Sangster usually preached more than forty minutes.

What made Sangster such a tremendous figure? First, his personality. He was a born leader. He swayed not by autocracy but by sheer compelling power. He did not demand the will of others; in response to his unspoken command, they gave up their wills. Second, Sangster was a tireless, energetic worker. Third, he was passionately interested in people. He preached with urgency and warm, direct, personal appeal. Fourth, like his Master and like Wesley, "he went about doing good" as a person, as a pastor. Fifth, he long sought sanctity, and there was much of it in him. Not once in his life as a minister of the gospel did he utter a word of criticism of another minister.

The essence of his power in the pulpit lay in prayer. But this power found its expression in his passion, his unforgettable delivery, and his dramatic gestures. Pastoral work fueled his sermons. His sixteen years at Westminster Chapel included five years as overseer of the air-raid shelters under his 3,000-seat preaching hall and in other blitzed streets of London. Above all, Sangster loved to preach.

Passion and urgency marked all his ministry. His greatest ability in preaching was his power of illustration.* This was no happy knack; it was the result of many years of careful preparation. His strong, human examples were vital to his popular pulpit acclaim on both sides of the Atlantic.

He was elected president of British Methodism, then became General Secretary of Home Missions. He initiated the Prayer Cell Movement. He died on Wesley Day, 1960, prematurely spent by progressive muscular atrophy. Throughout his ministry, he wrote a number of books, including works on preaching, evangelism, and devotional life.

His preaching was personal, positive, warm, pastoral. His examples propelled his sermons. His urgent illustrations replaced the traditional "should," "ought," and "must" exhortations of many ministers. His sense of concern always made him a caring pastor—compassionate, emotional, personal, and direct. He shared his work and his preaching.

Sangster, W. E., The Craft of Sermon Illustration, 1950; The Craft of Sermon Construction, 1951; Power in Preaching, 1958.

                                    RALPH L. LEWIS

Savonarola, Girolamo.

(1452–1498) The reformer-prophet of Renaissance Florence was born in Ferrara, Italy. At 23, he entered the Convent of San Domenico, of the strict observance of the Order of Friars Preachers, in Bologna. Upon completion of his philosophical and theological studies at the Dominican university in 1482, he was assigned as Reader in San Marco in Florence. He earned the respect of his fellow friars for his scriptural learning, but his preaching style was unpleasing, and his voice and Ferrarese accent sounded harsh to Florentine ears. Convinced that he had a preaching vocation, Savonarola persisted in his efforts to find his public voice. In 1484, he experienced a "sudden illumination": The church had to be scourged— and soon. He cited scripture as the basis of his certainty, although current widespread notions that 1484 was the beginning of a new religious era may also have played a part. Preaching in the Tuscan town of San Gimignano, Savonarola revealed his new message, expanding it to include the need for repentance and church reform before the last days.

After an absence of some three years, Savonarola was reassigned to Florence in 1490 upon the request of Lorenzo de' Medici and, through him, of the philosopher-prince, Pico della Mirandola. Pico had been impressed with the friar's piety and learning and wanted him as a spiritual counselor. With a new confidence in his powers, Savonarola launched into an exposition of the book of Revelation, elaborating his theme of the impending Last Days, filling his sermons with such terrifying images as the sword of the Lord suspended over Florence. His style included direct appeals to God, mock debates with members of his audience, and suspenseful pauses for rest. All of this conveyed intensity and spontaneity, in favorable contrast to the formal intricacies of the scholastic sermon and the rhetorical polish of current humanistic preaching. He also struck a response chord when he began to criticize tyrants who exploited the people with taxes and the rich who spent their money on palaces and prostitutes. Critics called him the "preacher of the desperate" and labeled his followers piagnoni, or snivellers, a name that stuck.

In the fall of 1494, King Charles VIII of France led a huge army into Italy bent on the conquest of the Kingdom of Naples. Piero de' Medici, who had succeeded his father as unofficial ruler of Florence, surrendered to Charles's demands for control of Florentine border fortresses and ports, which led the Florentines to expel Piero and his family. In their perplexity and terror, the Florentines turned to Savonarola, who, having warned them of the coming of a New Cyrus to scourge Italy, now more than ever appeared to be God's prophet. The friar held two interviews with the king, after which the French left the city unharmed, enhancing Savonarola's status as Florence's savior. This success also inspired him to a new prophetic vision. Preaching almost daily, he announced the divine plan as it unfolded in a series of scriptural images. Florence must begin the work of religious and moral reform: as the New Jerusalem, her spiritual leadership would radiate through the world; Charles VIII was God's instrument for scourging the church, conquering the Infidel, and reducing the world to a single sheepfold under one shepherd. For its part, Florence must have civic peace (no revenge against supporters of the Medici) and establish a Great Council in which the middling level of male citizens would legislate and choose their magistrates.

With the adoption of this "Venetian model," Savonarola was hailed as the father of the new popular republic. He now pressed his religious program, which largely consisted of puritanical legislation and the organization of the laity, especially of the city's youth, under the direction of the San Marco friars. Pagan books and objects of art were destroyed in public bonfires and processions, and unwelcome speech was punished by torture and execution. Certain lay confraternities became nuclei of Savonarolan-style puritanism and devotion, while female Dominican houses came under San Marco's direction. A fundamental reform was the curtailment of the patronage system by which ecclesiastical benefices were exchanged for money or political influence rather than clerical merit or need.

Having alienated Rome by his refusal to bring Florence into an anti-French alliance and by disregarding papal directives, Savonarola was ordered to stop preaching. At first he adhered to the ban, then defied the papal order. He was excommunicated, and Florence was threatened with an interdict if it continued to harbor him. This compounded his domestic difficulties. Despite his continued assurances, the French did not fulfill their prophetic role, while plague and severe economic depression mocked his promise that Florence would be "richer, more powerful, more glorious than ever." At this point, Savonarola was challenged to prove his divinely sanctioned mission by walking through fire. His lieutenant, Fra Domenico of Pescia, impetuously accepted on his behalf. For this most medieval of trials, the two sides met in the central square of Florence on April 8, 1498, before a vast, excited crowd; but hours of squabbling over procedure and a downpour persuaded the Signoria to suspend the ordeal. The onus of the canceled miracle seem to fall on Savonarola. A mob attacked San Marco. The Signoria intervened to arrest and imprison Fra Girolamo, Fra Domenico, and Fra Silvestro

Maruffi. Under torture, Savonarola confessed that he had faked his visions and falsified his prophecy. With the acquiescence of a papal commission, the three friars were burned at the stake on May 23, 1498.

Savonarola's influence survived his death despite the Medici's return in 1512. In 1527, the Medici were again driven out and a new revolution proclaimed the republic and the New Jerusalem. With the return of the Medici with Imperial backing in 1530, the fate of the Piagnoni movement was sealed, although the image of Savonarola as apostle of liberty and spiritual leader survived to surface among liberal and Catholic nationalists in the Risorgimento and again among Christian Democrats after World War II. Abroad, Savonarola's writings inspired Catholic evangelicals and Spanish contemplatives, while Protestant reformers hailed him as a forerunner, more for his bold criticism of the Roman Church than for any major departure from doctrinal orthodoxy (*see* History of Preaching).

Cordero, F., *Savonarola*, 4 vols., 1986–88. **Ridolfi, R.,** *The Life of Girolamo Savonarola*, 1959. **Weinstein, D.,** *Savonarola and Florence: Prophecy and Patriotism in the Renaissance*, 1970.   DONALD WEINSTEIN

Scherer, Paul Ehrman.

(1892–1969) Paul Scherer was educated at the College of Charleston in South Carolina and at the Lutheran Theological Seminary in Philadelphia, where he later became an instructor in homiletics. From 1920 to 1945, he was pastor of Holy Trinity Lutheran Church in New York City. In 1945, he became Brown Professor of Homiletics, Union Theological Seminary, in New York City, and remained there until his retirement in 1960. Following his retirement, he served as visiting professor at Union Theological Seminary in Richmond, Virginia, and at Princeton Theological Seminary.

A crucial element of Scherer's legacy was his concern with relating homiletical practice to theological understanding, a matter that led him to full participation in the theological movement begun by Karl Barth.* Acclaimed for his elegant and poetic style, he took it as a major task to restore theological integrity to the American pulpit, by which he meant a reinterpretation for his time of classic Christian faith and doctrine. The development of his legacy and the implementation of his self-appointed task may be explored in *For We Have This Treasure*, his Lyman Beecher lectures in 1943, and *The Word God Sent*, his last published work (1965). The Beecher lectures are more typical of books on preaching in their attention to the details of sermon preparation, their exposition of biblical texts, with relatively less attention to theological debate and issues. His later volume presents the summary of a career devoted to a theological interpretation of preaching and a detailed analysis of how Christian preaching so grounded should appropriately engage twentieth-century culture. It is divided into two sections: one devoted to theory, the other to sermons governed by the theory.

Although he barely referred to Harry Emerson Fosdick* in his published work, Scherer carried on a polemic against the "life-situation" preaching of which Fosdick was a master and which he made popular. Fosdick's method, Scherer feared, could lead preachers to do no more than "find out what people want, or think they must hear, and give it to them . . . where in a thousand pulpits the gospel is reduced to a plaintive warning, with a vague promise, held together with a bit of advice." Such preaching might give "religious" answers to "secular" questions—an impossible correlation—if in fact "the word of God lays hold on the stuff of human existence and reshapes it." Preaching, therefore, could be understood not as an attempt to answer or deal directly with human needs, crises, questions but only as God's "relentless moving in upon our lives," bringing new understandings, new questions, new needs, and affecting its own issues. The preacher

should not seek thus to be "relevant"; rather, the word declares its own relevance with its inherent power. It is, he insisted, unnecessary "to sneak up on the congregation, and slip in an apostle when nobody is looking. Use the inductive method.* Maneuver everybody into a corner—and who among them will not resent being cornered?—when there is nothing else for them to do but to turn to the fourteenth chapter of John or to the tenth of Isaiah" (Scherer 1965, 7, 11, 18, 19). Sermons faithful to the gospel do not answer human troubles so much as they communicate the troubling presence of God.

Christian sermons, for example, interpret texts that are beautiful, filled with angels, carols, mother, the little child, but they have a "beauty that demands something of us." Easter sermons are properly aimed, not just at assuaging the fear of death but at the manifestations of greater dimensions of life calling us to great tasks and visions:

> Mark says that the women "went out quickly, and fled from the sepulchre; . . . for they were afraid" (Mark 16:8). One can understand very simply why he wrote that. You would have been afraid too. But I keep asking myself, "Afraid of what? Afraid of death, or afraid of life?" (Scherer 1965, 86).

The impact of Scherer's interpretation of the gospel and the principles that he exercised in its communication in sermons may be sensed most immediately in their introductions. From the very first, interest in the gospel message being proclaimed is assumed. Here the very presence of God begins to make its way into human consciousness. He incisively describes his own methodology in an analysis of the preaching of a beloved Union Seminary colleague, Reinhold Niebuhr:* "From the very start both the preacher and his hearers are inescapably involved. There is no dependence on any tawdry storytelling for the arousing of interest . . . he pays his congregations the compliment of believing that matters of obviously profound and vital concern need no more at the outset than to be announced" (Kegley and Bretall 1956, 323).

For Paul Scherer "the Word in search of words" always involved God as subject, not as object. The shape and structure of sermons should give expression and illumination to the presence of God. *Word*, theologically and commonly understood, partakes of communion, personal address, or as Martin Buber, another contemporary, would have had it: an I-thou encounter (*see* Word of God). Lutheran sensibilities to faith as personal trust in God infuse the entire Scherer corpus. Indeed Niebuhr is gently chided over a resurrection sermon "in which the thought never really breaks through from the realm of idea" into the classic Johannine heralding of "that heard . . . seen . . . looked upon . . . touched . . . that . . . we proclaim also to you" (1 John 1:1–3) (Kegley and Bretall 1956, 330).

A more adequate understanding of how this preacher communicated God's personal address in the sermon requires a memory of Paul Scherer's presence itself: expressed in his deep melodious voice, delivering carefully crafted proclamations with hardly a glance at a manuscript, resounding for his hearers the depths and mystery of God.

Kegley, C. and R. Bretall, eds., *Reinhold Niebuhr, His Religious, Social, and Political Thought*, 1956. **Scherer, P. E.,** *For We Have This Treasure*, 1944; *The Word God Sent*, 1965. JOHN M. STAPLETON

NO EASY GOSPEL
Paul Ehrman Scherer

All along in Job, from the drawn-out bitterness of his heart, through the lurid flashes of blasphemy on his lips, you can watch that kind of faith being shaped by those great compassionate hands. And it hurt, and the hurt was an offense to Job. You can fairly see him losing his neat little God and coming up before that Other who *himself would put the questions* without bothering too much to answer any, except by being there and being himself. . . .

That isn't loveless power, and it isn't powerless love. It's something more disturbing than either of them. It's the power in love—in love with us!—that spares neither itself nor its object, like a potter with his wheel, day after day, turning out a human soul.

God knows it isn't an easy gospel. I think we have never heard it until we've been offended by it. If by nothing else, then by its divine effrontery. Over against the vast mysteries of life it stands. Have you ever looked into the face of them? Thousands upon thousands of years back, millions of them, and other thousands—or millions—to come: and you here in the vastness of such a universe, touching the surface of that stream as with a swallow's wing! Over against the dark mysteries of life, only the love of Christ. Over against the ceaseless rebuttals of the world, only the power of one who keeps saying, "Behold, I stand at the door, and knock. If any man will open the door"—You do it of course at your peril! There's never any knowing. He may deny you peace to give you glory.

From *The Word God Sent* (New York: Harper & Row, 1965), 176–77.

Schleiermacher, Friedrich D. E.

(1768–1834) Often called the "father of modern theology," Schleiermacher was also one of the leading preachers of his day in the Evangelical Church of the Prussian Union. Born of a long line of clergymen on both his mother's and his father's sides, Schleiermacher received his early education among the Moravian Pietists, first at their school in Niesky and later at the seminary in Barby. He continued his studies at the University of Halle in 1787. After serving as court preacher to the family of Count Dohna in Schlobitten (1790–1793), he took his first pastorate in Landsberg. Later, he became the Reformed pastor at the Charité hospital in Berlin (1796–1801), pastor of a church in Stolp, and professor of theology and university preacher at Halle University (1804–1806). He spent the majority of his career, however, as the Reformed pastor of Trinity Church, Berlin (1809–1834), and professor of theology in the city's new university.

Schleiermacher received public attention with the publication of his first book, *On Religion: Speeches to Its Cultured Despisers* (1799), in which he presents himself as a "preacher" to the cultured elite of Prussia. Already in this work, he reveals much of what would become his mature views on homiletics, although they receive more explicit attention in his *Brief Outline on the Study of Theology* (1811, 2d ed., 1830), *The Christian Faith* (1821–22, 2d ed., 1830–31), and the posthumously published lectures on *Practical Theology* (1850).

Schleiermacher understood the task of preaching in the context of his views on religious language. There are, he argued, three kinds of religious speech: the poetic, the rhetorical, and the descriptively didactic, and these roughly correspond to scripture, preaching, and theology, respectively. Poetic speech is a presentation of the religious affections that spring immediately from a moment of exaltation, enthusiasm, or inspiration. Rhetorical speech is representational and seeks to stir the religious affections of others; it is purely stimulative. The descriptively didactic form is the most abstract, as it seeks to describe with the greatest possible precision what is meant by the first-order language (poetic and rhetorical) of the faith (*see* Language, Theories of). Since Schleiermacher took preaching to be rhetorical language, he could rule out certain types of sermons that would have been common in his day. Enlightenment preaching, for example, which took its task to be the moral education of the congregation, was not adequate in his eyes since it failed to understand the representational character of preaching. Similarly, the dogmatic sermons of Protestant orthodoxy, laden as they were with technical theological terms, did not rightly distinguish rhetorical and descriptively didactic speech. Preaching, Schleiermacher believed, must take the form of testi-

mony to one's own experience with the Redeemer and the word of scripture, and it must seek to incite that experience in others. In fact, following in the tradition of Calvin's* sacramental understanding of preaching, Schleiermacher saw the sermon as the locus for Christ's work of reconciliation. An effective sermon is an epiphany: an appearance of Christ in the community of faith.

Schleiermacher's reflections on preaching, however, ranged beyond these prolegomena on religious language. True preaching, he maintained, is addressed to the community of faith, and as such it presupposes a genuine interest on the part of the congregation.* It is not the purpose of preaching to spark conversion experiences; rather, preaching is for the edification or upbuilding of faith already present in the congregation. Sound preaching, he insisted, must be exegetical: that is, it must be evidently based upon a certain passage of scripture. It should also conform to the confessional tradition of the preacher's church. Finally, sermons must be adapted to the needs and abilities of the audience they address. There is no such thing as a generically good sermon: in preaching, the relationship between persons is the prism through which the testimony of faith is refracted. Preaching is an intensely personal act; it involves the personalities of the preacher and the hearers alike.

Schleiermacher believed firmly in the distinction between an oral and a written style. He did not write out his sermons before delivering them but worked from very sketchy outlines. The ten volumes of sermons in his collected works were either composed by him specifically for publication or were taken down by scribes who attended his church. His custom was to preach serially through books of the Bible at the early service and to preach topical sermons on readings from the lectionary at the main service. Schleiermacher's own preaching is difficult to characterize in a few lines. Perhaps what is most evident is his attempt subtly to shape the theological consciousness of his hearers. Throughout the sermons, he takes up difficult theological topics—election, resurrection, justification, to name but a few—and in decidedly nontheological language, he grapples with them along with his congregation. During the time of the Napoleonic wars, Schleiermacher was famous for his patriotic preaching. He also preached a series of sermons on the Christian household that came to be widely circulated in Germany for many years. Perhaps most peculiar, given his Reformed heritage, was his decided dislike for the Old Testament. Out of the thousands of published sermons, fewer than thirty treat an Old Testament text, and most of these are on Psalms and Proverbs.

Contemporary accounts suggest that Schleiermacher was an exceptionally charismatic preacher who attracted a wide following among his fellow Berliners. His funeral procession was attended by some 20,000 mourners, most of whom would have known him as preacher. His own sermons, as well as his homiletic theory, are important texts for present-day preachers. They display keen theological sophistication communicated with deceptive simplicity.

Gerrish, B. A., *A Prince of the Church: Schleiermacher and the Beginnings of Modern Theology*, 1984. Redeker, M., *Schleiermacher's Life and Thought*, 1973. Schleiermacher, F., *Selected Sermons of Schleiermacher*, trans. M. F. Wilson, 1890; *Servant of the Word: Selected Sermons of Friedrich Schleiermacher*, trans. and ed. D. De Vries, 1987.   DAWN DE VRIES

THE LIGHT OF CHRIST
Friedrich Schleiermacher
It is not in vain that scripture compares the Word of God, in its nature and effects, to light. The sun's light shines down upon us pure and colorless; but it breaks forth from earthly objects only in a variety of colors, and all of them contribute to the beauty of our earth. Where these colors stand next to one another in their natural arrangement, and sparkle and play upon

one another, there we see the rainbow—the arch of peace—resplendent in its perfect beauty. Only when we reunite the various broken rays is pure and colorless light again restored. So it is with the Word of God. It has shone upon earth through the Son of God, pure in its heavenly splendor. But in every person it becomes a unique light, breaking forth in an individual color. The beauty of Christ's church consists in the fact that, in the fellowship of believers, all these colors are harmoniously united, all the diverse human views and representations of the one salvation gently flow together. That is what it means to seek the truth in love. And when it finally comes about that each understands others, and they him, the purity of the heavenly light is completely restored through this confluence of all the variety.

From "Christ in the Temple," in *Servant of the Word: Selected Sermons of Friedrich Schleiermacher*, trans. and ed. D. De Vries (Philadelphia: Fortress Press, 1987), 127.

Robert H. Schuller.

(1926–) In *The Varieties of Religious Experience*, William James wrote that "The advance of liberalism . . . in Christianity . . . may fairly be called a victory of healthy-mindedness within the church over the morbidness with which the old hell-fire theology was more harmoniously related" (James, 89). James wrote in 1902, but he might well have been describing the remarkable ministry of Robert H. Schuller, the advocate of possibility-thinking based on a theology of self-esteem. One important difference is that Schuller would not describe himself as a liberal, but as an evangelical within a mainline Protestant denomination, the Reformed Church in America (RCA). More to the point, Schuller defines himself as "one who communicates spiritual reality to the unchurched who . . . are not at all prepared to listen to 'someone with God-talk' "(Schuller, 12). Unlike many evangelicals, however, he eschews talk of sin and strongly criticizes fellow preachers for emphasizing sin and guilt in "scolding sermons from angry pulpits" (Schuller, 113). Instead, his worship leadership and preaching are carefully constructed to build "positive pride" and enhance individual dignity, self-worth, self-respect, and self-esteem, which he believes to be "the deepest of all human needs" (Schuller, 34).

Whether such themes address universal needs or not, they do have particular affinity with persons living in a culture of abundance, as has been true of the message of other advocates of "healthy-minded religion"—what more recently has been called "supply-side spirituality" (Delattre, 84ff.)—from Ralph Waldo Emerson to Norman Vincent Peale,* from various New Thought movements to New Age spirituality. These persons and movements emphasize a positive view of human nature and a way of life that is affirming, optimistic, and confident, often combined with a view of America as a special place. Schuller inhabits this tradition, melding it with traditional Christian themes.

Schuller's religion of healthy-mindedness may seem out of character for one born into an Iowa farm family of Dutch immigrant background and staunch members of the RCA. Growing up during the Great Depression, Schuller was nurtured on the doctrines of John Calvin.* A graduate of his denomination's Hope College and Western Theological Seminary, Schuller produced for his senior thesis a 285-page scriptural and topical index of Calvin's *Institutes*. While Calvinist orthodoxy may have permeated his formative experiences, Schuller has said that the seeds of possibility-thinking were sowed early in his life in a resolve to surmount the harshness of the Depression (Voskuil, 7).

Following seminary graduation in 1950, Schuller served a pastorate in Riverdale, Illinois, for four and a half years, when a call from the RCA Classis of California to organize a new congregation in Garden Grove drew him to that rapidly growing area. There he found few RCA transplants around whom to build a church; there were, however, large numbers of other newcomers, many with no church affiliation.

The development of the congregation progressed from services at a drive-in theater, where Schuller preached from the roof of the refreshment stand, to formal organization of the Garden Grove Community Church in 1958, and purchase of property on which a church building was erected. Along the way, Schuller was aided by endorsements and a personal appearance by Norman Vincent Peale, Schuller's immensely popular fellow RCA minister, whose book, *The Power of Positive Thinking*, was a national best seller and who has had an obvious influence on Schuller's own espousal of possibility-thinking. Schuller continued his drive-in theater ministry while also conducting services in the new building.

In 1961, the congregation constructed new facilities, designed so that worshipers could be inside the sanctuary or remain in their cars or on benches outside. Schuller was visible to those outside through a massive section of a glass wall that swung open to give a clear view of the pulpit. The congregation and its ministries of worship, education, counseling, and community outreach grew rapidly and were soon housed in a multistoried Tower of Hope, containing offices, meeting rooms, and a Chapel in the Sky, topped by a ninety-foot cross.

The most recent stage of church building was completed in 1980 with the dedication of the Crystal Cathedral, a spectacular glass-paned structure built in the shape of a four-pointed star and seating almost 3,000 people with room for hundreds more outside, who worship in their cars or on benches in a parklike space. Birds flutter and chirp in live trees around the inside walls of the sanctuary. A huge indoor fountain can be turned off as the service begins.

In addition to the many ministries undertaken on-site at the church, Schuller preaches to millions more on a nationally syndicated television* program, "The

Hour of Power," begun in the late 1960s. He also conducts regular seminars for pastors and lay leaders through the Robert Schuller Institute for Successful Church Leadership, and he has been a principal force in the formation of Churches United in Global Mission, a coalition of large congregations from across the denominational spectrum that supports various missionary activities, generally bypassing traditional denominational mission boards.

Schuller's approach to preaching, especially at the several morning services of the Crystal Cathedral, is decisively influenced by his view of himself as a "pre-evangelist" to the unchurched who have been turned off by traditional worship and sermons. "I am," he told one interviewer, "something like a show barker who cries out to the non-churched, 'come in here, there's something good inside for you'" (Shoemaker, 354). Once inside, they hear Schuller proclaim his gospel of possibility-thinking in sermons that are unerringly upbeat and positive. Sermons are oriented to hearers' need for self-worth, self-respect, and self-esteem and should, he believes, never address controversial issues. The latter strategy he defends with the argument that preaching is one-way conversation and that controversial social or political issues should be addressed where dialogue and debate are possible.

The sermons themselves are loosely based on a scriptural text whose main function is as a platform to launch his positive message. Messages are simple to grasp and easy to remember because they are cloaked in alliteration, slogans, and formulaic "catch-phrases" that serve as mnemonics: "inch by inch, everything's a cinch"; "there is no gain without pain"; "it takes guts to leave the ruts"; "turn your scars into stars." In a televised sermon (January 2, 1994), Schuller tells of being stopped in an airport by a man who recited the three points of a sermon that Schuller had preached several years earlier: "A commitment must be made, a plan must be laid, a price must be paid."

That formula, the man reported, had changed his life. In addition to the various mnemonic devices, the sermons are replete with stories, often of well-known individuals whose personal successes illustrate the power of possibility thinking and a healthy self-image. Many of these individuals join Schuller in the pulpit prior to the sermon and give their personal testimonies during an informal conversation with Schuller. These stories and those that Schuller tells in his preaching aim, he said in an interview about his preaching, at inspiring his hearers with the witness to personal experiences that come from the heart and not from the head (*Wittenburg Door*, June–July 1975).

Schuller's preaching style is dramatic. He gestures frequently and smiles almost constantly. His voice ranges from whispers to booming affirmations. During his television broadcasts, he may hold in view his latest book or some other object that is offered as a gift to those who contribute to his ministry.

Criticisms of Schuller's theology and ministry abound, and many seem justified. They include lack of depth and variety in his almost one-track message of possibility-thinking; his near total inattention to sin, especially its institutional and systemic dimensions; his refusal to address in sermons serious public moral concerns that are an offense to the gospel; his inordinate emphasis on success, especially wealth, which often seems for him to be more a contributor to self-esteem than its byproduct; and his tendency at times to identify the Christian way with the American way.

Schuller has answered many of these criticisms both in interviews and in his book *Self-Esteem: The New Reformation*, his most complete statement of his theology and ministry strategy. His answers often reveal a theological depth and ethical sensitivity that are not evident in his preaching or in many of his other books. Furthermore, his church's program, as Schuller and several of his critics have noted, extends considerably beyond the upbeat, noncontroversial Sunday morning services, inviting seekers and members to participate in serious Bible study, discussions of theology and ethical issues, and outreach in the community. Thus, one must look beneath the surface to these more substantive themes and programs to get a more balanced view of Schuller's ministry. At the same time, however, it seems fair to observe that the "body language of his ministry," as one commentator puts it (Voskuil, 143), is unlikely to lead many of his hearers beneath the surface of his upbeat message to engage the deeper truths of a gospel whose good news of resurrection and new possibilities comes only by way of the cross.

These criticisms notwithstanding, Schuller is an influential contributor to religious life and culture in the United States. Not only have his insights and techniques of church leadership been widely acclaimed, even by his critics (Barr, 424–27), but his particular brand of the "religion of healthy-mindedness," combined with themes from his evangelical heritage, has attracted a large following, especially among those seeking a spirituality attuned to a culture of abundance.

Barr, B., "Finding the Good at Garden Grove," The Christian Century, May 4, 1977, 424–27. Delattre, R. A., "Supply-Side Spirituality," in R. A. Sherrill, Religion and the Life of the Nation, 1990. Editors, The Wittenburg Door, June–July 1975, 11–13. James, W., The Varieties of Religious Experience, 1902. Schuller, R. H., Self-Esteem: The New Reformation, 1982. Shoemaker, D. E., "Schuller Shooting," Theology Today 31:4, 350–55. Voskuil, D. A., Mountains Into Goldmines: Robert Schuller and the Gospel of Success, 1983.   JACKSON W. CARROLL

Sermon. A sermon is an oral interpretation of scripture, usually in the context of worship. Sermons are interpretations of scripture. Communities of faith employ and acknowledge other forms of edifying discourse, but a sermon properly understood interprets a sacred text for the life of a community and its members.

The interpretation may be direct and explicit or implicit, may begin with the text or begin with a situation, but some conversation between contemporary concerns and scripture is included in every sermon.

Sermons are oral literature, whether the text for the sermon is written out or not. Sermons happen in the preaching rather than in the writing. Usually they are occasional, intended to provide insight for a particular people at a particular time. Though sermons may be published, anthologized, or circulated, such uses are secondary to the fundamental job of the sermon, which is to speak a direct, immediate, and timely word.

Because scripture has many forms and functions and because congregations have many needs and interests, sermons will have a variety of functions and a variety of forms. Building in part on work by H. Grady Davis,* this article seeks to classify sermons according to their functions and their forms (see Form). Scripture itself suggests a variety of functions for faithful speech, and the genres of scripture may further suggest some appropriate forms for the sermon (Davis, 98–138).

The Functions of Sermons

*Sermons may be kerygma, proclamation.** In the world of the New Testament, the kerygma was often the message proclaimed by a messenger, and behind much of the New Testament we find evidence of preaching whose major function is to herald the good news of what God has done in Jesus Christ—especially in Jesus' cross and resurrection (Acts 2:14–36; 3:12–26 and the understanding of preaching behind 1 Cor. 2:1–5). The purpose of such preaching is to call people to the decision of faith, whether for the first time or in a renewal of intention and commitment.

*Sermons may be didache, teaching.** Much of the material of Hebrew scripture and of the New Testament consists in instruction. Some of that instruction is doctrinal, dogmatic: In what does right faith consist? Some of that instruction is more directly related to questions of right conduct for people in covenant relationship to God: How are the faithful to live? The legal material of the Pentateuch provides instructions in fidelity as do the Sermon on the Mount in Matthew's Gospel and the Sermon on the Plain in Luke's Gospel. It is likely that every sermon will include some instruction—about the biblical text in its context if nothing else. The purpose of some sermons, however, will be primarily to inform the congregation in matters of faith and practice.

Sermons may be paraklesis. In the New Testament *parakaleo* can mean either "I exhort" or "I comfort." The exhortations of the Pauline epistles include both the urgent plea with Christians to live out their salvation in hope and love and the promise that it is in fact possible for them to do so. The exhortation to be faithful is itself comforting in its call to genuine fidelity. The comfort of God's grace and the guidance of the Spirit constrains toward a life of greater courage and compassion. Some sermons will have as their intent comfort and encouragement. Other sermons will have as their purpose encouragement and persuasion—not to believe some new thing or follow some new demand—but to live out what is already believed and understood.

Sermons may be anamnesis, remembrance. Paul begins his discussion of the Lord's Supper in 1 Corinthians with the call of his readers to recall what they already know, the awesome and saving story of the night of the Lord's betrayal (*see* Liturgical Preaching; Sacraments and Preaching). Much of the Pentateuchal discourse and much of the book of Psalms consists in the rhetoric of recall, to re-present the story of God's saving goodness in such a way that the listeners affirm that goodness as a present reality in their own lives. The purpose of sermons that function as *anamnesis* is to strengthen the congregation's or believer's sense of identity—defined, strengthened, and shaped by the memories embodied in text and tradition.

Sermons may be makarism, bless-ing. They may delight in God's own goodness and in the divine grace poured out on the faithful. Psalm 103 pronounces blessing upon God: "Bless the Lord, O My soul, and all that is within me, bless his holy name" (Ps. 103:1). The Sermon on the Mount begins with Jesus' announcement of blessing for those who follow him faithfully: "Blessed are the poor in spirit, for theirs is the kingdom of heaven" (Matt. 5:3). The element of celebration in much African-American preaching lays hold of the biblical delight in blessing God and receiving God's blessing. The purpose of sermons whose function is blessing is to inspire gratitude and delight.

Sermons may be sophia, wisdom. Biblical books like Proverbs in the Hebrew Bible and the Epistle of James in the New Testament point people to the orders of God's creation. They appeal to common sense: to a sense of how things go in the ordinary way of the world. To a shared sense of values and perceptions within a faithful community. Sermons that address social and personal problems often explicitly or implicitly are preached from a perspective influenced by biblical wisdom material. The purpose of such sermons is to inspire attention to God's working in the world and to commend prudential behavior that serves the sanctity of the self, the neighbor, the community: "All things are lawful for me, but not all things are beneficial" (1 Cor. 6:12); "Knowledge puffs up, but love builds up" (1 Cor. 8:1b).

Sermons may be propheteia, prophecy. For both Old and New Testaments, prophecy apparently often included experiences of direct revelation from the Spirit of God. Because preaching in the context of synagogue and church is understood as interpretation of the biblical text, the element of direct inspiration will have less play in most contemporary faith traditions than it did in biblical prophecy. Like biblical prophecy, however, contemporary preaching may attend to God's movement in human history and look toward God's judgment for good or ill as the future toward which history moves. The purposes of such prophetic sermons is not primarily to induce guilt or to stir controversy but to place human responsibility within the framework of the divine commitment to justice and compassion. Often prophetic sermons move to a call to repentance and renewal, for preacher and congregation alike.

Sermons may be parabole, parable. Like Jesus' parables,* they may use metaphor or simile drawn from common experience to show forth the uncommon dealings of God with humankind. Like the longer stories told by Nathan in 2 Sam. 12:1–6 or by Jesus in Luke 10:25–37 and 15:11–32, they may invite listeners to place themselves with biblical characters to let their lives be shaped by the conflicts and hopes revealed or hidden in the biblical plots.

The Form of Sermons

To a large extent, the form of the sermon may be determined by the sermon's purpose and by the kind of text that the sermon interprets. Again, H. Grady Davis has provided a suggestive beginning in his description of various sermonic forms (Davis, 139–62).

A sermon may tell a story. Sometimes the sermon will retell the biblical story on which it is based. Interpretation will always be part of the retelling, or the preacher would simply read the story again (and of course the way the story was read would also be interpretation). Sometimes the story is retold in a contemporary setting. (Clarence Jordan's *Cotton Patch Gospels* can be read as such a retelling, an extended sermon on the canonical Gospels.) Sometimes the sermon retells the story in biblical garb but with questions, implications, and applications drawn from the concerns of the congregation into the telling itself. Sometimes a story sermon will consist of stories related to the biblical text that do not simply repeat it, paraphrase it, or elaborate on it but that provide a kind of foil, a lens for hearing the biblical text. (Fred B. Craddock* and Frederick Buechner provide in different ways models of this kind

of preaching in the latter part of this century.) Many sermons include a considerable component of story but move out of that mode either to make a case or to discuss a subject. The risk and gift of preaching that relies exclusively on story is that it leaves interpretation openended. The hearer draws his or her own implications and responds accordingly (*see* Narrative Preaching).

A sermon may make a case. Both political rhetoric* and high school and college debate teams help preachers and congregations to see persuasion as an appropriate feature of public rhetoric. Such sermons often move from the conclusion backwards. The preacher knows what the congregation is supposed to believe, decide, or do at the end of the sermon and then finds the propositions or enticements that will help move the congregation from where they are to where the preacher believes they should be. Classically, such persuasion depends on reasoned argument, and such sermons may be highly propositional and nearly syllogistic. Arguments may be based on scripture, reason,* the experience of the congregation, or some combination of the three, but they move step-by-step to what the preacher hopes will be the nearly unavoidable conclusion. This is close to what John Killinger calls the "developmental sermon," the traditional way of preaching in many American churches (Killinger, 52–53). In an age more pervaded by advertisement as persuasion than by the traditions of debate, sermons may make their case more metaphorically, imagistically, or impressionistically, seeking to entice the heart more than to convince the mind. Such sermons are less apt to move in a linear direction from the first thesis to the inevitable conclusion and more apt to move along a variety of appeals, in the hope that the cumulative effect of the moves will be conviction on the part of the hearers (*see* Style; Figures of Speech).

A sermon may examine a subject, as a dog worries a bone: "This subject of which I speak is a noun subject without any hint of a predicate; it carries no suggestion at all of what is to be said" (Davis, 141). Typically, such a sermon will begin with a fairly straightforward topic sentence introducing the subject of the discourse. Because sermons are interpretations of biblical texts, central to any such discussion is attention to the biblical passage or passages that provide faith perspective on the subject. Preachers with strong reputations as problem-preachers often center their preaching on a subject that resonates with the concerns of their congregations—psychologically and ethically. While such sermons often include considerable teaching, they may also draw on the tradition of empirical observation that lies behind the biblical understanding of wisdom and may move toward exhortation—*paraklesis* (*see* Topical Preaching).

A sermon may meditate on an image. Thomas Troeger writes of appropriate exposition for imaginative preaching: "Do not assume that the clear grammatical sense of the words is what will flash in the mind's eye of the listener. Reach your way into the meaning of the words by grabbing hold of the images that they awaken" (Troeger, 16). Such preaching will attend both to the images, nuances, allusions, and connotations of the text and to the images, nuances, hidden grace, quirky implications of the experiences, and words of people in the congregation. Almost by definition, such preaching will play image against image, nuance against nuance. The sermon will seldom stop to explain, to make explicit what imagination* provides. Such preaching seeks not so much to persuade as to illumine and delight. To delight not in the cleverness of the preacher but in the splendor of God. At its most effective, it moves from blessing toward blessing.

A sermon may explicate a text, verse by verse. The records we have of the preaching of Luther* and Calvin* suggest that most often they proceeded in this way, and the sermons of Karl Barth* often follow a similar pattern. It is obvious that such preaching has a strong compo-

nent of *didache*, but the further purpose of exposition will depend on the purposes of the text. Often the epistles* of the New Testament, the Psalms* of the Hebrew Bible, with their dense style (and in the case of the epistles, complicated syntax), lend themselves to a careful explication, verse by verse. The challenge for the preacher is to find in the passage sufficient unity so that the sermon will be one discourse and not an oral series of notes for further development (*see* Expository Preaching; Exegesis).

A sermon may move dialectically. Samuel Proctor advocates sermons that have a dialectical form. For Proctor, preaching often moves from an antithesis (the condition of the world, the community, the congregation) to thesis (the scriptural word over against our condition) to synthesis: the word embodied in hopeful living within the world. The major work of the sermon comes in developing that synthesis persuasively (Proctor, 116–29).

A sermon may seek to answer a question. One of Robert J. McCracken's most helpful books of sermons is titled *Questions People Ask* (1951), and the series of sermons is set as a collection of helpful answers to deeply felt questions. Sermons that follow this form are deliberately dialogical. Not only the topic but the development of the sermon depends on the preacher's willingness to take seriously the questions and puzzles of the listener. The preacher works by listening to the other side of an implicit conversation and shaping the sermon as a direct, almost conversational response (*see* Inductive Preaching).

A sermon may move from indicative to imperative (in classical terms, from gospel to law). There are excellent biblical models for this rhetorical form. The Pentateuch moves from exodus to Torah, the Sermon on the Mount from beatitude to responsibility, Paul's letter to the Romans from an affirmation of God's inclusive gospel to a reminder of the church's responsibility to inclusiveness. Such preaching begins in affirmation and moves toward implication, application. Obviously, sermons whose function is *paraklesis* may include both these moves. The first move, however, may also be grounded in the kerygmatic function of preaching or in *anamnesis*. The power of such preaching depends on the organic connection between indicative and imperative, so that the application seems not tagged on but to be both implied and empowered by the gospel (*see* Law and Gospel).

Henry Mitchell claims that from a variety of structures black preaching usually moves toward a conclusion in celebration. At its best, such celebration grows directly out of the preceding sermon but ". . . the climax consists of a kind of positive reinforcement. The hearer is permitted to relax a bit from reaching after new spiritual insight and to lift up in confirmation and gratitude what he has already received" (Mitchell, 188) (*see* African-American Preaching).

Obviously the function of the sermon and the function of the text on which it is based will suggest forms for the sermon, but the connection is suggestive rather than mandatory. Sermons that tell stories may be particularly appropriate to parabolic texts and parabolic purposes. Sermons that meditate on an image may be especially appropriate to the Psalms and may function to elicit blessing. Sermons whose function is *anamnesis* may seek to recall a text to us, verse by verse. Yet each text is hospitable to a variety of sermons and a variety of forms, and even the different functions of a sermon can be realized in a variety of ways.

What does seem to strengthen preaching is clarity about a sermon's function and its form and a wholehearted intention to shape the sermon with integrity, to let the sermon do what it may with this text and this occasion, and to leave other forms and functions for other sermons, other days.

Davis, H. G., *Design for Preaching*, 1958. Killinger, J., *Fundamentals of Preaching*, 1985. Long, T. G., *The Witness of Preaching*, 1989. Mitchell, H. H., *Black Preaching*, 1979. Proctor, S., *Preaching About Crises in the Community*, 1988. Troeger, T., *Creating Fresh Images for Preaching: New Rungs for Jacob's Ladder*, 1982.

DAVID L. BARTLETT

The Sermon on the Mount.

To preach the Sermon on the Mount is both a boon and a bane. It is a boon because of the sermon's power to shape Christian life. It is a bane because the sermon is vulnerable to moralization: the inclination to present it as a list of precepts that congregants are challenged to observe by dint of personal effort. The purpose of this article is to assist in the preaching and teaching of the Sermon on the Mount by attending, respectively, to its place within Matthew's Gospel, the capacity in which Jesus delivers it, the audience to whom it is addressed, its structure and central theme, and the practicability of living its ethic (*see* Law).

In the beginning of his story (1:1–4:15), Matthew introduces Jesus to the reader. Preeminently, Jesus is the son of God in whom God is decisively at work to save (1:21; 9:13–17). In his coming, Jesus inaugurates the eschatological age of salvation (1:23).

Matthew situates the Sermon on the Mount in the first phase of Jesus' public ministry to Israel (4:17–11:1). In this phase Jesus, through a ministry of teaching, preaching, and healing (4:23; 9:35; 11:1), summons Israel to repentance in view of the salvation that he, as the bearer of God's eschatological rule, already makes available (4:17). Within the context of Jesus' ministry, the Sermon on the Mount (5:1–7:29) is the first and most imposing of the five great discourses Jesus delivers (10; 13; 18; 24—25) and constitutes the parade example of his eschatological teaching (5:2; 7:28–29).

In sharp contrast to the religious leaders, who are "without authority" (7:29), Jesus, son of God, ascends the mountain and authoritatively delivers the Sermon on the Mount to the "crowds" and the "disciples" (5:1; 7:28–29). The crowds are potential disciples, for Jesus strives until the close of his public ministry (26:1) to win them to his side. The disciples who hear the sermon number, strictly speaking, only four; these four are the fishermen whom Jesus has just called to follow him (4:18–22). The very smallness of their number suggests that Matthew envisages yet another audience as hearing the sermon: the Christians of his missionary "church" (16:18; 18:17), who constitute the eschatological people of God (21:43). These Christians are those who have heard the gospel of the kingdom (24:14; 26:13), have been baptized (28:19), and have become disciples of Jesus (28:19). As Jesus' disciples, they form a new "family" (12:48–50), for they have themselves become "sons of God" (5:9) and "brothers" of Jesus (23:8; 28:10) and they, too, know God as "Father" (5:45; 6:9). It is these Christians whom Jesus declares in the sermon to be "blessed": Theirs is the joy that springs from the firm assurance that the consummated kingdom of the future already reorders present circumstances (5:3–10). It is likewise these Christians whom Jesus calls the "light of the world": By the lives they lead, they attest to all that they are the handiwork of God wrought by God's son (5:14–16).

As an address to the church, the Sermon on the Mount may be divided into five parts: (1) Introductions: On Those who Practice the Greater Righteousness (5:3–16); (2) On Practicing the Greater Righteousness Toward the Neighbor (5:17–45); (3) On Practicing the Greater Righteousness Toward God (6:1–18); (4) On Practicing the Greater Righteousness in Other Areas of Life (6:19–7:12); and (5) Conclusion: Injunctions on Practicing the Greater Righteousness (7:13–27). As is apparent, the central theme of the Sermon on the Mount is that of the "greater righteousness" (5:20).

The "greater righteousness" is that style of life that characterizes Christian disciples. At 5:48, Jesus asserts, "You, therefore, must be perfect, as your heavenly Father is perfect." What being perfect means here is not to be morally flawless but, as Deuteronomy 18:13 explains, to be "wholehearted in your service of the Lord your God." Accordingly, to be perfect is to be wholehearted in doing God's will as taught by Jesus (7:21) and this, in turn, is to love God first of all and the neighbor second of all (22:34–40; 7:12). If Christian disciples love God and neighbor, they will approach God in prayer like that modeled in the Lord's Prayer and petition God to satisfy their spiritual, moral, communal, and physical needs (6:9–13); they will eschew ostentation in their piety (6:1–18); and they will not deal with family, community, or others on the basis of ill-tempered anger or hatred, marital infidelity, quick divorce, empty oaths, an "eye for an eye," or "us vs. them" (5:22–48). This latter kind of mentality is no mark of Christian disciples.

It should be clear from the preceding that the Sermon on the Mount does not expound an ethic for the public at large or society as a whole. The ethic of the greater righteousness is intended for the church of Jesus, son of God, God's eschatological people. Even so, is it practicable? Is it an ethic that Christian disciples can actually live? The answer is, yes. On what grounds? On the grounds that the risen Jesus has, in baptism, summoned Christian disciples to live in the sphere of God's eschatological rule where they know God as Father, as Son, and the Holy Spirit as the power by which Jesus enables them, through the word of his story and the eucharist, to be "like him" (28:19–20; 26:26–28). The purpose of the Sermon on the Mount is to describe, through striking images drawn from various facts of human experience, the "kind of life" that disciples of Jesus lead. Does this mean, then, that Matthew is oblivious to sins of little faith, to human frailty, or to the difficulty of living the ethic of the greater righteousness? Not at all. For the Jesus who delivers the Sermon on the Mount is none other than the Jesus who accomplishes salvation, at the heart of which is the forgiveness of sins (1:21; 26:28). In a word, then, the ethic of the greater righteousness, in summoning Christian disciples to be "like Jesus," summons them to look to Jesus himself for the spiritual power by which to love God wholly (5:48; 22:37), to receive from God the gift of forgiveness (6:12), and, in their dealings with others, to extend to them this same gift of love (6:12; 7:12; 22:39) (*see* Ethics; Jesus as Preacher).

Augustine, "Our Lord's Sermon on the Mount," *The Preaching of Augustine*, trans. F. Cardman, 1973. **Betz, H. D.,** *Essays on the Sermon on the Mount*, 1985. **Davenport, G. L.,** *Into the Darkness: Discipleship in the Sermon on the Mount*, 1988. **Davies, W. D.,** *The Setting of the Sermon on the Mount*, 1964. **Guelich, R. A.,** *The Sermon on the Mount: A Foundation for Understanding*, 1982. *Interpretation* 41 (April 1987), 117–69. **Kingsbury, J. D.,** *Matthew*, 1986. **Kissinger, W.,** *The Sermon on the Mount: A History of Interpretation*, 1975.

JACK DEAN KINGSBURY

Sheen, Fulton John. (1895–1979)

Fulton Sheen was a Roman Catholic bishop whose pioneering career as a radio* and television* preacher made him one of the most famous Catholic priests of twentieth-century America.

Following his education at St. Viator College and Seminary at Bourbonnais, Illinois, and St. Paul Seminary in Minnesota, Sheen was ordained to the priesthood in the diocese of Peoria in 1919. Because of his intellectual talents, he was sent for further theological study to the Catholic University of America, and the University of Louvain, where he earned his Ph.D. in 1923. He was also the first American to be awarded the prestigious "Agrégé en Philosophie" degree; his doctoral dissertation, *God and Intelligence in Modern Philosophy*, was published in 1925.

Sheen launched his academic career in 1926 when he was appointed to the faculty at the Catholic University of America, teaching theology and scholastic philosophy until 1950. His reputation as a dynamic orator and apologist for the Catholic faith soon won him national acclaim, and his energies were focused on a wider audience beyond the traditional classroom. He preached regularly from the pulpit at St. Patrick's Cathedral in New York City and lectured across the nation on world affairs as well as religion.

When the National Council of Catholic Men was presented with the opportunity to sponsor a religious program on the NBC radio network, Fulton Sheen was chosen as the featured speaker on the "Catholic Hour Broadcasts." From 1930–1952, he delivered a regular Lenten series on a wide range of subjects, interpreting religion at its highest and its best, in a nonsectarian manner, to an audience of over four million listeners. Sheen's popularity soared; he received thousands of letters requesting copies of his sermons, which were then printed in pamphlet form. "The Eternal Galilean" (1934), "Peace: The Fruit of Justice" (1940), and "The Crisis in Christendom" (1943) were among the most popular.

As a radio preacher, Sheen was able to overcome a good deal of misunderstanding and prejudice by making the doctrines of the Catholic Church better known to the American people. As well known for his common touch as he was for his scholarship and eloquence, he reawakened an interest in the spiritual and made religion intelligible to the masses. Fulfilling his priestly role—the salvation of souls—was another measure of his success, testified to by his fame as an instructor of converts. Many prominent figures sought him out, and he welcomed into the ranks of the church such celebrities as Congresswoman Clare Boothe Luce and former Communist Louis Budenz.

The decade of the 1950s marked the height of Bishop Sheen's influence and popularity, as the church made its way into the American mainstream during the postwar religious revival. His basic message was often a combination of Catholic social reform and the church's crusade against communism. Speaking as an American, he blended patriotism with piety, condemning communism as the epitome of both irreligion as well as un-Americanism.

As National Director of the Society for the Propagation of the Faith (1950–1966), Sheen led the American Church's evangelization and missionary efforts around the world. As an author, he achieved best-seller status with two books in the religious/inspirational genre: *Peace of Soul* (1949) and *Life of Christ* (1958). For many Americans, Sheen was the first association they could make with the Catholic church, and he projected a warm, friendly, and intelligent image. And it was his projection of that image through the new medium of television that best explains the unique 1950s phenomenon of "Bishop Sheen, Television Star."

From 1951–1957, Sheen was the star of "Life Is Worth Living," which appeared on the Dumont and ABC networks and was watched by an audience of over 30 million viewers. Relying on a popular lecture format, aided only by a blackboard, Sheen dramatically popularized religion through the power of his voice and personality. On his premier show, Sheen sounded an ecumenical note, announcing his intention to supply the spiritual, moral, and intellectual demands of the American people with a basic message of Christian ethics: love of God, love of neighbor, and love of country. He inspired and instructed an entire generation while achieving celebrity status, winning an Emmy award, and gracing the cover of *Time* magazine in 1952. As a "microphone missionary," Sheen was described as the most famous preacher in the United States and certainly America's best-known Roman Catholic priest.

In 1966, Sheen was appointed Bishop of Rochester, New York. Determined to implement the reforms of the Second Vatican Council, he embarked on a path of controversial innovation. After a short and stormy tenure, he resigned in 1969; he was best remembered for his ecumenical style, focusing the nation's attention on the plight of the poor in the inner city, and calling for the United States government's withdrawal from Vietnam.

Sheen's retirement, the final decade of his life, was devoted to continued lecturing, writing, reflecting on his life as a priest, and achieving the status of a "living legend." He died of heart disease in New York City at the age of 84.

In reflecting on the creativity of his vocation as a priest, Sheen said simply: "Everything that I have said can be summed up in the preaching of Christ and Him Crucified" ("Preaching as a Saving Event," unpublished 1972 manuscript, Fulton Sheen Archives, Rochester, New York). He recycled his radio and television sermons in book form; as a speaker, he never used a script, preferring to master his materials, aided by study and meditation. Always, Sheen remained a teacher determined to reach the largest possible audience by a life of Christian witness. The strength of his style could be found in his intense spirituality and his persistent critique of secularism as he insisted on the relevance of religion. Seeking to bridge the gap separating the church from the modern world, Sheen employed the new technology in carrying on a biblical tradition. He said that radio made it possible to address more souls in the span of thirty minutes than St. Paul did in all his missionary journeys: Broadcast and television were the distant echoes of the gospel.

At the time of his death, Bishop Fulton Sheen was remembered as the most eloquent exponent and effective champion of the Catholic faith, the greatest evangelizer in the history of the American Catholic Church, and one of the greatest preachers of the twentieth century.

Fields, K. R., "Bishop Fulton J. Sheen: An American Catholic Response to the Twentieth Century," Ph.D. diss., University of Notre Dame, 1988. **Sheen, F.,** *The Electronic Christian: 105 Readings from Fulton J. Sheen*, 1979; *Treasure in Clay*, 1980.

KATHLEEN L. RILEY

FOLLY
Fulton J. Sheen
If love is equivalent to sacrifice, and all sacrifice from the world's point of view is

foolishness, Christ on the cross is the supreme folly. From the standpoint of the world He was the greatest failure in history; in the ledger of the world's estimate of things, He suffered the greatest defeat . . . if He were God, why did he not try to win the favor of Pilate when he said, "Know you not that I have the power to release you?" He could have won his freedom by ingratiating himself with the Roman government, and He did not.

"Folly," cries the world.

If He is all powerful, why does He not strike dead those who scourge and mock Him?

"Folly," again cries the world.

If He could raise up children of Abraham from the stones, why could not He raise up his friends at the moment of arrest?

"Folly," cries the world.

If He could have won his release from Herod with just a miracle, why did He not work one?

"Folly," cries the world.

If the magic touch of His hands could restore sight to the blind and hearing to the deaf, why did He permit hard nails to pierce them?

"Folly," cries the world.

If He could have proven His divinity by coming down from the cross, "Let Him now come down from the cross and we will believe Him," why did He not step down as a king from His throne?

"Folly," cries the world.

As a demagogue He would have succeeded; as a God He was crucified. The cross is a folly and Christ a failure.

Hence it is that every lover of Christ and Him crucified must share His folly. The law is no different for the disciple than for the Master. The world calls everyone a fool who leaves his riches and his friends, his wine and his song, for the cloister or the convent, and exchanges his silks and satins for the hair shirt and discipline. . . . The world brands him as a fool who hangs himself on the cross of mortification when he might come down and shake dice with the soldiers even for the garments of a God.

Yes, but "the foolishness of God is wiser than men," and "the wisdom of this world is foolishness with God." It is only from the world's point of view that we are a fool as our Master was before the court of Herod. In the sublime words of St. Paul, "We are fools for Christ's sake."

From "The Folly of the Cross," in *The Life of All Living: The Philosophy of Life* (New York: The Century Co., 1929). Reprinted in 1950 by Garden City Books, 154–59.

Sockman, Ralph W.   (1889–1970)

Ralph Sockman served Christ Church Methodist, New York City, for 44 years, his sole pastoral appointment. He came to New York City from Ohio to do graduate work in political science and law. He joined Christ Church as a layman in 1911 and in 1913 became a student assistant while studying theology at Union Theological Seminary. In 1917, having graduated from Union, and while pursuing a doctorate at Columbia University, he was appointed senior pastor at Christ Church. He stayed there until he retired in 1961. His career there spanned two world wars, an economic depression, and several recessions.

His considerable homiletical skills and energies were channeled into weekly preaching at Christ Church; a weekly radio program, the National Radio Pulpit; a weekly newspaper column; and frequent preaching in other churches of all denominations across the country.

His sermons were generally topical,* featuring classical homiletical argument: a thesis statement and a lucid, three-point outline supporting the thesis. He constructed models of logical organization and quoted extensively from his voracious reading habit. As a result, his sermons fed the inquiring mind and used emotion sparingly. He usually preached without notes, except for quotations written for accuracy. Sockman wrote, "I try to deliver my sermon as if I were thinking along with the congregation" (Bishop, 53).

His delivery and style endeared him to his audiences. He studied public speaking extensively at Ohio Wesleyan College where he developed an engaging presence, cultured voice with a wide range, and a warm and relaxed delivery.

Theologically, he was eclectic, embracing a wide variety of theological, ethical, political, social, and aesthetic positions. He cherished the Apostles' Creed but accepted his congregation's varied interpretations of it. As World War II approached, he vacillated on the necessity of military action to stop Hitler's aggression but finally emerged as a patriot and a champion of American culture.

He emphasized personal and social needs in his preaching and believed the church and American culture were working together to make America great. The church had a moral and ethical responsibility to the nation and had to work closely with culture to unify the country and preserve a free, democratic society.

At his retirement in 1961, *Time* named him the finest Protestant preacher in the United States. His 5,000-member congregation attested to his preaching abilities. He was a twentieth-century practitioner of America's unique civil religion and was consistently rated foremost among America's great preachers.

Bishop, J., "Ralph W. Sockman: Twentieth-Century Circuit Rider," *Preaching* (July–August 1990). **Lawrence, W. B.,** "Ralph Sockman: The Compleat Methodist," *Quarterly Review* 5:4 (Winter 1985). **Sockman, R. W.,** *Live for Tomorrow*, 1939; and *The Highway of God*, 1942.   GRANVILLE E. TYSON

TODAY IS OURS
Ralph W. Sockman
Some keep their minds much too open on the rearward side. They continue to look back at yesterday's decisions, wondering whether they have reached the right conclusions and spending their energy in retrying cases. A popular essayist tells of a young minister who was so successful in his first parish that he received

an invitation to another. But being firmly rooted in the affections of his people, he declined the call. Then his troubles began, for thereafter when anything went wrong he thought of the delightful church he had refused. Some years later he did take a new parish. Then after the excitement of moving was over, his troubles began again, for whenever any difficulty was encountered he thought of the "dear old place" he had left. Thus the poor fellow allowed the energy and enjoyment of the present to escape through the mental door left open in the rear. Today's peace of mind is secured by closing the gate to keep out yesterday's yelping pack of hounding worries. Today's executive efficiency depends on the ability to shut the door on yesterday's decisions. This is the truth which Jesus drove home by such remarks as, "No man, having put his hand to the plough, and looking back, is fit for the Kingdom of God," or the sharper surgical one, "Let the dead bury their dead."

Preached in 1939 on the National Radio Pulpit, from a sermon titled, "Today Is Ours." Reprinted with the permission of Macmillan Publishing Company from *Live for Tomorrow* by Ralph W. Sockman. © 1939 by The Macmillan Company, renewed 1967 by Ralph W. Sockman.

Sojourner Truth. (ca. 1797?–1883) Formerly Isabella Van Wagener, Sojourner Truth was an African-American woman who gained a reputation as a preacher-prophet because of her itinerant* ministry as an anti-slavery and women's rights lecturer. Born to slave parents Elizabeth (or Mau-Mau) Bett and James (called Baumfree) in Ulster County, New York, she was legally property and was sold several times. While owned by John Dumont, she was married to a slave named Thomas and bore him at least five children, four of whom survived. During her lifetime, she bore thirteen children. In 1827, shortly before total emancipation in New York, she ran away from Dumont and was taken in by

Quakers, Isaac and Maria Van Wagener of Wagondale, Dutchess County, who gave her the name Isabella Van Wagener and her freedom. As Isabella Van Wagener, she successfully won a court case at Kingston, New York, that resulted in the return of her son Peter who had been illegally sold out of New York State to a slaveholder in Alabama.

Isabella spoke Dutch as her first language and was taught the Lord's Prayer in Dutch. Years later when lecturing on slavery, she spoke English with a Dutch accent. Though exposed to the influence of the Dutch Reformed religious culture, she sought out the sanctuary of a wooded place by a stream during her enslavement and conducted "talks with God." Her earliest religious conceptions were a combination of mysticism and deism. Isabella (or Bell, as she was called) experienced visions and heard voices she attributed to divine origin. She also attended Methodist camp meetings.

In about 1828, Isabella took her two youngest children and went to New York City, where she worked in domestic service. She initially attended John Street Methodist Church but soon withdrew to join the Zion African Methodist Church. An ecumenical independent who held no distinct religious creed, Isabella preached in the Bowery at the Magdalene Asylum, where she met Elijah Pierson, a former Presbyterian elder and Baptist deacon who operated the asylum for prostitutes. In 1832, she began to work as a maid in the Pierson household. A self-appointed prophet who called himself Elijah the Tishbite and later John the Baptist, Pierson taught the ritual of reciprocal washing of feet and the need for holding all material goods in common. He organized a religious commune called the Retrenchment Society.

While employed by the Pierson family, Isabella met Robert Matthews, another religious visionary. Matthews had a Millerite background, changed his name to Matthias, and gradually assumed the role of religious potentate. His bizarre behavior and teachings included ritual baths administered by other members of the commune and the spirit-matching of men and women contrary to the customary practice of marriage. When Pierson died in 1834, Matthias was suspected of poisoning him. Accused of being an accomplice, Isabella won a slander suit in 1834 against Ann Folger, the wife of a businessman who was a member of the "kingdom" and had been spirit-matched to Matthias. Isabella became disenchanted with the commune, sought employment elsewhere, and in 1843 left New York City.

She had some contact with the Shakers but soon set off on her own pilgrimage under the leading of the "Spirit" or "Holy Wind" and made her way to Northampton, Massachusetts. Isabella was now calling herself Sojourner Truth because she believed God had called her to travel up and down the land showing people their sins, especially the sin of chattel slavery. She urged everyone to accept the teachings of the Bible about God's goodness and love of all people. At Northampton, Sojourner temporarily resided in a utopian community where she learned of the organized abolitionist movement. There she met William Lloyd Garrison and Frederick Douglass, and later purchased a small lot and house near Northampton, Massachusetts. Though she kept the property until 1857, Sojourner left Northampton in 1851 to travel westward with a team of lecturers led by the Hon. George Thompson, M. P., the noted British abolitionist.

Though Sojourner Truth did not learn to read or write, she spent the next 25 years preaching and singing, on her own or in the company of other abolitionists. She spent two years in Ohio, where she gained notoriety for a speech delivered in 1851 at a women's rights convention in Akron that has become known as "Ain't I a Woman." Harriet Beecher Stowe spoke of Sojourner Truth's "subtle, controlling personal power," and referred to her as "the Libyan Sibyl." More than six feet tall, gaunt, yet stately in bearing, Sojourner Truth readily captured the attention of her audiences as she stood to denounce slavery in a compelling and melodious voice. Olive Gilbert, a friend and New England abolitionist, published the first edition of the *Narrative of Sojourner Truth* in 1850. In 1878, it became Part I of a 320-page, two-part edition reprinted by Francis W. Titus, an admirer from Battle Creek, Michigan. The Titus edition is composed of the biography, speeches of, and articles about Sojourner Truth. Sojourner sold copies of her narrative to support her travels, which criss-crossed Ohio, Indiana, Michigan, and other midwestern states as well as points back east. She often spoke on the theme "When I Found Jesus" and at times drove her own horse and buggy, giving out card photographs of herself, saying "I'll sell the shadow to support the substance."

The Charles Merrit family, Quakers in Battle Creek, Michigan, hosted Sojourner when she was not on her travels. In 1857, she purchased a small barn from the Merrits and used it as her permanent residence until her death in 1883. She continued to testify on behalf of the oppressed slaves, and after the Supreme Court's ruling in the Dred Scott case she countered Frederick Douglass's despair with the famous remark, "Frederick, is God dead?" During the Civil War, Sojourner spoke out against the Copperheads, went to Washington, D.C., where she helped integrate streetcars, and in 1864 met President Abraham Lincoln. She spent five months working for the National Freedman's Relief Association in a contraband camp called Freedman's Village at Arlington, Virginia.

After the war, she cared for the sick and injured in a Freedmen's Hospital, sought to recruit laborers from among the emancipated slaves of the south for northern employers, and then returned to Battle Creek, where she attempted to reunite her children and grandchildren. In the 1870s, Sojourner Truth advocated the resettlement of former slaves on public lands in the west. She went to Kansas to help distribute food and clothing to needy migrants among the Exodusters who had

fled the south. She continued to speak on behalf of the Temperance and women's rights causes. In 1875, Sojourner returned to Battle Creek. A year later her grandson Samuel died at the age of 24. He had been her traveling companion for many years, and his death affected her deeply. She died on November 26, 1883, and was buried by the Congregational and Presbyterian Church in Battle Creek.

The excerpt that follows this is from the testimony Sojourner Truth gave at the 1851 Akron Women's Rights Convention. It was recorded by Frances Dana Gage, the Ohio feminist who presided at the convention. Sojourner, wearing a gray dress and a white turban, "surmounted," Gage tells us, "with an uncouth sun-bonnet," marched up the aisle of the Universalist Church of Akron "with the air of a queen" and took a seat on the pulpit steps. On the second day, angered by theological arguments of the clergy that granted superior rights and privileges to men, Sojourner rose slowly from her seat and, after the tumult of objections had subsided, began to speak. Before she was done, she had, in the opinion of Frances Gage, "subdued the mobbish spirit of the day." She also transformed the debate by exposing the racism and patriarchal currents that ran deep within American reform (*see* African-American Preaching; Women as Preachers).

Bernard, J., *Journey Toward Freedom: The Story of Sojourner Truth,* 1967. **Fauset, A. H.,** *Sojourner Truth,* 1938. **Pauli, H.,** *Her Name Was Sojourner Truth,* 1962. **Titus, F. W.,** *Narrative of Sojourner Truth: A Bondswoman of Olden Time,* 1878.

MILTON C. SERNETT

AIN'T I A WOMAN?
Sojourner Truth

Well, children, where there is so much racket there must be somethin' out o' kilter. I think that 'twixt the Negroes of the South and the women of the North, all talkin' 'bout rights, the white men will be in a fix pretty soon. But what's all this here talkin' about?

That man over there say woman needs

to be helped into carriages, and lifted over ditches, and to have the best place everywhere. Nobody ever helps me into carriages, or over mud puddles, or gives me any best place! [*And raising herself to her full height, and her voice to a pitch like rolling thunder, she asked*] And ain't I a woman? Look at me! Look at my arm! [*and she bared her right arm to the shoulder, showing her tremendous muscular power*]. I have ploughed and planted, and gathered into barns, and no man could head me! And ain't I a woman? I could work as much and eat as much as a man—when I could get it—and bear the lash as well! And ain't I a woman? I have borne thirteen children, and seen them most all sold off to slavery, and when I cried out with my mother's grief, none but Jesus heard me! And ain't I a woman?

Then they talks about this thing in the head; what's this they call it? [*"Intellect,"* whispered someone near.] That's it, honey. What's that got to do with woman's rights or Negroes' rights? If my cup won't hold but a pint, and yours holds a quart, wouldn't you be mean not to let me have my little half-measure full? [*And she sent a keen glance at the minister who had made the argument. The cheering was long and loud.*]

Then that little man in black there, he say women can't have as much rights as men, 'cause Christ wasn't a woman! Where did your Christ come from? [*Rolling thunder couldn't have stilled that crowd, as did those deep, wonderful tones, as she stood there with outstretched arms and eyes of fire. Raising her voice still louder, she repeated*] Where did your Christ come from? From God and woman! Man had nothin' to do with Him. [*Oh, what a rebuke that was to that little man.*]

[*Turning again to another objector, she took up the defense of Mother Eve. I cannot follow her through it all. It was pointed, and witty, and solemn; eliciting at almost every sentence deafening applause; and she ended by asserting this:*] If the first woman God ever made was strong enough to turn the world upside down all alone, these women together [*and she*

glanced her eye over the platform] ought to be able to turn it back, and get it right side up again! And now they is askin' to do it, the men better let 'em. [*Long-continued cheering greeted this.*] Obliged to you for hearin' on me, and now old Sojourner hain't got nothin' more to say.

> From *History of Woman Suffrage,* ed. E. C. Stanton, S. B. Anthony, and M. J. Gage. Vol. 1, 1848–1861 (New York: Fowler & Wells, 1900), 115–17. Reprinted by Ayer Company, Publishers, Salem, New Hampshire (spelling altered).

Donald O. Soper. (1903–) A Methodist minister and member of the British House of Lords, Donald Soper is best known for his weekly dialogues at Tower Hill, London. Beginning in 1929, he preached and conversed with the crowds in the open air for more than thirty-six years. A socialist and pacifist throughout World War II, his intellectual honesty, commitment to the Christian faith, and consummate ability to articulate that faith ranked him with Leslie Weatherhead* and W. E. Sangster* as one of the most distinguished Methodist preachers in twentieth-century England. He received an M.A. from Cambridge and a Ph.D. from the London School of Economics. In 1929, he was appointed to the Central London Mission, where his congregation was experiencing the harsh reality of the Depression. The Depression left an indelible mark on Soper's psyche and thereby on his preaching. In 1936, he was appointed superintendent of the West London Mission. Self-described as a "social evangelist," Soper believed the kingdom of God was real and attainable and would be accomplished through social justice and moral responsibility. In these principles, he combined individual and social redemption. They provided him a lifelong agenda for his preaching.

Soper's contribution to homiletics lies in his extensive experience as an open-air preacher. Preaching to a crowd of reluctant listeners puts the listener in control of the communication. Yet Soper was successful in communicating his ideas to the crowd, honing his ability to sense quickly the point of human need and subtly yet forcefully to bring the gospel to bear on it (see Itinerant and Open-Air Preaching).

As a preacher in one of London's most significant pulpits, his approach remained focused on the gospel's relevance and reality. Fearing the church was becoming an irrelevant institution, he advocated preaching that was centered on the life and teachings of Christ and on human needs.

A champion of high oratory in preaching, Soper abhorred flamboyant and exhibitionistic substitutes. As an advocate of education in speech techniques and the use of television and tape recordings in homiletics training, he was ahead of his time. He believed that true evangelistic preaching can take place only in the context of the Communion service, where the worshiper is motivated not by guilt or the force of intellectual ideas but by the self-giving love and grace of God revealed in the sacrifice of Jesus Christ. When the penitent's needs intersect the liturgy in the imagery and symbolism representing the sacrifice of Jesus Christ, the gospel is proclaimed.

Soper's experiences with open-air preaching, combined with his high view of liturgy, made for a range and breadth found in few preachers. His ministry conveyed to the church and to the field of homiletics the benefits of preaching that meets the worshiper at his or her point of need as it is disclosed by the Eucharistic service and evokes a total response from the hearer.

Purcell, W., *Portrait of Soper*, 1972. **Soper, D.,** *Christian Politics: An Introduction*, 1977; and *The Advocacy of the Gospel*, 1961.

GRANVILLE E. TYSON

Spener, Philipp Jakob. (1635–1705). A Lutheran Pietist leader in seventeenth-century Germany, Spener was born into a pious and privileged home at Rappoltsweiler in Alsace. At nearby Strassburg University, Spener did his undergraduate and theological studies, receiving his doctor of theology degree in 1664.

Spener held three major pastorates. In Frankfurt am Main (1666–86), he was the senior minister of the Lutheran church, with many administrative responsibilities. Between 1686 and 1691, he was the Saxon court preacher in Dresden. From 1691 to 1705, he was dean of the Lutheran churches and pastor of St. Nicholas Church in Berlin.

In 1675, Spener published his *Pia Desideria*, expressing a heartfelt desire for church reform. His best-known publication, the *Pia Desideria* contains three sections. The first describes the corruptions in the church. The second reveals Spener's postmillennial, optimistic hope for "better times for the Church on earth." The conclusion consists of six reform proposals—the last two of which involve theological education and preaching.

Spener quarreled not with the theology but the life of his church. He criticized the frequent debauchery and ecclesiastical irresponsibility of the nobles; clergy professionalism, contentiousness, and worldliness; and lay coarseness manifested in drunkenness, lawsuits, and spiritual poverty.

For Spener, the correction of these ills depended upon reform of the clergy. His fifth proposal calls for clergy university training to include spiritual formation and instruction in pastoral praxis. His sixth proposal is "that sermons be so prepared by all that their purpose (faith and its fruits) may be achieved in the hearers to the greatest possible degree" (Spener, 115). At Halle University, founded in 1691 largely through Spener's influence at the Prussian court, the Pietists under August Hermann Francke (1663–1727) developed a theological education bent upon producing reborn clergy who would do such vital preaching.

Spener's own ministry departed from customary homiletical practices. He significantly modified lectionary* usage. Restriction to the same texts for each Sunday of the church year limited a congregation's familiarity with the whole Bible. The requirement that the sermon be drawn from each Sunday's Gospel lesson was even more serious—since preaching about faith and its fruits could better be done from the epistles. In Frankfurt am Main, Spener's departure from the lectionary resulted in a published series from the Pauline epistles. Spener's Dresden sermons were based on the Sunday Gospel lections and were published in three noteworthy collections: *Die Evangelische Glaubenslehre* (The Evangelical Doctrines), 1688; *Die Evangelischen Lebenspflichten* (The Evangelical Practical Duties), 1692; and *Der Evangelische Glaubenstrost* (The Evangelical Consolation), 1695. In Berlin his 66 famous sermons on the new birth were published in 1696 under the title *Der Hochwichtige Articul von der Wiedergeburt* (The Highly Important Article of the New Birth). Spener was the first to treat Lutheran orthodoxy in a sermon series and thereby to distinguish between dogma, ethics, and consolation doctrines.

Spener likewise resisted the florid and erudite preaching style of his day. He perceived a danger in eloquent preaching. Form must follow substance and not the reverse: "The pulpit is not the place for an ostentatious display of one's skill. It is rather the place to preach the Word of the Lord plainly but powerfully" (Spener, 116). Spener avoided using lengthy Greek and Latin quotations in his sermons, thus accentuating Pietism's stress upon making the gospel more accessible to the common people.

A powerful advocate of catechetical training and confirmation of the young, Spener preached brief catechism sermons at Frankfurt am Main. He firmly believed that catechism and preaching would reinforce each other in communicating the gospel.

Spener's sermons were heavily exegetical. Topical preaching had no appeal for him. He sought to explain the Bible as he preached. Textual analysis was of the highest priority. The scriptures have their authority from God, who speaks through them like a king making a proclamation to his subjects. The church is the messenger that brings us the king's letter. Preaching is necessary to inform those who are not well versed in scripture.

Generally, Spener's tightly structured sermons were divided into five parts: introduction, explanation of the text, doctrinal application, admonition, and comfort. There was often overlap between the first two sections. One notes in the latter three the Lutheran concern for correct doctrine and the necessary balance between law and gospel.*

Spener would not be deemed a popular preacher today. His sermons, frequently lasting about two hours, were excessively long even for his day. Intent upon careful exposition of scripture, he made little use of illustrations and similies. He occasionally referred to events in secular or church history. Quotations from Luther and other figures in church history appear in his sermons but rarely any personal or contemporary life experiences. It has been suggested that his sermons were more like treatises and that he had a schoolmasterly way of preaching.

A manuscript preacher, Spener read over his sermon text three times before delivering it. His delivery was dry and unexciting. He appealed to people's understanding much more than to their feelings.

Nevertheless, Spener's sermons were influential. Laypersons urged their publication. Those who heard and read them felt themselves addressed by the Word of God from the biblical text and by the deep personal faith and moral earnestness of the preacher. The Pietist movement in Lutheran Germany was strengthened by Spener's preaching.

Brown, D., *Understanding Pietism*, 1978. Erb, P. C., ed., *Pietists: Selected Writings*, 1983. **Spener, P. J.,** *Die Evangelische Glaubenslehre*, 1688; and *Pia Desideria*, 1675, 1964. **Stein, K. J.,** *Philipp Jakob*

Spener: Pietist Patriarch, 1986. **Stoeffler, F. E.,** *The Rise of Evangelical Pietism*, 1971.

K. JAMES STEIN

COMFORT
Philipp Jakob Spener

The comfort is that from the New Birth Christianity becomes easy for us. When we have once denied ourselves in true repentance and have come to New Birth and to living faith, the latter effects the rest by itself—just as a healthy root by itself produces fruit. If Christ would have commanded that we should give rebirth to ourselves, we would have to despair because such goes beyond our abilities. But God himself desires to work everything within all. Wherever out of the power of the New Birth we have stepped into a true Christian life so that we now live no longer for ourselves but for God and Christ, we will find that such a life is indeed happier than that of a person of the world, who still lives according to the flesh. Reason grasps this situation somewhat. We need only to remember the worries, the anxieties, the despair, the fear, and other unpleasantness with which such poor people of the world are tormented; whereas, the life of the children of God is led in quiet spirit. Although we still remain weak people after the New Birth, we are nevertheless comforted in that what is asked of us in our Christianity becomes possible for us through the New Birth; for if a person is not able by his or her own power to live according to God's commandments, Christians are able to do this out of the power of the New Birth. Thus, the yoke of Christ becomes gentle and his burden light (Matt. 11:30). And the commandments of God are no longer difficult for those who fulfill them out of love (1 John 5:3). What was difficult for us for a time becomes continually easier through practice, for the power of the Spirit increases. In this New Birth the old person and the fleshly nature have been weakened, but they have survived. They, therefore, make things difficult for the new person because sin still clings to us and makes us sluggish. It is the greatest cross of even upright Christians

that they speak with Paul, "Miserable man that I am. Who will deliver me from this body of death?" (Rom. 7:24). However, there will still be another New Birth, which is a New Birth into that blessed eternity, where the flesh and the old nature have been laid aside completely and everything in eternity will become completely new (Matt. 19:28). Then the shortcomings of the present New Birth will be completely erased.

From "Die Notwendigkeit der Wiedergeburt" (The Necessity of the New Birth, trans. K. Luckert), in *Der Hochwichtige Articul von der Wiedergeburt* (Frankfurt am Mayn: In Verlegung Johann David Zunners, 1696), Vol. I, 13–14.

Spirituality of the Preacher. The spirituality of the preacher is centered in the word of God.* The minister of the word is called to live in that word and out of that word, must struggle with, enflesh, and act on that word. Preaching is not so much a function of one's ministry but an integral dimension of one's identity. To be grounded in the reality "I am a preacher" keeps the focus on the word, not just for proximate preparation to preach but in remote preparation as well. One's daily choices and decisions become the factor that makes a difference in the preaching moment. A holistic understanding of spirituality, therefore, is essential for the preacher of the word of God.

Spirituality is a much-discussed term with varieties of definitions and expressions. Theologian Anne Carr defines it this way: "Spirituality can be described as the whole of our deepest religious beliefs, convictions, and patterns of thought, emotion, and behavior in respect to what is ultimate, to God" (Carr, 49). Or one might say that spirituality is the way persons live out their conviction of who they are in relation to God, self, others, and creation.

A central theme for the spirituality of the preacher is *Ephphatha*, "be opened," as found in Mark 7:32–37. Moved with compassion, Jesus healed the hearing-impaired, speech-impaired man. Accompanying the call to preach is the call to be open, to have open ears, eyes, lips, heart, hands; to be open to experience, to beauty, to relationships, to life. This call of *Ephphatha* is utilized by many traditions in the baptismal rite as a call to the initiated to flesh out the word of God in life. A stance of openness, of receptivity to all the ways the mystery of God is revealed, is a difficult challenge. Such is the vocation and spirituality of the baptized. Such is the vocation and spirituality especially of the preacher.

Open ears are fundamental to a preacher's spirituality. "The Lord God has given me the tongue of a teacher, that I may know how to sustain the weary with a word. Morning by morning he wakens—wakens my ear to listen as those who are taught. The Lord God has opened my ear" (Isa. 50:4–5a). The word must be allowed to do its transforming action in the preacher first. There must be personal wrestling with the questions What is God's word for me? What is God's word for us? This will enable the word to be the creative, healing, challenging, life-giving *dabar* that will not return to God empty (Isa. 55:11). Herein lies the difference between placid, prosaic preaching and preaching with power. The disciple is called not only to listen to God in the word but to listen to the people of God in the world and enable the connection of those two realities. The preacher must have *open eyes* and an *open mind* to study, to seek the truth wherever it is found, to reflect on that truth.

Needless to say, the preacher, like Jeremiah (20:9), like Jesus (John 12:49; Mark 1:38), must have *open lips* to birth the word of truth and love that has taken flesh within. As Mary of Magdala discovered, that word may not always be accepted or believed, but it must be spoken to all who are in upper rooms afraid, disillusioned, without hope.

The challenge to speak the word in season and out of season, regardless of its reception, requires the preacher to pray for the gift of a profound love for God and God's people. The spirituality of the preacher, therefore, calls for an *open heart* that can be stretched to encompass all of God's people. The vulnerability and disciplined study required of a preacher and the constant attentiveness to God's word and God's people in the here and now can only be motivated by grace and passionate love.

The image of *open hands* reflects another critical factor in the spirituality of the preacher, for word and deed must go together. Even though the fullness of the word preached may not yet be integrated in the preacher's life, it must be clear to the congregation that the preacher takes this word seriously and desires the grace to embody it, as it was embodied in the Master: "Today this scripture has been fulfilled in your hearing" (Luke 4:21).

Openness to life, relationships, and to experience is another dimension of a preacher's spirituality. One must be willing to risk entering into the world of those who are different from oneself in regard to culture, class, religion, race, and politics. Jesus opened himself to this kind of vulnerability with a rich young man, a poor widow, the Pharisees, the Sadducees, the Canaanite and the Samaritan woman, a Zacchaeus, and a Bartimaeus.

Finally, an *openness to beauty* is an essential element in a preacher's spirituality. Allowing oneself to be nurtured by art, music, poetry, and drama feeds the imagination and human desires. It puts one in touch with myth and symbol, which is crucial if the preacher is to communicate to human depths.

When one accepts the call to preach, one embraces a way of life, a spirituality, that is centered in God's word, is concerned about truth, is caring about people, and is convinced that, with the overshadowing of the Spirit, the word will become flesh anew for God's people (*see* Prayer).

Burghardt, W. J., S.J., *Preaching: The Art and the Craft*, 1987. **Carr, A.,** "On Feminist

Spirituality," in *Women's Spirituality: Resources for Christian Development*, ed. J. W. Conn, 1986. **Ruane, E., O.P.,** and **R. Siegfried, A.S.C.,** eds., *In the Company of Preachers*, 1992.   JOAN DELAPLANE, O.P.

Spurgeon, Charles Haddon

(1835–1892) Victorian-Age London pastor-evangelist of what was then the largest regular congregation in the world, C. H. Spurgeon was an internationally renowned preacher whose sermons and other volumes still form the largest body of evangelical writings in the English language.

The Essex-born grandson of an Independent clergyman, Spurgeon found personal salvation at 15 when, driven to shelter in a tiny Colchester chapel by an unexpected Sunday snowstorm, he listened to a simple gospel sermon delivered by a Primitive Methodist lay preacher. In the same year he abandoned his Congregational heritage to confess his faith through believers' baptism, then volunteered as a leader in a Cambridge Baptist Sunday school. In 1852, Spurgeon left his local vocation as an assistant schoolteacher to begin as the village pastor of the Baptist Chapel in the small village of Waterbeach where, under his mature preaching, attendance exploded from a mere handful of hearers to 400 within just one year.

At age 19 (in 1854), New Park Street Baptist Church in central London called him to serve its meager congregation of 100. The chapel's 800 seats filled rapidly until at 23 he became London's most popular preacher, often gathering huge congregations in large public auditoriums, such as Exeter Hall. In 1856, he gathered 12,000 for services at the Surrey Gardens Music Hall, and on October 7, 1857, 23,654 crushed in to hear him at London's Crystal Palace. In 1876, 20,000 attended a service at the Agricultural Hall, Islington. He often worked 18-hour days and, with his regular excursions outside of London, it was not uncommon for him

to have addressed a total of 30,000 persons during any particular week.

In 1861, Spurgeon moved his New Park Street Baptist Church to the new 6,000-seat Metropolitan Tabernacle, which opened debt-free at Newington in South London. He filled it twice each Sunday, gathering 3,000 each Thursday evening, and baptizing hundreds of converts each year. The pastor spent many day and evening hours each week in his church vestry personally leading inquirers seeking baptism and church membership into an individual assurance of salvation. His ministry stretched over 35 years with no diminishing of his power or appeal to the masses. Several times each year he asked members of his regular congregation to vacate their seats so that the tabernacle could be filled with invited guests from the local poor and other visitors to hear a special gospel message.

Spurgeon baptized his twin sons in 1874. Charles, Jr., became pastor at Greenwich and, in 1884, Thomas succeeded his father in the London pulpit, sustaining a successful ministry for 14 years, rebuilding the Tabernacle after its destruction by a disastrous fire. During 23 years of his preaching life, Spurgeon suffered severely from arthritic gout, a condition that finally resulted in his death from kidney failure in 1892.

American evangelists D. L. Moody,* R. A. Torrey, and J. Wilbur Chapman and British preachers John McNeill, F. B. Meyer, F. W. Boreham, G. Campbell Morgan,* and D. Martyn Lloyd-Jones represent but a few of the many evangelical pulpit giants who acknowledged the stimulation of his ministry upon their own.

Preaching. With the aid of secretaries, he spent all week "foraging for the pulpit," researching materials from his extensive library, often building a sermon skeleton and choosing one text (as a vehicle to share his understandings) as late as Saturday evening and Sunday afternoon. His sermons may best be defined as topical and textual; yet they are always anchored firmly in biblical revelation and include much of its substance. The phenomenal originality of his interpretations and the variety and diversity of his subjects consistently leave most who examine the sermon collections quite aghast. Yet for all this, his messages of comfort for saints and of instruction for seekers explore cardinal biblical themes with incredible simplicity and relevance. Many still adapt his sermonic ideas with great effectiveness in their current ministries and find his emphases to be timelessly relevant.

A preacher who chose fresh approaches and unusual texts, Spurgeon clearly sensed the pulse of his age by using current situations as hooks for his gospel preaching. These included a mine disaster, a cholera epidemic, and business and financial crises. He phrased his sermons with an uncommon clarity to hook into hearers' needs, bending novelty, humor, and emotive sense-appeal images to fresh ends. He communicated lucidly and logically and regularly used allusions to the natural world to illustrate his ideas. All this brought fresh air into the worship experiences of thousands. His sermons were styled to appeal to the masses in contrast to the unpalatable and indigestible theological essays so typical of many Victorian Age pulpits. His effective command of plain, precisely articulated, Anglo-Saxon language, and his bell-like silvery tenor voice combined to supply communications dynamics of unusual interest. He disciplined his oral interpretations and delivery by pacing and projecting his voice with such effect that speech teachers and dramatic coaches sent their students to observe his skills. In this sense he must be regarded a great preacher of sermons as much as a preacher of great sermons.

In the pulpit, Spurgeon balanced the relevance and evangelical fervor of his preaching with a mystical power of public prayer, which revealed the tenderness of his pastoral heart and a memory full of scripture. Many said that the quality of his extemporaneous prayers during worship exceeded that of his sermons. During the five funeral services held at the Tabernacle on the day of his death, his own devotional Bible lay open on the closed casket, at his favorite Old Testament book, the Song of Solomon, with many passages heavily annotated and underlined in his own hand. For some, this supported the impression that his preaching reached its greatest and most moving heights when it interpreted biblical analogies and metaphors.

Publications. Many of his sermons, taken down in shorthand, were edited and published one week later in a "penny pulpit" series that sold from the newsstands and the railroad stations at a rate of 25,000 per week. Many of these were translated into forty languages. Publication of his sermons in annual volumes continued after his death until 1917. The current official publishers' guide lists over two hundred publications authored or edited by C. H. Spurgeon still in print today, including his sixty-three-volume set of 4,000-plus sermons, which outsells all other sermon collections today. Reputable scholars have estimated that the publications he personally wrote total 23 million words—the equivalent of the twenty-seven volumes of the ninth edition of the *Encyclopaedia Britannica*! The many millions of copies of his sermons that have now been distributed defy computation, but the student who plans to read just one sermon a day from Spurgeon's main volumes will take ten years to complete the task. Spurgeon's most scholarly work was a seven-volume commentary on the Psalms titled *The Treasury of David*, still available from a variety of publishers and now collated into three volumes.

Social Conscience. The world today largely forgets the breadth of Spurgeon's concern for the practical issues of his day. His Tabernacle initiated 35 different philanthropic organizations. He attacked slavery. He publicly advocated workers' rights, supported struggles against alcohol abuse, and directed massive grams of social outreach, including an evening school for uneducated city youths, an orphanage enrolling 500, and almshouses for the indigent and the aged. He founded, staffed, and supported 23 mission halls in London's slums, which ministered to the social and economic ills of the city. Spurgeon opened his own private purse so deeply for the support of these institutions that he died without leaving any significant estate except the ownership of his own home.

Because the national universities were open only to members of the established church, he often gave Friday evening educational lectures on subjects ranging from historical biography to natural science and travel experiences, and he started a theological school. During the twelve final years of Spurgeon's own ministry, his Pastors' College students baptized 39,000 persons. Before his death in 1892, his graduates had erected 200 church buildings in the London area, and today the enrollment at Spurgeon's College makes it the largest seminary student body in all of Britain.

Theology. A self-taught theologian who built his understanding from the writings of the Reformers and Puritans, Spurgeon's orthodoxy centered on the sovereignty of God, the reality of forgiveness available to all through Christ, and the power of the indwelling Holy Spirit to transform those who commit themselves to faith. While essentially Calvinistic, he nevertheless advocated a balanced system that also embraced the responsibility of individuals to respond to God's free grace. He worked in a personal library of 12,000 volumes, one-third of which are on display at William Jewell College in Liberty, Missouri. His addresses to Church of England clergy, his regular ministries at annual denominational meetings other than Baptist, and his presence at many interdenominational gatherings all illustrate a spirit of broad fellowship.

Recent research (Skinner, 1984) clearly documents the origin of fundamentalism within the Spurgeon context many years before its emergence in America. The use of the word itself in its original English expression and the characteristics of the English movement confirm its genesis as a popular reaction to extremist liberal emphases. Fresh links have also been established between the English origins of fundamentalism and subsequent American developments that illumine the latter as a distortion of the original.

Drummond, L., *Charles Haddon Spurgeon: Prince of Preachers*, 1992. **Skinner, C.,** *Lamplighter and Son: The Forgotten Story of Thomas Spurgeon and His Famous Father, C. H. Spurgeon*, 1984. **Spurgeon, C. H.,** *The Metropolitan Tabernacle Pulpit*, Vols. 7–63, 1965–1980.   CRAIG SKINNER

SONGS IN THE NIGHT
Charles Haddon Spurgeon

But none saith, Where is God my Maker, who giveth songs in the night? (Job 35:10). Any fool can sing in the day. When the cup is full, man draws inspiration from it; when wealth rolls in abundance round about him, any man can sing to the praise of a God who gives a plenteous harvest, or sends home a loaded argosy. It is easy enough for an Aeolian harp to whisper music when the winds blow; the difficulty is for music to come when no wind bloweth. It is easy to sing when we can read the notes by daylight; but the skillful singer is he who can sing when there is not a ray of light to read by—who sings from his heart, and not from a book that he can see, because he has no means of reading, save from that inward book in his own living spirit, whence notes of gratitude pour out in songs of praise. No man can make a song in the night by himself; he may attempt it, but he will feel how difficult it is. Let all things go as I please—I will weave songs, weave them wherever I go, with the flowers that grow upon my path; but put me in a desert, where no flowers are, and wherewith shall I weave a chorus of praise to God? How shall I make a crown for him? Let this voice be free, and this body be full of health, and I can sing God's praise; but stop this tongue, lay me upon the bed of languishing; and it is not easy to sing from the bed, and chant high praises in the fires. Give me the bliss of spiritual liberty, and let me mount up to my God, get near the throne, and I will sing, ay, sing as sweet as seraphs; but confine me, fetter my spirit, clip my wings, make me exceeding sad, so that I become old like the eagle—ah! then it is hard to sing. It is not in man's power to sing, when all is adverse. It is not natural to sing in trouble—"Bless the Lord, O my soul, and all that is within me bless his holy name."

It is marvelous, brethren, how the sweet word of God will make whole songs for Christians. One word of God is like a piece of gold, and the Christian is the gold-beater, and he can hammer that promise out for whole weeks. I can say myself, I have lived on one promise for weeks, and want no other. I want just simply to hammer that promise out into gold-leaf, and plate my whole existence with joy from it. The Christian gets his songs from God: God gives him inspiration, and teaches him how to sing: "God my Maker, who giveth songs in the night."

From "Songs in the Night," in *The Protestant Pulpit*, ed. A. Blackwood (New York: Abingdon-Cokesbury, 1947), 114–17.

Steimle, Edmund A. (1907–1988)

Born in Allentown, Pennsylvania, Edmund Steimle was recognized as an author, an editor, and an innovative teacher of preaching, but he was best known as a radio preacher. His sermons on the Lutheran series "The Protestant Hour," which he preached from 1955 until 1974, were broadcast on several hundred radio stations in North America, creating a steady stream of letters from listeners, requests for printed copies of his sermons, and invitations to preach and speak around the world.

Steimle was educated at Princeton University, the Lutheran Theological Seminary in Philadelphia, and the University of Pennsylvania. Upon graduation from the seminary in 1935, he served as a Lutheran pastor for seventeen years, first in Jersey City, New Jersey, and then in Cambridge, Massachusetts. In 1952, his academic career began when he returned to the Lutheran Seminary in Philadelphia as the Hagan Professor of Practical Theology, a position he held until 1961, when he joined the faculty of Union Theological Seminary in New York City as the Brown Professor of Homiletics.

Steimle's appeal and effectiveness as a preacher was the result of a number of aspects of his approach to preaching. First, he was one of several notable preachers of his era who instinctively understood the demands and opportunities of radio. Rather than thinking of a radio audience in terms of thousands of people and therefore lifting his voice to speak to a multitude, Steimle knew that radio communication was quite personal and individual. People were listening to his sermons by themselves, in kitchens and automobiles, in hospital rooms, and on the bedside clock radio. So he spoke conversationally, dialogically. His voice was firm, but quiet and reasoned. He sounded as if he were across the breakfast table, sipping coffee as he talked. For emphasis, he would not raise his voice, but lower it. Where other preachers would shout or infuse frenetic excitement into their delivery, Steimle would insert a weary sigh, a deep pause, or an audibly exhaled breath.

His dialogical manner was not, however, simply a delivery technique; it was also a matter of theological conviction. Steimle was influenced by the New Testament scholar Amos Wilder, whose study of the rhetoric of the New Testament had led him to understand that the Bible itself spoke dialogically because of the inherently dialogical character of revelation. Thus, Steimle was persuaded that if the gospel itself was dialogical, then preaching ought to be as well. For a while, in order to contrast his style of preaching with that of others, Steimle even called his "Protestant Hour" homilies "conversations" instead of "sermons," and they were rich with the sounds of exchange with the hearer. It was a common feature of Steimle's sermons to end a paragraph with a phrase such as "This is true for us, isn't it so?"

Steimle was a biblical preacher. Most of his "Protestant Hour" sermons were based upon the text selections found in the Lutheran lectionary and were the products of careful exegesis and an awareness of the most recent biblical texts as parts of a larger biblical story of human failure and divine grace, of tragedy and redemption, of law and gospel.*

His view of the sweep of the biblical story and his Lutheran theological tradition led him often to build his sermons in two broad sections or movements. In the first section (theologically, a law section), he would give voice to the experience of estrangement. Steimle did not announce the law—he cried out as a human being under the law, expressing the doubt, rage, despair, and bitterness of the human predicament. Then, at some point, his sermons would inevitably turn from law to gospel, from cynicism to hope. This turn, this second movement, was never glib or easy but the expression of a truthful, half-doubting, half-believing person clinging tenaciously, if sometimes desperately, to the promises of his faith. Indeed, it was Steimle's refusal to be casually pious, his rigorous, sometimes even brutal, honesty as he struggled to hold on to the gospel, that gave his preaching much of its edge and power.

Steimle's sermons were also filled with references to the headlines in the newspaper and the major issues and cultural developments of the day. A sermon that begins in the Bible and ends in the Bible, he maintained, is not a biblical sermon. So, he spoke of Watergate, racial integration in the schools, the Vietnam War, the Black Manifesto, and Woodstock. He cited U.S. Presidents by name, found something to admire in the "flower children" of the 1960s, responded to the charismatic movement, described Broadway plays, quoted current novels and essays, and repeated lines from popular television sitcoms. His illustrations were never canned or placed in the sermon simply to teach a point. They were, rather, gritty and streetwise epiphanies, moments taken from human experience that breathed, amid the ambiguity, the air of divine presence and grace.

People who heard Steimle for the first time were sometimes shocked by his candor, his willingness to wrestle with doubt and anxiety, his distaste for piety. After one Sunday sermon, he was told at the door of the church by a parishioner, "You ought to have your mouth washed out with soap!" Once, when he was preaching in a university chapel, his sermon was interrupted by an outraged student, who shouted, "This is a lot of atheistic nonsense. God is very much alive and present. This man is a false prophet." Steimle looked out at the young man and said, characteristically, "That may very well be. But hear me out, and we'll see."

Those who did hear him out were almost always rewarded by receiving a sermon of biting authenticity, intellectual rigor, and profound hope and faithfulness. As a preacher, Steimle anticipated a trend in American preaching toward dialogue, narrative, and fluid sermon form, and his preaching style served as a model for a generation of preachers. In 1966, he edited *Renewal in the Pulpit*, an anthology of sermons by younger preachers, many of whom had been deeply influenced by him. He served as the consulting editor of the Fortress Press series, The Preacher's Paperback Library, and four collections of his own "Protestant Hour" sermons were published. With Charles Rice and Morris Niedenthal, he wrote *Preaching the Story*, a homiletical textbook.

Long, T. G., "Edmund Steimle and the Shape of Contemporary Homiletics," *The Princeton Seminary Bulletin* 11 (1990), 253–69. Steimle, E. A., *Are You Looking for God?*, 1957; *Disturbed by Joy*, 1967; *God the Stranger: Reflections About Resurrection*, 1979.   THOMAS G. LONG

AND HOW DOES IT ALL END?

Edmund A. Steimle

Early one summer morning, a New York policeman delivered a child in a dimly lighted Brooklyn tenement, and, less than three hours later, and only six blocks away, shot and killed a stick-up man who was pulling his gun on him. At the end of the day both the child and the gunman were still nameless. Anonymous birth and anonymous death—and the whole mystery of life and what it's all about caught up in a story of a policeman's tour of duty early one summer morning.

What *is* life all about? What's your life all about? And what question remains unanswered until you have faced up to the end of it? We may think that we know how the gunman's life ended, but how will that new baby's life end? And yours? And mine?

The Bible—as realistic a book as you'll find anywhere—presents two possibilities. The first is in the mouth of Job: "Man that is born of a woman is of few days and full of trouble. He comes forth like a flower and withers. . . ." That is a dark picture, of course. We can say it came out of Job's depression and bitterness and may well reflect our moments of bitterness too. But it's more than that. What of the death of the gunman? Or of the peasants at My Lai? Or drop in on a ward for terminal illness or into any shoddy nursing home. And, frankly, what does it look like? "Man that is born of a woman is of few days and full of trouble. He comes forth like a flower and withers. . . ."

But Paul, of course, gives us a brighter prospect: "We wish you not to remain in ignorance, brethren, about those who sleep in death; you should not grieve like the rest of men, who have not hope. We believe that Jesus died and rose again; and so it will be for those who died as Christians; God will bring them to life with Jesus."

But isn't that pretty much whistling in the dark of these days? For who can really believe any longer in a resurrection from the dead or in a life after death? Remember: Paul is not talking about an immortal soul that goes on living no matter what, some untouchable part of me which is indestructible. Paul is talking about a miracle; that we die, as Jesus died, every last bit of us. And then the miracle: "We believe that Jesus died—and rose again." And as for the rest of us who die: "God will bring them to life with Jesus."

From "And How Does It All End?" in *From Death to Birth* (Philadelphia: Fortress Press, 1973), 3–4. Used by permission.

Stewart, James Stuart.   (1896–1990)

James S. Stewart was born in Dundee, Scotland. His father William had given up a career in business to work there for the YMCA, where he taught an influential Bible class for thirty years. As R. S. Barbour noted of Stewart in his memorial address, "He was brought up in that strong atmosphere of evangelical piety reinforced by intellectual rigour which has done so much to make Scotland what she is today." Barbour adds that it was both in preparation for the ministry and for their own sake "that he [Stewart] assimilated so brilliantly the classical scholarship and the love of English literature which stood then . . . at the heart of what we call an education in the Arts." Stewart received both the M.A. and the B.D. from St. Andrews University and did postgraduate study at Bonn. He was pastor successively at Church of Scotland parishes in Auchterader (Perthshire), Beechgrove in Aberdeen, and at North Morningside in Edinburgh. He then became professor of New Testament language, literature, and theology at New College (the faculty of divinity) of the University of Edinburgh, where his lecture halls were nearly as crowded as his churches once had been. In 1953, at Yale, he delivered the Lyman Beecher Lectures on preaching. In 1963, he spent a year as moderator of the General Assembly of the Church of Scotland. He retired from New College in 1966.

For all its wide range—through scripture, history, literature, poetry, and biography—Stewart's preaching was intensely personal. When he took aim at grave matters of culture, politics, or current events, the ultimate purpose was still help for the individual spirit of the hearer. Challenge, comfort, vision, hope, consolation: these were what he sought to impart; and he did not give them out of his own strength or experience, but rather he promised them with authority to all those who would reach out for that companionship of God, that daily fellowship with Christ, toward which he was always turning his hearers' thoughts and hearts.

Ironically, a great strength of this deeply personal preaching was Stewart's almost extreme shyness. He made no claims for himself, put no trust in his own experience, made no move to surround himself with disciples or otherwise to aggrandize. One went to Stewart's preaching with an unthinking trust that he would not exalt himself at the hearer's expense. Given his powerful rhetorical gifts, his deep Christ-mysticism, his almost romantic imaging of scenes from scripture or common life, this self-abnegation became, perhaps, the most potent of all his attributes as a preacher. Before and after his half-hour in the pulpit, Stewart was self-effacing nearly to a fault; when he stepped into it and the first notes of his soft, melodic Scottish voice sounded forth, ringing like a gong, sounding like battle trumpets, ravishing as a melody by Mendelssohn, one witnessed an awesome transformation. What one saw in the street or study or at luncheon was but a smoldering wick; in the pulpit there leapt forth a powerful flame. Yet one felt that the charm, the ravishing, the exultation induced by the words were not intended to reflect glory on the preacher. All the emotion he could call forth was directed not to him but to the God for whom he spoke.

Whether he was piling up images and pictures or sending out wave after wave of metaphorical representations of truths and events, Stewart's pulpit rhetoric made stunning use of picture language and of the force of repetition. These reiterating waves of his imagery and logic would often finally crest in a very simple

yet quite unexpected phrase or sentence that capped it all, leaving one breathless with gratitude for a new insight that so exactly fit the situation. In a sermon preached in St. Giles's, Edinburgh, in the early 1960s, on the troubled state of today's church, Stewart realistically portrayed the current situation and the church's weaknesses and failures in the face of it. He then carried the mind's eye back to two contrasting but unnamed figures: a prisoner in a dungeon, writing letters—by the light of a guttering lamp—to minuscule, struggling, little churches nearly buried under the splendor and sin of a mighty empire. Meanwhile, far above him, sat another man, enthroned, wearing the purple, at whose command armies were dispatched to the corners of the known world. "Looking at them," he inquired, "to whom would you have said the future would belong?" A pause, and then J. S. Stewart's words sang forth, a simple, shimmering blade: "Yet today, men call their dogs Nero, but their sons Paul."

He got one to see the great truths of the faith, standing, embodied, before the mind's eye. One had believed it before but, unimagined, it had no hold. Stewart brought his hearers to see that to which they had already assented. This passage from a sermon on the peace of God describes his method beautifully. To find that peace, he says, one must fix on three basic facts:

Fact number one—*the sovereignty of God.* The Bible says, Build on that rock. The Lord God omnipotent reigneth. You confess it every time you say your creed, "I believe in God the Father Almighty." You acknowledge it every time you repeat the Lord's Prayer, "Thine is the kingdom, the power and the glory." Well, then, believe your own faith! The trouble is that we may believe it theoretically without ever *seeing it, imagining it, realizing it in its exciting dramatic reality* ("The Pressure of Life and the *Peace of God*," 1975, 39; latter emphasis added).

This was, perhaps, his greatest single strength as a preacher: he helped one to see, imagine, and realize the reality of what one already believed; in the force of that imagining, he could carry one very nearly to the gate of heaven itself and into the presence of the Lamb for sinners slain.

Stewart, J. S., *The Strong Name*, 1941; *A Faith to Proclaim*, 1953; and *King Forever*, 1975.   DONALD F. CHATFIELD

| THE ASCENSION OF CHRIST
| *James S. Stewart*
| Notice, in the second place, that it [the Ascension] was expedient for *the universalizing of the Gospel.* Consider how Christianity began. A Child is born to a peasant woman; a young Man toils at a bench; half a dozen fishermen suddenly leave their boats and nets; among a few out-of-the-way villages a fire of religious revival is kindled, flares up, and dies away; a table is spread for a family meal in an upper room; in the obscurity of a wooded glade a bowed Figure wrestles in prayer; on an insignificant hillock a cross is raised; in a garden a tomb stands empty. It all sounds so local—does it not?—a tale from an unimportant backwater of history, far removed from the main stream of the rushing years and the surge and thunder of the deeds of men, a sequestered story of long ago and far away, lovely but irrelevant. Yet it is this that in the providence of God has leapt the barriers of the centuries and the frontiers of every nation under heaven. It is this that from its hidden beginnings has stormed the mind and conscience of the world, and pounded at the battlements of ancient prejudice, and broken down like matchwood the stubbornest defences that men have raised against the fire and tempest of its coming. . . .

It was for this that it was expedient that Jesus went away. While He was with His followers visibly, He could not belong to all the world. While He was ministering to the needy folk of Galilee, He could not be equally the possession of mankind without distinction, barbarian, Scythian, bond

and free. Only by departing from the vision of the privileged few could He reign by His Spirit in the hearts of all.

Have you ever considered how many deeds of help and healing Jesus in His earthly ministry had to leave undone? . . . To any man with a conscience, that is bound to be a difficult and perplexing experience. What, I wonder, did it mean to Jesus? . . . [But] the day would come when the closing of this first stage of His ministry would be the opening of another, and it would be given to Him to be no longer the Companion and the Succourer of the few but the Friend of all and the Saviour of the world.

| From "The Gospel of the Ascension," in
| *The Strong Name*, Scribner, 1941, 50.

Style. "Style," as a characteristic of a sermon text, is its texture and design. A complete treatment of preaching style would, of necessity, consider its place within the dynamic of the preacher, the assembly, and the texts of scripture and sermon. Who and how one speaks; who hears and how they listen; what is spoken and in what space and for what occasion—all characterize the style of preaching. To cast the net even wider, the historical relationship between preaching and style would also have to consider other forms of preaching like iconography, drama, and architecture. The scope of this essay is restricted to a focus on the artifact of preaching, the sermon text read or delivered orally.

The principal element of a sermon's style is its language, the words and sentences selected by the author, their arrangement or distortion in order to produce some effect upon the hearer. Every sermon, whether uttered spontaneously or written in advance or after delivery, reveals through its composition textures and designs that can be named and evaluated. Particular texts, the entire canons of particular preachers, the preaching of particular traditions, theologies, and histories lend themselves to stylistic definition and identification. This essay connects the subject of preaching style to its historical roots in Hellenistic and early Christian rhetoric.* Finally, it defines some of the common elements of sermon design (*see* Form).

Scripture is the natural starting place for any discussion about preaching style. The imperative to preach permeates all of scripture; the reliance on Jewish models of preaching by Jesus and the disciples is singularly evident. The discourses attributed to Jesus build on the customary Jewish practice of uttering a sacred text and following with an explanation or interpretation. Jesus inaugurates his ministry in Luke 4:16–22 by adopting this model, one that provides the framework for a myriad of stylistic variations of New Testament speeches. The message of Jesus varies far less from gospel to gospel than does the texture of his message: parables from Matthew, poetry from John.

Scripture, then, can be read as a primer for identifying the breadth of choices available to the preacher. For every figure of thought and speech, for every trope listed and defined in handbooks of Greek and Roman rhetoric, there are corresponding examples within the canons of scripture. Two sermons recorded in the book of Acts illustrate the contrasting styles of the earliest preachers, both adopting the familiar models of Jewish preaching for their kerygmatic purposes. A focus on the conclusions of Peter's sermon at Pentecost (Acts 2:14–36) and Stephen's discourse (Acts 7:2–53) illustrates the point.

Both preachers indict their Jewish hearers for complicity in the death of Jesus, but the style of their conclusion or peroration is markedly different; the effect, significantly so. Peter concludes, "Therefore let the whole house of Israel know for certain that God has made him both Lord and Messiah, this Jesus whom you crucified." We are told that Peter's hearers are "cut to the heart" by his message. The success of Peter's preaching is confirmed and measured by those "three thousand" who repent and are baptized.

The relationship between the design or style of this discourse and Peter's success is made more striking by the contrasting style of Stephen's effort to proclaim essentially the same message. Stephen completes his sermon:

> You stiff necked people, uncircumcised in heart and ears, you always oppose the Holy Spirit; you are just like your ancestors. Which of the prophets did your ancestors not persecute? They put to death those who foretold the coming of the righteous one, whose betrayers and murderers you have now become. You received the law as transmitted by angels, but you did not deserve it.

Stephen's fate is well known. The design of Stephen's speech, especially its hyperbolic conclusion, both underscores and anticipates the anger of the hearers and the subsequent fate of the martyr. Indeed, the scriptures are not only inspired texts; they are also a rich tapestry of design and texture for the contemporary preacher's edification. But these sacred texts do not push far beyond the conventional limits of Jewish models.

As the disciples proclaim their message for non-Jewish hearers, the familiar rhetorical forms and commonplaces of Jewish preaching prove inadequate. The movement of the gospel, in part, depends upon new movements, new strategies for new communities. The most familiar illustration of this direction in Christian preaching is Paul's speech before Athenians at the Areopagus (Acts 17:22–31). In addressing the Gentile assembly, Paul draws upon his knowledge of Hellenistic culture. He cites the Athenians' altar "to an Unknown God" to create an antithesis between their unknowing worship of distant gods and Christians' familiar intimacy with the God "who is not far from any of us." This device as well as his allusion to Greek poetry reveal Paul's conscious adaptation of his preaching style to the needs of his hearers. By breaking convention and drawing upon examples from pagan religion and poetry, Paul also forecasts a protracted debate among Christian preachers about the suitability of using the rhetorical arts of pagans to spread the gospel.

As the earliest Christian preachers find themselves outmatched and overwhelmed by the artistry and skill of pagan orators who assault them, converted Christian rhetoricians like Augustine,* Basil, and John Chrysostom* mount a campaign to meet their opponents on a level playing field, armed with their own rhetorical skills, now refashioned for the gospel.

Augustine harnesses the pagan arts for the preacher in *On Christian Doctrine*. Book IV of this treatise, completed in 426, makes explicit the Christian preacher's debt to Cicero for providing the foundation upon which Christian eloquence might flourish. What Augustine adopts and adapts from Cicero in his handbook for preachers remained for centuries the clearest and most influential guidance for preachers. Understanding the historical relationship between preaching and style requires that Augustine's theory merit particular attention. Most homiletic theories merely echoed Augustine until the development of the *ars praedicandi* in the twelfth century. Even so, these handbooks concerned themselves almost exclusively with topics for invention and their arrangement or division. Elaborations on style are, for the most part, conspicuously absent or merely revisions of Augustine's theory. Thus, Augustine's prescriptions on style hold hegemony until well into the modern period and, for that reason, bear examination.

Borrowing from the tenets of Greek and Roman rhetoric, Augustine and similarly educated Christian rhetoricians understood style to be among the five offices or activities of the orator: invention, arrangement, style, delivery,* and memory.* While he dwells primarily on style in Book IV of *On Christian Doctrine*, to isolate that section from the previous three books would seriously distort Augustine's intention. His detailed analysis of the rules and ways for mining the truths of scripture in Books I through III reminds the preacher that scripture alone provides the matter for invention and determines other choices about sermon composition.

Any treatment of preaching style rested upon two presumptions: a relationship between style and the preacher's character* and a correspondence between style and the appropriateness of occasion or assembly. On the first point, Augustine adapts from Greek and Roman rhetoric the necessity of eloquence united to wisdom. Cicero's *De Oratore* (III, 14, 51) asserted that eloquence without wisdom was like a sword in the hands of a madman. Cicero taught that eloquence and wisdom were inexorably allied in a dynamic search for the most probable truth. But the Christian orator, according to Augustine, has now been given the truth in scriptures; therefore, preachers merely employ rhetorical devices in order to lead hearers to the wisdom that is Christ. Augustine emphasizes this in Book IV of *On Christian Doctrine* (27, 59): "However, the life of the speaker has greater weight in determining whether he is obediently heard than any grandness of eloquence." This corruption of Ciceronian rhetoric—that is, the presumption that wisdom or truth could actually be discovered, known, and taught without eloquence—gets at the heart of the historical controversy about the purpose of style in preaching.

From a modern and contemporary perspective it would seem that the growth of Christianity's cultural and religious dominance would obviate the need for elaborately constructed arguments on behalf of the faith. Similarly, those preachers who believe in the immediacy of scriptural truth, its accessibility to all believers, and its irresistible call to obedience, would rely less on crafting sermons with designs and textures that would teach, move, and delight their hearers. The ability of reason to apprehend truth short-circuits the need for services rendered by allegory or metaphor. Indeed, an extreme example of this occurred in seventeenth-century England with the collision of British empiricism and religion. English Latitudinarian preachers, in keeping with secular prose style, avoided ornaments and embellishments in favor of language that is "close, naked, and natural." Their Quaker contemporaries rejected the corruptions of human speech for the occasional utterance of inspiration; barring this, they chose silence.

This suspicion about language and its artifices explains, in large measure, why so little attention is given to the topic of style in preaching manuals after Augustine. But it is Augustine himself who, curiously, provides the most persuasive and persistent argument for learning and using the rhetorical figures. For him, obedience to wisdom is manifested through a successful interpretation of the literal and figurative signs of scripture, which culminates in the experience of love, *caritas*. The fact that scripture itself is replete with figures and ambiguities justifies the usefulness of these for preachers.

The second presumption that is a cornerstone for Augustine's theory is the link between style and propriety. Book IV elaborates on the conventional divisions of plain, middle, and grand style. These styles, rooted in ancient rhetorical distinctions, are distinguished by the sparse or copious use of figures of speech and thought. According to Augustine, each style has an appropriate use, depending on the purpose of the sermon: One *taught* in the plain style, *pleased* in the middle style, and *moved* in the grand style. Much of Book IV provides examples for each style, culminating with this admonition:

Thus those three ends which we described above for a man who speaks wisely if he would also speak eloquently, that is, that he should so speak that he is heard intelligently, willingly, and obediently, are not to be taken so that one of the three styles is attributed to each one so that the subdued style pertains to understanding, the moderate style to willingness, and the grand style to obedience; rather, there is such a way that the orator always attends to all three and fulfills them all as much as

he can, even when he is using a single style (IV, 26, 53).

Augustine imitates his Greek and Roman rhetorical ancestors by describing and defining the stylistic characteristics of effective speech, not sacred speech. To a greater rather than lesser degree, Augustine's precepts simply tell what works for hearers and what does not, and this changes little throughout the history of preaching.

Some presumptions that underlie Augustine's homiletic theories on style clearly fall short of actual experience. First, Augustine directed his treatise to those preachers who knew or could learn the principles of rhetoric, including the virtues of style and the numerous figures of diction and thought available to the orator. Only with the Council of Vaison in 529 was permission to preach extended to priests and deacons, most of whom relied exclusively on reading or imitating patristic sermons provided for their assemblies. For centuries, few preachers had access to the literary and technical training afforded the earliest Christian preachers.

Second, Augustine's prescriptions for preachers rest upon a primitive psychology that does not adjust readily to diversity among hearers. Oddly enough, Augustine's claim that each level of style corresponds to an appropriate audience (e.g., the plain style being suitable for the uneducated) finds support and expression in preaching manuals well into the twentieth century.

Third, when Augustine limits the functions of style to the service of revelation, he does not account for its role in the discovery of wisdom through the experience of preaching. For example, while Augustine would use allegory to illumine the truth of scripture, monastic preachers would later exploit allegory in order to draw listeners into the mysteries of the text. The Cistercian monk Bernard of Clairvaux* (1090–1153) aimed at producing within his brother monks the actual experience of praise, thanksgiving, or contemplation. His series of sermons on the "Canticle of Canticles," for example, extends the scriptural allegory with the copious uses of imagery and poetics, provoking within the monks an *experience* of *caritas*, which leads to contemplation rather than speculation.

This monastic insistence on the use of image to mediate experience found extended use by mendicant preachers in the thirteenth century. Franciscan* friars, in particular, brought the recreation of religious experience out of the monastery and into the fields and urban centers of Europe. By drawing upon the idiom and experiences of popular culture, their exempla, visual effects, and high drama gave these itinerant* preachers notoriety for creating the immediacy of religious experience.

The high drama of these friars coexisted with Augustine's inheritors, the scholastic preachers. Their thematic sermons sought to drive out heresy and teach correct doctrine by clear and precise development of propositions supported by arguments, authorities, and anecdotes. The Order of Preachers, or Dominican* friars, most closely claimed affinity with Augustine. For example, the Dominican Humbert of Romans* (1200?–1277) wrote a treatise on the formation of preachers in which Augustine is frequently cited for authority. Most telling in this work is the brief treatment given to the use of artistry in preaching: "Other arts are a matter of ingenuity, but in this art of preaching there is serious business for the mind to deal with. A sick man does not look for an eloquent doctor. If the doctor who can cure him can also make an eloquent speech about what has to be done, that is like having an expert helmsman who is also handsome" (Tugwell, 220).

The late medieval and early Renaissance preachers continue along parallel currents, producing both richly adorned sermons for the papal court and plainly simple sermons for the Lollards of England, choosing or rejecting from among the same range of choices as their ancestors. The discoveries and reforms of the sixteenth century, however, had major consequences for the relationship between preaching and style.

Thus far in the history of preaching, style had been more or less integrated with sermon invention. Essential to the preacher's choice of topic were correlative choices about how the matter for the sermon would be arranged and by what manner it would be conveyed. As diminished a role as style had within the handbooks on preaching, preachers had reserved for themselves the same duties as that for the secular orator: invention, arrangement, style, delivery, and memory. But, for a number of reasons, the traditional methods and forms failed to meet the demands of the modern age.

Peter Ramus (1515–1572) is generally credited with advancing a new logic intended to cope with the social and religious chaos of his time. In essence, the deductive methods of scholastic reasoning failed those searching for a method appropriate to the inductive reasoning of the new science. Similarly, Protestants like Ramus found the commonplaces of Catholic preaching inadequate for their reformed theologies.

The influence of Ramus on rhetoric and consequently on preaching is evident in the work of Abraham Fraunce, whose *Arcadian Rhetorike* (1588) leaves to rhetoric only style and delivery. By assigning to this new logic the offices of invention and arrangement, Ramistic philosophers greatly diminished the need for persuasion. Instead, they enlarged the notion that truth could be apprehended if observed in each of its components, divided and subdivided as necessary. The premise that truth need only be observed in order to be understood left to rhetoric nothing substantial.

With only style and delivery left to rhetoric, sacred or secular, inevitable corruptions followed. Robbed of their system of thought, rhetoric and homiletics had little to offer by way of subject matter: lists of figures and guidance for delivery. Designing the sermon seemed less an activity of invention than an afterthought, like embellishing or decorating an artifact. Predictably, the stylistic pendulum continued to swing between extremes of excess and aridity. By the eighteenth century, the elocutionary movement had taken on its own life, relegating to style not only the proper language of the sermon but also the proper manner of utterance and gesture.

The uses and abuses of style in preaching have followed a circuitous but traceable path. Current discussions about narrative or story preaching would have been unimaginable in a pre-Ramistic era. Yet a rhetoric or homiletic composed only of style and delivery lends itself to such preoccupations.

When crafted well, the sermon is always a memorable discourse composed of figures and moves that do not call attention to themselves; rather, they advance the preacher's intention. Consciously or not, preachers depend upon certain figures of speech* and thought in order to create their desired effect. The distinction between figures of thought and speech is itself not significant. Simply put, the figures of speech are semantic distortions designed for effect; figures of thought are syntactic arrangements for the same purpose.

In most instances, preachers choose to texture their sermons for one of three reasons: to advance, to emphasize, or to amplify. No matter how plain or how grand the style, sermons embody devices that aim at one or more of those ends. To achieve these intentions, the skilled preacher can draw upon any number of devices; several of these are described below.

Figures to Advance. *Defining* the subject of a sermon is a commonly used launching device: "The good witch is he or she that by consent in a good league with the deuill, doth vse his helpe, for the doing of good onely" (William Perkins, in Chandos, 132).

Preachers often use the *litotes* to create a sympathetic bond between themselves and the hearers: "Beloved Brethren, Though my profession of a cordwinder be something unsuitable to this Teacher-Calling, yet my text is not, as I have served seven years apprenticeship in the one, and full as many in the other" (Chandos, 525).

The *rhetorical question* is that for which the preacher expects no answer, presuming that it is already known by the hearers. Yet this device provides an excellent transition from point to point: "But, it may be asked, Did Christ hold out no hope for those who had lived in sin?" (Newman, 1673).

Figures to Emphasize. *Anaphora* is the repetition of beginning words or phrases to create a striking effect: "Let freedom ring from the mighty mountains of New York. Let freedom ring from the heightening Alleghenies of Pennsylvania. Let freedom ring . . ." (King, 220).

Asyndeton creates a forceful effect by omitting conjunctions: "If God calls us to greater renunciation of the world, and exacts a sacrifice of our hopes and fears, this is our gain, this is a mark of His love for us, this is a thing to be rejoiced in" (Newman, 1574).

Gradatio, as its name implies, creates a climax by graduating from one step to another:

. . . That man knows nothing of nature, or providence, or Christianity, or the rewards of virtue, of the nature of its constitution, or the infirmities of man, or the mercies of God, or the arts and prudence of his loving kindness, or the rewards of heaven, or the glorification of Christ's exalted humanity, or the precepts of the Gospel, who is offended at the mercy of sufferings in the cause of righteousness; . . . (Jeremy Taylor, in Chandos, 491).

Above all, preachers search for ways to amplify their subjects. Erasmus's dictum that the sermon is "wisdom speaking copiously" implies that the wise preacher can draw upon any number of ways to illustrate and extend the point so that the hearer in time may ponder or grasp it.

The piling on of images by using the *accumulatio* is a type of repetition that attenuates an idea: "The right rich man, that duly deserveth that name, is not known by his possessions, by his costly fare and costly building, by his sumptuous palace, by his plate, jewels and substance, but by considering the poor and needy" (Henry Smith, in Chandos, 90).

The *analogy* is a simple form of comparison that expands an idea convincingly: "Like the ever-flowing waters of a river, life has its moments of drought and its moments of flood. Like the ever-changing cycle of the seasons, life has the soothing warmth of the summers and the piercing chill of its winters. But through it all, God walks with us" (King, 223) (*see* History of Preaching).

Augustine, *On Christian Doctrine,* trans. D. W. Robertson, 1958. **Chandos, J.,** ed., *In God's Name: Examples of Preaching in England, 1534–1662,* 1971. **King, M. L., Jr.,** *A Testament of Hope,* ed., J. M. Washington, 1986. **Newman, J. H.,** *Parochial and Plain Sermons,* 1987. **Tugwell, S., O.P.,** ed., *Early Dominicans: Selected Writings,* 1982.

MARY E. LYONS

Sunday, William ("Billy"). (1862–

1935) Billy Sunday was the best-known preacher in America from 1908–1925. It is estimated that from 1908 to 1920, he preached to more than one hundred million people, with about one million personal responses of commitment to Christ or some pledge to a higher standard of Christian living. His evangelistic crusades were national news, and he was a friend of the great and powerful both in business and politics. He was even considered seriously as a presidential candidate. His social concern was broad and sincere, and his patriotism was unquestioned. But his great strength lay in the uniqueness of his preaching built on his experiences as a professional baseball player.

Billy Sunday was an evangelist and revivalist, one of a long line of preachers that includes George Whitefield,* Jonathan Edwards,* Dwight L. Moody,* J. Wilbur Chapman (who hired Billy Sunday as an assistant), Charles G. Finney,* Charles E. Fuller, and Billy Graham.* Like these others, he was evangelical and ecumenical, attempting to involve as broad a spectrum of ecclesiastical groups as possible. Some Christians were offended by Sunday's style; some felt his theology was too conservative; some deplored his method; but millions eagerly flocked to hear him preach.

Billy Sunday's preaching was so uniquely personal that it can only be understood through his life story. He emerged from a difficult childhood. His father died in the Civil War when Billy was five weeks old. He was placed in a Soldiers' Orphanage at ten, left it at fourteen, and was hired by the Chicago Whitestockings from Marshalltown, Iowa, when he was eighteen. He was converted at the Pacific Garden Mission in 1886, turned his life around, began Bible study at the Chicago YMCA, and was soon in demand to give his testimony as one who was both a Christian and a premier base-stealing ballplayer. His wife Nell affirmed in him the call of God to a full-time ministry in the Chicago YMCA. He left baseball in 1891. He preached constantly and in 1896 began tent meetings on his own. These continued with limited success until 1907, when his wife became the manager of the enterprise. The numbers attending and responding increased dramatically, and invitations for his crusades poured in.

His preaching was theologically conservative, and he sided with the fundamentalists on major doctrines. He had no place for what he termed "modernists." He was the constant foe of the liquor industry and undoubtedly aided the passage of prohibition. His views on the major social issues did not change appreciably during his lifetime, but it can be argued that his social views were serious attempts to remain true to biblical Christianity as he saw it.

His use of sawdust on the dirt floor of his tents and tabernacles is the origin of "sawdust trail," and the thousands of people who came to shake hands with him were "trail hitters." Though such statistics are hard to evaluate and often suspect, the growth of churches following the meetings was enough to impress hundreds of pastors of the validity of the evangelistic effort.

The preaching of Billy Sunday was breathtaking in its dramatic intensity. It was in a rhetorical style that did not capture all listeners in the first quarter of the twentieth century and would probably do much worse today. It was argued then that people would not listen to such an outmoded style of preaching, yet people came to hear by the thousands. He worked tirelessly on his sermons, and he repeated them in many places. But his hearers could not help but appreciate the total commitment of the preacher, his uninhibited style that seemed dedicated to his purpose, his fearlessness, and his folksy humor. When Billy would run like a cat from one side of the platform to the other, slide into "home," and shout the call, "Safe!" or when he would mount a chair and then the pulpit and wrap himself in an American flag to rally people to the war effort or against the liquor industry, the performance was unforgettable. A *New York Times* reporter wrote this:

He raced up and down the green-carpeted platform . . . waving his hands, kicking up one knee now and again, like a park-walking horse, brandishing a chair, standing with one foot on a chair and another on the pulpit, bending over backward like a springy sword blade, bobbing back and forth and waving a handkerchief between his legs as he reeled off one of his amazing long lists of vituperative epithets and displaying as much energy, determination and virtuous enthusiasm as Douglas Fairbanks.

This kind of preaching is best discovered today in many African-American pulpits. It may not match the vigor of black preaching, but it certainly continues the rhetorical artifice. Such preaching produces the hypnotic effect of a long list of adjectives or the cumulative power of repeated phrases or refrains. It features the alliterated descriptions, crescendos, repetition, and all else that contributes to effective performance. None of this was invented by Billy Sunday, but he possessed a natural gift for it that is rarely seen.

His preaching was not homiletically distinctive. He used clear, plain, manageable outlines and was ruled by what he termed "progressive orthodoxy." As an evangelist, he leaned to the Arminian side of the debate with Calvin. As a citizen, he marched with the Republican party, favored the Great War, raised one hundred million dollars in war bonds, and showed respect and concern for minorities (though he never shook the racist idea that blacks neither wanted nor should have "social equality").

He was never the victim of sexual scandal, but he foundered on the shoals of money. It was not that he did wrong, but he failed to protect himself from criticism with prudence in his financial affairs. In fact, he was extremely generous. After a ten-week New York revival, he gave away the entire love offering that could have been his—$120,500. Yet the necessary "expenses" and the elegant lifestyle of the evangelist and his wife and family did not escape public notice.

Mass evangelism went into eclipse in America following Billy Sunday, but it emerged again in Billy Graham, who duplicated many of the successes and avoided the pitfalls of the Billy Sunday story (*see* Evangelism; Revivals).

Dorsett, L. W., *Billy Sunday and the Redemption of Urban America,* 1991. **McLoughlin, W. G., Jr.,** *Billy Sunday Was His Real Name,* 1955.

ROBERT N. SCHAPER

EVERYDAY POWER
Billy Sunday
I don't care if a church has two thousand members. What I ask is, how much power have they? Nine times out of ten you blame the evangelist when there are

no conversions, instead of the God-forsaken, booze-hitting, card-playing church members. There were places where Jesus could do no mighty works because of unbelief where there should have been faith. As unbelief increases faith decreases, and that's the trouble with too many churches today. What the church needs isn't pipe organs. They're all right, but they won't bring power. You can never move any mountains with them. I think God ought to have the finest buildings and the finest decorations. I believe in them. Nothing can ever be too fine for him, but faith is the only thing that can ever roll the mountains into the sea.

Faith is to us what a trolley is to a streetcar. The trolley is the means by which the power gets from the dynamo to the motor, and the motor is what makes the car go. I cannot touch God with my hands, but I can touch you. You are material; God is spiritual. Faith is the hand of the soul, and it is with it we must touch God. There is a law of faith as positive as the law of electricity. We get results from electricity, when we obey its law, whether we understand it or not. We do as electricity commands, and it gives us power without stint. When we obey God's spiritual laws just as fully—and by these I mean the laws of faith—he will take up our mountains and throw them into the sea for us. When we obey the law of electricity we have physical power, and when we obey the law of faith we have spiritual power. That's all there is to it. One is as certain as the other, for the same God is back of both. It is the most common-sense thing in the world, this religion. You say you don't understand it to send a telegraph message, or talk over the telephone. So do what God tells you in religion, whether you understand it or not, and you will get results that will convince and satisfy you.

From "Sermon on Faith," in *The Real Billy Sunday*, ed. E. Brown (Dayton: Otterbein, 1914), 123–24.

Taylor, Gardner C.   (1918–)

Described by *Time* magazine as "the dean of the nation's black preachers" and by *Ebony* as "One of the greatest preachers in American history," Gardner C. Taylor perseveres in a ministry that has spanned more than five decades. After serving congregations in Ohio and his native Louisiana, in 1948 he assumed the pastorate of the Concord Baptist Church of Christ in Brooklyn, where he remained until retirement in 1990. During his long and fruitful tenure there, Taylor traveled around the world both as a representative of American Baptist churches and as one of the recognized masters of the contemporary pulpit. His national prominence was symbolized by his invitation to preach at the Presidential Inaugural Prayer Service in 1993.

Taylor has served as a role model and inspiration for two generations of African-American* preachers, not only as an orator but also as a fully engaged urban pastor whose Brooklyn congregation has maintained a nursing home, credit union, elementary school, clothing exchange, retirement center, and community uplift endowment. Taylor himself has served on the City of New York's Board of Education and has been otherwise deeply involved in urban affairs.

He maintained pastoral involvement in the civil rights movement of the 1950s and 1960s and, along with other New York ministers, succeeded in raising large sums of money for the early southern efforts of Martin Luther King Jr.* One of the most controversial episodes in Taylor's career occurred in the early years of the civil rights movement when, with King's support, he attempted to unseat the leadership of the National Baptist Convention. Its president, Joseph H. Jackson, had been critical of King's civil rights activities and had effectively obstructed King's dream of harnessing the enormous train of the Convention to his own civil rights organization. At the tumultuous Convention in 1960, the Taylor-King insurgency was beaten back, and the Jackson forces prevailed, leaving Taylor and King little choice but to form a new denomination, the Progressive National

Baptist Convention, which Taylor later served as president.

Taylor is also widely credited with exercising great influence on the preaching of King, and it is true that, as a long-time King family friend, Taylor was in a position to teach and encourage the younger King by his example. What King and many young preachers besides would have learned from Taylor was the genius for channeling evangelical doctrine and the great stories of the Bible into socially progressive and prophetic utterance. Taylor learned his progressive vocabulary from the great homiletical voices of the nineteenth and twentieth centuries—F. W. Robertson,* whom he greatly admires, Brooks,* Fosdick,* Scherer,* and many others. With them he shares the commitment of making sense of the Christian faith for modern people and the challenge of making sense of the modern world by means of the Christian faith. His Beecher lectures, *How Shall They Preach?*, are peppered with anecdotes from and the wisdom of the modern preaching tradition.

This tradition he has molded and shaped by his (and his race's) own distinctive experience in America, first as a black man from Louisiana, then as an eloquent combatant in the urban war zones of the North. The Taylor method features the selection of a great preaching text of the Bible, from which he proceeds to "seek my footing in the Word of God." (He has preached on the good Samaritan and the prodigal son countless times.) He moves through the story, tarrying over the telling phrase in order to use it as a stimulus for observations of the human condition and exhortations to his congregation. Although he is at his best when recollecting the lore of his Louisiana childhood, Taylor is not so much a storyteller as an incisive interpreter of the text and a commentator on the state of the human soul. "Human" is never restricted to "black" in Taylor's sermons, but the suffering and triumphs of Africans in America lend to his sermons the poignancy of their example, as well as a point

or focus for his mighty perorations. His progressivism never obscures the gospel of God's lordship over all schemes for human improvement, and his prophetic voice never overrides Christ's exclusive power to redeem human failure. When listening to Taylor, one has the impression that the formulas of the black church still live and work both in the preacher and among his hearers.

The Taylor style relies on a voice like a pipe organ; its stunning vocal range produces an equally impressive emotional range but one that never degenerates into posturing or histrionics. Taylor is able to achieve profound emotional contact through his natural timbre; he can soar in a disciplined tremolo, use his resonators to toy with sounds, and he can gravel, when provoked, like Louis Armstrong. In comparison with the most acclaimed preachers, Taylor's high baritone is purer, his low more richly resonant, and the mastery of his vocal instrument more complete. His use of that instrument is such that he can elicit applause from an audience by reading the text. On one occasion, as he read some of the proper names in Luke 3—Tiberius, Ituraea, Trachonitis—members of the congregation were heard to respond, "My Lord, My Lord!" His rhetorical flourishes regularly engage his hearers in a lively dialogue, as in his Presidential inaugural sermon in which he enjoined his audience to recognize "the splendor and the squalor, the grandeur and the grime, the everlastingness and the temporality in our humanity."

Taylor has mastered the inventory of African-American pulpit rhetoric—the ponderous ingratiation, the understatement, parallelism, antithesis, the prophetic stutter, the peroration, and, perhaps above all, the adroit manipulation of thematic set pieces. Taylor manages all this, however, without a hint of artificiality or obvious art and always in service to the message of the God of the Bible. His is the grand style advocated by Augustine but absent from all but a few contemporary pulpits.

Taylor, G. C., *How Shall They Preach?*, 1977.
                                                       RICHARD LISCHER

WE ARE CLIMBING JACOB'S LADDER
Gardner C. Taylor

I am among the last of the living links with the great aspirations of the fathers. I shared a public platform with Mordecai Johnson and Benjamin Mays and Charles Wesley, to name but three. I knew some blacks who had fought in the Union Army. My grandfather fought in the Civil War, but I did not know him directly. And I remember on what we call Declaration Day—really Memorial Day—how they would gather at the National Cemetery at Port Hudson and put on those old blue uniforms with GAR on it—Grand Army of the Republic—and even though bent of limb and slow of step, how proudly they would look back upon their aspirations, upon the fact that they had fought for their liberty.

I knew people, as I said, who came out of that tragic time with the almost rancid odor of slavery in their spirits. But, my God, they were not defeated nor beaten down. I can see them now across the chasm of the years in their little churches on the plantations and the cane breaks and the cotton fields. Gnarled hands, wrinkled brows, bent shoulders, with all of the disallowances and the intimidations, Nathan Bedford Forrest's Ku Klux Klan in its first wave of terrorism—all of that. You know what they were singing? I wish you could have heard them—"We Are Climbing Jacob's Ladder." Hardly with ground to stand upon, disallowed in the society, called "Nigger" on every hand—we are climbing Jacob's ladder. With no number to speak of, "every round going higher and higher." Looking at the long road ahead of them they raised the question, "Do you think I'll make a soldier?" "Do you think"—they'd sing it three times—"I'll make a soldier, soldier of the Cross?" And they were not talking about any indifference, any capitulation, any laziness. They went on, "Rise! Shine! Give God the glory, Soldier of the Cross." Then they'd sing that last line—"Do you want your freedom, soldier of the Cross?" They did not use the sickle and hammer, it was not the stars and bars, it was not the stars and stripes, it was Soldier of the Cross. And with that they marched, opened their little schools, started their little grocery stores and their insurance companies, built their churches. Soldier of the Cross! It was their confidence that in Jesus Christ there is power.

> He is light for darkness.
> Strength for weakness.
> Peace for confusion.
> Hope for despair.
> Bread for the hungry.
> Water for the thirsty.
> And at last the way to a taller town
>   than Rome
>   and an older place than Eden.

From "Another Look at the Crucifixion," a sermon delivered at Howard University on March 8, 1992. Used by permission of Gardner C. Taylor.

Teaching and Preaching. The New Testament at times appears to draw a distinction between preaching and teaching. In these cases preaching is proclaiming or announcing the good news to those who have never heard it. Teaching is instruction to those who have accepted the good news so they might be informed of its implications for them and their lives. For example, Jesus preaches the gospel openly to the crowds but reserves his teaching for his disciples (Mark 8:31–32). Likewise, the apostles teach those who have accepted their preaching (Acts 2:42; Col. 1:25).

The Christian preaching of a homily* (Greek) or sermon* (Latin) is rooted in synagogue practice (Luke 4:16; Acts 13:14), where it is understood as instruction or the exposition of scripture by a rabbi or teacher.

Apostolic preaching after the New Testament, however, makes no neat distinctions. Typically, sermons declare the story of God's action in Jesus, share Jesus' teachings, and interpret their meaning and significance. The overwhelming evidence is that congregations met weekly for worship in which the oral tradition concerning the life, death, and resurrection of Jesus, as well as his teaching, were repeated for the purpose of instruction.

Tertullian (ca. 160–ca. 220) in a lapidary phrase wrote, "Christians are made, not born." The way for making or fashioning Christians was named catechesis. Rooted in baptism, catechesis—literally "to echo" or reproduce the Word, namely Jesus—in English became "christening." Catechesis is all the means and processes of conversion and nurture used by the church in cooperation with the Holy Spirit to shape Christlike persons and communities.

Insofar as catechesis is derived from a word that also means "to sound from above," it became associated with a homily or sermon within the context of a liturgy or ritual action intended to contribute to the formation of Christians.

Moreover, catechesis is a word St. Paul employs frequently to describe the giving of oral instruction in order to illumine and enlighten his listeners concerning the content of the Christian faith and life. John Chrysostom,* the "golden-mouthed" (354–407), Bishop of Constantinople, marks the summit of sacred rhetoric. As a preacher, he poured his profound knowledge of scripture and his great learning into eloquent, detailed expositions of scripture.

By the close of the third century, preaching and teaching appear to be synonymous. However, after the birth of Christendom in the fourth century, with the exception of missionary preaching, preaching was increasingly neglected entirely. Numerous attempts were made to address this neglect. For example, Alcuin (730–804), Deacon and Abbot of Tours, rekindled the light of learning in the church and compiled a collection of instructional homilies to be used by parish priests. In the thirteenth century, Dominic (1170–1221) founded an Order of Preachers whose lives were devoted to teaching, thereby both reestablishing the importance of preaching and reconnecting preaching and teaching in the church (see Dominicans). During the Protestant Reformation in the sixteenth century, the preacher became known as the teaching elder, and the sermon, typically an exposition of scripture, became a primary means of instruction in the church.

So it is that the expository or instructional sermon became the dominant understanding of preaching, an understanding that by the twentieth century has fallen into neglect.

Types of Preaching. Three expressions of the ministry of the word can be discerned in the New Testament. There is *kerygma*, missionary preaching to the unconverted. There is *didache*, the instruction of new converts and of the baptized in the Christian life of faith (ethics* and doctrine*). And there is *paraklesis*, a renewal and deepening of the apprehension of the *kerygma*. A good example of the latter is the Epistle to the Hebrews.

The *kerygma* is the proclamation* of an event and a person, Jesus Christ, the eschatological redemptive act of God in the establishment of God's reign of justice and reconciliation. The aim of this proclamation (evangelical preaching) is not to secure intellectual assent to propositional truth but to evoke faith, a gift to those who have been enabled to have both an encounter with the person proclaimed and an experience of what is proclaimed. Such preaching is addressed to the outsider and aims at decision and conversion.

The aim of *paraklesis* (liturgical preaching,* in the context of the celebration of the Eucharist) is to announce the action of God that is to occur in and through the liturgical action culminating in the communion of the people. Such preaching is addressed to the baptized and aims at renewal.

The aim of *didache* (instructional preaching) is to aid in the understanding of scripture and the devotional, ethical, and doctrinal implications of the Christian life of faith. Increasingly, there is not only a dire need but a hunger for instruction from adults who were baptized as infants and attended church school, but find themselves biblically, theologically, and ethically illiterate.

An instructional sermon, however, is not to be confused with other forms of instruction. In an instructional sermon, while teaching is an intended by-product, its primary purpose remains the response of faith. The aim of an instructional sermon is not to help persons know more about scripture, Christian doctrine, or Christian ethics. It is, rather, to deepen their life of faith by helping them to comprehend the implications of the gospel, to live more faithfully, and to become apologists for the faith.

Instructional preaching, then, is instruction of a homiletical character. That is, it is teaching in a preaching mode, it is preaching in a teaching mode. Traditionally, in Anglicanism the instructional homily was delivered after Evening Prayer on Sunday. For many mainline Protestants, the Wednesday night liturgy included an instructional sermon. Typically, these practices and the use of the instructional sermon have become rare.

Instructional preaching is a progression of logical thought that makes God's revelation as contained in the scriptures intelligible, meaningful, and clear. Instructional preaching is intentional. In one sense, every sermon teaches—in that *how* we preach communicates as much as what we preach. The sermon reveals what the preacher believes is faithful theological reflection and moral decision-making. For example, how reason* is or is not employed in a sermon teaches people the place of reason in making judgments about faith and life. The role scripture plays in the sermon models the place it is intended to play in persons' lives.

Instructional preaching is personal. It remembers that sermons are delivered to people who have particular needs, abilities, interests, concerns, questions, life experiences, knowledge, and the like. It takes seriously the personhood of the preacher. Others' learning is dependent upon the preacher's knowledge, enthusiasm, convictions, and commitments.

Therefore, the study and prayer life of the instructional preacher is especially important.

Instructional preaching can be either deductive or inductive. In either case, it is fundamentally expository. Deductive instructional preaching is designed to engage listeners and bring forth the insights of a biblical passage and its implications for their lives. It is the logical organization of thought for the most persuasive communication of the gospel message.

Inductive instructional preaching is designed to engage by shaping an experience that interacts with the hearers, as do other art forms that lead their audiences to discover insights and implications for their lives. In either mode, the insights and implications are taken from scripture.

Fuller, R. *What Is Liturgical Preaching?* 1957. **Williamson, C.,** and **R. Allen,** *The Teaching Ministry,* 1991. **Worley, R.,** *Preaching and Teaching in the Early Church,* 1967.

JOHN H. WESTERHOFF

Television and Preaching. Since World War II, the explosion in television technology and programming has greatly transformed the context for preaching in many parts of the world. The tube has introduced millions of congregants to a myriad of disparate preaching styles and messages, heightening the confusion and competition among liturgical and ecclesiastical traditions. In addition, the phenomenal growth in electronic media has fostered a "secondary orality" (Ong) in American culture, favoring preaching styles that are more informal, narrational, and emotional. These developments have helped religious traditions steeped in orality—such as Pentecostalism and other Holiness traditions—while frustrating preachers from traditions that emphasize systematic theology, formal creeds and confessions, rationalistic apologetics, and academic approaches to homiletics.

The first truly successful TV preacher was Roman Catholic Bishop Fulton J.

Sheen.* During the 1950s, Sheen on prime-time American television combined a folksy homiletical style with popular moralisms and a simple Thomistic apologetic. The result was not only a widely viewed half-hour program but more significantly the first and perhaps the greatest religious TV personality of all time. Sheen's popularity proved that the new technology could confer considerable status on gifted performers, thereby transforming parish pastors into national celebrities.

During the 1960s and 1970s, television preaching exploded in all directions. The difference between worship and entertainment was increasingly tenuous, as were the lines between preaching and teaching and preaching and personal storytelling. Cable television and satellites rapidly expanded the theological and homiletical scope of preaching available to viewers around the globe. Locally, many mainline congregations televised their worship services, often under the sponsorship of church federations, with broadcast time provided without charge by stations. Regionally, and to some extent nationally, a growing number of evangelicals such as independent Baptist Jerry Falwell and Pentecostal Jimmy Swaggart purchased air time for presenting their home-church worship services to distant audiences. Meanwhile, other evangelical preachers began creatively combining preaching with various forms of television entertainment, including the variety show (Oral Roberts and Robert Schuller*) and the talk show (M. G. "Pat" Robertson, Jim and Tammy Bakker, and Paul and Jan Crouch). For some popular evangelical TV preachers, the medium became largely a fund-raising vehicle, and preaching itself became personal storytelling about the ministry's past accomplishments, visionary hopes, and current economic woes.

By the 1980s, TV preaching had become largely a competitive, high-stakes enterprise dominated by talented entrepreneurs from evangelicalism. Local mainline presentations were compara-tively dull and lifeless, and many of them disappeared from the airways. Through on-air practice, evangelicals became glib orators, folksy talk-show hosts, and flamboyant faith healers (e.g., Ernest Angley and Benny Hinn). Perhaps 15 million Americans regularly watched TV preachers, and nearly everyone else occasionally tuned in a Billy Graham* crusade or happened upon a TV preacher while flipping through the cable TV channels. The most popular syndicated personalities, such as Schuller and Swaggart, attracted weekly audiences of about two million adults, while daily talk shows such as Robertson's "700 Club" drew less than a million cable and broadcast viewers. Audiences dropped temporarily in the late 1980s, however, when a series of financial and sexual scandals rocked televangelism. Swaggart, the highest-rated weekly televangelist, was defrocked by the Assemblies of God, and Bakker was sent to federal prison for fraud.

There is little doubt that mainline parish preachers were put on the defensive by the growth of religious television. For one thing, the tube introduced many mainline Protestants and Roman Catholics to captivating, fervent, and sometimes compelling evangelical preaching. Even the charismatic movement, which swept across American denominations during the 1970s and 1980s, was fostered considerably by TV preaching from neo-Pentecostal personalities such as Robertson, whose Christian Broadcasting Network had considerable appeal among Protestants and Catholics. Rhetorically speaking, parish pastors could no longer take their congregations for granted; parishioners increasingly compared their own pastors with the talented performers on the screen. Partly because of this competition, millions of unhappy or discontented mainline Protestants and Roman Catholics may have left their churches to join evangelical congregations, including the new independent "megachurches," whose preaching and liturgy most closely resembled television-styled religion. Not surprisingly, megachurches were leaders in videotaping and televising their services, and frequently their sanctuaries were designed for high-quality TV production.

By the 1990s, this dilemma in mainline parish preaching was but one manifestation of a larger national problem in many religious traditions. Television exacerbated declining denominationalism brought about by social and cultural change, including geographic mobility and increased ideological polarization within churches. The cacophony of public preaching on television reflected, and perhaps helped bring about, widespread congregational confusion over the proper role and style of worship, including parish proclamation. Should preaching teach the Bible? Should it theologize? exegete? evangelize? catechize? psychologize? politicize? Should it entertain? amuse? astonish? Television preaching did every one of these things, and more.

Televisual Intimacy. Television's power to legitimize various types of preaching is largely a product of the medium's technological distinctiveness. Whereas pulpit preaching is primarily theatrical, using a combination of voice and body on the pulpit "stage," TV preaching is distinctively televisual. The only images that communicate effectively on the tube are close-up shots of the human face. Other images create the setting for the viewer, while facial shots deliver the emotionality of character* that makes television effective as a dramatic medium. All successful types of programming are dependent on creating effective persona through facial close-ups. Without the tight shots of the preacher, TV preaching is uninspiring at best and stilted at worst.

This technological characteristic makes television a particularly intimate medium. Viewed and heard in the privacy of the home, televised faces are about the same size and sound as real faces in the same room. Compared with theatrical film, there is much less aesthetic distance between audience and actor, and compared with stage and parish pulpit, con-

siderably less spatial distance. Such fabricated intimacy contributed enormously to the popularity of some TV preachers who used the medium to elicit financial contributions from "friends" of the ministry. Precisely for this reason, older and lonely or emotionally distraught viewers are especially attracted to TV preachers.

Compared with parish preaching, effective TV preaching depends upon the management of ethos. Parish preachers' ethos is determined largely by the pastor's overall life—how he or she interacts with congregants and with the rest of the community before the eyes of the parish. Preaching alone will not easily establish a parish pastor's ethos. A TV preacher's ethos, by contrast, is almost totally the construction of the program itself, since distant viewers are unlikely ever to meet, let alone get to know, the preachers.

Program producers and writers create an ethos for the TV preacher by managing the visual and aural elements of the show. This includes camera angles (e.g., shooting up at the preacher, giving him or her a sense of stature or even godliness), pace (e.g., fast cuts from one shot to another during exciting moments to create a sense of the preacher's dynamism and power), audience-reaction shots (e.g., capturing on screen the close-ups of particular "live" congregants whose faces suggest they are being deeply moved by the preacher's message), music (e.g., background music to elicit audience emotions), and zoom shots (e.g., tighter and tighter shots of the preacher leading to the sermon clincher, the altar call, the healing ceremony or the fund-raising pitch). Because cameras determine what the viewers will see, they can manage the audience's focus much more effectively than a parish preacher can shape a real congregation's attention.

Television tends to create, intentionally or unintentionally, personality cults composed of viewers who are particularly susceptible to the preacher's ethos. Oddly enough, in spite of the high degree of control that the medium puts in the hands of program producers, television preachers are significantly at the mercy of audiences' own interpretations of messages. Regardless of how careful a particular TV preacher might be to safeguard against communicating an exaggerated sense of his or her own power, authority, wisdom, or godliness, the technology tends to breed an influential and persuasive ethos. A little bit of positive ethos goes a long way on the tube, which amplifies that ethos through the contrived intimacy of the preacher-viewer relationship.

Of all of the dangers of TV preaching, personality cults are certainly the most common, as well as the most resistant to common-sense antidotes. Even if a TV preacher eschews being placed on a pedestal by viewers, there is little that can be done to prevent it from happening with some viewers. TV pulpiteers who ask viewers not to put their trust in the preacher himself are likely to be seen by some viewers as even more genuine and friendly than other TV preachers. Self-disclosure, whether genuine or contrived, enhances the medium's inherent intimacy. This is why religious TV talk-show hosts can move from TV pulpit to TV sofa without damaging their ethos as preachers; on TV, each of those roles feeds the persona of the other, thereby building the total ethos. Of course the TV preacher has the option of stepping completely out of the TV persona by getting to know audience members personally, but this is totally impractical except for local cable TV or low-power TV, where the broadcast audience lives within a few miles of the transmitter.

In the U.S., personality cults enable TV preachers to transfer their authority from one topic or issue to a different one and from distinctly religious or confessional ones to more broadly public ones. Even a successful exegetical or doctrinal TV preacher frequently can mobilize his or her audience in response to a perceived moral or political threat. This occurs regularly among evangelical preachers when public sentiment is focused on morally charged cultural conflict. In the 1980s, for example, Robertson and Falwell moved back and forth between evangelistic preaching and political sermonizing on such issues as abortion and prayer in public schools. Robertson even sought the Republican nomination for U.S. President in 1988. There is little doubt that the New Religious Right, formed in the 1970s and escalating throughout the 1980s, and represented by such groups as the Religious Roundtable and Falwell's Moral Majority, depended heavily on the power of personality cults generated through TV preaching and other religious broadcasting. There is also little doubt that the relative weakness of the religious left, organized largely through the mainline National Council of Churches, was the result of an abundance of bureaucratic authority and a dearth of media-generated charismatic authority. The American political left, with the exception of the black urban church, is highly suspicious of religiously affiliated personality cults.

Television confers the status of personality cults upon even low-profile denominational broadcasters. Especially in evangelical circles, a denomination's TV preacher carries an inordinately large amount of power within the organization. The TV preacher is able to communicate regularly with large numbers of members, and more important, to bypass official denominational channels by appealing directly to the people. Charles Stanley of Atlanta, for instance, was a leader in the conservative movement within the Southern Baptist Convention during the divisive 1980s and 1990s. For this reason, TV preachers are generally a two-edged sword in denominations. On the one hand, such charismatic figures may bring in new members and ably represent the ideals of the denomination to the outside world, as well as to the members themselves. When this occurs, denominational TV preachers are often well-liked and highly esteemed symbols of the members' fervent hopes. On the other hand, individualistic or reactionary TV preachers are often a thorn in the side of denominational prelates, who are jealous of the TV orator's authority even while opposing his or her power within the church.

Since the 1970s, there have been periodic concerns among both mainline and evangelical pastors that TV preachers may begin establishing their own denominations, thereby even further weakening the older denominations. There is very little evidence to support these concerns. Even the most popular TV preachers of recent years have shown a tendency to stay within an existing denomination rather than to start their own. Denominations are often a hindrance to individualistic, entrepreneurial TV preachers, but they can also provide a ready-made constituency, publicity, and even financial support during the formative years of TV ministries. The most widely represented denomination among TV preachers has been the Assemblies of God, which included Swaggart and Bakker, as well as dozens of influential regional TV pastors.

Regardless of TV preachers' commitments to denominations, their remarkable popularity is based on a loyal constituency that often acts like a denominational following. For example, TV preachers are among the best-selling authors of religious books and the most sought-after evangelical convention speakers. Their endorsements sell products and services, from new editions of the Bible to seminary degrees. Although the major TV preachers hardly support ecclesiastical hierarchies, their own broadcast ministries create a privileged place for themselves in the religious marketplace. Televised religious ethos is a valuable commodity, especially in American religion.

Orality and Television. Probably the greatest impact of television on modern preaching is the technology's role in fostering the emergence of secondary orality.* As Walter Ong, Harold Adams Innis, Marshall McLuhan,* and others have suggested, the dominant medium in a society tends to frame the cultural environment

in which all communication takes place. Dominant technologies "massage" (McLuhan) the message, making some types of public and private communication more effective than other types. This bias (Innis) in communication media spreads from one area of life (e.g., entertainment) to another (e.g., parish worship), causing some social institutions to grow in authority and others to decline. Religious organizations, from local churches to denominations, ecumenical groups, and parachurch ministries, have been influenced by the growth of the video revolution. Of all affected parties, however, preachers probably feel the direct effect more than any other religious workers.

Research on the rise of the electronic media, especially television, suggests that these technologies challenge literate modes of discourse and foster a secondary orality similar to the primary orality of the Old Testament culture and extant in nonliterate developing countries. In short, literate cultures are characterized by objective, analytical, formal, logical communication evident in activities such as scientific investigation, bureaucratic organization, business management, news reporting, and systematic theology. Oral cultures, in contrast, display subjective, informal, and narrative forms of communication evident especially in personal and collective storytelling. While the print media helped to usher in the Enlightenment, the electronic media have challenged Enlightenment beliefs with postmodern emphases on personal experience, cultural pluralism, and nonrational discourse. To the average parishioner and pastor, this theory of secondary orality may not seem too significant or even valid. After all, daily social intercourse may not seem to be affected. Behind the appearance of cultural continuity, however, is a fundamental shift in psychological and sociological conditions. Like the proverbial fish in water, residents of secondary orality live in a new world increasingly defined by subjective experience and moralistic story rather than objective truth and argument. The results of this shift in modes of communication are crucial for understanding the context of contemporary preaching.

First, popular public communication is biased theologically. Theologies that are consonant with postmodern, secondary orality will increasingly dominate religious discourse on the tube and in the pews. This enhances the effectiveness of Pentecostal and charismatic orators over virtually all other modes of preaching. These preachers usually offer the kinds of experiential validation and personalized storytelling that communicate effectively on the tube as well as in the culture shaped by secondary orality. The least effective preaching is shaped by dispassionate, highly systematic theologies associated with scholasticism, whether German Lutheranism or American Presbyterianism.

Second, seminary education is biased toward literate rather than oral modes of discourse. Seminarians are far more likely to learn to do academic theology and lecture-style preaching than they are to communicate in the new cultural environment. Seminary education tends to be literate in terms of both curriculum and pedagogy. This is evident in such things as the way the curricula are organized logically into discrete subject areas; the way homiletics and preaching are isolated from the more "academic" subjects like systematic theology and church history; the way lectures dominate pedagogy;* the way students' personal experience of the faith is often separated from each class's study of the faith; the way professors generally prefer manuscript preaching over more distinctly oral and personal styles; the way new preachers are discouraged from using first-person language or even personal anecdotes; the ways that student sermons are analyzed and evaluated as "objective" messages apart from the impact they have on real congregations; and the ways that sermons are actually interpreted by those audiences.

Third, the whole megachurch phenom-

enon and much of the independent church movement in the U.S. is predicated on reclaiming orality in worship, especially preaching. In an attempt to win new members by appealing to the market of unchurched people, these new churches are willing to discard traditional modes of communication that seemingly have lost their meaning for many people. They seek to integrate drama, personal testimony, anecdote, spontaneous singing, and other elements of orality into contemporary worship. Even their exegetical preaching tends to be guided less by distinctly literary concerns than by common-sense observations about the parallel relevance of biblical stories for today's world. Above all, these congregations tend to be nondoctrinal and ahistorical. They are far more interested in communicating a relevant message for immediate spiritual growth than they are in maintaining cultural and theological continuity with church beliefs and traditions of the past. All of these characteristics reflect attempts to integrate orality into church life.

Fourth, the steady influx to America of immigrants from Asia and Latin America is creating considerable church growth among populations with residual primary orality. Especially in Latin America, which has perhaps the fastest-growing Protestant churches in the world, the television age emerged prior to extensive literacy. Swaggart was far more popular in Central America, for instance, than he ever was in the United States, attracting to his show over half of all churched adults in the region. Secondary and primary orality have combined rapidly to shape the cultural milieu of immigrants from this type of area. When these people migrate to North America, their homegrown orality infuses especially urban churches with a stronger desire for emotional, spontaneous, and personally relevant preaching for themselves and especially for their children, who often face enormous peer and media pressure to conform to American consumerism and morality. Unless North American denominations provide a hospitable seminary and ecclesiastical environment for young pastors of these growing churches, immigrants will form their own denominations more attuned to the needs of oral cultures (see Homiletics and Preaching in Latin America).

Fifth, the growth of secondary orality in the television age tends to foster moralistic modes of discourse that give religious life a fundamentalistic edge. Narrativity and personal subjectivity, in particular, create popular characterizations of good and bad, right and wrong. There is little room in this oral universe for fine distinctions or nuances of meaning—characteristics of literate cultures. Some preachers on TV and in the pulpit take advantage of this situation by promoting particular agendas within denominational politics or even by advocating certain public policies associated with morality. This moralistic mode of discourse, however, is also shaping popular biblical interpretation, which tends to divide believers into opposing camps of righteousness and wickedness with regard to currently polarized public issues. Nonpolemical preaching is much more difficult to do successfully in an oral culture.

Contemporary preachers inherit opportunities along with limitations imposed by the television age. Preachers who learn an effective oral style will find not only eager listeners but also a great potential for communicating old truths in new ways to diverse audiences. They may also discover that the flamboyant TV preacher is no match for a parish pastor who integrates relational ministry with the oral style of public presentation. But some vexing questions remain about the TV environment: How can the fruits of academic theology be communicated to congregations? How can preaching be reclaimed as dramatic oral event, especially in traditions that are heavily steeped in the complex creeds, confessions, and theologies of literate culture? How can seminaries prepare students to preach in the television age when seminaries themselves are so grounded in academic modes of discourse based on Enlightenment epistemologies?

Market-Driven Preaching. The United States has always been host for a dynamic religious marketplace in which religious orators competed for adherents. Television, however, increases the rhetorical stakes. It is the only visual medium for reaching a national and increasingly international audience. Moreover, the medium is enormously expensive, both theologically and financially. In order to elicit necessary contributions in the tens of millions of dollars, some of the national TV ministries tune their sermons to the marketplace. They tell likely contributors what such potential patrons want to believe—namely, that God can be a means to financial gain and physical health, an instrument of prosperity.

Parish preachers in North America increasingly work in a religious environment shaped by this "health-and-wealth gospel," or "prosperity gospel." Religious television does not convert people to Christianity or other religions as much as it changes believers' notions of their faith, often leading them to the prosperity gospel. Viewers of religious television are among the most active and dedicated parishioners, as well as the most loyal financial supporters of both their local churches and the broadcast ministry. These viewers help spread the TV messages to their own churches by encouraging friends to watch, by distributing print, video, and audio materials obtained from the ministry, and, most important of all, by adjusting their own expectations of parish preaching and worship to the models they see and hear on television. In the U.S., these models are increasingly market-driven expressions of the prosperity gospel.

Although there are various strains of prosperity theology, they all share American culture's emphases on individualism and materialism. It is typically the individual believer, not the parish or church, who will reap the rewards of the faith. Viewers are addressed as needy individuals who can manufacture a miracle for themselves. Their miracles are generally for improved physical or emotional health, for direct financial gain from a new job, or more likely, for an unpredictable windfall that presumably only God can control, such as winning the lottery. While this type of message has fairly broad appeal, it elicits viewer responses from the primary audience of religious television: older, female viewers with lower incomes and less formal education than television viewers of the population overall. Variations of this message have been preached by televangelists such as Jim Bakker, Oral Roberts, Robert Tilton, Kenneth Copeland, and Benny Hinn.

Because the broader American culture is itself so oriented toward immediate gratification, the prosperity gospel will spread wherever the American Dream is alive and well. Part of the task of the parish preacher in the television age, then, will be to maintain a prophetic voice in the midst of TV-fostered pressure to conform to the culture's implicit religious ideals. It appears that modern preachers, like Old Testament prophets, must challenge some of the beliefs learned by congregants from the surrounding culture, including television.

Babin, P., with **M. Iannone,** *The New Era in Religious Communication,* trans. David Smith, 1991. **Hoover, S. M.,** *Mass Media Religion: The Social Sources of the Electronic Church,* 1988. **Innis, H. A.,** *The Bias of Communication,* 1951. **McLuhan, M.,** *Understanding Media: The Extensions of Man,* 1966. **Ong, W.,** *The Presence of the Word,* 1967; and "Worship at the End of the Age of Literacy," in *Faith and Contexts,* Vol. 1, 1992, 175–88. **Peck, J.,** *The Gods of Televangelism: The Crisis of Meaning and the Appeal of Religious Television,* 1993. **Postman, N.,** *Amusing Ourselves to Death,* 1985. **Schultze, Q. J.,** *Televangelism and American Culture: The Business of Popular Religion,* 1991.   QUENTIN J. SCHULTZE

Temple, William. (1881–1944) William Temple was successively Bishop of Manchester, Archbishop of York, and Archbishop of Canterbury. Immense as his influence was in the Church of England and in the global Anglican communion, he was also highly regarded as a pioneer ecumenist and leading figure in the movement that resulted in the World Council of Churches. Beginning his career as an Oxford philosophy don, Temple published a prodigious number of books and articles and played a leading role in the intellectual life of his times.

His early development was strongly shaped by his father Frederick, also Archbishop of Canterbury. His theological outlook was given significant direction by Professor Edward Caird and by Bishop Charles Gore, who taught him that Christians animated by an incarnational faith were to be ever and vigorously active in the world, addressing social problems from the vantage point of the gospel. His famous observation, that Christianity is the most materialistic of religions, reflects his university training and his lifelong devotion to the Christian socialism propounded by Frederick Denison Maurice in the mid-nineteenth century. Temple's major philosophical mentor was Plato. In *Mens Creatrix* he attempted to show that platonic idealism not only allowed for but virtually required an incarnation of the Logos. A subsequent volume, *Christus Veritas,* presented the revelational goal of the philosophical quest. The spirit of Plato also informs his celebrated Gifford lectures, *Nature, Man and God.*

Temple's preaching style was congruous both with the English context and with his academic background. Ever the teacher, he calmly laid out the truths of the Christian faith as constituting a rational and coherent philosophy of life. To drive home his points, he eschewed contrived rhetoric, theatrical posturing, and emotional excess. Instead, he relied on the suasive power of language, including the poetical, backed by candor, authority, and conviction. One commentator remarked on his "effortless, oracular delivery." He typically used none or the sparsest of outlines: His extraordinarily retentive mind was able nimbly to clothe themes, ideas, and illustrations with sentences at once eloquent and clear. He had a special gift for tailoring his message to fit the audience, whether it be made up of workers in a shipyard, young boys at a public school, or the whole nation in wartime when he spoke over radio at the invitation of the BBC.

An anecdote illustrates both his suppleness of mind and his sensitivity to his hearers. On one occasion, Temple was making his way to the pulpit in St. Mary's Cathedral, Edinburgh, when he chanced to see in the congregation a certain bishop. This man, Temple remembered, had been in another church in which Temple had preached the very sermon he was about to deliver. Thereupon he scrapped his original plan and offered an entirely different homiletical effort, described by his biographer as "fine." This move should be recommended, of course, only to those whose mental depth matches the Archbishop's.

Temple took as his master text for preaching a clause from John 14:9, in which Jesus says "Whoever has seen me has seen the Father." The fourth Gospel was his lifelong favorite; he wrote a commentary on it and named its author, as well as Robert Browning and Plato, as having made the greatest impact on his thinking. The central fact of the universe is that the divine creative principle has taken on the human condition in Jesus of Nazareth. This identification of Creator with creature comes to supreme expression at Calvary, where is revealed "the innermost heart of God, the anguish of his baffled love." It is not only, therefore, that Jesus is divine but that God is Jesuslike. The cross, however, is for Temple a symbol not only of redemption but also of the believer's willingness to suffer. As we focus on the concerns of others and as they become our own, we are molded more and more in the image of Christ, who came to serve, not to be served. Christianity is a way of life and teacher of values; it is heroic striving in the way of virtue, cooperating with the indwelling Spirit to abet the kingdom's coming. These were pervasive themes in Temple's preaching.

As already mentioned, his emphasis on the kingdom had an especially strong social focus that was an integral part of nearly every sermon. For the Christian, being joined to the "Hero-Master" in faith entailed an earnest sympathy with the less fortunate. "It is Christ," said the socialist prelate, "who is crushed by the pressure of our absurd social system; . . . if because they are cheap I buy goods made under conditions which destroy the character of those who make them, I am like Judas, for I have sold Christ for money" (Temple 1913). As Temple attempted to inculcate "high thinking" and moral uplift in his hearers, he never failed to let the cries of the dispossessed ring in their ears.

William Temple's influence on the men and women of his generation, through creativity of thought and felicity of expression, was enormous. Yet it was perhaps the person himself, his virile faith, patent goodness, and deep love of God, that left the most indelible impression. Many came away from his sermons feeling not that they had heard another stellar preacher but that they had been in the presence of a saint.

Iremonger, F. A., *William Temple, Archbishop of Canterbury*, 1948. **Temple, W.,** *Repton School Sermons*, 1913; *Studies in the Spirit and Truth of Christianity*, 1914; and *The Preacher's Theme To-Day*, 1936.

BRUCE WOLLENBERG

Theology of Preaching.

Theology of preaching is concerned with the role and place of preaching in the life of the Christian church. It is frequently considered in relation to various other theological issues, including theology of revelation, ecclesiology, soteriology, missiology, and theologies of liturgy and sacraments. Theology of preaching struggles with the question of what the church is doing when it preaches; that is, a theology of preaching is concerned with the expectations of preaching. Major issues within a theology of preaching include the authority* of the preacher, the relationship of the Bible to preaching, and the historical, social, and liturgical contexts of preaching.

Expectations of preaching range from proclaiming the Word of God, to liberating the oppressed, to providing pastoral counseling on a group scale. Although the range is broad, generally expectations for preaching fall into two major groupings: those that expect preaching principally to play a role in the sanctification of the people of faith and those that expect it principally to play a role in the justification of human beings before God.

Preaching and Sanctification. For much of the history of Christian preaching, up to the present day, preaching has instructed persons of faith on the Christian life and exhorted them to live accordingly. The focus of preaching has been the sanctification of the Christian. Preaching for sanctification aims at leading the Christian person and community toward a more fitting Christian life. As artfully as possible, the sermon explicates some aspect of Christian faith and applies it to living in the present.

The phrase "practice what you preach" could well apply to preaching aimed at sanctification, because of a focus on faithful practice. Although it may not be necessary for the preacher to be flawless, there is concern over the person of the preacher. The office of the preacher is ideally preserved for those who are capable of careful and faithful interpretation of the traditions of the church. He or she is to have enough training and character to promote a fitting Christian style of life, to explicate the sources of the Christian faith, and to apply them meaningfully to the present setting. Efforts to strengthen the skills of preachers through training in rhetoric* and doctrine have flourished.

Biblical texts play a prominent role as the principal source of Christian teaching and witness. The extent of authority granted to the Bible varies among confessional traditions. For some, the Bible is one among several sources of revealed truth. For others, it is *the* source and norm for all of Christian life and is to be consulted for wisdom and direction. For still others, the Bible is the infallible direct address of God. It provides the strict rule of faith and life.

The context of preaching is centrally important for sanctification preaching. The hearer's situation is the place to work out the faith that is addressed. Preaching in this vein gives moral guidance and frequently involves instruction or preparation for receiving the sacraments,* especially the Eucharist.

Preaching and Justification. A decisive element of the Reformation was the assertion that the Word of God was efficacious for justification. With this assertion, the reformers elevated the status of preaching from an edifying discourse to a revealing word of grace. God, through the Holy Spirit,* effects the salvation of Christ for the hearer of the word. Until the Reformation, this power had been held to adhere in the ecclesially administered sacraments. Clearly, there was preaching, even strong biblical preaching, prior to the Reformation; it is only that the Reformation posited a more autonomous character of the word (*see* Luther, Martin; Calvin, John).

If the word of God* has such power, and if the word of God can be uttered by human preachers, then the preacher's voice can be God's voice. Such an assertion raises concern for the proper authority of the preacher. Although there continues to be concern over the person of the preacher, the greater issue is the audacity of the preaching office. If God is to speak in human words, who are we to decide who can speak for God? On the other hand, whether a preacher who is part of sinful humanity can preach a word of salvation is a perennial problem.

Because the Bible is also the word of God, its relationship to preaching is essential. Preaching is derived from biblical texts. It is derived in the sense of being founded on explication of a particular scriptural passage. However, it is also derived in the sense that what is expected from biblical texts is similarly expected from preaching. The connection between the biblical texts and the preacher's words becomes a central focus in theologies of preaching. A theology of preaching becomes inseparably linked to theories of biblical interpretation (*see* Hermeneutics).

The liturgical* context of preaching may receive diminished attention for preaching in this vein. At points, liturgy is nearly eclipsed by preaching. The centrality and prominence of pulpits* in many Reformed churches bears physical witness to the place of preaching. While it is quite likely one will discover a Protestant church debating the frequency of celebrating the Lord's Supper, quarterly preaching services would be inconceivable. In recent years, something of a liturgical revival in Protestantism has attempted to reconnect preaching and liturgy.

The historical and social contexts of preaching become most important as the point of contact between the word of God in the Bible and the word of God in the sermon. Because in Christian faith the word of God is made flesh, the social and historical context is the location of God's self-revelation. The old adage, that the preacher should have a Bible in one hand and a newspaper in the other, describes the role social context plays for preaching.

Differing Theologies: Differing Expectations for Preaching. A major fruit of the Reformation's emphasis on preaching is a heightened sense of expectation for preaching. A brief survey of major theological figures and traditions indicates vastly different expectations of preaching.

The influential Protestant theologian Friedrich Schleiermacher* understood preaching to play an important role in shaping the hearer's experience of God. For Schleiermacher, religion is founded on an immediate feeling of the infinite and eternal. All people, whether they are conscious of it or not, have an experience of God. It is this universal experience of God that forms the connection between the world of the biblical materials and the

contemporary world. Contingencies of place and time produce variations in the expression of the underlying experience of God, but these are only variations in the expression and not variations of the consciousness itself. The Bible, referring as it does to this universally held experience of the divine, may awaken in its readers their own "slumbering consciousness."

Similarly, preaching may appropriately be expected to awaken a consciousness of God among the hearers of a sermon. Calling on powerful expressions of God-consciousness in the biblical text, the preacher brings this same experience to the congregation. Schleiermacher says: "As regards the feeling of absolute dependence in particular, everyone will know that it was first awakened in him in the same way, by the communicative and stimulative power of expression or utterance." Preaching awakens the experience of the divine.

If Schleiermacher focused on the subjective experience of God in the hearers of the sermon, Karl Barth* stressed the objective character of preaching. What is to be expected of preaching is nothing short of God speaking, the revelation of God.

Barth sees revelation in the threefold form of the word: the word proclaimed by the church, the word witnessed in the scripture, the word revealed in Jesus and the history of Israel. Each of these is to be seen as a unity and each of them has the same reference. The reference of the word of God is God. God is the subject of the sermon, not just in the sense of the subject matter but also in the sense of the speaker or actor in a sentence. What is to be expected of preaching is that it is to serve as a medium through which God reveals God. Preaching is functionally the same thing as the biblical text, namely the revelation of God by God. For Barth, preaching is not stating the meaning of the Bible but is itself revealing the word of God, because in the very human words of preaching, God is speaking.

In Karl Barth the pendulum swings toward a high view of preaching. As his theology has been appropriated, it has tended to elevate preaching beyond the reach of the congregation. The relevance of preaching to a congregation could be given short shrift in the name of speaking God's word.

The theologian Jürgen Moltmann has tried to establish a theological foundation that would give greater significance to relevance and remain faithful to the gospel. Like Barth, Moltmann begins with the doctrine of revelation. He has tried to understand revelation not as an uncovering of something hidden but as the creation of something altogether new. Moltmann sees revelation as a promise of a radically new reality, the new reality of the eschaton. For Moltmann, the God revealed in the Bible does not uncover God's present glory but promises God's future glory. The Bible speaks not so much of what is, but of what is to come. The world that the biblical texts refer to is a world that does not yet exist, a world that is on the horizon of history. This means that for those who suffer in the present, the Bible is not irrelevant but addresses their suffering. It does not ignore it but names it and promises a hopeful horizon beyond the current suffering.

For Moltmann, the connection between the biblical text and the contemporary setting is through a shared future. The eschaton, because it has not yet come, is a future reality for both the biblical texts and the contemporary congregation. The coming reign of God of which the Bible speaks is the same future to be anticipated by the congregation. The text's future and the congregation's future can thus become the common ground between two divergent worlds.

What is to be expected of preaching is the creation of communities that expect the future of the eschaton. Preaching does not uncover something hidden in the present but creates the expectation of a new future. Preaching gives hope to the forsaken by proclaiming the promise of a new future guaranteed in God's faithfulness. Preaching creates the church, the community that hopes for God's new future, God's coming reign.

The introduction of eschatology into a contemporary theology of preaching is shared by several theologies of liberation.* These recent theologies understand eschatology as the promised reign of God that stands as a judgment against present injustice, poverty, and oppression. They reject notions of eschatology that serve as an otherworldly pacifier for present complaints.

Gustavo Gutiérrez, a Latin American theologian, claims that the eschatological hope of the church calls forth a ministry of prophecy. In one aspect, that prophecy is denunciation. The church is to denounce all that is opposed to what is human. The prophecy cannot be abstract or disconnected from the concrete sufferings of the people of God. Especially the preaching of the gospel, which is good news to the poor, denounces all that contributes to impoverishment of the marginal ones. Prophetic denunciation of evil in concrete terms is matched by annunciation of communion with God. As the denunciation must be in concrete terms, so too must be the annunciation. The good news of the gospel, the coming reign of God, is to be wrought in the gifts of life for the dying, bread for the hungry, freedom for the imprisoned. Unless the preaching of the church is spoken in the concrete realities of the everyday for the poor and oppressed, it is a false hope.

Gutiérrez's theology discerns in the Bible critical tools for unmasking the self-interest of the voices of social, political, and economic domination. The recurring stories of oppression and liberation in the Bible become paradigmatic for preaching. Arguing that social location plays a powerful role in claims to truth, he pleads for the recovery of the voices of the poor as authentic voices of good news. The preachers of the church may not be those who wear robes and stoles but those who know suffering and redemption.

Listening to the voices of the marginalized and oppressed is a unifying theme in theologies of liberation. It is a strong theme in feminist* theologies. Observing that the sanctioned preachers of the church have long been male, feminist theologies are urging the preaching of the gospel in a different voice. From the first witnesses to the resurrection to the present there has been a largely hidden stream of women preachers. A call to claiming the distinctive voice of women, finding a more inclusive language for the church's life and practice, and a recovery of the hidden histories of women of the faith is being sounded by many feminist authors.

American feminist theologian Sallie McFague has made the point that the language the church uses in preaching, liturgy, and teaching shapes its theology. For McFague there is no direct language for God, only indirect language of image and metaphor. She argues that metaphors for God have been unduly limited by a male-dominated culture. The result is an impoverished concept of God. By recovering lost metaphors and expanding the images and models for God, it is possible to be liberated from the constraints of dehumanizing religious practices and beliefs. For McFague, many liberating metaphors are to be found in the Bible and tradition. However, it is also necessary to go outside the tradition to discover fresh images for God that can serve to critique the tradition.

Themes of liberation have long been themes of many African-American churches. Henry Mitchell has observed characteristic principles in what he has identified as a black preaching tradition. One of two major principles he identifies is the necessity of declaring the gospel in the language and culture of the people. Mitchell notes that many of the cultural marks of this preaching tradition have roots in the religious life of Africa. Through generations of slavery and racial oppression, the preaching of the church has developed while maintaining continuity with these cultural themes and practices.

A rich cultural heritage embodied and repeatedly performed in the worship and preaching of a congregation does more than provide a religious experience for the Christian. In a larger sense, it works to form a community. The formation of a community that is not tied solely to the Sunday service, but that from the preaching and performance of the word of God reaches into the everyday lives of the people, is an expectation of African-American preaching.

This leads to Mitchell's second major principle, the necessity of preaching to deal directly with human needs. The concrete needs of the people cannot be ignored or abstracted but must be concretely named and addressed.

Historically, preaching in the Roman Catholic Church has been focused on sanctification. The Second Vatican Council highlighted the centrality of preaching and broadened the place of the theologies of the word. The result has been a greater convergence in Protestant and Roman Catholic theologies of preaching, with a shift toward justification preaching in the Roman Catholic Church. Theologians like Karl Rahner, Hans Küng, and Edward Schillebeeckx have been major contributors to the theological foment since Vatican II.* In their own way, they have provided philosophical and theological foundations for new understandings of preaching.

The problem of human suffering plays a prominent role in the theology of Edward Schillebeeckx. In it, he describes what he calls contrast experiences, or the experience of events that fall short of the ideal of human life. These experiences, which are experiences of suffering, are in themselves revelatory. They provide a view of the world that is not just, and they fuel efforts for a world that is just. Drawing on the theological work of Schillebeeckx, Mary Catherine Hilkert has proposed a theology of preaching that understands preaching as naming of grace. According to Hilkert, preaching does not solely describe the grace-filled moments of life, as if preaching were to paint a rosy picture of Christian successes. Rather, in naming both the gracious moments and the contrast experiences, preaching makes it possible to communicate anew the presence of God.

Although many bemoan the actual practice of preaching as it takes place Sunday after Sunday, preaching remains a central theological issue. The Reformation claim, that in preaching something is not just being said but is being done by God, is now widely recognized. Exactly what is being done, how it is being done, and to what end it is done remain the areas of lively debate in the theology of preaching.

Barth, K., *Homiletics*, trans. G. W. Bromiley and D. E. Daniels, 1991. **Cooke, B.**, *Ministry to Word and Sacraments: History and Theology*, 1976. **Craddock, F.**, *Preaching*, 1985. **Gutiérrez, G.**, *A Theology of Liberation: History, Politics, and Salvation*, trans. and ed. C. Inda and J. Eagleson, with new Introduction, 1988. **Lischer, R.**, *A Theology of Preaching: The Dynamics of the Gospel*, rev. ed., 1992. **McFague, S.**, *Metaphorical Theology: Models of God in Religious Language*, 1982. **Mitchell, H.**, *Black Preaching: The Recovery of a Powerful Art*, 1990. **Moltmann, J.**, *Theology of Hope*, trans. J. W. Leitch, 1967. **Ritschl, D.**, *A Theology of Proclamation*, 1960. **Schleiermacher, F.**, *The Christian Faith*, English trans. of 2d German edition, ed. H. R. Macintosh and J. S. Stewart, 1928. DAVID M. GREENHAW

Thielicke, Helmut. (1908–1986)

Helmut Thielicke was one of the most popular and influential twentieth-century German Protestant theologians and preachers. Born in Wuppertal-Barmen, the young Thielicke studied philosophy and theology and, after graduation in both disciplines, looked toward an academic career in Heidelberg. However, the National Socialists prohibited him from speaking, writing, or traveling, whereupon Thielicke went to Württemberg as pastor and director of the theological office of the regional Lutheran Church. Soon crowds streamed to Thielicke's preaching—held mostly in Stuttgart—primarily in search of inner support in the midst of military and political collapse. Thielicke the preacher was born in these war years.

In 1945 Thielicke was called to Tübingen as professor of systematic theology. From 1954 until his retirement, he taught at the University in Hamburg. Mostly through his voluminous *Theological Ethics*—composed during the 1950s and 1960s—Thielicke shaped the postwar generation of preachers and theologians.

In discussion with Karl Barth* and dialectical theology, this Lutheran theologian found the question that would occupy him throughout his life: What happens in the realm of personal life, the state, and culture when humanity finds itself addressed by the word of God? Proclamation and theology should place themselves both in dialogue with and in opposition to the various challenges of history. His exploration of humanity and human reality became a distinctive mark of his life as a preacher. As early as the foreword to his famous *Discourses on the Lord's Prayer* in 1944–45, which went through numerous editions after the war, Thielicke described what became characteristic for his style: "The speaker saw written in his listeners' faces the destiny from which they came or which awaited them.... Everything he read there and all that filled him to the utmost as their co-participant is contained in his addresses. The Lord's prayer could encompass it all." With a metaphor typical of Thielicke, the mask of destiny could only assume fatherly traits in the face of Christ. Humanity could again learn to believe and pray in and through the prayer of Jesus.

For Thielicke the caring solidarity of the preacher with the listener is the basic presupposition that the revelation of God in Christ to be preached will "come home" in a credible way to the listener. This dialogical structure shapes the practical and often anecdotal vividness of Thielicke's preaching style. In his opinion the preaching of his day had no contagious power because it was beyond people's experience of the actual realities of their lives.

In the years after 1945, Thielicke enjoyed an enormously wide influence as preacher. He became a "political preacher." His Good Friday sermon of 1947, delivered with a large patriotic gesture, became famous. As a teacher and pastoral caregiver of the church, he vehemently attacked the denazification practice of the Allied Forces. Broad public support followed. The debate over collective guilt for Nazi war crimes stirred the German public at the time. In more than just this sermon, Thielicke cast himself on the side of the majority in church and society who were not interested in processing the recent German past.

For many years Thielicke the preacher captivated his hearers in the great St. Michael's Church in Hamburg. Even the news magazine *Der Spiegel* devoted a title article to the Thielicke phenomenon in 1955. His thematically arranged sermon series on the Creation stories and the Sermon on the Mount and his sermons on the catechism, which took seriously the intellectual problems of the modern age, became an aid to faith for many.

Thielicke spoke to persons from all parts of society. He did not want his hearers to think that the gospel has nothing to do with the practical questions of life. That is why his sermons usually have broad introductions in which he gathers up his hearers, where they live and with their questions of faith and life, with a kind of missionary intent. At the same time, the well-read Thielicke quotes his way through world literature and art. He appropriated what philosophers, poets, painters, sculptors, and musicians had expressed about anxiety, care, despair, protest, and meaninglessness in view of the abyss of human existence and the many attempts at escape into another world, and he used them as illustrative material for human existence as it is played out between judgment and grace. Thielicke's sermons follow a particular dramatic technique. By their end, the heart of the listener is addressed in a well-aimed manner.

Thielicke had a rich range of rhetorical tools at his disposal. He did not hesitate to employ provocative formulations and daring images to reach his listeners. Thus, his sermonic style not infrequently had an emotional effect.

Thielicke the preacher lifted up the peculiarity of the biblical text, its strangeness as well as its offensiveness and its foolishness. In the process he revealed a great familiarity with scripture as a whole. At its center stands the justification of the sinner by God, an alienated humanity's return home to the fatherly hand of God.

In his self-appraisal as a preacher, Thielicke felt himself closest to Charles Haddon Spurgeon,* to whom he devoted one of his books.

Thielicke, H., *Encounter with Spurgeon,* 1963; *The Trouble with the Church,* 1965; *The Waiting Father,* 1959; *Our Heavenly Father: The Prayer That Spans the World,* 1960.

ANDREAS RICHTER-BÖHNE

THE RICH MAN IN HELL
Helmut Thielicke

Very likely there were times, perhaps in the night hours whose loneliness even the best foam-rubber beds cannot banish, when the rich man felt clearly that there was something wrong about his life. And then the anxious images would loom up in his mind. The miserable wretches would troop past him, staring at him, and suddenly his fine villa became a dirty hovel. What he repressed during the day came out in his dreams and accused his hard, unfeeling heart. So he did what most people do in such cases: he looked for a moral alibi. He tried to prove to himself and to others that he actually *did* have a heart for the poor, that he really was an open-handed fellow. So he begins to contribute to charity balls, which produce not only a lot of high jinks but also considerable sums for charitable purposes. He also forks out considerable contributions from his bank account to the social missions and the organized charities of his city. And finally, he also allows himself to be chosen the chairman of a welfare committee, though he has one of his men represent him at the meetings. He likes to keep himself in the background as a contributing and supporting member of these social and humanitarian endeavors. This, people say, is attributable to his modesty. But in reality he wants a protective medium between himself and misery. He is evading any "personal" contact with Lazarus. . . .

But then the process goes on ineluctably. What happens is what must happen to every one of us with a mortal certainty: the rich man dies. And when he thus quite literally "comes to an end" he sees that he is absolutely separated from God. Now it becomes apparent how dreadfully different are the standards by which *God* measures our life. How foolish was our own assessment of ourselves and how foolishly we allowed ourselves to be assessed by others!

There the rich man is in hell, and from there he looks at his own funeral. Often during his lifetime he had allowed himself to imagine in pleasant moments of vanity what a splendid affair it would be. How many charitable societies would be in the procession, and surely the best preacher in the town would praise him to the skies while the poor whom he had showered with a thousand benefactions were sobbing in their handkerchiefs. But now he actually sees his own funeral. He sees it, however, from the viewpoint of hell and, suddenly and mysteriously, this alters the whole thing. It's all so oppressively different from the way it appeared to his coquettish fantasy. True, it is a magnificent funeral. But it no longer pleases him. It only gives him a pain because it is in such screaming contradiction to his real state.

He hears a shovelful of earth come thumping down on his coffin and one of his best cronies saying, "He lived life for its own sake." And he wants to interject (though nobody hears him): "I failed to live; I am in anguish in this flame."

Then the second shovelful falls and again the clods of earth come thudding down on his mahogany casket. "He loved the poor in the city," says another voice. And the rich man wants to shriek, "Oh, if

you only suspected what the truth is; I am in anguish in this flame."

Then the minister, the popular and beloved "abbé" of society, casts the third shovelful: "He was so religious. He donated bells, windows, and a seven-branched candlestick. Peace be to his ashes." And again the clods of earth come rumbling down on his coffin. Or is it the rumbling of the crater of hell? "I am in anguish in this flame."

How different, how dreadfully different are the judgments of God!

| From "The Parable of the Rich Man and Lazarus," *The Waiting Father* (New York: Harper & Brothers, 1959), 44–46. Used by permission.

Thurman, Howard. (1900–1981)

Howard Thurman was a Baptist clergyman, chapel dean, educator, theologian, and writer. Born and reared in Daytona Beach, Florida, he was the third child and only son of Saul Solomon and Alice (Ambrose) Thurman. His legacy as the grandson of former slaves informed his theology and preaching during a long and effective ministry that was interracial, ecumenical, and international in scope.

Thurman grew up in a community where no black was privileged to continue school beyond the seventh grade, but he was coached by a concerned black educator and became the first black child in Daytona Beach to receive an eighth-grade certificate. High school studies followed at Florida Baptist Academy (later Florida Normal Institute) in Jacksonville (1915–1919), after which he distinguished himself as a student at Morehouse College. He graduated in 1923 as class valedictorian with an A.B. degree in economics. While in college he worked, headed the college YMCA chapter, edited the yearbook, and was on the debate team headed by then-instructor Benjamin Elijah Mays. Thurman received his seminary degree from Colgate-Rochester Theological Seminary, where, because of the school's racial policy at that time, he was one of two blacks admitted annually. An apt learner and active in the black church, Thurman was ordained a Baptist minister a year before graduating from seminary in 1926. Marriage followed (to Katie Kelley), and he began ministry as pastor of the Mount Zion Baptist Church in Oberlin, Ohio. The pastorate lasted a brief period of two years because of his wife's failing health, which caused them to return to the south. During her prolonged illness, Thurman taught religious studies and was director of religious life at Morehouse College and nearby Spelman College in Atlanta. In 1929 a Kent Fellowship from the National Council on Religion in Higher Education provided support for independent study, and he spent some months of in-depth study of mysticism as a special student of Rufus Jones, the Quaker philosopher-mystic, at Haverford College. Thurman remained with the Atlanta colleges for two years after his wife Katie died, but left in 1932 to join the Howard University faculty in Washington, D.C., to teach theology and to chair the University Committee on Religious Life. Appointed dean of the university's Andrew Rankin Chapel in 1936, Thurman's pulpit ministry there brought him increased distinction on a national and international scale. As worship leader, he also introduced new practices, including meditation moments and liturgical dance, to the traditional order of the service of worship.

A pivotal experience in Thurman's life occurred in 1935 when, during a leave from the Howard campus, he headed a four-member team that visited the nations of India, Ceylon, and Burma on a "Pilgrimage of Friendship" sponsored by the World Student Christian Federation. During this time of touring and speaking at educational centers, he met with Mohandas K. Gandhi and others who were expressing their disapproval of Western Christianity's acceptance and sponsorship of segregation. The conversations with Gandhi pressed Thurman to restudy the teachings of Jesus with respect to the Master's ethic regarding human relations and to apply that ethic to the problem of

segregation in church and society. His developed statement was later published in the now-classic *Jesus and the Disinherited* (1949), and his stance and insights on the subject of interracial interaction steadily informed his vision, planning, and ministry.

The India visit left Thurman stirred by a vision to establish and lead a truly interracial church in America. Feeling the necessity to do so, he requested a leave of absence from Howard University in 1944 and became copastor (with Alfred G. Fisk) of a newly formed religious fellowship in San Francisco. Within nine years, The Church for the Fellowship of All Peoples, as it was named, had increased in numbers from fewer than forty to more than 300 members, with white Anglo-Saxon Protestants, African Americans, and Asian Americans sharing there a common commitment, worship, life, and witness—the first congregation of its kind in the nation. With an additional 1,000 "members-at-large," a group of persons beyond San Francisco who shared the dream of such a fellowship, the membership of Fellowship Church was not only interracial and intercultural but also international. Howard Thurman remained with Fellowship Church until 1953 when he became Dean of Marsh Chapel and Professor of Spiritual Disciplines and Resources in the Boston University School of Theology (the first black full-time professor in the university's history). Through the university's chapel, Boston University President Harold Case wanted to make available within an increasingly diverse campus setting the message and modeling of racial inclusiveness that had brought Fellowship Church, under Thurman's leadership, into national focus and prominence. When he left, The Church for the Fellowship of All Peoples named Thurman its minister-at-large.

Over the next decade of his life, Howard Thurman's star continued to rise, and his witness was increasingly recognized and valued. The April 6, 1953, issue of *Life* magazine identified him as one of the nation's twelve greatest preachers. Perceptive articles steadily appeared in print about his work, while his own writings included several articles and books growing out of his insights and experiences. Two of the twenty-one books Thurman wrote comprise sermons from his regular pulpit ministry at Marsh Chapel: *The Growing Edge* (1956), which was a Pulpit Book Club selection, and *Temptations of Jesus* (1962). Thurman retired from the Boston University chapel deanship in 1965 and thereafter gave leadership to an educational trust founded in his name to assist needy students, schools, and community programs. His schedule continued to include periodic appearances in the United States and beyond as a renowned preacher, lecturer, and respected spiritual leader.

Thurman was notable for his insights and the eloquence by which they were shared. He presented his message in such a way that fused its subject matter with his personality. Substance and style were one. For many, the experience of hearing Thurman preach was accompanied by a sense of presence, due in part to his preferred method of shaping the mood by prefacing his sermon with a focused meditational reading and partly by his own spirit of worship.

Typical of his approach is a passage from a sermon, "Concerning Prayer":

Pressure should not be put upon God. The right place for pressure is upon me, upon you, to bring my life, your life, in its totality, to an exposure to God. Not to give God orders. Not to presume that we are omniscient and can always understand what is best for us—tempting and natural as this is. We must ingather the fragments of our lives, the concerns of our spirits, the loves of our hearts—all of the aspects and dimensions of our living—we must ingather these and hold them in exposure to God. That is the ultimate responsibility of the human spirit. The Spirit of God, brooding over this stuff of our lives, will knead it and fashion it, infuse it with life, or withdraw vitality

from some aspects of it. All of that is the divine prerogative. Our obligation is to make the exposure! (Thurman 1956, 52).

His preaching was aided by training in rhetoric, a gift for imagery, apt illustrations, deliberate timing, sincerity, a rich baritone voice, and an expressive manner. Dorothy Henderson aptly summarized Thurman's pulpit artistry in these words:

When Howard Thurman holds up an idea for you to look at, it becomes like a brilliant jewel. He turns it for you this way and that, and as he throws differing lights on its many facets, you see things there you've never seen before. Soon from the heart of it you come to see Truth, and not only Truth, but you yourself in relation to that Truth (163).

Thurman's preaching was not primarily textual but thematic, although he generally read from scripture at the beginning of a sermon. Although an able expositor of biblical texts and numbered among front-rank expositors of biblical thought, he did not use biblical texts as the center of his consideration but dealt with philosophical and religious aspects of experience as he understood their correspondence to biblical truths. He focused on the universals of religious experience. His sermons are best described as religious tracts that treat the many facets of personal life in the light of God.

Thurman was a master exemplar of the one-point or single-phase model of the sermonic form. His typical sermon pattern is a single idea or insight, one point to which every aspect of the sermon directly and logically related. In each sermon a single concern is stated. The meaning of that concern is underscored by voicing a specific religious principle, assisted by pertinent phrases and illustrations. Its logic is then applied to the common quest or journey of the hearer. He dealt with large and strategic themes, often in a series of sermons and always without the use of a manuscript. He went about his task with the insights of a mystic, the joy of a believer, the rich articulateness of a teacher, and the deep concerns of a pastor.

With respect to form, Thurman's sermons reflect an "idea-flow" rather than a strict "idea-frame." He did not follow the classical sermon style in which several points are discussed as aspects of an idea. Nor did he totally follow the traditional black preaching style, which sometimes involves reiteration, rhythmic tonality, and upbeat cadences with which the sermon is expected to close (*see* African-American Preaching). Yet his sermons were celebratory, the controlling concern being the insight, which he explored by all means possible—graphic words, arresting expressions, strategic silence, pregnant pauses, germane gestures, poetic lines, and the insinuated tension of guided listening. He let the truth or text being treated set its own terms, and he worked to release in words what was inside that truth or text. Such was Howard Thurman's style in preaching, a style he developed in seeking to be always at one with his sermon and the idiom of his own soul.

Massey, J. E., "Thurman's Preaching: Substance and Style," in *God and Human Freedom: A Festschrift in Honor of Howard Thurman*, ed. H. J. Young, 1983. **Thurman, H.,** *With Head and Heart: The Autobiography of Howard Thurman*, 1979; *The Growing Edge*, 1956; and *Temptations of Jesus: Five Sermons*, 1962. **Yates, E.,** *Howard Thurman: Portrait of a Practical Dreamer*, 1964.

JAMES EARL MASSEY

Tillich, Paul. (1886–1965) Tillich emigrated to the United States after being discharged from his university chair in Germany by the Nazi government in 1932. He spent the rest of his career as a professor, teaching in the United States at Union Seminary (N.Y.), at Harvard, and at Chicago. Educated in German universities, Paul Tillich earned doctorates in philosophy and theology. He was or-

dained to the ministry of the Lutheran state church of which his father was also a minister and an official. He served five years as a chaplain in the German army in World War I.

Tillich characterized himself as an "apologetic theologian" and his theology as an "answering theology." He saw the task of theology as that of making Christian faith relevant to the contemporary situation. He was deeply interested, then, in the relationship between theology and culture, and he gave particular attention to issues in philosophy, art, depth psychology, and social structures.

Tillich's theological position is set forth most fully and clearly in the three volumes of his *Systematic Theology*, which is organized in five sections: Reason and Revelation, Being and God, Existence and the Christ, Life and the Spirit, and History and the Kingdom of God. In each pair of terms, the first represents the question of the human situation explored philosophically and the second the Christian theological answer, drawn from the Bible and the Christian heritage. The norm for the theological answer is the New Being, which is in Jesus as the Christ.

Tillich's theology is presented in more popular form in several series of lectures, the best known of which are *The Courage to Be* (1951) and *Dynamics of Faith* (1957). He regularly preached at Union Seminary and on college and university campuses but wrote, he confessed, only two or three sermons a year. Three collections of his sermons were published: *The Shaking of the Foundations* (1948), *The New Being* (1955), and *The Eternal Now* (1963).

Tillich believed that the task of preaching was to communicate the gospel, "making possible a definite decision for or against it" (Tillich 1959, 202). He also held that in today's world an apologetic style of preaching was required, taking account of the situation of the hearers and communicating in language adapted to their situation.

To do this, Tillich used biblical texts, bringing the biblical world to life in terms of human experience and bringing hearers in their present world into connection with the ways of God as manifest in scripture. The sermons rarely "translate" into philosophical, psychological, or scientific language as the *Systematic Theology* often does, but they connect human experience, human longing for God, and human awareness of the transcendent found in the Bible with those realities in the listeners to the sermon.

The major themes with which Tillich deals in the sermons center on God's response to the brokenness of human life, both personal and social. The sermons in *The Shaking of the Foundations* (1948), drawn in many cases from the prophets, reflect the situation in the time of World War II and its aftermath. Human anxiety about the world is countered by the proclamation of the existence of two orders, the order of human destruction and God's providential order, which is hidden and yet revealed. Human personal anxiety is met by the proclamation of divine forgiveness and acceptance, which one needs only to receive. The best known of the sermons in this first collection is "You Are Accepted," which has been for many people the telling word of grace in their lives.

In *The New Being* (1955), the sermons are divided into three groups: the New Being as Love, as Freedom, and as Fulfillment. Here one hears of forgiveness for guilt, reconciliation from enmity, healing for disease, and reunion in the fact of separation. These are the dimensions of the New Being, which is mediated and manifested in Jesus as the Christ, who is portrayed in the Gospels and letters of the New Testament and who is received by faith. Faith is multiform. It is the acceptance of grace. It is the courage to act through one's anxiety. It is always accompanied by doubt, and serious doubt is an element in faith. It is a gift of the Spirit.

The Spirit is central in the sermons of *The Eternal Now* (1963), which takes its title from one sermon, but whose substance Tillich suggests is more clearly seen in the sermon "Spiritual Presence." The three groups of sermons are designated "The Human Predicament," "The Divine Reality," and "The Challenge to Man." The latter group more than any other of the sermons calls the hearers to serious response to the gracious gift, a response that is made possible by the work of the Spirit.

The sermons are varied in form. Some are simple expositions of a passage. Others are drawn from a collection of texts. Some are for special occasions such as Advent, Christmas, Good Friday, and Easter. Some have a clear structure, either expository or narrative. Some are almost like stream-of-consciousness sharing. All are marked by a vivid awareness of the concrete and experiential. And all show the gifts of precision in language and of imagination.

One is struck by the aptness and pointedness of the concluding words of the sermons, for example, in "The New Being":

> Reconciliation, reunion, resurrection—this is the New Creation, the New Being, the New state of things. Do we participate in it? The message of Christianity is not Christianity, but a New reality. A New state of things has appeared, it still appears; it is hidden and visible, it is there and it is here. Accept it, enter into it, let it grasp you (1955, 24).

In "Who Are My Mother and My Brothers?" he concludes,

> . . . we know that even the image of God can be distorted by the images of father and mother, so that its saving power is almost lost. This is the danger of all religion and a serious limit for our religious work. But it is not a danger for God, who again and again breaks through the images we have made of Him, and who has shown us in Christ that He is not only father and mother to us, but also child, and therefore in him the inescapable conflicts of every family are overcome. The Father who is also child is more than a father as He is more than a child. Therefore we can

pray to the Father in heaven without transferring our hostility against the father image to Him. Because God has become a child it is possible for us to say the Our Father (1955, 109).

In such passages one sees the insight, the passion, and the relevance of Tillich's preaching.

Knupp, R. E., "The Apologetic Preaching of Paul Tillich," *Encounter* 42:3 (Fall 1981), 395–407. **Pauck, W.** and **M.,** *Paul Tillich: His Life and Thought, Volume I: Life,* 1976, esp. 227–32 on Tillich's preaching. **Tillich, P.,** *The Eternal Now,* 1963; *The New Being,* 1955; *The Shaking of the Foundations,* 1948; *Theology of Culture,* 1959.

C. BENTON KLINE, JR.

BORN IN THE GRAVE
Paul Tillich
In the Nuremberg war-crime trials a witness appeared who had lived for a time in a grave in a Jewish grave-yard, in Wilna, Poland. It was the only place he—and many others—could live, when in hiding after they had escaped the gas chamber. During this time he wrote poetry, and one of the poems was a description of a birth. In a grave nearby a young woman gave birth to a boy. The eighty-year-old gravedigger, wrapped in a linen shroud, assisted. When the new-born child uttered his first cry, the old man prayed: "Great God, hast Thou finally sent the Messiah to us? For who else than the Messiah Himself can be born in a grave?" But after three days the poet saw the child sucking his mother's tears because she had no milk for him.

This story, which surpasses anything the human imagination could have invented, has not only incomparable emotional value, but also tremendous symbolic power. When I first read it, it occurred to me more forcefully than ever before that our Christian symbols, taken from the gospel stories, have lost a great deal of their power because [they are] too often repeated and too superficially used. It has been forgotten that the manger of Christmas was the expression of utter poverty and distress before it became the place

where the angels appeared and to which the star pointed. And it has been forgotten that the tomb of Jesus was the end of His life and of His work *before* it became the place of His final triumph. We have become insensitive to the infinite tension which is implied in the words of the Apostles' Creed: "suffered . . . was crucified, dead, and buried . . . rose again from the dead." We already know, when we hear the first words, what the ending will be: "rose again"; and for many people it is no more than the inevitable "happy ending." The old Jewish gravedigger knew better. For him, the immeasurable tension implicit in the expectation of the Messiah was a reality, appearing in the infinite contrast between the things he saw and the hope he maintained.

From "Born in the Grave," in *The Shaking of the Foundations* (New York: Charles Scribner's Sons, 1948), 165–66. Used by permission.

Tillotson, John. (1630–1694) Tillotson was born into the strict Puritan family of a Yorkshire clothier and educated at Cambridge where he came under the influence of not only the leading Puritans of the day but also of the more liberal-minded Cambridge Platonists. He remained for a while within the Puritan camp but, being of a naturally irenic disposition and willing to consider a number of points of view, was ordained by a bishop and served various appointments within the Church of England. His fame began to build when he was in his early thirties and he preached on Sunday to the lawyers at Lincoln's Inn and on Tuesdays in the important city parish of St. Lawrence Jewry. At the latter parish he assisted John Wilkins, later Bishop of Chester, who was the leading force in founding the Royal Society and who in 1646 had published *Ecclesiastes; or, The Gift of Preaching,* the first homiletical textbook advocating the new plain style in preaching. The two were to become associated in many ventures, and Tillotson married Wilkins's stepdaughter, a niece of Oliver Cromwell. In time, preferment came to Tillotson; he became a chaplain of Charles II; a prebendary and then dean of Canterbury; and a canon of St. Paul's. Although he was among those who opposed James II's efforts to promote toleration for Roman Catholicism, he was not sent to the Tower because he was not yet a bishop. Nor was he one of those who signed the invitation to William and Mary to take over the throne. Yet as a close friend of William, he preached in court three days after their coronation. Although Tillotson had no desire to be a bishop, William prevailed upon him to accept Canterbury after Archbishop Sancroft joined the Nonjuror schism. He was very uncomfortable in that office because of attacks on the orthodoxy of his Latitudinarian theology and lived to occupy it for only three years (*see* Court Preachers).

It has been said of him that he was "the only Primate of All England to enjoy the reputation of being the greatest preacher of his day." After the Civil War and Commonwealth, people no longer had a taste for either the witty preaching of the Metaphysicals or the logic-chopping exegesis of the Puritans.* Instead, they craved something that was very clear and concerned more with morals than theological polemic. Although both Robert South and Isaac Barrow preceded Tillotson somewhat in satisfying the new taste encouraged by Wilkins's textbooks, it was Tillotson whose practice set the norm for over a century. The plain speech he modeled would hardly be recognized as such today, but it represented a change in the social group whose speech set the standard for the church; that group ceased to be the court and nobility and became "gentlemen," the squirearchy and mercantile class of Augustan England.

In the Age of Reason, England's anticipation of the Enlightenment, Tillotson was punctilious in not trying to move his audience by anything other than the clarity and cogency of his thought. He eschewed any effort to sway the emotions either by beauty of language or by drama of delivery. Instead, he personified "the

calm that breath'd o'er Eden." Nor was his thought either too demanding or profound; he wished to make sure that his audience could follow him every step of the way. He would begin a sermon with a short introduction that raised the issues he planned to discuss and showed their importance. Then he listed the divisions into which his subject fell and went on to discuss the issues thus raised like a woodsman methodically chopping a log into stove-sized pieces. At the end there was no stirring peroration, no emotional appeal. When he finished presenting his case, he left it to stand on its own merits.

Thus described, his homiletical method sounds rather dull, and indeed even the scholars who have studied his work most closely seem at a loss to explain his appeal. Yet there is no doubt of its popularity for some decades afterward. His style was aped by all who wished to be esteemed as preachers; his sermons were recycled by others for their own use; and he was considered to be the exemplar of elegant prose by secular writers as well as ecclesiastics. Addison, Steele, and Dryden seem to have profited from his example, and his sermons sold more copies than their essays. Perhaps, as has been suggested, one of the greatest reasons for his appeal to other writers was that his style was so very imitable.

There seems to be some connection between his homiletical style and his theology, which was the Latitudinarianism of the time. It has been said that his sermons communicated little beyond "a general impression that it was more prudent on the whole to believe the gospel, in a modified sort of way, than not." After him, English preaching seems to have degenerated into moral essays delivered orally. Yet in the age to which he spoke, this may have been as much of the gospel as people were able to hear (*see* History of Preaching).

Downey, J., *The Eighteenth-Century Pulpit: A Study of the Sermons of Butler, Berkeley, Secker, Sterne, Whitefield, and Wesley,* 1969. **Simon, I.,** *Three Restoration Divines: Barrow, South, Tillotson: Selected Sermons,* 2 vols., 1967–76. **Smyth, C.,** *The Art of Preaching: A Practical Survey of Preaching in the Church of England, 747–1939,* 1940.

O. C. EDWARDS, JR.

Titles. If one were to read the Sunday sermon titles in the nation's Saturday newspapers over a period of years, he or she would be led to several conclusions. One is that sermons are often titled to catch the eye in an attempt to be "brief, breezy, bright, and brotherly," as a certain type of sermon and worship was once described. Preachers who speak around the county in ministers' conferences, conventions, and the like are asked months in advance for sermon subjects. One has the impression that the more artful—or deceptive—of these luminaries learn to submit subjects that are so broad and general that any specific sermon direction might be subsumed under the vague title. Now and again sermon titles turn out to be far removed from the actual message of the sermon. In such instances, it may not be frivolous to conclude that the purpose of the title is to mislead, a kind of homiletic scam. The situations mentioned above are offset by the great majority of instances in which preachers seek to deal honorably and honestly in choosing their sermon titles.

John Henry Jowett in his Beecher lectures in 1912 insisted that "no sermon is ready for preaching, not ready for writing out, until we can express its theme in a short, pregnant sentence as clear as a crystal" (Jowett, 133). Jowett was wise in stressing the latter since subordinate clauses and the like in sentences can make the maxim a protracted procedure.

Perhaps it is not going too far to apply this principle to the sermon subject. To the extent that it can be done, the sermon title ought to be a contraction of the theme, which in turn ought to be a contraction of the sermon. Like the sermon introduction,* the title ought to attempt to be the sermon concealed, as the sermon ought to be the title revealed.

In these matters, one must not attempt to be overly dogmatic because at its highest the sermon is art, if by that term is meant the setting forth of a vision. In such matters of art, creativity and innovation are vital. Along that line, Paul Scherer once said that all the rules of sermon preparation and delivery may be valorously violated if one knows what she or he is doing. Fifty years have not dimmed the memory of so noble a preacher as Harold Cooke Phillips doing just that in a sermon titled "The Angel in the Sun." The text was from Revelation 19:17. At the outset the preacher stated that the text would not be treated in faithfulness to its context or its generally accepted meaning. The title and sermon were therefore shorn of what they would logically suggest. The Cleveland preacher then preached a memorable and telling sermon, *but* here was a master craftsman of his generation at work.

There is much to be learned about the importance of a title by recalling some of the notable sermons in the history of preaching. F. W. Robertson's* "An Israelite's Grave in a Foreign Land" dealt with Joseph's poignant request that in the deliverance to come his bones would be borne back to his own land. The title touches on our transience in the earth and our longing for home, deeply moving emotions. The arresting title doubtless helped to secure the sermon's place in the literature of the pulpit. Sometimes unforgettable titles that touch the depths of human experience grow out of apparently trivial incidents. Thomas Chalmers's great sermon on "The Expulsive Power of a New Affection" is supposed to have been born in the incident of a coachman who was driving Chalmers and who flicked his whip at the ears of the brace of horses in order to divert their attention from the annoyance of flies buzzing around their ears. What an example of huge oaks from small acorns!

Arthur Gossip's most memorable sermon was very likely "When Life Tumbles In, What Then?" It was wrung out of his agony at what he described as the first sermon preached after his wife's "dramatically sudden death." One of the most notable black preachers of the first half of the twentieth century, Lacey Kirk Williams of Chicago, gave a New Year's sermon in Olivet Church, Chicago, titled "God Ahead in 1926." The subject suggested the occasion and was a condensation of the text: "And the Lord, he it is that doth go before thee, he will not fail thee, neither forsake thee: Fear not, neither be dismayed." What a happy confluence of occasion, title, and text.

In the South, one of the best-known sermon titles was that of Robert G. Lee of Memphis, "Pay Day Some Day." People in other lands found the sermon a bit too gaudy, but the title was gripping and became a legend in the religious life of the American South.

Even a superficial study of the history of Christian preaching will reveal an incalculably rich vein of mental power touched and fired by worthy emotion in service to the incomparably rigorous and inexpressibly tender terms of the Christian gospel. Joseph Fort Newton was right when he wrote that "glorious is the history of the pulpit . . . consecrated as it is by so much of genius, power and beauty" (Newton, 465). Given the rare intellects and incandescent personalities possessed by a bright, long succession of Christian preachers, among the most amazing aspects of sermon preparation and sermon delivery, including titles, is the awareness that the sixty-six books in the canon and particularly the twenty-seven "pamphlets" in the New Testament have sustained twenty centuries of preaching with not the faintest suggestion of exhaustion.

Jowett, J., *The Preacher, His Life and Work*, 1912. Newton, J. F., *The New Preaching*, 1930.   GARDNER C. TAYLOR

Topical Preaching.

The topical sermon gives a systematic or integrated *treatment* of a theme considered worthy of discussion. Such a sermon may or may not be biblical. Whether a sermon is bibli-

cal does not depend on the degree to which it relies on particular texts from the Bible. Rather, that depends on faithfulness to the great themes of the Bible, "the characteristic and essential biblical ideas" (John Knox). Therefore, a topical sermon may be thoroughly biblical, even though it is not expository* or textual. By the same token, a so-called expository or textual sermon may not be biblical.

What will a good topical sermon look like? It will be *integrative;* it will reach out in all relevant directions for substance and form in order to make the best possible case for the matter under consideration. Understandably, the topical sermon will rely on scripture, for the Bible is the common ground on which both preacher and congregation normally meet. However, the problem or issue that gives impetus to a topical sermon may begin at a great distance from the Bible and be led ultimately, almost inevitably, to the scriptures. Personal problems of the hearers, controversial issues in the local community, ethical issues of national and international scope, denominational debates, matters of cultural and aesthetic concern, and congregational challenges—any and all of these fields of inquiry suggest proper topics for preaching (*see* Ethics). At the same time, it should be obvious that inordinate and narrow preoccupation with such themes could leave the preacher stranded in the desert of merely "weary, stale, flat, and unprofitable" ideas. Proper attention to the Bible, however, can render many of these themes profitable "for teaching, for reproof, for correction, and for training in righteousness, so that everyone who belongs to God may be proficient, equipped for every good work" (2 Tim. 3:16b–17).

Harry Emerson Fosdick* deplored the topical preaching of those who, as he put it, "search contemporary life in general and the newspapers in particular for subjects. . . . Instead of starting with a text, they start with their own ideas on some subject of their choice, but their ideas on that subject may be much farther away from the vital interests of the people than a great text from the Bible" ("What Is the Matter with Preaching?" *Harper's Magazine*, July 1928). Fosdick himself has been recognized as a topical preacher— but with a difference. He focused on people and their needs, rather than on subjects for discussion. This approach led to the scriptures for ultimate answers to problems, with such topics as "The Hope of the World in Its Minorities," "The Means Determine the End," "Are We Part of the Problem or of the Answer?" In similar fashion, Paul Scherer* used a line from Hemingway: "Life All the Way Up"; Ralph W. Sockman* asserted: "Fears May Be Liars"; Walter J. Burghardt offered: "The Other, the Others, and You." In every case, the truth of scripture was highlighted and embraced.

Not only is it of basic importance to attend to the word of scripture, it will be meaningful also to consider how God's people throughout history have dealt with troubling problems and issues. Tradition, of course, is subject to the authority and judgment of scripture, but God did not retire when the canon was closed. Augustine,* Francis of Assisi,* Luther,* Calvin,* Wesley,* and many others have made effective contemporary preachers their debtors.

Also, various modern-day disciplines contribute to preaching that can be at once biblical *and* topical. For example, the fields of philosophy, psychology, biology, and sociology can assist in making the biblical message more understandable and applicable.

The preaching of Jesus* demonstrated how a topical approach can, in certain situations, proclaim the word of God as surely as verse-by-verse explanation and application of scripture. He gave his parables in response to "topical" situations, and the authoritative words came at the end as the hearers perceived the relevant truth of God in what he said. In topical preaching at its best, there is an incarnational element: God's message in human garb, half-hidden, though perhaps more effectively present, in the raiment of rhetoric, philosophical inquiry, ethical debate, or political protest. If it is incarnational, can it be anything less than passionate, anything less than relevant? It is "truth through personality," which makes it both full of risk and full of promise.

Augustine* is credited with making the first formal defense of the use of the art of rhetoric in Christian preaching. It seems that until then preachers gave a running commentary on scripture lessons, explaining and applying the meaning as they went. As a teacher of the rhetorical art, Augustine was prepared to bring to his preaching creative innovation. Perhaps most of his preaching was expository in the traditional sense; however, many examples of what came to be called the sermon are extant in his writings. Here is Augustine's rationale:

> For since by means of the art of rhetoric both truth and falsehood are urged, who would dare to say that truth should stand in the person of its defenders unarmed against lying, so that they who wish to use falsehoods may know how to make their listeners benevolent, or attentive, or docile in their presentations, while the defenders of truth are ignorant of that art? (*On Christian Doctrine* IV, 2.3).

Everything that Augustine said in favor of the art of rhetoric in preaching can be said in favor of topical preaching—and for similar reasons.

Allen, R., Jr., *Preaching the Topical Sermon,* 1992. **Cox, J. W.,** *A Guide to Biblical Preaching,* 1976; and *Handbook of Themes for Preaching,* 1991.   JAMES W. COX

Vatican II. In line with its pastoral purpose, Vatican Council II (1962–1965) emphasized as no other council before it, the church's responsibility of preaching. Pope John XXIII set the tone for the renewal of preaching in his opening speech, declaring, "The substance of the ancient doctrine of the deposit of faith is one thing, and the way in which it is presented is another."

Consequently, the council imposed the duty of preaching on both pastors and lay people. Its duty devolved upon bishops first of all, priests as their coworkers, deacons wherever there was a scarcity of priests, and all lay people of the church in virtue of its missionary thrust (Decree on the Missionary Activity of the Church, 1–2, 5).

The Constitution on the Sacred Liturgy, the first of the sixteen conciliar documents to come under deliberation and discussion, stated that "the ministry of preaching is to be fulfilled with exactitude and fidelity" (35). The Decree on the Ministry and Life of Priests would have the people of God hear the word of the living God from the lips of priests who have "as their primary duty the proclamation of the gospel of God to all" (4). The phrases "primary duty" and "ministry" of the word were rather unfamiliar to Catholic ears.

Evangelization. If the renewal (and reform) of the church was to take place, it had to start with the word of scripture. Initially, God is revealed in the history of salvation through wonderful works. Then the scriptural message draws attention to God and God's works, and preaching follows in the service of the word.

The Dogmatic Constitution on Divine Revelation, in step with the biblical movement, promoted the ministry of the word. As the Bible sprang from preaching, so it should return to preaching. The church must add the living word of proclamation in order to vivify the mystery of Christ, to draw wholesome nourishment for itself, and to bear fruit in holiness. Ministry includes pastoral preaching, catechetics, and all other Christian instruction.

For the wider, deeper, and richer understanding of the sacred scriptures, the church was to enact by conciliar decree a set (three-year) cycle of scriptural readings in its liturgy.

Though the council did not favor a biblicism or a biblical preaching alone, it did seem to allow theological and spiritual tradition to recede into the background. Tradition, however, is transmission by word of mouth—the witness of speech. The preacher is to be a mystagogue who evangelizes people into spiritual ways of living.

The "law" of all evangelization is appropriately to accommodate preaching to the grasp of all and to the needs of the learned. Evangelization is "to penetrate and perfect the temporal sphere with the spirit of the gospel." It also and particularly implants the church. Hence it is related to the cultures and religions of non-Christian peoples. From an ecumenical point of view too, evangelical preaching must urge a renewal of conduct (Decree on the Church's Missionary Activity, 5, 6) (*see* Missions).

Restoration of the Homily. The homily* revives the first form of evangelization as found in the Gospels. The sacred text lends itself throughout the liturgical year to an exposition of the mysteries of the faith and the guiding principles of the Christian life. The homily is not only a part of the liturgy; it should have an exceptional place in it and should not be omitted without a serious reason (Constitutions on the Divine Revelation and Sacred Liturgy, 23, 52, respectively).

The homily is developed from the scriptural readings in the liturgy and the liturgy itself. It is both a proclamation and an instruction (recalling the combination of kerygma and didache in the early church). Preachers are both "heralds of the gospels" and "educators in the faith." They are to so contemporize Christ as to make him present and active among his followers. Actually, preaching is a gift from Christ and the Spirit (Decree on the Ministry and Life of Priests, 4, 6, 8; Constitution on the Sacred Liturgy, 35) (*see* Liturgical Preaching).

The council called for additional homiletic preaching in the ministry of all seven sacraments.* They serve the people throughout the Christian life: "The preaching of the Word is needed for the very administration of the sacraments . . . of faith, and faith is born of the Word and nourished by it" (Decree on the Ministry and Life of Priests, 4).

Minuses and Pluses of Preaching. The same decree sees preaching as dialogic, but therein too lies its difficulty. For his or her task, the preacher has to have the experience of faith. Otherwise the preacher may succumb to the evils of human society and lose the power of communication with it.

The challenge is to apply the perennial truth of the gospel to the concrete circumstances of modern life. The Pastoral Constitution on the Church in the Modern World invites the use of literature and the arts for the preaching of the gospel to clarify itself and show its relevance to the conditions of human life (62).

The last conciliar document, the Declaration on Religious Freedom, explains how the duties of preachers and hearers cohere. While the church is to teach authoritatively the truth that is Christ himself and confirm it with moral principles that originate in human nature itself, the Christian faithful are to accept that teaching for the formation of their consciences (14). To an even wider audience of all people of good will, the church must use and guide the communications media according to the norms of morality, in order to extend the kingdom of God (Decree on the Instruments of Social Communication, 1, 3, 24).

Abbott, W. M., S.J., ed. *The Documents of Vatican II,* 1966. **Fichtner, J., O.S.C.,** *To Stand and Speak for Christ: A Theology of Preaching,* 1981. **Vorgrimler, H.,** ed., *Commentary on the Documents of Vatican II,* 4 vols., 1968.   JOSEPH FICHTNER, O.S.C.

Voice. The voice is one of the least understood or appreciated gifts of the minister. The voice is the vehicle for the message. Without a dynamic, natural voice, it is difficult to obtain and maintain the attention of the listener. Normally, without any special effort, the voice is easily manipulated up and down the pitch range, altering between loud and quiet, fast-paced and leisurely, and modulating quality to add variety. This control over the many dimensions of sound should be treasured.

Voice production should be a natural and effortless task. The addition of excessive vocal effort or altering natural voice production from the pulpit can lead to voice disorders, vocal fatigue, and hoarseness. Voice production is a combination of the processes of breathing, phonation, and resonance. These three components should work in synchrony to create an interesting and effective delivery system for the message.

Breathing for speech differs from ordinary breathing employed during sleep or other nonvocal activities. Speech utilizes expiratory air, which vibrates the vocal folds and produces sound. The irregularity of speech breathing means speakers inhale more sharply and less often than when they are silent. Abdominal muscles and the chest wall expand, and the body automatically replenishes its power source. Common breathing problems of the minister include: (1) speaking too long without a pause for breath, (2) pausing long enough for a short gasp only, and (3) placing too much attention on breathing by using shoulder and neck muscles rather than the efficient abdominals, resulting in a strained, unnatural voice. The key to breath control is allowing the body to perform without any special effort. This entails developing a sense of how many words may be said in one breath and then planning to pause before that limit is reached. During a proper break in the speech stream, the body will inhale sufficient air for speech to continue.

Breath controls voice loudness as well. A quiet voice expends much less air than a full volume of overly loud voice. Changes in situation dictate alterations in vocal loudness and are natural and necessary for an intelligible, vibrant message. Appropriate loudness in the pulpit might be inappropriate in a small group or in one-on-one interaction. Excessive vocal intensity in such situations might be perceived as intimidating or hostile. Too little loudness conveys insecurity, lack of confidence, or an ill-prepared message. Within a sermon, loudness as well as pitch, pacing, and resonance should vary. Choosing too many points to emphasize at the same loudness level can dull the vigor of a sermon as a whole. However, a natural change from conversational loudness level to increased or decreased vocal intensity will build emphasis on the main aspects of the message.

Phonation, the second component of voice, occurs in the larynx, or voice box. The breath stream passes through the trachea into the larynx and sets the vocal folds, or cords, in motion. The vocal folds vibrate as the air moves through, and a sound similar to that of a plucked guitar string is produced. This sound should be relaxed and effortless, with pleasing pitch and pitch variety. A monotone voice is difficult to tolerate for any great length of time, and it conveys a lack of enthusiasm about the message as well.

Pitch is determined by the length, mass, and balance of tension in the vocal folds. For example, a small woman would have smaller vocal folds and therefore produce a higher pitch than a large man. Thus, our natural pitch is inherent since it is related to gender and body frame. But other factors such as stress or stage fright add tension to the vocal folds and can result in an elevated, strained voice (*see* Anxiety in the Pulpit).

The minister is at risk of a voice problem if he or she fails to keep the vocal folds in good condition. Misuses of the vocal folds include (1) frequent throat-clearing, (2) speaking while suffering an upper respiratory infection, (3) lack of exercise and stress reduction, (4) dehydration of the vocal mechanism by limited intake of water or excess of caffeine, and (5) speaking over noise without sufficient amplification or to compensate for a poor acoustic environment. These vocal stressors can accumulate and lead to temporary voice disturbance or a more serious voice disorder, such as vocal polyps, nodules, or swelling of the vocal tissues.

Resonance, the process of enriching and adding timbre to sound, occurs in the throat, mouth, and nasal cavities above the vocal folds. Sound is reflected within the walls of the throat and adds a fullness of voice. A relaxed, open-mouth posture gives a rich, full tone, while a tense jaw and throat can render the voice thin and strident. These voice acoustics can be compared to the acoustics of a room. When one speaks in a bare-walled gymnasium, sound echoes and carries. But a carpeted sanctuary filled with people absorbs sound quickly. A simple tip to improve overall resonance is to open the mouth, thereby increasing the distance between the upper and lower jaw to allow better oral-nasal balance and quality. For just as a cavernous room reflects sound more fully, so does an open oral cavity.

Vocal resonance while speaking the English language is determined by articulation standards. For example, the sounds *m, n,* and *ng* resonate appropriately in the nasal cavities. All other sounds in English resonate in the oral cavity. An imbalance between oral and nasal resonance might be perceived as lazy, affected, or congested delivery. Dialect, while an appropriate part of a personal delivery style, also has a significant effect on resonance. For example, midwesterners would be expected to have more nasal resonance than southerners. An imbalance or overt nasal resonance might distract listeners from the message, and consideration should be given to both the makeup of the audience and the formality of the setting.

To counteract a resonance problem such as hypernasality, a speaker should strive for appropriate vocal focus. The range may be visualized as a four-point axis, extending from the chest through the head and from the front of the mouth through the back. The voice focus is the point along this axis most involved in resonance. A balance must be struck between a voice focused too low in the throat, which sounds husky, guttural, and low, and an overly vertical focus in the nose, which is whining, sharp or unpleasant. A voice focused too far forward in the mouth might sound immature and effeminate, while a focus too far back sounds adenoidal and constricted. A vertical, forward focus yields a voice that is open, rich, and full. A speaker with poor voice focus is likely placing undue strain on the larynx and risks inaccurately representing both the speaker and the message.

Understanding and nurturing the voice are essential to the longevity and effectiveness of a minister's livelihood. Developing a natural and dynamic style of speaking will ensure a voice that will be reliable and effective for a lifetime (*see* Delivery of Sermons).

Boone, D. R., *Is Your Voice Telling on You? How to Find and Use Your Natural Voice,* 1991. **Colton, R. H.,** and **J. K. Casper,** *Understanding Voice Problems: A Physiological Perspective for Diagnosis and Treatment,* 1990.   CHRISTINE E. PARTON

Weatherhead, Leslie Dixon

(1893–1976) Leslie Weatherhead was a British Methodist minister who spent the larger part of his preaching ministry (1936–1960) at the famed City Temple, a Congregational church in London. He followed a distinguished line of preachers at the City Temple, including Joseph Parker, Joseph Fort Newton, and F. W. Norwood.

Weatherhead's outstanding effectiveness as a preacher is substantially documented. Edgar DeWitt Jones classifies him as a "modern master of pulpit discourse." Weatherhead delivered the Lyman Beecher Lectures on Preaching at Yale Divinity School in 1949. Horton Davies said that Weatherhead was "unrivaled as a twentieth-century physician of souls and preacher of the integration of personality through Christ" (Davies, 138).

Weatherhead's career as an effective preacher began in 1916 as a missionary pastor and military chaplain in India. Upon his return to England in 1922, he assumed the pastorate of the Oxford Road Wesleyan Church in Manchester. He was greeted on his first Sunday in Manchester by a congregation of thirty people. When he left Manchester in 1925, the sanctuary, which seated over 1,000, was practically full. While in Manchester,

Weatherhead attended Manchester University, where he completed a master's degree in nineteenth-century English poetry.

At age 32, Leslie Weatherhead became the pastor of the large Brunswick Methodist Church in Leeds. His concern there was not mustering a crowd as in Manchester but maintaining one already established in a strong preaching tradition. During his eleven years at Leeds he published eleven of his thirty-six books. Three thousand people gathered to hear his last sermon at Leeds.

Weatherhead began his ministry at the City Temple in London on October 4, 1936, only ten days prior to his forty-third birthday. Throughout his twenty-four years in London, including the devastating years of World War II, he drew overflow crowds to his services. His influence as a preacher and doctor of souls became widely known.

The prospect and subsequent reality of war occupied much of Weatherhead's attention during the first half of his tenure at the City Temple. While struggling with his own pacifist leanings, he wrestled with the evil personified in Hitler. He felt that preaching *about* the war itself was useless. He preached to meet the varying needs produced *by* the war, not the least of which were psychological. It was this commitment to the psychological health of persons that led him in 1950, at the age of 57, to complete the doctor of philosophy degree in psychology at the University of London. Upon his retirement at age 67, Weatherhead was made Minister Emeritus of the City Temple. His most significant contributions to the preaching task were sympathetic insight and the mastery of simple language, both evidence of his ability to identify with his listeners. An intense interest in the relationship between psychology and religion as well as a graduate education in nineteenth-century English poetry were seminal in Weatherhead's development of sympathy and simplicity in the pulpit. W. E. Sangster,* one of Weatherhead's fellow Methodist ministers in London, said of his sympathetic insight: "if I were driven to put the secret of his power into one word, I should use the word 'caring.' He cares for people: honestly, personally, and in a most costly way" (Weatherhead 1975, 67).

Very early in his career, Weatherhead set a sympathetic tone for his preaching that characterized his sermons throughout his ministry. He felt that the tests of a sermon were its contact with human life and its fidelity to the character of Jesus. In his book *The Transforming Friendship*, he underscored this sympathetic approach by suggesting certain test questions for a sermon: Is it going to help people to live? Does it actually touch life and come to grips with things people are facing? Does it send them out with new courage and hope for living? Weatherhead felt that the preacher must not be satisfied until people go away saying to themselves, "That made a difference to *me*; that's going to help *me*; that makes life more meaningful to *me*" (Weatherhead 1932, 82).

No less significant for preaching was Weatherhead's concern for simple, understandable language in the sermon. He addresses this concern in a sermon contained in *When the Lamp Flickers:*

The commonest criticism that I hear of sermons is that they do not deal with the problems ordinary men and women are facing, that they talk a language remote from everyday living, that much of the sermon time is given to biblical and theological problems which do not seem to bear upon life at all, and that the language used is often a preacher's jargon which means little to the layman. In a word, that religion is not apparently related to life, and that is a damning indictment (Weatherhead 1948, 13).

Simplicity was the hallmark of Weatherhead's own use of language in preaching. He drew his words from the common stock of everyday vocabulary. His sentence structure also reveals a distinct preference for simple style. Weatherhead

had the unique ability to communicate profound subjects and concerns through clear, simple language.

Davies, H., *Varieties of English Preaching 1900–1960,* 1963. **Odom, S. A.,** ed., *Steady in an Unsteady World: Sermons by Leslie Weatherhead,* 1986. **Weatherhead, K.,** *Leslie Weatherhead: A Personal Portrait,* 1975. **Weatherhead, L.,** *The Transforming Friendship,* 1932; and *When the Lamp Flickers,* 1948.   STEPHEN A. ODOM

THE INEVITABLE ENCOUNTER
Leslie Weatherhead

Perhaps the best-known and most quoted of all the sayings of Saint Augustine is, "Thou has made us for Thyself and our hearts are restless until they find rest in Thee."

Some situations give to an imaginative mind a curious and satisfying sense of poignant rightness. If I stand watching a stream flowing into the sea, I get that feeling. For the stream is fulfilled and complete, following its ordained plan. I get the same feeling by repeating aloud those lines from Stevenson's "Requiem":

Here he lies where he longed to be;
Home is the sailor, home from the sea,
And the hunter, home from the hill.

. . . I call it a sense of poignant rightness. The glove fits the hand because it was made to do so. The key opens only that lock for which it was constructed. If we saw life completely, we would get the same feeling when, in what I am calling the inevitable encounter, the soul made its peace with God and found an inner harmony otherwise unattainable.

. . . We feel intuitively that the soul and God *must* find one another, for until they do there is disharmony, and surely that must be temporary. Perhaps the idea of Judgment Day which the church has always taught owes part of its appeal to the thought that an encounter between the soul and God is inevitable. It is a pity that so many people associate Judgment Day with horror and terror. I am quite sure that if one can really speak of it as a day at all—since it is supposed to take place in a timeless world—it will be for some people the happiest day of their lives. For the first time *they will be really understood;* for the first time they will be confronted by a knowledge which is absolutely and utterly penetrating, but equally and utterly loving and carrying all the sympathy which knowledge and love bring. As a result of this experience, many people will be surprised, not by fear, but by an incredible joy. They will find it hard to believe that such joy can ever be associated with a religious experience. Finally, the sense of incompletion and frustration, of purposelessness and monotonous wandering, will give way to the sense of completion, harmony, and home. The stream finds the ocean at last. The nestling is mothered when the night comes, however lonely the day may have been. The prisoners escape at last. The hunter is home from the hill. The sailor is home from the sea.

> From "The Inevitable Encounter," in *Steady in an Unsteady World: Sermons by Leslie Weatherhead,* ed. S. A. Odom (Valley Forge: Judson Press, 1986), 103–5.

The Wedding Sermon. (Protestant) The Christian wedding ceremony is a Christian worship service. Therefore, preaching the gospel is an integral part of the service. While some wedding services have not included a brief message, more preachers are taking this opportunity to address the couple and congregation regarding Christian marriage. In some traditions it is called a wedding homily. The sermon may be directed primarily to the couple being married or to the congregation in general. When the sermon is addressed to the couple, referring to the bride and groom by name in the sermon, the members of the congregation may "overhear" the gospel and find the message even more meaningful than if addressed directly to them. The wedding sermon should be personal without becoming sentimental. It comes either just after the opening prayer or just before the vows.

The wedding sermon will vary in length according to the occasion. While some ministers preach a forty-five-minute wedding sermon, most wedding sermons are from five to ten minutes in length. If the wedding party is seated at the front of the church for the sermon, then it may be longer than if the wedding party is standing. When the wedding vows follow a Sunday morning worship service, as is common in the Church of Scotland, then the sermon may be its usual length.

The wedding sermon may be either topical or expository. Or it may deal with some aspect of the wedding ceremony, such as the vows. In the latter case, the sermon will explain the meaning of the vows and actions of the wedding. When the sermon is expository in nature it may be based on texts such as the creation story, or Jesus' words about marriage in Matt. 19:4–6. In 1 Peter 3:7, there is the assurance that we are joint heirs of the grace of life, another suggestive text for a wedding sermon. The epistles are rich with texts appropriate for a wedding. However, care must be given in interpreting some of the texts that reflect a patriarchal society's view of marriage. In a Christian marriage there should be quality and mutual respect. The Old Testament is also a fertile source of texts for a wedding sermon. Among the best known are the words of Ps. 127:1, which declare that unless the Lord builds the house (marriage and family), those who build it will labor in vain.

One of the best-known passages of the Bible is 1 Cor. 13–14:1, the hymn of love. (Note that vs. 4–7 are full of wisdom for a marriage relationship.) The passage ends with a charge to make love your aim, an especially fitting charge to give a couple being married.

The wedding sermon will be heard not only by the couple being married but also by young people in the wedding party and the congregation who are considering marriage and by couples who have been married for years. The wedding sermon can be not only a message to help prepare people for Christian marriage but also a call to renewal of marriage vows made earlier. This invitation to renew wedding vows may be given in one or two sentences.

The wedding sermon might also describe the marriage ceremony as a rite of passage in which two individuals move from being separate individuals to a new relationship. When the lighting of candles is part of the wedding ceremony, the wedding sermon may interpret the ritual, making it clear that the bride and groom are not merging their personalities into one but are being joined in a new relationship created by God.

Other suggestive texts are found in the Sermon on the Mount, especially those relating to forgiveness, which is the key to sustaining any relationship. The description of life in the kingdom set forth in this sermon can be used to describe the ideals for a marriage relationship.

One should not overlook the opportunity for giving a kind of prelude to the wedding sermon at the rehearsal, as the minister describes the purpose of the rehearsal and wedding itself. The seriousness of the occasion can be emphasized by remarks at the rehearsal in which the minister guides the wedding party in thinking about the biblical understanding of marriage.

The wedding sermon should recognize that in the marriage service the bride and groom form a covenant for life. While there are contractual aspects in a marriage, with each person agreeing to perform certain duties, marriage itself is a dynamic, organic covenant. The exchange of vows should be done with the couple facing each other, joining right hands while looking into each other's eyes. The wedding sermon might point toward these vows as the heart of the wedding ceremony itself (where the Eucharist is not celebrated). The minister witnesses to what the couple promises, as does the congregation. But the couple *marry* each other. The wedding sermon

should help convey this to the couple as well as to the assembly.

Biddle, P. H., Jr., *Abingdon Marriage Manual, rev. ed.,* 1987; *The Goodness of Marriage,* 1984. **Stein, M. K.,** *The Catholic Wedding Book,* 1988.   PERRY H. BIDDLE

Wesley, John.

(1703–1791) Wesley was the founder of the Methodist movement within the Church of England and is considered to be the "father" of the Methodist family of denominations worldwide. Born in Epworth, England, he was the second surviving son of Samuel and Susanna Wesley, who gave him a solid grounding in learning and religion. He attended Charterhouse School in London (1713–1720) before entering Christ Church, Oxford, where he received his baccalaureate degree in 1724. Wesley's vocational interests led him to seek ordination as deacon and as priest in 1725 and 1728, and a fellowship at Lincoln College in 1726. Those events led him to become more serious about religion and learning, and he began to preach in many of the churches in and around Oxford, as well as in his father's parish.

A group of Oxford students soon began to gather around Wesley to share his "method" of holy living and Arminian theology. He began to form small societies at Oxford to promote his vision of Christian living, a development he later called "the first rise of Methodism." Going then as a missionary and priest to Oglethorpe's new colony in Georgia at the end of 1735, Wesley hoped to preach to the Indians but spent most of his time serving the needs of parishioners in Savannah and Frederica. Upon his return to England in 1738, he helped form a religious society with the Moravian, Peter Böhler, under whose tutelage Wesley experienced an assurance of faith, which he had been seeking for years as the hallmark of the Christian experience.

As he prepared to sail for America in 1735, Wesley had written to a friend, "My tongue is a dedicated thing." For more

than a half century, his life would continue to exhibit this conviction that
preaching was a central feature of his
vocation. After his contact with the Mo-
ravians, his adoption of their radical emphasis upon faith caused him to be excluded from many of the pulpits. Wesley
therefore followed the lead of his close
friend George Whitefield* and, in Bristol
in April 1739, began to preach outdoors.
This practice of field-preaching served to
invest the Methodist revival with new vitality and gave Wesley exposure to vast
crowds of unchurched people. His constant concern, however, was to provide
nurture for those who were moved by the
preaching. Wesley enhanced the combination of evangelism* and nurturance
through the formation of Methodist societies, which provided for fellowship and
discipline within the movement (see Itinerant and Open-Air Preaching).

The Wesleyan movement ministered
largely to the working classes, to whom the
Oxford don conveyed the Christian message by exhibiting his faith through works
of love and concern, especially for the
poor. He kept in touch with his expanding movement by constantly traveling
throughout the British Isles, preaching
in church services, at society meetings,
and in the open air. He made extensive
use of laypersons within the growing network of societies throughout the land, relying heavily upon lay* preachers to convey
the gospel to the farthest reaches of the
realm.

Wesley attempted to maintain a high
degree of unity and uniformity in the
movement by establishing sets of rules
and guidelines for his preachers and people. Among the doctrinal standards that
emerged were the sermons in his first
four volumes of *Sermons on Several Occasions*, which contained what he felt to be
the "essential doctrines." His preachers
were required to preach no other doctrines than those contained therein and in
his Bible commentary, *Explanatory Notes
upon the New Testament*. Although he
constantly claimed unity with the Church
of England and its doctrinal standards, he

emphasized three points as the "grand
doctrines" of Methodism: (1) repentance,
which he called the "porch" of religion,
(2) justification by faith, the "door" of
religion, and (3) sanctification or holiness, "religion itself." His mature theology is perhaps best exemplified in his sermon, "The Scripture Way of Salvation"
(1767).

Wesley's style of preaching is typified
by his own characterization: "plain truth
for plain people." His biblical texts were
generally directed toward soteriological
themes, which he saw collectively as "the
analogy of faith" that gives unity to the
Bible. Scriptural themes, imagery, and
language are the sum and substance of
most of his sermons. His published sermons (the majority of the 151 extant
texts) tend to resemble theological treatises, while his oral preaching (some forty
to fifty thousand occurrences) contained
more anecdotal material. All of his homiletical endeavors were aimed toward the
application of the gospel message of faith
working through love in the lives of Christians everywhere.

Contemporaries differed in their perspective on Wesley. Their view of his
preaching often was determined by
whether or not they agreed with his theology. It appears, for instance, that his reputation as an "enthusiast" was worse than
the reality. A story is told about Wesley,
after preaching at Peasholm Green one
Sunday, going to the parish church, as was
his custom. The parish priest saw from
Wesley's clerical garb that he was a clergyman and, without knowing who he was,
offered him the pulpit. After the service,
the priest asked the clerk who the preacher
was. "Sir," said the clerk, "he is the vaga-
bond Wesley, against whom you warned
us." "Aye, indeed!" said the astonished rector. "We are trapped; but never mind, we
have had a good sermon."

John Wesley may not have been the
most impressive orator, as a Swedish visitor once noted, but he did reflect in his
person many of the primary ideals he
held. "He has no great oratorical gifts, no
outward appearance," said Professor J. H.

Liden after he heard Wesley preach in 1769, "but he speaks clear and pleasant. . . . He looks as the worst country curate in Sweden, but has learning as a bishop and zeal for the glory of God which is quite extraordinary. . . . He is the personification of piety, and he seems to me as a living representative of the loving Apostle John."

When he died in his eighty-seventh year, his obituary in the *Gentleman's Magazine* noted that Wesley was "one of the few characters who outlived enmity and prejudice, and received, in his latter years, every mark of respect from every denomination," and added that "he must be considered as one of the most extraordinary characters this or any age ever produced."

Heitzenrater, R. P., "Spirit and Life: John Wesley's Preaching," chap. 8 in *Mirror and Memory: Reflections on Early Methodism,* 1989. **Wesley, J.**, *John Wesley's Sermons: An Anthology,* ed. A. C. Outler and R. P. Heitzenrater, 1991; and *Sermons,* ed. A. C. Outler, vols. 1–4 in *The Works of John Wesley,* 1984–87.   RICHARD P. HEITZENRATER

White, Ellen G. (1827–1915) Ellen

White was a formative leader and spokeswoman of the Seventh-day Adventist Church. Her historical significance as a preacher has been largely ignored despite the fact that her leadership was an integral part in the birth and development of this indigenous American denomination. Even though she never published a formal work on homiletical theory, she preached extensively and wrote on the subject throughout her life. Her thoughts on preaching are found in some seventy books and 60,000 pages of manuscripts in the form of letters, articles, and diary material located in the Ellen G. White Estate.

Ellen Harmon was reared in the Methodist Episcopal Church and in the early 1840s came under the influence of William Miller, who advocated the imminent Second Advent of Christ in 1843 and 1844. She fervently embraced the teach-

ings of the early Millerites and left the Methodists in 1843. In 1846 she married James White and traveled extensively in the east and midwest to encourage the scattered Adventist believers who had gone through the bitter disappointments of 1843 and 1844, when the predicted date of October 22, 1844, passed without Christ's return.

Ellen White's emergence as a nineteenth-century preacher was influenced by three major factors. First, her "visions" and role as a "messenger from God" carried significant authority with the early Adventists. Second, her emergence coincides with the "Final Emergence" of women on the lecture-and-reform circuit of the mid-nineteenth century (1850–1865). Third, with the extended sickness and ultimate death of her husband James White in 1881, she assumed an even larger role in leadership and preaching within the newly organized Seventh-day Adventist (1863) community.

Among the 471 sermons known to exist from the period of 1865 to 1915, the majority deal with the subject of Christian faith and life (284). The rest cover a wide range of topics, such as ministry (65), education (39), medicine (31), miscellaneous topics (28), health and temperance (20), and publishing (4).

Ellen White advocated that the *authority* of preaching was based upon God's "ordination" and "appointment." She viewed the *purpose* of preaching as being "the salvation of souls," while her thoughts on the *function* of the sermon evolved over her lifetime. Her early years viewed the *function* as arousal, conviction, and persuasion, but by the 1880s, in line with the prevailing homiletical theorists of her day, she added the element of instruction. This kept the Seventh-day Adventist ministry from following the revivalistic/pentecostal preaching that characterized much of early Adventism. The *source* of the preacher's message was not fully stated until the 1880s and 1890s when numerous articles appeared urging the minister to "preach the word." She clearly encouraged the preacher to avoid the literalistic interpretation of scripture so prevalent in her day. Instead, she proposed an interpretive method that recognized: (1) truth is progressive; (2) difficulties exist in scripture; (3) historical and cultural conditioning; (4) contextual understanding; (5) scripture is its own interpreter; (6) the use of symbols, types, and figures; and (7) the "common-sense" approach. With this approach she departed from the simplistic methodology and wooden literalism of William Miller.

Ellen White advocated and practiced a simple and unadorned style of delivery that was devoid of any humor or sensationalism. Her sermons were characterized by a plain style and used simple language that was clear and direct. She used striking phrases, comparative figures of speech, repetition, and a varying sentence structure to heighten her simple use of language. All intentional ornamentation was avoided. She preferred an extemporaneous delivery without notes since this guaranteed her freshness of style, directness, and availability to the moving influence of the Spirit. Her arrangement followed a conversational style in which one idea tended to suggest another. Ellen White's style of delivery, however, was very popular both inside and outside the developing Adventist community since it flowed from the deep conviction and *ethos* of a formative leader and "prophetic" spokeswoman with a "message from God."

Turner, R. E., *Proclaiming the Word: The Concept of Preaching in the Thought of Ellen G. White*, 1980.   R. EDWARD TURNER

Whitefield, George.   (1714–1770)

Religious revivals* in the sense of local revitalizations and "seasons of grace" (when larger than usual numbers of converts would enter a particular church) are as old as religion itself. In New England and the Middle Colonies, they occurred with cyclical regularity, often corresponding to the coming of age of a new generation or, in the case of the Scots Presbyteri-

ans, sacramental renewals. But translocal mass revivals, incorporating thousands of people across state and even continental lines, were something entirely different. They did not exist before the Great Awakening of 1740. Indeed, they were what made the Great Awakening "great."

The catalyst for these mass revivals was a young 24-year-old English Anglican itinerant preacher named George Whitefield (1714–1770). Such was the breadth of his appeal that entirely new audiences appeared, as if by magic, to hear him preach the good news of the new birth. Wherever he preached, crowds of unprecedented size and inclusivity would appear. Friends and enemies alike could do anything, it seemed, but stay away. In the course of his career, Whitefield preached to audiences that must have numbered in the millions. Often he would spend up to forty hours a week *in the pulpit*.

Whitefield introduced innovations into the pulpit that had no precedent and perhaps no equal since. These innovations can be grouped in two central categories: pulpit presentation and communications media.

Pulpit Presentation. Before Whitefield, preaching was defined in medieval and classical categories as an extension of the classical oration. The preacher's craft, like the university lecturer's craft, was to inject learning into discourse in such a way that heads would be filled with information and hearts warmed to the logical truths of scripture. Apart from a handful of renegades and radicals, no serious preacher had ever dreamed of upsetting the divine balance between mind and emotion and using the passions to reach the minds and souls of his hearers; no one, that is, before Whitefield. In Whitefield's hands, preaching came to be something entirely new and different from virtually all that preceded him. It became, in a word, dramatic and theatrical.

Until Whitefield, everybody knew the difference between preaching and theater. With Whitefield, it was no longer so clear. He would turn his back on classical models of preaching. Contained within these classical models of oratory articulated by Cicero, Quintilian, and later Augustine* was an implicit or sometimes explicit psychology of the self that proclaimed the sovereignty of the mind over the emotions and passions and insisted that responsible rhetoric,* be it civil or pastoral, must address itself first to the head and then, through the process of logical and rational argumentation, the heart. Preachers did not ignore the heart, to be sure, but agreed that the avenue to the heart must be through the mind and the understanding (*see* Drama).

In terms of the presentation of self in the pulpit, this preaching model featured what today we would call "talking heads": preachers whose embodied self was generally hidden from the congregation by robes, elevated pulpits, and scripts, and whose motions were limited largely to hand movements punctuating the doctrines of the sermon. Speaker and hearer were fixed within the physical space of the church. University and church were the only two places where knowledge was transmitted.

Part of Whitefield's genius, inspired by a childhood career on the stage, was to invert this order and speak directly to the passions. Instead of the university lectern, Whitefield's model was the stage and the actor. What happens if we take the stage as our model and metaphor rather than the university lectern? First, and most important, the actor/preacher must speak to the passions and imaginary experience rather than to the understanding and the mind. Embodied empathy rather than doctrinal understanding is the key to a passion-based ministry.

If passion is the key to homiletics, how are passions raised? Here too we see a great reversal in Whitefield's preaching. As reason* and intellect are the keys to the mind and doctrinal understanding, so the body is the window to the passions. For dramatic preaching to realize its potential, the body must be freed from pulpits and texts. The story does not have to be profound, but the body has to be

moved. Consider great opera. Often the story lines are hopelessly juvenile and manipulative. But through song and dance—through embodied performance —opera can bring tears to the eyes of the most hardened intellectual. For passions to connect, the performer's body must be the fundamental point of contact. Voice, gesture, movement, and control of facial muscles are essential. The passion-based minister must preach as the actor strides the stage, with no script in hand and with all portions of the body registering the proper emotion. This is exactly what Whitefield achieved through the innovations of outdoor preaching in an extemporaneous mode. He was the first in a long line of embodied, evangelical preachers who would dispense with written text and fixed liturgy and speak as the spirit moved in close emotional concord with his audience. Accounts of Whitefield's sermons almost invariably registered tears, sweating, and violent agitations to the body as he strove to work himself—his *body*—to a fever pitch that perfectly conveyed the passion he was feeling or the passion his dramatic text called forth.

Communications. Besides his pulpit innovations, Whitefield proved to be a master at the art of self-promotion in a dawning age of mass media. Instead of building his revivals around the traditional institutional supports in the established or nonconforming churches, Whitefield built his revivals around the press. Just as the eighteenth century was a dawning age of commerce and marketing, so also did it mark the infancy of the weekly newspapers and magazines that would soon grow into a mass media revolution. From the start of his spectacular career, Whitefield enlisted friendly editors and baited antagonistic editors in a large campaign to publicize himself and his revivals. He didn't care if the coverage was wildly enthusiastic or wildly angry and threatened, as long as it played to the press. Wherever he preached, Whitefield worked with advance men who would send notices to local papers describing his past triumphs and future itineraries in their regions.

Before Whitefield, newspapers did not typically include religion in their subject matter except to present essays on morality and aesthetics. To traditional churchmen, the secular newspapers represented an alien presence, at best indifferent and at worst a threat to traditional religious print. But to Whitefield, it represented a novel form of public outreach that could reach customers and consumers who eluded the nets of printed sermons and settled churches. Again, we see a commercialization and commodification of preaching and ministry. In utilizing the secular newspapers and magazines, Whitefield was presenting religion as a popular commodity that could compete not so much against other churches as against the goods and services of this world.

Alongside his efforts to appear in the secular press, Whitefield promoted publishing endeavors of his own. Most important were cheap editions of his more popular sermons and his journal. The printed sermons were of value less for the quality of their literature (they could never match the power of his live delivery) than as icons and tokens of his preaching. And the journal served, much like Benjamin Franklin's *Autobiography*, as a vehicle to create a self—an *individual*—that would appeal to his popular audiences. Not coincidentally, Benjamin Franklin would be Whitefield's greatest American publisher and publicist and, in time, his greatest American friend.

To solidify a transatlantic, international community centered around his revivals, Whitefield augmented his sermons and journals with a novel magazine, *The Weekly History*, that carried letters and accounts of Calvinist revivals occurring simultaneously in England, Scotland, and the colonies. While Whitefield was always at the center of accounts describing the new and sensational revivals, he was not alone. Soon contemporary innovators and imitators surfaced, all transcending denominational boundaries and preaching the new birth to outdoor, voluntary audiences.

The effect of Whitefield's passion-based, mass media revivals was, in effect, to introduce religion to the marketplace. His mass revivals were not really a church, nor were they connected to local communities and congregations. The audiences changed with every meeting, evincing no permanent structure or leadership aside from Whitefield's own charismatic ministry and his network of media promoters. In addition, the audiences were routinely enjoined to support their local congregations and parishes, even as they were assured of bigger things afoot. In reality, Whitefield's audiences, publishers, and loyal supporters represented powerful new "parachurches"—groups of otherwise disconnected individuals bound in voluntary religious associations based on a marketplace organization and destined to characterize Pan-Protestant "evangelical" organizations in the nineteenth and twentieth centuries. His competition was not so much with other churches and denominations as it was with the neutral space of the market. His spiritual "goods" he placed alongside all of the goods and services of this world in an effort to compete for "market share" in the marketplace of commodities and entertainments (*see* Television and Preaching).

Whitefield's appeal to experience would touch something deep within the emerging democratic personality of an individualistic age. Subsequent generations would eventually forget his genius, and even his name; such is the fate of innovators who leave no institutional legacy. But in the eighteenth century, there was only one Whitefield, only one preacher capable of transcending his craft to become, in effect, a culture hero—a celebrity—who happened to be in the business of preaching rather than entertainment or politics. More than any other English-language preacher, he ensured that the pulpit would never again be quite the same (*see* History of Preaching).

Stout, H. S., *The Divine Dramatist: George Whitefield and the Rise of Modern Evangelicalism*, 1991. **Whitefield, G.**, *Fifteen Sermons*, 1794; and *Journals*, 1737–41.

HARRY S. STOUT

THE BINDING OF ISAAC
George Whitefield
Did you weep just now, when I bid you fancy that you saw the altar, and the wood laid in order, and Isaac bound on the altar? Look up by faith, behold the blessed Jesus, our all-glorious Immanuel, not bound, but nailed on an accursed tree: see how he hangs crowned with thorns, and had in derision of all that are round about him. See how the thorns pierce him, and how the blood in purple streams trickles down his sacred temples! . . . Isaac is saved, but Jesus, the God of Isaac, dies; a ram is offered up in Isaac's room, but Jesus has no substitute; Jesus must bleed, Jesus must die . . . And now where are all your tears? shall I say, refrain your voice from weeping? No, rather let me exhort you to look to him whom you have pierced, and mourn, as a woman mourneth for her first born: for we have been the betrayers, we have been the murderers of this Lord of glory. . . . Having so much done, so much suffered for us, so much forgiven, shall we not love much? O! let us love him with all our hearts, and minds, and strength, and glorify him in our souls and bodies; for they are his. . . . Remember, Abraham your father was tried so before you: think, O think, of the happiness he now enjoys, and how he is incessantly thanking God for tempting and trying him when here below. Look up often by the eye of faith, and see him sitting with his dearly beloved Isaac in the world of spirits. Remember, it will be but a little while, and you shall sit with them also, and tell one another what God has done for your souls. There I hope to sit with you, and hear this story of his offering up his son from his own mouth, and to praise the Lamb that sitteth upon the throne, for what he hath done for all our souls, for ever and ever.

From "Abraham's Offering Up His Son Isaac," in *The Character, Preaching, Etc. of the Rev. Whitefield,* B. Colman and W. Cooper, eds. (Boston, [1749?], 111–15.

Willard, Frances. (1839–1898) Willard was a noted educator, social reformer, proponent of the women's movement, and leader of the temperance crusade. Born in Churchville, New York, of New England stock, Willard graduated from the North Western Female College in Evanston, Illinois, in 1859. Raised in a devout Christian home, she joined the Methodist Church in 1861. She taught school, wrote, and traveled in Europe and the Middle East before becoming president of the newly founded Evanston College for Ladies in Illinois in 1871 and then dean of the college when it united with Northwestern University in 1873. It was not until after her resignation from college administration in 1874, however, that Willard became a leader in the Temperance Movement that would catapult her to fame.

As president of the Chicago Woman's Christian Temperance Union (WCTU), Frances Willard discovered she had a talent and love for preaching. Speaking mostly to unemployed men and boys, she read and expounded passages of scripture. Elected corresponding secretary of the national WCTU in 1874, Willard found herself increasingly drawn to public speaking and, in 1877, resigned the presidency of the Chicago WCTU to join the staff of the renowned evangelist Dwight L. Moody.* As an evangelist, she presided at "ladies meetings," frequently giving homilies to overflow crowds.

In 1897, Willard was elected national president of the WCTU, an office she held until her death. She reorganized the union and oversaw the WCTU's growth into the largest women's society in the nation. Under her leadership, the WCTU broadened its concerns to include women's suffrage, politics, peace, and labor and economic reform. As Willard gained national and then international notoriety, the press routinely reported her statements on religion and politics. In 1891, Willard was elected president of the World's Woman's Christian Temperance Union.

A firm believer in politics as a means of accomplishing desired goals, Willard promoted numerous petitions and was instrumental in the founding of the Prohibition Home Protection Party in 1882. The WCTU's political alliances—termed by Willard "gospel politics"—were not always well received by observers and members, but Willard's charisma and parliamentary agility kept the WCTU largely united behind her.

Willard became an advocate of liberal Christianity and the Social Gospel, eventually embracing Christian socialism. For her, Christianity was more a life than a creed and was best realized in acts of love and compassion. Her efforts in the realms of temperance, suffrage, "social purity" (laws protecting women and girls from seduction and rape), and economic and labor reform were all rooted in a progressive Christianity that looked for the fulfillment of God's kingdom on earth (see Rauschenbusch, Walter).

In 1880, Willard attended the Methodist General Conference to bring greetings from the WCTU and solicit support. Some delegates to the conference were so adamantly opposed to granting a woman the privilege of the floor that Willard chose not to speak. An active churchwoman, Willard was elected to the General Conference of the Methodist Episcopal Church eight years later, but strenuous opposition arose again, and that body refused to seat women delegates.

Willard, who personally desired ordination and longed for the acceptance of women pastors, took up the cause of women's leadership in the church and published *Woman in the Pulpit* in 1888. She countered the strong opposition to women's ecclesiastical leadership by appealing to the Bible and the church's need for the gifts of women. If the church was

to proclaim a potent and faithful gospel, she believed, it would need to open itself to women exegetes and preachers. "The mother-heart of God," she insisted, "will never be known . . . until translated into terms of speech by mother-hearted women." Despite the strong opposition she experienced, Willard predicted that women would, before long, enter the pulpit to preach the message of salvation (*see* Women as Preachers; Feminist Preaching).

Considered by many the leading woman speaker of her day, Willard used her personal magnetism, eloquence, and wit to enthrall her listeners. Willard frequently memorized her speeches before delivery to allow for a sense of spontaneity, and she used hyperbole and drama to heighten the urgency of her message. Most notable was her ability to coin a phrase, such as "Home Protection," to capture the essence of her message.

As WCTU president, Willard traveled incessantly, frequently spending only a few weeks at home per year. On these journeys, she gave numerous lectures and pulpit addresses on such topics as temperance, suffrage, prostitution, diet, and health. By envisioning all these concerns as an expansion of the Christian woman's concern for domesticity, Willard was able to appeal to many conservative women who would otherwise have dismissed these issues as outside their purview. Under the banner of home protection, Willard worked to promote the advance of God's kingdom through the efforts of women.

Bordin, R., *Frances Willard: A Biography,* 1986. **Earhart, M.,** *Frances Willard: From Prayers to Politics,* 1944.

BRADLEY J. LONGFIELD

THE MASTER'S CALL
Frances Willard
John 11:28. The last words in this verse are, "The Master has come and calleth for thee." Each principal word in the phrase is like a telescope pointing to a star, luminous and bright. One sister long ago bore

this message to another, even as I would gladly carry it to you. Christ himself asked the question, how can ye serve two masters? "Be not many masters," that is the curse of life. "One is your master, even Christ," The Master. Unity is a prerequisite of power. In the pictures of Raphael and other great masters, there is not a line, there is not a shade, there is not an accessory of the composition that does not lead the eye and the thought directly to the central figure, and so these great pictures have no fascination so potent as their unity.

. . . This which is so true in the fine arts, is most of all true in that finest of arts, character. Unless there is a predominating and overmastering purpose to which all the accessories and incidents of life contribute, the character will be weak, irresolute, uncertain. This is just what Christ is for, to impart to us a predominant motive of character that shall be the highest, the most lasting, and the most beneficent, to replace indefiniteness by clearness, and aimless reverie by resolute aim.

He is first of all the great Teacher, the Master, not a master. . . . If you would learn to play on the piano you must give your hand to the key-board, make it a bond-slave of the instrument; that is consecration. . . . You give up your will to your teacher as far as that key-board is concerned, and that is faith founded upon reason. If he were not a helpful master you would never give to him your will, and if the instrument were not true to its own laws you would never give to it your hand. Let us remember then that Christ is the Master, chosen out from all others, not a master contesting the palm with several others; He can never be to us what He must be if we are to attain a Christian character until He is the autocrat of our heart's mystic realm.

From "A Bible Talk: The Master Calleth for Thee" (Chicago: Woman's Temperance Pub. Assn., 1889), 2.

Wisdom Literature. "Wisdom Literature" is usually reserved for the books of Proverbs, Job, and Ecclesiastes, and among the so-called Apocrypha, Sirach, and the Wisdom of Solomon. There also seems to be "wisdom influence" on other books (e.g., Pss. 37, 73). While the five books may not be foremost among the lectionary selections, they deal with important life experiences. Their primary characteristic is that they do not make use of the typical Israelite traditions (promises to the fathers, exodus, Sinai, etc.). Instead, they are oriented to human experience: What does it teach us? What are the lessons handed down from generation to generation, especially within the family?

The literary types and the messages differ from book to book. Proverbs 1—9 consists of wisdom poems encouraging the youth to pursue wisdom with ardor (perhaps the most famous poem is the personification of wisdom in Proverbs 8). The rest of the work is an assembly of collections of two-line sayings: 10:1; 22:17; 24:23; 30:1; 31:1; and 31:10 carry titles indicating separate collections.

Sometimes the sayings may seem banal; at other times, subtle. The range of topics is enormous: from farm to court, vice to virtue (or folly to wisdom). The outlook is optimistic: virtue succeeds, and wickedness fails. The perspective, of course, is this life, since there is no life with God beyond death. There is only Sheol, where all were gathered, sinner and saint alike.

This situation makes the problem of Job all the more searing. Why is Job, obviously innocent, suffering? Where is the justice of God? The issue is debated between Job and his friends but is never resolved. Even though the Lord appears and questions Job in magnificent poetry (39—42), the mystery remains. But the appearance of the Lord to Job is enough for him (42:5); he yields to the Lord and the mystery of suffering.

Ecclesiastes, or Qoheleth (ca. 250 B.C.E.), proposed the thesis that everything is "vanity" (*hebel*). He tested several "values" in life such as riches, labor, pleasure, and wisdom, and found them all wanting. The best one can hope for is that God may dispense some joy and happiness to a person. But one cannot count on this, because no one knows what God is up to. The divine action is totally unintelligible (3:11; 7:13; 8:7; 11:5). Qoheleth simply accepts God on God's terms, as he understands them. No one has underscored the mystery of God more emphatically.

Sirach (also Ecclesiasticus) was written by Ben Sira near the beginning of the second century. His grandson's Greek translation of the fifty-one chapters replaced the Hebrew original, which was soon lost to the Western world. But within the last century, about two thirds of the Hebrew has been found, and the NRSV is a sound translation of a difficult text. The message itself is very orthodox and pious, following generally both the optimism and the style of the two-line sayings of Proverbs. But the sayings are usually blended together in relatively lengthy treatments of various topics: friendship, death, riches, control of the tongue—the customary topics of wisdom's concern.

The Wisdom of Solomon was written in Greek in the first century B.C. and is concerned with three principal topics: the gift of a blessed immortality (1—6), the glory of personified Wisdom (7—9), and the role of wisdom in salvation history, especially evidenced in the plagues of Egypt (10—19).

One may presume that a Christian audience would remember a couple of proverbs from their past, the story of Job, Qoheleth's phrase about vanity, and probably very little of the two apocryphal works. If this is true, as it very probably is, a biblical workshop in these books seems more necessary than an occasional sermon. However, one might also argue that the very novelty of these books presents an opportunity for breaking through mistaken notions to new insights. The obstacles are formidable but worth the effort. The homilist may note the following advantages:

1. This literature represents Israel's effort to understand and communicate with God through the medium of daily experience. There is what has been called "the mysticism of everyday things" (Rahner). God is found in everyday life (Prov. 14:31). Such is the area biblical wisdom addresses, the area in which most people live—at home, at work, in leisure, in relationships of all kinds. The objective for the biblical sage was formation of character, learning to cope with life and its ambiguities, its benefits and reversals—and inculcation of self-control.

2. The perspective of wisdom literature is on *this* life, and it provides a necessary ballast to Christians, many of whom are too much concerned about the next life, "super-eschatologized," as it were. Encountering God in the here and now, in suffering as well as in joy, without the perspective of eternity—that was the situation of the Old Testament person. Christians need to incorporate this attitude—without denying the gift of a blessed immortality—into their daily existence. The question that Satan put to God should ring in their ears: "Does Job fear God for nothing?" (1:9).

3. While the mystery of suffering is directly confronted in Isaiah 53 and in the person of Jesus Christ, an intimate knowledge of Job, his despair and his faith, his agony and his hope, is a splendid preparation for coping with this mystery.

4. The Christian audience will more easily learn of the historicity of revelation and its development. In a sense, Christians will realize that their eschatological timetable is out of sync with the Old Testament doctrine of Sheol. This is all to the good. Instead of asking why the Old Testament person could believe in God in such circumstances, they can learn to purify their own faith and motivation for love of God. Love is its own justification, not reward. There will be no erroneous sermons to be heard about such texts as Job 19:25 and Ecclesiastes 12:7.

The preacher may elect to preach from these books in a series of sermons, allowing the word to sink more deeply into the hearts of the audience. Among other benefits will be an increased appreciation of Jesus Christ, whom Paul called "the Wisdom of God" (1 Cor. 1:24), as the wisdom teacher that Jesus truly was.

Brown, R. E., J. A. Fitzmyer, and R. E. Murphy, *The New Jerome Biblical Commentary*, 1990, 447–522. Bultmann, R., *The History of the Synoptic Tradition*, 1963. Murphy, R. E., *The Tree of Life: An Exploration of Biblical Wisdom Literature*, 1990.

ROLAND E. MURPHY, O. CARM.

Women as Preachers.

The role of preacher has been grudgingly assigned to women only in recent years, and then not fully. The appearances of women in nearly 2,000 years of Christian preaching have been extremely rare. The bias against the use of their formidable gifts for communicating the gospel is one of the most appalling ethical failures in all of Christian history. Even with the World Council of Churches' designation of the "Ecumenical Decade of Churches in Solidarity with Women" (1988–1998), it may not now be assumed that the right of women to preach is an idea whose time has fully come.

In the United States, this issue is as old as the early colonies. Without particular concern for ordination as such, meaningful movements were led by women who preached. Such was Anne Hutchinson (1591–1642), self-styled interpreter of John Cotton's preaching. She was expelled from Massachusetts, where great numbers had followed her. She then launched a settlement in Rhode Island and was later slain by Indians in New York.

Until after the Revolutionary War, women preachers were largely among Quakers, who did not ordain anyone. Two of them, Ann Austin and Mary Fisher, were sent as missionaries to New England in 1656, where they were impris-oned and whipped for challenging the status quo. Other women missionaries who followed them were martyred.

By the late seventeenth century, religious revivals were breaking out in private circles. Evangelists included women. Eventually, these cottage-hosted evangelical revivals merged with the First Great Awakening" (Ruether and Keller, Vol. 2, 318). Sarah Osborn, a Newport Congregationalist and schoolteacher, drew hundreds to her preaching in her own home (1760–1796) but was never ordained or given a parish. Likewise, Barbara Ruckle Heck (1734–1804), "Mother of American Methodism," was catalyst in 1766 for the organization of the first Methodist Society in the United States, the John Street Church in New York. But she was never ordained as a preacher and pastor (Ruether and Keller, Vol. 2, 366). Still another historically noted preacher was Jarena Lee (1783–1836), widow of an African Methodist Episcopal pastor. While Bishop Allen praised her preaching gifts, he declined to ordain her on the basis of the Methodist Discipline.

During and after the Second Great Awakening (ca. 1800–1840), there were even more women preachers, but the respect and placement accorded them was never comparable to that given male pastors and evangelists. In 1814, at a meeting of the forerunner of the "Christian" Church (now in the United Church of Christ), Abigail Roberts was converted. Until her death in 1841, she conducted innumerable frontier revivals and organized new churches. But she was never accorded the recognition of ordination.

Born a slave, Amanda Berry Smith of Pennsylvania (1837–1915) was a widely hailed Holiness and Methodist camp meeting preacher in the United States, Britain, Africa, and India (Ruether and Keller, Vol. 1, 18). In spite of her unusual international following, she never received ordination.

It is generally accepted that the first woman to be fully ordained by a church of a major denomination was Antoinette Brown. She was ordained a Congregationalist and assigned to a small church in Butler, New York, in 1853. The first woman ordained by an action above the level of a local congregation was Olympia Brown (1835–1926), who was ordained Universalist (Ruether and Keller, Vol. 1, 214).

In the late nineteenth century, a powerful women's suffrage movement began to challenge prevailing biblical prohibitions of women's ordination. Several denominations with local congregational autonomy led in the ordination of women: Congregationalists, Christian Church (Disciples), and Unitarians. In the Holiness tradition, new groups such as the Church of God (Anderson, Indiana), the Church of the Nazarene, the Wesleyan Methodists, the Free Methodists, and the Salvation Army were launched with recognition of the ordination of women (Zikmund, 6). The momentum has increased and continued to the present, albeit with some national denominational bodies still holding out against the ordination of members of their female majorities.

The first Methodists of America to ordain women to the full eldership were the African Methodist Episcopal Zions, who ordained Mary J. Small in 1898 and Julia Foote in 1900. The African Methodist Episcopal Church licensed women to preach as early as 1884 but did not grant full ordination until 1948. The Christian Methodist Episcopal Church finally ordained women in 1954. And the body known as United Methodists, who gave local ordination to women for many years (Georgia Harkness in 1938), did not grant full ordination until 1956.

The Northern (now American) Baptists were the first Baptist group to recognize full ordination for women. While the decision was always local, the openness to women was manifest to some degree as early as 1851 (Libbie Cilley Griffen). Progressive National Baptists, organized in 1961, tend generally to recognize the ordination of women, but the rest of the African-American Baptist bodies and the huge Southern Baptist Convention all prohibit female ordination by rigid cus-

tom, if not by ecclesiastical law. All these national bodies, however, contain a few local exceptions.

The Cumberland Presbyterians were the first of their group to ordain women, in 1889, with the Presbyterians of the North (PCUSA) not following until 1955. The Presbyterians of the South (PCUS) authorized ordination of women in 1964 (Zikmund, 5).

Both the American Lutheran Church and the Lutheran Church in America first ordained women in 1970, while other Lutheran bodies in the U.S. are still opposed. Presently in the Evangelical Lutheran Church in America, women make up approximately 7 percent of the clergy. Without official denominational approval, eleven Episcopalian women were ordained in 1974. The denomination changed canon law to admit women into the priesthood in 1976.

While the trend is definitely toward greater acceptance of women, large bodies such as the Southern Baptists mentioned above and the Church of God in Christ (the largest black Pentecostal body), are still firmly committed to restricting women from full ordination and pastoral duties. Yet even in the most rigid denominations there are exceptions. There is no group, not even the Church of Jesus Christ of Latter-day Saints or the Roman Catholic Church, in which *all* women are content to accept less than full options for service. The agitation for change is enhanced by the fact that many of today's Protestant seminaries have student bodies that are nearly half female. Added to this is the pressure of federal laws enforcing the equality of women in every aspect of secular life. No denomination will likely survive far into the twenty-first century without finding some way to conform to the popular doctrine of equality and to the word of the apostle Paul, who said that in Christ there is neither male nor female (Gal. 3:28).

Howard, R., "Women and Preaching: A Bibliography," *Homiletic* 17:2, 7–10. **Hunter, E.,** and **D. A. Farmer,** eds., *And Blessed Is*

She, 1990. **James, J. W.,** ed., *Women in American Religion,* 1980. **Ruether, R. R.,** and **R. S. Keller,** eds., *Women and Religion in America,* 3 vols., 1981, 1983, 1986. **Zikmund, B. B.,** "Preachers in Petticoats," unpublished manuscript, 1989.

ELLA PEARSON MITCHELL

DARE TO PREACH
Barbara Brown Taylor

From the beginning of time the speaking of God's word has been an act of great power. God said, "Let there be light," and there was light. Moses delivered the Law to Israel, and Torah became the covenant of their life together. John the Baptist cried in the wilderness, "Prepare the way of the Lord" and the way was prepared, his very words paving the desert where Jesus would walk.

Sometimes the power of the Word is not so evident. Jeremiah was a laughing stock; Hosea, a cuckold; and Ezekiel, an exile— which may be God's way of telling us that no one can judge the power of God's word by its results. God is in charge of the results. It is enough for us to proclaim the word and to believe that in doing so we change the world whether the world knows it or not, whether we know it or not, simply by standing and speaking the words we have been given to say, words of love and challenge, words of judgment and grace, words of such truth and terrible clarity that sometimes we tremble to say them out loud. You don't need a grand pulpit to utter them from; any old housetop will do. Take the sun room at the nursing home, where you stand by the piano surrounded by wheelchairs full of old people, some of them dozing, some of them whimpering to go back to their rooms, less than half of them even aware that you are there. Say "resurrection" in their presence. Say "life everlasting." Say "remember." Just let those words loose in the room, just utter them in the light and trust them to do their work. Or speak to a support group for people with AIDS. Worship with them if you can, lay hands on their heads and pray for their healing. Say "mercy" to them. Say "hope." Say "be-loved children of God." Set those words free in their hearing and trust in their power to make people whole. Or let something you care about land you on the steps of city hall, where you stand staring into television cameras wondering what in the world you have gotten yourself into. Say "justice." Say "peace." Say "the righteousness of God," and never mind what other people say. Never mind that they walk past you without reading your sign or put you in the back of a paddy wagon and take you away. God is in charge of the results.

Wherever you are and whatever happens to you, just speak the word that has been given you to say, whatever it may be. Never forget that the very act of speaking sets God's word into motion, that your own willingness to utter it out loud is the best proof that it is an active word, as true and lively now as it was when it separated light from darkness and filled the earth with living things. Dare to create a new world with God's words. Give the people who listen to you new images of a new earth full of new people. And be careful of the power you have been given. Treat it as carefully as a stick of dynamite and use it with as much respect. Learn all that you can about the word you proclaim: study it, argue with it, fear it, love it, live it. Then let it go. Set it free.

From "Words We Tremble to Say Out Loud." © Barbara Brown Taylor, 1990. Used by permission.

Word of God. In the Old Testament, God's Word (Hebrew *dabar*) is understood not as mere descriptive speech but as creative, efficacious power turned outward toward the world (Isa. 55:10–11). God's Word is thus the active agent in creation (Gen. 1:3–29; Isa. 48:13; Ps. 33:6–9), the vehicle of God's covenant with Israel (Ex. 34:27; Deut. 30:14–20), and the guiding force behind history (Isa. 44:26–28; Jer. 1:9–10).

The Word of God is generally made manifest through the medium of human proclamation. Moses functions as the bearer of the divine Word to Israel (Ex. 4:10–16; 5:1–2; 19:3–9). The ministry of the prophets is likewise established and authorized by the Word. To them the divine Word "comes" (Hos. 1:1; Micah 1:1–2; Isa. 2:1; cf. Luke 3:2), acting as an irresistible force that enlists them in God's service and compels their proclamation (Amos 3:8; Jer. 6:11; 20:7–9).

Central among New Testament understandings of the Word of God (Greek *rhema*, or *logos*) is the confession of Jesus himself as God's Word incarnate in human flesh (John 1:14; Heb. 1:2). Jesus'* own proclamation, consequently, exhibits many of the features that characterize the Old Testament understanding of the divine Word: it possesses power to accomplish that for which it is sent (Mark 1:27–28; 4:35–41; Matt. 9:1–8); it stands over and has authority to reinterpret the covenant word (Matt. 5:21–48); it mediates judgment (Luke 6:47–49; John 12:48); and it is the source of eternal life (John 5:24).

Consequently, the New Testament generally sees an extremely close relationship obtaining between the church's proclamation of Christ, Jesus' own words, and the Word of God. So Jesus tells his disciples, "Whoever listens to you, listens to me, and whoever rejects you rejects me, and whoever rejects me rejects the one who sent me" (Luke 10:16; cf. John 12:49–50; Gal. 1:11–12; 1 Thess. 2:13; 1 Peter 4:11). The Apostolic office is thus understood as a ministry of the divine Word (Luke 1:2; Acts 6:2–4; Col. 1:24–26), and the proclaimed gospel comes to be identified with, and announced as, the Word of God given for the redemption of sinful humanity (Acts 10:44; 17:11; Rom. 10:8; 10:17; 1 Peter 1:23–25).

The identification of Christian preaching with the Word of God continues into the patristic period and early Middle Ages. Augustine,* for instance, can speak quite matter-of-factly about Christians as people who are "spiritually born of the same seed as ourselves, namely, the Word" (*On Christian Doctrine* II, 12).

With the decline of the preaching office in the centuries following Augustine and Chrysostom,* understandings of the sermon as the Word of God receded from prominence. This trend was dramatically reversed, however, with the advent of the Protestant Reformation.

Luther's* challenge to the authority of pope and council was supported throughout by an understanding of the Word of God as *the* preeminent ground of the church's faith and life. As in earlier centuries, the Word of God was here identified with the content of Christian proclamation,* with an additional emphasis, perhaps, on the Word of God as the ground of church *authority.**

The Word of God is closely tied to the scriptures in the understanding of the Protestant Reformers, though it is not identical to them. Lutherans and Reformed alike stressed the interdependence and inseparability of word and Spirit: It is precisely where the written gospel is proclaimed and heard under the guidance and illumination of the Holy Spirit* that the true and living Word of God enters into human hearts and lives. Thus, the Reformers understood the work of the Spirit to be one of leading Christians to the Bible, enabling believers to hear in it the word of personal address that God speaks in the present moment.

It is in light of just this understanding that Luther stresses the primacy of the proclaimed word as the preeminent locus where God meets believers in personal address and encounter: "through this instrument God works with us, does everything, and offers to us all his riches" (WA, *Tischreden*, 4:517). Preaching thus emerges in the Protestant Reformation as the heart and center of the church's life, the locus of the divine-human encounter between believers and the living Word of God.

The middle decades of the twentieth century have seen a resurgence of this Reformation emphasis on the role of the divine Word in preaching, particularly among the neo-orthodox "Word of God" theologians. Their ranks include figures such as Martin Kähler, Emil Brunner,

Gerhard Ebeling, and perhaps preeminently, Karl Barth.*

Barth draws on Reformation sources in formulating the threefold account of the Word of God that appears in the first volume of his *Church Dogmatics*. Beginning with a consideration of the Word of God *preached*, Barth makes very strong claims for identifying the words of human proclamation with the real and authentic Word of God. This identification is never automatic, however, but comes about only as the freely given gift of divine grace. Human speech has absolutely no power in itself to reveal God or to mediate the divine presence. It is only as God in gracious freedom chooses to reveal God in and through the church's proclamation that the words of human speech become also and at the same time God's Word and God's self-giving. Barth thus sees the Word of God as the gracious *event* of God's self-giving encounter with fallen humanity, here taking place in and through the church's preaching.

Such preaching does not stand on its own authority, however; nor is it rooted in the church's self-consciousness or inward experience. Rather, the church's preaching is anchored and grounded in the Bible, the Word of God *written*. The text of the Bible stands as the church's historic recollection of God's past revelation and promises, which in turn form the basis for its expectation of God's revelation in the present and future. Barth constantly stresses the contingency of the divine Word: the scriptures can function as the authentic recollection and testimony of God's revelation for the believing community only by the free and gracious decision of God, who gives himself through the human words of the biblical testimonies.

The scriptures, likewise, do not stand on their own authority, but derive their special status precisely as the authoritative witness to the Word of God *revealed*. The event of God's revelatory self-giving *to* humankind is, in the deepest sense, none other than Jesus Christ himself, the Word made flesh. So Christ stands as the

unifying ground in which the Word of God revealed, written, and proclaimed all have their anchor and focus (*see* Theology of Preaching).

Barth, K., *Church Dogmatics, Volume I: The Doctrine of the Word of God,* ed. G. W. Bromiley and T. F. Torrance, 1975. **Crowe, F. E.,** *Theology of the Christian Word: A Study in History,* 1978. **Kittel, G.,** *Theological Dictionary of the New Testament,* Vol. 4, trans. G. W. Bromiley, 1967, s.v. *lego.* **Lischer, R.,** *A Theology of Preaching,* rev. ed. 1992.

P. MARK ACHTEMEIER

Wycliffe, John. (ca. 1329–1384) John Wycliffe was a controversial English theologian, preacher, and scholar whose writing, teaching, and preaching contributed to the formation of most of the major tenets of the Protestant Reformation, both in England and continental Europe. For this reason he was called "Morning Star of the Reformation" by the sixteenth-century polemicist John Bale. He was instrumental in encouraging the production of an early English translation of the Bible, and his insistence on the preeminent authority and truth of scripture earned him the honorific "Doctor Evangelicus." One contemporary witnessed to his reputation among many as "the grettist clerk that thei [they] knewen lyvynge upon erthe." In contrast, one of his detractors called him *execrabilis seductor,* and a notable at the Council of Constance wrote of Wycliffe as "a man deformed by the devil, a heretic by instinct."

Such contrasting assessments stem from the fact that Wycliffe's work laid the foundation for the English heretical movement known as Lollardy. This widespread popular movement questioned, among other orthodox ideas, the substantial presence of Christ in the Eucharist; the power of the pope to excommunicate and clergy to absolve sin; the value of fasting, images, and pilgrimages; the integrity of mendicant orders and other manifestations of "private religion." As Wycliffe himself had done in treatises and in sermons, Lollard preachers continually called for the disendowment of the church and advocated that laity have access to scripture in the vernacular. Lollardy was associated with civil uprisings as well, notably the Peasants' Revolt of 1381 and Sir John Oldcastle's rebellion in 1414.

Lollardy continued to be a force in English life long after Wycliffe's death, but its ideas were often indiscriminately associated with Wycliffe himself. For this reason, scholars of the period must draw careful distinctions between Wycliffe's own work, that of his followers, and posthumous developments. Wycliffe was a careful if contentious scholar and preacher, not the intentional leader of a popular revolution. The connection between Wycliffe and Lollardy is clear but in many cases indirect. The message of the Lollards, however, was carried throughout England by itinerant "poor preachers" whose vernacular sermons often were derived from a sermon cycle written by Wycliffe himself and available in Latin and English reportations (*see* Itinerant and Open-Air Preaching).

A habitué of Oxford for most of his adult life, John Wycliffe arrived at the university from Yorkshire around 1354. He became Master of Balliol College around 1360, and was appointed Warden of Canterbury Hall in 1365, a post he held briefly until he was expelled in 1367 by Archbishop Simon Langham, who reestablished Benedictine control there. Wycliffe took his doctorate in 1372 and won international acclaim for his teaching and defense of realist philosophy against the *via moderna* of nominalism. Early in his teaching career, he wrote a commentary on the entire Bible, the only one that survives from that period. He also wrote a number of controversial works on theology and church polity, including treatises on civil and divine dominion, the power of the pope, the truth of sacred scripture, and the doctrine of the Eucharist.

Wycliffe's career shows him to have incurred royal favor as early as 1374, when he was among the English envoys who conferred with papal authorities at Bruges on the issue of papal provisions. In addition to teaching, Wycliffe held various parochial livings from 1361, the last of these (1374) being at Lutterworth, to which he retired in 1381. He continued, however, to be present at Oxford until his death in 1384.

Contemporary accounts note that Wycliffe expressed his views "unclothed and openly" (*nude et aperte*) when he preached. Although Wycliffe's own teaching and preaching was not as inflammatory as that of his followers, he was nevertheless under constant scrutiny and attack by the established church of his time, in part because it fired the imagination and activity of those who were disgruntled by the magisterial orthodoxy of Christianity in late medieval Europe. In 1377, he was called to answer for his ideas, chiefly about clerical wealth, expressed in his treatise *On Civil Dominion* and in his preaching, but the proceedings were interrupted by wrangling between convener Thomas Courtenay (then bishop of London) and Wycliffe's powerful supporters, John of Gaunt and Henry Percy.

In that same year, eighteen propositions drawn from his work were condemned in a series of bulls issued by Pope Gregory XI, none of which were enforced. In 1380, Oxford officials enjoined him to cease teaching what they deemed dangerous eucharistic doctrine. Wycliffe retired from Oxford the next year but was subjected to further condemnation in 1382 at the so-called Earthquake Council at Blackfriars in London, where twenty-four additional propositions from his writings were variously termed heretical or erroneous.

Wycliffe was able to weather this storm as well and was never excommunicated or put under any penalty more severe than house arrest. The Council of Constance, determined to demonstrate the authority of a unified papacy against heresy, recognized the connection between Wycliffe's thought and that of John Hus and ordered that Wycliffe's bones be exhumed and burned. Philip Repingdon, a one-time disciple of Wycliffe and bishop of Lincoln until 1424, declined to follow the council's decree, which was carried out in 1428.

John Wycliffe's Latin sermons were published in four volumes for the Wyclif Society between 1887 and 1890. Subsequent research has revealed that they consist in the main of a long sermon cycle of nearly 300 sermons on the epistles and Gospels for Sundays of the church year, written by Wycliffe after 1381 and principally intended for use by other preachers. English versions based on this cycle are also extant. In addition, a set of forty sermons (*Sermones Quadraginta*) survive that Wycliffe himself preached in London and Oxford (*see* History of Preaching).

Hudson, A., *The Premature Reformation,* 1988; *Selections from English Wycliffite Writings,* 1978. **Kenny, A.,** *Wyclif,* 1985. **McFarlane, K. B.,** *John Wycliffe and the Beginnings of English Nonconformity,* 1952.

JOHN R. ARCHER

Zwingli, Huldrych (Ulrich)

(1484–1531) Zwingli was pastor at the Great Minster in Zurich and the Protestant reformer of German-speaking Switzerland. Born in the Toggenburg region of northeast Switzerland, a son of the local magistrate, Zwingli was educated as a humanist in many of the leading educational centers of Europe, including Bern, Vienna, and Basel, which colored his preaching and reforming work throughout his life by committing him to scripture in his theologizing and preaching. As a Swiss patriot, Zwingli also sought to apply the gospel to concrete social and political situations.

He began his pastoral work in 1506 in Glarus, where he steeped himself in the works of the fathers of the church and came eventually under the influence of the pacifist Erasmus of Rotterdam. Convinced of the negative impact of foreign wars on the life of his people, he began preaching against Swiss involvement in the mercenary service, which elicited severe criticism, thereby forcing him to leave Glarus after ten years of service. Zwingli later consistently claimed it was about this time, while reading a poem by Erasmus—"Jesus Expostulating with a Sinner Perishing Through His Very Own Fault"—that he came to an understanding of the sole mediatorship of Christ. He further developed a spiritual understanding of true religion, one opposed to the manifestations of false and idolatrous religion characteristic of the medieval church of his day. This religious perspective, combined with its application within the socio-political realm, was to serve as a foundation for Zwingli's reformation work.

After spending two years in Einsiedeln as preacher to the pilgrims, Zwingli began his service at the Great Minster in Zurich on January 1, 1519, having already achieved some recognition as an influential preacher. He announced his intention to begin preaching through the Gospel of Matthew rather than following the assigned pericopes for the day. According to Zwingli, the method of following the lections had led to poor preaching and had obscured the glory of God. According to his biographer and friend Myconius, he indicated that he would expound the text not according to human reason, "but according to the purpose of the Spirit, which through diligent collating of the Scriptures, and through fervent prayers from the heart, he doubted not that he should be given to understand" (Myconius 1:8–9). The response to his method was mixed. Some rejoiced; others were unhappy. When his opponent, Canon Hoffman, complained that Zwingli was creating innovations for the pulpit, the reformer replied that he was only returning to the ancient practice of the early church, notably that of Chrysostom* and Augustine* (*see* Lectionary Preaching).

Ancient though it may have been, it *was* an innovation for the day. Zwingli intended to let the Spirit guide his interpretation of scripture, wherever that might take him. In 1522, he had occasion to describe and defend his preaching in the *Archeteles*, a response to the bishop of Constance. After preaching through Matthew, he said he turned to Acts so "that the Church of Zurich might see in what way and with what sponsors the Gospel was carried forth and spread abroad" (*Latin Works*, 238). Next came 1 Timothy, Galatians, both epistles of Peter, and then Hebrews, "that they might recognize more plainly the goodness and glory of Christ." Zwingli's preaching was centered on Christ, whom he set against the practices and regulations of the church. He professed a simple contextualization in his approach:

> I have not, I say, used any false nostrums or tricks or exhortations, but in simple words and terms native to the Swiss I have drawn them to the recognition of their trouble, having learned this from Christ himself, who began his own preaching with it (*Latin Works*, 239).

There were likely few instances in the Reformation when preaching was to play such a decisive role as it did in Zurich. There were few days in which Zwingli did not ascend the steps of the pulpit to expound the Word of God. Of the thousands of sermons he preached, only eight were printed. Unfortunately, there were not secretaries to record his preaching, as with Calvin. The published sermons are clearly written after the fact and have become theological treatises. They reflect characteristic concerns of Zwingli the reformer, and they demonstrate a consistent dependence on the Bible. Every page contains numerous scriptural allusions and quotations, all consistently interpreted within the framework of Zwingli's religious and social concerns. One of Zwingli's favorite methods was to contrast the antithetical manifestations of false and true religion. For example, his sermon "The Shepherd" (March 1524) contrasted the false shepherd with the true. His method of preaching straight

through books of the Bible was an enduring contribution to modern preaching. He facilitated exegetical preaching by organizing a theological school in the Great Minster that met daily to work through the consecutive books of the Bible on the basis of the original languages. Zwingli was concerned for the reformation of the whole community of Zurich in accordance with the gospel, and he directed his preaching to that end.

Pipkin, H. W., "The Making of a Pastor: Huldrych Zwingli's Path from Humanism to Reformation," *Reformed Review* 37:2 (1984), 54–67. **Potter, G. R.**, *Zwingli*, 1976. **Wandel, L. P.**, "Brothers and Neighbors: The Language of Community in Zwingli's Preaching," *Zwingliana* 17:5 (1988), 361–74.   H. WAYNE PIPKIN

THE SHEPHERD
Huldrych Zwingli

The Shepherd should begin to preach as Christ began: "Repent!" Now no one will repent who does not know how evil he is. Therefore here must sin be preached first, and then salvation. . . . For the illness must always be recognized before one takes the medicine. . . . However, the recognition of sin . . . brings nothing other than despair in ourselves and drives us powerfully to the mercy of God. Of that mercy we are certain, for God has given his son for us. . . . See! Here the gospel and repentance are connected; for no one really rejoices in the gospel who has not previously rightly recognized the disease of sin.

Now if a person has recognized his misery and found . . . salvation in Christ Jesus, it is not seemly any longer to live in sin. For since we have died to sin in Christ, we may no longer live in sin (Romans 6:2). Therefore the shepherd must also carefully prevent the washed sheep's falling again in the excrement; that is, after the believers have come into knowledge of their savior and have experienced the friendly grace of God, they should thereafter lead a blameless life so that they no longer walk in death. Just as Christ, having risen from the dead dies no more, so also they, having laid aside the old being, should put on a new being. . . . For whoever does not change his life from day to day, after he has been redeemed in Christ, mocks the name of Christ and disparages and disdains it before unbelievers. . . . We see that it is not enough only to take possession of salvation, it is also necessary to take care so that one does not lose or despise it.

Most helpful toward that end is the shepherd's doing in practice what he teaches in words, which Christ demands most clearly. . . . This is certain: it is only hypocrisy when one speaks beautifully of God but does not form one's life according to him. . . . Here the shepherd should carefully guard against putting on a hypocritical dress for the true one, so that he decks himself out with cowls and hooded mantles while he is inwardly full of avarice—as for the most part the monks and theologians of this time do. They bow low, but they have an arrogant disposition; they wear a white shirt, but are more unchaste than the wild boar; high shoes and hats, but are full of envy and hatred; murmur many psalms, but leave the clear word of God, etc. The simple people learn by such works to live a life of hypocrisy only, while inwardly temptations remain with them. Therefore the shepherd must not let himself be shaped according to humanly created teaching but according to the word of God which he preaches, or else he plants nothing but hypocrisy. And since Christ is a perfect model, the shepherd must see that he relies only on *his* example.

From "The Shepherd" (March 1524), in *Huldrych Zwingli: Writings.* Vol. II, trans. and ed. H. W. Pipkin (Allison Park, Pa.: Pickwick Publications, 1984), 90–91.

CPSIA information can be obtained at www.ICGtesting.com
Printed in the USA
LVOW062152100113

315241LV00003B/270/A